The Golf Guide
Where to Play, Where to Stay
in Britain & Ireland

2011

Over 2,800 Clubs, Courses plus Accommodation

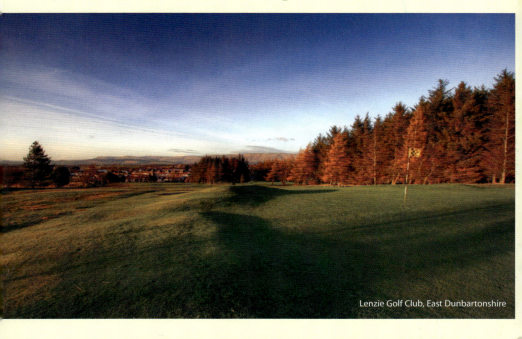

Lenzie Golf Club, East Dunbartonshire

© FHG Guides Ltd, 2011
ISBN 978-1-85055-433-2

Maps: ©MAPS IN MINUTES™ / Collins Bartholomew 2007

Typeset by FHG Guides Ltd, Paisley.
Printed and bound in China by Imago.

Distribution. Book Trade: ORCA Book Services, Stanley House,
3 Fleets Lane, Poole, Dorset BH15 3AJ
(Tel: 01202 665432; Fax: 01202 666219)
e-mail: mail@orcabookservices.co.uk
Published by FHG Guides Ltd., Abbey Mill Business Centre,
Seedhill, Paisley PA1 ITJ (Tel: 0141-887 0428 Fax: 0141-889 7204).
e-mail: admin@fhguides.co.uk

The Golf Guide, *Where to Play, Where to Stay* is published by FHG Guides Ltd,
part of Kuperard Group.

Cover design: FHG Guides
Cover Pictures: Old Thorns Manor Hotel, Golf & Country Estate, Liphook, Hampshire

Acknowledgements

The Publishers wish to acknowledge the assistance of Mike Harris of Golf Monthly and The Professional Golfers' Association regional golfing correspondents in the preparation of this 34th edition of
The Golf Guide, *Where To play, Where To stay.*

Photographs
We wish to thank Mike Harris (p5), Peter Godsiff (p14, 15), Jennifer Prentice (p184), David Birtill (p248),
Lough Erne Resort , Enniskillen (p501).
plus all Golf Clubs for sending all photographs used.

We wish to thank all our advertisers and, finally, the Club Secretaries, Professionals and others who have
co-operated in the annual updating of the golf club directory entries which are the essential ingredients of
The Golf Guide, *Where To play, Where To stay.*

Contents

Foreword
Mike Harris *(Golf Monthly)* 5

Golf Tours & Golfing Products 7

Golf Events 2011 9

Golfing Around Britain 10

How to use The Golf Guide 13

Golf in the West
Peter Godsiff 14

Golf in the South
Iain Pearson 66

Golf in the East
John H. Smith 139

Golf in the Midlands
Jennifer Prentice 183

Golf in the North
David Birtill 247

Golf in Scotland
Nick Rodger 337

Golf in Wales
Chris Smart 454

Golf in Ireland
Tony McGee 499

Clubs & Courses

ENGLAND
West 17
South 69
East 143
Midlands 185
North 249

SCOTLAND 343

WALES 457

IRELAND 507

THE ISLE OF MAN 555

CHANNEL ISLANDS 556

Driving Ranges 559

Index of Clubs and Courses 583

Index of Advertisers/Hotels 618

HolidayGuides.com

Foreword

by Mike Harris

Editor of *GOLF MONTHLY*

Not since the halcyon days of the 80s and 90s when Faldo, Lyle and Woosnam ruled the golfing globe, has homegrown golf looked quite so strong. As I write this introduction in the week before the US PGA Championship, half of the world's Top 10 are British or Irish and there are four more placed between number 10 and 25. Multiple wins have been chalked up on both sides of the Atlantic and at the moment few would bet against a European team, packed full of British and Irish golfers, recapturing the Ryder Cup at Celtic Manor this October.

The year started well when Ian Poulter battled through to victory in the WGC Accenture Matchplay (seeing off fellow Englishman Paul Casey in the final), Rhys Davies then announced himself on the scene with a win in Morocco, Lee Westwood yet again challenged down the stretch in a Major, this time at Augusta and three weeks later Rory McIlroy blew the field away with an incredible final round, 62, at Quail Hollow. Victories for Simon Khan at Wentworth and Luke Donald in Spain in consecutive weeks at the end of May signed off a sensational spring.

The first week of June saw Justin Rose triumph at one of the PGA Tour's biggest events, The Memorial Tournament – coming just a few hours after Graeme McDowell had won the Wales Open! And Lee Westwood made it back-to-back wins for the Brits on the PGA Tour as he won a play-off for the St Jude Classic.

Better was still to come when McDowell showed talent and determination at Pebble Beach in equal measure to win the US Open by cannily plotting his way round the course and seeing off Woods, Mickelson, Els and co. Justin Rose then won for the second time this season in the US, David Horsey chalked up his maiden win in Germany, and at St Andrews there were four British players in the top 10 with Westwood, McIlroy and Casey all further underlining their credentials as future Major Champions.

The first week of August saw Ross Fisher become the 10th different homegrown winner of the year when he was victorious in the Irish Open at Killarney.

The versatility of our top pros is rooted in the fact that as young amateur golfers they played such a wide variety of courses in the UK during their formative years.

They, and indeed all good players, understand the benefit to their game of teeing it up at as many different golf courses as possible. The shots and skills you need to tackle a coastal links are very different to those you'll need top get round a tree-lined parkland layout, for example. Learn how to tackle those different challenges and you will become a more complete golfer.

The good news for us British and Irish golfers is that we are truly spoilt by the fantastic variety of courses we have on our doorstep. There is something for every ability and, importantly in these cost conscious times, every budget.

To help you plan your next golfing away day or holiday, there is no better companion than **The Golf Guide,** *Where to Play, Where to Stay.*

Now in its 34th year of publication, **The Golf Guide,** *Where to Play, Where to Stay* includes comprehensive details on almost 2800 courses, along with information on local accommodation, providing the travelling golfer with all they need to know to play and stay anywhere in the UK and Ireland.

I hope, like me, you are inspired by the endless possibilities and that you will while away many happy hours planning your next golfing getaway.

Golf Tours & Products

Gleneagles is one of the most beautiful places in the world to play golf. The PGA Centenary Course is the venue for the 2014 Ryder Cup. We recommend Gleneagles to all our clients.

Morton Golf Holidays have been arranging golf packages for clients from all over the world for 20 years – contact us today and we will arrange the trip of a lifetime for your group.

Member of SIGTOA (Scottish Incoming Golf Tour Operators)
Member of GTS (Golf Tourism Scotland)
Tel: +44(0) 1577 866716
Fax: +44(0) 1577 866996
e-mail: info@mortongolf.com
www.mortongolf.com

putting your needs to the fore

Light, compact and very warm, these fantastic packs will keep you on top of your game all winter long!

Banish frozen fingers and keep playing in the worst that British weather can throw at you! Available from all good Pro shops.

Mycoal Warm Packs Ltd.
Tel: 023 8051 3300
Email: sales@mycoal.co.uk

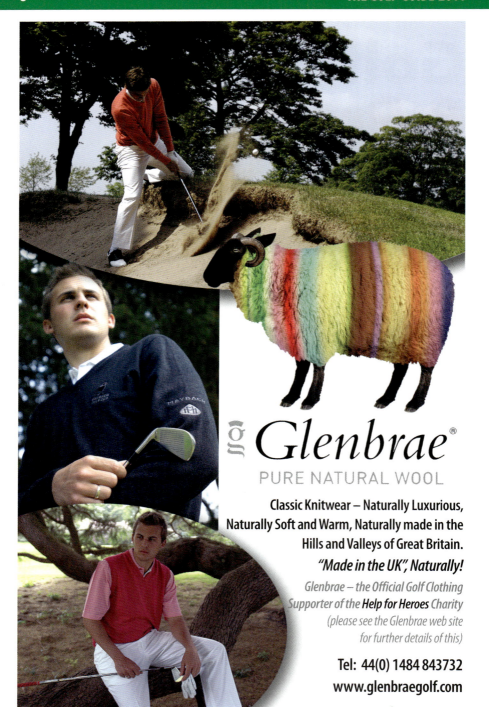

What's happening in Golf in 2011

APRIL

Scottish Boys' Championship
Dunbar — *April 11-16*

Peter McEvoy Trophy
Copt Heath — *April 13-14*

Lytham Trophy
Royal Lytham & St Anne's — *April 29-May 1*

MAY

Irish Open Stroke Play Championship
Royal Dublin — *May 6-8*

Welsh Open Stroke Play Championship
Saint Pierre — *May 20-22*

Scottish Open Stroke Play Championship
Blairgowrie, Lansdowne — *May 27-29*

JUNE

English Seniors' Championship
Northants County, Northants — *June 1-3*

St Andrews Links Trophy
St Andrews — *June 3-5*

Welsh Seniors' Championship
Aberdovey — *June 7-9*

Ladies' British Open Amateur Championship
Royal Portrush — *June 7-11*

British Amateur Championship
Hillside & Hesketh — *June 13-18*

Berkshire Trophy
Berkshire — *June 18-19*

Welsh Open Seniors' Championship
Rhuddlan — *June 21-23*

English Men's Stroke Play Championship (Brabazon Trophy)
Burnham & Berrow — *June 23-26*

Scottish Seniors' Championship
Irvine (Bogside) — *June 29-July 1*

JULY

Open Championship
Royal St George's — *July 14-17*

South of Ireland Open Championship
Lahinch — *July 23-27*

English Amateur Championship
Woburn — *July 25-30*

Scottish Amateur Championship
Western Gailes — *July 25-30*

Welsh Amateur Championship
Aberdovey — *July 26-30*

Ricoh Women's British Open 2011
Carnoustie — *July 28-31*

AUGUST

Boys' Home Internationals
Royal St Davids — *August 2-4*

British Seniors' Amateur Championship
Royal Portrush — *August 3-5*

Home Internationals
County Sligo — *August 10-12*

British Boys' Championship
Burnham & Berrow/ Enmore Park — *August 9-14*

SEPTEMBER

Walker Cup
Royal Aberdeen — *September 10-11*

Senior Home Internationals
Woodhall Spa — *September 13-15*

For full details of convenient accommodation near clubs and courses

www.holidayguides.com

Golfing around Britain

Where to Play and Where to Stay around the Golfing Regions

As this guide is produced early enough to be in the shops as a gift for Christmas, the result of the 2010 Ryder Cup was not known before we went to press, and therefore we were unable to include congratulations (or commiserations) to the European team. We did witness, however, a somewhat surprising result when the Open Championship returned to the 'Home of Golf', St Andrews. The runaway victor of the 2010 title was a relatively unknown South African Lodewicus Theodorus Oosthuizen (known as Louis). This helped to prove that unlike many other sports, golf still has the ability to throw up unexpected winners (Tom Watson just failing to turn the clock back the previous year was another example). It is almost impossible for anyone outside the top few favourites to win the FA Championship or Wimbledon but golf still has the ability to surprise and delight. In 2011 the 140th Open Championship will take place at Royal St George's golf club in Kent and we are all keen to see if a UK player will emulate Louis.

For the club player the handicap system in golf also provides a relatively even playing field for players of all ages and abilities. Where else could an average standard 15-handicap player have a competitive game against a top quality scratch golfer?

The Golf Guide, *Where to Play, Where to Stay* caters for every type of golfer including the professional, the club golfer, casual golfer, lady or junior. All will hopefully enjoy the comprehensive details of the wide variety of courses spread throughout the UK and Ireland. Using this guide it is possible to plan a trip taking in a wide variety of courses, including seaside links, parkland, moorland, hilly and flat, each with its own challenge, difficulties and enjoyments, stopping off overnight at the excellent accommodation recommended for golfers featured throughout the guide.

We have laid out the guide in a manner we hope will make finding the courses you are interested in as easy as possible. We have worked with the PGA Regional Professionals who have supplied articles about their regions, giving a summary of what is happening in the area and highlighting some of the accommodation and courses of particular interest to give you a brief idea of what is available. We have worked our way through the country starting across the south of the UK from the West Country to the South Region, then to the East and the Midlands, up to Northern England and following that with the countries of Wales, Scotland and Ireland.

At the back of the guide we have included

detailed indexes to make it as easy as possible to find any of the 2800 individual courses and the wide choice of hotels featured in this, the most comprehensive of guides.

All golfers can benefit from finding information on what courses are available in different areas, which ones will accept visitors and what the likely cost will be. Making full use of this guide can give all kinds of golfers, whether they play every day of the year or only on the occasional golfing holiday, the details they need to get the most enjoyment from the game.

Remember that golf need not be just a summer game, playing out of season can have many advantages. There is something special about teeing off on a crisp winter morning with the sun sparkling on the grass, at a time of year when hotels are often willing to offer discount rates for short breaks. Enjoy a challenging game of golf, followed by a relaxing evening spent in one of the many hotels featured in this guide, and where comfort and good food is par for the course.

No matter where you go, remember to take your copy of **The Golf Guide, *Where to Play, Where to Stay*** with you, and we would appreciate it if you could mention the guide when you contact Courses or Accommodation.

Henbury Golf Club, Bristol, Gloucestershire

Golfing National Regions

England & Wales

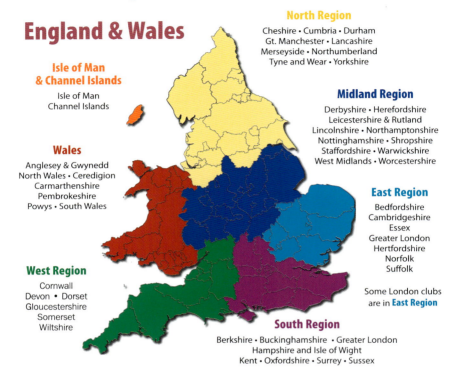

Isle of Man & Channel Islands
Isle of Man
Channel Islands

Wales
Anglesey & Gwynedd
North Wales • Ceredigion
Carmarthenshire
Pembrokeshire
Powys • South Wales

North Region
Cheshire • Cumbria • Durham
Gt. Manchester • Lancashire
Merseyside • Northumberland
Tyne and Wear • Yorkshire

Midland Region
Derbyshire • Herefordshire
Leicestershire & Rutland
Lincolnshire • Northamptonshire
Nottinghamshire • Shropshire
Staffordshire • Warwickshire
West Midlands • Worcestershire

East Region
Bedfordshire
Cambridgeshire
Essex
Greater London
Hertfordshire
Norfolk
Suffolk

Some London clubs are in **East Region**

West Region
Cornwall
Devon • Dorset
Gloucestershire
Somerset
Wiltshire

South Region
Berkshire • Buckinghamshire • Greater London
Hampshire and Isle of Wight
Kent • Oxfordshire • Surrey • Sussex

Scotland

Borders • Central • Dumfries and Galloway
Fife • Highland • Lothians
Orkney and Shetland
Strathclyde • Tayside
Western Isles

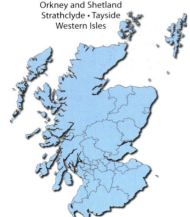

Northern Ireland

Antrim • Armagh • Co. Down
Fermanagh • Londonderry • Tyrone

Republic of Ireland

Carlow • Cavan
Clare • Cork
Donegal • Dublin
Galway • Kerry
Kildare • Kilkenny
Laois • Leitrim
Longford • Louth
Mayo • Meath
Monaghan
Offaly • Roscommon
Sligo • Tipperary
Waterford • Westmeath
Wexford • Wicklow

How to use this Golf Guide

The Golf Guide, *Where to Play, Where to Stay* contains up to date basic information on every course (as far as we know) in Britain and Northern Ireland plus clubs in the Irish Republic. Details are provided by the clubs themselves.

The guide carries entries from hotels, guest houses and other accommodation convenient to specific courses or areas. These are generally 'paid' entries and usually follow a recommendation from a club.

The Golf Guide, *Where to Play, Where to Stay* in association with Golf Monthly, is usually available for sale in golf clubs through the Professional and/or the Secretary, as well as bookshops etc.

• Golf Course Information

For virtually every course you will find the following details, updated annually:

1. Name, address and telephone number.   2. Location.   3. Brief description.

4. Number of holes, length and Standard Scratch Score.   5. Green fees.

6. Details of facilities for visitors – individuals, groups and societies.

7. Name and telephone number of the Professional and the Secretary.

The accuracy of details published depends on the response of the clubs and to our best knowledge is correct at the time of going to press (September 2010). Where entry details have not been confirmed an asterisk (*) is shown.

• Choosing a Course

The golf clubs and courses are listed alphabetically by nearest town or village within the appropriate region and county section for England, Scotland, Wales, Ireland, the Isle of Man and the Channel Islands. We have chosen to classify by place-name rather than club or course name since this seems more straightforward and recognisable to the majority.

If you want to find a club or course by its name, you should simply refer to the Index where you will see the page number of the listing. In each entry the name of the club or course is always shown in bold type after the place-name heading.

• Accommodation

Most of the accommodation advertised has been recommended by the local golf club, and the entries are placed as near a particular club or course as possible. A full index is provided.

The location details supplied with each entry should get you there and if you are in any doubt at all you should ask directions from the club itself.

Please mention **The Golf Guide,** *Where to Play, Where to Stay* when you make a hotel booking or play at courses after using our guide.

Golf in the West

Peter Godsiff

Cornwall • Devon • Dorset
Gloucestershire • Somerset • Wiltshire

Dartmouth Golf & Country Club, Devon – hotel across the 18th green

After a two-year postponement because of the recession, the West Country should have its own European Tour event again at St Mellion this year. The English Open is scheduled for August and Crown Golf, owners of the complex first developed by the Bond Brothers, is confident sufficient finance will be in place to stage one of only two Tour events in England on the championship course that Jack Nicklaus built back in 1990.

Since the last tour event 15 years ago the resort in Cornwall, on the doorstep of Plymouth, has undertaken many changes. St Mellion International Resort unveiled the final phase of redevelopment with the official opening of the £2 million revamped Kernow course last year. The £20 million development includes a new hotel, and unrivalled leisure, spa and meeting facilities. It is also offering deals to attract visiting golfers.

The Benson and Hedges International Open had been played over the original course, but was soon established on the first Nicklaus course in England and was staged from 1990 to 1995.

Cornwall, the favourite destination for so many holidaymakers, also boasts golf resorts at Trevose, China Fleet, Lanhydrock, Bowood Park at Camelford and Trethorne, while Bude offers fantastic golfing deals and the links course is perfect for winter golf breaks.

Dartmouth Golf and Country Club opened in 1991 and is now a quality 27-hole complex four miles inland from the famous naval town that attracts thousands of visitors. It is the hub of the South Devon Golf Tour portfolio, allowing golfers on short breaks to play eight special and contrasting courses. Visitors play on the Championship course at Dartmouth and have unlimited use of the par-33 nine-hole course. They then have the choice of two rounds at Bigbury, Dainton Park, Churston, China Fleet, The Warren at Dawlish or Bovey Castle at Moretonhampstead, where the up-market hotel and championship golf course attract patrons from all over the world. The golf tours are based at Dartmouth and the hotel, golf and leisure resort is the perfect base to explore everything South Devon has to offer.

Woodbury Park has now become the new home to the PGA West Region. The hotel and leisure facilities and two golf courses, originally developed by Nigel Mansell, have become an impressive feature in East Devon. Other stay-and-play venues in Devon include Ashbury, the holiday complex near Okehampton that caters for everyone and offers unlimited golf on several courses, and Teign Valley, under new ownership.

Serious golfers head for the historic links at Burnham and Berrow, Saunton, Royal North Devon and St Enodoc. All regularly stage the major amateur championships. This year the Brabazon Trophy and British Boys' Championships are being held at Burnham.

But many other lesser-known clubs demand attention and are playable at most attractive rates. Brean, with its new holes, and Taunton Vale are worth a try.

The centre for golf in Dorset is the Bournemouth-Poole area. As one of the favoured holiday destinations, hotels are in abundance. So are golf courses - from the long-established Big Three, Ferndown, Parkstone and Broadstone, to

5th hole, Tewkesbury Park, Gloucestershire

probably the best two publicly-owned (but now privately-run) courses in the country at Meyrick Park and Queens Park. The favoured destination for societies and travelling golfers is the Dorset Golf and Country Club, in the heart of the county near Wareham. Stay in a Scandinavian-type lodge or the functional hotel and play as long as you wish over the 27 holes.

The Georgian city of Bath and, 12 miles away, Bristol, the gateway to the West, are served by two dozen golf courses and every conceivable type of accommodation is available to suit all price ranges.

There are some classic parkland designs in Wiltshire, among them the prestigious Manor House Hotel Golf Club at Castle Combe, and Bowood, created by Dave Thomas, and now offering attractive deals in the new hotel. Wrag Barn is the favoured course in the Swindon area while High Post, near Salisbury, is viewed by many as the county's major course.

Moving towards the Midlands, Bristol and Clifton and Long Ashton are viewed as premier courses in Bristol while Thornbury Golf Centre not only offers 11 bedrooms but also two courses and a driving range. Stinchcombe Hill in the heart of Gloucestershire is nearby.

Whether travelling into or out of the West there is an abundance of both hotels and golf. Hotels with golf courses stand out in the Cotswold area of Gloucestershire. Tewkesbury Park, an 82-room hotel has an 18-hole and six-hole course, while Puckrup Hall is just three miles away. The Ramada Gloucester Hotel and Country Club – probably just as famous for its dry-ski slope – is a perfect venue, with 97 rooms and a quality golf course.

There are so many places to stay and play in this stunning region, the country's favourite holiday destination. Just try it.

Cornwall

BODMIN. **Lanhydrock Hotel & Golf Club,** Lostwithiel Road, Bodmin PL30 5AQ (01208 262570; Fax: 01208 262579). *Location*: 1½ miles outside Bodmin on B3269. Parkland with generous tees and greens, easy walking, with many natural water features. 18 holes, 6100 yards, 5600 metres, Par 70, S.S.S. 70. Practice range. *Green Fees*: information not available. One week unlimited golf pass available. *Eating facilities*: all day catering available in bar. Bistro open for lunch and dinner. *Visitors*: welcome, booking advised. Pro shop, golf buggies available. 44-bedroom luxury hotel, conference facilities. *Society Meetings*: welcome by arrangement, private suite available. Professional: Richard O'Hanlon. Manager: Graham Bond.*
e-mail: info@lanhydrockhotel.com
website: www.lanhydrockhotel.com

BUDE. **Bude and North Cornwall Golf Club,** Burn View, Bude EX23 8DA (01288 352006; Fax: 01288 356855). *Location*: seaside links course situated in the centre of the town adjacent to beaches. 18 holes, 6006 yards. S.S.S. 70. Practice net and grounds. Buggy hire. *Green Fees*: weekdays £30.00 per day; weekends £30.00 per round. *Eating facilities*: restaurant and bar snacks. *Visitors*: welcome without reservation. Snooker, billiards and pool. *Society Meetings*: catered for by bookings. Professional: Mark Yeo (01288 353635). Secretary: Mrs Pauline Ralph (01288 352006).

CAMBORNE. **Tehidy Park Golf Club,** Cot Road, Camborne TR14 0HH (Tel & Fax: 01209 842208). *Location*: A30 via Blackwater and Camborne by-passes to sign for Portreath. Parkland, wooded, lakes. 18 holes, 6241 yards. S.S.S. 71. *Green Fees*: weekdays £30.00, weekends £40.00. *Eating facilities*: bar snacks, à la carte restaurant except Mondays. *Visitors:* welcome with Handicap Certificate. *Society Meetings:* by arrangement; early booking essential. Catering Manager: M&K Hoyle (01209 842557). Professional: J. Lamb (01209 842914). Secretary/Manager Ian Veale (Tel & Fax: 01209 842208).
secretary-manager@tehidyparkgolfclub.co.uk
website: www.tehidyparkgolfclub.co.uk

CAMELFORD. **Bowood Park Hotel & Golf Club,** Lanteglos, Camelford PL32 9RF (01840 213017; Fax: 01840 212622). *Location:* M4, M5, A30, A39 through Camelford, turn right to Boscastle/Tintagel before BP garage, then left after Park Lane Motors. Well groomed, parkland course set in 230 acres of rolling hills and woodland with 26 ponds and lakes. 18 hole, par 72. Covered driving range and Golf School. *Green Fees:* price on application. *Eating facilities:* full restaurant and bar facilities. *Visitors:* welcome. Large, well-stocked Pro Shop. Buggies for hire. Hotel accommodation available in 31 spacious en suite rooms, most with golf views. *Society Meetings:* society and corporate days welcome by arrangement. Professional: Chris Kaminski. Director of Golf: Josh Greenaway.
e-mail: golf@bowood-park.co.uk
website: www.bowood-park.co.uk

CARLYON BAY. **Carlyon Bay Hotel Golf Course,** Beach Road, Carlyon Bay, St Austell PL25 3RD (Hotel: 01726 812304; Golf Club: 01726 814250). *Location:* St Austell A390. Clifftop course running into parkland. 18 holes, 6597 yards. S.S.S. 71. Six acre practice ground. *Green Fees:* information not available. *Eating facilities*: bar open 11am to 11pm, food available during high season 10am to 9pm Tuesday to Friday, 10am to 6pm Saturday to Monday. *Visitors:* welcome, must phone Professional for starting times. Accommodation available in 4 star hotel. *Society Meetings:* catered for by arrangement. Professional: Mark Rowe (01726 814228). Director of Golf: Paul Martin (01726 814250).
e-mail: golf@carlyonbay.com
website: www.carlyonbay.com

THE APPEARANCE OF AN ASTERISK (*) AT THE END OF A CLUB OR COURSE ENTRY INDICATES THAT UP-TO-DATE INFORMATION HAS NOT BEEN SUPPLIED

CORNWALL'S GREATEST GOLFING GETAWAY

A luxurious hotel with panoramic bay views. Superb facilities and award-winning cuisine. An all-new Health & Beauty Spa. And right next door, a spectacular private 18 hole clifftop course, free to hotel guests. It can only be The Carlyon Bay Hotel, Cornwall's greatest golfing getaway. Call 01726 812 304 today.

CARLYON BAY HOTEL
SPA & GOLF RESORT

18 Cornwall / WEST REGION — THE GOLF GUIDE 2011

Play golf at Falmouth Golf Club!
Situated on the cliff tops of Falmouth Bay, this beautiful location offers glorious views whilst you enjoy the finest parkland golf on the South Cornwall coast. With a par of 71 and a length of just under 6000 yards, the course is hard to beat.
After playing, what could be better than recounting your game over a good meal and a bottle of wine. Falmouth Clubhouse offers traditional British food at its best, in a friendly and congenial atmosphere.
For Corporate Days or membership please call Steve Burrows on 01326 314296.
To book a round, telephone Nick Rogers, PGA Professional, on 01326 311262 or contact Falmouth Golf Club Swanpool Road, Falmouth TR11 5BQ

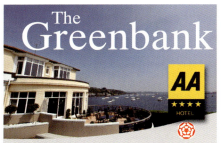

Here at the Greenbank Hotel we like to do things differently.
Overlooking the Fal estuary the setting is truly enviable, our hotel staff superbly trained and as anybody who has lived beside the sea will know, the fresh seafood is sublime! Cornwall is renowned for its feel good vibe and fresh produce, and a short stay or holiday at our luxury Four Star hotel will give you the break you deserve.

The Greenbank Hotel, Harbourside, Falmouth, Cornwall TR11 2SR
Telephone: +44 (0) 1326 312440
www.greenbank-hotel.co.uk

FALMOUTH. **Budock Vean Golf and Country House Hotel,** Near Mawnan Smith, Falmouth TR11 5LG (01326 250288; Fax: 01326 250892). *Location:* near Mawnan Smith, Falmouth – area of Helford River. 9 holes/18 tees, 5227 yards. Par 68. S.S.S. 65. *Green Fees:* information not available. *Eating facilities:* two bars, two restaurants, lunchtime bar menu. *Visitors:* daily only for outside visitors who are most welcome, but must have Handicap Certificate and book start time. Hotel accommodation. Secretary: D. McFarlane (01326 252102). Golf Manager: A. Ramsden.*

FALMOUTH. **Falmouth Golf Club,** Swanpool Road, Falmouth TR11 5BQ (01326 311262 / 314296; Fax: 01326 317783). *Location:* quarter of a mile west of Swanpool Beach, Falmouth, on the road to Maenporth. Magnificent course with stunning sea and coastal views. 18 holes, 5903 yards. S.S.S. 70, Par 71. Driving range. *Green Fees:* please ring for rates. *Eating facilities:* excellent catering and bar all year round. *Visitors:* welcome at all times, except during major competitions. *Society Meetings:* always welcome. Professional: Nick Rogers. Director: Steve Burrows.

HELSTON. **Helston Golf,** Redruth Road, Wendron, Helston TR13 0LX (Golf: 01326 572228; Restaurant: 01326 565103). *Location:* one mile out of Helston on B3297 Redruth Road. Parkland course. 18 holes, 2000 yards. S.S.S. 54. Nets and practice green. *Green Fees:* £8.50 per 18 holes, day card £11.50. Membership £165 per year. *Eating facilities:* licensed bar with meals and snacks. *Visitors:* welcome; family course, all ages welcome, pay and play; playable all weather. Club and ball hire £1.50. *Society Meetings:* all welcome, please book. Proprietor: A. Burns.

HELSTON. **Mullion Golf Club,** Cury, Helston TR12 7BP (01326 241176). *Location:* from Helston on the A3083 past Culdrose Air Station, take first right past roundabout; signposted three miles. Cliff top and links. Indoor Golf Teaching Academy. 18 holes, 6083 yards. S.S.S. 70. *Green Fees:* information not available. *Eating facilities:* bar and catering available each day. Caterers: (01326 241231). *Visitors:* welcome, with Handicap only. *Society Meetings:* by prior arrangement. Professional: Ian Harris (01326 241176). Secretary/Treasurer: G. Fitter (01326 240685).*

HELSTON. **RNAS Culdrose Golf Club,** Royal Naval Air Station, Helston TR12 7RH (01326 552413). *Location:* A3083 one mile from Helston towards Lizard. Flat parkland course built around part of the airfield. 18 holes, 6132 yards. S.S.S. 70. Large practice area. *Visitors:* members only. President: RNAS Culdrose.*

Please mention THE GOLF GUIDE when you enquire about clubs or accommodation

THE GOLF GUIDE 2011 — WEST REGION / Cornwall

LAUNCESTON. Launceston Golf Club, St Stephen's, Launceston PL15 8HF (01566 773442). *Location:* one mile north of town on Bude road (B3254). Parkland. 18 holes, 6385 yards. S.S.S. 70. *Green Fees:* weekdays £30.00 per round, £40.00 per day. 2010 rates (subject to review). *Eating facilities:* available. *Visitors:* welcome. *Society Meetings:* catered for. Professional: J. Tozer (01566 775359). Secretary: P. M. Jones (01566 773442; Fax: 01566 777506).
e-mail: secretary@launcestongolfclub.co.uk
website: www.launcestongolfclub.co.uk

LAUNCESTON. Trethorne Golf Club, Kennards House, Launceston PL15 8QE (01566 86903). *Location:* 200 yards off A30. Set in a picturesque valley with mature trees and water. 18 holes, 6432 yards. S.S.S. 68/69/71. Driving range, putting green. *Green Fees:* from £17.00. *Eating facilities:* bar, lounge bar and restaurant seating 100. *Visitors:* welcome, please ring for tee times. Accommodation available in 30 en suite bedrooms at the Club. Driving range available. *Society Meetings:* welcome. Groups of 12 or more. Professional: Wayne Basford. Proprietor: Jon Grainger.
e-mail: reservations@trethornegolfclub.com
website: www.trethornegolfclub.com

LOOE. Looe Golf Club, Bindown, Looe PL13 1PX (01503 240239; Fax: 01503 240864). *Location:* three miles east of Looe on A387. Downland/parkland, panoramic views over countryside to sea; designed by Harry Vardon. 18 holes, 5940 yards. S.S.S. 69. Large practice ground. *Green Fees:* information not available. *Eating facilities:* catering available. *Visitors:* most welcome, phone for tee reservations. Clubs, buggies and electric trolleys for hire. Golf tuition available. *Society Meetings:* welcome by arrangement. Professional: Barrie Evans. Secretary: Tony Day.
e-mail: enquiries@looegolfclub.co.uk
website: www.looegolfclub.co.uk

LOSTWITHIEL. Lostwithiel Hotel, Golf and Country Club, Lower Polscoe, Lostwithiel PL22 0HQ (01208 873550; Fax: 01208 873479). *Location:* off A390, Lostwithiel. Parkland course. 18 holes, 5984 yards. S.S.S. 71. Driving range and practice area. *Green Fees:* £34.00 to £40.00. *Eating facilities:* bar and restaurant. *Visitors:* welcome by prior arrangement. 27-bedroom 3 Star Hotel. *Society Meetings:* welcome by prior arrangement.
e-mail: reception@golf-hotel.co.uk
website: www.golf-hotel.co.uk

NEWQUAY. Newquay Golf Club, Tower Road, Newquay TR7 1LT (01637 874354). *Location:* 400 yards from Newquay Town Centre. Gently undulating seaside course running parallel to the beach and open to wind. Breathtaking views. 18 holes, 6155 yards, S.S.S. 69. *Green Fees:* £31.00 Mon-Frid, £36.00 weekends and Bank Holidays. *Eating facilities:* full catering facilities available. *Visitors:* welcome at all times, please telephone. *Society Meetings:* catered for, restricted availabilty at weekends. Saturdays and Sundays. Professional: J.R. Cant (01637 874830). Secretary: J. Gilbert (01637 874354; Fax: 01637 874066).

NEWQUAY. Treloy Golf Club, Newquay TR7 4JN (01637 878554). *Location:* five minutes' drive from Newquay on the A3059 Newquay to St. Columb Major road. Parkland. 9 hole Executive golf course. First of its kind in Cornwall – sculptured greens, American Pencross grass, extensive mouldings and bunkers. 9 holes, 2143 yards, 1955 metres. Par 32. Practice green. *Green Fees:* information not available. *Eating facilities:* available, bar. *Visitors:* welcome. *Society Meetings:* welcome. Changing facilities, golf shop, club hire and buggy hire. Secretary: Jane Paull.*

For full details of convenient accommodation near clubs and courses
www.holidayguides.com

- Par 71 with tree-lined fairways and water hazards
- Specialists in Group Bookings
- Preferential Green Fees at other local courses
- Free-draining USGA greens • 30 en suite rooms
- Big-screen SKY TV & Ten Pin Bowling • Late Bar
- Breaks from £99.00 for 2 nights, unlimited golf, Dinner, Bed & Breakfast

01566 86903 for further details
Trethorne Golf Club
Kennards House, Launceston PL15 8QE
www.trethornegolfclub.com
reservations@trethornegolfclub.com

20 Cornwall / WEST REGION — THE GOLF GUIDE 2011

stayplay

www.tregloshotel.com www.merlingolfcourse.co.uk

TREGLOS
CONSTANTINE BAY
CORNWALL
Tel: 01841 520727

MERLIN
GOLF & COUNTRY CLUB
MAWGAN PORTH
CORNWALL
Self-catering available
Tel: 01841 540222

NEWQUAY. **Holywell Bay Golf,** Holywell Bay, Near Newquay TR8 5PW (01637 832916). *Location*: take A3075 out of Newquay then follow signs to Holywell Bay and Cubert. Par 3 Links course. 18 holes, 2784 yards. Pitch and putt. "Best in Cornwall". Open 7 days a week, all year round. *Green Fees*: information not available. *Eating facilities*: bar and club house open April to October. *Visitors*: welcome at all times. Accommodation at Trevornick Holiday Park. *Society Meetings*: all welcome, ring for special prices. Contact: Jack Johnson (01637 832916).
website: www.holywellbaygolf.co.uk

NEWQUAY. **Merlin Golf Club and Driving Range,** St Eval Road, Mawgan Porth, Newquay TR8 4DN (01841 540222; Fax: 01841 541031). *Location*: on coast road between Newquay and Padstow, after Mawgan Porth take St Eval Road, golf course on right. Heathland, fairly flat course. 18 holes, 6210 yards. S.S.S. 71. Covered driving range. *Green Fees*: £20.00-£25.00 for 18 holes. *Eating facilities*: catering and bar all year round. *Visitors*: very welcome, some restrictions during club competitions. Buggies, carts and clubs for hire. Luxury self-catering apartments available all year. *Society Meetings*: very welcome. Secretary: Richard Burrough.

NEWQUAY near. **Carvynick Golf and Country Club,** Carvynick, Summercourt, Near Newquay (01872 510716; Fax: 01872 510172). *Location*: turn off the A30 at Summercourt then take B3058 towards Newquay. Half a mile on left. Parkland and wooded course. 9 holes, 1246 yards. S.S.S. 27. *Green Fees*: information not available. *Eating facilities*: at 16th century village inn and restaurant. *Visitors*: welcome all year. Sauna, gym, indoor swimming pool and badminton court. Luxury holiday cottages available.*
e-mail: info@carvynick.co.uk
website: www.carvynick.co.uk

PADSTOW. **Trevose Golf and Country Club,** Constantine Bay, Padstow PL28 8JB (01841 520208; Fax: 01841 521057). *Location*: M5 to A30 to A39 to B3274. At St Merryn turn right for golf club. Links course, superb test of golf in lovely coastal setting. H. Colt designed Championship course 18 holes, 7068 yards. S.S.S. 73. 9 hole full length course (Par 35) and one 9 hole short course (Par 29). *Green Fees*: information not available. *Eating facilities*: Club house with bar and restaurant providing à la carte catering facilities. *Visitors*: welcome if arranged by telephone beforehand; Handicap Certificate required. Accommodation, three tennis courts, heated swimming pool in summer. *Society Meetings*: welcome if arrangements have been made. Head Professional: Gary Lenaghan (01841 520261). Secretary: Nick Gammon (01841 520733).
e-mail: info@trevose-gc.co.uk
website: www.trevose-gc.co.uk

Please mention THE GOLF GUIDE when you enquire about clubs or accommodation

- Suitable for all ages and abilities
- Open 7 days a week, rain or shine
- Spectacular views overlooking Gull Rocks
- No dress code
- Club and trolley hire
- Groups welcome

Holywell Bay,
Newquay,
Cornwall TR8 5PW
Tel: 01637 832916

Holywell Bay Golf

www.holywellbaygolf.co.uk

THE GOLF GUIDE 2011   WEST REGION / Cornwall   21

PENZANCE. **Cape Cornwall Golf & Country Club,** Cape Cornwall, St Just, Penzance TR19 7NL (Tel & Fax: 01736 788611). *Location:* A30 to Land's End, A3071 from Penzance to St Just, turn left at clock tower to Cape Cornwall. Cliff top course with spectacular coastal views. 18 holes, 5650 yards. S.S.S. 69, Par 69. Practice putting green and golf area. *Green Fees:* information not available. *Eating facilities:* restaurant open daily; extensive à la carte evening menu Tues-Sat evenings incl. *Visitors:* welcome anytime. Accommodation available on site. Leisure facilities: gymnasium, indoor heated swimming pool, sauna, tanning suite. Golf shop now permanently on site. *Society Meetings:* welcome; prior booking advisable. PGA Professional: Scott Richards. Resort Director: Steven Brown.*
e-mail: info@capecornwall.com
website: www.capecornwall.com

PENZANCE **Praa Sands Golf & Country Club,** Germoe Crossroads, Near Penzance TR20 9TQ (01736 763445; Fax: 01736 763399). *Location:* midway between Helston and Penzance on A394. Parkland - beautiful sea views from all holes. 9 holes, 4050 yards. S.S.S. 60 men, 65 ladies, Par 62. Putting green and net. *Green Fees:* information not provided. Telephone for tee times. *Eating facilities:* restaurant, bar snacks. *Visitors:* welcome at all times without Handicap Certificate except Sunday mornings. Must be suitably attired. Clubs and trolleys for hire. *Society Meetings:* catered for by arrangement. Secretary: Mrs Anna Harry. Proprietors: The Haulfryn Group.

PERRANPORTH. **Perranporth Golf Club,** Budnic Hill, Perranporth TR6 0AB. Seaside links course overlooking Perranporth and beach. 18 holes, 6296 yards. S.S.S. 72. Par 72. Practice green. *Green Fees*: information not available. *Eating facilities*: lunch, dinner and breakfast. *Visitors*: welcome without reservation. Accommodation and buggies available. *Society Meetings*: catered for with advance notice; concessionary rates. Professional: D. Michell (01872 572140). Secretary: David Mugford (01872 572454). website: www.perranporthgolfclub.co.uk

www.holidayguides.com
for accommodation near golf clubs

It's more than just golf...

THE COURSES
• Championship Course - 7068 yards - Par 72 - SS 73.
• Nine hole Headland Course over 3106 yards - par 35.
• Nine hole short Course - excellent test and ideal for beginners.

THE ACCOMMODATION
• New for 2010, the state-of-the-art 'Fairways' apartments
• Self-Catering Apartments, Bungalows & Flats
• Free WiFi - Broadband internet in all rooms

THE FACILITIES
• Restaurant & Bar   • Tennis Courts & Heated Pool
• Therapy Room   • Games & Snooker Rooms
• Golf Shop & Boutique   • Children's Play Area

Call us on: **01841 520208**

www.trevose-gc.co.uk
Trevose Golf & Country Club, Constantine Bay, Padstow, North Cornwall, PL28 8JB

REDRUTH. **Radnor Golf and Leisure,** Radnor Road, Treleigh, Redruth TR16 5EL (01209 211059). *Location*: two miles north east of Redruth, signposted from A3047 at Treleigh and North Country crossroads. Purpose-built Par 3 - interesting layout. 9 holes/18 tees, 1312 yards. S.S.S. 52. Covered driving range. *Green Fees:* information not available. *Eating facilities:* Bar/Restaurant. *Visitors:* welcome. Indoor ski training machine. Small touring caravan site and static holiday homes. Professional: John Rule.*

Perranporth Golf Club
The Clubhouse
Budnic Hill, Perranporth TR6 0AB
Tel: 01872 572454
Email: secretary@perranporthgolfclub.co.uk
www.perranporthgolfclub.co.uk

This really is the perfect location for your golf breaks or golf holidays in Cornwall...

A sensational championship course, luxury mobile homes and excellent food – what better way is there to enjoy a golfing break away from it all? Nestled within the dunes of one of Cornwall's finest links courses our select site comprising just twelve luxury mobile homes assures you of the peace and quiet you deserve in this, the perfect getaway location.

By providing that 'home-from-home' feel we know that our spacious luxury homes (which provide either six- or eight-berth accommodation) will help you feel at ease from the moment you arrive. And with a well equipped kitchen, colour TV and roomy and tastefully furnished living area, you can be assured that our holiday accommodation is just perfect for golfing and non-golfing couples, groups and families alike.

22 Cornwall / WEST REGION — THE GOLF GUIDE 2011

St Mellion International Resort

- Championship Nicklaus Course
- Newly redeveloped Kernow Course
- Driving Range & Practice Grounds
- 4 Star Hotel Accommodation
- Multiple Dining Outlets
- Extensive Leisure Facilities
- Luxury Elemis Spa

www.st-mellion.co.uk
01579 352001

St Mellion

ST AUSTELL. **St Austell Golf Club,** Tregongeeves, Tregongeeves Lane, St Austell PL26 7DS (01726 74756; Fax: 01726 71978). *Location:* one mile west of St Austell on A390 St Austell to Truro road. Parkland course. 18 holes, 6091 yards. S.S.S. 69. Floodlit driving range. *Green Fees:* telephone for details. *Eating facilities:* bar and restaurant – meals can be arranged. *Visitors:* welcome with reservation. *Society Meetings:* catered for weekdays by arrangement. Professional: Tony Pitts (01726 62681). Secretary: Peter Clemo (01726 74756; Fax: 01726 71978).

ST IVES. **Tregenna Castle Hotel Golf and Country Club,** St Ives TR26 2DE (01736 797381). *Location:* on the main road between Carbis Bay and St Ives, half a mile from town centre. Parkland, 73 acres of grounds with beautiful sea views overlooking St Ives Harbour and Atlantic coast – a very tricky course. 14 holes, 1846 yards. Par 42. *Green Fees:* information not available. *Visitors:* welcome. Accommodation available in the hotel if booked. *Society Meetings:* welcome.*

ST IVES. **West Cornwall Golf Club,** Church Lane, Lelant, St Ives TR26 3DZ (Tel & Fax: 01736 753401). *Location:* two miles from St Ives, in village of Lelant; take Church Road, course situated approximately quarter of a mile past Lelant Church. True links course - wonderful coastal views. 18 holes, 5884 yards. S.S.S. 69. Practice ground, putting green. *Green Fees:* £40.00 Wed and Sat, £35.00 all other days. Five Day ticket £125.00, Seven Day ticket £150.00. *Eating facilities:* bar with bar menus and à la carte dining room. *Visitors:* must be golf club members with Handicap Certificate. Trolleys for hire. Home of "Long" Jim Barnes, first American Professional Champ 1916, Open Champion USA 1921, British Open Champion 1925 and World Champion of Golf 1921–1925. *Society Meetings:* welcome, written application required. Professional: Jason Broadway (01736 753177). Secretary: Gareth Evans (01736 753401).
e-mail: secretary@westcornwallgolfclub.co.uk
website: www.westcornwallgolfclub.co.uk

SALTASH. **China Fleet Country Club,** Saltash PL12 6LJ (01752 848668). *Location*: one mile from Tamar Bridge. Parkland course with beautiful river views. 18 holes, 6551 yards, S.S.S. 72. 28 bay floodlit driving range. *Green Fees:* information on request. *Eating facilities:* bars and bar meals, full restaurant facilities, coffee shop. *Visitors:* welcome, Handicap Certificate required. Other facilities include large Pro Shop, full leisure facilities and 40 apartments. *Society Meetings:* welcome, minimum number 12 persons. Professional: Dominic Rehaag (01752 854665; Fax: 01752 848456). Golf Manager: Linda Goddard (01752 854657; Fax: 01752 848456).

SALTASH. **St Mellion International Resort,** Near Saltash PL12 6SD (01579 351351; Fax: 01579 350537). *Location*: A38 to Saltash, A388 from Saltash to Callington. Parkland. Nicklaus Course: 18 holes, 6651 yards, par 72, S.S.S. 72 - designer Jack Nicklaus. Venue of the Benson & Hedges International Open 1990-1995 and host to the English Open from 2011. Old Course: 18 holes, 5782 yards, par 68. S.S.S. 68 - designer J. Hamilton-Stutt. Practice range. *Green Fees:* information not available. *Eating facilities:* Bewdern Brasserie and An Boesti Restaurant. *Visitors:* welcome at all times. Leisure club includes two indoor swimming pools, gymnasium, dance studio, sauna, steam room, spa pool, sports hall, creche. Skincare and spa centre. Founder member of the Premier Golf Clubs of Great Britain. *Society Meetings:* welcome. Accommodation available in Hotel overlooking 18th fairway, and in Fairway Lodges in the grounds. Head Professional: David Moon (01579 352002).*
e-mail: stmellion-golfdays@crown-golf.co.uk
website: www.st-mellion.co.uk

TORPOINT. **Whitsand Bay Hotel Golf Club,** Portwrinkle, Torpoint PL11 3BU (01503 230276). *Location*: on coast six miles from Torpoint. Clifftop course. 18 holes, 5770 yards. S.S.S. 68. *Green Fees:* information not available. *Eating facilities:* hotel. *Visitors:* welcome at all times with Handicap Certificate. Swimming/leisure complex. *Society Meetings:* catered for and hotel accommodation arranged on application to hotel (01503 230276; Fax 01503 230329). Professional: S. Dougan (01503 230778). Secretary: J. M. Fisher (01752 814171).*
e-mail: whitsandbayhotel@btinternet.com

THE APPEARANCE OF AN ASTERISK (*) AT THE END OF A CLUB OR COURSE ENTRY INDICATES THAT UP-TO-DATE INFORMATION HAS NOT BEEN SUPPLIED

St Mellion Golf Breaks

St Mellion Golf Breaks is the number one provider of self-catering golf breaks at St Mellion in south east Cornwall. Stay in spacious luxury accommodation in stunning surroundings and enjoy a fantastic deal at the same time. Our breaks include...

- luxurious and spacious accommodation (some with course views).
- Great value golf starting at £60ppp.
- Use of superb leisure facilities.
- We can accommodate from 2-20.
- One all in price with nothing extra to pay.

Contact us on 01579 383917
or info@stmelliongolfbreaks.co.uk
www.stmelliongolfbreaks.co.uk

View of the Nicklaus 12th from Fairways Cottage on the Oakridge Estate

CUTKIVE WOOD HOLIDAY LODGES

You can easily reach 25 golf courses from our peaceful family-owned country estate. Set on the edge of bluebell woods with lovely rural views, there are six well-equipped cedar-clad lodges and a practice golf field. Relax and enjoy yourself in this tranquil and idyllic setting. There is so much to see and do for all the family – memorable beaches, wonderful coasts, walking the moors, inspiring gardens and Eden, theme attractions, historic gems. Dogs welcome. Ideally situated to enjoy golf, coast and country holidays whatever the time of year.

St Ive, Liskeard, Cornwall PL14 3ND • Tel: 01579 362216
www.cutkivewood.co.uk • e-mail: holidays@cutkivewood.co.uk

Looking for accommodation near golf clubs?, then visit
www.holidayguides.com
for where to stay when playing golf around the regions

Cornwall / WEST REGION

POLLAUGHAN COTTAGES
Within easy reach of some of Cornwall's best Golf Courses

An award winning escape, hidden away in the beautiful Roseland Peninsula in a peaceful rural setting yet minutes from some of the best sandy beaches in Cornwall. Children just love it here and all are welcome to join the daily feeding of our friendly animals.
You'll find our cottages beautifully presented, family friendly, yet really relaxing with stunning views and safe gardens.
Oh... and then there's the home cooked Aga meals delivered to your door.
All Weather Tennis Court.
Green Tourism Gold.
Valerie & Tim Penny, Pollaughan Cottages, Portscatho, Truro TR2 5EH
Tel : 01872 580150
holidays@pollaughan.co.uk
www.pollaughan.co.uk

TRURO. **Killiow Golf Club & Driving Range,** Kea, Near Truro TR3 6AG (01872 270246; Fax: 01872 240915). *Location:* take A39 Truro to Falmouth road, turn right into club at first Playing Place roundabout (2½ miles). 18 holes, Par 72. All-weather floodlit driving range open 8am to 9pm weekdays (weekends until 6pm). *Green Fees:* information not available. *Eating facilities:* bar and restaurant. *Visitors:* only restricted by competitions; phone for availability. Secretary: John Crowson (01872 266876).
e-mail: info@killiow.co.uk
sec@killiow.co.uk
website: www.killiowgolf.co.uk

TRURO. **Truro Golf Club,** Treliske, Truro TR1 3LG (01872 272640). *Location:* one mile west of Truro on A390 to Redruth. Undulating parkland with magnificent views. 18 holes, 5306 yards. S.S.S. 66. *Green Fees:* weekdays £25.00 per day or round, weekends and Bank Holidays £30.00 per day or round. *Eating facilities:* restaurant and bar snacks available. *Visitors:* welcome with Handicap Certificates. Buggies and carts available. *Society Meetings:* welcome – special rates on application. Professional: N. Bicknell (01872 276595). Secretary: L. Booker (01872 278684; Fax: 01872 225972).

WADEBRIDGE. **Roserrow Golf and Country Club,** Roserrow, St Minver, Near Wadebridge PL27 6QT. *Location:* between Wadebridge and Polzeath off the B3314. Undulating wooded valley. 18 holes, 6226 yards, 5951 metres. S.S.S. 71. 15 bay driving range,

KILLIOW GOLF

The 18-hole Killiow Golf Club is set in the magnificent grounds of historic Killiow Estate and presents a challenge to golfers of all standards. Only 5 minutes from the cathedral city of Truro, Killiow offers the visiting golfer a true Cornish welcome and affords the best of hospitality for your enjoyment.
• Modern clubhouse • Driving range
• 18-hole course • 4-hole Academy Course

Killiow Golf, Kea, Truro, Cornwall TR3 6AG • Tel: 01872 270246
info@killiow.co.uk • sec@killiow.co.uk • www.killiowgolf.co.uk

This renowned 17th century inn is situated in an unspoilt fishing cove on the rugged North Coast of Cornwall. The beach is just 50 yards from the front door and the Coastal Path offers miles of breathtaking scenery. For a relaxing break with a friendly atmosphere you need look no further. Golf, fishing, sailing and riding are all nearby.

Pets welcome in the Inn and Self-catering accommodation.

Port Gaverne Hotel
Near Port Isaac, Cornwall PL29 3SQ
Tel: 01208 880244 • Fax: 01208 880151

WEST REGION / Cornwall

practice putting green. *Green Fees:* £30.00 May-September, £25.00 April and October (also Christmas and Easter), £20.00 November-March. *Eating facilities:* restaurant, bar food available. *Visitors:* always welcome, phone for tee times. Luxury self-catering accommodation on site. Indoor swimming pool, fitness suite, sauna, jacuzzi, steam room, solarium, outdoor tennis courts. Buggies and trolleys for hire. *Society Meetings:* welcome by arrangement. Club Manager: Hayley Carter (01208 863000; Fax: 01208 863002).
e-mail: golfmanager@roserrow.co.uk
website: www.roserrow.co.uk

WADEBRIDGE. **St Enodoc Golf Club,** Rock, Wadebridge PL27 6LD (01208 863216; Fax: 01208 862976). *Location:* take the B3314 from Wadebridge, signposted Rock (three miles). Seaside links. Two courses: Church Course 18 holes, 6547 yards. S.S.S. 70; Holywell Course 18 holes, 4103 yards. S.S.S. 61. Practice range, putting greens, etc. *Green Fees:* Church £65.00 weekdays, £75.00 weekends and Bank Holidays. Holywell £20.00 weekdays, weekends and Bank Holidays. *Eating facilities:* restaurant and bar snacks. *Visitors:* Handicap Certificates (24 and below) required for Church Course; no restrictions for Holywell Course. *Society Meetings:* all welcome by arrangement with the General Manager. Professional: Nick Williams (01208 862402).
e-mail: enquiries@st-enodoc.co.uk
website: www.st-enodoc.co.uk

WADEBRIDGE. **St Kew Golf Club,** St Kew Highway, Near Wadebridge, Bodmin PL30 3EF (Tel & Fax: 01208 841500). *Location:* on the main A39, two-and-a-half miles from Wadebridge towards Camelford. Parkland course, 9 holes (18 tees), 4543 yards. S.S.S. 62. Covered driving range, practice chipping/bunker area. *Green Fees:* information not available. *Eating facilities:* coffee shop and restaurant; licensed bar. *Visitors:* welcome. No restrictions. *Society Meetings:* discounts for eight or more. Professional: Mike Derry (Tel & Fax: 01208 841500). Secretary: John Brown.*

ISLES OF SCILLY

ST MARY'S. **Isles Of Scilly Golf Club,** Carn Morval, St Mary's, Isles of Scilly TR21 0NF (01720 422692). *Location:* one mile from Hugh Town, St Mary's. Heathland links course with magnificent views. 9 holes, 18 tees, 5898 yards. S.S.S. 69. Par 73. *Green Fees:* £22.00 per day. 2010 rates (subject to review). *Eating facilities:* lunches and evening meals available. *Visitors:* welcome.

Other useful guides to holidays in Britain from FHG Guides

PUBS & INNS
300 GREAT HOTELS
SHORT BREAK HOLIDAYS
The original PETS WELCOME!
500 GREAT PLACES TO STAY
SELF-CATERING HOLIDAYS
BED & BREAKFAST STOPS
CARAVAN & CAMPING HOLIDAYS
FAMILY BREAKS

Published annually: available in all good bookshops or direct from the publisher:
FHG Guides, Abbey Mill Business Centre, Seedhill, Paisley PA1 1TJ
Tel: 0141 887 0428 • Fax: 0141 889 7204
e-mail: admin@fhguides.co.uk
www.holidayguides.com

Visit www.holidayguides.com
for convenient accommodation when playing golf around the regions

---

GREAT BODIEVE FARM BARNS

Four spacious, luxury barns close to the Camel Estuary. Furnished and equipped to a very high standard: dishwashers, wide-screen TV/video/DVD/Freeview. Most bedrooms en suite (king-size beds). Sleep 2-8. Excellent area for sandy beaches, spectacular cliff walks, golf, Camel Trail and surfing. One mile from Wadebridge towards Rock, Daymer and Polzeath.

*Contact: Thelma Riddle or Nancy Phillips, Great Bodieve Farm Barns, Molesworth House, The Showground, Wadebridge, Cornwall PL27 7JE
enquiries@great-bodieve.co.uk • www.great-bodieve.co.uk
Tel: 01208 814916 • Fax: 01208 812713*

Devon

AXMOUTH. Axe Cliff Golf Club, Squires Lane, Axmouth, Seaton EX12 4AB (01297 21754; Fax: 01297 24371). *Location:* A35 from Sidmouth to Lyme Regis, turn right on to B3172 at junction with A358 Seaton. Clifftop course. 18 holes, 5969 yards, 5460 metres. S.S.S. 70. *Green Fees:* £20.00 weekdays, £25.00 weekends and Bank Holidays. *Eating facilities:* bar and small restaurant. *Visitors:* welcome without reservation, course closed until 11am on Sundays, Wednesdays till 10.30am and Fridays till 9.30am. Handicap Certificate not required. Electric cart hire, golf buggies, pull trolleys and clubs for hire. *Society Meetings:* societies very welcome. More details on website. Secretary: (01297 21754).
website: www.axecliff.co.uk

BARNSTAPLE. Portmore Golf Park, Landkey Road, Barnstaple EX32 9LB (01271 378378). *Location:* A361 just east of Barnstaple, turn right to Landkey 200 yards, turn right Newport, turn right again after a mile. Two parkland courses. The Landkey, Par 3. The Barum, Par 71. 24 bay floodlit golf range, chipping green, bunker, putting green. *Green Fees:* information not available. *Eating facilities:* full catering available. *Visitors:* welcome at all times, must telephone for tee times. Full dress code applies for Barum course. Tuition and buggy hire available. *Society Meetings:* welcome with prior booking, group rates available. Professional: Darren Everet.*
website: www.portmoregolf.co.uk

BIDEFORD near. Hartland Forest Golf Club, Near Clovelly, Bideford EX39 5RA (01237 431777). *Location:* between Bideford and Bude A39, signposted from main A39 road. Parkland with water hazards. 18 holes, 6004 yards. S.S.S. 70. Par 71. *Green Fees:* £15.00 for 18 holes. *Visitors:* welcome at all times. Buggies for hire. *Society Meetings:* welcome. Secretary: A. Cartwright.
e-mail: hfgolf@googlemail.com
website: www.hartlandforestgolf.co.uk

BIGBURY. Bigbury Golf Club Ltd, Bigbury-on-Sea TQ7 4BB (01548 810557). *Location:* off main Plymouth to Kingsbridge road, turn right at Harraton Cross. Undulating cliff top course. 18 holes, 6035 yards. S.S.S. 70. *Green Fees:* please see website. *Eating facilities:* catering facilities available every day. *Visitors:* welcome, Handicap Certificate not essential. Holiday bungalow available all year. *Society Meetings:* catered for by prior arrangement. Professional: Tracy Loveys. Director of Golf: Nigel Blenkarne. Pro Shop: (01548 810557 opt 2), Office: (01548 810557 opt 5)
website: www.bigburygolfclub.com

BRIXHAM. Churston Golf Club Ltd, Dartmouth Road, Churston, Near Brixham TQ5 0LA (01803 842751; Fax: 01803 845738). *Location:* A379 from Torquay to Brixham. At Windy Corner take A3022 to Brixham. Club situated half-a-mile on. Downland/parkland course stretching westward along the cliffs towards Brixham. 18 holes, 6219 yards. S.S.S. 70. *Green Fees:* information not available. *Eating facilities:* restaurant, bar and separate function room. *Visitors:* welcome, must be members of recognised club. Conference facilities available. Handicap Certificate preferred. *Society Meetings:* catered for by arrangement. Mondays, Thursdays and Fridays only. Professional: Rob Butterworth (01803 843442; Fax: 01803 845738). Manager: S.R. Bawden (01803 842751; Fax: 01803 845738).*

BUDLEIGH SALTERTON. East Devon Golf Club, Links Road, Budleigh Salterton EX9 6DG (01395 443570). *Location:* exit M5 Junction 30; follow A376 and B3179 for Exmouth/Budleigh Salterton. Cliff top and heathland; special features: Superb greens, spectacular views over English Channel. 18 holes, 6239 yards. S.S.S. 70. *Green Fees:* information not available. *Eating facilities:* full bar and restaurant. *Visitors:* anytime by prior arrangement. Handicap Certificate required. Ladies' Day Tuesdays. *Society Meetings:* catered for Thursdays only by arrangement. Professional: T. Underwood (01395 445195). Secretary: Julian Reynolds (01395 443570).*

PLEASE NOTE

All the information regarding Golf Clubs in this guide is given in good faith in the belief that it is correct. However, the publishers cannot guarantee the facts given in these pages, neither are they responsible for changes in ownership or facilities, such as green fees, that may take place after the date of going to press. Readers should always satisfy themselves that the facilities they require are available and that the terms, if quoted, still apply.

CHITTLEHAMHOLT. Highbullen Hotel Golf & Country Club, Chittlehamholt, Umberleigh EX37 9HD (01769 540561; Fax: 01769 540492). *Location*: M5 Tiverton Exit 27, A361 to South Molton, B3226 five miles. Right uphill following tourist signs through Chittlehamholt. Undulating parkland setting amongst mature specimen trees and water hazards, spectacular views to Exmoor and Dartmoor. 18 holes, 5562 yards. S.S.S. 67. Practice ground, golf simulator, indoor putting green. *Green Fees:* information not available. *Eating facilities:* restaurant, brasserie and bars. *Visitors:* welcome, check availability. Accommodation on site at Highbullen Hotel. New leisure complex and health spa with full shower and changing facilities. *Society Meetings:* golf societies welcome subject to availablilty. Professional: Paul Weston (01769 540530). Secretary: John Ayres (01769 540664).*
e-mail: club@highbullen.co.uk
website: www.highbullen.co.uk

CHULMLEIGH. Chulmleigh Golf Course, Leigh Road, Chulmleigh EX18 7BL (Tel & Fax: 01769 580519). *Location:* approximately midway between Barnstaple and Crediton on A377. North Devon's only tailor-made short game course. Undulating parkland course. 18 holes, 1450 yards Summer, 2353 yards Winter for 18 holes. S.S.S. 54. *Green Fees:* from £9.50. *Eating facilities:* licensed bar, bar snacks. *Visitors:* welcome. No Handicap Certificate required. Suitable for experienced golfers to improve short game, ideal for beginners, Juniors and retired golfers. Teaching available for beginners, juniors and adults by arrangement. Holiday cottage available. *Society Meetings:* welcome by prior arrangement. Secretary: Roy Dow. Proprietors: Mr and Mrs R.W Dow.
e-mail: chulmleighgolf@aol.com
website: www.chulmleighgolf.co.uk

CREDITON. Downes Crediton Golf Club, Hookway, Crediton EX17 3PT (01363 773025; Fax: 01363 775060). *Location:* off Crediton-Exeter road. Part flat, part hilly course featuring woods and water. 18 holes, 5962 yards. S.S.S. 70. *Green Fees:* weekdays £35.00 summer, £28.00 winter; weekends £40.00 summer, £32.00 winter. *Eating facilities:* available from 10.30am to one hour before bar closes. *Visitors*: welcome, advisable to phone first and must produce Handicap Certificate. *Society Meetings:* by arrangement. Professional: Barry Austin (01363 774464). Golf Administrator: Robin Goodey.

CREDITON near. Waterbridge Golf Course, Down St Mary, Near Crediton EX17 5LG (01363 85111). *Location:* on the A377 north of Crediton (one mile north of Copplestone). Attractive, gentle parkland course in a beautiful setting. 9 holes (18 tees), 3910 yards, S.S.S. 64. *Green Fees:* weekdays £9.00 9 holes, £14.50 18 holes; weekends £10.00 9 holes, £16.00 18 holes. 12.5% discount on parties of 10 and over. *Eating facilities:* café bar, lunches. *Visitors:* welcome. Club and trolley hire available. *Society Meetings:* welcome. Professional: David Ridyard. Secretary: Mrs A. Wren.
website: www.waterbridgegc.co.uk

CULLOMPTON. Padbrook Park Golf Club, Padbrook Park, Cullompton EX15 1RU (01884 836100). *Location:* one mile from Junction 28 M5. Picturesque parkland course with interesting water hazards, natural woodland and rolling fairways. 18 holes, 6500 yards. S.S.S. 72. 10 bay driving range. Large chipping and putting area. *Green Fees:* £25.00 all week. Juniors half price. *Eating facilities:* two bars and Ripleys Restaurant. *Visitors:* always welcome. Indoor bowls, fishing; full conference and meeting facilities. Health and Fitness studio. 40 bedroom hotel, crazy golf. *Society Packages:* welcome by prior arrangement. Professional: Stuart Disney (01884 836100). Directors: Susan and Garry Scargill (Fax: 01884 836101).
e-mail: info@padbrookpark.co.uk
website: www.padbrookpark.co.uk

DARTMOUTH. Dartmouth Golf and Country Club, Blackawton, Near Dartmouth TQ9 7DE (01803 712686; Fax: 01803 712628). *Location:* five miles from Dartmouth on the A3122. Undulating parkland course with lakes, rock faces and multiple tees. Dartmouth Course: 9 holes, 2583 yards. S.S.S. 33. Championship Course: 18 holes, 7191 yards. S.S.S. 74. 15-bay driving range. *Green Fees:* information not available. *Eating facilities:* full restaurant and lounge bar. *Visitors:* welcome daily, Handicap Certificate not essential. 3 Star hotel accommodation in 35 en suite bedrooms. Leisure suite with pool, gym and beauty therapy etc. Buggies available. *Society Meetings:* welcome daily. Professional: Rob Glazier (01803 712650). Secretary: Tony Chappell (01803 712016).*
e-mail: info@dgcc.co.uk
         golfoperations@dgcc.co.uk
website: www.dgcc.co.uk

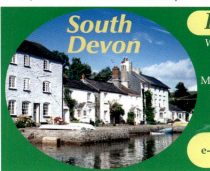

South Devon

Dart Valley Cottages

We have a fine selection of self-catering holiday cottages situated in the Dart Valley, including Dartmouth, Dittisham and along the coast. Many of our cottages have river views and log fires.
Close to Dartmouth Golf & Country Club, Thurlestone, Bigbury and Churston.

Please phone or e-mail for brochure.
Tel: 01803 771269
e-mail: enquiries@dartvalleycottages.co.uk
www.dartvalleycottages.co.uk

DAWLISH. Warren Golf Club, Dawlish Warren EX7 0NF (01626 862255). *Location:* 12 miles south of Exeter off A379. Links golf course lying on a spit of land between the sea and Exe Estuary. A challenging course situated in an internationally renowned conservation area. 18 holes, 5968 yards. S.S.S. 70. *Green Fees:* weekdays £35.00, weekends and Bank Holidays £40.00 (includes insurance). *Eating facilities:* bar and full catering available. *Visitors:* welcome, please call for reservations. *Society Meetings:* welcome by arrangement, Special Packages available. Professional: D. Prowse (01626 864002). Golf Co-ordinator Mike Davis (01626 862255).
e-mail: golf@dwgc.co.uk
website: www.dwgc.co.uk

EXETER. **Exeter Golf and Country Club,** Countess Wear, Exeter EX2 7AE (Tel & Fax: 01392 874139; Course Information: 01392 876413). *Location:* near M5, exit Junction 30, take main Plymouth/Torquay Road. Turn left Topsham, 300 yards left. Flat parkland course, many trees. 18 holes, 6023 yards. S.S.S. 69. Large practice ground. *Green Fees:* information not available. *Eating facilities:* sports bar, lounge bar, diningroom. *Visitors:* welcome except Tuesdays (Ladies' Day) and Saturdays very busy course, booking sheet in operation, Bookings taken one week prior subject to availability. Booking number 01392 876303. Function suite. *Society Meetings:* catered for Thursdays only. Professional: Gary Milne (01392 875028; Fax: 01392 874914). Secretary: Eddie Grant (01392 874639; Fax: 01392 874914).*

THE GOLF GUIDE 2011 — WEST REGION / Devon

EXETER. Woodbury Park Hotel and Golf Club, Woodbury Castle, Woodbury, Near Exeter EX5 1JJ (01395 233382; Fax: 01395 233384). *Location*: six miles east of Exeter between Sidmouth and Exmouth. Parkland with many water hazards. 18 hole championship course and 9 hole course. 18 holes, 7314 yards. S.S.S. 73. Tee of the day 6578 yards, Par 72. Handicap required. 9 hole-front 9, Par 32, 2297 yards. Pay & Play, no Handicap required. 16-bay driving range, practice green. *Green Fees:* information not provided. *Eating facilities:* two restaurants, two bars. *Visitors*: welcome at all times. Buggies for hire. Leisure Centre, Health and Beauty Spa and conference facilities. Five chalet-style luxury lodges ideal for four/eight golfers in each. 56-bedroom hotel. *Society Meetings:* welcome, Golf Packages available. Bookings please ring (01395 233500). Professional: Allan Perry. Golf Manager: Alan Richards.
e-mail: golfbookings@woodburypark.co.uk

EXETER near. Fingle Glen Hotel, Golf and Country Club, Tedburn St. Mary, Near Exeter EX6 6AF (01647 61817; Fax: 01647 61135). *Location*: A30 five miles from Exeter on the Okehampton Road. Parkland with streams and lakes. 18 holes, 5511 yards. S.S.S. 68. Golf academy, 12 bay floodlit driving range. *Green Fees:* information not available. *Eating facilities:* restaurant, bar snacks, sun terrace. *Visitors:* welcome at all times. En suite accommodation available. *Society Meetings:* welcome at all times. Pro Shop/Teaching Professional: Mark Hurst. Secretary: Danny Hoskins. Manager: A. Bridgeman.

EXETER near. Teign Valley Golf Club, Christow, Near Exeter EX6 7PA (01647 253026). *Location:* four miles off the A38 Devon Expressway between Exeter and Plymouth. Varied and interesting course set in beautiful valleys in the Dartmoor National Park. 18 holes, 6000 yards. *Green Fees:* information not available. *Eating facilities:* a welcoming spirit in the friendly clubhouse offering tasty bar snacks and a choice of real ales. *Visitors:* welcome. Clubhouse extension with 16 en suite double bedrooms, gymnasium and treatment rooms. *Society Meetings:* welcome. Conference facilities for 40 available.*
e-mail: reception@teignvalleygolf.co.uk
website: www.teignvalleygolf.co.uk

HOLSWORTHY. Holsworthy Golf Club, Killatree, Holsworthy EX22 6LP (01409 253177). *Location:* leave Holsworthy on the Bude road, A3072; one and a half miles on left. Parkland - gentle undulating hills. 18 holes, 6062 yards. S.S.S. 69. Practice area. *Green Fees:* information not provided. *Eating facilities:* bar, dining room. *Visitors:* welcome anytime. *Society Meetings:* welcome, special reductions for parties of 12 or more. Professional: Dan Wood (01409 255390). Secretary: (01409 253177).
e-mail: info@holsworthygolfclub.co.uk
website: www.holsworthygolfclub.co.uk

HONITON. Honiton Golf Club, Middlehills, Honiton EX14 9TR (01404 44422). *Location:* one mile south of town proceed from A35 at Tower Cross to Farway. Flat parkland. 18 holes; 5910 yards, S.S.S. 68 (men); 5659 yards, S.S.S. 73 (ladies). Small practice ground. *Green Fees:* visit website for details. *Eating facilities:* bar and restaurant. *Visitors:* bona fide members of other clubs welcome, with restrictions on Wednesdays (Ladies' day) and weekends (club competitions). Facilities for 10 touring caravans during summer months with electrics. *Society Meetings:* by prior arrangement. Professional: Adrian Cave (01404 42943). Administration Office: (01404 44422; Fax: 01404 46383).
e-mail: secretary@honitongolfclub.fsnet.co.uk
website: www.honitongolfclub.co.uk

HONITON. Otter Valley Golf Centre, Upottery, Honiton EX14 9QP (Tel & Fax: 01404 861266). *Location*: Take the A303 from Honiton, continue one and a half miles, turn off left at Upottery and Rawridge. Rolling parkland course. 9 holes, 1500 yards. Par 29. Four indoor practice bays, large putting green, eight tees on the driving range, chipping green. *Green Fees*: information not available. *Eating facilities*: snacks and refreshments, hot and cold drinks. Lounge with TV. *Visitors*: welcome, no restrictions. Holiday cottages, video analysis, lessons. *Society Meetings*: Societies and Company Days very welcome. Please phone for information. Professional: Andrew Thompson. Manager: Ryan Eaton.*
e-mail: andrewthompson@otter-golf.co.uk
website: www.otter-golf.co.uk

Teign Valley Golf & Hotel — situated in the beautiful Teign Valley within the Dartmoor National Park

We offer luxurious, contemporary accommodation, scrumptious food, real ales, and a superb wine list, in a relaxed and easy going atmosphere.

- Family run eco-friendly Hotel
- Challenging 18 hole Golf course
- Fully stocked Pro shop • Restaurant / Bar
- Gymnasium / Games room

www.teignvalleygolf.co.uk

Teign Valley Hotel & Golf, Christow, Exeter, Devon, EX6 7PB · To book call: 01647 253026

ILFRACOMBE. Ilfracombe Golf Club, Hele Bay, Ilfracombe EX34 9RT. *Location*: on main coastal road between Ilfracombe and Combe Martin. Undulating parkland with spectacular views of sea and moors from every tee and green. 18 holes, 5893 yards. S.S.S. 68. 9 hole practice area and driving range. *Green Fees*: weekdays £27.50, weekend £33.00. *Eating facilities*: catering available all day. *Visitors*: welcome, advance booking preferred. Members only before 10am weekends. *Society Meetings*: welcome, advance booking preferred. Bookings: (01271 862176 Option 1). Catering: (01271 862176 Option 3). Professional: Office: (01271 862176 Option 2).

ILFRACOMBE. Ilfracombe and Woolacombe Golf Range, Woolacombe Road, Ilfracombe EX34 7HF (01271 866222). *Location*: on main road between Ilfracombe and Woolacombe. Flat course. 1343 yards. 300 yard driving range with covered bays, 18-hole putting course, golf shop. Tennis court. *Green Fees*: 18 holes £4.50. *Eating facilities*: pre-packed snacks, drinks and cream teas available. *Visitors*: everyone is welcome. Secretary: David Crocker-White.

IVYBRIDGE. McCaulay's Fitness and Golf, Ivybridge Golf Club (aka Dinnaton Golf Club), Ivybridge PL21 9HU (01752 892512; Fax: 01752 698334). *Location*: from the Ivybridge turn off on A38, we are just two minutes' drive, please follow the brown tourist signs. 9 holes, 2028 yards. Par 32. *Green Fees*: information not available. *Visitors*: always welcome. No Handicap Certificate required. Other facilities offered include gym, 25m heated swimming pool, aerobics studio, tennis, squash, sauna, solarium and steam room. Contact: Jamie Phillips.*
website: www.mccaulays.com

MORETONHAMPSTEAD. Bovey Castle, Moretonhampstead TQ13 8RE (01647 445000; Fax: 01647 440961). *Location*: Junction 31 from M5, B3212 for two miles. Parkland with rivers and narrow fairways. 18 holes, 6303 yards, 5450 metres. S.S.S. 70. Golf academy. *Green Fees*: information not available. *Eating facilities*: brunch service, bar. *Visitors*: welcome. Please book in advance, golf shoes must be worn. Accommodation in 5 star Hotel, tennis courts; carts available. *Society Meetings*: by prior arrangement. Professional/Secretary: Richard Lewis (01647 445009; Fax: 01647 445020).*
website: www.boveycastle.com

NEWTON ABBOT. Stover Golf Club, Bovey Road, Newton Abbot TQ12 6QQ (01626 352460; Fax: 01626 330210). *Location*: A382 three miles north of Newton Abbot. Wooded parkland course with river in play on 8 holes. 18 holes, 5952 yards. S.S.S. 70. *Green Fees*: £32.30. *Eating facilities*: full catering daily from 11am. *Visitors*: welcome on production of Handicap Certificate or membership card of county affiliated golf club. Must telephone in advance. *Society Meetings*: catered for on Thursdays. Professional: James Langmead (01626 362078). Secretary: Will Hendry (01626 352460).

STOVER GOLF CLUB
The Club House, Stover, Newton Abbot, Devon TQ12 6QQ
Tel: 0326 352460 • Fax: 01626 330210
e-mail: info@stovergolfclub.co.uk • www.stovergolfclub.co.uk

Stover Golf Club is one of the most popular courses in South Devon, set in parkland with some of the prettiest golf holes in the county. Extensive mature woodlands and water feature on a number of holes, and the 5952 yards, par 69 course provides an interesting and enjoyable challenge to golfers of all abilities.

Visitors are most welcome and will appreciate the setting, warm welcome and friendly and intimate atmosphere of the Club.

A sporting resort and club with luxurious accommodation, superb cuisine and romantic ambience. Bovey castle, built 1907 in the heart of the National Park has a championship golf course designed in 1926 as a companion to Gleneagles and Turnberry. Numerous sporting activities include fly-fishing, equestrian, tennis, falconry, boating and more. An exceptional new spa and pool, cinema, children's pursuits and beautiful walks. Castle Lodges available for rent.

Bovey Castle, North Bovey, Dartmoor National Park, Devon TQ13 8RE
Fax: 01647 440 961   E-mail: enquiries@boveycastle.com

Telephone us on
01647 445 000

visit **www.boveycastle.com**

32 Devon / WEST REGION — THE GOLF GUIDE 2011

NEWTON ABBOT. **Dainton Park Golf Club,** Totnes Road, Ipplepen, Newton Abbot TQ12 5TN (01803 815000). *Location:* on A381 between Newton Abbot and Totnes. Undulating parkland course. 18 holes, 6400 yards. S.S.S. 71. Driving range and practice area. *Green Fees:* Monday to Thursday £26.00, Friday to Sunday £29.00. *Eating facilities:* full catering and licensed bar. *Visitors:* unrestricted. *Society Meetings:* welcome by arrangement.
website: www.daintonparkgolf.co.uk

NEWTON ABBOT. **Hele Park Golf Club,** Ashburton Road, Newton Abbot TQ12 6JN (01626 336060; Fax: 01626 332661). *Location:* A383 on Newton Abbot to Ashburton road, one and a half miles from Newton Abbot town centre. Parkland course. 9 holes, 5168 yards. S.S.S. 65 (for 18 holes). Floodlit driving range. *Green Fees:* from £11.50 for 9 holes and £20.00 for 18 holes. *Eating facilities:* bar and restaurant. *Visitors:* welcome. Booking advised. Normal dress rules apply. Pay as you play and members' club. *Society Meetings:* welcome, special rates on application. Professionals: Duncan Arnold, Malcolm Craig, Ben Martin. Manager: Wendy Stanbury.
e-mail: info@heleparkgolf.co.uk
website: www.heleparkgolf.co.uk

OKEHAMPTON. **Okehampton Golf Club,** Off Tors Road, Okehampton EX20 1EF (01837 52113). *Location:* from A30 take turning from centre of Okehampton then follow the signposts. Parkland. 18 holes, 5294 yards. S.S.S. 67. *Green Fees:* £25.00. *Eating facilities:* bar and dining room. *Visitors:* welcome; contact by telephone or letter. *Society Meetings:* welcome by prior arrangement. Professional: Ashley Moon (01837 53541). Secretary: Beverley Lawson.
e-mail: secretary@okehamptongolfclub.co.uk
website: www.okehamptongolfclub.co.uk

OKEHAMPTON near. **Ashbury Hotel,** Higher Maddaford, Ashbury, Near Okehampton EX20 4NL (01837 55453; Fax: 01837 55468). *Location:* signposted "Ashbury" off the B3079, three miles west of Okehampton. Hilly, wooded courses. Ashbury, seven courses: Pines 18 holes, 6400 yards, Par 72; Beeches 18 holes, 5765 yards, Par 69; Willows 18 holes, Par 3. Oakwood Course 18 holes, 5400 yards, Par 67; Kigbeare 18 holes, 6461 yards, Par 72. Forest 18 holes, 6140 yards, Par 71; Ashbury 18 holes, 5804 yards, Par 69. Practice area, putting green and 8-bay covered driving range. *Green Fees:* information not available. *Eating facilities:* fully licensed bar, bar snacks 12 noon to 5pm. *Visitors:* welcome, please telephone to arrange a tee time. Buggies, clubs and trolleys for hire. Coaching available. Accommodation in 2 star hotel; tennis, snooker, swimming (01837 53053). Secretary: Simon James.
website: www.ashburygolfhotel.co.uk

PLYMOUTH. **Elfordleigh Hotel, Golf and Leisure Club,** Colebrook, Plympton, Plymouth PL7 5EB (01752 336428; Fax: 01752 344581). *Location:* one mile from Plympton. Woodland course in picturesque countryside. 18 holes, S.S.S. 67. Practice area. *Green Fees:* information not available. *Eating facilities:* Churchill Restaurant; bar meals available from Brasserie. *Visitors:* welcome. Hotel accommodation available. *Society Meetings:* catered for, contact Golf Manager. Professional/Director of Golf: Nick Cook (01752 348425).*
website: www.elfordleigh.co.uk

PLYMOUTH. **Sparkwell Golf Club,** Sparkwell, Plympton, Plymouth PL7 5DF (Tel & Fax: 01752 837219). *Location:* Sparkwell village centre. Parkland course. 9 holes, 5772 yards, S.S.S. 68. Practice area, pitch and putt. *Green Fees:* information not available. *Eating facilities:* restaurant and bar. *Visitors:* all welcome; pay-as-you-play course. *Society Meetings:* all welcome. Secretary: J. J. Sandiford.*

PLYMOUTH. **Staddon Heights Golf Club,** Staddon Heights, Plymstock, Plymouth PL9 9SP (01752 402475). *Location:* from A38/city centre follow signs to Kingsbridge (A379), then Turnchapel then Bovisand. Cliff top course with spectacular views over Plymouth Sound and the City. 18 holes, 6164 yards. S.S.S. 70. Practice range and short game area. *Green Fees:* weekdays £28.00, weekends and Bank Holidays £32.00; reductions for groups of eight or more; twilight golf available April-October. *Visitors:* welcome. *Eating facilities:* full bar and restaurant service available. *Society Meetings:* welcome. Secretary: Tim Aggett (01752 401475).
e-mail: golf@shgc.uk.net
website: www.staddonheightsgolf.co.uk

www.holidayguides.com

For full details of convenient accommodation near clubs and courses

ELFORDLEIGH
Hotel, Golf & Country Club

Perfect Location...
For that somewhere truly extra special, why look anywhere else? You are warmly invited to relax, unwind and savour the unique atmosphere that is, the Elfordleigh.

Golf...
Elfordleigh is a golfers paradise, offering 18 superb holes of golf set deep in the secluded Plym valley. Measuring just over 5500 yards, this picturesque golf course offers a challenge to all.

Dining...
We pride ourselves on offering the finest food and wines. At the very heart of the hotel is the spacious and comfortable Brasserie serving light meals and tempting snacks throughout the day. Just a step or two away is the classically styled Churchill's Restaurant. With its adjoining airy conservatory, this elegant restaurant provides the perfect setting for fine dining, with menus to suit even the most discerning palate.

Oasis Leisure...
The pool stands at 15 meters by 9 meters (5ft deep) and provides a perfect jewel of the Oasis. Our extensive range of Life Fitness equipment is situated in our fitness suite.

ELFORDLEIGH
Hotel, Golf & Country Club
Colebrook | Plympton | Plymouth PL7 5EB
www.elfordleigh.co.uk

01752 336428 | reception@elfordleigh.co.uk

SAUNTON. **Saunton Golf Club,** Saunton, Braunton EX33 1LG (01271 812436; Fax: 01271 814241). *Location:* eight miles west of Barnstaple. Two traditional links courses. East course 18 holes, 6779 yards. S.S.S. 72. West course 18 holes, 6403 yards. S.S.S. 71. Practice ground and covered practice range. *Green Fees:* information not available. *Eating facilities:* full catering available. *Visitors:* welcome, Handicap Certificate required. Prior booking recommended. *Society Meetings:* welcome with prior booking. Professional: A.T. MacKenzie (01271 812013; Fax: 01271 812126). General Manager: P. McMullen (01271 812436; Fax: 01271 814241). e-mail: di5@sauntongolf.co.uk
website: www.sauntongolf.co.uk

SIDMOUTH. **Sidmouth Golf Club,** Cotmaton Road, Sidmouth EX10 8SX (01395 513451; Fax: 01395 514661). *Location:* half a mile from town centre, 12 miles south east of M5 Junction 30. Parkland with breathtaking views over Sid Valley and Lyme Bay. 18 holes, 5068 yards. S.S.S. 67. *Green Fees:* £30.00. Summer and winter packages available. Society packages on request. *Eating facilities:* catering available everyday. *Visitors:* welcome anytime depending on tee reservations. *Society Meetings:* by arrangement. Club Manager: Jonathan Lee (01395 513451).
e-mail: secretary@sidmouthgolfclub.co.uk

SOUTH BRENT. **Wrangaton Golf Club,** Golf Links Road, Wrangaton, South Brent TQ10 9HJ (01364 73001). *Location:* A38 from Exeter (Wrangaton Cross turn off), from Plymouth A38 Ivybridge turn off via Bittaford. Parkland course, first 9 holes on Dartmoor. 18 holes, 6065 yards. S.S.S 69. Practice ground, putting green and net. *Green Fees:* £25.00 weekdays and weekends. *Eating facilities:* full catering and bar facilities available. *Visitors:* welcome at all times but telephone first in case of club competition. *Society Meetings:* all welcome, written notice required. Professional: Glenn Richards (01364 72161). Secretary: Bob Clark (Tel & Fax: 01364 73229).

TAVISTOCK. **Hurdwick Golf Club,** Tavistock Hamlets, Tavistock PL19 0LL (01822 612746). *Location:* one mile north of Tavistock on the Brentor Road. Parkland. 18 holes, 5300 yards. S.S.S. 66. *Green Fees:* information not available. *Eating facilities:* fresh sandwiches, licensed bar. *Visitors:* welcome anytime. *Society Meetings:* (10 or more) welcome. Secretary: Roger Cullen.*

The Foxhunters Inn West Down, Near Ilfracombe EX34 8NU
- 300 year-old coaching Inn conveniently situated for beaches and country.
- Bar and Restaurant serving food all day every day.
- 8 en suite bedrooms, all with TV and tea/coffee making. • Large car park.
- Large choice of golf clubs in the area including Saunton Sands.

Tel: 01271 863757 • Fax: 01271 879313 • www.foxhuntersinn.co.uk

Welcome to the Saunton Experience...
Two Championship Links Courses

- Visitors and societies welcome.
- Excellent bar and restaurant facilities.
- East, Rated 60th in the world (Golf World June 2010).
- WINTER SPECIALS available November to March.

Saunton, Braunton EX33 1LG
Tel: 01271 812436
www.sauntongolf.co.uk
e-mail: gm4@sauntongolf.co.uk

WRANGATON GOLF CLUB — the best of both worlds...

Founded in 1895, Wrangaton Golf Club is unique – 9 moorland holes and 9 parkland holes. The moorland nine holes offer stunning views of the Devonshire countryside towards the sea 10 miles away and has no bunkers and no trees. The parkland nine is a complete contrast with its lush fairways bordered by hedgerows and trees. Two courses for the price of one!
We welcome visitors anytime and hope to see you soon.
Wrangaton Golf Club, Golf Links Road, Wrangaton, Devon TQ10 9HJ
Tel: 01364 73229 • e-mail(secretary): bob@wrangatongolfclub.co.uk • www.wrangatongolfclub.co.uk

TAVISTOCK. Tavistock Golf Club, Down Road, Tavistock PL19 9AQ (Tel & Fax: 01822 612344). *Location:* Whitchurch Down one mile from Tavistock. Moorland course with spectacular views. 18 holes, 6546 yards. S.S.S. 71. Practice ground. *Green Fees:* £40.00 per day. *Eating facilities:* all day catering and bar. *Visitors:* welcome, telephone first. *Society Meetings:* by prior arrangement, fees negotiable. Professional: S. Steel (01822 612316). Secretary: J. Coe (Tel & Fax: 01822 612344).
e-mail: info@tavistockgolfclub.org.uk
website: www.tavistockgolfclub.org.uk

TEIGNMOUTH. Teignmouth Golf Club, Haldon Moor, Teignmouth TQ14 9NY (01626 777070). *Location:* two miles north of Teignmouth on the Exeter Road - B3192. Level heathland course, designed by Dr Mackenzie (also designed Augusta National USA), with panoramic views. 18 holes, 6110 yards. S.S.S. 69. *Green Fees:* On application. *Eating facilities:* catering from 10am to 6pm. *Visitors:* welcome with reservation. *Society Meetings:* catered for Thursdays. Professional: Robert Selley (01626 772894). General Manager: Ian Evans (01626 777070; Fax: 01626 777304).

THURLESTONE. Thurlestone Golf Club, Thurlestone, Kingsbridge TQ7 3NZ (01548 560405). *Location:* turn off A379 near Kingsbridge. Undulating beside sandy beaches and over cliff tops, with superb coastal views. 18 holes, 6340 yards. S.S.S. 70. Practice area. *Green Fees:* information not available. *Eating facilities:* catering available from 10.00am until 5.30pm daily. *Visitors:* must produce Handicap Certificate, please telephone in advance. *Society Meetings:* not catered for. Professional: Peter Laugher (Tel & Fax: 01548 560715). Secretary: Terry Gibbons (01548 560405; Fax: 01548 562149).*

TIVERTON. Tiverton Golf Club, Post Hill, Tiverton EX16 4NE (01884 252187). *Location:* three miles east of Tiverton, Junction 27 of M5, proceed through Sampford Peverell and Halberton. Parkland, tree-lined fairways. 18 holes, 6346 yards. S.S.S. 71. *Green Fees:* on application. *Eating facilities:* snacks, lunches, teas and evening meals. *Visitors:* welcome, must ring Pro Shop in advance. *Society Meetings:* by arrangement with General Manager. Professional: Mike Hawton (01884 254836). General Manager: Richard Jessop (01884 252187).
e-mail: tivertongolfclub@lineone.net
website: www.tivertongolfclub.co.uk

TORQUAY. Torquay Golf Club, Petitor Road, St Marychurch, Torquay TQ1 4QF (01803 314591; Fax: 01803 316116). *Location:* north east of Torquay at St. Marychurch. Parkland. 18 holes, 6192 yards. S.S.S. 69. *Green Fees:* £40.00-£45.00. *Eating facilities:* lunches, teas and evening meals available. *Visitors:* welcome if members of a golf club with Handicap Certificate. *Society Meetings:* ring for rates. Professional: M. Ruth (01803 329113). Secretary: C.M. Nolan (01803 314591).
e-mail: info@torquaygolfclub.co.uk
website: www.torquaygolfclub.co.uk

TORRINGTON. Great Torrington Golf Club, Weare Trees, Torrington EX38 7EZ (01805 622229; Fax: 01805 623878). *Location:* one mile north of Torrington on Weare Giffard road. Heathland course with excellent views. 9 holes, 18 tees, 4419 yards. S.S.S. 63. Small practice area. *Green Fees:* information not available. *Eating facilities:* full meals and bar snacks available during bar hours. *Visitors:* welcome except on Tuesdays, Wednesdays, Saturdays and Sundays before noon and during club and open competitions. *Society Meetings:* catered for by arrangement. Secretary: Mrs J.M. Cudmore (01271 375927).*

UMBERLEIGH. Libbaton Golf Club, High Bickington, Umberleigh EX37 9BS (01769 560269; Fax: 01769 560342). *Location:* A377 Exeter to Barnstaple, turn off on B3227 to Torrington, at Atherington, turn off B3217 to High Bickington. Parkland with many lakes. 18 holes, 6481 yards. S.S.S. 71. Driving range, teaching centre. *Green Fees:* information not available. *Eating facilities:* bar, bar meals and first class restaurant. *Visitors:* always welcome, seven days a week. Dress code must be observed. *Society Meetings:* welcome by prior arrangement. Special Society Packages. Fully stocked golf shop. Secretary: Gerald Herniman (01769 560269).*

GET INTO THE SWING OF THINGS

A golfing experience that is hard to equal, anywhere in the West Country

Come and enjoy some of the best heathland links golf in Devon a traditional Mackenzie Design using the natural contours to full effect.

Book through the Pro Shop for two, three or four ball. Special rates particularly for evening play. Handicap Certificates or Proof of Playing ability required.

Extensive Clubhouse facilities

Teignmouth Golf Club
Haldon Moor, Teignmouth
01626 777070

THE APPEARANCE OF AN ASTERISK (*) AT THE END OF A CLUB OR COURSE ENTRY INDICATES THAT UP-TO-DATE INFORMATION HAS NOT BEEN SUPPLIED

Devon / WEST REGION

WESTWARD HO!. Royal North Devon Golf Club, Golf Links Road, Westward Ho!, Bideford EX39 1HD (01237 473817). *Location:* two miles North Bideford. Oldest links course in England. 18 holes, 6653 yards. S.S.S. 72. Practice area. *Green Fees:* information not available. *Eating facilities:* full catering available. *Visitors:* welcome with Handicap Certificate. Tee reservations should be made in advance. *Society Meetings:* catered for. Professional: Iain Parker (01237 477598; Fax: 01237 475347). Secretary: Darren Found (01237 473817; Fax: 01237 423456).
e-mail: info@royalnorthdevongolfclub.co.uk
website: www.royalnorthdevongolfclub.co.uk

WOOLACOMBE. Mortehoe & Woolacombe Golf Club at Easewell Holiday Park, Mortehoe, Near Woolacombe EX34 7EH (01271 870343). *Location:* M5 to J27, follow A361 to Barnstaple and then Ilfracombe; at Mullacott Cross roundabout take B3343 towards Woolacombe and turn off to Mortehoe. Course set on high ground overlooking fantastic countryside and sea views. 9 holes (18 tees), 4729 yards, Par 66. *Green Fees:* information not available. *Eating facilities:* clubhouse, cafe, takeaway and restaurant. *Visitors:* welcome dawn to dusk. *Society Meetings:* welcome.*
e-mail: goodtimes@woolacombe.com
website: www.woolacombe.com

WOOLACOMBE. Willingcott Valley Golf Club, Willingcott Valley, Woolacombe EX34 7HN (01271 8701730). *Location*: take the A361 north out of Barnstaple following the signs for Ilfracombe, passing through Braunton on the way. Turn left at Mullacott Cross Roundabout following the signs for Woolacombe. After 2 miles turn left to Georgeham & Croyde. After ¼ mile the road bends to the right and Willingcott Valley is on your left. There are brown Tourist Signs to assist you. 18 holes, 6452 yards, 5956 metres. S.S.S. 71. Putting green, chipping area, nets. *Green Fees:* information not available. *Eating facilities:* bar and restaurant. *Visitors*: welcome at all times. Inclusive golf holidays and breaks. Self-catering cottages. *Society Meetings:* welcome, prices on application. Professional: David Elliott. Secretary: Andy Hodge.*
e-mail: holidays@willingcott.com
website: www.willingcott.co.uk

YELVERTON. **Yelverton Golf Club,** Golf Links Road, Yelverton PL20 6BN (01822 852824). *Location*: eight miles north of Plymouth on A386 road. Testing moorland course with views across Dartmoor. 18 holes, 6353 yards. S.S.S. 71. Practice ground. *Green Fees:* weekdays £40.00 per day or part day; weekends and Bank Holidays £40.00 per day or part day. *Eating facilities:* full catering and bar facilities available. *Visitors:* welcome if member of a recognised golf club or golf society. Handicap Certificate required. Snooker. *Society Meetings:* catered for, welcome by arrangement with Secretary. Professional: T. McSherry (01822 853593). Secretary: S. M. J. Barnes (01822 852824; Fax: 01822 854869).
e-mail: secretary@yelvertongolf.co.uk
website: www.yelvertongolf.co.uk

Other useful guides to holidays in Britain from FHG Guides

**PUBS & INNS
300 GREAT HOTELS
SHORT BREAK HOLIDAYS
The original PETS WELCOME!
500 GREAT PLACES TO STAY
SELF-CATERING HOLIDAYS
BED & BREAKFAST STOPS
CARAVAN & CAMPING HOLIDAYS
FAMILY BREAKS**

Published annually: available in all good bookshops or direct from the publisher:
**FHG Guides, Abbey Mill Business Centre, Seedhill, Paisley PA1 1TJ
Tel: 0141 887 0428 • Fax: 0141 889 7204
e-mail: admin@fhguides.co.uk
www.holidayguides.com**

Royal North Devon Golf Club
Golf Links Road, Westward Ho!, Bideford, Devon EX39 1HD

e-mail: info@royalnorthdevongolfclub.co.uk
www.royalnorthdevongolfclub.co.uk
Tel: 01237 473817 • Fax: 01237 423456

At Royal North Devon Golf Club visitors will find a friendly and welcoming atmosphere. The recently extended clubhouse can seat up to 140 people and makes an ideal venue for a function. This is the oldest seaside links in England, and is steeped in history. Golfers on this unique and challenging course often find themselves sharing the greens with sheep and horses. Bullrushes and the roar of the Atlantic Ocean only a few metres away also provide a magnificent setting for this tough course and the experience of playing a fast running links in a stiff breeze still tests the very best in the game.

No. 77 in Golf World's Top 100 courses

Willingcott Valley . . .
. . . the best kept secret in North Devon

Why not have the convenience of taking a short break in one of our fantastic cottages, where you are free to come and go as you like, but with the added benefit of having your breakfast and evening meal cooked for you in our own restaurant.

We have eight different styles of cottages, offering different levels of comfort and price.

Sorry, no pets but we would be happy to recommend a local Kennel. Some cottages non-smoking. Our Bar & Restaurant is located in the old Willingcott Farmhouse which dates back to the 17th Century giving the bar area the feel of a traditional old Devon Pub.

Our cottages are set within a stunning Par 72 18 hole golf course, often described as the best parkland golf course in North Devon. The course is a tough test off the competition tees, yet the day tees offer all the visual impact, whilst allowing the visiting golfer a more relaxed game.

Willingcott Valley, Woolacombe, North Devon EX34 7HN
Tel: 01271 870173 • e-mail: holidays@willingcott.co.uk
www.willingcott.co.uk

Royal North Devon Golf Club, Westward Ho!

Dorset

BLANDFORD. **The Ashley Wood Golf Club,** Wimborne Road, Blandford Forum DT11 9HN (01258 452253; Fax: 01258 450590). *Location:* a mile south of Blandford on B3082. Downland with magnificent views over Tarrant and Stour valleys. 18 holes, 6308 yards. S.S.S. 70. Practice ground, putting green. *Green Fees:* weekdays £30.00; weekends £35.00 after 12 noon. *Eating facilities:* hot and cold snacks all day. *Visitors:* welcome during week; after 11am Saturday and Sundays. *Society Meetings:* welcome by arrangement. Professional: Jon Shimmons (01258 480379). Manager: Tim Salmon (01258 452253).
e-mail: generalmanager@ashleywoodgolfclub.com
website: www.ashleywoodgolfclub.com

BOURNEMOUTH. **Knighton Heath Golf Club,** Francis Avenue, Bournemouth BH11 8NX (01202 572633; Fax: 01202 590774). *Location:* A348 and A3049 roundabout exit Francis Avenue. Undulating heathland, 18 holes, 6094 yards. S.S.S. 69. *Green Fees:* weekdays £30.00 per round, £35.00 per day. *Eating facilities:* meals and bar snacks available daily. *Visitors:* welcome after 9.30am weekdays but please phone to check availability, Restrictions on competition days. Not at weekends unless with a member; Tuesdays and Thursdays £20.00 after 2pm. Handicap Certificate required. *Society Meetings:* catered for if arranged in advance. Professional: David Miles (01202 578275). Club Secretary: Guy Davis (01202 572633; Fax: 01202 590774).
e-mail: khgc@btinternet.com
website: www.khgc.co.uk

BOURNEMOUTH. **Meyrick Park Golf Club,** Central Drive, Bournemouth BH2 6LH (01202 786040). *Location:* one mile from Bournemouth town centre. Beautiful and challenging woodland course. 18 holes, 5802 yards. S.S.S. 68. Practice area. *Green Fees:* information not provided. *Eating facilities:* Pulse Cafe Bar and Summer Terrace. *Visitors:* welcome. Lodge on site offering 17 en suite bedrooms – golf breaks available. *Society Meetings:* welcome by prior arrangement. Professional: Marcus Urby (01202 786040).
website: www.theclubcompany.com

BOURNEMOUTH. **Queens Park (Bournemouth) Golf Club,** Queens Park West Drive, Bournemouth BH8 9BY (01202 437807). *Location*: off Wessex Way. Parkland course in centre of Bournemouth. 18 holes, 6090 yards. S.S.S. 69. Small practice area. *Green Fees:* Monday to Thursday £19.00; Friday to Saturday £25.00; Sunday £20.00. *Eating facilities:* restaurant and bar. *Visitors:* welcome anytime, last tee off times Sundays 12 noon. *Society Meetings:* welcome by prior arrangement. Secretary: Paul Greenwood (01202 302611), Bookings (01202 437807).

BOURNEMOUTH. **Solent Meads Golf Centre,** Rolls Drive, Hengistbury Head, Bournemouth BH6 4NA (01202 420795). *Location:* south of Christchurch, 2 miles from Bournemouth town centre. Seaside course. 18 holes, 2159 yards. S.S.S. 54. Driving range, 9 hole `Fun' pitch and putt. Lessons available. *Green Fees:* £8.00 for 18 holes, concessions available, groups welcome. *Eating facilities:* cafe. *Visitors:* no restrictions. Professional: Warren Butcher (01202 420795).
e-mail: solentmeads@yahoo.com
website: www.solentmeads.co.uk
             www.golflessonsbournemouth.com

BOURTON. **Bullpits Golf Club,** Bourton, Near Gillingham SP8 5AX (01747 840091). *Location:* off the A303 at Bourton and follow sign in village. Wooded parkland with streams and water, and River Stour. 12 holes, 18 tees, 3362 yards. S.S.S. 55. Putting green. *Green Fees:* visitors £10.00. *Eating facilities:* Bar; light refreshments by prior arrangement. *Visitors:* welcome at all times except early Sunday mornings. *Society Meetings:* welcome by appointment. Owners: Richard & Cathy Price.

THE APPEARANCE OF AN ASTERISK (*) AT THE END OF A CLUB OR COURSE ENTRY INDICATES THAT UP-TO-DATE INFORMATION HAS NOT BEEN SUPPLIED

Beaches, Blue Skies and...
BOURNE HALL HOTEL
14 Priory Road, West Cliff, Bournemouth BH2 5DN
Tel: 01202 299715 • Fax: 01202 552669

We would like to welcome you to this friendly hotel, which offers comfort, style and a very warm welcome • Just a few minutes' stroll from golden beaches and shops • Spacious bar and lounges with regular entertainment • Dining room offering buffet breakfasts and delicious evening menus • Special diets catered for • Lift to main bedrooms • All 50 bedrooms with full facilities, telephone and hairdryer • Free wireless internet • Reductions for children; cots and high chairs available • Special offers early and late season. AA ★★

e-mail: info@bournehall.co.uk • www.bournehall.co.uk

The Ashley Wood Golf Club
BLANDFORD FORUM • DORSET

Something of an unsung hero amongst Dorset's Golf Clubs, The Ashley Wood's 18 holes occupy some of the most outstanding landscape in the country!

Green Fees/Society Deals
from £25pp
Book now for 2011 and retain 2010 rates!

Deals available for Groups of 12 or more with the Society Organiser getting free golf!*

t: 0844 822 5560
'press option 5'

www.ashleywoodgolfclub.com
Wimborne Road, Blandford Forum,
Dorset DT11 9HN

*Terms and Conditions apply

Dorset / WEST REGION — THE GOLF GUIDE 2011

BRIDPORT. Bridport and West Dorset Golf Club, Burton Road, Bridport DT6 4PS (01308 421095). *Location*: one mile east of Bridport on B3157. Clifftop links course. 18 holes, 5729 yards. Par 70. Driving range and 9-hole pitch and putt course, 18 hole putting green May to September. *Green Fees*: information not available. *Eating facilities*: lounge and dining room, spikes bar. *Visitors*: welcome, but not before 9.30am Mondays, Wednesdays, Fridays and Saturdays, and after 1pm Tuesdays, Thursdays and Sundays. Members only 8am-9.30am daily and 11am-2pm weekends. Please check with Professional in advance. *Society Meetings*: catered for by prior arrangement. Clubhouse: (01308 422597). Caterer: (01308 421998). Professional: David Parsons (01308 421491). Secretary: Peter Ridler (Tel & Fax: 01308 421095).*
e-mail: secretary@bridportgolfclub.org.uk
website: www.bridportgolfclub.org.uk

BROADSTONE. Broadstone (Dorset) Golf Club, Wentworth Drive, Broadstone BH18 8DQ (01202 692595). *Location*: off A349 to B3072 to Broadstone. Heathland. 18 holes, 6419 yards. S.S.S. 71. Practice area. *Green Fees*: weekdays £58.00 per round, £88.00 per day. Weekend/Bank Holidays one round £70.00 (very limited). *Eating facilities*: full catering service. *Visitors*: welcome weekdays, weekends by prior arrangement, current Handicap Certificate required. *Society Meetings*: welcome by arrangement except weekends. Professional: Mathew Wilson (Tel & Fax: 01202 692835). Secretary: David Morgan (Tel & Fax: 01202 692595).
e-mail: admin@broadstonegolfclub.com
website: www.broadstonegolfclub.com

CHRISTCHURCH. Dudmoor Farm Golf Course, Dudmoor Farm Road, Christchurch BH23 6AQ. *Location:* off Fairmile road, near Christchurch Hospital. Wooded course. 9 holes. Longest hole 280 yards. *Green Fees:* 18 holes - £9.50 weekdays, £10.50 weekends and Bank Holidays. *Eating facilities:* tea, coffee, crisps, chocolate, ice cream. *Visitors:* welcome, no need to book. Riding instruction also available. (01202 473826; Fax: 01202 480207).

CHRISTCHURCH. Highcliffe Castle Golf Club, 107 Lymington Road, Christchurch BH23 4LA (01425 272953). *Location:* on the coastal road linking Lymington and Christchurch. Flat, wooded course. 18 holes, 4798 yards, 4387 metres. S.S.S. 63. Two practice nets. *Green Fees:* weekdays £27.50; weekends £30.00. Reductions during winter months and after 4pm in summer. Handicap Certificate preferred. *Eating facilities:* full bar/catering facilities. *Visitors:* welcome after 9.30am. Please phone to check tee reservations. *Society Meetings:* catered for by prior arrangement. Secretary: Graham Fisher (01425 272210).

CHRISTCHURCH. Parley Court Golf Club, Parley Green Lane, Hurn, Christchurch BH23 6BB (01202 591600). *Location:* opposite Bournemouth International Airport. Flat and challenging course. 9 holes (18 tees), 4938 yards (18 holes). S.S.S. 64, Par 68. Putting and chipping areas. *Green Fees:* information not available. *Eating facilities:* licensed bar; catering available. *Visitors:* welcome. No booking or Handicap Certificate required. Membership available. *Society Meetings:* welcome. Professional: Richard Hill. Secretary: S.D. Mitchell (01202 591600).*
e-mail: info@parleygolf.co.uk
website: www.parleygolf.co.uk

DORCHESTER. Came Down Golf Club, Came Down, Dorchester DT2 8NR (01305 813494). *Location*: two miles south of Dorchester. Downland course on chalk downs with excellent drainage and magnificent views. Birthplace of the Ryder Cup. Designed by Harry S. Colt. 18 holes, 6255 yards, 5720 metres. S.S.S. 70. Practice area and nets. *Green Fees:* £38.00 weekdays, £42.00 weekends. *Eating facilities:* full catering facilities. *Visitors:* welcome without reservation except Saturday and Sunday mornings - phone in advance. All visitors must have Handicap Certificate. Buggies for hire. Established in 1896. *Society Meetings:* Package from £29.50 includes golf and food. Professional: Nick Rodgers (01305 812670). Manager: Matthew Staveley (01305 813494; Fax: 01305 815122).
e-mail: manager@camedowngolfclub.co.uk
website: www.camedowngolfclub.co.uk

DORCHESTER. Charminster Golf Club, Wolfedale Golf Course, Dorchester DT2 7SG (01305 260186; Fax: 01305 257074). *Location:* Dorchester. Parkland course. 18 holes, 5467 yards. S.S.S. 67. 6 hole practice area. *Green Fees:* information not available. *Eating facilities:* Caddy Shack bar and restaurant. *Visitors:* welcome anytime. Sundays mainly competition days. *Society Meetings:* welcome. Professional: Tim Lovegrove (01305 260186; Fax: 01305 833668). Secretary: R. Walker.*

FERNDOWN. Dudsbury Golf Club, Christchurch Road, Ferndown BH22 8ST (01202 593499; Fax: 01202 594555). *Location:* Ferndown town centre. Follow signs for Poole on A348, turn left at first mini roundabout, turn left to Hurn Airport, 200 yards. Club on right hand side. Parkland course designed by Donald Steel, featuring six lakes in beautiful Dorset countryside rolling gently down to the River Stour. 18 holes, 6904 yards. S.S.S 73. 6 hole academy course, driving range. *Green Fees:* information not available. *Eating facilities:* two bars, spike bar, food served all day. *Visitors:* welcome at all times. Buggies and trolleys available. *Society Meetings:* welcome, phone Secretary for details. Professional: Steve Pockneall (01202 594488).

Came Down Golf Club
Came Down, Dorchester DT2 8NR Tel: 01305 813494
e-mail: manager@camedowngolfclub.co.uk
www.camedowngolfclub.co.uk
BIRTHPLACE OF THE RYDER CUP
Friendly club on chalk downs with magnificent views, designed by Harry S. Colt. Come and sample our hospitality. For golf in Dorset, there's nowhere better than Came Down.

THE GOLF GUIDE 2011 — WEST REGION / Dorset

FERNDOWN. Ferndown Golf Club, 119 Golf Links Road, Ferndown BH22 8BU (01202 653950). *Location*: off A31. Wooded heathland. 18 holes, 6453 yards. S.S.S. 71. 9 holes, 5651 yards. S.S.S. 68. Practice ground. *Green Fees:* information not available. *Eating facilities*: available. *Visitors:* welcome but prior permission recommended. Handicap Certificate required from a recognised golf club. Professional: Neil Pike (01202 653951/2). Secretary: Sean Malherbe (01202 653950; Fax: 01202 653960).*

FERNDOWN. Ferndown Forest Golf Club, Forest Links Road, Ferndown BH22 9PH (01202 876096; Fax: 01202 894095). *Location:* off main A31 trunk road. Flat, wooded parkland. 18 holes, 5200 yards, Par 68. Covered, floodlit driving range; large practice putting green. *Green Fees:* information not available. *Eating facilities:* licensed bar and patio serving breakfast, lunch, dinner. *Visitors*: all welcome. *Society Meetings*: welcome. Professional: Graham Howell. Secretary: Chris Lawford.

HALSTOCK. Halstock Golf Club, Common Lane, Halstock BA22 9SF (01935 891689; Fax: 01935 891839). *Location:* six miles south of Yeovil near Sutton Bingham Reservoir, signposted in village. Flat parkland course, short, tight but challenging. 18 holes, 4481 yards. S.S.S. 63. 12 bay driving range. *Green Fees:* information not available. *Eating facilities:* light refreshments available, bar, restaurant (01935 891747). *Visitors:* welcome at all times. Please telephone for booking. *Society Meetings:* catered for by prior arrangement. Secretary: John Page.*

LYME REGIS. Lyme Regis Golf Club, Timber Hill, Lyme Regis DT7 3HQ (01297 442963). *Location:* between Lyme Regis and Charmouth (A35). Cliff top course (not hilly) with fine coastal views. 18 holes, 6283 yards. S.S.S. 70. Practice ground, chipping area and bunker. New Driving Range open, tokens from Pro Shop. *Green Fees:* £36.00 per round. *Eating facilities:* bars (normal hours) and catering every day. *Visitors:* welcome, but not before 9.30am weekdays and Saturdays, Thursdays after 2.15pm and Sundays after 12 noon. Best to check with Professional. Handicap Certificate or proof of membership of a golf club required. *Society Meetings:* Tuesdays and Wednesdays, minimum for Tee Booking 14. Professional: Duncan Driver (01297 442963 select option 1). Secretary: Miss Sue Davidge (01297 442963). e-mail: secretary@lrgc.eclipse.co.uk
website: www.lymeregisgolfclub.co.uk

POOLE. Parkstone Golf Club, 49a Links Road, Parkstone, Poole BH14 9QS (01202 707138). *Location*: off A35 Bournemouth to Poole. Wooded heathland. 18 holes, 6251 yards. S.S.S. 71. *Green Fees:* April to October weekdays £60.00 per round, £85.00 per day; weekends and Bank Holidays £70.00 per round, £95.00 per day. November to March weekdays £35.00 per round, weekends £45.00. 2010 rates (subject to review). *Eating facilities:* comprehensive. *Visitors:* welcome with booking and Handicap Certificate. *Society Meetings:* catered for. Professional: Martyn Thompson (01202 708092). General Manager: Gary Peddie (01202 707138). e-mail: admin@parkstonegolfclub.co.uk

---

Pay & Play on our 18 hole Golf Course

No Handicap Certificate needed • New Beginners Course
Excellent Pro Shop • Equipment Hire Available

NCG Discount for:
Adults pay **£13.50**
Over 60's Senior **£9.80**
Under 17 Junior **£7.50**
18 Holes until May 7th

**Season Tickets
Bar & Restaurant
Facilities open to everyone**

Charminster, Dorchester, Dorset

01305 260186 Shop • 01305 262486 Bar

We believe we have one of the best golf courses in the South West and one of the finest locations in all Britain. The course occupies a cliff top site with coastal views to Portland Bill. Although on the top of a plateau the course itself is not actually hilly and golfers can enjoy an exhilarating round of golf and some magnificent views. We have a new driving range, and a separate chipping area and practice bunker close to the first tee. Visitors are most welcome.

Lyme Regis Golf Club
Timber Hill, Lyme Regis, Dorset DT7 3HQ
Tel: 01297 442963 • e-mail: secretary@lrgc.eclipse.co.uk
www.lymeregisgolfclub.co.uk

Dorset / WEST REGION

POOLE near. **Bulbury Woods Golf Club,** Bulbury Lane, Lytchett Minster, Poole BH16 6HR (01929 459574; Fax: 01929 459000). *Location:* just off A35, one mile after the Bakers Arms roundabout, three miles from Poole centre. Excellent woodland course, superbly manicured, panoramic views across Poole harbour and the Purbeck Hills. 18 holes, 6000 yards, par 71. Practice ground. *Green Fees:* information not available. *Eating facilities:* fully licensed bar and restaurant. *Visitors:* welcome anytime subject to availability. *Society Meetings:* societies and corporate days by prior arrangement.*

SHERBORNE. **Sherborne Golf Club,** Higher Clatcombe, Sherborne DT9 4RN (01935 814431; Fax: 01935 814218). *Location*: one mile north of Sherborne off the B3145 to Wincanton. Parkland with extensive views. 18 holes, 6414 yards. Par 72. S.S.S. 71. Practice ground. *Green Fees:* £40.00. *Eating facilities:* snacks, lunches, suppers, teas; dinners to order. *Visitors:* as commitment allows, telephone in advance. Handicap Certificates required. Thursday is Ladies' Day. *Society Meetings:* catered for Monday, Tuesday, Wednesday and Friday. Professional: Alistair Tresidder (Tel & Fax: 01935 812274).
e-mail: secretary@sherbornegolfclub.co.uk
website: www.sherbornegolfclub.co.uk

SOUTH PERROTT. **Chedington Court Golf Club,** South Perrott DT8 3HU (01935 891413). *Location:* three miles south east of Crewkerne on A356. Parkland course surrounded by woods, very picturesque, several ponds. 18 holes, 5924 yards, S.S.S. 70. 5-acre practice area. *Green Fees:* £25.00 weekdays, £30.00 weekends. *Eating facilities:* restaurant and bar open all day; new dining facility. *Visitors:* all welcome. Dress restrictions. Trolleys, buggies and clubs for hire. *Society Meetings:* all welcome, special rates available.
e-mail: info@chedingtoncourtgolfclub.com
website: www.chedingtoncourtgolfclub.com

STUDLAND. **Isle of Purbeck Golf Club,** Studland, Swanage BH19 3AB (01929 450361). *Location:* A351 towards Swanage, at Corfe Castle turn onto B3351 to Studland. Heathland courses with wonderful views. Purbeck - 18 holes, 6295 yards. S.S.S. 70. Dene - 9 holes, 2022 yards. S.S.S. 30. *Green Fees:* information not provided. *Eating facilities:* bar and restaurant. *Visitors:* welcome. Buggies available. *Society Meetings:* catered for by arrangement, minimum 8. Professional: Philippe Bonfanti (01929 450354). Secretary: Mrs C. Robinson (01929 450361; Fax: 01929 450501).
e-mail: iop@purbeckgolf.co.uk
website: www.purbeckgolf.co.uk

VERWOOD. **Crane Valley Golf Club,** The Clubhouse, Verwood BH31 7LE (01202 814088; Fax: 01202 813407). *Location:* on B3081 Verwood to Cranborne Road. Parkland featuring lakes and River Crane. 18 holes, 6400 yards. S.S.S. 71. 9 hole woodland course, 2100 yards. Covered driving range. *Green Fees:* Valley Course - weekdays £30.00, weekends £35.00. Woodland Course - weekdays £8.00, weekends £9.00. *Eating facilities:* restaurant and spikes bar. *Visitors:* welcome at all times. Accommodation adjoining course at West Farm. *Society Meetings*: by appointment. Secretary/Manager: Andrew Blackwell.

"Welcome to one of the most beautiful places in England. I can't take credit for the glorious views and the beaches. But I am proud to provide a comfortable and relaxing hotel with good food and attentive but informal service, to give you the break you deserve."

Andrew Purkis

Manor House Hotel, Studland, Dorset, BH19 3AU • T - 01929 450288
• W - www.themanorhousehotel.com E - info@themanorhousehotel.com

WAREHAM. **Wareham Golf Club,** Sandford Road, Wareham BH20 4DH (01929 554187; Fax: 01929 557993). *Location*: adjoining A351 north of Wareham. Partly wooded course with splendid views over Purbeck Hills and Poole Harbour. 18 holes, 5766 yards, S.S.S. 68. Practice ground, putting green. *Green Fees*: please telephone the Secretary for further information. *Eating facilities*: excellent bar and restaurant. *Visitors*: welcome, after 9.30am weekdays and after 1pm weekends. Handicap Certificate preferred. *Society Meetings*: very welcome, special packages available.
e-mail: warehamgolf@tiscali.co.uk
website: www.warehamgolfclub.com

WAREHAM. **The Dorset Golf & Country Club,** Hyde, Bere Regis, Near Wareham BH20 7NT (01929 472244; Fax: 01929 471294). *Location*: take A352 off Wareham by-pass, enter Puddletown Road, Worgret Heath or the Wool road from Bere Regis. After 4 miles, the Club is clearly signposted. A fantastic Golfing Complex. The courses have 27 holes with mixes of the three 9 holes. From 7027 yards Lakeland and Parkland, to 5901 yards Parkland and Woodland courses. Par 72 and Par 69. Driving range and Pro Shop. *Green Fees*: weekdays £39.00; weekends £43.00. *Eating facilities*: excellent bar and restaurant. *Visitors*: welcome anytime with prior tee reservation. *Society Meetings:* welcome by advance booking. The Dorset Golf Hotel overlooks course – 16 en suite bedrooms and 12 luxury Scandinavian log homes for rent. Professional: Scott Porter (01929 472244). Secretary: Graham Packer (01929 472244; Fax: 01929 471294).
e-mail: admin@dorsetgolfresort.com
website: www.dorsetgolfresort.com

Purbeck House Hotel & Louisa Lodge
91 High Street, Swanage, Dorset BH19 2LZ
Tel: 01929 422872 • Fax: 01929 421194

- A 38-bedroom, family-run hotel, close to the town centre, the sea and a clean, sandy beach.
- Superbly appointed en suite rooms have views across Swanage Bay, Victorian gardens, and to the Purbeck Hills beyond.
- Luxurious surroundings and fine dining in our two superb restaurants
- **Approximately 2 miles from Isle of Purbeck Golf Club.**

reservations@purbeckhousehotel.co.uk • www.purbeckhousehotel.co.uk

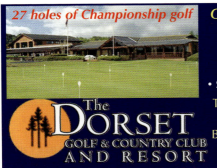

27 holes of Championship golf

Golf Breaks in 5 Star Luxury Lodges
- 4 star Dormy Golf Lodge
- Lakeland, Woodland & Parkland Golf Courses
- USGA Specification Greens & Tees
- 16 Bay Floodlit Driving Range
- Seasonal Specials • Individually Tailored Packages

Tel: 01929 472644 • Fax: 01929 471294
e-mail: admin@dorsetgolfresort.com
Bere Regis, Near Poole, Dorset BH20 7NT
www.dorsetgolfresort.com

Wareham Golf Club
Eighteen holes of challenging golf in the beautiful Dorset countryside.
Visitors and societies welcome
Membership also currently available
01929 554147
www.warehamgolfclub.com

Dorset / WEST REGION

WEYMOUTH. Wessex Golf Centre, Radipole Lane, Weymouth DT4 9HX (01305 784737). *Location:* Wessex roundabout off Weymouth by pass, behind football stadium. Flat public course. 9 holes, 1432 yards. Par 3. Large driving range, putting green, practice bunker. *Green Fees:* information not available. *Visitors:* welcome; public course. Shop. Professional: Jon Bevan.*

WEYMOUTH. Weymouth Golf Club Ltd, Links Road, Weymouth DT4 0PF (0844 9809909); Fax: 01305 788029). *Location:* A354 from Dorchester, take last exit at Manor roundabout then second left at Chafeys roundabout. Undulating parkland. 18 holes, 6044 yards. S.S.S. 70. Practice area. *Green Fees:* weekdays £34.00 per day, weekends and Bank Holidays £45.00. £20.00 after 4pm. Half price playing with a member. Juniors half price. 2010 rates (subject to review). *Eating facilities:* full restaurant and bar. *Visitors:* welcome, but only with EGU or Club Handicap Certificate. *Society Meetings:* welcome by prior arrangement except weekends. Special rates for Society, Company/ Corporate Days. Conference facilities and local transport arranged. Professional: Des Lochrie (01305 773997). Manager: Stuart Elliott (0844 9809909; Fax: 01305 788029).
e-mail: weymouthgolfclub@aol.com
website: www.weymouthgolfclub.co.uk

WIMBORNE. Canford Magna Golf Club, Knighton Lane, Wimborne BH21 3AS (01202 592552; Fax: 01202 592550). *Location:* off A341, near Bear Cross roundabout on the main A348 Ringwood Road. Three courses: Parkland – 18 holes, 6519 yards; Riverside – 18 holes, 6173 yards; Knighton – 9 holes, 1377 yards, Par 3. 6-hole academy course and driving range, practice area. *Green Fees:* Knighton – 9 holes from £7.00; Riverside - 18 holes from £19.50; Parkland – 18 holes from £23.50. Under 18s £12.00. 2010 rates, (subject to review). *Eating facilities:* two bars, meals served throughout day; restaurant. *Visitors:* welcome. Prior booking advisable (one week in advance). Club hire and lessons; Pro Shop. Handicap Certificate not required. Conference facilities. Professionals: 4 full-time professionals headed by PGA Pro David Cooper. General Manager: Stuart Hudson.
e-mail: admin@canfordmagnagc.co.uk
website: www.canfordmagnagc.co.uk

WIMBORNE. Canford School Golf Club, Canford School, Canford Magna. Wimborne BH21 3AD (01202 841254; Fax: 01202 881009). *Location:* close to Wimborne, Poole and Bournemouth. Flat Parkland course. 9 (x2) holes, 5934 yards, S.S.S. 69. *Green Fees*: information not available. *Society Meetings*: Contact Secretary. Secretary: Mark Burley (01202 841254; Fax: 01202 881009).*

WIMBORNE. Sturminster Marshall Golf Club, Moor Lane, Sturminster Marshall, Wimborne BH21 4AH (01258 858444; Fax: 01258 858262). *Location:* Poole to Blandford Forum road, A350 signposted at village. Flat parkland course, suits golfers of all abilities. 9/18 holes, Par 64. Practice net. *Green Fees:* information not available. *Eating facilities:* fully licensed snack bar. *Visitors:* welcome, no restrictions. *Society Meetings:* welcome. Professional/Secretary: Mike Dodd.*

Other useful guides to holidays in Britain from FHG Guides

PUBS & INNS
300 GREAT HOTELS
SHORT BREAK HOLIDAYS
The original PETS WELCOME!
500 GREAT PLACES TO STAY
SELF-CATERING HOLIDAYS •
BED & BREAKFAST STOPS
CARAVAN & CAMPING HOLIDAYS
FAMILY BREAKS

Published annually: available in all good bookshops or direct from the publisher:
FHG Guides, Abbey Mill Business Centre, Seedhill, Paisley PA1 1TJ
Tel: 0141 887 0428 • Fax: 0141 889 7204
e-mail: admin@fhguides.co.uk
www.holidayguides.com

PLEASE MENTION THIS GUIDE WHEN YOU ENQUIRE ABOUT CLUBS OR ACCOMMODATION

Gloucestershire

BRISTOL. **Bristol and Clifton Golf Club,** Beggar Bush Lane, Failand, Bristol BS8 3TH (01275 393474). *Location:* M5 Junction 19 - A369 towards Clifton, turn right at A.T.S. into Beggar Bush Lane. Parkland course. 18 holes, 6294 yards. S.S.S. 70. Practice ground. *Green Fees:* weekdays £50.50; weekends £60.50. *Eating facilities:* full restaurant. *Visitors:* welcome weekdays without reservation, must have current golf club Handicap. *Society Meetings:* most welcome, Thursdays. Professional: Paul Mitchell (Tel & Fax: 01275 393031). Secretary: James MacPherson (01275 393474; Fax: 01275 394611).
e-mail: mansec@bristolgolf.co.uk
website: www.bristolgolf.co.uk

BRISTOL. **Chipping Sodbury Golf Club,** Trinity Lane, Chipping Sodbury, Bristol BS37 6PU (01454 319042). *Location:* 12 miles north of Bristol, nine miles from Junction 14 on M5 and three miles from Junction 18 on M4. Parkland course. 6786 yards. *Green Fees:* 18-hole course weekdays £32.00; weekends £45.00. *Eating facilities:* full catering available. *Visitors:* welcome except Saturday/Sunday morning and Bank Holidays. *Society Meetings:* catered for by prior arrangement weekdays only. Professional: Mike Watts (01454 314087). Secretary: Bob Williams.
e-mail: info@chippingsodburygolfclub.co.uk
website: www.chippingsodburygolfclub.co.uk

Please mention THE GOLF GUIDE when you enquire about clubs or accommodation

BRISTOL. **Filton Golf Club,** Golf Course Lane, Filton, Bristol BS34 7QS (0117 969 4169; Fax: 0117 931 4359). *Location:* off A38 north of Bristol and only 3 miles from J15 of M5. Interesting, undulating and challenging mature parkland course on high ground to the north of the City. Established 1909 and regular host to County events. 18 holes, 6174 yards, Par 70, S.S.S 70. Excellent practice facilities. *Green Fees:* weekdays £36.00 per round, £40.00 per day. 2010 rates (subject to review). Weekends only as guest of member. Buggies and trolleys for hire. *Eating Facilities:* excellent menu of bar and main meals. *Visitors:* welcome subject to programme of club events. *Society Meetings:* welcome - usually available Monday, Wednesday and Friday - information pack on request. Advance booking essential. Professional: Daryl Kelley (0117 969 6968). Managing Secretary: Trevor Atkinson (0117 969 4169; Fax: 0117 931 4359).
e-mail: secretary@filtongolfclub.co.uk
website: www.filtongolfclub.co.uk

BRISTOL. **Henbury Golf Club,** Henbury Road, Westbury-on-Trym, Bristol BS10 7QB (0117 9500044). *Location:* north M5 Junction 17 A4018 to Westbury-on-Trym; right at traffic lights (Henbury Road), top of hill turn left. Wooded parkland, very picturesque;usually in superb condition; short distance from City Centre and M5. 18 holes, 6007 yards. S.S.S. 69. Practice ground. *Green Fees:* £36.00. *Eating facilities*: bars and dining room. *Visitors*: welcome weekdays and weekends, Handicap required. Clubs and trolleys for hire. *Society Meetings:* Tuesdays and Fridays normally. Professional: Nick Riley (Tel & Fax: 0117 9502121) Secretary: Derek Howell (0117 9500044; Fax: 0117 9591928).
e-mail: thesecretary@henburygolfclub.co.uk

BRISTOL & CLIFTON GOLF CLUB • www.bristolgolf.co.uk
New members and visitors always welcome at this superb parkland course. First-class catering throughout the day.
Excellent practice facilities incl. short game and driving range.
Contact James MacPherson on 01275 393474 • e-mail: mansec@bristolgolf.co.uk

Henbury Golf Club

Henbury is a beautiful parkland course in mature woodland bordering the famous Blaise Castle Estate. The course provides a number of different challenges including the par 3 7th hole over the River Trym. It is a popular venue within 5 minutes of the M5 (junction 17) and only 15 minutes from the centre of Bristol.
The experienced greenkeeping team maintain the course in excellent condition throughout the year and our fine greens are the envy of many clubs.
Henbury hosts the prestigious City & County of Bristol Championship each September.
The clubhouse offers excellent dining and comfortable surroundings for a relaxed drink after your game.
It is an ideal society venue with many groups returning year after year. Visitors are welcome 7 days a week.
Henbury Road, Westbury-on-Trym, Bristol, Gloucestershire BS10 7QB
Managing Secretary: Derek Howell 0117 9500044 • Professional: Nick Riley 0117 9502121
e-mail: thesecretary@henburygolfclub.co.uk • www.henburygolfclub.co.uk

Gloucestershire / WEST REGION

BRISTOL. The Kendleshire Golf Club, Henfield Road, Coalpit Heath, Bristol BS36 2TG (0117 956 7007; Fax: 0117 957 3433). *Location:* five minutes from Junction 1 M32. Parkland with water features including the "Island Green" 11th hole. 27 holes, from 6001 to 6507 yards. S.S.S. 71. Practice range, academy course and golf buggies available. *Green Fees:* information not available. *Eating facilities:* Golfers bar and sun-loving patio overlooking the 18th green, numerous function rooms. *Visitors:* welcome but prior booking essential. *Society Meetings:* welcome weekdays, packages available. Professional: Tony Mealing. Secretary: Patrick Murphy.
e-mail: info@kendleshire.com
website: www.kendleshire.com

BRISTOL. Knowle Bristol Golf Club, Fairway, West Town Lane, Brislington, Bristol BS4 5DF (0117 977 0660). *Location:* three miles south of city centre, left off Wells Road. A4 – Bath. Parkland course. 18 holes, 6006 yards. S.S.S. 69. Practice field, putting green. *Green Fees:* information not available. *Eating facilities:* bar/dining room, dinners by arrangement with Steward. *Visitors:* welcome with Handicap Certificate. *Society Meetings:* Thursdays only. Professional: Rob Hayward (0117 977 9193). Secretary: Viv Butler (0117 977 0660; Fax: 0117 972 0615).
website: www.knowlegolfclub.co.uk

BRISTOL. Thornbury Golf Centre, Bristol Road, Thornbury, Bristol BS35 3XL (01454 281144; Fax: 01454 281177). *Location:* five miles A38 north from Junctions M4/M5 at Almondsbury. Parkland course overlooking River Severn. 18 holes, 6308 yards. S.S.S. 70. Par 3 course. 25 bay floodlit driving range. *Green Fees:* information not available. *Eating facilities:* restaurant and licensed bar. *Visitors:* welcome seven days. Smart casual clothing desirable. Tuition. Golf Lodge available with 11 rooms. Stay and play packages. Conference and private function facilities. *Society Meetings:* welcome seven days. Professional: Mike Smedley. General Manager: Kevin Pickett.*
e-mail: info@thornburygc.co.uk
website: www.thornburygc.co.uk

BRISTOL. Long Ashton Golf Club, Clarken Coombe, Long Ashton, Bristol BS41 9DW (01275 392229; Fax: 01275 394395). *Location:* three miles south-west of Bristol on the B3128 Clevedon/Bristol Road. Wooded parkland. 18 holes, 6193 yards. S.S.S. 70. Practice ground. *Green Fees:* weekdays £30.00 18 holes, £35.00 36 holes; weekends £35.00 18 holes. *Eating facilities:* full catering daily, bar open Monday to Sunday (11am to 10.30pm). *Visitors:* welcome, must have current Handicap Certificate. *Society Meetings:* by arrangement with Secretary. Professional: Mike Hart (01275 392229). Secretary: Victoria Rose (01275 392229).
e-mail: secretary@longashtongolfclub.co.uk
website: www.longashtongolfclub.co.uk

WEST REGION / Gloucestershire

BRISTOL **The Park Resort,** Tracy Park Estate, Bath Road, Wick, Near Bristol BS30 5RN (0117 937 1800; Fax: 0117 937 4288). *Location*: M4 Junction 18, A46 towards Bath, A420 towards Bristol. Turn left at bottom of steep hill for Lansdown/Bath. Wooded parkland, 400-year-old trees with water hazards and magnificent views of surrounding countryside. Two courses: Crown Course - 18 holes, 6252 yards, Par 69; Cromwell Course - 18 holes, 6246 yards, Par 71. 13 bay driving range. *Green Fees:* telephone for details. *Eating facilities:* full catering available all day. *Visitors:* welcome – telephone ahead. *Society Meetings:* welcome. 24 en suite bedrooms. Director of Golf: Stuart Leech. Tee reservations (0117 937 1783; Fax: 0117 937 4288).
e-mail: golf@tpresort.com
website: www.theparkresort.com

BRISTOL. **Shirehampton Park Golf Club,** Park Hill, Shirehampton, Bristol BS11 0UL (0117 982 2083). *Location*: two miles from Junction 18 on M5 on B4054 to Shirehampton. Parkland course with spectacular views across Avon Gorge. 18 holes, 5502 yards. S.S.S. 67. *Green Fees:* weekdays £24.00, weekends £28.00. *Eating facilities:* lunches, snacks, teas, etc available daily. *Visitors:* welcome. *Society Meetings:* catered for by prior arrangement. Professional: Jon Palmer (0117 316 7955 or 0117 982 2488). Club Secretary: Karen Rix (0117 982 2083).

BRISTOL. **Shortwood Lodge Golf Club,** Carsons Road, Mangotsfield, Bristol BS16 9LW (0117 9565501). *Location*: four miles M32 via Downend, one mile Warmley A420. Parkland, hilly course. 18 holes, 5337 yards, 4877 metres. S.S.S. 66. Small practice area. *Green Fees:* weekdays £14.00, weekends £16.00. *Eating facilities:* no restriction on food and drink. *Visitors:* welcome anytime, no restrictions. *Society Meetings:* catered for weekdays only. Professional/Secretary: David Knipe.

BRISTOL. **Woodlands Golf and Country Club,** Trench Lane, Almondsbury, Bristol BS32 4JZ (01454 619319). *Location*: Junction 16 M5 - A38 towards Bristol. Left off AZTEC roundabout, first left Woodlands Lane. Two magnificent parkland 18 hole courses with USGA greens. The Masters Course 6101 yards. S.S.S. 70, with water in play on 8 holes. The Signature Course 5533 yards S.S.S. 69, water in play on 9 holes, drop hole with island green. Putting green. *Green Fees:* weekdays £14.00 per round, weekends £16.00 per round. *Eating facilities:* bar/lounge meals, snacks. *Visitors:* welcome, no restrictions and hire of clubs available. Trolleys and buggies available £12.00 per round. *Society Meetings:* bookable in advance. Pro shop. Professional: Leigh Riddiford (01454 619319). Secretary: David Knipe (Fax: 01454 619397; Clubhouse: 01454 618121).
e-mail: info@woodlands-golf.com
website: www.woodlands-golf.com

BROADWAY. **Broadway Golf Club,** Willersey Hill, Broadway WR12 7LG (01386 853683; Fax: 01386 858643). *Location*: 1½ miles east Broadway (A44). 18 holes, 6211 yards. S.S.S. 70. *Green Fees:* weekdays £32.00, weekends £40.00. *Eating facilities:* available daily. *Visitors:* welcome; reservation advised. Handicap Certificates required. Saturdays (April/September) with member only before 2pm. October/March no restrictions. Affiliated to the "Gloucestershire Golf Union". *Society Meetings:* by arrangement. Professional: Martyn Freeman (01386 853275). Secretary: Vic Tofts. Office: (01386 853683).

CHELTENHAM. **Brickhampton Court Golf Complex,** Cheltenham Road, Churchdown GL2 9QF (01452 859444; Fax: 01452 859333). *Location*: midway between Cheltenham and Gloucester on B4063; 5 minutes from Junction 11 of M5. Rolling parkland courses featuring lakes, streams, strategic white sand bunkers, tree plantations and no steep hills. Two courses: Spa Course – 18 holes, 6449 yards. S.S.S. 71; Glevum Course – 9 holes, 1859 yards. Par 31. 28 bay floodlit covered driving range. *Green Fees:* Spa Course - £23.00 per round all days. Glevum Course - weekdays £9.00; weekends and Bank Holidays £11.00. *Eating facilities:* bar and restaurant offering varied menu and Sunday lunches. *Visitors:* welcome although pre-booking advised. Buggies and trolleys for hire. Two fully stocked Pro shops. Conference facilities and corporate and society Golf Days available, call for details.
e-mail: info@brickhampton.co.uk
website: www.brickhampton.co.uk

Willersey Hill, Broadway WR12 7LG

One of the Cotswolds' premier Courses

Located 850 ft above sea level on a Cotswold escarpment, with exceptional views over the Vale of Evesham. Characterised by rolling fairways, intersected by dry stone walls, with undulating greens that will test the best of golfers.
Winners of the Whyte & Mackay/Golf World 2007 award for the best 19th Hole in the UK, renowned for exceptional catering, bar facilities and ambience. Visitors, come and enjoy a splendid round of golf complemented by a superb culinary experience.
Visit our web site **www.broadwaygolfclub.co.uk** Or call for details on **01386 853683**
Junior and Social Membership currently available. (BGC is Golf and Club Mark accredited)

CHELTENHAM. **Cleeve Hill Golf Club,** Cleeve Hill, Near Cheltenham GL52 3PW (01242 672025). *Location:* three miles north of Cheltenham on B4632. Hilltop inland links with gorse and natural quarries. Outstanding views from the highest point in the Cotswolds. 18 holes, 6411 yards. S.S.S. 72. *Green Fees:* information not available. *Eating facilities:* full restaurant and bar facilities. *Visitors:* welcome with prior booking. *Society Meetings:* welcome with prior booking (01242 672025). Professional: Dave Finch (01242 672592). Secretary: Hugh Fitzsimons (01242 672025).*

CHELTENHAM. **Cotswold Hills Golf Club,** Ullenwood, Near Cheltenham GL53 9QT (01242 515264). *Location:* at Ullenwood, off the A436 south of Cheltenham (two miles from town). Undulating Cotswold country course, excellent drainage. 18 holes, 6557 yards. S.S.S. 72. Large practice ground. *Green Fees:* weekdays £36.00 18 holes; weekends £42.00 18 holes. *Eating facilities:* full restaurant and bars. *Visitors:* no restrictions as a rule, but it is wise to telephone. Handicap Certificate required. *Society Meetings:* catered for on Wednesdays and Fridays only by arrangement with Club Manager. Professional: James Latham (01242 515263). Club Manager: Annie Hale (01242 515264).
e-mail: contact.us@cotswoldhills-golfclub.com
website: www.cotswoldhills-golfclub.com

CHELTENHAM. **Lilley Brook Golf Club,** Cirencester Road, Charlton Kings, Cheltenham GL53 8EG (01242 526785). *Location:* two miles south-east of Cheltenham on main Cirencester road (A435). Parkland, 18 holes, 6212 yards. S.S.S. 70. *Green Fees:* information not available. *Eating facilities:* full catering available. *Visitors:* welcome weekdays, weekends subject to availability. *Society Meetings:* by arrangement. Professional: Simon Harrison (01242 525201). Office: (01242 526785).*

THE APPEARANCE OF AN ASTERISK (*) AT THE END OF A CLUB OR COURSE ENTRY INDICATES THAT UP-TO-DATE INFORMATION HAS NOT BEEN SUPPLIED

CHELTENHAM. **Naunton Downs Golf Club Ltd,** Naunton, Cheltenham GL54 3AE (01451 850092; Fax: 01451 850091). Rolling Cotswold countryside with a valley running through course. 18 holes, 6135 yards. S.S.S. 70. Practice ground. *Green Fees:* information not available. *Eating facilities:* available. *Visitors:* welcome, must book at all times. *Society Meetings:* welcome. Professional: Nick Ellis (01451 850092); Golf Manager: Nick Ellis (01451 850090); Club Stewards: Jodie Hart and Matt Beamish (01451 850093).*

CHELTENHAM. **Ullenwood Manor Golf Course,** National Star College, Ullenwood, Cheltenham GL53 9QU (01242 527631). *Location*: turn off A436 past junction with A417. Parkland course, 18 holes (using 9 fairways). 2980 yards S.S.S. 54. Designed by Norm Allen, opened 1975. *Green Fees*: £10.00 all day. *Eating facilities*: catering available at Air Balloon pub half mile away. *Visitors:* welcome anytime. *Society Meetings*: welcome anytime. Secretary: Richard Greenwell.
e-mail: rgreenwe@natstar.ac.uk

CIRENCESTER. **Cirencester Golf Club,** Cheltenham Road, Bagendon, Cirencester GL7 7BH (01285 652465; Fax: 01285 650665). *Location:* two miles north of Cirencester on A435 Cheltenham road. Scenic and free-draining Cotswold course. 18 holes, 6030 yards. S.S.S. 69. Driving range, Par 3 course. *Green Fees:* weekdays £35.00, weekends £40.00. *Eating facilities:* bar and restaurant - snacks available 10am to 6pm. *Visitors:* welcome, dress code applies. Buggies for hire. *Society Meetings:* catered for seven days a week. Professional: Ed Goodwin (01285 656124). Secretary/Manager: R. Collishaw (01285 652465).
website: www.cirencestergolfclub.co.uk

COLEFORD. **Forest Hills Golf Club,** Mile End Road, Coleford GL16 7QD (01594 810620). Pro Shop: 01594 810823. *Location:* 10 miles from Severn Bridge, six miles from Monmouth M5, M50. 20 minutes from M5 at Gloucester. Coleford town centre on Gloucester Road. Parkland with panoramic views to Welsh hills. 18 holes, 6300 yards. Par 72. Practice ground, driving range. *Green Fees:* available on request. *Eating facilities:* bar, restaurant. *Visitors:* welcome, no restrictions. Buggies and electric trolleys available. *Society Meetings:* very welcome. Golf Sales Manager: Gavin Butcher.

COTSWOLD HILLS GOLF CLUB

This friendly Club is set in the picturesque Cotswolds, three miles south of Cheltenham in open rolling countryside, and is regarded as one of Gloucestershire's premier courses. The club has hosted many Championships, including the English Ladies' Amateur Championship, and will host the English Boys' County Finals in 2012. Visitors of all abilities are welcome and will enjoy this beautiful and challenging course.

Cotswold Hills Golf Club, Ullenwood,
Cheltenham, Gloucestershire GL53 9QT
Club Manager : Annie Hale • Tel: 01242 515264
www.cotswoldhills-golfclub.com

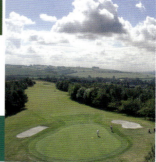

COLEFORD. Forest of Dean Golf Club, Lords Hill, Coleford GL16 8BE (01594 832583; Fax: 01594 832584). *Location:* quarter of a mile from Coleford town centre on B4431 Coleford to Parkend Road, 10 miles from Severn Bridge, M4, M5 and M50. Parkland course in Forest of Dean. 18 holes, 6033 yards. S.S.S. 69. Practice area. *Green Fees:* information not available. *Eating facilities:* food available all day - breakfast, coffee, lunches, teas and dinner. Table d'hôte restaurant, bar open all day. *Visitors:* always welcome, please book teeing-off times with Professional. Own 53 bedroom Hotel, golf shop on site, tennis court, bowling green, short mat bowling centre, golf cars available. *Society Meetings:* welcome. Professional: Stuart Jenkins (01594 833689). Secretary: Benn Jackson (01594 839356).

DURSLEY. **Stinchcombe Hill Golf Club,** Stinchcombe Hill, Dursley GL11 6AQ (01453 542015; Fax: 01453 549545). *Location*: M5 between Junctions 13 and 14, A38 to Dursley. At traffic lights in centre of Dursley turn right to enter May Lane, continue to top of Hill and turn right onto Golf Course. A gently undulating course situated on a hilltop at the southern edge of the Cotswolds, spectacular views. 18 holes, 5734 yards. S.S.S. 68. Practice and teaching areas. *Green Fees*: information not available. *Eating facilities*: full catering and bar service available. *Visitors*: welcome, please call the Professional in advance for availability. *Society Meetings*: Monday, Wednesday and Friday; other days by arrangement. Professional: Paul Bushell (01453 543878). Secretary: I. Crowther (01453 542015).*
e-mail: secretary@stinchcombehill.plus.com
website: www.stinchcombehillgolfclub.com

GLOUCESTER. **Ramada Hotel and Golf Resort,** Matson Lane, Gloucester GL4 9EA (01452 411331; Fax: 01452 302212). *Location:* follow signs off B4073. Stunning 18 hole, par 72 championship golf course, with breathtaking views of the surrounding countryside, complemented by challenging Par 3, 9-hole course, ideal for beginners and improvers, but a test to better players. Floodlit covered 12 bay golf academy with Callaway custom fit centre open 9.00am to 9.00pm, 7 days a week. Grass practice area with putting, chipping, pitching and bunker areas. *Green Fees:* information not available. *Eating facilities:* full catering and bar services available. *Visitors*: very welcome, please call for availability. Well-stocked and priced golf shop with all the leading brands, including Callaway, Ping and Taylormade. Hotel with 107 rooms with 5 suites. Extensive leisure complex with indoor swimming pool, gymnasium, sauna and solarium, health and beauty centre. Gloucester Ski Centre with qualified ski instructors. Golf breaks available, golf school with 2, 3 or 5 day programmes. Gloucester Golf Academy with team of registered PGA Golf Professionals. Pro-shop: (01452 411331/01452 874807)*
e-mail: gloucester@btopenworld.com
website: www.gloucestergolf.com

Forest Hills is a naturally undulating parkland course set in the beautiful Forest Of Dean, with panoramic views over the old market town of Coleford to the Welsh hills beyond. Regarded as one of the finest courses in the area with outstandly good drainage, allowing play throughout the year. Societies and Visitors very welcome. Buggies available.

Forest Hills Golf Club
Mile End Road, Coleford,
Gloucestershire GL16 7QD
Tel: 01594 810 620
www.foresthillsgolfandleisure.co.uk

Rated by Henry Longhurst as being among the top most scenic courses in England, Stinchcombe Hill is a challenging 18-hole course with a scratch par of 68. Gently undulating fairways add an additional interest to almost every shot. Members' and guests' facilities are of the highest standards, and arrangements can be made for whole day events for visiting groups. There can be few better places to spend a day, especially with a golf club in your hand.

Established 1889

Stinchcombe Hill Golf Club
Dursley, Gloucestershire GL11 6AQ
Tel: 01453 542015 • www.stinchcombehillgolfclub.com

Gloucestershire / WEST REGION

GLOUCESTER. Rodway Hill Golf Course, Highnam, Gloucester GL2 8DN (01452 384222). 18 holes, 6040 yards. S.S.S. 69. Driving range. *Green Fees:* £17.00 weekdays, £19.00 weekends. *Eating facilities:* cosy bar and restaurant. *Visitors:* all welcome - pay as you play. *Society Meetings:* welcome, special rates available.
website: www.rodway-hill-golf-course.co.uk

LYDNEY. Lydney Golf Club, The Links, off Lakeside Avenue, Lydney GL15 5QA (01594 842614). *Location:* between by-pass and the town, note - no access off by-pass, enter the town and take Hams Road off the main thoroughfare of Newerne Street. Lakeside Avenue is the 7th road on the left hand side. Flat meadowland with views over the River Severn. 9 holes, 5298 yards. S.S.S. 66. Small practice area. *Green Fees:* information not available. *Eating facilities:* snack meals only. *Visitors:* welcome weekdays, only with a member at weekends/Bank Holidays. *Society Meetings:* welcome by prior arrangement (maximum 36). Hon. Secretary: D.A. Barnard (01594 843940).*

MINCHINHAMPTON. Minchinhampton Golf Club (New Courses), Minchinhampton, Stroud GL6 9BE (01453 833866; Fax: 01453 837360). *Location:* five miles south-east of Stroud. Two exceptional courses set high on the Cotswolds in an Area of Outstanding Natural Beauty enjoying views over glorious countryside. Avening Course: 6311 yards S.S.S. 70. Superb parkland course featuring specimen trees, lakes. Cherington Course: 6459 yards S.S.S. 71. Inland links in style with challenging greens. Host to Open Championship Regional Qualifying 2002 to 2007, English Mid Amateur Championship 2007. Good practice facilities including covered Driving Range for use by members and green fee visitors only. *Green Fees:* weekdays £40.00, weekends £50.00. *Eating facilities:* fine Cotswold stone clubhouse offering good food - dining room and bar. *Visitors:* welcome, telephone booking essential on 01453 833840. Handicap Certificate required. *Society Meetings:* welcome weekdays, details on application. Professional: Chris Steele (01453 837351). Secretary/Manager: Robert East (01453 833866). Society/Corporate Bookings: Alan Green (01453 833866).
website: www.minchinhamptongolfclub.co.uk

MINCHINHAMPTON. Minchinhampton Golf Club (Old Course), Minchinhampton, Stroud GL6 9AQ (01453 832642). *Location*: three miles east of Stroud. Easy walking course. 18 holes, 6088 yards. S.S.S. 70. Practice area. *Green Fees:* weekdays £18.00, weekends and Bank Holidays £22.00. *Eating facilities:* bar and restaurant available. *Visitors:* welcome. *Society Meetings:* most welcome by arrangement. Admin Manager: A.P. Dangerfield (01453 832642). Shop: (01453 836382).
e-mail: alan@mgcold.co.uk
website: www.gcold.co.uk

PAINSWICK. Painswick Golf Club, Golf Course Road, Painswick, Near Stroud GL6 6TL (01452 812180). *Location:* one mile north of Painswick village on A46 turn left. Hilltop, wooded course. 18 holes, 4900 yards. S.S.S. 65. *Green Fees:* information not available. *Eating facilities:* lunches at clubhouse bar Tuesday to Sunday, evening meals in restaurant Tuesday to Saturday subject to availability of tables. *Visitors:* welcome weekdays and Saturday mornings. Saturday afternoons, Sunday mornings and Public Holidays only with member. *Society Meetings:* welcome weekdays. Secretary: Ann Smith.*
website: www.painswickgolf.com

TETBURY. Westonbirt Golf Course, c/o Jack Doyle, Westonbirt School Ltd, Westonbirt, Near Tetbury GL8 8QG (01666 880 242). *Location:* three miles south from Tetbury on A433 to Bath. Parkland. 9 holes, 4504 yards. S.S.S. 61. Practice area and green. *Green Fees:* information not available. *Eating facilities:* tea and refreshments from seasonal caravan. *Visitors:* welcome without reservation. *Society Meetings:* welcome.*
e-mail: doyle@westonbirt.gloucs.sch.uk
website: www.westonbirt.gloucs.sch.uk

Quality all ground floor accommodation. "Kilmorie" is Grade II Listed (c1848) within conservation area in a lovely part of Gloucestershire. Mostly en suite double, twin, family or single bedrooms, all having tea tray, colour digital TV, radio. Very comfortable guests' lounge, traditional home cooking is served in the separate diningroom overlooking large garden. Choice of golf nearby. Perhaps walk waymarked farmland footpaths which start here. We have ponies and "free range" hens. Rural yet perfectly situated to visit Cotswolds, Royal Forest of Dean, Wye Valley and Malvern Hills. Children over five years welcome. Hartpury College 3 miles. Ample parking.

Bed and full English Breakfast from £26 per person

**S.J. Barnfield, "Kilmorie Smallholding", Gloucester Road, Corse, Staunton, Gloucester GL19 3RQ
mobile: 07840 702218 • e-mail: sheila-barnfield@supanet.com**

THE GOLF GUIDE 2011 — WEST REGION / Gloucestershire

TEWKESBURY. **Hilton Puckrup Hall,** Puckrup, Tewkesbury GL20 6EL (01684 296200; Fax: 01684 850788). *Location:* leave M5 at Junction 8. Take M50 one mile to Junction 1, leave and bear left taking A38 towards Tewkesbury, Puckrup is half a mile along on the right. Undulating parkland with water hazards, spectacular views of the Malverns. 18 holes, 6219 yards. S.S.S. 70. Practice ground. *Green Fees:* information not available. *Eating facilities:* choice of bars and restaurants. *Visitors:* welcome, subject to golfing ability and course availability. Buggies available. 112 bedroomed hotel with full leisure facilities. Golfing Breaks available. *Society Meetings:* welcome, (min. 16 players). Professional: Mark Fenning (01684 271591). Secretary: Russell Lazenby (01452 840133).*
website: www.tewkesbury.hilton.com

TEWKESBURY. **Sherdons Golf Centre,** Tredington, Tewkesbury GL20 7BP (01684 274782; Fax: 01684 275358). *Location:* follow brown sign directions from A38 two miles south of Tewkesbury or A46 two miles east. Parkland course with bunkers, water and trees, and gentle slopes. 9 holes, 5308 yards. S.S.S. 66. 26 bay floodlit driving range. *Green Fees:* Information not provided. *Eating facilities:* restaurant, bar, coffee and light snacks available. *Visitors:* welcome at all times. *Society Meetings:* by arrangement. Special weekday society deals. Professionals: Philip Clark and John Parker (01684 274782). Secretary: Richard Chatham (01684 274782; Fax: 01684 275358).
website: www.sherdons.co.uk

TEWKESBURY. **Tewkesbury Park Hotel Golf and Country Club,** Lincoln Green Lane, Tewkesbury GL20 7DN (01684 295405; Fax: 01684 292386). *Location:* off Junction 9 of M5 through Tewkesbury on A38 - signposted. Parkland. 18 holes, 6533 yards. S.S.S. 71. Golf range, and pitching and chipping greens. *Green Fees:* information not available. *Eating facilities:* full Hotel facilities. *Visitors:* welcome, reservation required. Valid Handicap Certificate required. 82-bedroom hotel plus leisure section. *Society Meetings:* all welcome by prior arrangement. Professional: Marc Cottrell (01684 272320; Fax: 01684 292386).*
e-mail: tewkesburypark@foliohotels.com
website: www.tewkesburyparkgolfclub.co.uk

WOTTON-UNDER-EDGE. **Cotswold Edge Golf Club,** Upper Rushmire, Wotton-under-Edge GL12 7PT (01453 844167). *Location:* eight miles from Junction 14 M5, on B4058 Tetbury road. Fairly flat course with magnificent views. 18 holes, White Tees - 6170 yards. S.S.S. 71; Yellow Tees - 5816 yards. S.S.S. 69. *Green Fees:* information not provided. *Eating facilities:* good lunch time catering service, usual bar facilities. *Visitors:* welcome weekdays. Telephone call in advance advisable. *Society Meetings:* by arrangement with Secretary. Professional: Rod Hibbitt (01453 844398). Secretary: E. Johnson (01453 844167; Fax: 01453 845120).

Painswick Golf Club

PLAYER'S CHOICE • *"This is ancient links golf at its best, in my view, a challenge not to be missed. The golf is terrific - about as much fun as you can have without actually laughing. The 1st hole needs a 3-wood (trust me), then there's a mad, blind par 3 up and over the hill at the 4th or 5th (can't recall), where you have to shout 'Fore!' the moment you let it go. Well worth the trip."* - DAN COLBOURNE

Golf Course Road, Painswick, Gloucs GL6 6TL (01452 812180)

Floodlit Driving Range & Golf Course
www.sherdons.co.uk

**4 PGA Professionals • Tuition for groups and individuals at all levels
Clubhouse with bar and refreshments/meals • Conference room
Visitors always welcome • Special weekday society deals
Tredington, Tewkesbury • Tel: 01684 274782**

EXCITING GOLF AND PAMPER BREAKS NOW AVAILABLE

Come for tee

Do you live, breathe, eat and sleep golf? If so, we have the hotel for you.

Set in 140 acres of beautiful parkland between the Cotswolds and the Malverns, the four star Hilton Puckrup Hall has so much to enjoy, including 112 luxury bedrooms, conference facilities, a fully equipped health and leisure club, and a sumptuous restaurant, that you'll be forgiven for hardly venturing outside. That is until you see our 6219 yard, par 70 Championship Golf Course.

With mature trees and water hazards, and set in the lea of the Malverns, the course presents an exciting golf challenge for both the experienced and the novice golfer. Visitors are very welcome, with Green Fees starting at £30 per round weekdays, £40 for the day, and just £5 more at weekends. Society and Corporate packages (minimum of 16 players), start from £25pp.

So if you'd like the happy dilemma of the perfect golf hotel and the perfect golf course, you know where to come. For details of golf membership, to make a tee reservation, or to enquire about an appointment to view all this hotel has to offer, telephone:

01684 296200
01684 271591 Golf Shop

Hilton
PUCKRUP HALL
Tewkesbury
Gloucestershire GL20 6EL
Tel 01684 296200 Fax 01684 850788
www.tewkesbury.hilton.com

Somerset

BATH. **Bath Golf Club,** Sham Castle, North Road, Bath BA2 6JG (01225 425182). *Location:* off A36, one mile south-east of Bath City Centre. Hilltop, undulating downland course with views of Bath and the surrounding countryside. 18 holes, 6442 yards, 5891 metres. S.S.S. 71. *Green Fees:* information not available. *Eating facilities:* catering every day. *Visitors:* with bona fide Handicap welcome. *Society Meetings:* catered for Wednesday and Friday. Professional: Russell Covey (01225 466953). Club Secretary: Debbie Cole (01225 463834; Fax: 01225 331027).*
e-mail: proshop@bathgolfclub.org.uk
debbiecole@bathgolfclub.org.uk

BATH. **Entry Hill Golf Club,** Entry Hill, Bath BA2 5NA (01225 834248). *Location:* one mile south of city centre, off A367 road to Wells. Hilly parkland course with many young trees. 9 holes, 2103 yards, 1922 metres. S.S.S. 61 (18 holes). Practice net. *Green Fees:* information not available. *Eating facilities:* Spacious cafe serving excellent hot meals and snacks. *Visitors:* no restrictions but pre-booking up to one week in advance essential. *Society Meetings:* reduced green fees for pre-booked groups of 10 or more. Professional: T. Tapley (01225 834248). Secretary: J. Sercombe (01225 834248).*

BATH. **Fosseway Golf Club and Best Western Centurion Hotel,** Charlton Lane, Midsomer Norton, Bath BA3 4BD (01761 412214; Fax: 01761 418357). *Location:* off A367 Bath to Wells/Shepton Mallet. Beautiful, tree-lined parkland course on the edge of the Mendips. 9 holes, 2323 yards. S.S.S. 63. *Green Fees:* weekdays £9.00, weekends £10.00. *Eating facilities:* full à la carte restaurant, bar with bar meals. *Visitors:* welcome except Sunday mornings and Wednesday evenings. Accommodation available, gym, sauna, steam, Jacuzzi, swimming and bowls (outdoor). *Society Meetings:* welcome. General Manager: Mark Manley
e-mail: centurion@centurionhotel.co.uk
website: www.centurionhotel.co.uk

BATH. **Lansdown Golf Club,** Lansdown, Bath BA1 9BT. *Location:* M4 Junction 18, A46 towards Bath, follow signs for Lansdown Park and Ride, adjacent Bath Racecourse. Flat parkland, 800ft above sea-level, panoramic views. 18 holes, 6428 yards. S.S.S. 70. Practice ground. *Green Fees:* weekdays £32.00, weekends £40.00. *Eating facilities:* dining room for 100, snacks, lunch or dinner. *Visitors:* welcome, Handicap Certificate preferred. Trolleys and buggies for hire. *Society Meetings:* welcome weekdays. Professional: Scott Readman (01225 420242; Fax: 01225 483597). Secretary: Erica Bacon (01225 422138; Fax: 01225 339252).
e-mail: admin@lansdowngolfclub.co.uk
website: www.lansdowngolfclub.co.uk

Golf for all
at Bath Public Golf Facilities
www.aquaterra.org/golf

**Beginners welcome • Professional lessons & tuition • Great value pay & play
Membership & season tickets available • Concession discounts available**

Entry Hill Golf Course
Entry Hill, Bath, BA2 5NA
01225 834248

- 9 hole pay & play
- Club hire
- Golf shop
- Café

Bath Approach Golf Course
Weston Road, Bath, BA1 2DS
01225 331162

- 12 or 18 holes
- Free club hire
- Golf equipment available
- Refreshments

aqua terra leisure

Bath & North East Somerset Council

Somerset / WEST REGION

BATH. The Park Resort, Wick, Near Bath BS30 5RN (0117 937 1800; Fax: 0117 937 4288). *Location:* easily accessible from all parts of the South West. From J18 on the M4 we are situated 4 miles from Bath and 8 miles from Bristol. The entrance to The Park is just off the A420 east of the village of Wick. Parkland course. *HSBC/Golf Monthly* Top 200 Gold Award. Crown Course: 18 holes, 6252 yards, Par 69. Cromwell Course: 18 holes, 6246 yards, Par 71. Driving range, short game area. *Green Fees:* information not available. *Eating facilities:* clubhouse, brasserie, Oakwood Restaurant. *Visitors:* welcome, subject to availability. Tuition, buggy and trolley hire, club rental. On site hotel accommodation including function rooms for up to 150 guests. Golf holidays/breaks available. *Society Meetings:* welcome, subject to availability. Corporate/ Society Days a speciality. Director of Golf: Stuart Leech (0117 937 1780; Fax: 0117 937 4288).
e-mail: golf@tpresort.com
website: www.tpresort.com

BATH/BRISTOL. Farrington Golf and Country Club, Marsh Lane, Farrington Gurney, Near Bristol BS39 6TS (01761 451596; Fax: 01761 451021). *Location:* 12 miles south of Bristol, 10 miles east of Bath (through Midsomer Norton) at the junction of the A37 and A362 roads. Wooded, undulating 27 hole complex, 6 lakes, USGA-spec greens (no temporaries), tees up to 800 square yards, irrigated. Duchy Course - 18 holes, (White tees) 6629 yards, S.S.S. 72; (Yellow tees) 6328 yards, S.S.S. 71; (Green tees) 5972 yards, S.S.S. 68; (Ladies' Red tees), 5595 yards, S.S.S 73 . Manor Course - 9 holes, 3002 yards, par 54, S.S.S. 53. Floodlit, covered driving range, 300 yard practice ground, two extensive putting greens, chipping green, one practice bunker, video professional teaching. *Green Fees:* Duchy Course £22.00 Monday to Thursday, £25.00 Fridays, £30.00 weekends and holidays. Special twilight offers. Manor Course (9 holes): £6.00 weekdays, £7.00 weekends. 2010 rates (subject to review.) *Eating facilities:* Large clubhouse of character, full meals service, Sunday lunches, bars, dining room, patio and courtyard. Horizon Banqueting and Function Suite and King Charles Hall both licensed for civil weddings. *Visitors:* most welcome, 2 for 1 vouchers accepted, booking essential. *Society Meetings:* packages available. Pro Shop (01761 451046). Owner: Paul Harwood. Director of Golf: (for society and membership enquiries): Jon Cowgill (01761 451596).
e-mail: jon@farringtongolfclub.net
website: www.farringtongolfclub.net

BRIDGWATER. Cannington Golf Course, Cannington Centre For Land Based Studies, Cannington, Bridgwater TA5 2LS (01278 652394; Fax: 01278 652479). *Location:* M5 Junction 24, off A39 Bridgwater to Minehead road. Flat, with slight undulations, on parkland turf; exposed to sea breezes. 9 holes (18 tees to 9 greens), 6072 yards. S.S.S. 70. Small practice area. 10 bay floodlit driving range. *Green Fees:* information not available. *Eating facilities:* College restaurant. *Visitors:* pay and play course. *Society Meetings:* by arrangement with Professional/ Course Manager. Professional/Course Manager: Ron Macrow (01278 655050; Fax: 01278 655055).*

BRIDGWATER. Enmore Park Golf Club, Enmore, Bridgwater TA5 2AN (01278 672100). *Location:* M5 Exit 23/24, left at lights on A39 after Morrisons to Spaxton, course then signposted left to Enmore after approximately 1 mile. Wooded parkland course on Quantock foothills. 18 holes, 6411 yards, 5862 metres. S.S.S. 71. Large practice ground. *Green Fees:* £37.00 every day. 2010 rates (subject to review). *Eating facilities:* available 9am to 5pm daily. *Visitors:* welcome weekdays and weekends. Buggies available. *Society Meetings:* welcome by arrangement with office. Professional: Nigel Wixon (01278 672100, Option 3). Manager: Steve Varcoe (01278 672100, Option 4; Fax: 01278 672101).
e-mail: manager@enmorepark.co.uk
website: www.enmorepark.co.uk

BRISTOL. Mendip Spring Golf Club, Honeyhall Lane, Congresbury, Bristol BS49 5JT (01934 852322; Fax: 01934 853021). *Location:* between Congresbury and Churchill off B3133 (A370 and A38). Fairly flat courses with a lot of water hazards. Brinsea Course: 18 holes, 6412 yards. S.S.S. 71 men, 76 ladies; Lakeside Course: 9 holes, 2329 yards, S.S.S. 70 men and 75 ladies. 15 bay floodlit driving range, putting green. *Green Fees:* Brinsea: weekdays £30.00 – £40.00 per day, weekends £40.00. Lakeside: weekdays £9.50 per 9 holes, £19.00 per day; weekends £10.00 per 9 holes, £20.00 per day. *Eating facilities:* full restaurant and bar facilities. *Visitors:* welcome at any time. Tuition available. Buggies

THE GOLF GUIDE 2011 — WEST REGION / Somerset

available April to September. *Society Meetings:* welcome, corporate days available by arrangement. Secretary: A. Melhuish.

BRISTOL. **Stockwood Vale Golf Club,** Stockwood Lane, Keynsham, Bristol BS18 2ER (0117 9866505). *Location:* one mile from Hicks Gate - Bristol Ring Road. Testing parkland course set in beautiful surroundings. 18 holes, 6055 yards. S.S.S. 69. Driving range, practice green/bunker. *Green Fees:* £17.25 weekdays, £21.00 weekends. *Eating facilities:* licensed bar and restaurant. *Visitors:* welcome at all times, must reserve start times. GPS buggies available from £8.50. *Society Meetings:* welcome weekdays, prior booking essential; packages available. Secretary: M. Edenborough (0117 9860509; Fax: 0117 9868974).
website: www.stockwoodvale.com

BRISTOL. **Tall Pines Golf Club,** Cooks Bridle Path, Downside, Backwell, Bristol BS48 3DJ (01275 472076). *Location:* between A370 and A38 to Bristol Airport. Parkland. 18 holes, 6049 yards, 5420 metres. S.S.S. 70. Practice ground, putting green. *Green Fees:* £20.00. *Eating facilities:* fully licensed bar and restaurant. *Visitors:* welcome at all times, bookings at weekends. *Society Meetings:* welcome, weekends after 1.00pm. Professional: Alex Murray. Secretary: T. Murray (01275 472076; Fax: 01275 474869).

BRISTOL. **Woodspring Golf & Country Club,** Yanley Lane, Long Ashton, Bristol BS41 9LR (01275 394 378; Fax: 01275 394473). *Location:* located on the A38 4 miles south west of Bristol city centre. From M5 exit Junction 8 follow signs for Bristol Airport, from M4 exit Junction 19 onto M32 follow signs to Bristol Airport. Very attractive, 235-acre parkland course designed by Donald Steel, Peter Alliss and Clive Clark, with great views from high holes. Water on many holes. 27 holes, 3 x 9 hole loops giving a varying combination of yardage. 26 bay floodlit driving range, 15 automated. *Green Fees:* weekdays £32.00, weekends £36.00; fairway rate £16.00 weekday, £18.00 weekends. *Eating facilities:* food and drinks always available in large clubhouse. *Visitors:* always welcome. *Society Meetings:* always welcome, must book in advance. Tuition available from resident Professionals. Buggies for hire. Professional: David Morgan. Secretary: David Knipe.
e-mail: info@woodspring-golf.com
website: www.woodspring-golf.com

BURNHAM-ON-SEA. **Brean Golf Club at Brean Leisure Park,** Coast Road, Brean, TA8 2QY (Tel & Fax: 01278 752111). *Location:* leave M5 at Junction 22, follow signs for Brean Leisure Park (five miles). Flat moorland, easy access to five mile sandy beach (400 yards via path). 18 holes, 5715 yards. S.S.S. 67 (Par 69). Practice area, green and bunker. *Green Fees:* information not available. Reduced rates with a member. *Eating facilities:* snacks at bar, meals in main restaurant. *Visitors:* welcome weekdays and after 11am weekends/Bank Holidays. Prior booking advised to Pro Shop (01278 752111). Buggy and trolleys for hire. *Society Meetings:* welcome by prior booking. Professional: David Haines*.
e-mail: golf@brean.com
website: www.breangolfclub.co.uk

Brean Golf Club

Brean Leisure Park, Coast Road, Brean, Burnham-on-Sea TA8 2QY
Tel: 01278 752111 • e-mail: golf@brean.com • www.breangolfclub.co.uk

Brean Golf Club is located at Brean Leisure Park, four miles north of Burnham-on-Sea, and five miles from Junction 22 of the M5. The 18-hole, 5715 yards, Par 69 course is situated in 100 acres of meadowland. Water features come into play on many of the holes, providing formidable hazards. The course is well-drained and seldom closed. The resident PGA Professional offers a range of services including coaching and club repair, as well as a comprehensive range of golf equipment at competitive prices. Adjoining the Pro Shop are changing rooms and the Club Room. There is a fleet of luxury lodges and caravans both on site and at the adjoining Holiday Park - packages are available which include golf, accommodation and meals.

ENMORE PARK Golf Club

Enmore, Bridgwater, Somerset TA5 2AN

This fabulous championship golf course is a hidden gem of the South West set within the lower slopes of the glorious Quantock Hills. A parkland course near Bridgwater in Somerset which, from its highest point offers extensive views over nearby hills and across the Bristol Channel to Wales. Enmore Park offers a stern but enjoyable test of golf to all levels of golfer. Societies welcome by arrangement.

Professional: Nigel Wixon
Manager: Steve Varcoe • 01278 672100 • Fax: 01278 672101
e-mail: manager@enmorepark.co.uk • www.enmorepark.co.uk

Somerset / WEST REGION

BURNHAM-ON-SEA. Burnham and Berrow Golf Club, St Christopher's Way, Burnham-on-Sea TA8 2PE (01278 785760; Fax: 01278 795440). *Location:* one mile north of Burnham-on-Sea. Leave M5 at Exit 22. Seaside links. 18 holes, 6616 yards. S.S.S. 73; 9 holes, 5819 yards. S.S.S. 69. *Green Fees:* £70.00 weekdays, £85.00 Saturdays; 9 hole course £20.00 weekdays, £25.00 on Saturdays. *Eating facilities:* catering available daily 8am to 6pm (other meals by arrangement). *Visitors:* welcome with reservation if members of a recognised golf club and with Handicap Certificate. Dormy House accommodation, sleeps up to 8. *Society Meetings:* catered for. Professional: M. Crowther-Smith (01278 785760). Managing Secretary: M. Blight (01278 785760). e-mail: secretary.bbgc@btconnect.com
website: www.burnhamandberrowgolfclub.co.uk

CHARD. Windwhistle Golf Club, Cricket St Thomas, Near Chard TA20 4DG (01460 30231; Fax: 01460 30055). Established 1932. *Location:* on A30 between Chard and Crewkerne, opposite Warner's Hotel. Parkland course with breathtaking views. 18 holes, 5969 yards Par 70, S.S.S. 69. Driving range. Golf Shop. *Green Fees:* 18 holes; weekdays £25.00, weekends £30.00. *Eating facilities:* bar service, snacks and cooked meals daily. *Visitors:* welcome; starting time system in operation, bookings accepted up to seven days in advance. Squash courts available. *Society Meetings:* welcome. Professional: Paul Deeprose. Secretary: Ian Dodd.
website: www.windwhistlegolfclub.co.uk

CLEVEDON. Clevedon Golf Club, Castle Road, Walton, Clevedon BS21 7AA (01275 874057; Fax: 01275 341228). *Location:* M5 Junction 20, follow signs "Portishead", turn left into Holly Lane. Spectacular scenic parkland course overlooking Bristol Channel. 18 holes, 6557 yards. S.S.S. 72. Practice area. *Green Fees:* £35.00 weekdays, £45.00 weekends and Bank Holidays. 2010 fees (subject to review). *Eating facilities:* full catering every day. *Visitors:* welcome, please telephone Professional beforehand. Handicap Certificate essential. *Society Meetings:* welcome by prior arrangement. Professional: Robert Scanlan (01275 87470).
website: www.clevedongolfclub.co.uk

FROME. Orchardleigh Golf Club, Frome BA11 2PH (01373 454200; Fax: 01373 454202) *Location:* A362 Frome - Radstock. Parkland. 18 holes, 6824 yards. S.S.S. 73. Three practice greens, driving range. *Green Fees:* information not available. *Eating facilities:* bar menu; society and groups menu. *Visitors:* welcome anytime except before 11.00am Saturday and Sundays. *Society Meetings:* all very welcome, competitive rates. Professional: Ian Ridsdale (01373 454200). Club Secretary/Manager: Dave Forrest.*

LANGPORT near. Long Sutton Golf Club, Long Sutton, Near Langport TA10 9JU (01458 241017; Fax: 01458 241022). *Location:* from Podimore roundabout on A303 towards Langport turn left for Long Sutton. Gently undulating course. 18 holes, 6368 yards. S.S.S. 71. Floodlit driving range. *Green Fees:* information not available. *Eating facilities:* bar and food. *Visitors:* welcome at all times, phone for tee reservations at weekends. Golfing breaks available. *Society Meetings:* welcome. Professional: Andrew Hayes.*

FHG Guides

publish a large range of well-known accommodation guides. We will be happy to send you details or you can use the order form at the back of this book.

Berrow Links House

Enjoy bed & breakfast in our family home adjacent to the famous Burnham & Berrow golf links (the 12th hole is directly opposite the front of the house), with views across the Somerset Levels to the Mendip Hills. Four bedrooms, guest lounge and conservatory and private parking. Set in an acre of glorious gardens complete with stream and pond, and an abundance of wildlife. Just a short walk from miles of sandy beach. The proprietors are both keen golfers and will be happy to advise about courses in the area.

Coast Road, Berrow, Burnham-on-Sea TA8 2QS • Tel: 01278 751422
email: lisa.warren@towens.co.uk • www.berrowlinkshouse.co.uk

Burnham & Berrow Golf Club
St Christopher's Way, Burnham on Sea, Somerset TA8 2PE

The Dormy House

The Dormy House, a self contained detached property situated within the grounds of the Golf Club, is the perfect place to stay when playing at Burnham and Berrow. Over the years, it has been appreciated by scores of guests, many of whom return each year for a golfing break at this Championship course. The Dormy House can accommodate up to 8 guests in 4 twin bedded rooms; three are en suite and the fourth has an adjacent bathroom. There is a large lounge with comfortable seating and television and a fully equipped kitchenette. Your meals are served in the Clubhouse where Dormy guests have complimentary use of the snooker room, television and the bar facilities.

- One minute's walk to the clubhouse and first tee
- Golf and reserved tee times for your party included in the price
- Catering available throughout the day
- Forget the car, it's all on the doorstep.

Bed and Breakfast and 2 Rounds of Golf on the Championship Course from £115pppn. Special Winter rate £85pp.

Bookings for the Dormy House and Course are made via the Assistant Secretary who can be contacted by phone on **+44(0)1278 785760** or by e-mail on
secretary.bbgc@btconnect.com
www.burnhamandberrowgolfclub.co.uk
quote FHG

Somerset / WEST REGION

MINEHEAD. Minehead and West Somerset Golf Club, The Warren, Minehead TA24 5SJ (01643 702057). *Location:* beside the beach at eastern end of the town, three-quarters of a mile from town centre. Flat seaside links. 18 holes, 6153 yards. S.S.S. 69. *Green Fees:* information not provided. *Eating facilities:* available at clubhouse, bar open every day. *Visitors:* welcome with tee reservation at Pro shop. *Society Meetings:* welcome with tee reservations. Special golf and meal deals available to groups of four or more. Wide wheel trolleys only. Trolley and equipment hire available. Professional: Ian Read.
e-mail: secretary@mineheadgolf.co.uk
website: www.minehead-golf-club.co.uk

SALTFORD. Saltford Golf Club, Golf Club Lane, Saltford, Bristol BS31 3AA (01225 873513; Fax: 01225 873525). *Location:* A4 between Bristol and Bath. Wooded parkland course. 18 holes, 6398 yards. S.S.S. 71. Practice area, chipping green. *Green Fees:* information not available. *Eating facilities:* restaurant, bar service. *Visitors:* welcome, restricted to one round of golf per day weekends and during Summer. *Society Meetings:* accepted by arrangement, please call the Club Secretary's office for further details. Professional: Darren Read (01225 872043). Club Secretary: Mike Penn (01225 873513).
e-mail: mike@saltfordgolfclub.co.uk4).

SHEPTON MALLET. The Mendip Golf Club, Gurney Slade, Radstock, Shepton Mallett BA3 4UT (01749 840570). *Location:* three miles north of Shepton Mallet (A37). Downland, undulating course. 18 holes, 6383 yards. S.S.S. 71. Practice ground. *Green Fees:* information not provided. *Eating facilities:* bar and restaurant open seven days a week. *Visitors:* welcome every day, telephone Professional to check availability. *Society Meetings:* catered for Mondays to Fridays by arrangement. Professionals: John Goymer and Kevin Pitts (01749 840793). Secretary: Jim Scott (01749 840570).
e-mail: secretary@mendipgolfclub.com
website: www.mendipgolfclub.com

SOMERTON. Wheathill Golf Club, Wheathill, Somerton TA11 7HG (01963 240667; Fax: 01963 240230). *Location:* on B3153 three miles west of Castle Cary. Flat parkland. 18 holes, 5381 yards (white). S.S.S. 65, Par 68. Large practice ground, 8 hole academy course, driving range. *Green Fees:* £20.00; £15.00 after 4pm, £10.00 after 6pm. *Eating facilities:* bar and restaurant. *Visitors:* welcome. *Society Meetings:* welcome. Professionals: Mark Luckett and Mark Singleton. Secretary: Andrew England.
website: www.wheathillgc.co.uk

STREET. Kingweston Golf Club, (Millfield School), Street TA11 6PP (01458 444320). *Location:* one mile south of Butleigh Village, near Street, Somerset. Flat course - trees. 9 holes, 2307 yards. S.S.S. 61. Practice area. *Green Fees:* information not available. *Eating facilities:* pub half a mile. *Visitors:* welcome only with a member. Secretary: G.L. Frisby (01458 832068).*

TAUNTON. Oake Manor Golf Club, Oake, Taunton TA4 1BA (01823 461993; Fax: 01823 461995). *Location:* seven minutes' drive from Junction 26 of the M5 - take A38 towards Taunton and follow signs to Oake. Enjoyable and challenging parkland course with water features on 10 of the 18 holes. Magnificent setting with views of the Blackdown and Quantock Hills. 18 holes, 6109 yards. S.S.S 69. Driving range, practice holes. *Green Fees:* information not available. *Eating facilities:* catering/bar snacks available all day. *Visitors:* welcome any day but booking tee time essential. Ideal course to play en route to, or returning from golf in Devon and Cornwall. Function rooms (seat up to 300). *Society Meetings:* by arrangement, contact Golf Manager. Golf Manager & Professional: Russell Gardner (01823 461993).*
e-mail: russell@oakemanor.com
website: www.oakemanor.com

TAUNTON. Taunton and Pickeridge Golf Club, Corfe, Taunton TA3 7BY (01823 421537). *Location:* four miles south of Taunton on B3170. Undulating parkland. 18 holes, 6109 yards. S.S.S. 70. Practice ground, indoor swing nets. *Green Fees:* £35.00. *Eating facilities:* restaurant and bar. *Visitors:* welcome. *Society Meetings:* by arrangement. Professional: Simon Stevenson (01823 421790).
e-mail: mail@tauntongolf.co.uk
website: www.tauntongolf.co.uk

For full details of convenient accommodation near clubs and courses
www.holidayguides.com

Minehead & West Somerset Golf Club
www.minehead-golf-club.co.uk
The Warren, Minehead TA24 5SJ
Play this traditional links course all year round. No temporary tees or greens. Fantastic scenic views of the hills of Exmoor and across the Bristol Channel to Wales.
Tel: 01643 702057 • e-mail: secretary@mineheadgolf.co.uk

WEST REGION / Somerset

TAUNTON. Taunton Vale Golf Club, Creech Heathfield, Taunton TA3 5EY (01823 412220; Fax: 01823 413583). *Location:* just off A361 at Junction with A38 between Junctions 24 and 25 of M5; easily accessible. Parkland. Two courses. 18 holes, 6234 yards. S.S.S. 70. 9 holes, 1943 yards. S.S.S. 32. 10 bay floodlit driving range. *Green Fees:* see website for details. *Eating facilities:* two bars, dining room and conservatory. *Visitors:* welcome, telephone for bookings essential. *Society Meetings:* welcome by arrangement. For all the latest information see our website. Professional: Martin Keitch (01823 412880). Secretary: Joanne Wyatt (01823 412220; Fax: 01823 413583).
e-mail: admin@tauntonvalegolf.co.uk
website: www.tauntonvalegolf.co.uk

TAUNTON. Vivary Golf Course, Vivary Park, Taunton TA1 3JW (01823 289274). *Location:* turn into Wilton Road at side of police station. Turn left at Vivary Arms Inn. Flat parkland course with ponds and trees. 18 holes, 4533 yards. S.S.S. 63. Practice area. *Green Fees:* information not available. *Eating facilities:* licensed bar and restaurant. Available for private functions. *Visitors:* always welcome. Professional: James Smallacombe (01823 333875). Secretary: (01823 289274).*

TICKENHAM. Tickenham Golf Club, Clevedon Road, Tickenham BS21 6RY (01275 856626). *Location:* M5 Junction 20, signposted Nailsea on left after Tickenham. Challenging championship style contoured greens. 9 holes, 2000 yards. S.S.S. 58, Par 60. 24 bay floodlit driving range, power tees, putting green, bunkers. *Green Fees:* off-peak - 9 holes £8.00, 18 holes £12.00; peak times - 9 holes £10.00, 18 holes £15.00. *Eating facilities:* 19th hole licensed bar, snacks. *Visitors:* welcome. *Society Meetings:* welcome, telephone for rates. Professionals: A. Sutcliffe, S. Jarrett, A. Johnston, S. Lloyd.

WEDMORE. Isle of Wedmore Golf Club, Lineage, Lastcot Hill, Wedmore BS28 4QT (01934 712222). *Location:* from A38 Bristol/Bridgwater Road, take Wedmore Road from Lower Weare. Parkland, gently undulating fairways with magnificent views. Practice area. 18 holes, 6057 yards. S.S.S. 69. Small practice area, putting green. *Green Fees:* Winter: £22.00 per round, Winter 4 Ball £16.00 per person; Summer: £26.00 per round, Summer 4 Ball £18.00 per person. Twilight rates available. *Eating facilities:* full bar and restaurant (open 7 days a week), upstairs function/society room. Fairway Catering (01934 713649). *Visitors:* always welcome. Soft spikes only. *Society Meetings:* welcome. Professional: Nick Pope (01934 712452). Manager/ Director: Andrew Edwards (01934 712222).Contact: Chantelle White (01934 712222).
e-mail: info@wedmoregolfclub.com
website: www.wedmoregolfclub.com

WELLS. Wells (Somerset) Golf Club Ltd, Blackheath Lane, East Horrington, Wells BA5 3DS (01749 675005). *Location:* one mile east of city centre off B3139. Parkland, wooded. 18 holes, 6018 yards. S.S.S. 69. Practice area. 12 bay floodlit driving range open to the public. *Green Fees:* information not available. *Eating facilities:* restaurant and bar. *Visitors:* welcome, no play before 9.30am weekends and Public Holidays. *Society Meetings:* full packages available at all times. Professional: Adrian Bishop (01749 679059). Secretary: Eira Powell (01749 675005; Fax: 01749 683170).
e-mail: secretary@wellsgolfclub.co.uk
website: www.wellsgolfclub.co.uk

WESTON-SUPER-MARE. Weston-Super-Mare Golf Club, The Clubhouse, Uphill Road North, Weston-Super-Mare BS23 4NQ (01934 626968). *Location:* M5 Junction 21 - on the sea front. Flat links course with excellent greens. 18 holes, 6251 yards. S.S.S. 70. Practice area plus nets. *Green Fees:* information not provided. *Eating facilities:* full bar and catering facilities. *Visitors:* welcome weekdays and weekends. Handicap Certificate required. *Society Meetings:* catered for weekdays. Professional: Mike LaBand (Tel & Fax: 01934 633360). Secretary: (01934 626968; Fax: 01934 621360).
e-mail: secretary@westonsupermaregolfclub.com
website: www.westonsupermaregolfclub.com

TAUNTON VALE GOLF CLUB
Creech Heathfield, Taunton, Somerset TA3 5EY

Taunton Vale Golf Club is probably the most accessible club in the county, little more than a 5-minute drive from Junctions 24 or 25 of the M5. It comprises 27 holes of parkland course set amidst the gently rolling Somerset countryside. The Club has a 10-bay floodlit driving range, a fully stocked Pro Shop, and an excellent clubhouse offering a variety of menus. Societies are most welcome, with a package to suit all from small groups to large corporate events.

**For more details contact 01823 412220 or
e-mail: admin@tauntonvalegolf.co.uk**   www.tauntonvalegolf.co.uk

Somerset / WEST REGION

WESTON-SUPER-MARE. Worlebury Golf Club, Monks Hill, Worlebury, Weston-Super-Mare BS22 9SX (01934 625789). *Location:* from M5 (Junction 21) then A370 and first exit left onto old Bristol Road to town for two miles. Turn right into Baytree Road and continue to top of Milton Hill. Hill top with extensive views of the Severn Estuary and Wales. 18 holes, 5936 yards. S.S.S. 68. Practice ground and putting green. *Green Fees:* information not available. *Eating facilities:* bar and restaurant. *Visitors:* welcome without reservation. *Society Meetings:* catered for by arrangement. Professional: Gary Marks (01934 418473). Office: (01934 625789; Fax: 01934 621935).*
e-mail: secretary@worleburygc.co.uk

WINCANTON. Wincanton Golf Club, The Racecourse, Wincanton BA9 8BJ (01963 435850; Fax: 01963 34668). *Location:* middle of the racecourse, half a mile from the town centre. Very flat course, testing layout; large bunkers protecting very well maintained greens. 9 or 18 holes, 6266 yards. S.S.S. 69. Good practice facilities. Teaching/coaching on individual or group basis; hire of clubs/trolley/buggy. *Green Fees:* weekdays 9 holes £10.00; 18 holes £15.00, weekends 9 holes £12.00; 18 holes £17.00, juniors 9 holes £5.00; 18 holes £9.00. *Eating facilities:* licensed coffee shop. *Visitors:* welcome at all times. Overnight accommodation available. *Society Meetings:* can be catered for if booked in advance. Professional: Andrew England.

YEOVIL. Yeovil Golf Club, Sherborne Road, Yeovil BA21 5BW (01935 422965). *Location:* on A30, one mile from town centre towards Sherborne on right before Babylon Hill. Parkland. 18 holes, 6087 yards. S.S.S. 70. 9 holes, 4856 yards. S.S.S. 65. Putting green. 20-bay floodlit range. *Green Fees:* Old Course – £40.00. 9-hole Newton course – £25.00. *Eating facilities:* bars and dining room with full menu every day. *Visitors:* welcome, Handicap Certificates preferred for 18 hole course, telephone Pro shop to check times. *Society Meetings:* welcome weekdays. Professional: G. Kite (01935 473763; Fax: 01935 478605). General Manager (01935 422965; Fax: 01935 411283).
website: www.yeovilgolfclub.com

Taunton Vale Golf Club, Taunton

Wiltshire

BRADFORD-ON-AVON. **Cumberwell Park Golf Club,** Bradford-on-Avon BA15 2PQ (01225 863322; Fax: 01225 868160). *Location*: on A363 between Bath and Bradford-on-Avon, close to J17 and J18 off M4. Recognised as one of the top courses in the west country, encompassing 400 acres of parkland, enhanced by nine lakes, 34 acres of forest and streams. 36 holes (4 x 9), S.S.S. 72. Practice greens, 10 acre driving range. *Green Fees*: Monday to Thursday £31.00, Friday to Sunday £40.00. *Eating facilities*: private dining rooms and spikes bar. *Visitors*: always welcome; accommodation can be arranged nearby. *Society Meetings*: packages including catering available from £26.00 winter, from £39.00 summer. Golf days tailored to individual requirements. Professional: John Jacobs.
e-mail: enquiries@cumberwellpark.com
website: www.cumberwellpark.com

CALNE. **Bowood Hotel, Spa and Golf Resort,** Derry Hill, Calne SN11 9PQ (01249 822228; Fax: 01249 822218). *Location:* A4 between Marlborough and Chippenham, signposted off M4 Junction 17. Grade I listed, Capability Brown landscaped, parkland. 18 holes, 7317, 6890, 6566: 6027 yards. S.S.S. 74, 73, 71: 75. Ladies 6015 yards, S.S.S. 75. Three academy holes, floodlit driving range, two putting greens. *Green Fees*: information not provided. *Eating facilities*: public restaurant, private dining for up to 200. *Visitors*: welcome at all times except before 12 noon at weekends, bookings required. New 43-room luxury hotel and spa, 4-bedroom (double/twin) lodge in centre of course; banqueting, conferences, weddings etc catered for. Buggies, trolleys and clubs for hire; fully stocked Pro shop. *Society Meetings*: welcome, special packages available. Head Professional: Paul McLean. Proprietor: The Marquis of Lansdowne.
website: www.bowood.org

Please mention THE GOLF GUIDE when you enquire about clubs or accommodation

CASTLE COMBE. **The Manor House Hotel and Golf Club,** Castle Combe SN14 7JW (01249 782982; Fax: 01249 782992). *Location:* on the B4039 midway between M4 Junction 17 and 18. Parkland course situated in a series of wooded valleys in an Area of Outstanding Natural Beauty. 18 holes, 6500 yards. S.S.S. 71. Practice range. *Green Fees:* information not available. *Eating facilities:* full restaurant and bar facilities. *Visitors:* welcome by prior arrangement provided they have a club Handicap Certificate. The luxurious Manor House Hotel (four red stars) adjoins the course offering exceptional accommodation and an award-winning restaurant. *Society Meetings:* welcome by prior arrangement. Professional/Director of Golf: Steve Slinger (01249 782982; Fax: 01249 782992). General Manager: Paul Thompson (01249 782982; Fax: 01249 782992).*

CHIPPENHAM. **Chippenham Golf Club,** Malmesbury Road, Chippenham SN15 5LT (01249 652040). *Location:* A350 one mile from Chippenham, two miles from M4 (Junction 17). Parkland. 18 holes, 5570 yards. S.S.S. 67. *Green Fees:* £28.00 Mon-Fri, £35.00 Weekends and Bank Holidays. Special 4 for 3 offer. *Eating facilities:* snacks and evening à la carte (not Mondays). *Visitors:* welcome, prior arrangement necessary. *Society Meetings:* catered for Mondays, Tuesdays, Thursdays and Fridays only. Premier Travel Inn overlooking first fairway. Professional: Bill Creamer (01249 655519). Secretary: P. Dawson (01249 652040).
e-mail: chippenhamgolf@btconnect.com
website: www.chippenhamgolfclub.com

CHIPPENHAM. **Monkton Park Golf Club,** Monkton Park, Chippenham SN15 3PE (01249 653928). *Location:* centre of Chippenham, two miles from M4 Junction 17. Parkland Par 3 course. Probably the best Par 3 course in the south west of England. 9 holes, 979 yards. S.S.S. 27. Crazy golf. *Green Fees:* information not available. *Eating facilities:* tearoom now open. *Visitors:* always welcome 364 days of the year! Golf clubs available. *Society Meetings:* welcome. Secretary: Mrs W. Claridge.*
website: www.pitchandputtgolf.com

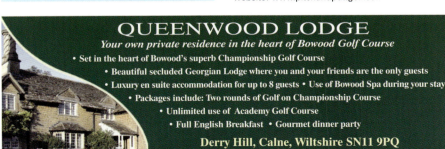

QUEENWOOD LODGE
Your own private residence in the heart of Bowood Golf Course

- Set in the heart of Bowood's superb Championship Golf Course
- Beautiful secluded Georgian Lodge where you and your friends are the only guests
- Luxury en suite accommodation for up to 8 guests • Use of Bowood Spa during your stay
- Packages include: Two rounds of Golf on Championship Course
- Unlimited use of Academy Golf Course
- Full English Breakfast • Gourmet dinner party

Derry Hill, Calne, Wiltshire SN11 9PQ
Tel: 01249 822228 • Fax: 01249 822218
www.bowood.org • e-mail: queenwood@bowood.org

CORSHAM. **Kingsdown Golf Club,** Corsham SN13 8BS (01225 743472). *Location:* five miles east of Bath. Downland. 18 holes, 6445 yards, 5891 metres. S.S.S. 71. *Green Fees:* information not available. *Eating facilities:* lounge bar and diningroom. *Visitors:* welcome except at weekends and Bank Holidays and must have current Handicap Certificate. *Society Meetings:* catered for by arrangement. Professional: Andrew Butler (01225 742634). Secretary: Neil Newman (01225 743472).*

CRICKLADE. **Cricklade Hotel & Country Club,** Common Hill, Cricklade SN6 6HA (01793 750751; Fax: 01793 751767). *Location*: A419 8 miles north of Swindon, B4040 out of Cricklade town by half a mile. Undulating course set around hotel. 9 holes, 1830 yards. S.S.S. 58 (18 holes). *Green Fees*: information upon request. *Eating facilities*: full à la carte restaurant and bar with snacks available. *Visitors*: guests of hotel welcome at all times, tee times must be booked at weekends. Weekends members and hotel guests only. 46-room hotel on site. *Society Meetings*: on application. Secretary: Colin Withers. Hotel General Manager: Paul Butler.
e-mail: reception@crickladehotel.co.uk
website: www.crickladehotel.co.uk

DEVIZES. **Erlestoke Golf Club,** Erlestoke, Near Devizes SN10 5UB. *Location:* six miles east of Westbury on B3098. Downland course, on two levels, spectacular 7th hole, 170 yards Par 3, with green 100ft below, one of the finest short holes in the West Country. 18 holes, 6406 yards. S.S.S. 71, Par 73. Large practice ground. *Green Fees:* information not available. *Eating facilities:* full catering service, lounge, bar and diningroom. *Visitors:* welcome (01380 831069). *Society Meetings:* welcome. Fabulous views and excellent food served from 11am.*

DEVIZES. **North Wilts Golf Club,** Bishop's Cannings, Devizes SN10 2LP (01380 860257). *Location:* one and a half miles from A4 east of Calne. Four miles from Devizes. Downland, undulating course with spectacular views. 18 holes, 6414 yards. S.S.S. 71. Practice ground. *Green Fees:* information not available. *Eating facilities:* full catering service. *Visitors:* welcome, except on club days. *Society Meetings:* catered for by prior arrangement. Professional: Graham Laing (01380 860330; Fax: 01380 860061). Secretary: Mrs Trish Stephenson (01380 860627; Fax: 01380 860877).*

HIGHWORTH. **Highworth Community Golf Centre,** Swindon Road, Highworth SN6 7SJ. *Location:* on A361 just south of the town. Undulating parkland. 9 holes, 3120 yards, 2851 metres. Par 35. 9 hole pitch and putt, 4 hole practice course. *Green Fees:* information not available. *Eating facilities:* vending machines. *Visitors:* municipal course, no restrictions. *Society Meetings:* welcome any day. Professional: Charles Pears (01793 766014). Secretary: Geoff Marsh.

HIGHWORTH. **Wrag Barn Golf and Country Club,** Shrivenham Road, Highworth, Swindon SN6 7QQ (01793 861327; Fax: 01793 861325). *Location:* just six miles off the M4. Undulating, set in beautiful Wiltshire countryside, three lakes and moat around 17th green. 18 holes, 6622 yards. S.S.S. 72. 11-bay driving range, practice area. *Green Fees:* weekdays £30.00; weekends £40.00. *Eating facilities:* spike bar. restaurant, function rooms. *Visitors:* welcome weekdays and after 12 noon weekends. Buggies and trolleys for hire. *Society Meetings:* welcome any weekday. Professional (01793 766027; Fax: 01793 861325). Director of Golf: Ian Ridsdale. Secretary/General Manager: Tracey Lee (01793 861327; Fax: 01793 861325).
website: www.wragbarn.com

MARLBOROUGH. **Marlborough Golf Club,** The Common, Marlborough SN8 1DU (01672 512147; Fax: 01672 513164). *Location:* about one mile north of Marlborough town centre on A346 towards Swindon. Seven miles south of J15 of the M4. Downland with panoramic views into the Og Valley and over the Marlborough Downs. 18 holes, 6514 yards, 5952 metres. S.S.S. 71, Par 72. Large practice ground and putting green. *Green Fees:* information not available. *Eating facilities:* full restaurant facility, plus bar snacks open all day. *Visitors:* welcome generally, but it is best to telephone in advance; some restrictions at weekends. *Society Meetings:* discounted rates and packages available. Essential to book in advance. Professional: Simon Amor (01672 512493; Fax: 01672 513164). General Manager: Les Trute (01672 512147; Fax: 01672 513164).*
e-mail: contactus@marlboroughgolfclub.co.uk

www.holidayguides.com
for accommodation near golf clubs

WRAG BARN Golf & Country Club
Shrivenham Road, Highworth, Swindon, Wiltshire SN6 7QQ
Tel: 01793 861327 • Fax: 01793 861325 • Pro Shop: 01793 766027
e-mail: info@wragbarn.com • www.wragbarn.com

"THE PERFECT GOLF SOCIETY VENUE"

Challenging Par 72 of 6622 yards. Friendly and welcoming.
Corporate, Conference and Society Days a speciality.
Golf clinic, scoring analysis, full conference facilities on request.
Traditional style clubhouse with shop, locker rooms and the Spike Bar open all day for food and drink. Our Banbury and Bellingham Suite facilities offer an unrivalled combination of superb food and the perfect setting adaptable for any style of event. Our location is perfect. The Thames Valley is just 6 miles north of Swindon and only ten minutes from Junction 15 of the M4.

Set in the Vale of the White Horse, the views of the Wiltshire Countryside around the course are truly superb. For a successful and memorable occasion plan your next golf day at Wrag Barn Golf Club.

WRAG BARN

SALISBURY. **Hamptworth Golf and Country Club,** Hamptworth Road, Hamptworth, Near Landford SP5 2DU (01794 390155). *Location:* off A36 Salisbury to Southampton Road, turning off B3079. Parkland, wooded course with river running through. 18 holes, 6004 yards. S.S.S. 69. Driving range, open to the public. *Green Fees:* please telephone for prices. *Eating facilities:* clubhouse with full catering and bar. *Visitors:* welcome, must have tee reservation. Buggies available to hire. No temporary greens or mats. *Society Meetings:* welcome.

SALISBURY. **High Post Golf Club Ltd,** Great Durnford, Salisbury SP4 6AT (01722 782356; Fax: 01722 782674). *Location:* midway between Salisbury and Amesbury on A345. Championship down-land course, hosted National and International major amateur events. Peter Allis rates the 9th in his dream 18 holes. An excellent inland links course. 18 holes, 6305 yards. S.S.S. 70. *Green Fees:* information not provided. *Eating facilities:* full catering and bars available. *Visitors:* welcome weekdays no restrictions, weekends and Bank Holidays require Handicap Certificate. *Society Meetings:* catered for weekdays only. Professional: Tony Isaacs (01722 782219). Manager: Peter Hickling (01722 782356). e-mail: manager@highpostgolfclub.co.uk
website: www.highpostgolfclub.co.uk

SALISBURY. **Rushmore Golf Club,** Tollard Royal, Salisbury SP5 5QB (01725 516326). *Location:* off the B3081 between Tollard Royal and Sixpenny Handley. Parkland and wooded course. 18 holes, 6131 yards. S.S.S. 70. Covered driving range and large practice area. *Green Fees:* from £30.00. *Eating facilities:* Spike Bar plus restaurant, home cooked food seven days a week. *Visitors:* welcome any time. *Society Meetings:* welcome by prior arrangement. Professional: Jason Sherman.

SALISBURY. **Salisbury and South Wilts Golf Club,** Netherhampton, Salisbury SP2 8PR (01722 742131). *Location:* on A3094, two miles from Salisbury, Wilton, opposite Netherhampton village. Parkland. 27 holes, 6528 yards. S.S.S. 71. Practice ground. *Green Fees:* £35.00 weekdays, £50.00 weekends. *Eating facilities:* full catering service and bar. *Visitors:* welcome without reservation at all times. Can also cater for conferences, social events and weddings. *Society Meetings:* catered for by prior arrangement. Professional: Jon Waring (01722 742645 ext 4). Secretary: Alex Taylor (01722 742645; Fax: 01722 742676).
e-mail: mail@salisburygolf.co.uk
website: www.salisburygolf.co.uk

SHRIVENHAM. **Shrivenham Park Golf Club,** Penny Hooks Lane, Near Swindon SN6 8EX (01793 783853/4). *Location:* M4 Exit 15. Follow signs to Shrivenham, go through village, golf club on left. A delightful parkland course in excellent condition. 18 holes, 5713 yards. S.S.S 69. Practice area. *Green Fees:* information not available. *Visitors:* open to all, Handicaps not required. *Society Meetings:* packages available. Professional: Richard Jefferies. Director of Golf: George Platt (01793 783853).*

SWINDON. **Broome Manor Golf Complex**, Pipers Way, Swindon SN3 1RG (01793 495761; Fax: 01793 433255 (Manager)). *Location:* two miles from Junction 15, M4 (follow signs to Swindon Town Centre then follow signs for "Golf Complex"). Wooded parkland. Two courses, 18 holes, 6283 yards, Par 71, S.S.S. 70. 9 holes, 5380 yards, Par 66, S.S.S. 66. 32 bay floodlit covered driving range. *Green Fees:* Information not available. *Eating facilities:* spike bar, conference facilities, restaurant. *Visitors:* welcome, no restrictions, booking essential for 18 hole course. *Society Meetings:* catered for weekdays. Professional: Barry Sandry (01793 491911; Fax 01793 433255). Manager: Dave Buckingham (01793 495761; Fax: 01793 4332553.*

FHG Guides publish a large range of well-known accommodation guides. We will be happy to send you details or you can use the order form at the back of this book.

Peter Allis rates High Post so highly he once said he would include the par 4 ninth hole on his 'Dream 18'. In the 1997 *Golf Monthly* described the course as a 'hidden gem'.

High Post has hosted the South West Amateur Championship in 1998, the prestigious Carris Trophy in 1999, the Wiltshire County Championship on countless occasions and more recently, the English Boys' Open in 2008.

If further proof were needed of High Post's pedigree, how about some of the past winners/participants of the High Post Open, including Andrew Sherbourne, David Howell, Zane Scotland and Justin Rose, all of whom are now established stars in the world of professional golf.

High Post's great strength is its all year round playability. The free-draining chalk downland enables golfers to enjoy summer greens and tees even in the depth of winter.

High Post, Salisbury, Wiltshire SP4 6AT Tel: 01722 782219 • Fax: 01722 782674
e-mail: manager@highpostgolfclub.co.uk • www.highpostgolfclub.co.uk

SWINDON. **Ogbourne Downs Golf Club,** Ogbourne St. George, Marlborough SN8 1TB (01672 841287). *Location:* A346, four miles south of Junction 15 (M4), three miles north of Marlborough. Downland course with extensive views. 18 holes, 6422 yards. S.S.S. 71. Practice area, baskets of practice balls for hire. *Green Fees:* weekdays £25.00; weekends £35.00. *Eating facilities:* full catering and bar service. *Visitors:* welcome weekdays, phone Professional at weekends for starting times. Buggy hire. *Society Meetings:* welcome, packages available. Professional: Mark Shipley (01672 841287). Manager: Geoff Scott. Office: (01672 841327).

SWINDON. **The Wiltshire**, Wootton Bassett, Swindon SN4 7PB (01793 849999). *Location*: through Wootton Bassett, head for Calne A3102, one mile on left hand side out of town. 27 holes designed by Peter Alliss and Howard Swann. 18 hole Lake Course with water features. 6782 yards. S.S.S. 72. 9 hole Garden Course 3214 yards. S.S.S. 71. Halfway House Practice area, Putting Green. Driving Range, Chipping green. *Green Fees*: weekdays £22.00 per round, weekends £30.00 per round. *Eating facilities*: bars and restaurant. *Visitors*: welcome, booking advised. Club, buggy and trolley hire. Club repairs and fitting. Indoor pool with spa, sauna and steam room. Hotel with 58 en suite bedrooms. Golf Breaks available. *Society Meetings*: conference and residential packages available. Professional: Richard Lawless.
e-mail: reception@the-wiltshire.co.uk
website: www.the-wiltshire.co.uk

TIDWORTH. **Tidworth Garrison Golf Club,** Bulford Road, Tidworth SP9 7AF (Tel & Fax: 01980 842301). *Location:* A338 Salisbury to Marlborough Road, golf course off Bulford Road. Undulating downland course. 18 holes, 6320 yards. S.S.S. 70. Practice driving area, chipping and putting greens. *Green Fees:* information not available. *Eating facilities:* full bar and catering facilities. *Visitors:* welcome at all times, except Friday mornings and normally after 2pm at weekends and Bank Holidays. *Society Meetings:* catered for Tuesdays, Wednesday and Thursdays. Professional: Terry Gosden (Tel & Fax: 01980 842301).
e-mail: tidworthgolfclub@btconnect.com
website: www.tidworthgolfclub.co.uk

UPAVON. **Upavon Golf Club,** Douglas Avenue, Upavon SN9 6BQ (01980 630787; Fax: 01980 635419). *Location:* off A342 Upavon to Andover Road, one-and-a-half miles out of Upavon. Undulating chalk downland course. 18 holes, 6402 yards. S.S.S. 71. Two practice areas. *Green Fees:* information not provided. *Eating facilities:* bar and catering every day. *Visitors:* visitors and societies welcome at Wiltshire's friendliest club. All County Cards and 2-fore-1 accepted. Daily course information line: 08712 300 800. Professional: Richard Blake (01980 630281). Secretary: Les Mitchell (01980 630787).
e-mail: play@upavongolfclub.co.uk
website: www.upavongolfclub.co.uk

Ogbourne Downs Golf Club

Located in the rolling countryside of the Marlborough Downs you will find real test of your playing ability, with stunning views of the Wiltshire countryside. In addition to the course, the Club offers a number of other excellent facilities, including a driving range, clubhouse and a well stocked Pro Shop.
If you are thinking of becoming a member or just visiting for the day, a warm welcome always awaits you.
Ogbourne Downs Golf Club, Ogbourne St George, Marlborough, Wiltshire SN8 1TB
Telephone: 01672 841327 • ogbournedowns@btconnect.com • www.ogdgc.co.uk

Planning a Society Golf Day?
A friendly fourball?
Or considering membership at a course that plays all year?
Whatever you are looking for
Upavon Golf Club
provides the answer.

Upavon Golf Club
Douglas Avenue
Upavon, Wiltshire SN9 6BQ

VISITORS AND SOCIETIES ARE ASSURED OF A WARM WELCOME AND EXCELLENT VALUE
Superb Society Rates • A limited number of memberships are currently available.
Located off the A342 midway between Devizes and Andover
When you discover Upavon Golf Club you will discover the friendliest club in Wiltshire!
Tel: 01980 630281/630787 • e-mail: play@upavongolfclub.co.uk • www.upavongolfclub.co.uk

WARMINSTER. West Wilts Golf Club, Elm Hill, Warminster BA12 0AU (Office: 01985 213133; Bar: 01985 212702). *Location*: one mile off the A350 north of Warminster, signposted to the town centre. Established 1891, a chalk downland course 200 metres above sea level, designed by J.H. Taylor. 18 holes, 5754 yards. S.S.S. 68. Indoor and outdoor practice facilities available. *Green Fees*: information not available. *Visitors*: welcome except Saturdays. *Society Meetings*: welcome mainly Wednesday to Friday, contact Secretary. Professional: Rob Morris (Tel & Fax: 01985 212110). Secretary: Geoff Morgan. House Manager: Sandra Frankle.*
e-mail: sec@westwiltsgolfclub.co.uk
website: www.westwiltsgolfclub.co.uk

High Post Golf Club, Salisbury

Golf in the South

Iain Pearson
Tournament Controller, PGA South Region

Berkshire • Buckinghamshire
Greater London • Hampshire & The Isle of Wight
Kent • Oxfordshire • Surrey • Sussex

A highlight for every golfer, whether they be a single-figure handicapper or an infrequent 'weekend warrior', is to follow in the footsteps of the world's greats. Very few get the chance to tread the same fairways as the legends but for those determined to give it a go then any visit to the south of England has to incorporate at least one of the 'big name' venues.

Top of the list is Royal St George's in Sandwich, Kent - the Open Championship venue for 2011 and a superb example of links golf. Scene of rookie American Ben Curtis' shock victory in 2003 and Greg Norman's brilliant defeat of Nick Faldo 10 years earlier, St George's is as tough a test as you could expect to find anywhere. Only three Open winners, Curtis, Norman and Bill Rogers in 1981 have broken par in lifting the Claret Jug there, so the best advice is to head to Sandwich with the intention of enjoying the experience rather than playing your best golf.

But if the rarefied exclusivity of St George's is a little bit out of your range then try the next best thing next door - Prince's Golf Club, itself a former Open venue and now Local Final Qualifying venue for 2011. The club has 27 holes consisting of three loops of nine, known as the Shore, Dunes and Himalayas courses, each starting and finishing beside the clubhouse. Prince's has recently undergone a full bunker renovation plan in order to maintain it at a

Play both Royal Ashdown's classic heathland courses this summer for **only £70** weekdays
Quote Ref. FHG

ROYAL ASHDOWN FOREST GOLF CLUB
FOUNDED 1888
Forest Row, East Sussex RH18 5LR   Tel: 01342 822018
www.royalashdown.co.uk

7th at Dale Hill Golf Club, Wadhurst, East Sussex

Championship Standard. But links golf is not just restricted to Sandwich, as just down the road lies Royal Cinque Ports Golf Club in Deal which will host the Amateur Championship in 2013 alongside Prince's Golf Club. It has an abundance of sand dunes and undulating fairways which make just standing up straight a challenge. Throw in the many steep bunkers and fast greens and this former Open venue provides another enjoyable seaside challenge - as does Littlestone further down the south-east coast near New Romney.

If you prefer to play your golf among resplendent greenery then head further inland and be spoiled for choice. Continuing the celebrity golf feel, Sunningdale in Berkshire (venue for both Open and US Open qualifying) and Wentworth (BMW PGA Championship) in Surrey both offer high quality, history-laden facilities at a premium, as well as Walton Heath, former Ryder Cup venue and host of US Open Qualifying. The Old Course plays to a championship length of 7462 yards and a par of 72 and is ranked in the world's top 100 golf courses.

Sittingbourne and Milton Regis Golf Club, Sittingbourne, Kent

Delve a little deeper and there are a number of hidden gems which are equally as pleasing to play at a fraction of the cost. The London Club, designed by Jack Nicklaus, lies to the south-west of London just outside the M25. It is an absolute delight and highly regarded by professionals and amateurs alike. Nick Faldo's Chart Hills in Kent, picturesque venue for the Ladies' European Tour's English Open, has 200-year-old oaks, an island green and 138 bunkers for the more discerning golfer.

For uniqueness why not try Hampton Court Palace - the only golf club in the UK to be situated inside a Royal Park. Being a Grade I Listed Home Park means wandering fallow deer and untamed rough are just two of the challenges for the inland links course, redesigned by Willie Park and with USPGA specification greens.

There are more than 500 venues in the region, which means there are almost unlimited options for a golfing itinerary taking in the very best and most challenging and enjoyable courses in southern England, with a budget to suit everyone. Some of those worthy of a visit include The Drift in Surrey, Sweetwoods Park on the Sussex-Kent border or the nine-hole par-30 Effingham Park, situated in the grounds of Copthorne Effingham Park Hotel. For something a little different, try the testing par-three course at Burgess Hill Golf Centre in West Sussex.

The choice is endless!

3rd hole at Burnham Beeches Golf Club, Burnham, Buckinghamshire

London (Central & Greater)

BEXLEYHEATH. Barnehurst Public Pay and Play Golf Course, Mayplace Road East, Bexleyheath, Kent DA7 6JU (01322 523746; Fax: 01322 523860). *Location:* 10 minutes from M25, follow signs for Erith. Mature inland course in traditional woodland setting. 9 holes, 2737 yards. S.S.S. 68 (for 18 holes). Designed by five times Open Champion James Braid in 1903. Practice ground. *Green Fees:* Information not available. *Eating facilities:* fully licensed bar with catering facilities. *Visitors:* welcome, no restrictions. Newly refurbished club house. *Society Meetings:* catered for. Large function rooms. Golf Manager: Freda Sunley.*

BROMLEY. Bromley Golf Centre, Magpie Hall Lane, Bromley, Kent BR2 8JF. *Location:* off A21 Bromley to Farnborough road. Open course with many trees and water. 9 holes, 2795 yards. S.S.S. 67. Putting green and teaching facilities. New 20 bay floodlit driving range. *Green Fees:* Information not available. *Eating facilities:* food available. *Visitors:* no booking required as this is a public course. Professional: Peter Remy (0208 462 7014)*

DULWICH. Dulwich and Sydenham Hill Golf Club, Grange Lane, College Road, London SE21 7LH (020 8693 3961). *Location:* off South Circular, Dulwich Common. 18 holes, 6079 yards. S.S.S. 69. *Green Fees:* Information not available. *Eating facilities:* lunch every day. *Visitors:* welcome, prior arrangement advised. *Society Meetings:* catered for. Professional: David Baillie. Secretary: Mark Hickson.*

ELTHAM. Eltham Warren Golf Club, Bexley Road, Eltham SE9 2PE (0208 850 4477). *Location:* off East Rochester Way (A2) at Falconwood, then onto A210 Bexley Road. Parkland course, narrow fairways. 9 holes, 5840 yards. S.S.S. 68. Practice ground. *Green Fees:* £30.00 per day; with member £15.00. *Eating facilities:* dining room and bar. *Visitors:* welcome weekdays only, weekends with member only. *Society Meetings:* welcome weekdays, please phone for details. Professional: Gary Brett (020 8850 4477). Secretary: D.J. Mabbott (0208 850 4477). website: www.elthamwarrengolfclub.co.uk

ELTHAM. Royal Blackheath Golf Club, The Clubhouse, Court Road, Eltham SE9 5AF. *Location:* M25, A20 exit London bound, second set of traffic lights turn right, 600 yards up hill on right. Parkland, wooded with water. 18 holes, 6219 yards. S.S.S. 70. Practice area. *Green Fees:* £55.00 per round, £75.00 per day. *Eating facilities:* excellent dining room and two bars. *Visitors:* welcome weekdays, weekends only if introduced by and playing with member. Museum. *Society Meetings:* catered for midweek, prior booking essential. Professional: Matt Johns (020 8850 1763). Secretary: (020 8850 1795; Fax: 020 8859 0150).
e-mail: info@rbgc.com
website: www.royalblackheath.com

HAMPTON WICK. Hampton Court Palace Golf Club, Hampton Wick, Kingston-upon-Thames KT1 4AD (020 8977 2658). *Location:* between Hampton Court and Kingston Bridge, entrance at Kingston Bridge roundabout. An historic course, redesigned by Willy Park. Parkland and inland links. 18 holes, 6513 yards. S.S.S. 71. *Green Fees:* Information not available. *Eating facilities:* New Clubhouse, full bar and dining facilities. *Visitors:* welcome; booking one week in advance through Pro Shop. *Society Meetings:* catered for by arrangement. Professional: Edward Litchfield (020 8977 2658). Contacts: (020 8977 2423)*
e-mail: hamptonwickpalace@crown-golf.co.uk

LONDON. London Scottish Golf Club, Windmill Enclosure, Wimbledon Common SW19 5NQ (020 8788 0135). *Location:* just off A3 – Tibbetts Corner – just south of Putney SW15. Wooded commonland. 18 holes, 5458 yards. S.S.S. 66. *Green Fees:* information not available. *Eating facilities:* bar and catering. *Visitors:* welcome weekdays only. Check with Professional recommended. Red top must be worn, no jeans or sweatshirts. *Society Meetings:* welcome. Professional/Secretary: Stephen Barr (020 8789 1207/7517).*

LONDON. Richmond Park Golf Club, Roehampton Gate, Richmond Park, London SW15 5JR (020 8876 1795; Fax: 020 8878 1354). *Location:* set within parkland in Richmond. Two courses (36 holes), 6036 yards and 5868 yards. S.S.S. 68/68/67. Driving range. *Green Fees:* information not available. *Visitors:* welcome every day. *Society Meetings:* all welcome. Secretary: Tony Gourvish (020 8876 3205).*

LONDON. Thamesview Golf Centre, Fairway Drive (off Summerton Way), Thamesmead North, London SE28 8PP (020 8310 7975; Fax: 020 8312 0546). Delightful, undulating Public Pay & Play Course, founded 1991. Water hazards and a mixture of new and mature trees. The 4th hole is a challenging 515 yards down a narrow fairway. 9 holes, 5414 yards, par 70. S.S.S. 66. Floodlit 30-bay driving range, putting green. *Green Fees:* information not provided. *Eating facilities:* restaurant, bars and function room. *Visitors*: no restriction. Fully stocked Pro Shop, club hire. *Society Meetings*: welcome, book by telephone or in writing. Head Professional: Gary Stewart. Site Manager: Stephen Lee.
e-mail: golf@tvgc.co.uk
website: www.tvgc.co.uk

**PLEASE NOTE
Some London golf clubs are listed in the EAST REGION
(see pages 143-148)**

London (Central & Greater) / SOUTH REGION

ROEHAMPTON. Roehampton Club, Roehampton Lane, London SW15 5LR (020 8480 4200; Fax: 020 8480 4265). *Location:* just off South Circular Road between Sheen and Putney. Parkland. 18 holes, 6065 yards. S.S.S. 69. *Green Fees:* members and guests only. *Eating facilities:* restaurant, club café, juice bar. *Visitors:* welcome as members' guest only, Handicap Certificate required at weekends. *Society Meetings:* catered for by arrangement. Professional: Richard Harrison (020 8876 3858). Chief Executive: Marc Newey (020 8480 4207).

SHOOTERS HILL. Shooters Hill Golf Club Ltd, "Lowood", Eaglesfield Road, Shooters Hill, London SE18 3DA (020 8854 6368; Fax: 020 8854 0469). *Location:* off A207 between Blackheath and Welling. Hilly wooded course with fine views. 18 holes, 5721 yards. S.S.S. 68. *Green Fees:* weekdays £35.00 per round, £45.00 per day; weekends with a member only. *Eating facilities:* bar and diningroom. *Visitors:* Buggies available. *Society Meetings:* catered for Tuesdays and Thursdays only. Professional: David Brotherton (020 8854 0073). Secretary: Office (020 8854 6368).

SOUTHWARK. Aquarius Golf Club, Beachcroft Reservoir, Marmora Road, Honor Oak SE22 0RY (020 8693 1626). *Location:* nearest main road - Forest Hill Road. The course is situated on and around a reservoir, testing first and eighth holes. 9 holes, 5246 yards. S.S.S. 66. *Green Fees:* information not available. *Eating facilities:* limited. *Visitors:* welcome with member only. Professional: F. Private. Secretary: Jim Halliday.*
e-mail: aquariusgolfclub@btopenworld.com

SUNBURY ON THAMES. Hazelwood Golf Club Ltd, Croysdale Avenue, Sunbury on Thames TW16 6QU (01932 770932; Fax: 01932 770933). *Location:* Junction 1 of M3. Parkland course. 9 holes, 2785 yards. Practice putting green, 36 bay driving range, bunker and chipping practice. *Green Fees:* information not available. *Eating facilities:* bar/food. *Visitors:* welcome every day. *Society Meetings* welcome. Professional: Robert Catley-Smith.*

WEST DRAYTON. Heathpark Golf Club, Stockley Road, West Drayton, Middlesex UB7 9NA (01895 444232). *Location:* in grounds of Crown Plaza Hotel, Junction 4 M40. Undulating parkland course. 9 holes, 2245 yards. S.S.S. 62. *Green Fees:* information not available. *Eating facilities:* catering and bars. *Visitors:* welcome, dress code. Sundays after 11.30 am. *Society Meetings:* welcome at all times. Contact: B. Sharma.*

WIMBLEDON. Royal Wimbledon Golf Club, 29 Camp Road, Wimbledon SW19 4UW. *Location:* one mile west of War Memorial in Wimbledon Village. 18 holes, 6348 yards. S.S.S. 70. *Visitors:* weekdays by prior arrangement. *Society Meetings:* Wednesdays and Thursdays only, by arrangement. Professional: David Jones. Secretary: Norman Smith (020 8946 2125; Fax: 020 8944 8652).
e-mail: secretary@rwgc.co.uk
website: www.rwgc.co.uk

WIMBLEDON. Wimbledon Common Golf Club, 19 Camp Road, Wimbledon Common, Wimbledon SW19 4UW (020 8946 0294; Fax: 020 8947 8697). *Location:* Wimbledon Common. Wooded course. 18 holes, 5438 yards. S.S.S. 66. Par 68. *Green Fees:* Monday £30.00, Tuesday to Friday £35.00. *Eating facilities:* bar, full catering every day except Mondays. *Visitors:* welcome weekdays, only with a member at weekends. Dress code – pillar box red upper garment must be worn. *Society Meetings:* welcome, groups of up to 50 catered for. Professional: J.S. Jukes (020 8946 0294; Fax: 020 8947 8697). Office Manager (020 8946 7571).
e-mail: office@wcgc.co.uk

WIMBLEDON. Wimbledon Park Golf Club, Home Park Road, Wimbledon, London SW19 7HR (020 8946 1002; Fax: 020 8944 8688). *Location:* Church Road, Arthur Road and Home Park Road from Wimbledon High Street, or by District Line to Wimbledon Park Station where signposted. Parkland, wooded around a lake. 18 holes, 5492 yards. S.S.S. 66. *Green Fees:* information not available. *Eating facilities:* information not available. *Visitors:* welcome on production of letter of introduction or Handicap Certificate. *Society Meetings:* welcome. Professional: Dean Wingrove (020 8946 4053). General Manager: Patrick Shanahan (020 8946 1250; 020 8944 8688).*
e-mail: patrick@wpgc.co.uk
website: www.wpgc.co.uk

PLEASE NOTE

All the information regarding Golf Clubs in this guide is given in good faith in the belief that it is correct. However, the publishers cannot guarantee the facts given in these pages, neither are they responsible for changes in ownership or facilities, such as green fees, that may take place after the date of going to press. Readers should always satisfy themselves that the facilities they require are available and that the terms, if quoted, still apply.

Berkshire

ASCOT. **The Berkshire Golf Club,** Swinley Road, Ascot SL5 8AY (01344 621495). *Location*: on A332 between Bagshot and Ascot. Heathland (wooded) course. 36 holes. Blue Course: 6358 yards, S.S.S. 71, Par 71. Red Course: 6452 yards, S.S.S. 71, Par 72. Practice facilities. *Green Fees:* information not available. *Eating facilities:* dining room open daily except Monday, snack bar open daily; bar open every day. *Visitors:* welcome weekdays only by application to the Secretary. *Society Meetings:* catered for by prior bookings. Professional: P. Anderson (01344 622351). Secretary: Lt. Col. J.C.F. Hunt (01344 621496).*

ASCOT. **Lavender Park Golf Centre,** Swinley Road, Ascot SL5 8BD (01344 893344). *Location:* Ascot to Bracknell Road, half a mile from racecourse. Very pleasant flat 9 hole, Executive course, 8 Par 3s and one Par 4. 9 holes, 1104 yards. S.S.S. 28. 23-bay driving range. *Green Fees:* information not available. *Eating facilities:* bar snacks. *Visitors:* welcome at all times; pay and play. 8 table snooker hall. *Society Meetings:* welcome. Director of Golf/Master Professional: David Johnson (01344 893344). website: www.lavenderparkgolf.co.uk

ASCOT. **Mill Ride Golf & Country Club,** Mill Ride, Ascot SL5 8LT (01344 891494; Fax: 01344 886820). *Location*: off Junction 3 of M3 or Junction 6 of M4, one mile west Ascot Racecourse. Championship golf course designed by Donald Steel. 18 holes, 6900 yards. S.S.S. 73. Driving range. *Green Fees:* information not available. *Eating facilities:* bar food. *Visitors:* welcome for private events and golf days. Professional: Terry Wild (01344 886777; Fax: 01344 886820). Manager: Stuart Gillett (01344 891494; Fax: 01344 886820).*
e-mail: info@mill-ride.com
website: www.mill-ride.com

ASCOT. **Royal Ascot Golf Club,** Winkfield Road, Ascot SL5 7LJ (01344 625175; Fax: 01344 872330). *Location:* Winkfield Road is off Ascot High Street (A329). Parkland; new 18-hole course. 18 holes, 6293 yards. S.S.S. 70. Par 70. *Green Fees:* information not available. *Eating facilities:* full catering available. *Visitors:* welcome only as guests of members. *Society Meetings:* catered for by agreement, maximum 40. Professional: Alistair White (01344 624656). Secretary: Mrs Sheila Thompson (01344 625175).*
e-mail: secretaries@royalascotgolfclub.co.uk
website: www.royalascotgolfclub.co.uk

ASCOT. **Swinley Forest Golf Club,** Coronation Road, Ascot SL5 9LE (01344 620197). *Location:* between Ascot and Bagshot. Wooded heathland course. 18 holes, 6001 yards. S.S.S. 69. *Green Fees:* information not provided. *Eating facilities:* lunches served. *Visitors:* welcome with a member or by special arrangement. *Society Meetings:* catered for. Professional: Stuart Hill (01344 295282). Secretary: Stewart Zuill (01344 259283; Fax: 01344 874733).

BINFIELD. **Blue Mountain Golf Centre,** Wood Lane, Binfield, Bracknell RG42 4EX (01344 300220; Fax: 01344 360960). *Location:* two miles north of M4 near Bracknell/Wokingham. Parkland course with numerous lakes. 18 holes, 6097 yards. S.S.S 70. 33 bay covered floodlit range. *Green Fees:* information not available. *Eating facilities:* fully licensed restaurant/ bar, Blues Bar with live jazz and food. *Visitors:* welcome any time. *Society Meetings:* always welcome, please call for details. Professional: Chris Lilleystone (01344 300220).*

BURNHAM. **Huntswood Golf Club**, Taplow Common Road, Burnham SL1 8LS (01628 667144; Fax: 01628 663145). *Location:* Junction 7 of M4, at roundabout turn left onto A4, then at Sainsburys roundabout turn right. Go straight over next two roundabouts, Huntswood Golf Club is quarter of a mile on the left. 18 holes, Par 69. *Green Fees:* information not available. *Eating facilities:* bar and dining facilities after 7am. All-day breakfast, Sunday lunch. All types of functions catered for. *Visitors:* very welcome, Pay and Play open to all. Smart golf attire required, strictly no jeans on course. Buggy, trolley, club hire available. *Society Meetings:* welcome, please phone for information. Professional: Graham Beynon.*
website: www.huntswoodgolf.com

CROWTHORNE. **East Berkshire Golf Club**, Ravenswood Avenue, Crowthorne RG45 6BD (01344 772041; Fax: 01344 777378). *Location*: M3 Junction 3 - Bracknell turn off, follow signs to Crowthorne, Ravenswood Avenue opposite Railway Station. Heathland course. 18 holes, 6344 yards. S.S.S. 70. *Green Fees:* £40.00 per round, £60.00 day ticket. *Eating facilities:* bar snacks. *Visitors:* welcome weekdays by prior notification. *Society Meetings:* Thursdays and Fridays only. Professional: Jason Brant (01344 774112). Secretary: Colin Day (01344 772041; Fax: 01344 777378).

THE APPEARANCE OF AN ASTERISK (*) AT THE END OF A CLUB OR COURSE ENTRY INDICATES THAT UP-TO-DATE INFORMATION HAS NOT BEEN SUPPLIED

72 Berkshire / SOUTH REGION

HURLEY. **Temple Golf Club,** Henley Road, Hurley, Near Maidenhead SL6 5LH (01628 824248; Fax: 01628 828119). *Location:* exit M4 Junction 8/9 or M40 at Junction 4. From M4 or M40 take A404 then A4130 signposted Henley. Chalk Downland course - exceptional drainage. 18 holes, 6210 yards. S.S.S. 71. Excellent practice area, putting and chipping green. *Green Fees:* weekdays £45.00 per round, £55.00 per day; weekends and Public Holidays £50.00 per round, £60.00 per day. Twilight rates available after 5pm. *Eating facilities:* bar and bar snacks available daily; lunch and dinner available by prior arrangement. *Visitors:* welcome by prior arrangement. Handicap Certificate required. *Society Meetings:* welcome weekdays and occasionally at weekends by prior arrangement; booking accepted one year in advance; minimum number 12, maximum 40. Professional: James Whiteley (01628 824254; Fax: 01628 828119). Secretary: Keith G.M. Adderley (01628 824795; Fax: 01628 828119).
e-mail: secretary@templegolfclub.co.uk
website: www.templegolfclub.co.uk

MAIDENHEAD. **Maidenhead Golf Club,** Shoppenhangers Road, Maidenhead SL6 2PZ (01628 624693; Fax: 01628 780758). *Location:* adjacent to Maidenhead Station (south side), one mile from M4. Level parkland course with irrigated fairways. 18 holes, 6364 yards. S.S.S. 70. *Green Fees:* weekdays £37.00. *Eating facilities:* restaurant and bar meals Tuesday to Friday. *Visitors:* welcome weekdays, no visitors after 12 noon Fridays. Handicap Certificate required. *Society Meetings:* welcome Tuesday pm, Wednesday and Thursday. Professional: Steve Geary (01628 624067). Secretary: J.D Pugh.
e-mail: manager@maidenheadgolf.co.uk
website: www.maidenheadgolf.co.uk

MAIDENHEAD. **Winter Hill Golf Club,** Grange Lane, Cookham SL6 9RP (01628 527613). *Location:* M4 Junction 8/9, four miles from Maidenhead. Parkland with extensive views of the Thames. 18 holes, 6408 yards - white tees, 6228 yards - yellow tees. S.S.S. 71. Large practice area. *Green Fees:* information not provided. *Eating facilities:* lunches and snacks available every day. *Visitors:* welcome weekdays; preliminary enquiries advisable, and with member at weekends. *Society Meetings:* may be accepted by application to the Secretary; minimum number 16, maximum 40. Dress rules: strictly no jeans, trainers on course or in clubhouse. PGA Club and Teaching Professional: Julian Goodman (01628 527610). Secretary: Hilary Spears (01628 527613).

MAIDENHEAD near. **Bird Hills (UK) Ltd.,** Drift Road, Hawthorn Hill, Near Maidenhead SL6 3ST (01628 771030; Fax: 01628 631023). *Location*: M4 Junction 8/9, take A308 then A330 to Bracknell. Gently undulating parkland course. 18 holes, 6176 yards. S.S.S. 69. 36 bay floodlit driving range. *Green Fees*: from £10.00. *Eating facilities*: club bar, restaurant, members bar, barbecue, private function hall. *Visitors:* always welcome, open every day except Christmas Day. Large golf shop. Conference facilities. *Society Meetings*: always welcome. Professional: Nick Slimming. Secretary: Hannah Edwards.
website: www.birdhills.co.uk

NEWBURY. **Deanwood Park Golf Club,** Stockcross, Newbury RG20 8JP (Tel & Fax: 01635 48772). *Location*: 200 yards off the A4 west of Newbury towards Stockcross village. Two miles from Newbury town centre. Undulating parkland/wooded course. 9 holes, 2114 yards, 1932 metres. S.S.S. 60 (18 holes). 7 bay driving range, practice net, practice bunker and putting green. *Green Fees:* information not available. *Eating facilities:* Lounge/bar/restaurant facilities; food served all day. *Visitors:* welcome at all times but must book in advance. Standard golf dress code applies, no jeans allowed on the course. Trolley, club and buggy hire available. *Society Meetings:* Society/Company groups welcome at all times; mix and match price structuring for golf and catering. Professional: Claire Waite. Secretary: John Bowness (Tel & Fax: 01635 48772).
e-mail: info@deanwoodpark.co.uk
website: www.deanwoodpark.co.uk

NEWBURY. **Donnington Grove Country Club,** Grove Road, Newbury RG14 2LA (01635 581000; Fax: 01635 552259). *Location:* northwestern outskirts of Newbury 3 miles from M4 J13. From the A4 running through Newbury take the B4494 (signposted Wantage) at Waitrose roundabout. After 600 yards turn left at mini roundabout. Dave Thomas designed, USGA specification greens, championship standard course. Parkland with lakes and other features; 18 holes, 7108 yards. Practice range for members, guests and visitors only. *Green Fees:* Monday and Tuesday £20.00 (excluding Bank Holidays), Wednesday and Thursday £25.00, Friday £30.00, weekends and Bank Holidays £40.00. 2010 rates (subject to review). *Eating facilities:* hotel with bar snacks and restaurant. *Visitors:* welcome anytime weekdays, after 11am weekends. *Society Meetings:* catered for; several packages available - phone for information. Professional: Gareth Williams (01635 551975). Secretary: Dave Allen (01635 581000).
e-mail: enquiries@donnington-grove.com
website: www.donnington-grove.com

NEWBURY. **Donnington Valley Hotel & Golf Club,** Snelsmore House, Snelsmore Common, Newbury RG14 3BG (01635 568140; Fax: 01635 568141). *Location:* Junction 13 of M4, then A34 towards Newbury. Take first exit off A34, follow signs to Donnington Castle, entrance on the right. 18 holes, 6353 metres. Practice net, computer analysis of swing. *Green Fees:* see website for details. *Eating facilities:* two bars and a restaurant. *Visitors:* welcome, must have own shoes. Accommodation in 4-star 111-bedroom hotel with a brand new Health Club and Spa. *Society Meetings:* welcome. Professional: Martin Balfour (01635 568142; Fax: 01635 568141). Secretary: Peter Smith (01635 568140; Fax: 01635 568144).
e-mail: golf@donningtonvalley.co.uk
website: www.donningtonvalley.co.uk

THE GOLF GUIDE 2011   SOUTH REGION / Berkshire   73

NEWBURY. **Newbury and Crookham Golf Club Ltd,** Bury's Bank Road, Greenham, Newbury RG19 8BZ (01635 40035). *Location:* on south side of Newbury; Junction 13 on M4. Varied and interesting with woods or trees on almost every hole. 18 holes, 5961 yards. S.S.S. 69. *Green Fees:* weekdays £40.00 per round, £50.00 per day. *Eating facilities:* restaurant/bar. *Visitors:* welcome, except weekends and Bank Holidays unless with a member. *Society Meetings:* welcome. Buggies available. Professional: Martin Balfour (01635 31201). Club Manager: Stephen Myers MBE (01635 40035).
website: www.newburygolf.co.uk

NEWBURY. **Newbury Racecourse Golf Centre,** The Racecourse, Newbury RG14 7NZ (01635 551464); Fax: 01635 528354). *Location*: one mile south east of Newbury. Challenging flat links course for all standards. Good conditions throughout the year. 18 holes, 6500 yards, S.S.S. 71. Pro Shop, Driving range, practice area and green. *Green Fees:* information not available. *Eating facilities:* bar food. *Visitors:* welcome to pay and play. *Society Meetings:* all welcome. Professional: Nick Mitchell (01635 551464). Manager: N. Mitchell (01635 40015; Fax: 01635 528354).*

NEWBURY. **The West Berkshire Golf Course,** Chaddleworth, Newbury RG20 7DU (01488 638574). *Location:* M4 Junction 14. A338 towards Wantage, then follow signposts to RAF Welford. Downland. 18 holes, 7022 yards. S.S.S. 74. Two practice grounds, tuition available. *Green Fees:* information not provided. *Eating facilities:* full catering available. *Visitors:* welcome weekdays; restricted to afternoons weekends, reservation required. Trolleys and buggies available. *Society Meetings:* welcome by arrangement. Professional: Paul Simpson (01488 638851). Secretary: Mrs C.M. Clayton (01488 638574; Fax: 01488 638781).
website: www.thewbgc.co.uk

READING. **Calcot Park Golf Club, Bath Road, Calcot, Reading RG31 7RN (0118 9427124; Fax: 0118 945 3373).** *Location:* off Exit 12, M4 along A4 towards Reading, approximately one and a half miles. H. Colt parkland course. 18 holes, 6216 yards. S.S.S. 70. Three practice areas. *Green Fees:* weekdays £50.00 per day, £40.00 after 2pm. Eating facilities: fully licensed restaurant, snacks available, three bars. *Visitors:* welcome on provision of Handicap Certificate. County card accepted. Not weekends or Bank Holidays. Advisable to ring first to check availability. *Society Meetings:* catered for midweek. Professional: Mark Grieve (0118 942 7797; Fax: 0118 945 3373). Secretary: Kim Brake (0118 942 7124; Fax: 0118 945 3373).
e-mail: info@calcotpark.com
website: www.calcotpark.com

READING. **Hurst Golf Club,** Sandford Lane, Hurst, Reading RG10 0SU (01189 344355). *Location:* five miles Reading towards Wokingham. Parkland by the side of a large lake. 9 holes, 3154 yards. S.S.S. 70. *Green Fees:* information not available. *Eating facilities:* bar and restaurant seating for 30. *Visitors:* unrestricted, bookings accepted. *Society Meetings:* welcome. Manager: P. Priddle.*

READING. **Pincents Manor Golf,** Pincents Lane, Calcot, Reading RG31 4UQ (01734 323511; Fax: 01734 323503). *Location:* Junction 12 M4 behind Savacentre. Parkland. Two courses: Manor Course - 18 holes, 6028 yards. S.S.S. 69; Lodge Course - 9 holes, 2600 yards. S.S.S. 68. Par 3 course. *Green Fees:* information not available. *Eating facilities:* Orchard Restaurant, Oak Bar, cruck barn. *Visitors:* welcome on Lodge Course, members only on Manor Course. Accommodation available in three bedrooms. *Society Meetings:* welcome. Professional: Alistair Thatcher.*

READING. **Reading Golf Club,** 17 Kidmore End Road, Emmer Green, Reading RG4 8SG (0118 947 2909). *Location:* two miles north of Reading off the Peppard Road (B481). Parkland. 18 holes, 6212 yards. S.S.S. 70. Practice facilities. *Green Fees:* Monday to Friday £40.00 per round, £50.00 per day. *Eating facilities:* available. *Visitors:* welcome Monday to Friday, weekends after 4pm. *Society Meetings:* catered for by arrangement Tuesdays, Wednesdays and Thursdays. Buggies available. Professional: Will Alsop (0118 947 6115). Secretary: Andrew Chaundy (0118 947 2909).
website: www.readinggolfclub.com

READING. **Sonning Golf Club,** Duffield Road, Sonning RG4 6GJ (01189 693332; Fax: 01189 448409). *Location*: left off A4 at Sonning Roundabout, then left again. Parkland. 18 holes, 6366 yards. S.S.S. 70. *Green Fees:* on application. *Eating facilities:* Restaurant - phone for booking 01189 272055. *Visitors:* welcome, must be member of a recognised golf club with an official Handicap; weekends with members only. *Society Meetings:* catered for Wednesdays. Professional: R. McDougall (01189 692910). General Manager: G. Stacey.

READING. **Wokefield Park Golf Club,** Mortimer, Reading RG7 3AE (0118 9334018; Fax: 0118 9334031). *Location:* 10 minutes Junction 11 M4, 20 minutes Junction 5 M3. Championship parkland course with winding streams, 9 lakes and large bunkers. 18 holes, 6961 yards. S.S.S. 73. Practice facilities. *Green Fees:* information not available. offers. *Eating facilities:* bar and two restaurants. *Visitors:* welcome at all times. Hotel with 322 en suite bedrooms; leisure facilities. *Society Meetings:* contact Golf Sales Team (0118 933 4018). Professional: Gary Smith (0118 9334078; Fax: 0118 9334162). Secretary: Norman West.*
website: www.verve-venues.com

SINDLESHAM. **Bearwood Golf Club,** Mole Road, Sindlesham RG41 5DB (0118 976 0060). *Location*: on B3030 from Winnersh to Arborfield. Flat, wooded course. 9 holes, 2802 yards. S.S.S. 68 (18 holes). Driving range 7.30am to 7.30pm every day. *Green Fees:* information not provided. *Eating facilities:* food available all day. *Visitors:* welcome weekdays and weekends after 3pm. *Society Meetings:* maximum of 21 catered for. Thursday only. Professional: Bayley Tustin; Manager: Barry Tustin (0118 976 0060). Shop: 0118 976 0156.

SLOUGH. Datchet Golf Club, Buccleuch Road, Datchet SL3 9BP (Tel & Fax: 01753 541872; Clubhouse: 01753 543887). *Location:* within two miles of both Windsor and Slough. 9 holes, 6087 yards. S.S.S. 69. *Green Fees:* £25.00 per round, £35.00 per day. 2010 rates (subject to review). *Visitors:* welcome weekdays and after 2.00pm weekends during BST. *Society Meetings:* welcome. Professional: Paul Cook (01753 545222) Secretary/Manager: Keith Smith (Tel & Fax: 01753 541872). e-mail: secretary@datchetgolfclub.co.uk
website: www.datchetgolfclub.co.uk

STREATLEY ON THAMES. **Goring and Streatley Golf Club,** Rectory Road, Streatley on Thames RG8 9QA (01491 873229; Fax: 01491 875224). *Location:* 10 miles north west of Reading off A417 Wantage Road. Downland course on Berkshire Downs. 18 holes, 6355 yards. S.S.S. 70. *Green Fees:* information not available. *Eating facilities:* full restaurant and bar meals. Restaurant (01491 875122). *Visitors:* welcome on weekdays by telephone booking. *Society Meetings:* catered for. Professional: Jason Hadland (01491 873715). Secretary: A.B.W. James (01491 873229).*
website: www.goringgc.org

SUNNINGDALE. **Sunningdale Ladies' Golf Club,** Cross Road, Sunningdale SL5 9RX (01344 620507). *Location:* second left going west on A30, past Sunningdale level crossing. Heathland. 18 holes, 3705 yards. S.S.S. 61, Men S.S.S. 58. *Green Fees:* £40.00 per round weekdays, £45.00 weekends/Bank Holidays. 2010 rates (subject to review). *Eating facilities:* light lunches available. *Visitors:* welcome. *Society Meetings:* associations, societies and events welcome.
e-mail: golf@sunningdaleladies.co.uk
website: www.sunningdaleladies.co.uk

WARGRAVE. **Hennerton Golf Club,** Crazies Hill Road, Wargrave RG10 8LT (0118 940 1000; Fax: 0118 940 1042). *Location:* halfway between Maidenhead and Reading off the A321 to Henley, follow "Golf Club" signs from Wargrave High Street. Challenging scenic course overlooking the Thames Valley. 18 holes, 4430 yards. Par 65. Driving range. *Green Fees:* see website for details. *Eating facilities:* clubhouse with full facilities. *Visitors:* welcome anytime, phone Pro Shop. *Society Meetings:* telephone for details. Professional/Manager: Glenn Johnson (0118 940 1000; Fax: 0118 940 1042).
e-mail: info@hennertongolfclub.co.uk
website: www.hennertongolfclub.co.uk

WOKINGHAM. **Bearwood Lakes Golf Club,** Bearwood Road, near Sindlesham, Wokingham RG41 4SJ (0118 979 7900; Fax: 0118 979 2911). *Location:* just off M4 at Reading. Wooded 18 hole golf course. 6892 yards, S.S.S. 72. *Green Fees:* information not available. *Eating facilities:* restaurant, bar, function room, dining club. *Visitors:* must be the guest of a member. A limited number of day members tee times are now available on application Practice ground available. Professional: Steve Harden (0118 978 3030). Manager: Carl Rutherford (0118 979 7900).*

WOKINGHAM. **Sand Martins Golf Club,** Finchampstead Road, Wokingham RG40 3RQ (0118 9792711; Fax: 0118 9770282). *Location:* off Nine Mile Ride, two miles from Wokingham town centre. Parkland, links/wooded course. 18 holes, 6235 yards. S.S.S. 70. Practice area including bunker/pitching area. *Green Fees:* information not available. *Eating facilities:* Half-Way House, bar and restaurant. *Visitors:* welcome weekdays and at selected times at weekends. *Society Meetings:* welcome weekdays. Professional: Andrew Hall (0118 9029964). Club Secretary: James McDonald (0118 9029965; Fax: 0118 9770282).*
e-mail: info@sandmartins.com

Buckinghamshire

AMERSHAM. **Harewood Downs Golf Club,** Cokes Lane, Chalfont St Giles HP8 4TA (01494 762184; Fax: 01494 766869). *Location:* off A413, two miles east of Amersham. Rolling, tree lined. 18 holes, 6028 yards. S.S.S. 70. Practice ground. *Green Fees:* weekdays £40.00 per round, £50.00 per day; weekends £45.00 per round, £50.00 per day. Special rates, winter golf. *Eating facilities:* full restaurant and bar. *Visitors:* welcome on weekdays with current Handicap, weekends by prior arrangement only. *Society Meetings:* welcome, mainly Thursdays and Fridays. Professional: G. Morris (01494 764102). Secretary: S.J. Thornton (01494 762184).

AYLESBURY. **Aylesbury Park Golf Club,** Andrews Way, Aylesbury HP17 8QQ (01296 399196). *Location:* Just outside Aylesbury town centre off the A418. Historic parkland course. 18 holes, 6146 yards. S.S.S. 69. 9-hole short course now open. *Green Fees:* information not available. Numerous green fee special offers take place throughout the year - call for details. *Visitors:* welcome at all times. No Handicap Certificate required. *Society Meetings:* please call for details.

AYLESBURY. **Chiltern Forest Golf Club,** Aston Hill, Halton, Aylesbury HP22 5NQ (01296 631267; Fax: 01296 632709). *Location:* five miles south-east of Aylesbury, signposted St. Leonards. Wooded, hilly course. 18 holes, 5765 yards. S.S.S. 69. *Green Fees:* £36.00 weekdays; £18.00 with a member. *Visitors:* weekdays unrestricted. *Society Meetings:* welcome, preferably Monday to Friday. Professional: Simon Perks. General Manager: Anthony Roberts (01296 631267; Fax: 01296 632709).
e-mail: secretary@chilternforest.co.uk
website: www.chilternforest.co.uk.

FHG GUIDES
www.holidayguides.com

AYLESBURY. **Ellesborough Golf Club,** Butlers Cross, Aylesbury HP17 0TZ (01296 622375). *Location:* on B4010 one-and-a-half miles from Wendover. Chiltern Hills course. Undulating links. 18 holes, 6360 yards, 5815 metres. S.S.S. 71. Practice net/ground. *Green Fees:* information not available. Eating facilities: full catering available. *Visitors:* welcome except Tuesday mornings and competition days, weekends with a member only. Must provide Handicap Certificate. *Society Meetings:* catered for by arrangement. Professional: Mark Squire (Tel & Fax: 01296 623126). General Manager: (Tel & Fax: 01296 622114).
website: www.ellesboroughgolf.co.uk

AYLESBURY. **Weston Turville Golf Club,** New Road, Weston Turville, Near Aylesbury HP22 5QT (01296 424084; Fax: 01296 395376). *Location:* two miles south east of Aylesbury off A41. Easy walking course at the foot of the Chiltern Hills. 18 holes, 6008 yards. S.S.S. 69. *Green Fees:* weekdays £25.00, weekends £30.00. *Eating facilities:* meals, snacks and visitors' bar. *Visitors:* truly welcome. *Society Meetings:* especially catered for. Professional: Gary George (01296 425949; Fax: 01296 395376). General Manager: David Allen (01296 424084; Fax: 01296 395376).
e-mail: enquiries@westonturvillegolfclub.co.uk

BEACONSFIELD. **Beaconsfield Golf Club,** Seer Green, Near Beaconsfield HP9 2UR (01494 676545; Fax: 01494 681148). *Location:* from A40 at Beaconsfield, A355 Amersham Road, one mile turn right to Jordans, one mile signposted. Parkland course. 18 holes, 6508 yards, Par 72. Large practice ground, driving range. *Green Fees:* information not available. *Eating facilities:* dining room or bar menu; two bars. *Visitors:* welcome weekdays with accredited introduction – check with Pro. Handicap Certificate required. *Society Meetings:* catered for Tuesdays and Wednesdays. Professional: Mike Brothers (01494 676616). Secretary: K.R. Wilcox (01494 676545).*
e-mail: secretary@beaconsfieldgolfclub.co.uk
website: www.beaconsfieldgolfclub.co.uk

The Warmest Welcome in Golf
where quality and value are standard

Situated two miles south east of Aylesbury off A41, this is an easy walking course at the foot of the Chiltern Hills. 18 holes, 6008 yards. S.S.S. 69.

Green Fees – weekdays £25.00; weekends £30.00

Visitors are truly welcome and Society Meetings are especially catered for.
Meals, snacks and visitors' bar.

Weston Turville Golf Club
New Road, Weston Turville, Near Aylesbury HP22 5QT
Tel: 01296 424084 • Fax: 01296 395376

Professional: Gary George
01296 425949• Fax: 01296 395376
General Manager: David Allen
01296 424084 • Fax: 01296 395376

BUCKINGHAM. **Buckingham Golf Club,** Tingewick Road, Buckingham MK18 4AE (01280 815566; Fax: 01280 821812). *Location*: two miles south west of Buckingham on A421. Undulating parkland - eight holes affected by river. 18 holes, 6162 yards. S.S.S. 70. Practice ground. *Green Fees:* £40.00 per round. County card accepted. *Eating facilities:* seven day catering - bars, lunch and evening (01280 813282). *Visitors:* welcome weekdays only. Pro shop (01280 815210). *Society Meetings:* pre-booked on Tuesdays or Thursdays. Assistant Secretary: Linda Sirett (01280 815566; Fax: 01280 821812). Professional: Gregor Hannah (01280 815210).
e-mail: admin@buckinghamgolfclub.co.uk
website: www.buckinghamgolfclub.co.uk

BURNHAM. **Burnham Beeches Golf Club,** Green Lane, Burnham, Slough SL1 8EG (01628 661448; Fax: 01628 668968). *Location*: Junction 7 on M4. Parkland/ wooded course. 18 holes, 6449 yards. S.S.S. 71. *Green Fees:* weekdays 18 holes £45.00, 36 holes £60.00. *Eating facilities:* bar and restaurant. *Visitors:* welcome weekdays. *Society Meetings:* welcome Wednesdays to Fridays all year round. Professional: R. Bolton (01628 661661). Secretary: P. Dawson (01628 661448).

BURNHAM. **The Lambourne Golf Club,** Dropmore Road, Burnham SL1 8NF (01628 666755; Fax: 01628 663301). *Location:* take M4 to Exit 7; take M40 to Exit 2. Parkland course, six lakes. 18 holes, 6798 yards. S.S.S. 73. Practice facilities available. *Green Fees:* Monday to Friday £60.00. *Eating facilities:* snack bar, half-way hatch, restaurant. *Visitors:* welcome. Handicap Certificate required. Golf Director: (01628 606717). Professional/General Manager: David Hart (01628 606717; Fax: 01628 663301).

CHALFONT ST GILES. **Oakland Park Golf Club,** Three Households, Chalfont St Giles HP8 4LW (01494 871277 Office). *Location*: off main A413 towards Amersham, 10 minutes from J2, M40. Parkland course. 18 holes, 5246 yards. S.S.S. 66. Practice range, green and bunkers. *Green Fees*: information not available. *Eating facilities*: clubhouse bar, full catering all week. *Visitors:* welcome 7 days (after midday at weekends and Bank Holidays). *Society Meetings*: welcome. Professional: Alistair Thatcher (01494 877333; Fax: 01494 874692). General Manager: Ian Donnelly.*
website: www.oaklandparkgolf.co.uk

CHESHAM. **Chartridge Park Golf Club,** Chartridge, Chesham HP5 2TF (01494 791772). *Location*: M25 Junction 18, Amersham, Chesham, three miles from roundabout by pond. Flat parkland course with wooded areas, two water holes and views over the Chiltern Valley. 18 holes, 5409 yards, S.S.S. 66. Chipping and putting area, driving nets. *Green Fees*: information not available. *Eating facilities*: snacks and cooked food available seven days a week; bar. *Visitors & Societies*: welcome, restrictions apply. Functions, Weddings, Corporate Events; Private, spacious suite available for hire. RGA Professional: Jeremy Reilly (07979 497465). General Manager: Eric Roca.*

CHESHAM. **Chesham and Ley Hill Golf Club,** Ley Hill, Chesham HP5 1UZ (01494 784541). *Location:* off A41 on B4504 to Ley Hill, nearest town - Chesham. Wooded parkland. 9 holes, 5296 yards. S.S.S. 65. *Green Fees:* information not available. *Eating facilities:* licensed bar, food available at certain times. *Visitors:* welcome Mondays and Thursdays all day; Wednesdays after 12 noon; Fridays up to 4pm. *Society Meetings:* Thursdays only by prior arrangement. Secretary: J. Short (01494 784541).*
website: www.cheshamgolf.co.uk

DENHAM. **Buckinghamshire Golf Club,** Denham Court, Denham Court Drive, Denham UB9 5PG (01895 835777; Fax: 01895 835210). *Location:* Junction 1 M40 off Denham roundabout, follow signs to Denham Country Park. Gently undulating parkland, River Colne and River Misbourne run through course. 18 holes, 6880 yards. S.S.S. 73. Practice range with ball dispenser and collection. *Green Fees:* Information not available. *Eating facilities:* Heron Restaurant, spike bar; food served all day. *Visitors:* welcome Mondays to Thursdays; advance bookings only. *Society Meetings:* welcome, golf company days up to 80 – details on application. Professional: Paul Schunter. Golf Director: John O'Leary. Enquiries: Gemma Griffiths.*
website: www.buckinghamshiregc.com

THE GOLF GUIDE 2011 — SOUTH REGION / Buckinghamshire

DENHAM. **Denham Golf Club,** Tilehouse Lane, Denham UB9 5DE (01895 832022; Fax: 01895 835340). *Location:* off A412 near Uxbridge. Parkland - undulating. 18 holes, 6462 yards, 5903 metres. S.S.S. 71. Practice ground. *Green Fees:* information not available. *Eating facilities:* diningroom, bar snacks. *Visitors:* welcome Monday to Thursday by prior arrangement only. Handicap Certificate. *Society Meetings:* catered for Tuesdays, Wednesdays and Thursdays. Professional: Stuart Campbell (01895 832801). Secretary: J. W. Tucker (01895 832022; Fax: 01895 835340).*
e-mail: club.secretary@denhamgolfclub.co.uk
website: www.denhamgolfclub.co.uk

GERRARDS CROSS. **Gerrards Cross Golf Club,** Chalfont Park, Gerrards Cross SL9 0QA (01753 883263; Fax: 01753 883593). *Location:* alongside A413 (to Amersham) about three miles from junction with A40 (London to Oxford road). Wooded parkland course. 18 holes, 6295 yards. S.S.S. 70. Practice nets and putting green. *Green Fees:* information not available. *Eating facilities:* lunch, bar snacks, afternoon tea always available, evening meals to order. *Visitors:* welcome except at weekends and Public Holidays but must produce a letter of introduction or current Handicap Certificate. Tuesday is Ladies' Day. *Society Meetings:* catered for Thursdays and Fridays, maximum number 100. Professional: M. Barr (01753 885300). Secretary/Manager: (01753 883263).*

HIGH WYCOMBE. **Flackwell Heath Golf Club Limited,** Treadaway Road, Flackwell Heath, High Wycombe HP10 9PE (01628 520929; Fax: 01628 530040). *Location:* M40 Exit 3 from London, Exit 4 from Oxford. 2 miles High Wycombe. Undulating heath and woodland. 18 holes, 6211 yards. S.S.S. 70. *Green Fees:* weekdays £36.00 per round, £50.00 per day; weekends with member only – £20.00. *Eating facilities:* restaurant and bars daily. *Visitors:* welcome weekdays with Handicap Certificate, weekends with member only. *Society Meetings:* catered for by arrangement Monday to Friday; contact Secretary. Professional: Simon Quilliam (01628 523017). Secretary: Peter J. Clarke (01628 520929, Option 2)).
e-mail: secretary@fhgc.co.uk
website: www.fhgc.co.uk

HIGH WYCOMBE. **Hazlemere Golf Club,** Penn Road, Hazlemere, Near High Wycombe HP15 7LR (01494 719300; Fax: 01494 713914). *Location*: from M40 North: Junction 2, via Beaconsfield and Penn on B474; from M40 South: Junction 4, through High Wycombe on A404. Undulating parkland course with a number of feature water holes. Practice area. 18 holes, 5833 yards. S.S.S. 69. *Green Fees:* information not available. *Eating facilities:* coffee shop and bar. *Visitors:* welcome 7 days a week (after midday weekends). *Society Meetings:* welcome weekdays. Professional: Gavin Cousins (01494 719306). Secretary: (01494 719300).*

HIGH WYCOMBE. **Wycombe Heights Golf Centre,** Rayners Avenue, Loudwater, High Wycombe HP10 9SZ (01494 816686; Fax: 01494 816728). *Location:* one mile south-east of High Wycombe off A40. Impressive tree-lined parkland course with panoramic views of Chilterns. Challenging final loop from 15th to 18th. 18 holes, 6265 yards, Par 70, S.S.S. 72. 18-hole, Par 3 course, practice green and bunker, 24-bay floodlit driving range. *Green Fees:* information not provided. *Visitors:* welcome, booking in advance is essential. *Society Meetings:* welcome 7 days, telephone or write for details. In house Golfing Academy.

IVER. **Iver Golf Club,** Hollow Hill Lane, Off Langley Park Road, Iver SL0 0JJ (01753 655615; Fax: 01753 654225). *Location:* near Slough. Situated on the right off Langley Park Road leaving the town of Langley and heading towards Iver. Flat parkland, easy walking with natural ditches and ponds. 9 holes, 5628 yards. S.S.S. 67. 18 bay driving range, practice area, putting green, bunker area onto a green. Plus new 9 hole short course. *Green Fees:* information not available. *Eating facilities:* food available 8.30am until 2.30pm seven days. *Visitors:* always welcome, best to phone on day of play for booking. We have a new Junior section, a Vet society every Tuesday and are willing to accommodate most requests. Senior Members' competitions Thursday mornings. *Society Meetings:* always welcome. Professional (01753 655615; Fax: 01753 654225).

IVER. **Richings Park Golf Club,** North Park, Iver SL0 9DL (01753 655370; Fax: 01753 655409). *Location:* M4 Junction 5. Flat parkland. 18 holes, 6269 yards. S.S.S. 70. Practice area, two putting greens, bunker and chipping area. *Green Fees:* information not available. *Eating facilities:* bar, restaurant, and spike bar. *Visitors:* welcome with restrictions at weekend. *Society Meetings:* welcome, minimum 12. Professional/Secretary/General Manager: Steve Coles (01753 655352).*

LITTLE CHALFONT. **Little Chalfont Golf Club,** Lodge Lane, Little Chalfont HP8 4AJ (01494 764877). *Location:* Junction 18 M25, two miles towards Amersham on A404, first left past garden centre. Undulating parkland. 9 holes, 5752 yards S.S.S. 68. *Green Fees:* information not available. *Eating facilities:* full bar and restaurant. *Visitors:* always welcome. *Society Meetings:* welcome midweek. Professional: J.M. Dunne (01494 762942). Secretary: Michael Dunne (01494 764877).*

MARLOW. **Harleyford Golf Club,** Harleyford Estate, Henley Road, Marlow SL7 2SP (01628 816161; Fax: 01628 816160). *Location:* two miles from Marlow on the A4155 to Henley. Parkland course designed by Donald Steel. 18 holes, 6708 yards, S.S.S. 72. Excellent practice range and green available. *Green fees:* information not provided. *Eating facilities:* restaurant, lounge and bar. *Visitors:* book via Pro Shop (01628 816162). *Society Meetings:* welcome by arrangement Tuesday, Wednesday and Friday, contact Events Office (01628 816178). Professional: Graham Finch (01628 816162). General Manager: Trevor Collingwood (01628 816164).
e-mail: info@harleyfordgolf.co.uk
website: www.harleyfordgolf.co.uk

Buckinghamshire / SOUTH REGION

MILTON KEYNES. Abbey Hill Golf Centre, Monks Way, Two Mile Ash, Milton Keynes MK8 8AA (01908 563845). *Location:* 2 miles west of town centre, just off the A5 on the H3. Undulating parkland course with mature trees and impressive backdrops. Water comes into play on seven holes. 18 holes, 6025 yards. S.S.S. 69, Par 71. Additional Par 3 course, putting green, 21-bay floodlit driving range. *Green Fees:* weekdays £19.50, weekends and Bank Holidays £25.75. *Eating facilities:* full clubhouse facilities. *Visitors:* welcome, booking in advance advisable. *Society Meetings:* welcome, telephone or write for details. Professional: Nick McNally PGA. Manager: Gordon Forster.
website: www.abbeyhillgc.co.uk

MILTON KEYNES. **Kingfisher Country Club,** Buckingham Road, Deanshanger, Milton Keynes MK19 6JY (01908 562332; Fax: 01908 260857). *Location*: twixt Milton Keynes/Buckingham on A422. Mature course setting - wooded - lakes and ponds major feature. 9 holes, 5471 yards. S.S.S. 67. 10-bay covered range. *Green Fees:* information not available. *Eating facilities:* full club house overlooking lake. *Visitors:* welcome weekdays and weekends; no restrictions on Sundays and Public Holidays. *Society Meetings:* welcome. Director: D.M. Barraclough.*

MILTON KEYNES. **Three Locks Golf Club,** Great Brickhill, Milton Keynes MK17 9BH (01525 270050 golf; Tel & Fax: 01525 270470). *Location:* A4146 Bletchley to Leighton Buzzard. Parkland with lakes and water hazards. 18 holes, 6400 yards. S.S.S. 71. Practice ground. *Green Fees:* information not provided. *Eating facilities:* hot bar food. *Visitors:* welcome every day. Golf buggies for hire. *Society Meetings:* all welcome. Professional: visiting Professional. Secretary: Caroline France (01525 270470).

MILTON KEYNES. **Wavendon Golf Centre,** Lower End Road, Wavendon, Milton Keynes MK17 8DA (01908 281811; Fax: 01908 281257). *Location:* from Junction 13 M1, A421, follow signs to Woburn Sands. Parkland with six small lakes as hazards. Three courses: 18 holes, 5608 yards. S.S.S. 69. 9 holes, 1424 yards. S.S.S. 27, pitch and putt course, Par 26, 536 yards. 36 bay driving range, practice course. *Green Fees:* weekdays £16.50, weekends £22.00; Mondays £10.00. *Eating facilities:* fully licensed bar and carvery restaurant. *Visitors:* always welcome. Buggies. *Society Meetings:* welcome. Professional/Secretary: Greg Iron (01908 281811).
e-mail: wavendon@hotmail.co.uk

MILTON KEYNES. **Windmill Hill Golf Centre,** Tattenhoe Lane, Bletchley, Milton Keynes MK3 7RB (01908 630660; Tee reservations 01908 631113. 7 days in advance). *Location:* M1 South Junction 14/M1 North Junction 13 A421 towards Buckingham. 32 bay covered floodlit driving range, seven grassed bays. Two putting greens; practice area. *Green Fees:* information not available. *Eating facilities:* restaurant, cafeteria, bars, function room; pool and games room. *Opening hours:* 7.30am till 11pm. *Society Meetings:* welcome (after 11am weekends and Bank Holidays); weekday and weekend packages. Three teaching Professionals, tuition, Pro shop. Professional: Colin Clingan (01908 378623). Secretary: (Hon) Di Allen (Tel & Fax: 01908 366457).*
e-mail: info@golfinmiltonkeynes.co.uk
website: www.golfinmiltonkeynes.co.uk

MILTON KEYNES. **Woburn Golf Club,** Little Brickhill, Milton Keynes MK17 9LJ (01908 370756; Fax: 01908 378436). *Location:* four miles west of Junction 13 M1. Three courses, 54 holes: Duke's Course 6976 yards, S.S.S. 74; Duchess' Course 6651 yards, S.S.S. 72; Marquess Course 7214 yards, S.S.S. 74. Practice facilities. *Green Fees:* information

WAVENDON GOLF CENTRE
Lower End Road, Wavendon, Milton Keynes MK17 8DA

Three courses over parkland with six small lakes • Pitch and putt; 36-bay driving range, practice, putting and bunker • Fees: weekdays £16.50, weekends £22.00, Monday rate £10.00.
• Fully licensed bar and carvery restaurant • Visitors and societies welcome.

CONTACT SECRETARY/PROFESSIONAL GREG IRON: 01908 281811

Tel: 01908 281811 • Fax: 01908 281257
e-mail: wavendon@hotmail.co.uk

PLEASE MENTION THIS GUIDE
WHEN YOU ENQUIRE ABOUT CLUBS
OR ACCOMMODATION

not provided. *Eating facilities:* restaurant; breakfasts and lunches; dinner by prior arrangement. *Visitors:* welcome weekdays by prior arrangement. Weekends restricted to members and their guests only. *Society Meetings:* catered for, details on application. Secretary: Mrs G. Beasley (01908 370756). Professional: L. Blacklock (01908 626600). e-mail: golf.enquiries@woburn.co.uk
website: www.woburn.co.uk/golf

PRINCES RISBOROUGH. **Princes Risborough Golf Club,** Lee Road, Saunderton Lee, Princes Risborough HP27 9NX (01844 346989. Fax: 01844 274938). *Location:* A4010, Princes Risborough, turn off at Rose and Crown Inn, one mile on right. Parkland course, slightly undulating, water hazards and has beautiful views. 9 holes, 5552 yards. S.S.S. 67. Practice area and nets. *Green Fees:* information not available. *Eating facilities:* restaurant and bar. *Visitors:* always welcome properly attired. Memberships available. *Society Meetings:* welcome. Outside functions, wedding receptions, parties and Christmas dinners catered for. Professional: Simon Lowry (01844 274567). Secretary/Proprietor: J.F. Tubb.*
website: www.prgc.co.uk

PRINCES RISBOROUGH. **Whiteleaf Golf Club Ltd,** Upper Icknield Way, Whiteleaf HP27 0LY (01844 274058/343097). *Location:* A4010 from Princes Risborough turn off at signpost for Whiteleaf into Upper Icknield Way. Hilly course with beautiful Chiltern views. 9 holes, 5391 yards. S.S.S. 66. Practice area. *Green Fees:* £25.00 weekdays and weekends, weekends only with a member. *Eating facilities:* full catering facilities, except Mondays. *Visitors:* always welcome; probably better to phone Secretary in case of disappointment. *Society Meetings:* on Thursdays – apply to Secretary. Professional: Ken Ward (01844 345472). Secretary: Derek Hill (01844 274058).

SLOUGH. **Farnham Park Pay and Play Golf Course,** Park Road, Stoke Poges, Slough SL2 4PJ (Tel & Fax: 01753 643332). *Location:* just off A355, two miles north of A4. Challenging parkland course with water. 18 holes, 6172 yards. S.S.S. 71. Short game practice facilities. *Green Fees:* weekdays £16.50, weekends £22.50. Reductions for Juniors and Seniors. *Eating facilities:* hot and cold food always available. *Visitors:* welcome. Pro shop with hire facilities. *Society Meetings:* welcome, special packages available, from as little as £20.00 per person. Professional: Nigel Whitton (01753 643332). Operated by South Bucks District Council. Secretary: Mrs M. Brooker, M. Inst. GCM (01753 647065).

STOKE POGES. **The Lanes Golf Academy,** Stoke Road, Stoke Poges SL2 4NL (01753 554840). *Location:* half-a-mile from Slough Railway Station in direction of Stoke Poges. Parkland course ideal for the less experienced player. 9 holes. 2400 yds. S.S.S. 62 (18 holes). 18 bay driving range. *Green Fees:* information not available. Professional/Manager: Nigel Whitton (01753 554840). Operated by South Bucks District Council.*

STOKE POGES. **Stoke Park,** North Drive, Park Road, Stoke Poges SL2 4PG (01753 717171; Fax: 01753 717181). *Location:* one mile north of Slough, eight miles from Heathrow. Parkland course. 27 holes, 6670 yards. S.S.S. 72. Practice ground. *Green Fees:* Monday to Friday open to non-members (subject to Golf Director's discretion). *Eating facilities:* Orangery, Dining Room and President's Bar. *Visitors:* welcome if playing with a member, Handicap Certificate must be produced. 49 bedrooms now available, conference facilities. *Society Meetings:* catered for. Club Director: Giammario Ragnoli (01753 717171; Fax: 01753 717181). Director of Golf: Stuart Collier. Club Shop: 01753 717184. Secretary: Kelly Ford (01753 717116).
e-mail: info@stokepark.com
website: www.stokepark.com

STOWE. **Silverstone Golf Club,** Silverstone Road, Stowe MK18 5LH (01280 850005; Fax: 01280 850156). *Location:* A43 half mile south of Silverstone Grand Prix Circuit. A parkland course with maturing copses divided by woodland. 18 holes, Par 72. 6558 yards. S.S.S. 71. Putting area, covered driving range. *Green Fees:* information not available. *Eating facilities:* meals at all times, licensed bar. *Visitors:* welcome, booking seven days in advance. Conference facilities. Corporate days. *Society Meetings:* welcome. Professional: Rodney Holt. Manager: Scott Barnes.
e-mail: enquiries@silverstonegolfclub.co.uk
website: www.silverstonegolfclub.co.uk

..:: Farnham Park Golf Course ::..

Set in 130 acres of attractive mature wooded parkland, Farnham Park is the ideal venue for a relaxing game of golf. Our 18 hole course is one of the finest public golf facilities in the South Of England and has been described as "The best kept secret in Buckinghamshire". The Colt/Hawtree design is both challenging and rewarding with a memorable selection of holes that would grace the finest championship layout. The friendly clubhouse offers an extensive menu in comfortable surroundings.

A value for money golfing experience
that will exceed your expectations.
Park Road, Stoke Poges, Buckinghamshire SL2 4PJ
Shop: 01753 643332
Manager/PGA Professional:
Mr Nigel Whitton: 01753 643332
E-mail: farnhamparkgolf@southbucks.gov.uk
www.farnhamparkgolfcourse.co.uk

STOWE. **Stowe Golf Club,** Stowe, Buckingham MK18 5EH (01280 816264). *Location:* situated at Stowe School, four miles north of Buckingham. Parkland course with follies and lakes. 9 holes, 2189 yards. S.S.S. 63. *Green Fees:* information not available. *Visitors:* only as a guest of a member. *Society Meetings:* catered for by appointment. Secretary: Di Procter (01280 818282).

WEXHAM. **Wexham Park Golf Course,** Wexham Street, Wexham, Slough SL3 6ND (01753 663271; Fax: 01753 663318). *Location:* M40 to Beaconsfield, A40 to Gerrards Cross, direction Fulmer on right hand side, near Wexham Park Hospital. Undulating parkland courses. 18 holes, 5251 yards. S.S.S. 66. Also 9 hole course, 2727 yards, par 34; and 9 hole course, 2219 yards, par 32. Driving range and short game practice area. *Green Fees:* from £9.50 per 9 holes, £16.00 for 18 holes. 2010 fees (subject to review). *Eating facilities:* clubhouse bar and full kitchen facilities. *Visitors:* welcome, Pay and Play, open to all. *Society Meetings:* 7 days a week by prior arrangement. Professional: John Kennedy (01753 663271). Secretary: G. McIntyre.

WOOBURN COMMON. **Hedsor Golf Course,** Pay & Play, Broad Lane, Wooburn Common HP10 0JW (01628 851285). *Location:* from Junction 2 of M40, take A355 to Slough, turn right at Hedsor Golf Course sign, then follow golf arrows to course. Easy walking course in mature parkland; many water hazards. 9 holes. Par 34. 18 holes S.S.S 64. *Green Fees:* information not available. *Eating facilities:* bar and catering available. Professional: Stuart Cannon.*

THE APPEARANCE OF AN ASTERISK (*) AT THE END OF A CLUB OR COURSE ENTRY INDICATES THAT UP-TO-DATE INFORMATION HAS NOT BEEN SUPPLIED

Farnham Park Pay and Play Golf Course, Slough

Hampshire

ALDERSHOT. **Army Golf Club,** Laffan's Road, Aldershot GU 11 2HF (01252 337272). *Location:* access from Eelmoor Bridge off A323 Aldershot Fleet Road - second oldest course in Hampshire. 18 holes, 6550 yards. S.S.S. 71. *Green Fees:* information not available. *Eating facilities:* bar snacks, restaurant/ dining room. *Visitors:* weekdays only, members' guests anytime. *Society Meetings:* catered for. Professional: G. Cowley (01252 336722). Manager: John Hiscock (01252 337272; Fax: 01252 337562).*
e-mail: secretary@armygolfclub.com

ALRESFORD. **Alresford Golf Club,** Cheriton Road, Tichborne Down, Alresford SO24 0PN (01962 733746; Fax: 01962 736040). *Location*: on B3046 south of A31, two miles north A272. Rolling downland, wooded. 18 holes, 5973 yards, 5461 metres. S.S.S. 69. Practice area. *Green Fees:* weekdays £32.00 per round; weekends and Bank Holidays £40.00 per round. *Eating facilities:* full catering. *Visitors*: welcome but not before 12 noon weekends/Bank Holidays. *Society Meetings*: welcome weekdays only, by arrangement. Professional: Malcolm Scott (Tel & Fax: 01962 733998). Secretary: David Maskery (01962 733746; Fax: 01962 736040).
e-mail: secretary@alresfordgolf.co.uk
website: www.alresfordgolf.co.uk

ALTON. **The Alton Golf Club,** Old Odiham Road, Alton GU34 4BU (01420 82042). *Location:* off B3349 (turn off at Golden Pot). Undulating meadowland, wooded course. 9 holes, 5744 yards. S.S.S. 68. Practice area, putting green. *Green Fees:* information not available. *Eating facilities:* bar, hot and cold snacks all day. *Visitors:* welcome any time without reservation. Buggies for hire. Club Professional available. *Society Meetings:* welcome weekdays only. *

ALTON. **Blacknest Golf & Country Club,** Blacknest Road, Blacknest, Alton GU34 4QL (01420 22888). *Location*: Bently exit of A31, between Farnham and Alton. Parkland course with several water features. 18 holes, Par 69; also Par 3 course. *Green Fees:* information not available. *Eating facilities:* bar and dining available from 8am to 4pm. *Visitors:* welcome by arrangement. *Society Meetings:* welcome.*

ALTON. **Worldham Golf Club,** Cakers Lane, East Worldham, Alton GU34 3BF (01420 544606). *Location:* B3004 Alton to Bordon road, one mile from Alton. Parkland course with views of the Wey Valley. 18 holes, 6199 yards. S.S.S. 70. 14-bay driving range.

Green Fees: weekdays £18.00, Fridays £20.00, weekends £22.00. *Eating facilities:* spike bar with hot and cold food, lounge area. *Visitors:* welcome - pay and play. Booking required at weekends. Professional shop. *Society Meetings:* welcome any day. Professional: Adam Harnett (01420 543151). General Manager: Ian Yates (01420 544606).

AMPFIELD. **Ampfield Golf Club,** Winchester Road, Ampfield, Near Romsey SO51 9BQ (01794 368480). *Location:* A31 Winchester to Romsey road, next door to White Horse Public House. Parkland course designed by Sir Henry Cotton. Home of Short Course PGA Championships. 18 hole Par 3 course, 2478 yards. S.S.S. 53. Practice area. *Green Fees:* information not available. *Eating facilities:* excellent food served Tuesday to Sunday. Weddings and private parties up to 120 guests catered for. *Visitors:* welcome 7 days a week; golf shoes must be worn. Pro Shop. Disabled access. *Society Meetings:* welcome 7 days a week; excellent value packages. Managing Director: Mark Hazell. Events Manager: Julia Francis (01794 368750).
e-mail: juliahazell@ampfieldgolf.com
website: www.ampfieldgolf.com

ANDOVER. **Andover Golf Club,** 51 Winchester Road, Andover SP10 2EF (01264 323980). *Location:* Stockbridge Exit from A303, left towards Andover, quarter of a mile on right. Gently sloping downland course with views over town and country. 9 holes, 6096 yards. S.S.S. 69. *Green Fees:* information not available. *Eating facilities:* full catering available. *Visitors:* welcome, check tee reservations with Professional. *Society Meetings:* welcome, please phone for availability. Professional: (01264 324151). Secretary:(01264 358040). Clubhouse Manager: (01264 323980).*
e-mail: secretary@andovergolfclub.co.uk
website: www.andovergolfclub.co.uk

ANDOVER. **The Hampshire Golf Club,** Winchester Road, Goodworth Clatford, Andover SP11 7TB (01264 357555; Fax: 01264 356606). *Location:* one mile south of Andover on A3057 Stockbridge Road. Downland with new trees and lakes. 18 holes, 6145 yards. S.S.S. 71. 10 bay covered driving range. *Green Fees:* weekdays £25.00, weekends £30.00. 9 hole, Par 3 course £5.00 weekdays, £6.00 weekends. Telephone for special deals. *Eating facilities:* full catering facilities, bar seven days a week. *Visitors:* always welcome. *Society Meetings:* welcome. Professional: Tim Baker (01264 357555). Secretary: Jan Miles (01264 356462; Fax: 01264 356606).

Alresford Golf Club
- Traditional 'members' club maintained to a very high standard.
- Free draining course on chalk downland for all-year-round play.
- Regular host to County amateur and PGA events.
- Visitors and Societies welcome.

Cheriton Road, Tichborne Down, Alresford SO24 0PN • 01962 733746 • www.alresfordgolf.co.uk

- Memberships -
- Society Days -
- Green Free Players welcomed -
- Driving Range -
- Twilight from 15:00pm -
- Golf Tuition -
- Wedding Receptions/Party Hire -
- Meeting Room Hire -
- Restaurant Facilities -

To book please call 01256 320347 - to get an exclusive discount please quote TGGCW

Weybrook Park Golf Club, Rooksdown Lane, Basingstoke, Hampshire. (just off A339 Newbury road) RG24 9NT
www.weybrookpark.co.uk
caroline.wilkes@weybrookpark.co.uk

BARTON-ON-SEA. **Barton-on-Sea Golf Club,** Milford Road, New Milton BH25 5PP (01425 615308; Fax: 01425 621457). *Location*: one mile from centre of New Milton on B3058 towards Milford-on-Sea. Cliff top links with easy walking; superb views of Isle of Wight and Christchurch Bay. 27 holes. S.S.S. 72 any 18 holes. *Green Fees:* £44.00 per day weekdays; £55.00 weekends and Bank Holidays. *Eating facilities:* lunch, snacks and teas daily, full bar service. *Visitors:* welcome after 8.30am weekdays; weekends and Bank Holidays after 8.45am; evening green fees after 5pm. Handicap Certificate required. Buggies for hire. *Society Meetings:* welcome by arrangement Mondays, Wednesdays and Fridays. Professional: P. Rodgers (01425 611210). Secretary/Manager (01425 615308).
website: www.bosgc.co.uk

BASINGSTOKE. **Basingstoke Golf Club,** Kempshott Park, Basingstoke RG23 7LL (01256 465990; Fax: 01256 331793). *Location:* M3 Junction 7, A30 one mile from motorway on right. Parkland course – easy walking. 18 holes, 6350 yards. S.S.S. 70. Small practice ground. *Green Fees:* £42.00 per round, £52.00 per day. *Eating facilities:* dining room, lounge and bar. *Visitors:* welcome weekdays. Buggies, trolleys for hire. *Society Meetings:* catered for Wednesdays and Thursdays. Professional: R. Woolley (01256 351332). Secretary: S.E. Lawrence (01256 465990; Fax: 01256 331793).
e-mail: office@basingstokegolfclub.co.uk

BASINGSTOKE. **Bishopswood Golf Course LLP,** Bishopswood Lane, Tadley, Basingstoke RG26 4AT (01189 408600). *Location:* six miles north of Basingstoke off the A340. Parkland/wooded course. 9 holes, 6474 yards. S.S.S. 71. 12 bay floodlit driving range open seven days a week. *Green Fees:* 9 holes £15.00, 18 holes £23.00. *Eating facilities:* lounge and spike bars - snacks, bar meals and 50 seater restaurant facility. *Visitors:* welcome. Tee reservation required. *Society Meetings:* welcome by arrangement. Professional: S. Ward (01189 408601). Manager: Kevin Pickett.
e-mail: kevinpickett@googlemail.com
website: www.bishopswoodgc.com

BASINGSTOKE. **Sandford Springs Golf Club,** Sandford Springs, Kingsclere RG26 5RT (01635 296800; Fax: 01635 296801). *Location:* on north side of A339 Basingstoke to Newbury road at Kingsclere. Three scenic loops of 9 holes combines woodland, parkland and lakes quite beautifully. 27 holes. S.S.S. 69/70/71. Driving range and putting green. *Green Fees:* Monday to Thursday £35.00; Friday, Saturday and Sunday £40.00 after 1.00pm. *Eating facilities:* available all day; also conference and banqueting facilities. *Visitors:* welcome every day, subject to availability. *Society Meetings:* welcome, subject to availability. Professional: Neal Granville (01635 296808).

BASINGSTOKE. **Test Valley Golf Club,** Micheldever Road, Overton, Near Basingstoke RG25 3DS (01256 771737; Fax: 01256 771285). *Location*: on the C79, one mile north of A303 signposted Overton. Downland course; easy walking; beautiful countryside views; excellent drainage, playable all year. 18 holes, 6663 yards. S.S.S. 72. Full practice facilities, short game practice area and 10 bay covered driving range. *Green Fees:* information not available. *Eating facilities:* spike bar; main bar, full dining facility. *Visitors:* welcome weekdays, or weekends after 12.00pm. *Society Meetings:* welcome weekdays. Professional/Manager: Alastair Briggs (01256 771737). Venue for Hampshire Open and Lombard Top Club Trophy.
website: www.testvalleygolf.com

BASINGSTOKE. **Weybrook Park Golf Club,** Rooksdown Lane, Basingstoke RG24 9NT (01256 320347; Fax: 01256 812973). *Location:* two miles north west of Basingstoke town centre, A339 Newbury Road, turn at first crossroads on A339. Parkland course with magnificent views, pleasantly undulating and picturesque landscape, excellent chalk drainage ensures continuous play. 18 holes, 6468 yards, 5914 metres. S.S.S. 71. Driving range, practice area. *Green Fees:* information not available. *Eating facilities:* bar with restaurant and spike bar. *Visitors:* welcome, advisable to telephone in case of competitions. All players must have their own clubs, suitable casual/smart attire must be worn. *Society Meetings:* welcome, telephone for booking and costs. Professional: Anthony Dillon (01256 333232; Fax: 01256 334242). Secretary: P. M. Shearman (01256 320347; Fax: 01256 812973).*
website: www.weybrookpark.co.uk

Hampshire / SOUTH REGION

BASINGSTOKE near. **Dummer Golf Club,** Dummer Village, Near Basingstoke RG25 2AD (01256 397950; Fax: 01256 397889). *Location:* at Junction 7 of M3. A downland course designed by Peter Alliss – easy walking, panoramic views, free draining; genuine all-year-round course. Par 72, 6533 yards. S.S.S. 71. 10 bay covered driving range plus teaching studios and practice facilities. *Green Fees:* see website for current green fees. *Eating facilities*: Spike Bar, conservatory and dining room. *Visitors*: welcome every day. *Society Meetings*: welcome. Professionals: Andrew Fannon, Darren Lovegrove and David Holman.
website: www.dummergolfclub.com

BORDON. **Blackmoor Golf Club,** Firgrove Road, Whitehill, Bordon GU35 9EH (01420 472775; Fax: 01420 487666). *Location:* lies midway between Petersfield and Farnham on A325. Parkland, wooded course. 18 holes, 6164 yards. S.S.S. 69. *Green Fees:* weekdays £45.00 per round, £60.00 36 holes. *Eating facilities:* dining room. *Visitors:* welcome weekdays, Handicaps necessary, Sat/Sun no visitors for golf but open for catering. Suitable dress code – no jeans in club or on course. Trolleys available. *Society Meetings:* catered for on weekdays. Morning coffee, lunch, evening meal. Golf Manager/Professional: Stephen Clay (01420 472345). Administration Manager: Mrs Jackie Dean (01420 472775; Fax: 01420 487666).
e-mail: admin@blackmoorgolf.co.uk

BORDON near. **Dean Farm Golf Course,** Main Road, Kingsley, Near Bordon GU35 9NG (01420 489478). *Location*: B3004 off A325 Farnham to Petersfield road. 9 holes Pay and Play. Ideal for novice to seasoned golfers. *Green Fees*: information not available. Trolley and club hire available. Acting Secretary: S. Parrott.

BROCKENHURST. **Brokenhurst Manor Golf Club,** Sway Road, Brockenhurst SO42 7SG (01590 623332). *Location:* one mile from Brockenhurst. Beautiful New Forest forest course. 18 holes, 6222 yards. S.S.S. 70. Practice ground. *Green Fees:* information not provided. *Eating facilities:* restaurant and bar. *Visitors:* welcome by arrangement. Handicap Certificate required. *Society Meetings:* welcome Thursdays by arrangement. Professional: Bruce Parker (01590 623332). Secretary: Neil Hallam Jones (01590 623332).
e-mail: secretary@brokenhurst-manor.org.uk
website: www.brokenhurst-manor.org.uk

CRONDALL. **Oak Park Golfing Complex,** Heath Lane, Crondall, Near Farnham, Surrey GU10 5PB (01252 850880; Fax: 01252 850851). *Location:* one and a half miles off A287 Farnham-Odiham road, five miles from Junctions 4, 4a and 5 of M3 motorway. Gently undulating parkland course. Woodland Course - 18 holes, 6247 yards. S.S.S. 70; Village Course - 9 holes, 3279 yards. Par 36. 16 bay covered driving range, putting green, chipping green and practice bunker. *Green Fees:* information not available. *Eating facilities:* restaurant, available for private hire and special occasions. Bar snacks available. V*isitors:* welcome; must book through Professional; reserved tee system at all times. *Society Meetings:* by arrangement. Professional: Paul Archer (01252 850066; Fax: 01252 850851). Manager: Richard Pilbury (01252 850850).*

DENMEAD. **Furzeley Golf Club,** Furzeley Road, Denmead PO7 6TX (023 9223 1180). *Location:* A3(M) Exit for Waterlooville, follow the B2150 to Denmead. Parkland course. 18 holes, 4488 yards. S.S.S. 62. *Green Fees:* information not available. *Eating facilities:* restaurant. *Visitors:* welcome anytime - Pay and Play and membership available. *Society Meetings:* always welcome. Professional: Derek Brown (023 9223 *

DIBDEN. **Dibden Golf Centre,** Main Road, Dibden, Hythe, Southampton SO45 5TB Bookings: (023 8020 7508). *Location:* half-mile off A326 Totton to Fawley road, on the road to Hythe. Parkland course with views over Southampton Water. 18 holes, 5965 yards, 5455 metres. S.S.S. 69. 9 hole course, 24 bay floodlit driving range. *Green Fees:* information not available. *Eating facilities:* full catering facilities available. *Visitors:* welcome. *Society Meetings:* welcome by prior booking. Catering: Clare Flowers (02380 845060) Professionals: John Slade/ Paul Smith (023 8084 5596).*
website: www.nfdc.gov.uk/golf

In the heart of the New Forest
THE WATERSPLASH HOTEL
The Rise, Brockenhurst SO42 7ZP • Tel: 01590 622344

Family-run hotel in two acres of grounds, located in the New Forest village of Brockenhurst with shops, pubs and amenities. Families find that they are particularly welcome here and guests return year after year to enjoy the country house atmosphere and the very high standards of accommodation, service and good food. There are 23 en suite bedrooms of varying sizes, including two four-poster rooms, four large family rooms with baby listening service; cots and high chairs available on request. There are also three ground floor rooms suitable for disabled guests. There is a range of leisure facilities in the surrounding area, including walking, golf (12 courses within easy reach) and horseriding, and south coast beaches are also easily reached. AA ★★

e-mail: bookings@watersplash.co.uk • www.watersplash.co.uk

SOUTH REGION / Hampshire

EASTLEIGH. Fleming Park Golf Course, The New Club House, Passfield Avenue, Eastleigh SO50 9HL (023 8061 2797). *Location*: two miles off M27 Eastleigh Airport turning. Parkland. 18 holes, 4524 yards. S.S.S. 62. *Green Fees:* information not available. *Eating facilities:* bar. *Visitors:* welcome, book on day or one week in advance. *Society Meetings:* all welcome. Professional: I. Warwick (023 8061 2797). Secretary: A. Wheavil (023 8061 2797).*

FAREHAM. Cams Hall Estate Golf Club, Fareham PO16 8UP (01329 827732; Fax: 01329 827111). *Location:* Junction 11 M27 follow signs to Fareham/Portchester, take A27 to Portchester. 18 hole creek course links, 9 hole parkland course; five lakes, 99 bunkers, Fareham Creek. Creek course 18 holes, 6244 yards. S.S.S. 71; Park Course 9 holes, 3247 yards. S.S.S. 36. Practice ground, putting green, chipping green. *Green Fees*: information not available. *Eating facilities*: Bar food. *Visitors*: welcome. Luxurious clubhouse, spacious locker rooms, sauna. *Society Meetings:* Societies/Groups welcome. Professional: Sam Pleshette (01329 827732; Fax: 01329 827111). Sales Manager: Heather Tubb (01329 827222; Fax: 01329 827111). General Manager: Ben Beagley.*
e-mail: camshall@crown-golf.co.uk

FAREHAM. Southwick Park Golf Club, Pinsley Drive, Southwick, Fareham PO17 6EL (023 92 380131; Fax: 0871 855 6809). *Location:* near Southwick village (B2177). Parkland. 18 holes, 5884 yards. S.S.S. 69. Practice area, 6 hole pitch and putt, short-game area. *Green Fees:* weekdays £26.00, weekends £29.00. *Eating facilities:* bar and snacks available. *Visitors:* weekdays. *Society Meetings:* book through Manager. Professional: E. Rawlings (023 9238 0131). Manager: S. Searle (023 9238 0131)
e-mail: southwickpark@btconnect.com
website:www.southwickparkgolfclub.co.uk

FAREHAM. Wickham Park Golf Club, Titchfield Lane, Wickham, Fareham PO17 5PJ (01329 833342; Fax: 01329 834798). *Location:* 2 miles north of Fareham, J10 of M27. Undulating parkland course. 18 holes, 5733 yards. S.S.S. 67. 12-bay covered driving range and dedicated short game area. *Green Fees:* information not available. *Eating facilities:* full menu. *Visitors:* welcome at all times but must pre-book. *Society Meetings:* welcome Monday to Friday - please telephone to book in advance. Professional: James Pitcher. Manager: Rob Gumbrell.*

FARNBOROUGH. Southwood Golf Course, Ively Road, Cove, Farnborough GU14 0LJ (01252 548700). *Location:* approximately half a mile west of A325. Flat parkland. 18 holes, 5669 yards. S.S.S. 67. Putting green. *Green Fees:* information not available. *Eating facilities:* bar and diningroom available. *Visitors:* welcome, bookable at all times. *Society Meetings:* catered for by arrangement. Professional: Chris Hudson. Club Manager: Ian Attoe.*

FLEET. North Hants Golf Club, Minley Road, Fleet GU51 1RF (01252 616443). *Location:* B3013 off A30, M3 Junction 4a. 400 yards from railway station. Heathland. 18 holes, 6472 yards. S.S.S. 72, Par 70. Practice ground. *Green Fees:* information not available. *Eating facilities:* lunch daily, evening meals by prior arrangement. *Visitors:* welcome weekdays only by prior arrangement, Handicap Certificates required, Thursdays Ladies' Day. *Society Meetings:* Tuesdays and Wednesdays only. Professional: Steve Porter (01252 616655). Secretary: Chris Donovan (01252 616443; Fax: 01252 811627)*
e-mail: secretary@north-hants-fleetgc.co.uk
website: www.northhantsgolf.co.uk

FOUR MARKS. Four Marks Golf Club, Headmore Lane, Four Marks GU34 3ES (01420 587214; Fax: 01420 587313). *Location*: A31 to Four Marks, follow brown signs to golf course. Parkland course. 9 holes, 2300 yards, S.S.S 62. Practice nets. *Green Fees*: weekdays £8.95, weekends and Bank Holidays £9.95. *Eating facilities*: bar snacks and drinks available. *Visitors*: welcome at all times. Tuition by Professional available. *Society Meetings*: welcome at any time. Professional: Stephen Bussill (01420 587214).

GOSPORT. Fleetlands Golf Club, DARA Fleetlands, Fareham Road, Gosport PO13 0AW (023 9254 4492). *Location*: two miles south of Fareham on Fareham/Gosport Road. Flat/wooded Course. 9 holes, 4852 yards. S.S.S. 64. *Green Fees:* information not available. *Eating facilities:* bar/clubhouse. *Visitors:* by appointment with member only. *Society Meetings:* by appointment with member only. Secretary: Mr R. Sheehan (023 9254 4903).*

GOSPORT. Gosport and Stokes Bay Golf Club, off Fort Road, Haslar, Gosport PO12 2AT (023 9258 1625). *Location*. A32 to Gosport, course is one mile east of Stokes Bay, near Gilkicker Point. Water course, natural hazards. 9 holes, 5957 yards. S.S.S. 70. Nets and putting green. *Green Fees:* information not provided. *Eating facilities:* full catering service, fully licensed bar. *Visitors:* welcome all week, restricted Sundays and Thursdays. *Society Meetings:* by arrangement. Secretary/Manager: M. Chivers (Tel & Fax: 023 9252 7941). Tee Shop (023 9258 7423).
secretary@gosportandstokesbaygolfclub.co.uk
website: www.gosportandstokesbaygolfclub.co.uk

HARTLEY WINTNEY. Hartley Wintney Golf Club, London Road, Hartley Wintney, Hook RG27 8PT (01252 844211; Fax: 01252 844211). *Location:* on A30 between Camberley and Basingstoke. Parkland, wooded. 18 holes, 6240 yards. S.S.S. 71. Practice area, indoor teaching studio. *Green Fees:* £38.00 per weekday round, £50.00 per day. *Eating facilities:* full catering facilities available. *Visitors:* please telephone in advance. *Society Meetings:* catered for weekdays. Professional: Martin Smith (01252 844211). Secretary: Paul Gaylor (Tel & Fax: 01252 844211).

Please mention this guide when enquiring about clubs or accommodation

86 Hampshire / SOUTH REGION — THE GOLF GUIDE 2011

HAVANT. **Rowlands Castle Golf Club,** 31 Links Lane, Rowlands Castle PO9 6AE (023 9241 2216). *Location:* four miles north of Havant or Horndean/ Rowlands Castle Junction from A3M. Flat parkland, wooded course. 18 holes, 6639 yards White Tees, 6395 yards Yellow Tees. S.S.S. 72 (White), 70 (Yellow). *Green Fees:* weekdays £40.00 per round/day; weekends £45.00. 2010 rates ((subject to review). *Eating facilities:* full catering and bar facilities. *Visitors:* welcome, except Saturdays unless playing with a member, maximum 12 visitors on a Sunday and Bank Holidays. *Society Meetings:* catered for Tuesdays and Thursdays, bookings through Secretary. Professional: Peter Klepacz (023 9241 2785). Secretary: K.D. Fisher (023 9241 2784).

HAYLING ISLAND. **The Hayling Golf Club,** Links Lane, Hayling Island PO11 0BX (023 9246 4491). *Location:* A3023 five miles south of Havant. Seaside links. 18 holes, 6531 yards, 5965 metres. S.S.S. 71. *Green Fees:* weekdays £52.00 per round; weekends £60.00 per round. Concessions for Juniors. *Eating facilities:* breakfasts, lunches and afternoon teas available and dinners by arrangement. *Visitors:* welcome with current Handicap Certificate and must be members of recognised clubs. *Society Meetings:* Tuesdays and Wednesdays by arrangement with the Secretary. Professional: Mark Treleaven (023 9246 4491). General Manager: Ian Walton (023 9246 4446).
e-mail: members@haylinggolf.co.uk
website: www.haylinggolf.co.uk

HOOK. **Tylney Park,** Rotherwick, Hook RG27 9AY (01256 762079; Fax: 01256 763079). *Location*: two-and-a-half miles from M3 J5. Approx. 9 miles south of M4 J11 via A33. 18 holes, Par 72 scenic English Heritage registered parkland course with specimen mature trees including 5 lengths of tees from 5429 to 7017 yards. Championship course with USGA free draining sand based tees and greens, re-built in 2005 and designed by the leading duo Donald Steele and Tom Mackenzie. *Green Fees:* refer to website. *Eating facilities:* catering and bar available. *Visitors:* weekdays unrestricted, weekends and Bank Holidays contact the Pro shop for availablility. *Society Meetings*: welcome, very competitive prices. Hotel facilities adjoining with English Heritage Grade II listing, indoor and outdoor pools, gym and ladies' beauty treatments. PGA Professional: Alasdair Hay.
e-mail: contact@tylneypark.co.uk
website: www.tylneypark.co.uk

LEE-ON-THE-SOLENT. **Lee-On-The-Solent Golf Club,** Brune Lane, Lee-on-the-Solent PO13 9PB (023 92 551170). *Location:* M27 Exit 9 eastbound, Exit 11 westbound, three miles south of Fareham. Flat parkland course. 18 holes, 5962 yards. S.S.S. 69. Practice range. *Green Fees:* Monday to Sunday £30.00. *Visitors:* welcome weekdays, Handicap Certificate required. *Society Meetings:* welcome weekdays, Handicap Certificate required. Professional: Rob Edwards. Manager: Rob Henderson (023 92 551170; Fax: 023 92 554233).
website: www.leegolf.co.uk

LIPHOOK. **Liphook Golf Club,** Wheatsheaf Enclosure, Liphook GU30 7EH (01428 723271; Fax: 01428 724853). *Location:* one mile south of Liphook on B2070 (old A3). Heathland. 18 holes, 6167 yards. S.S.S. 69. *Green Fees:* contact Club for details. *Eating facilities:* bar and restaurant. *Visitors:* welcome, Handicap Certificate required, check with Secretary. Buggy available for hire. *Society Meetings:* catered for Wednesdays to Fridays. Professional: Ian Mowbray (01428 723271). Secretary: (01428 723785; Fax: 01428 724853).
e-mail: secretary@liphookgolfclub.com
website: www.liphookgolfclub.com

LIPHOOK. **Old Thorns Golf & Country Estate,** Griggs Green, Liphook GU30 7PE (01428 724555). *Location:* A3 to Griggs Green then 500 yards on right. Parkland, wooded, with natural streams and lakes. 18 holes, 6471 yards. S.S.S. 71. Practice range, putting green, buggies, Pro shop. *Green Fees*: information on request. *Eating facilities*: Greenview Restaurant with open modern brasserie menu; bar menu. *Visitors*: welcome at all times. Facilities: 85 en suite bedrooms, indoor swimming pool, sauna, solarium, steam room, fitness centre, treatment rooms, tennis court, conference and banqueting rooms. *Society Meetings:* a range of golf days available for booking. Range of individual and corporate membership available. Co. Secretary: Greg Knights.
website: www.oldthorns.com

LYNDHURST. **Bramshaw Golf Club,** Brook, Lyndhurst SO43 7HE (023 8081 3433). *Location:* M27 (Interchange 1) one mile from M27 (north) at Brook. Two courses: one parkland, one woodland. Both 18 holes. Forest Course 5774 yards. S.S.S. 68. Manor Course 6527 yards. S.S.S. 71. Practice facilities. *Green Fees:* from £30.00. *Eating facilities:* clubhouse and restaurant, also Bell Inn close by. *Visitors:* welcome. Accommodation in 27-bedroom hotel. *Society Meetings:* welcome by arrangement. Professional: Clive Bonner (023 8081 3434). General Manager: Ian Baker (023 8081 3433).
e-mail: golf@bramshaw.co.uk
website: www.bramshaw.co.uk

LYNDHURST. **New Forest Golf Club Ltd,** Southampton Road, Lyndhurst SO43 7BU (023 8028 2752; Fax: 023 8028 4030). *Location:* on the A35 between Ashurst and Lyndhurst. Forest heathland course. 18 holes, 5772 yards. S.S.S. 67. Practice ground. *Green Fees:* information not available. *Eating facilities:* bar, dining room. *Visitors:* welcome, restrictions may apply. Please telephone. *Society Meetings:* advance booking only. Professional: (023 8028 3094). Secretary: (023 8028 2484; Fax: 023 8028 4030).*
e-mail: secretarynfgc@aol.com
website: www.newforestgolfclub.co.uk

www.holidayguides.com
for accommodation near golf clubs

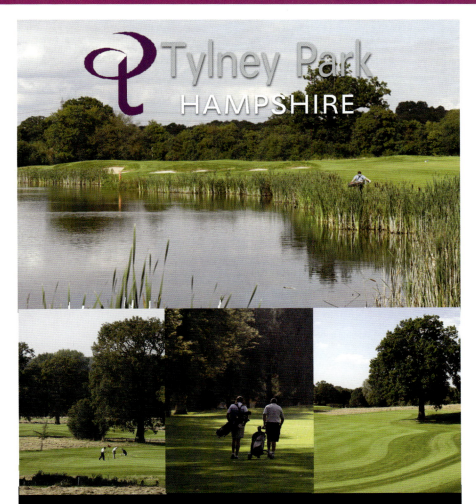

PETERSFIELD. **Petersfield Golf Club,** Tankerdale Lane, Liss GU33 7QY. *Location:* from the north, first turning left past the Liss exit on the Petersfield by-pass; from the south, leave by-pass at the Liss turn off (B3006), join the Southern dual carriage way then take the first turning left. Members club in Area of Outstanding Natural Beauty, gently undulating and wooded. 18 holes. White, 6450 yards, S.S.S. 71, Par 72. Yellow, 6000 yards, S.S.S. 69, Par 69. Red, 5447 yards, S.S.S. 71, Par 72. Practice ground, nets and putting green. *Green Fees:* weekdays £32.00 per round, weekends £42.00. Booking required at weekends. *Eating facilities:* full bar and catering service. *Visitors:* welcome, Handicap Certificate or proof of club membership required. Booking required for weekends via Professional. *Society Meetings:* welcome, see our website for details of packages. Professional: Greg Hughes (01730 895216). General Manager: Peter Badger (01730 261675; Fax: 01730 894713).
e-mail: manager@pgc1892.net
website: www.petersfieldgolfclub.co.uk

PORTSMOUTH. **Great Salterns Golf Course,** Burrfields Road, Portsmouth PO3 5HH (023 9266 4549). *Location:* public golf course and home of Southsea Golf Club. South on A2030 off M27 signposted "Southsea". Flat meadow-land course. 18 holes, 5620 yards. S.S.S. 67. Floodlit driving range. *Green Fees:* information not provided. *Eating facilities:* full bar and catering service at Farmhouse Pub next door. *Visitors:* always welcome, tee time booking required one week ahead. Innlodge Hotel overlooks 18th green (73 bedrooms). *Society Meetings:* welcome, administered by James Blatch. Professional: Terry Healy (023 9266 4549; Fax: 023 9265 0525). Secretary (Southsea Golf Club): Roger Collinson (023 9269 9110)
e-mail: roger.collinson@ntlworld.com

PORTSMOUTH. **Portsmouth Golf Club (1926),** Crookhorn Lane, Widley, Waterlooville PO7 5QL (023 9237 2210). *Location:* two thirds of a mile from junction of B2177 and A3. Hilly course with views of harbour; outstanding 6th hole. 18 holes, 6139 yards. S.S.S. 70. Practice ground, putting green. *Green Fees:* information not available. *Eating facilities:* full restaurant and bar. *Visitors:* welcome, tee bookings required. *Society Meetings:* welcome by prior arrangement with Pro Shop. Professional: (023 9237 2210 ext. 24). Secretary: S. Richard (023 9220 1827 ext. 21).*

PORTSMOUTH. **Waterlooville Golf Club,** Cherry Tree Avenue, Cowplain, Waterlooville PO8 8AP (023 9226 3388; Fax: 023 9224 2980). *Location:* off A3 or A3 (M), 10 miles north of Portsmouth. Parkland course. 18 holes, 6602 yards. S.S.S. 72. *Green Fees:* £40.00 per round/day. *Eating facilities:* full catering service available, bar facilities. *Visitors:* welcome weekdays and weekends by prior arrangement with Professional. *Society Meetings:* Thursdays only by prior arrangement. Professional: John Hay (Tel/Fax: 023 9225 6911). Secretary: David Nairne.
website: www.waterloovillegolfclub.co.uk

RINGWOOD. **Burley Golf Club,** Cott Lane, Burley, Ringwood BH24 4BB (01425 402431; Fax: 01425 404168). *Location:* A31 from Ringwood and turn right at Picket Post and on through Burley Street. Open heathland course in the New Forest. 9 holes, 6151 yards. S.S.S. 70, Par 71. *Green Fees:* weekdays £20.00 per round (£10.00 with member), £25.00 per day; weekends and Bank Holidays £25.00 per round (£15.00 with member), £30.00 per day. Under 18s £9.00 per round weekdays, £10.00 per round weekends. Weekly ticket £90.00. *Eating facilities:* bar open, food available every day. *Visitors:* welcome, but not before 4pm Saturdays, 8am Sundays, and 1.45pm Wednesdays. Handicap Certificates preferred. *Society Meetings:* limited to 20 players (by arrangement). Secretary: L.J. Harfield (01425 402431; Fax: 01425 404168).
e-mail: secretary@burleygolfclub.co.uk
website: www.burleygolfclub.co.uk

RINGWOOD. **Moors Valley Golf Course,** Horton Road, Ashley Heath, Ringwood BH24 2ET (01425 479776). *Location*: signposted from A338/A31 roundabout. Heathland course set in the valley of the Moors River. Awarded Silver Medal by HSBC/Golf Monthly course rankings. 18 holes, 6337 yards. S.S.S. 70. 4 hole short course, full size pitching green and practice nets. *Green Fees:* information not available. *Eating facilities:* spikes bar and bar. *Visitors:* welcome. *Society Meetings:* welcome by arrangement. Manager: Desmond Meharg (01425 479776).*
e-mail: golf@moorsvalleygolf.co.uk
website: www.moors-valley.co.uk/golf

ROMSEY. **Dunwood Manor Golf Club,** Danes Road, Awbridge, Near Romsey SO51 0GF (01794 340549; Fax: 01794 341215). *Location:* four miles from Romsey off A27. Undulating parkland. 18 holes, 5655 yards. S.S.S. 68. Practice area. *Green Fees:* weekdays £37.00, weekends £49.00. *Eating facilities:* full catering, all day bar. *Visitors:* welcome by prior arrangement. Self-catering accommodation for up to 32 people available. *Society Meetings:* welcome by prior arrangement. Professional: Heath Teschner (01794 340663; Fax: 01794 341215). Secretary: Hazel Johnson (01794 340549; Fax: 01794 341215).
e-mail: admin@dunwood-golf.co.uk
website: www.dunwoodgolf.co.uk

ROMSEY. **Paultons Golf Centre,** Old Salisbury Road, Ower, Near Romsey SO51 6AN (023 8081 3345; Fax: 023 8081 3993). *Location:* off M27 at Junction 2, A36 towards Salisbury, at first roundabout take first exit, then first right at the Vine Public House. Parkland/woodland laid out within the original grounds of Paulton House, landscaped by Capability Brown. 18 holes, 6200 yards, 5670 metres. S.S.S. 71. 9-hole academy course. 24-bay floodlit driving range. *Green Fees:* information not available. *Visitors:* welcome anytime. *Society Meetings:* welcome anytime with prior booking. Professional: M. Williamson.*

ROMSEY. **Wellow Golf Club,** Ryedown Lane, East Wellow, Romsey SO51 6BD (01794 322872; Fax: 01794 323832). *Location:* M27 Junction 2 - A36 Salisbury, one mile right to East Wellow, one mile right Ryedown Lane. Parkland. 27 holes (three loops of 9 holes). S.S.S. 69, 70, 68. Large practice ground. *Green Fees:* weekdays £22.00; weekends £27.00. *Eating facilities:* full catering and bar facilities available all day. *Visitors:* welcome – advise phone to confirm availability. Correct dress code must be observed. *Society Meetings:* all welcome. Professional: Neil Bratley (01794 323833). Secretary: Mrs C. Gurd.

SHEDFIELD. **Marriott Meon Valley Hotel and Country Club Resort,** Sandy Lane, Shedfield, Southampton SO32 2HQ (01329 833455; Fax: 01329 834411). *Location:* leave M27 at Exit 7, take A334 to Botley then towards Wickham. Sandy Lane is 2 miles on the left. Wooded course. 18 holes, 6520 yards. S.S.S. 71. 9 holes, 2714 yards. S.S.S. 34. Covered practice area. *Green Fees:* information not available. *Eating facilities:* Treetops Restaurant, The Long Weekend Restaurant and three bars. *Visitors:* welcome, no restrictions. Handicap Certificates required to play. 113-bedroom 4 Star Hotel. *Society Meetings:* welcome, arranged in advance. Professional: Rod Cameron (01329 832184; Fax: 01329 834411). Director of Golf: George McMenemy (01329 833455; Fax: 01329 834411).*

SOUTHAMPTON. **Botley Park Golf Club,** Winchester Road, Botley, Southampton SO32 2UA (01489 780888; Fax: 01489 789242). *Location:* approximately two miles from Junction 7 on M27. Parkland. 18 holes, 6341 yards. S.S.S. 70. Driving range. *Green Fees:* information not available. *Eating facilities:* two bars, main restaurant and club lounge. *Visitors:* welcome by prior booking by phone. Handicap Certificate required. 100 bedroomed hotel on site; tennis, squash, swimming, sauna, solarium, steam room, fitness suite, beauty spa. Dance studio. *Society Meetings:* weekdays only. Professional: Mark Smith (01489 789771; Fax: 01489 789242). Director of Golf: Mark White (01489 789771).*

SOUTHAMPTON. **Chilworth Golf Club,** Main Road, Chilworth, Southampton SO16 7JP (02380 740544). *Location*: situated off the A27. Parkland course. 18 holes, 5915 yards, S.S.S. 68. Covered driving range. *Green Fees*: information not available. *Eating facilities*: bar. *Visitors*: welcome, must follow dress code, please telephone for details. Pro shop. Tuition available. Professional: Darren Newing. Secretary: Fred Bendal.
e-mail: info@chilworthgolfclub.com

SOUTHAMPTON. **Corhampton Golf Club,** Shepherds Farm Lane, Corhampton, Southampton SO32 3GZ (01489 877279; Fax: 01489 877680). *Location:* one mile from Corhampton on Bishops Waltham to Corhampton road (B3135). Free draining downland course. 18 holes, 6398 yards. S.S.S. 71. Large practice ground. *Green Fees:* weekdays £28.00 per round, £40.00 per day; weekends £16.00 with a member only. *Eating facilities:* full catering. *Visitors:* welcome Monday to Friday; weekends and Bank Holidays with a member. Buggies and trolleys for hire. *Society Meetings:* Mondays and Thursdays. Professional: Ian Roper (01489 877638; Fax: 01489 877680). Secretary: Bob Ashton (01489 877279).
e-mail: secretary@corhamptongc.co.uk

SOUTHAMPTON. **Romsey Golf Club Ltd,** Nursling, Southampton SO16 0XW (023 8073 4637; Fax: 023 8074 1036). *Location:* two miles south east of Romsey on A3057, M27/M271 Junction 3. Well wooded, undulating course with extremely good views. 18 holes, 5718 yards. S.S.S. 68. *Green Fees:* on application. *Eating facilities:* bar and restaurant. *Visitors:* welcome weekdays only. *Society Meetings:* welcome weekdays. Professional: James Pitcher (023 8073 6673). Secretary: Michael Batty.

SOUTHAMPTON. **Stoneham Golf Club,** Monks Wood Close, Bassett, Southampton SO16 3TT (023 8076 9272). **Location:** A33/M27 north of Southampton find Chilworth roundabout, take road to Airport (A27), half mile on left. Undulating parkland course, used for Brabazon Trophy 1993, English County Finals 1998, English Ladies' Championship 2001, English Ladies' Senior Matchplay 2008. 18 holes, 6392 yards. S.S.S. 71. **Green Fees:** weekdays £48.00 per round, £55.00 per day; weekends £55.00 per round, £65.00 per day. **Eating facilities:** full catering, bar open all day. **Visitors:** welcome, except competition days. **Society Meetings:** catered for Monday, Tuesday afternoons, Thursday and Friday by arrangement. Professional: Ian Young (023 8076 8397). Manager: Richard Penley-Martin (023 8076 9272; Fax: 023 8076 6320).
e-mail: richard@stonehamgolfclub.org.uk
website: www.stonehamgolfclub.org.uk

An undulating parkland and heathland course, only three miles from the centre of Southampton, providing a good challenge to golfers of all abilities. Visitors, Societies and Corporate Golf welcome.
Special green fee rates for visiting golfers.

Stoneham Golf Club, Monks Wood Close, Bassett, Southampton SO16 3TT
Tel: 023 8076 9272
E-mail: richard@stonehamgolfclub.org.uk
www.stonehamgolfclub.org.uk

Hampshire / SOUTH REGION

SOUTHAMPTON. Southampton Golf Club (Play over the Municipal Golf Course), Golf Course Road, Bassett, Southampton SO16 7AY (023 8076 0546). *Location:* off Bassett Avenue. Parkland course. 18 holes, 6218 yards, S.S.S. 70. 9 hole Par 32. Practice area and putting greens. *Green Fees:* information not available. *Eating facilities:* bar and full catering (023 8076 7996). *Visitors:* welcome but must book at weekends; three and four ball play only at weekends. Professional: Andy Gordon (02380 760388). Secretary: E. Hemsley (07765 856267). Bookings: (023 8076 0546).*

WINCHESTER. Hockley Golf Club, Twyford, Near Winchester SO21 1PL (01962 713165; Fax: 01962 713612). *Location:* 100 yards Junction 11 M3 motorway. Downland with excellent views of Winchester and surrounding areas. James Braid designed course, long vistas. 18 holes, 6420 yards. S.S.S. 72. Large practice ground. *Green Fees:* April to September £35.00 per 18 holes, £45.00 per day; October to March £38.00 per 18 holes, £48.00 per 36 holes. *Eating facilities:* full catering and bar facilities. *Visitors:* welcome. Handicap Certificate preferred. *Society Meetings:* welcome by prior arrangement. Professional: (01962 713678). Secretary: Mrs Lyn Clash.
e-mail: secretary@hockleygolfclub.com
website: www.hockleygolfclub.com

WINCHESTER. Otterbourne Golf Centre, Poles Lane, Otterbourne, Winchester SO21 2EL (Tel & Fax: 01962 775225). Parkland course. 9 holes, 1939 yards, S.S.S. 30. 10 bay uncovered driving range. *Green Fees:* information not available. *Visitors:* welcome, pay as you play. Tuition available. *Society Meetings:* open to discussion. Professional: Darren Newing.

WINCHESTER. The Park Golf Course, Avington, Winchester SO21 1DA (01962 779945; Fax: 01962 779530). *Location:* 5 miles east of Winchester. Mature parkland course. 9 holes, 1907 yards, S.S.S. 58. *Green Fees:* information not available. *Visitors:* always welcome, please telephone to book. website: www.avingtongolf.co.uk

WINCHESTER. Royal Winchester Golf Club, Sarum Road, Winchester SO22 5QE (01962 852462). *Location:* from Junction 11 M3 follow signs to Oliver's Battery. At Pitt roundabout follow signs to Winchester then left into Kilham Lane. At end turn right into Sarum Road. Traditional downland course. 18 holes, 6387 yards. S.S.S. 72. *Green Fees:* information not available. *Eating facilities:* full catering and bar facilities available. *Visitors:* welcome weekdays, Handicap Certificate required. *Society Meetings:* by prior arrangement. Professional: Steven Hunter (01962 862473). Secretary: Andrew Buck (01962 852462; Fax: 01962 865048).*
e-mail: manager@royalwinchestergolfclub.com
website: www.royalwinchestergolfclub.com

WINCHESTER. South Winchester Golf Club, Romsey Road, Pitt, Winchester SO22 5QX (01962 877800; Fax: 01962 877900). *Location:* situated between Winchester and Hursley in the village of Pitt. Championship links-style course - home of the Hampshire PGA. 18 holes, 7086 yards. S.S.S. 74. Driving range. Chipping green, practice bunker and practice green. *Green Fees:* information not available. *Eating facilities:* two bars, one dining room, one conservatory/dining room, food available all day. *Visitors:* visiting golfers welcome. Golf days for non members by arrangement with the Professional. Professional: Richard Adams (01962 840469). General Manager: Laurence Ross.*
website: www.crown-golf.co.uk

4th hole at Stoneham Golf Club, Southampton

Isle of Wight

COWES. **Cowes Golf Club,** Crossfield Avenue, Cowes, Isle of Wight PO31 8HN (Tel & Fax: 01983 292303). *Location:* entrance adjacent Cowes High School. Parkland with sea views. 9 holes, 5934 yards. S.S.S. 68. *Green Fees:* information not available. *Eating facilities:* snack meals available in bar in summer. Bar open 11am to 2pm summer months. *Visitors:* welcome except Sunday before 1pm and Thursday, Ladies' Day (11.30am to 3pm). *Society Meetings:* welcome Mondays to Wednesdays by arrangement with Secretary. Society rates by arrangement. Secretary: C.J. Laley (01983 292303) Steward (01983 280135).*

EAST COWES. **Osborne Golf Club,** Osborne House Estate, East Cowes PO32 6JX (01983 295421). *Location:* off A3021 south-east of East Cowes. One mile from Southampton/East Cowes ferry terminal; 4 miles from Portsmouth/Fishbourne ferry terminal. Parkland. 9 holes, 6372 yards. S.S.S. 70. Practice area. *Green Fees:* weekdays £25.00; weekends and Bank Holidays £30.00. 2010 rates (subject to review). *Eating facilities:* catering available each day, bar facilities. *Visitors:* welcome except Tuesday, Saturday and Sunday before noon. Telephone for tee availability. *Society Meetings:* catered for (24 maximum).
e-mail: osbornegolfclub@tiscali.co.uk
website: www.osbornegolfclub.co.uk

FRESHWATER. **Freshwater Bay Golf Club,** Afton Down, Freshwater (Tel & Fax: 01983 752955). *Location*: western end of Island, approximately half-a-mile east of Freshwater Bay on coast road to Ventnor. Links type course on chalk uplands. 18 holes, 5725 yards. S.S.S. 68. *Green Fees:* information not available. *Eating facilities:* licensed bar, catering. *Visitors:* welcome. *Society Meetings:* welcome by arrangement. Secretary: Terry Riddett.*
e-mail: tr.fbgc@btopenworld.com

NEWPORT. **Newport (Isle of Wight) Golf Club,** St Georges Down, Near Shide, Newport PO30 3BA Founded 1895. *Location*: one mile south east of Newport, taking Sandown road. Testing downland course. 9 holes, 5704 yards. S.S.S. 68. Driving range available to visitors. *Green Fees*: information not available. *Eating facilities*: full catering available-breakfast, lunches, evening dinners. *Visitors:* welcome anytime except Wednesday 12pm-3pm, Saturday before 3pm and Sunday before noon. *Society Meetings:* groups of 12 plus welcome by arrangement weekdays except Wednesdays and not before 3pm on Saturdays or noon on Sundays. Secretary: Dave Boon (01983 525076).*
website: www.newportgolfclub.co.uk

RYDE. **Ryde Golf Club,** Binstead Road, Ryde, Isle of Wight PO33 3NF. *Location:* on A3054 Ryde to Newport Road, just outside Ryde. Parkland course. 9 holes, extended June 2002 to 5772 yards. Par 70. S.S.S. 69. *Green Fees:* information not available. *Eating facilities:* bar and catering available all day April to September; lunchtime only October to March. *Visitors:* welcome, restrictions Wednesdays and Sundays. *Society Meetings:* catered for. Limited Pro Shop on site. Secretary: Richard Dean (01983 614809; Fax: 01983 567418).*
e-mail: ryde.golfclub@btinternet.com
website: www.rydegolf.co.uk

SANDOWN. **Shanklin and Sandown Golf Club,** The Fairway, Lake, Sandown PO36 9PR (01983 404424/403217). *Location:* from Sandown travel towards Shanklin. Soon after Heights Leisure Centre turn right into The Fairway. One mile to Club. A traditional, beautiful heathland County Championship course. The 13th hole is one of the best in Southern England. 18 holes, 6062 yards. S.S.S. 69. Practice ground. *Green Fees:* £36.00 weekdays; £40.00 weekends. Three day ticket weekdays £81.00. *Eating facilities:* full catering and bar facilities. *Visitors:* welcome. Handicap Certificate preferred. *Society Meetings:* welcome by arrangement. Professional: Peter Hammond (01983 404424). Secretary: A. Creed (01983 403217).
e-mail: club@ssgolfclub.com

UPPER VENTNOR. **Ventnor Golf Club,** Steephill Down Road, Upper Ventnor PO38 1BP (01983 853326). *Location:* northwest boundary of Ventnor. Downland undulating with side slopes overlooking the sea. 12 holes, 5767 yards. S.S.S. 68. *Green Fees:* information not available. *Eating facilities:* bar snacks only. *Visitors:* welcome, Sundays after 1pm, Ladies' Day Monday . Secretary: Stewart Blackmore.*
website: www.ventnorgolfclub.co.uk

Looking for accommodation near golf clubs?, then visit www.holidayguides.com for where to stay when playing golf around the regions

Kent

ASH. **London Golf Club,** Stansted Lane, Ash, near Brands Hatch TN15 7EH (01474 879899; Fax: 01474 879912). *Location*: 1 mile east of Brands Hatch on A20, turn left after motorway underpass when leaving West Kingsdown. 36 holes Heritage Course: Nicklaus design 7250 yards, S.S.S. 74. International course: 7005 yards, S.S.S. 74. Practice range (350 yards), covered bays and grass tees; practice chipping and bunker facilities, 2x practice putting greens. *Green Fees*: information not provided. *Eating facilities*: restaurant, terrace bar, spike bar, plus private rooms, full changing facilities. *Visitors:* Heritage Course: members and guests only. International Course: visitors and corporate days by prior arrangement. General Manager: Austen Gravestock. Director of Golf/Head Professional: Paul Stuart. Marketing: Kate Brewer. Golf Events: Gordon Frost. Events Co-ordinator: Carole Jacques. Membership Secretary: Henry Fairweather.
e-mail: golf@londongolf.co.uk
website: www.londongolf.co.uk

ASH. **Redlibbets Golf Club,** Manor Lane, West Yoke, Ash TN15 7HT (01474 879190). Undulating woodland 18 hole course. Practice range, practice short game area, putting green and indoor net room. *Green Fees*: information not available. *Eating facilities*: Bar and restaurant. Secretary: R. Taylor.*

ASHFORD. **Ashford Great Chart Golf & Leisure,** Great Chart, Ashford (01233 645858). *Location*: Junction 9 off M20; A28 to Great Chart, follow signs. 9 hole main course, family pitch and putt course. 26 bay floodlit covered driving range. *Green Fees*: information not available. *Eating facilities*: bar/cafe. Function room; weddings catered for. *Visitors*: welcome, juniors and families welcome. Video tuition, shop, practice bunkers. Volley ball/ beach soccer sand pitch; paintball. Professional: James Sheldrick. Secretary: Grant Kay/John Kay.*

ASHFORD. **Ashford (Kent) Golf Club,** Sandyhurst Lane, Ashford TN25 4NT (01233 620180). *Location:* just off A20, one and a half miles west of Ashford. Parkland - stream cutting through course. 18 holes, 6261 yards. S.S.S. 70. *Green Fees:* information not available. *Eating facilities:* available every day. *Visitors:* welcome. Handicap Certificate required. *Society Meetings:* catered for Tuesdays and Thursdays by arrangement. Professional: Hugh Sherman (01233 629644). Secretary: A.H. Story (Tel & Fax: 01233 622655).*

THE APPEARANCE OF AN ASTERISK (*) AT THE END OF A CLUB OR COURSE ENTRY INDICATES THAT UP-TO-DATE INFORMATION HAS NOT BEEN SUPPLIED

ASHFORD. **Chart Hills Golf Club,** Weeks Lane, Biddenden, Ashford TN27 8JX (01580 292222; Fax: 01580 292233). *Location:* M25, M20 Leeds Castle turn off (B2163), A274 to Tenterden. Parkland course designed by Nick Faldo. 18 holes, 7119 yards. S.S.S. 74. Short game area, golf academy. *Green Fees:* information not available. *Eating facilities:* restaurant, bar snacks, bar, conference facilities. *Visitors:* welcome, after 1pm at weekends. *Society Meetings:* Tuesday and Thursday only.
e-mail: info@charthills.co.uk
website: www.charthills.co.uk

ASHFORD. **The Homelands Golf Centre,** Ashford Road, Kingsnorth, Ashford TN26 1NJ (01233 661620). *Location:* take exit 10 off M20, follow A2070 course signposted from second roundabout to Kingsnorth. 9 hole parkland course. 2499 yards. Par 68. S.S.S. 64. *Green Fees:* information not provided. *Visitors:* welcome at all times. Buggies, trolleys and clubs available for hire. *Society Meetings:* welcome with prior notice. Professional: Howard Bonaccorsi.
e-mail: info@ashfordgolf.co.uk
website: www.ashfordgolf.co.uk

BECKENHAM. **Beckenham Place Park Golf Club,** Beckenham Hill Road, Beckenham. *Location:* on A222 north of Bromley. Parkland. 18 holes, 5722 yards. S.S.S. 68. Practice ground, nets, putting green. *Green Fees:* visit website for information. *Eating facilities:* bar and cafeteria. *Visitors:* welcome but must book in advance. *Society Meetings:* catered for. Other facilities include tennis courts and putting green. Professional: J. Good (020 8650-2292). Secretary: J. Kemp.
website: www.glendale-golf.com

BECKENHAM. **Braeside Golf Club,** Beckenham Place Park, Beckenham Hill, Beckenham (020 8650 2292). Parkland course. 18 holes, 5722 yards, 5230 metres. S.S.S. 69. Practice area, putting green and nets. *Green Fees:* information not available. *Eating facilities:* cafe and bar. *Visitors:* welcome, will need to book weekends. Secretary: Mr Nicholas Wilkins.*

BECKENHAM. **Langley Park Golf Club,** Barnfield Wood Road, Beckenham BR3 6SZ (020 8658 6849). *Location:* one mile from Bromley South station. Flat wooded parkland. 18 holes, 6469 yards, 5916 metres, S.S.S. 71. Practice areas and nets. *Green Fees:* £40.00, £60.00 per day, County Card £25.00. *Eating facilities:* bar snacks, restaurant/dining room. *Visitors:* welcome weekdays by arrangement with Pro Shop. Handicap Certificate required. *Society Meetings:* Wednesdays and Thursdays by arrangement with the Club Manager. Other days considered. Professional: Colin Staff (020 8650 1663). Club Manager: Rodger Pollard (020 8658 6849).

Chart Hills Golf Club

The spectacular Nick Faldo designed golf course sits in the northern reaches of the Weald of Kent, just 20 miles from the M25. Recently recognised as one of the top courses in Europe by the prestigious Peugeot Golf Guide 2008-2009, you have the recipe for success and a quality golfing experience on and off the course. With nearly 140 bunkers, copious amounts of Oak woodland and water, Chart Hills will let you open your shoulders and test your skills.

Chart Hills Golf Club, Weeks Lane, Biddenden, Kent TN27 8JX
01580 292222   www.charthills.co.uk

BEXLEYHEATH. **Bexleyheath Golf Club,** Mount Road, Bexley Heath DA6 8JS (020 8303 6951). *Location:* adjacent to A2. Hilly parkland. 9 holes, 5239 yards, 4788 metres. S.S.S. 66. *Green Fees:* £25.00 (approximately). Weekends with member only. *Eating facilities:* catering available. *Visitors:* weekdays only. Professional: To be appointed. Secretary: Mrs J. Smith.
e-mail: bexleyheathgolf@aol.com

BIGGIN HILL. **Cherry Lodge Golf Club,** Jail Lane, Biggin Hill TN16 3AX (01959 572250; Fax: 01959 540672). *Location:* A233 to M25 Junction 5, Bromley, eight miles. Undulating Parkland 600 ft. above sea level with panoramic views of surrounding countryside. 18 holes, 6652 yards, 6084 metres. S.S.S. 73. Extensive practice ground. *Green Fees:* information not provided. *Eating facilities:* bar snacks all day, Sunday lunches. *Visitors:* welcome weekdays except Bank Holidays. *Society Meetings:* welcome weekdays (except Bank Holidays) by arrangement. Professional: Craig Sutherland (01959 572989).
e-mail: info@cherrylodgegc.co.uk
website: www.cherrylodgegc.co.uk

BROADSTAIRS. **North Foreland Golf Club,** The Clubhouse, Convent Road, Broadstairs CT10 3PU (01843 862140). *Location:* Broadstairs Station, A2, M2, A299, A253, A256, B2052. Cliff top, chalk based, free draining. 18 holes, 6382 yards. S.S.S. 71. Short Course: 18 holes, 1752 yards. Par 3. *Green Fees:* main course: weekdays £40.00 per round, £55.00 per day; weekends £40.00 per round. Par 3 course: weekdays £8.00 per day; weekends £10.00 per day. *Eating facilities:* bar, dining room and "Halfway House". *Visitors:* welcome weekdays and weekend afternoons with current Handicap Certificate. Tennis. *Society Meetings:* Wednesdays and Fridays by prior arrangement with Secretary. Professional: Darren Parris (01843 604471; Fax: 01843 862663). Secretary: Tony Adams (01843 862140).
website: www.northforeland.co.uk

BROMLEY. **Magpie Hall Lane Municipal Golf Club,** Magpie Hall Lane, Bromley. *Location:* off Bromley Common on A21. 9 holes, 5590 yards, 5014 metres. S.S.S. 67. *Green Fees:* information not available. *Eating facilities:* Food available. *Visitors:* welcome anytime without reservation.*

BROMLEY. **Shortlands Golf Club,** Meadow Road, Shortlands, Bromley BR2 0DX (020 8460 2471; Fax: 020 8460 8828). *Location:* car park and entrance in Ravensbourne Avenue, off the main Beckenham to Bromley Road, adjacent Shortlands B.R. Station. 9 holes, 5261 yards. S.S.S. 66. *Green Fees:* £15.00 for 18 holes, £10.00 for 9 holes. *Eating facilities:* available. *Visitors:* restricted to playing with a member. *Society Meetings:* only when member involved. Professional: (020 8464 6182). Manager: P.S. May (020 8460 8828).

BROMLEY. **Sundridge Park Golf Club,** Garden Road, off Plaistow Lane, Bromley BR1 3NE (020 8460 0278). *Location:* five minutes' walk from Sundridge Park station. Wooded parkland. 36 holes. East 6493 yards. West 5973 yards. S.S.S. 71 and 69. Two practice grounds. *Green Fees:* information not available. *Eating facilities:* restaurant, spike bar, lounge bar, members' bar and snack bar. *Visitors:* welcome weekdays only, with Handicap Certificate. *Society Meetings:* catered for by arrangement. Professional: Stuart Dowsett (020 8460 5540). General Manager: Robert J. Walden (020 8460 0278; Fax: 020 8289 3050).*
e-mail: info@spgc.co.uk
website: www.spgc.co.uk

CANTERBURY. **Broome Park Golf Club,** Broome Park Estate, Barham, Near Canterbury CT4 6QX (01227 830728; Fax: 01227 832591). *Location:* off the A2 at the A260 in the direction of Folkestone, half a mile on right. Undulating parkland, lake in front of 18th green. 18 holes, 6580 yards, S.S.S. 71. Driving range and practice ground. *Green Fees:* weekdays £30.00; weekends £40.00. *Eating facilities:* available all week. *Visitors:* welcome. Handicap Certificate required. *Society Meetings:* welcome weekdays by arrangement. Professional: Tienie Britz (01227 831126). Golf Manager: Mrs Del Burtenshaw (01227 830728; Fax: 01227 832591).
e-mail: golf@broomepark.co.uk
website: www.broomepark.co.uk

CANTERBURY. **Canterbury Golf Club,** Scotland Hills, Littlebourne Road, Canterbury CT1 1TW (01227 453532; Fax: 01227 784277). *Location:* one mile from centre of Canterbury on the A257 road to Sandwich. Parkland and wooded course. 18 holes, 6272 yards. S.S.S. 70. Practice ground and Driving

BROOME PARK Golf Club
Barham, Near Canterbury CT4 6QX

Don't miss this gem of a golf course
on your way to Dover.
4 Ball 'Specials' available.
Ring 01227 831126 to book.
Easy access from M2/A2
or M20/A20.
e-mail: golf@broomepark.co.uk
www.broomepark.co.uk

Range. *Green Fees:* Information not available. *Eating facilities:* full bar and catering service (snacks, sandwiches, lunches, dinners). *Visitors:* welcome without reservation but Handicap Certificate necessary (or evidence that visitor is bona fide playing member of another club). *Society Meetings:* catered for Tuesday, Thursday and Friday. Professional: Paul Everard (01227 462865). Secretary: John Morgan (01227 453532).

CHISLEHURST. **Chislehurst Golf Club,** Camden Park Road, Chislehurst BR7 5HJ (020 8467 2782). *Location:* between Bromley and junction of A222 and Sidcup bypass. Parkland. 18 holes, 5128 yards. S.S.S. 66. *Green Fees:* information not available. *Eating facilities:* catering available. Large parties by prior arrangement. *Visitors:* welcome but restricted to weekdays (except Wednesday mornings) and only with a member at weekends. *Society Meetings:* catered for by arrangement. Professional: (020 8467 6798). Secretary: Mark Hickson (020 8467 2782; Fax: 020 8295 0874). Caterer: L. de Bruyn.*

CHISLEHURST. **World of Golf,** A20 Sidcup Bypass, Chislehurst BR7 6RP (020 8309 0181). *Location:* six miles from Junction 3 on M25 heading towards London on A20. Parkland. Short game practice area, 54-bay driving range, adventure putting. *Green Fees:* information not available. *Eating facilities*: licensed cafe/bar. *Visitors:* welcome, no restrictions. Tennis courts. *Society Meetings:* welcome. Head Golf Professional: David Young.*
e-mail: sc.worldofgolf@dsl.pipex.com
website: www.worldofgolf.biz

CRANBROOK. **Hemsted Forest Golf Club,** Golford Road, Cranbrook TN17 4AL (01580 712833; Fax: 01580 714274). *Location:* two miles south of Sissinghurst. Parkland, a beautiful tree lined course in superb condition. 18 holes, 6305 yards. S.S.S. 71. *Green Fees:* weekdays £28.00 per round, weekends £40.00 per round. *Eating facilities:* open all day, special menus catered for. *Visitors:* welcome weekdays after 8.30am and weekends after 11am. *Society Meetings:* available weekdays and weekends. Professional: Henry Law (01580 712833; Fax: 01580 714274). Secretary: Karl Stevenson (01580 712833; Fax: 01580 714274).

DARTFORD. **Dartford Golf Club Ltd.,** The Clubhouse, Heath Lane (Upper), Dartford DA1 2TN (01322 223616). *Location:* backing on to A2, one mile from Dartford Tunnel and M25. Flat heathland. 18 holes, 5718 yards. S.S.S. 69. *Green Fees:* weekdays £26.00 per round, £37.00 per day; weekends (accompanied by member): one round £17.00, two rounds £27.00. *Eating facilities:* catering available. *Visitors:* welcome on weekdays with reservation, must be member of another golf club. *Society Meetings:* welcome on Mondays and Fridays by prior arrangement with Secretary. Professional: John Gregory (01322 226409). Secretary: Amanda Malas (Tel & Fax: 01322 226455).
e-mail: dartfordgolf@hotmail.com
website: www.dartfordgolfclub.co.uk

DARTFORD. **Fawkham Valley Golf Club,** Gay Dawn Farm, Valley Road, Fawkham, Longfield DA3 8LY (01474 707144). *Location:* off the A2 East of Dartford/off A20 North of Brands Hatch. Wooded course (tree lined), special feature being lakes in front of the 3rd and 6th greens. 9 holes, 6547 yards. S.S.S. 72. Practice area and putting green. *Green Fees:* information not available. *Eating facilities:* members' bar. *Visitors:* welcome anytime. *Society Meetings:* welcome Mondays, Wednesdays and Fridays. Professional: Nigel Willis. Secretary: Jo Marchant.
e-mail: fvgolfcourse@googlemail.com
website: www.fawkhamvalleygolf.com

DEAL. **Royal Cinque Ports Golf Club,** Golf Road, Deal CT14 6RF (01304 374007; Fax: 01304 379530). *Location:* A258 from Sandwich. In Upper Deal leave for Middle Deal Road, left turn into Albert Road, Western Road, on to Golf Road (or from Dover, A258 via Sea front and Godwin Road). Championship 18 hole links course. 18 holes, 6942 yards. S.S.S. 73. Par 72. Large practice area. *Green Fees:* information not available. *Eating facilities:* hot and cold comprehensive bar snack menu. *Visitors:* welcome, 4 ball rounds may be played on Tuesdays and Thursdays. Special packages available. Handicap Certificate required (max 22); times must be pre-booked. Buggies (with medical certificate); cart and caddies by arrangement. *Society Meetings:* by arrangement. Professional: Andrew Reynolds (01304 374170; Fax: 01304 379530). Secretary: (01304 374007; Fax: 01304 379530).*
e-mail: rcpgc.office@royalcinqueports.com
website: www.royalcinqueports.com

DEAL. **Walmer and Kingsdown Golf Club,** The Leas, Kingsdown, Deal CT14 8EP (01304 373256). *Location:* take A258 from Dover (A2) to Deal, Kingsdown club signposted at village of Ringwould. Downland course on the White Cliffs of Dover overlooking the English Channel. 18 holes, Par 72. Practice ground. *Green Fees:* weekdays £32.00. *Eating facilities:* full catering and bar service. *Visitors:* welcome after 9.30am weekdays and 12 noon at weekends. *Society Meetings:* catered for by arrangement. Professional: Jude Read (01304 363017). Secretary: Reg Harrison (01304 373256; Fax: 01304 382336).
e-mail: info@kingsdowngolf.co.uk
website: www.kingsdowngolf.co.uk

DEANGATE. **Deangate Ridge Golf Club,** Duxcourt Road, Hoo, Rochester ME3 8RZ (01634) 254481). *Location*: three miles from Rochester off A228 towards Isle of Grain. Municipal course – wooded. 18 holes, 6300 yards. S.S.S. 70. 11-bay driving range. *Green Fees:* information not available. Special rates for Senior Citizens. *Eating facilities:* available. *Visitors:* welcome without reservation, bookings required for weekends. *Society Meetings:* catered for, book through Professional. Professional: Richard Fox (01634 251180). Manager: (01634 254481). Club Members Secretary: Mrs C.J. Williams (01634 251950).*

www.holidayguides.com

EDENBRIDGE. **Kent and Surrey Golf and Country Club,** Crouch House Road, Edenbridge TN8 5LQ (01732 867381; Fax: 01732 867167). *Location:* from M25 take A25, at Limpsfield take B2026 to Edenbridge. Parkland. Old Course 18 holes, 6577 yards. S.S.S. 72. 20-bay floodlit driving range. *Green Fees:* information not available. *Eating facilities:* bar and restaurant. *Visitors:* welcome, call for start time. Buggies and carts available. Five tennis courts. *Society Meetings:* societies welcome weekdays and weekends. Conference facility seats up to 65. *
e-mail: info@thekentandsurrey.com
website: www.thekentandsurreygolf.com

ETCHINGHILL. **Etchinghill Golf Club,** Canterbury Road, Etchinghill CT18 8FA (01303 863863; Fax: 01303 863210). *Location:* one mile north of M20 Junction 12 on B2065. 27 holes, 6121 yards. S.S.S. 69. 9 hole Par 3 course. Covered and floodlit driving range. *Green Fees:* information not available. *Eating facilities:* full range of catering facilities available. *Visitors:* welcome. Professional: Roger Dowle (01303 863966).*
website: www.pentlandgolf.co.uk

EYNSFORD. **Austin Lodge Golf Club,** Upper Austin Lodge Road, Eynsford DA4 0HU (01322 863000; Fax: 01322 862406). *Location:* Enysford - 10 minutes' drive from Junction 3 of M25, M20, A20. Secluded rolling countryside with lakes. 18 holes, 6575 yards Yellow Tees, 7118 yards White Tees. S.S.S. 73. Practice ground. *Green Fees:* information

WALMER & KINGSDOWN GOLF CLUB
The Leas • Kingsdown • Deal • Kent CT14 8EP

Set atop the White Cliffs of Dover, our James Braid designed downland golf course founded in 1909, offers stunning views of the English Channel on every hole, and is a beautiful place to play golf. Visitors are always made welcome at this friendly members' golf club.

18 Holes Par 72 • White 6471• Yellows 6291 • Reds 5892

Food and Drink served all day
Visitors' green fees: 18 holes £32 Monday to Friday

Great Clubhouse facilities including changing rooms, a lounge and bar.

Secretary and Steward: 01304 373256
Pro: Jude Read: 01304 363017
e-mail: info@kingsdowngolf.co.uk
www.kingsdowngolf.co.uk

1909-2009
100 years of golf for everyone at Walmer and Kingsdown Golf Club

not available. *Eating facilities:* bar, restaurant with light meals all day. *Visitors:* welcome weekdays, and after 12noon weekends. Buggies available. *Society Meetings:* welcome, telephone booking only. Professional/Manager: Greg Haenan.*

FARNBOROUGH. **High Elms Golf Club,** High Elms Road, Downe BR6 7SL (01689 853232). *Location:* two miles from Farnborough Hospital on A21, turn right at Shire Lane, second on left. Beautiful parkland. 18 holes, 6210 metres. S.S.S. 70. *Green Fees:* information not available. *Eating facilities:* food available every day. *Visitors:* welcome, no restriction but should phone in advance. *Society Meetings:* apply to Catering Manager: Jacki Saxby. Professional: Jon Dummett (01689 858175). Secretary: Mrs P. O'Keeffe.*

FAVERSHAM. **Boughton Golf Club,** Brickfield Lane, Boughton, Faversham ME13 9AJ (01227 752277; Fax: 01227 7523610. *Location:* north-east of Boughton, near M2/A2 interchange; six miles west of Canterbury 18 holes, 6452 yards. S.S.S. 71. Driving range. *Green Fees*: information not available. *Eating facilities:* available. *Visitors:* welcome. Manager: G. Haenan.*

FAVERSHAM. **Faversham Golf Club Ltd.,** Belmont Park, Faversham ME13 0HB (01795 890561). *Location:* M2 Faversham Exit (A251) to A2 junction, left to Brogdale Road, left to Belmont. Long established (1902) very attractive parkland course in rural surroundings. 18 holes, 5965 yards. S.S.S. 69. *Green Fees:* £35.00 per round, £45.00 per day.

Eating facilities: full catering. *Visitors:* welcome weekdays (Handicap Certificate required); weekends with member only. *Society Meetings:* catered for on weekdays only. Professional: S. Rokes (01795 890275). Secretary: J. Edgington (01795 890561; Fax: 01795 890760).
e-mail: themanager@favershamgolf.co.uk

FOLKESTONE. **Sene Valley Golf Club,** Sene, Folkestone CT18 8BL (01303 268513). *Location:* M20 Junction 12, take A20 to Ashford turn left at first roundabout. Downland course with magnificent views over English Channel. 18 holes, 6271 yards. S.S.S. 70. Practice area. *Green Fees:* call for details. *Eating facilities:* snacks, meals on request. *Visitors:* welcome, Handicap Certificate required. Preferable to book in advance. *Society Meetings:* welcome by prior arrangements. Professional: Nick Watson (Tel & Fax: 01303 268514). Manager: John Hemphrey. e-mail: senevalleygolf@btconnect.com
website: www.senevalleygolfclub.co.uk

GILLINGHAM. **Gillingham Golf Club Ltd.,** Woodlands Road, Gillingham ME7 2AP (01634 850999). *Location*: on old A2 Gillingham. Flat parkland. 18 holes, 5514 yards, 5042 metres. Par 67. Practice nets. *Green Fees:* available weekdays, rates on application. *Eating facilities:* available. *Visitors:* welcome at all times except weekends. Must have proof of Handicap or membership of another club. *Society Meetings:* welcome by prior arrangement. Professional: (01634 855862). Office (01634 853017; Fax: 01634 574749).

The Kent & Surrey Golf & Country Club
Crouch House Road, Edenbridge, Kent TN8 5LQ
Tel: 01732 867381
info@thekentandsurrey.com

18-hole parkland golf course available to members of the public seven days a week (subject to availability). Comfortable clubhouse with bar and restaurant. 16-bay floodlit driving range with practice putting and chipping greens. Golf packages available.

www.thekentandsurreygolf.com

Gillingham Golf Club *Private Members' Club est.1905*

A lovely 18-hole parkland course set in the heart of the Medway Towns, just 10 minutes from the M2. Playable all year round on some of the best greens in Kent, this delightful short course is one not to be missed!
Open to visitors on weekdays.
Membership available - no joining fee.
Gillingham Golf Club Ltd, Woodlands Road,
Gillingham, Kent ME7 2AP
01634 853017/855862
e-mail: golf@gillinghamgolf.idps.co.uk
www.gillinghamgolfclub.co.uk

GRAVESEND. **Mid-Kent Golf Club,** Singlewell Road, Gravesend DA11 7RB (01474 352387). *Location:* A227 off A2. Parkland. 18 holes, 6106 yards. S.S.S. 70. *Green Fees:* information not available. *Eating facilities:* breakfast, dinner by arrangement, lunch every day, bar 11am to 11pm. *Visitors:* welcome weekdays except competition days with Handicap Certificate. *Society Meetings:* catered for Tuesdays only. Professional: Mark Foreman (01474 332810). Secretary: P. Gleeson (01474 568035; Fax: 01474 564218).*
e-mail: secretary@mkgc.co.uk
website: www.mkgc.co.uk

GRAVESEND. **Southern Valley Golf Course,** Thong Lane, Shorne, Gravesend DA12 4LF (01474 568568; Fax: 01474 360366). *Location:* take J4 off A2 (not M2), signposted "Inn on the Lake/Thong", at top of slip road turn left into Thong Lane at T-junction. Golf course is approx. one mile along on right-hand side. Undulating greens and rolling fairways. 18 holes, 6100 yards. Par 69. Practice area, putting green. *Green Fees:* information not available. *Eating facilities:* fully licensed bar and restaurant. *Visitors:* all welcome. No jeans or tracksuits; golf shoes must be worn. Tuition available; golf shop; buggies for hire all year round (depending on weather). *Society Meetings:* welcome, telephone in advance. Professional: Larry Batchelor.*
e-mail: larry@southernvalley.co.uk

HALSTEAD. **Broke Hill Golf Club,** Sevenoaks Road, Halstead, Kent TN14 7HR (01959 533225; Fax: 01959 532680). *Location:* four minutes from M25 Junction 4, A21, four miles from Bromley and two miles from Orpington. Parkland course, with strategically placed bunkers and 5 holes where water comes into play. 18 holes, 6415 yards. S.S.S. 71. Two practice grounds. *Green Fees:* information not available. *Eating facilities:* lounge bar, restaurant and banqueting facilities. *Visitors:* welcome weekdays only, strict dress code applies. Soft spikes. Golf buggies and carts available. *Society Meetings:* weekdays only. Professional: Iain Naylor (01959 533810; Fax: 01959 532680). General Manager: Jon Pleydell (01959 533225; Fax: 01959 532680).*

HAWKHURST. **Hawkhurst Golf Club,** High Street, Hawkhurst TN18 4JS (01580 752396; Fax: 01580 754074). *Location:* on A268 from Flimwell to Hawkhurst. Undulating parkland. 9 holes, 5751 yards. S.S.S. 68. Practice ground. *Green Fees:* information not available. *Eating facilities:* bar, spike bar, dining room. *Visitors:* welcome. Handicap Certificate recommended. Squash courts. Trolleys and buggies are available for hire. *Society Meetings:* welcome. Professional: Peter Chandler (Tel & Fax: 01580 752396).*
e-mail: hawkhurstgolfclub@tiscali.co.uk
website: www.hawkhurstgolfclub.org.uk

HEADCORN. **Weald of Kent Golf Course,** Maidstone Road, Headcorn TN27 9PT (01622 890866; Fax: 01622 890070). *Location:* Junction 8 M20, five miles south of Maidstone on A274. Scenic undulating parkland course featuring a range of natural hazards, including waterways, lakes and ditches. 18 holes, 6310 yards. S.S.S. 70. *Green Fees:* from £23.00 per person for 18 holes. *Eating facilities:* spacious architect designed clubhouse, extensive bar menu available 7.00am till 9.30pm. Banqueting and conference facilities also available (30 to 200 delegates). *Visitors:* welcome anytime, bookings available seven days in advance (01622 890866). Hotel accommodation. Golf Breaks available (01622 890866). *Society Meetings:* welcome 7 days, weekends subject to availability; booking required in advance, minimum 12. Director of Golf: Rob Golding.

HERNE BAY. **Herne Bay Golf Club,** Eddington, Herne Bay CT6 7PG (01227 373964). *Location:* off the New Thanet Way. Parkland/links course. 18 holes, 5567 yards. S.S.S. 68. Practice ground. *Green Fees:* information not available. *Eating facilities:* bar meals, restaurant by arrangement. *Visitors:* welcome weekdays unrestricted, weekends and Bank Holidays after 12 noon only. Handicap Certificate required. *Society Meetings:* welcome by prior arrangement. Professional: D. Ledingham (01227 374727).*

HEVER. **Hever Castle Golf Club,** Hever, Edenbridge TN8 7NP (01732 700771; Fax: 01732 700775). *Location:* from M25 Junction 5 or 6 follow signs to Hever Castle. The golf club is one mile east of the castle on the same road. Parkland, wooded. 27 holes. Kings and Queens course (Championship Course): 18 holes, 7002 yards. S.S.S. 74. Princes course: 9 holes, 2784 yards. S.S.S. 67 (for 18 holes). Large practice range, chipping and pitching areas, practice bunker, putting green. *Green Fees:* Championship Course - £40.00 Monday to Thursday, £50.00 Friday to Sunday. *Eating facilities:* restaurant and bars. *Visitors:* welcome by appointment. *Society Meetings:* welcome by prior arrangement; competitive rates available. Head PGA Professional: Peter Parks. General Manager: Jon Wittenberg.
website: www.hever.co.uk

HYTHE. **Mercure Hythe Imperial Hotel Spa & Golf Club,** Princes Parade, Hythe CT21 6AE (01303 267441). *Location:* come off M20 Junction 11, directions for Hythe A261. Flat seaside course. 9 holes, 5533 yards. S.S.S. 67. Practice ground. *Green Fees:* information not available. *Eating facilities:* available at the hotel. *Visitors:* welcome at all times except weekends up to 1pm. *Society Meetings:* welcome, please call for more information. Professional: Simon Wood. Professional Shop: (01303 233745).*

LYDD. **Lydd Golf Club and Driving Range,** Romney Road, Lydd, Romney Marsh TN29 9LS (01797 320808; Fax: 01797 321482). *Location:* B2075 within half a mile of Lydd Airport. Traditional links course with added water hazards. 18 holes, 6517 yards. S.S.S. 71. 20 bay floodlit driving range. *Green Fees:* information not provided. *Eating facilities:* bar and restaurant. *Visitors:* no restrictions. Pull trolleys, electric trolleys and golf carts. *Society Meetings:* welcome, discount rates available. Pro Shop: (01797 321201). Secretary: Keith Osbourne (01797 320808; Fax: 01797 321482).

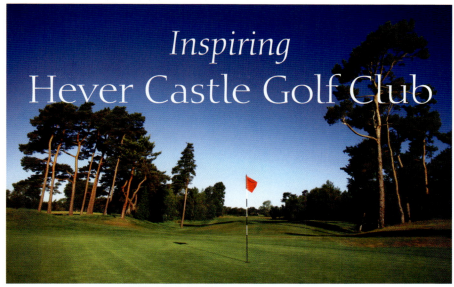

We invite you to visit us and experience the full range of outstanding facilities that we have to offer:

- 27 Holes of stunning golf on the Hever Estate: The Championship 18 Hole Course & Princes 9.
- Full Practice Facilities including: Driving Range, Chipping Area, Putting Green.
- Group Golf Packages available all year round.
  Organisers complimentary with groups of 21 or more.
- Luxury Accommodation at Hever Castle, including private entrance via golf buggy to the Club.
- Membership with some of the best benefits available to club golfers.
- Bar, lounge, restaurant and large function facilities open to all.

For more information please contact us on
01732 700771

100 Kent / SOUTH REGION

MAIDSTONE. Bearsted Golf Club, Ware Street, Bearsted ME14 4PQ (01622 738198). *Location:* Junction 7 off M20, turn right to Bearsted and follow signs. Undulating parkland course with view of North Downs. 18 holes, 6320 yards, 5739 metres. S.S.S. 71. Practice area, putting green, net. *Green Fees:* £34.00/£42.00 weekdays; weekends with a member. *Eating facilities:* bar/restaurant, open all day. *Visitors:* welcome weekdays, weekends must be with members. Current Handicap Certificates required. *Society Meetings:* catered for Mondays to Fridays by prior arrangement. Professional: Tim Simpson (01622 738024). Secretary: S. Turner (01622 738198; Fax: 01622 735608).

MAIDSTONE. Cobtree Manor Park Golf Club, Chatham Road, Sandling, Maidstone ME14 3AZ (01622 753276). *Location:* M20, A229 Chatham (not Maidstone). Undulating course with trees, and interesting 12th hole over lake. 18 holes, 5611 yards. S.S.S. 69. Tuition, practice, putting. *Green Fees:* information not available. *Eating facilities:* restaurant and bar. *Visitors:* welcome, book six days in advance through Professional. *Society Meetings:* welcome phone (01622 751881). Professional: Cameron McKillop (01622 753276).*

MAIDSTONE. Leeds Castle Golf Course, Leeds Castle, Near Maidstone ME17 1PL (01622 767828). *Location:* M20 Junction 8, A20 near Maidstone. Situated in the grounds of Leeds Castle, parkland. 9 holes, 2681 yards. S.S.S. 33. Putting green and practice nets. *Green Fees:* information not available. *Eating facilities:* Leeds Castle Restaurant on Leeds Castle Estate. *Visitors:* welcome anytime, bookings taken from six days in advance. Correct dress must be worn - no denim jeans allowed, golf shoes preferred. *Society Meetings:* welcome weekdays. Professional: Steve Purves.*

MAIDSTONE. Marriott Tudor Park Hotel and Country Club, Ashford Road, Bearsted, Maidstone ME14 4NQ (01622 734334). *Location:* east of Maidstone, on A20 at Bearsted. Off Junction 8 of M20. Parkland. 18 holes, 6085 yards. S.S.S. 69. Practice area. *Green Fees:* information not available. *Eating facilities:* restaurants and bars. *Visitors:* Hotel with 120 bedrooms, leisure and conference facilities. *Society Meetings:* Societies and Company Days catered for. Professional: to be arranged (01622 739412). Secretary: John Ladbrooke (01622 737119). Golf Director: Tim Hayman.*
website: www.marriotttudorpark.co.uk

MAIDSTONE. The Ridge Golf Club, Chartway Street, East Sutton, Maidstone ME17 3JB (01622 844382; Fax: 01622 844286). *Location:* Junction 8 M20, past Leeds Castle on Sutton Valence Road to A274 turn left and first turning on left. 18 holes, 6254 yards. S.S.S. 71. Driving range. *Green Fees:* on request. *Eating facilities:* bar snack menu and full menu. *Visitors:* welcome. *Society Meetings:* welcome Monday to Sunday. (01622 844382).

THE GOLF GUIDE 2011

MAIDSTONE. West Malling Golf Club, London Road, Addington, West Malling ME19 5AR (01732 844785). *Location:* M20, A228 turn off. Parkland/wooded course. Spitfire Course - 18 holes, 6142 yards. S.S.S. 70. Hurricane Course - 18 holes, 6300 yards. S.S.S 70. Practice ground. *Green Fees:* information not available. *Visitors:* welcome weekdays anytime, weekends after 12 noon. Conference/function facilities available. Buggies available. *Society Meetings:* catered for byprior arrangement. Professional: Duncan Lambert (01732 844022). Secretary: Mike Ellis (01732 844785).

NEW ROMNEY. Littlestone Golf Club, St Andrews Road, Littlestone, New Romney TN28 8RB (01797 362231; Fax: 01797 362740). *Location:* M20 Junction 10 (Ashford), B2070 to Brenzett - New Romney, one mile from New Romney. Seaside Championship links course. Local final qualifying venue for The Open in 2011. 18 holes, Blue tees 6676 yards, S.S.S. 73, White tees 6486 yards, S.S.S 72. Practice range, practice ground, chipping and putting greens. *Green Fees:* weekdays £65.00. *Eating facilities:* full dining room and bar. *Visitors:* Handicap Certificate required. Visitors restricted at weekends. 4-balls on Wednesdays; singles and foursomes at all other times. Caddie cars available. *Society Meetings:* welcome. Professional: Andrew Jones (01797 362231). Secretary: Stuart Fullager (01797 363355; Fax: 01797 362740).
e-mail: secretary@littlestonegolfclub.org.uk
website: www.littlestonegolfclub.org.uk

NEW ROMNEY. Littlestone Warren, St Andrews Road, Littlestone, New Romney TN28 8RB (01797 362231; Fax: 01797 362740). *Location:* one mile from New Romney off A259, down B2070; 20 minutes from J10 on M20. Undulating seaside links crisscrossed with dykes. 18 holes, 5126 yards. S.S.S. 67. Practice range. *Green Fees:* weekdays £22.00. *Eating facilities:* bar and restaurant. *Visitors:* welcome. *Society Meetings:* welcome by arrangement. Professional: Andrew Jones. Secretary: Stuart Fullager.
website: www.littlestonegolfclub.org.uk

ORPINGTON. Chelsfield Lakes Golf Centre, Court Road, Orpington BR6 9BX (01689 896266; Fax: 01689 824577). *Location:* M25 Junction 4, A224 Court Road. Gently undulating course with hazards and sandtraps; played through some orchards. 18 holes, 6077 yards. S.S.S. 69. 9 holes, 1188 yards. Par 3. 40 bay floodlit driving range, practice area. *Green Fees:* information not available. *Eating facilities:* bar and restaurant. *Visitors:* welcome, pay as you play facility, non members can book 7 days in advance. Pro shop. *Society Meetings:* welcome. Professionals: Nigel Lee, Bill Hodkin.*

ORPINGTON. Cray Valley Golf Club, Sandy Lane, St. Paul's Cray, Orpington BR5 3HY. *Location:* Ruxley roundabout A20; turn off into Sandy Lane, half a mile on left. Parkland. 18 holes, 5624 yards. S.S.S. 67. Also 9 hole course. *Green Fees:* information not available. *Eating facilities:* hot meals available lunchtimes, also bar. *Visitors:* welcome all week. *Society Meetings:* welcome. Professional: Gary Stewart (01689 837909). General Manager: Tom Ashman (01689 839677).*

www.holidayguides.com

Littlestone Golf Club

Come to Littlestone Golf Club for links golf at its very best. The Championship Course will again be a local final qualifying venue for The Open in 2011.

01797 363355

secretary@littlestonegolfclub.org.uk
www.littlestonegolfclub.org.uk

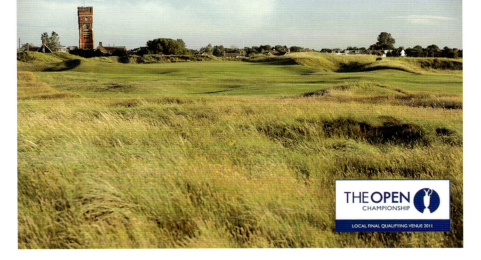

ORPINGTON. **Lullingstone Park Golf Club,** Park Gate Road, Chelsfield, Near Orpington, Kent BR6 7PX (01959 533794). *Location:* two miles from Junction 4 off M25, fifth exit on left (signposted). Undulating parkland. 18 holes, 6734 yards. S.S.S. 72. 9 holes, 2379 yards. Par 33. 22 bay driving range, pitch and putt course, putting green. *Green Fees:* information not available. *Eating facilities:* cafeteria and bar. *Visitors:* bookings welcome. *Society Meetings:* very welcome, telephone Professional for package details. Professional: Mark Watt (01959 533793; Fax: 01959 534129). Secretary: Chris Pocock.*

ORPINGTON. **Orpington Golf Centre,** Sandy Lane, St. Pauls Cray, Orpington BR5 3HY (01689 871490; Fax: 01689 891428). *Location:* off old A20 at Ruxley Corner. 53 holes, Par 71, 71, 32 and Academy course. 28 bays, covered, floodlit, grassed. *Green Fees:* information not available. *Eating facilities:* breakfast, lunch available, bar open all day. *Society Meetings:* welcome all week. Head Professional: Brad McLean. General Manager: Russell Mayne.*

ORPINGTON. **West Kent Golf Club**, Milking Lane, Downe, Near Orpington BR6 7LD (01689 851323). *Location:* from Downe village south along Luxted Lane, 600 yards turn right into West Hill. 18 holes, 6426 yards. S.S.S. 70. *Green Fees:* £45.00 per round, £55.00 per day. *Eating facilities:* meals by arrangement. *Visitors:* welcome weekdays only with recognised Handicap. Casual golfers should phone at least 24 hours in advance. *Society Meetings:* catered for. Professional: C.W. Forsyth (Tel & Fax: 01689 856863). Secretary: Sean Trussell (01689 851323).

RAMSGATE. **Manston Golf Centre,** Manston Road, Manston, Ramsgate CT12 5BE (01843 590005). *Location:* a quarter mile east of Manston village on the B2050. Flat seaside course with superb views across the English Channel. 9 holes, 4958 yards. Par 66. *Green Fees:* weekdays £8.00 9 holes; weekends £10.00 for 9 holes. 20-bay floodlit covered driving range. Grass tees and shortgame area with bunkers and two putting greens. Four "Positive Impact" PGA qualified coaches. *Eating facilities:* snacks and drinks. *Visitors:* unrestricted. *Society Meetings:* groups of 8 or more. Secretary. Professional: Philip Sparks (01843 590005).
e-mail: philip@manstongolf.co.uk
website: www.manstongolf.co.uk

RAMSGATE. **St Augustine's Golf Club,** Cottington Road, Cliffsend, Ramsgate CT12 5JN (01843 590333; Fax: 01843 590444). *Location*: two miles south-west of Ramsgate – approaching from A253 or A256 follow signs to St Augustine's Cross. Entrance 75 yards beyond Cross by railway bridge. Mainly parkland, flat - tight and challenging course. 18 holes, 5129 yards. S.S.S. 65. *Green Fees*: information not available. *Eating facilities*: usual bar facilities; catering available 9am to 3.30pm daily; Fridays also 6.30pm to 10.30pm. *Visitors*: welcome, advisable to ring Professional the day before to check periods booked for matches; booking necessary Saturdays and Sundays (Sundays visitors only after 1pm). To book golf phone Professional shop (01843 590222). *Society Meetings*: catered for, book through Secretary. Dormy flat available - ring Secretary. Professional: D. Scott (01843 590222). Secretary: R. F. Tranckle (01843 590333).
website: www.staugustinesgolfclub.co.uk

Golf from £8. Pay and Play nine hole links-style course and 20-bay range, only 7 miles from the 2011 Open venue at Royal St George's Golf Club, Sandwich.
Book tee times on 01843 590005
www.manstongolf.co.uk

Manston Golf Centre
Manston, Ramsgate, Kent CT12 5BE

St. Augustine's Golf Club is a private members club that prides itself on being very warm and welcoming to visitors. Compact and well maintained, it is reasonably flat, with some challenging holes. Visitors are welcome; special off-peak rates.
Friendly bar and restaurant.

St.Augustines Golf Club
Cottington Road, Cliffsend, Ramsgate, Kent CT12 5JN
Tel : 01843 590333 • Fax : 01843 590444
email : info@staugustinesgolfclub.co.uk • www.staugustinesgolfclub.co.uk

SOUTH REGION / Kent

RAMSGATE. Stonelees Golf Centre, Ebbsfleet Lane, Near Ramsgate CT12 5DJ (01843 823133); Fax: 01843 850569). *Location:* near junction of A256 and B2048 (Ebbsfleet Lane). Undulating seaside/ parkland courses. Three 9 hole courses. The Executive, 1471 yards, S.S.S. 29; The Par 3, 1159 yards, S.S.S. 27; The Heights, a full length 9-hole course, 2908 yards, S.S.S. 34, Par 35. Excellent teaching facilities, 22 bay driving range, Golf simulator, practice putting green, chipping area, miniature putting course. Function/conference room, showers, changing rooms, American Golf Shop. *Green Fees:* Executive – weekdays £7.10 9 holes, £10.80 18 holes; weekends £7.70 9 holes, £11.40 18 holes. Par 3 – weekdays £5.10 9 holes, £8.50 18 holes; weekends £6.10 9 holes, £9.60 18 holes. Heights – weekdays £9.50 9 holes, £14.50 18 holes, weekends £12.00 9 holes, £16.50 18 holes. 2010 rates (subject to review). Junior rates and membership discounts available. *Eating facilities:* licensed bar, restaurant. *Visitors:* always welcome, no restrictions. *Society Meetings:* small societies/groups welcome. Professional: David Bonthron. Manager: R.J. Chapman.
e-mail: stonelees@stonelees.com
website: www.stonelees.co.uk

ROCHESTER. Rochester and Cobham Park Golf Club, Park Pale, by Rochester ME2 3UL (01474 823411; Fax: 01474 824446). *Location:* A2, Shorne, Cobham turn off. Open championship regional qualifying course. Undulating parkland. 18 holes, 6597 yards. S.S.S. 72. Extensive practice facilities. *Green Fees:* weekdays £40.00 per round, £50.00 per day. *Eating facilities:* morning coffee, lunch, tea, dinner available, two bars. *Visitors:* welcome midweek only with Handicap Certificate. *Society Meetings:* welcome Tuesdays and Thursdays, must be pre-booked. Professional: Warren Wood (01474 823658). Manager: John Aughterlony (01474 823411; Fax: 01474 824446).

SANDWICH. Royal St. George's Golf Club, Sandwich CT13 9PB (01304 613090; Fax: 01304 611245). *Location:* one mile from Sandwich on the road to Sandwich Bay. From Canterbury A257, from Dover A258. Links. 18 holes, Championship 7204 yards, Medal 6630 yards. S.S.S. Championship 74, Medal 72. Practice ground. *Green Fees:* £140.00 for one round, £180.00 for two rounds weekdays. 2010 rates (subject to review). *Eating facilities:* snack bar and dining room. *Visitors:* welcome weekdays only, must be pre-booked. No visitors at weekends or on Public Holidays. Must have Handicap Certificate (under 18) and be member of club affiliated to EGU. Caddies to be booked in advance, trolleys available. *Society Meetings:* catered for by arrangement. All players must meet requirements for visitors. Professional: A. Brooks (01304 615236). Secretary: H.C.G. Gabbey (01304 613090; Fax: 01304 611245). Caddiemaster: (01304 626931).

SANDWICH BAY. Prince's Golf Club, Prince's Drive, Sandwich Bay, Sandwich CT13 9QB (01304 611118; Fax: 01304 612000). *Location:* four miles from Sandwich through the Sandwich Bay Estate. Seaside links. 27 holes arranged as 3 loops of 9 holes named "Dunes", "Himalayas", "Shore". D & H 6262 - 6776 yards, Par 71, S.S.S. 70-73. H & S 6238 - 6813 yards, Par 71, S.S.S. 70-73. S & D 6466-7204 yards, Par 72, S.S.S. 71-73. Championship 7204 yards. Driving range, full practice facilities. *Green Fees:* information not provided. *Eating facilities:* breakfast, lunch, available every day; bar; light snacks throughout the day. Dinner by arrangement. *Visitors & Societies:* welcome without restriction, Company days and private parties catered for. Brochure available on request. Professional: Rob McGuirk (01304 613797). Information & Bookings: David Holder (01304 611118). General Manager: Michael Lovett (01304 626909; Fax: 01304 612000).
e-mail: office@princesgolfclub.co.uk
website: www.princesgolfclub.co.uk

SEVENOAKS. Knole Park Golf Club, Seal Hollow Road, Sevenoaks TN15 0HJ (01732 452150; Fax: 01732 463159). *Location:* one mile north-east of Sevenoaks town centre. Deer Park; beautiful, natural course. Second to none in the South East. 18 holes, 6246 yards. S.S.S. 70. Practice ground and nets. *Green Fees:* weekdays only, £42.00 per round, £52.00 per day. 2010 rates (subject to review). *Eating facilities:* full bar and catering. *Visitors:* welcome by appointment, Handicap Certificate required. Squash courts. *Society Meetings:* catered for by arrangement only. Professional: (01732 451740). General Manager: Robert Brewer (01732 452150; Fax: 01732 463159).
website: www.knoleparkgolfclub.co.uk

SEVENOAKS. Wildernesse Club, Park Lane, Seal, Sevenoaks TN15 0JE (01732 761199). Location: A25 between Sevenoaks and Borough Green. Park and woodland. 18 holes, 6532 yards. S.S.S. 71. Large practice ground. *Green Fees:* £60.00 per round. *Eating facilities:* by arrangement. *Visitors:* welcome weekdays only by prior arrangement; Handicap Certificate required. *Society Meetings:* catered for Mondays, Thursdays and Fridays. Professional: Craig Walker (01732 761527). Secretary: Major (Retd) K.P. Loosemore (01732 761199).

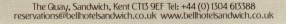

the bell hotel sandwich — A short iron from Kent's best courses.
The Quay, Sandwich, Kent CT13 9EF Tel: +44 (0) 1304 613388
reservations@bellhotelsandwich.co.uk   www.bellhotelsandwich.co.uk

Kent / SOUTH REGION

SEVENOAKS. Darenth Valley Golf Course Ltd, Station Road, Shoreham, Near Sevenoaks TN14 7SA (01959 522944; Fax: 01959 525089). *Location:* A225 between Otford and Eynsford, approximately four miles north of Sevenoaks. Pay and play parkland course. 18 holes, 6193 yards. S.S.S. 72. Practice area, putting green. *Green Fees:* weekdays £20.00; weekends £25.00. *Eating facilities:* bar snacks and meals; functions up to 150 covers. *Visitors:* welcome with reservation through Pro shop. *Society Meetings:* welcome by arrangement. Professionals Shop: (01959 522922). Clubhouse Manager: Deborah Terry (01959 522944; Fax: 01959 525089).
e-mail: enquiries@dvgc.co.uk
website: www.dvgc.co.uk

SEVENOAKS. Woodlands Manor Golf Club, Tinkerpot Lane, Woodlands, Near Otford, Sevenoaks TN15 6AB (01959 523806). *Location:* Junction 3, M25 take "Brands Hatch" sign on A20, seven miles. Parkland, designated Area of Outstanding Natural Beauty. 18 holes, 6100 yards. S.S.S. 69. Six acre practice ground. *Green Fees:* information not available. *Eating facilities:* bar daily. *Visitors:* welcome weekdays, weekends after 1pm. Buggies for hire. *Society Meetings:* welcome by arrangement Monday to Friday. On-line booking system. Professional: Philip Womack. Secretary: C.G. Robins (01959 523806).*
website: www.woodlandsmanorgolf.co.uk

SEVENOAKS. Wrotham Heath Golf Club, Seven Mile Lane, Comp, Sevenoaks TN15 8QZ (01732 884800). *Location:* on B2016 half-a-mile south of junction with A20. Woodland/heathland. 18 holes, 5994 yards. S.S.S. 70. *Green Fees:* information not available. *Eating facilities:* bar and snacks, meals by arrangement, except Mondays. *Visitors:* welcome on weekdays with Handicap Certificate, but not Bank Holidays. *Society Meetings:* catered for Thursdays and Fridays only, no more than 30 people. Professional: H. Dearden (01732 883854). Secretary: J. Hodgson (01732 884800).

SHEERNESS. Sheerness Golf Club, Power Station Road, Sheerness ME12 3AE (01795 662585). *Location:* follow A249 then A250 towards Sheerness. Flat marshland/meadowland; numerous water hazards. 18 holes, 6390 yards. S.S.S. 71. Practice area. *Green Fees:* weekdays £22.00 per round, £31.00 per day; weekends £28.00 per round (by appointment only). *Eating facilities:* available. *Visitors:* weekdays only except with member. *Society Meetings:* catered for weekdays by previous arrangement. Secretary: D. Nehra.
e-mail: secretary@sheernessgolfclub.co.uk

SIDCUP. Sidcup Golf Club, rear of Hurstmere School, Hurst Road, Sidcup DA15 9AW. *Location:* A222 near Sidcup Station. Parkland. 9 holes, 5571 yards. S.S.S. 68. *Green Fees:* on application. *Eating facilities:* restaurant and bar. *Visitors:* welcome Monday to Thursday except Bank Holidays. *Society Meetings:* not catered for. Secretary: Steve Armstrong (020 8300 2150).
e-mail: sidcupgolfclub@googlemail.com
website: www.sidcupgolfclub.co.uk

SITTINGBOURNE. The Oast Golf Centre Ltd, Church Road, Tonge, Sittingbourne ME9 9AR (01795 473527). *Location:* one mile north A2 between Faversham and Sittingbourne, take the turning to Tonge at Bapchild. 9-hole par 3 course. 17 bay covered floodlit driving range. *Green Fees:* 9 holes £6.00, 18 holes £8.00. *Eating facilities:* sandwiches, rolls. *Visitors:* welcome. Tuition available, golf shop. Two short mat bowls facility. *Society Meetings:* welcome. Professional: David Chambers. Secretary: Sally Chambers.
e-mail: info@oastgolf.co.uk

SITTINGBOURNE. Sittingbourne and Milton Regis, Wormdale, Newington, Sittingbourne ME9 7PX (01795 842261). *Location:* Junction 5 M2, follow signs to Danaway Chestnut Street, three quarters of a mile, first left over Bridge to Wormdale. Gently undulating tree-lined course. 18 holes, 6291 yards, 5771 metres. S.S.S. 70. *Green Fees:* 18 holes £32.00, 36 holes £42.00. No visitors weekends. *Eating facilities:* available. *Visitors:* welcome weekdays. *Society Meetings:* catered for Tuesdays and Thursdays by arrangement. Professional: J. Hearn (01795 842775). Manager: Charles Maxted.

SITTINGBOURNE near. Upchurch River Valley Golf Courses, Oak Lane, Upchurch, near Sittingbourne ME9 7AY (01634 360626; Fax: 01634 387784). *Location:* M2, Junction 4 (A278) or Junction 5 (A249) onto A2 between Rainham and Newington, Oak Lane (opposite Little Chef). Undulating parkland with ponds and panoramic views. 18 holes, 6237 yards, 5701 metres. S.S.S. 70. 9 holes, 1596 yards,

Darenth Valley
GOLF COURSE

Ideally situated for access from J3, 4, 5 of M25 and M20, we specialise in value pay and play golf on our excellently maintained, picturesque 18 hole parkland course.
A warm welcome is offered to individuals, society and corporate groups.
Advance booking essential either by phone or online.

www.dvgc.co.uk

Station Road, Shoreham, Near Sevenoaks, Kent TN14 7SA
T: 01959 522922 (Pro Shop) • T: 01959 522944 (Clubhouse)

Par 30. Driving range. *Green Fees:* information not available. *Eating facilities:* 120 seater à la carte restaurant, all day food and drinks lounge. *Visitors:* unrestricted. Swimming pool. *Society Meetings:* welcome weekdays. Professional: Roger Cornwell (01634 379592). Secretary: (Members only) D. Candy (01634 260594). Course Controller: URVGC Ltd.*

SNODLAND. **Oastpark Golf Course,** Sandhole, Malling Road, Snodland ME6 5LG (01634 242661). *Location*: half a mile from M20, two miles from M2; five miles from Maidstone. Easy walking, good test of golf, lots of water/sand/trees. 9 holes, 3150 yards. S.S.S. 70. Extensive practice facilities. Floodlit driving range. *Green Fees:* information not available. *Eating facilities:* full bar and catering service. *Visitors:* welcome, no restrictions. No jeans, tracksuits; golf shoes must be worn. *Society Meetings:* all welcome weekdays, and weekends after 11am. Professional: David Porthouse (01634 242661). Secretary: Mrs Lesley Murrock (01634 242818; Fax: 01634 240744).*

SWANLEY. **Pedham Place Golf Centre,** London Road, Swanley BR8 8PP (01322 867000; Fax: 01322 861646). *Location:* 300 yards east of Junction 3 M25, on A20 towards Brands Hatch. Two elevated links-style courses. 18 holes, 6444 yards. S.S.S. 71, Par 72; 9 holes, 1165 yards, Par 3. 40-bay floodlit driving range, putting green, practice facilities. *Green Fees:* information not available. *Eating facilities:* bar snacks to full meals; licensed bar. Modern marquee for larger groups. *Visitors:* all welcome. Thursday morning Ladies' day, Wednesday morning Veterans. Appropriate clothing/footwear must be worn. Buggy hire available. *Societies:* welcome, special rates available. Sales: Beverley Smith. Head Professional: John Woodroffe.*
e-mail: golf@ppgc.co.uk
website: www.ppgc.co.uk

TATSFIELD. **Park Wood Golf Club,** Chestnut Avenue, Tatsfield, Near Westerham TN16 2EG (01959 577744; Fax: 01959 577765). *Location:* on B2024 Croydon road which becomes Clarks Lane. At Church Hill junction join Chestnut Avenue. In an area of natural beauty, flanked by an ancient woodland, with superb views across Kent and Surrey. Undulating course, tree-lined and with some interesting water features. Playable in all weather. 18 holes, 6835 yards. Par 72. S.S.S. 72. Course record 66. *Green Fees:* information not available. *Visitors:* telephone in advance. May not play on Bank Holidays. *Societies:* apply in writing/ telephone (01959 577744). Professional: Nick Terry.
e-mail: john@parkwoodgolf.co.uk
website: www.parkwoodgolf.co.uk

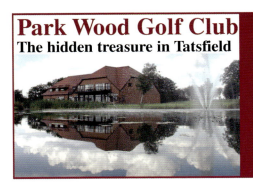

TENTERDEN. **Tenterden Golf Club,** Woodchurch Road, Tenterden TN30 7DR (Tel & Fax: 01580 763987). *Location*: 15 minutes from J9 M20 - A28 - Tenterden. 30 minutes from Channel Tunnel and west of Ashford International Station, on B2067 Woodchurch Road, Tenterden. Parkland course set in beautiful undulating Wealden countryside. 18 holes, 6152 yards. S.S.S. 70. Practice ground. *Visitors:* welcome. 2-4-1 accepted, buggies available, check website for special offers. *Eating facilities:* available, breakfast on request, lunch, snacks and dinner, all day bar. *Society Meetings:* telephone for details.
e-mail: enquiries@tenterdengolfclub.co.uk
website: www.tenterdengolfclub.co.uk

TENTERDEN. **London Beach Golf Club,** Ashford Road, Tenterden TN30 6HX (01580 766279; Fax: 01580 763884). *Location*: A28 Tenterden. Parkland course. 9 holes, 3018 yards. S.S.S. 71 (18 holes). Putting, pitch and putt, driving range (members only). *Green Fees:* information not available. *Eating facilities:* restaurant and bar. *Visitors*: welcome; restrictions Tuesday, Wednesday and Sunday before midday. Tuition available, book in advance. Hotel accommodation; golf breaks catered for. *Society Meetings:* welcome by arrangement. Professional: Mark Chilcott. Secretary: Pierre Edmonds.*
e-mail: enquiries@londonbeach.com
website: www.londonbeach.com

TONBRIDGE. **Hilden Golf Centre,** Hilden Park, Rings Hill, Hildenborough, Tonbridge TN11 8LX (01732 833607; Fax: 01732 834484). *Location*: take exit off A21 for Tonbridge North/Hildenborough; take second turning right (Watts Cross Road), follow road past station to bottom of the hill, golf centre is on the left. 36 bay covered, floodlit driving range with PowerTee. *Green Fees:* information not available. *Eating facilities:* fully licensed cafe bar open 8am to 10pm. all year round. Opening hours: Monday to Thursday 8am to 10pm, Friday to Sunday 7.30am to 9pm. Five PGA professionals (tuition available), large golf shop, 9 hole golf course and putting green. Leisure centre and crèche. Teaching academy and large golf discount store stocking all the top brands at discount prices. Professionals: Nick McNally, Karl Steptoe, Oliver Brown, Nicky Way and Rupert Hunter. Secretary: Jan Parfett (01732 834404; Fax: 01732 834484).*

TONBRIDGE. **Nizels Golf Club,** Nizels Lane, Hildenborough, Near Tonbridge TN11 8NU (01732 833833; Fax: 01732 833492). *Location:* M25 B245 off A21. Take signs to Tonbridge North, club one mile, Nizels Lane. Undulating parkland, several holes where water comes into play, many mature trees. 18 holes, 6361 yards off white tees. S.S.S. 71. Par 72. Limited practice area. *Green Fees:* information not available. *Eating facilities:* bar snacks and fine dining available. *Visitors:* welcome weekdays after 9.30am. Pro shop. *Society Meetings:* weekdays only after 9.30am. Professional: Ashley Weller (01732 838926). General Manager: Patrick Ferguson.*
website: www.theclubcompany.com

TONBRIDGE. **Poult Wood Public Golf Centre,** Higham Lane, Tonbridge TN11 9QR (01732 364039). *Location:* signposted from the A26 between Hadlow and Tonbridge. Parkland, very wooded. 18 holes, 5569 yards. S.S.S. 67. 9 hole course, driving range. *Green Fees:* visit website for details. *Eating facilities:* restaurant, bar, snack bar. *Visitors:* welcome every day. *Society Meetings:* welcome by booking only (01732 366180). Squash court. Professional: David Copsey (01732 364039).
website: www.poultwoodgolf.co.uk

TUNBRIDGE WELLS. **Lamberhurst Golf Club,** Church Road, Lamberhurst TN3 8DT (01892 890591; Fax: 01892 891140). *Location:* A21 from Tunbridge Wells to Hastings, take 3rd exit on roundabout towards Lamberhurst village, turn left prior to descending hill to Lamberhurst and golf club is on the right. Attractive parkland course. 18 holes, 6423 yards. S.S.S. 71. Small practice ground. *Green Fees:* available from website. *Eating facilities:* full catering by arrangement. *Visitors:* welcome after 8am weekdays, 12 noon weekends and Bank Holidays. Handicap Certificate required. *Society Meetings:* catered for Monday to Friday by arrangement. Professional: Brian Impett (01892 890552). Secretary: Mrs S. Deadman (01892 890591; Fax: 01892 891140).
e-mail: secretary@lamberhurstgolfclub.com
website: www.lamberhurstgolfclub.com

TUNBRIDGE WELLS. **Nevill Golf Club,** Benhall Mill Road, Tunbridge Wells TN2 5JW (01892 525818; Fax: 01892 517861). *Location:* off Forest Road, south of Tunbridge Wells. Parkland course with trees. 18 holes, 6349 yards. S.S.S. 70. Practice ground. *Green Fees:* weekdays £44.00 per round, £60.00 per day; weekends and Bank Holidays £60.00. *Eating facilities:* lunches at club by prior arrangement. *Visitors:* welcome with 48 hours notice. Handicap Certificate required. Trolley hire. *Society Meetings:* welcome with previous booking. Professional: Nick Duc (01892 532941). Secretary: F. Prescott (01892 525818; Fax: 01892 517861).
e-mail: manager@nevillgolfclub.co.uk
website: www.nevillgolfclub.co.uk

TUNBRIDGE WELLS. **Tunbridge Wells Golf Club,** Langton Road, Tunbridge Wells TN4 8XH (01892 523034). *Location:* adjoining Spa Hotel on A264. Parkland. 9 holes, 4725 yards. S.S.S. 62. *Green Fees:* information not available. *Eating facilities:* menu choices available daily best to check requirements in advance. *Visitors:* welcome anytime subject to availability. *Society Meetings:* welcome, contact the Secretary for details. Secretary: (01892 536918).*

WESTERHAM. **Westerham Golf Club,** Valence Park, Brasted Road, Westerham TN16 1LJ (01959 567100; Fax: 01959 567101). *Location*: midway between Westerham and Brasted on the A25. Mainly wooded with some parkland. 18 holes, 6270 yards. S.S.S. 72. Driving range and short game area. *Green Fees*: information not available. *Eating facilities*: bar and catering facilities available. *Visitors*: welcome

weekdays and weekends after 12 noon. Buggies and carts available for hire. *Society Meetings*: welcome any time weekdays, after 1pm weekends. Professional: James Marshall. General Manager: Rob Sturgeon.*
e-mail:caroline.waker@westerhamgc.co.uk
website: www. westerhamgc.co.uk

WESTGATE ON SEA. **Westgate and Birchington Golf Club,** 176 Canterbury Road, Westgate on Sea CT8 8LT. *Location:* seaside course between Westgate on Sea and Birchington (A28). Seaside links course. 18 holes, 4926 yards, 4547 metres. S.S.S. 63. *Green Fees:* weekdays £20.00, weekends and Bank Holidays £22.00 (includes £1.00 compulsory insurance). *Eating facilities:* available by prior arrangement with Steward. *Visitors:* welcome after 9.30am. *Society Meetings:* by arrangement with Secretary. Professional: M. Young (01843 831115). Secretary: T.J. Sharp (01843 831115).

WEST MALLING. **King's Hill Golf Club,** Discovery Drive, King's Hill, West Malling ME19 4GF (01732 875040; Fax: 01732 875019). *Location*: Junction 4 of M20. Heathland course. 18 holes, 6622 yards. S.S.S. 72. *Green Fees*: information not provided. *Eating facilities*: restaurant and bar open all day. *Visitors*: welcome seven days a week. Tuition available. *Society Meetings*: welcome Monday to Friday. Professional: David Hudspith (01732 842121). Secretary: Margaret Gilbert (01732 875040; Fax: 01732 875019).
e-mail: khatkhgolf@aol.com
website: www.kingshillgolf.co.uk

WHITSTABLE. **Chestfield (Whitstable) Golf Club,** 103 Chestfield Road, Chestfield, Whitstable CT5 3LU (01227 794411). *Location:* half a mile south of Old Thanet Way (A2990). Parkland with sea views. 18 holes, 6208 yards. S.S.S. 70. *Green Fees:* £36.00 midweek, £40.00 weekends. *Eating facilities:* lunchtime snacks, bar 11am to 11pm. Halfway House open for hot/cold snacks 7 days a week. *Visitors:* welcome. *Society Meetings:* welcome and catered for weekdays. Professional: David Ledingham (01227 793563).
e-mail: secretary@chestfield-golfclub.co.uk
website: www.chestfield-golfclub.co.uk

WHITSTABLE. **Whitstable and Seasalter Golf Club,** Collingwood Road, Whitstable CT5 1EB (01227 272020). *Location:* course adjoins town centre, take Nelson Road turning off main street. Flat seaside links. 9 holes, 5357 yards. S.S.S. 65. Practice net. *Green Fees:* information not available. *Eating facilities:* bar snacks. Secretary: M.D. Moore.*

THE APPEARANCE OF AN ASTERISK (*) AT THE END OF A CLUB OR COURSE ENTRY INDICATES THAT UP-TO-DATE INFORMATION HAS NOT BEEN SUPPLIED

Non-members and beginners welcome
"A genuine learning experience"
Teaching Academy
No temporary greens or tees
5 minutes from Junction 4 M20
Advance booking available
Pro Shop 01732 842121

Kings Hill Golf Club, Fortune Way, Kings Hill, West Malling, Kent ME19 4GF • Tel: 01732 875040
www.kingshillgolf.co.uk

Visit **www.holidayguides.com**
for convenient accommodation
when playing golf around the regions

Oxfordshire

ABINGDON. **Frilford Heath Golf Club,** Abingdon OX13 5NW (01865 390864; Fax: 01865 390823). *Location:* on A338 Oxford/Wantage Road seven miles south-west of Oxford, four miles west of Abingdon. Flat, wooded heathland. Red course: 18 holes, 6617 yards yellow tees, 6884 white tees. S.S.S. 71/73; Green course: 18 holes, 5763 yards yellow tees, 6006 white tees. S.S.S. 69; Blue course: 18 holes, 6379 yards yellow tees, 6728 white tees. S.S.S. 71/72. Three practice areas. *Green Fees:* Summer: weekdays £75.00, weekends and Bank Holidays £90.00; Winter: weekdays £55.00, weekends and Bank Holidays £70.00. *Eating facilities:* first class restaurant and bars. *Visitors:* welcome weekdays with Handicap Certificate, phone ahead for weekends and Bank Holidays. *Society Meetings:* welcome weekdays, enquire at office. Professional: D.C. Craik (01865 390887). General Manager: A.B.W. James (01865 390864).
e-mail: events@frilfordheath.co.uk

BANBURY. **Banbury Golf Club,** Aynho Road, Adderbury, Banbury OX17 3NT (01295 810419; Fax: 01295 810056). *Location*: 6 miles south of Banbury on B4100. M40 junction 10 or 11. Undulating wooded course with water features. 18 holes, 6597 yards, S.S.S. 71. *Green Fees*: information not available. *Eating facilities*: bar menu and three-course meals available. *Visitors*: welcome at all times. Tuition available. *Society Meetings*: welcome at all times. Professional: (01295 812880; Fax: 01295 810056). Secretary: Angela Prestidge.*
e-mail: office@banburygolfclub.co.uk
website: www.banburygolfclub.co.uk

BANBURY. **Cherwell Edge Golf Club,** c/o Cherwell Edge Course, Chacombe, Banbury OX17 2EN (01295 711591). *Location:* half-a-mile off M40 at Banbury. Parkland. 18 holes, 6085 yards. S.S.S. 69 men, 69 ladies. Practice area. *Green Fees:* information not available. *Eating facilities:* restaurant and bar. *Visitors:* welcome, some time restrictions. *Society Meetings:* welcome, some time restrictions. Professional: Jason Newman (01295 711591). Manager: Dave Bridger (01295 711591).*

e-mail: enquiries@cherwelledgegolfclub.co.uk
website: www.cherwelledgegolfclub.co.uk

BANBURY. **Rye Hill Golf Club,** Milcombe, Banbury OX15 4RU (01295 721818; Fax: 01295 720089). *Location:* six miles from Junction 11 M40 at Banbury, turn off A361 and follow signs through to Milcombe. Naturally free draining course. 18 holes, 6919 yards. S.S.S 73. Practice ground and Junior Golf Parc. *Green Fees:* information not available. *Eating facilities:* spike bar and restaurant, conference venue for up to 300. *Visitors:* welcome, no restrictions. Booking advisable at weekends. Buggies available. Trolleys can always be used. *Society Meetings:* welcome; various packages available. Professional: T. Pennock.*
website: www.ryehill.co.uk

BANBURY. **Tadmarton Heath Golf Club,** Wigginton, Banbury OX15 5HL (01608 737278; Fax: 01608 730548). *Location:* off M40 Junction 11, off A422, off B4035, five miles west of Banbury. Flat links; heathland. 18 holes, 5936 yards. S.S.S. 69. Practice area. *Green Fees:* weekdays £45.00; weekends £25.00 with a member only. 2010 rates (subject to review). *Eating facilities:* full catering and bars. *Visitors:* welcome weekdays (restrictions Thursdays); weekends with member only. Must be member of another golf club with Handicap Certificate. Hand carts and buggies available. *Society Meetings:* welcome weekdays by prior arrangement. Professional: John Stubbs (01608 730047). Secretary: John Cox (01608 737278; Fax: 01608 730548).
e-mail: secretary@tadmartongolf.com
website: www.tadmartongolf.com

BICESTER. **Bicester Country Club,** Chesterton, Near Bicester OX26 1TE (01869 241204). *Location:* five minutes from Junction 9 M40, one mile off A421, Bicester/Oxford. Two miles south-west of Bicester. Flat parkland course. 18 holes, 6255 yards. S.S.S. 71. Driving range, bunker area and putting green. *Green Fees:* Monday to Friday £30.00, weekends £35.00. *Eating facilities:* fine dining

Frilford Heath Golf Club
Abingdon, Oxfordshire OX13 5NW

All telephone enquiries: 01865 390864
E-mail: reception@frilfordheath.co.uk • www.frilfordheath.co.uk

Frilford Heath is Oxfordshire's finest golf club, and one of the best in the south of England. Situated on 600 acres of glorious undulating heathland it is one of very few clubs with three full-length golf courses - 54 holes of top quality golf. Visitors are always welcome. Generally you can turn up and play, but it might be worth checking with the office first.

Green Fees
Weekdays £75.
Weekends &
Bank Holidays £90.
Juniors £20.

restaurant and bar meals available daily. *Visitors:* welcome at all times, telephone bookings up to four days ahead. *Society Meetings:* welcome by prior arrangement.
website: www.bicestercountryclub.com
www.bicesterhotelgolfandspa.com

BURFORD. **Burford Golf Club,** Burford OX18 4JG (01993 822583). *Location:* A40 - Burford roundabout. Flat parkland with superb greens. 18 holes, 6401 yards. S.S.S. 71. *Green Fees:* £40.00 per day weekdays. *Eating facilities:* full catering. *Visitors:* welcome weekdays and weekends by arrangement with the Secretary. *Society Meetings:* catered for on application. Professional: Michael Ridge (01993 822344). Secretary: Robin Thompson (01993 822583; Fax: 01993 822801).

CHIPPING NORTON. **Chipping Norton Golf Club,** Southcombe, Chipping Norton OX7 5QH (01608 642383; Fax: 01608 645422). *Location:* Junction of A3400 and A44, 18 miles from Oxford, 20 miles from Stratford-on-Avon. Downland with lakes and trees and four Par 3s. 18 holes, 6316 yards, 5830 metres. S.S.S. 70. Practice ground and putting green. *Green Fees:* information not available. *Eating facilities:* diningroom and bars - new clubhouse. *Visitors:* welcome Monday to Friday but not Bank Holidays. *Society Meetings:* welcome Mondays to Fridays by arrangement. Professional: Neil Rowlands (01608 643356; Fax: 01608 645422). Secretary/Manager: Neil Clayton (01608 642383; Fax: 01608 645422).*
website: www.chippingnortongolfclub.com

CHIPPING NORTON. **The Wychwood Golf Club,** Lyneham, Chipping Norton OX7 6QQ (01993 831841; Fax: 01993 831775). *Location:* six miles from Burford off the A361 Burford to Chipping Norton Road. Parkland, several interesting water holes. 18 holes, 6844 yards, 6099 metres. S.S.S. 72. Practice range (15 bays). Motorised buggies available for hire. *Green Fees:* information not available. *Eating facilities:* bar, dining room, lounge. *Visitors:* always welcome, can book start time three days in advance. *Society Meetings:* welcome, various packages available, assistance available for starting, score cards, notice board, etc. Licensed for Civil Ceremonies and available for private parties and receptions. Professional: Adam Souter. Administrator: Susan Lakin.

DIDCOT. **Hadden Hill Golf Club,** Wallingford Road, Didcot OX11 9BJ (01235 510410). *Location:* on A4130, half-a-mile east of Didcot on the Wallingford road. Well drained parkland with superb greens - never closed for rain! 18 holes, 6563 yards. S.S.S. 71. 6-hole Par 3 course now open. 20-bay floodlit driving range. *Green Fees:* weekdays £20.00 18 holes; £12.50 9 holes, weekends £25.00 18 holes; £15.00 9 holes. *Eating facilities:* good food all day, every day. *Visitors:* book tee times online or telephone Pro Shop. *Society Meetings:* very welcome anytime. Professional: Ian Mitchell (01235 510410). Secretary: Adrian Smith (01235 510410; Fax: 01235 511260).
website: www.haddenhillgolf.co.uk

DRAYTON. **Drayton Park Golf Course,** Steventon Road, Drayton, near Abingdon OX14 4LA (01235 528989; Fax: 01235 525731). *Location:* A34 Didcot turn off, through Steventon to Drayton (south of Oxford). 18 hole Par 70 golf course, 9 hole Par 3 course. Driving range. *Green Fees:* weekdays £20.00; weekends £26.00. *Eating facilities:* full catering and bar facilities. Clubhouse open to visitors. *Visitors:* welcome. Clubhouse available for conferences and weddings; large function room. *Society Meetings:* welcome. Professional: J. Draycott (01235 550607). Secretary: I. Rhead (01235 528989).
e-mail: draytonpark@btclick.com.

FARINGDON. **Carswell Golf and Country Club,** Carswell Home Farm, Carswell, Faringdon SN7 8PU (01367 870422). *Location*: just off A420 between Oxford and Swindon, near Faringdon. Parkland course with many trees and water hazards. 18 holes, 6200 yards. S.S.S. 72. 19-bay floodlit driving range, practice area with putting green. *Green Fees:* weekdays £20.00, weekends £28.00. Twilight fees available, telephone for more details and prices. *Eating facilities:* clubhouse bar serving varied menu. *Visitors:* welcome, soft spikes preferred. Golf shop; club, cart and buggy hire. Clubhouse accommodation - four en suite rooms. *Society Meetings:* all welcome weekdays, please telephone for information on packages. Health Club on site, call for details. Secretary: Sarah Sample (01367 870422).
e-mail: info@carswellgolfandcountryclub.co.uk
website: www.carswellgolfandcountryclub.co.uk

Burford Golf Club

Burford Golf Club, Burford, Oxfordshire OX18 4JG
Secretary/Manager:
Robin Thompson: 01993 822583
E-mail:
secretary@burfordgolfclub.co.uk
www.burfordgolfclub.co.uk

Burford Golf Club opened for play in 1936 and offers challenging first-class parkland golf. Noted for its high-quality greens, the Club proves a popular venue for visitors - individuals or small groups wishing to play should telephone the Pro Shop (01993 822344).

HENLEY-ON-THAMES. **Badgemore Park Golf Club,** Badgemore, Henley-on-Thames RG9 4NR (01491 637300). *Location*: one mile from Henley town centre on road to Rotherfield Greys. Mature parkland course. 18 holes, 6129 yards. S.S.S. 69. Chipping green, two putting greens, practice net, bunker practice. *Green Fees:* midweek £30.00, weekends £39.00. *Visitors*: always welcome, weekends after 11am. Professional lessons available. Large car park. Accommodation on site. *Society Meetings*: welcome Wednesdays, Thursdays, Fridays; weekend afternoons. Professional: Jonathan Dunn (01491 574175). Secretary: J. Connell (01491 637300; Fax: 01491 576899).

HENLEY-ON-THAMES. **Henley Golf Club,** Harpsden, Henley-on-Thames RG9 4HG (01491 575781). Centenary Year 2007. *Location*: from centre of Henley-Reading, one mile from Harpsden Way to clubhouse. Parkland with many trees. 18 holes, 6264 yards. S.S.S. 70. *Green Fees:* weekdays £45.00; weekends with member only £20.00. *Eating facilities:* bar snacks at all times, meals by arrangement. *Visitors:* welcome weekdays, weekends and Bank Holidays with a member only. Handicap Certificate required. *Society Meetings:* catered for Wednesdays and Thursdays. Professional: Mark Howell (01491 575710). Manager: Gary Oatham (01491 575742; Fax: 01491 412179).
e-mail: manager@henleygc.com
website: www.henleygc.com

HENLEY-ON-THAMES. **Huntercombe Golf Club,** Nuffield, Henley-on-Thames RG9 5SL (01491 641207). *Location:* A4130, six miles west of Henley-on-Thames. Downland wooded course. 18 holes, 6271 yards. S.S.S. 70. Practice ground. *Green Fees:* information not available. *Eating facilities:* catering and bar facilities. *Visitors:* welcome by prior arrangement only. *Society Meetings:* Tuesdays and Thursdays by arrangement. Professional: Ian Roberts (01491 641241). Secretary: Nick Jenkins (Fax: 01491 642060).*
e-mail: office@huntercombegolfclub.co.uk
website: www.huntercombegolfclub.co.uk

KIRTLINGTON. **Kirtlington Golf Club,** Lince Lane, Kirtlington OX5 3JY (01869 351133; Fax: 01869 351143). *Location:* A4095, Witney/Bicester, half a mile outside Kirtlington. Undulating, dry, open parkland course with well contoured greens. 18 holes, 6107 yards. S.S.S. 69. Covered and grassed driving range, pitching/putting. Academy 9-hole course and fully equipped clubhouse. Conference/corporate days available. *Green Fees:* weekdays £25.00; weekends £30.00. Special rates on application. *Eating facilities:* available. *Visitors:* very welcome. *Society Meetings:* welcome. Secretary: Pamela Smith.
e-mail: info@kirtlingtongolfclub.com
website: www.kirtlingtongolfclub.com

MAPLEDURHAM. **The Club at Mapledurham,** Chazey Heath, Mapledurham, Reading RG4 7UD (01189 463353; Fax: 01189 463363). *Location:* leave Reading on A4074 towards Mapledurham,

Welcome to Hinksey Heights - The Oxford Golf Course
'An inland links course with the most remarkable views of Oxford's dreaming spires'

- 18-hole Championship course (7000 yards) - undulating heathland, links type, with a series of interesting and distinctive holes, testing yet fair to all standards of golfer.
- Spires: 9 hole course.
- Par 3 course.
- Licensed Clubhouse and Restaurant.
- Golf societies and company days welcome.
- Golf Shop. • Professional tuition.

Hinksey Heights Golf Course, South Hinksey, Oxford OX1 5AB
Tel: 01865 327775
e-mail: sec@oxford-golf.co.uk
www.oxford-golf.co.uk

SOUTHFIELD GOLF CLUB

With golf played here since 1922 and with views of the city's 'dreaming spires', this undulating parkland course with many fine mature trees will provide the visitor with a delightful golf experience in beautiful surroundings.

- Superb Harry Colt Course within 3 miles of City Centre
- Well drained course in excellent condition ALL YEAR
- Visitors and Societies welcome • Recently refurbished Clubhouse and Restaurant

Hill Top Road, Oxford OX14 1PF • Tel: 01865 242158 • Fax: 01865 250023
E-mail: sgcltd@btopenworld.com
Visit our Website: www.southfieldgolf.com

Woodcote and Wallingford, club is on the right immediately after leaving built up area. Parkland. 18 holes, 5700 yards. Par 69. Academy area. *Green Fees:* information not available. *Eating facilities:* bar/lounge, food available. *Visitors:* welcome, no restrictions. Facilities include fully equipped gym, sauna, steam room, spa and swimming pool. *Society Meetings:* welcome. Professional: Tim Gilpin. Manager: Rob Davies.*

OXFORD. **Hinksey Heights Golf Club,** South Hinksey OX1 5AB (01865 327775; Fax: 01865 736930). *Location:* on the Southern bypass of the A34, 4km west of Oxford. 18 hole Championship Course, 6936 yards, S.S.S. 73. An undulating inland links course with the most remarkable views of Oxford's dreaming spires. Spires Course, 2617 yards. 9 hole course, 939 yards. Driving range, short game practice area and large putting green. *Green Fees:* call for information. *Eating facilities:* spike bar, bar and restaurant. *Visitors:* welcome including weekends. *Society Meetings:* welcome but must book in advance. Director of Golf/Head Professional: Dean Davis. Club Secretary: Hilary Hester.
e-mail: sec@oxford-golf.co.uk
website: www.oxford-golf.co.uk

OXFORD. **Southfield Golf Club,** (home of Oxford City Golf Club, Oxford Ladies Golf Club, Oxford University Golf Club), Hill Top Road, Oxford OX4 1PF. *Location*: one mile from BMW Works, along Cowley Road, turn right into Southfield Road, then right at end of road. A challenging Harry Colt designed parkland course, well drained and suitable for year-round play. 18 holes, 6328 yards. S.S.S. 70. Practice ground available. *Green Fees:* £40.00 per day. *Eating facilities:* recently refurbished clubhouse and restaurant. *Visitors:* welcome. *Society Meetings*: welcome by arrangement (not weekends or Bank Holidays). Professional: Tony Rees (01865 244258). Admin. Secretary: Colin Whittle (01865 242158).
e-mail: sgcltd@btopenworld.com
website: www.southfieldgolf.com

OXFORD. **Studley Wood Golf Club**, The Straight Mile, Horton cum Studley, Oxford OX33 1BF (01865 351144; Fax: 01865 351166). *Location*: four miles east of Oxford. Superb, gently undulating, picturesque, mature woodland course. 18 holes, 6722 yards, S.S.S. 72. 15 bay covered driving range, putting lab, short game academy. *Green Fees:* £39.00; weekends after midday only. *Eating facilities:* function room, restaurant and bar. *Visitors:* welcome at all times weekdays, afternoons only at weekends, must play to Handicap standard. Tee time bookings taken four days in advance. Buggies available. Golf breaks available staying at local hotels. S*ociety Meetings:* welcome any time Mondays to Thursdays, and Friday mornings. Packages from £30.00 per person. Professional: Matthew Avann (01865 351122). Managing Director: Ken Heathcote.
e-mail: admin@studleywoodgolfclub.co.uk
website: www.studleywoodgolfclub.co.uk

Visit Studley Wood
the premier golf club in Oxfordshire

A superb golf course reputed to have some of the best greens in the country

- Set in a 177 acres of tranquil Oxfordshire countryside.
- 18 hole, 6722 yards, SSS72 winding around a 30-acre wood.
- Excellent practice facilities which include a 15 bay covered driving range, putting & chipping green.
- A sumptuous clubhouse, restaurant and bar with superb panoramic views.
- Visitors welcome at all times weekdays (weekends not before noon.

Studley Wood, a modern golf club with traditional values

For more information contact
ken@studleywoodgolfclub.co.uk
The Straight Mile, Horton-cum-Studley, Oxon OX33 1BF.
Tel: 01865 351144 Fax: 01865 351166
www.studleywoodgolfclub.co.uk

Oxfordshire's Hidden Gem   Studley Wood . . . *for everything golf*

OXFORD. **North Oxford Golf Club,** Banbury Road, Oxford OX2 8EZ (01865 554415; Fax: 01865 515921). *Location:* just north of Oxford on the Banbury Road to Kidlington. Flat parkland course with tree-lined fairways - six Par 3 holes. 18 holes, 5689 yards, S.S.S. 67. Indoor driving bay in Pro shop. *Green Fees:* information not available *Eating facilities:* dining room, lounge and stud bar. *Visitors:* welcome weekdays and after 12 noon weekends and Bank Holidays. *Society Meetings:* welcome, details on request.Professional: L. Jackson (01865 553977). General Manager: R.J. Harris (01865 554924; Fax: 0845 2805262).*
e-mail: generalmanager@nogc.co.uk
website: www.nogc.co.uk

OXFORD. **Waterstock Golf Club & Driving Range,** Thame Road, Waterstock, Oxford OX33 1HT (01844 338093; Fax: 01844 338036). *Location:* on Junction 8 and 8A, M40, at the Wheatley Service Station, five minutes from Thame and Oxford, 30 minutes from London and Birmingham. Rolling parkland with 15,500 trees. 18 holes, 6535 yards, Par 72, S.S.S 71. Practice bunkers and putting facilities, 22 bay driving range. *Green Fees:* 9 holes weekdays £13.00, weekends £15.50; 18 holes weekdays £23.00, weekends £28.00; twilight weekdays £15.00, weekends £17.50; per day £30.00 weekdays, £35.00 weekends. Winter fees (November 1st to end February): 9 holes weekdays £11.50, weekends £13.50; 18 holes £20.00; after 11.00am weekdays £15.00, weekends £19.00. *Eating facilities:* full bar and restaurant. *Visitors:* no restrictions, welcome at all times. Changing rooms. *Society Meetings:* fully catered for, packages available on request. Head Professional: Paul Bryant. Secretary: Andrew Wyatt.
e-mail: wgc_oxfordgolf@btinternet.com
website: www.waterstockgolf.co.uk

OXON/BUCKINGHAMSHIRE. **Magnolia Park Golf & Country Club,** Arncott Road, Boarstall, Bucks HP18 9XX (01844 239700). *Location:* B4011 south from Bicester or north from Thame; two miles north of Oakley turn to Boarstall. Parkland and landscaped terrain with seven lakes. 18 holes. Par 72. Excellent practice facilities. *Green Fees:* information not available. *Eating facilities:* Bar and dining 8am to 8pm (to 6pm during winter), function room available. *Society Meetings:* societies and corporate days welcome. Professional: Dusan Gavrilovic. General Manager: (01844 239700; Fax: 01844 238991)*
e-mail: info@magnoliapark.co.uk
website: www.magnoliapark.co.uk

THAME. **The Oxfordshire Golf Club,** Rycote Lane, Milton Common, Thame OX9 2PU (01844 278300; Fax: 01844 278003). *Location:* from south Junction 7 M40, A329 to Thame. From north Junction 8 M40, A418 to Thame then A329. A combination of mounded fairways and lakes offers American-style target golf. 18 holes, 6856 yards. S.S.S. 74. 28-bay driving range, practice area. *Green Fees:* information not available. *Eating facilities:* spike bar, Lakes Lounge and Oaks Restaurant offering light snacks to Continental and Japanese cuisine. Private rooms available for conferences, weddings and private dining. Luxurious changing facilities with Japanese ofuro baths. *Visitors:* welcome subject to availability, call reservations 01844 278300. Electric trolleys, pull trolleys and caddies (reserved in advance) available from well stocked Pro shop. *Society Meetings:* on application. PGA Professional: Justin Barnes (01844 278505).*
e-mail: info@theoxfordshiregolfclub.com
website: theoxfordshiregolfclub.com

13th hole at Southfield Golf Club, Oxford

SOUTH REGION / Oxfordshire

WALLINGFORD. The Springs Hotel and Golf Club, Wallingford Road, North Stoke, Wallingford OX10 6BE (01491 836687; Fax: 01491 836877). *Location*: two miles south-west of Wallingford on the B4009. M40 Junction 6. 18 holes, 6470 yards. par 72. *Green Fees*: £30.00 weekdays; £35.00 weekends; telephone for latest green fee offers. *Eating facilities*: restaurant and clubhouse. *Visitors*: by arrangement. Professional: Jamie Clutterbuck (01491 827310; Fax: 01491 827312).
e-mail: info@thespringshotel.com
proshop@thespringshotel.com
website: www.thespringshotel.com

WITNEY. Witney Lakes Golf Club, Witney Lakes Resort, Downs Road, Witney OX29 0SY (01993 893011; Fax: 01993 778866). *Location*: two miles west of Witney town centre, turn into Downs Road. From B4095. Parkland with five large lakes. 18 holes, 6500 yards. S.S.S. 71. 22-bay floodlit covered driving range, practice area. *Green Fees*: information not available. *Eating facilities:* Greens Sports Bar and Greens Restaurant. *Visitors:* no restrictions. Rawles - Hairdressers. Retreat Spa and Beauty Salon. Function/conference room; health and fitness club includes swimming pool, gymnasium and sauna. *Society Meetings:* all welcome. Teaching Professionals: (01993 893011; Fax: 01993 778866). Golf Desk (01993 893011; Fax: 01993 778866).
e-mail: golf@witney-lakes.co.uk
website: www.witney-lakes.co.uk

Other useful guides to holidays in Britain from FHG Guides

**PUBS & INNS
300 GREAT HOTELS
SHORT BREAK HOLIDAYS
The original PETS WELCOME!
500 GREAT PLACES TO STAY
SELF-CATERING HOLIDAYS
BED & BREAKFAST STOPS
CARAVAN & CAMPING HOLIDAYS
FAMILY BREAKS**

Published annually: available in all good bookshops or direct from the publisher:
**FHG Guides, Abbey Mill Business Centre, Seedhill, Paisley PA1 1TJ
Tel: 0141 887 0428 • Fax: 0141 889 7204
e-mail: admin@fhguides.co.uk
www.holidayguides.com**

The Springs Hotel & Golf Club
Wallingford Road, North Stoke
Wallingford, Oxfordshire, OX10 6BE
Tel: 01491 836 687 • Fax: 01491 836 877
e-mail: sales@thespringshotel.co.uk
www.thespringshotel.com

The Springs is an attractive Tudor style country house hotel nestled in the heart of the Thames Valley. Set in 133 acres of Parkland and overlooking a spring fed lake, it offers the perfect setting for a relaxing break away and has the added benefit of a stunning 18 hole par 72 golf course. Other Facilities include: 32 individually designed en suite bedrooms, welcoming oak panelled lounge with stone fireplace, 3 period reception/function rooms with natural daylight, wifi and views over the grounds, AA Rosette Lakeside Restaurant, sauna, outdoor pool, coarse fishing on the Thames, croquet, putting green, newly refurbished Clubhouse with Bar '19' serving fresh, homemade meals.

Golf Breaks from as little as £75 per person on one night stays and £180 per person on two night stays, including Dinner, B&B and 36 holes. See website for all Special Offers.

Surrey

BAGSHOT. **Pennyhill Park Hotel,** London Road, Bagshot GU19 5EU (01276 471774; Fax: 01276 473217). *Location*: just off A30 at Bagshot. Beautiful, undulating 9-hole par 3 course, 2000 yards. S.S.S. 64. *Green Fees*: complimentary for guests. *Eating facilities*: 'Michael Wignall at the Latymer' fine dining restaurant, brasserie, Ascot Bar, five red-star hotel with 123 luxury bedrooms, 45,000 sq ft spa with 8 indoor and outdoor pools, gym and treatment rooms, clay pigeon shooting, tennis court and archery. *Visitors*: prior booking required. *Society Meetings*: welcome. General Manager: Julian Tomlin.

BAGSHOT. **Windlesham Golf Club,** Grove End, Bagshot GU19 5HY. *Location*: A30 west from Sunningdale at Junction of A30 and A332 or Junction 3 from M3 and take the A322 to Bracknell then junction of A30/A332. Challenging parkland course designed by Tommy Horton - USPGA, greens and tees of highest specification. 18 holes, 6650 yards. S.S.S. 72. Practice range with three covered bays, practice green. *Green Fees:* information not available. *Visitors:* welcome, please ring first on weekdays, weekends, Bank Holidays after 12 noon. Teaching Academy School; carts available. Professional Lee Mucklow (01276 472323). Secretary: Richard Griffiths (01276 452220; Fax: 01276 452290).*
website: www.windleshamgolf.com

BANSTEAD. **Cuddington (Banstead) Golf Club Ltd,** Banstead Road, Banstead SM7 1RD (020 8393 0952; Fax: 020 8786 7025). *Location*: 200 yards from Banstead Railway Station. 18 holes, 6614 yards. S.S.S. 71. *Green Fees*: information not available. *Visitors*: welcome with reservation. *Society Meetings*: catered for on Thursdays and some Tuesdays pm. Professional: M. Warner. Secretary: Mrs. S. Burr.
e-mail: secretary@cuddingtongc.co.uk
website: www.cuddingtongc.co.uk

BLETCHINGLEY. **Bletchingley Golf Club,** Church Lane, Bletchingley RH1 4LP (01883 744666; Fax: 01883 744284). *Location*: off A25, three miles west from Junction 6 M25. Parkland course, sand based. 18 holes, 6513 yards. S.S.S. 71. Practice ground. *Green Fees*: information not provided. *Eating facilities*: lounge/dining room, large function room, bar. *Visitors:* welcome. Carts available. *Society Meetings*: welcome. Professional: Golf Manager/PGA Pro: Steven Cookson (01883 744848; Fax; 01883 742943).
e-mail: stevec1412@yahoo.co.uk
website: www.bletchingleygolf.co.uk

THE APPEARANCE OF AN ASTERISK (*) AT THE END OF A CLUB OR COURSE ENTRY INDICATES THAT UP-TO-DATE INFORMATION HAS NOT BEEN SUPPLIED

CAMBERLEY. **Camberley Heath Golf Club,** Golf Drive, Portsmouth Road, Camberley GU15 1JG (01276 23258; Fax: 01276 692505). *Location*: south of the M3 on the A325 Portsmouth Road, near Frimley. Heathland and pine, designed by Harry Colt - his best, established 1913. 18 holes, 6426 yards, 5876 metres. S.S.S. 71. Practice ground. *Green Fees*: £60.00. *Eating facilities:* restaurants and Teppan Yaki (Japanese Steak Bar). *Visitors*: welcome Monday to Thursday only by prior arrangement. *Society Meetings*: welcome by prior arrangement weekdays only; various packages available. Professional: Steve Speller (01276 27905). General Manager: Chris Donavon (01276 23258).
e-mail: info@camberleyheathgolfclub.co.uk
website: www.camberleyheathgolfclub.co.uk

CARSHALTON. **Oaks Sports Centre Ltd,** Woodmansterne Road, Carshalton SM5 4AN (020 8643 8363; Fax: 020 8661 7880). *Location:* on the B2032 past Carshalton Beeches Station, Oaks Sports Centre signposted north of A2022, half way between A217 and A237. Open 7am, 7 days, 364 days per year. Meadowland course. 18 holes, 6026 yards. S.S.S 69. 9 holes, 1497 yards. S.S.S 28. 18 bay golf range. *Green Fees:* information not provided. *Eating facilities:* bar lounge and cafeteria. *Visitors:* public course, everyone welcome. *Society Meetings:* by arrangement. Professionals: M. Pilkington. C. Mitchell. Secretary: D.J. Capper.
e-mail: info@theoaksgolf.co.uk
website: www.theoaksgolf.co.uk

CATERHAM. **Surrey National Golf Club,** Rook Lane, Chaldon, Caterham CR3 5AA (01883 344555). *Location*: M25, Junction 7 (M23) towards Croydon. After two miles turn right into Dean Lane and then left into Rook Lane, entrance on the left. Mature landscape with stunning views of South Downs. 18 holes. 6850 yards. Par 72. *Green Fees*: £22.00 weekdays (2 Fore! 1 rate); £35.00 weekends. *Eating facilities*: bar and catering facilities available. *Visitors*: welcome weekdays at anytime and weekends after 11am. Buggies and carts available for hire. *Society Meetings*: welcome weekdays at anytime and weekends after 11am. Professional: Matthew Stock. General Manager: Simon Hodsdon.
e-mail: caroline@surreynational.co.uk
website: www.surreynational.co.uk

CATERHAM near. **Woldingham Golf Club,** Halliloo Valley Road, Woldingham, near Caterham CR3 7HA (01883 653501; Fax: 01883 653502). *Location:* Caterham, Junction 6 M25, 3 miles. Downland course. 18 holes. 6393 yards. S.S.S. 71. Putting greens, practice ground. *Green Fees:* information not provided. *Eating facilities:* Function suite, Spike bar. *Visitors:* welcome anytime with seven days prior notice. *Society Meetings:* welcome Monday to Sunday (after 10.30am on weekends). Buggy hire. Professional: Frazer Amey (01883 653501).
e-mail: info@woldingham-golfclub.co.uk
website: www.woldingham-golfclub.co.uk

ALTONWOOD
The Golf Group

www.addingtongolf.com
Tel: 0208 777 1055

www.surreynational.co.uk
Tel: 01883 344 555

www.woldingham-golfclub.co.uk
Tel: 01883 653 501

www.westerhamgc.co.uk
Tel: 01959 567 100

Altonwood boasts five fine golf courses all within easy driving distance of each other for all standards of golfer. The four courses pictured above offer excellent club houses and facilities. First class service and beautiful surroundings make the Altonwood clubs the perfect setting for any event.

Book online and save up to 30%

116 Surrey / SOUTH REGION

CHERTSEY. Barrow Hills Golf Club, Longcross, Chertsey KT16 0DS (01344 635770). *Location:* four miles west of Chertsey, adjacent to M3 at Longcross. 18 holes, 3090 yards. S.S.S. 53. *Green Fees:* information not provided. *Visitors:* only with a member. Secretary: R. Hammond (01483 234807 home).

CHERTSEY. Laleham Golf Club, Laleham Reach, Mixnams Lane, Chertsey KT16 8RP (01932 562188; Fax: 01932 564448). *Location:* M25 to Junction 11, follow directions to Thorpe Park, entrance opposite roundabout. Flat but interesting parkland course with water features. 18 holes, 6291 yards. S.S.S. 70. *Green Fees:* information not available. *Eating facilities:* full restaurant and bar facilities. *Visitors:* welcome weekdays; weekends after 2pm in summer and 12.30pm in winter. Please phone to ensure no tee reservations. *Society Meetings:* catered for at competitive rates. Acting Secretary: Pauline Kennett (01932 564211; Fax: 01932 564448).*
e-mail: manager@laleham-golf.co.uk
website: www.laleham-golf.co.uk

CHESSINGTON. Chessington Golf Centre, Garrison Lane, Chessington KT9 2LW (020 8391 0948). *Location:* off A243, 500 yards from Chessington World of Adventure. Opposite Chessington South Station, Junction 9 M25. Parkland course. 9 holes, 1741 yards. S.S.S. 28. Covered floodlit driving range. *Green Fees:* weekdays £9.00, weekends £11.00. *Eating facilities:* bar, coffee, catering available. *Visitors:* welcome. Facilities open to public 8am until 10pm (8pm Saturday and Sunday). *Society Meetings:* welcome. Professional: Mark Janes (020 8391 0948; Fax: 020 8397 2068). Secretary: Martin Bedford (020 8391 0948; Fax: 020 8397 2068).

CHESSINGTON. Surbiton Golf Club, Woodstock Lane, Chessington KT9 1UG (020 8398 3101; Fax: 020 8339 0992). *Location:* two miles east of Esher, off A3 at Ace of Spades roundabout. Undulating parkland. 18 holes, 6055 yards. S.S.S. 69, Par 70. Practice area. *Green Fees:* information not available. *Eating facilities:* snacks and lunches to order by reservation weekdays. *Visitors:* at weekends play with member only. *Society Meetings:* catered for Monday and Friday only. Professional: Paul Milton (020 8398 6619). Secretary: Chris Cornish (020 8398 3101).*
e-mail: surbitongolfclub@hotmail.com

CHIDDINGFOLD. Ramsnest Golf Club, Petworth Road, Chiddingfold GU8 4SL (01428 685888). *Location:* Exit 10 off M25, A3 towards Portsmouth, take A283 turn off, golf course quarter-of-a-mile past Chiddingfold village. Parkland. 18 holes, 5500 yards. Par 70 S.S.S. 67. *Green Fees:* information not available. *Visitors:* welcome seven days, including Bank Holidays. Manager/Secretary: Moreno Pascolini.
e-mail: ramsnestgolfltd@btconnect.com

CHIPSTEAD. Chipstead Golf Club Ltd, How Lane, Coulsdon CR5 3LN (01737 555881; Fax: 01737 555404). *Location:* by Chipstead Station (Chipstead Valley Road). Parkland. 18 holes, 5504 yards, 5332 metres. S.S.S. 67. *Green Fees:* information not available. *Eating facilities:* full catering 7 days a week, bar. *Visitors:* welcome weekdays except Tuesday mornings. *Society Meetings:* welcome full or half days. Director of Golf: Gary Torbett (01737 554939).*

COBHAM. Silvermere Golf and Leisure Complex, Redhill Road, Cobham KT11 1EF (01932 584300). *Location:* half a mile from Junction 10 of M25 at A3. Wooded, parkland course with water on two holes. 34 bay driving range. *Green Fees:* information not available. *Eating facilities:* half-million pound new lakeside clubhouse serving food all day from 7am to 9pm, bar meals, snacks and lunches. *Visitors:* welcome every day but not early weekend mornings. *Society Meetings:* welcome, contact Secretary for details. Professional: Doug McClelland PGA (01932 584348). Secretary: Pauline Devereux (01932 584306; Fax: 01932 584301).*

COULSDON. Coulsdon Manor Hotel and Golf Centre, Coulsdon Court Road, Coulsdon CR5 2LL (020 8668 0414; Fax: 020 8668 0342). *Location:* off J7 of M25 through Coulsdon towards Caterham B2030 turning left via Stoneyfield Road and left in Coulsdon Court Road. Parkland. 18 holes, 6037 yards. Par 70. S.S.S. 68. *Green Fees:* information not available. *Eating facilities:* Terrace Bar/Orangery and Manor House Restaurant. *Visitors:* welcome, subject to availability. *Society Meetings:* welcome Mondays, Tuesdays, Thursdays and Fridays. Extensive banquet and conference facilities, 35 luxurious bedrooms, all en suite. Professional: Matt Asbury (020 8660 6083; Fax: 020 8668 3118). General Manager: Tom Hindle.*

COULSDON. Woodcote Park Golf Club, Meadow Hill, Bridle Way, Coulsdon CR5 2QQ. *Location:* south of Croydon, off A237. Parkland course. 18 holes, 6720 yards. S.S.S. 72. *Green Fees:* information not available. *Eating facilities:* meals at all times. *Visitors:* welcome with reservation. *Society Meetings:* up to 90 catered for, by arrangement. Professional: Wraith Grant. Secretary: A. Dawson (020 8668 2788; Fax: 020 8660 0918).*
e-mail: info@woodcotepgc.com
website: www.woodcotepgc.com

CRANLEIGH. The Cranleigh Golf and Leisure Club, Barhatch Lane, Cranleigh GU6 7NG (01483 268855; Fax: 01483 267251). *Location:* Guildford A281 Horsham take Cranleigh turn-off. Interesting parkland course. 18 holes, 5644 yards. S.S.S. 67. Covered driving range, practice ground. *Green Fees:* information not available. *Eating facilities:* bar, bar snacks, banqueting facilities available. *Visitors:* welcome weekdays and weekends except Thursday before 11am. Weekends subject to availability. *Society Meetings:* welcome weekdays and weekends after 11.30am. Professional: Trevor Longmuir (01483 277188). Secretary: Mike Kateley (01483 268855; Fax: 01483 267251).*

THE GOLF GUIDE 2011   SOUTH REGION / Surrey

CRANLEIGH. **Wildwood Country Club,** Horsham Road, Alfold, Cranleigh GU6 8JE (01403 753255; Fax: 01403 752005). *Location:* 10 miles from Guildford on the A281 to Horsham, near Cranleigh. Only 40 minutes from London on the A3. Championship parkland course with mature woodland and water hazards. An exhilarating challenge to all golfers. 27 holes, 6655 yards. S.S.S. 72. All-weather practice range and 9 hole course. *Green Fees:* weekdays 18 holes £40.00, weekends 18 holes £60.00. Discounted rates in winter. *Eating facilities:* two bars/restaurant. Function Room to seat 140 people. *Visitors:* welcome. Gymnasium. *Society Meetings:* welcome, corporate days organised. Accommodation available locally. Director of Golf: Phil Harrison.

CRONDALL. **Bowenhurst Golf Centre Ltd,** Mill Lane, Crondall, Near Farnham GU10 5RP (01252 851695). *Location:* public golf course, south of M3, 5 miles from exit 5 Farnham side on A287 (behind garage). Parkland course with mature trees and lakes. 3658 yards S.S.S. 60. 20 bay floodlit driving range, two practice putting greens, practice bunker. *Green Fees:* information not available. *Visitors:* welcome at any time. Pro shop. *Society Meetings:* welcome, rates on application. Professional: Alaister Hardaway (01252 851344). Secretary: Geoffrey Corbey.*

CRONDALL. **Oak Park Golfing Complex,** Heath Lane, Crondall, Near Farnham, Surrey GU10 5PB (01252 850880; Fax: 01252 850851). *Location:* one and a half miles off A287 Farnham-Odiham road, five miles from Junctions 4, 4a and 5 of M3 motorway. Gently undulating parkland course. Woodland Course - 18 holes, 6247 yards. S.S.S. 70; Village Course - 9 holes, 3279 yards. Par 36. 16 bay covered driving range, putting green, chipping green and practice bunker. *Green Fees:* information not available. *Eating facilities:* restaurant, available for private hire and special occasions. Bar snacks available. *Visitors:* welcome; must book through Professional; reserved tee system at all times. *Society Meetings:* by arrangement. Professional: Paul Archer (01252 850066; Fax: 01252 850851). Manager: Richard Pilbury (01252 850850).*

CROYDON. **Addington Court Golf Ltd,** Featherbed Lane, Addington, Croydon CR0 9AA (020 8657 0281; Fax: 020 8651 0282). *Location*: two miles east of Croydon. Leave B281 at Addington Village. Dry, well-drained, wooded parkland course. Four courses: Championship 5755 yards, S.S.S. 67. Falconwood 5513 yards, S.S.S. 67. Lower 9 hole course S.S.S 62. 18 hole, Par 3 course. 32-bay floodlit driving range. *Green Fees*: information not available. *Eating facilities*: restaurant, bar. *Visitors:* welcome anytime, no restrictions, public courses. *Society Meetings*: welcome. Professional: Tony Healy (020 8657 0281).*

CROYDON. **The Addington Golf Club,** 205 Shirley Church Road, Croydon CR0 5AB (020 8777 1055; Fax: 020 8777 6661). *Location:* Croydon, Surrey, 30 minutes from centre of London. Heath and woodland as set out by the famous J.F. Abercromby with the world renowned 13th Par 3. 18 holes, 6338 yards. S.S.S. 71. *Green Fees:* information not available. *Eating facilities:* bar and restaurant with full snack menu. *Visitors:* welcome, weekends restricted. *Society Meetings:* by prior arrangement. Assistant Manager: Oliver Peel (020 8777 1055).*
e-mail: info@addingtongolf.com
website: www.addingtongolf.com

CROYDON. **Addington Palace Golf Club,** Gravel Hill, Addington, Croydon CR0 5BB (020 8654 3061). *Location:* two miles east of Croydon Station. Undulating parkland course. 18 holes, 6404 yards. S.S.S. 71. *Green Fees:* information not provided. *Eating facilities:* bar all day, catering 10am to 5pm. *Visitors:* welcome weekdays; at weekends and Bank Holidays must be accompanied by a member. Buggies available. *Society Meetings:* welcome on Mondays, Tuesdays, Wednesdays and Fridays. Professional: Roger Williams (020 8654 1786).
e-mail: kim@addingtonpalacegolf.co.uk
website: www.addingtonpalacegolf.co.uk

CROYDON. **Croham Hurst Golf Club,** Croham Road, South Croydon CR2 7HJ (020 8657 5581; Fax: 020 8657 3229). *Location:* midway between Croydon and Selsdon. Parkland. 18 holes, 6290 yards. S.S.S. 70. *Green Fees:* information not available. *Eating facilities:* lunches, teas, snacks. *Visitors:* welcome with reservation on weekdays. *Society Meetings:* catered for booked one year ahead. Professional Shop: (020 8657 5581).
e-mail: secretary@chgc.co.uk
website: www.chgc.net

CROYDON. **Shirley Park Golf Club Ltd,** 194 Addiscombe Road, Croydon CR0 7LB (020 8654 1143; Fax: 020 8654 6733). *Location:* on A232 one and a half miles from East Croydon Station. Parkland. 18 holes, 6210 yards. S.S.S. 69. Practice area. *Green Fees:* information not available. *Eating facilities:* seven day catering, two bars. *Visitors:* welcome, see website for special offers. Trolleys and buggies available. Reduced accommodation charges available from Croydon Park Hotel if booked through the Secretary. *Society Meetings:* welcome Mondays, Tuesdays, Thursdays and Fridays. Professional: Michael Taylor (020 8654 8767; Fax: 020 8654 6733). Secretary: Steve Murphy (020 8654 1143; Fax: 020 8654 6733).
e-mail: secretary@shirleyparkgolfclub.co.uk
website: www.shirleyparkgolfclub.co.uk

Please mention this guide when enquiring about clubs or accommodation

118 Surrey / SOUTH REGION — **THE GOLF GUIDE 2011**

CROYDON. **Selsdon Park Hotel & Golf Club,** Addington Road, Sanderstead, South Croydon CR2 8YA (020 8657 8811; Fax: 020 8651 6171). *Location:* three miles south of Croydon on A2022 Purley-West Wickham road. Parkland course, designed by J.H. Taylor. 18 holes, 6473 yards. S.S.S. 71. Practice ground. *Green Fees:* information not available. *Eating facilities:* hotel bars, restaurant and grill. *Visitors:* welcome all week with pre-bookable tee-off times. Buggies. *Society Meetings:* welcome by prior arrangement. PGA Professional: Chris Baron (020 8768 3116). Golf Enquiries: (020 8657 8111 Ext. 3116).
website: www.principal-hayley.com

DORKING. **Betchworth Park Golf Club,** Reigate Road, Dorking RH4 1NZ (01306 882052). *Location*: on A25 one mile east of Dorking on Reigate Road. Established parkland course. 18 holes, 6329 yards, Par 69,. S.S.S 70. *Green Fees*: £50.00 Monday to Thursday, Friday to Sunday £75.00. *Eating facilities*: snacks available daily. *Visitors:* welcome, by arrangement. *Society Meetings*: welcome Mondays and Thursdays. Professional: A. Tocher (01306 884334). Manager: Richard Hall (01306 882052; Fax: 01306 877462).
e-mail: manager@betchworthparkgc.co.uk
website: www.betchworthparkgc.co.uk

DORKING. **Dorking Golf Club,** Deepdene Avenue, Dorking RH5 4BX (01306 886917). *Location:* on A24 half-a-mile south of junction with A25. Parkland/downland. 9 holes, alternative tees second 9, 5158 yards. S.S.S. 65. *Green Fees:* information not available. *Eating facilities:* full catering. *Visitors:* weekdays only without reservation. *Society Meetings:* catered for up to 48. Professional/Manager: A. Smeal.*

DORKING. **Gatton Manor Hotel & Golf Club,** Standon Lane, Ockley RH5 5PQ (01306 627555; Fax: 01306 627713). (Home of the PGA Surrey Open Championships 2010-2012). *Location:* to the west of the village of Ockley on the A29 between Dorking and Horsham, easy access from M25 Junction 9. 18 hole championship length course in parkland, makes good use of the many rivers and lakes to make it a picturesque but challenging course. 18 holes, 6653 yards. S.S.S. 72. Additional practice facilities. *Green Fees:* Summer fees - weekdays £35.00, weekends £45.00. Discounted green fee schemes accepted subject to conditions. *Eating facilities:* full à la carte restaurant and bar with bar meals. *Visitors:* a warm and friendly welcome anytime except Sunday mornings. Refurbished changing rooms. Hotel with 18 bedrooms all en suite, conference suites and, gym. Fishing and tennis available. *Society Meetings:* welcome weekdays only. Ideal society/ corporate day venue. 7 and 5 day memberships available. Golf bookings: (01306 627555). Secretary: Patrick Kiely (01306 627555; Fax: 01306 627713).
e-mail: golf@gattonmanor.co.uk

EAST HORSLEY. **Drift Golf Club,** The Drift, East Horsley KT24 5HD (01483 284641). *Location:* the club is located just off the Drift Road which runs between Ockham Road (B2039) and Forest Road, East Horsley. Picturesque woodland course set in the heart of Surrey countryside. 18 holes, 6425 yards, 5877 metres. S.S.S. 72. Golf Academy, driving range and

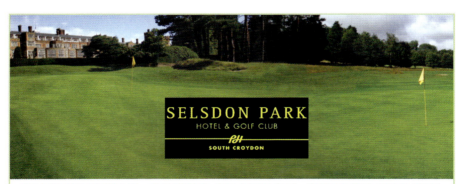

SANDERSTEAD, SOUTH CROYDON, SURREY CR2 8YA

Pay & Play parkland course, designed by J H Taylor.
18 holes, 6473 yards/5854 metres, Par 73. S.S.S. 71
Practice ground • Buggy hire • Pre-bookable tee times • Green fees
Corporate Golf Days, Society Meetings, Golfing Breaks
Restaurant, grill and private dining • 204 de luxe en suite bedrooms
Superb conference/meeting facilities • Golf Academy
Golf Tuition • PGA Professional: Chris Baron

*Golf Enquiries: 020-8657-8811 Ext 3116
Pro Shop: Tel: 020-8768-3116 • Fax: 020-8657-3401*
www.principal-hayley.com

putting green. *Green Fees:* information not available. *Eating facilities:* full bar, lounge, restaurant and bar snacks. *Visitors:* welcome Monday to Friday, and after midday at weekends. Bookings accepted up to seven days in advance. *Society Meetings:* catered for weekdays. (01483 284641).*

EFFINGHAM. **Effingham Golf Club,** Guildford Road, Effingham KT24 5PZ (01372 452203; Fax: 01372 459959). *Location:* A246 between Guildford and Leatherhead. Downland course with magnificent views towards London. 18 holes, 6542 yards. S.S.S. 71. *Green Fees:* information not provided. *Eating facilities:* full bar and catering facilities. *Visitors:* welcome Monday-Friday. Handicap Certificate required. *Society Meetings:* welcome Wednesdays, Thursdays, Fridays. Professional: Steve Hoatson (01372 452606). Secretary: Robin Easton (01372 452203). website: www.effinghamgolfclub.com

EPSOM. **Epsom Golf Club,** Longdown Lane South, Epsom KT17 4JR (01372 721666; Fax: 01372 817183). *Location:* off A240 into B288, 200 yards south of Epsom Downs Station. Downland, links-type course with fast, undulating greens. 18 holes, 5656 yards. S.S.S. 67. Par 69. Practice nets, putting green and chipping area. *Green Fees:* Information not available. *Eating facilities:* bar snacks available from two bars; dining room. *Visitors:* welcome anytime except am on Tuesday, Saturday and Sunday. *Society Meetings:* always welcome with similar exceptions to visitors. Professional and Tee Reservations: R. Goudie (01372 741867).*
e-mail: enquiries@epsomgolfclub.co.uk
website: www.epsomgolfclub.co.uk

EPSOM. **Horton Park Golf & Country Club,** Hook Road, Epsom KT19 8QG (020 8393 8400). Location: Junction 9 of M25 four miles. Epsom Town and station five minutes car or taxi. Attractive parkland course situated within a picturesque country park with water hazards and lakes. 18 holes, 5728 yards. S.S.S. 68. *Green Fees:* information not available. Eating facilities: bar food, restaurant and function room. Visitors: welcome. Society Meetings: welcome weekdays and weekend afternoons. Pro shop (020 8394 2626). Professional: John Terrell.*

ESHER. **Cranfield Golf at Sandown,** More Lane, Esher KT10 8AN. *Location:* signposted from A3, centre of Sandown Park Racecourse. Three golf courses; floodlit 33-bay driving range, plus grassed area. Cranfield Golf Academy. *Green Fees:* information not available. *Eating facilities:* bar and snacks. *Visitors:* welcome. *Society Meetings:* welcome. General Manager: David Parr (01372 461234; Fax: 01372 461203).*

ESHER. **Moore Place Golf Club,** Portsmouth Road, Esher KT10 9LN (01372 463533). *Location:* half a mile from Esher town centre on Portsmouth Road. Undulating parkland course with featured trees - recently lengthened. 9 holes, 2148 yards. S.S.S. 62. *Green Fees:* information not available. *Eating facilities:* bar and restaurant. *Visitors:* welcome, unrestricted. Smart casual dress; golf shoes required, hire available. *Society Meetings:* welcome anytime, 10% reduction for groups of 10 or more. Professional: Morgan Palmer (01372 463533). Hon. Secretary: Reg Egan (07860 133606).
website: www.moore-place.co.uk

ESHER. **Thames Ditton and Esher Golf Club,** Portsmouth Road, Esher KT10 9AL (020 8398 1551). *Location:* "Scilly Isles" roundabout(s), Junction Kingston by-pass, A3. Wooded commonland. 9 holes played twice from different tees, 5149 yards. S.S.S. 65. Practice nets. *Green Fees:* information not available. *Eating facilities:* bar snacks, meals by arrangement. *Visitors:* welcome except Sunday mornings. Trolleys. *Society Meetings:* always welcome, phone the Professional. Professional: Rob Jones. Secretary: Allan Barry.*

FARNHAM. **Farnham Golf Club Ltd,** The Sands, Farnham GU10 1PX (01252 782109; Fax: 01252 781185). *Location:* off A31 at Seale or Runfold slip roads. Follow signs to The Sands situated at junction of Sands Road and Blighton Lane. Mixture of wooded parkland and heathland. 18 holes, 6613 yards. S.S.S. 72. Large practice ground. *Green Fees:* weekdays £45.00 round, £65.00 day; weekends with a member £25.00, visitors at restricted times £45.00. May to August twilight rate £25.00 inclusive, after 5.30pm. County Cards Monday to Friday £22.50. *Eating facilities:* two bars and diningroom, full high standard catering. *Visitors:* welcome weekdays. Telephone for availability. *Society Meetings:* welcome by prior booking. Professional: Rob Colborne (01252 782198; Fax: 01252 781185). Secretary: Grahame Cowlishaw (01252 782109; Fax: 01252 781185).
website: www.farnhamgolfclub.co.uk

Farnham Golf Club

Farnham Golf Club in Surrey was founded in 1896 and is located on the outskirts of Farnham. The course is a mix of parkland, pine and heather with gentle rolling undulations. We can guarantee a friendly and intimate atmosphere with quality of service, food and golf, all at realistic prices. We look forward to welcoming you for a round soon.

**Farnham Golf Club Ltd, Blighton Lane,
The Sands, Farnham, Surrey GU10 1PX
Tel: 01252 782109 • Pro Shop: 01252 782198
e-mail: farnhamgolfclub@tiscali.co.uk • www.farnhamgolfclub.co.uk**

FARNHAM. Hankley Common Golf Club, Tilford Road, Tilford, Farnham GU10 2DD (01252 792493; Fax: 01252 795699). *Location:* off A3, right at lights at Hindhead. Off A31 (Farnham by-pass) left at lights, three miles beyond level crossing. Heathland, dry and sandy links-type course. 18 holes, 6702 yards. S.S.S. 72. Practice ground. *Green Fees:* weekdays £75.00 per round, £85.00 per day; weekends £85.00 per round after 2pm. *Eating facilities:* full range available, restaurant and two bars. *Visitors:* welcome by appointment with Secretary. Handicap Certificate required. *Society Meetings:* catered for on Tuesdays and Wednesdays. Professional: Peter Stow (01252 793761). Secretary: (01252 792493).

GODALMING. West Surrey Golf Club, Enton Green, Godalming GU8 5AF (01483 421275). *Location*: off the A3 south of Guildford, half mile past Milford Station/crossing. Wooded parkland. 18 holes, 6482 yards. S.S.S. 71. Practice ground. *Green Fees*: information not available. *Eating facilities*: bar, diningroom. *Visitors*: welcome, must be member of recognised golf club and have current Handicap Certificate. *Society Meetings:* catered for by prior arrangement. Professional: A. Tawse (01483 417278). Secretary: S.L. Sheppard (01483 421275).*
e-mail: office@wsgc.co.uk
website: www.wsgc.co.uk

GODALMING near. Hurtmore Golf Club, Hurtmore Road, Hurtmore GU7 2RN (01483 426492; Fax: 01483 426121). *Location:* A3 Guildford, M25 (15 minutes) A3 exit Guildford to Portsmouth. Undulating parkland with seven large lakes. 18 holes, 5530yards. S.S.S. 67 men, 68 ladies. Practice nets and putting green. *Green Fees:* weekdays £17.00, weekends £23.00. Twilight available from £12.00. 2010 rates (subject to review). *Eating facilities:* bar, restaurant. *Visitors:* welcome at all times, pay and play course with 200 members. Bookings taken by telephone. *Society Meetings:* welcome by prior booking. Professional and General Manager: Maxine Burton.

GODSTONE. Godstone Golf Club, Streete Court, Rooks Nest Park, Godstone RH9 8BZ (01883 742333; Fax:01883 740227). *Location:* 800 yards drive from junction 6 of the M25. A testing ccourse of exception quality with three new lakes. 9 holes (18 tees), 3000 yards. *Green Fees:* information not available. *Eating facilities:* club shop open all day for snacks and refreshments. *Visitors:* welcome. Buggy hire.*
e-mail: info@godstone-golfclub.co.uk

GUILDFORD. Bramley Golf Club, Bramley, Near Guildford GU5 0AL (01483 892696; Fax: 01483 894673). *Location:* three miles south of Guildford on the Horsham road, A281. Parkland. 18 holes, 5930 yards. S.S.S. 69. Practice area, driving range. *Green Fees:* £40.00; weekends with member only. *Eating facilities:* catering from 7.30am to 9pm, bar from 11am to 10pm. *Visitors:* welcome Monday to Friday. *Society Meetings:* by prior arrangement with the Club. Professional Shop: 01483 893685. General Manager: Mark Walden (01483 892696).
e-mail: secretary@bramleygolfclub.co.uk
website: www.bramleygolfclub.co.uk

GUILDFORD. Guildford Golf Club, High Path Road, Merrow, Guildford GU1 2HL (01483 563941). Steward: (01483 5631842). *Location:* from Guildford take Epsom Road (A246) turn right at the third set of traffic lights. Downland course. 18 holes, 6090 yards. S.S.S. 70. Practice area. *Green Fees:* information not available. *Eating facilities:* snacks and restaurant service. *Visitors:* welcome weekdays, with member weekends. *Society Meetings:* catered for Tuesday to Friday. Professional: A.R. Kirk (01483 566765). Secretary: B.J. Green (01483 563941; Fax: 01483 453228).*
e-mail: secretary@guildfordgolfclub.co.uk
website: www.guildfordgolfclub.co.uk

GUILDFORD. Merrist Wood Golf Club, Holly Lane, Worplesdon, Guildford GU3 3PB (01483 238890; Fax: 01483 238896). *Location:* three miles from Guildford, off A323 to Aldershot. 18 holes, 6909 yards. S.S.S. 73. *Green Fees:* information not available. *Visitors:* welcome; after 11.30am at weekends. Please call for up to date specials. *Society Meetings:* welcome. Professional: Greg Brodie (01483 238897). Golf Manager: Ben Beagley.*

GUILDFORD. Puttenham Golf Club, Heath Road, Puttenham, Guildford GU3 1AL (01483 810498; Fax: 01483 810988). *Location:* On B3000 between Farnham and Guildford, signposted off Hog's Back (A31). Wooded/heathland course. 18 holes, 6220 yards. S.S.S. 70. Practice ground. *Green Fees:* on application. *Eating facilities:* dining room, bar and 19th. *Visitors:* welcome weekdays only by prior arrangement. (Weekends playing with a member). *Society Meetings:* catered for Wednesdays, Thursdays and some Fridays. Secretary and Professional: Gary Simmons.
e-mail: enquiries@puttenhamgolfclub.co.uk
website: www.puttenhamgolfclub.co.uk

GUILDFORD. Roker Park Golf Club, Holly Lane, Worplesdon, Guildford GU3 3PB (01483 236677 Fax: 01483 232324). *Location:* from A3 Guildford take A323 to Aldershot, course two miles on right. Flat parkland course. 9 holes, 3037 yards. S.S.S.69. Driving range. *Green Fees:* information not available. *Eating facilities:* restaurant and bar. *Visitors:* welcome, pay and play course. *Society Meetings:* welcome weekdays only, reductions for parties over 12. Professional: Adrian Carter. Manager: Mrs C. Tegg (Tel & Fax: 01438 232324). *

GUILDFORD near. Sutton Green Golf Club, New Lane, Sutton Green, Near Guildford GU4 7QF (01483 766849). *Location:* midway between Guildford and Woking, just off A3. Easy walking parkland course, co-designed by Laura Davies, water features on nine holes. 18 holes, 6300 yards. S.S.S. 70. Practice ground. *Green Fees:* information not available. *Eating facilities:* fully air conditioned bar and restaurant. *Visitors:* welcome midweek, weekends after 2pm. Golf buggies and carts available; changing room. *Society Meetings:* welcome midweek. Professional: Paul Tedder (01483 766849; Fax: 01483 750289). Secretary: John Buchanan (01483 747898; Fax: 01483 750289).*
e-mail: admin@suttongreengc.co.uk
website: www.suttongreengc.co.uk

THE GOLF GUIDE 2011 SOUTH REGION / Surrey 121

HINDHEAD. The Hindhead Golf Club, Churt Road, Hindhead GU26 6HX (01428 604614; Fax: 01428 608508). *Location:* one and a half miles north of Hindhead on A287 to Farnham. The course is played over heathland and wooded valleys. Open Championship regional qualifying venue 2000-2005. 18 holes, White Tees 6356 yards, S.S.S. 71; Yellow Tees 6106 yards, S.S.S. 70. *Green Fees:* weekdays £60.00 per round, £70.00 per day; weekends £70.00 per round, £80.00 per day. *Eating facilities:* restaurant, snack bar, summer bar and members' bar. *Visitors:* welcome with Handicap Certificate, weekends by appointment. *Society Meetings:* Wednesdays and Thursdays only. Professional: Ian Benson (01428 604458). Secretary: Mrs C. Davison. e-mail: secretary@the-hindhead-golf-club.co.uk website: www.the-hindhead-golf-club.co.uk

KINGSTON UPON THAMES. Coombe Hill Golf Club, Golf Club Drive, off Coombe Lane West, Kingston KT2 7DF (020 8336 7600; Fax: 020 8336 7601). *Location:* from A3 take A238 to Kingston. Heathland/Parkland mix, highly manicured course with quick greens. 18 holes, 6401 yards. S.S.S. 71. *Green Fees:* information not provided. *Eating facilities:* dining room 8am to 3.30pm weekdays, bar (varying hours). *Visitors:* weekdays only, with a member at weekends. *Society Meetings:* please contact Office. Professional: Mark Lawrence (020 8336 7615). Chief Executive: Colin Chapman.

KINGSTON UPON THAMES. Coombe Wood Golf Club, George Road, Kingston Hill KT2 7NS (020 8942 0388). *Location:* from A3 take A308(east) or A238(west). Wooded course. 18 holes, 5312 yards. S.S.S. 65. *Green Fees:* information not available. *Eating facilities:* catering all week. *Visitors:* welcome; weekends afternoons only. *Society Meetings:* by arrangement Monday, Wednesday, Thursday and Friday. Professional: P. Wright (020 8942 6764). Office: Mrs C. Butler (020 8942 0388; Fax: 020 8942 5665). e-mail: info@coombewoodgolf.com website: www.coombewoodgolf.com

KINGSWOOD. Kingswood Golf and Country Club, Sandy Lane, Kingswood, Tadworth KT20 6NE (01737 832188; Fax: 01737 833920). *Location:* just off A217, 10 minutes from Junction 8, M25. James Braid's finest parkland course in England. 18 holes, 6916 yards. S.S.S. 73. Putting green and driving range. *Green Fees:* visit website for details. *Eating facilities:* bar snacks plus extensive catering options for society/corporate days. *Visitors:* welcome anytime, restricted tee times at weekends. Snooker tables available. *Society Meetings:* Society and Corporate Golf Days. Professional: Terry Sims (01737 832334). Club Secretary: Mark Stewart (01737 832188).
e-mail: sales@kingswood-golf.co.uk
website: www.kingswood-golf.co.uk

LYTHE HILL
HOTEL & SPA

Nestled deep within the Surrey countryside the Four Star Lythe Hill Hotel and Spa is a unique and very special venue, where traditional values of hospitality and service meet with the opulence and ease of modern facilities.

- Award-Winning Restaurant
- 41 Beautifully Furnished Bedrooms and Suites
- Fourteenth Century Tudor House
- Extensive Conference and banqueting Facilities
- Civil Marriages and Wedding Facilities

- Amarna – Health, Beauty & Fitness Spa
- Sauna, Steam room and Cold Temple Shower
- Wide range of luxurious Beauty Treatments
- Fully eqipped techno gym with Cardio Theatre

Special weekend leisure breaks available inclusive of 3 course à la carte dinner, accommodation, full English breakfast and full use of the Amarna Spa facilities.

Lythe Hill Hotel & Spa, Petworth Road, Haslemere, Surrey, GU27 3BQ
t: **01428 651 251** e: lythe@lythehill.com www.lythehill.co.uk

LEATHERHEAD. Leatherhead Golf Club, Kingston Road, Leatherhead KT22 0EE (01372 843966; Fax: 01372 842241). *Location:* off Junction 9 of M25, onto A243 to Kingston. Parkland, many mature trees. 18 holes, 6203 yards. S.S.S. 70. Practice ground, putting green. *Green Fees:* Monday to Friday £38.00 18 holes, £57.00 36 holes; Saturday and Sunday £43.00 18 holes. *Eating facilities:* à la carte restaurant, cafe/brasserie and lounge bar. *Visitors:* welcome, no visitors Saturday or Sunday mornings. *Society Meetings:* welcome, from 16 to 100 by reservation. Head Professional: Timothy Lowe (01372 849413). e-mail: sales@lgc-golf.co.uk
website: www.lgc-golf.co.uk

LEATHERHEAD. Pachesham Park Golf Centre, Oaklawn Road, Leatherhead KT22 0BP (01372 843453). *Location:* half a mile outside Leatherhead just off A244, quarter of a mile off Junction 9 M25. Undulating parkland course. 9 holes, 2806 yards. S.S.S. 67. 33 bay floodlit driving range, putting green, chipping area. *Green Fees:* weekdays £10.00 9 holes; weekends £14.00 9 holes. *Eating facilities:* fully licensed bar, restaurant. *Visitors:* welcome, bookings taken two days in advance. *Society Meetings:* welcome. Professional/Secretary: Phil Taylor.
e-mail: enquiries@pacheshamgolf.co.uk

LEATHERHEAD. Tyrrells Wood Golf Club Ltd, Leatherhead KT22 8QP (01372 376025). *Location:* south-east on A24 Leatherhead by-pass, half a mile left to Headley, then 200 yards right. Hillside, wooded course with glorious views. 18 holes, 6234 yards. S.S.S. 70. Small practice ground. *Green Fees:* information not available. *Eating facilities:* catering by arrangement with Manager. *Visitors:* no visitors Saturday or Sunday mornings. *Society Meetings:* catered for by arrangement with Manager. Professional: Simon Defoy (01372 375200). Secretary: Luke Edgcumbe (01372 376025).*

LINGFIELD. Lingfield Park Golf Club, Racecourse Road, Lingfield Park, Lingfield RH7 6PQ (01342 834602; Fax: 01342 836077). *Location:* A22 turn off at Blindley Heath, six miles from M25 Junction 6. Parkland/wooded course with streams. 18 holes, 6472 yards. S.S.S. 72. Driving range and practice ground. *Green Fees:* information not available. *Eating facilities:* lounge, dining room, spike bar.

Visitors: welcome midweek only by arrangement. Changing rooms. *Society Meetings:* catered for. Professional/ Secretary: C.K. Morley (01342 832659; Fax: 01342 836077).*

MILFORD. Milford Golf Club, Station Lane, Milford, Near Godalming GU8 5HS (01483 419200; Fax: 01483 419199). *Location:* five minutes from Guildford on the A3, follow signs to Milford train station, just this side of it. Parkland course which plays like a links in the wind, mixture of attractive water holes. 18 holes, 5960 yards. S.S.S. 68. Excellent practice facilities. *Green Fees:* information not available. *Eating facilities:* restaurant and pleasant bar area. *Visitors:* welcome at most times, must phone for reservations. *Society Meetings:* all welcome, packages available, please phone Sales Manager (01483 419200). Professional: Paul Creamer (01483 416291). General Manager: Robert Brewer.*

MITCHAM. Mitcham Golf Club, Carshalton Road, Mitcham Junction CR4 4HN (Fax: 020 8648 4197). *Location:* Carshalton Road, aim for Mitcham Junction Station. Flat course. 18 holes, 6022 yards. S.S.S. 69. *Green Fees:* information not available. *Eating facilities:* meals and snacks available. *Visitors:* welcome, book times via Professional. *Society Meetings:* catered for, book through Secretary. Professional: P. Burton (020 8640 4280). Secretary: D. Tilley (Tel & Fax: 020 8648 4197).*
e-mail: mitchamgc@hotmail.co.uk
website: www.mitchamgolfclub.co.uk

NEWDIGATE. Rusper Golf Club, Rusper Road, Newdigate RH5 5BX (Tel & Fax: 01293 871456). *Location:* Dorking-Horsham A24. Beare Green roundabout left to Newdigate, through Newdigate, right to Rusper, course on right. Parkland course with mature woodland and natural water features.18 holes, 6724 yards. S.S.S. 73. Driving range. *Green Fees:* please contact club for details. *Eating facilities:* fresh food and daily specials available every day. Full bar. *Visitors:* welcome every day, times bookable in advance. No Handicaps required. Golf Shop (01293 871871). *Society Meetings:* welcome, groups up to 50, various packages. Professional: Janice Arnold. Secretary: Mrs Jill Thornhill.
e-mail: nikki@ruspergolfclub.co.uk
website: www.ruspergolfclub.co.uk

Founded in 1903 Leatherhead Golf Club celebrated its centenary in 2003.

- 18 hole parkland course
- Practice ground
- Professional's shop
- Visitors welcome

Kingston Road, Leatherhead KT22 0EE
Telephone: (01372) 843966 • Fax: (01372) 842241
e-mail: sales@lgc-golf.co.uk
www.lgc-golf.co.uk

NEW MALDEN. **Malden Golf Club,** Traps Lane, New Malden KT3 4RS (020 8942 0654; Fax: 020 8336 2219). *Location:* half a mile from Malden Station - near A3, between Wimbledon and Kingston. Fairly flat parkland. 18 holes, 6295 yards. S.S.S. 70. *Green Fees:* information not provided. *Eating facilities:* restaurant and bar. *Visitors:* welcome weekdays, restricted weekends and Bank Holidays. Advisable to telephone Professional. Buggies and trolleys for hire. *Society Meetings:* catered for Wednesday and Thursdays. Professional: Robert Hunter (020 8942 6009). Club Manager: Neil Coulson (020 8942 0654; Fax: 020 8336 2219).

OTTERSHAW. **Foxhills,** Stonehill Road, Ottershaw KT16 0EL (01932 872050; Fax: 01932 874762). *Location:* Exit 11 M25, follow signs to Woking, right at roundabout, left at next roundabout, left at junction into Stonehill Road. Parkland course (Bernard Hunt) 18 holes, 6734 yards, S.S.S. 72. Wooded course (Longcross) 18 holes, 6417 yards, S.S.S. 71. Par 3 course (9 holes). *Green Fees:* information not available. *Eating facilities:* Bar XIX open from 7am - midnight serving everything from boiled eggs to three course à la carte menu. Manor House restaurant for breakfast, lunch and fine dining in the evening. Summerhouse brasserie from 11am. *Visitors:* welcome from 7.30am weekdays and after 12 noon at weekends. 70 rooms; health spa, 11 tennis courts, 3 squash courts, 4 swimming pools, 6 conference rooms and a large function room. *Society Meetings:* bookings for weekdays only. Head Professional: Richard Summerscales; Professional: Bernard Hunt MBE (01932 704465). Golf Operations Manager: Roger Hyder PGA (01932 704466).*

OXTED. **Limpsfield Chart Golf Club,** Westerham Road, Limpsfield, Oxted RH8 0SL (01883 722106). *Location:* on A25 between Westerham and Oxted. Heathland, now well wooded plus heather, gorse. Second/eleventh is played over an old gravel pit, a carry of 140 yards. 9 holes - alternate tees for 18 holes, 5718 yards. S.S.S. 68. Small practice area, practice net, putting green. *Green Fees:* information not provided. *Eating facilities:* snacks available; breakfast, lunch, dinner by prior arrangement. *Visitors:* welcome weekdays, Thursdays after 3pm, weekends by appointment. *Society Meetings:* catered for by prior arrangement. Secretary: R. Smitherman (01883 723405).

OXTED. **Tandridge Golf Club,** Oxted RH8 9NQ (01883 712274; Fax: 01883 730537). *Location:* from M25 Junction 6 take A22 south to A25 east, two miles. Parkland with flat first nine and undulating second nine. 18 holes, 6250 yards. S.S.S. 70. *Green Fees:* information not provided. *Eating facilities:* full catering facilities. *Visitors:* welcome Monday, Wednesday and Thursday only. *Society Meetings:* catered for Mondays, Wednesdays and Thursdays. Professional: Chris Evans (01883 713701). Secretary: A.J. Tanner.
e-mail: secretary@tandridgegolfclub.com
website: www.tandridgegolfclub.com

PIRBRIGHT. **Goal Farm Golf Course,** Gole Road, Pirbright, Woking GU24 0PZ (01483 473183). *Location:* public course between Woking and Guildford, off A322. Challenging, picturesque course. 9 holes, 1273 yards. S.S.S. 48. Practice net, putting green, bunker. *Green Fees:* information not available. *Eating facilities:* licensed bar and cafe. *Visitors:* welcome, restrictions Saturday and Thursday mornings (Club Competitions). Lessons available from Professional. Clubs available for hire. Professional: Peter Fuller. Secretary: Graham Williams (01483 473182).*

PURLEY. **Purley Downs Golf Club,** 106 Purley Downs Road, South Croydon CR2 0RB (020 8657 8347). *Location:* three miles south of Croydon, one mile east of A235. Undulating downland course. 18 holes, 6308 yards. S.S.S. 70. Practice area, nets. *Green Fees:* information not provided. *Eating facilities:* dining room, bar snacks, two bars. *Visitors:* welcome weekdays. *Society Meetings:* catered for all days except Tuesday mornings and Mondays. Professional: (020 8651 0819). Office: (020 8657 8347; Fax: 020 8651 5044).
e-mail: info@purleydowns.co.uk
website: www.purleydownsgolfclub.co.uk

REDHILL. **Redhill Golf Centre,** Canada Avenue, Redhill RH1 5BF (01737 770204). *Location:* in the grounds of East Surrey Hospital. Parkland. 9 holes, 1533 yards. S.S.S. 56 (18 holes); 28 (9 holes). 37 bay floodlit driving range. *Green Fees:* weekdays £5.00, weekends £6.00. *Eating facilities:* available locally. Open 8am to 10pm; weekends 9pm. *Visitors:* welcome no restrictions. Sponsored by Golf Foundation to give free junior coaching. *Society Meetings:* welcome. Professional: Declan Malone. Manager: Steven Furlonger.

REDHILL. **Redhill and Reigate Golf Club,** Clarence Lodge, Pendleton Road, Redhill RH1 6LB (Office: 01737 240777; Shop 01737 244433). *Location:* one mile south of Reigate between A23 and A25 – Junction 8 M25. Flat, well wooded parkland course. 18 holes, 5272 yards, 4978 metres. S.S.S. 68. Small practice area. *Green Fees:* information not provided. *Eating facilities:* available seven days a week. *Visitors:* welcome Monday to Friday from 9.30am, Saturday/Sunday after 10.00am. Telephone in advance. *Society Meetings:* by arrangement with Secretary (01737 240777; Fax: 01737 242117). Clubhouse Manager: Simon Ibbotson. Please contact for function bookings (01737 244626).
e-mail: mail@rrgc.net
website: www.rrgc.net

REIGATE. **Reigate Heath Golf Club,** The Clubhouse, Reigate Heath, Reigate RH2 8QR (01737 242610). *Location:* south of A25 on western boundary of Reigate. Heathland. 9 holes, 5658 yards. S.S.S. 68. *Green Fees:* information not available. *Eating facilities:* lunches and snacks available. *Visitors:* welcome weekdays and weekends after midday. Advisable to telephone before arrival. *Society Meetings:* packages of 9, 18, 27 or 36 holes available weekdays. Manager: Richard Arnold (01737 242610).*
e-mail: manager@reigateheathgolfclub.co.uk
website: www.reigateheathgolfclub.co.uk

REIGATE. **Reigate Hill Golf Club,** Gatton Bottom, Reigate RH2 0TU (01737 654477; Fax: 01737 642650). *Location*: J8, M25 (two minutes). Parkland. 18 holes, 6212 yards. S.S.S. 71. *Green Fees:* weekdays £27.00, weekends and Bank Holidays £32.00; twilight rates available from 2pm. 2010 rates (subject to review). *Eating facilities:* Extensive bar menu, spike bar, lounge bar. *Visitors*: Monday - Friday no restrictions; weekends and Bank Holidays after 12pm. *Society Meetings:* welcome. Professional: Mike Lovegrove (01737 646070). Administrator: H. Issom.
website: www.reigatehillgolfclub.co.uk

RICHMOND. **The Richmond Golf Club,** Sudbrook Park, Richmond TW10 7AS (020 8940 4351; Fax: 020 8332 7914). *Location:* off A307 two miles south of Richmond, end of Sudbrook Lane. Parkland. 18 holes, 6100 yards. S.S.S. 70. Practice driving range. *Green Fees*: information not available. *Eating facilities*: lunches available Monday to Friday. *Visitors:* welcome weekdays without reservation. *Society Meetings:* welcome Tuesdays, Thursdays and Friday mornings only by arrangement with General Manager. Professional: Steve Burridge (020 8940 7792; Fax: 020 8332 6694). General Manager: J.R. Maguire (020 8940 4351; Fax: 020 8332 7914).*

RICHMOND. **Royal Mid-Surrey Golf Club,** Old Deer Park, Richmond TW9 2SB (020 8940 1894; Fax: 020 8939 0150). *Location:* entrance on A316, five minutes from Richmond station. Parkland links designed by J.H. Taylor. Two 18 hole courses, Inner: 5544 yards, S.S.S. 67 men, 71 ladies; Outer: 6385 yards, S.S.S. 71 men, 73 ladies. Practice ground, putting green, pitching green. *Green Fees:* weekdays £75.00 and £65.00 (inner) (£50.00 after 1pm and in winter). *Eating facilities:* bars and dining areas. *Visitors:* welcome weekdays only. *Society Meetings:* corporate and society golf days welcome. Professional: Matthew Paget (020 8939 0148). Secretary: Peter Foord (020 8940 1894).

SUNNINGDALE. **Sunningdale Golf Club,** Ridgemount Road, Sunningdale, Ascot SL5 9RR (01344 621681; Fax: 01344 624154). *Location:* 350 yards west of station, off A30, 25 miles from London. Heathland, 36 holes, 2 courses. *Green Fees:* Information not provided. *Eating facilities:* diningroom and three bars. *Visitors:* require introduction from Secretary of own club plus Handicap Certificate on weekdays. Fridays and weekends with member only. *Society Meetings:* accepted Tuesdays, Wednesdays and Thursdays only, by arrangement. Professional: Keith Maxwell (01344 620128). Secretary: Stephen Toon. Golf Operations for bookings (01344 298036).

SUTTON. **Banstead Downs Golf Club,** Burdon Lane, Belmont, Sutton SM2 7DD (020 8642 2284; Fax: 020 8642 5252). *Location:* A217 (10 minutes from Belmont Station). 18 holes, 6192 yards. S.S.S. 69. *Green Fees:* contact Pro Shop. *Eating facilities:* lunches served at Club every day. *Visitors:* welcome Monday, Tuesday, Wednesday, Thursday; on Friday, Saturday, Sunday with member. *Society Meetings:* catered for all day Thursdays. Professional: Ian Golding (020 8642 6884). General Manager: Reunert Bauser.
e-mail: secretary@bansteaddowns.com
website: www.bansteaddowns.com

TADWORTH. **Walton Heath Golf Club,** Deans Lane, Walton-on-the-Hill, Tadworth KT20 7TP (01737 812060). *Location:* Junction 8 M25, A217 towards London, B2032 towards Dorking, turning right hand side Deans Lane. Two 18 hole heathland courses. Old: 7462 yards, S.S.S. 75. New: 7171 yards, S.S.S. 74. Large putting green; indoor nets and small outdoor practice facilities. *Green Fees:* information not available. *Eating facilities:* restaurant and two bars. *Visitors:* welcome by previous arrangement, Handicap Certificate or letter of introduction required; limited play weekends. *Society Meetings:* catered for by arrangement. A variety of packages available for both summer and winter. Professional: Simon Peaford (01737 812152). Secretary: Mike Bawden.*

VIRGINIA WATER. **Wentworth Club Ltd,** Wentworth Drive, Virginia Water GU25 4LS (01344 842201; Fax: 01344 842804). *Location:* 21 miles south-west of London, just off the A30 at junction with A329 to Ascot. M25 and M3 three miles. Wooded heathland. West course - 18 holes, 7308 yards, S.S.S. 74; East course - 18 holes, 6201 yards, S.S.S. 70; Edinburgh course - 18 holes, 7004 yards, S.S.S. 74; Executive course - 9 holes. Driving range. *Green Fees:* information not available. *Eating facilities:* dining room, ballroom, private rooms, bar. *Visitors:* welcome weekdays only by appointment. Handicap Certificates required: Ladies 32, Men 24. Accommodation available. *Society Meetings:* welcome by prior arrangement. Director of Golf: Stephen Gibson (01344 846306). Managing Director: Julian Small (01344 842201). Director of Operations: Stuart Christie (01344 846313).*

WALTON-ON-THAMES. **Burhill Golf Club,** Burwood Road, Walton-on-Thames KT12 4BL. *Location:* M25 Junction 10, take A3 London turn off, A245 Weybridge, right into Seven Hills Road and again into Burwood Road. Two 18 hole parkland courses both differing in character, Old Course 6479 yards. S.S.S. 71, New Course 6940 yards, S.S.S. 72 - opened May 2001. Full irrigation on both courses. Practice area, driving range, putting green and short game practice area. *Green Fees:* weekdays per round – £75.00 New Course, £85.00 Old Course; £110.00 per day. Special rates November to March. *Eating facilities:* Orangery Restaurant, Captains Bar, Honours Bar, Iveagh Lounge, Barnes Wallis suite for private dining and special occasions. *Visitors:* welcome Monday to Friday. *Society Meetings:* catered for Monday to Friday. Golf Days organised to suit your particular requirements. Professional: Michael Evans (01932 221729; Fax: 01932 252533). General Manager: David Cook (01932 227345; Fax: 01932 267159). Sales Manager: Gill Fee (01932 227345; Fax: 01932 267159). Director of Golf: Pip Elson.
e-mail: info@burhillgolf-club.co.uk

WARLINGHAM near. **Farleigh Court Golf Club**, Old Farleigh Road, Farleigh CR6 9PX (01883 627711); Fax: 01883 627722). *Location:* south of Croydon. Exciting course utilising two landscaped valleys with many natural features. 27 holes (18 holes members, 9 hole pay and play). 9155 yards, 8368 metres. Practice bunker, chipping green, putting green and 285 yard practice range. *Green Fees:* information not available. *Eating facilities:* full catering facilities available (seven days). *Visitors:* welcome anytime after 10am weekdays or weekends on members course and anytime on 9 hole pay and play. *Society Meetings:* welcome anytime. Professional/Secretary: Scott Graham.*

WEST BYFLEET. **West Byfleet Golf Club**, Sheerwater Road, West Byfleet KT14 6AA (01932 343433). *Location:* Junction 10 M25 onto A245 – half a mile west of West Byfleet. Easy walking, woodland course. 18 holes, 6197 yards. S.S.S. 70. *Green Fees:* weekdays £49.00 per round, £74.00 per day. *Eating facilities:* lunches, bar snacks, teas and evening meals available. Catering: (01932 353525). Bar: (01932 343433). *Visitors:* welcome weekdays with reservation, weekends with member only. *Society Meetings:* catered for, advance bookings, minimum group size 12. Professional: David Regan (01932 343433). General Manager: I.Attoe (01932 343433).

WEST CLANDON. **Clandon Regis Golf Club Ltd**, Epsom Road, West Clandon GU4 7TT (01483 224888); Fax: 01483 211781). *Location:* between Guildford and Leatherhead on A246. Parkland setting, fairly mature for new course, four areas of water. Course designed by David Williams. 18 holes, 6485 yards. S.S.S. 72/69. Indoor practice nets, full length driving area, putting green, chipping area. *Green Fees:* weekdays £40.00; weekends £50.00 (limited). *Eating facilities:* bar meals, restaurant available for booking. *Visitors:* welcome weekdays, weekends depending on club bookings. *Society Meetings:* welcome weekdays only. Professional: Steve Lloyd (01483 223922). General Manager: Paul Napier.

WEYBRIDGE. **New Zealand Golf Club**, Woodham Lane, Woodham, Addlestone KT15 3QD (01932 345049). *Location:* junction Woodham Lane and Sheerwater Road on A245. Traditional club with secluded heathland course in heather and woodland setting. 18 holes, 6075 yards. S.S.S. 69. *Green Fees:* information not available. *Eating facilities:* lunch available Tuesdays to Fridays. *Visitors:* welcome by prior arrangement. *Society Meetings:* catered for Tuesday, Wednesday, Thursday, Friday. Professional: V.R. Elvidge. Secretary: R.A. Marrett.*

WEYBRIDGE. **St George's Hill Golf Club**, Golf Club Road, St. George's Hill, Weybridge KT13 0NL (01932 847758; Fax: 01932 821564). *Location:* M25, Junction 10 take A3 towards London, turn off towards Byfleet (A245) then B374 Brooklands Road, entrance to St. George's Hill estate one mile on right. Hilly, Surrey heathland - well wooded with plentiful heather and rhododendron. 27 holes, 6513 yards. S.S.S. 71. *Green Fees:* information not provided. *Eating facilities:* dining room, two bars. *Visitors:* welcome Wednesdays, Thursdays. Fridays only by prior arrangement with Secretary's office. *Society Meetings:* catered for on Wednesdays, Thursdays and Fridays by prior arrangement. Professional: A.C. Rattue (01932 843523). Secretary: J. Robinson (01932 847758).

WOKING. **Chobham Golf Club**, Chobham Road, Knaphill, Woking GU21 2TZ (01276 855584; Fax: 01276 855663). *Location:* on A3046 one mile outside Chobham village, ten minutes from M3 Junction 3. Wooded parkland course. 18 holes, 5863 yards, S.S.S. 69. Practice area, putting green. *Green Fees:* information not provided. *Eating facilities:* bar snacks and restaurant. *Visitors:* welcome, handicap required. Must pre-book teetime with Pro shop. *Society Meetings:* welcome. Professional: Michael Harrison (01276 855748).
e-mail: info@chobhamgolfclub.co.uk
website: www.chobhamgolfclub.co.uk

WOKING. **Hoebridge Golf Centre**, Old Woking Road, Old Woking GU22 8JH (01483 722611). *Location*: the three Hoebridge courses are laid on mature parkland of 560 acres including 190 acres of environmental grassland and 60 acres of woodland. The course natural free draining soil allows all year playability in all weather conditions. Hoebridge Course – 18 holes, white 6536 yards, Par 72, Yellow Tees 6178 yards, Par 72, red tees 5842 yards, Par 73. Shey Copse – 9 holes, 2294 yards, Par 33. Maybury – 18 holes, 2181 yards, Par 54. Undercover 36 bay floodlit driving range. 75 yard constructed external chipping range. *Green Fees:* see website. *Eating facilities*: full bar and restaurant facilities. *Visitors*: welcome. Pay and Play facility. Golfing Academy, Golf Shop. Custom fitting and Launch monitor testing. Clubs for hire. Membership, societies. Centre Manager: Mike O'Connell
e-mail: info@hoebridgegc.co.uk
website: www.hoebridgegc.co.uk

WOKING. **Traditions Golf Course 1999,** Pyrford Road, Pyrford, Woking GU22 8UE (01932 350355; Fax: 01932 350234). *Location:* into West Byfleet and turn at traffic lights into Pyrford Road. Peter Alliss design with tree-lined holes, lakes and many streams. 18 holes. Par 71. *Green Fees:* information not available. *Eating facilities:* from 7am to 10pm (to 6pm in winter). Professional: Adam Whatford. *

WOKING. **West Hill Golf Club**, Bagshot Road, Brookwood GU24 0BH (01483 474365). *Location:* M3, Junction 3, A322 entrance adjacent railway bridge Brookwood. Heathland, wooded course. Golf World "Top 100 courses in UK" listed. 18 holes, 6350 yards. S.S.S. 71. Practice range and net. *Green Fees:* contact the club. *Eating facilities:* bar snacks available, meals including dinner by prior arrangement. *Visitors:* members' guests only at weekends. Buggies by arrangement. *Society Meetings:* catered for by arrangement through the Secretary. Professional: Guy Shoesmith (01483 473172). Secretary: Gina Rivett (01483 474365; Fax: 01483 474252).
e-mail: secretary@westhill-golfclub.co.uk
website: www.westhill-golfclub.co.uk

WOKING. Windlemere Golf Club, Windlesham Road, West End, Near Woking GU24 9QL (01276 858727). *Location:* off A322. Well designed parkland course. 9 holes, 2673 yards. S.S.S. 33. Floodlit 12-bay driving range. *Green Fees:* per 9 holes - weekdays £12.00, weekends £13.50. Seniors/Juniors weekdays £10.00, weekends £11.50. 2010 rates (subject to review). *Eating facilities:* bar with light menu, normal clubhouse facilities. *Visitors:* always welcome, may book up to one week in advance. Snooker, pool facilities. *Society Meetings:* welcome to book. Professional: Dave Thomas. Secretary: M. Walsh (01276 858727).

WOKING. Woking Golf Club, Pond Road, Hook Heath, Woking GU22 0JZ (01483 760053; Fax: 01483 772441). *Location:* via Hollybank Road and Golf Club Road or Hook Heath Road and Pond Road. Traditional heathland course. 18 holes, 6340 yards. S.S.S. 70. Practice ground. *Green Fees:* information not available. *Eating facilities:* lunches and snacks available. *Visitors:* welcome but only by prior arrangement, Handicap Certificate required. *Society Meetings:* welcome by prior arrangement. Professional: C.I. Bianco (01483 769582). Secretary: G.T. Ritchie.*
website: www.wokinggolfclub.co.uk

WOKING. Worplesdon Golf Club, Heath House Road, Woking. *Location:* off A322, six miles from Guildford and six miles from Junction 3 (M3). Wooded heathland course. 18 holes, 6431 yards. S.S.S. 71. *Green Fees:* information not available. *Eating facilities:* lunches served at club. *Visitors:* weekdays only. *Society meetings:* by arrangement. Professional: Jim Christine (01483 473287) Secretary: C.K. Symington (01483 472277; Fax: 01483 473303).*

WOKING near. Pyrford Golf Club 1993, Warren Lane, Pyrford, Near Woking GU22 8XR (01483 723555; Fax: 01483 729777). *Location:* A3 - Ripley turn off, turn next to Mitsubishi garage, continue for approximately two miles, on the right Warren Lane. Inland water links, 23 acres of water. 18 holes, 6230 yards. Par 72. Practice range, putting green. *Green Fees:* information not provided. *Eating facilities:* bar snack menu available all day. *Visitors:* welcome anytime Monday to Friday and after 12 noon at weekends, tee times MUST be booked. *Society Meetings:* welcome weekdays and weekend afternoons. Professional: Andrew Blackman (01483 751070). Secretary: Andrew Lawrence.
e-mail: pyrford@crown-golf.co.uk

WOLDINGHAM. North Downs Golf Club, Northdown Road, Woldingham, Caterham CR3 7AA (01883 652057). *Location:* Wapses Lodge roundabout at Caterham. Two miles Woldingham Road. 18 holes, 5857 yards, S.S.S. 68. *Green Fees:* £35.00 per round, £20.00 after 2pm, £15.00 after 4pm, £50.00 per day. *Eating facilities:* full restaurant facilities. *Visitors:* welcome with Handicap Certificate Monday to Friday (Thursdays after 12 noon only). *Society Meetings:* catered for. Professional: M. Homewood (01883 653004). Secretary/Manager: D. Sinden (01883 652057).

YATELEY. Blackwater Valley Golf Centre, Chandlers Lane, Yateley GU46 7SZ (01252 874725). *Location:* Junction 4 of M3. Into Yateley to White Lion pub roundabout, into Vicarage Road, then Vicarage Lane. Parkland course with lakes and mature trees. 9 holes. Par 34. Driving range. *Green Fees:* information not provided. *Eating facilities:* from 11am to 10pm (to 5pm during winter). Professional: Richard Lock.

Coombe Wood Golf Club, Kingston upon Thames

East Sussex

BATTLE. **Battle Golf Club,** Netherfield Hill, Battle TN33 0LH (Tel & Fax: 01424 775677). *Location*: A2100, just 1½ miles outside historic town of Battle. Parkland, woodland course. Panoramic views, gently undulating. 9 holes, 18 tees, 5941 yards. S.S.S 68. Practice ground. *Green Fees*: information not available. *Eating facilities:* large bars, 3-course meals and bar snacks available. *Visitors:* welcome daily from 7am. Strict dress code. En suite B&B in rooms overlooking the course available throughout the year. Accommodation available plus 2, 3 or 5 days of golf with tuition. Excellent golfing breaks midweek and weekends - stay and play; B&B with free golf £50.00pp weekdays, £65.00 weekends. Special midweek offers available; for more information phone or view website. Tuition available for individuals and groups. *Society Meetings*: welcome, special rates, please telephone for details. PGA Professional: Mike Egan. Club Secretary: Clare Lyons (01424 775677).*
e-mail: clare@battegolfclub.co.uk
website: www.battlegolfclub.co.uk

BEXHILL-ON-SEA. **Cooden Beach Golf Club,** Cooden Sea Road, Bexhill-on-Sea TN39 4TR (Tel & Fax: 01424 842040). *Location:* A259 Eastbourne to Hastings road, follow `Cooden Beach' sign at Little Common roundabout (one mile). Seaside course, slightly undulating. 18 holes, 6500 yards. S.S.S. 72. Practice facilities. *Green Fees:* weekdays £40.00; weekends and Bank Holidays £46.00. *Eating facilities:* catering and bar every day. *Visitors:* welcome, preferably by prior arrangement. Buggies for hire. *Society Meetings:* prior booking necessary. Professional: Jeffrey Sim (01424 843938; Fax: 01424 842040). Secretary: Keith Wiley (Tel & Fax: 01424 842040). Caterers: Steve Ede (01424 843936).
e-mail: enquiries@coodenbeachgc.com
website: www.coodenbeachgc.com

FHG GUIDES www.holidayguides.com

BEXHILL-ON-SEA. **Highwoods Golf Club,** Ellerslie Lane, Bexhill-on-Sea TN39 4LJ (01424 212625). *Location:* off A259 north west of town. Parkland, wooded course. 18 holes, 6218 yards. S.S.S. 70. *Green Fees:* from £35.00 all day, £25.00 with member. *Eating facilities:* snacks, lunches and teas always available. *Visitors:* welcome Monday to Saturday. Sunday mornings with member only. *Society Meetings:* welcome by arrangement. Professional: M. Andrews (01424 212770). Office: (01424 212625; Fax: 01424 216866).
e-mail: highwoods@btconnect.com
website: www.highwoodsgolfclub.co.uk

BRIGHTON. **Brighton and Hove Golf Club,** Devil's Dyke Road, Brighton BN1 8YJ (01273 507861). *Location:* A27 Brighton bypass exit for Devil's Dyke, club 1½ miles north of A27. Downland course with sea views. 9 holes, 5704 yards. S.S.S. 68. Practice area. *Green Fees:* (18 holes) weekdays £24.00; weekends and Bank Holidays £30.00. *Eating facilities:* bar and restaurant daily, limited on Mondays. *Visitors:* welcome, phone call advisable Wednesday after 12 noon, Friday after 11am, Saturday and Sunday after 12 noon. *Society Meetings:* catered for; up to 30, eating 60. Director of Golf: Phil Bonsall (01273 556482). Shop (01273 556686).

BRIGHTON. **The Dyke Golf Club,** Devil's Dyke, Devil's Dyke Road, Brighton BN1 8YJ (01273 857296; Fax: 01273 857078). *Location:* A23 onto A27 (New Brighton By-pass) heading west to Worthing, turn off for Devil's Dyke and follow signs for same. Brighton's premier downland course. 18 holes, 6627 yards. S.S.S. 72. Practice fairway and putting green. *Green Fees:* information not available. *Eating facilities:* full restaurant and bar available. *Visitors*: welcome with reservation, not before 12 noon Sundays. *Society Meetings:* catered for by appointment, from £42.00 inclusive of breakfast and lunch/evening meal (other meal arrrangements can be made). Professional: Mark Stuart-William (01273 857260; Fax: 01273 857564). Secretary: Stephen Wise (01273 857296; Fax: 01273 857078).*
e-mail: office@dykegolfclub.co.uk

Brighton's premier downland course
Full Restaurant and Bar. Practice facilities.
Visitors and Societies welcome by appointment.
Devil's Dyke, Devil's Dyke Road,
Brighton, East Sussex BN1 8YJ
Tel: 01273 857296 • Fax: 01273 857078
e-mail: office@dykegolfclub.co.uk
www.dykegolf.com

The Dyke Golf Club
Brighton, Sussex

East Sussex / SOUTH REGION

BRIGHTON. **East Brighton Golf Club,** Roedean Road, Brighton BN2 5RA (01273 604838). *Location:* one and a half miles east of Palace Pier, just off A259, behind the Marina. Undulating downland course offering superb views over the Channel. 18 holes, 6426 yards. S.S.S. 71 (white tees.) Putting green. *Green Fees:* weekdays £30.00, weekends £35.00. *Eating facilities:* restaurant, diningroom, bars. *Visitors:* welcome from 9am weekdays, after 11am weekends and Bank Holidays. Handicap Certificate not required. Buggy hire available. *Society Meetings:* welcome, full day's golf and catering from £43.00 per person. General Manager: George Mckay (01273 604838; Fax: 01273 680277).

BRIGHTON. **Hollingbury Park Golf Club,** Ditchling Road, Brighton BN1 7HS (01273 552010). *Location:* between A23 and A27. 18 holes, 6429 yards. S.S.S. 71. *Green Fees:* information not available. *Visitors:* welcome. All bookings through Professional. *Society Meetings:* catered for weekdays only. Professional: Graeme Crompton (01273 500086). Secretary: (Tel & Fax: 01273 552010)*

BRIGHTON. **Waterhall Golf Club,** Saddlescombe Road, Brighton BN1 8YN (01273 508658). *Location:* off A27 Brighton bypass, take Devil's Dyke turn off, course on the right. Downland course. 18 holes, 5773 yards, 5328 metres. S.S.S. 68. Practice area. *Green Fees:* information not available. *Visitors:* welcome except weekends. *Society Meetings:* catered for except weekends or Bank Holidays by prior arrangement with Secretary. Professional: Graeme Crompton (01273 555529). Secretary: L.B. Allen.*

CROWBOROUGH. **Crowborough Beacon Golf Club,** Beacon Road, Crowborough TN6 1UJ (01892 661511). *Location:* nine miles south of Tunbridge Wells on the A26. Heathland, superb views to the sea and South Downs (on clear days). 18 holes, 6273 yards. S.S.S. 70. *Green Fees:* information not available. *Eating facilities:* restaurant available. *Visitors:* welcome weekdays, Handicap Certificate or letter of introduction essential. Please contact either the Professional or Secretary. *Society Meetings:* bookings welcome through the Secretary's office. Professional: D.C Newnham (01892 653877). Secretary: Mrs V. Harwood (01892 661511).*
e-mail: secretary@cbgc.co.uk
website: www.cbgc.co.uk

DITCHLING. **Mid-Sussex Golf Club,** Spatham Lane, Ditchling BN6 8XJ (01273 846567; Fax: 01273 847815). *Location:* five minutes from A23, one mile east of Ditchling. Mature parkland course with superbly contoured greens and strategic bunkers. 18 holes, 6431 yards. S.S.S. 71. Practice ground, driving range and short game areas. *Green Fees:* information not available. *Eating facilities:* full bar/ restaurant facilities. *Visitors:* welcome weekdays, weekends restricted. Buggies available. *Society Meetings:* welcome weekdays only. Professional: Neil Plimmer. General Manager: Andy McNiven.*
website: www.midsussexgolfclub.co.uk

Crowborough Beacon Golf Club

**Beacon Road,
Crowborough,
East Sussex TN6 1UJ
Tel: 01892 661511
Fax: 01892 611988**

This well established 18 hole heathland course, founded in 1895, stands some 800 feet above sea level and with views on clear days of the Downs, Eastbourne and the sea, it must have arguably one of the finest panoramas in Sussex. Pine and fir trees are scattered around the course and there is plenty of heather and gorse. This course will test your accuracy rather than length off the tee!

Situated 8 miles south of Tunbridge Wells, on the A26, Crowborough Beacon extends a warm welcome to golfing societies and green fee visitors.

e-mail: secretary@cbgc.co.uk
www.cbgc.co.uk

East Sussex / SOUTH REGION

EASTBOURNE. **Eastbourne Downs Golf Club,** East Dean Road, Eastbourne BN20 8ES (01323 720827; Fax: 01323 412506). *Location*: half a mile west of Eastbourne on A259. Downland course with spectacular views to the South Downs and over the sea. 18 holes, 6601 yards. S.S.S. 71. Practice area. *Green Fees*: weekdays £20.00 per round; weekends £25.00 per round. *Eating facilities*: two bars; restaurant open seven days a week 8am to 6pm. *Visitors*: welcome unrestricted after 9am weekdays and 11.15am weekends. Trolleys for hire. *Society Meetings*: welcome - full day with coffee, lunch and two-course dinner - £40.00. Professional: Terry Marshall (01323 732264). Admin Manager: (01323 720827; Fax: 01323 412506).

EASTBOURNE. **Eastbourne Golfing Park,** Lottbridge Drove, Eastbourne BN23 6QJ (Tel & Fax: 01323 520400). *Location:* end of A22; half a mile south of Hampden Park and one mile north of the sea. Pleasant easy walk, a fairly short flat course but with water on seven of the nine holes it tests the accuracy of any golfer. 9 holes, 5178 yards. S.S.S. 66. 22-bay floodlit driving range. *Green Fees:* weekdays 9 holes £11.00, 18 holes £17.00, weekends 9 holes £12.00, 18 holes £19.00. Senior Citizens and Juniors reduced rates. *Eating facilities:* full bar and restaurant open to all. *Visitors:* welcome at all times. Equipment hire available. *Society Meetings:* all welcome, please ring to book. Professionals: Barry Finch, Alan Williamson and Mitch Harrison. Secretary: Maggie Garbutt (Tel & Fax: 01323 520400).

EASTBOURNE. **Royal Eastbourne Golf Club,** Paradise Drive, Eastbourne BN20 8BP (01323 744045). *Location:* one mile from town centre via Meads Road and Compton Place Road. Undulating downland and parkland. Devonshire course:18 holes, 6077 yards. S.S.S. 69. Hartington course: 9 holes, 2147 yards. S.S.S. 61. *Green Fees:* information not available. *Eating facilities:* full catering. *Visitors:* welcome. Handicap Certificate required Long Course only. Cottage accommodation for four people. *Society Meetings:* catered for. Professional: Alan Harrison (Tel & Fax: 01323 736986). Secretary: (01323 744045).*

EASTBOURNE. **Willingdon Golf Club,** Southdown Road, Willingdon, Eastbourne BN20 9AA (01323 410983). *Location:* north of Eastbourne, one mile from station, just off A22 at traffic lights (signposted). Downland course of particular beauty. 18 holes, 6158 yards. S.S.S. 69. Practice ground and nets. *Green Fees:* weekdays £20.00 per round winter, £24.00 per round summer. *Eating facilities:* diningroom, lounge and casual bar. *Visitors:* welcome weekdays after 9am. Buggies and trolleys available. *Society Meetings:* welcome, book well in advance. Professional: Troy Moore (01323 410984; Fax: 01323 411510). Secretary: Mrs Jacqueline Packham (01323 410981; Fax: 01323 411510).

EAST GRINSTEAD. **Sweetwoods Park Golf Club,** Cowden, Edenbridge TN8 7JN (01342 850729; Fax: 01342 850866). *Location:* directly off the A264 at Holtye, 5 miles east of East Grinstead. Wooded, parkland course with many water features. 18 holes, 5343-6515 yards, S.S.S. 70-73, Par 73. Practice ground, driving range and carts provided. *Green Fees:* weekday £40.00, weekends £48.00. Twilight rates available. *Visitors:* welcome anytime, can book up to 8 days in advance. *Society Meetings:* welcome Monday to Friday; Saturday and Sunday pm. Professional: (01342 850729).
website: www.sweetwoodspark.com

FOREST ROW. **Royal Ashdown Forest Golf Club (Old Course)** Chapel Lane, Forest Row, Near East Grinstead RH18 5LR (01342 822018; Fax: 01342 825211). *Location:* 3 miles south of East Grinstead to Forest Row. Take B2110 to Tunbridge Wells in the middle of village (left at second mini-roundabout) then take fourth turning on right into Chapel Lane, turn sharp left at top of Chapel Lane then bear right through golf course to Clubhouse. Undulating heathland. 18 holes, 6518 yards. S.S.S. 71. Selected to host regional qualifier until 2009 Open Championship. *Green Fees:* weekdays £65.00 per round; £80.00 per day; weekends £80.00 per round. *Eating facilities:* lunch and tea, bar snacks. *Visitors:* welcome by prior arrangement. *Society Meetings:* welcome on Wednesday, Thursday and Friday; prior reservation essential. Steward: (01342 823014). Professional: Martyn Landsborough (01342 822247) Secretary: Douglas Neave (01342 822018; Fax: 01342 825211).
e-mail: office@royalashdown.co.uk
website: www.royalashdown.co.uk

FOREST ROW. **Royal Ashdown Forest Golf Club (West Course)** Chapel Lane, Forest Row, East Sussex RH18 5LR (01342 824866; Fax: 01342 825211). *Location:* four miles south of East Grinstead to Forest Row. Take B2110 to Tunbridge Wells in the middle of village (left at second mini-roundabout) then take fourth turning on right into Chapel Lane, turn sharp left

Play both Royal Ashdown's classic heathland courses this summer for only £70 weekdays
Quote Ref. FHG

ROYAL ASHDOWN FOREST GOLF CLUB
FOUNDED 1888
Forest Row, East Sussex RH18 5LR   Tel: 01342 822018
www.royalashdown.co.uk

at top of Chapel Lane then bear right through golf course to Clubhouse. 5606 yards, S.S.S. 67, a shorter, but not easier, version of the Old Course with, according to the late Henry Longhurst, "one of the finest par fours in the South of England" as its closing hole. *Green Fees:* weekdays £30.00 per round, £40.00 per day; weekends £35.00 per round, £47.00 per day. *Eating facilities:* full dining facilities and bar snacks available all day. *Visitors and Societies:* welcome 7 days a week by prior arrangement. Professional: M. Landsborough (01342 822247).
e-mail: office@royalashdown.co.uk
website: www.royalashdown.co.uk

HAILSHAM near. **Wellshurst Golf and Country Club,** North Street, Hellingly, Near Hailsham BN27 4EE (01435 813636; Fax: 01435 812444). *Location:* two miles from the A22 roundabout at Hailsham on the A267. Parkland course. 18 holes, 6084 yards, S.S.S. 68. 16 bay driving range with two bunker bays. *Green Fees:* 18 holes weekdays £24.00, weekends £28.00. *Eating facilities:* bar and restaurant open 7 days a week. *Visitors:* no restrictions, pay as you play course; advisable to book at weekends. Conference/wedding suite. *Society Meetings:* all welcome at any time, good rates. Professional: Richard Hollands (01435 813456). Secretary: M. Adams.

HASTINGS. **Beauport Park Golf Course Ltd,** Battle Road, St. Leonards-on-Sea TN37 7BP (01424 854245; Clubhouse functions 01424 851165). *Location:* A2100 between Hastings and Battle, in the heart of 1066 Country in an Area of Outstanding Natural Beauty. Scenic, tree-lined undulating parkland course said to be among the best in Southern England and a very good test for all handicaps. 18 holes, 6180 yards. S.S.S. 70. 9 hole Par 3 short course, 14-bay driving range. *Green Fees:* information not available. *Eating facilities:* clubhouse, restaurant and bar. *Visitors:* unrestricted, but booking advised at weekends. Professional coaching, beginners and Junior coaching groups. Adjacent riding stables and leisure centre. Other facilities and accommodation available at Bannatyne Spa Hotel. *Society Meetings:* welcome; special rates available on request for societies/Corporate Days. Course Manager: Charles Giddins.*
e-mail: info@beauportparkgolf.co.uk
website: www.beauportparkgolf.co.uk

HEATHFIELD. **Horam Park Golf Course,** Chiddingly Road, Horam, near Heathfield TN21 0JJ (01435 813477, Fax: 01435 813677). *Location:* 13 miles north of Eastbourne, seven miles east of Uckfield. Follow signs to Heathfield and turn right onto the Eastbourne Road A267, go through Horam village, club on right hand side. A delightful parkland course with wooded areas and several lakes and ponds. 9 holes (18 tees), 6128 yards, S.S.S. 69. Floodlit driving range, 5-hole Par 3 course, large putting green. *Green Fees:* information not available. *Eating facilities*: restaurant and bar facilities open seven days a week, also spike bar. *Visitors:* all facilities at Horam Park are open to the general public with no restrictions, everybody welcome. Sky Sports available. Golf tuition available from PGA Pros seven days a week. *Society Meetings*: welcome seven days a week. Professional: Giles Velvick (01435 813477). Secretary: Angie Briggs.

HOVE. **West Hove Golf Club Ltd,** Badgers Way, Hangleton, Hove BN3 8EX (01273 419738; Fax: 01273 439988). *Location:* A27 adjacent to Brighton bypass, take Hangleton Interchange exit. Downland course overlooking the sea. 18 holes, 6260 yards. S.S.S. 70. Practice/driving range, putting green. *Green Fees:* weekdays £25.00; weekends £30.00. *Eating facilities:* bar and catering all day. *Visitors:* welcome. Phone Professional for tee times. *Society Meetings:* welcome, phone for prices. Professional: (01273 413494). Secretary: Gary Salt (01273 419738; Fax: 01273 439988).
e-mail: info@westhovegolfclub.co.uk
website: www.westhovegolfclub.co.uk

LEWES. **Lewes Golf Club,** Chapel Hill, Lewes BN7 2BB (01273 473245). *Location:* east of town centre from A27 and A26. Downland course with spectacular views of Sussex countryside. 18 holes, 6224 yards. S.S.S. 70. Practice ground, practice putting green. *Green Fees:* £30.00 per round, £42.00 per day weekdays and weekends. 2010 rates (subject to review). *Eating facilities:* hot and cold food available from 11am seven days a week, bar open from 10am. *Visitors:* welcome, no green fees after 2pm Tuesdays (Summer months) or before 2pm (11am Winter) at weekends. *Society Meetings:* welcome, special rates available. Professional: Tony Hilton (01273 483823). Secretary: Joan Raffety (Tel & Fax: 01273 483474).

NEWHAVEN. **Peacehaven Golf Club,** The Clubhouse, Brighton Road, Newhaven BN9 9UH (01273 514049). *Location:* one mile from Newhaven on the right hand side of A259 towards Brighton. Downland course, short but challenging. 9 holes, 5488 yards. S.S.S. 66. *Green Fees:* information not available. *Eating facilities:* snacks, meals, full bar. *Visitors:* welcome but not before 11am weekends. *Society Meetings:* welcome except weekends, from £22.00 including lunch. Professional: Alan Tyson (01273 512602). Manager: Dawn Corke (01273 512571).*

ROTHERFIELD. **Dewlands Manor Golf Course,** Dewlands Manor, Rotherfield TN6 3JN (01892 852266; Fax: 01892 853015). *Location:* three quarters of a mile south of village of Rotherfield, just off B2101. Challenging undulating course on second highest point of Sussex. Very high quality greens with fine bents and fescue. No temporary greens used. 9 holes, 3186 yards (18 - 6372 yards). Par 72. Practice hole. *Green Fees:* information not provided *Eating facilities:* bar lunches/snacks on request. *Visitors:* welcome at all times by telephone booking. Tee times set at 15 minute intervals (optional). Handicap not required. Dress and etiquette a prerequisite. Indoor teaching with computer analysis. Buggies, trolleys for hire. *Society Meetings:* welcome. Professional: Nick Godin. Course Director: Trevor Robins (01892 852266).

RYE. **Rye Golf Club,** Camber, Rye TN31 7QS (01797 225241/225460). *Location:* A259 from Rye, take Camber road to coast. Seaside links. Old Course: 18 holes, 6308 yards. S.S.S. 71. Jubilee Course: 9 holes, 6118 yards. S.S.S. 71. *Green Fees:* information not provided. *Eating facilities:* lunch only. Bars. *Visitors:* welcome, only on introduction by a member. Dormy house accommodation available – contact I. Rayson (01797 227882). Professional: Michael Lee (01797 225218). Secretary: J.H. Laidler (01797 225241; Fax: 01797 225460).
e-mail: links@ryegolfclub.co.uk
website: www.ryegolfclub.co.uk

East Sussex / SOUTH REGION

SEAFORD. Seaford Golf Club, Firle Road, East Blatchington, Seaford BN25 2JD (01323 892442; Fax: 01323 894113). *Location:* turn inland at War Memorial in Seaford, follow the road for one and a quarter miles. Downland course with magnificent views over Seaford Head and The Channel. 18 holes, 6546 yards, 5986 metres. S.S.S. 71. Practice ground. *Green Fees:* information not available. *Eating facilities:* bar and dining room open all day. Dormy House, 10 twin bedded rooms with en suite facilities. *Visitors:* welcome weekdays other than Tuesdays. Telephone first. *Society Meetings:* catered for Wednesdays and Thursdays. Professional: Chris Lovis (01323 894160). Secretary: Lawrence Dennis-Smither (01323 892442; Fax: 01323 894113).
e-mail: secretary@seafordgolfclub.co.uk
website: www.seafordgolfclub.co.uk

SEAFORD. Seaford Head Golf Club, Southdown Road, Seaford BN25 4HR (01323 894843). *Location:* midway between Eastbourne and Brighton on A259, signposted on entering Seaford. Downland course along cliff edge with view of "Seven Sisters". 18 holes, 5848 yards. S.S.S. 68. *Green Fees:* information not provided. *Eating facilities:* bar snacks and catering for Society Meetings. *Visitors:* welcome. *Society Meetings:* welcome, bookings with Professional. Professional: F. Morley (01323 890139). Secretary: R. W. Andrews (01323 894843).

SEDLESCOMBE. Sedlescombe Golf Club, Kent Street, Near Battle, TN33 0SD (01424 871700). Home of The James Andrews School of Golf. *Location:* 1066 Country, 5 miles north of Hastings on the A21, 3 miles from Battle. Gently undulating parkland course, 18 holes, 6269 yards. S.S.S. 70. 24 bay floodlit driving range, 4 practice putting greens, academy hole and bunkers. Residential golf school with 2, 3 and 5 day intensive courses for all ages and abilities. 5 PGA Professionals. Facilities include indoor video and computer analysis centre, on-site hotel, golf shop and tennis courts. *Green Fees:* information not available. *Eating facilities:* bar and restaurant open seven days. *Visitors:* course open to public. *Society Meetings:* welcome. Head Professional: James Andrews (01424 871700). Club Secretary (01424 871700). Golf School (01424 871717).*
website: www.golfschool.co.uk

UCKFIELD. East Sussex National Golf Resort and Spa, Little Horsted, Uckfield TN22 5ES (01825 880088; Fax: 01825 880066). *Location:* off the A22 Eastbourne road following the Uckfield by-pass, 30 minutes from Gatwick. American style, wooded, bent grasses. Two Championship courses; West: 18 holes, 6760 yards. S.S.S. 72; East: 18 holes, 6638 yards. S.S.S. 72. 3 hole Teaching Academy, Driving Range. *Green Fees:* Sunday to Thursday £45.00, Friday and Saturday £60.00. *Eating facilities:* three restaurants available. *Visitors:* welcome anytime. Luxury accommodation available on site in the 104 bedroom 4 star hotel which includes Health Club with indoor pool and Spa. General Manager: Derek Howe.
e-mail: reception@eastsussexnational.co.uk
website: www.eastsussexnational.co.uk

UCKFIELD. Piltdown Golf Club, Piltdown, Uckfield TN22 3XB (01825 722033; Fax: 01825 724192). *Location:* one mile west of Maresfield off A272, signposted. Undulating gorse and heather. 18 holes, 6076 yards. S.S.S. 69. Practice ground, putting green. *Green Fees:* information not available. *Visitors:* welcome; some time restrictions. Jacket and tie obligatory in diningroom. Smart dress on course. *Society Meetings:* catered for by prior arrangement. Professional: Jason Partridge (01825 722389). Secretary/ General Manager: I. Wallace (01825 722033).
e-mail: secretary@piltdowngolfclub.co.uk
website: www.piltdowngolfclub.co.uk

WADHURST. Dale Hill Golf Club, Ticehurst, Wadhurst TN5 7DQ (01580 201090 Fax: 01580 201249). *Location:* on B2087, one mile off A21 to west of Flimwell, 50 miles south of London, 16 miles north of Hastings. Open front nine and wooded back nine. 18 holes, 5856 yards. S.S.S. 68. Ian Woosnam Course (buggy only), 18 holes, 6512 yards. S.S.S. 72. Designed by Ian Woosnam to championship standards. Practice area and green, driving range. *Green Fees:* information not provided. *Eating facilities:* bar and brasserie. *Visitors:* welcome after 7.30am. 35 room luxury hotel, gym and swimming pool. Conference facilities. Buggies, trolleys. *Society Meetings:* catered for by prior arrangement. Secretary: (01580 201800).
e-mail: info@dalehill.co.uk
website: www.dalehill.co.uk

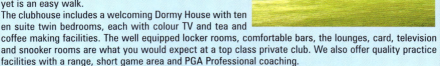

SEAFORD GOLF CLUB
Firle Road, Seaford, East Sussex BN25 2JD
Tel: 01323 892442 • Fax: 01323 894113

Seaford Golf Club has possibly the finest downland course in Sussex, offering glorious views of the Channel and Downs, yet is an easy walk.
The clubhouse includes a welcoming Dormy House with ten en suite twin bedrooms, each with colour TV and tea and coffee making facilities. The well equipped locker rooms, comfortable bars, the lounges, card, television and snooker rooms are what you would expect at a top class private club. We also offer quality practice facilities with a range, short game area and PGA Professional coaching.
e-mail: secretary@seafordgolfclub.co.uk • www.seafordgolfclub.co.uk

West Sussex

ALBOURNE. **Singing Hills Golf Course Ltd,** Albourne BN6 9EB (01273 835353; Fax: 01273 835444). *Location:* on the B2117 just off the A23. Gently undulating parkland course with spectacular views of the South Downs. 3 x 9 hole courses. S.S.S. 70. 15 bay driving range, putting green. *Green Fees:* information not provided. *Eating facilities:* Pavilion Restaurant, large bar. *Visitors:* welcome, no restrictions. *Society Meetings:* welcome, variety of golf and food packages for minimum 12 players. Professional: Wallace Street. Assistant Professional: Arron Trott. Secretary: Michael Whitty.
e-mail: info@singinghills.co.uk
website: www.singinghills.co.uk

ANGMERING. **Ham Manor Golf Club Ltd,** Angmering BN16 4JE (01903 775653). *Location:* on A259 between Worthing and Littlehampton. Flat parkland course. 18 holes, 6216 yards. S.S.S. 70. *Green Fees:* £35.00. *Eating facilities:* lunches every day. *Visitors:* welcome. Handicap Certificate required. *Society Meetings:* catered for thursdays only. Professional: Simon Buckley (01903 783732). Secretary: Paul Bodle (01903 783288).

BILLINGSHURST. **Foxbridge Golf Club,** Foxbridge Lane, Plaistow Road, Kirdford, Billingshurst RH14 0LB (Tel & Fax: 01403 753303). *Location:* B2133, A281 Guildford to Horsham Road. Parkland course with eight lakes. 9 holes, 6236 yards. S.S.S. 70. Practice ground. *Green Fees:* information not available. *Eating facilities:* restaurant and bar. *Visitors:* welcome. Buggies and carts available. *Society Meetings:* welcome. Professional: Neil Burke. Secretary: Elaine Purton (01403 753303; Fax: 01403 751975).

BOGNOR REGIS. **Bognor Regis Golf Club,** Downview Road, Felpham, Bognor Regis PO22 8JD (01243 865867; Fax: 01243 860719). *Location:* turn north at traffic lights on A259 at Felpham village. Flat parkland, many dogleg holes and water hazards. 18 holes, 6238 yards. S.S.S. 69, Par 70. Practice area. *Green Fees:* see web site for current offers. *Eating facilities:* bar open every day; hot and cold snacks available weekdays, light snacks available weekends. *Visitors:* welcome weekdays (Ladies' Day Tuesday), weekends when available. Handicap Certificate required. *Society Meetings:* welcome by arrangement (minimum 16). Professional: (01243 821929). Secretary: (01243 821929; Fax: 01243 860719).
e-mail: sec@bognorgolfclub.co.uk
website: www.bognorgolfclub.co.uk

BRIGHTON. **Pyecombe Golf Club,** Clayton Hill, Pyecombe, Brighton BN45 7FF (01273 845372; Fax: 01273 843338). *Location:* four miles north of Brighton on A273 Burgess Hill Road. Downland with magnificent views. 18 holes, 6251 yards, 5716 metres. S.S.S. 70. Two practice areas. *Green Fees:* information not available. *Eating facilities:* catering/bars from 10.30am daily. *Visitors:* welcome, after 9.15am weekdays. *Society Meetings:* welcome weekdays by prior arrangement. Professional: J. Bowen (01273 845398; Fax: 01273 843338). Secretary: J.M. Wilkinson (01273 845372; Fax: 01273 843338).*

Dale Hill Golf Club, Wadhurst, East Sussex

SOUTH REGION / West Sussex

BURGESS HILL. The Burgess Hill Golf Centre, Cuckfield Road, Burgess Hill RH15 8RE (01444 258585; Fax: 01444 247318). *Location:* on the B2036 north of Burgess Hill, on the Burgess Hill to Cuckfield road. An excellent short course in undulating wooded, parkland setting. 9 holes, 1250 yards. Par 3. 28 bay floodlit driving range, practice area, PGA teaching academy, Pro shop. *Green Fees:* information not provided. *Eating facilities:* bar and restaurant. *Visitors:* welcome, open from 8am to 9pm. Professional/Secretary: Mark Collins (01444 258585; Fax: 01444 247318).
website: www.burgesshillgolfcentre.co.uk

CHICHESTER. Chichester Golf Club, Hunston Village, Chichester PO20 1AX (01243 533833). *Location:* take B2145 south of Chichester, on left hand side after Hunston Village. 45 hole golf complex. Cathedral Course 18 holes, 6442 yards, Par 72; Tower Course 18 holes, 6109 yards, Par 69. Separate family golf centre: Par 3, 829 yards short course, mini golf, Golf Academy with video analysis and 27-bay floodlit driving range including automated power tee system. *Green Fees:* information not available. *Eating facilities:* fully licensed non-smoking bar and restaurant. *Visitors:* welcome anytime. *Society Meetings:* welcome. Well stocked golf shops. Head Professional: James Willmott (01243 528999). Proprietor: Sally Haygarth (01243 536666; Fax: 01243 539922). *
e-mail: enquiries@chichestergolf.com
website: www.chichestergolf.com

CHICHESTER. Golf at Goodwood, The Kennels, Goodwood, Chichester PO18 0PN. *Location:* one mile north of Chichester at east end of Chichester Bypass (A27). Architect James Braid (1914), renovated Howard Swan (2005). Undulating downland. 18 holes, 7104 yards. S.S.S. 74. Practice ground, nets, putting greens. *Green Fees:* information not available. *Eating facilities:* full catering and bar. *Visitors:* members only. *Society Meetings:* members only. Professional: Damon Allard (01243 755135). Secretary: (01243 755130; Fax: 01243 755135).*
e-mail: golf@goodwood.co.uk
website: www.goodwood.co.uk

CHICHESTER. Selsey Golf Club, Golf Links Lane, Selsey, Chichester PO20 9DR (01243 608935). *Location:* B2145, seven miles south of Chichester. Flat course. 9 holes playing 18, 5532 yards. S.S.S. 68. *Green Fees:* information not available. *Eating facilities:* lunches and snacks served in club. *Visitors:* welcome with bona fide Handicap Certificate or playing with a member. *Society Meetings:* small societies catered for weekdays only. Professional: P. Grindley (01243 608936). Secretary: B. Rogers (01243 608935; Fax: 01243 607101).
e-mail: secretary@selseygolfclub.com
website: www.selseygolfclub.co.uk

COWDRAY PARK Cowdray Park Golf Club, Petworth Road, Midhurst GU29 0BB (01730 813599; Fax: 01730 815900). *Location:* one mile east of Midhurst on A272 between Midhurst and Petworth. A testing parkland course with scenic views of the Downs and polo fields and Cowdray ruins. 18 holes, 6265 yards. S.S.S. 70. Driving range and Par 3 Academy. *Green Fees:* information not available. *Eating facilities:* restaurant and bar snacks. *Visitors:* welcome. Dormy house. *Society Meetings:* catered for. Professional: Scott Brown. Secretary: Malcolm Upfield. *
e-mail: enquiries@cowdraygolf.co.uk
website: www.cowdraygolf.co.uk

CRAWLEY. Copthorne Golf Club, Borers Arms Road, Copthorne, Crawley RH10 3LL (01342 712033). *Location:* off Exit 10 M23, one mile on A264 towards East Grinstead. Flat wooded course. 18 holes, 6505 yards. S.S.S. 71. Practice area. *Green Fees:* weekdays £40.00; weekends £45.00. *Eating facilities:* catering all day, bar. *Visitors:* welcome weekdays without reservation, after 1pm weekends. *Society Meetings:* welcome with advance bookings. Professional: Joe Burrell (01342 712405). Secretary: J. Pyne (01342 712508; Fax: 01342 717682)

CRAWLEY. Ifield Golf Club, Rusper Road, Ifield, Crawley RH11 0LN (01293 520222). *Location:* outskirts of Crawley near A23 to Gossops Green. Undulating parkland. 18 holes, 6314 yards. S.S.S. 70. Practice ground. *Green Fees:* £25.00 per round weekdays; Sundays pm only. *Eating facilities:* fully licensed bar, à la carte restaurant. *Visitors:* welcome, please telephone. Trolley and buggies for hire. *Society Meetings:* welcome. Professional: Jon Earl (01293 523088; Fax: 01293 612973). Office (01293 520222).

CRAWLEY. Pease Pottage Golf Centre, Horsham Road, Pease Pottage, Crawley RH11 9SG (01293 521706; Fax: 01293 521706). *Location:* M23 Junction 11, Pease Pottage, Black Swan. Wooded areas surrounding golf course. 9 holes, 1864 yards. S.S.S. 60, Par 4/3. 22 bay floodlit driving range, open from dawn 'till dusk. *Green Fees:* weekdays £8.50; weekends £10.00 for 18 holes. Senior Citizens £6.00. *Eating facilities:* restaurant, coffee shop. *Visitors:* welcome, no restrictions. Two PGA Professionals available for tuition. Full on site repair service. Right Sided Golf Academy. Professionals: Luke Ringrose, Steve Fenn (01293 521706). Secretary: Natalie Leszczar.

CRAWLEY. Tilgate Forest Golf Centre, Titmus Drive, Tilgate, Crawley RH10 5EU (01293 530103). *Location:* Crawley, five minutes from Junction 11 M23. Wooded parkland. 18 holes, 6167 yards, 5643 metres. Par 72. 35 bay floodlit driving range. Par 3 course. *Green Fees:* information not provided. On-line booking available. *Eating facilities:* restaurant and bar. *Visitors:* welcome at all times but there is a booking system in operation. *Society Meetings:* welcome, phone for details. Professional: William Easdale (01293 530103; Fax: 01293 523478).
website: www.glendale-golf.com

THE APPEARANCE OF AN ASTERISK (*) AT THE END OF A CLUB OR COURSE ENTRY INDICATES THAT UP-TO-DATE INFORMATION HAS NOT BEEN SUPPLIED

CRAWLEY. **Cottesmore Golf and Country Club,** Buchan Hill, Pease Pottage, Crawley RH11 9AT (01293 528256; Fax: 01293 522819). *Location:* one mile west of Junction 11 off M23 on road through Pease Pottage. Two mature golf courses set in 247 acres of rolling Sussex countryside. The fairways are lined with rhododendrons, silver birch, oak and chestnut trees. Four holes over lakes. Griffin Course 18 holes, 6248 yards. S.S.S. 70, par 71. Phoenix Course 18 holes, 5514 yards. S.S.S. 66, par 69. Practice ground, putting greens. *Green Fees:* information not available. *Eating facilities:* restaurant, coffee shop, two bars. *Visitors:* welcome. Health Club including indoor heated pool, tennis courts and gymnasium; en suite accommodation (21 rooms) also available. Trolleys and buggies available. *Society Meetings:* welcome, advance bookings required. Professional: Calum Callan (01293 861777; Fax: 01293 522819). General Manager: (01293 528256).*

CUCKFIELD. **Cuckfield Golf Centre,** Staplefield Road, Cuckfield RH17 5HY (01444 459999). *Location:* one mile north of Cuckfield village. Undulating open parkland course with outstanding views in an Area of Outstanding Natural Beauty. 9 holes, 18 tees. 5066 yards. Par 71. Putting green. *Green Fees:* 9 holes weekdays £10.00; weekends £11.00; 18 holes weekdays £14.00; weekends £16.00; £1.00 discount Juniors and Senior Citizens. *Eating facilities:* new clubhouse with fully licensed cafe bar. *Visitors:* always welcome. Pay and play; no Handicap Certificate required. Hire clubs, buggies and trolleys, please phone for availability. PGA teaching academy and practice facilities available. *Society Meetings:* always welcome. Head Professional: R. Dickman. Director of Teaching: N. Perryman-Best. Secretary: Mrs L. Dickman.
e-mail: lucy@cuckfieldgolf.co.uk
website: www.cuckfieldgolf.co.uk

EAST GRINSTEAD. **Chartham Park,** Felcourt Road, Felcourt, East Grinstead RH19 2JT (01342 870340; Fax: 01342 870719). *Location:* Felcourt Road off A22 on north side of East Grinstead. Parkland. 18 holes, 6680 yards. S.S.S. 72. Driving range, putting green. *Green Fees:* information not available. *Eating facilities:* restaurant, light snacks and bar all day. *Visitors:* pre-booking required. Golf carts and trolleys can be hired. *Society Meetings:* by prior arrangement. Professional: David Hobbs. General Manager: Nicky Briggs.

EAST GRINSTEAD. **Holtye Golf Club,** Holtye Common, Cowden, Near Edenbridge TN8 7ED (01342 850635). *Location:* four miles east of East Grinstead on A264, seven miles west of Tunbridge Wells. Undulating forest course; alternate tees. 9 holes, 5325 yards. S.S.S. 66. Large practice ground. *Green Fees:* weekdays £16.00; weekends £18.00. Lower rates in afternoon. *Eating facilities:* available every lunchtime, some evenings in summer season. *Visitors:* welcome, restrictions Wednesday, Thursday and weekend mornings. *Society Meetings:* catered for. Professional: Kevin Hinton (01342 850635). Secretary: Mrs D. M. Botham (01342 850635).

Cottesmore is a 36-hole golf club set in 247 acres of rolling, tree-edged Sussex countryside. Situated in Pease Pottage in the beautiful Sussex countryside, the course provides a great location for a relaxing game of golf in tranquil surroundings, with several mature trees and water that comes into play on several holes.

The course is only one mile from the M23 and just 15 minutes from Gatwick Airport, making it a great meeting point for friends and family. Try out your skills on the shorter Phoenix course or the more challenging Griffin course. The atmosphere in the club, leisure facilities and comfortable bedrooms encourages you to relax and enjoy your visit.

COTTESMORE Golf & Country Club
Buchan Hill, Pease Pottage, Crawley, West Sussex RH11 9AT
Tel: 01293 528256 • Fax: 01293 522819
e-mail: cottesmore@crown-golf.co.uk • www.cottesmoregolf.co.uk

EFFINGHAM. Effingham Park Golf Club, West Park Road, Copthorne RH10 8AL (01342 716528). *Location:* Junction 10 M23, two miles east on A264. Parkland (wooded), large lake in play over four holes. 9 holes, 1815 yards. S.S.S. 57 (18 holes). *Green Fees:* information not available. *Eating facilities:* club bar and restaurant. *Visitors:* welcome, restricted Tuesday evenings, Wednesday and Thursday mornings. Five star Hotel on site and leisure club. *Society Meetings:* catered for anytime weekdays, weekends after 12 noon. Club Professional: Mark Root. Secretary: Ian McRobbie. *

HASSOCKS. Hassocks Golf Club, London Road, Hassocks BN6 9NA . *Location:* on the A273 between Burgess Hill and Hassocks. Gently undulating pay and play course. 18 holes, 5703 yards, 5215 metres. S.S.S. 68. Driving range, irons only. *Green Fees:* weekdays £20.00; weekends £25.00, twilight rates available on application. *Eating facilities:* restaurant, bar, stud bar. *Visitors:* welcome anytime. Buggy for hire, £20.00. *Society Meetings:* welcome. Professional: Michael Ovett (01273 846990). Manager: Hamish Chambers (01273 846630; Fax: 01273 846070).
e-mail: hassocksgolfclub@btconnect.com
website: www.hassocksgolfclub.co.uk

HAYWARDS HEATH. Haywards Heath Golf Club, High Beech Lane, Haywards Heath RH16 1SL (01444 414457). *Location:* two miles north of Haywards Heath. Parkland. 18 holes, 6216 yards. S.S.S. 70. Practice areas. *Green Fees:* weekdays £32.00 per round, £47.00 for 36 holes; weekends and Bank Holidays £42.00 for 18 holes, £53.00 for over 18 holes. 2010 rates (subject to review). Packages for societies. *Eating facilities:* bar and catering both available. *Visitors:* welcome, by arrangement, phone Professional; Handicap Certificate required. *Society Meetings:* catered for Wednesdays and Thursdays by arrangement with the Secretary. Professional: M.P. Henning (01444 414866). Secretary: G.K. Honeysett.

HORSHAM. Horsham Golf and Fitness, Worthing Road, Horsham RH13 0AX (01403 271525; Fax: 01403 274528). *Location*: A24 Horsham bypass (southwest roundabout), 200 yards towards Horsham. Parkland with several water features. 9 holes, 4122 yards. S.S.S. 60. Driving range. *Green Fees*: from £6.00. *Eating facilities*: restaurant/bar open all day. *Visitors*: welcome at all times. Large well stocked shop, fitness suite on site. *Society Meetings*: welcome with booking. Professional/ Secretary: Chris Purton.

HORSHAM. Mannings Heath Golf Club, "Fullers", Hammerpond Road, Mannings Heath, Near Horsham RH13 6PG (01403 210228; Fax: 01403 270974). *Location:* off J11 M23, three miles south of Horsham off A281. Undulating wooded course with featured streams. Waterfall: 18 holes, 6683 yards (Gold tees). S.S.S. 72; Kingfisher Course: 18 holes, 6217 yards. S.S.S. 70. Driving range, two practice putting greens, chipping green. *Green Fees*: Waterfall Course, members and residents only; Kingfisher Course £30.00 weekdays (please call for current offers). On-line booking available. £45.00pp weekends. *Eating facilities*: luxurious clubhouse "Fullers", full bar, restaurant and spike bar facilities. *Visitors*: welcome; book online, or 4 weeks in advance by phone. Conference/ meeting facilities. *Society Meetings*: welcome at all times, full/half day. Professional: Neil Darnell. General Manager: Steve Slinger.
e-mail: enquiries@manningsheath.com
website: www.manningsheath.com

HORSHAM near. Slinfold Golf and Country Club, Stane Street (A29), Slinfold, Near Horsham RG13 7RE (01403 791154; Fax: 01403 791465). *Location:* situated on the A29, four miles west of Horsham with good road links to the M23 and East/West on the A272. A gently undulating parkland course with many interesting water features and mature trees. 18 Hole Championship Course, 6418 yards. 9 Hole course. S.S.S. 71. 19 bay floodlit driving range. *Green Fees:* information not available. *Eating facilities:* purpose built clubhouse with restaurant and bar. *Visitors:* welcome subject to tee time availability. Reservations can be made up to seven days in advance. No handicap required. *Society Meetings:* welcome weekdays and weekends. Professional: Ryan Fenwick (01403 791154). General Manager: Andy McNiven (01403 791154).

LINDFIELD. Lindfield Golf Club, East Mascalls Lane, Lindfield RH16 2QN (01444 484467; Fax: 01444 482769). *Location*: take Lewes Road out of Lindfield village one mile then left. Downland with water and River Ouse. 18 holes, 5957 yards. S.S.S. 68. Practice ground, putting green. *Green Fees*: weekdays £20.00, weekends £15.00. 2010 rates (subject to review). *Eating facilities*: restaurant and bar. *Visitors*: welcome daily. Trolleys. *Society Meetings*: welcome every day. Professional: Paul Lyons. General Manager: Louise Marks.
website: www.thegolfcollege.com

Looking for accommodation near golf clubs?, then visit
www.holidayguides.com
for where to stay when playing golf around the regions

West Sussex / SOUTH REGION

LITTLEHAMPTON. **Littlehampton Golf Club,** 170 Rope Walk, Riverside West, Littlehampton BN17 5DL (01903 717170; Fax: 01903 726629). *Location:* leave A259 one mile west of Littlehampton at sign. Seaside links. 18 holes, 6244 yards. S.S.S. 70. *Green Fees:* information not available. *Eating facilities:* restaurant and two bars. *Visitors:* welcome weekdays, weekends after 1pm, but phone prior to arrival. *Society Meetings:* societies only, minimum number 12. Professional: Stuart Fallow (01903 717170 ext 225). Secretary: Steven Graham.*
e-mail: lgc@talk21.com
website: www.littlehamptongolf.co.uk

PETWORTH. **Petworth Golf Course,** "Osiers Farm", London Road, Petworth GU28 9LX (Tel & Fax: 01798 344097; mobile: 07932 163941). Open all year round. *Location:* 2 miles north of Petworth on A283, heading northbound towards Guildford. Undulating natural farmland course, plenty of hedges and ditches. 18 holes, 6191 yards, S.S.S. 71. Nets and course practice holes. *Green Fees:* information not available. *Eating Facilities*: clubhouse catering for up to 80 people. *Visitors*: welcome anytime, B&B on site. Tuition available. *Society Meetings*: welcome. Professional: Steve Hall (01798 873487). Manager: Andy Long (01798 344097). Secretary: Matt Harrison (01798 343518).*
e-mail: info@petworthgolfcourse.co.uk
website: www.petworthgolfcourse.co.uk

PULBOROUGH. **West Sussex Golf Club,** Golf Club Lane, Wiggonholt, Pulborough RH20 2EN (01798 872563). *Location:* between Storrington and Pulborough on the A283. Heathland. 18 holes, 6264 yards. S.S.S. 70. Driving range. *Green Fees:* summer: weekdays £70.00 18 holes, £90.00 36 holes; weekends £80.00 18 holes, £100.00 36 holes. Winter: £70.00 weekdays, £80.00 weekends. *Eating facilities:* lunch and tea daily, bars. *Visitors:* welcome by prior arrangement (not Fridays). No three or four balls. *Society Meetings:* catered for Wednesdays and Thursdays. Professional: T. Packham (01798 872426). Secretary: A. Stubbs (01798 872563; Fax: 01798 872033).
e-mail: secretary@westsussexgolf.co.uk
website: www.westsussexgolf.co.uk

RUSTINGTON. **Rustington Golf Centre,** Golfers Lane, Angmering BN16 4NB (01903 850790; Fax: 01903 850982). *Location:* on A259 at Rustington, near Littlehampton. 18 holes, 5735 yards, S.S.S. 70. 9 hole Par 3 course, three hole academy course, putting green, 30 bay floodlit driving range (15 automated). *Green Fees:* information not available. *Eating facilities:* coffee shop and licensed bar. *Visitors:* welcome at all times. Cranfield Golf Academy available for tuition of all standards. Large Golf Store. *Society Meetings:* societies and corporate days welcome by appointment. Centre Manager: Stuart Langmead (01903 850790; Fax: 01903 850982).

WEST CHILTINGTON. **West Chiltington Golf Club,** Broadford Bridge Road, West Chiltington RH20 2YA (01798 813574; Fax: 01798 812631). *Location:* A29 Bognor to London Road, right at Adversane village B2132 then signposted. Gently undulating parkland with spectacular views of South Downs. 18 holes, 5967 yards. S.S.S. 69. 9 holes, 1360 yard short course ideal for beginners. 13-bay driving range. *Green Fees:* information not available. *Visitors:* always welcome, smart dress. Tee times may be booked through Pro Shop (01798 812115). *Society Meetings:* welcome, apply to Secretary. Secretary: Debbie Haines. General Manager: Richard Gough.*
website: www.westchiltgolf.co.uk

WORTHING. **Hill Barn Golf Club,** Hill Barn Lane, Worthing BN14 9QF (01903 237301). *Location:* signposted on the roundabout at the top of Broadwater, Worthing on the A27. Downland course with a few trees but generally fairly open. 18 holes, 6229 yards. S.S.S. 70. Small practice area (balls not provided) and putting green. *Green Fees:* information not available. *Eating facilities:* clubhouse and bar. *Visitors:* welcome, no restrictions or Handicap required. *Society Meetings:* welcome. Manager: Kevin Black (01903 237301).*
e-mail: info@hillbarngolf.com

WORTHING. **Worthing Golf Club,** Links Road, Worthing BN14 9QZ (01903 260801; Fax: 01903 694664). *Location:* on A27 250 yards east of junction with A24 (Offington Roundabout). Two downland courses. Lower course: 18 holes, 6505 yards. S.S.S. 72. Upper course: 5211 yards. S.S.S. 65. *Green Fees:* weekdays £55.00 per day; weekends and Bank Holidays £50.00/£40.00 per round. *Eating facilities:* dining room, lounge and bar. *Visitors:* welcome, check in advance with Pro Shop. *Society Meetings:* catered for by arrangement. Professional: Stephen Rolley (01903 260718; Fax: 01903 694613). General Manager: John Holton (01903 260801; Fax: 01903 694664).

For full details of convenient accommodation near clubs and courses
www.holidayguides.com

Please mention this guide when enquiring about clubs or accommodation

Golf in the East

John Smith • Regional Secretary, PGA East

Bedfordshire • Cambridgeshire • Essex
Greater London • Hertfordshire • Norfolk • Suffolk

PGA East Region offers some wonderful golfing opportunities with plenty of variety in some 350 clubs where golfers are spoilt for choice.

Suffolk and Norfolk include some heathland and links gems while the counties of Essex, Hertfordshire, Cambridgeshire, Bedfordshire and Middlesex have some magnificent parkland courses, many of them well over 100 years old.

Stunning views at Sheringham, the clifftop course at Royal Cromer and the magnificent fast greens at Hunstanton, which has hosted so many top events over the years, can provide many long-lasting memories. There is a new championship course near Hunstanton called

Cambridge National Golf, (Cambridge Meridian Golf Club)

Crews Hill Golf Club, Enfield (London)

Heacham Manor which is owned by Searle's Leisure Group. The four-star boutique hotel on the course is now up and running complete with a spa, pool and gymnasium. The course may be new but the hotel is a charming converted house dating back to the 16th century and provides an ideal base for spending a few days in Norfolk.

King's Lynn Golf Club was founded in 1923 but only moved to Castle Rising in 1975. The new course, designed by Dave Thomas and Peter Alliss, was carved out of a pine and silver birch forest not far from the Royal Sandringham Estate. It compares with the best in the land and reminds many people of Woburn.

In Suffolk two gems within three miles of one another are Aldeburgh and Thorpeness, Aldeburgh providing perhaps one of the toughest tests in the region. Some of the gorse has been cut back but some new championship tees have been installed. The greens are fast and true and the fairways drain so well that winter rules are virtually unknown. The coastal heathland course at Thorpeness was designed by James Braid in 1922. It is built on sandy soil and also drains well. It is an excellent winter course that caters for short breaks at the superb on-site hotel. Accommodation is available at the club. Haverhill, in West Suffolk, has an original nine holes round the River Stour and the new nine have matured well. Furthermore the club has some of the best greens in the region.

Essex can boast some top class parkland courses. Stock Brook Country Club, which hosts the PGA Virgin Atlantic Classic professional tournament, provides a real test of golf in scenic surroundings with plenty of mature trees. The venue, which has a superb Health Club, is also the ideal location for your dream wedding reception or dinner/dance. Colchester, designed by James Braid, Chelmsford and Thorndon Park are other top quality venues.

Golf by the seaside can be found at Frinton and Clacton, the venue of the PGA East Region Virgin Atlantic Summer Classic. Both provide intriguing tests which can become very tricky indeed on a windy day. Clacton is the older by three years, having been founded in 1892, but both courses are thoroughly enjoyable, with a warm welcome in the professionals' shops and club houses.

Nazeing, thriving under new ownership, is notable for some well-placed water hazards. The par three 13th is the signature hole, with water to the right and out of bounds to the left, testing the best.

An amazing number of courses are found on the outskirts of London. They provide areas of tranquillity away from the hustle and bustle found immediately outside the gates. Bush Hill Park, Grim's Dyke, Hendon, Wanstead, Crews Hill, West Middlesex, South Herts, Woolston Manor and the wooded and hilly West Essex are prime examples.

Chigwell, founded in 1925, is a most attractive private members' club with willow trees a feature on several holes. Hainault Forest, a pay and play club, has new owners, ensuring that it will be restored to its former glories. There are two courses, the Upper and the Lower, both designed by the great J H Taylor in 1905 and 1923 respectively. The 12th hole on the Lower course, a 386-yard par four, is renowned as one of the best holes in the entire country.

Bishop's Stortford, on the Essex-Hertfordshire border, is headquarters of the PGA East Region, and hosted the PGA East Anglian Open. The club celebrated its centenary year in 2010, and visitors are assured of a friendly welcome at this parkland course, an ideal venue for a tremendous society day or green fee. East Herts Golf Club in glorious

Essex Golf & Country Club, Colchester, Essex

Hamels Park, just north of Puckeridge on the A10, hosts the Weston Homes Plc Classic. It is a joy to play over the rolling parkland, with wonderfully mature trees, many planted in the late 18th century.

Knebworth Golf Club, host to the PGA Order of Merit, is a good test of golf for the tournament professional or the aspiring amateur. The traditional parkland layout was designed by Willie Park Jnr and opened in 1908, but a great many trees have been introduced over the past 50 years and the new clubhouse facilities are superb. Brocket Hall has two splendid courses, the Melbourne and the Palmerston, named after former Prime Ministers who once lived there. The Melbourne, designed by Peter Alliss and Clive Clark, has a ferry over the lake at the 18th hole.

A jewel in Bedfordshire's crown is John O'Gaunt founded in 1948. Choose between the John O'Gaunt course which is 6531 yards, or the Carthagena, only 5869 yards. Both provide a real test for golfers before they relax in the club house, a mansion built in 1859.

If you play on the parkland course at Ely City there are wonderful views of the 12th century cathedral.

The Links at Newmarket, on the other side of the road from the Rowley Mile race course, attracts many of the racing fraternity. It was founded by Colonel Henry McCalmont, MP for Newmarket East and owner of 1893 Derby winner Isinglass so that he could entertain his racing friends. It was redesigned by Colonel Hotchkin of Woodhall Spa fame.

There is a wealth of choice for those wanting to play golf in the East of England. Don't miss the opportunity.

Happy golfing!

Brocket Hall Golf Club, Welwyn Garden City, Hertfordshire

London (Central & Greater)

ASHFORD. **Ashford Manor Golf Club,** Fordbridge Road, Ashford, Middlesex TW15 3RT (01784 424644; Fax: 01784 424649). Parkland course, flat with narrow fairways. 18 holes, 6351 yards. S.S.S. 71. *Green Fees:* weekdays £45.00 per round. 2010 rates (subject to review). *Eating facilities:* dining room and snacks. *Visitors:* welcome weekdays; it is advisable to ring in advance, Handicap Certificate required. May not play at weekends other than with a member. *Society Meetings:* welcome. Professional: (01784 424645). Manager: Peter Dawson (01784 424644; Fax: 01784 424649).
e-mail: secretary@amgc.co.uk

BARNET. **North Middlesex Golf Club,** The Manor House, Friern Barnet Lane, Whetstone N20 0NL (020 8445 1604; Fax: 020 8445 5023). *Location:* five miles south of Junction 23 of M25. 18 holes, 5594 yards. S.S.S. 67. *Green Fees:* weekdays £25.00, weekends after 1pm £30.00. *Eating facilities:* luncheons, snacks and dining facilities. *Visitors:* welcome weekends after 12 noon. Advisable to telephone Professional to book time. *Society Meetings:* catered for. Professional: Freddy George (020 8445 3060). General Manager: Howard Till (020 8445 1604; Fax: 020 8445 5023)
e-mail: manager@northmiddlesexgc.co.uk
website: www.northmiddlesexgc.co.uk

BARNET. **Old Fold Manor Golf Club,** Old Fold Lane, Hadley Green, Barnet, Herts EN5 4QN (020 8449 1650). *Location:* Junction 23 M25 - A1000 one mile north of Barnet. Heathland course. 18 holes, 6447 yards. S.S.S. 71. Practice ground and putting green. *Green Fees:* information not available. *Eating facilities:* restaurant and bar. *Visitors:* welcome weekdays, discount Green Fee days Monday/Wednesday; special visitors' concessions at weekends by arrangement. *Society Meetings:* catered for Monday-Friday. Professional: Peter McEvoy (020 8440 7488). Manager: Brian Cullen (020 8440 9185; Fax: 020 8441 4863).*
website: www.oldfoldmanor.co.uk

CHINGFORD. **Chingford Golf Club,** 158 Station Road, Chingford E4 7AZ (020 8529 2107). 18 holes, 6342 yards. S.S.S. 70. *Green Fees:* information not available. *Visitors:* welcome weekdays only, an article of red must be worn. Pro shop: 020 8529 5708. Professional: Andy Traynor. Secretary: Bryan Woods.

CHINGFORD. **Royal Epping Forest Golf Club,** Forest Approach, Chingford, London E4 7AZ (020 8529 2195). *Location:* 200 yards east of Chingford (BR) Station. A private club on a public course. Wooded. 18 holes, 6342 yards. S.S.S. 71. *Green Fees:* information not available. *Eating facilities:* public snack bar. *Visitors:* may play course but may not use clubhouse. Must wear red garment (trousers or shirt/sweater). Professional: Andy Traynor (020 8529 5708). Secretary: D. Bright-Thomas (020 8529 2195).*

CHINGFORD. **West Essex Golf Club,** Bury Road, Sewardstonebury, Chingford, London E4 7QL (020 8529 7558; Fax: 020 8524 7870). *Location:* two miles north of Chingford BR Station. M25 (Junction 26) and Waltham Abbey follow directions to Chingford (Daws Hill on left). Parkland, wooded, hilly. 18 holes, 6289 yards. S.S.S. 70. Driving range (for members, members' guests and societies). *Green Fees:* information not available. *Visitors:* welcome weekdays except Tuesday mornings. Phone first. *Society Meetings:* catered for by arrangement Mondays, Wednesdays and Fridays. Professional: Robert Joyce (Tel & Fax: 020 8529 4367). Secretary: (020 8529 7558; Fax: 020 8524 7870).
e-mail: sec@westessexgolfclub.co.uk
website: www.westessexgolfclub.co.uk

EDMONTON. **Leaside Golf Club,** Lee Valley Leisure Centre, Pickett's Lock Lane, Edmonton N9 0AS (020 8803 3611; Fax: 020 8884 4975). *Location:* M25 Juntion 25, nearest town Enfield. Flat parkland course, lake on first 9 holes, good drainage; short but challenging course. 18 holes, 4811 yards (yellow). S.S.S. 64 (yellow). 20 bay driving range, practice ground. *Green Fees:* information not available. *Eating facilities:* cafe and bar. *Visitors:* welcome everyday. Trolleys available. Professional: Richard Gerken (020 8803 3611). Membership/Secretary: David Campbell (020 8364 7782)*

EDMONTON. **Lee Valley Leisure Golf Course,** Meridian Way, Edmonton N9 0AR (020 8803 3611). *Location:* off Meridian Way between north Circular Road and Ponders End. Flat parkland course with lake and River Lea as water hazards. Short but challenging. 18 holes, 5204 yards. S.S.S. 65. *Green Fees:* information not available. *Visitors:* welcome, pay and play everyday. *Society Meetings:* small societies welcome, prior booking. Professional: R.G. Gerken (020 8803 3611).*

PLEASE MENTION THIS GUIDE WHEN YOU ENQUIRE ABOUT CLUBS OR ACCOMMODATION

ENFIELD. **Crews Hill Golf Club (1920) Ltd**, Cattlegate Road, Crews Hill, Enfield EN2 8AZ (020 8363 6674). *Location*: off Junction 24 M25, follow directions to Crews Hill. H.S. Colt designed parkland course. 18 holes, 6281 yards. S.S.S. 70. *Green Fees*: information not available. *Eating facilities*: full bar and snacks available, restaurant by arrangement. *Visitors*: welcome weekdays. Handicap Certificate required. Weekends by prior booking. *Society Meetings*: by arrangement. Professional: C. Parker (020 8366 7422). Club Manager: Pauline Cullen (020 8363 6674; Fax: 020 8363 2343).
e-mail: info@crewshillgolfclub.com
website: www.crewshillgolfclub.com

ENFIELD. **Enfield Golf Club,** Old Park Road South, Enfield, Middlesex EN2 7DA (020 8363 3970; Fax: 020 8342 0381). *Location:* off Junction 24, M25; follow directions to Enfield. Parkland; designed by James Braid. 18 holes, 6154 yards. S.S.S. 70. *Green Fees:* Monday £20.00; Tuesday to Friday £28.00; weekends and Bank Holidays £36.00. *Eating facilities*: full bar and catering facilities. *Visitors:* welcome weekdays, limited availability at weekends. Please telephone Professional Shop before travelling. *Society Meetings:* welcome weekdays by prior arrangement. Professional: Martin Porter (020 8362 3223). Secretary: Peter Monument (020 8363 3970; Fax: 020 8342 0381).
e-mail: secretary@enfieldgolfclub.co.uk
website: www.enfieldgolfclub.co.uk

ENFIELD. **Whitewebbs Golf Club,** Clay Hill, Beggars Hollow, Enfield EN2 9JN (020 8363 2951). *Location:* A10 off M25, north of Enfield. Parkland course. 18 holes, 5863 yards. S.S.S. 68. Practice area, separate 9 hole pitch and putt. *Green Fees:* information not available. *Eating facilities:* public cafe on site. *Visitors:* welcome, public course, no restrictions. *Society Meetings:* contact the Secretary. Professional: Gary Sherrif (020 8363 4454). Secretary: Stephen Pyke (020 8363 2951).*

FINCHLEY. **Finchley Golf Club,** Nether Court, Frith Lane, Mill Hill NW7 1PU (020 8346 2436; Fax: 020 8343 4205). *Location:* close A1/M1, near Mill Hill East underground station. Parkland course, tree lined, designed by James Braid. 18 holes, 6411 yards. S.S.S. 71. *Green Fees:* weekdays information not available. *Eating facilities:* two bars and catering. *Visitors:* welcome weekdays except Tuesdays, Thursdays and weekend mornings. Clubs, shoes, trolleys and carts for hire. Excellent 19th century Manor House. *Society Meetings:* catered for Mondays, Wednesdays and Fridays. Professional: David Brown (020 8346 5086). Secretary: M. Gottlieb (020 8346 2436).*
e-mail: secretary@finchleygolfclub.co.uk

GREENFORD. **Ealing Golf Club,** Perivale Lane, Greenford, Middlesex UB6 8TS. *Location:* on Western Avenue A40 half a mile from Hanger Lane Gyratory System. Parkland. 18 holes, 6191 yards. S.S.S. 70. *Green Fees:* information not available. *Eating facilities:* spike bar, mixed lounge, restaurant - lunch, dinner and bar snacks. Conference room. *Visitors:* welcome weekdays with reservation through Professional Shop. *Society Meetings:* catered for Monday to Friday. Professional: Ricky Willison (020 8997 3959). General Manager: Guy Stacey (020 8997 0937).*
e-mail: info@ealinggolfclub.co.uk

GREENFORD. **Horsenden Hill Golf Club,** Greenford, Middlesex UB6 0RD. *Location:* two miles from A40; off Whitton Avenue East, next door to Sudbury Golf Course. Situated on Horsenden Hill Conservation Area. Undulating parkland course, eight Par 3, one Par 4. 9 holes, 1632 yards. S.S.S. 28. Practice area, nets and putting green. *Green Fees:* information not available. *Eating facilities:* bar/cafe. *Visitors:* welcome at all times, public course. Membership available. Trolley hire. *Society Meetings:* welcome. Professional: Jeff Quarshie (020 8902 4555). Golf Course Manager: Parks, Countryside and Events Service (020 8825 6999).*

GREENFORD. **Perivale Park Golf Club,** Stockdove Way, Argyle Road, Greenford, Middlesex. *Location:* A40, turn off at sign for Ealing and Perivale. Entrance to golf club is at Stockdove Way, Perivale. Flat, riverside course set amongst the meadows of Brent River Park. Internal out of bounds areas. 9 holes (18 holes), 2733 yards (white tees). S.S.S. 65. Practice area. *Green Fees:* information not available. *Eating facilities:* cafeteria. *Visitors:* welcome at all times. Public course. Membership available. Professional: P. Bryant (020 8575 7116). Golf Course Manager: Ray Peters: (07989 243219).*

HAMPTON HILL. **The Fulwell Golf Club,** Wellington Road, Hampton Hill, Middlesex TW12 1JY. *Location:* opposite Fulwell Railway Station and bus garage. Stunning parkland course. 18 holes, 6544 yards. S.S.S. 71. Practice ground. *Green Fees:* information not available. *Eating facilities:* bar lunches and teas. *Visitors:* welcome weekdays, weekends by prior arrangement. *Society Meetings:* welcome Monday, Thursday and Friday. Professional: Nigel Turner (Tel & Fax: 020 8977 3844). Secretary: Mark Walden (020 8977 2733; Fax: 020 8977 7732).*
e-mail: secretary@fulwellgolfclub.co.uk
website: www.fulwellgolfclub.co.uk

Crews Hill Golf Club Cattlegate Road, Crews Hill, Enfield EN2 8AZ
Tel: **020 8363 6674** • Fax: **020 8363 2343** • **www.crewshillgolfclub.com**

Probably one of the best kept secrets in north London, Crews Hill Golf Club boasts wonderful scenery, a testing Harry Colt designed golf course and genuine hospitality only 3.2 miles from J24 of the M25. To book your golf day, rent our facilities or to enquire about membership please contact the Crews Hill Office on **020 8363 6674**

HAMPSTEAD. Hampstead Golf Club, Winnington Road, London N2 0TU (020 8455 6420). *Location:* off Hampstead Lane adjacent to Spaniards Inn. Undulating parkland with mature trees. 9 holes, 5812 yards. S.S.S. 68. *Green Fees:* information not available. *Eating facilities:* bar meals/snacks and afternoon teas. *Visitors:* welcome weekdays (not Tuesdays); limited at weekends, telephone Professional. Professional: P J. Brown (020 8455 7089). Secretary: (020 8455 0203).*

HANWELL. Brent Valley Golf Club, Church Road, Hanwell, London W7. *Location*: one mile from Uxbridge Road, off Greenford Avenue, entrance at Church Road. Situated in a picturesque valley in the Brent River Park, 18 holes, 5446 yards. S.S.S. 67. Pay and Play. Nets and practice area. *Green Fees*: information not available. *Eating facilities*: bar/cafe. *Visitors* :welcome at all times. Membership available Public course. *Society Meetings*: welcome. Professional: V. Santos (020 8567 1287). Golf Course Manager: Ray Peters (07989 243219).*

HENDON. Hendon Golf Club, Ashley Walk, Devonshire Road, Mill Hill, London NW7 1DG (020 8346 6023) *Location:* leave M1 southbound at Junction 2. Turn off A1 into Holders Hill Road, first circle , take first left into Devonshire Road, golf club approx. 50 metres on the left. 10 miles north of London. Parkland, wooded, well bunkered. 18 holes, 6289 yards. S.S.S. 70. *Green Fees:*information not available. *Eating facilities:* full bar and catering facilities. *Visitors:* welcome weekdays (limited at weekends and Bank Holidays), book through Pro Shop. *Society Meetings:* catered for by arrangement Tuesdays to Fridays, book through Secretary's office. Professional: Matt Deal (020 8346 8990). Secretary: Clive Bailey (020 8346 6023; Fax: 020 8343 1974).*
e-mail: hendongolfclub@globalnet.co.uk
website: www.hendongolfclub.co.uk

HIGHGATE. Highgate Golf Club, Denewood Road, Highgate, London N6 4AH (020 8340 1906). Founded 1904. *Location:* near A1, turn down Sheldon Avenue, opposite Kenwood House and first left. Parkland. 18 holes, 5985 yards. S.S.S. 69. *Green Fees:* information not provided. *Eating facilities:* bar, restaurant. *Visitors:* welcome weekdays except Wednesdays. Telephone Pro Shop before travelling. *Society Meetings:* catered for Tuesdays, Thursdays (pm only), and all day Friday. Book through Secretary's office. Professional: Robin Turner (020 8340 5467). Secretary: Nick Higginson (020 8340 3745).
website: www.highgategc.co.uk

HILLINGDON. Hillingdon Golf Club, 18 Dorset Way, Hillingdon, Uxbridge, Middlesex UB10 0JR (01895 239810). *Location:* near A40, adjacent to RAF Uxbridge. Gently undulating wooded parkland course sloping down to river. 9 holes, 5490 yards, 5068 metres. S.S.S. 67. *Green Fees:* information not available. *Eating facilities:* bar meals available Tuesday to Friday. *Visitors:* welcome Mondays, Tuesdays and Fridays; Thursdays - Ladies' Day. *Society Meetings:* catered for by special arrangement only with Committee through Club Secretary. Professional: Phil Smith (01895 460035). Secretary: B.L. Russell (01895 233956).*

HOUNSLOW. Airlinks Golf Club, Southall Lane, Hounslow, Middlesex TW5 9PE (020 8561 1418; Fax: 020 8813 6284). *Location:* Junction 3 on M4, A312 to Hayes. Same entrance as D. Lloyd Tennis Centre. Parkland course with water holes and doglegs. 18 holes, 6000 yards. S.S.S. 68. Floodlit driving range. *Green Fees:* information not available. *Eating facilities:* full catering and bar facilities/ restaurant area. *Visitors:* weekdays no restrictions, some restrictions weekends, bookings advised seven days in advance. Membership, including 5 and 7 day, now open. *Society Meetings:* catered for all week. Professional: Tony Martin. Secretary: Stefan Brewster.*

HOUNSLOW. Hounslow Heath Golf Centre, Staines Road, Hounslow TW4 5DS (020 8570 5271). *Location:* Staines Road A315 between Hounslow and Bedfont. Heathland course with water hazards, tight fairways. 18 holes, 5901 yards. S.S.S. 68. Practice area. *Green Fees:* information not available. *Eating facilities:* snacks; teas and coffee. *Visitors:* welcome at all times, bookings seven days in advance for weekends and Bank Holidays. *Society Meetings:* by arrangement. Professional: Del Taylor.*
e-mail: golf@hhgc.uk.com
website: www.hhgc.uk.com

PLEASE NOTE
Some London golf clubs are listed in the CENTRAL REGION (see pages 69-70)

Highgate Golf Club Denewood Road, London N6 4AH
Wonderful, friendly members club, nearest 18-hole course to the centre of London.
It boasts a ready welcome in the clubhouse, grand views, a competitive
Pro Shop for all your golfing needs, a practice net and putting green.
Nick Higginson • Tel: 020 8340 3745
Fax: 020 8348 9152 • e-mail: nick@highgategc.co.uk
www.highgategc.co.uk

ISLEWORTH. **Wyke Green Golf Club,** Syon Lane, Osterley, Isleworth, Middlesex TW7 5PT (020 8560 8777). *Location:* situated half-a-mile north of A4 near Gillettes Corner. Fairly flat parkland. 18 holes, 6182 yards. S.S.S. 70. *Green Fees:* information not available. *Eating facilities:* full catering restaurant and halfway house. *Visitors:* welcome; weekends only with member until after 4pm. *Society Meetings:* catered for by arrangement, minimum 12. Professional: Neil Smith (020 8847 0685) Secretary: David Pearson (020 8560 8777; Fax: 020 8569 8392).*
e-mail: office@wykegreengolfclub.co.uk
website: www.wykegreengolfclub.co.uk

LONDON. **Dukes Meadows Golf and Tennis,** Dukes Meadows, Dan Mason Drive, London W4 2SH (020 8994 3314; Fax: 020 8995 5326). *Location:* next to Chiswick Bridge on the A316, one mile south of the Hogarth roundabout. 9 holes. Parkland course, greens to USGA standard. Golf Range with 50 covered floodlit bays. 5 hole Academy Course for young players accompanied by adult golfers. *Green Fees:* on request, no membership required. *Eating facilities:* restaurant area. *Visitors:* welcome, tee times up to 7 days advance booking. 12 teaching PGA professionals, trolleys available. *Society Meetings:* Welcome by arrangement. Professional: Van Phillips (020 8994 3314).
 www.dukesmeadows.com

LONDON. **Mill Hill Golf Club,** 100 Barnet Way, Mill Hill, London NW7 3AL (020 8959 2339). Est. 1925. *Location:* A1, south half a mile before Apex Corner left into clubhouse car park – signposted. Wooded parkland. 18 holes, 6247 yards, 5697 metres. S.S.S. 70. Practice ground. *Green Fees:* information not available. *Eating facilities:* restaurant and bar. *Visitors:* welcome Monday to Friday; weekends and Bank Holidays prior bookings recommended. Two snooker tables. *Society Meetings:* welcome weekdays with prior booking. For green fees ring the Pro Shop (020 8959 7261); for society and membership enquiries ring Club Office (020 8959 2339). Professional: D. Beal. Secretary: R. Bauser.*

LONDON. **Trent Park Public Golf Course,** Bramley Road, Southgate, London N14 (020 8367 4653). *Location:* opposite Oakwood Tube Station. Undulating parkland. 18 holes, 6176 yards. S.S.S. 69. Modern heated, floodlit 36 bay driving range. *Green Fees:* information not available. *Eating facilities:* restaurant and snacks. *Visitors:* open to public at all times. Bookings advised on weekdays and necessary at weekends. Golf superstore. *Society Meetings:* welcome any day. Professional: Ray Stocker. Secretary: Richard Flint.*

MUSWELL HILL. **Muswell Hill Golf Club,** Rhodes Avenue, London N22 7UT (020 8888 2044; Fax: 020 8889 9380). *Location:* North Circular/Bounds Green tube station one mile. Mature parkland. 18 holes, 6438 yards. S.S.S. 71. *Green Fees:* enquire for details. *Eating facilities:* restaurant open seven days. *Visitors:* welcome weekdays, weekends pre-booked with Professional. *Society Meetings:* welcome weekdays; terms on request. Professional: D. Wilton (020 8888 8046). Manager: A. Hobbs (020 8888 1764).

NORTHWOOD. **Northwood Golf Club Ltd,** Rickmansworth Road, Northwood, Middlesex HA6 2QW (01923 821384; 01923 840150). *Location:* on A404 between Pinner and Rickmansworth. Parkland/wooded course. 18 holes, 6535 yards. S.S.S. 71. *Green Fees:* information not available. *Eating facilities:* restaurant and bar snacks, lounge bar. *Visitors:* welcome weekdays, except Tuesdays; with members only at weekends. *Society Meetings:* by arrangement, details from the Secretary. Professional: C.J. Holdsworth (01923 820112). Secretary: T. N. Collingwood (01923 821384).*

NORTHWOOD. **Sandy Lodge Golf Club,** Sandy Lodge Lane, Northwood, Middlesex HA6 2JD. *Location:* adjacent to Moor Park Underground Station. Sandy Lodge Golf Club is a member of the Hertfordshire Golf Union and situated on the Moor Park Estate close to Moor Park, Batchworth Park.

"Probably the most convenient course to Central London"

Situated between Heathrow Airport and Marble Arch, this flat, parkland course, built in 1926 (designed by Hawtree and Taylor), offers a good challenge to every calibre of golfer, particularly the seven par 4 holes in excess of 420 yards. Enjoy the warm, friendly surroundings of the clubhouse as well as enjoying a 'quick bite' at our famous 'Halfway House'. Societies and Corporate days welcome between Mondays & Fridays.

**Tel: 020 8560 8777 • Fax: 020 8569 8392
e-mail: office@wykegreengolfclub.co.uk
www.wykegreengolfclub.co.uk**

Wyke Green Golf Club

• WYKE GREEN GOLF CLUB, SYON LANE, ISLEWORTH, MIDDLESEX TW7 5PT •

Chorleywood and Rickmansworth. Inland links. 18 holes, 6328 yards. S.S.S. 71 (white). *Green Fees:* see website for details. *Eating facilities:* full catering and bar service available. *Visitors:* weekdays only, please telephone in advance. Handicap Certificate required. *Society Meetings:* by prior written arrangement. Professional: Jeff Pinsent (01923 825321). Manager: Clive Bailey (01923 825429; Fax: 01923 824319). website: www.sandylodge.co.uk

PINNER. **Grim's Dyke Golf Club,** Oxhey Lane, Hatch End, Pinner, Middlesex HA5 4AL (020 8428 4539). *Location:* on A4008 Watford to Harrow (2 miles north of Harrow). Undulating parkland, tree-lined, testing greens. 18 holes, 5600 yards. S.S.S. 67. Practice area. *Green Fees:* information not available. *Eating facilities:* bar snacks, lunches available on request. *Visitors:* must produce Certificate of Handicap. Buggies available. Phone Pro shop for tee times. *Society Meetings:* catered for Mondays to Fridays. Professional: Lee Curling. Office & Pro: (020 8428 4539; Fax: 020 8421 5494).*

PINNER. **Pinner Hill Golf Club,** Southview Road, Pinner Hill HA5 3YA (020 8866 0963; Fax: 020 8868 4817). *Location:* one mile west Pinner Green. Parkland course with magnificent views over London. 18 holes, 6392 yards. S.S.S. 71. *Green Fees:* Monday, Tuesday and Friday £35.00; Wednesday and Thursday £19.50. 2010 rates (subject to review). *Eating facilities:* bar and catering available at all times; parties by prior arrangement please. *Visitors:* welcome with Handicap Certificate. *Society Meetings:* weekdays. Professional: Greg Smith (020 8866 2109). General Manager: Alan Findlater (020 8866 0963).
e-mail: phgc@pinnerhillgc.com
website: www.pinnerhillgc.com

RUISLIP. **Ruislip Golf Club,** King's End, Ickenham Road, Ruislip, Middlesex HA4 7OQ (01895 638081). *Location:* two and a half miles from Junction 1, M40, first left after M40/A40 merge, onto B467, then left at T-Junction onto B466. Parkland course. 18 holes, 5571 yards. Par 69. Driving range (40 bays). *Green Fees:* information not provided. *Eating facilities:* full restaurant facilities. *Visitors:* welcome, booking system at all times. *Society Meetings:* welcome by arrangement. Professional: Paul Glozier (01895 638835). Secretary: N. Jennings (07899 663534).

SHEPPERTON. **Sunbury Golf Centre,** Charlton Lane, Shepperton TW17 8QA (01932 772898). *Location:* two miles south-west of M3 Junction 1; south-east of Queen Mary Reservoir between villages of Charlton and Upper Halliford. Two parkland courses. 18 holes, 5103 yards. S.S.S. 65, Par 68. 9 holes, 2444 yards, Par 33. 32 bay floodlit driving range (8am to 10pm), practice puttting green. *Green Fees:* information not available. *Eating facilities:* snacks, meals and bar. *Visitors:* welcome, no restrictions. Booking up to one week in advance essential. Buggies and trolleys for hire. *Society Meetings*: welcome at all times; advance booking required; special packages available. Professional: Adrian McColgan. General Manager: Patrick Dawson (01932 771414; Fax: 01932 789300).*

SOUTHALL. **West Middlesex Golf Club,** Greenford Road, Southall, Middlesex UB1 3EE (020 8574 3450). *Location:* junction of Uxbridge Road (A4020) and Greenford Road. 18 holes, 6119 yards. S.S.S. 69. *Green Fees:* please telephone the Pro Shop on 020 8574 1800. *Visitors:* welcome weekdays and at weekends after 2.00pm, except on competition days. *Society Meetings:* catered for by prior arrangement. Professional: T. Talbot. Secretary: Miss R. Khanna (020 8574 3450; Fax: 020 8574 2383).
e-mail: westmid.gc@virgin.net
website: www.westmiddxgolfclub.com

STANMORE. **Stanmore Golf Club,** 29 Gordon Avenue, Stanmore, Middlesex HA7 2RL (Tel & Fax: 020 8954 2599). *Location:* turn off A410 by church to Old Church Lane, Gordon Avenue is to the right. Wooded, parkland course. 18 holes, 5879 yards. S.S.S. 68. Practice and putting areas. *Green Fees:* information not available. *Eating facilities:* restaurant facilities available *Visitors:* welcome. No jeans or trainers. Jacket and tie after 7pm. *Society Meetings:* catered for by prior booking only. Professional: James Reynolds. Secretary: Allan Knott. Caterer: (0203 113 2088).*
e-mail: secretary@stanmoregolfclub.co.uk
website: www.stanmoregolfclub.co.uk

STANMORE. **Stanmore & Edgware Golf Centre,** Brockley Hill, Stanmore HA7 4LR (020 8420 6222; Fax: 020 8420 6333). *Location:* Junction 4 M1, A41. Parkland course. 9 holes, 1007 metres. S.S.S. 27. Covered and floodlit 2-tier driving range including 18 automated "Powertees". *Green Fees:* adults - 9 holes £6.50, 18 holes £9.00. Juniors/Seniors - 9 holes £5.00, 18 holes £7.00. £1.00 reduction on prices for Golf Card holders. 2010 rates (subject to review). *Visitors:* welcome anytime - pay as you play. Shop - Direct Golf UK. *Society Meetings:* welcome on application. Professionals: Cranfield Golf Academy.

TOTTERIDGE. **South Herts Golf Club,** Links Drive, Totteridge N20 8QU (020 8445 2035). *Location:* off Totteridge Lane N20, one mile from Whetstone, nearest underground station Totteridge & Whetstone. Parkland. 18 holes, 6432 yards. S.S.S. 71. *Green Fees:* information not provided. *Eating facilities:* lunch, high tea (breakfast and dinner by arrangement). *Visitors:* welcome with reservation Monday to Friday and Sunday pm. *Society & Corporate Meetings:* welcome Monday to Friday. Professional: R.Y. Mitchell (020 8445 4633). Secretary: John Charlton (020 8445 2035; Fax: 020 8445 7569).
website: www.southhertsgolfclub.co.uk

TWICKENHAM. **Amida Golf Course and Teaching Academy,** Staines Road, Twickenham TW2 5JD (020 8783 1698; Fax: 020 8941 9134). *Location*: at end of M3, on A305 near its junction with 35. Golf teaching academy. *Green Fees:* information not available. *Eating facilities:* Golfers' Bar and Indoor Virtual Golf. *Visitors*: welcome, play and pay. Function room available. *Society Meetings*: welcome. Professional: Suzy Watt (020 8783 1698; Fax: 020 8941 9134)*
website: www.amidaclubs.com

TWICKENHAM. Strawberry Hill Golf Club, Wellesley Road, Strawberry Hill, Twickenham TW2 5SD (020 8898 2082). *Location:* near Twickenham Green, 200 yards Strawberry Hill Station. Flat parkland. 9 holes, 4762 yards. S.S.S. 63. *Green Fees:* 18 holes £25.00; with a member £15.00. 9 holes £15.00, with a member £10.00. *Eating facilities:* restaurant and bar. *Visitors:* welcome, restrictions weekends and competition days. *Society Meetings:* welcome weekdays, small parties only. Professional: Peter Buchan (020 8898 2082). Secretary: Paul Astbury (020 8894 0165).
e-mail: secretary@shgc.net

UXBRIDGE. Stockley Park Golf Club, Stockley Park, Uxbridge UB11 1AQ (020 8813 5700; Fax: 020 8813 5655). *Location:* Junction 4 M4, Heathrow Airport turnoff, A408 to Uxbridge. Parkland course, designed by Robert Trent Jones Snr. 18 holes, 6754 yards. S.S.S. 71. Practice nets, chipping and putting greens. *Green Fees:* information not available. *Eating facilities:* balcony restaurant and bar. *Visitors:* all welcome. Trolleys available all year round. *Society Meetings:* welcome. Professional: Stuart Birch. Adminstration: Jackie Hickey.*
website: www.stockleyparkgolf.com

UXBRIDGE. Uxbridge Golf Course, The Drive, Harefield Place, Uxbridge UB10 8AQ (01895 237287; Fax: 01895 810262). *Location*: off Swakeleys Junction - M40. Undulating parkland. 18 holes, 5753 yards. S.S.S. 68. *Green Fees:* information not available. *Eating facilities*: bars, carvery restaurant. *Visitors*: welcome anytime, booking required at weekends. Function suite. *Society Meetings*: welcome. Professional: Phil Howard (01895 237287). Secretary: Anne James (01895 272457).*

WANDSWORTH. Central London Golf Centre, Burntwood Lane, Wandsworth SW17 0AT (020 8871 2468; Fax: 020 8874 7447). *Location:* turn right through the Wandsworth town centre into Garrat Lane, Burntwood Lane is off Garrat Lane. Short course with three good Par 3s and several good Par 4s. 9 holes, 2223 yards. S.S.S. 31. Large practice putting green. 14 bay driving range. *Green Fees:* information not available. *Eating facilities:* full bar and restaurant; function room. *Visitors:* welcome, no restrictions. Special disabled putting green. Trolleys for hire. *Society Meetings:* welcome, special terms on request. Professional: Jeremy Robson (020 8871 2468).*
e-mail: golf@clgc.co.uk
website: www.clgc.co.uk

WANSTEAD. Wanstead Golf Club, Overton Drive, Wanstead E11 2LW (020 8989 3938; Fax: 020 8532 9138). *Location:* one mile from junction of A12 and A406. Parkland bordering Epping Forest with featured lake. 18 holes, 6109 yards. S.S.S. 69. *Green Fees:* information not available. *Eating facilities:* dining room and bars. *Visitors:* welcome weekdays by prior arrangement with the Secretary. Handicap Certificate required. Weekends with member only. *Society Meetings:* welcome, apply Secretary: Bill Cranston (020 8989 3938; Fax: 020 8532 9138).*

WEMBLEY. Sudbury Golf Club Ltd, Bridgewater Road, Wembley, Middlesex HA0 1AL (020 8902 3713). *Location:* junction of A4005 (Bridgewater Road) and A4090 (Whitton Ave East). Undulating parkland. 18 holes, 6282 yards. S.S.S. 70. Practice ground. *Green Fees:* information not provided. *Eating facilities:* dining room and bars. *Visitors:* welcome weekdays with Handicap Certificate. *Society Meetings:* catered for. Professional: Neil Jordan (020 8902 7910). General Manager: Neil Cropley.

WINCHMORE HILL. Bush Hill Park Golf Club, Bush Hill, Winchmore Hill, London N21 2BU (020 8360 5738; Fax: 020 8360 5583). *Location:* half a mile south of Enfield town (off London Road). Parkland. 18 holes, 5825 yards. S.S.S. 68. Practice ground and nets. *Green Fees:* weekdays £29.50 per round, weekends by arrangement. *Eating facilities:* restaurant, bar, bar snacks. *Visitors:* welcome weekdays, Handicap Certificate required. *Society Meetings:* catered for Mondays, Tuesdays, Thursdays and Fridays. Professional: Lee Fickling (020 8360 4103). Manager: Martin Berry (020 8360 5738; Fax: 020 8360 5583).

Other British holiday guides from FHG Guides

**PUBS & INNS · 300 GREAT HOTELS · SHORT BREAK HOLIDAYS
The bestselling and original PETS WELCOME! · 500 GREAT PLACES TO STAY
SELF-CATERING HOLIDAYS · BED & BREAKFAST STOPS
CARAVAN & CAMPING HOLIDAYS · FAMILY BREAKS**

Published annually: available in all good bookshops or direct from the publisher:
**FHG Guides, Abbey Mill Business Centre, Seedhill, Paisley PA1 1TJ
Tel: 0141 887 0428 • Fax: 0141 889 7204
e-mail: admin@fhguides.co.uk • www.holidayguides.com**

Bedfordshire

AMPTHILL. **The Millbrook Golf Club,** Millbrook, Ampthill MK45 2JB (01525 840252; Fax: 01525 406249). *Location:* just off A507 Ampthill to Woburn Road, near Junction 13 of M1. Rolling links situated on the Greensand Ridge overlooking Bedfordshire. 18 holes, 6966 yards. Par 73. S.S.S. 73. Two practice areas. *Green Fees:* information not available. *Eating facilities:* bar/restaurant, breakfasts, lunches, dinners. *Visitors:* welcome midweek. *Society Meetings:* welcome. Professional & Tee Time bookings: Rob Brightman (01525 402269). Manager: Derek Cooke (01525 840252; Fax: 01525 406249).*
e-mail: info@themillbrook.com
website: www.themillbrook.com

ASPLEY GUISE. **Aspley Guise and Woburn Sands Golf Club,** West Hill, Aspley Guise MK17 8DX (Tel & Fax: 01908 583596). *Location*: two miles west of Junction 13 M1, between Aspley Guise and Woburn Sands. Undulating parkland, 18 holes, 6079 yards. S.S.S. 70. *Green Fees*: information not available. *Eating facilities*: catering service, bar. *Visitors*: welcome weekdays with bona fide handicaps - check with Secretary. *Society Meetings*: Wednesdays and Fridays. Professional: Colin Clingan (01908 582974). Secretary: Richard Norris (Tel & Fax: 01908 583596).*

BEADLOW. **Beadlow Manor Hotel, Golf and Country Club,** Beadlow, Near Shefford SG17 5PH (01525 860800). *Location*: from M1 (J12) take A5120 east to Ampthill, then A507 to Shefford. From A1 (J10) take A507 west to Ampthill. Challenging, rolling parkland with water hazards. Two courses (Baron and Baroness): 18 holes, 6819 yards. S.S.S. 72; 18 holes, 6072 yards. S.S.S 69. Covered 25 bay floodlit driving range, practice area. *Green Fees*: information not provided. *Eating facilities*: restaurant, three bars, snacks, refreshments, two function rooms. *Visitors*: welcome at all times. Residential Golf Breaks available. Professional academy and shop. Special mid-week and weekend Breaks for Society and Company Groups. All reservations through Sales and Marketing Office. General Manager: Graham Wilson.

BEDFORD. **The Bedford Golf Club,** Great Denham Golf Village, Biddenham, Bedford MK40 4FF (01234 320022; Fax: 01234 320023). *Location*: two miles west of Bedford on A428. American-style course with 90 bunkers and eight water features, built on free-draining sandy soil. 18 holes, 6478 yards. S.S.S. 72. Practice range and putting green. *Green Fees:* information not available. *Eating facilities*: restaurant and bar meals; course refreshments. Function room. *Visitors*: always welcome - excellent rates. Buggies for hire. *Society Meetings*: welcome midweek and weekend. Manager: Geoff Swain.*
e-mail: info@thebedfordgc.com
website: www.thebedfordgc.com

BEDFORD. **Bedford and County Golf Club,** Green Lane, Clapham, Bedford MK41 6ET (01234 352617). *Location:* off the old A6 road north of Bedford just before the village of Clapham. Parkland. 18 holes, 6420 yards. S.S.S. 70. *Green Fees:* call for availability and prices. *Eating facilities:* full catering facilities and bar. *Visitors*: welcome. *Society Meetings:* welcome. Professional: R. Tattersall (01234 359189). General Manager: S. Edwin (01234 352617; Fax: 01234 357195).
website: www.bandcgc.co.uk

BEDFORD. **Bedfordshire Golf Club,** Spring Lane, Stagsden, Bedford MK43 8SR (01234 822555; Fax: 01234 825052). *Location:* one mile west of Bedford town centre on the A422. Wooded parkland, flat. 18 holes, 6565 yards. S.S.S. 71. 9-hole course. 24-bay driving range. *Green Fees:* weekdays £32.00, weekends £40.00. *Eating facilities:* bar and catering; evening meals by arrangement. *Visitors:* welcome at any time. *Society Meetings:* welcome. Pro Shop: (01234 826100). Professional/Manager: Geraint Dixon (01234 822555).
e-mail: office@bedfordshiregolf.com
website: www.bedfordshiregolf.com

BEDFORD. **Mowsbury Golf Club,** Cleat Hill, Kimbolton Road, Bedford MK41 8BJ (01234 772700). *Location:* on B660 at northern limit of city boundary. 18 holes, 6451 yards. S.S.S. 71. Driving range. *Green Fees:* on request. *Eating facilities:* meals and bar snacks until 3pm; evening meals if booked in advance. *Visitors:* welcome. Squash courts. *Society Meetings:* by arrangement with the Professional. Professional: Malcolm Summers (01234 772700), for tee reservations and fees. Secretary: T.W. Gardner (01234 771041).

BEDFORD. **Pavenham Park Golf Club,** Pavenham, Bedford MK43 7PE (01234 822202; Fax: 01234 826602). *Location:* take the A6 out of North Bedford, from Clapham follow signs to Pavenham. Parkland course with fast and contoured greens. 18 holes, 6400 yards. S.S.S. 71. Practice ground. *Green Fees:* information not available. *Eating facilities:* bar and catering available. *Visitors:* welcome midweek; weekends after 12pm. Must adhere to dress code. Buggies and carts available. *Society Meetings:* welcome, excellent rates. Professional: Steve Vinnicombe. Secretary: Lee Pepper.*
e-mail: pavenhampark@o2.co.uk
website: www.pavenhampark.com

CADDINGTON. **Caddington Golf Club,** Chaul End Road, Caddington LU1 4AX (01582 415573 Fax: 01582 415314). *Location:* Ten minutes from Junctions 9 or 11 M1. Gently undulating parkland. 18 holes, 6240 yards. S.S.S.70. *Green Fees:* information not available. *Eating facilities:* bar with catering available. *Visitors:* welcome anytime midweek; weekends by arrangement. *Society Meetings:* welcome, special deals available. Secretary: David Isger. *
e-mail: info@caddingtongolfclub.co.uk

Bedfordshire / EAST REGION

COLMWORTH. Colmworth and North Bedfordshire Golf Club, New Road, Colmworth MK44 2NN (01234 378181; Fax: 01234 376678). *Location:* north of Bedford just off B660 and only 10 minutes from the A1 at Wyboston. Fast maturing, well drained course in its 19th year offering easy walking yet challenging golf all year round. 18 holes, 6459 yards. S.S.S. 71. 9-hole Par 3 course. 8 bay driving range. *Green Fees:* information not available. *Eating facilities:* licensed clubhouse with bar. *Visitors:* no restrictions. All inclusive golf breaks from £80.00 midweek.*
website: www.colmworthgolfclub.co.uk

DUNSTABLE. Dunstable Downs Golf Club, Whipsnade Road, Dunstable LU6 2NB (01582 604472; Fax: 01582 478700). *Location:* on B4541; one and a half miles from town centre. Downland course with exceptional views. 18 holes, 5903 yards. S.S.S. 70. Practice ground. *Green Fees:* information not provided. *Eating facilities:* bar and restaurant. *Visitors:* welcome weekdays, weekends with member only. Handicap Certificate required. Carts for hire. *Society Meetings:* Mondays, Tuesdays and Thursdays, limited availability on Fridays. Professional: Darren Charlton (01582 662806). Secretary/Manager: Alan Sigee (01582 604472; Fax: 01582 478700).

DUNSTABLE. Tilsworth Golf Centre, Dunstable Road, Tilsworth, Leighton Buzzard LU7 9PU (01525 210721; Fax: 01525 210465). *Location:* two miles north of Dunstable off A5, Tilsworth turn-off. Parkland course, water hazards on three holes! 18 holes, 5306 yards. S.S.S. 67, Par 69. 30 bay floodlit driving range. *Green Fees:* information not provided. *Eating facilities:* bar snacks and restaurant available. *Visitors:* welcome any time except Sundays before 10am. Bookings taken up to seven days in advance. *Society Meetings:* welcome by prior arrangement. Professional: Nick Webb.

HENLOW. Mount Pleasant Golf Course, Station Road, Lower Stondon, Henlow SG16 6JL (01462 850999). *Location:* three-quarters of a mile west of A600 (Hitchin to Bedford) at Henlow Camp roundabout. Undulating meadowland. 9 holes (alternative tees for second 9 holes), 6185 yards, 5656 metres. S.S.S. 70. Practice chipping, putting and nets. New clubhouse and conference facilities opening July 2010. *Green Fees:* weekdays £10.00 for 9 holes, £18.00 for 18 holes; weekends and Bank Holidays £12.50 for 9 holes, £22.00 for 18 holes. Reductions for Senior Citizens and Juniors. 2010 rates (subject to review). *Eating facilities:* spike bar, dining room. Group catering by prior arrangement. *Visitors:* welcome anytime, booking required for weekends and summer evenings. *Society Meetings:* welcome on weekdays and weekend afternoons. Professional: Glen Kemble. Proprietor: David Simkins.
website: www.mountpleasantgolfclub.co.uk

LEIGHTON BUZZARD. Aylesbury Vale Golf Club, Stewkley Road, Wing, Leighton Buzzard LU7 0UJ (01525 240196). *Location:* four miles west of Leighton Buzzard on Stewkley to Wing road. Gently undulating course with water hazards. 18 holes, 6622 yards, S.S.S. 72. 9-bay driving range. *Green Fees:* weekdays £23.00; weekends £30.00 up to 11am, £25.00 after 11am. Please telephone for availability. Senior Citizens £12.00 Tuesdays and Thursdays. 2010 rates (subject to review). *Eating facilities:* first floor bar and balcony, ground floor bar and restaurant. *Visitors:* welcome any time, no restrictions apart from correct dress. Telephone in advance. Individual lessons from £15.00. *Society Meetings:* welcome, competitive rates, Monday to Friday anytime, weekends afternoons only. Professional: Terry Bunyan (07731 966749); Secretary: Chris Wright (01525 240196).

LEIGHTON BUZZARD. Leighton Buzzard Golf Club, Plantation Road, Leighton Buzzard LU7 3JF (01525 244800). *Location:* off A5 between Dunstable and Milton Keynes at village of Heath and Reach. Wooded parkland course. 18 holes, 5904 yards. S.S.S. 69. Practice ground. *Green Fees:* weekdays, please call for current prices; weekends with members only. *Eating facilities:* available - dining room and three bars. *Visitors:* welcome weekdays. (Tuesday Ladies' Day). Weekends and Bank Holidays with member only. *Society Meetings:* catered for weekdays only, except Tuesdays. Professional: M. Campbell (01525 244815). Secretary: D. Mutton (01525 244800; Fax: 01525 244801).
e-mail: secretary@leightonbuzzardgolf.net
website: www.leightonbuzzardgolf.net

LEIGHTON BUZZARD near. Ivinghoe Golf Club, Wellcroft, Ivinghoe, Near Leighton Buzzard LU7 9EF (01296 668696; Fax: 01296 662755). *Location:* leave A41 at Tring and take B488 to Ivinghoe. When approaching the village, the church is on the left, and Vicarage Lane is on the right. Go down the lane to the Rose & Crown pub and turn right up to the club. Gently rolling parkland course in lee of Ivinghoe Beacon. 9 holes, 4508 yards. S.S.S. 62. Pro shop, tuition available. *Green Fees:* 9 holes £6.00, 18 holes £10.00. *Eating facilities:* bar meals anytime. *Visitors:* welcome except before 8am Monday to Saturday and 9am Sundays; dress code in operation. *Society Meetings:* catered for. Professional: Mark Flitney (01296 668696). Secretary: Mrs S.E. Garrad (01296 668696). Steward: B. Burton (01296 661186).

LEIGHTON BUZZARD near. Mentmore Golf and Country Club, Mentmore, Near Leighton Buzzard LU7 0UA (01296 662020; Fax: 01296 662592). *Location:* between Leighton Buzzard and Aylesbury in village of Mentmore. Rolling parkland, mature trees and with many water features. Two courses - Rothschild and Rosebery. 36 holes, 6777 and 6763 yards. S.S.S. 72. Driving range. *Green Fees:* information not available. *Eating facilities:* restaurant, two bars, spike bar; function room. *Visitors:* welcome. Also available swimming pool, sauna, jacuzzi and steam room, two tennis courts, full gymnasium and aerobics studio. *Society Meetings:* welcome everyday, please telephone for details. General Manager: Kevin Whitehouse. Sales Manager: Matthew Darley. Professional: Robert Davies.*

EAST REGION / Bedfordshire

LUTON. South Beds Golf Club, Warden Hill Road, Luton LU2 7AE (01582 591500). *Location:* on east side A6, two and a half miles north of Luton. Undulating chalk downland course. 18 holes, 6401 yards. S.S.S. 71. Also 9 holes, 4704 yards. S.S.S. 63. Practice fairway and chipping area. *Green Fees:* weekdays 9 hole course £10.00 for 18 holes, 18 hole course £23.00; weekends 9 hole course £13.00 for 18 holes, 18 hole course £32.00. *Eating facilities:* three-course meals (must be booked), snacks at all times. *Visitors:* welcome anytime on 9-hole course, weekdays and limited weekends on 18-hole course. Handicap Certificate essential for 18-hole course. Tuesday is Ladies' Day. *Society Meetings:* catered for by arrangement on Mondays, Wednesdays and Thursdays. Professional: Michael Davis (01582 591209). Secretary: Ray Wright (01582 591500; Fax: 01582 495381).

LUTON. Stockwood Park Golf Club, London Road, Luton LU1 4LX (01582 431788). *Location:* adjacent Exit 10/10A of M1 exit for Luton Airport. Parkland. 18 holes, 6049 yards. S.S.S. 69. Driving range, par 3 nine hole course. *Green Fees:* information not available. *Eating facilities:* two bars and restaurant. *Visitors:* always welcome, municipal Golf Centre run by Active Luton Trust. Changing rooms. *Society Meetings:* catered for by prior arrangement. Professional: Matt Green. Club Administrator: Brian E. Clark (01582 413708).*
e-mail: spgc@hotmail.com

SANDY. John O'Gaunt Golf Club, Sutton Park, Sandy SG19 2LY (01767 260360; Fax: 01767 262834). *Location:* on B1040 off A1 two miles north of Biggleswade. Parkland courses. Two 18 hole courses: John O'Gaunt Course 6513 yards S.S.S. 71 and Carthagena Course 5869 yards S.S.S. 69. Small practice area. *Green Fees:* information not available. *Eating facilities:* restaurant and bar. *Visitors:* welcome weekdays, Handicap Certificate required. *Society Meetings:* welcome weekdays. Professional: Lee Scarbrow (01767 260094). Secretary: Simon Davis (01767 260360).*
website: www.johnogauntgolfclub.co.uk

SHARNBROOK. Colworth Golf Club, Colworth House, Sharnbrook MK44 1LQ (01933 353269). *Location:* off A6 between Bedford and Rushden through Sharnbrook village. Parkland course, narrow fairways, tree lined. 9 holes, 5210 yards. S.S.S. 66. *Green Fees:* information not provided. *Eating facilities:* none. *Visitors:* with members only. Secretary: E.W. Thompson (01933 353269).

TODDINGTON. Chalgrave Manor Golf Club, Dunstable Road, Toddington, Near Dunstable LU5 6JN (01525 876556). *Location:* two minutes from Junction 12 M1 (Toddington Services), on main A5120 between Toddington and Houghton Regis. Rolling, open course with many natural undulations; four holes with water features. 18 holes, 6417 yards, 5892 metres. S.S.S. 71. Practice areas. *Green Fees:* weekdays £23.00 per round, weekends £35.00 per round. Apply online for free loyalty card for £5.00 discount weekdays, £10.00 weekends. Day tickets available. *Eating facilities:* meals available every day, licensed bar. *Visitors:* booking not required. No starting times before 11am weekends and Bank Holidays, no restrictions midweek. *Society Meetings:* welcome weekdays by prior arrangement. Secretary: Steve Rumball (01525 876554).
e-mail: steve@chalgravegolf.co.uk
website: www.chalgravegolf.co.uk

WYBOSTON. Wyboston Lakes Golf Course, Great North Road, Wyboston Lakes, Wyboston, Bedfordshire MK44 3AL (01480 223004). *Location:* one mile south of St Neots at the junction of the A1 and the A428 east. Flat parkland with five lakes. 18 holes, 6000 yards. S.S.S. 68. Driving range. Putting green. *Green Fees:* phone for details. *Eating facilities:* available. *Visitors:* welcome, bookings required for weekends and Bank Holidays. Hotel on site. *Society Meetings:* catered for seven days. Professional: P.G. Ashwell (01480 223004; Fax: 01480 407330). Secretary: D. Little (01480 212625; Fax: 01480 223000).

Visit
www.holidayguides.com
for convenient accommodation when playing golf around the regions

Cambridgeshire

CAMBRIDGE. **Cambridge Golf Club,** Station Road, Longstanton, Cambridge CB24 3DS (01954 789388). *Location:* 10 minutes from city, off A14 at Bar Hill, turn right to Longstanton B1050. Parkland course. 18 holes, 6736 yards, S.S.S. 73. 9 bay floodlit grassed driving range, 9 holes pitch and putt. *Green Fees:* information not available. *Eating facilities:* clubhouse; 50-seat function room available for hire. *Visitors:* welcome, may need to book on competition days. Coaching by appointment. *Society Meetings:* catered for. Professional: Geoff Hugget.*

CAMBRIDGE. **Cambridge Meridian Golf Club,** Comberton Road, Toft, Cambridge CB23 2RY (01223 264700). *Location:* 5 minutes from Junction 12 of M11 onto B1046. Heavily landscaped championship design set in 250 acres with six lakes and 108 bunkers. 18 holes, 6707 yards. S.S.S. 72. Practice ground and putting green. *Green Fees*: information not provided. *Eating facilities:* available all day. *Visitors:* welcome at all times (subject to availability). Buggies and trolleys for hire. *Society Meetings:* corporate and society golf days catered for. Professional: Craig Watson (01223 264702). Golf Administrator: Steve Creighton. Tee Time Booking: (01223 264702)
e-mail: meridian@golfsocieties.com

CAMBRIDGE. **Girton Golf Club,** Dodford Lane, Girton, Cambridge CB3 0QE (01223 276169; Fax: 01223 277150). *Location:* two miles north of Cambridge. Flat parkland. 18 holes, 6012 yards. S.S.S. 69. Large practice area. *Green Fees:* Monday to Friday £25.00. *Eating facilities:* diningroom, lounge and bar. *Visitors:* weekdays only. *Society Meetings:* welcome Tuesdays to Fridays. Professional: S. Thomson (01223 276991). Secretary: Miss V. Webb (01223 276169; Fax: 01223 277150). website: www.girtongolf.co.uk

CAMBRIDGE. **Gog Magog Golf Club,** Shelford Bottom, Cambridge CB22 3AB (01223 247626; Fax: 01223 414990). *Location:* Two miles from the A11-A1307 roundabout, Colchester - Cambridge Road. Open, undulating chalkland hill course. Old Course - 18 holes, 6367 yards, S.S.S. 71. Wandlebury Course - 18 holes, 6750 yards, S.S.S. 73. Large driving range and practice areas, with ball hire available. *Green Fees:* weekdays £46.00 per round. *Eating facilities:* diningroom, bar meals, large bar area with lounge and spike bar. *Visitors:* welcome, only with members at weekends and Bank Holidays, Handicap Certificate required. *Society Meetings:* catered for Tuesdays and Thursdays. Professional: I. Bamborough (01223 246058). Secretary: K. Mader (01223 247626).
e-mail: secretary@gogmagog.co.uk
website: www.gogmagog.co.uk

CAMBRIDGE. **Menzies Cambridgeshire Hotel & Golf Club,** Bar Hill, Cambridge CB23 8EU (01954 780098). *Location:* five miles north from Cambridge on A14 Huntingdon Road, Junction 29. Well established Championship parkland course with many mature trees. 18 holes, 6750 yards. Par 72. S.S.S. 73. Practice facilities. *Green Fees:* information not available. *Eating facilities:* one restaurant and two bars. *Visitors:* welcome anytime by prior phone call. 136 bedroom 4-star Hotel with excellent conference facilities. Full leisure facilities including gym, heated pool, sauna, solarium, steam rooms and tennis courts. *Society Meetings:* Society and Corporate days welcome. Golf Manager: Tom Turner (01954 780098; Fax: 01954 780010).
e-mail: cambridge.golfpro@menzieshotels.co.uk
website: www.menzieshotels.co.uk

Please mention THE GOLF GUIDE when you enquire about clubs or accommodation

Named after the Greenwich Meridian Line which runs through the course. Over 6,700 yards from the members' tees and built to USGA championship course standards, a challenge for aspiring champions while being pleasantly playable for all.

We welcome visitors on weekdays and weekends.
Weekday - £20.00 per round or £35.00 per day
Weekend - £28.00 per round or £48.00 per day

Cambridge Meridian Golf Club
Comberton Road, Toft, Cambridge CB23 2RY
Tel: 01223 264 700 • Fax: 01223 264 701
Pro Shop Tel: 01223 264 702
E-mail: meridian@golfsocieties.com
www.golfsocieties.com

ELY. **Ely City Golf Course Ltd,** 107 Cambridge Road, Ely CB7 4HX (01353 662751). *Location:* on southern outskirts of city on A10 if heading towards Cambridge. Parkland course, undulating, magnificent views of the 12th century cathedral. 18 holes, 6627 yards. S.S.S. 72. Practice area. *Green Fees:* weekdays £36.00, weekends £42.00. *Eating facilities:* full bar, catering and restaurant facilities. *Visitors:* welcome anytime with a member or if in possession of a valid Handicap Certificate. Jeans, T-shirts and trainers not allowed. Well equipped Pro Shop. Snooker. *Society Meetings:* welcome Monday to Friday inclusive by arrangement. Professional: Andrew George (01353 663317). General Manager: Cameron Renton (01353 662751; Fax: 01353 668636) e-mail: info@elygolf.co.uk
website: www.elygolf.co.uk

HUNTINGDON. **Brampton Park Golf Club,** Buckden Road, Brampton, Huntingdon PE28 4NF (01480 434705). *Location*: three-quarters of a mile off A1, travelling north take first Huntingdon turn, south take second sign for "RAF Brampton". Picturesque with many water hazards, wooded areas and prolific wildlife – swans, badgers, muntjac deer, Canada geese, water fowl, etc. 18 holes, 6300 yards. S.S.S. 72. 10-bay driving range. *Green Fees:* information not available. *Eating facilities*: bar snacks, restaurant, two bars and on-course refreshments. *Visitors*: welcome at all times, no restrictions, telephone for tee reservations prior to arrival. Accommodation and business conference facilities available plus banqueting for up to 120 people. Buggies available. *Society Meetings*: Society and Corporate events welcome. Professional: Alisdair Currie (Tel & Fax: 01480 434705). Club Manager: Lisa Charlton (01480 434700; Fax: 01480 411145).*
e-mail: admin@bramptonparkgc.co.uk
website: www.bramptonparkgc.co.uk

HUNTINGDON. **Hemingford Abbots Golf Club,** Cambridge Road, Hemingford Abbots, Huntingdon PE28 9HQ (01480 495000; Fax: 01480 496000). *Location:* two miles south of Huntingdon on the A14. Gently undulating parkland with trees. 9 holes, 2680 yards. S.S.S.68. *Green Fees:* information not available. *Visitors:* welcome, no restrictions. Comfortable clubhouse with bar. *Society Meetings:* welcome. 'The Friendly One', all standards welcome. Alternative tee positions on back nine. Secretary: Dennis Brown. Proprietor: R. D. Paton.*

HUNTINGDON. **Lakeside Lodge Golf Centre,** Fen Road, Pidley, Huntingdon PE28 3DF (01487 740540; Fax: 01487 740852). *Location*: on the B1040 St Ives to Warboys Road. Course has 8 lakes and considerable landscaping. Three courses - Lodge Course: 18 holes, 6437 yards. S.S.S. 73; Manor Course: 9 holes, 2601 yards; Church Course: 6 holes, 1645 yards. Driving range and Teaching Academy. *Green Fees:* weekdays £18.00 for 18 holes, £10.00 for 9 holes; weekends £27.00 for 18 holes, £14.00 for 9 holes; after 12.30pm weekends £19.00. *Eating facilities:* full bar serving all day snacks and meals. *Visitors:* welcome but best to book. Ten pin bowling. Accommodation available in 64 twin en suite bedrooms adjoining the course. *Society Meetings:* all welcome. Professional: Scott Waterman PGA (01487 741541). Secretary: Mrs Jane Hopkins (01487 740540; Fax: 01487 740852).
e-mail: info@lakeside-lodge.co.uk
website: www.lakeside-lodge.co.uk

HUNTINGDON. **Ramsey Golf and Bowls Club,** 4 Abbey Terrace, Ramsey, Huntingdon PE26 1DD (01487 812600; Fax: 01487 815746). *Location:* 20 minutes from A1, 12 miles south of Peterborough, 10 miles north of Huntingdon. Flat parkland with a river running full length which comes into play on many holes. 18 holes, 5998 yards. S.S.S. 69. Two practice grounds, chipping area. *Green Fees:* information not provided. *Eating facilities:* bar and full catering service available. *Visitors:* welcome weekdays, with member weekends. Six rink county standard bowling green. *Society Meetings:* welcome by prior arrangement. Professional: Stuart Scott (01487 813022). Secretary/Administrator: John Bufton (01487 812600; Fax: 01487 815746).
e-mail: admin@ramseyclub.co.uk
website: www.ramseyclub.co.uk

MARCH. **March Golf Club Ltd,** Frogs Abbey, Grange Road, March PE15 0YH (01354 652364). *Location:* quarter of a mile west of March bypass (A141). Flat parkland. 9 holes, 6204 yards. S.S.S. 70. Six acre practice area. *Green Fees:* £22.00 per day weekdays, £26.00 weekends. *Eating facilities:* bar, bar meals. *Visitors:* welcome. *Society Meetings:* welcome midweek and Sundays. Professional: Alex Oldham. Secretary: Mrs M.A. Simpson.
website: www.marchgolfclub.co.uk

PETERBOROUGH. **Elton Furze Golf Club,** Bullock Road, Haddon, Peterborough PE7 3TT (01832 280189; Fax: 01832 280299). *Location*: four miles west of Peterborough on old A605 Oundle to Peterborough road. Opened April 1993. Scenic parkland, wooded. 18 holes, 6279 yards, 5715 metres. S.S.S. 70. Driving range. *Green Fees:* information not available. *Eating facilities:* new spacious bar and restaurant (holds 120). *Visitors:* welcome any time. Buggies available for hire. *Society Meetings:* welcome Monday to Friday - small groups only on Friday - need to pre-book. Contact: Secretary. (01832 280189).

PETERBOROUGH. **Orton Meadows Golf Course,** Ham Lane, Orton Waterville, Peterborough PE2 5UU (01733 237478). *Location*: three miles west of Peterborough on A605, at entrance to Nene Park. Parkland, lakes. 18 holes, 5613 yards. S.S.S. 68. with 12 hole pitch and putt course adjoining. *Green Fees*: weekdays £14.60, Juniors £6.00; weekends and Bank Holidays £19.50. Pitch and Putt weekends £3.60, Juniors £2.70. *Visitors*: welcome; unrestricted – Pay as you Play course. Catering at adjoining pub/restaurant. Bookings taken seven days in advance. *Society Meetings*: Golf Societies welcome, contact Pro Shop (01733 237478). Head Professional: Stuart Brown (01733 237478). Director of Golf: Roger Fitton. Secretary: W.L. Stocks
e-mail: enquiries@ortonmeadowsgolfcourse.co.uk
website: www.omgc.co.uk

PETERBOROUGH. **Peterborough Milton Golf Club,** Milton Ferry, Peterborough PE6 7AG. *Location*: on A47 west of Peterborough, three miles east of A1. Parkland. 18 holes, 6516 yards. S.S.S. 72. *Green Fees:* £40.00 per round. Societies £40.00 per day. *Eating facilities:* available daily except Mondays. *Society Meetings:* available by arrangement with Secretary. Professional: Jasen Barker (01733 380489). Secretary: Andy Izod (01733 380489).
e-mail: admin@pmgc.org.uk
website: www.pmgc.org.uk

PETERBOROUGH. **Thorney Golf Centre,** English Drove, Thorney, Peterborough PE6 0TJ (01733 270570). *Location:* approximately two miles off the middle roundabout, just off the Thorney Bypass; Thorney Golf Centre is one mile on the left. Fen Course - flat, ideal for beginners; Lakes Course - challenging links with lakes. 36 holes: Fen 18 holes, 6104 yards, S.S.S. 69; Lakes 18 holes, 6399 yards, S.S.S. 71. Driving range. *Green Fees:* weekdays Fen £11.00, Lakes £18.50; weekends Fen £13.75, Lakes £27.00. *Eating facilities:* three bars and restaurant. *Visitors:* welcome, no restrictions on Fen Course, Lakes Course contact in advance at weekends. *Society Meetings:* all welcome. Professional: Mark Templeman. Secretary: Jane Hind.

PETERBOROUGH. **Thorpe Wood Golf Course,** Thorpe Wood, Peterborough PE3 6SE (01733 267701). *Location*: two miles west of Peterborough on A47. Parkland. 18 holes, 7086 yards. S.S.S. 74. Practice ground. *Green Fees*: weekdays £15.50; Concessions; £9.50; Juniors £6.50. Weekends and Bank Holidays £21.00 (no concessions). Juniors £6.50. *Visitors*: welcome, unrestricted; Pay-as-you-Play course. Catering at adjoining pub/restaurant. Bookings taken 7 days in advance. *Society Meetings*: Golf Societies welcome – contact Jenny Walters (01733 267701). Head Coach: Gary Casey (01733 267701). Director of Golf: Simon Fitton.
e-mail: enquiries@thorpewoodgolfcourse.co.uk

Two Great Courses – Two Great Choices

Orton Meadows Golf Course
Orton Waterville, Peterborough PE2 5UU
Tel: 01733 237478
www.ortonmeadowsgolfcourse.co.uk

Thorpe Wood Golf Course
Thorpe Wood, Peterborough PE3 6SE
Tel: 01733 267701
www.thorpewoodgolfcourse.co.uk

- ☑ Pay as you play at affordable prices
- ☑ Club and Trolley Hire available
- ☑ You do not have to be a member or have a Handicap to play
- ☑ Large well-stocked Golf Shops
- ☑ 12-hole Pitch and Putt Course at Orton Meadows
- ☑ Golf Societies welcome
- ☑ Catering available at adjoining pub restaurants

**Looking for accommodation near golf clubs?, then visit
www.holidayguides.com
for where to stay when playing golf around the regions**

EAST REGION / Cambridgeshire

RAMSEY. **Old Nene Golf Club,** Muchwood Lane, Bodsey, Ramsey PE26 2XQ (01487 813519 or 815622). *Location:* three-quarters of a mile north of Ramsey towards Peterborough, halfway between Ramsey and Ramsey Mereside and half mile from Rainbow Superstore. Easy walking course with water hazards, quiet with wildlife – herons, swans, pheasants, partridges. 1996 Eastern Area Environmental Winner. 9 holes, 5605 yards, S.S.S. 68. Edrich driving range on site. *Green Fees:* information not available. *Eating facilities:* in clubhouse, open to all, fully licensed bar; bar snacks always available, meals to order. *Visitors:* welcome, telephone to avoid club tee closures. *Society Meetings:* welcome. Professional: Adrian Perkins. Secretary: G. Stoneman (01487 815622).*

ST IVES. **St Ives (Hunts) Golf Club,** Needingworth Road, St Ives PE27 4NB (01480 499920). *Location:* off A14. 18 holes, 6758 yards. S.S.S. 73. *Green Fees:* information not available. *Eating facilities:* full catering. *Visitors:* welcome weekdays. *Society Meetings:* welcome. Professional: Mark Pond (01480 499924). Manager: Mike Kjenstad (01480 499920; Fax: 01480 301489).
e-mail: manager@stivesgolfclub.co.uk

ST NEOTS. **Abbotsley Golf Club and Hotel,** Eynesbury Hardwicke, St Neots PE19 6XN (01480 474000; Fax: 01480 471018). *Location:* A428 St Neots bypass, turn towards St. Neots at Tesco's follow signs to Eynesbury Hardwicke and Abbotsley. Pleasantly undulating, parkland course with several water features. Two courses, 36 holes - Abbotsley 6311 yards, S.S.S. 72; Cromwell 6087 yards, S.S.S. 69. Floodlit covered driving range, 300 yard grass practice area. 9 hole Par 3 course. *Green Fees:* information not available. *Eating facilities:* 80 cover restaurant, three bars. *Visitors:* always welcome. 42 bedroom hotel. *Society Meetings:* welcome. General Manager: Nicky Briggs. Professional: Steve Connolly. Sales: (01480 474000; Fax: 01480 471018).*

ST NEOTS. **St Neots Golf Club,** Crosshall Road, St Neots PE19 7GE (01480 472363). *Location:* just off the A1, Junction B1048 heading for St Neots. Picturesque, undulating parkland course with water hazards and challenging greens. 18 holes, 6087 yards. S.S.S. 70. Practice ground, putting green. *Green Fees:* weekdays £35.00. *Eating facilities:* full catering and bar. *Visitors:* welcome, with Handicap Certificates; weekends with a member only. *Society Meetings:* welcome weekdays. Club Secretary: (01480 472363; Pro Shop: 01480 476513).
e-mail: office@stneots-golfclub.co.uk
website: www.stneots-golfclub.co.uk

WISBECH. **Tydd St Giles Golf & Leisure Estate,** Kirkgate, Tydd St Giles, Wisbech PE13 5NZ (01945 871007; Fax: 01945 870566). *Location*: A1101 from Wisbech to Long Sutton to Tydd Gote and follow the river to Tydd St Giles, one mile from this junction on right hand side. Slightly undulating course, fenland Grade 1 silt/loam free draining. Course always open. 18 holes, 6264 yards, S.S.S. 70. Indoor/outdoor floodlit driving range. *Green Fees*: midweek £19.00, weekends £22.00, prices for all day golf. Twilight £12.00 after 1pm (Monday-Sunday) all year. *Eating facilities*: all day snacks/grills. Full pub licence - everyone welcome. *Visitors*: welcome, please ring for a tee off time, dress code applies. Tuition available daily. *Society Meetings*: welcome, packages available.
e-mail: enquiries@tyddgolf.co.uk
website: www.tyddgolf.co.uk

THE APPEARANCE OF AN ASTERISK (*) AT THE END OF A CLUB OR COURSE ENTRY INDICATES THAT UP-TO-DATE INFORMATION HAS NOT BEEN SUPPLIED

Other British holiday guides from FHG Guides

**PUBS & INNS • 300 GREAT HOTELS
SHORT BREAK HOLIDAYS
The bestselling and original PETS WELCOME!
500 GREAT PLACES TO STAY
SELF-CATERING HOLIDAYS • BED & BREAKFAST STOPS
CARAVAN & CAMPING HOLIDAYS • FAMILY BREAKS**

Published annually: available in all good bookshops or direct from the publisher:
**FHG Guides, Abbey Mill Business Centre, Seedhill, Paisley PA1 1TJ
Tel: 0141 887 0428 • Fax: 0141 889 7204**
e-mail: admin@fhguides.co.uk • www.holidayguides.com

Essex

BASILDON. **Basildon Golf Centre,** Clay Hill Lane, Basildon SS16 5JP (01268 533532). *Location:* off A13 or A127 on A176 – Kingswood Roundabout. Undulating woodland. 18 holes, 6236 yards. S.S.S. 70. Practice area. *Green Fees:* information not available. *Eating facilities:* snacks, full meals, bar. *Visitors:* welcome anytime, booking system at weekends and Bank Holidays. *Society Meetings:* welcome, booking through Centre Manager: Steve Cunningham. (01268 533532).*

BENFLEET. **Boyce Hill Golf Club Ltd,** Vicarage Hill, South Benfleet SS7 1PD (01268 793625). *Location*: 1½ miles south of A13/A127. Hilly course, 18 holes, 6003 yards, 5489 metres. S.S.S. 69. *Green Fees*: £35.00 18 holes, £45.00 36 holes. *Eating facilities*: full bar and dining facilities daily. *Visitors*: welcome, except Tuesday mornings and weekends. 24 hours notice of booking and Handicap Certificate required. *Society Meetings*: catered for Thursdays only. Professional: G. Burroughs (01268 752565). Secretary: D. Kelly (01268 793625; Fax: 01268 750497).
e-mail: secretary@boycehillgolfclub.co.uk
website: www.boycehillgolfclub.co.uk

BILLERICAY. **Stock Brook Golf & Country Club,** Queens Park Avenue, Stock, Near Billericay CM12 0SP (01277 653616; Fax: 01277 633063). *Location*: nearest main roads A12 and A127, Billericay. Parkland - gently undulating with featured lakes. 18 hole championship course, 6905 yards. S.S.S. 72. Manor - 9 holes, 2997 yards. Driving range, putting green and three par 3 practice holes. *Green Fees:* weekdays £30.00. weekends (after 12 noon) £35.00. *Eating facilities:* bar meals available. *Visitors:* welcome weekdays, and Saturday/Sunday after 12 noon. Extensive conference and banqueting facilities. Country club, swimming pool, tennis courts, gym. *Society Meetings:* welcome. Professional: Craig Laurence (01277 658181). Membership, Corporate and Society enquiries: Sandra Johnson: (01277 653616).

BRAINTREE. **Braintree Golf Club,** Kings Lane, Stisted, Braintree CM77 8DD (01376 346079; Fax: 01376 348677). *Location:* A120 to Colchester, 300 yards east of Braintree by-pass, signposted Stisted and Golf Club. Parkland, with slopes down to the river, many specimen trees. 18 holes, 6241 yards, S.S.S. 70. Practice ground, pitching area. *Green Fees:* weekdays £50.00 per day, £35.00 per round; weekends and Bank Holidays after 2pm £50.00 per round; no visitors weekend mornings. Twilight after 5pm £20.00 per round. *Eating facilities:* available. *Visitors:* welcome Monday to Fridays (weekends must have Handicap Certificate). *Society Meetings:* catered for Wednesdays and Thursdays Professional: D. Woolger (01376 343465). Secretary: Mrs N. Wells (01376 346079; Fax: 01376 348677).

BRAINTREE. **Towerlands Golf Club,** Panfield Road, Braintree CM7 5BJ (01376 326802; Fax: 01376 552487). *Location*: off A120 into Braintree, then B1053. Undulating course. 9 holes, 2749 yards. S.S.S. 66. Practice area. *Green Fees:* information not available. *Eating facilities:* bar (part-time). *Visitors:* welcome. We have equestrian facilities, no accommodation. *Society Meetings:* by arrangement. Secretary: C. Cooper (01376 326802; Fax: 01376 552487).*

BRENTWOOD. **Bentley Golf Club,** Ongar Road, Brentwood CM15 9SS (01277 373179). *Location:* situated on A128 approximately five miles from Junction 28 of M25. Undulating parkland course, a great test of golf. 18 holes, 6709 yards, 6136 metres. S.S.S. 72. Practice field. *Green Fees:* information not available. *Eating facilities:* food and bar available all day. *Visitors:* welcome weekdays; Bank Holidays after 11am. *Society Meetings:* welcome by prior arrangement. Professional: Nick Garrett (01277 372933). Secretary: Andy Hall (01277 373179).*

BRENTWOOD. **Hartswood Golf Club,** (Play on Brentwood Municipal), King George's Playing Fields, Ingrave Road, Brentwood CM15 8AY (01277 218850). *Location*: one mile south of Brentwood on A128. Parkland, 18 holes, 6238 yards. S.S.S. 70. *Green Fees*: information not available. *Eating facilities*: full catering available. *Visitors*: welcome without reservation. Tee Reservation – 01277 214830. *Society Meetings*: unlimited weekdays. Professional: Stephen Cole (01277 218714).

BRENTWOOD. **South Essex Golf and Country Club,** Brentwood Road, Herongate, Brentwood CM13 3LW (01277 811006; Fax: 01277 811304). *Location:* Halfway House Exit (A128) from A127 (Junction 29 - M25). Gently rolling countryside incorporating established woodland. 27 holes, 6851 yards. S.S.S. 73. Covered 14 bay driving range. *Green Fees:* information not available. *Eating facilities:* restaurant and fully licensed bar. *Visitors:* welcome with appropriate dress. Buggies available. *Society Meetings:* welcome, including weekends. (01277 811289; Fax: 01277 811304).*

BRENTWOOD. **Thorndon Park Golf Club Ltd,** Ingrave, Brentwood CM13 3RH (01277 810345). *Location:* three miles south of Brentwood on A128. 18 holes, 6511 yards. S.S.S. 71. *Green Fees:* £65.00 per day, £50.00 per round weekdays, £55.00 per round after 1pm Sundays (if available). Saturday and Sunday morning with members only. 2010 rates. *Eating facilities:* lunches served at club. *Visitors:* welcome with reservation, weekdays subject to prior permission. *Society Meetings:* catered for. Professional: Brian White (01277 810736). Club Manager: Giles Thomas (01277 810345).
website: www.thorndonparkgolfclub.com

EAST REGION / Essex

BRENTWOOD. The Warley Park Golf Club, Magpie Lane, Little Warley, Brentwood CM13 3DX (01277 224891). *Location:* leave M25 at Intersection 29. A127 towards Southend. Turn left three-quarters-of-a-mile Little Warley, Hall Lane. Turn left into Magpie Lane. Parkland, 3 Courses, (27 holes). S.S.S. 70-70-69. Large practice area, putting greens. *Green Fees:* available on request. *Eating facilities*: lounge bar and restaurant/spike bar. *Visitors*: welcome Monday to Friday, must have Handicap Certificate. *Society Meetings*: catered for. Professional: K. Smith (01277 200441). Golf Manager: Nick Hawkins (01277 224891).

BRENTWOOD. Weald Park Golf Club, Coxtie Green Road, South Weald, Brentwood CM14 5RJ (01277 375101). *Location:* M25 and A12 junction (map available). Parkland course surrounded by countryside. 18 holes, 6612 yards. S.S.S. 72/70. *Green Fees:* information not available. *Eating facilities:* bar and restaurant. *Visitors:* welcome. *Society Meetings:* welcome Monday to Friday. Professional: Dean Vickerman (01277 375101; Fax: 01277 374888). General Manager: Darcy Tallon (01277 375101; Fax: 01277 374888).*

BULPHAN. The Langdon Hills Golf & Country Club, Lower Dunton Road, Bulphan RM14 3TY (01268 548444; Fax: 01268 490084). *Location:* eight miles from M25, Dartford River crossing, Basildon three miles between A127 and A13. Gently undulating parkland. Three loops of 9 holes – 27 holes: 6760 yards S.S.S. 72, 6537 yards S.S.S. 72, 6279 yards S.S.S. 71. Two putting greens. *Green Fees:* information not available. *Eating facilities:* restaurant, Function Suite available. *Visitors:* welcome at all times (except Saturday and Sunday morning), subject to availablity. Hotel accommodation and function suite available. *Society Meetings:* welcome. Professional: Terry Moncur (01268 544300; Fax: 01268 490084). Secretary: Keith Thompson (01268 548444; Fax: 01268 490084).*
website: www.golflangdon.co.uk

BURNHAM-ON-CROUCH. Burnham-on-Crouch Golf Club Ltd, Ferry Road, Creeksea CM0 8PQ (01621 782282). *Location:* Burnham-on-Crouch, one and a half miles before Burnham town. Undulating meadowland rolling alongside River Crouch. 18 holes, 6056 yards. S.S.S. 69. Par 70. Practice ground. *Green Fees:* information not provided. *Eating facilities:* bar, full catering. *Visitors:* welcome weekdays, and weekend afternoons, with Handicap Certificate. *Society Meetings:* welcome Mondays, Tuesdays, Wednesdays and Fridays. Club Managers: SK Golf (01621 782282; Fax: 01621 784489). Private members club.
e-mail: burnhamgolf@hotmail.com
website: www.burnhamgolfclub.co.uk

CANVEY ISLAND. Castle Point Golf Club, Somnes Avenue, Canvey Island SS8 9FG (01268 696298). *Location:* A13 towards Southend, A130 to Canvey Island, opposite sports centre. Links course, with views of Hadleigh Downs and Castle. 18 holes, 6176 yards. S.S.S. 69. Floodlit driving range. *Green Fees:* information not available. *Eating facilities:* clubhouse open to public – full catering. *Visitors:* welcome anytime, booking required at weekends. Changing room and showers; buggies available. Pro Shop (01268 510830). *Society Meetings:* welcome. Professional: Steve Richardson (01268 510830). Secretary: Belinda de Kuster (01268 692899).*

CHELMSFORD. Channels Golf Club, Belsteads Farm Lane, Little Waltham, Chelmsford CM3 3PT (01245 440005). *Location:* 3 miles north east of Chelmsford on A130. Reclaimed gravel workings, many lakes, hazards and an abundance of wild life. Two courses – Channels 6402 yards, S.S.S. 71; Belsteads 4779 yards, S.S.S. 63. *Green Fees:* Channels Course – weekdays only £40.00 per 18 holes; members and guests only at weekends. Belsteads Course – £15.00 9 holes, £20.00 18 holes, no restrictions weekends. *Eating facilities:* excellent restaurant in 13th century clubhouse. *Visitors:* welcome. *Society Meetings:* catered for weekdays. Professional: I.B. Sinclair (01245 441056). Secretary: Mrs S. Stubbings-Larner (01245 440005; Fax: 01245 442032).
e-mail: info@channelsgolf.co.uk
website: www.channelsgolf.co.uk

CHELMSFORD. Chelmsford Golf Club, Widford Road, Chelmsford CM2 9AP (Tel & Fax: 01245 256483). *Location:* A12–A414 to Chelmsford, first roundabout turn right. Parkland course. 18 holes, 5996 yards. S.S.S. 69. *Green Fees:* weekdays £40.00. *Eating facilities:* dining room and bar. *Visitors:* welcome Monday to Friday with reservation. *Society Meetings:* welcome, discounts available. Professional: Mark Welch (01245 257079). Secretary: G. Winckless.
e-mail: office@chelmsfordgc.co.uk
website: www.chelmsfordgc.co.uk

CHELMSFORD. The Regiment Way Golf Centre, Pratts Farm Lane, Little Waltham, Chelmsford CM3 3PR (01245 361100). *Location:* three miles north east of Chelmsford off A130. Flat parkland, ideal novice course. 9 holes, 2500 yards. S.S.S. 64. 22 bay floodlit driving range. *Green Fees*: weekdays £11.00 9 holes, £15.00 18 holes; weekends £12.00 9 holes, £17.00 18 holes. Student and Senior discount £2.00 9 holes, £3.00 18 holes. 2010 rates (subject to review). *Visitors:* pay as you play. *Society Meetings:* welcome. Professional: David March. Secretary: David Wallbank.

CHELMSFORD. Three Rivers Golf and Country Club, Stow Road, Cold Norton, Purleigh, Near Chelmsford CM3 6RR (01621 828631; Fax: 01621 828060). *Location:* four miles from South Woodham Ferrers, six miles from Maldon. Parkland with lakes and wooded copses; spectacular views. Two courses: 36 holes, 6403 yards Kings Course, 4501 Jubilee Course. Kings par 72/Jubilee par 64. *Green Fees:* Information not available. *Eating facilities:* bar meals available all day, carvery available Sunday lunchtime. *Visitors:* welcome. Function suites available. Buggies available. *Society meetings:* very welcome. Specialists in looking after companies and groups. Professional: Kevin Clark, individual and group lessons available. (01621 829781).*

CHIGWELL. Chigwell Golf Club, The Clubhouse, High Road, Chigwell IG7 5BH (020 8500 2059; Fax: 020 8501 3410). *Location:* on A113, 14 miles from London, seven miles from Exit 26 on the M25. Testing undulating parkland course. 18 holes, 6296 yards. S.S.S. 70. Practice bays and ground. *Green Fees:* information not available. *Eating facilities:* restaurant and bars available. *Visitors:* weekdays by prior arrangement, Handicap Certificate required and membership of authorised Golf Club. *Society Meetings:* weekdays by arrangement. Professional: J. Fuller (020 8500 2384). General Manager: James Fuller (020 8500 2059; Fax: 020 8501 3410).*
e-mail: info@chigwellgolfclub.co.uk
website: www.chigwellgolfclub.co.uk

CHIGWELL. Hainault Forest Golf Club, Romford Road, Chigwell IG7 4QW (020 8500 2097). *Location:* off A12 towards Hainault/Chigwell. Undulating parkland with tree-lined fairways. 36 holes: Lower 6545 yards. S.S.S. 72; Upper 5886 yards. S.S.S. 69. Driving range, practice hole and putting green. *Green Fees:* information not available. *Eating facilities:* fully licensed bar and restaurant, cafe. *Visitors:* welcome any time, all week. *Society Meetings:* welcome all week, enquiries welcome. Head Professional: Chris Hope. Secretary: Ben Jones.*

CHIGWELL. Woolston Manor Golf Club, Woolston Manor, Abridge Road, Chigwell IG7 6BX (020 8500 2549; Fax: 020 8501 5452). Private exclusive members' club - for membership enquiries call membership secretary on 020 8500 2549. *Location:* Junction 5, M11 one mile. Parkland, Neil Coles Championship design, 18 holes, 6435 yards. S.S.S. 71. Top golf driving range. *Green Fees:* information not available. *Eating facilities:* full catering available. *Visitors:* welcome weekdays after 10.30am and after 11.30am weekends. Handicap Certificate required. *Society Meetings:* welcome weekdays only. Professional: Paul Eady (020 8559 8272; Fax: 020 8501 5452). Secretary: Peter Spargo.*

CLACTON-ON-SEA. Clacton-on-Sea Golf Club, West Road, Clacton-on-Sea CO15 1AJ (01255 421919). *Location:* A12 then A120 and A133 to Clacton-on-Sea, follow signs for promenade/pier then turn right along promenade to sharp right hand bend. 250 metres on left. Seaside course. 18 holes, 6448 yards. S.S.S. 71. *Green Fees:* information not available. *Eating facilities:* full bar and catering facilities available from 11am. *Visitors:* welcome with reservation and current Handicap Certificate. Please check with Pro Shop prior to visit. *Society Meetings:* Monday to Friday catered for by arrangement. Professional: Stuart Levermore (01255 426304).*
e-mail: secretary@clactongolfclub.com
website: www.clactongolfclub.com

COLCHESTER. Birch Grove Golf Club, Layer Road, Colchester CO2 0HS (01206 734276). *Location:* on B1026, two miles south of town. Parkland - small but challenging. 9 holes, 4500 yards. Par 66. *Green Fees:* £11.00 per 9 holes, £16.00 per 18 holes. *Eating facilities:* hot meals and snacks are available during opening hours. *Visitors:* welcome without reservation Monday to Saturday and after 1pm Sundays. *Society Meetings:* catered for weekdays. Secretary: Mrs M. Marston.

COLCHESTER. Colchester Golf Club, Braiswick, Colchester CO4 5AU (01206 853396). *Location:* one mile north-west of Colchester North Station, on B1508. Parkland course with wooded areas. 18 holes, 6347 yards. S.S.S. 70. *Green Fees:* information not available. *Eating facilities:* catering available all day. *Visitors:* welcome except Saturday and Sunday mornings, must have Handicap Certificates. *Society Meetings:* catered for by prior arrangement. Professional: Mark Angel (01206 853920). Secretary: Ms J.A. Ruscoe (01206 853396; Fax: 01206 852698).*
e-mail: colchester.golf@btinternet.com

COLCHESTER. Colne Valley Golf Club, Station Road, Earls Colne, Colchester CO6 2LT (01787 224343; Fax: 01787 224126). *Location:* off the A1124, 10 miles from Colchester. Parkland course in the Valley of the River Colne. 18 holes, 6286 yards. S.S.S. 71. Practice ground. *Green Fees:* information not available. *Eating facilities:* two bars and restaurant facilities open all day. *Visitors:* welcome anytime but weekends only after 9.30am and please phone in advance to confirm. Carts for rental. *Society Meetings:* midweek anytime, weekends after 10.30am, packages available. Head Professional: Jamie Lowe.
website: www.colnevalleygolfclub.co.uk

COLCHESTER. The Essex Golf and Country Club, Earls Colne, Colchester CO6 2NS (01787 224466; Fax: 01787 224410). *Location:* B1024 off the A120 opposite Coggeshall. Flat parkland 18 hole/9 hole courses. 18 holes, 7090 yards. S.S.S. 73. Floodlit driving range. *Green Fees:* information not available. *Eating facilities:* Poolside Grill, sports brasserie, restaurant. *Visitors:* all welcome, no restrictions. Buggies and trolleys available. Full leisure facilities, indoor pool, sauna, steam room, gym, tennis courts. Full day nursery facilities available, conference and entertainment facilities. On site 42 bedroom hotel including two suites. *Society Meetings:* welcome.*
e-mail: info@theclubcompany.com
        essex.hotel@theclubcompany.com
website: www.theclubcompany.com

COLCHESTER. Lexden Wood Golf Club, Colchester and Lexden Golf Centre, Bakers Lane, Colchester CO3 4AU (01206 843333; Fax: 01206 854775). *Location:* one mile north west of Colchester, two minutes on the A12 northbound on A133. Undulating parkland with many water features. 27 holes –18 hole Par 70 5895 yards and 9 hole short course. *Green Fees:* £22.00 weekday, £30.00 weekend. *Eating facilities:* home cooked food always available during opening hours. *Visitors:* always welcome, please phone to book tee time. Floodlit covered driving range/putting green. *Society Meetings:* always welcome by prior arrangement. Professional: Phil Grice (01206 843333; Fax: 01206 854775).

EAST REGION / Essex

ELSENHAM. Elsenham Golf Centre, Hall Road, Elsenham CM22 6DH (01279 812865). *Location:* A120 Takley, turn towards Elsenham. Just past the "Jam Factory". Parkland, part wooded course. Dual 9 hole course, 5919 yards. Par 70. 18 bay floodlit driving range, 3 hole Academy Course. *Green Fees:* information not available. *Eating facilities:* bar, food. Open to non-members, children welcome. *Visitors:* always welcome. Changing facilities. Pro Shop. Teaching facility. *Society Meetings:* all welcome. Professional: Owen McKenna (01279 812865).*

EPPING. North Weald Golf Club, Rayley Lane, North Weald, Epping CM16 6AR (01992 522118; Fax: 01992 522881). *Location:* from M11 Junction 7 take A414 to Chelmsford, two miles to first roundabout, turn right. Club is 200 yards on left. Parkland and lakes. 18 holes, 6377 yards. S.S.S. 71. Driving range, putting green, chipping green and practice bunker. *Green Fees:* information not provided. *Eating facilities:* available. *Visitors:* welcome. *Society Meetings:* welcome by arrangement. Tee bookings (01992 522118). Club Manager: Stacey Smith (01992 522118; Fax: 01992 522881).
website: www.northwealdgolfclub.co.uk

EPPING. The Epping Golf Course, Flux Lane, Epping CM16 7NJ (01992 572282). *Location:* ½ mile from Tube station. By car: M25 to M11 (J7) Harlow, turn left to Epping; in Epping High Street turn south onto Station Road; Epping Golf one mile on left. "Quality golf without the price tag". Undulating parkland course with water features and extensive views. 18 holes, 5405 yards. S.S.S. 65. Putting green, chipping green, practice hole, golf range. Golf Foundation Starter Centre. Free lessons for adults and inexpensive Junior lessons - contact for details. *Green Fees:* weekdays £12.00, weekends £19.00. Special rates for Seniors Monday and Thursday. *Eating facilities:* new clubhouse with licensed bar and home cooking. Function room available. *Visitors:* welcome at all times; advisable to book by phone for weekend play. *Society Meetings:* welcome at any time - typical price for 18 holes + meal is £24.00. Professional: Gareth Williams (01992 572282). Secretary: Neil Sjoberg (07909 635549).
e-mail: neilsjoberg@hotmail.com
website: www.eppinggolfcourse.org.uk

EPPING. Theydon Bois Golf Club, Theydon Road, Epping CM16 4EH. *Location:* M25 Waltham Abbey/ Epping A121 London to Cambridge, turn right at Quality Hotel. Wooded course. 18 holes, 5490 yards. S.S.S. 67. Practice area. *Green Fees:* information not available. *Eating facilities:* restaurant and bar. *Visitors:* welcome except Wednesday and Thursday morning. *Society Meetings:* Monday, Tuesday and Friday. Professional: R. Hall (01992 812460). Manager: C. Stewart (01992 813054).*

FRINTON-ON-SEA. Frinton Golf Club, 1 Esplanade, Frinton-on-Sea CO13 9EP. *Location:* 17 miles east of Colchester, A12-A133, B1033. Flat seaside links-type course, strength of wind always a feature. Havers Course: 18 holes, 6265 yards. Par 71. Kirby Course 3062 yards. Indoor practice facilities. *Green Fees:* information not provided. *Visitors:* welcome, check with Pro Shop. Handicap Certificate required for Havers Course. *Society Meetings:* catering by arrangement. Professional: Peter Taggart (Tel & Fax: 01255 671618). Office: 01255 674618.
e-mail: secretary@frintongolfclub.com
website: www.frintongolfclub.com

HALSTEAD. Gosfield Lake Golf Club, Hall Drive, Gosfield, Halstead CO9 1SE. *Location:* off the A1017 four miles north of Braintree. Gently undulating parkland course with lakes and woods; designed by Sir Henry Cotton. Two courses: Lakes Course 18 holes, 6615 yards. S.S.S. 72; Meadows Course 9 holes (double teed to 18), 4990 yards S.S.S. 64. Practice facilities including putting, chipping, bunkers. *Green Fees:* please contact Pro Shop for information (01787 474488). *Eating facilities:* bar and catering facilities from 7am; bar menu. *Visitors*: welcome. Weekdays booking advisable, weekends from 12 noon (booking necessary). Handicap Certificate required for Lakes Course, Meadows Course ideal for beginners/ improvers. Trolley hire. Buggy hire (summer only). *Society Meetings:* welcome by prior arrangement. Professional: Richard Wheeler (01787 474488) Secretary: J.A. O'Shea (01787 474747; Fax: 01787 476044).
e-mail: gosfieldlakegc@btconnect.com.
website: www.gosfield-lake-golf-club.co.uk

HARLOW. Canons Brook Golf Club, Elizabeth Way, Harlow CM19 5BE (01279 425142). *Location*: Turn onto Elizabeth Way at Harlow Town Station on A414 from M11. Parkland course. 18 holes, 6745 yards. S.S.S. 73. *Green Fees*: information not provided. *Eating facilities*: available, open all day. *Visitors*: welcome weekdays, weekends with a member. *Society Meetings*: catered for Mondays, Wednesdays and Fridays. Professional: Alan McGinn (01279 418357). Secretary: Mrs S. Langton (01279 421482; Fax: 01279 626393).

HARWICH. Harwich and Dovercourt Golf Club, Station Road, Parkeston, Harwich CO12 4NZ (01255 503616; Fax: 01255 503323). *Location:* A120 then to Parkeston Quay, course marked on left hand side of Station Road. Flat course. 9 holes, 5742 yards. S.S.S. 68. *Green Fees:* with member – 18 holes £18.00, 9 holes £10.00; without member – 18 holes £24.00, 9 holes £13.00. *Eating facilities:* licensed clubhouse, catering available to order (not Thursdays). *Visitors:* welcome with Handicap Certificates. Saturdays, Sundays and Bank Holidays after 11am. *Society Meetings:* small groups welcome by arrangement. Hon. Secretary: P. J.Cole (01255 503616).

ILFORD. Fairlop Waters, Forest Road, Barkingside, Ilford IG6 3JA (020 8500 9911). *Location:* two miles north of Ilford, half a mile from A12, one and a half miles from southern end of M11. Covered, floodlit range, 36 bays. 18 hole golf course, 9 hole Par 3 course. Individual or group tuition available. *Green Fees:* information not available. Opening hours: 9am to 10pm. *Eating facilities:* bars and diner. Banqueting facilities and conferences. 38 acre sailing lake, 25 acre country park, children's play area. Professional: Paul Davies (020 8501 1881). General Manager: F. Taylor.*

160 Essex / EAST REGION

ILFORD. Ilford Golf Club, 291 Wanstead Park Road, Ilford IG1 3TR (020 8554 2930). *Location:* at end of M11, off A406. Parkland with winding river. 18 holes, 5299 yards. S.S.S. 66. *Green Fees:* weekdays £19.00 plus special offers, weekends £24.00. *Eating facilities:* restaurant and bar. *Visitors:* welcome weekdays, restricted times at weekends. *Society Meetings:* welcome. Professional: G. Cant (020 8554 0094). General Manager: Mrs J. Pinner (020 8554 2930; Fax: 020 8554 0822).

INGATESTONE. **Hylands Golf Complex,** Main Road, Margaretting, Ingatestone CM4 0ET (01277 356016; Fax: 01277 356056). *Location*: off A12. Parkland course. 9 holes 2445 yards, 18 holes 6604 yards. Driving range, practice bunker. *Green Fees:* information not available. *Eating facilities:* coffee and soft drinks available. *Visitors:* all welcome. New complex, pay and play only; no membership. Accommodation at Ivy Hill Hotel, Margaretting. Professional: Lee Porter (01277 356016; Fax: 01277 356056).*

LEIGH-ON-SEA. **Belfairs Golf Club,** Eastwood Road North, Leigh-on-Sea SS9 4LR (01702 526911). Park front 9, heavy woodland back 9; easy walking but challenging golf. Play over Belfairs Municipal course, 18 holes, 5857 yards. S.S.S. 68. *Green Fees:* information not available. *Visitors:* unrestricted on the course but no clubhouse facilities available. Bookings required (01702 525345). Secretary: B. J. Harvey (01702 714567).*

LITTLE BURSTEAD. **The Burstead Golf Club,** Tye Common Road, Little Burstead CM12 9SS (01277 631171; Fax: 01277 632766). Parkland course. 18 holes, 6275 yards, S.S.S. 70. Practice field, chipping area, putting green. *Green Fees*: information not available. *Eating facilities*: restaurant, bar and spike bar. *Visitors*: welcome 7 days; weekends and Bank Holidays after 11am. Tuition available. *Society Meetings*: welcome 7 days; weekends and Bank Holidays after 11am. Professional: Keith Bridges. Secretary: Lee Mence.*
website: www.thebursteadgolfclub.com

LOUGHTON. **Loughton Golf Club,** Clay's Lane, Debden Green, Loughton IG10 2RZ (020 8502 2923). *Location*: just north of Loughton, on edge of Epping Forest. Parkland, wooded. 9 holes, 4700 yards. S.S.S. 63. *Green Fees:* information not available. *Eating facilities:* bar, snacks available. *Visitors:* welcome, telephone to book. *Society Meetings:* welcome. Manager: Alan Day.*

MALDON. **Bunsay Downs Golf Club,** Little Baddow Road, Woodham Walter, Maldon CM9 6RW (01245 222648; Fax: 01245 223989). *Location:* 7 miles east of Chelmsford off A414 at Woodham Walter, left onto Little Baddow Road. Undulating landscaped partly wooded course. 9 holes, 2932 yards. S.S.S. 68. Par 3 course. *Green Fees:* information not available. *Eating facilities:* bar/grill restaurant. *Visitors:* welcome at all times. Gift shop. *Society Meetings:* small societies welcome. Professional: David Brooks. Secretary: M. Durham (01245 223258).*

MALDON. **Five Lakes Resort,** Colchester Road, Tolleshunt Knights, Maldon CM9 8HX (01621 868888; Fax: 01621 869696). *Location:* seven miles from A12 on B1026 north of Maldon and south of Colchester. Parkland. Two courses: Links Course - 18 holes, 6181 yards, S.S.S. 70; Lakes Course - 18 holes, 6751 yards, S.S.S. 72. Driving range, three putting greens. *Green Fees:* information not available. *Eating facilities:* three restaurants and two bars. *Visitors:* welcome at most times except before 10am weekend mornings. 194 en suite bedrooms, conference and banqueting facilities, indoor pool, air conditioned gym, health club, sauna, steam room and spa bath, tennis, squash and badminton. *Society Meetings:* catered for by appointment. Professional: Gary Carter (01621 862326; Fax: 01621 862320). Golf Consultant: James Taylor (01621 862307; Fax: 01621 862320).*

MALDON. Forrester Park Golf and Tennis Club, Beckingham Road, Great Totham, Near Maldon CM9 8EA (Tel & Fax: 01621 891406). *Location:* three miles off A12 Rivenhall turn-off, on B1022 in Great Totham, near Maldon between Compasses and Bull. Parkland course. 18 holes, 6073 yards. S.S.S. 69. Practice ground. *Green Fees:* weekdays £25.00 per round, weekends £26.00 after 12 noon only. 2010 rates (subject to review). *Eating facilities:* full catering and bar facilities. *Visitors:* welcome subject to prior booking, but not before 12 noon Tuesdays, Wednesdays and weekends. Trolley hire. Buggy hire. *Society Meetings:* welcome subject to prior booking. Professional: Gary Pike (07801 428174). Manager: Tim Forrester-Muir (Tel & Fax: 01621 891406).
e-mail: info@forresterparkltd.com

MALDON. **Maldon Golf Club,** Beeleigh, Langford, Maldon CM9 4SS (01621 853212). *Location:* B1019 two miles northwest of Maldon, turn off by the Museum of Power. Flat parkland. 9 holes, 6253 yards, 5718 metres. S.S.S. 70. *Green Fees:* Information not available. *Eating facilities:* full catering service, bar. *Visitors:* welcome weekdays. *Society Meetings:* catered for by arrangement. Secretary: V. Locke

MALDON. **Warren Golf Club,** Woodham Walter, Maldon CM9 6RW (01245 223198/223258; Fax: 01245 223989). *Location:* close to Chelmsford. A414 turn off to Maldon. Undulating wooded course. 18 holes, 6263 yards, S.S.S. 70. Large practice area. *Green Fees:* information not provided. *Eating facilities:* restaurant, bar, bar snack menu. *Visitors:* welcome with reservation weekdays except Wednesday mornings. Handicap Certificate required. Golf Academy. *Society Meetings:* catered for weekdays - up to 40 players. Professional: David Brooks (01245 224662). Managing Director: J.E. Durham.

NAZEING. **Nazeing Golf Club,** Middle Street, Nazeing EN9 2LW (01992 893915; Fax: 01992 893882). *Location:* from Waltham Abbey Town Centre – signposted. Parkland course, American design (sand based greens and tees). 18 holes, 6617 yards. S.S.S. 72. Continental style driving range. *Green Fees:* information not available. *Eating facilities:* available. *Visitors:* welcome anytime except weekend mornings, must ring and book through Pro shop. Buggies, trolleys available. *Society Meetings:* welcome. Professional: Robert Green (01992 893798; Fax: 01992 893882).

OCKENDON. **Belhus Park Golf Club,** Belhus Park, Aveley By-Pass, South Ockendon RM15 4QR (01708 852248 complex, 01708 854748 office). *Location:* on A13 London - Southend Road, approximately one mile from Dartford Tunnel. Parkland. 18 holes, 5350 yards. S.S.S. 69. Driving range. *Green Fees:* information not available. *Eating facilities:* cafe and bar. *Visitors:* welcome anytime (municipal course), but booking essential weekends and Bank Holidays. Swimming pool. *Society Meetings:* by arrangement, telephone complex. Professional: Jamie Gowan (01708 854260). Secretary: J. Cleary (01708 865645).*

ONGAR. **Toot Hill Golf Club,** School Road, Toot Hill, Near Ongar CM5 9PU (01277 365523; Fax: 01277 364509). *Location*: A128 to Ongar, A414 to Harlow, two miles left at Blake Hall Road. Parkland course, lakes and brook. 18 holes, 6197 yards, Par 70, S.S.S. 69. Practice range, putting and chipping green. *Green Fees:* information not provided. *Eating facilities:* available, clubhouse and spike bar. *Visitors:* welcome. *Society Meetings:* welcome, various packages. Professional: Mark Bishop (01277 365747). Secretary: Mrs C. Cameron.

ORSETT. **Orsett Golf Club,** Brentwood Road, Orsett RM16 3DS (01375 891352). *Location:* A13 Junction roundabout with A128. South towards Chadwell St Mary on A128. Heathland course. 18 holes, 6682 yards. S.S.S. 73. *Green Fees:* weekdays £35.00 per round, £45.00 all day. *Eating facilities:* full catering available. *Visitors:* welcome on weekdays only by arrangement. Must be members of a club and have Handicap. Proof must be produced. *Society Meetings:* welcome most days; contact for availability. Professional: R. Herring (01375 891797). Secretary: Gary Smith. Office (01375 891352; Fax: 01375 892471).

RAYLEIGH. **Hanover Golf and Country Club,** Hullbridge Road, Rayleigh SS6 9QS (01702 232377; Fax: 01702 231811). *Location:* A130, A127 Rayleigh. Parkland, gently undulating, with featured lakes. Spectacular views. 36 holes. Georgian Course 6669 yards. Par 73. Regency Course Par 68. Floodlit driving range. *Green Fees:* information not available. *Eating facilities:* bar meals available all day; Sunday carvery; function suites and restaurant. *Visitors:* welcome, Handicap Certificate required for Georgian Course. *Society Meetings:* welcome. Professional: A. Blackburn. Secretary: J. Court.*

ROCHFORD. **Rochford Hundred Golf Club,** Hall Road, Rochford SS4 1NW (01702 544302; Fax: 01702 541343). *Location:* A127 towards Southend on Sea, turning for Rochford. Flat parkland course, ancient clubhouse, course surrounds church. 18 holes, 6176 yards (white boxes). S.S.S. 71. *Green Fees:* information not available. *Eating facilities:* full restaurant and snack facilities; bars. *Visitors:* welcome, Tuesday mornings ladies only. Handicap Certificate necessary. *Society Meetings:* catered for except Tuesday mornings, Fridays and weekends. Professional: G. Hill (01702 548968). Secretary: M.A. Boon.*

ROCHFORD near. **Ballards Gore Golf Club,** Gore Road, Canewdon, Near Rochford SS4 2DA (01702 258917). *Location:* Southend Airport three miles, London via A127, club two miles from Rochford. Parkland with lakes. 18 holes, 6845 yards. S.S.S. 73. Practice area. *Green Fees:* information not avaialble. *Eating facilities:* diningroom (100 covers). Daily special menu available from £4.95. *Visitors:* welcome weekdays, except Tuesday mornings. *Society Meetings:* catered for by arrangement. Professional: Gary McCarthy (01702 258924; Fax: 01702 258924). Secretary: Iain Evans (01702 258917; Fax: 01702 258571).*

ROMFORD. **Maylands Golf and Country Club,** Harold Park, Romford RM3 0AZ (01708 341777). *Location:* turn off Junction 28 M25, directly on A12 between Romford and Brentwood. 18 holes, 6182 yards. S.S.S. 70. Driving range and putting green. *Green Fees:* information not available. *Eating facilities:* bar, spike bar, restaurant and bar snacks. *Visitors:* welcome midweek. *Society Meetings:* catered for Mondays, Wednesdays and Fridays. Professional: Darren Parker (01708 346466). Secretaryr: M. Gallop (Tel & Fax: 01708 341777). website: www.maylandsgolf.com

ROMFORD. **Risebridge Golf Centre,** Risebridge Chase, Romford RM1 4DG (01708 741429). Location: off Lower Bedfords Road, between Collier Row and Harold Hill, signposted from Gallows Corner (A12). Mature parkland course with some long tough holes. 18 holes, 6342 yards. S.S.S. 70. 9 hole Par 3 course, driving range, practice green. *Green Fees:* information not available. *Eating facilities:* cafe and spike bar. *Visitors:* welcome at all times. *Society Meetings:* all welcome, for details contact the Professional. Professional/Manager: Mr P. Jennings (Tel & Fax: 01708 741429).*

SAFFRON WALDEN. **Saffron Walden Golf Club,** Windmill Hill, Saffron Walden CB10 1BX (01799 522786). *Location:* end of town on B184 to Cambridge. 18 holes, 6632 yards. S.S.S. 72 (S.S.S. Red Tees 74). *Green Fees:* from £44.00 - offers available. Twilight green fees after 4pm. *Eating facilities:* wide range of homemade snacks, lunches and dinners, available to members, guests and visitors. *Visitors:* welcome with current Handicap Certificate Sunday to Friday. *Society Meetings:* on application, please contact General Office. Professional: Philip Davis. Club Manager: Stephanie Standen.
e-mail: office@swgc.com
website: www.swgc.com

162 Essex / EAST REGION — THE GOLF GUIDE 2011

STAPLEFORD ABBOTTS GOLF CLUB

Stapleford Abbotts Golf Club is the perfect venue for a golfing day out. With two championship 18-hole courses to choose from, a pleasant Clubhouse and a qualified events team - our society groups return year on year. The ideal location for a relaxing game of golf in tranquil surroundings.

**Stapleford Abbotts Golf Club
Horsemanside, Tysea Hill,
Stapleford Abbotts, Essex RM4 1JU
Tel: 01708 381108
staplefordabbotts@crown-golf.co.uk
www.staplefordabbottsgolf.co.uk**

Estuary views, sand based, year round play. 18 holes, 6474 yards. S.S.S. 71. 19 bay floodlit driving range, chipping and putting greens. 9 hole Par 3 course. *Green Fees:* information not provided. *Eating facilities:* bar; restaurant. *Visitors:* welcome, enquire about tee closures. *Society Meetings:* welcome anytime weekdays; weekends afternoons only. Please phone for details. Professional/Secretary: David Wood.

STAPLEFORD ABBOTTS. **Stapleford Abbotts Golf Club,** Horseman's Side, Tysea Hill, Stapleford Abbotts, Romford RM4 1JU (01708 381108; Fax: 01708 386345). *Location:* three miles from Junctions 28 and 29 of the M25, off main Ongar Road B175 at Stapleford Abbotts. Parkland course with many mature trees, large bunkers and water hazards. 18 holes, 6501 yards, S.S.S. 72. Par 3 9-hole course. Two practice grounds and practice nets. Also The Priors 18 hole pay-and-play course, 5878 yards, S.S.S 70. *Green Fees:* Abbots: £32.00 Monday to Thursday, £36.00 Friday, £40.00 weekends and Bank Holidays; Priors: £17.00 Monday to Friday, £23.00 weekends. *Eating facilities:* fully licensed bar, extensive menu. *Visitors:* welcome weekdays, weekends after 12 noon; welcome all week on 9-hole course. Correct golfing attire must be worn. *Society Meetings:* welcome, call 01708 381108 for more information. Pro Shop: 01708 381278 .
e-mail: staplefordabbotts@crown-golf.co.uk
website: www.staplefordabbottsgolf.co.uk

STAPLEFORD TAWNEY. **Abridge Golf and Country Club,** Epping Lane, Stapleford Tawney RM4 1ST (01708 688396). *Location:* A113 from London through Chigwell to Abridge, left at The Rodings, right after 300 yards. Two miles on. Parkland. 18 holes, 6704 yards. S.S.S. 72. *Green Fees:* information not available. *Eating facilities:* bar lunches, drinks, snacks available all week. *Visitors:* welcome but must be a member of a recognised golf club and produce evidence of current Handicap, weekdays and weekend afternoons. *Society Meetings:* catered for on Mondays, Wednesdays and Fridays only by arrangement. Professional: Stuart Layton (01708 688333). Secretary: M Gottlieb (Fax: 01708 688550)*.
e-mail:info@abridgegolf.com
website: www.abridgegolf.com

STOCK. **Crondon Park Golf Club,** Stock Road, Stock CM4 9DP (01277 841115; Fax: 01277 841356). *Location:* off the A12, on to B1007 towards Billericay. Set in parkland valley with trees, lakes and magnificent greens, longest hole in the country (18th 655yds). 18 holes, 6250 yards (Club). S.S.S. 70. 9-hole Par 3 course. Driving range and putting green. Academy Lessons. *Green Fees:* information not available. *Eating facilities:* bar, restaurant. *Visitors:* welcome weekdays; weekends afternoons only. Modern changing rooms, showers, etc. *Society Meetings:* welcome weekdays, Saturday and Sunday (pm) . Professional: Fred Sunderland (Head Pro), Chris Woods (01277 841887). Secretary: Paul Cranwell (01277 841115).*

SOUTHEND-ON-SEA. **Southend-on-Sea Golf Club,** Belfairs Lodge, Belfairs Park, Leigh-on-Sea SS9 4LR (01702 524836). *Location*: A127 London to Southend Road. Parkland/wooded course (Belfairs Municipal course). 18 holes, 5877 yards. S.S.S. 68. *Green Fees:* information not available. *Eating facilities:* restaurant in the park near Starter's Hut. *Visitors:* welcome, unrestricted, but bookings required by phone to Starter's Hut (01702 525345). Professional: Martin Foreman (01702 520202). Secretary: Alan Wood (01702 474737).*

SOUTHEND-ON-SEA. **Thorpe Hall Golf Club,** Thorpe Hall Avenue, Thorpe Bay, Southend-on-Sea SS1 3AT (Tel & Fax: 01702 582205). *Location:* one mile east of Southend-on-Sea. Parkland. 18 holes, 6290 yards. S.S.S. 70. *Green Fees:* information not provided. *Eating facilities:* Two restaurants and bars. *Visitors:* welcome weekdays with Handicap Certificate, weekends with members only. Squash, snooker and sauna available. *Society Meetings:* welcome. Professional: J. Fryatt (01702 588195). Secretary: Ms F. Gale (01702 582205; Fax: 01702 584498).
e-mail: sec@thorpehallgc.co.uk
website: www.thorpehallgc.co.uk

STANFORD LE HOPE. **St. Cleres Hall Golf Club,** St. Cleres Hall, London Road, Stanford le Hope SS17 0LX (Tel & Fax: 01375 361565). *Location*: from M25, A13 Stanford turnoff, Linford exit on roundabout, course half mile on left. Parkland course with Thames

STOKE BY NAYLAND. Stoke by Nayland Golf & Spa, Keepers Lane, Leavenheath, Colchester CO6 4PZ (01206 262836; Fax: 01206 265840). *Location:* just off A134 Colchester to Sudbury on B1068 towards Stoke by Nayland. Host venue to PGA Seniors' Championship. Undulating parkland with water hazards. Two courses (1) Gainsborough - 18 holes, 6561 yards. S.S.S. 72. (2) Constable - 18 holes, 6544 yards. S.S.S. 72. 20 bay covered range, practice area. *Green Fees:* information not provided. *Eating facilities:* full catering and bars. *Visitors:* welcome, please ring for availability and tee bookings. *Society Meetings:* welcome weekdays, book well in advance. Seasonal packages offered. Excellent golf and spa breaks. Extensive Health and Leisure Facility including gymnasium, pool, sauna, jacuzzi and spa; modern, spacious, en suite hotel rooms overlooking lake and fairways. Professional: Roly Hitchcock (01206 265812). Golf Secretary: Mike Verhelst (01206 265815).
e-mail: golfsecretary@stokebynayland.com
website: www.stokebynaylandclub.co.uk

UPMINSTER. Top Meadow Golf Club and Hotel, Fen Lane, North Ockendon, Upminster RM14 3PR (01708 852239; Fax: 01708 852598) *Location*: M25, A127, B186 towards North Ockendon - Fen Lane. Parkland course with panoramic views of Essex countryside. 18 holes, 6227 yards. S.S.S. 72. Practice range. On site hotel. *Green Fees*: information not available. *Eating facilities*: fully licensed bar and à la carte restaurant. *Visitors*: Visitors and Societies welcome Monday to Friday. Golfing holidays available midweek and weekends. Professional: Roy Porter (01708 859545). Secretary: Daniel Stock (01708 852239).*

UPMINSTER. Upminster Golf Club, 114 Hall Lane, Upminster RM14 1AU (01708 222788). *Location:* one mile (north) Upminster Station, one and a half miles west M25/A127 junction. Parkland/wooded – River Ingrebourne runs through the course. Beautiful Grade II Listed Clubhouse, rebuilt in 1654, with an official ghost – listed in the British Book of Ghosts. 18 holes, 6021 yards. S.S.S. 69. *Green Fees:* information not available. *Eating facilities:* full catering service every day. *Visitors:* welcome weekdays by arrangement except Tuesday mornings. *Society Meetings:* catered for Wednesdays, Thursdays and Fridays (max 60).

Professional: Jodie Dartford (01708 220000). Secretary: Russell Winmill (01708 222788; Fax: 01708 222484).
e-mail: secretary@upminstergolfclub.co.uk
website: www.upminstergolfclub.co.uk

WITHAM. Benton Hall Golf Club, Wickham Hill, Witham CM8 3LH (01376 502454 Fax: 01376 521050). *Location:* one mile from A12 between Chelmsford and Colchester. Wooded course with natural lakes. 18 holes 6495 yards. S.S.S. 72. 9 hole executive par three course. *Green Fees:* information not available. *Eating facilities:* Blackwater Suite function room, Waterside Bar and Restaurant. *Visitors:* welcome, not before 12 noon at weekends. *Society Meetings:* welcome. Director of Golf: Colin Fairweather. General Manager: James Gathercole.*

WITHAM. Braxted Park Golf Club, Braxted Park, Witham CM8 3EN (01376 572372; Fax: 01376 572372). *Location:* A12 south of Witham; from Chelmsford take Rivenhall turn-off, if travelling from Colchester take Silver End turn-off. Established 54 years, set in 18th century parkland. 9 holes, 5880 yards. Par 35, S.S.S. 34. Practice ground. *Green Fees:* information not available. *Eating facilities:* clubhouse (licensed), snacks. *Visitors:* welcome. Corporate entertainment available, activity days, wedding receptions. *Society Meetings:* welcome.*

WOODFORD GREEN. Woodford Golf Club, 2 Sunset Avenue, Woodford Green IG8 0ST (020 8504 3330). *Location*: near The Harvester (formerly The Castle), High Road, Woodford Green. Forest land. 9 holes, 5878 yards. S.S.S. 69. *Green Fees:* weekdays £18.00 per 18 holes, £12.00 per 9 holes; weekends £20.00 per 18 holes, £14.00 per 9 holes. 2010 rates (subject to review). *Eating facilities:* food available Tuesday to Saturday lunchtimes. Bar. *Visitors:* no green fees Tuesday mornings; tee times available on Saturdays by arrangement. Red (scarlet) clothing must be worn - trousers or top. *Society Meetings:* welcome. Professional: Adam Baker (020 8504 4254). Secretary: Peter Willett (020 8504 3330; Fax: 020 8559 0504).
e-mail: office@woodfordgolf.co.uk
professional@woodfordgolf.co.uk
website: www.woodfordgolf.co.uk

Woodford Golf Club
your friendly local golf club

Come and play our long-established (1890) course set in Epping Forest. Visitors are most welcome. Being 9 holes, it is well suited to those who have time restrictions (although you can play the full 18).
No handicap certificate required. We also offer a mix of membership schemes. Contact the secretary on 020-8504-3330 or the professional on 020-8504-4254, or visit our website **www.woodfordgolf.co.uk**

Hertfordshire

BARKWAY. **Barkway Park Golf Club,** Nuthampstead Road, Barkway SG8 8EN (01763 849070). *Location:* A10 north from M25 for 15 miles, B1368 to Barkway 8 miles. Inland links. 18 holes, 6997 yards. S.S.S. 74. Practice areas. *Green Fees:* information not available. *Eating facilities:* bar, restaurant. *Visitors:* welcome at all times. *Society Meetings:* always welcome. Professional: Jamie Bates. Secretary: Val Sadler. *

BARNET. **Arkley Golf Club,** Rowley Green Road, Barnet EN5 3HL (Fax: 020 8440 5214). *Location*: follow A411 from A1 Stirling Corner towards Barnet, left into Rowley Lane. Wooded parkland. 9 holes, 18 tees, 6046 yards. S.S.S. 69. Practice ground. *Green Fees:* weekdays £25.00 per round, £32.00 per day; weekends with a member only £20.00. *Eating facilities:* available. *Visitors:* welcome weekdays, please phone Professional. *Society Meetings:* catered for Wednesdays, Thursdays and Fridays; special rates available. Professional: Andrew Hurley (020 8440 8473). Secretary: A.N. Welsh (020 8449 0394).
website: www.arkleygolfclub.co.uk

BARNET. **Hadley Wood Golf Club,** Beech Hill, Near Barnet EN4 0JJ (020 8449 4328). *Location:* off the exit from M25 at Junction 24 on to A111 Cockfosters. Down hill, third turning on the right. Very attractive undulating parkland with lakes. Regional Open qualifying venue 2000 - 2005. 18 holes, 6514 yards. S.S.S. 71. Practice range open to members and green fees only. Chipping and putting areas. *Green Fees:* information not available. *Eating facilities:* available weekdays. *Visitors:* welcome weekdays, (not Tuesday a.m.), with club Handicap Certificate or letter of introduction. *Society Meetings:* corporate and society days catered for weekdays except Tuesday mornings and Wednesdays. Professional: Peter Jones (020 8449 3285). General Manager: Bill Beckett (020 8449 4328; Fax: 020 8364 8633).*
e-mail: gm@hadleywoodgc.com
website: www.hadleywoodgc.com

BERKHAMSTED. **Ashridge Golf Club,** Little Gaddesden, Berkhamsted HP4 1LY (01442 842244). *Location:* on B4506, five miles north west of Berkhamsted. Parkland. 18 holes, 6625 yards. Par 72. Practice area, putting green. *Green Fees:* information not available. *Eating facilities:* dining room and spike bar, two lounges. *Visitors:* welcome with reservation weekdays only. *Society Meetings:* catered for. Professional: Peter Cherry (01442 842307). Secretary: Martin S. Silver (01442 842244; Fax: 01442 843770).*
e-mail: info@ashridgegolfclub.ltd.uk
website: www.ashridgegolfclub.ltd.uk

BERKHAMSTED. **Berkhamsted Golf Club,** The Common, Berkhamsted HP4 2QB (01442 865832; Fax: 01442 863730). *Location*: A41 to Berkhamsted, up past the castle to the common. Heathland, wooded, grass bunkers. 18 holes, 6605 yards. S.S.S. 72. Two practice grounds. *Green Fees:* on application. *Eating facilities:* bar and restaurant. *Visitors:* welcome, best to phone first. Handicap Certificate required. *Society Meetings:* catered for Mondays, Wednesdays and Fridays. Professional: John Clarke (01442 865851). General Manager: Barry Hill (01442 865832)
e-mail: barryh@berkhamstedgc.co.uk
website: www.berkhamstedgolfclub.co.uk

BISHOP'S STORTFORD. Bishop's Stortford Golf Club, Dunmow Road, Bishop's Stortford CM23 5HP (01279 654715). Location: M11 Junction 8, follow signs for Bishop's Stortford, entrance quarter of a mile on left. Undulating parkland, fairly flat: well-established course and a true test of golf. 18 holes, 6404 yards. S.S.S. 71. Green Fees: weekdays £40.00 per round, £50.00 per day, weekends as guest of member. Eating facilities: restaurant and bar service. Visitors: welcome weekdays; weekends with member only. Valid Handicap Certificate required. Society Meetings: catered for weekdays except Tuesdays (minimum 12). Special rates available. Professional: Simon Sheppard (01279 651324). Secretary: Judy Barker (01279 654715; Fax: 01279 655215).
e-mail: office@bsgc.co.uk
website: www.bsgc.co.uk

BISHOP'S STORTFORD. **Great Hadham Golf and Country Club,** Great Hadham Road, Much Hadham, Near Bishop's Stortford SG10 6JE (01279 843558; Fax: 01279 842122). *Location:* two miles west of Bishop's Stortford on the B1004, four miles west of Junction 8 M11 motorway. Rolling meadowland course. 18 holes, 6854 yards. S.S.S. 73. Three Par 3 practice holes, practice bunker, 18 bay driving range. *Green Fees:* information not available. *Eating facilities:* well stocked bar, comfortable lounge and dining room/spike bar. *Visitors:* welcome weekdays (Ladies' Day Wednesday mornings), weekends after 12 noon. Health Club with fitness centre facilities. *Society Meetings:* welcome weekdays. See website. Professional: Kevin Lunt. Secretary: Ian Bailey.*
website: www.ghgcc.co.uk

EAST REGION / Hertfordshire

BROXBOURNE. The Hertfordshire Golf & Country Club, Broxbournebury Mansion EN10 7PY (01992 466666; Fax: 01992 470326). *Location:* 10 minutes north on A10 from Junction 25 of M25 take Broxbourne exit, third left Bell Lane, over A10 right hand side. 18 hole "Nicklaus" design set around a Grade II Listed clubhouse, full USGA Specifications - irrigated and drained. 18 holes, 6388 yards. S.S.S. 70. 30 bay floodlit driving range. *Green Fees:* information not available. *Eating facilities:* Spike Bar, Cocktail Bar. Health club, golf academy, indoor and outdoor tennis courts, indoor swimming pool. *Visitors:* welcome weekdays, weekends restricted. *Society Meetings:* welcome. Head Professional: James Jones. Pro Shop: (01992 441268). General Manager: Neil Dainton*

BUNTINGFORD. East Herts Golf Club Ltd, Hamels Park, Buntingford SG9 9NA (01920 821978). *Location:* one mile north of Puckeridge on A10. 18 holes, 6451 yards. S.S.S. 71. *Green Fees:* £36.00. *Eating facilities:* separate restaurant. *Visitors:* welcome, with members only at weekends. *Society Meetings:* catered for weekdays. Professional: D. Field (01920 821978). Secretary: Ms Alex McDonald (01920 821978; Fax: 01920 823700).
e-mail: secretary@eastherstgolfclub.co.uk
website: www.eastherstgolfclub.co.uk

BUSHEY. Bushey Golf and Country Club, High Street, Bushey WD23 1TT (020 8950 2215). *Location:* Junction 5 of M1 onto A41, south to second roundabout, turn right to Bushey Heath; take A411 towards Watford, entrance down hill on left. 9 holes. Par 70. 18 tee boxes. Driving range. *Green Fees:* Telephone to book. Twilight after 3pm weekdays unlimited golf £10.00 green fee. *Eating facilities:* bar and dining facilities open from 8am to 11pm. *Visitors:* welcome. *Society Meetings:* welcome. Professional: Martin Siggins.

BUSHEY. Bushey Hall Golf Club, Bushey Hall Drive, Bushey WD23 2EP (01923 222253; Fax: 01923 229759). *Location:* one mile from M1 Junction 5, off Aldenham Road roundabout. Undulating parkland. 18 holes, 6099 yards, 6670 metres. S.S.S. 69. Practice nets, putting green. *Green Fees:* midweek £25.00, weekend £35.00, twilight £15.00. *Eating facilities:* full catering available, two bars. *Visitors:* welcome, no restrictions. *Society Meetings:* catered for weekdays. Secretary/ Manager: Glen Halsey (01923 222253).
e-mail: info@golfclubuk.co.uk
website: www.busheyhallgolfclub.co.uk

BUSHEY HEATH. Hartsbourne Golf and Country Club, Hartsbourne Avenue, Bushey Heath WD2 1JW (020 8421 7272; Fax: 020 8950 5357). *Location:* five miles south east of Watford. Parkland. 18 holes, 6385 yards. S.S.S. 70. 9 holes, 5773 yards. S.S.S. 68. *Green Fees:* information not available. *Eating facilities:* restaurant and snack bar available. *Visitors:* guests of members only. *Society Meetings:* catered for Mondays and Fridays. Professional: Reeves Weedon (020 8421 7266). General Manager: Ian Thomas (020 8421 7272; Fax: 020 8950 5357).*

CHORLEYWOOD. Chorleywood Golf Club Ltd, Common Road, Chorleywood WD3 5LN (01923 282009; Fax: 01923 286739). *Location:* half a mile from Junction 18 of M25 via A404, three miles from Rickmansworth. A challenging mix of heath and woodland with natural hazards. 9 holes, 5686 yards. S.S.S. 67. *Green Fees:* £20.00 weekdays, £25.00 weekends. *Eating facilities:* meals available at most times. *Visitors:* welcome weekdays except Tuesday mornings, restricted at weekends. *Society Meetings:* contact Secretary for details. Secretary: Rod Botham (01923 282009; Fax: 01923 286739).
e-mail: secretary@chorleywoodgolfclub.co.uk

ELSTREE. Elstree Golf and Country Club, Watling Street, Elstree WD6 3AA (020 8953 6115; Fax: 020 8207 6390). *Location:* between Radlett and Elstree. Watling Street is also known as A5 (A5183) road. Close to M1, M25, A41, A1 (map available on request). Parkland course - undulating with ponds and ditches. 18 holes, 6556 yards. S.S.S. 72. 60 bay driving range. *Green Fees:* from £15.00. Please check for special offers. *Eating facilities:* bar, restaurant, conservatory available all day. *Visitors:* welcome weekdays anytime, weekends after 11.00am. Buggy and trolley hire, lockers/ showers; large car park. Function facilities. *Society Meetings:* welcome, information pack sent on request. Professional/General Manager: Marc Warwick (020 8238 6941). Club Secretary: Kathy Roberts (020 8238 6942).
e-mail: admin@elstree-golf.co.uk
website: www.elstree-golfclub.co.uk

HARPENDEN. Aldwickbury Park Golf Club, Piggottshill Lane, Harpenden AL5 1AB (01582 760112; Fax: 01582 760113). *Location:* east of Harpenden on the Wheathampstead Road, Luton and St. Albans 10 minutes' drive. Rolling parkland with mature woodland. Two courses. Park Course – 18 holes, 6350 yards. S.S.S. 70. Manor Course – 9 holes, 1000 yards. Par 3. Practice area. *Green Fees:* information not available. *Eating facilities:* licensed bar/restaurant and all day snack menu available. *Visitors:* welcome, call first; no weekend mornings play. PGA tuition, buggies and trolleys for hire. *Society Meetings:* welcome weekdays, please call for further details/prices. Professional: Robin Turley (01582 760112; Fax: 01582 760113). General Manager: Tristan Hall (01582 765112; Fax: 01582 760113).*
e-mail: info@aldwickburyparkgc.co.uk
website: www.aldwickburyparkgolfclub.com

HARPENDEN. Harpenden Golf Club, Hammonds End, Redbourn Lane, Harpenden AL5 2AX (01582 712580; Fax: 01582 712725). *Location:* turn off A1081, four miles after St. Albans on B487. Parkland course. 18 holes, 6377 yards. S.S.S. 70. *Green Fees:* weekdays £40.00 per round, £50.00 per day; weekends £45.00 per round. *Eating facilities:* snacks and lunches, order in advance. *Visitors:* welcome weekdays and weekends strictly by arrangement. *Society Meetings:* by arrangement only. Professional: Peter Lane (01582 767124; Fax: 01582 712725). General Manager: Frank Clapp.

Redcoats is a country house hotel, between Hitchin and Stevenage, with accommodation shared between the main house, the Stable courtyard and Milk Parlour. All rooms provide the same high standard of service, with direct dial telephone and wi-fi internet access. The restaurant offers the best in traditional fare, with an excellent selection of wines.

Redcoats Green, Near Hitchin,
Hertfordshire SG4 7JR
Tel : 01438 729 500
E-mail: info@redcoats.co.uk
www.redcoats.co.uk

AA ★★★ Small Hotel

HARPENDEN. **Harpenden Common Golf Club,** Cravells Road, East Common, Harpenden AL5 1BL (01582 711322; Fax: 01582 711321). *Location:* Harpenden half mile, St Albans 3 miles, Luton 6 miles. Wooded parkland course. 18 holes, 6214 yards. S.S.S. 70. Nets, putting green, chipping green. *Green Fees:* information not available. *Eating facilities:* restaurant and bar. *Visitors:* Monday-Tuesday after 1.30pm, Wednesday-Saturday after 3pm in Summer. Tuition available. *Society Meetings:* Thursdays and Fridays (Mondays by request). Professional/ Secretary: Daniel Fitzsimmons (01582 460655/711325; Fax: 01582 711321).
e-mail: manager@hcgc.co.uk
website: www.hcgc.co.uk

HATFIELD. **Brookmans Park Golf Club,** Golf Club Road, Brookmans Park, Hatfield AL9 7AT (01707 652487; Fax: 01707 661851). *Location:* A1000, just north of Potters Bar; M25 Junction 24. Parkland, two lakes. 18 holes, 6249 yards. S.S.S. 71. Practice ground and putting green. *Green Fees:* information not available. *Eating facilities:* bar snacks and lunches weekdays. *Visitors:* welcome weekdays; weekends with member only. *Society Meetings:* catered for Mondays, Wednesdays, Thursdays and Friday mornings. Professional: Ian Jelley (01707 652468). General Manager: Una Handley (01707 652487; Fax: 01707 661851).
e-mail: info@bpgc.co.uk
website: www.bpgc.co.uk

HATFIELD. **Hatfield London Country Club,** Bedwell Park, Essendon, Hatfield AL9 6HN (01707 260360; Fax: 01707 278475). *Location:* four miles south of Junction 4 A1(M), five miles north east of Junction 24 M25 Potters Bar. 9 holes Pitch and Putt. 36 holes (Old Course, 18 holes, 6808 yards, Par 72; New Course, 18 holes, 6938 yards, Par 72). Practice ground. *Green Fees:* information not available. *Eating facilities:* bar and restaurant with full catering available. *Visitors:* welcome, advance bookings only. *Society Meetings:* always welcome.*

HEMEL HEMPSTEAD. **Boxmoor Golf Club,** 18 Box Lane, Boxmoor, Hemel Hempstead HP3 0DJ (01442 242434). *Location*: two miles from Hemel Hempstead, three-quarters of a mile from Hemel Hempstead Station on A41. Hilly/moorland course, 9 holes, 4112 yards. S.S.S. 62. *Green Fees:* information not available. *Eating facilities:* ring Steward. *Visitors:* welcome without reservation, except on Sundays. *Society Meetings:* catered for on application. Secretary: Brian Swann.*

HEMEL HEMPSTEAD. **Little Hay Golf Complex,** Box Lane, Bovingdon, Hemel Hempstead HP3 0DQ (01442 833798). *Location*: just off A41, along Chesham Road from Hemel Hempstead. Parkland. 18 holes, 6678 yards. S.S.S. 72. 6 hole pitch and putt course, short game practice area, floodlit driving range. *Green Fees:* information not available. *Eating facilities:* available, open all day. *Visitors:* welcome. *Society Meetings:* welcome by arrangement. Professionals: Nick Allen and Michael Perry (01442 833798). Complex Manager: Chris Gordon (01442 833798).*

HEMEL HEMPSTEAD. **Shendish Manor Hotel & Golf Course,** London Road, Apsley, Hemel Hempstead HP3 0AA (01442 251806; Fax: 01442 230683). *Location:* two miles from J20 M25 on the west side of A4251 London Road (ex A41) between Kings Langley and Hemel Hempstead. Mature parkland course. 18 holes, 5660 yards. S.S.S. 67 (Par 70). *Green Fees:* information not available. *Eating facilities:* Coachhouse Bar and Restaurant. *Visitors:* no restrictions, please telephone to ensure tee time. Hotel, conference and full banqueting facilities. *Society Meetings:* welcome seven days a week. Secretary: Seema Patel.*

HERTFORD. **Brickendon Grange Golf Club,** Brickendon, Near Hertford SG13 8PD (01992 511258; Fax: 01992 511411). *Location:* three miles south of Hertford, one mile from Bayford Railway Station. Undulating parkland with specimen trees. 18 holes, 6458 yards. S.S.S. 71. Excellent practice area. *Green Fees:* information not available. *Eating facilities:* bar and restaurant, snack meals available lunchtimes. *Visitors:* welcome weekdays only, Handicap Certificate required. *Society Meetings:* catered for by arrangement. Professional: A. Clapp (01992 511218). General Manager: Jane Coulcher (01992 511258; Fax: 01992 511411).
e-mail: play@bggc.org.uk
website: www.bggc.org.uk

EAST REGION / Hertfordshire

HITCHIN. Chesfield Downs Golf Club, Jack's Hill, Graveley, Near Hitchin SG4 7EQ (01462 482929). *Location*: just off Junction 8 of the A1(M), approximately two miles along the B197. Parkland. Two Courses: Chesfield Downs–18 holes, 6646 yards. S.S.S. 72. Par 71. Lannock Links–Par 3. 9 holes, 975 yards. S.S.S. 27. 27 bay floodlit driving range/practice bunker, putting green. *Green Fees*: information not available. *Eating facilities*: "Chesfields Restaurant and Bar". *Visitors*: welcome, advance booking system available to reserve tee-off times. Geoff Budds Golf Emporium, Learn Golf Academy, changing facilities. Part of the Leisure Links International Group. *Society Meetings*: catered for by arrangement. Head Professional: Keith Bond. General Manager: Paul Barnfather.*

KNEBWORTH. Knebworth Golf Club, Deards End Lane, Knebworth SG3 6NL (01438 812752). *Location*: one mile south of Stevenage, off B197 (A1(M)) turnoff no. 7. Undulating parkland. 18 holes, 6518 yards. S.S.S. 71. *Green Fees*: weekdays £42.00. *Eating facilities*: full facilities available. *Visitors*: welcome weekdays, with members only at weekends. *Society Meetings*: welcome Mondays, Tuesdays, Thursdays and Fridays (£5.00 pp supplement). Professional: G. Parker (01438 812757). General Manager: S. Barrett (01438 812752).
e-mail: admin@knebworthgolfclub.com
website: www.knebworthgolfclub.com

LETCHWORTH. Letchworth Golf Club, Letchworth Lane, Letchworth SG6 3NQ. *Location:* **two miles from A1 (M) near village of Willian, adjacent to Letchworth Hall Hotel. Parkland course. 18 holes, recently extended to 6420 yards. S.S.S. 71. Large practice ground with 9 hole pitch and putt course.** *Green Fees:* **weekdays (except Mondays) £42.00 per round, £70.00 per day; Mondays £22.00 per round, £40.00 per day; weekends accompanied only.** *Eating facilities:* **bars and restaurant (limited menu Monday lunchtime only).** *Visitors:* **Handicap Certificate required.** *Society Meetings:* **catered for Wednesdays, Thursdays and Fridays. Professional: Karl Teschner (01462 682713). Secretary: Niki Hunter (01462 683203; Fax: 01462 484567).**

POTTERS BAR. **Potters Bar Golf Club,** Darkes Lane, Potters Bar EN6 1DE (01707 652020; Fax: 01707 655051). *Location*: one mile north of M25 exit 24 signposted Potters Bar, turn right at third traffic lights, club on left at end of shopping centre. Parkland course, well wooded, undulating, with streams. 18 holes, 6279 yards. S.S.S. 70. Small practice ground. *Green Fees:*Information not available. *Eating facilities:* luncheons and bar available from 11.30am. *Visitors:* weekdays only. *Society Meetings:* welcome weekdays, Wednesday afternoons only. Professional: Gary A'ris (01707 652987; Fax: 01707 655051). Secretary: J.D. Bowen (01707 652020; Fax: 01707 655051).*
e-mail: johnb@pottersbargolfclub.com

RADLETT. **Porters Park Golf Club,** Shenley Hill, Radlett WD7 7AZ (01923 854127; Fax: 01923 855475). *Location*: approximately 3 miles south west of Junction 22 (M25), three miles north-east Junction 5 (M1), half a mile north of Radlett Station on Shenley Hill. Undulating parkland with fine trees and a brook. 18 holes, 6362 yards. S.S.S. 71, Par 70. Open and Regional qualifying course. Three practice areas, putting. *Green Fees:* information not available. *Visitors:* welcome Monday to Friday. Handicap Certificate required. *Society Meetings:* catered for Wednesday and Thursday and Friday. Professional: David Gleeson (01923 854366). Managing Secretary: P.A. Marshall (01923 854127; Fax: 01923 855475).
e-mail: enquiries@porterspark.com

REDBOURN. **Redbourn Golf Club,** Kinsbourne, Green Lane, Redbourn AL3 7QA (01582 793493; Fax: 01582 794362). *Location:* one mile east of M1 Junction 9, four miles north of St. Albans, four miles south of Luton. Parkland course on which water comes into play on several holes. Two courses - Ver 18 holes. 6506 yards. S.S.S. 71. Kinsbourne Course - challenging Par 3, 9 holes, 1361 yards. S.S.S. 27. Driving range. *Green Fees:* information not available. *Eating facilities:* licensed bar, restaurant, snacks and hot meals readily available. *Visitors:* welcome weekdays, weekends and Bank Holidays after 12 noon. *Society Meetings:* welcome weekdays, and weekends after 12 noon. Professional: Stephen Hunter. Golf Secretary: Stuart Hatch (01582 794888).*
email: info@redbourngc.co.uk
website: www.redbourngolfclub.com

RICKMANSWORTH. **Batchworth Park Golf Club,** London Road, Rickmansworth WD3 1JS (01923 711400; Fax: 01923 710200). *Location:* situated five miles from Junction 17 M25 on the A404. Undulating parkland course. 18 holes, 6723 yards. S.S.S. 72. Practice range, putting green and chipping area. *Green Fees:* information not available. *Eating facilities:* bar, dining room - food served all day. *Visitors:* guests of members only. Professional: Stephen Proudfoot (01923 714922).*

RICKMANSWORTH. **Moor Park Golf Club,** Moor Park, Rickmansworth WD3 1QN (01923 773146; Fax: 01923 777109). *Location*: Junction 18 of M25 and follow A404, signs to Moor Park Golf Club. Parkland course with rolling fairways. High Course: 18 holes, 6717 yards (white), 6424 yards (yellow). S.S.S. 73 (white), 72 (yellow). West Course: 18 holes, 5833 yards (white), 5547 yards (yellow). S.S.S. 68 (white), 67 (yellow). Practice ground. *Green Fees:* weekdays High Course £85.00, West Course £55.00. *Eating facilities:* full catering available. *Visitors:* welcome by prior arrangement. *Society Meetings:* welcome weekdays only. Secretary: J. Moore.
e-mail: enquiries@moorparkgc.co.uk
website: www.moorparkgc.co.uk

RICKMANSWORTH. **Rickmansworth Public Golf Course,** Moor Lane, Rickmansworth WD3 1QL (01923 775278). *Location*: from town centre along A404 to Waterworks, left along B4504, then first right. Testing, undulating parkland course. 18 holes, 4656 yards, Par 65. *Green Fees:* information not available. *Eating facilities:* bars, restaurant. *Visitors:* welcome. *Society Meetings:* catered for, contact Professional. Professional: Dan Peck (01923 775278). Secretary: Tom Moore (01923 720008).*

ROYSTON. **Heydon Grange Golf and Country Club,** Heydon, Royston SG8 7NS (01763 208988; Fax: 01763 208926). *Location*: A505 10 minutes drive east of Royston and minutes from M11 Duxford. Parkland course, gently rolling countryside. 27 holes, 6512 yards. S.S.S. 71. Covered range. *Green Fees:* weekdays £20.00, weekends £25.00. *Eating facilities:* bar menu, bar, patio. *Visitors:* welcome all times. Buggies available. *Society Meetings:* welcome. Professional: Stuart Smith.
e-mail: enquiries@heydongrange.co.uk
website: www.heydongrange.co.uk

ROYSTON. **New Malton Golf,** Malton Lane, Meldreth, Royston SG8 6PE (01763 262200). *Location*: Junction 12 of M11, A603 West to Orwell, through village, right to Malton. 230 acres of beautiful, peaceful landscaped countryside, lightly wooded, with River Cam running through the course. Teeming with wildlife and flora. 18 holes, 6635 yards, S.S.S. 71. Buggies available for hire. Driving range, short game area. Coaching for golfers of all ages and abilities encouraged. Tee booking and enquiries (01763 262200). *Green Fees:* weekdays £15.00 (cheaper at certain times), weekends £20.00. Special rates for members. *Eating facilities:* clubhouse provides freshly prepared food and caters for up to 80 people; more in bbq style. *Visitors:* all welcome. *Society Meetings*: all welcome. Special package prices available on request. Professional: Brian Mudge.
e-mail: info@newmaltongolf.co.uk
website: www.newmaltongolf.co.uk

ROYSTON. **Royston Golf Club (Founded 1892),** Baldock Road, Royston SG8 5BG (01763 242696). *Location*: alongside the A505 on right hand side when approaching from Baldock, clubhouse at top of hill before entering town. Links - undulating heathland. 18 holes, 6086 yards. S.S.S. 69 yellow, 70 white. Practice fairway. *Green Fees:* from £15.00. *Eating facilities:* lounge bar – 19th hole bar, diningroom and bar meals. *Visitors:* welcome weekdays; weekends pm. *Society Meetings:* weekdays and weekends pm, book through Manager. Professional: S. Clark (01763 243476). Golf Club Manager: S. Clark (01763 242696).
e-mail: roystongolf@btconnect.com
website: www.roystongolfclub.co.uk

ST ALBANS. **Batchwood Golf and Tennis Centre,** Batchwood Drive, St Albans AL3 5XA (01727 844250; Fax: 01727 858506). *Location:* near City Hospital, close to St Albans town centre. Flat, parkland, wooded course. 18 holes, 6463 yards. S.S.S. 71. *Green Fees:* information not available. *Eating facilities:* bar and restaurant. *Visitors:* welcome. Society Meetings: welcome with reservation. Bookings: (01727 844250) PGA Professional: Mark Flitton (07797 386003). General Manager: Andy Smithard (017277 8444250).*

ST ALBANS. **Mid-Herts Golf Club,** Gustard Wood, Lamer Lane, Wheathampstead, Near St Albans AL4 8RS (01582 832242). *Location:* B651, six miles north of St Albans. Flat heathland, short and tight course. 18 holes, 6060 yards. S.S.S. 69. Course record 63. *Green Fees:* £35.00. *Eating facilities:* by arrangement. *Visitors:* welcome weekdays. *Society Meetings:* catered for by arrangement. Professional: Barney Puttick (01582 832788). Secretary: (01582 832242; Fax: 01582 834834).
e-mail: secretary@mid-hertsgolfclub.co.uk
website: www.mid-hertsgolfclub.co.uk

ST ALBANS. **Verulam Golf Club,** 226 London Road, St Albans AL1 1JG (01727 839016). *Location*: M25 Junction 22a or 22 to A1081 to St. Albans, course is off London Road (A1081) near railway bridge. Easy walking parkland course designed by James Braid. 18 holes, 6429 yards. S.S.S. 72. Practice ground, nets, putting and chipping green, bunker and driving tee. *Green Fees:* Monday £25.00, Tuesday-Friday £35.00, weekends O/A. *Eating facilities:* bar snacks from 11am to 4.30pm, other dining by prior arrangement. *Visitors:* welcome weekdays except Wednesday mornings. *Society Meetings:* welcome by prior arrangement with Manager – deposit required. Professional: Nick Burch (01727 861401). Manager: Robin Farrer (01727 853327; Fax: 01727 812201).
e-mail: gm@verulamgolf.co.uk
website: www.verulamgolf.co.uk

SAWBRIDGEWORTH. **Manor of Groves,** High Wych, Sawbridgeworth CM21 0JU (0870 4108833; Fax: 0870 4178833). *Location:* Junction 7 off M11 follow A414 to High Wych. Parkland/woodland course with water features. 18 holes, 6237 yards. S.S.S. 71. Practice ground. Soft spikes only. *Green Fees:* information not available. *Eating facilities:* hotel and golf club facilities, bar. *Visitors:* welcome anytime weekdays, advise phoning; weekends after 11am only. Accommodation available in our 80 bedroomed Hotel. Leisure facilities including pool, gym, aerobics studio, Thalgo beauty salon. *Society Meetings:* most welcome, special packages available. Golf Club Manager: Sarah Ward.

STEVENAGE. **Stevenage Golf Centre,** Aston Lane, Stevenage SG2 7EL (01438 880424). *Location*: turn off A1(M) at Stevenage South Junction onto A602 to Hertford, course signposted at Van Hagues Garden Centre. Water hazards on course. 18 holes, 6451 yards. S.S.S. 71. Par 72. 20 bay driving range. *Green Fees*: information not available. *Eating facilities:* restaurant and bar. *Visitors:* welcome. Municipal course, advance booking system available to reserve tee-off times. Shower facilities. *Society Meetings*: catered for by arrangement. Professional: Pat Winston (01438 880424). Secretary: Mr S. Green (01438 880322).*

WALTHAM CROSS. **The Cheshunt Golf Club,** The Clubhouse, Park Lane, Cheshunt EN7 6QD (01992 629777). *Location:* M25 Junction 25 to Hertford, A10 left at second set of traffic lights, turn right at mini roundabout then approximately quarter of a mile. Flat parkland course. 18 holes, 6608 yards. S.S.S. 71. Practice area. *Green Fees:* information not available. *Eating facilities:* public cafe. *Visitors:* welcome anytime. For tee-off times phone Pro Shop (01992 624009). Professional: D. Banks (01992 624009). Secretary: B. Furne (01992 629777).*

EAST REGION / Hertfordshire

WARE. **Briggens Park Golf Club,** Briggens Park, Stanstead Road, Stanstead Abbotts, Ware SG12 8LD (Tel & Fax; 01279 793867). *Location:* A414 near Harlow, Essex. Parkland course. 9 holes, 5582 yards. S.S.S. 69. Practice area. *Green Fees:* 9 holes £10.00 weekdays, £12.00 weekends; 18 holes £15.00 weekdays, £18.00 weekends. *Eating facilities*: coffee shop with snacks. *Visitors:* welcome anytime. *Society Meetings:* very welcome. Professional: (07711 609444). Secretary: Trevor Mitchell

WARE. **Chadwell Springs Golf Club,** Hertford Road, Ware SG12 9LE (01920 461447). *Location*: just off A10 Hertford to Ware. Heathland. 9 holes, 6418 yards. S.S.S. 71. Practice ground. *Green Fees*: Information not available. *Eating facilities*: bar, bar meals; function room. *Visitors*: welcome weekdays except Tuesday and Thursday mornings; weekends with member only. Carts available. *Society Meetings*: welcome weekdays by arrangement. Professional: David Smith. Secretary: David Robertson (01920 462075).*.

WARE. **Hanbury Manor Golf and Country Club,** Ware SG12 0SD (01920 487722; Fax: 01920 487692). *Location:* leave the M25 at Junction 25 and take the A10 towards Hertford, continue for 12 miles and Hanbury Manor is located on the left. Parkland and Championship course designed by Jack Nicklaus II. Host to 1997, 1998 and 1999 English Open. 18 holes, 7052 yards. S.S.S. 74 (blue tees). Putting green, practice ground. *Green Fees:* information not available. *Eating facilities:* two award-winning restaurants in five star Marriott Hotel which overlooks course. *Visitors:* golf available only to Club members or hotel guests. Club and buggy hire, golf shop. *Society Meetings:* Corporate Golf Days are available. Director of Golf: Mike Harrison.* website: www.hanbury-manor.com

WARE. **Whitehill Golf Club,** Whitehill Golf Centre, Dane End, Ware SG12 0JS (01920 438495; Fax: 01920 438891). *Location:* turn off A10 at Raj Villa, High Cross. Undulating course. 18 holes, 6618 yards. S.S.S 72. 25 bay floodlit driving range. *Green Fees:* information not available. *Eating facilities:* bar, restaurants and function room. *Visitors:* welcome. Snooker room. *Society Meetings:* welcome, groups of 12 or more. Professional: Matt Belsham. Secretary: Andrew Smith. *
e-mail: whitehillgolfcentre@btconnect.com

WATFORD. **Aldenham Golf and Country Club,** Church Lane, Aldenham, Watford WD25 8NN (01923 853929; Fax: 01923 858472). *Location:* three minutes from M1 Junction 5, off B462 to Radlett. Flat parkland course. 18 holes, 6500 yards. S.S.S. 71. 9 holes, 2350 yards. Practice area. *Green Fees:* weekdays £35.00, weekends £45.00. *Eating facilities*: full catering and bar facilities. *Visitors:* welcome, weekends after 1pm. Buggy cars for hire. *Society Meetings*: welcome byprior arrangement. Professional: Tim Dunstan (01923 857889). Secretary: (01923 853929).
e-mail: info@aldenhamgolfclub.co.uk
website: www.aldenhamgolfclub.co.uk

WATFORD. **West Herts Golf Club,** Cassiobury Park, Watford WD3 3GG (01923 236484). *Location:* off Rousebarn Lane from Links Way, A412 at Croxley Green. Parkland. 18 holes, 6612 yards. S.S.S. 72. *Green Fees:* information not available. *Eating facilities:* catering (including breakfast) available seven days a week. *Visitors:* welcome. *Society Meetings:* catered for. Professional: Charles Gough (01923 220352). General Manager: Ross McCue (01923 236484; Fax: 01923 222300).*
website: www.westhertsgolfclub.co.uk

WELWYN GARDEN CITY. **Brocket Hall Golf Club,** Welwyn Garden City AL8 7XG (01707 335241; Fax: 01707 390052). *Location*: A1(M) two minutes from Junction 4. 36 holes Melbourne Course, parkland course, 6616 yards, S.S.S. 72; Palmerston Course, woodland, 18 holes, 7080 yards, S.S.S. 73. Par 3 course, Palmerston Golf Academy. *Green Fees:* from £75.00. *Eating facilities*: available all day. *Visitors:* welcome on one course, subject to availability. Residential golf packages available.
e-mail: golfclubinfo@brocket-hall.co.uk
website: www.brocket-hall.co.uk

ALDENHAM GOLF & COUNTRY CLUB

Easily accessible from M1 and M25, this picturesque 18-hole parkland course and 9-hole course are situated in the pretty village of Aldenham.
Visiting societies are always welcome and we offer excellent "value for money" golfing packages throughout the year. For details phone

01923 853929
Church Lane, Aldenham, Watford WD25 8NN
www.aldenhamgolfclub.co.uk

Hertfordshire / EAST REGION

WELWYN GARDEN CITY. Mill Green Golf Club, Gypsy Lane, Welwyn Garden City AL7 4TY (01707 276900; Fax: 01707 276898). *Location:* from A1 North exit 4 (Hatfield) A414 to Hertford, take first slip road on left to A1000, left at lights, second right Ascots Lane, mini roundabout turn right into Gypsy Lane. Parkland course. Peter Alliss and Clive Clarke designed. 18 holes, 6615 yards. S.S.S. 72. Two contrasting loops of 9 holes. Front 9 open and elevated, back 9 long narrow fairways through woodland. Par 3 course, driving range, putting green. *Green Fees:* information not available. *Eating facilities:* full bar menu available and extensive conference and banqueting facilities. *Visitors:* Monday to Friday all day, after midday at weekends. *Society Meetings:* welcome Monday to Friday. Professional: Ian Parker. General Manager: Tim Hudson.
e-mail: millgreen@crown-golf.co.uk

WELWYN GARDEN CITY. **Panshanger Golf Complex,** Old Herns Lane, Panshanger, Welwyn Garden City AL7 2ED (01707 333350; Fax: 01707 390010). *Location*: just off Junction 6 A1(M), 10 minutes from M25. Parkland set in the Mimram Valley. 18 holes, 6347 yards. S.S.S. 70. Practice ground, 9 hole pitch and putt. *Green Fees:* information not available. *Eating facilities:* Fairway Tavern and cafe. *Visitors:* municipal course, pay as you play, all welcome, dress conditions. *Society Meetings:* welcome weekdays. Secretary: Trish Skinner (0798225 9475). General Manager: Gordon Dunn.*

WELWYN GARDEN CITY. **Welwyn Garden City Golf Club Ltd,** Mannicotts, High Oaks Road, Welwyn Garden City AL8 7BP (01707 325243). *Location*: from north Junction 5 on A1M and take B197 to Valley Road. From south Junction 4 on A1M to Lemsford Lane and Valley Road. Undulating parkland. 18 holes, 6200 yards. S.S.S. 69. Practice ground. *Green Fees:* £35.00 weekdays. *Eating facilities:* by order for lunches; sandwiches available. *Visitors:* welcome weekdays with Handicap Certificate; weekends with member only. *Society Meetings:* Mondays, Wednesdays and Thursdays only (£60.00 per person per day). Professional: R. May (01707 325525). General Manager: (01707 325243; Fax: 01707 393213).
website: www.welwyngardencitygolfclub.co.uk

WHIPSNADE. **Whipsnade Park Golf Club,** Studham Lane, Dagnall HP4 1RH (0144-284 2330/2331; Fax: 0144-284 2090). *Location:* between Dagnall and Studham. Junction 11 M1 (from north), Junction 9 (from south). Parkland. 18 holes, 6800 yards. S.S.S. 72. Large practice area. *Green Fees:* £35.00 per round, £45.00 two rounds weekdays, weekends after 1pm visitors welcome, (without member) £40.00. 2010 rates (subject to review). *Eating facilities:* restaurant open daily, two bars. *Visitors:* welcome weekdays with reservation. *Society Meetings:* welcome with reservation. Professional: Mark Day (0144-284 2310). Secretary: Ruth Whalley (0144-284 2330).
e-mail: secretary@whipsnadeparkgolf.co.uk
website: www.whipsnadeparkgolf.co.uk

Aldenham Golf & Country Club, Watford

Norfolk

CROMER. **Links Country Park Hotel and Golf Club,** Sandy Lane, West Runton, Cromer NR27 9QH (01263 838383). *Location:* midway between Cromer and Sheringham on the A149, turn left opposite the village inn. Undulating parkland with narrow fairways and tricky greens. Spectacular views. 9 holes, 4814 yards, S.S.S. 64. *Green Fees:* information not available. *Eating facilities:* clubhouse catering every day except Tuesday. *Visitors:* welcome weekdays, restrictions weekends. Adjoining Hotel offers free golf to residents; gym, sauna, solarium, swimming pool etc. *Society Meetings:* welcome. Professional/ Manager: Gary Potter (01263 838675; Fax: 01263 838264).*
e-mail: sales@links-hotel.co.uk
garypottergolf@hotmail.co.uk
website: www.links-hotel.co.uk

THE APPEARANCE OF AN ASTERISK (*) AT THE END OF A CLUB OR COURSE ENTRY INDICATES THAT UP-TO-DATE INFORMATION HAS NOT BEEN SUPPLIED

CROMER. **Royal Cromer Golf Club,** 145 Overstrand Road, Cromer NR27 0JH (01263 512884; Fax: 01263 512430). *Location:* one mile east of Cromer on B1159 Coast Road. Undulating cliff top course. 18 holes, 6528 yards. S.S.S. 72. Practice ground. *Green Fees:* £50.00 weekdays, £60.00 weekends; weekly tickets available. *Eating facilities:* full catering and bar snacks. *Visitors:* welcome, booking essential from 1st April to 31st October, Handicap Certificates required. *Society Meetings:* welcome. Professsional: Lee Patterson (Tel & Fax: 01263 512267). Secretary/ Manager: G. A. Richardson (01263 512884).

DEREHAM. **Dereham Golf Club,** Quebec Road, Dereham NR19 2DS (01362 695900; Fax: 01362 695904). *Location:* three-quarters of a mile from town centre on B1110. Wooded parkland. 9 holes (double tees), 6225 yards. S.S.S. 70, Par 71. Practice nets, practice ground. *Green Fees:* Information not available. *Visitors:* welcome with prior notice. Handicap Certificates required. *Society Meetings:* catered for with advance booking. Professional: Neil Allsbrook (01362 695631). Secretary: Maria Allsebrook (01362 695900).
e-mail: derehamgolfclub@dgolfclub.freeserve.co.uk

Set in 35 acres of coastal parkland, Norfolk's longest established Golf, Leisure, Wedding and Conference Hotel offers a traditional welcome, a peaceful escape from everyday pressures and the opportunity to relax in this unspoilt part of North Norfolk.
The hotel has its own superb 9-hole Par 33 golf course, which combines tight, hilly fairways with tricky greens – a challenge for players of all abilities.
All year-round golfing breaks offer and group discounts available – use of the golf course is **FREE** to guests.

The Links Country Park Hotel and Golf Club, West Runton, Cromer, Norfolk NR27 9QH
Tel: 01263 838383 • Fax: 01263 838264 • e-mail: sales@links-hotel.co.uk

Norfolk / EAST REGION

DISS. Diss Golf Club, Stuston Common, Diss IP21 4AA (01379 641025). *Location:* close to the town of Diss on the Suffolk/Norfolk border. Interesting parkland/heathland course with natural hazards abounding. A good test of golf for every standard of player. 18 holes, 6202 yards. S.S.S. 70, Par 70. Good practice facilities; driving range one mile. *Green Fees:* £32.00 per round, £40.00 per day. Summer and Winter Green Fee deals are available, phone for details. *Eating facilities:* good dining and bar facilities at the clubhouse. *Visitors:* always welcome, membership available. Lessons available; golf shop. *Society Meetings:* societies and groups always welcome. For all enquiries contact the Secretary Manager. Professional: (01379 644399). Secretary Manager: (01379 640125). Club Bar and Catering Manager: (01379 642847) after 11am.
e-mail: sec.dissgolf@virgin.net
website: www.club-noticeboard.co.uk/diss

DOWNHAM MARKET. Ryston Park Golf Club, Ely Road, Denver, Downham Market PE38 0HH (01366 382133); Fax: 01366 383834). *Location:* one mile south Downham Market on A10. 36 miles north Cambridge. Parkland with mature trees and water on three holes. 9 holes, 6330 yards, 5778 metres. S.S.S. 71. Practice ground, practice putting green, practice bunker. *Green Fees:* weekdays £25.00, weekends restricted – contact Club. *Eating facilities:* restaurant and bar. *Visitors:* welcome weekdays, weekends by prior arrangement. *Society Meetings:* welcome (up to 50 members). Secretary: Joe Flogdell (01366 382133).

FAKENHAM. Fakenham Golf Club, Gallow Sports Centre, Hempton Road, Fakenham NR21 7NY (01328 862867). *Location:* half-a-mile town centre on Swaffham Road. Parkland. 9 holes, 6245 yards. S.S.S. 70. Large practice area. *Green Fees:* information not available. *Eating facilities:* available in Sports Centre. *Visitors:* welcome by appointment. *Society Meetings:* welcome, reduced rates. Professional: Colin Williams (01328 863534). Secretary: G.G. Cocker (01328 855678).

GREAT YARMOUTH. Caldecott Hall Golf Club and Hotel, Beccles Road, Fritton, Great Yarmouth NR31 9EY (01493 488488; Fax: 01493 488561). *Location:* on the A143 just north of the village of Fritton. Parkland. 18 holes, 6685 yards, S.S.S. 73. 18-hole short course. Floodlit driving range, putting and pitching practice area. *Green Fees:* information not available. *Eating facilities:* bar, restaurant. *Visitors:* welcome at all times, starting sheets weekends and Bank Holidays. Luxury en suite rooms. Packages available. The Barnworks Leisure Spa; massage treatments. *Society Meetings:* welcome by arrangement. Professional: (01493 488488; Fax: 01493 488561).
website: www.caldecotthall.co.uk

GREAT YARMOUTH. Gorleston Golf Club, Warren Road, Gorleston, Great Yarmouth NR31 6JT (01493 661082). *Location:* A12 Lowestoft to Great Yarmouth. Seaside links, seventh green is the most easterly green in the British Isles. 18 holes, 6400 yards. S.S.S. 71. *Green Fees:* information not available. *Eating facilities:* restaurant/bars open seven days. *Visitors:* welcome, advisable to check in advance for details of restrictions. *Society Meetings:* catered for by prior arrangement (membership of recognised club required). Professional: Nick Brown (01493 662103). Secretary: J.E. Woodhouse (01493 661911).*

GREAT YARMOUTH. Great Yarmouth and Caister Golf Club, Beach House, Caister-on-Sea, Great Yarmouth NR30 5TD (01493 728699). *Location:* A149 coast road, two miles north of Great Yarmouth. Links. 18 holes, 6330 yards. S.S.S. 70. Practice ground. *Green Fees:* £20.00 weekdays; £25.00 weekends. *Eating facilities:* full range of catering; bar. *Visitors:* welcome, not before 11.30am Saturdays, Sundays and Bank Holidays. *Society Meetings:* catered for. Clubhouse Catering (01493 720214). Professional: Martyn Clarke (01493 720421). Secretary: Brian Lever.
e-mail: office@caistergolf.co.uk
website: www.caistergolf.co.uk

HEACHAM. Heacham Manor Golf Club, Hunstanton Road, Heacham PE31 7JX (01485 536030; Fax: 01485 533815). *Location:* take A149 from King's Lynn, continue straight ahead at Heacham traffic lights, take left hand turn before the approach of the hill to Hunstanton; Heacham Manor on the right. Links-style course with large raised greens and several lakes; plays across River Heacham. 18 holes, 6622 yards. S.S.S. 72. Driving range at sister course at Searles Resort. *Green Fees:* weekdays £20.00 per round, £35.00 per day; weekends £25.00 per round. *Eating facilities:* hotel bar and restaurant at Heacham Manor, serving fine cuisine and drinks. Country Club at Searles

Great Yarmouth & Caister Golf Club
Beach House, Caister-on-Sea, Great Yarmouth NR30 5TD

Founded in 1882, Great Yarmouth & Caister Golf Club is a traditional-style links course, set along the coast north of Great Yarmouth. Partly set among sand dunes, it is always well-drained and has challenging fairways and excellent greens. Golfers of all abilities will find something to test themselves here.
SOCIETIES AND VISITORS ARE MOST WELCOME. Various packages are available to societies from Monday to Friday. For details and bookings please call **01493 728699 (Secretary)** or **01493 720421 (Professional).**
For more information see our website or e-mail your enquiry.

Tel: 01493 728699 • Fax: 01493 728831
www.caistergolf.co.uk • office@caistergolf.co.uk

Club Lounge (10th tee). *Visitors*: welcome at any time with advance notice. *Society Meetings:* welcome any time with advance notice; reduced green fees with food. Special rates for groups of 10 or more. Professional: Ray Stocker (07850 330022). Secretary: Paul Searle.
e-mail: golf@heacham-manor.co.uk
website: www.heacham-manor.co.uk

HUNSTANTON. **Hunstanton Golf Club,** Golf Course Road, Old Hunstanton PE36 6JQ (01485 532811; Fax: 01485 532319). *Location*: off A149. Adjoins Old Hunstanton village, approximately half a mile north east of Hunstanton. Championship links course with excellent fast greens. 18 holes, 6735 yards. S.S.S. 72. Practice ground. *Green Fees*: information not available. *Eating facilities:* catering and bar facilities. *Visitors:* welcome but limited times available at weekends. Prior booking advisable. Visitors must be member of recognised golf club and hold a current Handicap. Play in two-ball format only. *Society Meetings*: welcome. Professional: Jim Dodds (01485 532751). Secretary: Derek Thomson (01485 532811).*

Norfolk / EAST REGION

HUNSTANTON. Searles Resort Golf Course, Searles Leisure Resort, South Beach Road, Hunstanton PE36 5BB (01485 536010; Fax: 01485 533815). *Location:* A149 from King's Lynn to Hunstanton; at roundabout on hill at Hunstanton take 2nd left down Oasis Way; at mini-roundabout straight over and immediate left into Leisure Resort; follow signs. Seaside links-style course. 9 holes, 2850 yards. S.S.S. 34. 10-bay covered driving range. Putting. *Green Fees:* adults £11.50, under-18s £8.00. *Eating facilities:* new clubhouse with bar, restaurant, shop, changing facilities etc. *Visitors:* welcome at all times. Lodges and cabin on site available for hire. Club hire. Fishing lake and bowling green. *Society Meetings:* all welcome. Secretary/Manager: Paul Searle.
e-mail: golf@searles.co.uk

KING'S LYNN. King's Lynn Golf Club, Castle Rising, King's Lynn PE31 6BD (01553 631654; Fax: 01553 631036). *Location:* four miles north-east of King's Lynn. Undulating wooded course. 18 holes, 6609 yards. Par 72, S.S.S. 73. Practice areas. *Green Fees:* please see website for information. *Eating facilities:* snacks, lunches, teas available; dinners by arrangement; two bars. *Visitors:* welcome on production of Handicap Certificate and by prior arrangement. *Society Meetings:* catered for by prior arrangement. Professional/Golf Manager: J. Reynolds (01553 631655). Secretary: M. Bowman.
e-mail: secretary@kingslynngc.co.uk
website: www.kingslynngc.co.uk

THE GOLF GUIDE 2011 — EAST REGION / Norfolk

KING'S LYNN. Eagles Golf Club, 39 School Road, Tilney All Saints, King's Lynn PE34 4RS (01553 827147). *Location:* off A47 between King's Lynn and Wisbech. Parkland. 9 holes, 4284 yards. S.S.S. 61. Par 3 course, driving range, practice bunkers and putting green. *Green Fees:* weekdays £12.00 9 holes, £15.00 18 holes; weekends and Bank Holidays £12.00 9 holes, £15.00 18 holes. Weekday special Seniors/Juniors £8.00 9 holes, £12.00 18 holes. *Eating facilities:* bar/restaurant. *Visitors:* welcome, restrictions at weekends. Dress code must be adhered to at all times. *Society Meetings:* apply to Secretary. Professionals: Nigel Pickerell, Sam Cubitt. Secretary: R. K. Shipman (01553 827147).

KING'S LYNN. Middleton Hall Golf Club, Middleton, King's Lynn PE32 1RY (Tel & Fax: 01553 841800). *Location:* on A47 King's Lynn to Norwich, 3 miles from King's Lynn. Undulating parkland. 18 holes, 6004 yards. Par 71. Floodlit driving range, practice greens. *Green Fees:* weekdays £25.00, weekends £30.00, day ticket £40.00. *Eating facilities:* full restaurant services. *Visitors:* welcome. *Society Meetings:* welcome, special rates available. Professional: Steve White (01553 841801). Secretary: J. Holland (Tel & Fax: 01553 841800). e-mail: enquiries@middletonhallgolfclub.com website: www.middletonhallgolfclub.com

KING'S LYNN. Royal West Norfolk Golf Club, Brancaster, Near King's Lynn PE31 8AX (01485 210087). *Location:* one mile off A149, Beach Road junction, seven miles east of Hunstanton. Seaside links. 18 holes, 6458 yards. S.S.S. 71. *Green Fees:* weekdays £85.00 per day. *Eating facilities:* available. *Visitors:* all visitors must be members of a recognised Golf Club, hold an official Handicap and must make prior arrangements with the Secretary to play. No visitors at weekends and no visitors in August. Maximum numbers in party 12. Professional: S. Rayner (01485 210616). Secretary: N.I Symington (Tel & Fax: 01485 210087).

MATTISHALL. Mattishall Golf Club, South Green, Mattishall, Dereham NR20 3JZ (01362 850111). *Location:* signposted from Mattishall Church. 9 hole (18 tees), flat course, 6170 yards, SSS 69. *Green Fees:* £10.00 for 9 holes. *Eating facilities:* small bar only. *Visitors:* welcome seven days. Secretary: Mrs Bridgette Hall.

NORWICH. Barnham Broom Hotel, Golf & Spa, Barnham Broom, Norwich NR9 4DD (01603 759393 (Hotel); 01603 757505 (Golf Shop); Fax: 01603 758224). *Location:* situated 10 miles west of Norwich off A47 and A11 trunk routes; follow brown tourist signs. Two 18 hole courses in 250 acres of the beautiful River Yare Valley. The Valley Course: 6483 yards, S.S.S. 71; The Hill Course: 6495 yards, S.S.S. 71. Exceptional practice facilities including 5-acre practice ground and three full length academy holes. GPS buggies available. Group and individual tuition at the Barnham Broom Golf School. *Green Fees:* information not provided. *Eating facilities:* Flints Restaurant, Sports Bar and Cafe (serving light meals and drinks throughout the day).Conference and private dining for up to 200 people. *Visitors:* welcome anytime. Hotel with 52 en suite bedrooms. Leisure Club. *Society Meetings:* welcome all year; corporate Golf Events. Contact Alan Hemsley (01603 757501). Bookings: (01603 759393) e-mail: golf@barnham-broom.co.uk website: www.barnham-broom.co.uk

NORWICH. Bawburgh Golf Club, Glen Lodge, Marlingford Road, Bawburgh, Norwich NR9 3LU (01603 740404; Fax: 01603 740403). *Location:* directly off Norwich Southern Bypass – exit follow Royal Norfolk Showground/Bawburgh. Rolling landscape mixture of heath and parkland. 18 holes, 6720 yards. S.S.S. 72. Driving range covered and floodlit, group tuition. *Green Fees:* weekdays £25.00; weekends £25.00 on application. 2010 rates (subject to review). *Eating facilities:* restaurant and bar, snacks. *Visitors:* welcome, advisable to ring in advance. *Society Meetings:* welcome on application, Corporate Days arranged. Professional: Mark Spooner (07545 948089). General Manager: Ian Ladbrooke. e-mail: info@bawburgh.com website: www.bawburgh.com

THE APPEARANCE OF AN ASTERISK (*) AT THE END OF A CLUB OR COURSE ENTRY INDICATES THAT UP-TO-DATE INFORMATION HAS NOT BEEN SUPPLIED

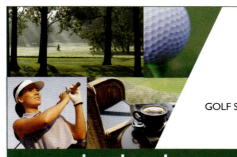

BARNHAM BROOM
Hotel, Golf & Spa

Two magnificent 18 hole Golf Courses with Driving Range, Practice Area with bunkers and a 3 hole Academy Course.
GOLF SOCIETIES, GOLF BREAKS and GOLF SCHOOLS
Golf Breaks price from £74 per person, Dinner, Bed & Breakfast plus two rounds of golf.
(based on two sharing and subject to availability)

www.barnham-broom.co.uk T: 01603 759393

NORWICH. **Costessey Park Golf Course,** Old Costessey, Norwich NR8 5AL (01603 746333). *Location:* off the A47 Norwich to King's Lynn road, in the village of Old Costessey (adjacent to Norwich). Set in river valley with some parkland. 18 holes, 5900 yards. S.S.S. 69. Par 71. Practice area. *Green Fees:* information not available. *Eating facilities:* bar and bar snacks; set meals available. *Visitors:* welcome anytime except weekends when visitors allowed only after 11am. Handicap Certificates required weekends only. Golf carts available for hire. *Society Meetings:* catered for by arrangement. Professional: Andrew Young (01603 747085).*

NORWICH. **De Vere Dunston Hall,** Ipswich Road, Norwich NR14 8PQ (Hotel: 01508 470444; Fax: 01508 470689; Shop: 01508 470178). *Location:* on A140 Ipswich Road. Parkland, wooded, with many water features. USGA spec. greens. 18 holes, 6319 yards. Par 71. 22 bay covered driving range, putting green. *Green Fees:* information not available. *Eating facilities:* three restaurants, two bars. *Visitors:* pay and play course, all welcome at any time. Golfing weekends; accommodation available in 130-bedroom Hotel; tennis courts; leisure centre with indoor pool, sauna, steam room and jacuzzi. *Society Meetings:* special packages available. Professional: Peter Briggs.*

NORWICH. **Eaton (Norwich) Golf Club,** Newmarket Road, Norwich NR4 6SF (01603 451686; Fax: 01603 457539). *Location:* off A11, one and a half miles from city centre. Parkland course – "the hidden gem". 18 holes, 6118 yards. S.S.S. 70. Practice areas available. *Green Fees:* weekdays £42.00, weekends £50.00. *Eating facilities:* full bar, snacks, lunches, dinners by arrangement. *Visitors:* welcome; only after 11.30am weekends. Handicap Certificate required. *Society Meetings:* welcome, details on request. Professional: Mark Allen (01603 251 394). Club Manager: Peter Johns (01603 451686; Fax: 01603 457539).
e-mail: admin@eatongc.co.uk
website: www.eatongc.co.uk
blog: http://egchiddengem.blogspot.com

NORWICH. **Marriott Sprowston Manor Hotel and Country Club,** Wroxham Road, Norwich NR7 8RP (0870 400 7229; Fax: 0870 400 7329). *Location:* off A1151 Norwich to Wroxham. £1.6 million Championship course set in mature parkland. Host to Sky Televised PGA Europro Tour 2004 & 2005. Full USGA specification greens and tees. Designed by Ross McMurray (European Golf Design), who has also designed the Marquess at Woburn and improvements at Celtic Manor for 2010 Ryder Cup. 18 holes, 6547 yards. S.S.S. 71. Putting green, chipping and bunker practice area. 26 bay floodlit driving range, PGA tuition including Explanar and GASP video analysis. *Green Fees:* information not available. *Eating facilities:* Zest café bar and grill. Four-star hotel on site. *Visitors:* always welcome. Bookings 10 days in advance. *Society Meetings:* special packages available - must be pre-booked. Preferential green fee rates and group packages available for residents. Professional: Guy Ireson (0870 400 7229). Secretary: A. Moule (0870 400 7229).
website: www.marriott.co.uk/nwigs

NORWICH. **Mundesley Golf Club,** Links Road, Mundesley, Norwich NR11 8ES (01263 720279; Fax: 01263 722849). *Location:* one mile from village centre. Undulating, testing downland course with fine panoramic views. 9 holes, 5377 yards. S.S.S. 66. Covered driving range, small practice area. *Green Fees:* information not available. *Eating facilities:* full catering facilities. *Visitors:* welcome, but course reserved for members until 11.30am at weekends and Bank Holidays and 10.30am to 2.30pm Wednesdays. *Society Meetings:* catered for, restrictions as for visitors. Professional: T.G. Symmons (01263 720279). Manager: T.E. Duke (01263 720095; Fax: 01263 722849). *
website: www.mundesleygolfclub.co.uk

NORWICH. **Royal Norwich Golf Club,** Drayton High Road, Hellesdon, Norwich NR6 5AH (01603 429928; Fax: 01603 417945). *Location:* centre of city and thence by A1067 Fakenham or via Ring Road, then 500 yards along A1067. Mature parkland. 18 holes, 6506 yards. S.S.S. 72. Large practice ground. *Green Fees:* weekdays and weekends £48.00 per day, weekdays £30.00 per round, weekends £40.00 per round. Discounted rates for groups of 12 and over £33.00 per day, £24.00 per round. Reduction if playing with a member, special winter rates available on request. 2010 fees (subject to review). *Eating facilities:* two bars, restaurant plus bar menu. Prior booking required for evening meals. *Visitors:* welcome weekdays after 9am, weekends by prior booking only. Handicap Certificate required. *Society Meetings:* welcome weekdays except Wednesday by prior arrangement. Golf Manager: Simon Youd (01603 429928). General Manager: Ryan O'Connor. e-mail: mail@royalnorwichgolf.co.uk
website: www.royalnorwichgolf.co.uk

NORWICH. **Wensum Valley Hotel, Golf and Country Club,** Beech Avenue, Taverham, Norwich NR8 6HP (01603 261012; Fax: 01603 261664). *Location:* five miles out of Norwich on the A1067 to Fakenham. Two courses. Parkland and very picturesque set in the valley. Wensum Course: 18 holes, 6922 yards S.S.S. 73. Valley Course: 18 holes, 6223 yards. S.S.S. 70. Covered, floodlit driving range. *Green Fees:* information not provided. *Eating facilities:* full catering and bar facilities. *Visitors:* always welcome. Hotel on site with en suite twin and double bedrooms. Special golf, fishing and leisure breaks available. *Society Meetings:* all welcome; package available. Professional: Brad Jordan. Secretary: Bridgette Hall (01603 261012).
e-mail: enqs@wensumvalleyhotel.co.uk
website: www.wensumvalleyhotel.co.uk

Please mention THE GOLF GUIDE when you enquire about clubs or accommodation

THE GOLF GUIDE 2011 — EAST REGION / Norfolk

NORWICH. Weston Park Golf Club, Weston Longville, Norwich NR9 5JW (01603 872998; Fax: 01603 873040). *Location:* nine miles north west of Norwich off the A1067 Norwich to Fakenham road. Parkland, wooded course. 18 holes, 6606 yards. S.S.S. 72. Practice ground and net. *Green Fees:* weekdays £40.00; weekends £42.00. 2010 rates (subject to review). *Eating facilities:* available. *Visitors:* welcome. Must book teeing off times. Handicap Certificate required. Two tennis courts and croquet lawn. *Society Meetings:* welcome. Professional: Michael Few (01603 872998). Sales Manager: C. E. Ashmore (01603 872363).
e-mail: info@weston-park.co.uk
website: www.weston-park.co.uk

REYMERSTON. The Norfolk Golf and Country Club, Hingham Road, Reymerston NR9 4QQ (01362 850297; Fax: 01362 850614). *Location:* Dereham B1135 five miles, Wymondham 10 miles. Parkland course. 18 holes, 6609 yards. S.S.S. 72. *Green Fees:* information not available. *Eating facilities:* clubhouse, bar, function room. *Visitors:* welcome subject to availability. Advisable to check in advance. Full leisure facilities in Leisure Centre; swimming pool, sauna, gym, spa bath. *Society Meetings:* society and conference packages available. Professional: Tony Varney (01362 850297; Fax: 01362 850614). Secretary: Jeff Smith.
website: www.thenorfolkgolfclub.co.uk

SHERINGHAM. Sheringham Golf Club, Weybourne Road, Sheringham NR26 8HG (01263 823488). *Location:* one mile west of town on Weybourne Road (A149). Clifftop course. 18 holes, 6456 yards. S.S.S. 71. Large practice area. *Green Fees:* Sunday to Friday per day £55.00 (April to Oct), £40.00 (Nov to March). Saturday per day £60.00 (April to Oct), £50.00 (Nov to March). 2010 rates (subject to review). Twilight and 3-day tickets available. *Eating facilities:* full catering to order. *Visitors:* welcome, telephone first, with reservation for members of other clubs, Handicap Certificate required. *Society Meetings:* catered for by prior arrangement with Secretary. Professional: M.W. Jubb (01263 822980). Secretary: R. Caldecott (01263 823488).
e-mail: info@sheringhamgolfclub.co.uk
website: www.sheringhamgolfclub.co.uk

SWAFFHAM. Swaffham Golf Club, Cley Road, Swaffham PE37 8AE (01760 721621). *Location*: two miles south-west of Swaffham Market Place (signposted) on Cley Road. Heathland course. 18 holes, 5728 yards Red, 6192 yards Yellow, 6525 yards White. S.S.S. 71. Practice ground. *Green Fees*: please call (01760 721621 option 2) for Summer/Winter deals. *Eating facilities:* bar and dining facilities available; full catering Tuesday-Sunday. *Visitors*: welcome weekdays; please call first to reserve a tee time. *Society Meetings*: society and group bookings weekdays by prior arrangement. Please phone or e-mail for booking pack. Professional: Peter Field. Club Manager: Chris Wellstead. Assistant: Nikki Strickland.
e-mail: manager@swaffhamgc.co.uk

SHERINGHAM GOLF CLUB

Located between the sea and the North Norfolk Steam Railway, in an Area of Outstanding Natural Beauty, Sheringham Golf Club offers clifftop golf at its best, and is rated in the top 100 clubs in England.

Handicap Certificate required.

Visitors and societies are welcome throughout the year.
Discounted fees and specials are available.
For all enquiries and bookings please contact the Secretary
01263 823488 • Fax: 01263 826129
e-mail: info@sheringhamgolfclub.co.uk • www.sheringhamgolfclub.co.uk
Sheringham Golf Club, Sheringham, Norfolk NR26 8HG

SWAFFHAM
GOLF CLUB

Cley Road,
Swaffham, Norfolk
PE37 8AE
Tel: 01760 721621
Fax: 01760 336998

This Breckland club was established in 1922, with an additional 9 holes created in 2001 in an area of mature woodland. The attractive and demanding course remains well drained throughout the year.
Host to corporate days, county fixtures and open days.
**e-mail: manager@swaffhamgc.co.uk
www.club-noticeboard.co.uk**

Norfolk / EAST REGION

THETFORD. **Feltwell Golf Club,** Thor Avenue, off Wilton Road, Feltwell, Thetford IP26 4AY (01842 827644). *Location:* take the B1386 off the A10 at Southery (five miles south of Downham Market). Inland links. 9 holes, 6488 yards, 6197 metres. S.S.S. 71. Practice range and nets. *Green Fees:* weekdays £20.00, twilight golf £15.00; weekends £30.00, twilight golf £18.00. *Eating facilities:* bar, hot and cold food available Tuesday through Sunday. *Visitors:* welcome at all times but check with Secretary. *Society Meetings:* welcome, packages available. Secretary/ Professional: Jonathan Moore (01842 827644).
e-mail: sec.feltwellgc@virgin.net

THETFORD. **Thetford Golf Club,** Brandon Road, Thetford IP24 3NE (01842 752258). *Location:* one mile west of Thetford on B1107 Brandon Road. Wooded breckland course. 18 holes, 6849 yards. S.S.S. 73. Practice ground. *Green Fees:* information not available. *Eating facilities:* catering and bar service. *Visitors:* welcome weekdays. April to October after 2pm weekends. *Society Meetings:* catered for Mondays, Wednesdays, Thursdays and Fridays – Handicap Certificate needed. Professional: Gary Kitley (01842 752662). Secretary: Mrs Diane Hopkins (01842 752169; Fax: 01842 766212).
e-mail: thetfordgolfclub@btconnect.com

WATTON. **Richmond Park Golf Club,** Saham Road, Watton, Thetford IP25 6EA (01953 881803; Fax: 01953 881817). *Location:* half a mile north west of Watton town centre. Parkland. 18 holes, 6289 yards. S.S.S. 71. Driving range. *Green Fees:* information not available. *Eating facilities:* bar, bar food, restaurant. *Visitors:* always welcome. Accommodation available on site. *Society Meetings:* welcome, excellent facilities available. Secretary: Simon Jessup.*

THE APPEARANCE OF AN ASTERISK (*) AT THE END OF A CLUB OR COURSE ENTRY INDICATES THAT UP-TO-DATE INFORMATION HAS NOT BEEN SUPPLIED

King's Lynn Golf Club. Norfolk

Suffolk

ALDEBURGH. **Aldeburgh Golf Club,** Saxmundham Road, Aldeburgh IP15 5PE (01728 452890). *Location:* A12 north from Ipswich; turn right on A1094 to Aldeburgh. Quality heathland course in excellent condition all year round, many challenging Par 4s. 18 holes, 6603 yards. par 68. S.S.S. 73; also 9 holes, 2030 yards. Par 30, S.S.S. 30. *Green Fees:* 18-hole: weekdays £70.00 per day, £55.00 after 12 noon; weekends £75.00 per day, £60.00 after 12 noon. *Eating facilities:* lunches, teas etc. *Visitors:* welcome by arrangement on 18-hole course; must have Handicap Certificate. No three or four balls allowed on 18-hole course. *Society Meetings:* by arrangement (any day). Professional: K.R. Preston (01728 453309). Secretary: G. Hogg (01728 452890). e-mail: info@aldeburghgolfclub.co.uk

BECCLES. **Beccles Golf Club,** The Common, Beccles NR34 9BX (01502 712244). *Location:* A146 Beccles by-pass, to town centre at Safeway roundabout, left over level crossing. Flat commonland. 9 holes, 5558 yards, 5084 metres. S.S.S. 67. *Green Fees:* information not provided. *Eating facilities:* bar snacks available. *Visitors:* welcome anytime. *Society Meetings:* catered for by prior arrangement. Secretary: Alan Ereira (01502 712244).

BUNGAY. **Bungay and Waveney Valley Golf Club,** Outney Common, Bungay NR35 1DS (01986 892337; Fax: 01986 892222). *Location:* a quarter mile from town centre and alongside A143. Flat, heath-type course. 18 holes, 6050 yards. S.S.S. 69. *Green Fees:* information not available. *Eating facilities:* available everyday. *Visitors:* welcome weekdays, weekends with member only. Must telephone (01986 892337) prior to a visit to book a tee time. *Society Meetings:* by arrangement with Secretary. Professional: Andrew Collison (01986 892337; Fax: 01986 892222). Secretary: John Lunniss (01986 892337; Fax: 01986 892222).*

BURY ST EDMUNDS. **Bury St Edmunds Golf Club,** Tut Hill, Bury St Edmunds IP28 6LG. *Location:* B1106 just off A14. Flat parkland. 18 holes, 6675 yards. S.S.S. 72; 9 holes, 2217 yards. S.S.S. 31. Practice facilities. *Green Fees:* information not available. *Eating facilities:* available. *Visitors:* welcome Monday to Friday on both courses; weekends on 9-hole course only. *Society Meetings:* catered for. Professional: Mark Jillings (01284 755978). Secretary: John Taylor (01284 755979; Fax: 01284 763288).*
e-mail: info@burygolf.co.uk

BURY ST EDMUNDS. **Flempton Golf Club,** Flempton, Bury St Edmunds IP28 6EQ (01284 728291). *Location:* follow A1101 from Bury St Edmunds towards Mildenhall for about four miles, course on right. 9 holes, 6184 yards. S.S.S. 70. *Green Fees:* £35.00 per round, £40.00 per day. *Eating facilities:* by arrangement. *Visitors:* welcome, except Bank Holidays. By prior arrangement and must produce Handicap Certificate. Professional: Kieran Canham (01284 728291). Secretary: M.S. Clark.

BURY ST EDMUNDS. **The Suffolk Hotel Golf and Country Club,** Fornham St Genevieve, Bury St Edmunds IP28 6JQ (01284 706777; Fax: 01284 706721). *Location:* Exit A14 at Bury St Edmunds West and travel north on B1106 for approx. 2 miles. Mature parkland, testing water hazards. Putting green and practice ground. 18 hole Genevieve course 6392 yards. S.S.S. 71. *Green Fees:* information not provided. *Eating facilities:* Bars and restaurant; residential packages available. *Visitors:* welcome, booking advised. Club, buggy and trolley hire. Indoor pool, with spa sauna and steam room. 41 bedroom en suite hotel. Conference facilities. *Society Meetings:* society packages available. Professional/Director of Golf: Stephen Hall.
e-mail: proshop.suffolkgolf@ohiml.com
website: www.oxfordhotelsandinns.com

DISS. **Diss Golf Club,** Stuston Common, Diss IP21 4AA (01379 641025). *Location:* close to the town of Diss on the Suffolk/Norfolk border. Heath and parkland course with natural hazards abounding, and 30 bunkers to avoid. A good test of golf for every standard of player. 18 holes, 6206 yards. S.S.S. 70, Par 70. Good practice facilities; driving range one mile. *Green Fees:* information not available. *Eating facilities:* good dining and bar facilities at the clubhouse. *Visitors:* always welcome, membership available. Lessons available; golf shop. *Society Meetings:* societies and groups always welcome. For all enquiries contact the Secretary Manager. Professional: (01379 644399). Secretary Manager: (01379 641025). Club Bar and Catering Manager: (01379 642847) after 11am.
e-mail: sec.dissgolf@virgin.net
website: www.club-noticeboard.co.uk/diss

FELIXSTOWE. **Felixstowe Ferry Golf Club,** Ferry Road, Felixstowe IP11 9RY (01394 286834). *Location:* one mile from town centre, follow signs to golf club from A14. Seaside links course named one of the Top 200 Clubs in Britain. Martello Course - 18 holes, 6379 yards. S.S.S. 71, Par 72. Kingsfleet Course - 2986 yards. S.S.S. 69, Par 70. Large practice area. *Green Fees:* Martello Course - weekdays £45.00 per day; £35.00 per round; weekends and Bank Holidays £50.00 after 2.30pm. Kingsfleet Course - £13.00 per day (twilight rates available). *Eating facilities:* diningroom and fully licensed bar. *Visitors:* Martello Course - welcome, but advisable to check first; Handicap Certificates required. Ladies priority Thursday mornings. Kingsfleet course - visitors welcome at any time. Two self-catering flats available, free golf included in charges. *Society Meetings:* catered for weekdays only. Professional: Ian MacPherson (01394 283975). Secretary/ Manager: Ray Baines (01394 286834).
e-mail: secretary@felixstowegolf.co.uk
website: www.felixstowegolf.co.uk

Suffolk / EAST REGION

FRAMLINGHAM. **Cretingham Golf Club,** Swans Lane, Cretingham, Woodbridge IP13 7BA (01728 685275). *Location:* off A1120, signposted to Cretingham, 10 miles north of Ipswich. Wooded inland course, challenging water holes. 18 holes, 5278 yards. Par 68. *Green Fees:* information not available. *Eating facilities:* restaurant and fully licensed bar. *Visitors:* always welcome, no restrictions. Please book in advance. Tennis available. Outdoor swimming pool. Caravans welcome. Log cabins available to let. *Society Meetings:* welcome. Professional: Neil Jackson (01728 685275). Secretary: Kate Jackson.*

HALESWORTH. **Halesworth Golf Club,** Bramfield Road, Halesworth IP19 9XA (01986 875567). *Location*: on A144 between Halesworth and Bramfield. 18 hole Blyth course, 6506 yards, par 72. 9 hole Valley course, 2280 yards, par 33. Practice area, putting green, 10 bay floodlit driving range. *Green Fees:* information not provided. *Eating facilities*: bar and restaurant. *Visitors*: welcome. *Society Meetings*: welcome. Buggies available.
e-mail: info@halesworthgc.co.uk

HAVERHILL. **Haverhill Golf Club Ltd,** Coupals Road, Haverhill CB9 7UW (Tel & Fax: 01440 761951). *Location:* Sturmer Road turn into Chalkestone Way, right into Coupals Road. Club is one mile on right. Undulating parkland with river. 18 holes, 5986 yards. S.S.S. 70. Practice ground. *Green Fees:* weekdays £30.00 per day, weekends and Bank Holidays £40.00. Half price if playing with a member. *Eating facilities:* clubhouse, snacks, hot meals, bar. *Visitors:* welcome at all times except when first tee booked for matches and societies. *Society Meetings:* welcome. Professional: Paul Wilby (01440 712628). Secretary: Linda Farrant (Tel & Fax: 01440 761951).

IPSWICH. **Fynn Valley Golf Club,** Witnesham, Ipswich IP6 9JA (01473 785267; Fax: 01473 785632). *Location:* two miles north of Ipswich on B1077. Attractive, undulating parkland along the Fynn Valley. 18 holes, 6391 yards. S.S.S. 71. 9 hole Par 3 course, 23 bay floodlit golf range (10 undercover), practice bunker and putting greens. *Green Fees:* £26.00 per round weekdays; £32.00 per round weekends (twilight discounts). *Eating facilities:* bar, terrace, gourmet restaurant. *Visitors:* welcome, members only Sunday mornings. Special rates for parties of 12 or more. Two golf shops. Teaching facilities, golf buggies, trolley hire. *Society Meetings:* welcome by prior arrangement. Professionals: Alastair Spink, Simon Dainty, Chris Smith (01473 785463). Secretary: A.R. Tyrrell (01473 785267; Fax: 01473 785632).
e-mail: enquiries@fynn-valley.co.uk
website: www.fynn-valley.co.uk
e-mail: enquiries@fynn-valley.co.uk
website: www.fynn-valley.co.uk

IPSWICH. **Hintlesham Golf Club,** Hintlesham, Ipswich IP8 3JG (01473 652761; Fax: 01473 652750). *Location:* four miles west of Ipswich on the A1071 to Sudbury. Parkland, championship standard - Architect: Martin Hawtree. 18 holes, 6638 yards. S.S.S. 72. Full practice facilities. *Green Fees:* information not available. *Eating facilities:* full catering facilities. *Visitors:* please telephone for tee off times. Accommodation available at Hintlesham Hall Hotel. *Society Meetings:* telephone enquiries welcome. We have a growing national reputation for the organisation of golf days. Professional: Henry Roblin.*
e-mail: sales@hintleshamgolfclub.com
website: www.hintleshamgolfclub.com

IPSWICH. **Ipswich Golf Club,** Purdis Heath, Bucklesham Road, Ipswich IP3 8UQ. *Location:* three miles east of Ipswich on Bucklesham Road. Heathland. 18 holes, 6439 yards. S.S.S. 72. 9 holes, 1930 yards. S.S.S. 59. *Green Fees:* weekdays £50.00 per round, £70.00 per day; weekends and Bank Holidays £55.00 per round, £75.00 per day. 9-hole course: weekdays £10.00 per day, weekends and Bank Holidays £15.00 per day. 2010 rates (subject to review). *Eating facilities:* full catering facilities available for visitors. *Visitors:* by prior arrangement for 18-hole course, and must produce Handicap Certificate or letter of introduction. No restriction for 9-hole course. *Society Meetings:* by special reservation only and on Society terms. Professional: (01473 724017). Secretary: N.M. Ellice (01473 728941)
e-mail: neill@ipswichgolfclub.com
website: www.ipswichgolfclub.com

IPSWICH. **Rushmere Golf Club,** Rushmere Heath, Woodbridge Road, Ipswich IP4 5QQ (01473 727109). *Location:* off A1214 north from Ipswich, 300 yards signposted. Heathland course. 18 holes, 6265 yards. S.S.S. 70. Practice facilities. *Green Fees:* £25.00 per round, £40.00 per day. *Eating facilities:* full catering available. *Visitors:* welcome except 4.30-5.30pm, weekends after 2.30pm. Handicap Certificate required. *Society Meetings:* welcome. Professional: Kelvin Vince (01473 728076). Secretary: R.W.G. Tawell (01473 725648).
e-mail: rushmeregolfclub@btconnect.com
website: www.club-noticeboard.co.uk/rushmere

LOWESTOFT. **Rookery Park Golf Club,** Beccles Road, Carlton Colville, Lowestoft NR33 8HJ (01502 509190; Fax: 01502 509191)). *Location:* A146 Beccles to Lowestoft road. Parkland. 18 holes, 6729 yards. S.S.S. 72. 9 hole Par 3 course. Practice ground. New driving range. *Green Fees:* information not available. *Eating facilities:* bar, restaurant. *Visitors:* welcome weekdays (Saturdays and Bank Holidays after 11am). Handicap Cards must be produced. *Society Meetings:* welcome. Professional: M. Elsworthy (01502 515103). Secretary/Manager: R.F. Jones (01502 509190; Fax: 01502 509191). *

THE APPEARANCE OF AN ASTERISK (*) AT THE END OF A CLUB OR COURSE ENTRY INDICATES THAT UP-TO-DATE INFORMATION HAS NOT BEEN SUPPLIED

EAST REGION / Suffolk

MILDENHALL. Royal Worlington and Newmarket Golf Club, Golf Links Road, Worlington, Bury St. Edmunds IP28 8SD (01638 712216; Fax: 01638 717787). *Location:* seven miles north east of Newmarket, signposted off A11 just south of Barton Mills roundabout. Inland links type course. 9 holes, 3105 yards. S.S.S. 70 (18 holes). Practice ground. *Green Fees:* weekdays £60.00 per day, £45.00 for 18 holes. *Eating facilities:* lunch and tea available with prior notice; no evening meals. *Visitors:* welcome weekdays only, Handicap Certificate or letter of introduction from home club required. 3 and 4 balls allowed with prior permission from Secretary. Trolleys for hire. Professional: (01638 715224). Secretary: Scott Ballentine (Tel & Fax: 01638 717787).

NEWMARKET. Links Golf Club, Cambridge Road, Newmarket CB8 0TG (01638 663000; Fax: 01638 661476). *Location:* one mile south-west of Newmarket, opposite racecourse. Relatively flat parkland. 18 holes, 6643 yards. S.S.S. 73. Two practice grounds. *Green Fees:* midweek £36.00 per round, £42.00 per day; weekends and Bank Holidays £42.00 per round, £46.00 per day. 2010 rates (subject to review). *Eating facilities:* restaurant and bar. *Visitors:* welcome. Handicap Certificate required. *Society Meetings:* by arrangement. Professional: John Sharkey (01638 662395). Secretary: M.L. Hartley (01638 663000; Fax: 01638 661476). website: www.club-noticeboard.co.uk/newmarket

RAYDON. Brett Vale Golf Club, Noakes Road, Raydon, Ipswich IP7 5LR (01473 310718). *Location:* midway between Colchester and Ipswich, just off A12 on B1070 to Hadleigh, head for Raydon Water Tower. Undulating countryside parkland course within Dedham Vale in natural valley setting. 18 holes, 5864 yards. S.S.S. 69. 5 bay outdoor Golf Academy, practice ground, putting green. *Green Fees:* information not available. *Eating facilities:* clubroom bar and restaurant; society/function room and bar. *Visitors:* welcome anytime. Pro shop; buggies and power trolley hire. *Society Meetings:* welcome anytime, various packages available.

SOUTHWOLD. Southwold Golf Club, The Common, Southwold IP18 6TB (01502 723234). *Location:* from A12 Blythburgh turn off on A1095 to Southwold. Flat common land with sea views. 9 holes, 6052 yards. S.S.S. 69. *Green Fees:* information not provided. *Visitors:* welcome, phone for availability. *Society Meetings:* welcome. Professional: B.G. Allen (01502 723790). Hon. Secretary: R. Wilshaw (01502 723248).
e-mail: mail@southwoldgolfclub.org
website: www.southwoldgolfclub.org

STOKE-BY-NAYLAND. Stoke-by-Nayland Golf & Spa, Keepers Lane, Leavenheath, Colchester CO6 4PZ (01206 262836; Fax: 01206 265840). *Location:* just off A134 Colchester to Sudbury on B1068 towards Stoke-by-Nayland. Host venue to PGA Seniors' Championship 2006. Undulating parkland with water hazards. Two courses (1) Gainsborough - 18 holes, 6561 yards. S.S.S. 72. (2) Constable - 18 holes, 6544 yards. S.S.S. 72. 20 bay covered range, practice area. *Green Fees:* information not provided. *Eating facilities:* full catering and bars. *Visitors:* welcome, please ring for availability and tee bookings. *Society Meetings:* welcome weekdays, book well in advance. Seasonal packages offered. Extensive Health and Leisure Facility including gymnasium, pool, sauna, jacuzzi and spa; modern, spacious, en suite hotel rooms overlooking lake and fairways. Professional: Roly Hitchcock (01206 265812). Secretary: Mike Verhelst (01206 265815). e-mail: golfsecretary@stokebynayland.com
website: www.stokebynaylandclub.co.uk

STOWMARKET. Stowmarket Golf Club Ltd, Lower Road, Onehouse, Stowmarket IP14 3DA (01449 736473; Fax: 01449 736826). *Location:* on B1508 from Stowmarket to Onehouse. Parkland. 18 holes, 6101 yards. S.S.S. 69. Driving range. *Green Fees:* information not available. *Eating facilities:* lunches, snacks all week. *Visitors:* welcome, avoid Wednesdays. Handicap Certificate required. *Society Meetings:* catered for Thursdays and Fridays only. Professional: D. Burl (01449 736392). Secretary: G.R. West (01449 736473).*

SUDBURY. Newton Green Golf Club, Newton Green, Sudbury CO10 0QN. *Location:* on A134 three miles east of Sudbury. Heath and parkland course. 18 holes, 5961 yards. Par 69. Practice ground. *Green Fees:* weekdays £23.00; weekends and Bank Holidays £27.00. Twilight weekdays £15.00 after 4pm and Sundays £20.00 after 2pm. *Eating facilities:* fully licensed bar, full catering facilities, separate dining room available. *Visitors:* welcome (except Sundays am and Tuesdays before 12.30pm); trolleys for hire. *Society Meetings:* welcome by arrangement. PGA Professional: Tim Cooper (01787 313215). Club Manager: Carole List (01787 377217).
e-mail: info@newtongreengolfclub.co.uk
website: www.newtongreengolfclub.co.uk

For full details of convenient accommodation near clubs and courses

www.holidayguides.com

THORPENESS. Thorpeness Golf Club and Hotel, Thorpeness, Leiston IP16 4NH (01728 452176; Fax: 01728 453868). *Location:* leave A12 at Aldeburgh turnoff. Heathland coastal course. 18 holes, 6271 yards. S.S.S. 71. *Green Fees:* £40.00 midweek, £45.00 weekends. *Eating facilities:* bar, restaurant, terrace and garden. *Visitors:* welcome on application, telephone Pro shop for times. One player is required to either hold a Handicap Certificate or be a member of a golf club to maintain pace of play. Accommodation available – 36 bedrooms. Snooker room, six tennis courts. *Society Meetings:* welcome. Professional: Frank Hill (01728 454926). Golf Manager: Christopher Oldrey (01728 452176).
website: www.thorpeness.co.uk

WOODBRIDGE. Best Western Ufford Park Hotel, Golf and Spa, Yarmouth Road, Melton, Woodbridge, Near Ipswich IP12 1QW (01394 383555; Fax: 01394 383582). *Location*: A12 northwards to A1152 to Melton. In Melton turn left at traffic lights, one mile on the right hand side. Challenging 120-acre parkland course. A "Top 10 Inland British Winter Course" for the last 5 years. 18 holes, 6312 yards. S.S.S. 71. Two storey floodlit driving range: 'American Golf and the Doctorgolf Academy'. *Green Fees:* weekdays £20.00; weekends and Bank Holidays £30.00. Special Golf Breaks available. *Eating facilities:* bar snacks, children's menu and restaurant. *Visitors:* welcome anytime, need to book tee time in advance. 87 en suite bedroom hotel. Ideal for groups; full Health Club with pool and gym, luxury Thermal Suite for spa experiences. Buggies for hire, tuition breaks available. *Society Meetings*: welcome, competitive rates, details on request. PGA Head Professional. Stuart Robertson (01394 383480 (The Doctorgolf Academy)). Secretary: Alan Knight (01394 382836; Fax: 01394 383582).
website: www.uffordpark.co.uk
        www.doctorgolf.co.uk

THE APPEARANCE OF AN ASTERISK (*) AT THE END OF A CLUB OR COURSE ENTRY INDICATES THAT UP-TO-DATE INFORMATION HAS NOT BEEN SUPPLIED

WOODBRIDGE, Seckford Golf Club, Seckford Hall Road, Great Bealings, Near Woodbridge IP13 6NT (01394 388000; Fax: 01394 382818). *Location:* between Martlesham and Woodbridge just off A12. Undulating parkland course maintained in excellent condition. 18 holes, 4981 yards. Par 68. Full length driving range and putting green. *Green Fees:* please call for rates and specials. *Eating facilities:* fully licensed bar and restaurant. *Visitors:* always welcome, telephone to book your place. Buggies, trolleys, clubs and shoes available for hire. *Society Meetings:* welcome by prior arrangement, packages available. PGA Professional: Simon Jay (01394 388000). GASP Video analysis.
e-mail: secretary@seckfordgolf.co.uk
website: www.seckfordgolf.co.uk

WOODBRIDGE. Waldringfield Golf Club, Newbourne Road, Waldringfield, Woodbridge IP12 4PT (01473 736768). *Location:* five miles north of Ipswich, off the old A12. Easy walking, picturesque heathland course with attractive water features. 18 holes, 6079 yards. S.S.S. 69. Limited practice area available. *Green Fees:* weekdays £23.00 + Food Voucher, weekends £28.00 + Food Voucher. Special rates available for societies by arrangement. *Eating facilities:* full service. *Visitors:* welcome weekdays and weekends. *Society Meetings:* welcome weekdays and weekends by arrangement. Course Administrator: (01473 736417). Manager: Pat Whitham (01473 736768. Fax: 01473 736793)
e-mail: enquiries@waldringfieldgc.co.uk

WOODBRIDGE. Woodbridge Golf Club, Bromeswell Heath, Woodbridge IP12 2PF (01394 382038; Fax: 01394 382392). *Location:* leave A12 at Melton Roundabout. After traffic lights, follow A1152 over level crossing, fork left at roundabout. Club is 400 yards on right. Heathland. 18 holes, 6299 yards. S.S.S. 71. 9 holes, 3191 yards. S.S.S. 71. Large practice ground. *Green Fees:* £42.00 18 hole course, £18.00 9 hole course. *Eating facilities:* main bar, casual bar and restaurant. *Visitors:* not before 9.30am, not at weekends on 18-hole course. Handicap Certificates mandatory on 18 hole course. No restriction on 9-hole course. Telephone call advisable. *Society Meetings:* by prior arrangement, maximum number 36. Professional: T. Johnson (01394 383213). Secretary: A.J. Bull (01394 382038; 01394 382392).

THORPENESS SUFFOLK

ROUND OFF A PERFECT DAY

Enjoy a break on the invigorating Heritage Coast. Play the challenging, mature 18-hole seaside course designed by the legendary James Braid.
Guests in the hotel can enjoy concessionary rates at Aldeburgh Golf Club, one of the top 100 courses in the British Isles.
A warm welcome, 36 comfortable en suite rooms and good food.

The Hotel & Golf Club, Thorpeness, Aldeburgh, Suffolk IP16 4NH
CALL NOW FOR YOUR FREE BROCHURE
Tel 01728 452176 Fax 01728 453868 www.thorpeness.co.uk

Golf in the Midlands

Jennifer Prentice

**Derbyshire • Herefordshire
Leicestershire & Rutland • Lincolnshire
Northamptonshire • Nottinghamshire • Shropshire
Staffordshire • Warwickshire • West Midlands
Worcestershire**

If a region's golfing strengths can be defined by the quality and accessibility of its golf courses, then the Midlands ranks high!

The exceptionally fine facilities, a good number widely recognised not only in this country but also throughout the world, attract visitors from far and wide.

The quality of the courses, as well as boosting the popularity of the region to golfers and tourists alike, also makes a major contribution to the expertise and development of the young golfers who play over them in their formative years. They are then well equipped to take on any challenges, however stiff, as amateurs or world ranking professionals if they choose to pursue golf as a career. Several current leading top professionals honed their skills on some of the Midlands' best known courses. Many golfers are eager to follow in their footsteps, even if not quite matching their prowess but just playing on a well deserved, enjoyable break, or as part of a longer family holiday.

Make no mistake, the Midlands offers plenty to attract all ages, with a multiplicity of other sporting activities and interests available close to golfing venues. There are great historic houses and sites, cultural venues such as theatres and galleries, and retail therapy highspots, along with a wide variety of accommodation in cities, or in beautiful, tranquil countryside. Value for money is supreme and here too the Midlands holds an enviable position, scoring well on feedback from visitors, whether staying in a golf hotel complex or in budget accommodation.

One of the biggest tournaments on the 2010 European Senior Tour was played at the luxurious Stapleford Park Hotel and Golf Course in rural Leicestershire. This course is the centrepiece of this world-renowned English sporting estate. The event attracted a powerful international field for the inaugural Handa Senior Masters with a £400,000 prize fund. There were two curtain raiser Pro/Ams too. Northants County Golf Club near Northampton staged the Seniors' PGA Professional Championship in late spring, the forth successive year the title has been decided there. The century-old heathland layout continues to pose a challenge to golfers of all abilities. Regional qualifiers for a number of top national PGA events included the Pro-Captain Challenge at De Vere Staverton Park Hotel and Golf Club, the Glenmuir PGA Championship qualifier at Little Aston, and two Midland courses were used for Open Championship regional qualifiers – Coventry and Enville.

The PGA Midland held several Order of Merit tournaments in 2010. The season opener – the Glazerite Trophy – was at Wellingborough; the PTS Invitational at South Staffs; the PDF Midland Masters at Kedleston Park; the Midland Open, supported by the Mark Group, at Birstall, near Leicester; the FineTurf Midland Professional Championship at De Vere Belton Woods; and the climax came with the Tour Championship at Cold Ashby – the highest spot in Northamptonshire.

Winter series events were held at the world-famous Belfry and at other hotel, golf and leisure venues, such as Marriott Forest of Arden in Warwickshire, and at Forest Pines, north Lincolnshire. Forest Pines hosted the final of the Skins PGA 4-Ball Championship with regional qualifying at Stapleford Park. The PGA Midland Assistants' Championship also had an autumn date – at Telford Hotel and Golf Resort, supported by Sky Caddie, and Breadsall Priory saw a Business Fort English PGA Championship qualifier. Golfers, including European Tour professionals, made a welcome return to the historic, highly attractive Nailcote Hall with its great amenities and a special atmosphere, for the British Par 3 Championship.

Many Midland hotels where facilities include golf courses, provide other first class services, not only for players, but also for their families, with plenty to enjoy either on-site or within a short distance, ensuring everyone is happy with their trip away, no matter the length of stay.

So whatever your taste in sport, well equipped gyms and pampering, the Midlands has it all!

12th green at De Vere Staverton Park Hotel & Golf Club, Northamptonshire

Derbyshire

ALFRETON. **Alfreton Golf Club,** Wingfield Road, Alfreton DE55 7LH (01773 832070). *Location:* B6024 (Matlock Road) one mile from Alfreton. Parkland course. 11holes, 5121 yards. S.S.S. 66. *Green Fees:* information not available. *Eating facilities:* bar snacks and fully licensed restaurant every day 10am - 9pm. *Visitors:* welcome Monday to Friday with reservation. *Society Meetings:* catered for. Lessons available from teaching professional by prior arrangement. Professional: (01773 831901). Secretary: S. Bradley. *

ASHBOURNE. **Ashbourne Golf Club Ltd,** Off Wyaston Road, Ashbourne DE6 1NB (01335 342078; Fax: 01335 347937). *Location:* Wyaston Road, Ashbourne, one and a half miles out of Ashbourne. Undulating parkland. 18 holes, 6402 yards. S.S.S. 70. Practice area. *Green Fees:* £30.00 weekdays, £35.00 weekends and Bank Holidays. Continuation of our special 2009 10th anniversary rate: weekday green fee £20.00 (not available with other green fee discount).Subject to review. *Eating facilities:* available daily; parties must make prior arrangement. *Visitors and Societies:* welcome by arrangement with Professional. Professional: Andrew Smith (01335 347960). Secretary: P.J. Mawdsley (01335 342078).
website: www.ashbournegolfclub.co.uk

BAKEWELL. **Bakewell Golf Club,** Station Road, Bakewell DE45 1GB (01629 812307). *Location:* Sheffield Road out of Bakewell, turn right up the hill after the river bridge. Parkland, scenic hillside course. 9 holes, 5240 yards. S.S.S. 68. *Green Fees:* information not available. *Eating facilities:* bar meals, formal catering except Mondays. *Visitors:* welcome weekdays; weekends by prior arrangement. *Society Meetings:* welcome by arrangement. Secretary: G. Holmes.*
website: www.bakewellgolfclub.co.uk

BRAILSFORD. **Brailsford Golf Club,** Pools Head Lane, Brailsford, Near Ashbourne DE6 3BU (01335 360096). *Location*: on the main A52 Derby to Ashbourne road, Derby 6 miles, Ashbourne 5 miles. Parkland course. 12 holes, planning permission granted for a further 6 holes. 5758 yards (18 holes), S.S.S. 68. Practice facilities and 15 bay covered, floodlit, driving range. *Green Fees*:information not provided. *Eating facilities*: available. *Visitors*: welcome at any time except Sunday mornings. Tuition available - two teaching Professionals. *Society Meetings*: welcome except Sunday mornings. Special rates available. Professional: David McCarthy (01335 360096).

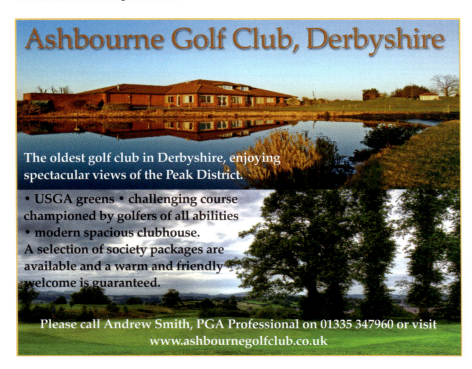

Derbyshire / MIDLANDS REGION

BURTON-ON-TRENT. Burton-on-Trent Golf Club, 43 Ashby Road East, Burton-on-Trent DE15 0PS (01283 544551). *Location:* three miles east of Burton-on-Trent on the A511 towards Ashby de la Zouch. Undulating parkland course with many trees, testing finishing hole. 18 holes, 6579 yards. S.S.S. 72. Practice ground. *Green Fees:* weekdays £40.00 per round, £50.00 per day; weekends and Bank Holidays £46.00 per round, £60.00 per day. Special rates by arrangement. *Eating facilities:* dining room, lounge bar. *Visitors:* welcome weekdays, restrictions at weekends and Bank Holidays. *Society Meetings:* welcome, apply in writing for terms. Professional: Gary Stafford (01283 562240). Secretary: Graham Duckmanton (01283 544251).
e-mail: thesecretary@burtonontrentgolfclub.co.uk
website: www.burtonontrentgolfclub.co.uk

BUXTON. Buxton and High Peak Golf Club, Town End, Waterswallows Road, Buxton SK17 7EN (Office: 01298 26263). *Location:* A6 one mile north of Buxton. Parkland, good positional play required. 18 holes, 5966 yards. S.S.S. 69. Practice facilities. *Green Fees:* weekdays £24.00 per round, £30.00 per day; weekends £30.00 per round, £36.00 per day. *Eating facilities:* full catering facilities. *Visitors:* welcome without reservation, ring at weekends. *Society Meetings:* welcome. Professional: John Lines (01298 26263). Secretary: Garry Bagguley.
e-mail: sec@bhpgc.co.uk
website: www.bhpgc.co.uk

BUXTON. The Cavendish Golf Club Ltd, Gadley Lane, Buxton SK17 6XD (01298 79708). *Location:* three quarters of a mile from town centre, on Leek Road A53, signposted. Parkland/moorland course, designed by Dr Alister Mackenzie who designed Augusta. Parkland/moorland course. 18 holes, 5833 yards. S.S.S. 68. Practice ground. *Green Fees:* information not available. *Eating facilities:* restaurant, usual bar hours, snacks, meals available at all times. *Visitors:* apply to Golf Shop. *Society Meetings:* catered for weekdays and Sundays, apply to the Secretary for booking arrangements. Admin: S. Davis (Tel & Fax: 01298 79708).

CHAPEL-EN-LE-FRITH. Chapel-en-le-Frith Golf Club, The Cockyard, Manchester Road, Chapel-en-le-Frith, High Peak SK23 9UH (01298 812118). *Location:* 13 miles southeast of Stockport, close to Buxton on the B5470. A true test of golf in a beautiful parkland setting. 18 holes, 6400 yards. S.S.S. 72. Practice ground. *Green Fees:* information not available. *Eating facilities:* bar snacks and à la carte menu. *Visitors:* welcome, small numbers without reservation. *Society Meetings:* tailor-made packages by arrangement. Professional: D. Cullen (01298 812118). Secretary: D. Goldfinch (01298 813943; Fax: 01298 814990).*
e-mail: info@chapelgolf.co.uk

CHESTERFIELD. Birch Hall Golf Club, Sheffield Road, Unstone, Near Chesterfield S18 5DH (01246 291979). *Location:* off A61 between Sheffield and Chesterfield. Moorland course with outstanding views. 18 holes, 6409 yards, 5860 metres. S.S.S. 71. Practice area. *Green Fees:* information not available. *Eating facilities:* bar with meals available. *Visitors:* welcome but prior booking essential. *Society Meetings:* welcome but prior booking essential. Hon. Gen. Secretary: E. Gallagher.*

CHESTERFIELD. Chesterfield Golf Club Ltd, Matlock Road, Walton, Chesterfield S42 7LA (01246 279256; Fax: 01246 276622). *Location:* two miles from Chesterfield town centre on Matlock road (A632); Junction 29 M1. Parkland with natural hazards. 18 holes, 6281 yards. S.S.S. 70. Practice ground, putting green. *Green Fees:* information not available. *Visitors:* welcome weekdays, and Sundays after 1.30pm; other times at weekend as members' guests only. Trolleys. Snooker. *Society Meetings:* catered for on application. Professional: Michael McLean (01246 276297). Secretary: Trevor Marshall.*

CHESTERFIELD. Grassmoor Golf Centre, North Wingfield Road, Grassmoor, Chesterfield S42 5EA (01246 856044; Fax: 01246 853486). *Location:* 4 miles M1 Junction 29 or A61 near Chesterfield. Heathland course incorporating water hazards, testing greens, testing par 3's for distance. 18 holes, 5723 yards, S.S.S. 68. 25 bay covered, floodlit range. 9 hole practice putting area and a practice area. *Green Fees:* weekdays £12.00, weekends £15.00. County Cards reduction. *Eating facilities:* excellent bar and restaurant facilities available 8am to 10pm. *Visitors:* welcome, weekends included, 6 days' advance booking system by phone. *Society Meetings:* group bookings and societies welcome, including at weekends. Lessons available with Senior PGA Professional. Open daily 8am to 10pm, everyone welcome. Professional: Gary Hagues. Club Manager: Helen Hagues (01246 856044).
website: www.grassmoorgolf.co.uk

CHESTERFIELD. Stanedge Golf Club, Walton Hay Farm, Chesterfield S45 0LW (01246 566156). *Location:* five miles south-west of Chesterfield, off B5057 near "Red Lion" public house. Course 1000ft above sea level, views of four counties. 10 holes, 5786 yards. *Green Fees:* information not provided. *Visitors:* welcome, before 4pm unless with member. *Society Meetings:* catered for by prior arrangement. Secretary: Chris Shaw (01246 566156).

CHESTERFIELD. Tapton Park Golf & Leisure Centre, Crow Lane, Chesterfield S41 0EQ (01246 239500; Fax: 01246 555140). *Location:* behind railway station. Wooded parkland course. 18 hole course, 9 hole course and pitch and putt course. 18 hole course - 6025 yards. S.S.S. 69; 9 hole course - 2595 yards, Par 34. Putting and pitching greens. *Green Fees:* information not available. *Eating facilities:* bar and restaurant open to the public. *Visitors:* welcome at all times, booking for 18 hole course taken six days in advance. Club/Trolley/Locker hire. *Society Meetings:* welcome on written application. Professional: Andrew Carnall. Secretary: (01246 273887; Fax: 01246 558024). *

THE GOLF GUIDE 2011 — MIDLANDS REGION / Derbyshire — 187

CODNOR. **Ormonde Fields Golf Club,** Nottingham Road, Codnor, Ripley DE5 9RG (01773 744157). *Location*: five miles M1 Junction 26 towards Ripley on A610. Parkland. 18 holes, 6504 yards. S.S.S. 72. Practice area, putting green. *Green Fees:* information not provided. *Eating facilities:* full restaurant available. *Visitors:* unrestricted. *Society Meetings:* catered for; book through Secretary. Professional: R. White (01773 742987). Secretary: K. Constable (01773 570043).

DERBY. **Allestree Park Golf Club,** Allestree Hall, Duffield Road, Allestree, Derby DE22 2EU (01332 552971). *Location*: 3 miles north of Derby city centre on A6. Municipal undulating parkland course with outstanding views. 18 holes, 5728 yards. Par 68, S.S.S. 68. Practice ground and putting green. *Green Fees:* weekdays £11.50, weekends £13.50. Off peak rates and discounts available. *Eating facilities:* full bar, catering available. *Visitors:* always welcome, call Pro Shop for booking a time. *Society Meetings:* available any time weekdays after 1pm, weekends – details on request. Professional: Leigh Woodward (01332 550616. Secretary: Clive Barker (01332 552971).
e-mail: Leigh.woodward@derby.gov.uk

DERBY. **Derby Golf Club,** Wilmore Road, Sinfin, Derby DE24 9HD (office: 01332 766323). *Location:* two miles city centre. Parkland. 18 holes, 6185 yards, 5653 metres. S.S.S. 70. Practice area. *Green Fees:* information not provided. *Eating facilities:* bar and catering available. *Visitors:* welcome at any time (Saturdays until 1pm reserved for club members). Phone Pro Shop for tee times. *Society Meetings:* welcome at any time (except Saturdays until 1pm). Professional: Leigh Woodward (01332 766462; Fax: 01332 769004). Hon. Secretary: D.P. Anderson (01332 766323).

DERBY. **Marriott Breadsall Priory Hotel and Country Club,** Moor Road, Morley DE7 6DL (01332 836016; Fax: 01332 836089). *Location:* turn off the A61 towards Breadsall, proceed on Croft Lane, turn left into Rectory Lane, then bear right onto Moor Road, continue past the Church for approximately one mile. Two courses - Priory is a parkland course and Moorland is a contrast of open moorland. Priory - 18 holes, 5875 yards. S.S.S. 68 off yellow tees; Moorland - 18 holes, 5820 yards. S.S.S. 68 off yellow tees. Practice area and putting green; floodlit driving range. *Green Fees:* information not available. *Visitors:* welcome any time subject to availability. *Society Meetings:* welcome at any time subject to availability. Hotel has 112 bedrooms, leisure club and conference facilities. Golf buggies. Professional: Darren Steels.

DUFFIELD. **Chevin Golf Club,** Golf Lane, Duffield Belper DE56 4ES (01332 841864). *Location:* five miles north of Derby on A6 at Duffield village. Hilly course, part parkland, part moorland with superb views. 18 holes, 6057 yards, 5451 metres. S.S.S. 69. Two practice areas. *Green Fees:* information not provided. *Eating facilities:* bar snacks and diningroom. *Visitors:* always welcome; Handicap Certificates required. Snooker. *Society Meetings:* welcome weekdays and weekends. Professional: W. Bird (01332 841112). Secretary: M.E. Riley (01332 841864; Fax: 01332 844028).

GLOSSOP. **Glossop and District Golf Club,** Sheffield Road, Glossop SK13 7PU (01457 865247). *Location:* off A57, one mile from town centre. Moorland course. 11 holes, 5800 yards. S.S.S. 68. *Green Fees:* information not provided. *Eating facilities:* full catering facilities available. *Visitors:* welcome with reservation through Professional, except Saturdays during playing season. *Society Meetings:* welcome, same restrictions as visitors. Professional: Philip Haynes (01457 853117). Secretary: K. Harrison.
website: www.glossopgolfclub.co.uk

Please mention THE GOLF GUIDE when you enquire about clubs or accommodation

---

ALLESTREE PARK AND SINFIN GOLF COURSES

Two contrasting mature 18-hole 'Pay and Play' golf courses in the city of Derby.
Allestree Park is undulating, and set in the former grounds of Allestree Hall, and **Sinfin**, established in 1923, is generally flat, and suitable for golfers of all ages.

Advance booking advisable; telephone bookings accepted.
GOLF SOCIETIES WELCOME by prior arrangement.
Please contact us for full details of our great value Society Day golf and meals packages.
GOLF TUITION AVAILABLE with PGA Golf Professionals. Beginners welcome.

Allestree Park
Golf Course
Allestree Hall
Duffield Road
Allestree, Derby
DE22 2EH
Tel: 01332 550616

Sinfin
Golf Course
Wilmore Road
Sinfin
Derby
DE24 9HD
Tel: 01332 766462

HORSLEY. **Horsley Lodge Golf Club and Hotel,** Smalley Mill Road, Horsley DE21 5BL (01332 780838; Fax: 01332 781118). *Location:* north of Derby on A61, past Little Eaton, right turn to Horsley – signposted. Parkland. 18 holes, 6381 yards. S.S.S. 70. Par 71. Driving range. *Green Fees:* information not available. *Eating facilities:* two bars, bar meals, à la carte restaurant; function room seats 140. *Visitors:* welcome weekdays and some weekends but not on competition days. Four-star accommodation available. *Society Meetings:* by appointment. Professional: Mark Whithorn (01332 780838; Fax: 01332 781118). Company Secretary: Richard Salt. Hon. Secretary (club): Dennis Wake (01332 780838).* website: www. horsleylodge.co.uk

ILKESTON. **Erewash Valley Golf Club Ltd,** Stanton-by-Dale, Near Ilkeston DE7 4QR (0115 932 3258). *Location:* Junction 25 of the M1, Stanton-by-Dale village. Parkland with two holes in an old quarry. 18 holes, 6557 yards, 5996 metres. S.S.S. 71. Driving, pitching and putting practice area. *Green Fees:* weekdays £37.00 per round, £48.00 per day; weekends and Bank Holidays £48.00 per round. DUGC Card reduced rate. *Eating facilities:* bar snacks available at all times, diningroom service on request. *Visitors:* welcome at all times subject to club events and society bookings. *Society Meetings:* welcome Monday, Wednesday and Friday only. Professional: Darren Bartlett (0115 932 4667). Secretary: Neil Cockbill (0115 932 3258).
e-mail: secretary@erewashvalley.co.uk
website: www.erewashvalley.co.uk

THE APPEARANCE OF AN ASTERISK (*) AT THE END OF A CLUB OR COURSE ENTRY INDICATES THAT UP-TO-DATE INFORMATION HAS NOT BEEN SUPPLIED

ILKESTON. **Ilkeston Borough Golf Club,** Peewit Municipal Golf Course, West End Drive, Ilkeston DE7 5GH (01602 304550). *Location:* one mile west of Ilkeston market place. Slightly hilly meadowland. 9 holes, 4116 yards. S.S.S. 60. *Green Fees:* information not available. *Eating facilities:* not available. *Visitors:* welcome, no restrictions. Secretary: B. Smith (01159 300824).

MATLOCK. **Matlock Golf Club,** Chesterfield Road, Matlock Moor, Matlock DE4 5LZ (01629 582191). *Location*: Matlock-Chesterfield road, A632, one mile out of Matlock, left hand side main road. Moorland with extensive views. 18 holes, yellow tees, 5808 yards. S.S.S. 68. *Green Fees:* £30.00 per round, £35.00 per day. *Eating facilities:* snacks available, luncheons and evening meals by arrangement. *Visitors:* welcome weekdays. *Society Meetings:* catered for Monday to Friday. Professional: C.J. Goodman (01629 584934). Secretary: M. Wain.

MICKLEOVER. **Mickleover Golf Club,** Uttoxeter Road, Mickleover, Derby DE3 9AD (Tel & Fax: 01332 516011). *Location:* three miles west of Derby on the A516/B5020 to Uttoxeter. Undulating course. 18 holes, 5705 yards, 5217 metres. S.S.S. 68. *Green Fees:* £30.00 Monday - Sunday. Societies £25.00. *Eating facilities:* full restaurant facilities. *Visitors:* welcome, no restrictions; telephone Professional before arrival. *Society Meetings:* Monday to Friday. Professional: Tim Coxon (01332 518662). Secretary: Graham Finney (01332 516011).

MICKLEOVER. **Pastures Golf Club,** Social Centre, Off Merlin Way, Mickleover DE3 0DQ (01332 521074). *Location:* four miles west of Derby, A516, half a mile past Mickleover Court Hotel. Undulating meadowland. 9 holes, 5014 yards. S.S.S. 64. Practice area, putting green. *Green Fees:* information not provided. *Eating facilities:* snacks; bar/lounge bar. *Visitors:* welcome, DUGC Card holders welcome. *Society Meetings:* welcome any weekday by arrangement, catering available. Secretary: C. Hunt (07766 098628).

Horsley Lodge
Golf Club • Restaurant • Hotel
18 spectacular holes on the edge of The Derbyshire Peak District.
Friday and Sunday night Golf Breaks from £50pp. (Bed, Breakfast and 18 holes of Golf)
VisitEngland ★★★★
Horsley Lodge, Horsley, Derbyshire DE21 5BL
Tel: 01332 780838 • www.horsleylodge.co.uk
Founded 1990

THE GOLF GUIDE 2011 — MIDLANDS REGION / Derbyshire

MORLEY. Morley Hayes Golf Club, Main Road, Morley DE7 6DG (01332 782000). *Location:* just north of Junction 25 of M1, on A608 between Derby and Heanor. Championship parkland course with water features and established trees, surrounded by mature woodland and deer park. Manor course, 18 holes, 6891 yards. Par 72. Tower course, 9 holes, 1614 yards, Par 30. 17 bay driving range. Pay and Play course. *Green Fees:* information not available. *Eating facilities:* two bars, bar meals, à la carte restaurant, function suites. Hotel, 32 bedrooms; golf breaks available. *Society Meetings:* company and society days welcome seven days a week. Professionals: James Whatley, Steve Astle. Golf Manager: Daniel Delaney (01332 782000).*
e-mail: enquiries@morleyhayes.com
website: www.morleyhayes.com

QUARNDON. Kedleston Park Golf Club, Kedleston, Quarndon, Derby DE22 5JD (01332 840035). *Location:* Derby, follow signs to Kedleston Hall. Parkland with lakes. 18 holes, 6731 yards. S.S.S. 72. *Green Fees:* weekdays £40.00 per round, £50.00 per day. *Eating facilities:* full catering, bars. *Visitors:* welcome Sunday to Friday. Carts available. *Society Meetings:* welcome Monday and Friday. Professional: Paul Wesselingh. General Manager: S.P. Kay (01332 840035).
e-mail: secretary@kedlestonparkgolfclub.co.uk
website: www.kedlestonparkgolfclub.co.uk

RISLEY. Maywood Golf Club, Off Rushy Lane, Risley, Draycott DE72 3SW (0115 939 2306). *Location*: between Derby and Nottingham at Risley, two minutes from Junction 25 M1. Parkland course. 18 holes, 6424 yards. S.S.S. 71. Practice area. *Green Fees:* information not available. *Eating facilities:* licensed bar and bar meals. *Visitors:* welcome, please phone to check availability. *Society Meetings:* rates on request. Professional: Simon Purcell-Jackson (0115 949 0043). Manager: Miss Tory Moon. Proprietors: Miss Tory Moon and Brian Tucker.
e-mail: maywoodgolfclub@btinternet.com
        torymoon@btinternet.com
website: www.maywoodgolfclub.com

SHEFFIELD. Renishaw Park Golf Club, Golf House, Mill Lane, Renishaw, Sheffield S21 3UZ (01246 432044). *Location:* A6135 Barlborough (Junction 30 M1) to Sheffield. Parkland/meadowland. 18 holes, 6262 yards. S.S.S. 70. Practice area. *Green Fees:* weekdays £25.00 per round, £38.00 per day; weekends £35.00 per round, £42.00 per day. *Eating facilities:* bar meals, full restaurant. *Visitors:* welcome without reservation (advisable to ring Pro prior to arrival). *Society Meetings:* by prior arrangement. Full day package available. Professional: N. Parkinson (01246 435484). Course and Club Manager: M. Nelson (01246 432044).

SHEFFIELD. Sickleholme Golf Club, Bamford, Hope Valley S33 0BN (01433 651306). *Location:* 3A625 west of Sheffield, right at Marquis of Granby, Bamford. Scenic wooded course in the Peak District. 18 holes, 6064 yards. S.S.S. 69. Practice ground, putting green. *Green Fees:* information not available. *Eating facilities:* bar snacks and restaurants. *Visitors:* no visitors Wednesday mornings; must be members of a recognised Golf Club; advance booking required. *Society Meetings:* welcome by prior arrangement. Professional/ Secretary: P. H. Taylor (01433 651306).*

SHIRLAND. Shirland Golf Club, Lower Delves, Shirland, Alfreton DE55 6AU (01773 834935). *Location*: one mile north of Alfreton off A61, three miles from M1 Junction 28 via A38. Tree-lined rolling parkland, 18 holes, 6072 yards. S.S.S. 69. Par 71. Practice ground. *Green Fees:* information not available. *Eating facilities:* bar meals. Conference and banquet rooms. *Visitors:* unrestricted weekdays, but must book through Manager at weekends. *Society Meetings:* welcome. Manager: A. Colton (01773 834935). Secretary: R. Lambert (07811 339068).*

STOCKPORT. The New Mills Golf Club, Shaw Marsh, New Mills, High Peak SK22 4QE (01663 743485). *Location:* signposted off the B6101 from Marple to New Mills, between Buxton and Stockport. Relatively flat upland course, magnificent views, excellent greens. 18 holes, 5604 yards. S.S.S. 67. Large practice area and driving range. New members accepted. *Green Fees:* information not provided. *Eating facilities:* full catering, very good value; wide range of food. *Visitors:* welcome any day but not competition days, contact the Professional for these dates. *Society Meetings:* welcome. Professional: Carl Cross (01663 746161). Secretary: John A. Abson (07764 192699).

FHG GUIDES
www.holidayguides.com

Two courses specifically designed to accommodate all levels of expertise.
The Manor Course 18 holes par 72, the Tower Course 9 holes Par 30.
Both are set within parkland with water features and established trees.
• 17-bay all weather driving range with Power Tees • Professional tuition
• Roosters Bar • Spike Bar • Dovecote Restaurant • 4★ Morley Hayes Hotel

Morley Hayes Golf Club, Main Road, Morley, Derbyshire DE7 6DG
Tel: 01332 782000 • Fax: 01332 781094 • www.morleyhayes.com • enquiries@morleyhayes.com

Herefordshire

BELMONT. **Belmont Lodge and Golf,** Belmont, Hereford HR2 9SA (01432 352666; Fax: 01432 358090). *Location:* one and a half miles south of Hereford, off A465 to Abergavenny. Parkland running alongside the River Wye offering tremendous views. 18 holes, 6369 yards. S.S.S. 72. *Green Fees:* information not available. *Eating facilities:* restaurant meals and bar snacks. *Visitors:* welcome at all times, advisable to check availability first. Other facilities available include a 30 bedroom hotel, tennis, fishing and walking; buggies and trolleys for hire. *Society Meetings:* catered for, special packages available. Professional: (01432 352717). Reception/Reservations: (01432 352666; Fax: 01432 358090). General Manager: Christopher T. Smith.*
e-mail: info@belmont-hereford.co.uk
website: www.belmont-hereford.co.uk

HAY-ON-WYE. **Summerhill Golf Course,** Clifford, Near Hay-on-Wye HR3 5EW (01497 820451). *Location:* half a mile out of Hay on B4350 for Clifford and Whitney Toll Bridge and Hereford Road A438. Parkland. 9 holes 2929 yards (18 holes, 5858 off white tees). S.S.S. 68. *Green Fees:* information not available. *Eating facilities:* restaurant, two bars and large function room. *Visitors:* welcome, not on Thursday evening or Sunday mornings. *Society Meetings:* welcome Monday, Wednesday and Friday. Professional: Will Dowd. Secretary: Mike Tom.*
website: www.summerhillgolfcourse.co.uk

HEREFORD. **Burghill Valley Golf Club,** Tillington Road, Burghill, Hereford HR4 7RW (01432 760456; Fax: 01432 761654). *Location:* three miles north-west of Hereford. From Worcester and North (avoiding Hereford city), take A4103 for two miles, first right after traffic lights. From south (via Hereford city) take A4110, turn left at traffic lights after Three Elms Inn and then first right. Follow signs to club. Pleasantly undulating parkland including two lakes, and easy walking with some interesting holes through mature cider orchards. 18 holes, 6224 yards. S.S.S. 70. Large practice area. *Green Fees:* on application. *Eating facilities:* bar and dining room with full catering available every day. *Visitors:* welcome at any time, must book tee time with Professional. *Society Meetings:* by prior arrangement with the Manager. Special rates available, please enquire. Professionals: Keith Preece PGA, Andy Cameron PGA (01432 760808; Fax: 01432 761654). General Manager: Keith Smith.
e-mail: info@bvgc.co.uk
website: www.bvgc.co.uk

HEREFORD. **The Herefordshire Golf Club,** Raven's Causeway, Wormsley, Hereford HR4 8LY (01432 830219). *Location:* six miles north-west of Hereford on a B road to Weobley. Undulating parkland course. 18 holes, 6055 yards. S.S.S. 70. *Green Fees:* information not provided. *Eating facilities:* catering available at all times. *Visitors:* all welcome. *Society Meetings:* Societies given a warm, friendly welcome. Catering available 7 days a week. Packages from £25.00pp. Please arrange through Pro Shop (01432 830465) or Secretary (01432 830219).
e-mail: herefordshire.golf@breathe.com
website: www.herefordshiregolfclub.co.uk

A Taste of Countryside on the edge of the City
Our restaurant and bar are open every day including Sunday

Contact 01432 352666 for full detail and membership forms
Email info@belmont-hereford.co.uk
www.belmont-hereford.co.uk

BELMONT LODGE & GOLF

Burghill Valley Golf Club
WELCOMES NEW MEMBERS, VISITORS & SOCIETIES

This beautiful Herefordshire course has developed into one of the leading clubs in the county, setting a challenge to players of all abilities. Excellent service, highly praised greens and a warm and friendly clubhouse atmosphere make all 19 holes a pleasure.

Tillington Road
Burghill
Hereford • HR4 7RW
Tel: 01432 760456
Fax: 01432 761654
e-mail: info@bvgc.co.uk
www.bvgc.co.uk

THE GOLF GUIDE 2011 — MIDLANDS REGION / Herefordshire

HEREFORD. **HMGC Golf Club,** Halo Golf, Hereford Leisure Centre, Holmer Road, Hereford HR4 9UD (01432 344376; Fax: 01432 266281). *Location:* follow A49 Leominster to Hereford road; north of city centre next to Leisure Centre. Flat parkland course with excellent greens all year round. 9 holes, 3060 yards. S.S.S. 68 for 18 holes. Large practice area, bunker and practice green. *Green Fees:* information not available. *Eating facilities:* full catering and bar in Leisure Centre. *Visitors:* welcome at all times. *Society Meetings:* welcome, prices on application. Professional: Gary Morgan (01432 344376; Fax: 01432 266281).*

KINGTON. **Kington Golf Club,** Bradnor Hill, Kington HR5 3RE (01544 230340). *Location*: one mile out of Kington, on B4355 to Presteigne. Easy walking hill course with superb greens and views over seven counties. Highest 18 hole course in England. 18 holes, 5966 yards. S.S.S. 69. *Green Fees:* weekdays £22.00 per round, £28.00 per day; weekends and Bank Holidays £28.00 per round, £34.00 per day. *Eating facilities:* full catering and bar facilities. *Visitors:* welcome. Please contact Professional to ensure course is available. Buggies available through the Professional. *Society Meetings:* by arrangement with the Professional. Professional: (01544 231320). Secretary: Glyn R. Wictome (01544 340270).
e-mail: kingtongolf@ukonline.co.uk
 glyn@wictome.com
website: www.kingtongolf.co.uk

LEOMINSTER. **Grove Golf & Bowl,** Ford Bridge, Leominster HR6 0LE (01568 610602). *Location:* three miles south of Leominster on A49. Two linked loops of 9 holes. Deer Run 6153 yards. S.S.S. 71. Badgers 4020 yards, S.S.S.60. Full USGA spec greens, challenging parkland courses with many water features. Floodlit, covered driving range. Golf shop, buggy and equipment hire. *Green Fees:* from £6.00 for 9 holes. *Eating facilities:* full catering and bars. *Visitors:* welcome anytime. 8 lanes 10-pin bowling. Professional: Pete Lowery (01568 615333).
website: www.grovegolfandbowl.co.uk

LEOMINSTER. **Leominster Golf Club,** Ford Bridge, Leominster HR6 0LE (01568 610055). *Location:* three miles south of Leominster on A49 bypass, clearly signed. Undulating parkland with some holes alongside River Lugg and extensive views over Herefordshire countryside. 18 holes, 6026 yards. S.S.S. 69. *Green Fees:* weekdays £20.00 per round, £25.00 per day; weekends £25.00 per round, £30.00 per day. *Eating facilities:* bar open daily, full catering daily. *Visitors:* welcome every day; please telephone to check availability. Trolley and buggy hire available. *Society Meetings:* most welcome. From £24.00 weekdays, £29.00 weekends, golf and catering. Professional: Nigel Clarke (01568 611402). Secretary: Ian Hamilton (Tel & Fax: 01568 610055). Manager: Jessica Kingswood.
e-mail: contact@leominstergolfclub.co.uk
website: www.leominstergolfclub.co.uk

The Herefordshire Golf Club

Tel: 01432 830219 • Professional: 01432 830465
Fax: 01432 830095 • Bar/Kitchen: 01432 830877

The Club provides comfortable changing accommodation, and an excellent Clubhouse in which to wine and dine. Visitors are welcome, and are assured of a friendly reception.

Ravens Causeway, Wormsley, Near Hereford HR4 8LY
e-mail: herefordshire.golf@breathe.com
www.herefordshiregolfclub.co.uk

The Highest Golf Club in England

Kington Golf Club

Kington Golf Club is the highest 18 hole golf course in England. Founded in 1925, it is located on Bradnor Hill, just outside the medieval town of Kington in the beautiful county of Herefordshire but nestling on the border of Wales. Members and Visitors to the golf club can enjoy first class facilities, with the well appointed lounge and dining room offering fine views of the outstanding finishing hole and the Brecon Beacons National Park.

Tel: 01544 230340 • Fax: 01544 231951
e-mail: kingtongolf@ukonline.co.uk • www.kingtongolf.co.uk
Bradnor Hill, Kington, Herefordshire HR5 3RE

Herefordshire / MIDLANDS REGION

ROSS-ON-WYE. The Ross-on-Wye Golf Club, Gorsley, Ross-on-Wye HR9 7UT (01989 720267; Fax: 01989 720212). *Location:* adjacent Junction 3 M50, five miles east of Ross-on-Wye. Tree lined, undulating parkland course. 18 holes, 6451 yards. S.S.S. 71. Driving range, practice area. *Green Fees:* please ring for details. *Eating facilities:* full restaurant catering, excluding Mondays. *Visitors:* welcome any day if prior arrangement made with Professional or Secretary. Buggies and trolleys available. Snooker tables (2). *Society Meetings:* welcome, minimum 16. Tee reservations Wednesdays to Fridays. Professional: P. Middleton (01989 720439). Secretary: Sarah Creighton (01989 720267; Fax: 01989 720212). e-mail: admin@therossonwyegolfclub.co.uk website: www.therossonwyegolfclub.co.uk

ROSS-ON-WYE. South Herefordshire Golf Club, Twin Lakes, Upton Bishop, Ross-on-Wye HR9 7UA (01989 780535; Fax: 01989 740611). *Location:* end roundabout of M50 at Ross take B4221 to Upton Bishop, in Upton Bishop turn right, club half a mile. Good test of golf for all standards with variety of holes. Superb views. Rarely on temporary greens in Winter. 18 holes S.S.S. 72. 16 bay covered, floodlit driving range. *Green Fees:* information not available. *Eating facilities:* fully licensed bar serving snacks and full meals. *Visitors:* always welcome, no restrictions. Ring to reserve tee time. Buggies and trolleys available. Fully qualified PGA Professional, club fitting centre, Pro shop. Free junior training Saturday mornings, group lessons available. *Society Meetings:* always welcome. Director of Golf: Lewis Hanney.*
e-mail: info@herefordshiregolf.co.uk
website: www.herefordshiregolf.co.uk

Leicestershire & Rutland

ASHBY DE LA ZOUCH. **Willesley Park Golf Club,** Measham Road, Ashby de la Zouch LE65 2PF (01530 414596). *Location:* on B5006 towards Tamworth, one mile from centre of Ashby. Wooded parkland, semi-heathland. 18 holes, 6290 yards. S.S.S. 71. *Green Fees:* weekdays £37.00, weekends £45.00. *Eating facilities:* dining room and bar. *Visitors:* welcome with reservation. *Society Meetings:* catered for Wednesday, Thursday and Friday. Professional: B.J. Hill (01530 414820). Secretary: Mrs T. Harlow (01530 414596).
e-mail: info@willesleypark.com
website: www.willesleypark.com

BIRSTALL. **Birstall Golf Club,** Station Road, Birstall LE4 3BB (0116 267 4450). *Location*: three miles north of Leicester on A6, adjacent to Great Central Steam Railway. Parkland with mature trees. 18 holes, 6239 yards. S.S.S. 71. Practice ground. *Green Fees*: £30.00 per round, £35.00 per day weekdays; £40.00 per round weekends. *Eating facilities*: all day bar menu. *Visitors*: Welcome. *Society Meetings*: minimum 20, catered for by prior arrangement from £27.00 per person. Professional: Dave Clark (0116 267 5245). Secretary: Mrs S.E. Chilton (0116 267 4322).
website: www.birstallgolfclub.co.uk

BLABY. **Blaby Golf Centre,** Lutterworth Road, Blaby LE8 4DP (0116 278 4804). Flat parkland. 9 holes, S.S.S. 68. Par 4 9-hole pitch and putt. *Green Fees*: 9 holes £7.00, 9 holes Pitch & Putt £4.00. 18 hole American Adventure Crazy Golf £4.00 per round. *Eating facilities*: cafe and outside terrace overlooking courses. *Visitors*: welcome.
website: www.blabygolfcourse.com

BOTCHESTON. **Forest Hill Golf and Country Club,** Markfield Lane, Near Botcheston LE9 9FH (01455 824800; Fax: 01455 828522). *Location*: close to Leicester, near M1 Junction 21a. An established, well presented course which has undergone a major investment. 18 holes, 6490 yards, Par 72. 26-bay floodlit driving range with new power tees; new 9-hole short game area. *Green Fees*: £26.00-£30.00. *Eating facilities*: available all day. *Visitors*: welcome. Buggy and trolley hire available. *Society Meetings*: welcome; packages available. PGA Professional: Richard Hughes.
website: www.foresthillgolfclub.co.uk

Please mention THE GOLF GUIDE when you enquire about clubs or accommodation

Cosby Golf Club, Cosby, Leicester

COSBY. **Cosby Golf Club,** Chapel Lane, off Broughton Road, Cosby, Leicester LE9 1RG (0116 2864759; Fax: 0116 2864484). *Location:* eight miles south of Leicester, four miles from Junction 21 M1. Undulating parkland. 18 holes, 6474 yards. S.S.S. 71. Floodlit driving range. *Green Fees:* £28.00 per round, £40.00 per day. *Eating facilities:* wide range of snacks and meals always available. *Visitors:* most welcome before 4pm weekdays. Handicap Certificates may be required for all visitors. *Society Meetings*: welcome, prior booking essential. Professional: Gary Coysh (0116 2864759). Secretary/ Manager: Peggy Remington (0116 2864759; Fax: 0116 2864484).
e-mail: secretary@cosbygolfclub.co.uk
website: www.cosbygolfclub.co.uk

EAST GOSCOTE. **Beedles Lake Golf Centre,** 170 Broome Lane, East Goscote LE7 3WQ (0116 260 7086). *Location:* off A46 just north of Leicester, through village of Ratcliffe on the Wreake. Fairly flat course in river valley, adjoining lake. 18 holes, 6641 yards, 6156 metres. S.S.S. 72. 17-bay floodlit driving range. *Green Fees:* weekdays £16.00, weekends £22.00. Twilight fees £12.00. 2010 rates (subject to review). *Eating facilities*: restaurant and bar available. *Visitors:* always very welcome. *Society Meetings*: welcome but with restricted tee-times at weekends. Steward: (0116 260 7086). Professional: Sean Byrne (0116 260 6759). Manager: Jon Coleman (0116 260 7086).
e-mail: joncoleman@jelson.co.uk
website: www.beedleslake.co.uk

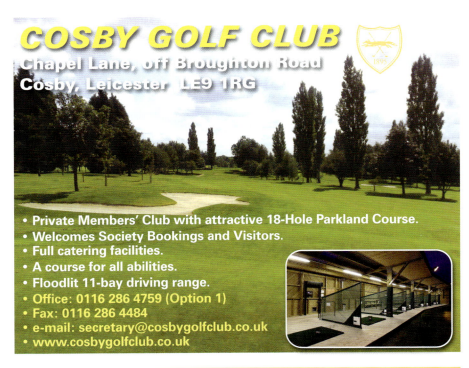

COSBY GOLF CLUB
Chapel Lane, off Broughton Road
Cosby, Leicester LE9 1RG

- Private Members' Club with attractive 18-Hole Parkland Course.
- Welcomes Society Bookings and Visitors.
- Full catering facilities.
- A course for all abilities.
- Floodlit 11-bay driving range.
- Office: 0116 286 4759 (Option 1)
- Fax: 0116 286 4484
- e-mail: secretary@cosbygolfclub.co.uk
- www.cosbygolfclub.co.uk

Beedles Lake Golf Centre

170 Broome Lane
East Goscote, Leicester LE7 3WQ
Tel: 0116 2607086
e-mail: joncoleman@jelson.co.uk
www.beedleslake.co.uk

A fine all-year parkland course situated in the heart of the Wreake Valley. We cater for all standards of golfer and offer value for money membership rates and green fees. Societies welcome. • Driving range with Power tee bays, putting green, chipping area • Excellent bar and catering facilities. • Resident PGA Professional
• Well stocked shop • Conference facilities, Weddings and functions catered for in our rooms and conservatory.
• Fishing on our Carp/Coarse fishing lake.
Visitors can always expect a very warm and friendly welcome and atmosphere at Beedles Lake.

ENDERBY. Enderby Golf Course, Mill Lane, Enderby LE19 4LX (0116 2849388) *Location:* two miles from M1/M69 Junction 21 roundabout. Gently undulating course with lakes and ditches. 9 holes. 2900/5800 yards. S.S.S. 71. Par 36/72. *Green Fees:* weekdays £9.95, weekends and Bank Holidays £12.25. *Eating facilities*: two bars, restaurants, open 9.30am to 10.30pm. *Visitors:* welcome at all times, no booking required. Leisure centre, bowls, squash, badminton, sauna, solarium, fitness suite, etc. Professional/Secretary: Chris d'Araujo.

HINCKLEY. Hinckley Golf Club, Leicester Road, Hinckley LE10 3DR (01455 615124; Fax: 01455 890841). *Location:* situated one mile from Hinckley, just off Hinckley's A47 perimeter road. Parkland with lakeside features. 18 holes, 6517 yards, 5959 metres. S.S.S. 71. Practice area for members. *Green Fees:* information not available. *Eating facilities:* bar meals daily except Sundays. *Visitors:* welcome except Tuesdays and weekends. *Society Meetings:* Mondays and Wednesdays by appointment. Professional: R. Jones (01455 615014). Finance and Administration Manager: Y. Watts (01455 615124).*
e-mail: rjones@hinckleygolfclub.com
website: www.hinckleygolfclub.com

KIRBY MUXLOE. Kirby Muxloe Golf Club, Station Road, Kirby Muxloe LE9 2EP (0116 2393457). *Location:* Junction 21a M1, just off A47 heading to Hinckley, towards Kirby Muxloe village. Parkland, 5th tee is set outside the course. 18 holes, 6428 yards. S.S.S. 71. Driving range, practice area and tuition from Professional. *Green Fees:* very competitive. *Eating facilities:* full restaurant and bar. *Visitors:* welcome every day except Tuesday and Saturday. Advisable to phone in advance. Snooker room. *Society Meetings:* by arrangement with Manager. Professional: B. Whipham (Tel & Fax: 0116 2392813).
e-mail: kirbymuxloegolf@btconnect.com

LEICESTER. Humberstone Heights Golf Club, Gipsy Lane, Leicester LE5 0TB (0116 276 1905). *Location:* A563 ring road, Uppingham side of Leicester. Parkland. 18 holes, 6343 yards. S.S.S. 70. 30 bay driving range, 9 hole pitch and putt course.

Green Fees: information not available. *Eating facilities:* bar, snacks; clubhouse closed Mondays. *Visitors:* welcome (Municipal Golf Course). Green Fee ticket gains entry to Clubhouse. *Society Meetings:* welcome. Professional/Course Manager: Dave Butler (0116 299 5570). Secretary: Margaret Weston (0116 288 2998).

LEICESTER. Kibworth Golf Club, Weir Road, Kibworth Beauchamp LE8 0LP (0116 2792301). *Location:* A6, four miles Market Harborough, 12 miles Leicester. Flat wooded course. 18 holes, 6354 yards. S.S.S. 71. Driving range. *Green Fees:* £32.00 per round, £40.00 per day. *Eating facilities:* catering available. *Visitors:* welcome, Handicap Certificate required or introduction from club member. *Society Meetings:* welcome, prior booking essential; reductions for large societies. Professional: Bryn Morris (0116 2792283). Secretary: (0116 2792301; Fax: 0116 2796434).
e-mail: secretary@kibworthgolfclub.freeserve.co.uk
website: www.kibworthgolfclub.co.uk

LEICESTER. The Leicestershire Golf Club, Evington Lane, Leicester LE5 6DJ (0116 2738825). *Location:* Evington Village, two miles from city centre off A6. Parkland. 18 holes, 6330 yards. S.S.S. 71. Practice area. *Green Fees:* information available on request. *Eating facilities:* available 7 days per week. *Visitors and Society Meetings:* welcome, advance booking required together with proof of handicap. Professional: Darren Jones. Secretary: Tim Stephens.
e-mail: secretary@theleicestershiregolfclub.co.uk
website: www.theleicestershiregolfclub.co.uk

LEICESTER. Scraptoft Golf Club, Beeby Road, Scraptoft, Leicester LE7 9SJ (0116 241 9000). *Location:* off A47 Scraptoft. Undulating. 18 holes, 6235 yards. S.S.S. 70. *Green Fees:* information not available. *Eating facilities:* full restaurant service seven days a week from April to October. *Visitors:* welcome, proof of Handicap required. *Society Meetings:* catered for on application weekdays only (contact Secretary). Professional: Simon Wood (0116 2419138).*

Forget "Par for the Course" - Go First Class!

• Centrally located, within a few miles of the M69, M1 and M6. • Extensive supervised car parking. • Competitively priced. • Flexibility, with packages to suit all requirements.
Green Fees: Weekdays £33 per round, £43 per day.

Hinckley Golf Club
Leicester Road, Hinckley LE10 3DR Tel: 01455 615124 • Fax: 01455 890841
Club Professional: Richard Jones 01455 615014
e-mail: rjones@hinckleygolfclub.com • www.hinckleygolfclub.com

LEICESTER. **Western Park Golf Club,** Scudamore Road, Braunstone Frith, Leicester LE3 1UQ. *Location:* four miles west of Junction 21 (M1) and M69. Flat, wooded course. 18 holes, 6486 yards (white), 5981 yards (yellow). S.S.S. 71. Practice area. *Green Fees:* Information not available. *Eating facilities:* full catering facilities. *Visitors:* welcome, book weekends (Tuesdays at 8am for Saturdays and Wednesdays at 8am for Sundays). Indoor school; carts for hire. *Society Meetings:* all welcome, contact Professional. Professional: Dave Butler (01162 995566; Fax: 01162 995567). Secretary: Paul Williams (0115 9114137).*
website: www.westernparkgc.co.uk

LEICESTER. **Whetstone Golf Club and Driving Range,** Cambridge Road, Cosby LE9 1SJ (Tel & Fax: 0116 286 1424). *Location:* 10 minutes off Junction 21 M1, between Cosby and Whetstone. Flat parkland. 18 holes, 5795 yards. S.S.S. 68. Driving range, putting green. *Green Fees:* information not available. *Eating facilities:* bar/lounge serving full range of meals. Smart casual dress please. *Visitors:* Handicap not required. Welcome by prior arrangement. Dress code to be observed. *Society Meetings:* welcome by prior arrangement. Professional: D. Raitt. Secretary: D. Dalby.

LOUGHBOROUGH. **Charnwood Forest Golf Club,** Breakback Road, Woodhouse Eaves, Near Loughborough LE12 8TA (01509 890259). Steward: 01509 890925. *Location:* A6 to B591 or M1 Junction 23–A512–Snells Nook Lane. Heather, gorse and bracken, no bunkers. Oldest golf club in Leicestershire played around volcanic rocks. 9 holes, 5972 yards. S.S.S. 69. *Green Fees:* weekdays £30.00 per 18 holes, £35.00 per day; weekends £40.00 per 18 holes. *Eating facilities:* full catering. *Visitors:* welcome except Tuesdays (Ladies' Day). *Society Meetings:* welcome by prior arrangement. Secretary: P.K. Field (01509 890259).
e-mail: secretary@charnwoodforestgolfclub.com
website: www.charnwoodforestgolfclub.com

LOUGHBOROUGH. **Longcliffe Golf Club,** Snell's Nook Lane, Nanpantan, Loughborough LE11 3YA (01509 239129; Fax: 01509 231346). *Location:* M1 Junction 23 – A512 Loughborough, first right, Snells Nook Lane. Wooded heathland, EGU Championship course. 18 holes, 6625 yards. S.S.S. 73. Practice ground. *Green Fees:* weekdays £35.00 per round, £45.00 per day. *Eating facilities:* bar and restaurant. *Visitors:* welcome weekdays. Handicap Certificate required. *Society Meetings:* welcome by arrangement Mondays, Tuesdays, Wednesdays, Thursdays and Fridays. Professional: D.C. Mee (01509 231450). Manager: Brian Jones (01509 239129; Fax: 01509 231286).
e-mail: longcliffegolf@btconnect.com
website: www.longcliffegolf.co.uk

LOUGHBOROUGH. **Park Hill Golf Club,** Park Hill, Seagrave, Loughborough LE12 7NG (01509 815454; Fax: 01509 816062). *Location:* 5 miles from J21a of M1 northbound. Just off the A46 northbound. Undulating parkland course with rolling tree-lined fairways and excellent views – the closing hole is a challenging par 5 with water protecting both sides of the green. Excellent playing conditions all year round! 18 holes, 7219 yards. S.S.S. 74. 9 hole Par 3 Academy Course now open. Large practice area and putting green. 20 bay fully covered floodlit driving range, including grass bays. *Green Fees:* weekdays £27.00, with a member £15.00; weekends and Bank Holidays £33.00, with a member £18.00. Seniors (55 years and over) Monday to Wednesday. Students £15.00 weekdays, £20.00 weekends. *Eating facilities:* lunch/ dinner/ bar snacks, fully licensed bar. *Visitors:* welcome at all times Monday to Friday, after 9am at weekends. Conference room for up to 120 people (function room). *Society Meetings:* all welcome by prior arrangement. Special rates for societies over 12 people. Professional: Matt Ulyett (01509 815775; Fax: 01509 816062). Secretary: Jonathan Hutson (01509 815454; Fax: 01509 816062).
e-mail: mail@parkhillgolf.co.uk
website: www.parkhillgolf.co.uk

LUTTERWORTH. **Lutterworth Golf Club,** Rugby Road, Lutterworth LE17 4HN. *Location:* Junction 20 M1; Junction 1 M6. Parkland course. 18 holes, 6243 yards. S.S.S. 70. Practice area, computerised indoor teaching academy. *Green Fees:* information not available. *Eating facilities:* catering available and bar facilities. *Visitors:* welcome all day Monday to Thursday, and Friday till noon. *Society Meetings:* welcome Monday to Thursday all day, and Friday mornings. Secretary: John Faulks (01455 552532). Professional: Lee Challinor (01455 557199). Bar/ Catering (01455 557141).*

LUTTERWORTH near. **Ullesthorpe Court Golf Club,** Frolesworth Road, Ullesthorpe, Near Lutterworth LE17 5BZ. *Location:* 10 minutes M1, M6, M69, A5; near Lutterworth between Leicester and Coventry. Open parkland course, with interesting greens, a fair test for all abilities; lakes on three holes. 18 holes, 6662 yards. S.S.S. 72. *Green Fees:* visitors £25.00. 2010 rates (subject to review). *Eating facilities:* à la carte restaurant, bar meals, club bar. *Visitors:* welcome weekdays, except Bank Holidays, and must book in advance. Hotel with 72 en suite bedrooms and full leisure centre. *Society Meetings:* five packages available, bookable in advance. Tel: Golf Office 01455 209023. Professional: Jonathan Salter (01455 209150; Fax: 01455 202537).
e-mail: bookings@ullesthorpecourt.co.uk

MARKET HARBOROUGH. **Market Harborough Golf Club,** Great Oxendon Road, Market Harborough LE16 8NB (01858 463684). *Location:* one mile south of Market Harborough on A508. Parkland. An excellent testing course, lovely views and lakes a feature of the course. 18 holes, 6095 yards. S.S.S. 69. Practice ground. *Green Fees:* information not provided. *Eating facilities:* bar snacks and full meals available. *Visitors:* welcome weekdays; weekends only with a member. *Society Meetings:* welcome on application. Professional: F. Baxter. Secretary: P. Weston (01858 463684).

MELTON MOWBRAY. **Melton Mowbray Golf Club**, Thorpe Arnold, Melton Mowbray LE14 4SD (Tel & Fax: 01664 562118). *Location:* approximately 1½ miles east of Melton Mowbray on A607 towards Grantham. Parkland, easy walking but challenging. 18 holes, 6279 yards, S.S.S. 70 (men), 72 (ladies). Practice area including mid iron, practice chipping and bunker play. Practice putting green. Floodlit 7-bay driving range. Golf lessons available. *Green Fees:* weekdays £27.00 per round, £38.00 per day; weekends and Bank Holidays £32.00 per round. *Eating facilities:* bar and restaurant. *Visitors:* welcome, contact Pro Shop to book. *Society Meetings:* packages available. No societies on Saturdays. Professional: Neil Curtis (01664 569629; Fax: 01664 562118). Secretaries: Sue Millward and Marilyn Connelly (Tel & Fax: 01664 562118 Option 2).
e-mail: meltonmowbraygc@btconnect.com
website: www.mmgc.org

MELTON MOWBRAY. **Six Hills Golf Club,** Six Hills, Melton Mowbray LE14 3PR (01509 881225). *Location*: on B676, half way between Melton Mowbray and Loughborough. Flat course. 18 holes, 5826 yards, S.S.S. 69. Practice green and ground. Driving range. *Green Fees*: £16.00 weekdays, £20.00 weekends. *Eating facilities:* cafe style; restaurant and bar. *Visitors*: no restrictions. Professional: James Hawley. Secretary: Mrs J. Showler.

NORTH KILWORTH. **Kilworth Springs Golf Club,** South Kilworth Road, North Kilworth LE17 6HJ (Clubhouse/office: 01858 575082; Pro-shop: 01858 575974; Fax: 01858 575078). *Location:* six miles from Junction 20, four miles M6 - A14 Junction. Links type, parkland course. 18 holes, 6718 yards. S.S.S. 72. Driving range. *Green Fees*: weekdays £15.00 9 holes, £24.00 18 holes; weekends £17.00 9 holes, £27.00 18 holes. Day rate £40.00. Special society rates for 12 people or over. *Eating facilities*: restaurant, bar, bar snacks. *Visitors*: welcome at all times subject to tee times being available. Buggies available. *Society Meeting*s: welcome. Professional: Anders Mankert. General Manager: Jeremy Wilkinson.
e-mail: admin@kilworthsprings.co.uk
website: www.kilworthsprings.co.uk

OADBY. **Glen Gorse Golf Club,** Glen Road, Oadby LE2 4RF (0116 271 4159). *Location:* on A6, four and a half miles south of Leicester between Oadby and Great Glen. Fairly flat parkland course, some ridge and furrow. 18 holes, 6648 yards, 6079 metres. S.S.S. 72. *Green Fees:* weekdays £30.00 per round, £35.00 per day (£15.00 with member); weekends £15.00 with member only. *Eating facilities:* bar and meals/snacks. *Visitors:* welcome weekdays, weekends with members only. Snooker room. *Society Meetings:* welcome Monday to Friday by prior arrangement. Professional: Dominic Fitzpatrick (0116 271 3748). Secretary: Mrs J. James (Tel & Fax: 0116 271 4159).
e-mail: secretary@gggc.org
website: www.gggc.org

OADBY. **Oadby Golf Course,** Leicester Road, Oadby, Leicester LE2 4AJ (0116 270 0215). *Location:* on A6 south of Leicester, one mile from City boundary, at Leicester Racecourse. Parkland. 18 holes, 6376 yards, 5827 metres. S.S.S. 71. Practice ground, coaching, driving bays. *Green Fees:* weekdays £10.00, weekends £12.00. 2010 rates (subject to review). *Eating facilities:* snacks always available, bar with meals on prior notice. *Visitors:* welcome, booking is advised at weekends and Bank Holidays. Please contact Golf Shop. *Society Meetings:* welcome, bookings taken through Golf Shop (0116 270 9052). Caterers (0116 270 0215).

ROTHLEY. **Rothley Park Golf Club,** Westfield Lane, Rothley, Leicester LE7 7LH (0116 2302809). *Location:* off A6, north of Leicester. Parkland. 18 holes, 6481 yards. S.S.S. 71. *Green Fees:* £50.00 per day (mid-week). *Eating facilities:* available daily. *Visitors:* welcome except Tuesdays, weekends and Bank Holidays, must be members of recognised golf club with Handicap. *Society Meetings:* as visitors' restrictions and by prior arrangement only. Professional: Katie Tebbet (Tel & Fax: 0116 2302809). General Manager: Danny Sallane (Tel & Fax: 0116 2302809).
e-mail: admin@rothleypark.co.uk
website: www.rothleypark.com

Melton Mowbray Golf Club
Parkland Course
Easy Walking
Catering & Bar
Driving Range
Visitors & Societies welcome

Melton Mowbray Golf Club, Thorpe Arnold
e-mail: meltonmowbraygc@btconnect.com
www.mmgc.org   Tel 01664 562118

RUTLAND. **Greetham Valley Hotel, Golf and Conference Centre,** Wood Lane, Greetham, Near Oakham, Rutland LE15 7SN (01780 460444; Fax: 01780 460623). *Location:* one mile off A1 between Stamford and Grantham on the B668. Four miles from Rutland Water. Parkland, undulating with many water features. Many holes playing over natural valley. 45 holes. "The Lakes" 6736 yards, S.S.S 72; "The Valley" 5595 yards, S.S.S. 68; Academy Course 9 holes, 1263 yards, S.S.S. 27. 14 bay floodlit driving range. *Green Fees:* £20.00 weekdays, £25.00 weekends. *Eating facilities:* excellent clubhouse, lounge, bar and restaurants. *Visitors:* welcome, please phone first for tee availability. Conference rooms, banqueting suite, pool table, quad biking, 4x4 off-roading, salmon and coarse fishing and bowls. Buggies and pull trolleys for hire. Hotel with 35 en suite bedrooms, 8 lodges; holiday cottage. Gym. Golf breaks welcome all year. *Society Meetings:* welcome. Professional: Neil Evans (01780 460666; Fax: 01780 460623). Secretary: Dee Hinch (01780 460444; Fax: 01780 460623).
e-mail: info@greethamvalley.co.uk
website: www.greethamvalley.co.uk

STAMFORD. **Luffenham Heath Golf Club,** South Luffenham Road, Ketton, Stamford, Lincolnshire PE9 3UU (01780 720205; Fax: 01780 722146). *Location:* 6 miles from Stamford and 1½ miles south-west of Ketton on the A6121. Undulating heathland, in conservation area for flora and fauna. 18 holes, 6563 yards. S.S.S. 72. Practice ground. *Green Fees:* £50.00 per round, £65.00 per day. 2010 rates (subject to review). *Eating facilities:* snacks available daily, full meals by arrangement. *Visitors:* Monday to Friday excluding Tuesdays. Weekends and Bank Holidays 10.30am-12 noon and after 2pm. Handicap Certificate required. *Society Meetings:* welcome, except Tuesdays and weekends/Bank Holidays. Details of packages on request. Professional: Ian Burnett (Tel & Fax: 01780 720298). Secretary: John R. Ingleby (01780 720205; Fax: 01780 722146).
e-mail: jringleby@theluffenhamheathgc.co.uk
website: www.luffenhamheath.co.uk

WOODHOUSE EAVES. **Lingdale Golf Club,** Joe Moore's Lane, Woodhouse Eaves, Near Loughborough LE12 8TF (01509 890703). *Location:* on B5300, Anstey – Shepshed road, three miles from Exit 23 on M1. Woodland and parkland – set in Charnwood Forest. 18 holes, 6545 yards. S.S.S. 71. Practice ground. *Green Fees:* weekdays £30.00 per round, £36.00 per day; weekends £37.50 per round, £49.00 per day. *Eating facilities:* full catering available. *Visitors:* welcome, but please telephone first. *Society Meetings:* welcome. Details and booking form available from Secretary. Professional: Peter Sellears (01509 890684). Managing Secretary: Terry Walker (01509 890703).

For full details of convenient accommodation near clubs and courses
www.holidayguides.com

Other British holiday guides from FHG Guides

**PUBS & INNS · 300 GREAT HOTELS · SHORT BREAK HOLIDAYS
The bestselling and original PETS WELCOME! · 500 GREAT PLACES TO STAY
SELF-CATERING HOLIDAYS · BED & BREAKFAST STOPS
CARAVAN & CAMPING HOLIDAYS · FAMILY BREAKS**

Published annually: available in all good bookshops or direct from the publisher:

**FHG Guides, Abbey Mill Business Centre, Seedhill, Paisley PA1 1TJ
Tel: 0141 887 0428 • Fax: 0141 889 7204
e-mail: admin@fhguides.co.uk • www.holidayguides.com**

Lincolnshire

ALFORD. **Woodthorpe Hall Golf Club,** Woodthorpe, Alford LN13 0DD (01507 450294). *Location:* on the B1373, 3 miles north of Alford, 8 miles SE of Louth. Undulating parkland. 18 holes, 5067 yards. S.S.S. 64. *Green Fees:* weekdays £12.00 per round; weekends and Bank Holidays £15.00 per round. *Eating facilities:* at Woody's Bar & Restaurant on site; conference rooms also available (01507 450079). *Visitors:* welcome, unrestricted. *Society Meetings:* by prior arrangement (01507 450294). Secretary: Mrs J. Smith. (Tel & Fax: 01507 450000).

BLANKNEY. **Blankney Golf Club,** near Metheringham, Lincoln LN4 3AZ (01526 320202). *Location:* near Metheringham on B1188 Lincoln to Sleaford Road. Parkland, slightly undulating. 18 holes, 6638 yards. Par 72. Centenary Year 2004, host to Midland PGA Tournament. Practice area, putting green and snooker. *Green Fees:* visit website. *Eating facilities:* dining room and bar meals. *Visitors:* welcome except Wednesday mornings, limited numbers at weekends. *Society Meetings:* welcome with prior booking. Professional/ Club Manager: G. Bradley (01526 320202). Admin Office (01526 320263; Fax: 01526 322521).
e-mail: manager@blankneygolfclub.co.uk
website: www.blankneygolfclub.co.uk

BLANKNEY. **Martin Moor Golf Club,** Martin Road, Blankney LN4 3BE (01526 378243). *Location:* off the B1189 between Martin and Metheringham. Gently undulating parkland course that offers challenges for players of all standards. 9 holes with 18 different tees, 'back nine' plays very differently to the front. 3 par 5s, 12 par 4s, 3 par 3s, 6345 yards. Par 72. Large practice area with driving nets, practice bunker and chipping area. *Green Fees:* 9 holes £7.50, 18 holes £11.00. *Eating facilities:* bar and restaurant, bar snacks and meals. *Visitors:* welcome. Warm changing rooms and hot showers. Lessons by arrangement. Buggy, trolley and club hire available. Functions catered for. *Society Meetings:* welcome. Rates negotiable. Various packages available. Catering on request. Secretary: Mrs Carole Roberts (01526 378243).
e-mail: enquiries@martinmoorgolfclub.co.uk
website: www.martinmoorgolfclub.co.uk

THE APPEARANCE OF AN ASTERISK (*) AT THE END OF A CLUB OR COURSE ENTRY INDICATES THAT UP-TO-DATE INFORMATION HAS NOT BEEN SUPPLIED

The Inn at Lea Gate
Lea Gate Road, Coningsby, Lincolnshire LN4 4RS

The Old Lea Gate Inn has been satisfying the hungry traveller since 1542, and still retains its essential period style, while also applying a modern approach to catering for customers' needs. The bar, with its ancient oak beams and inglenook fireplace is soaked in atmosphere and history, and this, combined with the eight bedroom hotel annex, a comfortable restaurant and the best of modern hospitality, must make the Lea Gate quite unbeatable.

Good Pub Guide • ETC ★★★★
Tel: 01526 342370 • Fax: 01526 345468
e-mail: theleagateinn@hotmail.com • www.the-leagate-inn.co.uk

---

Blankney Golf Club
Blankney, Lincolnshire LN4 3AZ • Tel: 01526 320202
e-mail: manager@blankneygolfclub.co.uk • www.blankneygolfclub.co.uk

Established in 1904, this superb 18 hole, Par 72 championship course is now considered to be one of the most challenging courses in Lincolnshire.

Societies and visitors are welcome by prior arrangement.

Lincolnshire / MIDLANDS REGION

BOSTON. **Boston Golf Club,** Cowbridge, Horncastle Road, Boston PE22 7EL (01205 350589; Fax: 01205 367526). *Location:* two miles north of Boston on B1183. Look for sign to right if travelling north. Parkland with featured water. 18 holes, 6415 yards, 5885 metres. S.S.S. 71. *Green Fees:* midweek £25.00 per round, £33.00 per day; round after 2.30pm £16.00. Weekends and Bank Holidays £31.00 per round. 2010 rates (subject to review). *Eating facilities:* daily by arrangement with resident Steward (01205 352533). *Visitors:* welcome without reservation. *Society Meetings:* welcome. Monday/Tuesday pm, Wednesday pm, Thursday/Friday/weekends after 2pm. Professional: N. Hiom (01205 362306). Company Secretary: S. Shaw (01205 350589).

BOSTON. **Boston West Golf Club,** Hubberts Bridge, Boston PE20 3QX (01205 290670; Fax: 01205 290725). *Location:* Junction of A1121 and B1392, 1½ miles west of Boston. Parkland course with 25,000 trees and shrubs planted, with water in play on five holes. 18 holes, 6411 yards. S.S.S. 71. 6 hole short course, putting greens, practice bunker. 20 bay floodlit driving range. *Green Fees:* information not available. *Eating facilities:* catering available all day in newly extended Clubhouse, with restaurant overlooking the course. *Visitors:* no restrictions but must book in advance. Lessons available from Sophie Hunter. VI Digital Coaching System available. Large discount store with custom fitting on site. Buggies available. 24-bedroom hotel on site. Golf packages available. *Society Meetings:* welcome at all times, including weekends. Special rates on request. Secretary: Mike Couture (01205 290670). *
e-mail: info@bostonwestgolfclub.co.uk
website: www.bostonwestgolfclub.co.uk

BOSTON. **Kirton Holme Golf Club,** Holme Road, Kirton Holme, Boston PE20 1SY (01205 290669). *Location:* four miles west of Boston, signposted off A52. Flat parkland. 9 holes, 2884 yards. S.S.S. 34. Small practice area includes net. *Green Fees:* weekdays £8.00 per 9 holes, £12.00 per 18 holes; weekends and Bank Holidays £9.00 per 9 holes, £13.00 per 18 holes. *Eating facilities:* bar open 11am to dusk, snack meals available. *Visitors:* always welcome, smart dress required. *Society Meetings:* by arrangement. Secretary: T. Welberry (01205 290669).

BOURNE. **The Toft Hotel Golf Club,** Toft, Near Bourne PE10 0JT (01778 590614; Fax: 01778 590264). *Location:* in Toft village on A6121 Stamford to Bourne road. Undulating course with natural lake. 18 holes, 6486 yards. S.S.S. 71. Practice area. *Green Fees:* information not available. *Eating facilities:* bar open all day; bar snacks and restaurant. *Visitors:* welcome at all times, prior booking essential. Hotel has 22 bedrooms. *Society Meetings:* welcome, prior booking essential. Professional: Mark Jackson (01778 590616). Secretary: Robin Jackson (01778 590616).*
website: www.thetofthotelgolfclub.com

BRIGG. **Elsham Golf Club,** Barton Road, Elsham, Brigg DN20 0LS (01652 680291; Fax: 01652 680308). *Location:* off M180 at J5 or A15 through Brigg to Barton. Wooded parkland course. 18 holes, 6426 yards. S.S.S. 72. Outdoor practice ground. *Green Fees:* weekdays only £30.00 for 18 holes, £40.00 for 36 holes. £15.00 (18 holes) with a member both during the week and at weekends. Special rates for societies of 12 or more. *Eating facilities:* full catering. *Visitors:* welcome weekdays. *Society Meetings:* catered for on weekdays. Steward (01652 688382). Professional: Stuart Brewer (01652 680432). Secretary: T. Hartley (01652 680291).
e-mail: office@elshamgolfclub.co.uk
website: www.elshamgolfclub.co.uk

BRIGG. **Forest Pines Hotel & Golf Resort,** Ermine Street, Broughton, Near Brigg DN20 0AQ (01652 650770). Golf Shop (01652 650756; Fax: 01652 650495). *Location:* 200 yards from Junction 4 M180 towards Scunthorpe. Three 9 hole courses – Forest, Pines, Beeches. Forest/Pines Championship Course: 6842 yards, S.S.S. 74. Pines/Beeches: 6653 yards, S.S.S. 73. Forest/Beeches: 6393 yards, S.S.S. 71. Practice range and practice green. *Green Fees:* Monday to Thursday £50.00 18 holes; Friday to Sunday £60.00 18 holes. *Eating facilities:* clubhouse, Pine Bar. *Visitors:* welcome; telephone in advance. Compulsory 'soft spikes' or dimples, no steel spikes. All facilities of The Forest Pines Hotel, golf course and spa available - 188 bedrooms. 29 electric buggies and carts for hire; residential golf schools, leisure club (swimming, gym, sauna and jacuzzi). *Society Meetings:* welcome. Various packages available. Residential Golfing Breaks available. Please call the

A warm welcome to old and new customers – 20 refurbished en suite bedrooms, all with flat screen TVs and tea/coffee making facilities. Weddings, Banquets and Conferences. 18 hole Golf Course with natural lake. New Driving Range. Practice Putting area.

Toft • Near Bourne • Lincs • PE10 0JT   T 01778 590614   F 01778 590264
www.tofthotelgolf.co.uk • tofthouse@btconnect.com

golf events team for details (01652 650770). Forest Pines will be the venue for the 2013 Boys Home Internationals and many other PGA events, including the National PGA 4 Ball Championships in 2010.
e-mail: forestpinesgolf@qhotels.co.uk
website: www.qhotels.co.uk

CLEETHORPES. **Cleethorpes Golf Club (1894) Ltd,** Golf House, Kings Road, Cleethorpes DN35 0PN (01472 816110). *Location:* approximately one mile south of Cleethorpes Leisure Centre. Mature coastal course, slight undulations give variation but local topography makes for easy walking. Presented to the highest standards the course provides a challenge to all level of players. 18 holes, 6272 yards. S.S.S. 71. Large and small practice areas. *Green Fees:* weekdays £25.00, £15.00 with member, weekends £30.00, £15.00 with member. Handicap Certificate preferred. *Eating facilities:* bar lunches, evening meals. *Visitors:* welcome anytime except Wednesdays. *Society Meetings:* welcome by arrangement with the Secretary. Attractive packages available Monday, Thursday, Friday and Sunday. Professional: P. Davies (01472 814060). Secretary: Andrew Thompson (01472 816110).
e-mail: secretary@cleethorpesgolfclub.co.uk
website: www.cleethorpesgolfclub.co.uk

GAINSBOROUGH. **Gainsborough Golf Club,** Thonock, Gainsborough DN21 1PZ (01427 613088); Fax: 01427 810172). *Location:* signposted from A631 Gainsborough to Grimsby Road. Thonock Park Course is a parkland course with many deciduous trees, Karsten Lakes Course is a Championship Course designed by Neil Coles (opened 1.4.97). Thonock Park Course - 18 holes, 6620 yards. Par 70, S.S.S. 71. Karsten Lakes Course - 18 holes, 6724 yards. Par 72, S.S.S. 72. 20 bay floodlit driving range. *Green Fees:* information not available. *Eating facilities:* restaurant and coffee shop, two bars. *Visitors:* welcome, seven days on both courses (tee time bookings available). *Society Meetings:* welcome (booking in advance necessary). Professional: Stephen Cooper. Manager: S. Keane.

GRANTHAM. **Belton Park Golf Club,** Belton Lane, Londonthorpe Road, Grantham NG31 9SH (01476 567399; Fax: 01476 592078). *Location:* two miles from Grantham. 250 acre Deer Park adjacent to the historical Belton House. Three loops of 9 holes each beginning and ending at the clubhouse: Brownlow Course 6472 yards (Championship). S.S.S. 71. Ancaster Course 6325 yards. S.S.S. 70. Belmont Course 6075 yards. S.S.S. 69. Two large practice areas. *Green Fees:* weekdays £37.00 per round, £42.00 per day; weekends and Bank Holidays £42.00 per round, £50.00 per day. Special winter rates November to March. *Eating facilities:* full restaurant facilities every day. *Visitors:* welcome without reservation. *Society Meetings:* catered for by arrangement weekdays only. Special day package. Professional: S. Williams. General Manager: S Rowley.
e-mail: greatgolf@beltonpark.co.uk

GRANTHAM near. **De Vere Belton Woods Hotel,** Belton, Near Grantham NG32 2LN (01476 593200; Fax: 01476 574547). *Location:* two miles from the A1. Belton Woods Hotel offers a golfers' paradise with two Championship courses and a Par 3 9-hole course. The Lakes Course - 6831 yards, Par 72; The Woodside Course - 6623 yards, Par 73; The Red Arrows Academy Course - 1116 yards. Practice facilities include a floodlit undercover 20-bay driving range, a chipping area with bunker and putting green. Tuition available on site from the golf Professionals. *Green Fees:* information not available. *Eating facilities:* two eating experiences: 19 Bar & Grill, an informal restaurant which serves food all day, and Stantons Restaurant, a formal brasserie-style menu. *Visitors:* welcome, please call to book in order to avoid disappointment. Accommodation in Hotel – 136 luxurious bedrooms including some luxury suites, with extensive leisure and conference facilities. Golf holidays, society and corporate events are our speciality. Please ring the hotel for any special offers on golfing breaks (01476 593200) and ask for Golf Sales or Golf Shop.

GRANTHAM. **Stoke Rochford Golf Club,** Stoke Rochford, Near Grantham NG33 5EW (01476 530275). *Location:* five miles south of Grantham on A1. Entrance at BP petrol station. Parkland. 18 holes, 6313 yards. S.S.S. 70. Small practice ground. *Green Fees:* £30.00 per round, £37.00 per day. *Eating facilities:* meals available daily, to be booked before playing. *Visitors:* cannot commence play before 10.30am at weekends or on Public Holidays. No visitors on Sundays November, December and January. Buggies and numerous trolleys for hire. Snooker room. *Society Meetings:* by prior arrangement. Professional: A.E. Dow (01476 530218). Secretary: J.Martindale (01572 756305).

GRANTHAM. **Sudbrook Moor Golf Club,** Charity Street, Carlton Scroop, Grantham NG32 3AT (01400 250796). *Location:* A607 Lincoln to Grantham, six miles north-east of Grantham in village location of Carlton Scroop. Private course in picturesque valley; easy walking parkland/ meadowland. 9 holes, 4827 yards. S.S.S. 63/64/65. Covered driving range bays. *Green Fees:* visitor's day ticket £12.00. *Eating facilities:* Spike Bar and dining room. Bistro menu, Monday-Saturday, closed Sunday. Catering (01400 250876). *Visitors:* welcome by appointment, no Society groups. All enquiries via Club Secretary's office. Professionals: Tim Hutton/Ben Hutton. Club Secretary: Judith M. Hutton (01400 250796).

GRIMSBY. **Grimsby Golf Club Ltd,** Littlecoates Road, Grimsby DN34 4LU (01472 342823). *Location:* two miles west of town centre, one mile from A180 and A46. Undulating parkland course. 18 holes, 6098 yards. S.S.S. 69. Practice ground, chipping area. *Green Fees:* information not available. *Eating facilities:* quality food available at all times and bar facilities. *Visitors:* welcome weekdays, must be members of golf clubs. *Society Meetings:* catered for Mondays and Fridays by arrangement with Secretary. Professional: Richard Smith (01472 356981). Secretary: D. McCully (01472 342630).*
e-mail: secretary@grimsbygc.fsnet.co.uk

Lincolnshire / MIDLANDS REGION

GRIMSBY. Manor Golf Club, Laceby Manor, Laceby, Grimsby DN37 7LD (01472 873468). *Location:* A18, half a mile on left hand side from Oaklands Hotel, situated at Laceby roundabout. Parkland - tree lined fairways, many water features including green surrounded by water. 18 holes, 6343 yards. S.S.S. 71. Netted driving range, putting green, chipping area. *Green Fees:* £22.00 weekdays, £25.00 weekends. Twilight weekdays £14.00, £16.00. *Eating facilities:* bar, lounge bar, dining area. *Visitors:* welcome any day. Booked tee system operated all days, non-members may book up to six days in advance. *Society Meetings:* welcome by prior arrangement. Club Manager: Judith MacKay (01472 873468).
e-mail: mackayj@grimsby.ac.uk
website: www.lmgc.co.uk

GRIMSBY. Waltham Windmill Golf Club, Cheapside, Waltham, Grimsby DN37 0HT (01472 824109). *Location:* off A16 main Louth to Grimsby road. Parkland course incorporating seven lakes. 18 holes, 6442 yards. S.S.S. 71. Practice ground. *Green Fees:* weekdays £27.00, with member £17.00; weekends £34.00, with member £24.00. Reductions for societies; minimum 12. *Eating facilities:* bar and restaurant. *Visitors:* welcome, telephone booking. *Society Meetings:* welcome, contact the Secretary. Professional: Mark Stephenson (01472 823963). Secretary: Ivor Williams (01472 824109; Fax: 01472 828391).

HORNCASTLE near. **Horncastle Golf Club,** West Ashby, Near Horncastle LN9 5PP (01507 526800). *Location:* just off A158 between Horncastle and Baumber. Parkland course - water features on 14 holes. 18 holes, 5800 yards. S.S.S. 70. *Green Fees:* information not available. *Eating facilities:* bars, restaurant. *Visitors:* welcome anytime but helpful to phone. Special package available golf range, golf course, food and drink. Ballroom and conference facilities. Accommodation available, caravan site. Carts. Fishing lakes. *Society Meetings:* please phone in advance. Professional: Alison Johns. Secretary: Chris Redfearn.*

IMMINGHAM. Immingham Golf Club, St Andrew's Lane, Church Lane, Immingham DN40 2EU (01469 575298; Fax: 01469 577636). *Location:* two miles off A180, behind St Andrew's Church, Immingham. Undulating parkland with water hazards. Drainage dyke comes into play for over half the holes. Excellent greens. 18 holes, 6215 yards, 5682 metres. S.S.S. 70. Small practice area. *Green Fees:* information not provided. *Eating facilities:* snacks; full catering (book in advance). *Visitors:* welcome anytime except Thursday pm. Handicap Certificate preferred. *Society Meetings:* welcome midweek during the day, limited availability at weekends. Professional: Nick Harding (01469 575493). Manager: C. Todd (01469 575298).
e-mail: immgc@btconnect.com
website: www.immgc.com

Immingham Golf Club

This member-owned 18-hole parkland course is situated on the outskirts of Immingham. We understand golf and golfers and can organise something special for companies and groups who really want to impress. Clubhouse with bar and restaurant.

Club Manager: Clive Todd   Tel: 01469 575298 Ext. 1
Secretary: Jody Webb
Immingham Golf Club. St Andrews Lane,
Church Lane, Immingham, N.E. Lincolnshire DN40 2EU
e-mail: immgc@btconnect.com • www.immgc.com

CANWICK PARK GOLF CLUB

GREAT GOLF ALL YEAR ROUND

Attractive parkland course of 6148 yards. SSS 69, located 2 miles east of Lincoln City Centre on the B1190, with panoramic views of Lincoln Cathedral. The 5th and 13th holes are testing Par 3s.
• Fully licensed bar and restaurant area •
• Golf Society and Corporate Golf Days a speciality •
• Canwick Park offers a warm welcome to all its visitors •

WASHINGBOROUGH ROAD, LINCOLN LN4 1EF
Manager: 01522 542912   •   Clubhouse: 01522 522166
e-mail: manager@canwickpark.org • www.canwickpark.org

MIDLANDS REGION / Lincolnshire

LINCOLN. Canwick Park Golf Club, Canwick Park, Washingborough Road, Lincoln LN4 1EF (Clubhouse: 01522 522166). *Location:* two miles east of Lincoln on B1190. Parkland, wooded course - two testing Par 3s (5th & 13th). 18 holes, 6148 yards, 5600 metres, S.S.S. 69. Practice ground on adjacent driving range. *Green Fees:* information not available. *Eating facilities:* bar snacks and meals to order. *Visitors:* welcome weekdays; weekends after 2:30pm without a member. Locker rooms. *Society Meetings:* welcome by prior arrangement. Manager: N. Porteus (01522 542912; Fax: 01522 526997).*
e-mail: manager@canwickpark.org
website: www.canwickpark.org

LINCOLN. Carholme Golf Club, Carholme Road, Lincoln LN1 1SE (01522 523725). *Location:* one mile from city centre on A57 to Worksop. Flat parkland. 18 holes, 5501 yards. S.S.S. 67. *Green Fees:* information not available. *Eating facilities:* full service. *Visitors:* welcome most days subject to restrictions regarding starting times, information available on request. *Society Meetings:* by prior arrangement only. Office: Tel/Fax: 01522 533733. Secretary: J. Lammin (01522 523725).
e-mail: info@carholme-golf-club.co.uk
website: www.carholme-golf-club.co.uk

LINCOLN. Lincoln Golf Club, Torksey, Lincoln LN1 2EG (Tel/Fax: 01427 718721). *Location:* A156 approx. 6 miles south of Gainsborough. Mature, testing championship standard course built on sandy subsoil. 18 holes, 6438 yards. S.S.S. 71. *Green Fees:* £35.00 per round, £45.00 per day. 2010 rates (subject to review). Winter packages available. *Eating facilities:* full facilities available. *Visitors:* welcome anytime except Tuesday mornings (Ladies' Day). *Society Meetings:* welcome by prior arrangement (not weekends). Professional: Ashley Carter (Tel/Fax: 01427 718273). Manager: Derek B. Linton (Tel/Fax: 01427 718721).
e-mail: info@lincolngc.co.uk
website: www.lincolngc.co.uk

LINCOLN. Pottergate Golf Club, Moor Lane, Branston, Lincoln LN4 1JA (01522 794867). *Location:* south of Lincoln on B1188 to Branston. Turn left onto Moor Lane. Parkland course. 9 holes. Par 34. Indoor golf simulator with 17 golf courses and driving range. Putting green. *Green Fees:* weekdays £10.00 9/18 holes, weekends and Bank Holidays £14.00 9/18 holes. *Eating facilities:* bar open 11am to 10pm, bar snacks and light meals. Closed Mondays. *Society Meetings:* welcome by prior arrangement. Professional: Lee Tasker. Proprietor: Robert Mawer.

LINCOLN. RAF Coningsby Golf Club, Coningsby, Lincoln LN4 4SY (01526 342581 Ext. 6828). *Location:* on the B1192 halfway between Tattershall Thorpe and Woodhall Spa, signposted RAF Woodhall. Parkland course. 9 holes (18 tees), 5354 yards, S.S.S. 66. *Green Fees*: £10.00, with member £8.00. 9 holes £6.00. Juniors £4.00. Day ticket £12.00. *Visitors:* welcome weekdays except Monday am (Ladies). *Society Meetings*: welcome weekdays by appointment. Secretary: J. Bramley (01526 347467).

LINCOLN. Welton Manor Golf Centre, Hackthorn Road, Welton, Lincoln LN2 3PA (01673 862827). *Location:* six miles north of Lincoln. Off A46 to Welton village, through Welton, turn left at mini roundabout signposted Spridlington, entrance half-a-mile on left. Gently undulating parkland with streams, ponds and tree-lined fairways. 10-bay floodlit driving range. *Green Fees:* information not available. *Eating facilities:* bar meals and The Falcon Restaurant, from 8am to 11pm. Licensed patio area. Caravan club site, fishing lake. *Visitors:* welcome, phone for tee closures, buggies available. Professional: Gary Leslie.*
e-mail: enquiries@weltonmanorgolfcentre.co.uk
website: www.weltonmanorgolfcentre.co.uk

LOUTH. Kenwick Park Golf Club, Kenwick Park, Louth LN11 8NY (01507 605134; Fax: 01507 606556). *Location:* two miles south of Louth on A157. 18 hole wooded parkland course with feature lakes, in an Area of Outstanding Natural Beauty. White tees 6715 yards S.S.S. 73, yellow tees 6257 yards S.S.S. 71, red tees 5764 yards S.S.S. 74. *Green Fees:* £40.00 weekdays, £50.00 weekends. *Eating facilities:* catering available. *Visitors:* welcome by prior arrangement. Driving range, teaching facilities, buggies available. Accommodation available at Kenwick Park Hotel (01507 608806). *Society Meetings:* welcome, contact Director of Golf. Professionals: Paul Spence & Michael Langford (01507 607161). Director of Golf: Eric Sharp.
e-mail: secretary@kenwickparkgolf.co.uk
website: www.kenwickparkgolf.co.uk

- 6438 yards, SSS 71
- Venue for English Seniors County Championship and Lincolnshire Open Championship
- Putting green
- Large practice area
- 3-hole pitch and putt
- Golf shop

Lincoln Golf Club
TORKSEY • LINCOLN • LN1 2EG

Founded in 1891, Lincoln is a mature, testing, championship standard course built on sandy subsoil offering a variety of holes from links-style to parkland with mature trees and some water features. We offer golfing packages in summer and winter, including a wide range of excellent snacks and meals.

Manager: John Cox
Tel/Fax: 01427 718721
Pro: Ashley Carter Tel/Fax: 01427 718273
e-mail: info@lincolngc.co.uk
www.lincolngc.co.uk

LOUTH. **Louth Golf Club,** 59 Crowtree Lane, Louth LN11 9LJ (01507 603681; Fax: 01507 608501). *Location:* western outskirts of Louth. Undulating parkland course in an Area of Outstanding Natural Beauty. 18 holes, 6411 yards. S.S.S. 71. Practice ground, putting green. *Green Fees:* information not available. *Eating facilities:* full catering 11am to 9pm (earlier to order). *Visitors:* welcome without reservation other than notification and dress rules. *Society Meetings:* catered for. Professional: Nick Taylor (01507 604648). General Manager: Simon Moody (01507 603681; Fax: 01507 608501). website: www.louthgolfclub.com

MABLETHORPE. **Sandilands Golf Club,** Roman Bank, Sandilands, Sutton-on-Sea LN12 2RJ (01507 441432). *Location:* A52 one mile south of Sutton-on-Sea. Seaside links adjacent to sea and sand. 18 holes, 6021 yards. S.S.S. 69. 40-acre practice area. *Green Fees:* information not available. *Eating facilities:* bar snacks available. *Visitors:* welcome. *Society Meetings:* welcome with reductions for numbers. Professional/Manager: Simon Sherratt (01507 441432).

MARKET RASEN. **Market Rasen and District Golf Club,** Legsby Road, Market Rasen LN8 3DZ (01673 842319). *Location:* A46 to Market Rasen - one mile east of town. Wooded heathland course. 18 holes, 6239 yards. S.S.S. 70. Practice ground. *Green Fees:* £28.00 per round, £39.00 per day. 2010 rates (subject to review). *Eating facilities:* available every day. *Visitors:* welcome weekdays with prior booking, must be members of a bona fide golf club, weekends with members only. *Society Meetings:* welcome weekdays with prior booking. Professional: A.M. Chester (01673 842416). Secretary: J.P. Smith (01673 842319). e-mail: marketrasengolf@onetel.net
website: www.marketrasengolfclub.co.uk

MARKET RASEN. **Market Rasen Racecourse 9-Hole Pay and Play Course,** Legsby Road, Market Rasen LN8 3EA (01673 843434; Fax: 01673 844532). *Location:* on A631 Market Rasen to Louth road, midway between Lincoln and Grimsby. Course is in centre of picturesque National Hunt racecourse. 9 holes, 2532 yards. S.S.S. 33. *Green Fees:* information not available. *Eating facilities:* hot and cold drinks and sweet shop available April to October. *Visitors:* no restrictions. Golf course is closed on race days. *Society Meetings:* welcome on application to Secretary. Secretary: Pip Adams*

SCUNTHORPE. **Ashby Decoy Golf Club,** Burringham Road, Scunthorpe, North Lincolnshire DN17 2AB (01724 866561; Fax: 01724 271708). *Location:* leave M181 Scunthorpe South, turn right, right again, third right by ASDA Superstore. Flat wooded, parkland course. 18 holes, 6281 yards. S.S.S. 70. Large practice area. *Green Fees:* £25.00 per round, £30.00 per day. *Eating facilities:* full catering and bar available. *Visitors:* welcome weekdays only. *Society Meetings:* Monday, Wednesday, Thursday, Friday. Professional: Andrew Miller (01724 868972). Secretary: Mrs J.A. Harrison (01724 866561; Fax: 01724 271708).
e-mail: info@ashbydecoygolfclub.co.uk
website: www.ashbydecoy.co.uk

SCUNTHORPE. **Grange Park Golf Club,** Butterwick Road, Messingham, Scunthorpe DN17 3PP (01724 762945). *Location:* five miles south of Scunthorpe between Messingham and East Butterwick, four miles south of Junction 3 of M180. Parkland course with interesting water features. 18 holes, 6146 yards. S.S.S. 69. Second 9 hole course – flat parkland course, 1300 yards. S.S.S 27. Floodlit driving range. Clubhouse offering full facilities. Pine Lodges available for golf holidays, societies/groups welcome. *Green Fees:* weekdays £16.00, weekends £18.00, Juniors 50% reduction. Memberships available. *Eating facilities:* full catering facilities available. *Visitors:* welcome at all times. Pro shop. Caravan site also available. *Society Meetings:* welcome, ring for details. Golf Professional: Jonathan Drury. Manager: Ian Cannon.
website: www.grangepark.com

SCUNTHORPE. **Holme Hall Golf Club,** Holme Lane, Bottesford, Scunthorpe DN16 3RF (Tel & Fax: 01724 862078). *Location:* M180 Exit 4 (Scunthorpe East). Heathland with sandy subsoil. 18 holes, 6413 yards. S.S.S. 71. *Green Fees:* £30.00 per round, £35.00 per 27 holes, £40.00 per day. *Eating facilities:* full catering and restaurant facilities available. *Visitors:* welcome Monday to Friday. *Society Meetings:* society and corporate packages available by arrangement. Professional: R. McKiernan (01724 851816). Secretary/Manager: R. Webster (01724 862078; Fax: 01724 862081).
e-mail: secretary@holmehallgolf.co.uk
website: www.holmehallgolf.co.uk

The Grange & Links Hotel
& Sandilands Golf Club
Tel: 01507 441334 • Fax: 01507 443033

Our own privately owned 18 hole (Par 70, SSS 69) links golf course. Two tennis courts, 4-acre garden, gymnasium, 2 snooker tables, croquet lawn.

The Hotel is renowned for its superb cuisine in most elegant surroundings. 'Arguably the finest value we've found' *Golf Monthly.*

Sandilands, Sutton-on-Sea, Lincs LN12 2RA
grangeandlinkshotel@btconnect.com • www.grangeandlinkshotel.co.uk

AA ★★★

Luxury Golf Breaks

in your own superb quality Pine Lodge, overlooking the magnificent 18-hole Grange Park golf course. Each 3-bedroom, 2-bathroom lodge (sleeps 6) has extensive views of the 16th hole, and is only a short two-minute walk to the first tee and Clubhouse.

Short Breaks available

Facilities include • 20-bay floodlit driving range • 5 tennis courts • Fishing • Restaurant & Bar

Grange Park,
Butterwick Road,
Messingham,
North Lincs
DN17 3PP
Tel: 01724 762945

www.grangepark.com

THE NORTH SHORE
HOTEL & GOLF CLUB

The North Shore Hotel with its very own magnificent 18 hole golf course has to be one of the finest venues on the Lincolnshire Coast. It has an unrivalled position, being the closest hotel to the sea in Skegness, enjoying views across the Wash to the Norfolk Coast, not to mention its fabulous views of the golf course. The North Shore Hotel is the ideal venue for your Wedding, Conference, Private Function, Golf Day or your Golfing Holiday.

NORTH SHORE HOTEL & GOLF CLUB
North Shore Road, Skegness, Lincolnshire PE25 1DN
Tel: 01754 763298
Email: info@northshorehotel.co.uk
www.northshorehotel.co.uk

SCUNTHORPE. **The Lincolnshire Golf Course,** Crowle, Scunthorpe DN17 4BU (01724 711619). *Location:* M180 Junction 2, A161 to Crowle Goole, course 800 yards on left. Flat parkland. 18 holes, 6430 yards. S.S.S.70. Practice green. *Green Fees:* information not available. *Eating facilities:* bar and restaurant. *Visitors:* welcome, no restrictions. *Society Meetings:* welcome, no restrictions. Proprietor: A. York. Secretary: J. Middlehurst.*

SCUNTHORPE. **Normanby Hall Golf Club,** Normanby Park, Near Scunthorpe DN15 9HU (01724 720226). *Location*: five miles north of Scunthorpe on B1130. Follow signs for Normanby Hall Country Park. Parkland. 18 holes, 6561 yards. S.S.S. 71. Practice area. *Green Fees*: information not available. *Eating facilities*: fully licensed Clubhouse, restaurant; meals most times. *Visitors*: welcome, check times in advance with Professional. *Society Meetings*: bookings taken for weekdays. Professional: Dean Worral (01724 720226). Manager: Nick Over (01724 720226).*

SKEGNESS. **North Shore Hotel and Golf Club,** North Shore Road, Skegness PE25 1DN (01754 763298; Fax: 01754 761902). *Location:* north of town one mile. Part links, part parkland, challenging course situated overlooking the sea. 18 holes, 6134 yards. S.S.S. 71. Putting green. *Green Fees:* from £31.00 per round. *Eating facilities:* formal restaurant, spike bar serving home cooked bar food 10am to 9 pm. Hotel accommodation on course 36 en suite bedroomed hotel. Special winter deals available. *Visitors:* welcome, prior notice required. Golf schools and instruction provided by professional; juniors welcome. *Society Meetings:* welcome, catering for between 4 and 200. Professional: John Cornelius (01754 764822). General Manager: M. McGrath. e-mail: golf@northshorehotel.co.uk
website: www.northshorehotel.co.uk

SKEGNESS. **Seacroft Golf Club,** Drummond Road, Seacroft, Skegness PE25 3AU (Tel & Fax: 01754 763020). *Location:* towards Gibraltar Nature Reserve. Seaside links course. 18 holes, 6492 yards. S.S.S. 72. *Green Fees:* weekdays £48.00 per round, £60.00 per day; Saturdays £60.00 per round, £70.00 per day; Sundays £60.00 per round, £75.00 per day. 2010 rates (subject to review). *Eating facilities:* available all day/evenings. *Visitors:* welcome after 9.30am if members of recognised club or society, Handicap Certificate required. *Society Meetings:* societies/ company golf days and groups catered for on any day. Professional: R. Lawie (01754 769624). Secretary: Richard England (Tel & Fax: 01754 763020). e-mail: richard@seacroft-golfclub.co.uk
website: www.seacroft-golfclub.co.uk

SKEGNESS. **Southview Golf Club,** Southview Leisure Park, Burgh Road, Skegness PE25 2LA (01754 760589; Fax: 01754 768455). *Location:* half a mile from Skegness towards Burgh Le Marsh A158. Flat parkland. 9/18 holes, 5126 yards. S.S.S. *Green Fees:* information not available. *Eating facilities:* full bar and meals service. *Visitors:* welcome. *Society Meetings:* welcome weekdays. Golf Manager: P. Cole.*

SLEAFORD. Sleaford Golf Club, Willoughby Road, Greylees, Sleaford NG34 8PL (01529 488273). *Location:* off A153, two miles west of Sleaford. Inland links-type course, fairly flat and lightly wooded. 18 holes, 6526 yards. S.S.S. 71. Practice field, 6 hole pitch and putt. *Green Fees:* weekdays £28.00 per round, £35.00 per day, Juniors £9.00 per round or day; weekends £36.00 per round or day. (2010 rates). *Eating facilities:* full catering. Bar open seven days. *Visitors:* welcome without reservation, except where weekends. Handicap Certificate may be required. *Society Meetings:* catered for weekdays and weekends only by prior arrangement. Professional: (01529 488644). Manager: N. Porteus (01529 488273).
e-mail: manager@sleafordgolfclub.co.uk
website: www.sleafordgolfclub.co.uk

SOUTH KYME. **South Kyme Golf Club,** Skinners Lane, South Kyme LN4 4AT (01526 861113; Fax: 01526 861080). *Location:* approximately four miles off A153 road from Sleaford to Horncastle, turn right before North Kyme. Four miles off A17 from Sleaford to Boston, turn left before East Heckington. An interesting "inland links" with excellent greens all year round. 18 holes, 6556 yards White, 6194 yards Yellow, 5389 yards Red. S.S.S. White 71, Yellow 69, Red 70. 6 hole Par 3 course, practice ground. *Green Fees:* from £18.00 per round. Check for seasonal 'special offers'. Society discount for 8 players or more. Expert golf instruction available, send for brochure. *Eating facilities:* bar and restaurant. Snacks available all day. Lunch menu available. *Visitors:* Tuesday and Thursday mornings limited tee availability. Advisable to call regarding all potential visits. *Society Meetings:* welcome with prior booking. PGA Director of Golf/Secretary: Peter Chamberlain.
e-mail: southkymegc@hotmail.com
website: www.skgc.co.uk

SPALDING. The Spalding Golf Club, Surfleet, Spalding PE11 4EA (01775 680474). *Location:* four miles from Spalding on A16 to Boston. Parkland course, water features on many of the holes with the drive on the second over the River Glen. 18 holes, 6527 yards. S.S.S. 72. Driving range and practice area. *Green Fees:* weekdays £30.00 per round, £35.00 per day, half rate with a member; weekends £40.00, £20.00 with a member. *Eating facilities:* full catering and bar facilities. *Visitors:* welcome, advisable to telephone in advance. Handicap Certificates required. *Society Meetings:* large groups on Thursdays, smaller groups of up to 16, any weekday April to October. Professional: John Spencer (01775 680474). Secretary: Carole Douglas (01775 680386).
e-mail: secretary@spaldinggolfclub.co.uk
website: www.spaldinggolfclub.co.uk

SPALDING. **Sutton Bridge Golf Club,** New Road, Sutton Bridge, Spalding PE12 9RQ (01406 350323). *Location:* off A17 between Long Sutton and King's Lynn, New Road leads off Sutton Bridge main street (Bridge Road), almost opposite church. Parkland course built around former Victorian dock basin. 9 holes. Small practice ground, driving range. *Green Fees:* April to September £25.00; October to March £15.00. £15.00 with a member. *Eating facilities:* bar and catering open Tuesday to Sunday. *Visitors:* welcome weekdays except Tuesday after 3pm, and Wednesday mornings. *Society Meetings:* welcome weekdays by arrangement; some restrictions, contact club for details. Special concessions for groups of 8 or more; package available. Professional: Antony Lowther (01406 351422). Secretary: T. Young.

SPALDING near. **Gedney Hill Golf Course,** West Drove, Gedney Hill, Near Spalding PE12 0NT (01406 330183). *Location:* six miles from Radar Tower near Crowland, off B1073 follow signs or follow 1066 off A47. Testing interesting course, Guinness Book of Records for longest hole in Britain (671 yards). 18 holes, 5357 yards. S.S.S. 66. Practice/putting area. *Green Fees:* information not available. *Eating facilities:* two bars (one casual spike bar), Chinese restaurant (70 seater). *Visitors:* welcome, no restrictions. Full snooker room/snookerette table, new restaurant conservatory. *Society Meetings:* all very welcome. Discount Golf shop: Neil Venters (01406 330922). Secretary: R. Newns.*

STAMFORD. **Burghley Park Golf Club,** St. Martins Without, Stamford PE9 3JX (01780 753789). *Location:* leave A1 at roundabout on B1081 south of Stamford, club one mile on right. Flat parkland. 18 holes, 6236 yards. S.S.S. 70. *Green Fees:* information not provided. *Eating facilities:* restaurant and bar. *Visitors:* welcome weekdays. Handicap Certificates required. Visit Burghley House, the greatest of Elizabethan mansions. *Society Meetings:* Tuesdays, Wednesdays and Thursdays only. Professional: (01780 762100). Secretary: (01780 753789).
e-mail: burghley.golf@lineone.net
website: www.burghley.golf.org

STAMFORD. **Rutland County Golf Club,** Pickworth, Stamford PE9 4AQ (01780 460330; Fax: 01780 460437). *Location:* heading north on A1 from Stamford, about one and a quarter miles after Texaco Garage/OK Diner, take Pickworth/Woolfox Depot off-slip, turn right under A1, turn left take second turning on right at mobile telephone masts. Heading south, after Ram Jam Inn, take off-slip marked Pickworth/ Woolfox Depot and turn left at mobile telephone masts. Inland links, easy walking. 18 holes, 6440 yards. S.S.S. 71. 9 holes short course. 20 bay floodlit driving range with powertees, floodlit putting green, practice bunker and chipping green. *Green Fees:* from £12.50 but call Course Manager's Office/ TeeBroker on 01780 460239 for outstanding four-ball offers. *Eating facilities:* bar meals, lounge bar, dining room. *Visitors:* very welcome. *Society Meetings:* very welcome, to book call Course Manager's Office/ Teebroker. *Director*: George Lowe.
e-mail: info@rutlandcountygolf.co.uk
website: www.rutlandcountygolf.co.uk

WOODHALL SPA
The Home of English Golf

Enjoy a round of golf on the Hotchkin Championship course - voted the 20th best golf course in the world and the number one inland course in the UK by Golf World magazine - or on the parkland Bracken course, an excellent complement to the Hotchkin.

GOLF WORLD — THE WORLD'S TOP 100 COURSES 2010

Summer rates from:
- Hotchkin £69.50
- Bracken £47.00

WOODHALL SPA
THE NATIONAL GOLF CENTRE

For further information, please contact the Booking Office, quoting **'TGG11'**:
T: 01526 352511
E: booking@englishgolfunion.org W: www.woodhallspagolf.com

The National Golf Centre, The Broadway, Woodhall Spa, Lincolnshire, LN10 6PU

WOODHALL SPA. The National Golf Centre, The Broadway, Woodhall Spa LN10 6PU (01526 352511; Fax: 01526 351817). *Location:* 19 miles from Lincoln, Boston, Sleaford; 23 miles from Skegness; 50 miles from Nottingham. The Hotchkin is a flat heathland course rated 'Best Inland Course in the UK' by *Golf World*; The Bracken is a parkland course opened in 1998. Hotchkin Course: 18 holes, 7080 yards. S.S.S. 75; Bracken Course: 18 holes, 6735 yards S.S.S. 74. Driving range, short game academy, grass tees, putting greens and 9-hole pitch and putt. *Green Fees:* Hotchkin – £83.00 per round (£69.50 EGU/EWGA members); Bracken – £56.00 per round, (£47.00 EGU/EWGA members). Daily rates and reduced rates for Juniors available. *Eating facilities:* clubhouse with restaurant and bar with all facilities. *Visitors:* welcome at all times, all tee times to be booked in advance. Handicap Certificates required. *Society Meetings:* welcome and catered for, but must book in advance. Please contact Golf Reservations (01526 352511).
e-mail: bookings@englishgolfunion.org
website: www. woodhallspagolf.com

For full details of convenient accommodation near clubs and courses

www.holidayguides.com

WOODHALL SPA, LINCOLNSHIRE LN10 6QG

After an enjoyable day's golf at the Woodhall Spa Golf Course, Petwood is the ideal setting in which to relax.
A unique hotel famous for its beautiful gardens and woodland, with 5 excellent golf courses within 30 minutes' drive.

HOTEL • WEDDINGS • CONFERENCES • RESTAURANT

Tel: 01526 352411 • Fax: 01526 353473 • www.petwood.co.uk

The Penny Farthing Inn
Station Road **01526 378359**
Timberland   www.pennyfarthingtimberland.co.uk
pennyfarthing@talktalkbusiness.net

9 minutes from Woodhall Spa

- *Traditional Inn with a warm & friendly atmosphere*
- *7 new large en suite rooms. 32" TVs - Free Internet*
- *All food cooked fresh - we cater for Gluten Free*
- *Good Cask Ales*   *Privately Owned Free House*

FHG Guides
publish a large range of well-known accommodation guides. We will be happy to send you details or you can use the order form at the back of this book.

Northamptonshire

CORBY near. **Priors Hall Golf Club,** Stamford Road, Weldon, Near Corby NN17 3JH (01536 260756). *Location:* on the A43, four miles from Corby on the Stamford Road. Parkland course. 18 holes, 6631 yards, 6063 metres. S.S.S. 72. Practice nets and ground. *Green Fees:* information not available. Certain concessions apply to local residents. *Eating facilities:* bar meals. *Visitors:* welcome at all times; pre-booking advisable; starting sheet in operation. *Society Meetings:* welcome by prior arrangement. Professional: Jeff Bradbrook. Secretary: Phill Ackroyd (01536 263722).*

\DAVENTRY. **Daventry and District Golf Club,** Norton Road, Daventry NN11 2LS (01327 702829). *Location:* on Borough Hill, site of Iron Age Fort and Roman Camp. 9 holes, 5812 yards. S.S.S. 68. *Green Fees:* £15.00 weekdays, £20.00 weekends *Visitors:* welcome weekdays and weekends except Sunday before 11.30am. *Society Meetings*: welcome with prior booking. Hon. Secretary: C. Long.

DAVENTRY. **Staverton Park Golf Club,** Daventry Road, Staverton, Near Daventry NN11 6JT (01327 302000; Fax: 01327 311428). *Location:* one mile from Daventry on A425 to Leamington Spa. Easy access from M1 Junctions 16 or 18. Undulating parkland. Championship course – 18 holes, 6609 yards. S.S.S. 73. Practice range, two putting greens. *Green Fees:* information not available. *Eating facilities:* full catering available at all times. *Visitors:* always welcome. Handicap Certificate required at weekends. Advance Tee Time (visitors) booking (01327 705506). 245-bedroom hotel with leisure and conference facilities. Residential golf packages available. Buggies, trolleys and clubs for hire. *Society Meetings:* welcome, for details please contact Lindi Rawden (01327 302000). Professional: Richard Mudge (01327 311119; Fax: 01327 312787). Secretary: Roy Patrick (01327 876020).*
e-mail: staverton@initialstyle.co.uk
website: www.verve-venues.com

HELLIDON. **Hellidon Lakes Golf Club,** Hellidon Lakes Hotel, Hellidon, Daventry NN11 6GG (01327 262550; Fax: 01327 262559). *Location:* one and a half miles from A361, six miles from Daventry, 12 miles from Banbury. Parkland. 27 hole championship course, putting green. *Green Fees*; information not available. *Eating facilities:* themed 100 seater casual bar and restaurant. AA rosette restaurant. *Visitors:* always welcome. 110 en suite bedrooms, leisure centre, tennis, health and beauty centre with salon, gym, sunbed, steam room, whirlpool bath and heated indoor swimming pool. Indoor golf simulator, 4-lane tenpin bowling. *Society Meetings:* all welcome. Professional: Joe Kingston (01327 262551).*
e-mail: hellidon@marstonhotels.com
website: www.hellidon@marstonhotels.com

KETTERING. **Kettering Golf Club,** Headlands, Kettering NN15 6XA (01536 511104). *Location:* off A14 (Junction 8) A43 to Kettering, right at 1st roundabout and follow signs for golf club. Flat parkland. 18 holes, 6057 yards, 5515 metres. S.S.S. 69. *Green Fees:* £36.00 per round. 2-Fore-1 accepted. *Eating facilities:* available. *Visitors:* welcome weekdays only. *Society Meetings:* catered for Wednesdays and Fridays only by arrangement. Professional: K. Theobald (01536 481014). Secretary: J. Gilding (01536 511104; Fax: 01536 523788).
e-mail: secretary@kettering-golf.co.uk
website: www.kettering-golf.co.uk

THE APPEARANCE OF AN ASTERISK (*) AT THE END OF A CLUB OR COURSE ENTRY INDICATES THAT UP-TO-DATE INFORMATION HAS NOT BEEN SUPPLIED

This 18 hole course was established in 1891, and with excellent greens it is regularly used for Men's and Ladies' County Events and Fixtures. There are two practice areas and a putting green. The well run and friendly Clubhouse is recognised as one of the best in the region for both snacks and main meals. Visitors welcome Monday to Friday.

Kettering Golf Club, Headlands, Kettering, Northamptonshire NN15 6XA
Tel: 01536 511104 or 08458 731215 • e-mail: secretary@kettering-golf.co.uk
www.kettering-golf.co.uk

MARKET HARBOROUGH near. Stoke Albany Golf Club, Ashley Road, Stoke Albany, Market Harborough LE16 8PL (01858 535208; Fax: 01858 535505). *Location:* A427, A14 five minutes away, Market Harborough 10 minutes. Undulating parkland. 18 holes, 6175 yards. S.S.S. 70. Practice area, putting green. *Green Fees:* weekdays £17.00; weekends £21.00 per round. *Eating facilities:* light meals, spike bar. *Visitors:* welcome, no restrictions. *Society Meetings:* all welcome, but booking is essential. Professional: Adrian Clifford. Secretary: R. Want.
e-mail: info@stokealbanygolfclub.co.uk
website: www.stokealbanygolfclub.co.uk

NORTHAMPTON. Brampton Heath Golf Centre, Sandy Lane, Church Brampton, Northampton NN6 8AX (01604 843939; Fax: 01604 843885). *Location:* signposted off A5099 five miles north of Northampton town centre. Undulating heathland course, excellent conditions all weathers. 18 holes, 6533 yards. S.S.S 71, par 72. 18 bay covered, floodlit driving range, PGA Short Course British Championships Par 3 course. *Green Fees:* information not available. *Eating facilities:* full facilities available from 7.30am. *Visitors:* welcome, no restrictions, advisable to book. Buggies and carts available all year round. Short course available - ideal for beginners. Golf superstore. *Society Meetings:* welcome seven days. Online booking available. Professional: Alan Wright. General Manager: Sally Carter-Jones.*
website: www.bhgc.co.uk

NORTHAMPTON. Cold Ashby Golf Club, Stanford Road, Cold Ashby, Northampton NN6 6EP (Tel & Fax: 01604 740548). *Location:* midway between Rugby, Leicester and Northampton, close to Junction 1 A14 and Junction 18 M1. Undulating parkland. 27 holes, 6308 yards. S.S.S. 71. Short game practice area. Driving range. *Green Fees:* £21.00 midweek, £28.00 weekends. *Eating facilities:* meals and bar snacks available daily. *Visitors:* welcome midweek anytime, weekends must reserve a starting time. *Society Meetings:* catered for weekdays and weekends. Professional: Shane Rose (01604 740099; Fax: 01604 740548). Secretary: David Croxton (01604 740548).
e-mail: info@coldashbygolfclub.com
website: www.coldashbygolfclub.com

NORTHAMPTON. Collingtree Park Golf Course Ltd, Windingbrook Lane, Northampton NN4 0XN (01604 700000; Fax: 01604 702600). *Location:* 2 minutes from Junction 15 off M1-A508. Johnny Miller design Championship Course with its signature 18th hole set on a stunning island green. Host to The British Masters 1995/96 and Europro Challenge Tour, and Mobile Cup Seniors Tournament 2005. 18 holes, 6692 yards. S.S.S. 72. Floodlit, covered 16 bay driving range. *Green Fees:* information not available. *Eating facilities:* members bar, Greens restaurant open to the public. *Visitors:* welcome, advised to book in advance. Handicap Certificates required. Indoor teaching facilities. *Society Meetings:* welcome, advisable to book in advance; discount for group bookings. Professionals: Geoff Pook and Brian Mudge (01604 701202/700000). Club Secretary: Les Pullan (01604 700000).*
e-mail: kmundy@collingtreeparkgolf.com

NORTHAMPTON. Delapre Golf Centre, Eagle Drive, Nene Valley Way, Northampton NN4 7DU (01604 764036; Fax: 01604 706378). *Location:* two miles from Junction 15 M1 on A45 towards Wellingborough. Parkland. Five courses: 18 hole main course; 9 holes course; two Par 3 courses; pitch and putt course and putting greens. 40 bay covered floodlit range. *Green Fees:* please visit website for information. *Eating facilities:* licensed bar and restaurant, coffee shop. Opening hours: 7am to 10pm daily. Digicards and meal deals available. *Visitors:* PGA qualified coaches available for private or group tuition; golf schools, video etc. Buggies for hire. *Society Meetings:* welcome. Centre Manager/PGA Professional: Andrew Coleman (01604 764036).
website: www.jackbarker.com

NORTHAMPTON. Kingsthorpe Golf Club, Kingsley Road, Northampton NN2 7BU. *Location:* off M1 and A43. Undulating parkland. 18 holes, 5903 yards. S.S.S. 69. *Green Fees:* weekdays £30.00 per round, £40.00 per day April-October; £20.00 per round, £30.00 per day November-March. *Eating facilities:* full catering. *Visitors:* welcome weekdays; weekends by arrangement. *Society Meetings:* catered for by arrangement, see website for packages; brochure available. Professional: Paul Armstrong (01604 719602). Office: (01604 710610).
e-mail: secretary@kingsthorpe-golf.co.uk
website: www.kingsthorpe-golf.co.uk

Stoke Albany Golf Club

Stoke Albany Golf Club has established itself as one of the most popular 18-hole courses in the Mid Counties. Nestling within the picturesque Welland Valley and set amid beautiful parkland, the course offers panoramic views over the surrounding countryside, with well laid out, individually contoured greens. A "Food 2 Go" catering service provides a range of snacks and drinks.
For further details and special offers call 01858 535208 or visit www.stokealbanygolfclub.co.uk
Stoke Albany Golf Club, Ashley Road,
Stoke Albany, Market Harborough LE16 8PL

NORTHAMPTON. **Northampton Golf Club,** Harlestone, Northampton NN7 4EF (01604 845102; Fax: 01604 820262). *Location:* on A428 north-west of Northampton in the village of Harlestone. Parkland with a lake coming into play 16th and 18th holes. 18 holes, 6515 yards. S.S.S. 72. Practice ground. *Green Fees:* information not provided. *Eating facilities:* restaurant and bar snacks. *Visitors:* welcome weekdays but must have a Certificate of Handicap. *Society Meetings:* weekdays except Wednesdays. Inclusive packages available. Professional: (01604 845167). Director of Golf: Barry Randall (01604 845155; Fax: 01604 820262).
e-mail: golf@northamptongolfclub.co.uk
website: www.northamptongolfclub.co.uk

NORTHAMPTON. **Northamptonshire County Golf Club,** Sandy Lane, Church Brampton, Northampton NN6 8AZ (01604 842951). *Location:* four miles north west of Northampton between A50 and A428. Heathland with woods, gorse and stream. 18 holes, 6505 yards, 5948 metres. S.S.S. 72. Practice ground. Recent addition of 3 extra holes and 6 holes Par 3 course with artificial tees and greens. *Green Fees:* £70.00 for 18 holes, £80.00 for 27 or 36 holes. Special rates for large groups - visit website for details. *Eating facilities:* restaurant and bar. *Visitors:* by prior arrangement, must have Club Handicap. *Society Meetings:* catered for Wednesdays, small groups on Thursdays. Professional: T. Rouse (Tel & Fax: 01604 842226). Secretary: (01604 843025; Fax: 01604 843463).
website: www.countygolfclub.org.uk

NORTHAMPTON. **Overstone Park Golf and Country Club,** Billing Lane, Northampton NN6 0AS (01604 647666; Fax: 01604 642635). *Location:* seven miles from Junction 15 M1 A508 merges with A45. Follow signs for Overstone from Billing turn off. Undulating parkland with some water features. 18 holes, 6478 yards. S.S.S. 72. Practice ground. *Green Fees:* telephone for up to date prices. *Eating facilities:* bar, brasserie/restaurant and spike bar. *Visitors:* welcome seven days - must pre book at weekends. *Society Meetings:* welcome Monday to Friday, special packages available. Accommodation available in 30 en suite rooms. Leisure Club. Professional: Stuart Kier (01604 643555). General Manager: Allan McLundie.
e-mail: enquiries@overstonepark.com
website: www.overstonepark.com

OUNDLE. **Oundle Golf Club,** Benefield Road, Oundle, Peterborough PE8 4EZ (01832 273267). *Location:* one mile from Oundle on Corby Road A447. Parkland course. Home of "The Oundle Putter".18 holes, 6265 yards. Par 72 S.S.S. 70. *Green Fees:* information not available. *Eating facilities:* bar meals/restaurant. *Visitors:* welcome, check with Professional. No visitors before 10.30am at weekends. *Society Meetings:* welcome by arrangement. Professional: R. Keys (01832 273267 Ext. 2). Secretary: D. Foley (01832 273267 Ext. 1; Fax: 01832 273008). GKInfoline: (01832 274882).*
e-mail: office@oundlegolfclub.com
website: www.oundlegolfclub.com

Overstone Park

Overstone Park Golf & Leisure Club is located on the outskirts of Northampton and occupies 165 acres of mature Victorian parkland.

- A unique venue ideally located for either society and corporate days or weekend breaks.
- The award-winning, 18-hole, Par 72 Championship course offers a 'fair but challenging' game to the novice or experienced golfer, with a number of attractive feature holes.
- The course also benefits from excellent drainage making it particularly suitable for winter golf.
- Hotel guests enjoy reduced green fees and FREE use of the leisure facilities.

Tel: 01604 647666

Overstone Park Hotel, Golf & Leisure Resort, Billing Lane, Overstone, Northampton NN6 0AS
e-mail: enquiries@overstonepark.com • www.overstonepark.com

Looking for accommodation near golf clubs?, then visit
www.holidayguides.com
for where to stay when playing golf around the regions

RUSHDEN. **Rushden Golf Club,** Kimbolton Road, Chelveston, Wellingborough NN9 6AN (01933 418511). *Location:* on B645 two miles east of Higham Ferrers. Undulating meadowland. 10 holes, 6249 yards. S.S.S. 70. Small practice area. *Green Fees:* weekdays £25.00, weekends restricted. *Eating facilities:* bar and dining area. *Visitors:* welcome except Wednesday afternoons. *Society Meetings:* small societies catered for weekdays. Secretary: Miss E.J. Williams (01933 418511).
e-mail: secretary@rushdengolfclub.org

TOWCESTER near. **Farthingstone Golf Club and Hotel,** Farthingstone, Near Towcester NN12 8NA (01327 361291; Fax: 01327 361645). *Location:* just a few minutes from Junction 16 of the M1, close to A5 and A45. Major towns within easy reach include Milton Keynes, Banbury, Oxford, Rugby and Northampton. Undulating wooded countryside. 18 holes, 6299 yards. S.S.S. 70 (Par). Practice area. *Green Fees:* information not provided. *Eating facilities:* bar snacks and restaurant. *Visitors:* welcome, advance bookings available. Rental of golf buggies. Hotel, squash court. *Society Meetings:* bookings welcome. Professional: Mike Gallagher (01327 361533). Secretary: Christian Donaldson.
website: www.farthingstone.co.uk

TOWCESTER near. **Whittlebury Park Golf and Country Club**, Whittlebury, Near Towcester NN12 8WP (01327 850000; Fax: 01327 850001). *Location:* on A413 south of Whittlebury village, 10 minutes from M1, J 15a (Northampton), 15 minutes from M1, J14 (Milton Keynes), 20 minutes M40, J10 (Banbury/Oxford). 36 hole Championship course in 4 loops of 9, each with its own distinctive character. Two tier driving range with extensive practice facilities. *Green Fees:* visit website. *Eating facilities:* bar/bistro within clubhouse plus special function suites. *Visitors:* individual golfers, societies and corporate guests welcome seven days. Other sports and activities offered. Indoor Golf Centre with astro turfed putting green and private teaching bays. *Society Meetings:* welcome seven days, by arrangement. Bookings: please contact Golf Shop on (01327 858588).
e-mail: enquiries@whittlebury.com
golfevents@whittlebury.com
website: www.whittlebury.com

WELLINGBOROUGH. **Wellingborough Golf Club**, Harrowden Hall, Great Harrowden, Wellingborough NN9 5AD (01933 677234; Fax: 01933 679379). *Location*: one mile out of Wellingborough on A509, turn right at crossroads by Great Harrowden Church. Undulating parkland. 18 holes, 6651yards, 6079 metres. S.S.S. 72. Practice ground. *Green Fees*: information not available. *Eating facilities*: bar with casual lunch or dinner menu, restaurant. *Visitors*: weekdays only. Buggies available. *Society Meetings*: welcome by appointment. Conference facilities available. Professional: David Clifford (01933 678752). General Manager: David Waite (01933 677234; Fax: 01933 679379). *
e-mail: info@wellingboroughgolfclub.com
website: www.wellingboroughgolfclub.com

PLEASE MENTION THIS GUIDE WHEN YOU ENQUIRE ABOUT CLUBS OR ACCOMMODATION

Farthingstone Hotel & Golf Course
Farthingstone, Near Towcester, Northants NN12 8HA
01327 361291 (Reception) • 01327 361533 (Golf Shop & Tee Bookings)
Fax: 01327 361645 • www.farthingstone.co.uk

This picturesque and challenging course (with country hotel and additional facilities) is tucked away at the head of a secluded valley. Established in 1973, it is a mature and satisfying course that abounds in interesting features. A popular venue for golfing breaks and golf days, Farthingstone offers a relaxed and informal atmosphere and a range of excellent offers, some of which include free beer!

WHITTLEBURY PARK

36 Hole Championship Golf Course
EuroPro Tour venue 2004, 2005 & 2006
Clubhouse of the Year 2007/8 & 2008/9

The impressive Atrium clubhouse overlooks the golf courses and the facilities onsite include:
- 36 Holes of Championship Golf.
- Corporate and Golf Society Days for members and non-members.
- Multi-Activity and Team Building events.
- Product Launches and Exhibitions.
- Accommodation available.

Visit our "Golf Academy."
- The most advanced indoor practice facility in the UK.
- Swing & Putting Analysis.
- 9 hole Southwestern putting green.
- For more information about pricing and promotions contact:

Whittlebury Park
Nr. Towcester, Northamptonshire. NN12 8WP
Tel: 01327 850000 Fax: 01327 850001
Email: golfevents@whittlebury.com   Web: www.whittlebury.com

WELLINGBOROUGH GOLF CLUB

**Harrowden Hall, Great Harrowden
Wellingborough,
Northamptonshire NN9 5AD**

Telephone 01933 677234

e-mail: info@wellingboroughgolfclub.com

'The house, rebuilt in 1719, has been in recent years restored and is now home to Wellingborough Golf Club, a private members' club and one of the best in the country. Wellingborough Golf Club, situated at Harrowden Hall in the heart of the English countryside, presents a magnificent golf course with facilities for conferences, business meetings and private functions. We cater for numbers from 4 to 80 at competitive inclusive rates.

★ All facilities within a short distance of the main motorway network. ★ Easy parking available.
★ Coffee on arrival. ★ Snacks available throughout the day. ★ Full lunch and dinner menus daily.

*Situated 2 miles from Wellingborough on the A509,
68 miles from London and 3 miles from A1/M1 link.*

**– For further details contact: David Waite on 01933 677234
Please visit our website at www.wellingboroughgolfclub.com**

Nottinghamshire

BULWELL. **Bulwell Forest Golf Club,** Hucknall Road, Bulwell NG6 9LQ. *Location:* A610 north of Nottingham, M1 Junction 26, three miles from course. Heathland or links type course. 18 holes, 5726 yards. S.S.S. 68. *Green Fees:* telephone for offers and twilight reductions. *Eating facilities:* bar snacks available, societies or parties catered to order. *Visitors:* welcome weekdays except Tuesday mornings (Ladies' Day) and Saturday morning. Flat green bowls, hard tennis court and children's playground all on site. *Society Meetings:* catered for every day, but book well in advance. Professional: Ian Brown (0115 9763172). Secretary/Manager: R.D. Savage (Tel & Fax: 0115 9770576).
e-mail: secretary@bulwellforestgolfclub.co.uk
website: www.bulwellforestgolfclub.co.uk

CALVERTON. **Ramsdale Park Golf Centre,** Oxton Road, Calverton NG14 6NU (01159 655 600; Fax: 01159 654 105). *Location:* leave M1 at J26 to Arnold, from there take the A60 to Doncaster, turn right onto B6366, Club is on right. Scenic parkland course offering exciting and testing golf, with spectacular views over Nottinghamshire. Seely Course, 18 holes, 6674 yards; Lee Course, 18 holes, Par 3 2844 yards. S.S.S. 54. 24-bay floodlit driving range and practice area. *Green Fees:* information not available. *Eating facilities:* comfortable and relaxing bar with heated patio, restaurant catering for group bookings. *Visitors:* welcome any time. PGA Teaching Academy. *Society Meetings:* welcome anytime, including weekends. Special rates and bespoke packages always available; please call for details. Professional: Robert Macey (01159 655 600). Secretary: Nick Birch (01159 655 600).
e-mail: info@ramsdaleparkgc.co.uk
website: www.ramsdaleparkgc.co.uk

CALVERTON. **Springwater Golf Club,** Moor Lane, Calverton, Nottingham NG14 6FZ (0115 965 4946). *Location:* off A6097. Moor Lane is one mile south east of Oxton roundabout, course one mile south east of Calverton. Parkland course set in an orchard with new and mature trees, four ponds, well drained. 18 holes, 6262 yards. S.S.S. 71. Floodlit driving range. *Green Fees:* £22.00 weekdays, £27 weekends. *Eating facilities:* fully licensed, bar food, and function rooms available every day. *Visitors:* welcome, weekdays and weekends off peak, seven day booking in advance for non-members. Dress code in operation. *Society Meetings:* weekdays and off peak weekends. Professional: Paul Drew (0115 965 4946). Secretary: Eddie Brady (0115 952 3956).

EAST LEAKE. **Rushcliffe Golf Club,** Stocking Lane, East Leake, Near Loughborough LE12 5RL (01509 852959). *Location:* on A60 signposted eight miles south of Nottingham. Wooded hills on edge of the Wolds. 18 holes, 6200 yards. S.S.S. 70. Practice ground. *Green Fees:* £25.00 per round. *Eating facilities*: full catering except Mondays when bar snacks only. *Visitors:* welcome with reservation, weekends without a member between 9.30am to 11am and 3pm to 4.30pm. *Society Meetings:* catered for Mondays, Wednesdays, Thursdays and Fridays strictly by prior booking. Professional: Chris Hall (01509 852701). Secretary: C. Bee (01509 852959).
e-mail: secretary@rushcliffegolfclub.com
website: www.rushcliffegolfclub.com

EDWALTON. **Edwalton Golf Courses,** Wellin Lane, Edwalton, Nottingham NG12 4AS (0115 923 4775). *Location:* follow Nottingham ring road, course signposted from roundabout on ring road. Gently sloping parkland. 9 holes, 3342 yards. S.S.S. 72. Also 9 hole par 3 course. Driving range (seasonal). *Green Fees:* information not available. *Eating facilities:* first class catering, bar open all day. *Visitors:* welcome, book in advance. Professional: Lee Rawlings (0115 923 4775). Secretary: Debbie (0115 923 5473 Mon-Fri 8.30am-12.30pm). *

HUCKNALL. **Hucknall Golf Centre,** Wigwam Lane, Hucknall, Nottingham NG15 7TA (0115 9642037; Fax: 0115 9642724). *Location:* 300 yards from Hucknall Railway Station (signposted). Parkland course. 18 holes, 6001 yards. S.S.S. 70. Driving range, putting green and chipping green. *Green Fees:* information not available. *Eating facilities:* "Swan" bar and restaurant. *Visitors:* always welcome. Handicap certificates not required. *Society Meetings:* always welcome. Manager: Richard Hanson.*

KIRKBY-IN-ASHFIELD. Notts. Golf Club Ltd, Hollinwell, Kirkby-in-Ashfield, Nottingham NG17 7QR (01623 753225; Fax: 01623 753655). *Location:* three miles from Exit 27 on M1, turn off M1 then left on A611. Testing heathland championship course. 18 holes, 7213 yards. S.S.S. 76. *Green Fees:* information not available. *Visitors:* welcome on production of Handicap Certificate (weekends and Bank Holidays on application only). Advisable to book beforehand. *Society Meetings:* welcome weekdays. Professional: Mike Bradley. General Manager: Brian Noble.*

LENTON LANE. Riverside Golf Centre, Trentside, Lenton Lane NG7 2SA. *Location:* A52 Nottingham to Grantham, two miles from Nottingham city centre, near Clifton Bridge. Flat course, easy to walk. 9 holes, 2000 yards. S.S.S. 31. Par 3 course. *Green Fees:* information not available. *Eating facilities:* licensed restaurant/bar. Excellent facilities. *Visitors:* welcome all week. Pay and play course, booking required. *Society Meetings:* very welcome. Professionals: Guy Meek, Russell Meek (0115 9862179; Fax: 01159 865989). Secretary: G. Meek (0115 9862220; Fax: 01159 865989).*

LONG EATON. Trent Lock Golf Centre, Lock Lane, Sawley, Long Eaton, Nottingham NG10 2FY (0115 9464398; Fax: 0115 9461183). *Location:* Sawley/ Long Eaton, two miles from M1 Junctions 24 and 25. Set in rural countryside with six lakes and River Trent. 18 holes, 5883 yards, Par 69. 9 hole Pay and Play, 2911 yards, Par 36. 22-bay floodlit driving range. *Green Fees:* information not provided. *Eating facilities:* à la carte restaurant (0115 9461184), bar food, 200 seater function room. *Visitors:* welcome anytime. Online "Virtuatour". The Business Venue - three purpose-built conference rooms. *Society Meetings:* all welcome. Professional: Mark Taylor. Director of Golf: E.W. McCausland (0115 9464398). e-mail: enquiries@trentlockgolf.com
website: www.trentlock.co.uk

MANSFIELD. Coxmoor Golf Club, Coxmoor Road, Sutton in Ashfield, Mansfield NG17 5LF (01623 557359). *Location:* exit Junction 27 M1, A611 for three miles. Testing heathland championship course. 18 holes, 6577 yards. S.S.S. 72. Practice area and nets. *Green Fees:* weekdays £45.00 per round, £58.00 per day. Golf/food packages available. *Eating facilities:* restaurant and bars. *Visitors:* welcome except weekends and Bank Holidays, pre-book through Professional. (Tuesday Ladies' Day). *Society Meetings:* catered for by prior application to Secretary. Professional: Craig Wright (01623 559906). Secretary: J. Chambers (01623 557359; Fax: 01623 557435).
e-mail: secretary@coxmoorgolfclub.co.uk
website: www.coxmoorgolfclub.co.uk

MANSFIELD. Mansfield Woodhouse Golf Club, Leeming Lane North, Mansfield Woodhouse NG19 9EU (01623 623521). *Location:* Junction 27 of M1, A60 Mansfield – Warsop. Flat parkland. 9 holes, 2446 yards. S.S.S. 64. *Green Fees:* information not available. *Eating facilities:* bar snacks. *Visitors:* welcome, unrestricted – pay and play. Professional: L. Highfield Jnr. (01623 623521). Manager/Secretary: S.L. Highfield (01623 623521).*

TRENT LOCK GOLF CENTRE
18 hole course par 69, 9 hole course par 36, short game area, 22 bay automated powertee golf range, golf club custom fitting centre, 120 seater Locks Bar, 100 seater Locks Restaurant, 200 seater function suite and the business venue incorporating 3 meeting rooms and self contained breakout zone with up to date equipment.
Contact: 0115 9464398
www.trentlock.co.uk • enquiries@trentlockgolf.com

PINE LODGE HOTEL
281 Nottingham Road, Mansfield,
Nottinghamshire NG18 4SE

Close to Coxmoor, Hollinwell and Sherwood Forest Golf Clubs, we offer quality, value, service – and a warm welcome – in addition to the good food, car parking and garden. Free wireless internet access. All bedrooms en suite – featuring r/c colour TV with Freeview and satellite stations, direct-dial phone and tea/coffee making facilities.

Tel: 01623 622308 • Fax: 01623 656819
e-mail: reception@pinelodge-hotel.co.uk • www.pinelodge-hotel.co.uk

MANSFIELD. **Sherwood Forest Golf Club,** Eakring Road, Mansfield NG18 3EW (01623 626689). *Location:* leave M1 at Exit 27, take signs for Mansfield, proceed via Southwell Road and Oak Tree Lane - course is located one mile east on Eakring Road. Traditional heathland course with an abundance of heather, pines and silver birch. 18 holes, 6860 yards. S.S.S. 74. Two practice grounds. *Green Fees:* £55.00 per round, £75.00 per day. *Eating facilities:* bar with snooker table, lounge and dining room; full catering service every day. *Visitors:* welcome by arrangement and must be member of a recognised golf club with a Handicap. *Society Meetings:* catered for by arrangement. Professional: K. Hall (01623 627403; Fax: 01623 420412).
e-mail: info@sherwoodforestgolfclub.co.uk

MAPPERLEY. **Mapperley Golf Club,** Central Avenue, Plains Road, Mapperley NG3 6RH (0115 9556672). *Location:* B684, four miles north east of centre of Nottingham. Hilly picturesque course. 18 holes, 6335 yards. S.S.S. 70. Practice ground. *Green Fees:* information not available. *Eating facilities:* bar and food all day. *Visitors:* welcome except Saturdays and Ladies' Day (Tuesdays). *Society Meetings:* catered for, please ring Professional for price. Ass. Professional: John Newham (0115 9556673). Secretary: Michael Mulhearn (0115 9556672). *

NEWARK. **Newark Golf Club,** Coddington, Newark NG24 2QX (01636 626282; Fax: 01636 626497). *Location:* off the A17 Sleaford road four miles east of Newark. Parkland, wooded course. 18 holes, 6444 yards. S.S.S. 71. Practice ground. *Green Fees:* £36.00 weekdays; weekends £42.00. *Eating facilities:* full catering, bar all day. *Visitors:* welcome with reservation. Restriction at peak times Saturday and Sunday, Ladies' Day Tuesday. Snooker. Professional tuition and computer/video analysis. *Society Meetings:* welcome except Tuesdays, weekends. Professional: Peter Lockley. Manager: David Collingwood.
e-mail: manager@newarkgolfclub.co.uk
website: www.newarkgolfclub.co.uk

NOTTINGHAM. **Beeston Fields Golf Club,** Old Drive, Wollaton Road, Beeston NG9 3DD (0115 925 7062). *Location:* Wollaton road off A52 Derby road, M1, Junction 25. Parkland. 18 holes, 6430 yards. S.S.S. 71. Practice ground and net available. *Green Fees:* weekdays £39.00, weekends £45.00. *Eating facilities:* available daily. *Visitors:* welcome, pre-booking recommended, Tuesday not until 2.30pm. *Society Meetings:* Mondays, Wednesdays and Fridays, telephone for society rates. Professional: Alun Wardle (0115 925 7062). Secretary: J. Lewis (0115 925 7062).
e-mail: info@beestonfields.co.uk
website: www.beestonfields.co.uk

NOTTINGHAM. **Chilwell Manor Golf Club,** Meadow Lane, Chilwell, Nottingham NG9 5AE (0115 925 8958; Fax: 0115 922 0575). *Location:* four miles from Nottingham on main Nottingham to Birmingham road. Flat parkland course. 18 holes, 6379 yards. S.S.S. 70. *Green Fees:* Winter (Nov-March) £20.00 per round; Summer (Apr-Oct) £25.00 per round. Winter packages available. *Eating facilities:* available. *Visitors:* welcome weekdays with reservation, restricted at certain busy times. *Society Meetings:* societies catered for by appointment (minimum 16). Professional: P. Wilson. Hon. Secretary: C. Lawrence.
e-mail: info@chilwellmanorgolfclub.co.uk

NOTTINGHAM. **Cotgrave Place Golf and Country Club,** Stragglethorpe, Nottingham NG12 3HB (0115 9333344; Fax: 0115 9334567). *Location:* ten minutes east of Nottingham on the A52 towards Radcliffe-on-Trent, 20 miles from M1. Lakeside and parkland course. Two courses: Open Course 18 holes, 6302 yards; Masters Course 18 holes, 5933 yards. 9 bay floodlit driving range, practice net, short game area, putting green. *Green Fees:* from £28.00. *Eating facilities:* newly refurbished restaurant and snack bar. *Visitors:* welcome at all times, subject to reservation. Conference facilities for up to 200 people. *Society Meetings:* welcome, please telephone for packages. Professional: Robert Smith. General Manager: Nick Leuty.
e-mail: cotgrave@crown-golf.co.uk
website: www.cotgraveplacegolf.co.uk

Beeston Fields Golf Club
Old Drive, Wollaton Road, Beeston, Nottingham NG9 3DD

Tel: 0115 925 7062 • e-mail: info@beestonfields.co.uk • www.beestonfields.co.uk

Close to the city centre and the M1, yet tucked away from the bustle of everyday life, Beeston Fields is a relaxing, calm oasis. Our challenging parkland golf course will test your skills, our historic clubhouse will entrance you and the whole ambiance will refresh and invigorate you.
Visitors welcome. Societies catered for Mondays, Wednesdays and Fridays. Golf packages available.

NOTTINGHAM. **Nottingham City Golf Club,** Norwich Gardens, Bulwell Hall Park, Nottingham NG6 8LF. *Location:* Exit 26 M1, at first roundabout follow signs for Bulwell. Parkland. 18 holes, 6218 yards. S.S.S. 69. *Green Fees.* telephone 01159 272767 for information. Secretary: G. Chappell (07740 288694).

NOTTINGHAM. **Oakmere Park Golf Club,** Oaks Lane, Oxton, Near Nottingham NG25 0RH (0115 965 3545; Fax: 0115 965 5628). *Location:* eight miles north east of Nottingham on A614. Heathland course. Admirals Course: 18 holes, 6739 yards, S.S.S. 73. Commanders Course: 9 holes, 6573 yards. S.S.S. 72. 20 bay floodlit driving range. *Green Fees:* Admirals Course from £24.00 weekdays and from £34.00 weekends. Commanders Course from £7.00 weekdays. *Eating facilities:* clubhouse bar, spike bar, restaurant and resident chef. *Visitors:* welcome at all times, phone to book. *Society Meetings:* welcome, weekend golf available, require maximum notice possible. Professional/ Director of Golf: Daryl St. John Jones.
e-mail: enquiries@oakmerepark.co.uk
website: www.oakmerepark.co.uk

NOTTINGHAM. **Ruddington Grange Golf Club,** Wilford Road, Ruddington, Nottingham NG11 6NB (0115 9214139). *Location:* M1 Junction 24 Nottingham road, A52 to Nottingham Knight island, right to Ruddington, half a mile outside Ruddington. Parkland. 18 holes, 6515 yards. Par 72. S.S.S. 72. *Green Fees:* information not provided. *Eating facilities:* full restaurant. *Visitors:* welcome all the time but at weekends members have priority. Tee times must be booked. *Society Meetings:* welcome Monday to Friday. Professional: R. Simpson (0115 9211951). Secretary: Paul Deacon.
e-mail: info@ruddingtongrange.co.uk
website: www.ruddingtongrange.co.uk

THE APPEARANCE OF AN ASTERISK (*) AT THE END OF A CLUB OR COURSE ENTRY INDICATES THAT UP-TO-DATE INFORMATION HAS NOT BEEN SUPPLIED

Ruddington Grange

**Ruddington Grange Golf Club Ltd,
Wilford Road, Ruddington, Nottingham NG11 6NB**

You get the best of both worlds at Ruddington Grange, a splendid golf course and an idyllic setting for weddings and conferences.
Golfers of all standards relish the challenge of a par-72 course that has rapidly developed into one of the finest in the country. Ruddington Grange is far more than just a golf course.
A village location just 3 miles from the centre of Nottingham, plus a choice of meeting & function rooms, make the Grange an ideal choice.

**Tel: 0115 921 1951 (Golf)
0115 921 4139 (Hospitality)
Fax: 0115 940 5165
www.ruddingtongrange.co.uk**

NOTTINGHAM. **Wollaton Park Golf Club,** Lime Tree Avenue, Wollaton Park, Nottingham NG8 1BT (0115 978 7574; Fax: 0115 970 0736). *Location:* entrance off slip road from A52 Derby Road at junction A614 Nottingham Ringroad. Traditional parkland course with many mature trees; two deer herds roam the course. 18 holes, 6445 yards. S.S.S. 71. Two practice areas and pitch and putt course. *Green Fees:* weekdays £38.00/£52.00; weekends £42.00/£58.00. 2010 rates (subject to review). Special rates on application for visiting societies. *Eating facilities:* full restaurant and snack bar. *Visitors:* welcome at all times except Wednesday mornings. *Society Meetings:* catered for Tuesdays and Fridays. Professional: John Lower (0115 978 4834). Secretary: Avril Jamieson (0115 978 7574).
e-mail: secretary@wollatonparkgolfclub.com

Oakmere Park Golf Club

"The All Weather Course"

Admiral's Course: 18 holes, 6739 yards, SSS 73
Commander's Course: 9 holes, 6573 yards, SSS 72
♦ Full clubhouse facilities ♦ Pro Shop
♦ Practice facilities with a premier learning academy.
♦ Societies welcome ♦ Package deals available
Green Fees from £24 weekdays, £34 weekends (Admiral's);
from £7 for 9 holes weekdays (Commander's)

Professional: Daryl St John Jones
**Oakmere Park Golf Club
Oaks Lane, Oxton, Nottingham NG25 0RH
Tel: 0115 965 3545 • Fax: 0115 965 5628**
enquiries@oakmerepark.co.uk • www.oakmerepark.co.uk

218 Nottinghamshire / MIDLANDS REGION — THE GOLF GUIDE 2011

RADCLIFFE-ON-TRENT. **Radcliffe-on-Trent Golf Club,** Dewberry Lane, Cropwell Road, Radcliffe-on-Trent NG12 2JH (0115 9333000). *Location:* A52 from Nottingham turn right at traffic lights on Cropwell Road; 400 yards along on left hand side. Flat, wooded parkland. 18 holes, 6374 yards. S.S.S. 71. Two large practice areas. *Green Fees:* weekdays £30.00 per round, £40.00 per day; weekends £37.00 per round, £45.00 per day (reductions for members' guests). *Eating facilities:* snacks, meals and bar. *Visitors:* welcome, confirm course availability with Professional or Secretary. *Society Meetings:* catered for on Wednesdays and Fridays. Professional: Craig George (l0115 9333000). Finance Manager: Les Wake (0115 9333000; Fax: 0115 9116991). Club Manager: Bill Dunn (0115 9333000; Fax: 0115 9116991)
e-mail: les.wake@radcliffeontrentgc.co.uk
        bill.dunn@radcliffeontrentgc.co.uk
website: www.radcliffeontrentgc.co.uk

RETFORD. **Retford Golf Club Ltd,** Brecks Road, Ordsall, Retford DN22 7UA (01777 711188). *Location:* one mile south off A620 midway between Worksop and Gainsborough. Wooded parkland. 18 holes, 6507 yards. S.S.S. 72, Par 72. Practice ground. *Green Fees:* information not provided. *Eating facilities:* meals available and licensed bar. *Visitors*: welcome, except Tuesday mornings. *Society Meetings:* welcome by prior arrangement. Professional: C. Morris (01777 703733). Secretary: (01777 711188; Fax: 01777 710412).

RUFFORD. **Rufford Park Golf & Country Club,** Rufford Lane, Rufford, Newark NG22 9DG (01623 825253; Fax: 01623 825254). *Location*: 400 yards off A614, two miles south of Ollerton roundabout. Map available on request. Scenic parkland course. 18 holes, 6368 yards. S.S.S. 71. 16-bay floodlit driving range, practice facilities. *Green Fees:* weekday £22.00, weekend £28.00. 2010 rates (subject to review). *Eating facilities:* clubhouse and restaurant with spectacular views. Large function suite and meeting rooms for up to 200 people. *Visitors:* always welcome; buggies for hire. *Society Meetings:* corporate hospitality and society days catered for. Professionals: James Thompson and John Vaughan. Secretary: Kay Whitehead.
website: www.ruffordpark.co.uk

SOUTHWELL. **Norwood Park Golf Course Ltd,** Norwood Park, Southwell NG25 0PF (01636 816626). *Location:* half-a-mile west of Southwell, off the road to Kirklington. American-style layout parkland course in beautiful grounds of stately home. Natural water features and large undulating greens. 18-acre grass practice ground. 18 holes, 6805 yards from the back tees. Par 72. New West Wood Academy Course opened April 2009. *Green Fees:* from £20.00; West Wood Green fees from £7.00. *Eating facilities:* available. *Visitors:* always welcome. 2-Fore-1 welcome any day. *Society Meetings:* always welcome. Conference facilities in stately home available. Professional: Rob Macey. Manager/Secretary: Paul Thornton.
e-mail: golf@norwoodpark.co.uk
website: www.norwoodpark.co.uk

SOUTHWELL. **Southwell Golf Club,** Southwell Racecourse, Rolleston, Newark NG25 0TS (01636 816501/813706). Flat parkland course with water features. 18 holes, 5772 yards. S.S.S. 68. Driving nets, pitching, putting green, practice area. *Green Fees*: weekdays £18.00, with member £10.00; weekends £21.00, with member £12.00. *Eating facilities:* full service all day. *Visitors:* welcome, please book in advance. 12 bedroom Motel on site. Professional: Chris White (01636 813706). Secretary: Mike Harness (01636 821651).
e-mail: southwellgolfclub@southwellgolfclub.com
       misylharness@btinternet.com

STANTON-ON-THE-WOLDS. **Stanton-on-the-Wolds Golf Club,** Golf Course Road, Stanton-on-the-Wolds NG12 5BH (0115 937 4885). *Location:* seven miles south of Nottingham, one mile west of main Nottingham-Melton road. Meadow land. 18 holes, 6184 yards, 5708 metres. S.S.S. 70 (yellow tees). Practice ground. *Green Fees:* information not available. *Eating facilities:* restaurant and bar. *Visitors:* welcome by prior arrangement with Secretary, weekends with member only. *Society Meetings:* catered for by arrangement with Secretary. Professional: Nick Hernon (0115 937 2390). Secretary: Michael J. Price (0115 937 4885).*
e-mail: info@stantongc.co.uk
website: www.stantongc.co.uk

WORKSOP. **Bondhay Golf Club & Academy,** Bondhay Lane, Whitwell Common, Worksop S80 3EH (01909 723608). *Location:* from Junction 30 M1, A619 towards Worksop; signposted Bondhay Lane after 3½ miles. Chatsworth Estate, on the ancient boundary of Derbyshire and Yorkshire. Flat with bordering woodlands. 18-hole Championship course, 6871 yards. S.S.S. 72. Par 3 Academy and family course, driving range, putting green and practice bunkers. PGA tuition; latest EZGO RXV buggies available. *Green Fees:* from £16.00 midweek, £26.00 weekends. *Eating facilities:* full catering and hospitality available. *Visitors:* welcome all year. *Society Meetings:* welcome all year with prior booking. Golf Professional: Michael Ramsden. Director: Mark Hardisty.
website: www.bondhaygolfclub.com

WORKSOP. **College Pines Golf Club,** Worksop College Drive, Worksop S80 3AL (Clubhouse 01909 488785; Pro Shop: 01909 501431). *Location:* situated on outskirts of town on B6034, Edwinstowe road adjacent to Worksop College. Heathland course surrounded by woodland; very well drained, with Winter play a speciality. 18 holes, 6801 yards. S.S.S. 73. Driving range and short game practice area. *Green Fees:* weekdays £16.00 per round, £10.00 with a member; weekends £22.00 per round, £15.00 with a member. 2010 rates (subject to review). *Eating facilities:* full facilities. *Visitors:* welcome by appointment; phone for starting times. *Society Meetings:* welcome by appointment. Golf Director/Professional: Charles Snell (01909 501431).
website: www.collegepinesgolfclub.co.uk

THE GOLF GUIDE 2011 — MIDLANDS REGION / Nottinghamshire

WORKSOP. Kilton Forest Golf Club, Blyth Road, Worksop S81 0TL (01909 486563). *Location:* main Worksop to Blyth road, right hand side. Undulating parkland. 18 holes, 6424 yards. S.S.S. 71, Par 72. Practice and putting areas. *Green Fees:* information not provided. *Eating facilities:* bar meals and restaurant area. *Visitors:* welcome, club competitions most Sundays – check with Professional. *Society Meetings:* by arrangement with Professional. Professional: Stuart Betteridge (01909 486563). Secretary: John Beeston.

WORKSOP. Lindrick Golf Club, Lindrick Common, Worksop S81 8BH (01909 485802). *Location*: on A57 four miles west of Worksop. M1 Junction 31 on to A57 Worksop. Heathland. 18 holes, 6612 yards, 6046 metres. S.S.S. 71. Two practice areas. *Green Fees:* information not available. *Eating facilities*: dining room and Ryder Cup Room. *Visitors*: welcome weekdays, except Tuesday mornings. Enquire re Sunday availability. Prior booking required. *Society Meetings:* catered for weekdays. Professional: John King (01909 475820). Secretary: Carol Kirk (01909 475282; Fax: 01909 488685).*
website: www.lindrickgolfclub.co.uk

WORKSOP. Worksop Golf Club, Windmill Lane, Worksop S80 2SQ (01909 477731; Fax: 01909 530917). *Location:* just off Worksop bypass (A57), take B6034 Edwinstowe immediately left; clubhouse 400 yards. Heathland with gorse, broom, birch and oak; easy walking. 18 holes, 6660 yards. S.S.S. 72. Practice ground. *Green Fees:* information not available. *Eating facilities:* dining room and bar. *Visitors:* welcome Mondays, Wednesdays and Fridays. Advise preliminary phone call to Professional. Snooker table. *Society Meetings:* weekdays only by arrangement with Professional. Not Bank Holidays. Professional: K. Crossland (01909 477731). Secretary: D.A. Dufall 01909 477731; Fax: 01909 530917).*

PLEASE NOTE

All the information regarding Golf Clubs in this guide is given in good faith in the belief that it is correct. However, the publishers cannot guarantee the facts given in these pages, neither are they responsible for changes in ownership or facilities, such as green fees, that may take place after the date of going to press. Readers should always satisfy themselves that the facilities they require are available and that the terms, if quoted, still apply.

Beeston Fields Golf Club, Nottingham

Shropshire

BRIDGNORTH. **Bridgnorth Golf Club,** Stanley Lane, Bridgnorth WV16 4SF (Tel & Fax: 01746 763315). *Location:* one mile from town centre on Broseley road. Parkland, alongside River Severn. 18 holes, 6582 yards. S.S.S. 73. Practice ground. *Green Fees:* information not available. *Eating facilities:* full catering available except Mondays. *Visitors:* welcome weekdays except Wednesday. Handicap Certificate or bona fide club membership required. *Society Meetings:* catered for Monday, Tuesday, Thursday, Friday only. Professional: Steve Russell. Secretary: B. Ayrey.*

BRIDGNORTH. **Chesterton Valley Golf Club,** Chesterton, Near Worfield, Bridgnorth WV15 5NX (01746 783682). *Location:* B4176 Dudley/Telford road. 18 holes, Par 71. *Green Fees:* £16.00. *Visitors:* no restrictions but can book 24 hours in advance. Professional/Secretary: Philip Hinton.

BRIDGNORTH. **Severn Meadows Golf Club,** Highley, Bridgnorth WV16 6HZ (01746 862212). *Location:* seven miles from Bridgnorth on B4555. Eight miles from Bewdley on B4194, then on to B4555. Signposted from village. Undulating woodland course. Severn Valley Steam Railway runs through the middle of the course, on the banks of the River Severn. 18 holes, 6357 yards. Par 72. *Green Fees:* weekday £15.00; weekend £20.00. *Eating facilities:* bar snacks, lunches daily, fully licensed bar. *Visitors:* welcome anytime weekdays but must book tee times at weekends. *Society Meetings:* welcome anytime. Professional/Secretary: Noel Woodman (01746 862212).

CHURCH STRETTON. **Church Stretton Golf Club,** Trevor Hill, Church Stretton SY6 6JH (01694 722281). *Location:* one mile west of A49, adjacent to Carding Mill Valley. Set on the lower slopes of the Longmynd Hills, with wonderful springy turf and panoramic views of the surrounding country. No winter greens. 18 holes, 5020 yards. S.S.S. 65. *Green Fees:* information not available. *Eating facilities:* meals and snacks available daily, full bar facilities. *Visitors:* welcome, Saturdays not between 9am and 10.30am and 1pm to 2.30pm (Winter 12noon to 1.30pm), Sundays not before 10.30am or between 1pm and 2.30pm (Winter 12noon to 1.30pm). *Society Meetings:* welcome. Contact Hon. Secretary or Professional to pre-book. Professional: James Townsend (01694 722281; mobile: 07973 762510). Hon. Secretary John Povall (01743 860679; mobile: 07817 538080).*
e-mail: secretary@churchstrettongolfclub.co.uk
website: www.churchstrettongolfclub.co.uk

CLEOBURY MORTIMER. **Cleobury Mortimer Golf Club,** Wyre Common, Cleobury Mortimer, Near Kidderminster DY14 8HQ (01299 271112). *Location:* two miles out of Cleobury on B4201. 27 hole course comprising three loops of nine holes. Badgers Sett 3271 yards, Foxes Run 2960 yards, Deer Park 3167 yards, giving three 18 hole courses with S.S.S. 71, 70, 69. *Green Fees:* information not available. *Eating facilities:* restaurant and Spike Bar. *Visitors:* welcome midweek; weekends by arrangement. Snooker room. Golf Buggies for hire, trolleys available, bookable in advance. *Society Meetings:* welcome by prior arrangement, ring for details. PGA Professional: Martin Payne (01299 271112). Director of Golf: Tim Hall. Secretary/Manager: Graham Pain (01299 271112; Fax: 01299 271468).*
e-mail: enquiries@cleoburygolfclub.com
website: www.cleoburygolfclub.com

LUDLOW. **Elm Lodge Golf Course,** Elm Lodge, Fishmore, Ludlow SY8 3DP (01584 872308; Fax: 01584 877397). *Location*: from the A49 Ludlow bypass turn towards Ludlow town centre at the roundabout junction A4117 Kidderminster road; after 1/3 mile turn right. Various types of terrain. 9 holes, 1051 yards, Par 3, S.S.S. 27. *Green Fees:* adults £5.00, under 16s £4.00. Discounts for groups of 10 or more. *Visitors:* welcome, pay-and play course. Accommodation available in Elm Lodge.
e-mail: info@elm-lodge.org.uk
website: www.elm-lodge.org.uk

At Cleobury Mortimer Golf Club we believe that a really enjoyable game of golf takes more than just a great golf course, and that your whole experience is part of a day that you'll remember. 27 holes set out in three individual 9-hole loops, covering 200 acres of Shropshire's most beautiful countryside. Each hole has its own character and challenge.

A Clubhouse with excellent facilities, choice of refreshment and dining areas to suit all tastes – open 7 days. Golf Shop with wide range of stock from all the leading brands.

Cleobury Mortimer Golf Club
Wyre Common, Cleobury Mortimer DY14 8HQ
Enquiries: 01299 271112 • Fax: 01299 271468
e-mail: enquiries@cleoburygolfclub.com • www.cleoburygolfclub.com

27 unique holes set in 200 acres of Shropshire's most beautiful countryside

LUDLOW. **Ludlow Golf Club,** Bromfield, Ludlow SY8 2BT (01584 856285; Fax: 01584 856366). *Location:* A49 one mile north of Ludlow bypass, turn right onto the Bridgnorth road. Well signposted. Heathland course based on sandy soil providing springy fairways and superb greens. 18 holes, 6277 yards. S.S.S. 70. Practice ground. *Green Fees:* weekdays £30.00 per round, £35.00 a day; weekends £35.00 per round (reductions with member). 2010 rates (subject to review). *Eating facilities:* full catering and bar service during normal hours. *Visitors:* welcome weekdays and weekends with prior booking. *Society Meetings:* call for details. Professional/ Administrator: R. Price (Pro Shop: 01584 856366; Admin: 01584 856285).

MARKET DRAYTON. **Market Drayton Golf Club,** Sutton, Market Drayton TF9 2HX (01630 652266). *Location:* A41 south towards Newport, turn left at crossroads just past Tern Hill Barracks. Parkland with exceptional views. 18 holes, 6214 yards, 5702 metres. S.S.S. 71. *Green Fees:* £30.00. *Eating facilities:* bar and high class catering open all day. *Visitors:* welcome weekdays only; first tee closed daily until 9.30am and from 12.30pm to 1.30pm. Tuesday Ladies' Day. On-course bungalow (sleeps 6) available from £30.00 per person per night including FREE golf. *Society Meetings:* catered for weekdays by prior arrangement. Professional: Russell Clewes (01630 656237). Secretary: Chris Stubbs (01630 652266). Steward: Gareth Hickman (01630 658083). e-mail: market.draytongc@btconnect.com

NEWPORT. **Aqualate Golf Centre,** Stafford Road, Newport TF10 9DB (01952 811699). *Location*: two miles east of Newport town centre; 400 yards from the junction with A41. Parkland course with gentle gradients and water hazards. 18 holes, 5659 yards. S.S.S. 67. 20 bay floodlit driving range, practice putting green. *Green Fees*: information not available. *Eating facilities*: coffee bar. *Visitors*: welcome at all times (pay and play), but advance booking advisable.

No handicap restrictions. PGA Professional tuition available by appointment - group and/or personal lessons. Golf Club Memberships available. *Society Meetings*: welcome by prior arrangement. Hire clubs and trolleys available. Opening hours: weekdays 9.00am to 10.00pm, weekends and Bank Holidays 7.30am to 9.00pm. Professional: Kevin Short (01952 811699). Director: H. Brian Dawes (01952 811699).*

NEWPORT. **Lilleshall Hall Golf Club,** Lilleshall, Near Newport TF10 9AS (01952 604776; Fax: 01952 604272). **Location:** at Lillyhurst turn north off Abbey Road, which joins Wellington Road near Lilleshall and the B4379 near Sheriffhales. Wooded parkland. 18 holes, 5813 yards. S.S.S. 68. Practice ground. **Green Fees:** £32.00 midweek, £42.00 weekends (with approval).**Eating facilities:** meals served 10am to 5.30pm, order in advance. **Visitors:** welcome on weekdays, check with Professional for tee restrictions. **Society Meetings:** catered for by prior arrangement with Secretary. Professional: R. Bluck. Secretary: A. Marklew.
e-mail: honsec@lhgc.entadsl.com
website: www.lilleshallhallgolfclub.co.uk

OSWESTRY. **Henlle Park Golf Club,** Henlle Lane, Gobowen, Oswestry SY10 7AX (01691 670680; Fax: 01691 652429). *Location:* Take the B5009 off the A5 trunk road just north of Gobowen Village, take first left and Henlle Park is on the right. Undulating Georgian Parkland with lakes and mature trees.New Clubhouse opened 2008. 18 holes, 6107 yards. S.S.S. 69. Practice ground, nets, putting green. *Green Fees:* information not available. *Eating facilities:* bar, restaurant for up to 100. Balcony. *Visitors:* welcome by arrangement with Secretaries' office, not before 10am. *Society Meetings:* see website. Golf Shop, Pro tuition available. Professional: David Skelton (01691 670680 ext 3). Secretary: Liz Williams (01691 670680ext 1).*
e-mail: enquiries@henllegolf.co.uk
website: www.henllegolf.co.uk

Once described as the Pine Valley of England, tucked away in rolling Shropshire countryside, this picturesque, relatively flat and easy walking course is a popular favourite with visiting golfers. A 5813 yard course set in 165 acres, with tight fairways cutting through mature trees with undulating greens. The back 9 is simply stunning.
Lilleshall Hall Golf Club, Lilleshall, Newport, Shropshire TF10 9AS
Tel: 01952 604776 Fax: 01952 604272
e-mail: honsec@lhgc.entadsl.com • www.lilleshallhallgolfclub.co.uk

Welcome to Brownhill Bungalow
INCLUDES FREE GOLF
Rates for 2010/2011:
1/2 nights £45 per person per night
3/4 nights £38 per person per night
5 nights or more £30 per person per night.
Please contact the Secretary on 01630 652266 for booking details

Market Drayton Golf Club
Sutton, Market Drayton, Shropshire TF9 2HX
A hidden gem set in the quiet rural Shropshire countryside and an enjoyable test for even the most proficient of players. Whether you are an individual or a member of a society you will truly enjoy a great round of golf at Market Drayton.
Please contact the Club Secretary on **01630 652266.**
e-mail: market.draytongc@btconnect.com • www.marketdraytongolfclub.co.uk
On-Course self-catering bungalow overlooking the 14th green available to rent.

Shropshire / MIDLANDS REGION

OSWESTRY. Llanymynech Golf Club, Pant, Near Oswestry SY10 8LB (01691 830542). *Location:* six miles south of Oswestry on A483, turn at Cross Guns Inn, Pant. Undulating lush hilltop course with extensive views, 15 holes in Wales, three in England. 18 holes, 6047 yards. S.S.S. 69. Practice area and putting green. *Green Fees:* weekdays £32.00 per round, £42.00 per day; weekends £40.00 per round. 2010 rates (subject to review). Half price with member. Reductions for Juniors. *Eating facilities:* restaurant and bar. *Visitors:* welcome weekdays; some weekends by prior arrangement; prior enquiry advisable. *Society Meetings:* weekdays by arrangement with Secretary. Professional: A.P. Griffiths (01691 830878). Secretary: Howard Jones (01691 830983).
website: www.llanymynechgolfclub.co.uk

OSWESTRY. Mile End Golf Club, Mile End, Oswestry SY11 4JF (01691 671246 (bookings); Fax: 01691 670580). *Location:* signposted off A5, one mile south-east of Oswestry. Gently undulating course with water features. 18 holes, 6233 yards. S.S.S. 70. Driving range. *Green Fees:* weekdays £20.00 per round, £30.00 per day; weekends £28.00 per round, £42.00 per day. 2010 rates (subject to review). *Eating facilities:* full bar/catering available. *Visitors:* welcome at all times subject to course availability. Extensively stocked quality golf shop with all top name brands. Hi-tech custom fitting service. New driving range and custom fit centre now open. *Society Meetings:* welcome weekdays by prior arrangement. Professional: Scott Carpenter (01691 671246). Secretary: Richard Thompson (01691 671246; Fax: 01691 670580).
e-mail: info@mileendgolfclub.co.uk
website: www.mileendgolfclub.co.uk

OSWESTRY. Oswestry Golf Club, Aston Park, Queen's Head, Oswestry SY11 4JJ. *Location:* a friendly members' club four miles south-east of Oswestry on A5. Mature parkland course with many feature trees, laid out by James Braid in rolling Shropshire countryside. Well drained soils ensure excellent year-round play. 18 holes, 6051 yards. S.S.S. 69. Practice ground. *Green Fees:* Sunday to Friday £35.00, Saturdays £41.00, Twilight £19.00. *Eating facilities:* dining room and bar. *Visitors:* welcome; must be member of another club with a recognised Handicap Certificate or playing with a member. Snooker table. *Society Meetings:* societies of 16 plus welcomed Wednesdays and Fridays by arrangement with the Secretary. Smaller groups catered for by arrangement with the Professional. Professional: Jason Davies (01691 610448). Secretary: Roger Stamp (Tel & Fax: 01691 610535).
e-mail: secretary@oswestrygolfclub.co.uk
website: www.oswestrygolfclub.co.uk

SHIFNAL. Shifnal Golf Club, Decker Hill, Shifnal TF11 8QL (Tel & Fax: 01952 460330). *Location:* one mile north east of Shifnal, one mile from A5, Junction 4 M54. Parkland course. 18 holes, 6504 yards. S.S.S. 71. *Green Fees:* £35.00 per round, £40.00 per day; weekends with member only. *Eating facilities:* full catering service. *Visitors:* welcome, phone first, not Thursdays, weekends or Bank Holidays. *Society Meetings:* catered for by arrangement with Secretary. Professional: D. Ashton (01952 461560). Secretary: N.R. Milton (Tel & Fax: 01952 460330).
e-mail: secretary@shifnalgolf.com
website: www.shifnalgolf.com

SHREWSBURY. Arscott Golf Club, Arscott, Pontesbury, Shrewsbury SY5 0XP (Tel & Fax: 01743 860114). *Location:* 10 minutes from Shrewsbury off the A488 Bishops Castle road. Set in mature parkland with stunning views of South Shropshire and Welsh Borders. 18 holes, 6158 yards. S.S.S. 69. Practice area, putting green and driving net. *Green Fees:* £24.00 weekdays; £29.00 weekends. *Eating facilities:* food and beverages available from 10.30am daily. *Visitors:* welcome at all times. Please telephone Shop to book tees. Self-catering cottage available. *Society Meetings:* by arrangement, please telephone. Secretary: Mrs Sian Hinkins (01743 860114 or 01743 860881).

SHREWSBURY. Hawkstone Park, Weston-under-Redcastle, Shrewsbury SY4 5UY (01948 841700; Fax: 01939 200311). *Location*: 14 miles north of Shrewsbury off A49. Hawkstone Course – parkland, 18 holes, 6491 yards (white). S.S.S. 71; Windmill Course – parkland (designed by Brian Huggett), 18 holes, 6476 yards (white). S.S.S. 71; Academy Par 3 Course – 6 holes, 741 yards. Par 18, S.S.S. 18. Target practice ground, putting green and short game area. Open all year. *Green Fees:* information not provided. *Eating facilities*: Terrace Room, all day bar and restaurant. *Visitors*: welcome. 66 room Hotel and historic park. *Society Meetings:* welcome. Reservations for bookings: 01948 841700. Professional: Stuart Leech (01948 841700).
e-mail: enquiries@hawkstone.co.uk
website: www.hawkstone.co.uk

SHREWSBURY. Shrewsbury Golf Club, Condover, Shrewsbury SY5 7BL (Tel & Fax: 01743 872977). *Location:* A49 two miles south west of Shrewsbury. Parkland first 9 holes, undulating back 9 holes with fine views of Longmynd. 18 holes, 6207 yards. S.S.S. 70. Large practice ground. *Green Fees:* information not available. *Eating facilities:* full facilities available seven days. *Visitors:* welcome at all times except Wednesday mornings and weekends before 10am. *Society Meetings:* welcome by arrangement. Professional: John Richards (01743 872977). Secretary: D.J. Knight (01743 872977).*
e-mail: info@shrewsbury-golf-club.co.uk

TELFORD. The Shropshire Golf Centre, Muxton, Telford TF2 8PQ (01952 677800; Fax: 01952 677622). *Location:* off Junction 4 of M54, follow signs for Muxton (signposted). Parkland course featuring many water hazards, wide, American-type fairways, and undulating well-bunkered greens. Three loops of 9 holes (Blue, Silver, Gold): 27 holes, 3286 yards, 3303 yards, 3334 yards, S.S.S. 71, 72, 72. 30 bay floodlit driving range, 12 hole short course, 18 hole putting green. *Green Fees:* information not available. *Eating facilities:* Greenkeeper Bar and Grill, Conservatory Restaurant. *Visitors:* welcome, no restrictions. Pay as you Play. Buggies available, golf academy. *Society Meetings:* very welcome, packages available. Professional: Mark Sutcliffe.*
website: www.theshropshire.co.uk

TELFORD. **Telford Golf & Spa Hotel,** Great Hay Drive, Sutton Heights, Telford TF7 4DT (01952 429977; Fax: 01952 586602). *Location:* turn off A442 between Bridgnorth and Telford, only two miles to M54 Junction 4. Hotel overlooks Ironbridge Gorge - a World Heritage site. Rolling parkland course with water features, suspended water table greens as at Augusta. 18 holes, 6741 yards (whites). S.S.S. 72. All-weather driving range, two putting greens. *Green Fees:* information not available. *Eating facilities:* bar and refreshments adjacent 18th green. 114 bedrooms, restaurant, leisure and spa suite and indoor heated pool (half Olympic size). *Visitors:* welcome, but advance booking essential. Handicap Certificates or membership of bona fide golf club essential. *Society Meetings:* by arrangement. Private rooms available. Professional: George Boden (01952 586052). Secretary: Ian Lucas (01952 429977).*
e-mail: telford@qhotels.co.uk

TELFORD. **Wrekin Golf Club,** Ercall Woods, Golf Links Lane, Wellington, Telford TF6 5BX (01952 244032; Fax: 01952 252906). *Location*: from M54 Junction 7 to Wellington, turn back along Holyhead road towards Wellington for three-quarters-of-a-mile. Golf Links Lane on right hand side. Undulating parkland. 18 holes, 5570 yards. S.S.S. 67. Small practice ground. *Green Fees*: midweek £27.50 per round, £35.00 per day, weekends £30.00 per round. *Eating facilities*: restaurant and bar facilities by arrangement with Stewardess. *Visitors:* welcome except weekends and Bank Holidays when limited. *Society Meetings*: by arrangement with the Secretary. Professional: O. Evans (01952 223101). Secretary: B.P. Everitt (01952 244032; Fax: 01952 252906).*
e-mail: secretary@wrekingolfclub.org.uk

WHITCHURCH. **Macdonald Hill Valley Hotel Golf and Country Club,** Terrick Road, Whitchurch SY13 4JZ (01948 667788; Fax: 01948 667373). *Location:* signposted from Whitchurch Bypass. Magnificent Alliss/Thomas Emerald Championship Course. 18 holes, 6628 yards. Par 73. Sapphire Course 4801 yards, Par 66. *Green Fees:* information not available. *Eating facilities:* full restaurant/bars, snacks available. *Visitors:* welcome without reservation. Luxury 90 bedroom 4-star hotel; leisure facilities also available. *Society Meetings:* please contact for details. Professional: Graeme Bagnall (01948 663032). Secretary: John Pickering (01948 860425).*
e-mail: general.hillvalley@macdonald-hotels.co.uk
website: www.hillvalleygolfclub.co.uk

WOLVERHAMPTON. **Patshull Park Hotel, Golf and Country Club,** Patshull Road, Pattingham, Near Wolverhampton WV6 7HR (01902 700100; Fax: 01902 700874). *Location:* take Junction 3 off M54, turn left on A41 back towards Wolverhampton and fork right into Albrighton. From main crossroads turn right along Cross Road, taking T-junction with A464 Wolverhampton/Shifnal Road and turning right towards Shifnal. Signposted Patshull Park Golf Course. Glorious parkland course set in landscapes by Capability Brown; John Jacobs designed course. 18 holes, 6345 yards. S.S.S. 69. Large practice area. *Green Fees:* information not available. *Eating facilities:* Lakeside Restaurant and two bars. Earl's Bar. *Visitors:* welcome on application. 49 bedroom hotel, country club and swimming pool, fishing lakes (80 acres). Residential Breaks. Buggies available. *Society Meetings:* corporate and society meetings welcome; special group rates and facilities. Professional: Richard Bissell (01902 700342).*
website: www.patshull-park.co.uk

WORFIELD. **Worfield Golf Club,** Roughton, Worfield, Near Bridgnorth WV15 5HE (01746 716541; Fax:01746 716302). *Location*: A454 Wolverhampton to Bridgnorth Road, three miles from Bridgnorth. Parkland course set on rolling countryside. 18 holes, 6440 yards. S.S.S. 71. Chipping area, practice area, putting greens. *Green Fees:* weekdays £20.00, weekends after 1pm £20.00 per person. *Eating facilities*: restaurant and bar meals all day. *Visitors:* welcome. Buggies available. *Society meetings:* all welcome. Professional: Nick Doody (01746 716541). Secretary: William Weaver (01746 716372; Fax: 01746 716302).

Staffordshire

BARLASTON. **Barlaston Golf Club,** Meaford Road, Stone ST15 8UX (01782 372795). *Location:* one mile south of Barlaston off A34; between Stoke and Stone. 18 holes, 5801 yards. S.S.S. 68. *Green Fees:* information not available. *Eating facilities:* dining room and bar snacks with lounge bar. *Visitors:* welcome anytime. *Society Meetings:* welcome weekdays. Professional: Ian Rogers (01782 372795). Admin (01782 372867; Fax: 01782 373648).*
e-mail: barlaston.gc@virgin.net
website: www.barlastongolfclub.co.uk

BURTON UPON TRENT. **The Branston Golf and Country Club,** Burton Road, Branston, Burton upon Trent DE14 3DP (01283 512211; Fax: 01283 566984). *Location:* A38 Junction A5121. Flat parkland adjacent to the River Trent, spectacular 18th hole, water on 13 holes (flowing). 18 holes, 6697 yards. S.S.S. 72. 9 holes 1856 yards, S.S.S. 58. Driving range. *Green Fees:* information not available. *Eating facilities:* restaurant, bar, spikes bar, private rooms. *Visitors:* welcome, two week advance booking system in operation, restrictions weekends. Buggy hire, trolleys available. Country Club has extensive leisure facilities. *Society Meetings:* welcome midweek, special rates. Professional: Iain Ross (01283 512211; Fax: 01283 566984). Golf Booking office (01283 528320).*

BURTON UPON TRENT. **The Craythorne,** Craythorne Road, Rolleston on Dove, Burton upon Trent DE13 0AZ (01283 564329; Fax: 01283 511908). *Location:* A38 first turning to Burton from Derby, A5121 signposted Stretton. Parkland. 18 holes, 5641 yards. S.S.S. 68 (gents), 70 (ladies). Floodlit driving range. *Green Fees:* £40.00 and under. *Eating facilities:* bars and restaurant open daily; function room. *Visitors:* welcome at all times, booking required at weekends. Special society and golfing packages. *Society Meetings:* welcome. Professional: Steve Hadfield **(01283 533745).** Managing Director: Tony Wright.
e-mail: admin@craythorne.co.uk
website: www.craythorne.co.uk

CANNOCK. **Beau Desert Golf Club,** Rugeley Road, Hazel Slade, Cannock WS12 0PJ (01543 422626; Fax: 01543 451137). *Location:* A460 Hednesford, signposted Beau Desert. Fowler-designed heathland course. 18 holes, 6310 yards. S.S.S. 71. Driving range, practice ground. *Green Fees:* information not available. *Eating facilities:* full catering and bar. *Visitors:* welcome anytime subject to availability. *Society Meetings:* catered for Monday to Thursday. Professional: Barrie Stevens (01543 422492). Manager: Steve Mainwaring.*
website: www.bdgc.co.uk

CANNOCK. **Cannock Park Golf Club,** Stafford Road, Cannock WS11 2AL (01543 578850). *Location:* on the A34 Stafford Road, quarter of a mile from Cannock town centre. Parkland course, playing alongside Cannock Chase. 18 holes, 5149 yards. S.S.S. 65. *Green Fees:* £11.50 weekdays; £15.00 weekends (am), £11.50 weekends (after 4pm). Phone bookings up to two weeks in advance. Reductions for Juniors. 2010 rates (subject to review). *Visitors:* welcome every day. Golf shop. *Society Meetings:* welcome weekdays. Bookings and enquiries (01543 578850).

CHEADLE near. **Whiston Hall Golf Club and Mansion Court Hotel,** Whiston, Near Cheadle ST10 2HZ (01538 266260). *Location:* A52 Stoke to Ashbourne road, 3 miles from Alton Towers. Scenic course set in beautiful countryside. 18 holes, 5784 yards. S.S.S. 69. *Green Fees:* information not available. *Eating facilities:* extensive clubhouse bar menu available from 8.00am onwards. *Visitors:* welcome at any time. Golfing theme rooms for all types of golfing breaks. Snooker, fly fishing. *Society Meetings:* all welcome 7 days a week. Packages available. Golf breaks also available. Secretary: R. Cliff.

LEEK. **Leek Golf Club,** Cheddleton Road, Birchall, Leek ST13 5RE (01538 384779). *Location:* one mile south of Leek on A520. Undulating parkland. 18 holes, 6218 yards. S.S.S. 70. *Green Fees:* weekdays £30.00; weekends and Bank Holidays £35.00. Twilight rates (after 4pm on Saturdays and Sundays) £15.00. 2010 rates (subject to review). *Eating facilities:* full catering facilities 11.30am, light refreshments from 10am. *Visitors:* welcome most times by prior arrangement. *Society Meetings:* catered for by arrangement Wednesdays (limited availability on Mondays and Fridays). Catering (01538 384779). PGA Professional: Fred Fearn. Secretary: David T. Brookhouse (Tel & Fax: 01538 384779).
e-mail: enquiries@leekgolfclub.co.uk
website: www.leekgolfclub.co.uk

LEEK. **Leek Westwood Golf Club,** Newcastle Road, Leek ST13 7AA (01538 398385). *Location:* A53 one and a half miles south of Leek. Moorland/ parkland. 18 holes, 6105 yards. S.S.S. 70. Practice area, nets, chipping green. *Green Fees:* telephone Professional for special offers. *Eating facilities:* full facilities. *Visitors/Society Meetings:* Monday to Friday. Professional: Greg Rogula (01538 398897). Secretary: A.J. Horton (Tel & Fax: 01538 398385; Fax: 01538 382485).

LICHFIELD. **The Seedy Mill Golf Club,** Elmhurst, Near Lichfield WS13 8HE (01543 417333; Fax: 01543 418098). *Location:* just off A51 north of Lichfield. Parkland with lakes, ponds and streams. The Mill: 18 holes, 6305 yards. S.S.S. 70; The Spires: 9 holes, Par 3. 26 bay floodlit driving range. *Green Fees:* information not available. *Eating facilities:* full clubhouse facilities open 7.30am to 11pm. *Visitors:* welcome at all times. *Society Meetings:* welcome weekdays and weekends. Professional: Simon Joyce. Secretary: Abi Burns. General Manager: Richard Gee.*

LICHFIELD. **Whittington Heath Golf Club,** Tamworth Road, Lichfield WS14 9PW (01543 432317). *Location:* on A51 Tamworth-Lichfield Road. Wooded heathland. 18 holes, 6490 yards. S.S.S. 71. Practice ground. *Green Fees:* weekdays £40.00 per round, £55.00 36 holes. *Eating facilities:* meals available at all times. *Visitors:* welcome weekdays only. Handicap Certificate or letter of introduction required. *Society Meetings:* catered for Monday, Tuesday and Friday afternoons and Wednesdays or Thursdays by arrangement. Professional: Mike Raj (01543 432261). Secretary: Mrs J.A. Burton (01543 432317; Fax: 01543 433962). Steward: 01543 432212.
e-mail: info@whittingtonheathgc.co.uk
website: www.whittingtonheathgc.co.uk

NEWCASTLE-UNDER-LYME. **Jack Barkers Keele Golf Centre,** Keele Road, Newcastle-under-Lyme ST5 5AB (01782 627596). *Location*: A525 Newcastle to Whitchurch, opposite University of Keele. Undulating parkland. 18 holes, 6396 yards, 5822 metres, S.S.S. 70. Driving range. *Green Fees*: weekdays £13.00, weekends £17.00. Juniors: weekdays £7.00, weekends £9.00 *Eating facilities*: available. *Visitors:* welcome at all times. Buggies, clubs and trolleys available for hire. *Society Meetings*: welcome by arrangement. Manager: N. Worrall.

NEWCASTLE-UNDER-LYME. **Newcastle-under-Lyme Golf Club,** Whitmore Road, Newcastle-under-Lyme ST5 2QB (01782 616583). *Location:* M6 Junction 15, one mile from Newcastle-under-Lyme. Parkland. 18 holes, 6395 yards white, 6276 yards yellow. S.S.S. 71 white, 70 yellow. *Green Fees:* £35.00 for 18 holes, £45.00 for 36 holes. *Eating facilities:* restaurant and bar meals. *Visitors:* welcome. Restrictions at weekends. *Society Meetings:* welcome most week days except Tuesdays by arrangement. Contact Secretary/Manager for details. Professional: David Cooper (01782 618526). Secretary/ Manager: Vicki Wiseman (01782 617006).

PENKRIDGE. **The Chase Golf Club,** Pottal Pool Road, Penkridge ST19 5RN (01785 712191). *Location:* M6 Junction 13, take the A449 to Wolverhampton, then left onto B5012 towards Cannock then onto Rugeley Road. Flat parkland with Links characteristics. 18 holes, 6613 yards. S.S.S. 71. 20 bay floodlit driving range and teaching academy. Putting green, bunker, and chip and run facility. *Green Fees:* information not available. *Eating facilities:* excellent clubhouse facilities. *Visitors:* please ring to book, members have priority. Fully stocked pro shop. *Society Meetings:* welcome at reduced rates. Professional: Michael Beaumont. General Manager: Sean Hall.*

RUGELEY. **Lakeside Golf Club,** Rugeley Power Station, Rugeley WS15 1PR (01889 575667). *Location:* nearest town Rugeley (between Lichfield and Stafford), course over power station grounds. Flat parkland adjacent River Trent. 18 holes, 5765 yards. S.S.S. 68. *Green Fees:* weekdays £15.00, weekends £20.00. *Eating facilities:* bar, lunchtime weekends and every evening. *Visitors:* welcome by arrangement with Professional. *Society Meetings:* welcome; arrange in advance with Professional. Secretary: T.A. Yates (01889 575667). Professional: P.J. Cary (07906 526061).

RUGELEY near. **St Thomas's Priory,** Armitage Lane, Armitage, Near Rugeley WS15 1ED (Tel & Fax: 01543 491911). *Location:* one mile south-east of Rugeley on A513, opposite Ash Tree Inn. Undulating parkland. 18 holes, 5969 yards. S.S.S. 70. Practice range area available. *Green Fees*: information not available. *Eating facilities*: full restaurant and bar facilities. *Visitors:* welcome weekdays, weekends. *Society Meetings*: by arrangement. Professional: M. Beaumont (Tel & Fax: 01543 491911).*

STAFFORD. **Brocton Hall Golf Club,** Brocton, Stafford ST17 0TH (01785 661901; Fax: 01785 661591). *Location:* off A34 Stafford to Cannock four miles south east of Stafford. Undulating parkland. 18 holes, 6095 yards. S.S.S. 69. *Green Fees:* information not available. *Society Meetings:* by arrangement Tuesdays, Thursdays and Fridays. Professional: Nevil Bland (01785 661485). Secretary: Jeremy Duffy (01785 661901).*

STAFFORD. **Ingestre Park Golf Club,** Ingestre, Near Stafford ST18 0RE (01889 270845; Fax: 01889 271434). *Location:* six miles east of Stafford, between Tixall and Great Haywood. Parkland. 18 holes, 6352 yards. S.S.S. 70. Extensive practice ground. *Green Fees:* 18 holes £40.00, £50.00 more than 18 holes weekdays. 2010 rates (subject to review). *Eating facilities:* lunch and dinner menu. *Visitors:* welcome weekdays before 3.30pm. Handicap Certificate required. Buggies available. *Society Meetings:* welcome with reservation except Wednesday. Special winter rates on application. Professional: Danny Scullion (01889 270304). Manager: Mrs D. Williams (01889 270845).

STAFFORD. **Stafford Castle Golf Club,** Newport Road, Stafford ST16 1BP (01785 223821). *Location*: M6 Junction 14, follow signs for town centre and Telford. Off A518 approximately one mile from town centre. Challenging parkland course set in the lee of Stafford Castle. 9 holes, (18 tees). 6383 yards. S.S.S. 70, Par 71. *Green Fees:* weekdays £18.00; weekends £22.00. *Eating* facilities: snacks and full catering available except Mondays. *Visitors*: welcome except Sunday mornings. Society Meetings: by arrangement. Contact: Sharon Calvert.
e-mail: staffordcastlegolfclub@btconnect.com

Please mention this guide when enquiring about clubs or accommodation

Staffordshire / MIDLANDS REGION

STOKE-ON-TRENT. **Burslem Golf Club Ltd,** Wood Farm, High Lane, Tunstall, Stoke-on-Trent ST6 7JT (01782 837006). *Location:* leave Burslem centre by Hamil Road, turn left at High Lane junction, one mile on right. Parkland. 9 holes, 5360 yards. S.S.S. 66. *Green Fees:* weekdays £10.00 per round, £16.00 per day. *Eating facilities:* meals and refreshments by arrangement except Wednesday and Sunday. *Visitors:* welcome weekdays with reservation. Bona fide golf club members only. *Society Meetings:* catered for.

STOKE-ON-TRENT. **Goldenhill Golf Course,** Mobberley Road, Goldenhill, Stoke-on-Trent ST6 5SS (01782 787678). *Location:* on A34 between Tunstall and Kidsgrove, north of Stoke city centre. Rolling parkland course, panoramic views of Mow Cop and Newchapple. 18 holes, 5957 yards, 5447 metres. S.S.S. 69. 24 bay floodlit range open 9 am to 9 pm. *Green Fees:* weekdays from £7.00; weekends from £10.00. *Eating facilities:* fully licensed bar and cafeteria. *Visitors:* visitors and societies welcome 7 days a week.

STOKE-ON-TRENT. **Jack Barker's Greenway Hall,** Stanley Road, Stockton Brook, Stoke-on-Trent ST9 9LJ (01782 503158). *Location:* M6 (Junction15) – A500 - A53 to Leek, right at crossroads in Stockton Brook. Countryside course with wooded areas and some beautiful scenic views. 18 holes, 5681 yards, 5194 metres. S.S.S. 67. *Green Fees:* information not available. *Eating facilities:* meals available from 10am to 11pm. *Visitors:* welcome. *Society Meetings:* welcome, packages available on request. Manager: Jonathan Latham.*

STOKE-ON-TRENT. **Parkhall Golf Course,** Hulme Lane, Weston Coyney, Stoke-on-Trent ST3 5BH (01782 599584). *Location:* one mile east of Longton. Tight unforgiving heathland course, great character, ideal for new golfers looking to improve their game. 18 holes, 2335 yards, 2136 metres. S.S.S. 54. Par 3. *Green Fees:* information not available. *Eating facilities:* chocolate, crisps, pop, tea and coffee. *Visitors:* all welcome. Golf clubs and trolley hire available. Seven days advance booking for weekends and Bank Holidays. *Society Meetings:* welcome. Professional: Joe Mortimore.*

STOKE-ON-TRENT. **Trentham Golf Club**, 14 Barlaston Old Road, Trentham, Stoke-on-Trent ST4 8HB (01782 658109). *Location:* off A34 travelling south of Newcastle (Staffs.). Left at Trentham Gardens onto Longton Road (A5035); right at National Westminster Bank. Open Championship Regional Qualifying course. 18 holes, 6632 yards. S.S.S. 72. Practice ground. *Green Fees:* information not available. *Eating facilities:* lunches and dinners available. *Visitors:* welcome weekdays, and Sundays after 2.30pm. Handicap Certificate required. *Society Meetings:* welcome by prior arrangement. Professional/ General Manager: S. Owen (01782 658109 ext 3/ext 1 office).
website: www.trenthamgolf.org

STOKE-ON-TRENT. **Trentham Park Golf Club,** Trentham Park, Trentham, Stoke-on-Trent ST4 8AE *Location:* off A34 adjoining Trentham Gardens near Junction 15 on M6. 18 holes, 6425 yards. S.S.S. 71. *Green Fees:* information not available. *Visitors:* welcome weekdays; weekends subject to course availability. *Society Meetings:* catered for

---

Stafford Castle Golf Club
Newport Road, Stafford ST16 1BP

Challenging 9 hole parkland course
(18 different tees) set in the lee of Stafford Castle,
one mile from Stafford town centre.
Snacks and full catering available (except Mondays), and visitors are welcome
(except Sunday mornings).

Tel: 01785 223821
e-mail: staffordcastlegolfclub@btconnect.com

Visit **www.holidayguides.com**
for convenient accommodation
when playing golf around the regions

Wednesdays and Fridays only. Professional: Simon Lynn (01782 642125; Fax: 01782 658800). Manager: Gordon Martin (Tel & Fax: 01782 658800).*
e-mail: admin@trenthamparkgolfclub.com
website: www.trenthamparkgolfclub.com

STONE. **Izaak Walton Golf Club,** Eccleshall Road, Cold Norton, Stone ST15 0NS (01785 760900). *Location:* on the B5026 linking Stone and Eccleshall. Testing course with many water features. 18 holes, 6370 yards. S.S.S. 72. Driving range. *Green Fees:* weekdays £25.00, weekends £35.00. Visit website for special offers. *Eating facilities:* available. *Visitors:* welcome. *Society Meetings:* welcome. Contact the Secretary for information. Professional: Rob Grier (01785 760900). Secretary: Charlie Lightbown.
e-mail: secretary@izaakwaltongolfclub.co.uk
website: www.izaakwaltongolfclub.co.uk

STONE. **Stone Golf Club,** The Fillybrooks, Stone ST15 0NB (01785 813103). *Location:* one mile north west of Stone on the A34 adjacent to the Walton Inn. Parkland. 9 holes, 6299 yards. S.S.S. 70. *Green Fees:* information not available. *Eating facilities:* full meals to order, snacks always available, bar. *Visitors:* welcome, not Bank Holidays. Snooker table. *Society Meetings:* catered for by arrangement. Secretary: D.M. Cole (01785 817746).

STOURBRIDGE. **Enville Golf Club Ltd,** Highgate Common, Enville, Stourbridge DY7 5BN (01384 872074). *Location:* leave A449 at Stewpony Hotel taking Bridgnorth Road A458, fork right after Fox Inn following signs for Halfpenny Green Airport. Two flat wooded heathland courses. Highgate Course: 18 holes, 6592 yards. S.S.S 73; Lodge Course: 18 holes, 6417 yards. S.S.S. 71. *Green Fees:* information not available. *Eating facilities:* meals available. *Visitors:* welcome weekdays, advisable to phone prior to visit. Ladies' Day Thursday; weekends with members only. *Society Meetings:* welcome except Thursdays and weekends. Professional: S. Power (01384 872585). Secretary/Manager: J.J. Bishop (01384 872074; Fax: 01384 873996).*
e-mail: secretary@envillegolfclub.com
website: www.envillegolfclub.com

STREETLY. **Little Aston Golf Club,** Roman Road, Streetly, Sutton Coldfield B74 3AN (0121-353 2066). *Location:* off A454. Parkland course. 18 holes, 6670 yards. S.S.S. 73. *Green Fees:* £80.00. *Eating facilities:* dining room and bars, lunch and dinner. *Visitors:* welcome on weekdays by prior arrangement, weekends with a member. *Society Meetings:* welcome Monday, Tuesday, Wednesday and Friday. Professional: Brian Rimmer (0121-353 0330). Manager: Glyn Ridey (0121-353 2942; Fax: 0121-580 8387).
e-mail: manager@littleastongolf.co.uk
website: www.littleastongolf.co.uk

TAMWORTH. **Drayton Park Golf Club,** Drayton Park, Fazeley, Tamworth B78 3TN (01827 251139; Fax: 01827 284035). *Location:* follow signs for Drayton Manor Park, adjacent drive at the top. Parkland with well defined wooded holes. 18 holes, 6473 yards. S.S.S. 71. Practice ground. *Green Fees*: information not available. *Eating facilities*: full catering facilities. *Visitors*: welcome weekdays except Wednesday mornings. *Society Meetings*: catered for Tuesdays and Thursdays, booked through General Manager. Professional: M.W. Passmore (01827 251478). General Manager: Jon Northover (01827 251139; Fax: 01827 284035).
website: www.draytonparkgc.co.uk

TAMWORTH. **Tamworth Golf Centre Limited,** Eagle Drive, Amington, Tamworth B77 4EG (01827 709303; Fax: 01827 709305). *Location:* Junction 10 M42 Tamworth, A5, towards Amington. Parkland course used by NAPGC for Juniors' and Ladies' Championships. 18 holes, 6488 yards. Par 73 S.S.S. 72. Practice area, putting green. *Green Fees:* information not available. *Eating facilities:* lounge bar with catering. *Visitors:* welcome. *Society Meetings:* function room available for meetings, parties, etc.*

UTTOXETER. **Manor Golf Club,** Leese Hill, Kingstone, Uttoxeter ST14 8QT (01889 563234). *Location*: A518, Uttoxeter to Stafford road, 3 miles from Uttoxeter. Grassland course. 18 holes, 6206 yards. S.S.S. 71. Practice range and putting green. *Green Fees*: weekdays £25.00; weekends £35.00. *Eating facilities*: bar meals available Monday to Friday from 12pm till 4pm, Saturday and Sunday from 11am to 4pm. *Visitors*: welcome every day, please book in advance for Saturdays and Sundays. Tuition available. *Society Meetings*: welcome 7 days a week, please call for rates. Course Manager: Ant Foulds.
e-mail: manorgc@btinternet.com
website: www.manorgolfclub.org.uk

UTTOXETER. **Uttoxeter Golf Club,** Wood Lane, Uttoxeter ST14 8JR (01889 566552; Fax: 01889 564884). *Location:* approximately half a mile past the main entrance to the racecourse. Undulating parkland, very picturesque scenery. 18 holes, 5801 yards. S.S.S. 69. Practice area and putting green. *Green Fees:* information not available. *Eating Facilities:* bar, clubhouse dining room. *Visitors:* welcome except on days of "major" competitions. A starting sheet operates at weekends. Buggies and trolleys available for hire. *Society Meetings:* welcome by arrangement (maximum 60), but not at weekends or on Bank Holidays. Professional: Adam McCandless (01889 564884; Fax: 01889 556552). Secretary: Roger Harvey (Tel & Fax: 01889 566552).*

WOLSTANTON. **Wolstanton Golf Club,** Dimsdale Old Hall, Hassam Parade, Wolstanton, Newcastle ST5 9DR (01782 622413; Fax: 01782 622718). *Location:* one mile north of Newcastle, turn right off A34 (Dimsdale Parade), first right (Hassam Parade) then right again 75 yards. Flat parkland. 18 holes, 5533 yards. S.S.S. 68. *Green Fees:* information not provided. *Eating facilities:* full catering service and bar. *Visitors:* welcome weekdays; weekends only as member's guest. Trolleys available. *Society Meetings:* catered for by arrangement. Professional: Simon Arnold (Tel & Fax: 01782 622718). Secretary: Valerie Keenan (01782 622413; Fax: 01782 622413).

Manor Golf Club
Leese Hill, Kingstone,
Uttoxeter, Staffs. ST14 8QT

A traditional English Golf Course which provides a challenge for both low and high handicaps.

Tel: 01889 563234
e-mail: manorgc@btinternet.com

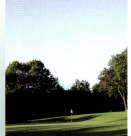

Uttoxeter Golf Club
welcomes societies and visitors

One of the best kept secrets in the country. A beautiful course with stunning views across Staffordshire and Derbyshire.

Club Secretary: 01889 566552
Club Professional: 01889 564884

Warwickshire

ATHERSTONE. Atherstone Golf Club, The Outwoods, Coleshill Road, Atherstone CV9 2RL (01827 713110). *Location:* off Coleshill Road, Atherstone, five miles north of Nuneaton and seven miles south of Tamworth. Undulating parkland. 18 holes, 6006 yards. S.S.S. 71. *Green Fees:* information not available. *Eating facilities:* bar and dining room. *Visitors:* welcome weekdays without reservation, Saturdays with member only, not Sundays. Ladies' Day Wednesday. *Society Meetings:* 12 and above by prior arrangement with Secretary. Secretary: D. Bond (01827 704948).

BERKSWELL. Nailcote Hall Golf Club, Nailcote Lane, Berkswell CV7 7DE (02476 466174; Fax: 02476 470720). Parkland setting. Cromwell Course - 9 holes, 1037 yards. *Green Fees:* information not available. *Eating facilities*: two restaurants and two bars. *Visitors:* welcome. Host venue to the "British Par 3 Championship". Mark Mouland Short Game and Junior Academy available for lessons. Accommodation in hotel and leisure club facilities. Professional: Mark McKay.*
website: www.nailcotehall.co.uk

BIDFORD. Bidford Grange Golf Club, Stratford Road, Bidford B50 4LY (01789 490319; Fax: 01789 490998). *Location:* 6 miles west of Stratford-upon-Avon on the B439. American links course with a variety of water holes. 18 holes, 7233 yards. S.S.S. 74. Driving range and putting green. *Green Fees:* information not available. *Eating facilities:* Spikes Bar and restaurant. *Visitors:* welcome any day, after 9am. On-site Hotel. *Society Meetings:* please call for details or view website. Secretary: Daniel Broadhurst.*
e-mail: enquiries@bidfordgrange.com
website: www.bidfordgrange.com

BRAILES. Feldon Valley Golf Course, Sutton Lane, Lower Brailes, Banbury OX15 5BB (01608 685633; Fax: 01608 685205). The home of Brailes Golf Club. *Location:* M40 Exit 11 Banbury, 10 miles west on B4035; A3400 Shipston on Stour, four miles east on B4035. Parkland/meadowland course. 18 holes, 6304 yards. S.S.S. 70. Practice ground. *Green Fees:* please call for details. *Eating facilities:* modern clubhouse; bar (11am to 11pm) and restaurant (8am to 9pm) facilities. *Visitors:* welcome. Tuition; buggies and trolleys for hire. *Society Meetings:* welcome subject to availability; from £23.95pp. Professional/General Manager: Steve Hutchinson (01608 685336).
e-mail: steve.hutchinson@feldonvalley.co.uk
website: www.brailesgolfclub.co.uk

COVENTRY. City of Coventry Brandon Wood Golf Course, Brandon Lane, Wolston, Near Coventry CV8 3GQ (024 7654 3141). *Location:* six miles south of Coventry off southbound carriageway A45. Parkland on banks of River Avon. 18 holes, 6521 yards. S.S.S. 71. Floodlit driving range. *Green Fees:* information not available. *Eating facilities:* bar and restaurant. *Visitors:* welcome anytime, unrestricted, bookings available up to seven days in advance, telephone Pro Shop. *Society Meetings:* phone Pro Shop for details. Professional/Secretary: Chris Gledhill (024 7654 3141). Stewardess: Paula Howson (024 7654 3133).*
website: www.brandonwoodgolfclub.co.uk

COVENTRY. Marriott Forest of Arden Hotel & Country Club, Maxstoke Lane, Meriden, Coventry CV7 7HR (0870 400 7272; Fax: 0870 400 7372). *Location:* take Junction 6 from M42, follow A45 to Coventry. After one mile turn left into Shepherds Lane, hotel is one and a half miles on left. Parkland and greenside water hazards. Home to 13 consecutive European Tour events. Two courses. The Arden - 7213 yards. S.S.S. 73; The Aylesford - 5801 yards. S.S.S. 68. Floodlit golf academy. *Green Fees:* information not provided. *Eating facilities:* bars and restaurants available. *Visitors:* welcome seven days subject to tee-time availability. 214-bedroom four star hotel with extensive conference and luxurious leisure facilities. *Society Meetings:* enquiries welcome. Professional: Philip Hoye (0958 632170). Director of Golf: Iain Burns.

HENLEY-IN-ARDEN. Henley Golf and Country Club, Birmingham Road, Henley-in-Arden B95 5QA (01564 793715; Fax: 01564 795754). *Location:* two miles from M40 Junction 16; 20 minutes from Birmingham, Solihull, Stratford-upon-Avon and Warwick. Parkland, with lovely countryside views. 18 holes, 6933 yards. S.S.S. 73. 9-hole Par 3 course. Practice range. *Green Fees:* information not available. *Eating facilities:* bar lounge menu, Brasserie. *Visitors:* no restrictions, but must book in advance. Smart casual dress required, no denim. *Society Meetings:* very welcome. Professional: Neale Hyde.*
e-mail: enquiries@henleygcc.co.uk

KENILWORTH. Kenilworth Golf Club Ltd, Crewe Lane, Kenilworth CV8 2EA (01926 854296; Fax: 01926 864453). *Location:* A429 Coventry to Kenilworth adjacent to A46 Coventry to Warwick Road. Parkland and wooded course. 18 holes, 6261 yards. S.S.S. 71. *Green Fees:* £40.00. *Eating facilities:* diningroom, bar snacks, bar. *Visitors:* must be members of another club with official Handicap Certificate. *Society Meetings:* groups (under 60 in number) weekdays, Societies (over 20). Professional: S. Yates (01926 512732). Secretary: R.J. Griffiths (01926 858517; Fax: 01926 864453).

230 Warwickshire / MIDLANDS REGION — THE GOLF GUIDE 2011

LEAMINGTON SPA. **Leamington and County Golf Club,** Golf Lane, Whitnash, Leamington Spa CV31 2QA (01926 425961). *Location:* three and a half miles from M40 south of town centre of Royal Leamington Spa. 18 holes, 6418 yards, 5869 metres. S.S.S. 72. *Green Fees:* weekdays £35.00 per round, £45.00 per day; weekends £40.00 per round. *Eating facilities:* luncheons, teas, evening meals and snacks. *Visitors:* welcome without reservation. *Society Meetings:* catered for. Professional: J. Mellor (01926 425961 option 3). Club Secretary/Manager: David M. Beck (01926 425961 option 2).

LEAMINGTON SPA. **Newbold Comyn Golf Club,** Newbold Terrace East, Leamington Spa CV32 4EW (01926 421157). *Location:* signposted off Willes Road. Parkland, front 9 hilly, back 9 flat. 18 holes, 6315 yards. S.S.S. 70. Practice area. *Green Fees:* weekdays per 18 holes: Seniors (60+) £6.60, over 18s £12.70, under 18s £5.40. Weekends per 18 holes: over 18s £15.65, under 18s £10.95. 2010 rates (subject to review). *Eating facilities:* Newbold Arms on site. *Visitors:* welcome, unrestricted, but please book. Leisure centre on site. *Society Meetings:* catered for, book through Professional. Professional: (01926 421157). Secretaries: L. Ryan (01926 429458), I. Shepherd (01926 313825).
e-mail: ian@viscount5.freeserve.co.uk

MERIDEN. **Stonebridge,** Somers Road, Meriden CV7 7PL (01676 522442; Fax: 01676 522447). *Location:* two minutes from NEC, M42 Junction 6, just off the A45. Parkland. 27 holes, 6102 yards. S.S.S. 70. 6073 yards S.S.S. 70, 5543 yards, S.S.S. 66. 21 bay floodlit driving range. *Green Fees:* weekdays £20.00, weekends £30.00. *Eating facilities:* Spike Bar 8am to 8pm, restaurant Wednesday to Saturday evenings, Sunday lunch. *Visitors:* welcome, seven day advance booking facility for tee-times. Conference and private function suites available. *Society Meetings:* welcome weekdays and weekends, packages available. Professional: Darren Murphy (01676 522442; Fax: 01676 522447).

NORTH WARWICKSHIRE. **Purley Chase Golf Club,** Ridge Lane, Near Nuneaton CV10 0RB (024 7639 3118; Fax: 024 7639 8015). *Location:* three miles off A5 between Atherstone and Nuneaton. Slightly undulating parkland. 18 holes, 6807 yards. S.S.S. 72. Conference and corporate. *Green Fees:* information not available. *Eating facilities:* restaurant. *Visitors:* welcome. *Society Meetings:* welcome, weekdays only. Special rates. Secretary: Linda Jackson (024 7639 3118; Fax: 024 7639 8015).*
website: www.purleychase.com

NUNEATON. **Bramcote Waters Golf Course,** Bazzard Road, Bramcote, Nuneaton CV11 6QJ (01455 220807). *Location:* approximately five miles from Nuneaton, off B4114. Undulating parkland. 9 holes, 2491 yards. S.S.S. 64. *Green Fees:* information not provided. Reductions for Juniors. *Visitors:* always welcome, pay and play or book up to one week in advance. *Society Meetings:* welcome. Professional: Nic Gilks. Secretary: S. Britain.

NUNEATON. **Nuneaton Golf Club,** Golf Drive, Whitestone, Nuneaton CV11 6QF (024 7638 3281). *Location:* Nuneaton Road, B4112 cross with two small roundabouts, Lutterworth Road. Wooded course. 18 holes, 6429 yards. S.S.S. 71. Practice ground. *Green Fees:* information not available. *Eating facilities:* catering available except Mondays; bar open usual hours. *Visitors:* welcome weekdays. *Society Meetings:* welcome - special days Wednesdays. Professional: Mr John Salter (024 7634 0201). Secretary: Mr P. Smith (024 7634 7810; Fax: 024 7632 7563).*

NUNEATON. **Oakridge Golf Club,** Arley Lane, Ansley Village, Nuneaton CV10 9PH (01676 541389; Fax: 01676 542709). *Location:* on outskirts of Nuneaton, approximately 15 minutes from town centre, 20 minutes from Coventry and 25 minutes from Tamworth. Woodland; undulating fairways with many water hazards. 18 holes, 6242 yards. S.S.S. 70. Practice area, Pro shop, putting green. *Green Fees:* information not provided. *Eating facilities:* à la carte restaurant, bar meals, lounge bar. *Visitors:* welcome. Snooker room. *Society Meetings:* welcome weekdays (Monday - Friday). Golf Shop: Tony Harper Golf (01676 540542). Secretary (Admin. and Society Bookings): Mrs S. Lovric; Mr K. Clegg (Golf Section Secretary).

RUGBY. **Rugby Golf Club,** Clifton Road, Rugby CV21 3RD (01788 544637). *Location:* one mile from Rugby town centre on the Clifton road. Parkland course. 18 holes, 5457 yards. S.S.S. 67. Practice ground. *Green Fees:* information not available. *Eating facilities:* bar open daily, dining - contact Steward (01788 544637). *Visitors:* welcome weekdays; weekends and Bank Holidays only with a member. Ladies' Day Wednesday. Carts for hire. Fairway Lounge available for meetings. *Society Meetings:* welcome if pre-booked. Professional: David Quinn (01788 575134). Manager: John Drake (Tel & Fax: 01788 542306).*

RUGBY near. **Whitefields Golf Club and Draycote Hotel,** London Road, Thurlaston, Near Rugby CV23 9LF (01788 815555; Fax: 01788 521695). *Location:* A45 near Rugby where it meets the M45. Undulating parkland course, with water feature; not hilly. Backdrops onto Draycote Water to the south. 18 holes, 6223 yards. S.S.S. 70, Par 71. 16-bay floodlit driving range. *Green Fees:* information not available. *Eating facilities:* restaurant, spike bar, 19th hole. *Visitors:* welcome. Accommodation available in 50 en suite bedrooms all with Sky TV. Five conference rooms available. Golf Shop (01788 815555; Fax: 01788 521695). *Society Meetings:* welcome. Special rates and packages available. Secretary: Brian Coleman (01788 815555; Fax: 01788 521695).*

THE APPEARANCE OF AN ASTERISK (*) AT THE END OF A CLUB OR COURSE ENTRY INDICATES THAT UP-TO-DATE INFORMATION HAS NOT BEEN SUPPLIED

The luxurious Menzies Welcombe Hotel Spa and Golf Club, Stratford-upon-Avon, offers some of the finest leisure facilities in the Midlands.

The par 70, 18 hole championship golf course, with its lakes and rolling countryside is challenging for the expert and exhilarating for the novice.

Take a luxury golfing break and enjoy our stylish golf clubhouse with superb Brasserie and bar. Then relax and rejuvenate at the luxurious Welcombe Spa.

MenziesWelcombe
Hotel Spa & Golf Club
Warwick Road
Stratford-upon-Avon
Warwickshire
CV37 0NR
Tel: 01789 413 800
welcombe.golfpro@menzieshotels.co.uk
www.welcombehotelstratford.co.uk

Golf Breaks from £69.00pp
18-hole par 72 Championship course
Golf Societies and visitors welcome.
www.ingonmanor.co.uk
info@ingonmanor.co.uk
Tel: 01789 731857

STONELEIGH. **Stoneleigh Deer Park Golf Club,** The Old Deer Park, Coventry Road, Stoneleigh CV8 3DR (024 7663 9991; Fax: 024 7651 1533). *Location:* A46 Stoneleigh Village, close to N.A.C. Stoneleigh. Parkland. 18 holes, 6056 yards. S.S.S. 69. 9 hole par 3 course; putting green and practice area. *Green Fees:* Monday to Thursday £20.00, Friday £22.00, weekends and Bank Holidays £30.00. *Eating facilities:* bar and restaurant with full catering. *Visitors:* welcome midweek, restrictions at weekends. *Society Meetings:* welcome midweek, restrictions at weekend. Professional: Matt McGuire (024 7663 9912). Secretary: Cherry Reay.

STRATFORD-UPON-AVON. **Ingon Manor Hotel & Golf Club,** Ingon Lane, Snitterfield, Stratford-upon-Avon CV37 0QE (01789 731857). *Location:* Junction 15 of M40, A46 to Stratford, then signposted 'Ingon Manor'. Undulating greens with stunning views across Welcombe Hills. 18 holes, 6575 yards. Par 72. Large practice area, putting green, driving range. *Green Fees:* information not provided. *Eating facilities:* available daily. Professional: Neil Evans.
e-mail: info@ingonmanor.co.uk
website: www.ingonmanor.co.uk

STRATFORD-UPON-AVON. **Menzies Welcombe Hotel, Spa and Golf Club,** Warwick Road, Stratford-upon-Avon CV37 0NR (01789 295252; Fax: 01789 414666). *Location:* exit M40 at Junction 15, follow signs to Stratford. Club is on A439 after five miles, or take A439 out of town and club is on left after one mile. Undulating parkland with mature trees, lakes and waterfall. 18 holes, 6288 yards. S.S.S. 70. Practice area and putting green. *Green Fees:* information not provided. *Eating facilities:* clubhouse with Atrium Brasserie and private function suites. *Visitors:* welcome, please telephone for starting times. Hotel on site, four star facilities. *Society Meetings:* welcome. Please contact Corporate Golf Office (01789 413800; Fax: 01789 262028).
e-mail: welcombe.golfpro@menzieshotels.co.uk
website: www.welcombehotelstratford.co.uk

STRATFORD-UPON-AVON. **Stratford-on-Avon Golf Club,** Tiddington Road, Stratford-upon-Avon CV37 7BA (01789 205749). *Location:* half a mile from town on B4086. Flat parkland. 18 holes, 6374 yards. S.S.S. 71. *Green Fees:* information not available. *Eating facilities:* full catering/bar service. *Visitors:* welcome any time subject to domestic commitments. *Society Meetings:* catered for Tuesdays and Thursdays. Professional: D. Sutherland (01789 205677). Secretary: C.J. Hughes (01789 205749).*

SUTTON COLDFIELD. **Marston Lakes Golf Club,** Lea Marston Hotel & Leisure Complex, Haunch Lane, Lea Marston, Sutton Coldfield B76 0BY (01675 470707; Fax 01675 470871). *Location:* from junction 9, M42 take A4097 signposted Kingsbury (KGBY) for one mile. Take second right hand turning into Haunch Lane, hotel and golf course 150 yards on right hand side. Beautifully laid out lake and parkland course built to USGA standards. 9 holes, 2059 yards (white tees), S.S.S. 61; 1840 yards (yellow tees), S.S.S. 59; 1695 yards (red tees), S.S.S.59 (over 18 holes). Putting green, 30 bay floodlit driving range. *Green Fees:* information not available. *Eating facilities:* Hathaways Bar/Restaurant serving snacks, hot beverages, lunches, dinners, also fully licensed restaurant in hotel. *Visitors:* welcome any time. 88 bedroom, four star hotel on site. Tuition, golf simulator, fully stocked golf shop. *Society Meetings:* welcome. Professional: Darren Lewis (01675 470707; Fax: 01675 470871). Secretary: Katya Townsend (01675 470468; Fax: 01675 470707).*
e-mail: info@leamarstonhotel.co.uk
membership@leamarstonhotel.co.uk
website: www.leamarstonhotel.co.uk

WARWICK. **Warwick Golf Club,** Warwick Golf Centre, Racecourse, Warwick CV34 6HW (01926 494316). *Location:* off M40, from A41/A46 junction, travel half a mile towards Warwick, turn right into racecourse. Flat parkland course. 9 holes, 2682 yards. S.S.S. 66. Driving range (floodlit). *Green Fees:* information not available. *Eating facilities:* bar open 7 to 10.30pm weekdays, no catering. *Visitors:* welcome any time except Sunday mornings. *Society Meetings:* accepted, must book in advance. Professional: P. Sharp (07879 611814). Secretary: R. Dunkley.

WARWICK. **The Warwickshire,** Leek Wootton, Near Warwick CV35 7QT (01926 409409; Fax: 01926 497911). *Location:* on B4115, just off A46, five minutes from M40 Junction 15. Parkland and woodland courses with many attractive holes over water. North/West Course: 18 holes, 7407 yards. S.S.S. 74. South/East Course: 18 holes, 7157 yards. S.S.S. 74. 9-hole Par 3 course, driving range, practice and putting greens. *Green Fees:* information not available. *Eating facilities:* bar and restaurant. *Visitors:* welcome at all times. Conference facilities available. *Society Meetings:* Golf Days arranged for groups from 12 to 300. Professional: M. Dulson (01926 409409). General Manager: Steve Dixon (01926 409409; Fax: 01926 408409).*

For full details of convenient accommodation near clubs and courses
www.holidayguides.com

Nailcote Hall, Berkswell

West Midlands

BIRMINGHAM. **Brandhall Golf Club,** Heron Road, Oldbury, Warley B68 8AQ (0121-552 2195). *Location:* Wolverhampton Road A4123 off Junction 2 M5; right at Hen and Chickens Junction. Wooded course, elevated tees. 18 holes, 5833 yards. S.S.S. 68. *Green Fees:* information not available. Senior Citizens cards. *Visitors:* welcome, ring course for details. Tuition available, buggies (summer only) for hire. *Society Meetings:* welcome by prior arrangement. Professional: Carl Yates.*

BIRMINGHAM. **Cocks Moors Woods Golf Club,** Alcester Road South, Kings Heath, Birmingham B14 4ER (0121-464 3584; Fax: 0121 441 1305). *Location:* A435 Alcester Road, three and a half miles from M42 Junction 3. Undulating woodland course, many meandering streams. 18 holes, 5769 yards, Par 69. S.S.S. 68. *Green Fees:* information not available. *Eating facilities:* adjacent to leisure centre offering excellent bar and catering facilities. *Visitors:* welcome at all times. Full range of leisure facilities within complex. *Society Meetings:* welcome during quiet times, please telephone. Professional: Steve Ellis. Secretary: D. W. Wincott (0121-777 7837).*

BIRMINGHAM. **Edgbaston Golf Club Ltd,** Church Road, Edgbaston, Birmingham B15 3TB (0121-454 1736; Fax: 0121-454 2395). *Location*: from Birmingham City Centre take A38 (Bristol Road). After one mile and at third set of traffic lights turn right into Priory Road, at end of which turn into Church Road; the club entrance is 80m on the left. Undulating parkland course set in the grounds of historic Edgbaston Hall, which is now the club house. Course designed by H.S. Colt in 1935. Ancient trees, sloping fairways and a large lake contribute to the challenge and enjoyment of the course which is also a conservation area. 18 holes, 6132 yards. S.S.S. 69, Par 69. Practice area. *Green Fees*: weekdays £47.00, weekends £57.00 (summer); weekdays £30.00 (winter). 2010 rates (subject to review). *Eating facilities*: fully licensed, lunches, teas daily and bar meals daily; other meals by prior arrangement. *Visitors*: welcome subject to some restrictions on starting times, and the production of Handicap Certificate. Facilities for business meetings/ seminars; snooker rooms; fully stocked shop, offering tuition, organisation of competitions, prizes, clinics. *Society Meetings*: welcome by arrangement with General Manager. Professional: Jamie Cundy (0121-454 3226; Fax: 0121-454 2395). General Manager: Adam Grint (0121-454 1736).
e-mail: secretary@edgbastongc.co.uk
website: www.edgbastongc.co.uk

BIRMINGHAM. **Fulford Heath Golf Club Ltd,** Tanners Green Lane, Wythall, Birmingham B47 6BH (01564 822806). *Location:* one mile from Alcester Road, via Tanners Green Lane. Parkland with two lakes and River Cole. 18 holes, 6179 yards. S.S.S. 70. Practice ground. *Green Fees:* weekdays £36.00 (Societies £30.00). 2010 rates (subject to review). *Eating facilities:* available. *Visitors:* welcome weekdays, not at weekends and Bank Holidays. Buggies for hire. *Society Meetings:* catered for on application. Professional: R. Dunbar (01564 822930). Secretary/ Manager: Mrs J. Morris (01564 824758; Fax: 01564 822629)

BIRMINGHAM. **Gay Hill Golf Club,** Hollywood Lane, Hollywood, Birmingham B47 5PP (0121-430 8544; Fax: 0121 436 7796). *Location:* M42 Junction 3, three miles. Parkland course. 18 holes, 6406 yards. S.S.S. 72. Practice area. *Green Fees:* information not provided. *Visitors:* welcome all week. *Society Meetings:* catered for by arrangement Thursdays. Professional: Chris Harrison (0121-474 6001). Secretary: Mrs Debbie O'Reilly (0121-430 8544).

BIRMINGHAM. **Great Barr Golf Club,** Chapel Lane, Great Barr, Birmingham B43 7BA (0121-357 1232). *Location:* six miles north-west of Birmingham M6 Junction 7. Parkland. 18 holes, 6523 yards. S.S.S. 72. *Green Fees:* information not available. *Eating facilities:* meals served, order in advance. *Visitors:* welcome weekdays, restricted at weekends. Weekends maximum handicap 18. Handicap Certificate required. *Society Meetings:* Packages available. Professional: R. Spragg (0121-357 5270). Secretary: D. Smith (0121-358 4376).*

BIRMINGHAM. **Handsworth Golf Club,** 11 Sunningdale Close, Handsworth Wood, Birmingham B20 1NP (0121-554 0599). *Location*: M5 Junction 1. A41 left at first lights, left at next set of lights, second left, second left/M6 Junction 7. A34 Birmingham Road, Old Walsall Road, Vernon Avenue, Westover Road, Craythorne Avenue. Parkland course. 18 holes, 6272 yards, 5733 metres. S.S.S. 70. Large practice area and putting green. *Green Fees*: information not available. *Eating facilities*: bar snacks to à la carte menu in restaurant. *Visitors:* welcome weekdays with Handicap Certificate. *Society Meetings*: catered for by arrangement with Secretary. Special packages available. Professional: L. Bashford (0121-523 3594). Secretary: PS. Hodnett (0121-554 3387; Fax: 0121-554 6144).*
e-mail: info@handsworthgolfclub.net

BIRMINGHAM. **Harborne Golf Club,** 40 Tennal Road, Harborne, Birmingham B32 2JE (0121-427 3058). *Location:* A4123, A456, B4124 three miles west Birmingham city centre. Undulating parkland/ moorland. 18 holes, 6210 yards. S.S.S. 70. *Green Fees:* weekdays £35.00. *Eating facilities:* bar and dining area daily. *Visitors:* welcome except weekends and Bank Holidays. Trolleys for hire. *Society Meetings:* welcome with pre-booking. Special rates for parties comprising over 20 players. Professional: Stuart Mathews (0121-426 0043). General Manager: Adrian Cooper (0121-426 0040).

BIRMINGHAM. **Harborne (Church Farm) Golf Club,** Vicarage Road, Harborne, Birmingham B17 0SN (0121-427 1204; Fax: 0121-428 3126). *Location:* signposted from Harborne Centre. Parkland, brooks a special feature on five holes. 9 holes, 2441 yards. S.S.S. 64. *Green Fees:* information not available. *Eating facilities:* canteen serves hot and cold snacks. *Visitors:* welcome anytime - phone call required as a booking system is in operation. *Society Meetings:* by arrangement with the Professional. Professional: Paul Johnson. Secretary: William Flanagan (0121-427 1204; Fax: 0121-428 3126).*

BIRMINGHAM. **Hatchford Brook Golf Club,** Coventry Road, Sheldon, Birmingham B26 3PY (0121-743 9821; Fax: 0121 743 3420). *Location:* on A45 3 miles from Junction 6 M42, next to Birmingham International Airport. Parkland course with wide fairways and large greens. 18 holes, 6143 yards. S.S.S. 69. Large practice area. *Green Fees:* £16.00 2010 rates (subject to review). *Eating facilities:* restaurant and bar in clubhouse. *Visitors:* welcome with some restrictions. *Society Meetings:* contact Professional. Professional: Mark Hampton (0121 743 9821). Secretary: Ian Thomson (0121 742 6643).

BIRMINGHAM. **Hilltop Public Golf Course,** Park Lane, Handsworth, Birmingham B21 8LJ (0121-554 4463). *Location:* Two miles from M5 J1, turn into Park Lane opposite West Bromwich Albion football ground. Wide fairways. 18 holes, 6254 yards. S.S.S. 70. *Green Fees:* information not available. *Eating facilities:* café serving drinks and hot meals. Licensed bar. *Visitors:* welcome, phone to book a starting time. Municipal course. *Society Meetings:* bookings available through Professional. Professional/Secretary: Kevin Highfield.*

BIRMINGHAM. **Kings Norton Golf Club Ltd.,** Brockhill Lane, Weatheroak, Alvechurch, Birmingham B48 7ED (01564 826706; Fax: 01564 826955). *Location:* M42 Junction 3, A435 to Birmingham, sign on left to Weatheroak, follow for one mile, over first crossroads. Club on right hand side. Parkland course. 27 holes, 7000 yards. S.S.S. 72, plus 12-hole par 3 course and 22-acre practice field. *Green Fees:* information on request. *Eating facilities:* excellent restaurant and bar snacks available. *Visitors:* welcome weekdays only, weekends with member. *Society Meetings:* catered for weekdays only; minimum number 16; special rates available. Buggies available. Professional: Kevin Hayward (01564 822635). Manager: Terry Webb (01564 826789).
e-mail: info@kingsnortongolfclub.co.uk
website: www.kingsnortongolfclub.co.uk

BIRMINGHAM. **Maxstoke Park Golf Club,** Castle Lane, Coleshill, Birmingham B46 2RD (01675 462158). *Location:* three miles north east of Coleshill on B4114, turn right for Maxstoke. Parkland with trees and lakes. Water-filled moat surrounding Maxstoke Castle. 18 holes, 6442 yards, S.S.S. 71. Two practice areas. *Green Fees:* information not available. *Eating facilities:* restaurant and bar. *Visitors:* welcome weekdays only, weekends with

Kings Norton Golf Club

Founded in 1892, Kings Norton Golf Club is considered as one of the premier golf courses in The Midlands, set in 220 acres of beautiful parkland and boasting 27 holes of championship standard, a par 3 short course, putting green and practice facilities. Visitors, Societies and Corporate Customers will find a traditional club with a friendly and welcoming atmosphere. We offer a challenging course, a majestic Clubhouse, a Professional's Shop and staff who are eager to make your visit memorable. We are confident that once you have played here you will want to return.

Brockhill Lane, Weatheroak, Alvechurch,
Birmingham B48 7ED
Tel: 01564 826706 • Fax: 01564 826955
info@kingsnortongolfclub.co.uk
www.kingsnortongolfclub.co.uk

member. Handicap Certificate required. *Society Meetings:* catered for Tuesdays/Thursdays. Professional: N. McEwan (01675 464915). Secretary: A. J. Brown (01675 466743; Fax: 01675 466185).*
e-mail: info@maxstokeparkgolfclub.com
website: www.maxstokeparkgolfclub.com

BIRMINGHAM. **Moseley Golf Club,** Springfield Road, Kings Heath, Birmingham B14 7DX (0121-444 2115). *Location:* from M42 take A435 north to Kings Heath, turn right into Wheelers Lane (A4040), left into Barn Lane crossing Addison Road into Springfield Road where the club is on the right hand side. Rolling parkland course with major water feature. 18 holes, 6300 yards. S.S.S. 70. Practice area. *Green Fees:* information not provided. *Eating facilities:* dining room and bar. *Visitors:* welcome midweek only by prior arrangement. Handicap Certificates required. *Society Meetings:* welcome, minimum of 12 players. Professional: Martin Griffin (0121-444 2063). General Manager: Michael W. Wake (0121-444 4957; Fax: 0121-441 4662).

BIRMINGHAM. **North Worcestershire Golf Club,** Frankley Beeches Road, Northfield, Birmingham B31 5LP (0121-475 1026). *Location:* A38 from Birmingham City Centre. Parkland, established inland course. 18 holes, 5959 yards. S.S.S. 68. *Green Fees:* information not provided. *Eating facilities:* catering facilities on request, normal bar opening hours. *Visitors:* welcome weekdays. *Society Meetings:* catered for Tuesdays and Thursdays. Professional: D. Cummins (0121-475 5721). Secretary: C.W. Overton (0121-475 1047; Fax: 0121-476 8681).

BIRMINGHAM near. **Rose Hill Golf Club,** Rose Hill, Rednal, Near Birmingham B45 8RR. *Location:* Lickey Hills Country Park, Junction 1 M42, Junction 4 M5. Established 1921, parkland, semi flat course. 18 holes, 5890 yards. S.S.S. 68. *Green Fees:* information not available. *Eating facilities:* no bars, restaurant all day. *Visitors:* welcome with prior bookings only via Professional. Old Rose and Crown Hotel on course. *Society Meetings:* welcome with prior booking via Professional. Professional: Mark Toombs (0121-453 3159). Secretary: A Cushing (07976 793698; Fax: 0121-250 1719).*

ANSTY GOLF CENTRE IS PROUD TO SPONSOR
STEVE WEBSTER PGA & EUROPEAN PRO.

- 18 Hole Course
- 9 Hole Academy Course
- Driving Range • Putting Green
- Fully Stocked Pro Shop
- PGA Tuition 7 days a week
- Tailor-made Golf Day packages
- Corporate Golf Days
- High quality on-site catering
- Fully Licensed Club House
- Family Room
- Course always open, regardless of weather
- One mile from Junc.2 M6 and M69

BRINKLOW ROAD, ANSTY, COVENTRY CV7 9JL
Tel: 024 7662 1341 or 024 7660 2568

COVENTRY. **Ansty Golf Centre,** Brinklow Road, Ansty, Coventry CV7 9JH (024 7662 1341; Fax: 024 7660 2568). *Location:* half a mile from Junction 2 M6 and parallel to the M69 is the B4065 signposted to Ansty. Parkland. 18 holes, 6150 yards. S.S.S. 69, Par 71. 9 hole par 3 course. Driving range. *Green Fees:* information not provided. *Eating facilities:* available 7 days a week; fully licensed restaurant with family room. *Visitors:* always welcome. Fully stocked Golf Shop, teaching academy, open 7 days regardless of weather, driving range, putting green, practice area. *Society Meetings:* welcome. Individual parties, corporate golf days and society golf days tailored to individual requirements 7 days a week. Professional: Mark Goodwin (024 7662 1341/024 7660 2568). Secretary: K. Smith (Tel & Fax: 024 7660 2671).

COVENTRY. **Copsewood Grange Golf Club,** Copsewood Sports Ground, Allard Way, Coventry CV3 1JP (024 7663 5452). *Location:* three miles from centre of Coventry on A4082 off the A428 road to Rugby, Lutterworth. 9 holes, 6048 yards. S.S.S. 71. *Green Fees:* weekdays guests £8.00 per round, £15.00 per day; visitors £15.00 per round, £20.00 per day. Sundays guests £10.00 per round, visitors £20.00 per round. *Visitors:* welcome except Saturdays or Sunday mornings. Secretary: R.E.C. Jones (07729 818249).

COVENTRY. **Coventry Golf Club,** St. Martins Road, Finham, Coventry CV3 6RJ (024 7641 4152; Fax: 024 7669 0131). *Location:* south Coventry off A45, one mile along B4113. Gently undulating parkland course designed by Vardon/Hawtree, an exciting challenge to all golfers. 18 holes, 6590 yards. S.S.S. 72. Practice ground. *Green Fees:* £50.00 per day. *Eating facilities:* full catering in lounge bar, restaurant (maximum 120). *Visitors:* welcome weekdays. Fully stocked shop. *Society Meetings:* welcome Wednesdays, Thursdays and some Fridays by prior arrangement with Secretary's Office. Handicap Certificates required. Group bookings accepted two years in advance. Professional: P. Weaver (024 7641 1298). Secretary: Anne Smith (024 7641 4152).

COVENTRY. **Coventry Hearsall Golf Club,** Beechwood Avenue, Coventry CV5 6DF (024 7671 3470; Fax: 024 7669 1534). *Location:* off A45 south of Coventry, one mile south of city centre. Flat parkland, easy walking. 18 holes, 6001 yards. S.S.S. 69, Par 70. *Green Fees:* information not available. *Eating facilities:* restaurant open six days a week; closed Mondays. *Visitors:* welcome weekdays, special request at weekends. Pull carts for hire. *Society Meetings:* welcome, must book in advance with Secretary. Professional: Michael Tarn (024 7671 3156). Secretary: Rachael Meade (024 7671 3470; Fax: 024 7669 1534).*
e-mail: secretary@hearsallgolfclub.co.uk
website: www.hearsallgolfclub.co.uk

COVENTRY. **Marriott Forest of Arden Hotel & Country Club,** Maxstoke Lane, Meriden, Coventry CV7 7HR (0870 400 7272; Fax: 0870 400 7372). *Location:* take Junction 6 from M42, follow A45 to Coventry. After one mile turn left into Shepherds Lane, hotel is one and a half miles on left. Parkland and greenside water hazards. Home to the British Masters 2003. Two courses. The Arden - 7213 yards. S.S.S. 73; The Aylesford - 5801 yards. S.S.S. 68. Floodlit golf academy. *Green Fees:* information not available. *Eating facilities:* bars and restaurants available. *Visitors:* welcome seven days subject to tee-time availability. 214-bedroom four star hotel with extensive conference and luxurious leisure facilities. *Society Meetings:* enquiries welcome. Professional: Philip Hoye (0958 632170). Director of Golf: Iain Burns.*

COVENTRY. **North Warwickshire Golf Club Ltd,** Hampton Lane, Meriden, Warwickshire CV7 7LL (01676 522915; Fax: 01676 523004). *Location:* on B4102, one mile from Stonebridge on A45, approximately midway between Birmingham and Coventry. Heathland. 9 holes, 6352 yards. S.S.S. 71. Small practice ground. *Green Fees:* £26.00 weekdays; weekends with member only. *Eating facilities:* snack lunch, meals by prior arrangement. *Visitors:* welcome weekdays without reservation except Thursdays, weekends by invitation. *Society Meetings:* catered for by prior arrangement, limited numbers. Professional: Andrew Bownes (01676 522259). Secretary: R.D. May (01676 522915; Fax: 01676 523004).
e-mail: nwgcltd@btconnect.com
website: www.northwarwickshiregolfclub.co.uk

COVENTRY. **Windmill Village Hotel, Golf and Leisure Club,** Birmingham Road, Allesley, Coventry CV5 9AL (024 7640 4041; Fax: 024 7640 4042). *Location:* A45 westbound, west of Coventry. Rolling parkland with water features. 18 holes, 5213 yards. S.S.S. 66. Course record 63 Pro, 66 Amateur. *Green Fees:* Monday to Thursday and Friday before 11.30am £18.00; Friday after 11.30am and Saturday/Sunday £20.00. 2-Fore-1 vouchers Mon-Fri

---

The Baginton Oak | Pub and Restaurant | Coventry

A warm welcome awaits you at
The Baginton Oak, Coventry,
a family friendly pub.
Nice relaxed environment with log fires,
table service, traditional ales and good
quality home cooked food. Large bar area
with comfy leather sofas and dining area.
Quality bed and breakfast accommodation,
13 full en suite rooms.

Celebrate in Style... **...Relax in Comfort**

Coventry Road | Baginton | CV8 3AU | Tel: 024 7651 8855 | 024 7651 8866
Email: thebagintonoak@aol.com | www.thebagintonoak.co.uk

£22.50. Twilight golf available. *Eating facilities:* food and drinks available all day. *Visitors:* welcome with booking. 4-star standard 100-bedroom hotel with leisure centre; conferences, weddings catered for. *Society Meetings:* welcome, special rates available. Professional: Robert Hunter. Managers: Marci Hartland and Stuart Perry.
e-mail: golfpro@windmillvillagehotel.co.uk
website: www.windmillvillagehotel.co.uk

DUDLEY. **Dudley Golf Club Ltd,** Turners Hill, Rowley Regis, Warley B65 9BD (01384 254020). *Location:* one mile south of Dudley town centre on Oakham Road. 18 holes, 5730 yards. S.S.S. 68. *Green Fees:* weekdays £15.00 per round, weekends by arrangement, £20.00 per round. *Eating facilities:* full catering facilities available. *Visitors:* welcome. *Society Meetings:* by prior arrangement. Professional: Gary Kilmister (01384 254020). Secretary: B. Whitcombe (01384 233877).
e-mail: secretary@dudleygolfclub.com
website: www.dudleygolfclub.com

DUDLEY. **Himley Hall Golf Centre,** Log Cabin, Himley Park, Himley Road, Dudley DY3 4DF (01902 895207). *Location:* just off A449 at Himley near Dudley. Parkland. Pay and Play course. 9 holes, 3145 yards. S.S.S. 35 for 9 holes. Practice ground, pitch and putt. *Green Fees:* information not provided. *Eating facilities:* hot and cold snacks. *Visitors:* welcome weekdays, weekends with booking. *Society Meetings:* midweek only. Professional: Mark Sparrow (01902 895207). Secretary: Bernard Sparrow (01902 894973; 07515 284196).

DUDLEY near. **Swindon Golf Club,** Bridgnorth Road, Swindon, Near Dudley DY3 4PU (01902 897031). *Location:* B4176 Dudley/Bridgnorth Road, three miles from A449 at Himley. Woodland and parkland course with exceptional views. 18 holes - 6121 yards. S.S.S. (18) 70. *Green Fees:* weekdays £25.00, weekends £30.00. *Eating facilities:* fully licensed bar and restaurant. Functions and weddings catered for. *Visitors:* always welcome, booking required. Buggies available. Fishing. *Society Meetings:* by arrangement 7 days a week. General Manager: M.R. Allen (01902 897031); Fax: 01902 326219).
e-mail: admin@swindongolfclub.co.uk
website: www.swindongolfclub.co.uk

DUDLEY. **Sedgley Golf Centre,** Sandyfields Road, Sedgley, Dudley DY3 3DL (01902 880503). *Location:* half a mile from Sedgley town centre near Cotwall End Valley Nature Reserve, just off the A463.

WINDMILL VILLAGE
HOTEL, GOLF & LEISURE CLUB

Stay and Play
The Whole in One
(Golf, Leisure Club, Indoor Pool, Steam, Sauna, Bar, Restaurant, Entertainment)
"Where Excellence Comes As Standard"

Golf Societies Welcome
Call Rob Hunter P.G.A. Golf Professional
For Your Personal Quote

Tel: 02476 404041
In the heart of the Warwickshire countryside.
Birmingham Road, Allesley
Coventry CV5 9AL • A45 west bound

www.windmillvillagehotel.co.uk

Undulating contours and mature trees with extensive views over surrounding countryside. 9 holes, 3147 yards. S.S.S. 70 (18 holes). Covered, floodlit, fully automated golf range. *Green Fees:* £8.00 9 holes, £10.00 18 holes. Reductions for Juniors and Senior Citizens. *Eating facilities:* hot and cold snacks available on request. *Visitors:* pay and play course throughout the week, booking advisable at weekends. *Society Meetings:* weekdays preferred by prior arrangement. Professional: Garry Mercer (01902 880503). Secretary: P. Willis (01902 880503).

HALESOWEN. **Halesowen Golf Club,** The Leasowes, Leasowes Lane, Halesowen B62 8QF (0121-501 3606). *Location:* exit Junction 3 M5, A456 (Kidderminster) two miles, Halesowen town centre one mile. Parkland course in the Midlands with a Grade I Listed clubhouse and park. 18 holes, 5754 yards. S.S.S. 69. *Green Fees:* information not available. *Eating facilities:* available every day. *Visitors:* welcome weekdays. *Society Meetings:* by arrangement. Secretary (0121 501 3606) or e-mail.
e-mail: office@halesowengc.co.uk
website: www.halesowengc.co.uk

Halesowen Golf Club, The Leasowes, Halesowen B62 8QF
The Club, which has been established for over 100 years, has an 18 hole course set in the only Grade 1 Listed Park in the Midlands, with excellent panoramic views of Worcestershire, and is always in excellent condition. Playing membership of over 500 but visitors and new members are always welcome. Places available with special rates.
Arrangements with the Secretary on 0121 501 3606, or Professional 0121 503 0593

REDNAL. **Lickey Hills Golf Club,** Rose Hill, Rednal, Birmingham B45 8RR (0121-453 3159; 0121-457 8779). *Location:* Three miles from M42 J1 or M5 J4 at the bottom of Rose Hill on Lickey Hills Country Park. Picturesque course with dramatic slopes and banks of pine trees. 18 holes, 5866 yards. S.S.S. 68. *Green Fees:* information not available. *Eating facilities:* cafe at clubhouse. *Visitors:* welcome. Professional: Mark Toombs.*

SOLIHULL. **Copt Heath Golf Club,** 1220 Warwick Road, Knowle, Solihull B93 9LN (01564 772650). *Location:* on A4141 half-a-mile south of Junction 5 with M42. Flat parkland. 18 holes, 6528 yards. S.S.S. 71. Full practice facilities available. *Green Fees:* weekdays £45.00. Weekends and Public Holidays by arrangement with Secretary or Professional. *Eating facilities:* lunch and evening meal available except Mondays. *Visitors:* no restrictions weekdays. *Society Meetings:* by arrangement with Secretary. Professional: Brian Barton. Secretary: Clive Hadley. e-mail: maria@copt-heath.co.uk
website: www.coptheathgolf.co.uk

SOLIHULL. **Ladbrook Park Golf Club Ltd,** Poolhead Lane, Tanworth-in-Arden, Solihull B94 5ED (01564 742220). *Location:* south from Junction 3 M42. Parkland, gently undulating. 18 holes, 6427 yards. S.S.S. 71. Practice ground. *Green Fees:* information not available. *Eating facilities:* excellent dining. *Visitors:* welcome weekdays, prior telephone call suggested. Weekends with member only. *Society Meetings:* catered for by prior arrangement with the Secretary. Professional: Richard Mountford (01564 742581). Secretary: M.R. Newman (01564 742264; Fax: 01564 742909).*

SOLIHULL. **Olton Golf Club Ltd,** Mirfield Road, Solihull B91 1JH (0121-705 1083; Fax: 0121-711 2010). *Location:* approximately two miles off Junction 5 (M42), A41 - Birmingham. Parkland. 18 holes, 6230 yards, 5697 metres. S.S.S. 70. *Green Fees:* from £40.00 weekdays. Discounts for large groups. *Eating facilities:* by arrangement. *Visitors:* welcome weekdays only except Wednesday mornings. *Society Meetings:* catered for by arrangement. Professional: C. Haynes (0121-705 7296). Hon. Secretary: Bob Gay (0121-704 1936; Fax: 0121-711 2010).

SOLIHULL. **Robin Hood Golf Club,** St. Bernards Road, Solihull B92 7DJ (0121-706 0061). *Location:* eight miles south of Birmingham, off A41 Birmingham to Warwick road. Flat parkland. 18 holes, 6635 yards, 6067 metres. S.S.S. 72. *Green Fees:* information not available. *Eating facilities:* by prior arrangement with Steward (0121-706 5010). *Visitors:* welcome weekdays only subject to limitations. Arrange with Secretary or Professional. *Society Meetings:* catered for by prior booking. Professional: A.R. Harvey (0121-706 0806). Manager: Martin Ward (0121 706 0061; Fax: 0121-700 7502).*
e-mail: manager@robinhoodgolfclub.co.uk

SOLIHULL. **Shirley Golf Club,** Stratford Road, Monkspath, Solihull B90 4EW (0121-744 6001; Fax: 0121-746 5645). *Location:* (A3400), Junction 4 M42, towards Birmingham. Parkland. 18 holes, 6507 yards. S.S.S. 71. Practice ground, putting area. Buggies available. *Green Fees:* visit website. *Eating facilities:* bar and restaurant. *Visitors:* welcome without reservation, must have Handicap. Trolleys available. *Society Meetings:* welcome by arrangement. Professional: Stuart Bottrill (Tel & Fax: 0121-746 5646). General Manager: Steve Wilkins (0121-744 6001; Fax: 0121-746 5645).
e-mail: enquiries@shirleygolfclub.co.uk
website: www.shirleygolfclub.co.uk

SOLIHULL. **Tidbury Green Golf Club,** Tilehouse Lane, Shirley, Solihull B90 1HP (01564 824460). *Location:* two miles from Shirley and three miles off the M42. To play over numerous ponds, lakes and the River Coal. 18 holes, 4792 yards, 4382 metres. S.S.S. 64. 15 bay driving range, 9 hole pitch 'n' putt.. *Green Fees:* information not available. *Eating facilities:* excellent bar and restaurant facilities. *Visitors:* welcome, no restrictions. Facilities for fishing. *Society Meetings:* catered for. Secretary: L.M. Broadhurst.*

SOLIHULL. **West Midlands Golf Club,** Marsh House Farm Lane, Barston, Solihull B92 0LB (01675 444 890). *Location:* located between Birmingham and Coventry, five minutes from National Exhibition Centre, Junction 4 of M6, Junction 6 of M42. Take A452 towards Leamington and Warwick (Balsall Common) and look for signs to club. USGA Golf Course over rolling parkland with island green. Putting green, open driving range, practice green. 18 holes, 6624 yards. S.S.S. 72. *Green Fees:* information not provided. *Eating facilities:* spike bar serving light meals and à la carte restaurant. *Visitors:* welcome. *Society Meetings:* please call for information, we will tailor a package to suit your needs. Secretary: Ron Guthrie.
website: www.wmgc.co.uk

West Midlands Golf Club
Located just 5 minutes from the NEC, between Meriden and Balsall Common, this superb course (6624 yards, par 72) has been built to the highest specification with USGA tees and greens. Several holes demand tee shots and approach shots over water, including the signature 18th hole, par 3 with island green.

Marsh House Farm Lane, Barston, Solihull,
West Midlands, B92 0LB
www.wmgc.co.uk 01675 444890

THE GOLF GUIDE 2011 — MIDLANDS REGION / West Midlands

SOLIHULL. Widney Manor Golf Club, Saintbury Drive (off Widney Lane), Widney Manor, Solihull B91 3SZ (0121-704 0704; Fax: 0121-704 7999). *Location:* exit M42 Junction 4 and follow signs for Shirley, then Monkspath. A challenging course for golfers of all abilities, set in parkland with mature oaks and water hazards. 18 holes, 5500 yards. 14-bay covered driving range. *Green Fees:* information not available. *Eating facilities:* normal bar hours, catering facilities available all day. *Visitors:* welcome at all times with advance booking available. Casual but smart dress code. *Society Meetings:* welcome any day. Tailor-made to suit the customer. Professional Tim Atkinson. Secretary: Ron Guthrie.*
website: www.wmgc.co.uk

STOURBRIDGE. Stourbridge Golf Club, Worcester Lane, Pedmore, Stourbridge DY8 2RB (01384 395566). *Location:* situated between Hagley and Stourbridge on Worcester road. Parkland. 18 holes, 6231 yards. S.S.S. 70. Small practice ground. *Green Fees:* information not available. *Eating facilities:* bar meals available, lunch, dinner. *Visitors:* welcome weekdays, weekends with member. *Society Meetings:* catered for. Professional: Mark Male (01384 393129). Secretary: Miss M. Kite (01384 395566); Fax: 01384 444660).*
e-mail: secretary@stourbridge-golf-club.co.uk
website: www.stourbridge-golf-club.co.uk

SUTTON COLDFIELD. Aston Wood Golf Club, Blake Street, Little Aston, Sutton Coldfield B74 4EU (0121-580 7803; Fax: 0121-353 0354). *Location:* situated on Blake Street off A5127 Lichfield to Sutton Coldfield Road. Gently flowing Allis-Clark designed course with many water hazards.18 holes, 6480 yards. S.S.S. 71. Practice area, bunker and green. *Green Fees:* information not available. *Eating facilities:* superb restaurant and bars open daily 7.30am-11pm. *Visitors:* weekdays only. Buggies. *Society Meetings:* corporate and societies welcome. Excellent packages available. Superb functions and conference facilities. Professional: Simon Smith (0121-580 7800). General Manager: Ken Heathcote (0121-580 7803).*

SUTTON COLDFIELD. Boldmere Golf Club, Monmouth Drive, Sutton Coldfield B73 6JL (0121-354 3379; Fax: 0121-355 4534). *Location:* off A452 (Chester road North), next to Sutton Park on Monmouth Drive. Flat parkland, wooded. 18 holes, 4463 yards. S.S.S. 62. Practice net and putting area. Shorter, lush course ideal for those who prefer a less tiring round of golf. *Green Fees:* information not provided. *Eating facilities:* cafe in clubhouse. *Visitors:* welcome, Link Card system in operation. *Society Meetings:* welcome at quiet times, to be arranged with the Professional. Professional: Trevor Short (0121-354 3379; Fax: 0121-354 4534). Secretary: Roy Leeson (0121-354 3379; Fax: 0121-354 4534).
e-mail: boldmeregolfclub@hotmail.com
website: www.boldmeregolfclub.co.uk

SUTTON COLDFIELD. Moor Hall Golf Club Ltd, Moor Hall Drive, Sutton Coldfield B75 6LN (0121-308 6130). *Location:* one mile east of Sutton Coldfield, A446. Parkland. 18 holes, 6293 yards. S.S.S. 70. Practice area. *Green Fees:* £45.00 per round, £60.00 per day. 2010 rates (subject to review). *Eating facilities:* available weekdays. *Visitors:* welcome weekdays only (not Thursday mornings). 4-star Moor Hall Hotel on golf estate (independently owned). *Society Meetings:* catered for. Professional: Cameron Clark (0121-308 5106). Secretary: D.J. Etheridge (0121-308 6130).

SUTTON COLDFIELD. Pype Hayes Golf Club, Eachelhurst Road, Walmley, Sutton Coldfield B76 8EP (0121-351 1014). *Location:* off the A38 Kingsbury Road, one and a half miles from Junction 9 M42. Flat wooded course with small greens, four demanding Par 3's. 18 holes, 5996 yards. S.S.S. 69. *Green Fees:* Information not available. *Eating facilities:* cafeteria. *Visitors:* welcome but must book via telephone. *Society Meetings:* welcome but must book via telephone. Professional: Joe Kelly. Secretary: C.R. Marson (0121-788 3450).*

SUTTON COLDFIELD. Sutton Coldfield Golf Club, Thornhill Road, Streetly, Sutton Coldfield B74 3ER (0121-353 9633; Fax: 0121-353 5503). *Location:* situated in Sutton Park, one mile off A452, seven miles from centre of Birmingham. Natural heathland. 18 holes, 6548 yards. S.S.S. 72. *Green Fees:* weekdays £35.00 per round, £45.00 all day; weekends £45.00 per round. *Eating facilities:* by arrangement with Chef (0121-353 2014). *Visitors:* welcome without reservation but please ring Pro to check availability. Handicap Certificate required. *Society Meetings:* special arrangements for societies by arrangement with Secretary. Professional: J.K. Hayes (0121-580 7878). Secretary: I.H. Phillips (0121-353 9633; Fax: 0121-353 5503).
website: www.suttoncoldfieldgc.com

SUTTON COLDFIELD. Walmley Golf Club, Brooks Road, Wylde Green, Sutton Coldfield B72 1HR (0121-373 0029; Fax: 0121-377 7272). *Location:* Birmingham/Sutton Coldfield main road, turn right at Green Hill Road. Parkland. 18 holes, 6585 yards. S.S.S. 72. Practice ground. *Green Fees:* information not available. *Eating facilities:* lunch and evening meals available. *Visitors:* welcome weekdays only. *Society Meetings:* catered for Wednesdays, Thursdays and some Fridays only. Professional: Chris Wicketts (0121-373 0029 Ext.3).*
e-mail: walmleygolfclub@aol.com

WALSALL. Bloxwich Golf Club (1988) Ltd, 136 Stafford Road, Bloxwich, Walsall WS3 3PQ (01922 476593; Fax: 01922 493449). *Location:* off main Walsall-Cannock road (A34). Semi parkland. 18 holes, 6257 yards. S.S.S. 71. *Green Fees:* Monday £30.00, Tuesday to Thursday £33.00, Friday £35.00 per round. *Eating facilities:* available. *Visitors:* welcome with or without reservation except weekends and Bank Holidays. *Society Meetings:* catered for midweek, reduced rates for 20 or more. Professional: R.J. Dance (01922 476889; Fax: 01922 493449). Secretary/Manager: R.J. Wormstone (01922 476593; Fax: 01922 493449).

West Midlands / MIDLANDS REGION

WALSALL. **Calderfields Golf Club,** Aldridge Road, Walsall WS4 2JS (01922 632243; Fax: 01922 640540). *Location:* A454 between Aldridge and Walsall, Junction 10 M6. Parkland, water hazards. 18 holes, 6509 yards, S.S.S. 73. 27 bay floodlit driving range, practice bunkers, putting green. *Green Fees:* information not available. *Eating facilities:* Lake View restaurant and bar. New function suite for all occasions, seating for 150. *Visitors:* welcome at all times. *Society Meetings:* packages available 7 days a week, subject to availability. Booking Tee Time (01922 632243).*
website: www.calderfieldsgolf.com

WALSALL. **Druids Heath Golf Club**, Stonnall Road, Aldridge, Walsall WS9 8JZ (01922 455595; Fax: 01922 452887). **Location**: off A452 near Little Aston – Aldridge. Testing undulating heathland course. 18 holes, 6665 yards. S.S.S. 73. Practice ground and net. **Green Fees**: £37.00 weekdays; £40.00 weekends after 2pm. **Eating facilities**: dining room and bar snacks. **Visitors:** welcome by prior arrangement. **Society Meetings**: catered for by prior arrangement. Professional: Glenn Williams (01922 459523). Secretary: K.I Taylor.
e-mail: admin@druidsheathgc.co.uk
website: www.druidsheathgc.co.uk

WALSALL. **The Walsall Golf Club,** Broadway, Walsall WS1 3EY (01922 613512; Fax: 01922 616460). *Location:* one and a half miles from M6/M5 junction. Wooded course. 18 holes, 6259 yards. S.S.S. 71. *Green Fees:* information not provided. *Eating facilities:* all facilities available. *Visitors:* welcome weekdays only. *Society Meetings:* catered for. Professional: R. Lambert (01922 626766). Secretary: P. Thompson (01922 613512).

WARLEY. **Warley Woods Golf Club,** The Pavillion, Lightwoods Hill, Smethwick B67 5EO (0121-429 2440; Fax: 0121-434 4430). *Location:* Hagley Road. Adjacent to Warley Woods. Warley water tower at top of course. Parkland course. 9 holes, 2686 yards. S.S.S. 66. *Green Fees:* information not available. *Eating facilities:* cafe. *Visitors:* welcome, advised to book in advance as this is a very busy club. *Society Meetings:* welcome during quiet times, telephone Course Manager for details. Course Manager: H. Hardman (0121-429 2440; Fax: 0121-434 4430). Secretary: Ron Simcox (0121-686 2619; Fax: 0121-241 3451).*

WEST BROMWICH. **Dartmouth Golf Club,** Vale Street, West Bromwich B71 4DW (0121-588 57461/ 2131). *Location:* one mile from West Bromwich town centre. All Saints Way A4031, turn right at McDonalds and follow signposts. Part flat, part undulating course, a good test for all categories. 9 holes, 6036 yards. S.S.S. 70. Practice area, putting green. *Green Fees:* weekdays 18 holes £20.00, 9 holes £12.00; with a member 18 holes £12.00, 9 holes £8.00, weekends 18 holes £25.00, with a member 18 holes £20.00. 2010 rates (subject to review). During 2010 Centenary Year ring for special green fee offers. *Eating facilities:* bar snacks always available, meals by prior arrangement. *Visitors:* welcome weekdays, weekends with a member only. *Society Meetings:* welcome by prior arrangement. Secretary: C.F. Wade (0121-532 4070).

WEST BROMWICH. **Sandwell Park Golf Club Ltd,** Birmingham Road, West Bromwich B71 4JJ (0121-553 4637; Fax: 0121-525 1651). *Location:* on A41 to Birmingham 200 yards from Junction 1 M5, turn left under footbridge. Wooded, heathland course. 18 holes, 6468 yards. S.S.S. 73. Two practice areas, chipping green. *Green Fees:* information not available. *Eating facilities:* full restaurant facilities and two bars. *Visitors:* welcome weekdays, weekend and Bank Holidays with a member only. Handicap Certificate required. *Society Meetings:* by prior arrangement with the Manager. Manager: A. Turner. Professional: Nigel Wylie (0121-553 4384). Secretary: D.A. Paterson (0121-553 4637).*
website: www.sandwellparkgolfclub.co.uk

WISHAW. **The Belfry,** Wishaw, Sutton Coldfield B76 9PR (01675 470301; Fax: 01675 470178). *Location:* leave M42 at Junction 9 and follow signs for Lichfield (A446). Three courses. The Brabazon - 18 holes, 7196 yards. S.S.S. 76. PGA National - 18 holes, 7053 yards. S.S.S. 72. The Derby - 18 holes, 6057 yards. S.S.S. 69. PGA National Golf Academy, 34 bay floodlit driving range, short game area, putting green. National Custom Fit Centre with 5 individual suites and clubs from the world's 9 leading manufacturers. Expert tuition from 20+ PGA Professionals. Buggies, carts and caddies available. *Green Fees:* The Brabazon Course from £70.00; PGA National Course from £40.00; The Derby Course from £25.00. Per person per round. 2010 rates

A challenging test of golf, hidden away in the heart of the West Midlands, together with a superb clubhouse and dining facilities

Visit our website for our latest green fee offers

www.walsallgolfclub.co.uk

The Walsall Golf Club
Broadway, Walsall, West Midlands WS1 3EY
Tel No: 01922 613512

(subject to review). *Eating facilities:* selection of bars and restaurants. *Visitors:* welcome. 324 bedrooms, 22 conference suites, leisure club, indoor heated swimming pool, sauna, solarium, Aqua Spa, gymnasium; squash and tennis courts, snooker and pool tables plus a day spa. Nightclub situated in the hotel grounds. *Society Meetings:* always welcome subject to availablity. Director of Golf: Gary Silcock. e-mail: enquiries@thebelfry.com
website: www.thebelfry.co.uk

WOLVERHAMPTON. **Oxley Park Golf Club Ltd,** Stafford Road, Bushbury, Wolverhampton WV10 6DE. *Location:* 1½ miles M54/A449 junction, 1½ miles Wolverhampton town centre. Undulating parkland. 18 holes, 6226 yards. S.S.S. 71. *Green Fees:* information not available. *Eating facilities:* available daily except Monday. *Visitors:* welcome weekdays, weekends by arrangement with Professional. *Society Meetings:* preferred day Wednesday; for alternatives please contact Secretary. Professional: Leslie Burlison (01902 425445). Secretary: (01902 773989; Fax: 01902 773981).*

WOLVERHAMPTON. **The South Staffordshire Golf Club,** Danescourt Road, Tettenhall, Wolverhampton WV6 9BQ (01902 751065). *Location:* A41 out of Wolverhampton (approx. three miles). Parkland. 18 holes, 6512 yards. S.S.S. 72. Practice area (approx. 10 acres). Driving range. *Green Fees:* £40.00 weekdays, weekends by arrangement. 2010 rates (subject to review). *Eating facilities:* snacks, buffets, three-course dinners available 10 hours per day. Catering Manager: Peter Finch (01902 751065 option 3). *Visitors:* welcome weekdays except Tuesdays. *Society Meetings:* by arrangement through Club Manager, Mrs Sue Lebeau (01902 751065 option 1). Professional Shop: (01902 751065 option 2). Club Administration: (01902 751065 option 5); Fax: 01902 751159).
e-mail: suelebeau@southstaffsgc.co.uk
website: www.southstaffordshiregolfclub.co.uk

Please mention THE GOLF GUIDE when you enquire about clubs or accommodation

West Midlands / MIDLANDS REGION

WOLVERHAMPTON. Penn Golf Club Ltd, Penn Common, Penn, Wolverhampton WV4 5JN (01902 341142). *Location:* two miles south west of Wolverhampton, off A449. Heathland. 18 holes, 6487 yards. S.S.S. 72. *Green Fees:* £25.00 per round, £30.00 per day. *Eating facilities:* full catering and bar facilities. *Visitors:* welcome weekdays. *Society Meetings:* catered for. Professional: G. Dean (01902 330472). Club Administrator: Mrs A. Rafferty (01902 341142).
e-mail: secretary@penngolfclub.org.uk
website: www.penngolfclub.org.uk

WOLVERHAMPTON. Perton Park Golf Club, Wrottesley Park Road, Perton, Wolverhampton WV6 7HL (01902 380073). *Location:* just off the A454 Bridgnorth Road or A41 Wolverhampton to Newport road. Parkland. 18 holes, 6560 yards, S.S.S. 72. Covered floodlit driving range, full practice facilities. *Green Fees:* please visit website. *Eating facilities:* bar and eating facilities open to the public. *Visitors:* always welcome, booking times available. Buggies and trolleys for hire. *Society Meetings:* welcome 7 days a week. General Manager: J. Harrold (01902 380073; Fax: 01902 326219).
e-mail: golf@pertongolfclub.co.uk
website: www.pertongolfclub.co.uk

WOLVERHAMPTON. Wergs Golf Club, Keepers Lane, Tettenhall, Wolverhampton WV6 8UA (01902 742225). *Location:* from centre of Wolverhampton, take A41 (to Newport), after two and a half miles turn right, half a mile on right. Open parkland. 18 holes, 6949 yards. S.S.S. 73. 20 acre practice area. *Green Fees:* weekdays £17.00; weekends and Bank Holidays £22.00. Senior Citizens and Juniors £14.50 weekdays, £19.00 weekends and Bank Holidays. *Eating facilities:* full catering and bar facilities. *Visitors:* always welcome. Membership available. *Society Meetings:* welcome anytime during week, after 10am at weekends. Secretary: Mrs G. Parsons.
e-mail: wergs.golfclub@btinternet.com

THE APPEARANCE OF AN ASTERISK (*) AT THE END OF A CLUB OR COURSE ENTRY INDICATES THAT UP-TO-DATE INFORMATION HAS NOT BEEN SUPPLIED

The Walsall Golf Club, Walsall

Worcestershire

BEWDLEY. **Little Lakes Golf Club,** Lye Head, Bewdley, Worcester DY12 2UZ (01299 266385; Fax: 01299 266178). *Location:* take Lye Head turn - off A456, three miles west of Bewdley. Parkland course with superb views, wonderful walks, undulating. 18 holes, 6298 yards. S.S.S. 71. Practice ground and short game academy. *Green Fees:* information not available. *Eating facilities:* bars, restaurant, cafe. *Visitors*: welcome most days by prior arrangement. Buggies available. *Society Meetings:* welcome by prior arrangement. All-day package includes breakfast, lunch, three-course carvery plus two rounds of golf. Professional: Mark Laing. Secretary: Mrs J. Dean (01562 741704).
e-mail: info@littlelakes.co.uk
website: www.littlelakes.co.uk

BEWDLEY. **Wharton Park Golf Club,** Long Bank, Bewdley DY12 2QW (01299 405163; Fax: 01299 405121). *Location:* A456 from Kidderminster, top of Bewdley by-pass. Championship course with woods and parkland. 18 holes, 6468 yards. S.S.S. 71, Par 71. Practice range. *Green Fees:* information not available. *Eating facilities:* full facilities available including "Greens" Restaurant open Wednesday, Thursday, Friday and Saturday evenings, plus Sunday lunchtimes. *Visitors:* welcome at all times. Functions/Conferences catered for. *Society Meetings:* welcome. Ring for details. Professional: Angus Hoare (01299 405163). Secretary: (01299 405163).*
website: www.whartonpark.co.uk

BLACKWELL. **The Blackwell Golf Club,** Blackwell, Near Bromsgrove B60 1PY (0121-445 1994). *Location:* approximately 10 miles south of Birmingham and three miles east of Bromsgrove. Parkland. 18 holes, 6230 yards. S.S.S. 71. *Green Fees:* weekdays only £70.00 per round, £80.00 per day. *Eating facilities:* bar snacks at all times, meals by arrangement. *Visitors:* welcome by arrangement. *Society Meetings:* catered for by arrangement through Secretary. Professional: Finlay Clark (0121-445 3113). Secretary: J.T. Mead (0121-445 1994; Fax: 0121-445 4911).
e-mail: info@blackwellgolfclub.com
website: www.blackwellgolfclub.com

Blackwell Golf Club

Formed in 1893 with a nine hole course, extended to eighteen holes in 1923, now measures 6260 yards with a par of 70 and a SSS of 71.

Blackwell is a club with a small membership and reflects the playing of golf on an uncrowded course of original and timeless character in an atmosphere of congenial company.

Blackwell has played host as a Regional Qualifying Course for the Open on six occasions, and is proud to have three English Amateur Champions as members during the past seventy years.

Visitors can play by prior arrangement on any weekday. No visitors are allowed at weekends unless playing with a member. Societies are welcome on Mondays, Wednesdays, Thursdays and Fridays and occasionally on Tuesday afternoons.

Blackwell's welcoming facilities are designed to gladden the hearts of all who play there.

**Blackwell, Near Bromsgrove, Worcs B60 1PY
Tel: 0121 445 1994 • e-mail: info@blackwellgolfclub.com
www.blackwellgolfclub.com**

BLAKEDOWN. **Churchill and Blakedown Golf Club,** Churchill Lane, Blakedown, Near Kidderminster DY10 3NB (01562 700018). *Location:* off A456 Birmingham/Kidderminster road at Blakedown. Undulating parkland, partially wooded course. 9 holes, 6491 yards. S.S.S. 71. *Green Fees:* call Secretary for details. *Eating facilities:* snacks and full meals except Monday. *Visitors:* welcome weekdays, weekends with member only. *Society Meetings:* weekdays only by arrangement through the Secretary: D. Higson (01562 700018). Catering: 01562 700200.

BRANSFORD. **Bransford Golf Club,** Bank House Hotel, Golf and Country Club, Bransford, Worcester WR6 5JD (Tel & Fax: 01886 833545). *Locatio*n: From Junction 7 M5 follow signs to Malvern, Ross then pick up signs to Hereford A4103, Hotel is approx. 2 miles on left of small traffic island. 'Florida' style golf course, flat, 14 lakes, island greens, dog legs, etc. 18 holes, 6172 yards. S.S.S. 71. 20 bay driving range and short game practice area. *Green Fees:* information not provided. *Eating facilities*: hotel and clubhouse bars. *Visitors:* welcome, not before 10am. Smart golf attire. Accommodation in 70 bedroom hotel, golf breaks available. *Society Meetings:* welcome, special packages available. Professional: Matt Nixon (01886 833621) (Tel & Fax:01886 833545).
e-mail: bransfordgolfclub@brook-hotels.co.uk

BROMSGROVE. **Bromsgrove Golf Centre,** Stratford Road, Bromsgrove B60 1LD (01527 575886; Course Reception 01527 570505; Conference and Restaurant 01527 579179). *Location:* easily located on the junction of the A38 and A448, one mile from Bromsgrove town centre. Just five minutes' drive from Junctions 4 and 5 of the M5 and Junction 1 of the M42 (exit west bound only). Gently undulating parkland course, large contoured greens with superb views over Worcestershire. 18 holes, 5969 yards. S.S.S. 68. New 29-bay automated driving range, large multilevel putting green. *Green Fees:* available on request. *Eating facilities:* friendly clubhouse with full bar and restaurant facilities available to non members. *Visitors:* most welcome. Tee times bookable up to seven days in advance. Golf shoes or similar, with socks, collared shirts, tailored trousers/shorts. Conference and function rooms, Golf Shop, Golf Academy. Wide range of tuition available with resident PGA Professionals (Tuition Fees list available). New "Teaching Studio" complete with state of the art computerised video systems. *Society Meetings:* welcome by prior arrangement, packages available on request. Head Professional: Graeme Long. Assistant Professional: Danny Wall. Secretary: John Brothwood.
e-mail: enquiries@bromsgrovegolfcentre.com
website: www.bromsgrovegolfcentre.com

BROMYARD. **Sapey Golf Club,** Upper Sapey, Worcester WR6 6XT (01886 853288). *Location:* situated six miles north of Bromyard on B4203. Parkland course with water features, outstanding views over Malvern Hills. The Rowan: 18 holes, 5935 yards. S.S.S. 68. The Oaks: 9-holes, 1203 yards. Practice, putting green. *Green Fees:* The Rowan – weekdays £27.00; weekends £32.00. The Oaks – weekdays £7.00. weekends £9.00. *Eating facilities:* bar and restaurant meals available seven days a week. *Visitors:* always welcome. Buggies, power trolleys, trolleys for hire. Fully stocked Pro Shop with PGA tuition available for all, including Junior coaching under the Golf Foundation Scheme. *Society Meetings:* always welcome. Professional: Chris Knowles (01886 853288). Secretary: Lynn Stevenson (01886 853506; Fax: 01886 853485).
e-mail: anybody@sapeygolf.co.uk
website: www.sapeygolf.co.uk

DROITWICH. **Droitwich Golf and Country Club Ltd,** Westford House, Ford Lane, Droitwich WR9 0BQ. Location: between Junction 5 of M5 and Droitwich just off A38. Parkland, undulating, wooded. 18 holes, 5976 yards. S.S.S. 69. Practice area. *Green Fees:* information not available. *Eating facilities:* full catering and bar facilities available. *Visitors*: welcome without reservation Mondays to Fridays (Ladies Day Tuesday, tee closed to 12 noon), weekends with member only. *Society Meetings*: catered for Wednesdays or Fridays. Professional: P. Cundy (01905 770207). Secretary: C.S. Thompson (01905 774344; Fax: 01905 797290).*

DROITWICH near. **Ombersley Golf Club,** Bishops Wood Road, Lineholt, Ombersley, Near Droitwich WR9 0LE (01905 620747; Fax: 01905 620047). *Location:* from A449, two and a half miles north of Ombersley, take A4025 then first left. High, though gently undulating course enjoying panoramic views over Severn Valley. 18 holes, 6139 yards. S.S.S. 69. Covered driving range, chipping green and bunker, putting green. *Green Fees:* information not available. *Eating facilities:* bar facilities, snacks and meals available. *Visitors:* all visitors welcome, bookable seven days in advance. Seventeen buggies, cart rental available. *Society Meetings:* welcome by arrangement – we specialise in corporate golf. Professional/General Manager: Graham Glenister.*

DROITWICH SPA. **Gaudet Luce Golf Club,** Middle Lane, Hadzor, Droitwich Spa WR9 7JR (Tel: 01905 796375; Fax: 01905 797245). *Location:* Junction 5 or 6 off M5, Droitwich Spa, located just off Tagwell Road. Undulating parkland course with a mixture of long and short holes offering a demanding challenge for all golfers. 18 holes, 5887 yards. S.S.S. 69. Par 3, 9 hole Academy Course, 12 bay Driving Range. *Green Fees:* information not available. *Eating facilities:* full clubhouse facilities including restaurant, lounge and bar. *Visitors:* welcome most days (essential to phone the Pro Shop before visit). Fully stocked Pro Shop with PGA tuition available for all, including Junior coaching under the Young Masters Golf. *Society Meetings:* welcome most weekdays by prior arrangement with Pro Shop. Professional: Russell Adams.*
e-mail: info@gaudet-luce.co.uk
website: www.gaudet-luce.co.uk

EVESHAM. **Evesham Golf Club,** Craycombe Links, Fladbury Cross, Pershore WR10 2QS (01386 860395). *Location:* M5 at Junction 6, A4538 and A44 to Evesham approximately 10 miles then towards Worcester for about three miles. Meadowland, tree-lined fairways. 9 holes (18 tees), 6415 yards, 5866 metres. S.S.S. 71. Practice area. *Green Fees:* information not available. *Eating facilities:* diningroom and bar. *Visitors:* must be members of a recognised club and have a certified Handicap. Tuesday Ladies' Day. *Society Meetings:* catered for by prior arrangement. Professional: Dan Clee (01386 861011). Secretary: Jerry Cain.*

HAGLEY. **Hagley Golf and Country Club,** Wassell Grove Lane, Hagley DY9 9JW (01562 883701; Fax: 01562 887518). *Location*: A456 Birmingham to Kidderminster Road. Wooded undulating course with many testing holes. 18 holes, 6553 yards. S.S.S. 72. 28-bay driving range. *Green Fees:* £34.00 per round, £39.00 per day. *Eating facilities:* restaurant and bars. *Visitors:* welcome to play Monday to Friday, weekends with a member only. Buggies available. *Society Meetings:* welcome weekdays by prior arrangement. Professional: Paul Johnson (01562 883852). Secretary: Graham F. Yardley

KIDDERMINSTER. **Habberley Golf Club,** Habberley, Kidderminster DY11 5RF. *Location*: north west side of Kidderminster. Undulating parkland course. 9 holes, 5401 yards. S.S.S. 68. *Green Fees:* £15.00; £12.00 with a member. Twilight golf available at reduced rates, after 4pm, including weekends. *Eating facilities:* food and bar available. *Visitors*: welcome weekdays, without reservation; weekends afternoons only. *Society Meetings:* welcome, on application. Secretary: D.S.McDermott (01562 745756).

KIDDERMINSTER. **Kidderminster Golf Club,** Russell Road, Kidderminster DY10 3HT (01562 822303; Fax: 01562 827866). *Location:* signposted off A449 Worcester–Wolverhampton Road. Wooded parkland course. 18 holes, 6422 yards. S.S.S. 71. Practice ground. *Green Fees:* information not available. *Eating facilities:* bar and restaurant available. *Visitors:* welcome weekdays only if bona fide member of another club, weekends if guest of member. Snooker room with bar. *Society Meetings:* Thursdays; small parties catered for other weekdays. Professional: (01562 740090). Secretary: (01562 822303; Fax: 01562 827866).*
e-mail: info@kidderminstergolfclub.com
website: www.kidderminstergolfclub.com

KIDDERMINSTER. **Wyre Forest Golf Club,** Zortean Avenue, Kidderminster DY11 7EX (01299 822682; Fax: 01299 879433). *Location:* from Kidderminster to Stourport-on-Severn on the A451. Flat inland links type course. Full practice facilities. 18 holes, 57901 yards. S.S.S. 68. *Green Fees:* information not provided. *Eating facilities*: clubhouse bar open until 9pm daily. *Visitors*: can book 6 days in advance. Must book at weekends. *Society Meetings*: catered for. Packages available. Professional/General Manager: C. Botterill.
e-mail: chris@wyreforestgc.co.uk

MALVERN WELLS. **The Worcestershire Golf Club,** Wood Farm, Malvern Wells WR14 4PP (01684 575992; Fax: 01684 893334). *Location:* two miles south of Great Malvern, near junction of A449 and B4209. Exceptionally scenic - Malvern Hills and Vale of Evesham. 18 holes, 6500 yards. S.S.S. 72. *Green Fees*: information not available. *Eating facilities*: available. *Visitors*: visitors unaccompanied by a member must provide a current Handicap Certificate. Weekends after 10am. *Society Meetings*: catered for Mondays, Thursdays and Fridays only on application. Professional: R. Lewis (Tel & Fax: 01684 564428). Secretary/Manager: David Wilson (01684 575992; Fax: 01684 893334).*
e-mail: secretary@worcsgolfclub.co.uk

PERSHORE. **The Vale Golf Club,** Hill Furze Road, Bishampton, Near Pershore WR10 2LZ (01386 462781; Fax: 01386 462597). *Location:* off the A44 road, between Evesham and Pershore at Fladbury crossroads. Feature lakes and wooded surrounds. Two courses: The Lenches, 9 holes, 2628 to 2918 yards. S.S.S 66 to 68; The International Championship Course, 18 holes, 6663 to 7174 yards. S.S.S. 72/74. Driving range. *Green Fees:* information not available. *Eating facilities:* Vale restaurant, spike bar, Sir William Lyons Suite. *Visitors:* welcome. *Society Meetings:* corporate and society days welcome. Professional: Richard Jenkins (01386 462520; Fax: 01386 462660). General Manager: Melanie Drake.*
e-mail: vale-sales@crown-golf.co.uk

REDDITCH. **The Abbey Hotel Golf & Country Club,** Hither Green Lane, Dagnell End Road, Redditch B98 9BE (01527 406500; Fax: 01527 406514). *Location:* on the northern boundary of Redditch town, between the villages of Beoley and Bordesley. From M42, junction 2, take A441 towards Redditch, signposted Redditch, turn left at first traffic lights, signposted Beoley, B4101. Turn right after approximately 500 metres into Hither Green Lane. The golf course is immediately on the left. Donald Steel designed parkland course. 18 holes, 6691 yards (white tees), S.S.S. 72, 6397 yards (yellow tees) S.S.S. 71, 5729 yards (red tees), S.S.S. 72. Golf range, putting green. *Green Fees:* information not provided. *Eating facilities:* Tawnys Bar serving bar snacks, hot beverages, lunches and dinners. Fully licensed restaurant in the hotel. *Visitors:* welcome alll week; bookings to be made 4 days or less in advance. Golf tuition, trolley and buggy hire, golf shop. 100 room, 4 star hotel on site. *Society Meetings:* welcome. Professional: Rob Davies (01527 406500; Fax: 01527 406514). Secretary: Mrs P. Williamson (01527 406538; Fax 01527 406914).
e-mail: info@theabbeyhotel.co.uk
       membership@theabbeyhotel.co.uk
       golfshop@theabbeyhotel.co.uk
website: www.theabbeyhotel.co.uk

Please mention THE GOLF GUIDE when you enquire about clubs or accommodation

REDDITCH. **Pitcheroak Golf Course,** Plymouth Road, Redditch B97 4PB (01527 541043). *Location*: 500 yards from bus/train stations. Hilly parkland course very tricky, lots of trees and bunker. 9 holes (18 tees), 4561 yards. S.S.S. 62. Practice grounds, nets, putting green. *Green Fees:* information not available. *Eating facilities:* bar and cafeteria facilities open all day. *Visitors:* welcome any time, municipal course. Changing rooms (ladies and gents). *Society Meetings:* welcome. Professional: C. Stanley (01527 541054). Secretary: Ray Barnett (01386 793370).*

REDDITCH. **Redditch Golf Club,** Lower Grinsty, Green Lane, Callow Hill, Redditch B97 5PJ (01527 543079; Fax: 01527 547413). *Location:* three miles west of Redditch town centre, off Redditch to Bromsgrove road (A448), or Astwood Bank to Redditch (A441), take Windmill Drive, look for Callow Hill signs. First 9 holes parkland, second 9 holes wooded. White - 18 holes, 6671 yards. S.S.S. 72. Two practice areas. *Green Fees:* information on website. *Eating facilities:* restaurant and bar with bar snacks except Mondays. *Visitors:* welcome, weekends with member. *Society Meetings:* catered for by arrangement. Professional: David Down (01527 543079 Option 2). Secretary: W. Kerr (01527 543079 Option 1; Fax 01527 547413).
website: www.redditchgolfclub.com

REDDITCH. **Redditch Kingfisher Golf Club,** Pitcheroak Golf Course, Plymouth Road, Redditch B97 4PB. *Location:* just up from the station. Hilly parkland course. 9 holes, 4561 yards. S.S.S. 62. Practice, nets, putting green. *Green Fees:* 9 holes £5.40. *Eating facilities:* full catering and bar facilities. *Visitors:* welcome at all times. Showers/ changing rooms. *Society Meetings:* welcome at all times. Professional: Chris Stanley (01527 541054). Secretary: Ray Barnett (01386 793370).

TENBURY WELLS. **Cadmore Lodge Golf and Country Club,** Berrington Green, Tenbury Wells WR15 8TQ (01584 810044). *Location:* two miles south of Tenbury Wells, just off A4112 to Leominster. Parkland with lake and streams in constant play. *Green Fees:* information not provided. *Eating facilities:* hotel bar and restaurant. *Visitors:* welcome, no restrictions. Hotel with AA Rosette restaurant and 14 en suite bedrooms. *Society Meetings:* welcome. Secretary: R.V. Farr (01584 810306 home).

WORCESTER. **Perdiswell Park Golf Club,** Bilford Road, Worcester WR3 8DX (01905 754668). *Location:* 600 yards from A38, north of the city centre. A testing 18 hole parkland course with many natural features. *Green Fees:* 9 holes £8.25 weekdays, £10.50 weekends; 18 holes £12.50 weekdays, £16.50 weekends. 2010 rates (subject to review). *Eating facilities:* food available. *Visitors:* welcome at any time, but advised to phone first. *Society Meetings:* welcome. PGA Professional: Mark Woodward (01905 754668). Secretary: Brian Hodgetts (01905 640456).

WORCESTER. **Ravenmeadow Golf Club,** Hindlip Lane, Claines, Worcester WR3 8SA (01905 757525; Fax: 01905 458876). *Location*: Junction 6 (M5 motorway) A449, leave at Blackpole exit; at main road turn right then first left into Hindlip Lane, entrance is half-mile on the left. Gently undulating course, with greens and tees to USGA standards; Barbourne Brook meanders through the course. 10 holes (18 tees). 5352 yards, S.S.S. 66. Excellent practice facilities: driving range, 9 hole pitch and putt, adults' and children's practice greens, chipping green. *Green Fees:* available 7 days a week. *Eating facilities:* Bar open 7 days, food available from 11am. *Visitors:* always welcome, telephone to reserve tee times. *Society Meetings*: welcome every day. Telephone (01905 575725) for special rates. Professional: Tommy Robinson (PGA) (01905 757525). Manager: Christian Davis (01905 757525; Fax: 01905 458876).
e-mail: info@ravenmeadowgolf.co.uk
website: www.ravenmeadowgolf.co.uk

WORCESTER. **Worcester Golf and Country Club,** Boughton Park, Worcester WR2 4EZ (01905 422555). *Location*: one-and-a-quarter miles west of city on A4103 (to Hereford). Parkland with lakes and specimen trees. 18 holes, 6251 yards. S.S.S. 70. Practice areas. *Green Fees:* information not available. *Eating facilities:* full catering available. *Visitors:* welcome weekdays, telephone Professional. Handicap Certificate required. *Society Meetings:* welcome, telephone Secretary. Professional: Graham Farr (01905 422044). Secretary: P. Tredwell (01905 422555).
e-mail: worcestergcc@btinternet.com
website: www.worcestergcc.co.uk

For full details of convenient accommodation near clubs and courses
www.holidayguides.com

Golf in the North

David Birtill

Cheshire • Cumbria • Durham Greater Manchester • Lancashire • Merseyside Northumberland • Tyne & Wear • Yorkshire

Maybe it's too presumptuous for the North West to describe itself as the second Home of Golf, but can any other region in the world claim to have hosted 10 major championships in 12 years?

With the three Royal clubs the jewels in the crown, it's not surprising that the powers-that-be rate the area so highly.

Next year sees the return of the greatest championship of all to this golfing Mecca - the Open at Royal Lytham & St Anne's, which will also stage the Walker Cup, the biennial contest between Great Britain & Ireland and the USA, in 2015.

Last summer the Ricoh Women's British Open was played out over the rolling dunes at Royal Birkdale, as it was at Lytham in 2009, and when Royal Liverpool was named as the 2012 venue the champagne hardly had time to go flat before it was announced that the Open Championship would be back at the Hoylake club two years later - and rightly so! The 2006 showpiece was justifiably hailed as the most memorable in recent times as it attracted record crowds in excess of 230,000.

The appropriately named England's Golf Coast certainly gets its share of the big occasions. Aside from the majors, the Curtis Cup and four Amateur Championships have been fought here since the start of the millennium.

The area extends from the Fylde, across the River Mersey and down to the Wirral, and contains without doubt some of the most scenic and testing links in the country, with a combination of sea, sand and the forces of nature offering an irresistible challenge for players of all levels.

One of the most wonderful aspects of this great game is that none of these iconic clubs is out of bounds to the public. While only the chosen few are entitled to boot a ball at Wembley or drive over for a try at Twickenham, anyone with a handicap can follow in the spike marks of golfing greats such as Henry Cotton, Jack Nicklaus and Seve Ballesteros.

But let's pull ourselves away from the coast because inland there are more delights, and hidden gems, awaiting the avid golfer – especially in Yorkshire.

Moorland or parkland – you'll be spoiled for choice. Ganton, one of the country's greatest inland links and a former Walker Cup venue, Alwoodley, Fulford, Sand Moor, Moor Allerton, Pannal, Lindrick and Catterick are all well established clubs which complement a host of new ones which have sprung up recently, including the excellent Aldwark Manor and Rudding Park.

Latest edition to this impressive list is Rockcliffe Hall, set in 360 acres of breathtaking countryside on the border with County Durham and destined to become one of the major resorts in the European game.

It's an obvious centre of excellence with a modern clubhouse plus practice academy, driving range, putting green and short game area and the hotel itself offers elegance and history with all the appropriate facilities essential in a five-star resort.

Speaking of hotels, the De Vere group have invested heavily since purchasing the former public course which envelopes their five-star Oulton Hall. The 27-hole layout has been upgraded to a high standard and a splendid new clubhouse adds to the ambience.

Last summer the Leeds Cup, the oldest in professional golf, returned there as De Vere renewed their previous long-running sponsorship of the event. They also restored their support for the PGA North Region Championship which was also back at its old home, De Vere Heron's Reach in Blackpool.

Now we've crossed the Pennines again, the rich parkland courses should be included in any itinerary. Mere, Stockport, Prestbury and Wilmslow have all been deemed suitable for Open Championship regional qualifying in Cheshire, as Clitheroe, Ormskirk and Pleasington have in Lancashire.

If you're heading North, stop off at Lancaster to savour the delights of this pretty course which has a dormy house attached. When you reach Cumbria take in Carlisle and Penrith, then maybe meander up the coast to Silloth, Seascale and Workington.

Apart from being probably England's most scenic countryside, Northumberland has a wealth of courses that blend in well with it. Slaley Hall, Burham Park, Longhirst Hall, Close House and Matfen Hall are comparatively recent developments which sit comfortably with the older Newbiggin, Whitley Bay, Prudhoe and Tynemouth.

That quality spills over into neighbouring Durham clubs Seaton Carew, South Shields, Bishop Auckland and Barnard Castle in Durham, giving the golfer an excellent choice of courses over a very wide area.

Seascale Golf Club, Cumbria, offers a serious test when the wind blows

Cheshire

ADLINGTON. **Adlington Golf Centre,** Sandy Hey Farm, Adlington, Macclesfield SK10 4NG (01625 850660). *Location*: 2 miles south of Poynton off A523. 9 hole Par 3 course plus 9 hole Academy Course. 24 bay covered, floodlit driving range. *Fees*: information not provided. *Eating facilities:* tea and coffee available. Reductions for Senior Citizens. Tuition available all the time. Proprietor: David Moss (01625 850660).

ALDERLEY EDGE. **Alderley Edge Golf Club,** Brook Lane, Alderley Edge SK9 7RU (01625 586200). *Location:* off A34. 9 holes, 5836 yards. S.S.S. 68. *Green Fees:* information not available. *Eating facilities:* meals served in clubhouse. *Visitors:* subject to restrictions on Tuesday mornings, Wednesday afternoons and weekends. *Society Meetings:* welcome on Thursdays. Professional: P. Bowring (01625 584493). Secretary: J. Dixon.*

ALSAGER. **Alsager Golf and Country Club,** Audley Road, Alsager, Stoke-on-Trent ST7 2UR (01270 875700; Fax: 01270 882207). *Location:* off M6 at Junction 16 onto A500 to Stoke, first left to Alsager, course is one and a half miles on right. Parkland. 18 holes, 6225 yards. S.S.S. 70. *Green Fees:* information not available. *Eating facilities:* restaurant and bar snacks. *Visitors:* welcome Mondays, to Thursdays and Fridays 8am to 12pm, without reservation. Wedding, conference and banqueting facilities. Bowls. *Society Meetings:* welcome Mondays, Wednesdays and Thursdays, packages arranged. Professional: Richard Brown (01270 877432; Fax: 01270 882207). Administration Manager: Margaret Davenport (01270 875700).*
e-mail: business@alsagergolfclub.com
website: www.alsagergolfclub.com

APPLETON. **Warrington Golf Club,** Hill Warren, London Road, Appleton, Near Warrington WA4 5HR (01925 261620). *Location:* M56 Junction 10, A49 Warrington one and a half miles on left. Parkland course. 18 holes, 6210 yards. S.S.S. 71. Practice ground. *Green Fees:* information not available.

Eating facilities: available every day except Mondays. *Visitors:* welcome with booking through Professional. *Society Meetings:* Wednesdays only, booked through Secretary. Professional: R. MacKay (01925 265431). Secretary: D.S. Macphee (01925 261775; Fax: 01925 265933).*
e-mail: secretary@warringtongolfclub.co.uk
website: www.warringtongolfclub.co.uk

CHEADLE. **Cheadle Golf Club,** Cheadle Road, Cheadle SK8 1HW (0161-428 2160). *Location:* one-and-a-half miles Junction 11 M63. Parkland. 9 holes, 5006 yards. S.S.S. 65. *Green Fees:* information not available. *Eating facilities:* by arrangement with the Steward. *Visitors:* welcome, must be members of a bona fide golf club; current Handicap Certificate to be produced; no visitors on Tuesdays or Saturdays. *Society Meetings:* catered for by arrangement with the Secretary. Professional: Anthony Millar (0161-428 9878). Secretary: J.V. Heyes (0161-491 4452).

CHEADLE. **Gatley Golf Club Ltd,** Waterfall Farm, Styal Road, Heald Green, Cheadle SK8 3TW (0161-437 2091). *Location:* from Gatley village to South down Styal Road and follow directions into Yew Tree Grove, then Motcombe Grove to Club entrance. Parkland course. 9 holes, 5934 yards. S.S.S. 68. *Green Fees:* information not available. Special rates by arrangement. *Eating facilities:* available except Monday, bar. *Visitors:* welcome Mondays, Wednesdays and Thursdays. *Society Meetings:* welcome Thursdays. Professional: Jon Cheetham (0161-436 2830). Secretary: G. Griffiths (0161-437 2091).*

CHESTER. **Aldersey Green Golf Club,** Aldersey, Near Chester CH3 9EH (01829 782157). *Location:* on A41 Chester to Whitchurch road five minutes from Broxton roundabout. Flat wooded parkland. 18 holes, 6159 yards. S.S.S. 69. Practice area. *Green Fees:* information not available. *Eating facilities:* bar with meals available. *Visitors:* welcome. *Society meetings:* welcome. Professional and Secretary: Stephen Bradbury.*

Nestled on the border of South Cheshire and North Staffordshire, this Par 70 and 6225 yard course is challenging for golfers of all abilities and is conveniently located two miles from Junction 16 of the M6. From the 13th green the panoramic views span across six counties.

Tel: 01270 875700 • Fax: 01270 882207
e-mail: business@alsagergolfclub.com

CHESTER. **Carden Park Hotel, Golf Resort & Spa,** Carden, near Chester CH3 9DQ (01829 731000; Fax: 01829 731032). *Location:* take A41 from Chester to Broxton roundabout, turn right onto A534 (Wrexham). Parkland courses with trees and superb views over the Cheshire countryside. Cheshire Course, 18 holes, 6824 yards. Par 72. Nicklaus Course, 18 holes, 7045 yards, Par 72. Driving range. *Green Fees*: information available on request. *Eating facilities:* Clubhouse. *Visitors:* welcome. No metal spikes allowed. Accommodation in 196-bedroom hotel. *Society Meetings:* welcome.
e-mail: reservations.carden@devere-hotels.com
website: www.cardenpark.co.uk

CHESTER. **Chester Golf Club,** Curzon Park, Chester CH4 8AR (01244 675130). *Location:* one mile south west of city centre. From Chester Castle take A483 (Wrexham) to first roundabout over Grovesnor Bridge. Turn right into Curzon Park North and follow signs. Parkland on two levels overlooking the River Dee. 18 holes, 6508 yards. S.S.S. 71. *Green Fees:* information not available. *Eating facilities:* full restaurant and bar facilities. *Visitors:* welcome most days but advisable to telephone first. *Society Meetings:* catered for by prior arrangement. Professional: Scott Booth (01244 671185). Secretary: V.F.C. Wood (01244 677760).*

CHESTER. **Eaton Golf Club,** Guy Lane, Waverton, Chester CH3 7PH (01244 335885). *Location*: three miles south east of Chester off A41. 18 holes, 6580 yards. S.S.S. 72. Substantial practice area. *Green Fees*: weekdays £35.00, weekends £40.00. *Eating facilities*: catering available seven days. *Visitors:* welcome at all times but with Handicap Certificate and prior checking with either Secretary or Professional. *Society Meetings*: welcome except Wednesdays. Society rates available on request. Professional: Bill Tye (01244 335826). Secretary: Kerry Brown (01244 335885; Fax: 01244 335782).
e-mail: office@eatongolfclub.co.uk
website: www.eatongolfclub.co.uk

CHESTER. **Mollington Grange Golf Club,** Townfield Lane, Mollington, Chester CH1 6NJ (01244 851185; Fax: 01244 851349). *Location:* A540, 5 minutes from end of M56 and two miles from Chester City. A superb undulating course with five lakes, 16 ponds and a Par 3 island green, providing a challenge for the advanced player while remaining friendly to the average player or beginner. 18 holes, 6400 yards. Par 71. Driving range. *Green Fees:* information not provided. *Eating facilities:* club house with warm and friendly atmosphere, lounge and bar area, restaurant and sports lounge/bar situated on the first floor. *Visitors:* welcome. Membership open, details on request. Fully stocked golf shop and comfortable changing facilities. *Society Meetings:* welcome. Corporate days and corporate membership catered for. Details available on request. Secretary: Gail Matthews.

CHESTER. **Pryors Hayes Golf Club,** Willington Road, Oscroft, Near Tarvin CH3 8NL (01829 741250; Fax: 01829 749077). *Location:* signposted; situated just off A54 between Kelsall and Tarvin. Flat, parkland course. 18 holes, 5915 yards. S.S.S. 69. Practice area. *Green Fees:* information not available. *Eating facilities:* restaurant and bar. *Visitors:* welcome every day subject to availability. *Society Meetings:* Societies/Companies/Groups all welcome. Professional: Martin Redrup (01829 740140; Fax: 01829 749077). Secretary: Joan Quinn (01829 741250; Fax: 01829 749077).*

CHESTER. **Upton-by-Chester Golf Club,** Upton Lane, Chester CH2 1EE (01244 381183; Fax: 01244 376955). *Location:* off A41, near Zoo turn-off traffic lights. Flat parkland course. 18 holes, 5807 yards. S.S.S. 68. *Green Fees:* information not available. *Eating facilities:* large restaurant and bar. *Visitors:* no restrictions except Competition Days. *Society Meetings:* welcome except Mondays, Tuesdays and weekends. Minimum number 16. Costings to suit numbers and catering requirements. Build your own package from our website. Professional: Stephen Dewhurst (01244 381183). Secretary: Fred Hopley (01244 381183; Fax: 01244 376955).*
website: www.uptonbychestergolfclub.co.uk

CHESTER. **Vicars Cross Golf Club,** Tarvin Road, Great Barrow, Chester CH3 7HN (01244 335174; Fax: 01244 335686). *Location:* four miles east of Chester on the A51. Undulating parkland course, wooded. 18 holes, 6411 yards. S.S.S. 71. Practice grounds/covered bays. *Green Fees:* £35.00 weekdays, £40.00 weekends and Bank Holidays, £25.00 after 3pm every day. 2010 rates (subject to review). *Eating facilities:* restaurant and bar snacks. *Visitors:* welcome every day except competition days - phone Secretary or Professional beforehand. *Society Meetings:* welcome Tuesday/Thursday and occasional Fridays. Conference facilities, lounge/ dining rooms available for hire. Professional: Gavin Beddow (01244 335595). Secretary: Mrs Katrina Hunt.
e-mail: manager@vicarscrossgolf.co.uk

CONGLETON. **Astbury Golf Club,** Peel Lane, Astbury, Near Congleton CW12 4RE (01260 272772). *Location:* on outskirts south of Congleton, leave A34 Congleton to Newcastle Road at Astbury Village. Parkland/meadowland, water feature on four holes. 18 holes, 6178 yards. S.S.S. 69. Large practice area. *Green Fees:* information not provided. *Eating facilities:* dining room and bar. *Visitors:* welcome

Guy Lane, Waverton, Chester CH3 7PH
e-mail: office@eatongolfclub.co.uk • www.eatongolfclub.co.uk
♦ Three miles south east of Chester off the A41 ♦ 18 holes, 6580 yards. S.S.S. 72. ♦ Visitors welcome at all times but with Handicap Certificate and prior checking with either Secretary or Professional
♦ Catering available seven days a week
Professional: 01244 335826 ♦ *Secretary: 01244 335885*

weekdays, weekend with a member only. Must be members of recognised golf club with bona fide Handicap. Smart casual dress in clubhouse, jackets expected when meal/presentation held. *Society Meetings:* Thursdays only. Professional: Neil Dawson (01260 272772). Secretary: Pete Bentley (01260 272772). Caterer: (01260 272772).

CONGLETON. **Congleton Golf Club,** Biddulph Road, Congleton CW12 3LZ (01260 273540). *Location:* one mile south of Congleton Railway Station on Biddulph Road. Parkland. 9 holes, 5119 yards. S.S.S. 65. *Green Fees:* £24.00 weekdays. *Eating facilities:* meals served daily. *Visitors:* welcome. *Society Meetings:* welcome Mondays and Thursdays by prior arrangement. Professional: Andrew Preston (07796 444321). Secretary: D. Lancake (01260 273540).

CREWE. **Crewe Golf Club Ltd,** Fields Road, Haslington, Crewe CW1 5TB (01270 584099). *Location:* off A534 between Crewe and Sandbach in the village of Haslington. Parkland course. 18 holes, 6424 yards. S.S.S. 71. *Green Fees:* information not available. *Eating facilities:* bar, diningroom. *Visitors:* welcome weekdays only, not Bank Holidays. Snooker room. *Society Meetings:* Tuesdays. Catering (01270 584227). Professional: David Wheeler (01270 585032). Secretary: Hayley Taylor (01270 584099; Fax: 01270 256482).*
e-mail: secretary@crewegolfclub.co.uk
website: www.crewegolfclub.co.uk

CREWE. **Onneley Golf Club,** Barr Hill Road, Onneley, Near Crewe CW3 5QF (01782 750577). *Location:* one mile from Woore on A525, 12 miles from Stoke-on-Trent. Parkland on gentle slope. 18 holes, 5728 yards. S.S.S. 68. Par 70. *Green Fees:* weekdays £20.00 per day, Saturday £25.00 per round. *Eating facilities:* dining room and bar snacks. *Visitors:* welcome weekdays unrestricted, Saturdays after 10am. *Society Meetings:* welcome (weekdays £15.00, Saturdays £20.00, Sundays limited availablity. Packages to suit, please enquire. Secretaty: Phil Robinson (01270 820127; 07802 389323).
website: www.onneleygolfclub.co.uk

CREWE. **Queens Park Golf Course,** Queens Park Drive, Crewe CW2 7SB (01270 662378). *Location:* next to Queens Park, one mile from Crewe Station. Parkland. 9 holes x 2, 4920 yards. S.S.S. 64. *Green Fees:* information not available. *Eating facilities:* bar with excellent bar snacks. *Visitors:* welcome, restrictions Sunday mornings to 11am. *Society Meetings:* welcome. Professional: Jamie Lowe (01270 666724). Secretary: Tom Weston (01270 662887).*

DISLEY. **Disley Golf Club Ltd,** Stanley Hall Lane, Disley, Stockport SK12 2JX (01663 764001). *Location:* off A6 at Disley Village. Open hillside/ parkland course. 18 holes, 6015 yards, 5832 metres. S.S.S. 69. *Green Fees:* £30.00 weekdays, £40.00 weekends. *Eating facilities:* available. *Visitors:* welcome. *Society Meetings:* catered for by arrangement. Professional: L. Thorneycroft (01663 764001). Secretary: Phil Housley (01663 764001).

FRODSHAM. **Frodsham Golf Club,** Simons Lane, Frodsham WA6 6HE (01928 732159; Fax: 01928 734070). *Location:* 10 minutes from Junction 12 M56. Parkland with views over Mersey estuary. 18 holes, 6328 yards. S.S.S. 70 (gents), 70 (ladies). Two practice areas, putting green, bunker and net. *Green Fees:* information not available. *Eating facilities:* clubhouse: dining room, lounge bar, spike bar, snooker room. *Visitors:* welcome weekdays only, guests of members only at weekends. *Society Meetings:* welcome weekdays. Professional: Graham Tonge (01928 739442; Fax: 01928 739037). Secretary: A. Webb (01928 732159; Fax: 01928 734070).*
e-mail: alastair@frodshamgc.co.uk
website: www.frodshamgolfclub.co.uk

HELSBY. **Helsby Golf Club,** Towers Lane, Helsby WA6 0JB (01928 722021; Fax: 01928 726816). *Location:* 7 miles south of Chester. M56 Junction 14 take B5117 to Helsby. Through traffic lights one mile, first right into Primrose Lane, then first right into Towers Lane (400 yards). James Braid designed parkland course. 18 holes, 6229 yards. S.S.S. 70. Practice area available. *Green Fees:* £27.50 weekdays; £17.00 with a member weekends. 2010 rates (subject to review). *Eating facilities:* full restaurant facilities. *Visitors:* welcome weekdays, weekends must play with a member. Snooker facilities. *Society Meetings:* welcome Tuesdays and Thursdays by arrangement. Professional: M. Jones (01928 722021; Fax: 01928 726816). Secretary: C.A. Stubbs (01928 722021).
e-mail: secretary@helsbygolfclub.org
website: www.helsbygolfclub.org

KNUTSFORD. **Heyrose Golf Club,** Budworth Road, Tabley, Knutsford WA16 0HZ (Tel & Fax: 01565 733664). *Location:* Junction 19 on M6 right at Windmill Pub to Pickmere, three-quarters of a mile right fork, half a mile further on right. Undulating parkland, wooded course. 18 holes, 6513 yards. S.S.S. 71. New 12 bay driving range, net and bunker, putting green. *Green Fees:* information not provided. *Eating facilities:* bar and restaurant. *Visitors:* no visitors on Saturdays before 3.30pm, Ladies priority Wednesdays, Seniors priority Thursdays. *Society Meetings:* welcome weekdays and Sundays. Professional: Philip Bills (Tel & Fax: 01565 734267). General Manager: Mrs Elizabeth Bridge (Tel & Fax: 01565 733664).
e-mail: info@heyrosegolfclub.com
website: www.heyrosegolfclub.com

KNUTSFORD. **Knutsford Golf Club,** Mereheath Lane, Knutsford WA16 6HS (01565 633355). *Location:* quarter of a mile from town centre. 9 holes, 6200 yards. S.S.S. 70. *Green Fees:* information not provided. *Eating facilities:* bar snacks, other meals by prior arrangement. *Visitors:* welcome with reservation except Wednesdays and Saturdays and Sundays before 10am. *Society Meetings:* catered for by prior arrangement. Professional: Tim Maxwell. Secretary: Neil Fergusson.

Cheshire / NORTH REGION

KNUTSFORD. Mere Golf and Country Club, Chester Road, Mere, Knutsford WA16 6LJ (01565 830155; Fax: 01565 830713). *Location*: one mile east of Junction 19 M6 and two miles west of Junction 7 M56. Parkland Championship course. A regional qualifying course for The Open Championship. 18 holes, 6817 yards. S.S.S. 73. Short game practice area, one 18 hole putting green, driving range (April to October). *Green Fees:* information not provided. *Eating facilities:* informal atrium spike bar and brasserie. *Visitors:* welcome by prior arrangement only. *Society Meetings:* Mondays, Tuesdays and Thursdays only by arrangement. Professional: Peter Eyre (01565 830219). Golf Bookings: Karen Gallagher (01565 830155). Secretary: Peter Whitehead.
e-mail: play@meregolf.co.uk
website: www.meregolf.co.uk

KNUTSFORD. Mobberley Golf Club, Burleyhurst Lane, Mobberley, Knutsford WA16 7JZ (01565 880178; Fax: 01565 880178). *Location*: exit 6 M56 to A538 Wilmslow, turn right at Mobberley Road. 9 hole course set in rolling Cheshire countryside. 5542 yards, S.S.S. 67. *Green Fees*: weekdays 9 holes £13.00, 18 holes £20.00; weekends 9 holes £14.00, 18 holes £24.00; under 18's 9 holes £5.00, 18 holes £10.00. *Eating facilities*: fully licensed facilities available. *Visitors*: welcome at all times. Dress code must be adhered to. No denims, tracksuits, collarless shirts. Golf shoes must be worn. *Society Meetings*: welcome at all times. Professional/Golf Director: Gary Donnison.
e-mail: info@mobgolfclub.com
website: www.mobgolfclub.co.uk

KNUTSFORD. The Wilmslow Golf Club, Great Warford, Mobberley, Knutsford WA16 7AY (01565 872148). *Location:* two miles from Wilmslow off the Knutsford Road. Parkland course. 18 holes, 6635 yards. S.S.S. 72. Practice facility. *Green Fees:* weekdays £45.00 per round, £55.00 per day; weekends £55.00 per round, £65.00 per day. 2010 rates (subject to review). *Eating facilities:* full catering, two bars. *Visitors:* welcome, Ladies' Day Wednesday. *Society Meetings:* Tuesdays, Thursdays, and occasionally Fridays. Professional: L. J. Nowicki (01565 873620). General Manager: (01565 872148); Fax: 01565 872172).
e-mail: info@wilmslowgolfclub.co.uk
website: www.wilmslowgolfclub.co.uk

KNUTSFORD near. Peover Golf Club, Plumley Moor Road, Lower Peover, Near Knutsford WA16 9SE (01565 723337; Fax: 01565 723311). *Location:* Junction 19 of M6, A556, Knutsford. Parkland course, 18 holes, 6702 yards. S.S.S. 72. Practice area, putting green. *Green Fees:* information not available. Subject to change. *Eating facilities:* bar food and function room. *Visitors:* always welcome. Please ring for a tee time. Buggy and trolley hire. *Society Meetings:* welcome.*
e-mail: mail@peovergolfclub.co.uk
website: www.peovergolfclub.co.uk

LYMM. Lymm Golf Club, Whitbarrow Road, Lymm WA13 9AN (Tel & Fax: 01925 755020). *Location:* five miles south east of Warrington, two and a half miles from Junction 20 on M6 and Junction 9 on M56. Parkland. 18 holes. White 6351 yards. S.S.S. 71. Yellow 6103 yards. S.S.S. 70. Red 5575 yards. S.S.S. 73. Practice ground. *Green Fees:* weekdays £36.00. *Eating facilities:* coffee, bar snacks, lunches and dinner, bar. *Visitors:* welcome with Handicap Certificates, no visitors at weekends, Bank Holidays or Thursdays until 2.30pm. *Society Meetings:* catered for with reservation. Professional: Steve McCarthy (01925 755054). Secretary: T.H.Glover (Tel & Fax: 01925 755020). Clubhouse (01925 752177).
website: www.lymm-golf-club.co.uk

MACCLESFIELD. Macclesfield Golf Club, The Hollins, Macclesfield SK11 7EA (01625 423227). *Location:* turn off A523 Leek Road into Windmill Street, half a mile fork right. Hillside course with extensive views. 18 holes, 5714 yards. S.S.S. 68. *Green Fees:* information not available. *Eating facilities:* full catering and bars. *Visitors:* welcome by arrangement. *Society Meetings:* welcome weekdays except Thursdays. Professional: Tony Taylor (01625 423227). Secretary: Bob Littlewood (01625 423227; Fax: 01625 260061).*
e-mail: secretary@Maccgolfclub.co.uk
website: www.Maccgolfclub.co.uk

MACCLESFIELD. The Tytherington Club, Dorchester Way, Tytherington, Macclesfield SK10 2JP (01625 506000; Fax: 01625 506040). *Location:* one mile north of Macclesfield off A523. Undulating parkland with numerous water features and ample woodland. 18 holes, 6765 yards. S.S.S. 74. Driving range, short game area. *Green Fees:* information not provided. *Eating facilities:* bar with brasserie-style food and private function rooms available. *Visitors:* welcome, by prior arrangement. Buggies available. *Society Meetings:* welcome weekdays only. Highly competitive packages available. Professional: Anthony Haste (01625 506013). General Manager: James Gathercole.
e-mail: tytherington.events@theclubcompany.com

NANTWICH. Alvaston Hall Golf Club, Alvaston Hall Hotel, Middlewich Road, Nantwich CW5 6PD (01270 628473; Fax: 01270 623395). *Location:* A530 Middlewich Road. Parkland course. 9 holes. S.S.S. 59. *Green Fees*: information not available. Professionals: Mark Taylor, Neil Bates. Secretary: John Walkington.*

Situated in the heart of Cheshire, close to the historic town of Knutsford, which makes it ideally accessible to golfers. Close to Junction 19 M6. Peover's 18-hole par 72 parkland course measures 6,702 yards off the back tees. One of its most attractive features is the Peover Eye River which winds its way through the centre of the course, coming into play on three of the holes, while the tees and greens are situated to maximise the benefits of the natural contours. Clubhouse facilities available. Bar/food. Function room. Locker rooms. VISITORS MOST WELCOME.

Plumley Moor Road, Lower Peover, Near Knutsford WA16 9SE • Tel: 01565 723337
Fax: 01565 723311 • e-mail: mail@peovergolfclub.com • www.peovergolfclub.co.uk

Mere Golf & Country Club

From the welcoming yet peaceful grounds, the friendly service, the five star food and wines and the fact that you are spoilt for choice when it comes to an unusually large venue with superb leisure facilities, including a fitness studio, swimming pools and tennis court, a golfing experience at Mere will be a memorable occasion.

For an exhilarating round of golf, it's hard to beat the 6,817 yard, par 71 course created out of 150 acres of Cheshire parkland in 1934 by none other than Open Champions James Braid and George Duncan.

It would be hard to find a more picturesque course than Mere, with its parkland setting alongside the beautiful lake which gives the course its name. Mere offers cleverly sited hazards and some of the best greens in Britain.

Over the years Mere has hosted several major events, including the 2001 Dan Technology Seniors and the Tournament of Champions, and was a regional qualifying course for the 2009 Open at Turnberry.

- Individual and Corporate Golfing Packages.
- Clubs, Trolleys and Buggies for hire. Caddies available.
- Unique Floating Golf Ball Range.
- Extensively stocked Professional Shop. • Resident Professional.
- First class Restaurant and Conference & Banqueting facilities

One of the most exclusive leisure and sporting facilities in the North West.

Mere Golf & Country Club
Chester Road, Mere
Knutsford, Cheshire WA16 6LJ
Telephone: 01565 830 155
Fax: 01565 830 713
e-mail: play@meregolf.co.uk
www.meregolf.co.uk

Cheshire / NORTH REGION

NANTWICH. **Reaseheath Golf Club,** Reaseheath College, Nantwich CW5 6DF. *Location:* B5074 just north of Nantwich. Flat parkland. 9 holes, 3736 yards. S.S.S. 58. Short challenging course (4 par 4s, 5 par 3s) with narrow fairways and well guarded greens. Two tee positions for most holes. Also used for training greenkeepers. *Green Fees:* £10.00 for 18 holes. *Visitors:* with a member or by prior approval. *Society Meetings:* subject to approval. Secretary: John H. Soddy (01270 629869; Mobile: 07909 641238; Fax: 01270 625665).

NORTHWICH. **Antrobus Golf Club,** Foggs Lane, Antrobus, Northwich CW9 6JQ (01925 730890). *Location:* two minutes from Junction 10 of M56 between Northwich and Warrington. Parkland course with lakes. 18 holes, 6220 yards. S.S.S. 72. Putting green and driving range. *Green Fees:* Monday to Friday £28.00, Sundays £30.00. 2010 fees (subject to review). *Eating facilities:* available. *Visitors:* welcome every day, except Saturdays. *Society Meetings:* welcome any day except Saturday. Ring for discounted rates. Professional: Paul Farrance (01925 730900). Secretary: (01925 730890).

NORTHWICH. **Delamere Forest Golf Club,** Station Road, Delamere, Northwich CW8 2JE (01606 883264). *Location:* opposite Delamere Station on the B5152 Tarporley to Frodsham road. Undulating heathland course suitable for play winter or summer. 18 holes, 6348 yards. S.S.S. 72. Two practice grounds. *Green Fees:* weekdays £50.00 18 holes; £65.00 per day, weekends £60.00 *Eating facilities:* bar meals, diningroom. *Visitors:* welcome most weekdays if no large parties booked. Some restrictions on four balls on Sundays. Prior booking with Pro advisable. *Society Meetings:* societies, corporate days, parties and small groups catered for. Professional: Martin Brown (01606 883800). Secretary: Michael Towers (01606 883800; Fax: 01606 889444).
e-mail: see@delameregolf.co.uk
website: www.delameregolf.co.uk

NORTHWICH. **Hartford Golf Club,** Burrows Hill, Hartford, Northwich CW8 3AP (01606 871162; Fax: 01606 872182). *Location:* Just off A49 and A556 near ICI at Winnington. Undulating parkland course with numerous water hazards. 9 holes, 2780 yards, Par 35. 26 bay driving range with automatic tees. *Green Fees:* weekdays £7.50, weekends £9.50. *Eating facilities:* available. Large golf shop, tuition available. *Society Meetings:* welcome. Professional: L. Percival (01606 871162; Fax: 01606 872182). Secretary: C. Maddock.

NORTHWICH. **Sandiway Golf Club,** Chester Road, Sandiway, Northwich CW8 2DJ (01606 883247). *Location:* off A556, Northwich by-pass. Undulating heavily wooded parkland. 18 holes, 6404 yards. S.S.S. 72. *Green Fees:* information not available. *Eating facilities:* lunches and teas served daily, full restaurant facilities. *Visitors:* welcome on weekdays with Handicap Certificate from home club. *Society Meetings:* Tuesdays - parties up to 90; Mondays, Wednesdays, Thursdays and Fridays - parties up to 24. Professional: William Laird (01606 883180). Manager: Keith Melia (01606 883247; Fax: 01606 888548). Caterer: (01606 882606).*

NORTHWICH. **Vale Royal Abbey Golf Club,** Whitegate, Northwich CW8 2BA (01606 301291; Fax: 01606 301784). Parkland championship course. 18 holes, 6463 yards, S.S.S. 71. Short game practice area, putting green, chipping green, practice range. *Green Fees:* information not available. *Eating facilities:* informal spike bar. Professional: David Ingman.
website: www.vragc.co.uk

POYNTON. **Davenport Golf Club,** Worth Hall, Middlewood Road, Poynton SK12 1TS (01625 876951; Fax: 01625 877489). *Location*: A6 from Stockport, Macclesfield Road at Hazel Grove, left at Poynton Church. Undulating parkland course. 18 holes, 6034 yards. S.S.S. 69. Putting green and practice ground. *Green Fees*: Summer: weekdays £32.00 (£13.50 with member), weekends £43.00 (£16.50 with a member); Winter: weekdays £27.00 (£11.00 with member), weekends £32.00 (£13.50 with a member). *Eating facilities*: bar snacks daily except Mondays; full meals by arrangement. *Visitors:* welcome, advisable to check with the Professional for availability of first tee. *Society Meetings*: catered for Tuesdays and Thursdays; other days by arrangement. Professional: Tony Stevens (01625 877319). Secretary: Chris Souter (01625 876951; Fax: 01625 877489).
website: www.davenportgolf.co.uk

POYNTON. **Shrigley Hall Hotel, Golf & Country Club,** Shrigley Park, Pott Shrigley, Near Macclesfield SK10 5SB (01625 575757; Fax: 01625 575437). *Location:* easily accessible from the M56, M62,M60, M6,A523 and A6, only 10 minutes from Manchester Airport. Parkland course with magnificent views. 18 holes, 6305 yards. S.S.S 71. *Green Fees:* information not available. *Eating facilities:* private rooms catering for 16-250 people, plus hotel Orangery Restaurant. *Visitors:* corporate, society and resident golfers welcome. 156-bedroom Four Star hotel. Secretary: Alex Brannigan (01625 576681).*

PRESTBURY. **De Vere Mottram Hall,** Wilmslow Road, Mottram St. Andrew, Prestbury SK10 4QT (01625 820064). *Location*: M56 and M6. Parkland/woodland course, well draining. 18 holes, 7006 yards, 6250 metres. Par 72. Practice area. *Green Fees:* please telephone for prices. *Eating facilities:* Golf Brasserie. *Visitors:* no restrictions. Accommodation available in 131 bedrooms. *Society Meetings:* no restrictions except for certain times at weekends. Professional: Matthew Turnock. Head of Golf Operations: Tim Hudspith.

PRESTBURY. **Prestbury Golf Club,** Macclesfield Road, Prestbury, SK10 4BJ (01625 828241). *Location*: between Wilmslow and Macclesfield. 18 holes, 6371 yards, 5825 metres. S.S.S. 71. Practice ground. *Green Fees:* information not available. *Eating facilities:* snacks, lunches, teas and dinners. *Visitors:* welcome on weekdays 9.30am to 11.30am and after 2.00pm; Tuesdays Ladies' Day until 2.30pm. Wednesdays Gentlemen members only until 2pm. Bank Holidays and weekends only with a member. *Society Meetings:* Thursdays only. Professional: Nick Summerfield (01625 828242). Secretary: N. Young (Tel & Fax: 01625 828241).
e-mail: office@prestburygolfclub.com
website: www.prestburygolfclub.com

RUNCORN. **Runcorn Golf Club,** Clifton Road, Runcorn WA7 4SU (01928 572093). *Location:* signposted The Heath, A557; M56 Junction 12. High parkland, easy walking course. 18 holes, 6035 yards, 5514 metres. S.S.S. 69. *Green Fees:* information not available. *Eating facilities:* bar snacks, lunches; dinner by arrangement. *Visitors:* welcome weekdays, Tuesday is Ladies' Day. No visitors weekends or Bank Holidays except with a member. Handicap Certificate required. *Society Meetings:* by arrangement Mondays and Fridays. Professional: K.Hartley (01928 564791). Secretary: B.R. Griffiths (Tel & Fax: 01928 574214)*

SANDBACH. **Malkins Bank Municipal Golf Course,** Betchton Road, Malkins Bank, Sandbach CW11 4XN (01270 765931). *Location:* M6, Junction 17 west on A534 for one mile, south on A533 for 400 metres, turn into Hassall Road (signposted). Parkland course. 18 holes, 5971 yards, S.S.S. 69. Practice area. *Green Fees:* information not available. All rates subject to review. *Eating facilities:* bar and food available. *Visitors:* welcome at all times, please pre-book (01270 765931). *Society Meetings:* welcome, please pre-book (01270 765931). Professional: Davron Hackney (01270 765931; Fax: 01270 76473)*

SANDBACH. **Sandbach Golf Club,** 117 Middlewich Road, Sandbach CW11 1FH (01270 762117). *Location*: two miles from Junction 17 of M6 on Middlewich Road. Meadowland course. 9 holes, 5397 yards. S.S.S. 67. Practice field. *Green Fees:* information not available. *Eating facilities:* available except Mondays and Thursdays. *Visitors:* welcome weekdays, weekends by invitation only. *Society Meetings:* catered for only by advance arrangement with Hon. Secretary. Secretary: H. Buckley.*

SOUTH WIRRAL. **Ellesmere Port Golf Centre,** Chester Road, Childer, Thornton, South Wirral CH66 1QF (0151-339 7689). *Location*: approximately six miles north of Chester on main A41 trunk road to Birkenhead. Wooded parkland with a lot of ponds. 18 holes, 6296 yards. S.S.S. 70. Practice ground. *Green fees*: information not available. Eating facilities: bar and catering facilities. *Visitors*: welcome anytime. *Society Meetings:* by arrangement with Centre. Golf Centre Manager: Malcolm Cooke (0151-339 7689).*

STALYBRIDGE. **Stamford Golf Club,** Oakfield House, Huddersfield Road, Carrbrook, Stalybridge SK15 3PY (01457 832126). *Location:* on B6175 off A6018. Moorland course. 18 holes, 5701 yards. S.S.S. 68. *Green Fees:* weekdays and weekends £25.00. Special rates for golf societies. *Eating facilities:* full meals except Monday (bar available). *Visitors:* welcome without restrictions. *Society Meetings:* catered for by appointment only. Golf Shop: (01457 832126). Secretary: J. Kitchen (01457 832126).
e-mail: admin@stamfordgolfclub.co.uk

STYAL. **Styal Golf Club,** Station Road, Styal SK9 4JN. (01625 530063). *Location:* Station Road, Styal, five minutes from Manchester Airport, Junction 5 M56, five minutes from Wilmslow. Flat, parkland course with many water hazards and interesting features. 18 holes, 6238 yards, 5704 metres. S.S.S. 70. 9 hole, par 3 course, 1242 yards, Par 27. 24-bay de luxe driving range. New 10-bay outdoor range. *Green Fees:* £24.00 midweek, £30.00 weekends. *Eating facilities:* fully equipped restaurant and bar. *Visitors:* welcome. *Society Meetings:* welcome; packages available. Professional: Simon Forrest (01625 531359). Director of Golf: Glynn Traynor (01625 530063 ext. 214). Golf booking line (01625 531359).
e-mail: gtraynor@styalgolf.co.uk
website: www.styalgolf.co.uk

SUTTON WEAVER (NEAR RUNCORN). **Sutton Hall Golf Club,** Aston Lane, Sutton Weaver WA7 3ED (01928 790747; Fax: 01928 759174). *Location:* M56, Junction 12 signposted Frodsham. Wooded, parkland course. 18 holes, 6618 yards. S.S.S. 72. Full practice ground, putting green. *Green Fees:* information not provided. *Eating facilities:* Club catering available all day. *Visitors:* welcome weekdays; by arrangement only at weekends. *Society Meetings:* welcome. Professional: Jamie Hope (01928 714872; Fax: 01928 759174). Secretary: Maxwell Faulkner.
e-mail: info@suttonhallgolf.co.uk

TARPORLEY. **Macdonald Portal Hotel, Golf & Spa,** The Championship Course, Cobblers Cross Lane, Tarporley CW6 0DJ (01829 734161; Fax: 0870 1942235). *Location:* half-a-mile from Tarporley on A49. Near Oulton Park. Donald Steel Championship course set in scenic parkland in the heartland of Cheshire with breathtaking panoramic views – lots of water! 18 holes, 7058 white yards. S.S.S. 74. Practice facilities, putting green. Indoor golf academy. *Green Fees:* information not provided. *Eating facilities:* excellent facilities with large banquet suite and bar area. *Visitors:* all visitors are required to book tee times in advance - seven day availability. Golf Shop, locker rooms, buggies. *Society Meetings:* welcome. Professional: Chris Knight. Director of Golf: Andrea Newton.

TARPORLEY. **Portal, The Premier Course,** Forest Road, Tarporley CW6 0JA (01829 733884). *Location:* half a mile from Tarporley on A49. Undulating parkland with scenic views of Cheshire Plains. 18 holes, 6600 yards. S.S.S. 71. Putting green. *Green Fees:* information not available. *Eating facilities:* bar and restaurant. *Visitors:* welcome. *Society Meetings:* welcome, except weekends. Professional: Judy Statham (01829 733703). Director of Golf: David Wills.*

WARRINGTON. **Alder Root Golf Club,** Alder Root Lane, Winwick, Warrington WA2 8RZ (01925 291919; Fax: 01925 291961). *Location*: M62 Junction 9, A49 2 miles north of Warrington. Flat, parkland course. 10 holes, 6152 yards. S.S.S. 69. Putting green. Practice ground. Lessons available. *Green Fees:* midweek 18 holes £15.00, 9 holes £10.00; weekends 18 holes £20.00, 9 holes £12.00. Two "Fore" one rates available. *Eating facilities:* available. *Visitors:* some restrictions, ring for details. *Society Meetings:* welcome. Professional: C. McKevitt (01925 291932; Fax: 01925 291961). Secretary: E. Lander (01925 291919; Fax: 01925 291961).
website: www.alderrootgolfclub.com

WARRINGTON. Birchwood Golf Club, Kelvin Close, Science Park North, Birchwood, Warrington WA3 7PB (01925 818819; Fax: 01925 822403). *Location:* Junction 11 off M62, follow A574 signs for Risley then Science Park North signs. Flat parkland course with numerous natural ponds and streams. 18 holes, 6727 yards. S.S.S. 72. Practice ground, putting green. *Green Fees:* information not available. *Eating facilities:* bar snacks throughout the day; restaurant facilities on request. *Visitors:* welcome on weekdays. Conference and banqueting facilities. Trolleys for hire. *Society Meetings:* Societies, companies and groups are welcome Mondays, Wednesdays and Thursdays if booked in advance. Professional: Paul McEwan (01925 825216; Fax: 01925 822403). Secretary: Barrie Wickens (01925 818819; Fax: 01925 822403).*

WARRINGTON. Leigh Golf Club, Kenyon Hall, Broseley Lane, Culcheth, Warrington WA3 4BG (01925 762943). *Location:* off A580 East Lancs Road to Culcheth Village. Parkland with tree-lined fairways. 18 holes, 5876 yards. S.S.S. 69. Three practice areas, practice nets. *Green Fees:* information not available. *Eating facilities:* two bars and restaurant. *Visitors:* check with Professional. *Society Meetings:* catered for Mondays, Tuesdays and Fridays. Professional: Andrew Baguley (01925 762013). Secretary: D.A. Taylor. See website for special offers.*
website: www.leighgolf.co.uk

WARRINGTON. Poulton Park Golf Club Ltd, Dig Lane, Cinnamon Brow, Warrington WA2 0SH (01925 812034). *Location:* M6 (Junction 21), off A574 (Warrington/Leigh) Crab Lane. 9 holes, 5651 yards. S.S.S. 69. Practice ground. *Green Fees:* information not available. *Visitors:* welcome most days, restricted at weekends. *Society Meetings:* catered for at any time if possible. PGA Professional: Ian Orrell (01925 825220). Secretary: D. N. Owen(01925 822802).*

WARRINGTON. Walton Hall Golf Club, Warrington Road, Higher Walton, Warrington WA4 5LU (01925 266775). *Location:* two miles south of Warrington off A56. Wooded parkland. 18 holes, 6801 yards. S.S.S. 73, Par 72. Practice ground. *Green Fees:* information not provided. *Eating facilities:* licensed clubhouse, meals and bar snacks. *Visitors:* unrestricted. *Society Meetings:* welcome, weekends after 1pm. Professional: J. Jackson (01925 263061). Secretary: John Diprose (01925 266775 or 01925 230860).
e-mail: theclub@waltonhallgolfclub.co.uk
website: www.waltonhallgolfclub.co.uk

WESTON. Wychwood Park Golf Club, Weston Crewe, CW2 5GP (01270 829200; Fax: 01270 829201). *Location:* 5 minutes from Junction 16 of M6 towards Nantwich. European PGA tour-standard course opened in 2002. 7191 yards off the championship tees. Water features throughout with a number of protected wildlife areas. Practice range, chipping and putting green. *Green Fees:* information not available. *Eating facilities:* superb modern clubhouse facility to cater for up to 150 people. *Visitors:* always welcome, handicap certificate requested. 108 en suite twin and double bedrooms, fitness suite. Meeting rooms for up to 160. *Society Meetings:* society and corporate welcome. Professional/Club Manager: Jon Farmer (01270 820955/820787).*
website: www.deverevenues.co.uk

WIDNES. Mersey Valley Golf & Country Club, Warrington Road, Bold Heath, Widnes WA8 3XL (0151-424 6060; Fax: 0151 257 9097). *Location:* two miles from Junction 7 off M62, on the A57 towards Warrington. Flat parkland course. 18 holes, 6511 yards. S.S.S. 71, Par 72. *Green Fees:* information not available. *Eating facilities:* full facilities available. *Visitors:* welcome at all times. Tuition available. Non-members welcome. Buggies available. *Society Meetings:* very welcome, special rates apply. Contact General Manager. Professional: Andy Stevenson PGA. General Manager: Chris Gerrard.*

WIDNES. Widnes Golf Club, Highfield Road, Widnes WA8 7DT (0151-424 2440; Fax: 0151-495 2849). *Location:* near town centre, five miles from M56 and M62. Parkland course. 18 holes, 5729 yards. S.S.S. 68 White, 69 Ladies. *Green Fees:* weekdays and weekends £20.00. *Eating facilities:* two bars and full catering service. *Visitors:* welcome weekdays; weekends by arrangement. Proof of Handicap required. *Society Meetings:* very welcome, special rates apply, contact Secretary (0151-424 2995). Professional: Jason O'Brien (0151-420 7647).

WINSFORD. Knights Grange Sports Complex, Grange Lane, Winsford CW7 2PT (01606 552780). *Location:* signposted "Knights Grange Sports Complex" from traffic lights Winsford Town Centre. 6 miles from M6, 16 miles from Chester. Set in beautiful Cheshire countryside on the outskirts of Winsford. A challenging course for golfers of all abilities. 18 holes - front 9 mainly flat but with water, ditches and other hazards. Back 9 take players deep into the countryside with many tees giving panoramic views of the course. There is also a lake and many mature woodland areas. Red Tees 5137 yards, S.S.S. 70; yellow tees 5270 yards, S.S.S. 66; white tees 5921 yards, S.S.S. 70. *Green Fees:* information not available. *Eating facilities:* snacks and hot drinks available from Complex. Public house adjacent. *Visitors:* unrestricted, advance booking (01606 552780). Tennis, football, athletics. *Society Meetings:* welcomed - booking in writing in advance to Manager. Manager: Mrs P. Littler (01606 552780).*

Highfield Road, Widnes WA8 7DT
- 18-hole parkland course five miles from M56 and M62
- Green Fees: weekdays £20, weekends £20.
- Visitors welcome (proof of Handicap required).

Tel: 0151-424 2995 • Fax: 0151-495 2849

Cumbria

ALSTON. **Alston Moor Golf Club,** The Hermitage, Middleton in Teesdale Road, Alston CA9 3DB (Tel & Fax: 01434 381675; Fax: 01434 381675). *Location:* one and three quarter miles from Alston on B6277 to Barnard Castle. Penrith, Hexham, Carlisle all within 30 miles. Parkland with panoramic views (highest golf course in England). 18 holes, 5456 yards. S.S.S. 66. Practice ground. *Green Fees:* information not available. *Eating facilities:* 19th Hole bar, May to October. *Visitors:* welcome anytime, prior notice required for groups. Competitions most Sundays, tee reserved 9am to 10am and 1pm to 2.30pm. *Society Meetings:* welcome by arrangement. Secretary: Paul Parkin (01434 381354).*

APPLEBY. **Appleby Golf Club,** Brackenber Moor, Appleby-in-Westmorland CA16 6LP (017683 51432). *Location:* off A66 at Coupland Beck, two miles east of Appleby. Moorland course. 18 holes, 5993 yards. S.S.S. 69. *Green Fees:* weekdays £25.00 per round, £32.00 per day; weekends and Bank Holidays £31.00 per round, £38.00 per day. *Eating facilities:* meals available each day. *Visitors:* welcome with Handicap Certificate without reservation. *Society Meetings:* catered for by prior arrangement. Handicap Certificate required. Secretary: J.M.F. Doig. website: www.applebygolfclub.co.uk

ASKAM-IN-FURNESS. **Dunnerholme Golf Club,** Duddon Road, Askam-in-Furness LA16 7AW (01229 462675/467421). *Location:* A595 Askam-in-Furness, over level crossing. Seaside links with stream on four holes, spectacular views from elevated 6th green. 10 holes (18 tees), 6154 yards. S.S.S. 70 White, 70 Red, 69 Yellow. Practice ground. *Green Fees:* information not available. *Eating facilities:* bar in evenings; meals not available. *Visitors:* welcome without reservation, excluding competition days. Competitions Saturday mornings and Sundays May to October. *Society Meetings:* catered for by prior arrangement. Secretary: A. Haines (01229 462675 day, 01229 826198 evenings).*

ASPATRIA. **Brayton Park Golf Club,** Lakeside Inn, Brayton, Aspatria CA7 3TD (016973 20840). *Location:* one mile east of Aspatria. Parkland course. 9 holes. S.S.S. 65 (18 holes). *Green Fees:* information not available. *Eating facilities:* available at Lakeside Inn. *Visitors:* always welcome. *Society Meetings:* welcome. Coarse fishing pond. Secretary: Mr J. Gibson (01697 322517).*

BARROW-IN-FURNESS. **Barrow Golf Club,** Rakesmoor Lane, Hawcoat, Barrow-in-Furness LA14 4QB (01229 825444). *Location:* one mile from Barrow town centre, approach via Dalton bypass, turn left at Bank Lane opposite "Kimberley Clarke" paper mill. Clubhouse at top of hill on left hand side. 18 holes, 6184 yards, 5679 metres. S.S.S. 70. *Green Fees:* information not available. *Eating facilities:* catering available by prior arrangement. *Visitors:* welcome without formal reservation. *Society Meetings:* welcome by prior arrangement, call Club Administrator or Secretary. Club Administrator: E. Payne (01229 825444). Secretary: S.G. Warbrick (01229 831358).*
e-mail: barrowgolf@supanet.com

BARROW-IN-FURNESS. **Furness Golf Club,** Central Drive, Walney Island, Barrow-in-Furness LA14 3LN (01229 471232). *Location:* A590 into Barrow via Dalton by-pass, follow sign to Walney Island, over bridge, straight on at lights. Clubhouse half-a-mile on right hand side. Seaside links. 18 holes, 6363 yards. S.S.S. 71. Practice area. *Green Fees*: please see website. *Eating facilities:* full catering (except Mondays), licensed bar. *Visitors*: parties by prior arrangement, others without reservation. Ladies' Day Wednesdays; Competition Days - Saturdays or Sundays in summer. *Society Meetings*: welcome (tee reservation by prior arrangement). Secretary: Mrs. S. Campbell.
e-mail: furnessgolfclub@chessbroadband.co.uk
website: www.furnessgolfclub.co.uk

Other British holiday guides from FHG Guides

PUBS & INNS • 300 GREAT HOTELS • SHORT BREAK HOLIDAYS
The bestselling and original PETS WELCOME! • 500 GREAT PLACES TO STAY
SELF-CATERING HOLIDAYS • BED & BREAKFAST STOPS
CARAVAN & CAMPING HOLIDAYS • FAMILY BREAKS

Published annually: available in all good bookshops or direct from the publisher:
FHG Guides, Abbey Mill Business Centre, Seedhill, Paisley PA1 1TJ
Tel: 0141 887 0428 • Fax: 0141 889 7204
e-mail: admin@fhguides.co.uk • www.holidayguides.com

Cumbria / NORTH REGION

BRAMPTON. **Brampton Golf Club,** Tarn Road, Brampton CA8 1HN (016977 2255). *Location*: situated on the Brampton-Castle Carrock road (B6413), approximately one and a half miles from Brampton. Rolling fell countryside, excellent views. 18 holes, 6407 yards. S.S.S. 71. Driving range/practice facilities available. *Green Fees:* weekdays £35.00 per round, £46.00 per day; weekends and Bank Holidays £42.00 per round, £52.00 per day. *Eating facilities:* catering available every day during playing season and on most days during winter period. *Visitors:* welcome without reservation but pre-booking is advisable. *Society Meetings:* very much catered for, limited numbers at weekends. Secretary and contact for visiting societies/party bookings: I.J. Meldrum (016977 2255). Professional: S. Wilkinson (016977 2000; Fax: 016977 41487).
e-mail: secretary@bramptongolfclub.com
website: www.bramptongolfclub.com

CARLISLE. **Carlisle Golf Club,** Aglionby, Carlisle CA4 8AG (01228 513029). *Location*: on A69 Newcastle Road, half a mile from Junction 43 of M6. Parkland course with wide variety of trees, strategic hazards, etc. 18 holes, 6263 yards. S.S.S. 70. Practice area. *Green Fees*: weekdays £40.00 per round, £60.00 per day; £50.00 per round Sundays only; Saturdays with member only. 2010 rates (subject to review). Package deals for parties of 20 or more. *Eating facilities:* bar meals, restaurant, two bars, etc. *Visitors*: welcome except on a Saturday (unless with a member), unless tee is reserved; visitor bookings (01228 513029). Trolley and buggy hire. *Society Meetings*: catered for Mondays, Wednesdays, Thursdays and Fridays. Professional: G. Lisle (01228 513241). Secretary: Roger Johnson (01228 513029; Fax: 01228 513303).
website: www.carlislegolfclub.org

CARLISLE. **Dalston Hall Golf Club & Holiday Park,** (aka Caldew Golf Club) Dalston Hall, Dalston, Carlisle CA5 7JX (01228 710165). *Location:* leave M6 at Exit 42, take road to Dalston; at Dalston take B5299, Carlisle road, course on the right after one mile. Scenic parkland course. 10 holes, (18 Tees) 5294 yards. S.S.S. 67. Practice area. *Green Fees:* £16.00 to £18.00 for 18 holes. *Eating facilities:* full catering and bar facilities *Visitors:* welcome, teereservation is required at Bank Holidays and weekends and after 4pm during the week. Pool table. *Society Meetings:* welcome by prior arrangement. Secretary: Paul Holder (01228 710165).
website: www.dalstonholidaypark.com

CARLISLE. **The Eden Golf Course,** Crosby-on-Eden, Carlisle CA6 4RA (01228 573003). *Location*: M6 Junction 44, A689 to Low Crosby. Parkland course with tree-lined fairways incorporating lakes, streams and River Eden. 18 holes, 6368 yards. S.S.S. 72. 9-hole Hadrian's Course, par 71, S.S.S. 71. *Green Fees*: Information not provided. *Eating facilities*: full restaurant and bar meals. *Visitors:* welcome at all times, telephone booking requested. *Society Meetings*: welcome at all times, telephone booking requested. 16 bay floodlit driving range and practice facilities. Professional: Steven Harrison.
e-mail: info@edengolf.co.uk
website: www.edengolf.co.uk

CARLISLE. **Stoney Holme Municipal Golf Course,** St Aidans Road, Carlisle (01228 33208). *Location:* off A69 between M6 Junction 42 and town. Parkland course, 18 holes, 6000 yards. S.S.S. 68. Large practice area, changing rooms. *Green Fees:* information not available. *Eating facilities:* bar and restaurant. *Visitors:* welcome without reservation, but booking advisable weekends and Bank Holidays. *Society Meetings:* welcome by prior arrangement. Professional: Stephen Ling (01228 625511).*

EMBLETON. **Cockermouth Golf Club,** The Clubhouse, Embleton, Near Cockermouth CA13 9SG (017687 76223/76941; Fax: 017687 76941). *Location:* three miles east of Cockermouth. Scenic fell land course. 18 holes, 5410 yards, S.S.S. 66. *Green Fees:* information not available. *Eating facilities:* bar, meals by arrangement with Secretary. *Visitors:* welcome except Wednesdays between 10am to 11am and 4pm to 6pm and Thursdays 8.45am-10am, some restrictions at weekends. Some trolleys for hire. *Society Meetings:* welcome as per visitors. Secretary: R.S.Wimpress (Tel & Fax: 017687 76941 mornings only weekdays).*
e-mail: secretary@cockermouthgolf.co.uk
website: www.cockermouthgolf.co.uk

The Eden Golf Club & Driving Range

CROSBY-ON-EDEN, CARLISLE, CUMBRIA CA6 4RA
TEL: 01228 573003

- 18-HOLE CHAMPIONSHIP PARKLAND COURSE
- 9-HOLE PAR 36, SSS 71 HADRIAN COURSE
- FLOODLIT COVERED DRIVING RANGE
- PITCHING GREENS AND PRACTICE BUNKERS
- EXCELLENT RESTAURANT AND LOUNGE BAR WITH OPEN FIRE

*The Eden Golf Club is a hidden gem situated along the banks of the River Eden. Tight tree-lined fairways and numerous natural water hazards mark this course out as a great test of golf.
Situated 5 miles from Junction 44 of M6, one hour from Newcastle. On the doorstep of the Lakes, Hadrian's Wall and Gretna Green.*

e-mail: info@edengolf.co.uk • www.edengolf.co.uk

Brampton Golf Club

**TALKIN TARN, BRAMPTON
CUMBRIA CA8 1HN**
www.bramptongolfclub.com

Consider the rest, play the best

Situated in a stunning corner of North Cumbria, the jewel of the region's crown boasts panoramic views of the Lake District, Southern Scotland and the Pennines. The undulating heathland Par 72 course offers both challenging golf and an idyllic setting which has been likened to a "mini Gleneagles".
The clubhouse provides a full range of first-class services and facilities. Visiting societies, corporate golf days and visitors most welcome, but pre-booking clearly recommended.

For societies/visiting party bookings please contact Ian Meldrum (Secretary) on 016977 2255 or
e-mail: secretary@bramptongolfclub.com. Other visitor enquiries contact the Professional on 016977 2000

GRANGE-OVER-SANDS. **Grange Fell Golf Club,** Fell Road, Grange-over-Sands LA11 6HB (015395 32536). *Location:* Cartmel Road from Grange one mile. Hillside course with panoramic views. 9 holes, 4840 metres. S.S.S. 66. *Green Fees:* weekdays £15.00, weekends and Bank Holidays £20.00. *Eating facilities:* bar. *Visitors:* welcome without reservation, closed most Sundays until 4pm during season. *Society Meetings:* not catered for. Secretary: Mr J. G. Park (015395 58513).

GRANGE-OVER-SANDS. **Grange-over-Sands Golf Club,** Meathop Road, Grange-over-Sands LA11 6QX (015395 33180; Fax: 015395 33754). *Location:* leave the A590 at roundabout signposted Grange, take the B5277 for approximately three miles. Flat parkland. 18 holes, 6065 yards. S.S.S. 69. Practice area, bunker, green. *Green Fees:* information not available. *Eating facilities:* dining room open every day; bar snacks and bar every day. *Visitors:* welcome without reservation weekdays and most weekends. *Society Meetings:* by arrangement with Secretary. Professional: Nick Lowe (015395 35937). Secretary: D.C. Booth (015395 33180).*

KENDAL. **Carus Green Golf Club,** Burneside Road, Kendal LA9 6EB (Tel & Fax: 01539 721097). *Location:* one mile north-east of Kendal on Burneside Road. Flat riverside parkland location. 18 holes, 5800 yards, Par 70. 160 yard practice ground, 300 yard automated driving range, putting green. *Green Fees:* information not available. *Eating facilities:* Full catering facilities and bar. *Visitors:* welcome anytime, restrictions on competition days. Tuition available from 2 PGA teaching professionals. Buggy hire. *Society Meetings:* packages available, please call for details. Large golf super-shop. Professional: David Turner and Andrew Pickering (Tel & Fax: 01539 721097). Secretary: Wayne Dand.*

KENDAL. **Kendal Golf Club,** The Heights, Kendal LA9 4PQ (01539 733708). *Location:* off A6 at Town Hall, signposted. Undulating parkland course with magnificent views in all directions. 18 holes, 5769 yards. S.S.S. 68. *Green Fees:* weekdays £25.00 per round, £32.00 per day; weekends £30.00 per round, £40.00 per day. *Eating facilities:* meals available all day; bar. *Visitors:* welcome with reservation. Buggy hire available. Professional: Ben Waller (01539 723499).
website: www.kendalgolfclub.co.uk

3rd fairway, Kirkby Lonsdale Golf Club

Cumbria / NORTH REGION — THE GOLF GUIDE 2011

KESWICK. Keswick Golf Club, Threlkeld Hall, Threlkeld, Keswick CA12 4SX (017687 79324; Fax: 017687 79861). *Location:* four miles from Keswick on A66 road to Penrith. Scenic fell and parkland course. 18 holes, 6225 yards. S.S.S. 70, Par 71. Extensive practice area. *Green Fees:* information not available. Subject to review. *Eating facilities:* bar and restaurant. *Visitors:* welcome, Ladies' Day Thursdays 11am to 2pm. *Society Meetings:* welcome by arrangement. Professional: Gary Watson. Administration Manager: May Lloyd.*

KIRKBY LONSDALE. Kirkby Lonsdale Golf Club, Scaleber Lane, Barbon, Kirkby Lonsdale, Carnforth, Lancs LA6 2LJ (015242 76365). *Location:* three and a half miles from Kirkby Lonsdale on the A683 Sedbergh Road. Parkland course in Lune Valley crossing Barbon Beck and along the banks of the River Lune. 18 holes, 6542 yards. S.S.S. 72. Par 72. Practice area, lessons. *Green Fees:* £35.00 per round, £40..00 per day. 2010 rates (subject to review). *Eating facilities:* full facilities. *Visitors:* welcome, no restrictions except on competition days. Handicap Certificate required or certificate of competence. *Society Meetings:* welcome by arrangement. Package deals available for groups of eight or more. Professional: Paul Brunt (015242 76366). Secretary: David Towers (015242 76365).
e-mail: klgolf@dial.pipex.com
website: www.kirkbylonsdalegolf.co.uk

KIRKBY LONSDALE near. Casterton Golf Course, Sedbergh Road, Casterton, Near Kirkby Lonsdale, Cumbria LA6 2LA (015242 71592). *Location:* from Junction 36 of M6 take A65 to Skipton, five miles to Kirkby Lonsdale, one mile north on A683. Undulating parkland course, scenic with wonderful views. 9 holes, 5726 yards. S.S.S. 68. Practice area and driving net. *Green Fees:* weekdays £15.00; weekends and Bank Holidays £18.00. *Eating facilities:* light refreshments and shop in clubhouse (licensed). *Visitors:* always welcome. Booking advisable. Clubhouse has well-stocked Pro Shop, changing facilities and toilets. Clubs and trolleys available for hire. Two holiday flats sleeping four/five. *Society Meetings:* parties of under 40 persons only. Professional: Roy Williamson. Secretary: Elizabeth Makinson. Course Manager: John Makinson.
e-mail: castertongc@hotmail.com
website: www.castertongolf.co.uk

MARYPORT. Maryport Golf Club Ltd, Bankend, Maryport CA15 6PA (01900 812605). *Location:* approximately one mile north of Maryport on B5300 towards Silloth. 9 holes links extended to 18 with new holes parkland type, exposed, relatively flat. 18 holes, 5982 yards. S.S.S. 69. *Green Fees:* information not provided. *Eating facilities:* available. *Visitors:* welcome, no restrictions. *Society Meetings:* catered for by prior arrangement. Secretary: Mrs L. Hayton.

PENRITH. Penrith Golf Club, Salkeld Road, Penrith CA11 8SG (01768 891919). *Location:* off Junction 41 M6 motorway, towards Penrith, golf course signposted. Parkland course. 18 holes, 6026 yards. S.S.S. 69. Range facilities. *Green Fees:* weekdays £32.00/£40.00; weekends £37.00/£45.00. *Eating facilities:* all day catering seven days a week. *Visitors:* welcome, book through Professional shop, tee times required at weekends. *Society Meetings:* by appointment with Secretary. Professional: Garry Key (Tel & Fax: 01768 891919). Secretary: Dennis Wright (Tel & Fax: 01768 891919).

ST BEES. St Bees Golf Club, Peckmill, Beach Road, St Bees (01946 824300). *Location:* four miles south of Whitehaven off A595. Hilly, seaside course. 9 holes, 5307 yards. S.S.S. 66. *Green Fees:* information not available. *Visitors:* welcome weekdays (except after 4pm Wednesdays). Only after 3pm weekends. Bar available April to September between 12 noon and 8pm. Secretary: B. G. Ritson.*

SEASCALE. Seascale Golf Club, Seascale CA20 1QL (Tel & Fax: 019467 28202). *Location:* B5344 off A595 to north of village. Links. 18 holes, 6450 yards. S.S.S. 72. 16-acre practice ground. *Green Fees:* information not available. *Eating facilities:* catering available every day. *Visitors:* welcome when no tee reservations in force. *Society Meetings:* catered for by arrangement with Secretary. Secretary: David Stobart (019467 28202).*
e-mail: seacalegolfclub@googlemail.com
website: www.seascalegolfclub.co.uk

KIRKBY LONSDALE GOLF CLUB
GOLF SOCIETIES & VISITING PARTIES

Golfing packages from £41.00 to include:
Coffee & Biscuits on arrival, Full Day's
Golf, Lunch and Evening Meal.

Telephone: 015242 76365

Scaleber Lane, Barbon, Kirkby Lonsdale, Carnforth LA6 2LJ
Telephone: Secretary 015242 76365 – Pro Shop 015242 76366 - Caterer 015242 76367
e-mail: klgolf@dial.pipex.com • www.kirkbylonsdalegolf.co.uk

THE GOLF GUIDE 2011 — NORTH REGION / Cumbria

Dale Head Hall Lakeside Hotel
and luxury self-catering suites

In the heart of the Lake District, in acres of mature gardens and woodland, award-winning Dale Head Hall sits alone on the shores of Thirlemere. With Helvellyn rising majestically behind, this family-run hotel and award-winning restaurant is an ideal base for exploring this most beautiful corner of England.

Superb views. Wildlife in abundance.
Luxury self-catering suites are also available.

Lake Thirlmere, Keswick CA12 4TN • Tel: 01687 72478 • Fax: 01687 71070
e-mail: onthelakeside@daleheadhall.co.uk • www.daleheadhall.co.uk

Situated in the attractive town centre of Penrith, The George Hotel is steeped in over 300 years of history, and provides the ideal base from which to explore the Lake District and Eden Valley. 35 comfortable en suite bedrooms. Meals available in the Devonshire Restaurant or bar. Discounted golf available.

Devonshire Street, Penrith, Cumbria CA11 7SU
Freephone: 0800 840 1242
E-mail: georgehotel@lakedistricthotels.net
www.lakedistricthotels.net

The George Hotel ❖ Penrith

SEASCALE GOLF CLUB
Play our challenging links course

Superb 6,495 yards traditional links. Reduced terms for daily parties of 8 or more. Any three consecutive days golf from £100. Bookings now being taken for 2011. Both midweek and weekend dates available. Societies and groups assured of a warm and friendly welcome.

For further details contact:
**David Stobart, The Secretary,
Seascale Golf Club, Seascale,
Cumbria CA20 1QL**
or phone 01946 728202

e-mail: seascalegolfclub@googlemail.com • www.seascalegolfclub.co.uk

Cumbria / NORTH REGION

SEDBERGH. **Sedbergh Golf Club,** Sedbergh LA10 5SS (015396 21551). *Location:* five miles J37, M6, one mile out of Sedbergh on road to Dent, well signposted. Superbly scenic course in Yorkshire Dales National Park. 9 holes, 5588 yards. S.S.S. 68. *Green Fees:* 18 holes £20.00, 9 holes £14.00. *Eating facilities:* full bar and basic catering facilities. *Visitors:* welcome, but prior booking advisable. Pro shop; hire trolleys available. *Society Meetings:* very welcome by prior arrangement. Manager: Craig Gardner (015396 21551).
website: www.sedberghgolfclub.com

SILECROFT. **Silecroft Golf Club,** Silecroft, Near Millom LA18 4NX (01229 774250). *Location:* three miles north of Millom on the coast. Near junction of A595 and A5093, eight miles west of Broughton-in-Furness. Seaside links course with good greens. 9 holes (18 tees), 5877 yards. S.S.S. 68 (67 off Yellow tees). *Green Fees:* information not available. *Eating facilities:* catering available at nearby public house (Silecroft Miners Arms), bar at club. *Visitors:* welcome, although access to the course may be restricted on Bank Holidays or on competition days. Secretary: Keith Newton (01229 770467).
e-mail: silecroftgcsec@aol.com

SILLOTH. **Silloth on Solway Golf Club,** The Clubhouse, Silloth, Wigton CA7 4BL (016973 31304). *Location:* from south - M6 Junction 41 B5305 Wigton, B5302 Silloth. From north and east - M6 Junction 43 A69 Carlisle, A595/596 Wigton, B5302 Silloth. Seaside links, rated in the best five links courses in England. 18 holes, 6641 yards. S.S.S. 72. Practice facilities. *Green Fees:* weekdays £45.00 per day, weekends and Bank Holidays £55.00 per round. 2010 rates (subject to review). Restriction, only one round allowed per day at weekends. *Eating facilities*: full bar and catering. *Visitors:* welcome without reservation. *Society Meetings:* welcome midweek, weekend times available on request. Professional: J. Graham (016973 32404; Fax: 016973 31782). Secretary: John Hill (016973 31304; Fax: 016973 31782).
website: www.sillothgolfclub.co.uk

SILVERDALE. **Silverdale Golf Club,** Redbridge Lane, Silverdale, Carnforth LA5 0SP (01524 701300). *Location*: 10 minutes from Exit 35 off M6 to Carnforth, then two miles west, adjacent to railway station and RSPB nature reserve. Interesting heathland course with rock outcrops, half course with wide open fairways, all with excellent views. 18 holes, 5535 yards. S.S.S. 67. *Green Fees*: weekdays from £25.00, weekends and Bank Holidays from £35.00 (20% reduction, ask about Silverdale Golf Ticket). 2010 rates (subject to review). *Eating facilities*: full catering (except Mondays) and bar facilities. *Visitors*: welcome except Sundays a.m. in the summer unless with a member. *Society Meetings*: welcome by arrangement with Secretary. Professional: Alyn Cousins. Secretary: Barbara Hebdon (01524 701300).
e-mail: info@silverdalegolfclub.co.uk
website: www.silverdalegolfclub.co.uk

ULVERSTON. **Ulverston Golf Club Ltd,** Bardsea Park, Ulverston LA12 9QJ (01229 582824). *Location:* Exit 36, M6. A590 to Barrow then A5087 to Bardsea village. Wooded parkland. 18 holes, 6191 yards. S.S.S. 70. *Green Fees:* information not available. *Eating facilities:* lunch and bar snacks. *Visitors:* welcome except Saturdays (competition day). Must be members of accredited golf club and have a Handicap. *Society Meetings:* welcome, write with reservation to the Secretary. Professional: P.A. Stoller (01229 582806). Acting Secretary: G. Brown.*

WHITEHAVEN. **Whitehaven Golf Club,** Red Lonning, Whitehaven CA28 8UD (01946 591177). *Location:* set in parkland above Whitehaven. Parkland course with spectacular views of the Lakeland fells. 18 holes, 6289 yards, Par 70. 16-bay floodlit driving range plus golf super store. *Green Fees:* information not available. *Eating facilities:* clubhouse and bar. *Visitors:* always welcome. Tees can be booked all year round, phone 01946 591144. 7 golf buggies available. Professional: Craig Hamilton.*
e-mail: craighamilton@whitehavengolfclub.com
website: www.whitehavengolf.com

Visit
www.holidayguides.com
for convenient accommodation
when playing golf around the regions

Windermere Golf Club IN THE ENGLISH LAKE DISTRICT

In the heart of the Lake District with spectacular views over Windermere and the surrounding fells • A friendly welcome for visitors and golf societies
Cleabarrow, Windermere LA23 3NB • 015394 43123
office@windermeregc.demon.co.uk • www.windermeregolfclub.co.uk

WINDERMERE. **Windermere Golf Club,** Cleabarrow, Windermere LA23 3NB (015394 43123). *Location:* one mile from Bowness-on-Windermere on Crook road, B5284. Idyllic National Park setting. 18 holes, 5151 yards, S.S.S. 65. Practice ground. *Green Fees:* information not available. *Eating facilities:* Restaurant. *Visitors:* made most welcome. *Society Meetings:* catered for by prior arrangement with the Secretary, numbers from 12 to 50, corporate days by arrangement. Professional: Simon Edwards (015394 43550). Secretary: Carol Slater (015394 43123).
e-mail: office@windermeregc.demon.co.uk
website: www.windermeregolfclub.co.uk

WORKINGTON. **Workington Golf Club Ltd**, Branthwaite Road, Workington CA14 4SS (01900 603460). Location: A596, two miles east of town centre. Meadowland. 18 holes, 6252 yards. S.S.S. 70. *Green Fees*: as applicable. *Eating facilities*: dining available six days per week. *Visitors*: welcome via tee reservation. Buggies available by prior arrangement. *Society Meetings*: accepted, contact Professional: Andrew Wells (01900 67828) or Club Secretary: P. Hoskin (01900 603460).
e-mail: secretary@workingtongolfclub.com

Holly-Wood
Guest House
Holly Road, Windermere LA23 2AF
Tel: 015394 42219

Holly-Wood is a beautiful, family-run Victorian house offering clean comfortable accommodation, set in a quiet position 3 minutes' walk from Windermere village amenities. It is the perfect place to unwind after a day exploring the Lakes.
• All rooms en suite • Private car park • Hearty traditional/vegetarian breakfasts • Non-smoking throughout • Help with walk planning available • All major credit cards accepted.

Bed & Breakfast from £35pppn.
Please contact Ian or Yana
for more information
We look forward to welcoming
you to Holly-Wood

e-mail: info@hollywoodguesthouse.co.uk
www.hollywoodguesthouse.co.uk

FHG Guides publish a large range of well-known accommodation guides. We will be happy to send you details or you can use the order form at the back of this book.

The Wild Boar
Inn, Grill & Smokehouse

The Wild Boar
Crook,
near Windermere
Cumbria LA23 3NF

08458 504604
thewildboarinn.co.uk

Discounted Green Fees for all guests

Nestling in a peaceful setting in the Gilpin Valley, the Wild Boar benefits from beautiful surrounding countryside, including its own private woodland and close to Lake and Windermere Golf Course, only 1 mile away.

A special venue for many an occasion, whether that be a romantic or adventurous break, family get-together, or intimate business meeting.

After undergoing a refurbishment the Wild Boar now offers individually designed bedrooms, Grill and Smokehouse.

16th hole at Seascale Golf Club

Durham

BARNARD CASTLE. **Barnard Castle Golf Club,** Harmire Road, Barnard Castle DL12 8QN (01833 638355 or 637237). *Location:* one mile north of Barnard Castle Town Centre on the B6278. Open parkland with a number of streams to be crossed and with maturing copses. 18 holes, 6406 yards. S.S.S. 71. Practice area. *Green Fees:* weekdays – 18 holes £27.00, 27 holes £30.00, 36 holes £35.00; weekends and Bank Holidays – 18 holes £30.00, 27 holes £35.00, 36 holes £40.00. After 6pm – £12.00 weekdays and £15.00 weekends. *Eating facilities:* full catering. *Visitors:* welcome, but formal booking system applies at weekends and Bank Holidays. *Society Meetings:* catered for by prior arrangement. Professional: Darren Pearce (01833 631980). Secretary: J. Saunders (01833 638355).

BEAMISH. **Beamish Park Golf Club,** Beamish, Stanley DH9 0RH (0191-370 1382; Fax: 0191-370 2937). *Location:* follow directions to Beamish Museum. Parkland, 18 holes, 6183 yards (white markers). S.S.S. 70. 5963 yards (yellow markers). S.S.S. 69. Two practice areas. *Green Fees:* information not available. *Eating facilities:* bar and à la carte menu. *Visitors:* welcome weekdays. Carts for hire. *Society Meetings:* welcome. Professional: Chris Cole (0191-370 1984). Hon. Secretary: Les Pickering.*

BILLINGHAM. **Billingham Golf Club**, Sandy Lane, Billingham TS22 5NA (01642 554494). *Location:* off A19 trunk road, one mile west of Billingham town centre. Undulating parkland. 18 holes, 6346 yards. S.S.S. 70. Practice area including pitching green and putting greens. *Green Fees:* information not available. *Eating facilities:* full catering. *Visitors:* welcome weekdays, prior booking advised. Buggies available. *Society Meetings:* catered for by prior arrangement with Secretary. Caterer (01642 554494). Professional: M. Ure (01642 557060). Secretary: W.E. Pattison (Tel & Fax: 01642 533816).*
e-mail: billinghamgc@btconnect.com
website: www.billinghamgolfclub.com

BISHOP AUCKLAND. **Bishop Auckland Golf Club,** High Plains, Durham Road, Bishop Auckland DL14 8DL (01388 661618). *Location:* leave Bishop Auckland Market Place on route to Spennymoor/ Durham, half a mile on left. Parkland, 18 holes, 6379 yards. S.S.S. 71 (Par 72). Practice fairways. *Green Fees:* information not provided. *Eating facilities:* bar, full catering facilities. *Visitors:* welcome mid-week only. Ladies' Day Tuesday. Two snooker tables. *Society Meetings:* catered for on application, official Handicap required. Special package start from £38.50 for parties of 8 or more, includes catering. Professional: M. Pilgrim (01388 661618). Secretary: M.S. Metcalf (01388 661618).
e-mail: enquiries@bagc.co.uk
website: www.bagc.co.uk

Bishop Auckland Golf Club

One of the finest parkland courses in the North East, excellent views, superb greens and fairways.
Catering and bar facilities available every day.
Green Fees: midweek £30 per round, £35 per day; weekends £35 per round, £40 per day.

**For special deals contact
Hon. Sec. M. Metcalf (01388 661618)
Fax: 01388 607005**
e-mail: enquiries@bagc.co.uk • www.bagc.co.uk

'A warm welcome awaits'

**Looking for accommodation near golf clubs?, then visit
www.holidayguides.com
for where to stay when playing golf around the regions**

BRANCEPETH. **Brancepeth Castle Golf Club,** The Clubhouse, Brancepeth, Durham DH7 8EA (0191-378 0075; Fax: 0191-378 3835). *Location:* A690 Durham to Crook, turn left at crossroads in Brancepeth village, take immediate left at the castle gates, 200 yards down lane. Parkland course designed by Harry Colt. 18 holes, 6400 yards, S.S.S. 70. Practice field, putting green. *Green Fees:* weekdays £35.00 per round, £40.00 per day; weekends by arrangement. *Eating facilities:* full bar and restaurant facilities. *Visitors and Society Meetings:* parties welcome weekdays and from 2pm at weekends. Good rates available; special rates on Mondays. Please contact us for details and bookings. Hon. Secretary: Arthur Chadwick; Office Manager: Leona Broom (0191-378 0075; Fax: 0191-378 3835).
e-mail: enquiries@brancepeth-castle-golf.co.uk
website: www.brancepeth-castle-golf.co.uk

CHESTER-LE-STREET. **Chester-le-Street Golf Club,** Lumley Park, Chester-le-Street DH3 4NS (0191 3883218). *Location:* half a mile east of Chester-le-Street adjacent to Lumley Castle. Fairly flat parkland. 18 holes, 6457 yards, 5535 metres. S.S.S. 71. Practice area. *Green Fees:* midweek £25.00 per round, £30.00 per day; weekends and public holidays £30.00 per round, £35.00 per day. *Eating facilities:* snacks, lunches, dinners. *Visitors:* welcome 9.30am to 12 noon, 1.30pm to 4.30pm weekdays; 10.30am to 12 noon, 2pm onwards weekends. Must be members of a golf club and have a Handicap. Hotel adjacent. *Society Meetings:* welcome except weekends and Public Holidays. Professional: D. Fletcher (0191 3890157; Fax: 0191 3881220). Secretary: Bill Routledge (0191 3883218).
e-mail: clsgcoffice@tiscali.co.uk
website: www.clsgolfclub.co.uk

CHESTER-LE-STREET. **Roseberry Grange Golf Club,** Grange Villa, Chester-le-Street DH2 3NF (0191-370 0670). *Location:* three miles west of Chester-le-Street on A693. Parkland course. 18 holes, 5809 yards. S.S.S. 68. Driving range. *Green Fees:* weekdays £16.00; weekends £22.00; visiting party packages. *Eating facilities:* bar meals 12 noon to 2pm and 7pm to 9.30pm. *Visitors:* welcome, no restrictions weekdays, Saturdays 7am to 10.30am, Sundays 7am to 11.30am. Professional: C. Jones (0191-370 0660). Secretary: Raymond McDermott (0191-370 2047).

CONSETT. **Consett and District Golf Club Ltd,** Elmfield Road, Consett DH8 5NN (01207 502186; Fax: 01207 505060). *Location:* 14 miles north of Durham on A691 (hidden turning on steep hill). 18 holes, 6041 yards. Par 71, S.S.S. 69. Parkland, undulating, excellent views over Derwent Valley. *Green Fees:* weekdays £20.00, weekends £25.00; reduced fees with member. *Eating facilities:* full catering available (limited on Mondays). *Visitors:* welcome most times, phone Secretary. *Society Meetings:* catered for by arrangement, enquiries welcomed through Secretary. Secretary/Treasurer: V. Kelly (01207 505060 Fax/ Answer machine)

CROOK. **Crook Golf Club,** Low Jobs Hill, Crook DL15 9AA (01388 762429). *Location:* eleven miles west of Durham City on A690. Scenic views; excellently conditioned course. 18 holes, 6102 yards, 5902 metres. S.S.S. 69. Practice area. *Green Fees:* available on request. *Eating facilities:* available, book in advance. *Visitors:* welcome but limited times at weekends. *Society Meetings:* welcome by arrangement with Secretary. Special packages available. Hon Secretary: Les Shaw (01388 762429).

DARLINGTON. **Blackwell Grange Golf Club,** Briar Close, Blackwell, Darlington DL3 8QX (01325 464464). *Location:* one mile south of Darlington on A66 turn into Blackwell. Signposts to Club. Parkland course. 18 holes, 5621 yards. S.S.S. 68. *Green Fees:* weekdays £25.00 per round, £35.00 per day; weekends and Bank Holidays £35.00 per round. *Eating facilities:* full menu except Sundays and Mondays. *Visitors:* welcome without reservation except weekends. *Society Meetings:* catered for except Wednesdays and weekends. Professional: Peter Raine (01325 462088). Secretary: Phil Wraith (Tel & Fax: 01325 464458).

THE APPEARANCE OF AN ASTERISK (*) AT THE END OF A CLUB OR COURSE ENTRY INDICATES THAT UP-TO-DATE INFORMATION HAS NOT BEEN SUPPLIED

BRANCEPETH CASTLE Golf Club
...a gem of a course designed by Harry Colt, situated 4 miles from the centre of historic Durham City and 5 miles from the A1(M).
Contact our friendly staff for more details
Tel: 0191 378 0075
www.brancepeth-castle-golf.co.uk enquiries@brancepeth-castle-golf.co.uk

DARLINGTON. **The Darlington Golf Club (Members) Ltd,** Haughton Grange, Darlington DL1 3JD (01325 355324). *Location:* northern outskirts of town, A1150 off A167, easy access from A1(M) or A19. Flat wooded parkland course designed by Dr Alister Mackenzie. 18 holes, 6209 yards. S.S.S. 70. 10 acre practice ground. *Green Fees:* information not available. *Eating facilities:* dining room, lounge and bar. *Visitors:* welcome weekdays and selected weekends with reservation. Must be members of recognised golf club. Buggies available for hire. *Society Meetings:* package deals by arrangement weekdays. Professional: Craig Dilley (01325 484198). Secretary: M. Etherington (01325 355324 Ext.1.)
e-mail: office@darlington-gc.co.uk
website: www.darlington-gc.co.uk

DARLINGTON. **Dinsdale Spa Golf Club,** Neasham Road, Middleton-St-George, Darlington DL2 1DW (01325 332222). *Location:* near Teesside Airport. Parkland. 18 holes; 6462 yards, S.S.S. 71 (white); 6107 yards, S.S.S. 69 (yellow). Large practice ground. *Green Fees:* £30.00 per day. Playing with a member £15.00. *Eating facilities:* bar, catering. *Visitors:* welcome weekdays, weekends with a member only. *Society Meetings:* catered for Wednesday, Thursday and Friday by advance booking. Professional: Martyn Stubbings (Tel & Fax: 01325 332515). Secretary: A. Patterson (01325 332297)

DARLINGTON. **Hall Garth Golf and Country Club Hotel,** Coatham, Mundeville, Darlington DL1 3LU (01325 300400; Fax: 01325 310083). *Location:* A1 J59, follow the A167 toward Darlington, after 300 yards turn left at Brafferton, entrance after 200 yards on right. Parkland course. 9 holes, 6621 yards. S.S.S. 72. *Green Fees:* information not available. *Eating facilities:* Stables Country Pub. *Visitors:* always welcome. *Society Meetings:* welcome; prices on request.*

DARLINGTON. **Stressholme Golf Club,** Snipe Lane, Darlington DL2 2SA (01325 461002; Fax: 01325 461002). *Location:* signposted off the A66 Teesside to Scotch Corner outside of Darlington. Parkland course with water features. 18 holes, 6431 yards. S.S.S. 71. 25 bay driving range with nets, chipping greens, distance markers, etc. *Green Fees:* information not provided. *Eating facilities:* bar in clubhouse with extensive catering facilities. *Visitors:* welcome all week. Professional/Secretary: Ralph Givens (Tel & Fax: 01325 461002).

DURHAM. **Durham City Golf Club,** Littleburn, Langley Moor, Durham DH7 8HL (0191 3780069). *Location:* from Durham City take A690 to Crook - course signposted in Langley Moor. Parkland, bordered by the River Browney. 18 holes, 6326 yards. S.S.S. 70. Large practice area. *Green Fees:* on application. *Eating facilities:* limited catering Mondays and Thursday evenings. *Visitors:* welcome at all times, only restrictions when club competitions are being held – ring Professional for details. *Society Meetings:* welcome Monday to Friday. Professional: S. Corbally (0191 3780029).

DURHAM. **Mount Oswald Manor and Golf Course,** South Road, Durham DH1 3TQ (0191-386 7527; Fax: 0191-386 0975; *Location:* A1(M) Junction marked Bowburn, A177 Durham City follow signs for Darlington. Parkland, partially wooded. 18 holes, 5991 yards. S.S.S. 69. *Green Fees:* information not available. *Eating facilities:* bar meals, Sunday lunches, set meals, etc. *Visitors:* welcome except Sunday mornings before 9.15am (members only). Bookings only at weekends and Bank Holidays. *Society Meetings:* welcome, same restrictions as visitors. Must order food. General Manager: Mr N. P. Galvin (0191-386 7527).*
e-mail: information@mountoswald.co.uk
website: www.mountoswald.co.uk

DURHAM. **Ramside Hall Hotel and Golf Club,** Carrville DH1 1TD (0191-386 9514; Fax: 0191- 386 9519). *Location:* two miles north-east of Durham on A690. A1 (M) Junction 62. 27 holes, 6217/6851 yards. S.S.S. 70/73. Driving range and golf academy. *Green Fees:* see website for current offers. *Eating facilities:* choice of three eating areas. *Visitors:* welcome. Professional: K. Jackson (0191-386 9514). Golf Operations Manager/Secretary: K. Jackson.

EAGLESCLIFFE. **Eaglescliffe Golf Club Ltd,** Yarm Road, Eaglescliffe, Stockton-on-Tees TS16 0DQ (01642 780238; Office: 01642 780238). *Location:* on A135 one mile north of Yarm and three miles south of Stockton. Hilly parkland course, sloping to River Tees. 18 holes, 6245 yards. S.S.S. 70. Practice area and putting green. *Green Fees:* weekdays £32.00 per round, £40.00 per day.; weekends and Bank Holidays £40.00 per round, £55.00 per day. *Eating facilities:* two bars, meals available, separate diningroom. *Visitors*: welcome weekdays, restriction on Tuesdays and Fridays. *Society Meetings*: societies and visiting parties catered for weekdays, some restrictions Tuesdays and Fridays. Professional: Graeme Bell (01642 780238). Secretary: A.W. McNinch (01642 780238).
e-mail: secretary@eaglescliffegolfclub.co.uk

HARTLEPOOL. **Castle Eden Golf Club,** Castle Eden, Hartlepool TS27 4SS (01429 836510). *Location*: two miles south of Peterlee, use exits from A19. Picturesque parkland course. 18 holes, 6262 yards. S.S.S. 70. Practice ground. *Green Fees:* weekdays £30.00, weekends and Bank Holidays £38.00. *Eating facilities:* restaurant, lounge and bar and snooker room. *Visitors:* welcome weekdays 9.30am-11.30am, 1.45pm-3.30pm. *Society Meetings:* only with reservation. Professional: Peter Jackson (01429 836510). Secretary: Steve Watkin (01429 836510).

HARTLEPOOL. **Hartlepool Golf Club Ltd,** Hart Warren, Hartlepool TS24 9QF (01429 274398; Fax: 01429 274129). *Location:* turn right off A1086 at Hart Station – north of town, signposted. Seaside links course. 18 holes, 6298 yards. S.S.S. 71. *Green Fees:* contact Professional for prices. *Eating facilities:* full catering available. *Visitors:* welcome, contact Professional. Buggies and caddy carts available for hire. *Society Meetings:* catered for by prior arrangement. Professional/Manager: G.I. Laidlaw (01429 267473).
website: www.hartlepoolgolfclub.co.uk

HARTLEPOOL. **High Throston Golf Club,** Hart Lane, Hartlepool TS26 0UG (01429 275325). *Location:* two miles from A19. Course designed by Jonathan Gaunt (USGA specification) with natural banks, rolling countryside with sea views - 7000 trees planted. 18 holes, 6247 yards, S.S.S. 71. Practice nets, putting green. *Green Fees:* information not available. *Eating facilities:* only light refreshments available at present. *Visitors:* welcome usually at all times. Secretary: Mrs J. Sturrock (01429 268071).*

HARTLEPOOL. **Seaton Carew Golf Club,** Tees Road, Seaton Carew, Hartlepool TS25 1DE (01429 266249). *Location:* two miles south of Hartlepool on A178. Championship seaside links. 22 holes. Old Course: 6658 yards. S.S.S. 72. Brabazon Course: 6900 yards. S.S.S. 73. Micklem Course: 6574 yards. S.S.S. 71. *Green Fees:* on application. *Eating facilities:* bar snacks, full catering to order. *Visitors:* welcome midweek and some weekends. Advance booking recommended. Buggies for hire. *Society Meetings:* catered for by arrangement. Professional: Clifford Jackson (01429 890660). Secretary: J. Hall (01429 296496).
e-mail: seatoncarewgolf@btconnect.com
website: www.seatoncarewgolfclub.co.uk

NEWTON AYCLIFFE. **Oak Leaf Golf Complex,** School Aycliffe Lane, Newton Aycliffe DL5 6QZ (01325 310820). Location: three miles from A1(M) and A68 on the outskirts of Newton Aycliffe. Rolling parkland. 18 holes, 5568 yards. S.S.S. 67. Driving range (floodlit), chipping and bunker practice. *Green Fees:* information not available. *Eating facilities:* bar and catering available at Oakleaf Golf Complex. Contact (01325 300600). *Visitors:* public course. Visiting parties by appointment. Showers/toilets/changing facilities. Squash/Indoor Bowls at Oakleaf Golf Complex. *Society Meetings:* all welcome by prior arrangement. Professional: Ernie Wilson (01325 310820) Secretary: B. Oliver (Club) (01325 316040).*

NEWTON AYCLIFFE. **Woodham Golf and Country Club,** Burnhill Way, Newton Aycliffe DL5 4PN (01325 320574; Fax: 01325 315254). *Location:* A167, one mile north of Newton Aycliffe on the Shildon road. Parkland, wooded with lakes. 18 holes, 6688 yards. S.S.S. 72. Practice grounds, putting green. *Green Fees:* information not available. *Eating facilities:* bar/restaurant. *Visitors:* welcome anytime, must book though on Friday, Saturday and Sunday. Buggies, trolleys available. *Society Meetings:* all welcome. Professional: Ernie Wilson (01325 315257; Fax: 01325 315254). Director of Golf: Glenn Lowery. Steward: (01325 301551).

SEAHAM. **Seaham Golf Club,** Shrewsbury Street, Seaham SR7 7RD (0191-581 2354). *Location:* Dawdon, two miles north east of A19 leave for Murton/Seaham. Heathland. 18 holes, 6017 yards. S.S.S. 69. Practice area. *Green Fees:* information not provided. *Eating facilities:* snacks available, meals on request. *Visitors:* welcome, unrestricted weekdays, booking for weekends. *Society Meetings:* welcome on application. Professional: Andrew Blunt (0191-513 0837). Secretary: Terry Johnson (0191-581 1268).
e-mail: seahamgolfclub@btconnect.com
website: www.seahamgolfclub.co.uk

SEDGEFIELD. **Knotty Hill Golf Centre,** Sedgefield, Stockton-on-Tees TS21 2BB (01740 620320; Fax: 01740 622227). *Location:* A1 (M) Junction 60, one mile north of Sedgefield A177. The 18 hole Princes Course 6433 yards, 5882 metres, S.S.S. 71, Par 72; and 18 hole Bishops Course, 6053 yards, 5535 metres, Par 70, are situated in mature parkland with strategically placed water hazards and bunkers, along with tree lined fairways, making accuracy a premium and the courses rewarding for all standards of play. The recently completed 9 hole Academy Course, 2494 yards, Par 32, is ideal for both young aspiring golfers and those who wish to take life at a more leisurely pace. Indoor Golf Academy, video and tuition range, high quality floodlit driving range, open grass tee area, chipping and putting greens, practice bunker. *Green Fees:* 9 holes £9.00, 18 holes £13.00. 2010 rates (subject to review). *Eating facilities:* restaurant, coffee shop. *Visitors:* welcome at all times. Buggy and cart hire. *Society Meetings*: welcome, information on request. Secretary: Mrs J. Reynolds (01740 620320).
website: www.knottyhill.com

FHG GUIDES
www.holidayguides.com

Woodham Golf and Country Club
Burnhill Way, Newton Aycliffe, Durham DL5 4PN
Tel: 01325 320574 • Pro Shop: 01325 315257
e-mail: woodhamgcc@gawab.com
www.woodhamgolfandcountryclub.co.uk

Opened in 1981, the course at Woodham Golf & Country Club is one of the most challenging in the North. Our 18-hole championship golf course is set in 229 acres of mature parkland, a lengthy 6,668 yards from the championship tees, with lakes and woodland forming part of the picturesque setting.
We welcome both members and visitors to our club and promise a friendly atmosphere at all times.

THE GOLF GUIDE 2011   NORTH REGION / Durham   269

STANLEY. **South Moor Golf Club,** The Middles, Craghead, Stanley DH9 6AG (01207 232848; Fax: 01207 284616). *Location:* eight miles north-west of Durham, seven miles west of A1 (M) from Chester-le-Street. Parkland and moorland. 18 holes, 6273 yards. S.S.S. 70. *Green Fees:* information not available. *Eating facilities:* available. *Visitors:* visiting parties between 10am and 11.30am and 2pm to 3.30pm. *Society Meetings:* catered for except Sundays. Professional: Shaun Cowell (01207 283525). Secretary: M. Brennan (01207 232848). e-mail: secretary@southmoorgc.co.uk

STOCKTON-ON-TEES. **Norton Golf Course,** Blakeston Lane, Norton, Stockton-on-Tees TS20 2SU (01642 676385; Fax: 01642 608467). *Location:* turn into Junction Road to Norton from A177 at Horse and Jockey, two miles north of Stockton roundabout. Slightly hilly course with five lakes. 18 holes, 5393 yards. S.S.S. 70. *Green Fees:* information not available. *Visitors:* must have golf shoes and own clubs; no jeans. Parties welcome weekdays. *Society Meetings:* rates on application. Contact (01642 676385).*

STOCKTON-ON-TEES. **Teesside Golf Club,** Acklam Road, Thornaby, Stockton-on-Tees TS17 7JS (01642 676249; Fax: 01642 676252). *Location*: A19 - A1130 to Thornaby, 0.7 miles on right hand side. Flat parkland. 18 holes, 6535 yards. S.S.S. 71. Practice ground, putting green. *Green Fees:* weekdays £30.00, weekends £34.00. *Eating facilities:* catering except Mondays, bar 11am to 11pm. *Visitors:* welcome midweek up to 4.30pm, weekends after 11am by arrangement. *Society Meetings:* Monday - Friday. Special rates and conditions for parties and guests. Professional: S. Pilgrim (01642 673822). Secretary: R. Ferri (01642 616516).
e-mail: teessidegolfclub@btconnect.com
website: www.teessidegolfclub.co.uk

Brancepeth Castle Golf Club, Brancepeth

Lancashire

ACCRINGTON. **Accrington and District Golf Club,** Devon Avenue, Oswaldtwistle, Accrington BB5 4LS (01254 231091). *Location*: on A679, 2 miles from Blackburn. 18 holes, 6060 yards. S.S.S. 69. *Green Fees*: information not provided. *Eating facilities*: lunches and evening meals. *Visitors*: welcome by prior arrangement. *Society Meetings*: prior bookings catered for. Professional: Mark Harling (01254 231091). Secretary: S. Padbury (01254 350112).
e-mail: info@accringtongolfclub.com

BACUP. **Bacup Golf Club,** Bankside Lane, Bacup OL13 1HY (01706 873170; Fax: 01706 87726). *Location:* one mile from Bacup centre. Moorland. 9 holes, 6018 yards. S.S.S. 69. *Green Fees:* information not available. *Eating facilities:* by arrangement except Mondays. *Visitors:* welcome without reservation except Mondays and Saturdays. Secretary: T. Leyland (01706 879644).*

BAXENDEN. **Baxenden and District Golf Club,** Wooley Lane, Baxenden BB5 2EA (01254 234555). *Location:* towards Accrington from M65, past Hollands Pies right, signposted. Golf course has fantastic views as far as the Fylde Coast and Ingleborough. 9 holes, 5702 yards. S.S.S. 68. *Green Fees:* information not provided. *Eating facilities:* available. *Visitors:* welcome weekdays only. *Society Meetings:* welcome by arrangement with Secretary. Secretary: N. Turner (01254 234555).
e-mail: baxgolf@hotmail.com
website: www.baxendengolf.co.uk

BLACKBURN. **Blackburn Golf Club,** Beardwood Brow, Blackburn BB2 7AX (01254 51122; Fax: 01254 665578). *Location:* off A677 within easy reach of M6 (Junction 31), M61 and M65; west end of Blackburn. Parkland with superb views of Lancashire coast and Pennine Hills. 18 holes, 6144 yards. S.S.S. 70. Par 71. Practice area. *Green Fees:* weekdays £32.00 (£12.00 with a member); weekends and Bank Holidays £38.00 (£12.00 with a member). *Eating facilities:* full catering and bar facilities (restricted Mondays). *Visitors:* welcome without reservation except on competition days. *Society Meetings:* catered for by arrangement. Professional: Alan Rodwell (01254 55942). Hon. Secretary: N. Readett (01254 51122; Fax: 01254 665578).

Mytton Fold Hotel & Golf Complex

Play golf to the backdrop of the stunning Ribble Valley and Forest of Bowland.
Golf Breaks from only £47pppn to include DB&B, 18 holes golf, based on two persons sharing twin/double room.
Summer Society Packages from £29.50pp.
Alternative packages available.
Contact: 01254 240662 for full details.

Winner Small Hotel of the Year 2009
Lancashire & Blackpool Tourist Board

Mytton Fold Hotel & Golf Complex, Whalley Road, Langho, Near Blackburn BB6 8AB
Hotel Tel: 01254 240662
Golf Shop: 01254 245392
e-mail: reception@myttonfold.co.uk
www.myttonfold.co.uk

BLACKBURN. **Great Harwood Golf Club,** Harwood Bar, Whalley Road, Great Harwood, Blackburn BB6 7TE (01254 884391). Flat wooded course. 9 holes, 6404 yards, 5856 metres. S.S.S. 71. Practice area. *Green Fees:* £24.00 weekdays, £30.00 weekends. *Eating facilities:* all meals catered for, bar hours 12-2pm, 4-11pm. *Visitors:* welcome Wednesday-Friday. *Society Meetings:* catered for by advance bookings. Secretary: J. Spibey (01254 884391).

BLACKBURN. **Mytton Fold Hotel & Golf Complex,** Whalley Road, Langho, Blackburn BB6 8AB (01254 245392/240662). *Location*: from Junction 31 of M6, follow A59 towards Whalley/Clitheroe for 10 miles. At second roundabout follow Whalley sign, entrance 500 yards on right. Undulating parkland with panoramic views over the Ribble Valley. 18 holes. Par 72. *Green Fees:* £26.00. 2010 rates subject to review). *Eating facilities*: bar open all day, food till 9.30pm. *Visitors:* prior booking essential. Buggies available. *Society Meetings:* welcome, from £23.50 per person (subject to review).
e-mail: reception@myttonfold.co.uk
website: www.myttonfold.co.uk

BLACKBURN. **Pleasington Golf Club,** Pleasington, near Blackburn BB2 5JF (01254 202177). *Location:* five minutes from Junction 3 of the M65. Undulating woodland. 18 holes, 6539 yards. S.S.S. 72. *Green Fees:* weekdays £48.00, weekends and Bank Holidays £55.00. *Eating facilities:* full catering available. *Visitors:* welcome by prior arrangement. *Society Meetings:* Mondays, Wednesdays, Thursdays and Fridays by arrangement. Professional: G.J. Furey (01254 201630). Secretary/ General Manager: C.J. Williams (01254 202177). Caterer: D. Whittam (01254 207346).
e-mail: secretary-manager@pleasington-golf.co.uk
website: www.pleasington-golf.co.uk

BLACKBURN. **Rishton Golf Club,** Eachill Links, Rishton BB1 4HG (01254 884442; Fax: 01254 887701). *Location:* between Junctions 6 and 7 M65 signposted from Rishton village centre. Moorland course. 10 holes, 6172 yards. S.S.S. 69. *Green Fees:* information not available. *Eating facilities:* full catering by prior arrangement. *Visitors:* welcome on weekdays and with a member at weekends and on Bank Holidays. *Society Meetings:* visiting parties welcome by prior arrangement, special rates can be obtained. Hon. Secretary: W. Shaw (07951 278690).*

BLACKBURN. **Wilpshire Golf Club Ltd,** 72 Whalley Road, Wilpshire, Blackburn BB1 9LF (01254 248260; Fax: 01254 246745). *Location:* A666 three miles north of Blackburn in the Ribble Valley on Blackburn to Whalley road. Parkland/moorland. 18 holes, 5961 yards. S.S.S. 69. Practice ground. *Green Fees:* information not available. *Eating facilities:* lunch, high tea, dinner except Mondays. *Visitors:* welcome, no restrictions except competition days. Buggies and trolley hire. *Society Meetings:* catered for by prior booking through Secretary. Professional: Walter Slaven (01254 249558; Fax: 01254 246745). Secretary: S.H. Tart.
e-mail: admin@wilpshiregolfclub.co.uk
website: www.wilpshiregolfclub.co.uk

BLACKPOOL. **Blackpool North Shore Golf Club,** Devonshire Road, Blackpool FY2 0RD (01253 352054; Fax: 01253 591240). *Location:* north Blackpool on A587 behind North Prom. Undulating parkland. 18 holes, 6431 yards. S.S.S. 71. *Green Fees:* weekdays £30.00 per round, £38.00 per day; weekends £36.00 per round, £45.00 per day. Society Package £49.00, *Eating facilities:* full catering and bar facilities. *Visitors:* welcome except Thursdays and Saturdays. Professional: Andrew Richardson (01253 354640). Secretary/Manager: Christine Woosnam (01253 352054).
e-mail: office@bnsgc.com
website: www.bnsgc.com

BLACKPOOL. **Blackpool Park Golf Club,** North Park Drive, Blackpool FY3 8LS (Tel & Fax: 01253 397916). *Location:* one mile east of Tower. MacKenzie-designed course. 18 holes, 6089 yards. S.S.S. 70. *Green Fees:* information not available. *Eating facilities:* full restaurant facilities. *Visitors/ Society Meetings:* welcome (bookings for tee reservations must be made on 01253 478176). Meal and Play packages available. Professional: B. Purdie (01253 391004). Secretary: Charles Wright (Tel & Fax: 01253 397916).
website: www.blackpoolparkgc.co.uk

BLACKPOOL. **De Vere Herons' Reach Golf & Leisure Resort,** East Park Drive, Blackpool FY3 8LL (01253 766156; Fax: 01253 798800). *Location*: leave M55 at Junction 4, follow signs for Stanley Park and Victoria Hospital. Designed by Peter Alliss & Clive Clark. Testing championship course with 10 man-made lakes- all year round play course. Heron's Reach Course -18 holes, 6461 yards, S.S.S. 70. 17 bay floodlit driving range, putting and chipping green. *Green Fees*: information not available. *Eating facilities*: Nineteen Bar serving from 7am daily and Brasserie open seven days. *Visitors:* welcome. 172 bedroomed hotel with extensive conference and banqueting facilities for up to 600 plus leisure complex. *Society Meetings*: welcome. Golf Centre: (01253 766156; Fax: 01253 798800).*
e-mail: paul.heaton@devere-hotels.com

BLACKPOOL. **Poulton-le-Fylde Golf Club,** Myrtle Farm, Breck Road, Poulton-le-Fylde, Blackpool FY6 7HJ (Tel & Fax: 01253 892444). *Location:* Junction 3 from M55, follow A585 signed Fleetwood. At River Wyre pub turn left at roundabout and follow signs. Parkland/wooded course. 9 holes, 3260 yards. Par 36. Practice and putting facilities. *Green Fees:* information not available. *Eating facilities:* breakfast and lunch served, all day bar in summer. *Visitors:* welcome anytime, even on weekends (01253 892444). Snooker. *Society Meetings:* welcome by prior booking. Professional: John Greenwood (Tel & Fax: 01253 892444). Secretary: John Greenwood (Tel & Fax: 01253 892444).*
website: www.poultonlefyldegolfclub.co.uk

Please mention THE GOLF GUIDE when you enquire about clubs or accommodation

Knott End Golf Club
1910-2010

A unique blend between links and parkland, our 18-hole golf course is a challenge for golfers of all abilities. Facilities include: bar, restaurant, Pro Shop. Buggy and trolley hire available. Great value packages available. Visiting parties welcome.

**Knott End Golf Club Limited,
Wyreside, Knott End On Sea,
Lancashire FY6 0AA
Secretary/Manager: Miss L.M. Freeman
Tel: (01253) 810576
e-mail: hilary@knottendgolfclub.com
www.knottendgolfclub.com**

BLACKPOOL. **Knott End Golf Club Ltd,** Wyre Side, Knott End-on-Sea, Poulton-le-Fylde FY6 0AA (01253 810576). *Location:* M55 Exit 3, A585 Fleetwood Road then A588 to Knott End. Scenic riverside course, slight undulations. 18 holes, 5849 yards. S.S.S. 69. Practice ground. *Green Fees:* £33.00 18 holes weekdays, weekends £41.00. *Eating facilities:* full catering and bar. *Visitors:* welcome, time sheet in use, contact Professional with 24 hours notice. Buggies for hire. *Society Meetings:* by arrangement weekdays and Sundays. Professional: Paul Walker (01253 811365). Manager: Louise Freeman (01253 810576; Fax: 01253 813446).
e-mail: hilary@knottendgolfclub.com
website: www.knottendgolfclub.com

BOLTON. **Bolton Open Golf Course,** Longsight Park, Longsight Lane, Harwood, Bolton BL2 4JX (01204 597659). *Location:* one and a half miles from Bolton town centre. Parkland, mature wooded, superb layout. 18 holes, 6000 yards. S.S.S. 68. 20 bay floodlit driving range. *Green Fees:* information not available. *Eating facilities:* one bar, all day catering. *Visitors:* no restrictions, everyone welcome at all times. *Society Meetings:* welcome anytime, discounts available.*

BOLTON. **Douglas Valley Golf Club,** A6 Blackrod By-Pass, Blackrod, Bolton BL6 5HX. *Location:* M61 Junction 6, off A6. Parkland greens. 9 holes, 2190 yards, 2004 metres. 22-bay floodlit driving range. *Green Fees:* weekdays - 9 holes £8.00, 18 holes £10.00, weekends - 9 holes £9.00, 18 holes £12.00. 2010 rates (subject to review). *Visitors:* welcome anytime. Bookings two days in advance. Fully stocked Pro Shop and Teaching Academy. *Eating facilities:* Portofino Italian Restaurant and Function Suite available, ring for details (01257 476012) or see website below. *Society Meetings:* society and corporate days available, ring for details. Company Secretary: Julie Downes (01257 474844).

BURNLEY. **Burnley Golf Club,** Glen View, Burnley BB11 3RW (01282 455266). *Location:* 300 yards from junction of A56 and A646. Moorland. 18 holes, 5943 yards, 5434 metres. S.S.S. 69. *Green Fees:* weekdays £25.00; weekends and Bank Holidays £30.00. *Eating facilities:* generally available, please telephone to check. *Visitors:* welcome except Saturdays. *Society Meetings:* catered for.
e-mail: burnleygolfclub@onthegreen.co.uk
website: www.burnleygolfclub.com

BURNLEY. **Towneley Golf Club,** Towneley Park, Todmorden Road, Burnley BB11 3ED (01282 415636). *Location:* Todmorden Road, Burnley, Top Gates to Towneley Park. Guarded greens (ie. bunkered) and internal O.B.B. 18 holes, 5811 yards. S.S.S. 68. Practice ground. *Green Fees:* information not available. *Eating facilities:* full licensed bar and catering (full meals). *Visitors:* welcome but make tee reservations in advance. *Society Meetings:* welcome, apply to course booking shop. Professional: James Major (01282 438473) Secretary: Bernard Walsh (01282 415636).*

CHORLEY. **Charnock Richard Golf and Country Club,** Preston Road, Charnock Richard, Chorley PR7 5LE (01257 470707). *Location:* on A49 between M6 turn-offs for Standish and Leyland, five minutes from Camelot Theme Park. Parkland with water features. 18 holes. Par 70. Buggy hire. *Green Fees:* information not provided. *Eating facilities:* Italian restaurant on site. Director of Golf: Alan Lunt.

CHORLEY. **Chorley Golf Club,** Hall o' the Hill, Heath Charnock, Chorley PR6 9HX (01257 480263; Fax: 01257 480722). *Location:* south of Chorley, just off the A673 at the junction with the A6. Scenic course with some of the finest views in Lancashire. 18 holes, 6269 yards. S.S.S. 70. *Green Fees:* weekdays £35.00. *Eating facilities:* restaurant and lounge bar. *Visitors:* welcome by prior arrangement except Bank Holidays or weekends. Two buggies and carts for hire. *Society Meetings:* catered for by arrangement. Professional: M.N. Bradley (01257 481245). Secretary: Mrs A. Green (01257 480263). Catering: (01257 474664).
e-mail: secretary@chorleygolfclub.freeserve.co.uk
website: www.chorleygolfclub.co.uk

THE GOLF GUIDE 2011 — NORTH REGION / Lancashire

CHORLEY. **Duxbury Park Golf Club (Municipal),** Duxbury Hall Road, Duxbury Park, Chorley PR7 4AS (01257 265380, 01257 241634). *Location:* one mile south of town centre off A6. Wooded parkland with water hazards on several holes. 18 holes, 6390 yards, 5843 metres. S.S.S. 70. Practice area. *Green Fees:* information not available. *Eating facilities:* Golf Cafe open 7 days a week, very reasonable prices. For details contact Paul (01257 277049). *Visitors:* welcome, book seven days in advance. *Society Meetings:* book in advance. Professional: (01257 265380). Secretary: F. Holding (01257 262209). Membership available, contact Secretary.*

CHORLEY. **Euxton Park Golf Centre,** Euxton Lane, Chorley PR7 6DL (01257 261601; Fax: 01257 261601). *Location:* Euxton Lane, between A6 and A49, next to Royal Ordnance factory. A short, yet challenging Par 3 course, ideal for beginners. 9 holes, Par 3. 40 bay driving range, practice bunkers. *Green Fees:* information not available. *Eating facilities:* fully licensed bar. *Visitors:* welcome every day, no need to book, pay and play course. *Society Meetings:* welcome, professionally catered for. Professional: Jon Haines (01257 233500). Secretary: T.R. Evans (Tel & Fax: 01257 261601).*

CHORLEY. **Shaw Hill Hotel Golf and Country Club,** Preston Road, Whittle-le-Woods, Chorley PR6 7PP (01257 269221; Fax: 01257 261223). *Location:* A6 between Chorley and Preston. (Near M6 J28 & M61 J8) Parkland course with many water hazards. 18 holes, 6283 yards. S.S.S. 71 yellow. Practice area. *Green Fees:* on request. *Eating facilities:* spike bar and formal bar, à la carte restaurant. *Visitors:* welcome, must hold current Handicap Certificate. Hotel with 30 bedrooms available. Golf trolleys and buggies also available. *Society Meetings:* catered for midweek only. Professional: David Clarke (01257 279222). General Manager: Mrs K. Tyrer. Secretary: L. Bateson.
e-mail: info@shaw-hill.co.uk
website: www.shaw-hill.co.uk

CLITHEROE. **Clitheroe Golf Club,** Whalley Road, Pendleton, Clitheroe BB7 1PP (Tel & Fax: 01200 422292). *Location:* A59, junction A671 (south of Clitheroe); 300m turn left (signposted Barrow) clubhouse 100m on right. Parkland with extensive countryside views. 18 holes, 6326 yards, 5785 metres. S.S.S. 71. Practice ground and range. *Green Fees:* information not available. *Eating facilities:* full service available. *Visitors:* welcome but restricted to times available. No jeans, trainers, track/shell suits. *Society Meetings:* catered for, maximum 48 Friday; maximum 24 Thursday. No parties weekends. Professional: Paul McEvoy (01200 424242). Secretary: (01200 422292).*
e-mail: secretary@clitheroegolfclub.com
website: www.clitheroegolfclub.com

CLITHEROE. **Whalley Golf Club,** Long Lease Barn, Clerk Hill Road, Whalley, Clitheroe BB7 9DR (01254 822236). *Location:* seven miles east of Blackburn on A59. Parkland. 9 holes, 6258 yards, 5727 metres. S.S.S. 71. *Green Fees:* £25.00 weekdays, £30.00 weekends and Bank Holidays. *Eating facilities:* full catering and bar facilities. *Visitors:* welcome except Thursday afternoons and Saturdays April to September. *Society Meetings:* welcome by appointment. Professional: Jamie Hunt (01254 824766).

COLNE. **Colne Golf Club,** Law Farm, Skipton Old Road, Colne BB8 7EB (01282 863391). *Location:* come off eastern end of M65. Carry on one mile to next roundabout and take first exit on left, signposted Lothersdale, Goup Hill. Flat scenic moorland course with trees. 9 holes, 6053 yards, 5535 metres. S.S.S. 69. Full practice facilities. *Green Fees:* £20.00 weekdays, £25.00 weekends and Bank Holidays. 2010 rates (subject to review). Parties of 12 or more £19.00 per person (not weekends, Thursdays or competition days). *Eating facilities:* available daily except Mondays. *Visitors:* welcome except on competition days; two-balls only on Thursdays. *Society Meetings:* welcome except weekends, Thursdays and competition days. Secretary: A. Turpin.

Welcome to *Shaw Hill Hotel Golf and Country Club*

With its own 18-hole parkland golf course, Shaw Hill is ideal for the golf enthusiast, with our golfing weekends, Society Days and Corporate Golf Days proving very popular throughout the year. Non-members are welcome Monday-Friday (although a Handicap Certificate will be required) Overlooking the breathtaking scenery of Shaw Hill Golf Course, Vardon's offers the finest of dishes at affordable prices. With its award-winning cuisine, it caters for every occasion, offering a choice of à la carte & table d'hôte menus. In the luxurious Leisure Complex, indulge yourself with a swim, sauna or a dip in the jacuzzi, a work out in the hi-tech gym, followed by a beauty treatment at Le Visage. *At Shaw Hill we offer everything you could ever want for a luxury day out.*

Enjoy 2 rounds on our Championship Course, one night's stay, use of our spa, sauna, pool and steam room plus a 3-course dinner on the night of your stay, all for just £75.00pp. Terms and conditions apply.

Preston Road, Near Chorley, Lancashire PR6 7PP • Tel: 01257 269221 • Fax: 01257 261223
e-mail: info@shaw-hill.co.uk • www.shaw-hill.co.uk

Lancashire / NORTH REGION

DARWEN. Darwen Golf Club, Winter Hill, Darwen BB3 0LB (01254 704267). *Location*: one-and-a-half miles from Darwen centre. Moorland. 18 holes, 6354 yards. S.S.S. 71. Large practice area. Golf Club of the Year 2009 finalist. *Green Fees*: Casual: weekend £30.00 per round, £40.00 per day, weekday £25.00 per round, £30.00 per day; Introduced: weekend £10.00 per round, £12.00 per day, weekday £10.00 per round/day; Junior Introduced: any day £6.00 per round/day. *Eating facilities*: full catering. *Visitors*: welcome, not Tuesdays (Ladies' Day) or Saturdays. *Society Meetings*: welcome, except Saturdays. Professional: W. Lennon (01254 776370). Secretary: M. J. Catterall (01254 704367).
e-mail: admin@darwengolfclub.com
website: www.darwengolfclub.com

FLEETWOOD. Fleetwood Golf Club Ltd., The Golf House, Princes Way, Fleetwood FY7 8AF (Tel & Fax: 01253 773573). *Location:* on Fylde Coast, eight miles from Blackpool, Coast Road Blackpool to Fleetwood, two miles west of Fleetwood Centre. Seaside, true links. White course 18 holes, 6557 yards, S.S.S. 72; Yellow course 18 holes, 6308 yards, S.S.S. 71. *Green Fees:* information not available. *Eating facilities:* full catering and bar service. *Visitors:* welcome weekdays and Sundays. Professional: Ian Taylor (01253 873661). Office Manager: Ernie Langford (01253 773573).*
e-mail: secretary@fleetwoodgolf.co.uk
website: www.fleetwoodgolf.co.uk

HEYSHAM. Heysham Golf Club, Trumacar Park, Middleton Road, Heysham LA3 3JH (01524 851011; Fax: 01524 853030). *Location:* five miles from M6 via Lancaster and Morecambe. Parkland, part-wooded. 18 holes, 6355 yards. S.S.S. 70. Driving range and chipping green. *Green Fees:* weekdays £30.00 per round, £35.00 per day; weekends/Bank Holidays £40.00. 2010 rates (subject to review). Special rates for parties. *Eating facilities:* full catering seven days, closed Mondays October to March. *Visitors:* welcome with Handicap Certificates. Tee reserved for members 1pm to 1.45pm. Buggy hire available. *Society Meetings:* catered for by arrangement. Professional: R. Done (01524 852000). Secretary: Mrs Gill Gardner (01524 851011).
e-mail: secretary@heyshamgolfclub.co.uk
website: www.heyshamgolfclub.co.uk

LANCASTER. Lancaster Golf Club Ltd, Ashton Hall, Ashton-with-Stodday, Lancaster LA2 0AJ (01524 751247). *Location:* three miles south of Lancaster on A588. Parkland. 18 holes, 6512 yards. S.S.S. 71. *Green Fees:* weekdays only £44.00 per round. *Eating facilities:* available (Caterer: 01524 751247). *Visitors:* welcome weekdays only unless staying in the Dormy House. Club has a Dormy House (part of Ashton Hall), single and twin rooms with en suite facilities, two nights minimum stay. Professional: David Sutcliffe (01524 751247). Secretary: B. Inglis (01524 751247).
e-mail: secretary@lancastergc.co.uk

LANCASTER. Lansil Golf Club, Caton Road, Lancaster LA1 3PE (01524 39269/61233). *Location:* A683, towards Lancaster from Junction 34 M6. Parkland. 9 holes, 5608 yards. S.S.S. 67. *Green Fees:* information not available. *Eating facilities:* bar meals available - contact Steward. *Visitors*: welcome weekdays, not before 1pm Sundays. *Society Meetings:* groups of 12 plus welcome weekdays by prior arrangement. Steward: 01524 39269.*

Darwen Golf Club

A mixture of parkland and moorland halves, this challenging 18-hole SSS 71 course is set in beautiful countryside with breathtaking views over the Ribble Estuary and Blackpool Tower; the Pennine Chain and Welsh Mountains are visible on clearer days. There is a large practice area, and visitors are welcome every day except Tuesdays (Ladies) and Saturdays (members comp.)

Darwen Golf Club Ltd, Duddon Avenue, Darwen BB3 0LB
Clubhouse: 01254 701287 • Secretary: 01254 704367 • Pro: 01254 776370
e-mail: admin@darwengolfclub.com • www.darwengolfclub.com

Fleetwood Golf Course is the only true links course on the **Fylde Coast**. It was opened in 1932 and designed to perfection by **James Steer**. Lancashire's 'oldest traditional links' is a must for keen golfers, offering a good challenge to golfers of all abilities. The area abounds in good accommodation for those travelling from inland.
Princes Way, Fleetwood, Lancashire FY7 8AF   **Tel: 01253 773573**
e-mail: secretary@fleetwoodgolf.co.uk   www.fleetwoodgolf.co.uk

LEYLAND. Leyland Golf Club Ltd., Wigan Road, Leyland, Preston PR25 5UD (01772 436457). *Location*: leave M6 at Exit 28, turn right to traffic lights, (200 yards) turn right onto the A49, course located one mile on left. Flat parkland. 18 holes, 6298 yards. S.S.S. 70. *Green Fees:* £34.00 weekdays. 2010 rates (subject to review). *Eating facilities:* full catering except Mondays in winter. *Visitors:* welcome weekdays; weekends only with a member. *Society Meetings:* welcome by arrangement. Professional: C. Burgess (01772 423425). Admin. Manager: Stephanie Drinkall (01772 436457).
e-mail: manager@leylandgolfclub.co.uk
website: www.leylandgolfclub.co.uk

LYTHAM ST ANNES. **Fairhaven Golf Club,** Oakwood Avenue, Lytham St Annes FY8 4JU (01253 736741). *Location:* on B5261, two miles from Lytham, eight miles from Blackpool. A final qualifying Open Championship course. 18 holes, 6883 yards. S.S.S. 73. Par 74. Practice ground, chipping and putting greens, and nets. *Green Fees:* information not available. *Eating facilities:* full catering service seven days a week. *Visitors:* welcome, advisable to reserve tee time. Handicap Certificate required. Well stocked Pro Shop; lessons available. *Society Meetings:* various packages can be arranged on Mondays, Tuesdays, Wednesdays and Fridays. Professional: A. Lancaster (01253 736976). Secretary: Bob Thompson (Tel & Fax:01253 736741).
e-mail: secretary@fairhavengolfclub.co.uk
website: www.fairhavengolfclub.co.uk

LYTHAM ST ANNES. **Lytham Green Drive Golf Club,** Ballam Road, Lytham St Annes FY8 4LE (01253 737390; Fax: 01253 731350). *Location*: one mile from town centre. Flat parkland course. 18 holes, 6305 yards. S.S.S. 70. *Green Fees:* from £35.00 per person, depending on group numbers. *Eating facilities:* catering available daily. *Visitors:* welcome. *Society Meetings:* welcome by prior arrangement. Professional: Simon Williamson (01253 737379). Secretary: I. Stewart (01253 737390; Fax: 01253 731350).
e-mail: secretary@lythamgreendrive.co.uk
website: www.lythamgreendrive.co.uk

LYTHAM ST ANNES. Royal Lytham and St Annes Golf Club, Links Gate, Lytham St Annes FY8 3LQ (01253 724206; Fax: 01253 780946). *Location:* within one mile of the centre of St Annes on Sea. Seaside Championship links course. 18 holes, 6334 yards. S.S.S. 71. Practice ground, chipping green, putting green. *Green Fees:* Mondays and Thursdays £140.00 including lunch, limited availability on Sundays £140.00 including lunch. 2010 rates (subject to review). *Eating facilities:* restaurant and bar. *Visitors:* welcome Mondays and Thursdays; limited availablity other days. Dormy House accommodation available. *Society Meetings:* by arrangement Mondays and Thursdays. Professional: Eddie Birchenough (01253 720094). Secretary: R.J.G Cochrane.
e-mail: bookings@royallytham.org
website: www.royallytham.org

LYTHAM ST ANNES. **St Annes Old Links Golf Club,** Highbury Road, Lytham St Annes FY8 2LD (01253 723597). *Location:* M55 via Blackpool South Shore, following airport signs. Past airport down to coast road, turn left and first left at next traffic lights. The only true links course in Lancashire. 18 holes, 6872 yards. S.S.S. 73. Practice ground, putting and chipping greens. *Green Fees:* weekdays from £60.00 per day, from £50.00 for 18 holes after 1.30pm. *Eating facilities:* restaurant and snack facilities, bar. *Visitors:* welcome, not Saturdays, restricted Sundays. Tuesday is Ladies' Day. *Society Meetings:* restricted to those with Handicaps and membership of other clubs. Professional: D. Webster (01253 722432). Secretary: J. Donohoe (01253 723597; Fax: 01253 781506).
e-mail: secretary@stannesoldlinks.com
website: www.stannesoldlinks.com

MORECAMBE. **Morecambe Golf Club Ltd.,** The Club House, Bare, Morecambe LA4 6AJ (01524 412841). *Location:* on A589 leaving Morecambe towards Carnforth. Parkland course affected by sea breezes and offering superb views. 18 holes, 5791 yards. S.S.S. 69. *Green Fees:* information not provided. *Eating facilities:* diningroom and bar snacks. *Visitors:* welcome at all times, tee reserved for members up to 9.30am and from 12 noon to 1.30pm. *Society Meetings:* welcome at all times. Professional: Simon Fletcher (Tel & Fax: 01524 415596). Secretary: Mrs Judith Atkinson (01524 412841; Fax: 01524 400088).
e-mail: secretary@morecambegolfclub.com
website: www.morecambegolfclub.com

NELSON. **Nelson Golf Club,** King's Causeway, Brierfield, Nelson BB9 0EU (01282 611834). *Location:* leave M65 at Junction 12, take A682 for Brierfield, turn left at Brierfield centre traffic lights, course on the right at top of the hill. Wooded moorland, good views of the surrounding Pendle Area. 18 holes, 6007 yards. S.S.S. 69. Large practice area. *Green Fees:* weekdays £30.00, weekends and Bank Holidays £35.00. *Eating facilities:* lunches, dinners by arrangement except Mondays. *Visitors:* weekdays except Thursdays (Ladies' Day), or Saturdays during Competition season. Carts. *Society Meetings:* daily except Monday, Thursday and Saturday. Rates for visiting parties from £41.00 per person. Professional: Simon Eaton (01282 617000). Business Manager: Richard Lees (01282 611834).

ORMSKIRK. **Mossock Hall Golf Club,** Liverpool Road, Bickerstaffe, Ormskirk L39 0EE (01695 421717). *Location:* one mile from Junction 3 of M58 or two miles from Junction 1 of M57, between Kirby and Ormskirk. Parkland course; USGA greens with water in play on four holes. 18 holes. Par 71. *Green Fees:* information available on (01695 421717). *Eating facilities:* licensed bar and restaurant. *Society Meetings:* catered for - advance bookings only, contact Manager Jackie Fray (01695 421717). Professional: Brad Millar.

Lytham Green Drive Golf Club

* Founded 1913 *

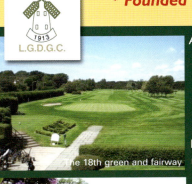
The 18th green and fairway

The Clubhouse

The 6th tee from the 1st green

The thirteenth hole is named "Harold's Beck" after the club's famous professional

At only 6,305 yards long this parkland course with links-like undulating fairways is small by modern standards, and very well-bunkered. Despite its modest length, it demands a wide variety of golf shots with its assortment of different challenges and approaches to most greens.

Laid out by 1902 Open Champion Alex Herd and re-designed in the 1940's, Lytham Green Drive is situated on the outskirts of Lytham next to the Green Drive.

This formidable little test was officially recognised when it was used as a final qualifying course for the 1974, 1979 and 1988 Open Championships held at nearby Royal Lytham & St Annes Golf Club.

Green Drive has a reputation as probably the friendliest and most sociable golf club on the Fylde. We encourage guests and the course is ideal for visitors - flat, pleasant parkland, but a bit more testing than you would expect.

Visiting parties are welcome on weekdays and Sundays. Golf packages for parties of 12 or more can be tailored to suit your requirements.

Ballam Road, Lytham St Annes, Lancashire FY8 4LE
Tel: 01253 737390
Fax: 01253 731350
e-mail:
secretary@lythamgreendrive.co.uk
www.lythamgreendrive.co.uk

Open Championship Qualifying Course 1974, 1979 and 1988

THE GOLF GUIDE 2011   NORTH REGION / Lancashire 277

ORMSKIRK. **Ormskirk Golf Club,** Cranes Lane, Lathom L40 5UJ (01695 572112). *Location:* two miles east of Ormskirk. Parkland course. 18 holes, 6358 yards. S.S.S. 70. *Green Fees:* weekdays £45.00 per round, £55.00 per day, Saturday £60.00 per round, Sunday £50.00 per round, £60.00 per day. *Eating facilities:* available except Monday. *Visitors:* welcome, Handicap Certificates required, notice advised with reservation. *Society Meetings:* catered for, book in advance. Professional: J. Hammond (01695 572074). Secretary: R.K. Oakes (01695 572227).

PRESTON. **Ashton and Lea Golf Club Ltd,** Tudor Avenue, off Blackpool Road, Lea, Preston PR4 0XA (01772 735282; Fax: 01772 735762). *Location:* on A5085, three miles west of Preston, turn opposite Toby Carvery. Parkland with water features. 18 holes, 6334 yards. S.S.S. 70. Practice ground. *Green Fees:* information not available. *Eating facilities:* full catering every day. *Visitors:* welcome but please telephone the Professional to reserve tee time. Conference and function facilities available. Reduced rates for groups of 12 or more. *Society Meetings:* catered for weekdays only, contact the Secretary. Professional: Mike Greenough (01772 720374). Secretary: (01772 735282).*
e-mail: secretary@ashtonleagolfclub.co.uk
website: www.ashtonleagolfclub.co.uk

PRESTON. **Fishwick Hall Golf Club,** Glenluce Drive, Farringdon Park, Preston PR1 5TD (01772 798300). *Location*: two minutes from Junction 31 M6, off A59 Blackburn to Preston Road. Parkland, part wooded, bounded by river. 18 holes, 6084 yards. S.S.S. 69. Small practice area. *Green Fees:* information not available. *Eating facilities:* bar, full catering available except Mondays in winter. *Visitors:* welcome unless club competition on. *Society Meetings:* welcome weekdays and Sundays. Professional: M. Watson (01772 795870). Secretary: R. E. Stamp (01772 798300; Fax: 01772 704600).*

PRESTON. **Ingol Golf Club,** Tanterton Hall Road, Ingol, Preston PR2 7BY (01772 734556; Fax: 01772 729815). *Location:* two miles from Junction 32 M6 (joins M55). Parkland. 18 holes, 6294 yards, Par 72. Chipping and putting practice areas. *Green Fees:* information not available. *Eating facilities:* bar/ restaurant. *Visitors:* welcome anytime, please telephone to check tee reservations. Buggies and trolleys available. Squash courts. Meeting room available. Stay and play packages. *Society Meetings:* welcome by arrangement. Professional: Ryan Grimshaw (01772 769646). Secretary: Marjorie Kenny (01772 734556; Fax: 01772 729815).*
website: www.ingolgolfclub.co.uk

PRESTON. **Longridge Golf Club,** Fell Barn, Jeffrey Hill, Longridge, Preston PR3 2TU (01772 783291; Fax: 01772 783022). Location: eight miles north-east of Preston off B6243. Moorland with extensive spectacular views. One of the oldest clubs in England

PENWORTHAM GOLF CLUB

On the outskirts of Preston in the heart of Lancashire, Penwortham prides itself on being a friendly and welcoming club.

Summer and Winter Golfing Packages available for groups of all sizes.

Blundell Lane, Penwortham, Preston PR1 0AX
Tel: 01772 744630
Pro Shop: 01772 742345
secretary@penworthamgc.co.uk
www.penworthamgc.co.uk

PARKLAND GOLF AT ITS BEST

(Est. 1877). 18 holes, 5975 yards. S.S.S. 69. Green Fees: weekday £17.00, weekend £25.00. Eating facilities: full catering and bars. Visitors: welcome. Society Meetings: welcome by prior arrangement. Professional: Stephen Taylor. Secretary: David Carling.
e-mail: secretary@longridgegolfclub.co.uk
website: www.longridgegolfclub.co.uk

PRESTON. **Penwortham Golf Club Ltd.,** Blundell Lane, Penwortham, Preston PR1 0AX (01772 744630; Fax: 01772 740172). *Location:* one mile west of Preston on main Southport to Liverpool road. Parkland. 18 holes, 5865 yards. S.S.S. 69. *Green Fees:* £29.00 weekdays; £39.00 weekends. *Eating facilities:* lunches and dinners served at Club. *Visitors:* welcome. *Society Meetings:* by arrangement Monday, Wednesday, Thursday, Friday only. Professional: Darren Hopwood (01772 742345). Secretary: Neil Annandale (01772 744630; Fax: 01772 740172).
e-mail: secretary@penworthamgc@co.uk
website: www.penworthamgc.co.uk

THE APPEARANCE OF AN ASTERISK (*) AT THE END OF A CLUB OR COURSE ENTRY INDICATES THAT UP-TO-DATE INFORMATION HAS NOT BEEN SUPPLIED

Lancashire / NORTH REGION

PRESTON. Preston Golf Club, Fulwood Hall Lane, Fulwood, Preston PR2 8DD (01772 700011; Fax: 01772 794234). *Location:* exit 32 on M6 marked Preston & Garstang, partway to Preston turning at Watling Street Road. Parkland course. Driving range. 18 holes, 6312 yards. S.S.S. 71. *Green Fees:* information not provided. *Eating facilities:* first class dining room, bars. *Visitors:* welcome weekdays, weekends or Bank Holidays must be accompanied by a member. *Society Meetings:* welcome except Tuesdays, weekends or Bank Holidays. Handicap Certificate required. Professional: Andrew Greenbank (01772 700022). Secretary: E. Burrow (01772 700011).

ROCHDALE. **Tunshill Golf Club Ltd,** Kiln Lane, Milnrow, Rochdale OL16 3TS (01706 342095). *Location:* two miles east of Rochdale, M62 J21. Hillside course adjacent to M62 motorway. 9 holes/18 tees, 5743 yards. S.S.S. 68. *Green Fees:* information not provided. *Visitors:* welcome during the week. *Society Meetings:* welcome.

ROSSENDALE. **Rossendale Golf Club Ltd.,** Ewood Lane Head, Haslingden, Rossendale BB4 6LH (01706 831686). *Location:* 14 miles north of Manchester, easy access from M66 and A56. 18 holes, 6293 yards. S.S.S. 71. *Green Fees:* please see website. *Eating facilities:* full catering except Mondays; bar. *Visitors:* welcome except Saturdays during season. *Society Meetings:* welcome. Professional: S.J. Nicholls (01706 213616). Hon. Secretary: K. Wilson (01706 831339; Fax: 01706 228669).
e-mail: admin@rossendalegolfclub.net
website: www.rossendalegolfclub.net

THE APPEARANCE OF AN ASTERISK (*) AT THE END OF A CLUB OR COURSE ENTRY INDICATES THAT UP-TO-DATE INFORMATION HAS NOT BEEN SUPPLIED

ST HELENS. **Houghwood, Billinge Hill,** Crank Road, Crank, St Helens WA11 8RL (Tel & Fax: 01744 894754). *Location:* ten minutes from M6. Parkland. 18 holes, 6268 yards. S.S.S. 69. Practice ground. *Green Fees:* weekdays £31.00, weekends £42.00, reduced rates for off peak. *Eating facilities:* spike bar open from 11am every day. First floor public restaurant with quality food, reasonable prices and superb views; soft spikes required by all. *Visitors:* always welcome. Snooker table. *Society Meetings:* welcome Mondays, Tuesdays and Thursdays. Professional: Paul Dickenson (01744 894444). Secretary: Julie Melling (Tel & Fax: 01744 894754).
e-mail: houghwoodgolf@btinternet.com
website: www.houghwoodgolfclub.co.uk

SCARISBRICK. **Hurlston Hall Golf & Country Club,** Hurlston Lane, Scarisbrick L40 8HB (01704 840400; Fax: 01704 841404). *Location:* six miles from Southport and two miles from Ormskirk along A570 trunk road; eight miles from M58. Parkland with several lakes and streams. 18 holes, 6540 yards. S.S.S. 72. Golf centre with 18-bay driving range, putting green. Flood-lit driving range. *Green Fees:* weekdays £40.00, weekends £45.00. For winter fees please telephone Golf Shop (01704 842829). *Eating facilities:* three bars; restaurant. *Visitors:* welcome, must book in advance. *Society Meetings:* Golf Societies welcome. Golf Centre and Driving Range (01704 842829). Director: Aoife O'Brien (01704 840400; Fax: 01704 841404).
e-mail: info@hurlstonhall.co.uk
website: www.hurlstonhall.co.uk

SILVERDALE. **Silverdale Golf Club**, Redbridge Lane, Silverdale, Carnforth LA5 0SP (01524 701300). *Location:* 10 minutes from Exit 35 off M6 to Carnforth, then two miles west, adjacent to railway station and RSPB nature reserve. Interesting heathland course with rock outcrops, half course with wide open fairways, all with excellent views. 18 holes, 5535 yards. S.S.S. 67. *Green Fees:* information not available. *Eating facilities:* full catering (except Monday), bar facilities. *Visitors:* welcome except Sundays a.m. in the summer unless with a member. *Society Meetings:* welcome by arrangement with Secretary. Secretary: Barbara Hebden (01524 701300; Fax: 01524 701986).*
e-mail: info@silverdalegolfclub.co.uk
website: www.silverdalegolfclub.co.uk

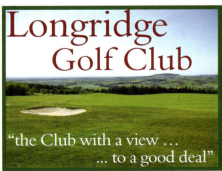

Longridge Golf Club

"the Club with a view ... ... to a good deal"

One of the oldest clubs in England, only 10 minutes from the M6 and 45 minutes from Manchester and Liverpool. Situated between the Ribble and Hodder Valleys, the Clubhouse offers magnificent views and the moorland course sits in an area of outstanding natural beauty. Visitors can be assured of a warm welcome. Full clubhouse facilities available.

Please book in advance.
**Fell Barn, Jeffrey Hill, Longridge, Preston, Lancashire PR3 2TU
Tel: 01772 783291
www.longridgegolfclub.co.uk**

HURLSTON HALL
GOLF & COUNTRY CLUB

Between Southport and Ormskirk, Hurlston Hall is set in 135 acres of peaceful undulating land with streams, lakes and fine views across to the Bowland Fells and Pennines.

The emphasis of this 18 hole, 135 acre, par 72 course is enjoyment. The strategic use of natural elevation, well placed traps and the finely sculpted contours of the greens, present an inspiring challenge.

The beautifully manicured practice putting area and a fully equipped floodlit driving range provide the perfect pre-match limber up.

Private booths allow for one on one coaching with the club's Professional, Tim Hastings. Extensive floodlighting allows for practice into the night during the darker months of the year.

A challenging round of golf on our picturesque course can be complemented by a relaxing afternoon in the fully equipped Leisure Club and Spa.

A luxurious clubhouse with 3 bars, excellent restaurant and function rooms complete an ideal venue for the discerning.

Visitors can also benefit from a wide variety of dining options with our Restaurant, Spike Bar and new Clubhouse Bistro serving a selection of locally sourced main meals and snacks.

The exciting and diverse range of facilities on offer at Hurlston Hall makes for a stimulating and enjoyable day out.

Hurlston Lane • Scarisbrick • Lancashire L40 8HB

For your golfing relaxation, corporate days, conference facilities
– just call **01704 840400**
e-mail: info@hurlstonhall.co.uk • www.hurlstonhall.co.uk

UPHOLLAND. Beacon Park Golf & Country Club, Beacon Lane, Dalton WN8 7RU (01695 625551). *Location:* ten minutes from J26 of M6. Follow signs for A577 Upholland. Undulating parkland course. Designed by Donald Steel. 18 holes, 6151 yards. S.S.S. 70. Driving range, practice ground. *Green Fees:* information not available. *Eating facilities:* fully licensed restaurant as part of the complex. *Visitors:* welcome, no restrictions, a six day advance booking system applies. Tuition available. *Society Meetings:* welcome, special deals on offer that include food and golf. Professional: Colin Parkinson (01695 622700). Secretary: Mark Prosser (01695 625551).*
e-mail: info@beaconparkgolf.com
website: www.beaconparkgolf.com

UPHOLLAND. Dean Wood Golf Club, Lafford Lane, Upholland, Skelmersdale WN8 0QZ (01695 622219). *Location:* Exit 26 from M6 signposted for Wigan. Follow A577 to Upholland, first right after church. Wooded parkland course. 18 holes, 6137 yards. S.S.S. 70. *Green Fees:* information not available. *Eating facilities:* daily catering available, bar. *Visitors:* welcome with reservation, not before 10.30am weekends and Bank Holidays. *Society Meetings:* catered for by prior arrangement. Professional: Stuart Danchin. Secretary: A.S. McGregor (01695 622219).*
e-mail: secretary@deanwoodgolfclub.co.uk*

WIGAN. Wigan Golf Club, Arley Hall, Haigh, Wigan WN1 2UH (01257 421360). *Location*: M6 Exit 27, two miles on B5329, east of Standish. Parkland. 18 holes, 6026 yards. Par 70. *Green Fees*: £30.00. *Eating facilities*: meals and bar snacks available. *Visitors*: welcome anytime except Tuesdays, Saturdays and Sundays. *Society Meetings*: catered for on Wednesdays, Thursdays and Fridays. Contact Assistant Secretary.
e-mail: info@wigangolfclub.co.uk

For full details of convenient accommodation near clubs and courses
www.holidayguides.com

Beacon Park Golf Club
Dalton, Upholland, West Lancs WN8 7RU
info@beaconparkgolf.com • www.beaconparkgolf.com
"One of the 10 best golf courses in the UK" – *The Independent 2006.*
Societies welcome • Pro Shop 01695 622700

Be prepared for a pleasant surprise

Shaw Hill Hotel, Golf & Country Club, near Chorley

Greater Manchester

ALTRINCHAM. **Altrincham Golf Club,** Stockport Road, Timperley, Altrincham, Cheshire WA15 7LP (0161-928 0761). *Location:* one mile east of Altrincham on A560. Parkland. 18 holes, 6190 yards, 5659 metres. S.S.S. 69. Driving range. *Green Fees:* information not available. *Eating facilities:* Old Hall Hotel attached to course. *Visitors:* welcome any time, book one week in advance. Public course. Professional: Scott Partington Secretary: C. J. Schofield.*

ALTRINCHAM. **Dunham Forest Golf and Country Club,** Oldfield Lane, Altrincham WA14 4TY (0161-928 2605; Fax: 0161-929 8975). *Location:* approximately 9 miles south of Manchester off A56. Wooded parkland. 18 holes, 6630 yards. S.S.S. 72. *Green Fees:* weekdays £58.00, weekends £68.00. 2010 rates (subject to review). *Eating facilities:* clubhouse restaurant and bar open daily. *Visitors:* welcome, but should telephone to check availability. *Society Meetings:* welcome by prior arrangement. Professional: I. Wrigley (0161-928 2727). Secretary: Mrs A. Woolf (0161-928 2605).

ALTRINCHAM. **Hale Golf Club,** Rappax Road, Hale, Altrincham WA15 0NU (0161-980 4225). *Location*: off Bankhall Lane near Altrincham Priory Hospital. Undulating parkland with River Bollin featuring on 3 holes. 9 hole course (played twice for a round), 5780 yards, S.S.S. 68. Practice ground. *Green Fees:* £30.00 per day. *Eating facilities:* by arrangement with Steward; lunches available, dinner; two bars. *Visitors:* welcome weekdays (except Thursday), weekends by arrangement with Hon. Secretary. Meetings: by arrangement with Hon. Secretary. Professional: Richard Booth (0161-904 0835). Hon. Secretary: Chris Wood (0161-980 4225).

ALTRINCHAM. **Ringway Golf Club Ltd,** Hale Road, Hale Barns, Altrincham WA15 8SW (0161-980 2630). *Location:* Junction 6, M56 then A538 signposted Hale and Altrincham, one mile. Parkland. 18 holes, 6482 yards. S.S.S. 71. Putting green, short game area and practice ground. *Green Fees:* weekdays £45.00, weekends and Bank Holidays £55.00. 2010 rates (subject to review). *Eating facilities:* full service except Mondays (snacks only). *Visitors:* generally not on Tuesdays, Fridays or Saturdays. *Society Meetings:* catered for by arrangement. Professional: Nick Ryan (0161-980 8432). Secretary: F. Cornelius (0161-980 2630; Fax: 0161-980 4414).

ASHTON-IN-MAKERFIELD. **Ashton-in-Makerfield Golf Club Ltd,** Garswood Park, Liverpool Road, Ashton-in-Makerfield, Wigan WN4 0YT (01942 727267). *Location:* M6, Junction 23 from south, Junction 24 from north. Parkland course. 18 holes, 6205 yards. S.S.S. 70. *Green Fees:* information not povided. *Eating facilities:* available. *Visitors:* welcome mid-week (except Wednesday) with reservation but not before 9.45am. *Society Meetings:* catered for Mondays, Tuesdays, Thursdays, Fridays and some Sundays by prior appointment. Professional: P. Allan (01942 724229). Secretary: G.S. Lacy (01942 719330).

ASHTON-UNDER-LYNE. **Ashton-under-Lyne Golf Club,** Gorsey Way, Ashton-under-Lyne OL6 9HT (0161-330 1537; Fax: 0161-330 6673). *Location*: three miles from town centre, Mossley Road, left at Queens Road, right at Nook Lane, Clubhouse top of St. Christopher's Road. Wooded course. 18 holes, 6209 yards. S.S.S. 70. Practice ground. *Green Fees*: information not available. *Eating facilities*: full catering except Mondays. *Visitors*: welcome weekdays except Wednesdays; members of recognised golf clubs welcome without reservation. *Society Meetings*: catered for on application: special daily rates. Professional: Mr Colin Boyle (0161-308 2095). Secretary: Mr A.H. Jackson.*
e-mail: info@ashtongolfclub.co.uk
website: www.ashtongolfclub.co.uk.

BOLTON. **Bolton Golf Club Ltd,** Lostock Park, Chorley New Road, Bolton BL6 4AJ (01204 843067). *Location:* off main road halfway between Bolton and Horwich. 18 holes, 6237 yards. S.S.S. 70. *Green Fees:* winter: (1 Nov-31 March) £25.00, summer (1 April-31 Oct) £36.00 per round, £44.00 per day. Fourball £120.00. *Eating facilities:* luncheons and evening meals. *Visitors:* welcome. *Society Meetings:* catered for weekdays except Tuesdays. Professional: D. Fitzgergald (01204 843073). Secretary: S. Higham (Tel & Fax: 01204 843067)

THE APPEARANCE OF AN ASTERISK (*) AT THE END OF A CLUB OR COURSE ENTRY INDICATES THAT UP-TO-DATE INFORMATION HAS NOT BEEN SUPPLIED

Ashton Under Lyne Golf Club
An enjoyable day's golf. A challenge for golfers of all abilities.
Green fees £27, weekends £27 with member only.
Visiting Societies welcome by arrangement. **Telephone: 0161 330 1537**
e-mail: **info@ashtongolfclub.co.uk** • **www.ashtongolfclub.co.uk**

BOLTON. **Bolton Old Links Golf Club Ltd,** Chorley Old Road, Montserrat, Bolton BL1 5SU (01204 842307). *Location:* on B6226, 400 yards north of roundabout on ring road. Championship course, moorland. 18 holes, 6479 yards. S.S.S. 72. Practice facilities, indoor net. *Green Fees:* £35.00 weekdays, £45.00 weekends. *Eating facilities:* available. *Visitors:* welcome except weekends. *Society Meetings:* packages available weekdays. Professional: P. Horridge (01204 843089). Secretary: Mrs J. Boardman (01204 842307).

BOLTON. **Breightmet Golf Club,** Red Bridge, Ainsworth, Bolton BL2 5PA (01204 399275). *Location*: leave Bolton on main road to Bury, turn left two miles on Milnthorpe road for the bridge. 18 holes, 6405 yards. S.S.S. 71. *Green Fees*: information not available. *Eating facilities*: lunches and light refreshments. *Visitors:* welcome, preliminary phone call advisable. *Society Meetings*: catered for on application. Secretary: I.D. Cooke.*

BOLTON. **Deane Golf Club,** Broadford Road, Deane, Bolton BL3 4NS (01204 61944). *Location:* one mile east of Junction 5 of M61 towards Bolton Centre. Rolling parkland with number of small ravines to cross. 18 holes, 5652 yards, 5168 metres. S.S.S. 68. *Green Fees:* weekdays £25.00; weekends £30.00. *Eating facilities:* lunches and evening meals by arrangement. *Visitors:* welcome. *Society Meetings:* Tuesdays, Thursdays and Fridays only. Professional: David Martindale. Secretary: P. Parry (01204 651808; Fax: 01204 652047).
e-mail: secretary@deanegolfclub.com
website: www.deanegolfclub.co.uk

BOLTON. **Dunscar Golf Club Ltd,** Longworth Lane, Bromley Cross, Bolton BL7 9QY (01204 303321). *Location:* one and a half miles north of Bolton on A666. Parkland, moorland course. 18 holes, 5995 yards. S.S.S. 69. Practice ground available. *Green Fees:* weekdays £27.50, weekends £33.00. *Eating facilities:* available. *Visitors:* welcome, on Sunday by arrangement. Carts available. *Society Meetings:* catered for by arrangement with the Secretary. Professionals: Andy Green and Mark Gregory (01204 592992). Secretary: Alison Jennings (01204 303321). e-mail: dunscargolfclub@uk2.net

BOLTON. **Great Lever and Farnworth Golf Club Ltd,** Plodder Lane, Farnworth, Bolton BL4 0LQ (01204 656650; Fax: 01204 656137). *Location:* A666 or M61 (Junction 4), two miles from Bolton town centre. Parkland. 18 holes, 5745 yards. S.S.S. 68. Practice ground. *Green Fees:* information not available. *Eating facilities:* restaurant and bar every day except Monday. *Visitors:* welcome, preferably by appointment. *Society Meetings:* welcome weekdays. Professional: Tony Howarth (01204 656650). Secretary: Mrs J. Ivill (Tel & Fax: 01204 656137).*

BOLTON. **Harwood Golf Club,** Roading Brook Road, Harwood, Bolton BL2 4JD (01204 522878). *Location:* situated just off the B6196 three miles east of Bolton between Harwood and Ainsworth. Parkland/ meadowland course. 18 holes, 5915 yards. S.S.S. 69. Par 70. Large practice area. *Green Fees:* £25.00, £12.00 with a member. *Eating facilities:* catering available Tuesday to Sunday (Monday by arrangement). *Visitors:* welcome weekdays only, weekends only with a member. Should be members of recognised golf club or society. Carts allowed. *Society Meetings:* Monday to Saturday by arrangement with the Secretary. Professional: Clive Loydell (01204 522878). Secretary: Harold Howard (01204 522878).
e-mail: haroldwendy.howard219@ntlworld.com
website: www.harwoodgolfclub.co.uk

BOLTON. **Regent Park Golf Club Ltd,** Links Road, off Chorley New Road, Lostock, Bolton BL6 4AF (01204 495421). *Location:* midway between Bolton and Horwich, A763. Parkland, stream and ditches cross five fairways, par 5 start, out of bounds to the left; 18 holes, 6217 yards. S.S.S. 69. Driving range and practice chipping to green; floodlit, automated golf driving range. *Green Fees:* £13.00 weekdays, £16.00 weekends and Bank Holidays. *Eating facilities:* meals/bar available. *Visitors:* welcome seven days, telephone Professional to book time slot. Buggies and club hire. *Society Meetings:* welcome every day. Book in advance. Professional: Neil Brazzel (01204 842336/ 495421). Secretary: K. J. Taylor (01204 652882).

Turton Golf Club

Wood End Farm,
Hospital Road,
Bromley Cross,
Bolton BL7 9QD
Tel: 01204 852235

One of the North Wests premier 18 hole golf courses

Challenging mixture of moorland and parkland • 18 holes, 6119 yards, Par 70
• Green Fees: April to October £32 day; weekends & BHs £40 day.
November to March £20 per day • Golf society packages
• Places of interest list • Call General Manager, Andrew Scully
e-mail: info@turtongolfclub.com • www.turtongolfclub.com

NORTH REGION / Greater Manchester

BOLTON. **Turton Golf Club,** Wood End Farm, Hospital Road, Bromley Cross, Bolton BL7 9QD (01204 852235). *Location:* three miles north of Bolton off the A666; follow signs for Last Drop Village, literally a few hundred yards up the hill from the Last Drop. Host to Bolton Championship 2003. An interesting and challenging 18 hole moorland golf course with stunning views across seven counties. 6119 yards. S.S.S. 69. Practice area. *Green Fees:* weekdays £32.00 per day; weekends £40.00 per day. Nov-March £20.00 per day. *Eating facilities:* Bar and restaurant. *Visitors:* welcome, Monday, Tuesday, Thursday, Friday and Sunday. Please call for availability on any day. *Societies:* welcome by arrangement. Changing facilities; lockers, pro shop, buggies and trolley hire. General Manager: A. Scully (01204 852235).
e-mail: info@turtongolfclub.com
website: www.turtongolfclub.com

BURY. **Bury Golf Club,** Unsworth Hall, Blackford Bridge, Bury BL9 9TJ (0161-766 4897; Fax: 0161-766 3480). *Location:* A56 between Whitefield and Bury. Semi-moorland course, tight fairways, good greens. 18 holes, 5927 yards. S.S.S. 69. Small practice area. *Green Fees:* weekdays £30.00, with a member £15.00; weekends £35.00, with a member £18.00. *Eating facilities:* restaurant and bar. *Visitors:* welcome, Tuesday is Ladies' Day. Handicap Certificate will be required prior to play. *Society Meetings:* welcome; check website for details. Professional: G. Coope (0161-766 2213). Secretary: D. Parkinson.
e-mail: secretary@burygolfclub.com
website: www.burygolfclub.com

BURY. **Greenmount Golf Club,** Greenhalgh Fold Farm, Greenmount, Bury BL8 4LH (01204 883712). *Location:* three miles north of Bury. Undulating parkland. 9 holes, 6214 yards. S.S.S. 70. *Green Fees:* information not available. *Eating facilities:* available, clubhouse closed all day Monday. *Visitors:* welcome, weekends with members only, Tuesday – Ladies' Day. *Society Meetings:* welcome. Secretary: David Beesley (0161 761 7609).*

BURY. **Lowes Park Golf Club Ltd,** Hill Top, Lowes Road, Bury BL9 6SU (0161-764 1231). *Location:* take A56 north from Bury, turn right at Sundial Inn into Lowes Road. Moorland course, exposed, easy walking. 9 holes, 6009 yards. S.S.S. 69. Small practice area. *Green Fees:* information not available. *Eating facilities:* full catering except Mondays. *Visitors:* welcome weekdays except Wednesdays (Ladies' Day); weekends, Sunday by appointment. *Society Meetings:* catered for by appointment. Secretary: Alan Taylor (0161-764 1231; Fax: 0161-763 9503).*
e-mail: lowesparkgc@btconnect.com

BURY. **Pike Fold Golf Club,** Hills Lane, Unsworth, Bury BL9 8QP (0161-766 3561). *Location:* just off the Whitfield turn off on the M60. New course with an abundance of water and USA specification greens. 18 holes, 6252 yards, Par 71. *Green Fees:* weekdays £30.00; Saturday £35.00. *Eating facilities:* restaurant and bar facilities available at all times. *Visitors:* welcome weekdays without reservation. *Society Meetings:* catered for Tuesday to Friday. Hon. Secretary: Martin Jeffs.
e-mail: secretary@pikefold.co.uk
website: www.pikefold.co.uk

BURY. **Walmersley Golf Club,** Garretts Close, Walmersley, Bury BL9 6TE (0161-764 1429). *Location:* leave A56 approximately two miles north of Bury at Walmersley Post Office into Old Road, right at Masons Arms Inn. Moorland course. 18 holes, 6064 yards, 5546 metres. S.S.S. 70. *Green Fees:* £40.00. *Eating facilities:* lunches and evening meals served except Mondays. *Visitors:* welcome weekdays except Tuesday afternoon. *Society Meetings:* weekdays. Professional: M. Eubank (0161-763 9050). Secretary: V. Slater (0161-764 1429).

DAVYHULME. **Davyhulme Park Golf Club,** Gleneagles Road, Davyhulme, Urmston M41 8SA (0161-748 2260). *Location:* one mile from M60/M62. Wooded parkland, flat course. 18 holes, 6237 yards. S.S.S. 70. *Green Fees:* information not available. *Eating facilities:* lunches and dinners. *Visitors:* welcome Tuesdays and Thursdays. *Society Meetings:* catered for Tuesdays and Thursdays. Professional: Dean Butler (0161-748 3931). Secretary: G.R. Swarbrick (0161-748 2260).*

DENTON. **Denton Golf Club,** Manchester Road, Denton M34 2GG (0161-336 3218; Fax: 0161-336 4751). *Location:* M60 Junction 24 to Manchester (A57), after quarter of a mile turn right at traffic lights. Parkland. 18 holes, 6443 yards, 5891 metres. S.S.S. 71. Practice area and putting green. Meeting facilities. *Green Fees:* weekdays £28.00; weekends and Bank Holidays £35.00. 2010 rates (subject to review). *Eating facilities:* catering by arrangement. *Visitors:* welcome with Club Handicap. *Society Meetings:* catered for on Wednesday to Friday. Professional: Michael Hollingworth (0161-336 2070; Fax: 0161-336 4751). Secretary (0161-336 3218; Fax: 0161-336 4751).
e-mail: info@dentongolfclub.com
website: www.dentongolfclub.com

DUKINFIELD. **Dukinfield Golf Club,** Lyne Edge, Yew Tree Lane, Dukinfield SK16 5GF (0161-338 2340). Location: six miles east of Manchester via Ashton-under-Lyne. Parkland. 18 holes, 5303 yards. S.S.S. 66. *Green Fees:* information not available. *Eating facilities:* full catering and bar facilities. *Visitors:* welcome except Wednesdays noon to 2pm and 4pm to 6pm and weekends. Times may be booked in advance by phoning Pro Shop. *Society Meetings:* catered for by prior arrangement; special package rates available. Professional: David Green. Secretary: Bob Winterbottom (0161-338 2760).

Please mention THE GOLF GUIDE when you enquire about clubs or accommodation

Greater Manchester / NORTH REGION

ECCLES. **Worsley Golf Club,** Stableford Avenue, Monton, Eccles M30 8AP (0161-789 4202). *Location:* A580 East Lancs Road, one mile from Junction 13 M60. Parkland. 18 holes, 6200 yards. S.S.S. 70. *Green Fees:* £30.00 weekdays; £35.00 weekends. *Eating facilities:* snacks, lunches and evening meals. *Visitors:* welcome, if past or present members of recognised golf clubs. *Society Meetings:* catered for Mondays, Wednesdays, Thursdays and Fridays. Professional: Andrew Cory. Hon. Secretary: M. Heath. Chief Executive: J.D. Clarke
e-mail: secretary@worsleygolfclub.co.uk
website: www.worsleygolfclub.co.uk

FLIXTON. **Acre Gate Golf Club,** Pennybridge Lane, Flixton, Manchester M41 5DX (0161 748 1226 (Sat/Sun). *Location:* off Flixton Road downside of Bird in the Hand public house. Flat parkland course. 18 holes, Par 64. Chipping area, putting green, practice net and bunkers. *Green Fees:* information not provided. *Eating facilities:* food and drink available at clubhouse by prior arrangement. *Visitors:* course is Municipal (William Wroe Golf Course) and bookings, in advance, with Golf Shop. William Wroe Golf Course Shop/Professional: (0161-748 8680).

HORWICH. **Horwich Golf Club,** Victoria Road, Horwich, Bolton BL6 5PH (01204 696980). *Location:* Junction 6 M61 - Chorley New Road - Victoria Road, Horwich. Tight tricky course, hilly with fast greens. 9 holes, 5286 yards, 4832 metres. S.S.S. 66. *Green Fees:* information not available. *Eating facilities:* dining and bar. *Visitors:* Wednesday Ladies' Day but tee times still available. Snooker room. *Society Meetings:* by arrangement. Professional: B. Sharrock. Secretary: C. Sherborne.*

HYDE. **Werneth Low Golf Club Ltd,** Werneth Low Road, Hyde, Cheshire SK14 3AF (0161-368 2503). *Location:* M67 to Hyde, through town to Gee Cross turn left to NLQC. Scenic, hilly course with excellent views, postage stamp greens, terrific test of golf. 18 holes,(7,4,7) 6550 yards. S.S.S. 70. *Green Fees:* information not available. *Eating facilities:* bar snacks daily, à la carte by arrangement. *Visitors:* welcome any time except Sunday before 4pm and Tuesday mornings and after 4pm. *Society Meetings:* catered for by prior arrangement. Professional: Tony Bacchus (0161-367 9376). Secretary: M. Gregg (0161-336 9496; Fax: 0161-320 0053).*
e-mail: mel.gregg@btinternet.com

LEIGH. **Pennington Golf Club (Municipal),** Pennington Golf Course, Pennington Country Park, off St Helens Road, Leigh WN7 3PA. *Location*: Junction 23 on M6 follow A580 towards Manchester, then follow signs for Pennington Flash. Flat parkland with water coursing through. 9 holes, 5638 yards. S.S.S. 67. Par 70. *Green Fees:* 9 holes: weekdays £5.40, weekends and Bank Holidays £6.70. *Eating facilities:* snack facilities. *Visitors:* welcome, no restrictions. Bookings: (01942 682852). Secretary: Mrs A. Lythgoe (01942 741873).

LITTLEBOROUGH. **Whittaker Golf Club,** Whittaker Lane, Littleborough OL15 0LH (01706 378310). *Location:* one mile from town centre along Blackstone Edge Old Road. Moorland course. 9 holes, 5632 yards. S.S.S. 67. *Green Fees:* weekdays £15.00, weekends and Bank Holidays £20.00. *Eating facilities:* bar only. *Visitors:* welcome without reservation, except Tuesday afternoons and Sundays. *Society Meetings:* weekdays and Saturdays only by prior arrangement with Secretary. Secretary: S. Noblett (01706 842541).

MANCHESTER. **Blackley Golf Club,** Victoria Avenue East, Blackley, Manchester M9 7HW (0161-643 2980). *Location:* five miles north from City Centre. Parkland. 18 holes, 6217 yards, 5708 metres. S.S.S. 69. *Green Fees:* £24.00. *Eating facilities:* diningroom/bar. *Visitors:* welcome, Thursdays and weekends with member only. *Society Meetings:* catered for. Professional: Craig Gould (0161-643 3912). Secretary: Brenda Beddoes (0161-654 7770; Fax: 0161 653 8300).

MANCHESTER. **Brookdale Golf Club Ltd,** Medlock Road, Woodhouses, Failsworth, Manchester M35 9WQ (Tel & Fax: 0161-681 4534). *Location:* five miles north of Manchester. Parkland course, hilly with river running through. 18 holes, 5874 yards. S.S.S. 68. Small practice ground. *Green Fees:* information not provided. *Eating facilities:* bar snacks available; evening meal by prior arrangement. *Visitors:* welcome, only with a member weekends. *Society Meetings:* welcome except Tuesdays (Ladies' Day). Package Deal £35.00 by arrangement. Professional: Tony Cuppello (0161-681 2655). Secretary: F. Woodworth (Tel & Fax: 0161-681 4534).
website: www.brookdalegolfclub.co.uk

MANCHESTER. **Chorlton-cum-Hardy Golf Club,** Barlow Hall Road, Chorlton-cum-Hardy M21 7JJ (0161-881 3139; Fax: 0161-881 4532). *Location:* near junction of A5145 and A5103 (M60) Barlow Moor Road, South Cemetery. Meadowland. 18 holes, 5980 yards. S.S.S. 69. *Green Fees:* information not available. *Eating facilities:* catering 7 days a week. *Visitors:* welcome without reservation, except on Competition days, must provide proof of recognised Handicap. *Society Meetings:* catered for Thursdays and Fridays by arrangement with Secretary. Professional: D.R. Valentine (0161-881 9911). Secretary: I.R. Booth (0161-881 5830).*

THE GOLF GUIDE 2011   NORTH REGION / Greater Manchester

MANCHESTER. **Didsbury Golf Club Ltd,** Ford Lane, Northenden, Manchester M22 4NQ (0161-998 9278). *Location:* Junction 5 on M60 to Palatine Road, to Church Road, to Ford Lane. Riverside parkland. 18 holes, 6276 yards. S.S.S. 70. Good practice facilities. *Green Fees:* information not available. *Eating facilities:* fully equipped bar and restaurant. *Visitors:* welcome 10am to 12 noon and 1.30pm to 4pm except competition times and match days. *Society Meetings:* catered for Mondays (pm), Thursdays, Fridays and Sundays (pm). Professional: P. Barber (Tel & Fax: 0161-998 2811). Manager: J. K. Mort (0161-998 9278; Fax: 0161-902 3060).*
e-mail: golf@didsburygolfclub.com
website: www.didsburygolfclub.com

MANCHESTER. **Ellesmere Golf Club,** Old Clough Lane, Worsley, Manchester M28 7HZ (Tel & Fax: 0161-790 2122). *Location:* off A580 East Lancs Road, adjacent to M60 (clockwise) northbound, (eastbound) access. Wooded parkland. 18 holes, 6247 yards. S.S.S. 70. *Green Fees:* information not available. *Eating facilities:* bar; catering available, with or without reservation. *Visitors:* members of recognised golf clubs welcome, but not during club competitions, contact Professional for restrictions. *Society Meetings:* catered for by appointment. Professional: Simon Wakefield (0161-790 8591). Secretary: A.T. Leaver (0161-799 0554).
e-mail: honsec.egc@btconnect.com

MANCHESTER. **Fairfield Golf and Sailing Club,** "Boothdale", Booth Road, Audenshaw, Manchester M34 5QA *Location:* off A635, five miles east of Manchester. Parkland bounded in part by reservoir. 18 holes, 6062 yards. S.S.S. 69. *Green Fees:* information not available. *Eating facilities:* available. *Visitors:* welcome, restrictions Wednesdays and weekends. *Society Meetings:* catered for by prior arrangement midweek. Professional: Steven Pownell (0161-301 4528). Manager: Jeff Johnson (0161-301 4528; Fax: 0161 301 4254).
e-mail: manager@fairfieldgolfclub.co.uk
website: www.fairfieldgolfclub.co.uk

MANCHESTER. **Flixton Golf Club,** Church Road, Flixton, Urmston M41 6EP (Tel & Fax: 0161-748 2116). *Location:* five miles from Manchester on B5213. Parkland. 9 holes, 6410 yards. S.S.S. 71. *Green Fees:* weekdays £18.00, with member £10.00; weekends and Bank Holidays £25.00, with member £15.00. *Eating facilities:* daily. *Visitors:* welcome, please contact Professional or Administrator. *Society Meetings:* catered for by arrangement. Professional: M. Williams. Hon. Secretary: A. Braithwaite (Tel & Fax: 0161-748 2116). Catering: (0161-749 8834).

MANCHESTER. **Heaton Park Golf Centre**, Middleton Road, Prestwich, Manchester M25 2SW (0161-654 9899; Fax: 0161-653 2003). *Location*: Junction 19 M60. Undulating mature parkland, J.H. Taylor designed. 18 holes, 5755 yards. S.S.S. 68. Also 18-hole Par 3 pitch and putt course. *Green Fees:* Main Course: adults weekdays £16.00 peak, £11.00 twilight; adults weekends £20.00 peak, £12.00 off-peak. Par 3 course: £6.00/£5.00 peak, £4.00/£5.00 off-peak. *Eating facilities:* spike bar and dining/function room; range of meals and snacks available. *Visitors*: welcome 7 days a week. Pro Shop, Teaching Academy and tuition available. *Society Meetings:* Society bookings a speciality. Professional: Gary Dermott. General Manager: Brian Dique.
e-mail: heatonpark@btconnect.com
website: www.mackgolf.co.uk

MANCHESTER. **Houldsworth Golf Club Ltd,** Houldsworth Street, Reddish, Stockport SK5 6BN (0161-442 1712). *Location*: off A6 between Manchester and Stockport, close to M60. Flat parkland with water hazards. 18 holes, 6209 yards. S.S.S. 70, Par 71. Practice area. *Green Fees:* information not available. *Eating facilities:* bar snacks, or full restaurant service. *Visitors:* must be pre-arranged with Professional or Office Manager. *Society Meetings:* Monday, Thursday and Friday, catered for on application to Professional. Professional: Daniel Marsh (0161-442 1714).
e-mail: secretary@houldsworthgolfclub.co.uk
website: www.houldsworthgolfclub.co.uk

Didsbury Golf Club

- Established parkland course • Par 70, 6210 yards
- Visitors and Societies welcome
  - Full food and beverage facilities
    - Easy access from M60 and M56
      - Manchester's 'friendly' club

Didsbury Golf Club, Ford Lane, Northenden, Manchester M22 4NQ • Tel: 0161 998 9278
e-mail: golf@didsburygolfclub.com
www.didsburygolfclub.com

Situated just off junction 19 of the new M60 motorway, The New North Manchester Golf Club at Rhodes provides a testing challenge for any golfer, regardless of ability. Its wealth of natural hazards, occasional lakes and abundance of trees, makes for an adventurous layout, coupled with picturesque views.

The New North Manchester Golf Club
Rhodes House
Manchester Old Road
Middleton, Manchester M24 4PE
Telephone: 0161 643 9033
Pro: 0161 643 7094
e-mail: tee@nmgc.co.uk
www.northmanchestergolfclub.co.uk

MANCHESTER. **The Manchester Golf Club Ltd.,** Hopwood Cottage, Rochdale Road, Middleton, Manchester M24 6QP (0161-643 3202). *Location:* M62 Junction 20 to Middleton. Moorland/parkland. 18 holes, 6491 yards, 5935 metres. S.S.S. 72. Large practice ground. Driving range. *Green Fees:* weekdays £50.00 per round, £60.00 per day; weekends £55.00 per round. *Eating facilities:* two bars; restaurant booking by arrangement. *Visitors:* welcome weekdays. *Society Meetings:* parties up to 120 catered for by arrangement. Professional: B. Connor (0161-643 2638). Secretary: S. Armstead (0161-643 3202).
e-mail: secretary@mangc.co.uk
website: www.mangc.co.uk

MANCHESTER. **New North Manchester Golf Club Ltd,** Rhodes House, Manchester Old Road, Middleton, Manchester M24 4PE (0161-643 2941). *Location:* A576, less than one mile from Junction 19 on M60. Rolling parkland including lakes. 18 holes, 6436 yards. S.S.S. 71. Large practice area. *Green Fees:* information not available. *Eating facilities:* catering every day. *Visitors:* welcome most days, please telephone for course availability. *Society Meetings:* welcome, contact Professional for details. Reductions available for societies over 12. Professional: J. Peel (0161-643 7094).Manager: G. Heaslip (0161-643 9033; Fax: 0161-643 7775).*
e-mail: tee@nmgc.co.uk
website: www.northmanchestergolfclub.co.uk

MANCHESTER. **Northenden Golf Club,** Palatine Road, Northenden, Manchester M22 4FR (0161-998 4738; Fax: 0161-945 5592). *Location:* half a mile off Junction 2 M56, half a mile off Junction 5 M60. Parkland with plenty of trees, first six tees on bank of river. 18 holes, 6452 yards. S.S.S. 71. Practice net. *Green Fees:* available on request. *Eating facilities:* available (0161-998 4738 opt.4). *Visitors:* welcome most days, preferably with reservation. Restrictions 11.30am to 1.30pm Monday to Friday, Thursday Ladies' Day. Trolleys available. *Society Meetings:* catered for Tuesdays and Fridays only. Professional: Grant Doyle (0161-945 3386; Fax: 0161-945 5592). Manager: (0161-998 4738; Fax: 0161-945 5592).

MANCHESTER. **Prestwich Golf Club,** Hilton Lane, Prestwich, Manchester M25 9XB (0161-772 0700). *Location:* one mile from Junction 17 of the M60 on the A6044. Parkland. 18 holes, 4819 yards. S.S.S. 64. *Green Fees:* information not available. *Eating facilities:* available Tuesday to Sunday (no catering on Mondays). *Visitors:* welcome weekdays. *Society Meetings:* catered for weekdays, special rates for parties of 16 and over. Professional: Mark Pearson (0161-773 1404). Exec. Member for Administration: Tom Walker (0161-772 0700).*
website: www.prestwichgolf.co.uk

MANCHESTER. **Stand Golf Club,** The Dales, Ashbourne Grove, Whitefield, Bury, Manchester M45 7NL (0161-766 2388). *Location:* M62 Exit 17, A56/A665 one mile. Undulating parkland with sandy subsoil, playable all year round. 18 holes, 6426 yards. S.S.S. 71. *Green Fees:* weekdays £35.00; weekends £40.00. Various Society packages; information on request. *Eating facilities:* meals served daily and bar except Mondays, order in advance. *Visitors:* welcome Monday to Friday; weekends by prior arrangement. *Society Meetings:* welcome Wednesday/Friday by prior arrangement. Professional: Mark Dance (0161-766 2214). Hon. Secretary: Trevor E. Thacker (0161-766 3197; Fax: 0161-796 3234).
website: www.standgolfclub.co.uk

MANCHESTER. **Swinton Park Golf Club,** East Lancashire Road, Swinton, Manchester M27 5LX (0161-794 1785). *Location:* on the A580 Manchester to Liverpool Road, five miles from Manchester centre. Parkland course. 18 holes. White tees 6726 yards – Yellow tees 6519 yards. Practice area. *Green Fees:* information not available. *Eating facilities:* full catering facilities available. *Society meetings:* welcome, please ring for details. Conferencing, meetings and banqueting facilities. Private hire also available Corporate golf days catered for. Professional: J. Wilson (0161-793 8077). General Manager: Barbara Wood (0161-794 0861; Fax: 0161-281 0698).*

MANCHESTER. **Withington Golf Club,** 243 Palatine Road, West Didsbury, Manchester M20 2UE (0161-445 9544). *Location:* three miles from Manchester city centre, adjacent M56 and M63. Flat parkland. 18 holes, 6410 yards. S.S.S. 70. *Green Fees:* information not available. *Eating facilities:* lunches and evening meals to order. Snacks available at all times. *Visitors:* welcome except Thursdays, and weekends which are by prior arrangement. Ring Professional for times. *Society Meetings:* catered for by arrangement with the Secretary. Professional: S. Marr (0161-445 4861). Secretary/Manager: Patrick Keane (0161-445 9544).*
e-mail: secretary@withingtongolfclub.org.uk

MARPLE. **Marple Golf Club,** Barnsfold Road, Marple, Stockport SK6 7EL (0161-427 2311). *Location:* off A6 at Hawk Green sign. Parkland. 18 holes, 5554yards. S.S.S. 67. Practice area. *Green Fees:* information not provided. *Eating facilities:* full meals available every day along with bar snacks. *Visitors:* welcome, not competition days or Tuesdays between 10am and midday or Thursdays between 11am and 3.30pm. *Society Meetings:* all welcome by arrangement with Professional. Professional: D. Myers (0161-427 1195). Secretary: W. Hibbert (Tel & Fax: 0161-427 2311).
e-mail: secretary@marple-golf-club.org.uk

OLDHAM. **Crompton and Royton Golf Club Ltd,** High Barn, Royton, Oldham OL2 6RW (0161-624 0986; Fax: 0161-652 4711). *Location:* near Junction 20 follow signs to Oldham/Royton. Heathland. 18 holes, 6186 yards. S.S.S. 70. Nets. *Green Fees:* Sunday and Bank Holidays £20.00 per round; all other times £17.50 per round. *Eating facilities:* lunches and meals served, except Mondays. *Visitors:* welcome without reservation, not on Saturdays. *Society Meetings:* catered for by arrangement with Steward. Professional: Martin Beaty (0161 624 0986). Hon. Secretary (0161-624 0986). Steward: (0161 624 0986 or mobile 07791 536785).

OLDHAM. **Oldham Golf Club,** Lees New Road, Oldham OL4 5PN (0161-624 4986). *Location:* B6194 between Ashton-under-Lyne and Oldham. Moorland course. 18 holes, 5122 yards. S.S.S. 65. *Green Fees:* weekdays £20.00, weekends £25.00. 2-Fore-1 vouchers welcome. *Eating facilities:* full catering available. No catering Mondays. *Visitors:* welcome, telephone to check for competitions, especially weekends. *Society Meetings:* catered for by prior arrangement with Secretary. Professional: J. Rowlands (0161-626 8346). Secretary: J. Brooks (0161-624 4986).
e-mail (club): info@oldhamgolfclub.com
e-mail (Pro): james-golfpro@hotmail.co.uk

OLDHAM. **Saddleworth Golf Club,** Mountain Ash, Ladcastle Road, Uppermill, Near Oldham OL3 6LT (01457 873653). *Location:* five miles from Oldham – M62. A moorland course with superb views of the Pennines. 18 holes, 6118 yards. S.S.S. 69. Practice area. *Green Fees:* information not provided. *Eating facilities:* snacks and meals available. *Visitors:* welcome weekdays. Ladies' Day Thursdays. Buggies available. *Society Meetings:* groups of 12 or more catered for except weekends. Professional: R.I. Johnson (01457 810412; Fax: 01457 820647). Secretary: Paul Green (01457 873653).

OLDHAM. **Werneth Golf Club,** 124 Green Lane, Garden Suburb, Oldham OL8 3AZ (0161-624 1190). 18 holes, 5363 yards. S.S.S. 66. Practice ground. *Green Fees:* £18.00 weekdays only. *Eating facilities:* full catering service available. *Visitors:* welcome, ring for details. *Society Meetings:* catered for, ring for details. Professional: James Matterson (Tel & Fax: 0161-628 7136). Secretary: John Barlow (0161-624 1190).

ROCHDALE. **Castle Hawk Golf Club,** Chadwick Lane, Castleton, Rochdale OL11 3BY (01706 640841; Fax: 01706 860587). *Location:* five minutes from exit 20 M62. Parkland course. 18 holes, 2699 yards. S.S.S. 55. 9 holes, 5398 yards, S.S.S. 66. Driving range. *Green Fees:* information not available. *Eating facilities:* fully licensed bar and restaurant. *Visitors:* welcome. Trolley and equipment hire. Tuition available, fully stocked Pro shop. *Society Meetings:* welcome. Professional: Andy Duncan. Secretary: Louise Entwistle.*
e-mail: teeoff@castlehawk.co.uk
website: www.castlehawk.co.uk

ROCHDALE. **Lobden Golf Club,** Whitworth, Near Rochdale OL12 8XJ (Tel & Fax: 01706 343228). *Location:* take A671 from Rochdale, turn right at Dog and Partridge Pub in Whitworth. Moorland. 9 holes, 5697 yards, 5212 metres. S.S.S. 68. *Green Fees:* weekdays £12.00; weekends £15.00, £10.00 at all times with a member. 2010 rates (subject to review). *Eating facilities:* by prior arrangement with Secretary. *Visitors:* welcome all week except Saturday. *Society Meetings:* catered for by arrangement. Secretary: B. Harrison (01706 852752).

Please mention THE GOLF GUIDE when you enquire about clubs or accommodation

---

Why not take this opportunity to play **Withington Golf Club.** Enjoy our wonderful parkland course with its beautiful greens. Full catering available. Spring/Summer Society Golf Packages.

For information & bookings telephone: 0161 445 9544
e-mail: secretary@withingtongolfclub.co.uk

Withington Golf Club, West Didsbury, Manchester M20 2UE

ROCHDALE. **Rochdale Golf Club,** The Clubhouse, Edenfield Road, Rochdale OL11 5YR (01706 643818; Fax: 01706 861113). *Location:* three miles from M62, Junction 20, on A680. Parkland. 18 holes, 6034 yards. S.S.S. 69. Practice ground, putting green. *Green Fees:* information not available. *Eating facilities:* meals and bar snacks available. *Visitors:* welcome, please check for tee closures. *Society Meetings:* catered for by prior arrangement Mondays, and Wednesdays. Professional: A. Laverty (01706 522104). General Manager: Phil Kershaw (01706 643818).*
e-mail: rochdale.golfclub@zen.co.uk

ROCHDALE. **Springfield Park Golf Club,** Springfield Park, Bolton Road, Marland, Rochdale OL11 4RE (01706 649801 weekends only). *Location:* A58 out of Rochdale, along Bolton Road on right. Parkland. 18 holes, 5237 yards. S.S.S. 66. *Green Fees:* information not available. *Visitors:* welcome, no restrictions weekdays, booking in advance weekends. Professional: D. Youd (01706 649801). Secretary: J. Wallis (01706 623570).*

SALE. **Ashton-on-Mersey Golf Club,** Church Lane, Ashton-on-Mersey, Sale M33 5QQ (0161 976 4390). *Location:* M60 Junction 7; 1½ miles, off Glebelands Road. Parkland course. 9 holes, 6242 yards. S.S.S. 69. *Green Fees:* £25.00 weekdays, £12.00 with a member. *Eating facilities:* available weekdays except Mondays. *Visitors:* welcome on weekdays. Saturdays, Sundays and Bank Holidays only with member. *Society Meetings:* welcome. Professional: K. Andrews (0161 962 3727). Secretary: R. Coppock (0161 976 4390).

SALE. **Sale Golf Club,** Sale Lodge, Golf Road, Sale M33 2XU (0161-973 1638; Fax: 0161-962 4217). *Location:* M60 Junction 6, A6144. Flat parkland course. 18 holes, 6301 yards. S.S.S. 70. Practice ground. *Green Fees:* £40.00. *Eating facilities:* catering and bar facilities 7 days. *Visitors:* welcome Mondays, Tuesdays, Wednesdays, Fridays and Sundays. Carts and buggies available for hire. *Society Meetings:* welcome by arrangement with Professional. Professional: Mike Stewart (0161-973 1730). Hon. Secretary: C.J. Boyes (0161-973 1638; Fax: 0161-962 4217).

SALFORD. **Brackley Golf Club,** Bullows Road, Little Hulton, Worsley M38 9TR (0161-790 6076). *Location:* off Captain Fold Lane. M61 to Junction 4 onto A6, left at roundabout onto A6 (Walkden), half a mile turn left at White Lion pub. Flat parkland course. 9 holes, 3003 yards, 2747 metres. S.S.S. 69. *Green Fees:* information not available. *Visitors:* welcome anytime. *Society Meetings:* welcome. Secretary: Gary Jones (0161-790 6076).*

STOCKPORT. **Bramall Park Golf Club,** 20 Manor Road, Bramhall, Stockport SK7 3LY (0161-485 3119). *Location:* 10 miles south of Manchester, one mile from Cheadle Hulme. Parkland. 18 holes, 6247 yards. S.S.S. 70. *Green Fees:* information not available. *Eating facilities:* full eating facilities except Mondays. *Visitors:* welcome, apply to Professional. *Society Meetings:* welcome, please contact Secretary's office. Professional: M. Proffitt (0161-485 2205). Secretary: D.E. Shardlow (Tel & Fax: 0161-485 7101).*

STOCKPORT. **Bramhall Golf Club,** The Clubhouse, Ladythorn Road, Bramhall, Stockport SK7 2EY (0161-439 6092). *Location:* half-a-mile from Bramhall Railway Station off Bramhall Lane South. Parkland with views of Pennines and Lyme Park. 18 holes, 6347 yards, 5801 metres. S.S.S 70. Practice ground. *Green Fees:* information available on request. *Eating facilities:* full bar and dining facilities and bar snacks. *Visitors:* welcome except Thursdays, weekends and Competition Days. *Society Meetings:* catered for Wednesdays, minimum 30; Fridays maximum 30. Professional: R. Green (0161-439 1171; Fax: 0161-439 0789). Secretary: (0161-439 6092).
e-mail: office@bramhallgolfclub.com
website: www.bramhallgolfclub.co.uk

STOCKPORT. **Hazel Grove Golf Club,** Buxton Road, Hazel Grove, Stockport SK7 6LU (0161-483 3978 clubhouse). *Location*: A6 to Buxton out of Hazel Grove, three miles south of Stockport. Parkland with tree-lined fairways. 18 holes, 6310 yards. S.S.S. 71. *Green Fees*: weekdays £35.00 per round; weekends and Public Holidays £40.00 per round. 2010 rates (subject to review). Society booking £38.00 for parties of 12 or more. *Eating facilities:* available daily. *Visitors*: welcome, ring Professional for booking of tee times. *Society Meetings*: catered for on Mondays, Thursdays and Fridays. Professional: James Hopley (0161-483 7272). Assistant Secretary: Jane Hill (0161-483 3978).

STOCKPORT. **Heaton Moor Golf Club,** Mauldeth Road, Heaton Mersey, Stockport SK4 3NX (0161-432 2134). *Location:* M56 to A34 or M60 Junction 1; near Glass Pyramid – Didsbury Road. Flat parkland course, tree lined fairways. 18 holes, 5970 yards. S.S.S. 69. Practice ground. *Green Fees:* weekdays £27.00 per round, £32.00 per day; weekends £35.00 per round, £40.00 per day. *Eating facilities:* lunches and evening meals available; bar. *Visitors:* welcome all times. Trolley hire. *Society Meetings:* catered for by arrangement. Professional: Simon Marsh (0161 432 0846). Secretary: D. Linsley (0161 432 2134).

STOCKPORT. **Mellor and Townscliffe Golf Club Ltd,** Gibb Lane, Mellor, Tarden, Stockport SK6 5NA (0161-427 9700 Clubhouse/Steward). *Location:* seven miles south-east of Stockport off A626. Parkland with trees/moorland. 18 holes, 5925 yards. S.S.S. 69. *Green Fees:* weekdays £24.00 per day, £11.00 with a member; weekends and Bank Holidays £32.00, with a member £13.00. *Eating facilities:* available daily except Tuesdays. *Visitors:* welcome weekdays, no casual visitors weekends. *Society Meetings:* catered for by prior arrangement. Professional: Gary R. Broadley (0161-427 5759). Secretary: J. Dixon (0161-427 2208).
website: www.mellorgolf.co.uk

STOCKPORT. **Reddish Vale Golf Club,** Southcliffe Road, Reddish, Stockport SK5 7EE (0161-480 2359). *Location:* one mile north east of M60 in central Stockport. Varied undulating heathland course, designed by Dr Alister MacKenzie. 18 holes, 6086 yards. S.S.S. 69. *Green Fees:* information not

THE GOLF GUIDE 2011 — NORTH REGION / Greater Manchester 289

available. *Eating facilities:* bar and catering. *Visitors:* welcome on weekdays (not 12.30-1.30pm). Buggies available. *Society Meetings:* catered for by arrangement, groups of eight or more. Professional: Andrew Myers (0161-480 3824). Secretary: R.G. Dean (0161-480 2359).*

STOCKPORT. **Romiley Golf Club Ltd,** Goosehouse Green, Romiley, Stockport SK6 4LJ (0161-430 2392). *Location:* B6104 off A560, signposted from Romiley village. Parkland. 18 holes, 6412 yards. S.S.S. 71. *Green Fees:* information not provided. *Eating facilities:* full catering by arrangement. *Visitors:* welcome all week except Saturdays. *Society Meetings:* catered for by prior arrangement with Secretary. Professional: Matt Ellis (0161-430 7122). Secretary: T. Smith (0161-430 2392).

STOCKPORT. **Stockport Golf Club Ltd,** Offerton Road, Offerton, Stockport, Cheshire SK2 5HL (Tel & Fax: 0161 427 8369). *Location:* one mile from lights at Hazel Grove, along Torkington Road. Parkland. 18 holes, 6326 yards. S.S.S. 71. *Green Fees:* weekdays £45.00; weekends £50.00. 2010 rates (subject to reveiw). *Eating facilities*: available, excellent. *Visitors:* welcome weekdays, contact Professional at weekends. *Society Meetings:* catered for. Professional: G. Norcott (0161 427 8369). Secretary: J.S. Howarth (0161 427 8369).

TRAFFORD. **William Wroe Municipal Golf Course,** Pennybridge Lane, off Flixton Road, Flixton, Trafford M41 5DC (0161-748 8680). Course and shop managed by Trafford Borough Council, Acre Gate Golf Club play over the course. *Location:* from M60 follow Urmston, Flixton Road to Bird i'th Hand pub. Flat parkland course. 18 holes, 4395 yards. S.S.S. 61. Driving range two miles from course. *Green Fees:* information not available. *Eating facilities:* at Bird i'th Hand Public House. *Visitors:* public course - book seven days in advance, weekend mornings some restrictions. *Society Meetings:* booking accepted in writing. Professional: Scott Partington (0161-928 0761).*

WESTHOUGHTON. **Westhoughton Golf Club,** Long Island, School Street, Westhoughton, Bolton BL5 2BR (01942 811085). *Location:* four miles south west of Bolton on A58. Parkland. 18 holes, 5918 yards. S.S.S. 69. *Green Fees:* information not provided. *Eating facilities:* bar meals and home cooking. *Visitors:* welcome weekdays except Tuesdays. Snooker room. *Society Meetings:* welcome weekdays except Tuesdays and Saturdays, maximum 32. Secretary: D. Moores (01942 811085). e-mail: honsec.wgc@btconnect.com

WHITEFIELD. **Whitefield Golf Club,** Higher Lane, Whitefield, Manchester M45 7EZ (0161-351 2700; Fax: 0161-351 2712). *Location:* Exit 17, off M60 then take road to Radcliffe for half a mile. 18 holes, 6063 yards. S.S.S. 69. *Green Fees:* information not available. *Eating facilities:* restaurant facilities every day. *Visitors:* welcome. *Society Meetings:* catered for. Professional: (0161-351 2709). Secretary: Mrs M. Rothwell (0161-351 2700; Fax: 0161-351 2712). e-mail: enquiries@whitefieldgolfclub.com

WIGAN. **Gathurst Golf Club,** Miles Lane, Shevington, Wigan WN6 8EW (01257 255235). *Location:* one mile south of Junction 27 M6. Parkland course. 18 holes, 6016 yards (from men's tee). S.S.S.69. *Green Fees:* £30.00; weekends with a member only. *Eating facilities:* available bar hours daily. *Visitors:* welcome Monday, Tuesday, Thursday and Friday with reservation. *Society Meetings:* catered for by appointment with Secretary. Professional: David Clarke (01257 255882). Secretary: Mrs. I. Fyffe (01257 255235).

WIGAN. **Haigh Hall Golf Club,** Haigh Country Park, Aspull, Near Wigan WN2 1PE (01942 831107). *Location:* well signposted from M6, Junction 27 and M61, Junction 5. Balcarres 18 hole course, 6358 yards. Par 70. Crawford course 9 holes, 1446 yards. Par 28. 18 hole Himalayan putting green and golf academy practice facilities. All U.S.G.A specification greens and tees. Brand new golf complex in the superb surroundings of Haigh Country Park. *Green Fees:* information not available. *Eating facilities:* full catering available, bar facilities and function rooms in The Stables Golf & Visitor Centre. *Visitors:* welcome at all times. *Society Meetings:* welcome at all times - packages available. Professional: Ian Lee (01942 831107). Members' Secretary: Steve Eyres (01942 833337).*
e-mail: secretary@haighhall-golfclub.co.uk
website: www.haighhall-golfclub.co.uk

WIGAN. **Hindley Hall Golf Club,** Hall Lane, Hindley, Wigan WN2 2SQ (01942 525020). *Location:* two miles east of Wigan, Junction 6 M61, or A58 to Ladies Lane/Hall Lane. 18 holes, 5913 yards. S.S.S. 68. *Green Fees:* information not available. *Eating facilities:* book before playing. *Visitors:* welcome without reservation if members of a recognised golf club. *Society Meetings:* catered for by arrangement with the Secretary. Professional: D. Clarke (01942 255991). Secretary: S. Tyrer (01942 255131).*
website: www.hindleyhallgolfclub.co.uk

WORSLEY. **Marriott Worsley Park Hotel & Country Club,** Worsley Park, Worsley, Manchester (0161 975 2043). *Location:* Junction 13 off M60, follow A575 to Worsley. Challenging new parkland course. 18 holes. Par 71. *Green Fees:* information not available. *Eating facilities:* bar and dining facilities 8am to 10pm. *Visitors:* welcome. Handicap Certificate is required. *Society Meetings:* details of golf and leisure breaks on request. Conference and banqueting facilities available. Superbly equipped country club, including 20-metre pool, spa bath, sauna, steam room and health and beauty salons. Professional: David Screeton.*
website: www.marriott.com/marriot/mangs

THE APPEARANCE OF AN ASTERISK (*) AT THE END OF A CLUB OR COURSE ENTRY INDICATES THAT UP-TO-DATE INFORMATION HAS NOT BEEN SUPPLIED

Merseyside

BIDSTON. **Bidston Golf Club Ltd,** Bidston Link Road, Wallasey, Wirral CH44 2HR (0151-638 3412). *Location:* M53 Junction 1 (from Chester direction) turn right at roundabout, course entrance 200 yards on dual carriageway. Parkland. 18 holes, 6140 yards. S.S.S. 70. Practice ground and nets. *Green Fees:* information not available. *Eating facilities:* restaurant, snacks, lounge bar. *Visitors:* welcomed weekdays and weekends. *Society Meetings:* welcome weekdays and weekends. Professional: Alan Norwood (0151-638 3412). Administrator: L. Letts.*
e-mail: linda@bidstongolf.co.uk
website: www.bidstongolf.co.uk

BIRKENHEAD. **Arrowe Park Golf Course,** Arrowe Park, Birkenhead CH49 5LW. *Location:* Mersey Tunnel into Brough Road, then Woodchurch Road, head for Arrowe Park roundabout, bear left approximately 400 yards, turn right into Arrowe Park. Flat tree-lined parkland. 18 holes, 6396 yards, 5885 metres. S.S.S. 71. 9 hole pitch and putt, putting green. *Green Fees:* information not available. *Eating facilities:* restaurant/cafe - bar. *Visitors:* welcome except weekends before noon. *Society Meetings:* by arrangement through Professional. Professional: Colin Disbury (0151-677 1527). Secretary: P. Hickey (0151-678 3296).*

BIRKENHEAD. **Prenton Golf Club,** Golf Links Road, Prenton, Birkenhead CH42 8LW (0151-609 3426). *Location:* M53 Junction 3, off A552 towards Birkenhead. Parkland course. 18 holes, 6411 yards. S.S.S. 71. *Green Fees:* prices on application. *Eating facilities:* full catering facilities available. *Visitors:* welcome, reservation advisable. *Society Meetings:* catered for Mondays, Wednesdays and Fridays. Professional: Robin Thompson (0151-608 1636). Secretary: N. Brown.

BIRKENHEAD. **The Wirral Ladies' Golf Club Ltd,** 93 Bidston Road, Oxton, Birkenhead CH43 6TS (0151-652 1255). *Location:* off the M53 Junction 1 or 3. Acid heath/gorse and heather course. 18 holes, 4948 yards (Ladies), 5182 yards (Men). S.S.S. 69 (Ladies), S.S.S. 65 (Men). Practice ground. *Green Fees:* £35.00 per round, £50.00 per day. *Eating facilities:* dining room, meals during day to order. *Visitors:* welcome weekdays; weekends after 11am Club Competitions permitting. Trolleys. *Society Meetings:* welcome weekdays only. Professional: Angus Law (0151-652 2468). Club Secretary: P. Greville (0151-652 1255; Fax: 0151-651 3775).

West Lancashire Golf Club
founded 1873

Hall Road West, Blundellsands, Liverpool L23 8SZ

West Lancashire invites you to come and play the historic links at Blundellsands. Visitors are welcome to use the facilities of Lancashire's oldest club. This true links course has hosted numerous championships.

The links are in fantastic condition all year round. The Yellow Tees, measuring 6239 yards, provide a course which is a fair test of golf. If you enjoy a challenge and wish to play some classic links golf on one of the top ten oldest courses in England why not pay us a visit. We are sure you will find the prices more than acceptable and the experience rewarding.

It could not be easier to arrange your visit to Blundellsands. With its perfect location, comfortable surroundings and excellent catering and bar facilities, the Clubhouse is a haven for the tired and hungry golfer.

Tel: 0151 924 1076 • e-mail: sec@westlancashiregolf.co.uk
Online booking available at www.westlancashiregolf.co.uk

BLUNDELLSANDS. West Lancashire Golf Club, Hall Road West, Blundellsands, Merseyside L23 8SZ (0151-924 1076; Fax: 0151-931 4448). *Location:* A565 Liverpool - Southport to Crosby, follow signs to West Lancashire Golf Club from Crosby. Links Course. 18 holes, 6767 yards. S.S.S. 73. Substantial practice ground. *Green Fees:* £80.00 weekday, £95.00 weekend. *Eating facilities:* full bar and catering available. *Visitors:* welcome on weekdays except Tuesdays. All subject to availability. *Society Meetings:* booking in advance with Secretary. Professional: Gary Edge (0151-924 5662). Secretary: Stewart King (0151-924 1076; Fax: 0151-931 4448).
e-mail: sec@westlancashiregolf.co.uk
website: www.westlancashiregolf.co.uk

BOOTLE. Bootle Golf Club, 3 Dunnings Bridge Road, Bootle L30 2PP (0151-928 1371). *Location:* five miles north of Liverpool, one mile from M57 and M58. Links course. 18 holes, 6362 yards. S.S.S. 70. *Green Fees:* weekdays £10.50; weekends £13.00. *Eating facilities:* full catering as required by arrangement. *Visitors:* welcome any time, Pay and Play Course. *Society Meetings:* by arrangement. Manager: Gary Howarth (0151-949 1815).

BROMBOROUGH. Bromborough Golf Club, Raby Hall Road, Bromborough, Wirral, Merseyside CH63 0NW(0151-334 2155). *Location:* Exit 4 Wirral Motorway M53. Parkland. 18 holes, 6547 yards. S.S.S. 72. *Green Fees:* information not available. *Eating facilities:* bar and full catering facilities. *Visitors:* welcome weekdays, but essential to ring in advance for weekends and Bank Holidays. *Society Meetings:* catered for by prior arrangement. Professional: G. Berry (0151-334 4499). Secretary: P. McMullen (0151-334 2155; Fax: 0151-334 7300).*

CALDY. The Caldy Golf Club Ltd, Links Hey Road, Caldy, Wirral CH48 1NB (0151 625 5660). *Location:* one mile south of West Kirby on the River Dee, 10 miles from Chester. Undulating heathland with cliff top, links, open aspect with views across the Dee to the North Wales hills. 18 holes, 6707 yards, 6133 metres. S.S.S. 73. Practice ground and putting green. *Green Fees:* weekdays £60.00 per round, £70.00 per day; weekends with member only. *Eating facilities:* bars and restaurant throughout the day. *Visitors:* welcome weekdays with advance booking and Handicap Certificate. Restrictions Tuesdays and Wednesdays. Jeans not allowed on course or in Clubhouse. *Society Meetings:* Thursdays by prior arrangement. Professional: Alan Gibbons (Tel & Fax: 0151-625 1818). Secretary/Manager: G.M. Copple (0151-625 5660; Fax: 0151-625 7394).
e-mail: secretarycaldygc@btconnect.com
        golfcaldygc@btconnect.com
website: www.caldygolfclub.co.uk

EASTHAM. Eastham Lodge Golf Club, 117 Ferry Road, Eastham Village, Wirral CH62 0AP (0151-327 3003; Admin office Ext 3). *Location:* exit Junction 5 M53 into Eastham Village from A41, follow signs for Eastham Country Park. Pleasant 18 hole woodland course. 5706 yards, Par 68. *Green Fees:* weekdays and weekends £30.50 per round. *Eating facilities:* full bar facilities, bar snacks, restaurant (advance booking only). *Visitors:* welcome. *Society Meetings:* most welcome, please contact Professional. £25.50 per round, by prior arrangement. Professional: Nick Sargent (0151 327 3003 Ext 2).
e-mail: easthamlodge.g.c@btinternet.com
website: www.easthamlodgegolfclub.co.uk

FORMBY. Formby Golf Club, Golf Road, Formby, Liverpool L37 1LQ (01704 872164). *Location:* one mile west of A565 by Freshfield Station. Seaside links, wooded. 18 holes, 7028 yards. S.S.S. 74. *Green Fees:* weekdays £100.00 per day, weekends £120.00 per day. 2010 rates (subject to review). *Eating facilities:* available. *Visitors:* welcome by arrangement with the Secretary, except before 10am Wednesdays, 3.30pm weekends or Bank Holidays. Handicap Certificate/ introduction required. "Dormy" accommodation available. *Society Meetings:* catered for Tuesdays, Thursdays and Fridays. Professional: Andrew Witherup (01704 873090). Secretary: (01704 872164; Fax: 01704 833028).
e-mail: info@formbygolfclub.co.uk

FORMBY. Formby Ladies' Golf Club, Golf Road, Formby, Liverpool L37 1YH (01704 873493; Fax: 01704 874127). *Location:* A565 (Southport Bypass) to Formby. Seaside links. 18 holes, 5374 yards, 4914 metres. S.S.S. 72. Practice area. *Green Fees:* £48.00 weekday, £55.00 weekend. *Eating facilities:* light lunches, afternoon teas. *Visitors:* by prior reservation. *Society Meetings:* catered for with prior reservation. Professional: Andrew Witherup (01704 873090). Secretary: Mrs A. Bromley (Tel: 01704 873493; Fax: 01704 874127).

HESWALL. Heswall Golf Club, Cottage Lane, Gayton, Wirral CH60 8PB (0151-342 1237). *Location:* off A540, eight miles north-west of Chester. Parkland on the banks of River Dee estuary overlooking Welsh coast and hills. 18 holes, 6882 yards, 6290 metres. S.S.S. 74. Large practice area. *Green Fees:* information not available. *Eating facilities:* bar snacks, full meals by arrangement. *Visitors:* welcome, subject to availability. Must have accredited Handicaps. *Society Meetings:* catered for fully on Wednesdays and Fridays only. Winter packages available October/March. Professional: Alan Thompson (0151-342 7431). Secretary: (0151-342 1237).*
e-mail: dawn@heswallgolfclub.com

THE APPEARANCE OF AN ASTERISK (*) AT THE END OF A CLUB OR COURSE ENTRY INDICATES THAT UP-TO-DATE INFORMATION HAS NOT BEEN SUPPLIED

Merseyside / NORTH REGION

HOYLAKE. Royal Liverpool Golf Club, Meols Drive, Hoylake, Wirral, Merseyside CH47 4AL (0151-632 3101). *Location*: 10 miles southwest of Liverpool on Wirral Peninsula. Approach from M6, M56 and M53 Junction 2. Championship links. Host to The Open Championship in 2006. 18 holes, 6847 yards. S.S.S. 75. Large practice area. *Green Fees*: on application. *Eating facilities*: food available on request. *Visitors*: welcome weekdays and Fridays. No visitor play at weekends. Proof of Handicap required (max 21). Caddies available by prior booking. *Society Meetings*: catered for Wednesdays and Fridays. Professional: John Heggarty (0151-632 5868). Secretary: David R. Cromie (0151-632 3101). e-mail: secretary@royal-liverpool-golf.com
website: www.royal-liverpool-golf.com

HUYTON. Bowring Municipal, Bowring Park, Roby Road, Knowsley L36 4HD (0151-489 1901). *Location*: Junction 5, M62 signposted. 200 metres. Parkland. 18 holes, S.S.S. 73. *Green Fees*: information not available. *Eating facilities*: limited. Private club facilities on site, bar. *Visitors*: no restrictions. *Society Meetings*: bookings required.*

HUYTON. Huyton and Prescot Golf Club Ltd, Hurst Park, Huyton Lane, Huyton, Liverpool L36 1UA (0151-489 3948). *Location*: from M57 Junction 2 follow B5199 signposted Huyton. Parkland. 18 holes, 5779 yards. S.S.S. 68 white, 67 yellow. *Green Fees*: information not available. *Eating facilities*: bar snacks and restaurant area 9am-5pm; normal bar hours. *Visitors*: welcome, midweek days 9.30am to 12.00pm, 2pm to 4pm, except Tuesdays. Snooker table. *Society Meetings*: catered for Mondays, Wednesdays, Thursdays and Fridays. Summer and Winter packages available. Professional: John Fisher (0151-489 2022). Secretary: David Hughes (0151-489 3948; Fax: 0151-489 0797).*

LIVERPOOL. Allerton Park Golf Club, Allerton Municipal Golf Course, Allerton Road, Liverpool L18 3JT (0151-428 8510). *Location*: end of M62, two miles to Allerton Road, one and a half miles along Allerton Road. Undulating parkland course. 18 holes, 5494 yards, 5023 metres. S.S.S. 67. 9 hole course 1685 metres. S.S.S. 34. *Green Fees*: information not available. *Eating facilities*: in clubhouse, (bar snacks only), licensed bar. *Visitors*: welcome anytime, booking system for all games. *Society Meetings*: welcome by prior arrangement with the Professional. Professional: Barry Large (0151-428 7490). Secretary: H. O'Neill.*

LIVERPOOL. The Childwall Golf Club Ltd., Naylors Road, Gateacre, Liverpool L27 2YB (0151-487 9982). *Location*: Exit 6 M62 to Liverpool, follow Huyton A5080 to second set of traffic lights, turn left into Wheathill Road. Parkland, flat, designed by James Braid. 18 holes, 6547 yards. S.S.S. 72. Practice area. *Green Fees*: weekdays £40.00; weekends £50.00. *Eating facilities*: bar, snacks and restaurant. *Visitors*: no visitors weekends and Tuesdays. *Society Meetings*: catered for on weekdays, contact the Manager. Professional: N.M. Parr (0151-487 9871). Manager: P. Bowen (0151-487 0654; Fax: 0151-487 0882). website: www.childwallgolfclub.co.uk

LIVERPOOL. Dudley Golf Club, Allerton Municipal Golf Course, Menlove Avenue, Allerton, Liverpool L18 3EE (0151-428 8510). *Location*: end of M62, then two miles on Allerton road, five miles from city centre. Wooded parkland. Two courses. (1) 18 holes, 5459 metres. S.S.S. 67. (2) 9 holes, 1685 metres. S.S.S. 34. *Green Fees*: information not provided. *Eating facilities*: licensed bar, bar snacks. *Visitors*: welcome at any time, please book in advance. *Society Meetings*: welcome by advance booking. Professional: Barry Large (0151-428 1046). Secretary: Brian L. Harris (01244 661511).

LIVERPOOL. Lee Park Golf Club, Childwall Valley Road, Liverpool L27 3YA (0151-487 3882; Fax: 0151-498 4666). *Location*: M62 J6, A5080 to Huyton, turn left at second set of lights (Wheathill Road), turn left at next lights (one mile), club on right 200 yards. Easy walking parkland course, a challenging test of golf with 6 doglegs and well protected raised greens. 18 holes, 5959 yards. Medal tees: 5721 yards. Front tees: S.S.S. 69. Ladies' tees: 5543 yards. S.S.S. 72. Driving nets, chipping/bunker practice green, practice area, and all-weather bay canopy *Green Fees*: weekdays £40.00, weekends £45.00. 2-fore-1/ Open Fairways - 50% discount one 4-ball per weekday. *Eating facilities*: informal Spike Bar for bar snacks, restaurant, formal main lounge for larger parties. *Visitors*: welcome Monday, Wednesday, Thursday, Friday, Saturday (12-2.15pm members and guests only). *Society Meetings*: catered for mainly Monday, Thursday, Friday only. Manager: Steve Settle (0151-487 3882; Fax: 0151-498 4666). e-mail: lee.park@virgin.net
website: www.leepark.co.uk

ROYAL LIVERPOOL GOLF CLUB, HOYLAKE *Founded 1869*

Visitors are welcome to use the full facilities of this long established Club, venue for 11 Open Championships, the most recent in 2006. Hoylake offers the challenge of a magnificent Championship Links as well as the chance to experience the history of a traditional Clubhouse with its impressive displays of golfing memorabilia. Green fees on application.

Meols Drive, Hoylake, Wirral CH47 4AL
Tel: 01516 323101 • Secretary: D.R.Cromie
www.royal-liverpool-golf.com

Host of the 2012 Ricoh Women's British Open and 2014 Open Championship

THE GOLF GUIDE 2011 — NORTH REGION / Merseyside

LIVERPOOL. **West Derby Golf Club,** Yew Tree Lane, West Derby, Liverpool L12 9HQ (0151-254 1034). Flat parkland course. 18 holes, 6275 yards. S.S.S. 70. *Green Fees:* weekdays £30.00, weekends £40.00. *Eating facilities:* soup and sandwiches, light meals available at lunch. Evening meals by prior arrangement. *Visitors:* welcome if members of a recognised golf club. *Society Meetings:* catered for only by arrangement with Secretary. Professional: Stuart Danchin (0151-254 1034). Secretary: A.P. Milne (0151-254 1034); Fax: 0151-259 0505).
e-mail: pmilne@westderbygc.freeserve.co.uk
website: www.westderbygc.co.uk

LIVERPOOL. **Woolton Golf Club,** Doe Park, Speke Road, Woolton, Liverpool L25 7TZ (0151 486 2298). *Location:* South Liverpool, one mile from Woolton Village. Parkland, rolling terrain, excellent springy fairways affording inviting lies. 18 holes, 5747 yards. S.S.S. 69. *Green Fees:* Information not available. *Eating facilities:* bar snacks daily, evening dining by arrangement. *Visitors:* welcome; few restrictions. *Society Meetings:* catered for by arrangement with the General Manager; various packages - information pack on request. Professional: D. Thompson (0151-486 1298). General Manager: Tracy Rawlinson (0151-486 2298; Fax: 0151-486 1664).
e-mail: golf@wooltongolf.co.uk
website: www.wooltongolfclub.com

MORETON. **Leasowe Golf Club,** Leasowe Road, Moreton, Wirral, Merseyside CH46 3RD (0151-677 5852; Fax: 0151-641 8519). *Location:* Exit 1 from M53, one mile towards Hoylake. Flat seaside links. 18 holes, 6263 yards, S.S.S. 71. Practice area. *Green Fees:* information not available. *Eating facilities:* dining room and bar snacks. *Visitors:* welcome anytime except Saturdays and Sunday mornings. Phone first. *Society Meetings:* available at discount, catered for except Saturdays , must book in advance. Professional: Andrew Ayre (0151-678 5460). Secretary/ Manager: L. Jukes (0151-677 5852).*

NEWTON-LE-WILLOWS. **Haydock Park Golf Club,** Newton Lane, Newton-le-Willows WA12 0HX (01925 228525). *Location:* off East Lancs Road (A580) and M6, three quarters of a mile from Newton-le-Willows High Street. Flat, wooded parkland course in beautiful setting. 18 holes, 6058 yards. S.S.S. 69. Large practice ground. *Green Fees:* weekdays £35.00; weekends £13.00 with member only. *Eating facilities:* restaurant and two bars. *Visitors:* welcome weekdays except Tuesdays. *Society Meetings:* catered for by arrangement. Professional: P. Kenwright (01925 226944). Secretary: D. Hughes (01925 228525).

RAINHILL. **Blundells Hill Golf Club,** Blundells Lane, Rainhill L35 6NA (0151-426 9040; Fax: 0151-426 5256). *Location:* three minutes from Junction 7 of M62, course lies adjacent to eastbound M62. Built on a gently sloping hill, created from some 120 acres of parkland surroundings with wide fairways, big bunkers and large undulating greens, several ponds, ditches and a beautifully landscaped lake. 18 holes, 6256 yards. S.S.S. 71. Practice ground, putting green. *Green Fees:* information not available. *Eating facilities:* licensed bar, restaurant, snooker room, function room, Sky TV. *Visitors:* all welcome, call 0151-430 0100 to pre-book tee times. No jeans, tracksuits, tee shirts, trainers, short socks, etc. Expert tuition. *Society Meetings:* welcome, packages available; call 0151-430 9551 for brochure. Professional: Richard Burbidge (0151-430 0100). Hon. Secretary: Andy Roberts (0151-430 9551; Fax: 0151-426 5256).*

RAINHILL. **Eccleston Park Golf Club,** Rainhill Road, Rainhill, Prescot L35 4PG (0151 493 0033). *Location:* Junction 7 of M62, follow A57 towards Prescot; at traffic lights after humpback bridge, turn right into Rainhill. Gently undulating open parkland layout. 18 holes. Par 70. *Green Fees:* information not available. *Eating facilities:* bar and dining from 8am to 11pm (9am to 6pm during winter). *Visitors:* Handicap Certificate required at weekends.*
e-mail: eccleston-sales@crown-golf.co.uk

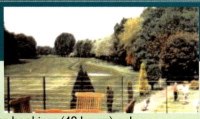

WEST DERBY GOLF CLUB
Yew Tree Lane, West Derby, Liverpool L12 9HQ

West Derby is one of Merseyside's finest offerings, offering a secluded 18 holes despite its inland setting. Always in first-class condition, this parkland course is a fantastic, easy-walking layout, and perfect for all levels of golf. Advance bookings (48 hours) only.

Tel: 0151 254 1034 • e-mail: pmilne@westderbygc.freeserve.co.uk
www.westderbygc.co.uk

294 Merseyside / NORTH REGION — THE GOLF GUIDE 2011

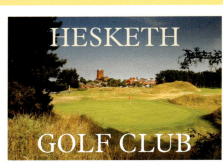

Professional championship golf has been played on these famous old links from the club`s earliest days, the course played host to the centennial Lancashire Championship in 2010 and will be co-hosting the Amateur Championship in 2011. Visitors, Societies and Corporate events are most welcome. On-Line Booking for Visitors and Open Events available.

For more information please call Gavin, Gill or Sue on 01704 536897 Ext 1.
Secretary@heskethgolfclub.co.uk
Hesketh Golf Club
Cockle Dick's Lane
Southport PR9 9QQ
www.heskethgolfclub.co.uk

ST HELENS. **Grange Park Golf Club,** Prescot Road, St. Helens WA10 3AD (Tel & Fax: 01744 26318). *Location:* one and a half miles south west of St. Helens on A58. Wooded parkland. 18 holes, 6422 yards. S.S.S. 71. Practice area. *Green Fees:* information not available. *Eating facilities:* full catering and bar facilities. *Visitors:* welcome anytime except Tuesdays and times are often not available at weekends/Bank Holidays; reservation through Professional recommended. *Society Meetings:* welcome except Tuesdays, Bank Holidays and weekends. Professional: Paul Roberts (01744 28785; Fax: 01744 26318). Secretary: Gavin R. Brown (Tel & Fax: 01744 26318).*
e-mail: secretary@grangeparkgolfclub.co.uk
website: www.grangeparkgolfclub.co.uk

ST HELENS. **Sherdley Park Municipal Golf Course and Driving Range,** Off Eltonhead Road, Sutton, St Helens WA9 5DE (01744 813149). *Location:* Exit 7 off M62, follow St Helens Linkway to second island, turn right for 300 yards, course on left hand side. Undulating parkland course. 18 holes, 5974 yards. S.S.S. 71. Driving range. *Green Fees:* information not available. *Eating facilities:* Licensed bar and Cafe in the Park open most times, phone (01744 815518) for more information. *Visitors/ Society Meetings:* welcome midweek and weekends (book early). Booking system operates up to six days in advance. Golf Professional: Danny Jones. Manager: Jeff Barston (01744 817967).*

SOUTHPORT. **Hesketh Golf Club,** Cockle Dick's Lane, Cambridge Road, Southport PR9 9QQ (01704 536897). *Location:* one mile north of town centre. Seaside links Championship course. 18 holes, 6655 yards. S.S.S. 72. Practice ground. *Green Fees:* information not available. *Eating facilities:* bar snacks and dining room; three bars. *Visitors:* welcome by prior arrangement with Secretary. *Society Meetings:* catered for by arrangement with Secretary; special rates for parties over 12 in number. Professional: Scott Astin (01704 530050). Secretary: Martyn G. Senior (01704 536897; Fax: 01704 539250).*
e-mail: secretary@heskethgolfclub.co.uk
website: www.heskethgolfclub.co.uk

SOUTHPORT. **Hillside Golf Club,** Hastings Road, Hillside, Southport PR8 2LU (01704 567169; Fax: 01704 563192). *Location:* three miles south of town centre on A565, Hillside station one mile. Championship links course. 18 holes, 6850 yards. S.S.S. 74. Practice ground. *Green Fees:* information not available. *Eating facilities:* bar and restaurant. *Visitors:* welcome, book through Office. Tuesday up to 2pm Ladies' Day; no visitors Saturdays, limited Sundays. Buggies and carts for hire. *Society Meetings:* welcome with prior reservations. Professional: B. Seddon (01704 568360). Secretary: Simon H. Newland (01704 567169; Fax: 01704 563192).*

SOUTHPORT. **Royal Birkdale Golf Club,** Waterloo Road, Birkdale, Southport PR8 2LX (01704 552020; Fax: 01704 552021). *Location:* one mile south of Southport town centre. Classic Links on the Open Championship rota. 18 holes, 6381 yards. S.S.S. 72. *Green Fees:* Information not available. *Visitors:* welcome but it is essential to make prior arrangements with the Secretary's office, official golf Handicap required. *Society Meetings:* catered for, dining room facilities. Professional: Brian Hodgkinson (01704 552030). Secretary: M.C. Gilyeat (01704 552020).
e-mail: secretary@royalbirkdale.com
website: www.royalbirkdale.com

SOUTHPORT. **Southport and Ainsdale Golf Club,** Bradshaw's Lane, Off Liverpool Road, Ainsdale, Southport PR8 3LG (01704 578000; Fax: 01704 570896). *Location:* south of Southport on A565. Links course. 18 holes, 6749 yards. S.S.S. 74. *Green Fees:* weekdays £75.00 per round, £100.00 per day; weekends £100.00. *Eating facilities:* full catering available. *Visitors:* welcome at all times; by arrangement at weekends. *Society Meetings:* catered for by arrangement. Professional: J. Payne (01704 577316). Secretary: M.J. Vanner (01704 578000; Fax: 01704 570896).
e-mail: secretary@sandagolfclub.co.uk
website: www.sandagolfclub.co.uk

NORTH REGION / Merseyside

SOUTHPORT. Southport Municipal Golf Club, Park Road West, Southport PR9 0JR (01704 55130). *Location:* Park Road West, north end of Promenade, near Marine Lake, Southport. Flat seaside links. 18 holes, 6139 yards. S.S.S. 70. *Green Fees:* information not available. *Eating facilities:* licensed cafe. *Visitors:* booking system operates up to seven days in advance (visitors unrestricted). *Society Meetings:* welcome, book in advance. Professional: William Fletcher (01704 35286)*

SOUTHPORT. Southport Old Links Golf Club, Moss Lane, Churchtown, Southport PR9 7QS (01704 228207). *Location:* end of Roe Lane, Churchtown, at the rear of Meols Hall. Tree-lined links course. 9 holes, (x2), 6450 yards. Par 72, S.S.S. 71. *Green Fees:* Monday to Friday 9 holes £16.00, 18 holes £26.00; Saturday, 9 holes £20.00, 18 holes £32.00. *Eating facilities:* available daily except Mondays. *Visitors:* welcome except Wednesdays, Sundays and Bank Holidays. *Society Meetings:* catered for by arrangement, letter of application required. Secretary: B. Kenyon (01704 228207; Fax: 01704 505353).
e-mail: secretary@southportoldlinksgolfclub.co.uk

WALLASEY. Wallasey Golf Club, Bayswater Road, Wallasey CH45 8LA (0151-691 1024; Fax: 0151-638 8988). *Location:* via M53 through Wirral or 15 minutes from Liverpool centre via Wallasey Tunnel. Championship seaside links. 18 holes, 6503 yards. S.S.S. 73. *Green Fees:* weekdays £75.00 per round, £95.00 per day; weekends and Bank Holidays £85.00 per round, £100.00 per day. *Eating facilities:* snacks and full catering facilities. *Visitors:* welcome with reservation. *Society Meetings:* catered for by arrangement. Professional: Mike Adams (0151-638 3888). Secretary: Trevor Barraclough (0151-691 1024)

WALLASEY. Warren Golf Club, The Grange, Grove Road, Wallasey CH45 0JA (0151-639 8323). *Location:* 300 yards Grove Road Station. Seaside links course, wonderful view over Mersey. 9 holes, 5914 yards. S.S.S. 68. *Green Fees:* information not available. *Visitors:* welcome Mondays to Saturdays. Course closed to public Sundays 7am to 11am. *Society Meetings:* welcome. Professional: Mark Eagles (0151-639 5730); Secretary: Kevin McCormack (0151-678 0330).*
e-mail: golfer@warrengc.freeserve.co.uk

WIRRAL. Brackenwood Golf Club, Bracken Lane, Bebington, Wirral L63 2LY (0151-608 5394). *Location:* M53 Clatterbridge roundabout Junction 4. Flat parkland. 18 holes, 6200 yards. S.S.S. 70. *Green Fees:* information not available. *Visitors:* welcome, weekends must be booked through Professional one week in advance. *Society Meetings:* welcome, book through Pro for tee times and Secretary for bar/catering. Professional: Ken Lamb (0151-608 3093). Secretary: R. B. Boyle (0151-653 6405).*

WIRRAL. Hoylake Golf Club, Carr Lane, Hoylake, Wirral CH47 4BG (0151 632 2956). *Location:* turn at roundabout Hoylake town centre, over railway. Part flat semi links. 18 holes, 6313 yards, 5780 metres. S.S.S. 70. *Green Fees:* information not provided. *Eating facilities:* cafe and bar. Phone in advance (0151 632 4883). *Visitors:* welcome, booking fee required in advance. *Society Meetings:* society bookings weekdays and after 1.30pm Saturday; after 12 midday Sunday. Professional: S.N. Hooton (0151-632 2956). Secretary: Peter Davies (0151 632 0523).

Looking for accommodation near golf clubs?, then visit www.holidayguides.com for where to stay when playing golf around the regions

---

PLEASE NOTE

All the information regarding Golf Clubs in this guide is given in good faith in the belief that it is correct. However, the publishers cannot guarantee the facts given in these pages, neither are they responsible for changes in ownership or facilities, such as green fees, that may take place after the date of going to press. Readers should always satisfy themselves that the facilities they require are available and that the terms, if quoted, still apply.

Northumberland

ALLENDALE. **Allendale Golf Club,** High Studdon, Allenheads Road, Allendale, Hexham NE47 9DH (0700 5808246). *Location:* B6295 Allendale to Allenheads Road, 10 miles south of Hexham. Parkland course, hilly but not too severe. 9 holes, 16 tees. 4501 yards. S.S.S. 64. Driving net and putting green. *Green Fees:* information not available. *Eating facilities:* new clubhouse with licensed bar, catering by arrangement. *Visitors:* welcome anytime other than August Bank Holiday Monday before 3pm. Secretary: Norman Harris (01434 683115).*
e-mail: norman@harris8484.freeserve.co.uk
website: www.allendale-golf.co.uk

ALNMOUTH. **Alnmouth Golf Club Ltd,** Foxton Hall, Alnmouth NE66 3BE (01665 830231). *Location:* four miles east of Alnwick. 18 holes, 6414 yards, 5855 metres. S.S.S. 71. *Green Fees:* £35.00 per round, £40.00 per day weekdays; £35.00 per round weekends. *Eating facilities:* diningroom and bars. *Visitors:* welcome Monday to Thursday and Sundays. Packages available. Dormy House accommodation available. Play and Stay packages available. *Society Meetings:* welcome Monday to Thursday and Sundays. Secretary: Peter Simpson (01665 830231; Fax: 01665 830922).
e-mail: secretary@alnmouthgolfclub.com
website: www.alnmouthgolfclub.com

ALNMOUTH. **Alnmouth Village Golf Club,** Marine Road, Alnmouth NE66 2RZ (01665 830370). *Location:* leave A1 from Alnwick to Alnmouth. Seaside links course. 9 holes, 6090 yards, 5572 metres. Par 71. S.S.S. 70. *Green Fees:* information not available. *Eating facilities:* available. *Visitors:* welcome, restrictions on club competition days. *Society Meetings:* must book in advance and only with official Golf Club Handicaps. Secretary: R.A Hill (01665 833189).*

ALNWICK. **Alnwick Golf Club,** Swansfield Park, Alnwick NE66 2AB (01665 602632). *Location:* signposted from the south A1 slip road. A friendly welcome awaits you at Alnwick Golf Club. Established in 1907, extended to 18 holes in 1995. Superb layout set in mature parkland, open grassland and gorse with panoramic views out to sea. 18 holes, 6250 yards. S.S.S. 70. *Green Fees:* weekdays £25.00 per round, £35.00 per day; weekends and Bank Holidays £27.50 per round, £35.00 per day. 2010 rates (subject to review). *Eating facilities*: catering and bar facilities available most times. *Visitors:* welcome most times, part restrictions during competitions. Buggies available. *Society Meetings:* welcome by prior arrangement with the Secretary. Secretary: Neil Foggon (01665 605725).
e-mail: neil@neil448.orangehome.co.uk
website: www.alnwickgolfclub.com

BAMBURGH. **Bamburgh Castle Golf Club,** The Club House, Bamburgh NE69 7DE (01668 214378). *Location:* midway between Alnwick and Berwick upon Tweed on A1, take B1341 or B1342 to Bamburgh village. Seaside course with outstanding views of Farne Islands, Holy Island and magnificent coastal area. 18 holes, 5621 yards, 5132 metres. S.S.S. 67. Practice area. *Green Fees:* information not available. Restricted play at weekends. *Eating facilities:* bar snacks, lunch, high tea, beverages, etc. *Visitors:* welcome except on competition days and Bank Holidays. Buggy hire. *Society Meetings:* welcome, by written application. Secretary: M. N. D. Robinson (01668 214321).*

BEDLINGTON. **Bedlingtonshire Golf Club,** Acorn Bank, Hartford Road, Bedlington NE22 6AA (01670 822457). *Location:* one mile south of Bedlington on A1068. Parkland. 18 holes, 6813 yards. S.S.S. 73. Practice ground and putting green. *Green Fees:* £27.00 per round midweek; £35.00 per round weekends and Bank Holidays. *Eating facilities:* catering, bar services, open all day. *Visitors:* welcome, but not before 9.00am weekdays and 10.00am weekends. *Society Meetings:* welcome, contact the Secretary. Professional: Marcus Webb (01670 822457). Secretary: (01670 822457).
e-mail: secretary@bedlingtongolfclub.com
website: www.bedlingtongolfclub.com

BELFORD. **The Belford,** South Road, Belford NE70 7DP (01668 213232; Fax: 01668 213282). *Location:* turn off A1 sign-posted Belford, first turning on right. Parkland course. 9 holes, 18 tee box, 6225 yards. S.S.S. 70, Par 72. Floodlit driving range. *Green Fees:* information not available. *Eating facilities:* catering available 9am - 9pm, 7 days a week. *Visitors:* welcome all year. Buggies available. *Society Meetings:* open all year round to non-members, visitors and societies. Secretary: A.M. Gilhome (01668 213433).*
website: www.thebelford.com

THE GOLF GUIDE 2011 — NORTH REGION / Northumberland

ALNMOUTH GOLF CLUB

Alnmouth Golf Club
Foxton Hall, Alnmouth NE66 3BE
Tel: 01665 830231 • Pro-Shop: 01665 830043
e-mail: secretary@alnmouthgolfclub.com • www.alnmouthgolfclub.com

Visitors are sure of a friendly Northumbrian welcome at what is widely regarded as one of the finest courses in the North East. A coastal club with parkland turf and fine quality greens. Dormy house accommodation available.

ALNWICK GOLF CLUB

GREEN FEES (2010 rates subject to review):
WEEKDAYS £25 per round, £35 per day
WEEKENDS & BANK HOLIDAYS £27.50 per round • £35 per day
2-Fore-1 and Bunkers vouchers accepted • Golf Passport.
Tel: 01665 602632 • SEE WEBSITE FOR SPECIAL OFFERS
e-mail: neil@neil448.orangehome.co.uk • www.alnwick-golfclub.co.uk

Point Cottages, Bamburgh

A cluster of cottages in a superb location next to a beautiful golf course only a short drive away from many other attractive Links courses. Bamburgh is an unspoilt coastal village dominated by a magnificent castle and is an ideal base for visiting historic Northumbria. In excellent order, warm, cosy and well-equipped. Overlooking the sea. Sandy beaches nearby. Large garden. Parking (two cars per cottage).

John and Elizabeth Sanderson, 30 The Oval, Benton, Newcastle-upon-Tyne NE12 9PP
Tel: 0191-266 2800 • Fax: 0191-215 1630
e-mail: info@bamburgh-cottages.co.uk • www.bamburgh-cottages.co.uk

WAREN LEA HALL

Budle Bay, Bamburgh
Luxurious Self-Catering Holiday Accommodation for families, golf parties and friends.

Short and long breaks on the beautiful coast of Northumberland.

Standing on the shore of beautiful Budle Bay, an Area of Outstanding Natural Beauty, central for 10 golf courses, lies WAREN LEA HALL (up to 14 guests). This wonderfully sited Old Hall, set in 2½ acres, enjoys spectacular views over the bay to Lindisfarne. In addition to the Hall there are two entirely self-contained apartments, GHILLIE'S VIEW (up to 10 guests) and GARDEN COTTAGE (up to 4 guests). ParSport 3 & 5 day discounts for 12 courses.

For further information please contact the owners:
Carolynn and David Croisdale-Appleby
Abbotsholme, Hervines Road
Amersham, Buckinghamshire HP6 5HS
Tel: 01494 725194 • Mobile: 07901 716136
e-mail: croisdaleappleby@aol.com
www.selfcateringluxury.co.uk

BELLINGHAM. **Bellingham Golf Club,** Boggle Hole, Bellingham, Hexham NE48 2DT (01434 220530). *Location:* 17 miles north of Hexham on B6320, in the picturesque North Tyne Valley between Hadrian's Wall and the Scottish Border. Rolling parkland course with an abundance of natural hazards. 18 holes, 6077 yards, 5557 metres. S.S.S. 70. Driving range. *Green Fees:* weekdays £24.00; weekends £30.00. *Eating facilities:* full bar and catering available throughout the year. *Visitors:* welcome at all times, daily starting sheet. Buggies for hire. *Society Meetings:* welcome by advance booking. Secretary: Craig Wright (01434 220530).
e-mail: admin@bellinghamgolfclub.com
website: www.bellinghamgolfclub.com

BERWICK-UPON-TWEED. **Berwick-upon-Tweed (Goswick) Golf Club,** Goswick, Berwick-upon-Tweed TD15 2RW (01289 387256; Fax: 01289 387392). *Location:* signposted off A1, five miles south of Berwick-upon-Tweed. Seaside links, undulating fairways, elevated tees. Open Regional Qualifying Course until 2012. 18 holes, 6686 yards. S.S.S. 72. Driving range, practice ground. *Green Fees:* weekdays £33.00 per round, £42.00 per day; weekends £38.00 per round, £48.00 per day. 2010 rates (subject to review). *Eating facilities:* full catering available. *Visitors:* welcome, restricted at weekends. Buggies and carts for hire. *Society Meetings:* welcome midweek and weekends. Professional: Paul Terras (01289 387380). Secretary: (01289 387256; Fax: 01289 387392).
e-mail: goswickgc@btconnect.com
website: www.goswicklinksgc.co.uk

BERWICK-UPON-TWEED. **Magdalene Fields Golf Club**, Magdalene Fields, Berwick-upon-Tweed TD15 1NE (01289 306130). *Location:* five minutes' walk from town centre and railway station. Seaside, parkland course with stunning scenic views. 18 holes, 6521 yards. S.S.S. 71. Practice area and putting area. *Green Fees:* information not available. *Eating facilities:* bar and dining area - first class meals. *Visitors:* welcome Monday to Saturday, restrictions on Sundays. Member of Parsport to Scenic Northumberland. *Society Meetings:* all welcome. Secretary: J. Gall (01289 306130).
website: www.magdalene-fields.co.uk

BLYTH. **Blyth Golf Club Ltd,** New Delaval, Blyth NE24 4DB. *Location:* 12 miles north of Newcastle near the coast. Flat parkland, water hazards. 18 holes, 6424 yards. S.S.S. 71. Large practice area and putting green. Host to Northumberland County Championships 2005. *Green Fees:* information not available. *Eating facilities:* full catering and bar. *Visitors:* welcome weekdays up to 4pm and weekends after 2pm. Starting times available in advance; please ring Professional. *Society Meetings:* welcome, packages available. Professional: Andrew Brown (01670 356514). Manager: Jim Wright (01670 540110).*
e-mail: clubmanager@blythgolf.co.uk
website: www.blythgolf.co.uk

Riverdale Hall Hotel
Bellingham Northumberland NE48 2JT
01434 220254

The Cocker Family's 32nd year

Opposite Bellingham Golf Course – host to county events and one of the most highly rated moorland courses in the north. Indoor pool and sauna and the only hotel in the north with Les Routiers Gold Plate Award for its restaurant. 28 bedrooms all en suite plus 5 self-catering cottages and apartments.

Nearby courses include Minto, Woll, Brampton, Dunstanburgh, Hexham and Matfen Hall

GOLF, BED AND BREAKFAST AND DINNER FROM £89.00 PER PERSON

www.riverdalehallhotel.co.uk
reservations@riverdalehallhotel.co.uk

CARLISLE. **Haltwhistle Golf Course,** Wallend Farm, Gilsland, Greenhead, Via Carlisle CA8 7HN (016977 47367). *Location*: off the A69 at the village of Greenhead on Gilsland Road, two and a half miles west of Haltwhistle. Undulating parkland course with wooded areas. 18 holes, 5532 yards. S.S.S. 68. Practice area. *Green Fees*: information not provided. *Eating facilities*: clubhouse bar, catering by prior arrangement. *Visitors*: welcome, no restrictions except Sundays 8am to 11am competition days. *Society Meetings*: welcome by prior arrangement. Secretary: K.L. Dickinson (01434 320708).

EMBLETON. **Dunstanburgh Castle Golf Club,** Embleton NE66 3XQ (01665 576562). *Location:* seven miles off A1, to the north-east of Alnwick. Seaside links course in area of outstanding natural beauty. Designed by James Braid. 18 holes, 6298 yards. S.S.S. 70. *Green Fees:* weekdays £26.00 per day; weekends £32.00 per round, £38.00 per day. *Eating facilities:* snacks, lunches, high teas; bar. *Visitors:* welcome without reservation. *Society Meetings:* welcome anytime. Secretary: P.F.C. Gilbert.
e-mail: enquiries@dunstanburgh.com
website: www.dunstanburgh.com

HEXHAM. **Hexham Golf Club,** Spital Park, Hexham NE46 3RZ (01434 603072; Fax: 01434 601865). *Location:* 20 miles west of Newcastle upon Tyne, one mile west of Hexham town centre. An undulating parkland course, one of the driest in the area, with superb views of the north and south Tyne valleys. 18 holes, 6294 yards. S.S.S. 70. *Green Fees:* weekdays £35.00 per round, £45.00 per day; weekends and Bank Holidays £45.00 per round only. Special packages available. *Eating facilities:* lunches and evening meals. *Visitors:* welcome without reservation. Preliminary booking advisable. *Society Meetings:* catered for Monday to Friday by arrangement. Professional: Andy Paisley (01434 603072). Secretary: Dawn Wylie (01434 603072; Fax: 01434 601865).
website: www.hexhamgolf.co.uk

Please mention THE GOLF GUIDE when you enquire about clubs or accommodation

Visitors are welcomed at **BERWICK-UPON-TWEED GOSWICK GOLF CLUB**
Signposted off the A1, south of Berwick, only 15 minutes from the centre. The club is open all year to non-members. • Anytime weekdays • Bookings weekdays and weekends • Bar service • Catering • Resident Pro
Secretary: Ian Alsop (01289 387256)   **Pro Shop: Paul Terras (01289 387380)**
e-mail: goswickgc@btconnect.com   e-mail: paul@pterras.freeserve.co.uk
• Please book via Professional • Full and Country Membership Available
www.goswicklinksgc.co.uk   Open Regional Qualifying Course 2008-2012

Magdalene Fields Golf Club
Magdalene Fields, Berwick-upon-Tweed TD15 1NE
5 minutes' walk from town centre and railway station • Seaside, parkland course with stunning scenic views • 18 holes, 6521 yards. S.S.S. 72 • Bar and dining area
• Visitors welcome Monday to Saturday, restrictions on Sundays • Club Manager: J. Gall.
Tel: 01289 306130 • www.magdalene-fields.co.uk • Secretary: J. Gall

Blyth Golf Club
Blyth
Northumberland NE24 4DB

Enjoy our superb 18 hole parkland course, host to the Northumberland County Championships 2005. Added to this, superb catering from our Stewardess, Christine, will ensure that you have a day to remember.
Genuine hospitality awaits you, here in Blyth!
Excellent package deals for Golf Societies & Company days. Ring Club Manager Jim Wright on the above number for details or e-mail clubmanager@blythgolf.co.uk

01670 540110   **www.blythgolf.co.uk**

300 Northumberland / NORTH REGION

HEXHAM. **Tynedale Golf Club,** Tynegreen, Hexham NE46 3HQ (01434 608154). *Location:* off A69 towards Hexham over Tyne Bridge, first roundabout turn right - golf course at the end of road. Flat, parkland course along the banks of the river. 9 holes, 5403 yards. S.S.S. 67. *Green Fees:* information not provided. *Eating facilities:* full catering available. *Visitors:* welcome, restricted Sunday mornings 11.30am members only. *Society Meetings:* welcome, discounts for parties over 10 people. Secretary: Trevor Hodge.

MATFEN. **Matfen Hall Golf Club,** Matfen, Newcastle upon Tyne NE20 0RH (01661 886400; Fax: 01661 886055). *Location:* 15 miles west of Newcastle, five miles north of Corbridge, off B6318 (Military Road). Lovely parkland setting directly in front of Matfen Hall, with natural and added water hazards. 27 holes, 6700 yards. S.S.S. 72. New Dewlaw course: full 9 hole course, approx 3400 yards. Old front 9 called Douglas, back 9 called Standing Stone. Covered driving range. *Green Fees:* information not provided. *Visitors:* very welcome any day; after 11am weekends. Good locker room facilities. 'Stay and Play' packages available at Matfen Hall Country House Hotel. *Society Meetings:* very welcome. Professional: John Harrison. Golf and Leisure Manager: Peter Smith.
e-mail: golf@matfenhall.com
website: www.matfenhall.com

MORPETH. **Burgham Park Golf and Leisure Club,** Near Felton, Morpeth NE65 9QP (01670 787898; Fax: 01670 787164). Home of the PGA North Region Championship 2006-2008. *Location:* 5½ miles north of Morpeth, ½ mile west of A1 on Longhorsley Road. 18 holes; 7065 yards championship tees, 6804 yards medal tees, 6403 leisure tees. S.S.S. 72. Practice area. *Green Fees:* £30.00 weekdays, £35.00 weekdays and Bank Holidays. 2010 rates (subject to review). *Eating facilities:* catering and bar available daily. *Visitors:* welcome; special rates for parties by arrangement. Secretary: William Kiely. Professional/Golf Manager: David Mather.
e-mail: info@burghampark.co.uk
website: www.burghampark.co.uk

MORPETH. **Longhirst Hall Golf Course,** Longhirst, Morpeth NE61 3LL (Tee Reservations: 01670 791562; Fax: 01670 791768). *Location:* on A1 3 miles north from Morpeth take B1337 Hebron road. Florida-style course with two 18-hole layouts (Dawson and Lakes courses) during the summer, and one layout in winter, with water featuring on many holes. Greens built to USGA specifications. Astro Turf driving range. Full spec chipping and putting green. Host of 2010 Euro Pro Tour. *Green Fees:* from £10.00. *Eating facilities:* bar. *Visitors:* welcome (advisable to pre-book). *Society Meetings:* welcome any day of the week. 75 bedroom hotel on site with sports village. Professional: Wayne Tyrie Golf School. Clubhouse Manager: Graham Chambers (01670 791562).
e-mail: enquiries@longhirstgolf.co.uk
website: www.longhirstgolf.co.uk

MORPETH. **Macdonald Linden Hall,** Longhorsley, Morpeth NE65 8XF (01670 500011; Fax: 01670 500001). *Location:* A697 from A1, half a mile from Longhorsley. Mature woodland parkland and rolling countryside with many water features. 18 holes, 6846 yards. S.S.S. 73. Driving range, pitching green, putting green. *Green Fees:* information not available. *Eating facilities:* Linden Tree (traditional country pub), Dobson Restaurant, function suites. *Visitors:* welcome, prior booking essential, packages available. *Society Meetings:* welcome, telephone for enquiries. Director of Golf: Geoff Dixon.*
e-mail: golf.lindenhall@macdonald-hotels.co.uk
website: www.macdonaldhotels.co.uk/lindenhall

MORPETH. **The Morpeth Golf Club Ltd.,** The Clubhouse, Morpeth NE61 2BT (01670 515675). *Location:* turn off A1 for Morpeth, A167 south side of town. Easy walking parkland. 18 holes, 6206 yards. S.S.S. 69. Practice area. *Green Fees:* information not available. *Eating facilities:* restaurant/bar meals/snacks etc. *Visitors:* welcome, weekdays after 9.30am, Handicap Certificates may be asked for. Venue for 1997 County Strokeplay and 2000 County Matchplay Championships. *Society Meetings:* catered for weekdays by prior arrangement; discounts available for large parties. Professional: M.R. Jackson (01670 515675). General Manager: T. Minett (01670 504942; Fax: 01670 504918).*

NEWBIGGIN-BY-THE-SEA. **Newbiggin-by-the-Sea Golf Club,** Clubhouse, Prospect Place, Newbiggin-by-the-Sea NE64 6DW (01670 817344; Fax: 01670 520236). *Location:* take signpost for Newbiggin off A189 (spine road from Tyne Tunnel). Clubhouse at most easterly point of village, adjacent to Church Point Caravan Park. Links course. 18 holes, 6452 yards, 5900 metres. S.S.S. 72. Practice area. *Green Fees:* information not provided. *Eating facilities:* restaurant, bar and lounge. *Visitors:* welcome, not before 10am or on competition days. *Society Meetings:* catered for by prior arrangement with Secretary. Secretary: Frank Fletcher (01670 817344).

NEWCASTLE UPON TYNE. **Arcot Hall Golf Club Ltd,** Arcot Hall, Dudley, Cramlington NE23 7QP (0191-236 2794). *Location:* seven miles north of Newcastle. Turn off A1 for Cramlington and then signposted. Flat, parkland – mostly tree lined. 18 holes, 6329 yards, 5788 metres. S.S.S. 70. Practice ground, chipping area, putting green. *Green Fees:* weekdays £28.00 (£23.00); weekends £32.00. *Eating facilities:* good restaurant, bar. *Visitors:* welcome, booking is essential due to popularity of the course. *Society Meetings:* catered for on application to Secretary. Professional: (0191-236 2794). Secretary: Brian Rumney (0191-236 2794).

NEWCASTLE UPON TYNE. **De Vere Slaley Hall Hotel, Golf Resort and Spa,** Hexham NE47 0BX (01434 673350; Fax: 01434 673152). *Location*: 20 miles west of Newcastle upon Tyne, seven miles south of Corbridge, signposted off A68. Set in parkland and moorland with an abundance of lakes and streams, woodland and heather. PGA European Tour Venue. Hunting Course:- Championship Standard, home of the Compaq European Grand Prix: 18 holes, 7088 yards (5903 yards - ladies). S.S.S. 74, 72. Priestman Course: Championship Standard, 18 holes, 6951 yards (5755 yards - ladies). S.S.S 72, 73. Golf academy and driving Range. *Green Fees:* information not available. *Eating facilities:* clubhouse

bar and restaurant; hotel bar and restaurant. *Visitors:* welcome, prior booking essential. 4-star hotel. Buggy hire. *Society Meetings:* welcome anytime, book through Golf Co-ordinator. Golf Reservations (01434 673154) Manager: Mark Stancer (01434 673350; Fax: 01434 673152).*
e-mail: slaley@dircon.co.uk

NEWCASTLE UPON TYNE. **Ponteland Golf Club,** Bell Villas, Ponteland, Newcastle upon Tyne NE20 9BD (01661 822689). *Location:* A696, one and a half miles north of Newcastle Airport. Parkland. 18 holes, 6611 yards. S.S.S. 72. Large practice area. *Green Fees:* £30.00 per day or round (inclusive VAT). *Eating facilities:* full menu in restaurant and bar. *Visitors:* welcome Monday to Thursday, weekends and Bank Holidays. Handicap Certificate required. *Society Meetings:* Tuesdays or Thursdays, catered for with pre-booking agreed by Secretary. Professional: Alan Robson-Crosby (01661 822689). Secretary: Chris Espiner (01661 822689).
e-mail: secretary@thepontelandgolfclub.co.uk
website: www.thepontelandgolfclub.co.uk

PRUDHOE. **Prudhoe Golf Club,** Eastwood Park, Prudhoe NE42 5DX (01661 832466; Fax: 01661 830710). *Location:* 10 miles west of Newcastle upon Tyne, off A695 to Hexham. Wooded parkland with scenic views of the Tyne Valley. 18 holes, 5839 yards. S.S.S. 69. Practice area. *Green Fees:* information not available. *Eating facilities:* bar facilities and bar meals available. *Visitors:* welcome midweek and after 4pm weekends. *Society Meetings:* welcome. Golf Manager: John Crawford (01661 832466).*

ROTHBURY. **Rothbury Golf Club**, Whitton Bank Road, Rothbury, Morpeth, Northumberland NE65 7RX (01669 621271). *Location:* 15 miles north of Morpeth, take A697 turn off at Weldon Bridge for Rothbury. On entering village turn left, cross river and turn immediately right. Club entrance few hundred yards on right, just past hospital. 18 holes, 6160 yards. Par 71, S.S.S. 70. Undulating course adjacent to River Coquet. Practice ground. *Green Fees:* information not available. *Eating facilities*: catering and bar facilities available. *Visitors:* welcome by arrangement. New Clubhouse with function room, showers etc. *Society Meetings:* welcome by arrangement. Secretary: F. Brown (01669 621271 or 0191 2150268).*
website: www.rothburygolfclub.com

SEAHOUSES. **Seahouses Golf Club,** Beadnell Road, Seahouses NE68 7XT (01665 720794). *Location:* 15 miles north of Alnwick, turn off A1 for B1340. Flat seaside links with water hazards. 18 holes, 5542 yards. S.S.S. 67. Practice ground. *Green Fees:* weekdays £24.00 per round, £32.00 per day; weekends £32.00 per round, £40.00 per day. *Eating facilities:* full catering and bar. *Visitors:* welcome all year, telephone club to arrange times. packages available. Buggy, trolley and equipment hire. *Society Meetings:* by arrangement. Secretary: Alan Patterson (01665 720794).
e-mail: secretary@seahousesgolf.co.uk
website: www.seahousesgolf.co.uk

STOCKSFIELD. **Stocksfield Golf Club,** New Ridley, Stocksfield NE43 7RE (01661 843041; Fax: 01661 843046). *Location:* 15 miles west of Newcastle on A69, and three miles east of A68. Half woodland, half parkland, slight hillside. 18 holes, 5991 yards. S.S.S. 69. Small practice areas. *Green Fees:* weekdays £20.00 per round, £25.00 per day; weekends and Bank Holidays £28.00 per round. 2010 rates (subject to review). 2-Fore-1 tickets accepted weekdays only. *Eating facilities:* available, also bar. *Visitors:* welcome except Wednesday mornings. Full size snooker table. Buggies, trolleys and clubs for hire. *Society Meetings:* catered for by prior arrangement. Professional: S. Harrison.

SWARLAND. **Percy Wood Golf & Country Retreat,** Coast View, Swarland, Morpeth NE65 9JG (01670 787940). *Location:* approximately one mile west of A1 trunk road, eight miles south of Alnwick. Parkland course within mature woodland. 18 holes, 6628 yards, 6060 metres. S.S.S. 72. *Green Fees:* information not available. *Eating facilities:* full dining facilities, bar meals, licensed bar. *Visitors:* welcome any day, but suggest telephoning to avoid club competitions on Sundays. Accommodation available on site. *Society Meetings:* welcome. Golf shop. Professional: Peter Ritchie (01670 787010).*

WARKWORTH. **Warkworth Golf Club,** The Links, Warkworth, Morpeth NE65 0SW (01665 711596). *Location:* off A1068 at Warkworth. Seaside links orginally designed by "Old Tom Morris" in 1891. 9 holes, 5986 yards, S.S.S. 70. Practice area. *Green Fees:* weekdays £15.00 per day, weekends £20.00 per day. *Eating facilities:* full catering facilities, bar open 7 days. *Visitors:* welcome except Tuesdays and Saturdays. *Society Meetings:* welcome by arrangement. Secretary: Mark Nicholson (01665 711596).
website: www.warkworthgolfclub.com

WOOLER. **Wooler Golf Club,** Dod Law, Doddington, Wooler NE71 6EA. *Location:* situated on the high ground named Dod Law to the east of the B6525 Wooler–Berwick road. The route is signposted from Doddington village. Hillside course with exceptional panoramic views. 9 holes (18 tees), 6411 yards. S.S.S. 71. Limited practice area. *Green Fees:* information not available. *Eating facilities:* bar open evenings (operated voluntarily). *Visitors:* always welcome except during all day competitions, check with Secretary. Buggies available. *Society Meetings:* welcome by arrangement with Secretary. Secretary: S. Lowrey (01668 281631).*

SEAHOUSES GOLF CLUB 18 HOLES, 5542 YARDS, S.S.S. 67.
Green Fees: £24 per round/£32 per day (weekdays), £32 per round/£40 per day (weekends & Bank Holidays). Full catering and bar. Visitors, Society meetings by arrangement.
For details Tel: Secretary 01665 720794
Beadnell Road, Seahouses, Northumberland NE68 7XT
e-mail: secretary@seahousesgolf.co.uk • www.seahousesgolf.co.uk

Tyne & Wear

BIRTLEY. **Birtley Golf Club,** Birtley Lane, Birtley DH3 2LR (0191-410-2207). *Location:* just off old Durham road and main A1. Parkland. 9 holes, 5740 yards. S.S.S. 67. *Green Fees:* £15.00 per round. *Eating facilities:* bar open after 7.15pm each evening and 11.45am to 5pm Saturday, 11.45 to 4pm Sunday; snacks available. *Visitors:* welcome weekdays; weekends and Bank Holidays with a member only. *Society Meetings:* welcome, must be pre-booked. Catering available. Secretary: Mrs Jackie Proud (0191 410 2207).
e-mail: birtleygolfclub@aol.com
website: www.birtleyportobellogolfclub.co.uk

CHOPWELL. **Garesfield Golf Club,** Chopwell NE17 7AP (Tel & Fax: 01207 561309; Bar and Catering 01207 561278). Sat Nav: NE17 7AP Clayton Terrace Road. *Location:* leave A694 at Rowlands Gill, follow signposts for Chopwell, after approximately three miles turn left at The Bute Arms; golf course is one mile up road on left. Undulating wooded parkland. 18 holes, 6043 yards. par 72. Practice ground, nets and putting green. *Green Fees:* from £15.00. *Eating facilities:* catering available. *Visitors:* welcome weekdays; weekends and Bank Holidays confirm availability. Buggies available. *Society Meetings:* welcome. Group rates (min. 12) check availability with Secretary. Professional: S. Cowell (01207 563082). Secretary: (01207 561309).
e-mail: garesfieldgc@btconnect.com
website: www.garesfieldgolfclub.co.uk

EAST BOLDON. **Boldon Golf Club Ltd,** Dipe Lane, East Boldon NE36 0PQ (0191-536 5360). *Location:* near Sunderland, approximately one mile from roundabout at junction of A19 and A184 highways. Fairly flat parkland. 18 holes, 6414 yards. S.S.S. 71. *Green Fees:* weekdays £22.50, with a member £15.00; weekends £25.50, with a member £15.00. *Eating facilities:* bar snacks and restaurant. *Visitors:* welcome, not between 9am and 10am. Not before 12 noon Saturdays or 1.30pm Sundays. *Society Meetings:* catered for. Professional: Phipps Golf (0191-536 5835; Fax: 0191-537 2270). Secretary: D.A. Greenfield (0191-536 5360; Fax: 0191-537 2270).
e-mail: info@boldongolfclub.co.uk
website: www.boldongolfclub.co.uk

GATESHEAD. **Heworth Golf Club,** Gingling Gate, Heworth, Gateshead. *Location:* A1 (M) south east boundary of Gateshead. Flat wooded course. 18 holes, 6422 yards. S.S.S. 71. Practice area. *Green Fees:* information not available. *Eating facilities:* diningroom, two bars. *Visitors:* weekdays up to 4pm, no visitors Saturdays; but after 10am on Sundays. *Society Meetings:* welcome mid-week only up to 4pm. Professional: A. Marshall (0191-438 4223). Secretary: C. J. Watson (0191-469 9832).*

GATESHEAD. **Ravensworth Golf Club Ltd,** 'Angel View', Longbank, Gateshead NE9 7NE (0191-487 6014). *Location:* two miles south of Gateshead town centre, near A1 (Angel of the North). Parkland course. 18 holes, 5825 yards. S.S.S. 69. *Green Fees:* information not available. *Eating facilities:* meals served with reasonable notice (not Mondays). *Visitors:* welcome, weekends very restricted. *Society Meetings:* catered for. General Manager: (0191-487 6014).*

HEDDON ON THE WALL. **Close House Hotel and Golf,** Heddon on the Wall, Newcastle upon Tyne NE15 0HT (01661 852255). *Location:* 10 miles west of Newcastle, signposted off A69 to Wylam. Set in picturesque parkland with panoramic views of the Tyne Valley. Undergoing £7.5 million development including Colt Course - new Championship Course due to open in June 2011. The essence and focus of the design is fun for all level of golfers. Much anticipated Turner-Macpherson designed course has been named as a tribute to the famous golf architect Harry Colt, and his courses have influenced the design. 18 holes, 6900 yards. Par 71. Filly Course - 18 holes, 6000 yards. Par 70. New state-of-the-art clubhouse and golf academy/custom fit centre with teaching bay, short game area, indoor and outdoor bays and cafe. Buggy hire. *Green Fees:* information not provided. *Eating facilities*: restaurant and bar menu. *Visitors*: welcome, booking is essential. 4-star hotel. *Society Meetings*: welcome, telephone with enquiries. Golf Operations Manager: John Glendinning (01661 852255).
e-mail: enquiries@closehouse.co.uk
website: www.closehouse.co.uk

HETTON-LE-HOLE. **Elemore Golf Course,** Elemore Lane, Hetton-Le-Hole (0191-517 3057; Fax: 0191 517 3054). *Location:* follow signs to Easington Lane, located off A1068, following signs to Elemore/Pittington. Flat meadowland Public Pay & Play golf course. 18 holes, 5947 yards. S.S.S. 69. Practice area. *Green Fees:* information not available. *Eating facilities:* clubhouse with bar/lounge serving snacks and meals. *Visitors:* welcome, no restrictions. Buggy Hire £12.00 per round. *Society Meetings:* welcome throughout the year. Contact Course Manager for advance bookings (14 days' notice required). Course Manager: Barbara Blenkinsop.*

GARESFIELD Golf Club
Chopwell, Tyne & Wear NE17 7AP

Packages available • Prices on application
For further details contact The Secretary
Mr A Teasdale on 01207 561309
garesfieldgc@btconnect.com

NORTH REGION / Tyne & Wear

HOUGHTON-LE-SPRING. Houghton-le-Spring Golf Club, Copt Hill, Houghton-le-Spring DH5 8LU (0191 5841198). *Location:* off A690 Durham road take Seaham road, course is situated at the top of Copt Hill Bank. Testing hillside course. 18 holes, 6120 yards, S.S.S. 71, Par 72. *Green Fees:* information not available. *Eating facilities:* excellent food available (not Mondays), bar open every day. *Visitors:* welcome every day except competition days (Sundays). Buggies available. *Society Meetings:* catered for by arrangement with Professional. Professional: Graeme Robinson (0191 5847421). Secretary: David Freeman (0191 5840048).*
e-mail: houghton.golf@virgin.net
website: www.houghtongolfclub.co.uk

NEWCASTLE UPON TYNE. City of Newcastle Golf Club, Three Mile Bridge, Gosforth, Newcastle upon Tyne NE3 2DR (0191-285 1775; Fax: 0191-284 0700). *Location:* B1318 three miles north of city. Flat woodland. 18 holes, 6528 yards. S.S.S. 71. *Green Fees:* Monday to Sunday £28.00, £36.00 per day. *Eating facilities:* bar, meals. *Visitors:* welcome without reservation, restricted times Fridays. *Society Meetings:* very welcome. Professional: S. McKenna (0191-285 5481; Fax: 0191-284 0700). Club Manager: A.J. Matthew (0191-285 1775).
e-mail: info@cityofnewcastlegolfclub.com
website: www.cityofnewcastlegolfclub.com

NEWCASTLE UPON TYNE. Gosforth Golf Club, Broadway East, Gosforth, Newcastle upon Tyne NE3 5ER (0191-285 0553). *Location:* three miles north of Newcastle near Great North Road, B1318. Parkland with stream. 18 holes, 6024 yards. S.S.S. 69. *Green Fees:* information not available. *Visitors:* welcome weekdays and weekends. *Society Meetings:* catered for by arrangement with the Secretary, including some weekends and Bank Holidays. Professional: G. Garland (0191-285 0553). Secretary: Greg Waugh (0191-285 3495; Fax: 0191-284 6274).*
e-mail: gosforth.golf@virgin.net
website: www.gosforthgolfclub.com

NEWCASTLE UPON TYNE. Hobson Golf Club, Hobson, Burnopfield, Newcastle upon Tyne NE16 6BZ (01207 271605). *Location:* on Newcastle to Consett road. Fairly flat, well designed course. 18 holes, 6403 yards, 5854 metres. S.S.S. 71. Practice area. *Green Fees:* information not available. *Eating facilities:* bar, lounge and restaurant. *Visitors:* no restrictions; booking system at weekends. Strict dress code in operation. *Society Meetings:* by prior arrangement with Professional (all bookings). Professional: J.W. Ord (01207 271605). Secretaries: A. Giles and T. Maguire.*

NEWCASTLE UPON TYNE. Newcastle United Golf Club, 60 Ponteland Road, Cowgate, Newcastle upon Tyne NE3 3JW (0191-286 9998). *Location:* two miles west of city centre in direction of airport. Moorland. 18 holes, 6617 yards, 6048 metres. S.S.S. 72. Practice area. *Green Fees:* information not available. *Eating facilities:* bar meals available. *Visitors:* no restrictions midweek, welcome weekends if no competitions. Book through the golf shop or see our website. *Society Meetings:* welcome, book through Secretary. Golf Shop: (0191-286 9998). Secretary: S. Darbyshire.*
website: www.nugc.co.uk

NEWCASTLE UPON TYNE. The Northumberland Golf Club Ltd, High Gosforth Park, Newcastle upon Tyne NE3 5HT (0191-236 2498). *Location:* off A1. 18 holes, 6680 yards. S.S.S. 72. *Green Fees:* £50.00 per round, £60 per day weekdays; £60.00 per round weekends. *Visitors:* club members are most welcome but should contact Secretary to avoid disappointment. *Society Meetings:* small groups can now be catered for on Mondays and at weekends. Secretary: Jamie Forteath (0191-236 2498; Fax: 0191-236 2036).
e-mail: sec@thengc.co.uk
website: www.thengc.co.uk

Other British holiday guides from FHG Guides

PUBS & INNS · 300 GREAT HOTELS
SHORT BREAK HOLIDAYS
The bestselling and original PETS WELCOME!
500 GREAT PLACES TO STAY
SELF-CATERING HOLIDAYS · BED & BREAKFAST STOPS
CARAVAN & CAMPING HOLIDAYS · FAMILY BREAKS

Published annually: available in all good bookshops or direct from the publisher:
FHG Guides, Abbey Mill Business Centre, Seedhill, Paisley PA1 1TJ
Tel: 0141 887 0428 • Fax: 0141 889 7204
e-mail: admin@fhguides.co.uk • www.holidayguides.com

NEWCASTLE UPON TYNE. **Parklands Golf Club,** High Gosforth Park, Newcastle upon Tyne NE3 5HQ (0191-236 4480). *Location:* three miles north of centre of Newcastle, off the A1 follow signs for Gosforth Park. Parkland. 18 holes, 6013 yards, 5742 metres. S.S.S. 69. 18 hole mini golf course, 28 bay floodlit driving range. *Green Fees:* information not available. *Eating facilities:* restaurant and bar. *Visitors:* welcome, no restrictions. *Society Meetings:* catered for. Complex Manager: David King (0191-236 3322). Secretary: Geoff Brown (0191-236 4480).*

NEWCASTLE UPON TYNE. **Tyneside Golf Club Ltd,** Westfield Lane, Ryton NE40 3QE (0191-413 2742; Fax: 0191-413 0199). *Location:* seven miles west of Newcastle upon Tyne, off B6317 in Ryton Village. Parkland, hilly with water hazards. Large practice area. 18 holes, 6103 yards. S.S.S. 70. Practice field. *Green Fees:* weekdays £35.00; weekends £42.00. *Eating facilities:* full catering. *Visitors:* bona fide golfers welcome by arrangement with the Golf Services Manager or Professional. *Society Meetings:* weekdays by arrangement with Golf Services Manager or Professional; possibly Sunday afternoons. Professional: Gary Vickers (0191-413 1600). Secretary: (0191-413 2742).

NEWCASTLE UPON TYNE. **Westerhope Golf Club,** Whorlton Grange, Westerhope, Newcastle-upon-Tyne NE5 1PP (0191-286 9125). *Location:* Stamfordham Road, Westerhope, near Jingling Gate Public House. Parkland/wooded. 18 holes, 6392 yards. S.S.S. 71. Two practice areas. *Green Fees:* £26.00 per round. *Eating facilities:* lunches and high teas. *Visitors:* welcome weekdays. *Society Meetings:* welcome weekdays and Bank Holidays. Professional: M. Nesbit (0191-286 0594). Secretary: D. Souter (0191-286 7636).

NEWCASTLE UPON TYNE. **Whickham Golf Club Ltd,** Hollinside Park, Fellside Road, Whickham, Newcastle upon Tyne NE16 5BA (0191-488 1576; Fax: 0191-488 1577). *Location:* on the east bank of the beautiful Derwent Valley, easily reached from the A1 Western By-pass. City centre 6 miles, Metro Centre 2.5 miles. Parkland course - undulating with attractive panoramic views. 18 holes, 6666 yards. Par 72. Practice grounds and putting green. *Green Fees:* weekdays £30.00, weekends £35.00. *Eating facilities:* lunches, teas, evening meals available by prior order, bar snacks all day. *Visitors:* welcome by arrangement with Professional. Smart casual wear on course and in clubhouse. *Society Meetings:* welcome by arrangement with Secretary. Professional: Simon Williamson (0191-488 8591). Secretary: M.E. Pearse (0191-488 1576; Fax: 0191-488 1577).
e-mail: enquiries@whickhamgolfclub.co.uk
website: www.whickhamgolfclub.co.uk

RYTON. **Ryton Golf Club,** Dr. Stanners, Clara Vale, Ryton NE40 3TD (0191-413 3253). *Location:* off A695 eight miles west of Newcastle at Crawcrook to Clara Vale. Flat parkland, wooded, running alongside River Tyne. 18 holes, 6042 yards, 5499 metres. S.S.S. 69. Practice area. *Green Fees:* information not available.

Eating facilities: available by arrangement with Steward. *Visitors:* welcome weekdays, weekends with member or by prior arrangement. *Society Meetings:* catered for by arrangement with Secretary. Secretary: Mrs H. Oliver (0191-413 3253; Fax: 0191-413 1642).*

SHIREMOOR. **Backworth Golf Club,** The Hall, Backworth, Shiremoor NE27 0AH (Course Information Service: 0191-268 9131; Club Steward: 0191-268 1048). *Location:* A191 Newcastle to Whitley Bay; at Shiremoor crossroads turn left one mile. Flat parkland, part wooded. 9 holes, 5800 yards. S.S.S. 68. Putting/chipping area. *Green Fees:* information not available. *Eating facilities:* dinner booked in advance; bar meals/snacks. *Visitors:* welcome by arrangement but not Tuesday (Ladies' Day), not Saturday until 5.30pm (Summer), not Sunday mornings. *Society Meetings:* welcome by prior arrangement only. Secretary: G.M. Sales (0191 268 8815).*
e-mail: backworth.miners@virgin.net

SOUTH SHIELDS. **South Shields Golf Club Ltd,** Cleadon Hills, South Shields NE34 8EG (0191-456 0475). *Location:* near A19 and A1 M, Cleadon Chimney prominent landmark. 18 holes, 6222 yards. S.S.S. 70. Excellent greens, heathland/links, practice area. *Green Fees:* information not available. *Eating facilities:* meals available at all times, bar. *Visitors:* welcome at all times without reservation. *Society Meetings:* catered for by arrangement. Professional: G. Jones. (0191-456 0110). Secretary: R. Stanness (0191-456 8942).*

SOUTH SHIELDS. **Whitburn Golf Club Ltd,** Lizard Lane, South Shields NE34 7AF (0191-529 4944). *Location:* between Sunderland and South Shields adjoining Coast Road. Parkland. 18 holes, 5899 yards, S.S.S. 69. *Green Fees:* information not available. *Eating facilities:* available. *Visitors:* welcome except on Sunday when competitions being held and restricted Tuesdays (Ladies' Day). *Society Meetings:* catered for on weekdays by prior reservations. Professional: (0191-529 4210). Secretary: R. Button (0191-529 4944).*
website: www.golf-whitburn.co.uk

SUNDERLAND. **Wearside Golf Club,** Cox Green, Sunderland SR4 9JT (0191-534 2518). *Location:* on south bank of River Wear, one mile west of A19. From A19 exit for A183, direction Chester-le-Street, at 100 yards turn right, signposted Offerton/Cox Green, then left at T junction, down hill over humped bridge. Parkland, bordered on north by River Wear, deep wooded gully traverses course. 18 holes, 6323 yards. S.S.S. 70. 4 holes Par 3 field and separate practice field. *Green Fees:* information not provided. *Eating facilities:* full catering and bar service. *Visitors:* welcome most times, telephone Professional for information. *Society Meetings:* by advance application. Professional: Doug Brolls (0191-534 4269). Secretary: P. Hall (0191-534 2518).

THE GOLF GUIDE 2011

NORTH REGION / Tyne & Wear

TYNEMOUTH. Tynemouth Golf Club Ltd, Spital Dene, Tynemouth NE30 2ER (0191 257 4578). *Location:* on A695. 18 holes, 6359 yards. S.S.S. 70. *Green Fees:* information not provided. *Eating facilities:* full range of catering available. *Visitors:* welcome Monday to Friday after 9.30am. Tuesday is Ladies' Day. *Society Meetings:* welcome Monday to Friday and after 1pm on Sundays. Professional: John McKenna. Secretary: T.J. Scott.

WALLSEND. Wallsend Golf Club, Rheydt Avenue, Wallsend NE28 8SU. *Location:* western boundary. Parkland. 18 holes, 6031 yards. S.S.S. 69. Driving range. *Green Fees:* weekdays £20.00, weekends and Bank Holidays £24.00. *Eating facilities:* meals available on request. *Visitors:* restricted weekends - not before 12.30pm April to October. *Society Meetings:* welcome. Golf Shop (0191-263 1538). Secretary: D. Souter (0191-262 1973).

WASHINGTON. George Washington Golf and Country Club, Stone Cellar Road, Washington NE37 1PH (0191-402 9988). *Location:* Washington New Town, one mile from A1M Junction A194. Parkland course with many tree-lined fairways. 18 holes, 6604 yards, 6038 metres. S.S.S. 72. 21 bay floodlit driving range, 9 hole Par 3 course. *Green Fees:* information not available. *Eating facilities:* fully licensed hotel on site. *Visitors:* welcome by arrangement. Special rates for visiting parties of over 12 midweek. Hotel with 103 bedrooms. *Society Meetings:* society/corporate golf days catered for. Professional/ Golf Manager: Graeme Robinson (0191-417 8346).*
e-mail: graeme.amanda@btopenworld.com

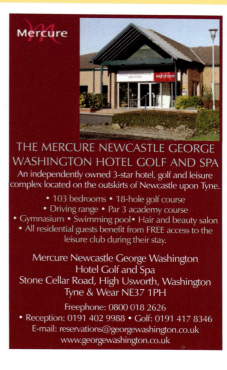

THE MERCURE NEWCASTLE GEORGE WASHINGTON HOTEL GOLF AND SPA

An independently owned 3-star hotel, golf and leisure complex located on the outskirts of Newcastle upon Tyne.

- 103 bedrooms • 18-hole golf course
- Driving range • Par 3 academy course
- Gymnasium • Swimming pool • Hair and beauty salon
- All residential guests benefit from FREE access to the leisure club during their stay.

Mercure Newcastle George Washington
Hotel Golf and Spa
Stone Cellar Road, High Usworth, Washington
Tyne & Wear NE37 1PH

Freephone: 0800 018 2626
• Reception: 0191 402 9988 • Golf: 0191 417 8346
E-mail: reservations@georgewashington.co.uk
www.georgewashington.co.uk

WHITLEY BAY. Whitley Bay Golf Club, Claremont Road, Whitley Bay NE26 3UF (0191-252 0180). *Location:* north side of town. Simulated links. 18 holes, 6529 yards. S.S.S. 71. *Green Fees:* weekdays £30.00 per round, £40.00 per day; weekends £35.00. Reductions for visiting societies. *Eating facilities:* full catering every day. *Visitors:* welcome every weekday, and Sunday afternoons. *Society Meetings:* catered for by arrangement. Professional: P. Crosby (0191-252 5688). Secretary: Frank Elliott (0191-252 0180).
e-mail: whtglfcclb@aol.com
website: www.whitleybaygolfclub.co.uk

THE APPEARANCE OF AN ASTERISK (*) AT THE END OF A CLUB OR COURSE ENTRY INDICATES THAT UP-TO-DATE INFORMATION HAS NOT BEEN SUPPLIED

Looking for accommodation near golf clubs?, then visit
www.holidayguides.com
for where to stay when playing golf around the regions

East Yorkshire

BEVERLEY. **Beverley and East Riding Golf Club,** Westwood, Beverley HU17 8RG (01482 867190). *Location:* one mile west of Beverley on Walkington Road. Common pastureland, undulating course with 18 distinctively different holes. 18 holes, 6127 yards. S.S.S. 69. *Green Fees:* £17.00 weekdays, £24.00 weekends and Bank Holidays. *Eating facilities:* bar snacks available 11.30am until 2pm, evening meals by arrangement. *Visitors:* welcome any time. Cart and club hire. *Society Meetings:* welcome weekdays by prior arrangement. Professional: Alex Ashby (01482 869519). Secretary: Mike Drew (Tel & Fax: 01482 868757).

BEVERLEY. **Cherry Burton Golf Club,** Leconfield Lane, Cherry Burton, Beverley HU17 7LU (Tel & Fax: 01964 550924). *Location:* off the B1248 3 miles north of Beverley. Parkland course with lakes. 9 holes and 18 tees, 6345 yards. Par 71. Driving range, putting green. *Green Fees:* information not provided. *Eating facilities:* licensed bar, light meals, sandwiches. *Visitors:* welcome. Pro shop, tuition, golf academy. *Society Meetings:* welcome, please telephone. Professionals: John Gray and John Wells (01964 550924; Fax: 01964 550924). Secretary: James Walmsley (Tel & Fax: 01964 550924).
website: www.cherryburtongolfclub.co.uk

BRIDLINGTON. **Bridlington Golf Club,** Belvedere Road, Bridlington YO15 3NA (01262 606367). *Location:* A165 main Hull to Bridlington Road. Flat parkland course with sea views, excellent greens with ponds, ditches, bunkers and trees. 18 holes, 6638 yards. S.S.S. 72. Practice facilities/area. *Green Fees:* information not available. *Eating facilities:* food available, bar meals and full menu/usual bar hours. *Visitors:* welcome seven days a week (advisable to book in advance). *Society Meetings:* excellent packages available for parties of 12 or more. Professional: Anthony Howarth (01262 674721). Admin Office: Claire Horrocks (01262 606367).*
e-mail: enquiries@bridlingtongolfclub.co.uk
website: www.bridlingtongolfclub.co.uk

BRIDLINGTON. **The Bridlington Links,** Flamborough Road, Marton, Bridlington YO15 1DW (01262 401584; Fax: 01262 401702). *Location:* on the B1255 between Bridlington and Flamborough. Links course on clifftop with spectacular views over Bridlington Bay. 18 holes, 6719 yards. S.S.S. 72. 9-hole course (seven par 3s and two par 4s). Driving range and Golf Academy. Golf schools weekly during Summer. *Green Fees:* weekday £18.00; weekend £22.00. *Eating facilities:* bar, function suite, and restaurant. *Visitors:* welcome at all times, no restrictions. *Society Meetings:* very welcome anytime, society packages available. Professional: Wayne Stephens.
e-mail: bridlingtonlinks@hotmail.co.uk
website: www.bridlington-links.co.uk

BROUGH. **Brough Golf Club,** Cave Road, Brough HU15 1HB (01482 667291; Fax: 01482 669873). *Location:* 10 miles west of Hull off A63. Parkland. 18 holes, 6075 yards. S.S.S. 69 (white tees). Practice facilities. *Green Fees:* on application. *Eating facilities:* full restaurant and bar snack menu available on request. *Visitors:* welcome Mondays, Tuesdays, Thursdays and Fridays after 9.30am. *Society Meetings:* on application. Director of Golf: G. Townhill (01482 667291).
e-mail: gt@brough-golfclub.co.uk
website: www.brough-golfclub.co.uk

BROUGH. **Cave Castle Golf Club,** South Cave, Brough HU15 2EU (01430 421286; Fax: 01430 421118). *Location:* minutes from M62/A63. Undulating parkland course in 150 acres. 18 holes, 6524 yards. S.S.S. 72. *Green Fees:* £20.00 per round, £25.00 per day weekdays; £25.00 per round, £30.00 per day weekends. 2010 rates (subject to review). *Eating facilities:* licensed clubhouse. *Visitors:* welcome anytime weekdays, after 11am weekends. Must have valid Handicap Certificate. Idyllic setting, superb hotel with 70 en suite bedrooms, restaurant, lounge bar, leisure complex. Golf break packages include unlimited golf, bed, breakfast, lunch and evening meal plus use of leisure complex. *Society Meetings:* Golf society packages also available. Professional: Stephen MacKinder (01430 421286). Golf administrator: Jane Simpson (01430 421286/ 01430 426259).

CONISTON. **Ganstead Park Golf Club,** Longdales Lane, Coniston, Near Hull HU11 4LB (Tel & Fax: 01482 817754). *Location:* A165 to Bridlington, five miles from Hull City Centre. Easy walking parkland course with lakes. 18 holes, 6801 yards. S.S.S. 71 yellow, 73 white, 73 red. Nets, chipping area, putting green. *Green Fees:* weekdays £24.00 per round, £30.00 per day; weekends £30.00 per round. 2010 rates (subject to review). Special rates for parties. *Eating facilities:* full facilities. *Visitors:* welcome, restrictions Wednesday and Sunday mornings. *Society Meetings:* welcome; apply to Secretary or Professional. Professional: Mike Smee (01482 811121). Secretary: Mike Milner (Tel & Fax: 01482 817754).
e-mail: secretary@gansteadpark.co.uk
website: www.gansteadpark.co.uk

THE APPEARANCE OF AN ASTERISK (*) AT THE END OF A CLUB OR COURSE ENTRY INDICATES THAT UP-TO-DATE INFORMATION HAS NOT BEEN SUPPLIED

Golf on the East Coast

Bridlington & the surrounding coast line proudly boasts four of Yorkshire's finest Golf Courses all located within a short distance of each other. All courses have stunning coastline views and offer Golfers of all abilities an excellent test on four very different and contrasting courses.

four Clubs have come together to create a new and vative golf pass which enables both individual and group ors to Bridlington and the East Yorkshire area the opportunity lay all four fantastic courses and at the same time enjoy edible savings of up to half the normal Green Fees.

can now apply for the **"Golf Coast Passport"** and get your ds on a unique opportunity to play eighteen holes at each of courses over a 7 day period (incl. Weekends & Bank Holidays).

special reduced cost of your Passport is:

£56 for 3 rounds of golf!
£68 for 4 rounds of golf!

NJOY EXCELLENT SAVINGS!!

How to apply for this great deal?

Simple, just contact the office at Bridlington Belvedere Golf Club, tel. 01262 606367 between 9am-2pm Monday to Friday or e-mail enquiries@bridlingtongolfclub.co.uk and your Passport will be sent to you with a validity of seven days from your chosen start date.

When you receive your Passport you can use it to book 3 or 4 courses at a convenient tee off time or alternatively let us take care of the arrangements for you.**

As a Golf Coast Passport holder you will automatically become a member of each club for the day of your visit, giving you full access to all their facilities including the Clubhouse for refreshments and even a game of pool or snooker.

Buggies are available at all clubs by prior arrangement.

*Terms and conditions apply   **Dates subject to availability   ***Offer not to be used in conjunction with any other offer.

BRIDLINGTON GOLF FESTIVAL
Check out one of the biggest golf festivals in the country. This 6 day event runs from Monday 2nd May until Saturday 7th May 2011. Further details visit:
www.bridlingtongolffestival.co.uk

---

dlington Belvedere Golf Club
edere Road, Bridlington • Tel: 01262 606367
our website: www.bridlingtongolfclub.co.uk

Flamborough Head Golf Club
Lighthouse Road, Flamborough • Tel: 01262 850333
Visit our website: www.flamboroughheadgolfclub.co.uk

The Bridlington Links Golf Club
Flamborough Rd, Marton, Bridlington • Tel: 01262 401784
Visit our website: www.bridlington-links.co.uk

Filey Golf Club
West Avenue, Filey • Tel: 01723 513293
Visit our website: www.fileygolfclub.com

The Revelstoke Hotel
1-3 Flamborough Road, Bridlington YO15 2HU

Three Day Golf Break
Only £149.00
nc. three rounds of golf & two nights bed & breakfast

Four Day Golf Break
Only £198.00
nc. four rounds of golf & three nights bed & breakfast

lay your golf at Bridlington Links, Bridlington Belvedere, Flamborough Head and Filey Golf Course

Offer Includes Weekends

Please contact us on 01262 672362
Email: info@revelstokehotel.co.uk

East Yorkshire / NORTH REGION

COTTINGHAM. **Hessle Golf Club,** Westfield Road, Raywell, Cottingham HU16 5ZA (01482 306844). *Location:* three miles south west of Cottingham. Parkland. 18 holes, 6621 yards, S.S.S. 72. Two practice areas. *Green Fees:* (2010 rates) weekdays £35.00 per round, £45.00 per day; weekends £45.00 per round. *Eating facilities:* snack lunches Tuesday to Sunday, set lunches by arrangement. *Visitors:* mid-week unrestricted except Tuesdays 8.30am - 12.30pm. Weekend visitors may play after 12.00 noon at Professional's discretion. *Society Meetings:* catered for weekdays and weekends after 2.00pm only by arrangement. Professional: G. Fieldsend (01482 306842). Secretary: Derrick Pettit (01482 306840; Fax: 01482 652679).

DRIFFIELD. **Driffield Golf Club,** Sunderlandwick, Beverley Road, Driffield YO25 9AD (01377 253116; Fax: 01377 240599). *Location:* from Driffield A164 to Beverley 300 yards from main roundabout on right. Mature parkland course within the attractive Sunderlandwick Estate. 18 holes, 6215 yards. S.S.S. 70. Two practice areas, practice green and two practice putting greens. *Green Fees:* Summer (1st April to 31st October): weekdays £30.00 per round, £40.00 per day; weekends £40.00 per round, £50.00 per day. Winter: weekdays £20.00 per round, weekends £24.00 per round. *Eating facilities:* full catering and bar service. *Visitors:* welcome by arrangement with the manager. Limited numbers on weekends and Bank Holidays. *Society Meetings:* welcome by prior arrangement. Professional: Kenton Wright (01377 241224). Manager: Simon Collingwood.

FLAMBOROUGH. **Flamborough Head Golf Club,** Lighthouse Road, Flamborough, Bridlington YO15 1AR (01262 850333). *Location:* situated five miles north-east of Bridlington on the Flamborough headland. Cliff tops links type course. 18 holes, 6189 yards. S.S.S. 70, Par 71. *Green Fees:* weekdays £22.00/£32.00, weekends £31.00/£38.00. *Eating facilities:* available; seafood a speciality in season. *Visitors:* welcome, limited Sunday and Wednesday mornings. *Society Meetings:* catered for, apply to Golf Co-ordinator at the above address.
e-mail: enquiries@flamboroughheadgolfclub.co.uk
websit: www.flamboroughheadgolfclub.co.uk

HORNSEA. **Hainsworth Park Golf Club,** Brandesburton, Near Driffield YO25 8RT (01964 542362). *Location:* eight miles north east of Beverley, just off A165 road to Bridlington, at the Brandesburton roundabout. Easy going, well drained parkland course with mature trees. 18 holes, 6362 yards. S.S.S. 71, Par 71. Practice area. *Green Fees:* weekdays £20.00-£24.00; weekends £24.00- £29.00. 2010 rates (subject to review). *Eating facilities:* bar and full catering. *Visitors:* welcome anytime, please phone. Hotel accommodation. *Society Meetings:* welcome. Professional: P. Myers (01964 542362). Secretary: R. Hounsfield (01964 542362).

HORNSEA. **Hornsea Golf Club,** Rolston Road, Hornsea HU18 1XG (Tel & Fax: 01964 532020). *Location:* follow signs for Hornsea Freeport – Golf Course 200 yards past Freeport. Flat parkland. 18 holes, 6661 yards. S.S.S. 72. Practice area. *Green Fees:* information not provided. *Eating facilities:* available every day. *Visitors:* welcome, please ring Professional for a time. Ladies' Day Tuesdays. Snooker room. *Society Meetings:* welcome by prior arrangement with the Secretary. Professional: S. Wright (01964 534989). Office: M. Moorhouse (Tel & Fax: 01964 532020).
e-mail: hornseagolfclub@aol.com
website: www.hornseagolfclub.co.uk

HOWDEN. **Boothferry Golf Club,** Spaldington Lane, Howden, Near Goole DN14 7NG (01430 430364). *Location:* two and a half miles from Junction 37 of the M62 on the B1228 road between Howden and Bubwith. Flat meadowland, with natural dykes and ponds. 18 holes, 6651 yards. S.S.S. 72. Large practice area. *Green Fees:* weekdays £20.00; weekends and Bank Holidays £24.00; after 4pm (all days) £12.00. *Eating facilities:* restaurant and bar facilities available. *Visitors:* welcome weekdays and weekends. No jeans, trainers or collarless shirts. *Society Meetings:* all Golf Societies and individual parties receive group discounts and are welcome with prior booking.
e-mail: info@boothferrygolfclub.co.uk
website: www.boothferrygolfclub.co.uk

HULL. **Burstwick Country Golf,** Ellifoot Lane, Burstwick, Hull HU12 9EF (01964 670112). *Location:* eight miles east of Hull. A63. A1033, then signposted. Modern parkland layout. USGA tees and greens, designed by Jonathan Gaunt. 18 holes, 6000 yards. S.S.S. 69. Floodlit driving range. *Green Fees:* weekdays £18.00, weekends £22.00; twilight (week nights) £10.00 per round. *Eating facilities:* restaurant, bar, cafe. *Visitors:* welcome. *Society Meetings:* welcome. 18 holes, bacon roll and buffet £22.00. Professional: Stewart Fraser (07852 973173). Secretary: Alan Key.
e-mail: info@burstwickcountrygolf.co.uk
website: www.burstwickcountrygolf.co.uk

HULL. **Cottingham Parks Golf & Country Club,** Woodhill Way, Cottingham HU16 5RZ (01482 846030; Fax: 01482 845932). *Location:* from the Humber Bridge to Beverley road, take the B1233 turnoff at the Skidby roundabout to Cottingham Golf Club turnoff. Mature parkland with several water hazards. 18 holes, 6459 yards. S.S.S. 71. Two tier driving range. *Green Fees:* information not available. *Eating facilities:* bar snacks and full dining room menu available. *Visitors:* welcome. *Society Meetings:* welcome with restrictions at weekends. Special packages available. Conference and social functions catered for; full leisure facilities including gym, 20 metre pool, steam room and jacuzzi. Professional: Chris Gray (01482 842394). Administrative Office: 01482 846030; Fax: 01482 845932.*
website: www.cottinghamparks.co.uk

Please mention this guide when enquiring about clubs or accommodation

Hessle Golf Club

18 hole Parkland Course • All Categories of Membership Available
including Corporate • Society Bookings welcome

Group or Individual Tuition Available from two fully qualified PGA Professionals

Fully equipped Pro Shop. Excellent golf club repair service including custom fitting

Golf Buggy and Trolley Hire

10-Bay Driving Range (6 Covered) for use by Day Members

Licensed Bar

Full dining facilities Tuesday-Sunday

Snooker Table

Professional 01482 306842 • Secretary 01482 306840 • Caterers 01482 306843
Hessle Golf Club, Westfield Road, Raywell, Cottingham, E Yorks HU16 5ZA • www.hessle-golf-club.co.uk

HAINSWORTH PARK GOLF CLUB

18-hole parkland course located 6 miles east of Beverley, just off A165 to Bridlington.

- Easy going, well drained parkland course with mature trees
- Weekdays £20-£24 • Weekends/Bank Holidays £24-£29
- Catering available • Societies welcome by arrangement
- Accommodation at Burton Lodge Hotel on the course.
- **For Golf: Tel: 01964 542362 • Hotel: Tel: 01964 542847 • Hotel: Fax: 01964 544771**

BURTON LODGE HOTEL, BRANDESBURTON, DRIFFIELD, E. YORKSHIRE YO25 8RT

Cottingham Parks golf and leisure club

Skidby Lakes golf club

two 18 hole golf courses · health and fitness centre · swimming pool · equestrian centre · business and conference facilities
corporate golf days · weddings · social events · timber lodge homes · hair and beauty · cafe bar and restaurant

Woodhill Way · Cottingham · East Yorkshire · HU16 5SW · 01482 846030   www.cottinghamparks.co.uk

HORNSEA GOLF CLUB

An established course of one hundred years set amongst mature trees and gorse with attractive water features and smooth, fast and subtly borrowed greens. An easy walking course with generous fairways, a feature of which are the undulations known locally as 'Lands' which were created by medieval farming methods. The course is ideal for corporate and society days, as well as for the casual visitors.

Measuring 6661 yards from the white tees (SSS 72) and with plenty of trouble awaiting the wayward tee shot or approach, the course is challenging for golfers of every standard and is highly rated throughout Yorkshire.

Hornsea Golf Club, Rolston Road, Hornsea, East Yorks HU18 1XG
Clubhouse: 01964 532020 • Pro: 01964 534989
www.hornseagolfclub.co.uk • e-mail hornseagolfclub@aol.com

East Yorkshire / NORTH REGION

HULL. **Hull Golf Club (1921) Ltd,** The Hall, 27 Packman Lane, Kirk Ella, Hull HU10 7TJ. *Location:* five miles west of Hull. Parkland and wooded. 18 holes, 6262 yards. S.S.S. 70. *Green Fees:* £30.00 per round, £40.00 per day. *Eating facilities:* available. *Visitors:* welcome weekdays except Wednesday. *Society Meetings:* by prior arrangement. Professional: David Jagger (01482 660972). General Manager: David Crossley (01482 660977). website: www.hullgolfclub.com

HULL. **Springhead Park Golf Club,** Willerby Road, Hull HU5 5JE (01482 614968 - Ticket Office). *Location:* off the M62/M18 onto the A63. Parkland surrounded by many trees, some undulating fairways, three ponds and many ditches around course. 18 holes, 6102 yards, 5680 metres. S.S.S. 71. Two practice areas. *Green Fees:* information not available. *Eating facilities:* mobile sandwich bar on course, restaurant and basket meals for club members and societies. *Visitors:* welcome. Tuition and club hire available. *Society Meetings:* welcome. Secretary: P. Smith (01482 654334 - Home, or phone clubhouse number 01482 656309).*

HULL. **Sutton Park Golf Club,** Saltshouse Road, Hull HU8 9HF (01482 374242). *Location:* A63, north ring road, Sutton Road, Leads Road, Robson Way. Flat parkland course. 18 holes, 6251 yards. S.S.S. 70. Practice area and nearby driving range. *Green Fees:* information not available. *Eating facilities:* restaurant/bar. *Visitors:* welcome, no restrictions. *Society Meetings:* welcome, bookings via Secretary. Professional: To be appointed. Secretary: Philip.*

KILNWICK PERCY. **KP Club,** Pocklington YO42 1UF (01759 303090). *Location:* one mile east of Pocklington off B1246. Unbelievably pretty parkland course overlooking the spectacular Yorkshire Wolds. A fantastic new clubhouse and major course improvements make KP an ideal day out for golfers of all abilities. 18 holes, 6140 yards. S.S.S. 70. *Green Fees:* £25.00 midweek, £30.00 weekends. *Eating facilities:* food available all day from award-winning chef. *Visitors:* welcome. Buggy, trolley and club hire; professional tuition available. Accommodation available on site. *Society Meetings*: packages available to suit your group's needs. Director of Golf: Aaron Pheasant (01759 303090). website: www.kpclub.co.uk

WITHERNSEA. **Withernsea Golf Club,** Egroms Lane, Withernsea HU19 2NT (01964 612078 or 612258). *Location:* 25 miles north-east of Hull on main road into Withernsea (signposted). Flat course. 9 holes, 6207 yards. S.S.S. 70. *Green Fees:* £15.00 per 18 hole round. *Eating facilities:* bar and meals available (except Monday). *Visitors:* welcome weekdays, weekends after 1pm Sunday. *Society Meetings:* by arrangement. Special rates available. Administrator: John Boasman (01964 612078). e-mail: info@withernseagolfclub.fsnet.co.uk

Hull Golf Club is a picturesque parkland course, designed by James Braid over 80 years ago. It offers a good challenge to golfers of all abilities, followed by a well-stocked bar and excellent catering in the fine Grade II Listed clubhouse. A warm welcome is extended to societies and visitors. Contact the General Manager, David Crossley, who will be happy to discuss your requirements.

Packman Lane, Kirk Ella, Hull HU10 7TJ
Tel: 01482 660977
www.hullgolfclub.com

FHG Guides publish a large range of well-known accommodation guides. We will be happy to send you details or you can use the order form at the back of this book.

North Yorkshire

ALDWARK. **Aldwark Manor Golf Club,** Aldwark, Alne, York YO61 1UF (01347 838353; Fax: 01347 833991). *Location:* in village of Aldwark, five miles south-east of Boroughbridge off A1 and 12 miles north-west of York off A19. Easy walking parkland with water hazards. 18 holes, 6187 yards. S.S.S. 70. Practice ground, putting green, practice bunker. *Green Fees:* information not available. *Eating facilities:* two restaurants and two bars. *Visitors:* always welcome weekdays, restricted weekends. 60 bedroomed hotel on the course. *Society Meetings:* societies and corporate meetings always welcome, restricted weekends. PGA Professional Alastair Grindlay (01347 838353; Fax: 01347 833991).*

BARNOLDSWICK. **Ghyll Golf Club,** Ghyll Brow, Barnoldswick, Colne, Lancs BB8 6JH (01282 842466). *Location:* M65 to Colne. A56 towards Skipton. 1 mile past Earby B6252 to Barnoldswick. Parkland course. York Course, 9 holes, 5770 yards, S.S.S. 68; Tudor Course, 9 holes, 6259 yards, S.S.S. 70. *Green Fees:* weekdays £15.00 per day (£10.00 with a member), weekends £20.00 per day (£15.00 with a member). *Eating facilities:* bar, evening only. *Visitors:* welcome except Sundays and some Saturdays. *Society Meetings:* catered for by arrangement. Secretary: Kenneth J. Wilkinson (01282 865582).

BEDALE. **Bedale Golf Club,** Leyburn Road, Bedale DL8 1EZ. *Location*: from A1 take A684 at Leeming Bar to Bedale; club is situated 400 yards out of town on the Leyburn Road. Undulating parkland with tree-lined fairways and water hazards. 18 holes, 6610 yards. S.S.S. 72. Practice facilities, fully stocked golf shop, lessons available. *Green Fees*: weekdays 18 holes £25.00, 27 holes £32.00; weekends 18 holes £36.00, 27 holes £36.00. 2010 rates (subject to review). *Eating facilities*: bar and catering always available. *Visitors*: welcome weekdays and weekends. *Society Meetings*: catered for weekdays by prior arrangement, limited availability on some Saturday afternoons; tailor-made packages and discounts available. Professional: Tony Johnson (01677 422443). Secretary: Jackie Wanless (01677 422451; Fax: 01677 427143).
e-mail: office@bedalegolfclub.com
website: www.bedalegolfclub.com

BENTHAM. **Bentham Golf Club,** Robin Lane, Bentham, Near Lancaster LA2 7AG (01524 262455). *Location:* B6480 north-east of Lancaster towards Settle. Parkland with magnificent views. 18 holes, 6033 yards. *Green Fees:* weekdays £30.00; weekends £35.00. *Eating facilities:* hot and cold snacks and meals available. *Visitors:* welcome all week. *Society Meetings:* welcome – contact Pro Shop: Chris Cousins (015242 62455).

Bedale Golf Club

www.bedalegolfclub.com

Visitors and visiting parties are very welcome at this mature parkland 18-hole Championship course with many interesting features. Packages including excellent food available to suit every budget. Close to the A1 and adjacent to the A168, just outside Wensleydale. Trolleys and buggies available for hire.

**Bedale Golf Club, Leyburn Road, Bedale, North Yorkshire DL8 1EZ
Office: 01677 422451 • e-mail: office@bedalegolfclub.com**

The Buck Inn
Thornton Watlass
Near Bedale, Ripon HG4 4AH
www.buckwatlass.co.uk
Tel: 01677 422461

- Traditional Country Inn overlooking cricket green
- Comfortable en suite accommodation
- Golf, Fishing and Race packages available
- Golf courses include Bedale, Masham, Catterick, Richmond and Romanby
- Choice of 5 real ales and over 40 malt whiskies
- Excellent food with friendly service

See our website for directions, accommodation, dining and beers

North Yorkshire / NORTH REGION

BROTTON. **Hunley Hall Golf Club & Hotel,** Brotton, Saltburn TS12 2QQ (01287 676216; Fax: 01287 678250). *Location:* off A174 at St. Margarets Way in Brotton. Signposted through housing estate, approximately half-a-mile to club. Picturesque 27 hole coastal courses adjacent to Heritage Coast. Morgan's Course 18 holes, 6918 yards, 6320 metres, S.S.S. 73. Millennium Course, 18 holes, 6510 yards, S.S.S. 68. Floodlit driving range, large practice and chipping area. *Green Fees:* information not available. *Eating facilities:* excellent facilities including two restaurants, lounge bar, spike bar, golfers' bar; quality food served daily 8am to 9.30pm. *Visitors:* always welcome. Three Star Hotel offering en suite rooms, etc. Club hire, buggy hire and tuition available. *Society Meetings:* welcome Monday to Saturday, packages available. Golfing Holidays and golf schools available. Professional: Andrew Brook (Tel & Fax: 01287 677444). Secretary: Liz Lillie (01287 676216; Fax: 01287 678250).*
e-mail: reservations@hunleyhall.co.uk
website: www.hunleyhall.co.uk

CATTERICK. **Catterick Golf Club,** Leyburn Road, Catterick Garrison DL9 3QE (01748 833268). *Location:* six miles south-west Scotch Corner, A1 turn off to Catterick Garrison. Undulating parkland/ moorland with spectacular views. 18 holes, 6329 yards, S.S.S. 71. Practice ground. *Green Fees:* from £10.00. E*ating facilities:* bar and restaurant. *Visitors:* welcome without reservation. *Society Meetings:* catered for by appointment only. Professional: Andy Marshall (01748 833671). Secretary: Mairi Young (01748 833268).

EASINGWOLD. **Easingwold Golf Club,** Stillington Road, Easingwold, York YO61 3ET (01347 822474). *Location:* 12 miles north of York, course one mile along Stillington Road. Flat, wooded parkland established 1930. 18 holes, 6717 yards, 6142 metres, S.S.S. 73. Practice ground. *Green Fees:* weekdays £28.00 per round, £35.00 per day; weekends and Bank Holidays £35.00, with a member £17.00; £15.00 1st November to 31st March. *Eating facilities:* available. *Visitors:* welcome, prior booking essential, contact Secretary. *Society Meetings:* prior booking essential, contact Secretary. Professional: John Hughes (01347 821964). Secretary: Tom Jenkinson (01347 822474).
e-mail: enquiries@easingwoldgolfclub.co.uk
website: www.easingwoldgolfclub.co.uk

FILEY. **Filey Golf Club**, The Clubhouse, West Avenue, Filey YO14 9BQ (01723 513293; Fax: 01723 514952). *Location:* one mile south of town centre. Links, parkland course. 18 holes, 6112 yards. S.S.S. 69. 9 holes, 1513 yards. Par 30. Two practice grounds. *Green Fees:* from £25.00 per person in winter. *Eating facilities:* full dining and bar facilities. *Visitors:* welcome, no restrictions. *Society Meetings:* welcome by arrangement. Professional: Darren Squire (01723 513134). Secretary: (01723 513293; Fax: 01723 514952).
website: www.fileygolfclub.com

HARROGATE. **Crimple Valley Golf Club,** Hookstone Wood Road, Harrogate HG2 8PN (01423 883485; Fax: 01423 881018). *Location:* one mile south from town centre. Turn off A61 at Nidd Vale Garage on to Hookstone Road, signposted to right. Gently sloping fairways in rural setting. 9 holes, 2500 yards. S.S.S. 33. *Green Fees:* information not available. *Eating facilities:* licensed bar, no eating facilities Monday or Sunday; breakfasts available Tuesday to Sunday. *Visitors:* welcome at all times. *Society Meetings:* special rates available. Club Proprietor: Kate Johnson.*

HARROGATE. **Harrogate Golf Club Ltd,** Forest Lane Head, Harrogate HG2 7TF (01423 862999). *Location:* two miles from Harrogate on the A59 Harrogate/Knaresborough Road. Parkland, wooded. 18 holes, 6241 yards, 5706 metres. S.S.S. 70. Large practice ground, covered net. *Green Fees:* weekdays £40.00 per round, £45.00 per day, weekends £50.00 per round/per day. *Eating facilities:* chef catering and bar menu, lounge and casual spike bars. *Visitors:* welcome subject to club events. *Society Meetings:* catered for weekdays except Tuesdays. Parties of 12 or more welcome. Professionals: G. Stothard/S. Everson (01423 862547). Secretary: Christine Calvert-Brown (01423 862999). Caterer: (01423 860278).
e-mail: secretary@harrogate-gc.co.uk
website: www.harrogate-gc.co.uk

HARROGATE. **Oakdale Golf Club,** Oakdale Glen, Harrogate HG1 2LN (01423 567162). ***Location***: five minutes from Harrogate town centre, off Ripon road into Kent Road, follow signs. Parkland, with featured stream. 18 holes, 6456 yards. S.S.S. 71. Practice ground. **Green Fees**: weekdays £45.00 per round, £61.00 for 36 holes; weekends £61.00 per round. ***Eating facilities***: first class restaurant, bar. ***Visitors***: welcome at all times, Tuesday Ladies' Day. ***Society Meetings***: welcome weekdays by arrangement. Professional: Clive Dell (01423 560510). Secretary: (01423 567162; Fax: 01423 536030).

HARROGATE. **Pannal Golf Club**, Follifoot Road, Pannal, Harrogate HG3 1ES (01423 872628; Fax: 01423 870043). *Location*: two miles south of Harrogate A61 (Leeds Road). 18 holes, 6614 yards. S.S.S. 72. Large practice ground with driving range facility. *Green Fees:* weekdays £55.00 per round, £65.00 per day; weekends and Bank Holidays £70.00 per round. 2010 rates (subject to review). *Eating facilities:* lunch available daily, dinner by arrangement. *Visitors:* welcome Monday to Friday, enquiry advised. Society Meetings: catered for Monday, Tuesday (pm only), Wednesday, Thursday and Friday. Professional: D. Padgett (01423 872628). Secretary: N.G. Douglas (01423 872628; Fax: 01423 870043).
e-mail: secretary@pannalgolfclub.co.uk
website: www.pannalgolfclub.co.uk

Filey Golf Club West Avenue, Filey, North Yorkshire YO14 9BQ
Overlooking Filey Bay on the Yorkshire coast. A challenging 18-hole course, and new 9-hole Academy course. Packages available. Visitors welcome.
Bookings tel: 01723 513134 • www.fileygolfclub.com

HARROGATE. **Rudding Park Golf,** Harrogate HG3 1JH (01423 872100; Fax: 01423 872286). *Location*: lies just off the A658 linking the A61 from Leeds to the A59 York Road. Parkland course designed to USGA specifications. 18 holes, 6883 yards, Par 72. Six hole Par 3 short course and Golf Academy incorporating extensive practice facilities. 18 bay floodlit driving range with three Professionals. *Green Fees:* Rates available throughout the year from £15.00 to £52.00 on the 18 hole Hawtree Course and from £6.00 to £16.00 on the 6 hole Repton Short Course. *Eating facilities*: clubhouse bar open all day, every day. *Visitors*: welcome at all times, must have a Handicap Certificate. Shop and buggies available all year round, with all-year-weather buggy tracks; caddies on request. Hotel on site with 4 Red Stars and AA 2 Rosette restaurant. *Society Meetings*: society and corporate days welcome. Professional: Mark Moore (01423 872100).
e-mail: golf@ruddingpark.com
website: www.ruddingpark.co.uk

KIRKBYMOORSIDE. **Kirkbymoorside Golf Club,** Manor Vale, Kirkbymoorside, York YO62 6EG (01751 431525). *Location:* on A170 through Kirkbymoorside. Undulating parkland. 18 holes, 6207 yards, 5676 metres. S.S.S. 69. Practice area, putting green. *Green Fees:* weekdays £24.00 per round, £30.00 per day; weekends and Bank Holidays £35.00 . Reduced fees in winter. *Eating facilities:* available every day. *Visitors:* welcome after 9am, not during weekend Medal competitions. *Society Meetings:* catered for by arrangement with Richard Carr, Clubhouse Manager. Professional: J. Hinchliffe (01751 431525).

KNARESBOROUGH. **Knaresborough Golf Club,** Boroughbridge Road, Knaresborough HG5 0QQ (01423 862690). *Location:* one-and-a-half miles from town centre, direction A1 Boroughbridge. Wooded parkland. 18 holes, 6780 yards. Par 72. Large practice area. *Green Fees:* £36.00 per round weekdays, £48.00 per round weekends. Please contact Secretary for further details. *Eating facilities:* full catering. *Visitors:* welcome but not before 9.30am weekdays and 2pm weekends and Bank Holidays. *Society Meetings:* welcome by prior arrangement. Professional: Andrew Turner (01423 864865). Secretary: M. Taylor (01423 862690).

MALTON. **Malton and Norton Golf Club,** Welham Park, Malton YO17 9QE (01653 697912). *Location:* off A64 to Malton between York and Scarborough. One mile south on Welham road turn right at Norton level crossing. 27 holes – longest 18: 6423 yards. S.S.S. 71. Medal Course: 6147 yards. S.S.S. 69 (Club). *Green Fees:* weekdays £30.00; weekends and Bank Holidays £35.00. *Eating facilities:* full bar and catering available. *Visitors:* welcome without reservation except club match days. *Society Meetings:* catered for by arrangement with Secretary. Professional: M. Brooks (01653 693882). Secretary: L. Gurnell (01653 697912).
e-mail: maltonandnorton@btconnect.com
website: www.maltonandnortongolfclub.co.uk

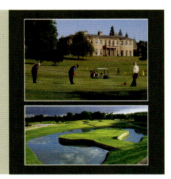

Rudding Park

- Award winning 4 red star hotel
- 50 contemporary bedrooms • 2 AA rosette Clocktower restaurant
- 18 hole parkland golf course
- 6 hole short course • Golf Academy
- 18 bay floodlit, covered Driving Range • Professional tuition

Rudding Park, Follifoot, Harrogate, North Yorkshire HG3 1JH
Tel: 01423 871250   Web: www.ruddingpark.co.uk

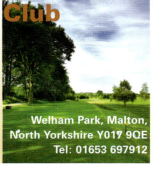

Malton & Norton Golf Club

A 27-hole course of three contrasting loops providing challenge and enjoyment for members and visitors alike. Ideally situated between York and Scarborough with marvellous views of the North Yorkshire Moors.

The club has a driving range which is available to both members and visitors, who are made most welcome. The quality of the course and the warm and friendly welcome is reflected in the fact that many of our visitors return time and time again.

e-mail: maltonandnorton@btconnect.com
www.maltonandnortongolfclub.co.uk

Welham Park, Malton, North Yorkshire YO17 9QE
Tel: 01653 697912

MIDDLESBROUGH. Middlesbrough Golf Club, Brass Castle Lane, Marton, Middlesbrough TS8 9EE (01642 311515; Fax: 01642 319607). *Location:* five miles south of Middlesbrough west, off the A172. Parkland course. 18 holes, 6328 yards. S.S.S./Par 70. Practice facilities available. *Green Fees:* weekdays £39.00 per day; weekends £44.00 per day. *Eating facilities:* lunches, teas and dinners. *Visitors:* welcome when tee not booked. Venue of the North of England Open Amateur Youth Golf Championship. Conference facilities. *Society Meetings:* welcome Mondays, Wednesdays, Thursdays and Fridays. Professional: Gordon Cattrell (01642 311766). Secretary: Ian Jackson (01642 311515).

MIDDLESBROUGH. Middlesbrough Municipal Golf Centre, Ladgate Lane, Middlesbrough TS5 7YZ (01642 315533; Fax: 01642 300726). *Location:* three miles south of Middlesbrough on A174. Parkland course with featured streams. 18 holes, 6333 yards. S.S.S. 71. Floodlit driving range, practice area and putting green. *Green Fees:* information not available. *Eating facilities:* lunches available seven days, snacks at all other times. *Visitors:* welcome anytime, but starting times must be booked in advance through Manager. *Society Meetings:* must be booked through Manager, special golf packages available. Professional: Alan Hope (01642 300720). Manager: M. Gormley (01642 315533). Hon. Secretary: J. Brannagan (01642 886706).*

NORTHALLERTON. Romanby Golf Course, Yafforth Road, Northallerton DL7 0PE. *Location:* west of Northallerton on the B6271 Richmond Road. Parkland course with formidable "Great Lake Complex" on the 2nd, 11th and 12th. 18 holes, 6663 yards. 12 bay floodlit driving range. *Green Fees:* information not available. *Visitors:* always welcome, best to telephone for tee times. *Society Meetings:* golf parties a speciality. Bookings telephone (01609 778855; Fax: 01609 779084).*
e-mail: mark@romanby.com
website: www.romanbygolf.com

REDCAR. Cleveland Golf Club, Majuba Road, Redcar TS10 5BJ (01642 471798; Fax: 01642 487691). *Location:* on entering town via A1042 or A1085 follow signs to Esplanade, course runs adjacent to beach on north side of town. Seaside links course. Practice ground. 18 holes. 6669 yards. S.S.S. 72. *Green Fees:* by arrangement. *Eating facilities:* available except Mondays. *Visitors:* welcome by arrangement; after 10am weekdays and Sundays. *Society Meetings:* by arrangement.
e-mail: majuba@btconnect.com
website: www.clevelandgolfclub.co.uk

REDCAR. Wilton Golf Club, Wilton, Redcar TS10 4QY (01642 465265). *Location:* eight miles east of Middlesbrough (A174), four miles west of Redcar. Parkland course, partly wooded. 18 holes, 6276 yards. S.S.S. 69. Small practice area. *Green Fees:* weekdays £26.00 per day; Sundays and Bank Holidays £34.00 per day. *Eating facilities:* lunches, including Sundays; evening meals by arrangement, lounge bar and 19th bar. *Visitors:* welcome except Saturdays; weekdays and Sundays not before 10am. Tuesdays ladies playing in competitions have priority on 1st tee. *Society Meetings:* welcome by arrangement, except Saturdays. Please contact the Club Secretary. Special rates for parties over 20. Professional: Miss P.D. Smillie (01642 452730). Secretary: Claire Harvey (01642 465265).
e-mail: secretary@wiltongolfclub.co.uk
website: www.wiltongolfclub.co.uk

RICHMOND. Richmond (Yorkshire) Golf Club, Bend Hagg, Richmond DL10 5EX (01748 825319). *Location:* Scotch Corner (A1). Wooded, parkland, some hills. 18 holes, 6073 yards. S.S.S. 69. Par 71. *Green Fees:* midweek £30.00 per day, £25.00 per round; weekends £35.00 per day, £30.00 per round. Special offer Mondays and Fridays £15.00 per round. *Eating facilities:* bar and catering. *Visitors:* welcome but not before 3.30pm Sundays. Pro Shop. *Society Meetings:* catered for, book with Professional. Professional: James Cousins (01748 822457). Secretary: Mrs A. Lancaster (01748 823231).

RIPON. Masham Golf Club, Burnholme, Swinton Road, Masham, Ripon HG4 4NS (01765 689379). *Location:* nine miles north of Ripon just off A6108. Parkland, River Burn flows through course and is featured in several holes. 9 holes, 6204 yards. S.S.S. 70. *Green Fees:* 18 holes £20.00, £25.00 per day. *Eating facilities:* mainly midday catering, bar all day. *Visitors:* welcome Monday-Friday; weekends and Bank Holidays by arrangement only. *Society Meetings:* by arrangement with Secretary. Office: (01765 688054).

RIPON. Ripon City Golf Club, Palace Road, Ripon HG4 3HH (01765 603640). *Location:* one mile north of Ripon on A6108 (Masham). Undulating parkland with magnificent views over Ure Valley, city of Ripon, Hambleton Hills. 18 holes, 6084 yards. S.S.S. White 69, Yellow 68. Nearby golf range. *Green Fees:* dependent on size of party. *Eating facilities:* available every day. *Visitors:* welcome (not Saturdays). *Society Meetings:* welcome. Professional: S.T. Davis (01765 600411). Secretary: M.J. Doig MBE (01765 603640).
e-mail: secretary@riponcitygolfclub.com
website: www.riponcitygolfclub.co.uk

Saltburn-by-the-Sea Golf Club
Hob Hill, Saltburn-by-the-Sea TS12 1NJ
Tel: 01287 622812 • Fax: 01287 625988
e-mail: secretary@saltburngolf.co.uk
www.saltburngolf.co.uk   Est.1894

A superb parkland course in lovely rural surroundings with outstanding views and tricky par 3s.
Visitors and parties welcome.

THE GOLF GUIDE 2011 — NORTH REGION / North Yorkshire

SALTBURN BY THE SEA. **Saltburn by the Sea Golf Club Ltd,** Hob Hill, Saltburn by the Sea TS12 1NJ (01287 622812). *Location*: east on A174, right at Quarry Lane roundabout, left at traffic lights; club one mile on right. Parkland course. 18 holes, 5974 yards. S.S.S. 70. *Green Fees:* weekdays, winter £21.00, summer £33.00; weekends winter £25.00, summer £37.00. *Eating facilities:* available. *Visitors:* welcome, limited Sundays and Thursdays and no visitors Saturdays. *Society Meetings:* catered for by arrangement. Professional: (01287 624653). Secretary: Mike Murtha (01287 622812).
e-mail: secretary@saltburngolf.co.uk
website: www.saltburngolf.co.uk

SCARBOROUGH. **Ganton Golf Club Ltd,** Ganton, Near Scarborough YO12 4PA (01944 710329; Fax: 01944 710922). *Location*: on A64, nine miles west of Scarborough. Heathland/links Championship course, host to Ryder Cup (1949), Walker Cup (2003), Curtis Cup (2000). 18 holes, 6734 yards. S.S.S. 73. *Green Fees*: weekdays £80.00 per round or day; weekends and Bank Holidays £90.00 per round or day. *Eating facilities*: available. *Visitors*: welcome by prior arrangement. *Society Meetings*: catered for with reservation. Professional: Gary Brown. Secretary: Paul Ware (01944 710329).
e-mail: secretary@gantongolfclub.com
website: www.gantongolfclub.com

SCARBOROUGH. **Scarborough North Cliff Golf Club,** North Cliff Avenue, Scarborough YO12 6PP (01723 355397; Fax: 01723 362134). *Location:* two miles north of Scarborough on coastal road to Whitby. Mainly parkland course with a cliff top start and finish; views of North Bay and Castle. 18 holes, 6493 yards. S.S.S. 71. Practice ground, chipping green, putting green. *Green Fees:* information not available. *Eating facilities:* available. *Visitors:* welcome (restrictions on competition days, not allowed Sundays before 10.30am). Must be members of golf club. Electric trolleys, carts available. *Society Meetings:* catered for, parties from 8 to 40. Prior booking through Secretary. Professional: S.N. Deller (01723 365920). Secretary: J. Barnfather (01723 355397).*
e-mail: info@northcliffgolfclub.co.uk

SCARBOROUGH. **Scarborough South Cliff Golf Club,** Deepdale Avenue, Scarborough YO11 2UE (01723 360522). *Location:* one mile south of Scarborough off Filey road. Parkland and clifftop with panoramic sea views. 18 holes, 6432 yards. S.S.S. 71 (white tees), 69 (yellow tees). Practice ground. *Green Fees:* £30.00 Monday to Thursday, £35.00 Friday to Sunday. *Eating facilities:* dining room, bar; full catering facilities. *Visitors:* welcome when course available. *Society Meetings:* catered for by prior arrangement. Professional: T. Skingle (01723 360525). Secretary: David Roberts (Tel & Fax: 01723 360522).
e-mail: clubsecretary@southcliffgolfclub.com
website: www.southcliffgolfclub.com

SELBY. **Selby Golf Club,** Mill Lane, Brayton Barff, Selby YO8 9LD (01757 228622). *Location:* off A64 Selby bypass. Links-type course, very well drained. 18 holes, 6374 yards. S.S.S. 71. Practice ground. *Green Fees:* £35.00 per round, £40.00 per day. *Eating facilities:* restaurant and bar. *Visitors:* welcome weekdays. Snooker tables. *Society Meetings:* welcome Wednesday to Friday. Professional: Nick Ludwell (01757 228785). Secretary: Neil Proctor.

SETTLE. **Settle Golf Club,** Buck Haw Brow, Giggleswick, Settle BD24 0DH (Tel & Fax: 01729 825288). *Location:* one mile north of Settle on B6480. Moorland. 9 holes, 6200 yards. S.S.S. 72. *Green Fees:* Information not available. *Eating facilities:* bar only on Sundays. *Visitors:* welcome, restrictions Sundays. *Society Meetings:* welcome with prior notice. Secretary: Alan Wright (01729 822858; Mobile: 07801 550358).*

SKIPTON. **Skipton Golf Club Ltd,** Short Lee Lane, Skipton BD23 3LF (01756 793922). *Location:* one and a half miles northwest of Skipton town centre on A65. Undulating, with panoramic views, some water hazards. 18 holes, 6090 yards. S.S.S. 69. Practice ground. *Green Fees:* £25.00 per round, £30.00 per day. *Eating facilities:* full bar; catering daily except Mondays. *Visitors:* welcome at all times, some restrictions weekends and Tuesdays. *Society Meetings:* welcome by prior arrangement. Special package rates. Professional: P. Robinson (01756 793257). Business Manager: Beverley Hardy (01756 795657; Fax: 01756 796665).

New Close Farm — FHG Diploma Award Winner

A supa dupa cottage on New Close Farm in the heart of Craven Dales with panoramic views over the Aire Valley. Excellent area for walking, cycling, fishing, golf and touring.

- Two double and one single bedrooms; bathroom.
- Colour TV, video and CD player.
- Full central heating and double glazing.
- Bed linen, towels and all amenities included in the price.
- Sorry, no young children, no pets.
- Non-smokers preferred.
- From £350-£400. Winter Short Breaks available.

The weather can't be guaranteed but your comfort can
Kirkby Malham, Skipton BD23 4DP
Tel: 01729 830240 • Fax: 01729 830179
e-mail: brendajones@newclosefarmyorkshire.co.uk
www.newclosefarmyorkshire.co.uk

STOCKTON-ON-TEES. **Teesside Golf Club,** Acklam Road, Thornaby, Stockton-on-Tees TS17 7JS (01642 676249; Fax: 01642 676252). *Location*: A19 - A1130 to Thornaby, 0.7 miles on right hand side. Flat parkland. 18 holes, 6535 yards. S.S.S. 71. Practice ground, putting green. *Green Fees:* information not available. *Eating facilities:* catering except Mondays, bar 11am to 11pm. *Visitors:* welcome midweek up to 4.30pm, weekends after 11am by arrangement. *Society Meetings:* Monday - Friday. Special rates and conditions for parties and guests. Professional: S Pilgrim (01642 673822). Secretary: R. Ferri (01642 616516).
e-mail: teessidegolfclub@btconnect.com
website: www.teessidegolfclub.com

TADCASTER. **Scarthingwell Golf Course,** Scarthingwell. Tadcaster LS24 9PF (01937 557878; Fax: 01937 557909). *Location*: 4 miles south of Tadcaster on the A162 Tadcaster/Ferrybridge Road approximately 3 miles from A1. Parkland course. 18 holes, 6642 yards. S.S.S.72. *Green Fees*: information not provided. *Eating facilities*: licensed clubhouse facilities and snooker table, restaurant. *Visitors*: welcome every day except before 2pm on Saturdays. *Society Meetings*: welcome, packages and special rates available. Professional: Simon Danby (01937 557864). Secretary: Kathryn Pick (01937 557878).
ben.burlingham@scarthingwellgolfcourse.co.uk
website: www.scarthingwellgolfcourse.co.uk

THIRSK. **Thirsk and Northallerton Golf Club,** Thornton-le-Street, Thirsk YO7 4AB (01845 525115). *Location:* on Northallerton Road (A168), two miles from Thirsk. Flat parkland with excellent views of Hambleton Hills. 18 holes, 6533 yards. S.S.S. 72. Practice ground. *Green Fees:* on application. *Eating facilities:* catering and bar. *Visitors:* welcome, phone before arrival. Trolleys, buggies for hire. *Society Meetings:* welcome. Professional: Robert Garner (01845 525115 ext 4). Secretary: C.I. Todd (01845 525115 ext 1).
e-mail: secretary@tngc.co.uk
website: www.tngc.co.uk

WHITBY. **Whitby Golf Club,** Sandsend Road, Low Straggleton, Whitby YO21 3SR (Tel & Fax: 01947 600660). *Location:* on the A174, one mile from Whitby. Picturesque coastal course on cliff tops, three holes over ravines. 18 holes, 6259 yards. S.S.S. 70. *Green Fees:* £30.00 weekends, £27.00 midweek. *Eating facilities:* dining room and bar. *Visitors:* welcome, parties by prior reservation. *Society Meetings:* catered for by prior arrangement. Professional: Tony Mason (01947 602719). Office: (Tel & Fax: 01947 600660).

YORK. **Forest of Galtres Golf Club,** Moorlands Road, Skelton, York YO32 2RF (01904 766198; Fax: 01904 769400). *Location:* two miles from the northern section of the ring road around the historic city of York. Parkland course, designed by Simon Gidman. 18 holes, 6534 yards. S.S.S. 71. Covered driving range and practice ground. *Green Fees:*

weekdays £26.00 per round, £32.00 all day; weekends and Bank Holidays £32.00 per round, £42.00 all day. Midweek Specials starting from £30.00 including food. Sunday Specials after 12 noon from £40.00. *Eating facilities:* full facilities available. *Visitors:* welcome any day. *Society Meetings:* welcome but must be pre-booked with Secretary. Advanced PGA Professional: Alastair Grindlay (Tel & Fax: 01904 766198). Secretary: Mrs Sue Procter (Tel & Fax: 01904 769400).
e-mail: secretary@forestofgaltres.co.uk
website: www.forestofgaltres.co.uk

YORK. **Forest Park Golf Club,** Stockton on Forest, York YO32 9UW (01904 400325). *Location:* one and a half miles from east end of York bypass, follow signs for Stockton on Forest. Flat 27 hole parkland course with trees and stream running through. 18 holes, 6673 yards. S.S.S. 71; 9 holes, 3186 yards. S.S.S. 70 (twice round). Open air driving range and 8 bay driving range, practice area. *Green Fees:* weekdays £10.00 for 9 holes, £25.00 per round, £32.00 per day; weekends £12.00 for 9 holes, £30.00 per round, £40.00 per day. 2010 rates (subject to review). Special party and package rates; quotation on request. *Eating facilities:* full bar and golf club catering facilities. *Visitors:* welcome mid week, limited availability weekends. *Society Meetings:* welcome by prior arrangement. Professional: Mark Winterburn (01904 400425). Secretary: Sally Crossley (01904 400688).
e-mail: admin@forestparkgolfclub.co.uk
website: www.forestparkgolfclub.co.uk

YORK. **Fulford (York) Golf Club Ltd,** Heslington Lane, York YO10 5DY *Location:* A19 (Selby) from city, turn left to Heslington (signposted to University). Heathland. 18 holes, 6864 yards. S.S.S. 74. Practice ground. *Green Fees:* information not available. *Eating facilities:* lounge, diningroom and bar. *Visitors:* welcome, prior reservation required. Snooker table. *Society Meetings:* Monday to Friday by arrangement with Manager. Professional: Guy Wills (01904 412882). General Manager: Gary Pearce (01904 413579; Fax: 01904 416918).*
e-mail: info@fulfordgolfclub.co.uk
website: www.fulfordgolfclub.co.uk

YORK. **Heworth Golf Club,** Muncaster House, Muncastergate, York YO31 9JY (01904 426156). *Location:* one and a half miles east of City Centre on A1036 Malton/Scarborough road. Parkland, easy walking. 12 holes, 6105 yards, 5635 metres. S.S.S. 69. Practice ground. *Green Fees:* information not provided. *Eating facilities:* bar (snacks), dining room. *Visitors:* generally welcome, advisable to telephone Professional in advance. Carts for hire. *Society Meetings:* by written arrangement with Professional. Professional: Stephen Burdett (Tel & Fax: 01904 422389). Secretary: Joe Baxter (Tel & Fax: 01904 426156).

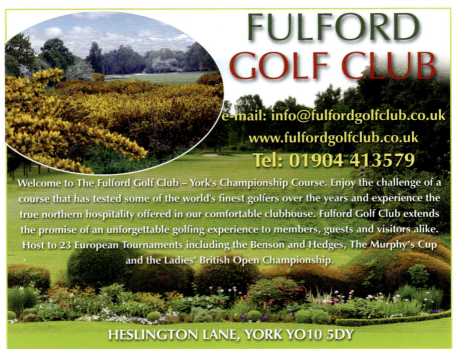

YORK. **The Oaks Golf Club and Spa,** Aughton Common, Aughton, York YO42 4PW (01757 288577; Fax: 01757 288232). *Location:* on the B1228 one mile north of Bubwith village. Wooded course with seven lakes that come into play. 18 holes, 6743 yards, 6035 metres. S.S.S. 72. Practice ground and Golf Academy. *Green Fees:* £32.00 per round. *Eating facilities:* lounge bar, normal meals, à la carte restaurant. *Visitors:* welcome weekdays. *Society Meetings:* Monday to Friday only. Head Professional: Graham Walker. Senior Professionals: Lysa Jones and John Mellor. Secretary: Sheila Nutt.
e-mail: sheila@theoaksgolfclub.co.uk
website: www.theoaksgolfclub.co.uk

YORK. **Pike Hills Golf Club,** Tadcaster Road, Askham Bryan, York YO23 3UW (01904 706566). *Location:* four miles from York on Tadcaster Road (A64), left hand side going east. Flat parkland surrounding wildlife reserve. 18 holes, 6146 yards. S.S.S. 70. *Green Fees:* £30.00 per round, £36.00 per day. *Eating facilities:* restaurant and bar facilities. *Visitors:* welcome except weekends or Bank Holidays. *Society Meetings:* welcome by arrangement. Professional: Ian Tailby (01904 708756). Secretary: Garry Dunn (Tel & Fax: 01904 700797).

YORK. **The York Golf Club,** Lords Moor Lane, Strensall, York YO32 5XF (01904 490304). *Location:* two miles north of York ring road (A1237). Wooded heathland. 18 holes, 6301 yards. S.S.S. 70. Practice ground; Professional shop. *Green Fees:* weekdays £44.00, weekends £54.00. *Eating facilities:* full catering. *Visitors:* welcome weekdays, but advisable to ring before visiting. *Society Meetings:* catered for weekdays and Sundays. Professional: Mark Rogers (01904 490304). Secretary: Mike Wells (01904 491840; Fax: 01904 491852).
e-mail: secretary@yorkgolfclub.co.uk
website: www.yorkgolfclub.co.uk

THE APPEARANCE OF AN ASTERISK (*) AT THE END OF A CLUB OR COURSE ENTRY INDICATES THAT UP-TO-DATE INFORMATION HAS NOT BEEN SUPPLIED

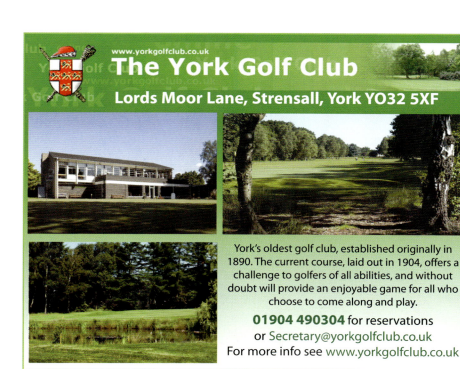

The York Golf Club
Lords Moor Lane, Strensall, York YO32 5XF

York's oldest golf club, established originally in 1890. The current course, laid out in 1904, offers a challenge to golfers of all abilities, and without doubt will provide an enjoyable game for all who choose to come along and play.

01904 490304 for reservations
or Secretary@yorkgolfclub.co.uk
For more info see www.yorkgolfclub.co.uk

South Yorkshire

BARNSLEY. **Barnsley Golf Club,** The Limes, Wakefield Road, Staincross, Barnsley S75 6JZ (01226 382856). *Location:* A61 three miles north of Barnsley, five miles south of Wakefield. Parkland course. 18 holes, 6048 yards, 5529 metres. S.S.S. 69. *Green Fees:* midweek £15.00 per round, weekends £17.00 per round. Ride-on buggies for hire, midweek £12.00 per round, weekends £14.00 per round. *Eating facilities:* full catering and licensing facilities every day. *Visitors:* welcome, no restrictions; booking through Professional. Professional: S. Wyke (01226 380358). Secretary: T. Jones (01226 382856).

BARNSLEY. **Sandhill Golf Club,** Middlecliffe Lane, Little Houghton, Barnsley S72 0HW (Tel & Fax: 01226 753444). Clubhouse (01226 755079). *Location:* 6 miles east of Barnsley, off A635. 18 holes, 6309 yards. S.S.S. 70. Floodlit golf range (01226 751775). *Green Fees*: on request. *Eating facilities*: licensed bar providing tea, coffee and meals at various prices. *Visitors*: welcome. Buggies available. *Society Meetings*: welcome with various packages on request. Winter Society Specials available. Secretary: Mrs V. Wistow.
website: www.sandhillgolfclub.co.uk

BARNSLEY. **Silkstone Golf Club,** Field Head, Elmhirst Lane, Silkstone, Barnsley S75 4LD (01226 790328). *Location:* one mile from Junction 37 (M1) along A628 (the road to Manchester). Parkland/downland course. 18 holes, 6648 yards, Par 73. Practice ground. *Green Fees:* weekdays £29.00 for 18 holes, £36.00 all day. *Eating facilities:* full catering facilities and bar. *Visitors:* welcome weekdays, Ladies' Day Tuesdays, with a member only at weekends and Bank Holidays. Caddie cart and buggy hire. *Society Meetings:* by arrangement. Professional: Kevin Guy (01226 790128). Secretary: A. Cook (01226 790328).

DONCASTER. **Bawtry Golf Club,** Cross Lane, Austerfield, Doncaster DN10 6RF (01302 711409). *Location:* two miles from Bawtry on the A614. Parkland. 18 holes, 6900 yards. S.S.S. 73. 10 bay floodlit golf range, practice ground. *Green Fees:* information not available. *Eating facilities:* bar snacks and full restaurant. *Visitors:* welcome without reservation. Trolley and cart hire; buggies. *Society Meetings:* welcome, special package rates. Professional: Daniel Gregory (01302 710841). Office: (01302 711409). Catering: (01302 711755).*

DONCASTER. **Crookhill Park (Municipal) Golf Club,** Carr Lane, Conisbrough, Doncaster DN12 2AH (01709 862979). *Location:* off A630 Doncaster to Rotherham road turn on A6094 (opposite castle), then one mile. 18 holes, 5846 yards. Parkland, special feature hole 11 (index 1) – approach to green over small wall to elevated green. S.S.S. 68. Practice area. *Green Fees:* information not provided. *Eating facilities:* hot lunches at club. *Visitors:* welcome; pre-book with Professional if specific time is required. Professional: Andy Martin (01709 862979). Hon. Secretary: M. Belk (07870 417467).

DONCASTER. **Doncaster Golf Club,** Bawtry Road, Doncaster DN4 7PD (01302 868316). *Location:* four miles south of Doncaster town centre on the A638. Wooded, heathland course. 18 holes, 6244 yards. S.S.S. 70. Practice area, putting green. *Green Fees:* information not available. *Eating facilities:* all day catering Monday to Saturday, up to 4pm Sundays. *Visitors:* welcome weekdays, Wednesday Ladies' Day; restricted tee times at weekends and Bank Holidays. *Society Meetings:* by arrangement, contact Secretary. Professional: G. Bailey (01302 868404). Secretary: D.E. James (01302 865632; Fax: 01302 865994).*
e-mail: doncastergolf@aol.com
website: www.doncastergolfclub.org.uk

Sandhill Golf Club
Middlecliffe Lane,
Little Houghton, Barnsley S72 0HW
- 18 hole golf course. Buggies available.
- Societies welcome with various packages on request.
- Weekend Society Specials available. • Licensed club house providing tea, coffee and meals at various prices.
- Floodlit Golf Driving Range • Tel: 01226 751775

Tel: 01226 753444 • www.sandhillgolfclub.co.uk
Clubhouse - Tel: 01226 755079

DONCASTER. **Doncaster Town Moor Golf Club,** Bawtry Road, Belle Vue, Doncaster DN4 5HU (01302 533778; Bar: 01302 533167). *Location:* clubhouse approx. 300 yards from racecourse roundabout travelling south towards Bawtry, same entrance as Doncaster Rovers Football Club. Flat parkland/lowland heath, centre of Doncaster racecourse. 18 holes, 5650 yards, S.S.S. 69. *Green Fees:* information not available. *Eating facilities:* restaurant and bar meals. *Visitors:* welcome by arrangement. *Society Meetings:* catered for by arrangement with Professional. Discount package available. Professional: Steve Shaw (01302 535286). Secretary: R. Smith (01302 533778).*

DONCASTER. **Hickleton Golf Club,** Lidgett Lane, Hickleton, Near Doncaster DN5 7BE (01709 896081; Fax: 01709 896083). *Location:* from Junction 37 A1(M) six miles on A635 to Barnsley, in Hickleton village turn right to Thurnscoe, 500 yards on right. Undulating parkland. 18 holes, 6434 yards, S.S.S. 71. Practice ground. *Green Fees:* information not available. *Eating facilities:* available seven days a week. *Visitors:* welcome by arrangement, restricted times at weekends. Buggies by arrangement with Professional. *Society Meetings:* welcome by arrangement. Professional: Paul Audsley (Tel & Fax: 01709 888436). Manager: John Little (01709 896081; Fax: 01709 896083).*
e-mail: john@hickletongolfclub.co.uk
website: www.hickletongolfclub.co.uk

DONCASTER. **Owston Hall**, Owston, Askern, Doncaster DN6 9JF (01302 722231; Fax: 01302 728885). *Location:* 7 miles north of Doncaster on the A19 from Doncaster to Askern, take the B1220 and turn right through the stone gates. Championship venue on the PGA Euro Pro Tour schedule. Parkland with mature trees. 18 holes, 6937 yards. S.S.S. 72. Putting Green, practice ground. *Green Fees:* weekdays £22.00; weekends £30.00. *Eating facilities:* bar lunches and full evening menu. *Visitors:* welcome, booking at weekends recommended. Function and conference rooms. Hotel with 63 de luxe bedrooms; swimming pool, spa, fitness suite. *Society Meetings:* packages available – please phone for brochure. Dress code applies – locker changing and shower facilities. PGA Instruction available. Professional: Jason Laszkowicz (01302 722231; Fax: 01302 728885). Secretary: Gerry Briggs (01302 722800).
e-mail: reservations@owstonhall.com
proshop@owstonhall.com
website: www.owstonhall.com

DONCASTER. **Serlby Park Golf Club,** Serlby, Doncaster DN10 6BA (01777 818268). *Location:* between Bawtry and Blyth. Parkland, wooded course. 9 holes, 5300 yards. S.S.S. 66. *Green Fees:* information not available. *Eating facilities:* catering and bar. *Visitors:* limited to playing with a member. *Society Meetings:* parties of 4 or more welcome any time if booked through Secretary. Secretary: K.J. Crook (01302 742280).*

DONCASTER. **Thorne Golf Club**, Kirton Lane, Thorne, Near Doncaster DN8 5RJ (01405 812084; Fax: 01405 741899). *Location*: M18 Junction 5, onto M180, take first junction onto A614 Thorne, follow signposts. Flat parkland with three ponds. 18 holes, 5366 yards. S.S.S. 66. Practice ground and putting green. *Green Fees*: weekdays £12.00 for 18 holes, weekends £13.00 for 18 holes. *Eating facilities*: snacks and meals available. *Visitors*: welcome, no restrictions. *Society Meetings*: welcome, please book in advance. Secretary/Professional: Edward Highfield. Proprietor: Richard Highfield.
e-mail: edward@highfield247.fsworld.co.uk
website: www.thornegolf.co.uk

DONCASTER. **Thornhurst Park Golf Course,** Holme Lane, Owston, Doncaster DN5 0LR (01302 337799). *Location:* 10 minutes from centre of Doncaster through Bentley on A19 to Selby. Flat, parkland course with excellent countryside views. 18 holes, 6490 yards. S.S.S. 71. Practice area, putting green. *Green Fees:* weekdays 18 holes £12.00; weekends 18 holes £15.00. 9 holes: weekdays £7.00, weekends £8.00. 2010 rates (subject to review). *Eating facilities:* restaurant, lounge bar, function room. *Visitors:* welcome every day, members have priority between 8am and 9am. *Society Meetings:* welcome any day. Professional: Kevin M. Pearce.

DONCASTER. **Wheatley Golf Club,** Armthorpe Road, Doncaster DN2 5QB (01302 831655). *Location:* follow East Coast route alongside Racecourse boundary to water tower at first crossroads. Flat parkland, water hazards between 10th and 18th holes. 18 holes, 6240 yards, S.S.S. 70 (yellow markers); 6405 yards, S.S.S. 71 (white markers). Practice area and putting green. *Green Fees:* weekdays £28.00 per round, £37.00 per day; weekends £38.00 per round. *Eating facilities:* restaurant and bars. *Visitors:* welcome if member of another club. *Society Meetings:* society days catered for weekdays only. Professional: S. Fox (01302 834085). Secretary: K. Gosden (01302 831655). Office Manager: Mrs S. Foy (01302 831655).
e-mail: secretary@wheatleygolfclub.co.uk
website: www.wheatleygolfclub.co.uk

ROTHERHAM. **Grange Park Golf Club,** Upper Wortley Road, Kimberworth Park, Rotherham S61 2SJ (01709 558884). Commercial golf club; superb layout, quality and value for money. *Location:* A629 from Rotherham, easy access from M1. Parkland. 18 holes, 6353 yards. S.S.S. 71. Practice ground, driving range. *Green Fees:* information not available. *Eating facilities:* licensed bar and full catering. *Visitors:* welcome without restriction. *Society Meetings:* contact Professional in first instance. Professional: Eric Clark (01709 559497). Secretary: Richard Townley (01709 559497 home, 01709 558884 club).*

Please mention THE GOLF GUIDE when you enquire about clubs or accommodation

South Yorkshire / NORTH REGION

ROTHERHAM. Phoenix Golf Club, Phoenix Sports and Social Club, Pavilion Lane, Brinsworth, Rotherham S60 5PA (Tel & Fax: 01709 363788). *Location:* M1 (J34) Tinsley roundabout, Bawtry Road, Pavilion Lane one mile on left. 18 holes, 6181 yards. S.S.S. 70. Practice area, 20-bay driving range. *Green Fees:* ring Professional for details. *Eating facilities:* snacks or full meals. *Visitors:* welcome anytime. *Society Meetings:* welcome weekdays, limited availability on Sundays. Professional: M. Roberts (01709 382624). Secretary: I. Gregory (Tel & Fax: 01709 363788).
e-mail: secretary@phoenixgolfclub.co.uk
website: www.phoenixgolfclub.co.uk

ROTHERHAM. Rotherham Golf Club Ltd, Thrybergh Park, Doncaster Road, Thrybergh, Rotherham S65 4NU (01709 850466). *Location*: three and a half miles east of Rotherham on A630. Wooded parkland. 18 holes, 6327 yards. S.S.S. 70. Practice ground. *Green Fees*: available on request. *Eating facilities*: full catering, bar and restaurant. *Visitors*: welcome all day with limitations. *Society Meetings*: welcome weekdays and weekends (after 2pm). Professional: Simon Thornhill (01709 850480). Manager: (01709 859500; Fax: 01709 859517).
e-mail: manager@rotherhamgolfclub.com
website: www.rotherhamgolfclub.com

ROTHERHAM. Roundwood Golf Club, Green Lane, Rawmarsh, Rotherham S62 6LA (01709 826134). *Location:* half a mile from the A633. Flat course, easy walking. 18 holes, 5568 yards, S.S.S. 67. *Green Fees:* information not available. *Eating facilities:* bar open seven days a week, food available Fridays and Saturdays. *Visitors:* welcome midweek and Sunday afternoons. *Society Meetings:* welcome weekdays and Sunday afternoons. Secretary: G. Billups (01709 525208).*

ROTHERHAM. Sitwell Park Golf Club, Shrogswood Road, Rotherham S60 4BY (01709 541046; Fax: 01709 703637). *Location:* A631 off M18, Bramley turn off to Rotherham thence to Sheffield, Exit 33 off M1, follow A631 to Bawtry. Undulating parkland. 18 holes, 6229 yards. Par 71. Practice ground. *Green Fees:* information not available. *Eating facilities:* restaurant and bar. *Visitors:* welcome with reservation, Saturdays only with member, Sundays after 11.30am. Buggies and carts available. *Society Meetings:* catered for if pre-arranged with Secretary. Not Saturdays; Sundays after 11.30am only. Professional: N. Taylor (01709 540961). Secretary: G. Hardy (01709 541046; Fax: 01709 703637).
e-mail: secretary@sitwellgolf.co.uk
website: www.sitwellgolf.co.uk

Sitwell Park Golf Club is a challenging undulating 18 hole course measuring 5955 yards from the Yellow Tees with a par of 71.

Sitwell Park offers all the amenities associated with a quality course. Our experienced Professional Nic Taylor is always on hand to look after your requirements, whether you need advice on purchasing golf equipment or wish to book a lesson to help improve your game. Visitors and societies welcome.

The Clubhouse offers a wide range of facilities including a conference room, large lounge with TV, a comfortable 19th with snooker tables and our new balcony overlooking the course. The dining room can seat up to 100, and our catering manager Brian Thickett & his staff can provide any type of catering you may require, from sandwiches to 5 course dinners. Bar available.

Sitwell Park Golf Club
Shrogs Wood Road, Rotherham, South Yorkshire S60 4BY
Tel: 01709 541046
E-mail: secretary@sitwellgolf.co.uk
www.sitwellgolf.co.uk

ROTHERHAM. **Wath Golf Club**, Abdy, Rawmarsh, Rotherham S62 7SJ (01709 872149). *Location:* A633 from Rotherham, through Rawmarsh, taking B6090 towards Wentworth, right along B6089 taking signed road to Clubhouse 300 yards on right. Flat parkland course with small greens, dykes and two ponds. 18 holes, 6086 yards. S.S.S. 70. Limited practice area. *Green Fees:* £36.00 per round or day. Golf/meal package £33.00/£38.00. 2Fore1 Monday to Friday. *Eating facilities:* lounge bar and dining area with seating for up to 100 people. *Visitors:* weekdays only. *Society Meetings:* welcome weekdays only by prior arrangement. Professional: Chris Bassett. Secretary: M. Godfrey (01709 878609; Fax: 01709 877097).

SHEFFIELD. **Abbeydale Golf Club,** Twentywell Rise off, Twentywell Lane, Dore, Sheffield S17 4QA (0114 2360763; Fax: 0114 2360762). *Location*: A621 five miles south of Sheffield. Parkland. 18 holes, 6241 yards. S.S.S. 70. Practice ground. *Green Fees*: information not available. *Eating facilities:* restaurant and bar meals. *Visitors*: welcome by arrangement. Starting time restrictions April-October. *Society Meetings*: catered for by arrangement. Golf Manager/Professional: N. Perry (0114 2365633). Office Manager: Mrs J. Wing (0114 2360763; Fax: 0114 2360762).

SHEFFIELD. **Beauchief Golf Club,** Abbey Lane, Beauchief, Sheffield S8 0DB (0114 236 7274). *Location:* near the junction with A621 Abbeydale Road 5 miles SW of Sheffield. Access from J33 or J29 via outer ring road. 'Pay and Play' parkland course with some hilly holes. 18 holes, 5452 yards,. S.S.S. 66. Practice area. *Green Fees:* information not provided. *Eating facilities:* cafe/bar, open daily from 11am to dusk. *Visitors:* welcome weekdays and after 10am at weekend. *Society Meetings:* welcome weekdays and after 10am weekend, contact Pro. Professional: M. Trippett (01142 367274). Secretary: Mrs B. Fryer (0114 236 5628).

SHEFFIELD. **Birley Wood Golf Club,** Birley Lane, Sheffield S12 3BP (0114 264 7262). *Location:* Junction 30 M1 then A616 to Sheffield. Undulating meadowland course with good views. Fairway Course: 18 holes, 5734 yards. Par 69, S.S.S. 68. Short Birley Course: 18 holes, 4906 yards. Par 66. S.S.S. 65. Practice field near course. Membership available. *Green Fees:* information not available. *Eating facilities:* restaurant and bar meals at adjacent Fairway Inn. *Visitors:* welcome anytime. *Society Meetings:* contact Mr N. Luety (0114 279 7451). Secretary: P. Renshaw (0114 265 3784).*

SHEFFIELD. **Concord Park Municipal Golf Course,** Shiregreen Lane, Shiregreen, Sheffield S5 6AE (0114 2577378). *Location:* M1 Junctions 34/35, one and a half miles north of junctions. Parkland, hilly, good views. 18 holes, 4872 yards, S.S.S. 64, Par 67. Driving range; buggies available. *Green Fees:* information not provided. *Eating facilities:* available in new clubhouse. *Visitors:* welcome any time; busy Saturday and Sunday mornings. *Society Meetings:* welcome. Professional: W. Allcroft (0114 2577378). Secretary: A. Martin (01709 877287).

SHEFFIELD. **Dore and Totley Golf Club,** The Clubhouse, Bradway Road, Bradway, Sheffield S17 4QR (0114 236 0492; Fax: 0114 235 3436). *Location:* leave M1 at Junction 33. Flat, easy walking parkland course. 18 holes, 6256 yards. S.S.S. 70. *Green Fees:* information not available. *Eating facilities:* bar catering facilities available except Mondays. *Visitors:* welcome. After 10am Tuesdays and Thursday; afternoons only Wednesdays and Sundays. No visitors on Saturdays. Handicap Certificates may be requested. *Society Meetings:* welcome by arrangement. Special all day price; catering by arrangement with Stewardess. Professional: Gregg Roberts (Tel & Fax: 0114 236 6844). Secretary: J. Johnson (0114 2369872).*

SHEFFIELD. **Hallamshire Golf Club Ltd,** Sandygate, Sheffield S10 4LA (0114 230 1007; Fax: 0114 230 2153). *Location:* A57 out of Sheffield, four miles out of city then fork left for Lodge Moor. Undulating moorland course. 18 holes, 6346 yards, 5800 metres. S.S.S. 71. *Green Fees:* visit website. *Eating facilities:* dining room/verandah, two bars. *Visitors:* welcome weekdays by arrangement, some weekends. Dress code. Snooker table. *Society Meetings:* catered for by arrangement with Secretary. Professional: Geoffrey Tickell (0114 230 5222). Secretary: Bob Hill (0114 230 2153; Fax: 0114 230 5413).

SHEFFIELD. **Hallowes Golf Club,** Hallowes Lane, Dronfield, Near Sheffield S18 1UR (01246 411196; Fax: 01246 413753). *Location:* six miles south of Sheffield on B6057 turn on to Hallowes Lane and to top of hill. Moorland/parkland. 18 holes, 6342 yards. S.S.S. 71. Large practice area and short game facility. *Green Fees:* weekdays £37.50 per round, £42.50 per day. *Eating facilities:* bars, dining room. *Visitors:* weekdays only, no visitors at weekends and Bank Holidays except with members. *Society Meetings:* EGU registered societies welcome. special reduced packages available. Professional: John Oates (01246 411196). Manager: Dr Nigel Ogden (01246 413734).

SHEFFIELD. **Hillsborough Golf Club Ltd,** Worrall Road, Sheffield S6 4BE (0114 234 9151 – Office; 0114 229 4103 – Steward). *Location:* three miles from city centre. Worrall Road via Middlewood Road, Dykes Hall Road. Undulating wooded parkland and heath. 18 holes, 6035 yards. S.S.S. 70. Practice field. *Green Fees:* weekdays £30.00, weekends and Bank Holidays £35.00. *Eating facilities:* snacks available; lunches, teas, evening meals by arrangement (not Fridays). *Visitors:* welcome weekdays, weekends with a member only. *Society Meetings:* catered for by arrangement with Professional. Professional: Lewis Horsman (0114 229 4100). Office: (0114 234 9151).

THE APPEARANCE OF AN ASTERISK (*) AT THE END OF A CLUB OR COURSE ENTRY INDICATES THAT UP-TO-DATE INFORMATION HAS NOT BEEN SUPPLIED

SHEFFIELD. **Lees Hall Golf Club Ltd,** Hemsworth Road, Norton, Sheffield S8 8LL (0114 255 4402). *Location:* three miles south of Sheffield, between A61 and A6102 ring road. Undulating parkland with extensive views over Sheffield. 18 holes, 6171 yards. S.S.S. 70. *Green Fees:* information not available. *Eating facilities:* available daily. *Visitors:* welcome, except Saturday and Sunday before 10.30am. *Society Meetings:* by arrangement only. Professional: Simon Berry (0114-250 7868). Secretary: (0114 255 4402).
e-mail: secretary@leeshallgolfclub.co.uk

SHEFFIELD. **Rother Valley Golf Centre,** Mansfield Road, Wales Bar, Sheffield S26 5PQ (0114 2473000; Fax: 0114 2476000). *Location:* centrally situated between Sheffield, Rotherham, and Chesterfield. Two miles from Junction 31 of M1, signposted. Parkland with water features. Island green at 7th hole and monster par 5 18th hole. Floodlit driving range and 9 hole pitch and putt course. Jack Barker golf school. 18 holes, 6602 yards. S.S.S. 72. *Green Fees:* information not available. *Eating facilities:* bar open 9am to 10.30pm. *Visitors:* welcome. *Society Meetings:* welcome including weekends. Phone for special offers. General Manager: Richard Hanson.

SHEFFIELD. **Stocksbridge and District Golf Club Ltd,** 30 Royd Lane, Deepcar, Sheffield S36 2RZ (0114 2882003). *Location:* 10 miles from Sheffield on A616 heading towards Manchester. Moorland course. 18 holes, 5200 yards. S.S.S. 65. Practice ground. *Green Fees:* information not available. *Eating facilities:* dining room and bars available. *Visitors:* welcome weekdays, restrictions weekends. *Society Meetings:* catered for during the week. Professional: Roger Broad (0114 2882779). Secretary: Dennis Haley (0114 2882003).*

SHEFFIELD. **Tankersley Park Golf Club Ltd,** High Green, Sheffield S35 4LG (0114 2468247; Fax: 0114 2457818). *Location:* M1 north to Junction 35a, A616, golf club on right. M1 south Junction 36, A61 Sheffield, left on A616, golf club on left. Parkland/wooded. 18 holes, 6212 yards. S.S.S. 70. Practice area and practice green. *Green Fees:* information not provided. *Eating facilities:* sandwiches, bar and evening meals. *Visitors:* welcome weekdays without reservation but not before 3pm weekends. *Society Meetings:* catered for by prior arrangement with Secretary. Professional: I. Kirk (Tel & Fax: 0114 2455583). Secretary: A. Brownhill (0114 2468247).

SHEFFIELD. **Tinsley Park Golf Club (Municipal),** High Hazels Park, Darnall, Sheffield S9 4PE (0114 2448974). *Location:* three miles from Junction 33 M1, exit – A6102. Wooded course. 18 holes, 6096 yards. S.S.S. 69. Practice facilities. *Green Fees:* information not available. *Eating facilities:* catering only available on Friday 8am-4pm, Saturday and Sunday 7am-5pm. *Visitors:* welcome without restriction, times booked through Professional up to 8 days in advance. *Society Meetings:* bookings through Professional. Professional: Wayne Yellott (0114 244 8974).*

SHEFFIELD. **Wortley Golf Club,** Hermit Hill Lane, Wortley, Sheffield S35 7DF (0114 288 8469; Fax: 0114 288 8488). *Location:* leave M1 Junction 36 or 35A - A616 or A61 to A629 leading to Wortley Village, through village turn right. Parkland. 18 holes, 6035 yards, 5520 metres. S.S.S. 69. Practice ground. *Green Fees:* weekdays £30.00 per round, £40.00 per day; weekends £35.00 per round. *Eating facilities:* order in advance, limited on Mondays. *Visitors:* welcome, no restrictions. Golf buggy, trolley and club hire available. *Society Meetings:* welcome, must pre-book. Professional: Ian Kirk (0114 288 6490). Office: (0114 288 8469).
e-mail: wortley.golfclub@btconnect.com
website: www.wortleygolfclub.co.uk

WORKSOP. **Lindrick Golf Club,** Lindrick Common, Worksop S81 8BH (01909 485802). *Location*: on A57 four miles west of Worksop. M1 Junction 31 on to A57 Worksop. Heathland. 18 holes, 6612 yards, 6046 metres. S.S.S. 71. Two practice areas. *Green Fees:* information not available. *Eating facilities*: dining room and Ryder Cup Room. *Visitors:* welcome weekdays, except Tuesday mornings. Enquire re Sunday availability. Prior booking required. *Society Meetings:* catered for weekdays. Professional: John King (01909 475820). Secretary: Carol Kirk (01909 475282; Fax: 01909 488685).*
website: www.lindrickgolfclub.co.uk

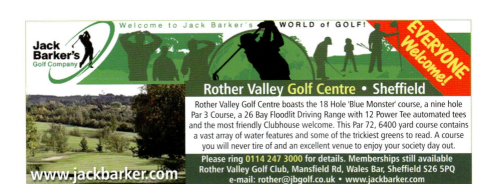

West Yorkshire

BINGLEY. **Bingley (St Ives) Golf Club,** The Golf Clubhouse, Harden, Bingley BD16 1AT (01274 562436; Fax: 01274 511788). *Location:* A650 Keighley/Bradford Road. Parkland/moorland. 18 holes, 6480 yards. S.S.S. 71. Practice ground. *Green Fees:* information not available. *Eating facilities:* daily. *Visitors:* welcome weekdays, limited availability weekends. *Society Meetings:* welcome, book through Professional. Professional: Nigel Barber (01274 562436). Manager: Ray Adams (01274 562436; Tel & Fax: 01274 511788).*
e-mail: secretary@bingleystivesgc.co.uk
website: www.bingleystivesgc.co.uk

BINGLEY. **Shipley Golf Club**, Beckfoot Lane, Bingley BD16 1LX (01274 568652). *Location*: One mile out of Bingley town centre on B265 heading towards Bradford. Parkland course. 18 holes, 6220 yards. S.S.S. 70. Practice ground including chipping area, putting green and bunker. Qualified PGA Professional onsite. Individual and group coaching offered. *Green Fees*: £39.00. Special offers throughout the year. Visit website for details. *Eating facilities*: bar menu or tailor-made to suit requirements. *Visitors*: welcome every day except Tuesday 8am - 2.30pm and Saturday. Buggies available during golfing season. *Society Meetings*: welcome most days. Packages available. Telephone for quotation. Professional: Nathan Stead (01274 563674). Secretary: Melanie Simpson (01274 568652).
e-mail: office@shipleygc.co.uk
website: www.shipleygolfclub.com

BRADFORD. **Baildon Golf Club,** Moorgate, Baildon, Shipley BD17 5PP (01274 584266). *Location:* five miles north-west of Bradford via Shipley. Moorland course. 18 holes, 6225 yards. S.S.S. 70. *Green Fees:* £18.00 per round, 7 days a week. *Eating facilities:* catering except Mondays. Bar and separate dining room. *Visitors:* welcome, restricted at weekends and Tuesdays. *Society Meetings:* welcome 7 days a week, contact Secretary with bookings. Professional: R. Masters (01274 595162). Secretary: Nick Redman.
e-mail: secretary@baildongolfclub.com
website: www.baildongolfclub.com

BINGLEY ST IVES GOLF CLUB
The Clubhouse, Harden, Bingley BD16 1AT

Superb course and facilities with magnificent views of the Aire valley. Visitors welcome, special package rates all year round.

Contact **Pro: 01274 562436** / **Manager: 01274 562436** *for details*
e-mail: secretary@bingleystivesgc.co.uk
www.bingleystivesgc.co.uk

BRADFORD. **Bradford Moor Golf Club,** Scarr Hall, Pollard Lane, Bradford BD2 4RW (01274 771716). *Location:* A658 two miles from top of M606. Moorland, undulating course. 9 holes, 5854 yards. S.S.S. 68. *Green Fees:* £12.00 (£9.00 with a member). *Eating facilities:* available by appointment only. *Visitors:* welcome weekdays. *Society Meetings:* welcome weekdays. Secretary: Chris Bedford (01274 771693).

BRADFORD. **Clayton Golf Club,** Thornton View Road, Clayton, Bradford BD14 6JX (01274 880047). *Location:* two miles south west of Bradford, via Thornton Road, then Listerhills Road. Parkland course. 9 holes, 6200 yards. S.S.S. 72. *Green Fees:* information not available. *Eating facilities:* diningroom – meals and snacks daily; evening meals by arrangement; two bars. *Visitors:* welcome at all times except before 4.00pm on Sundays. Snooker room. *Society Meetings:* catered for by arrangement. Secretary: D.A. Smith (01274 572311).*

BRADFORD. **East Bierley Golf Club,** South View Road, East Bierley, Bradford BD4 6PP (01274 683666). *Location*: situated about three miles east of Bradford on the Wakefield/Heckmondwike Road. Turn off at Bierley Bar and down South View Road. Parkland course. 9 holes, 5224 metres. S.S.S. 66. *Green Fees*: information not available. *Eating facilities:* lunchtime and evening catering (except Tuesdays). *Visitors*: welcome, not Mondays after 4pm. Secretary: Mr R.J. Welch (01274 683666). Hon. Secretary: R.J. Welch. Steward: (01274 680450).

BRADFORD. **Headley Golf Club,** Headley Lane, Thornton, Bradford BD13 3LX (01274 833481). *Location:* five miles west of Bradford. Undulating parkland, excellent views. 9 holes, 4914 yards. S.S.S. 65. *Green Fees:* information not available. *Eating facilities:* dining room and bar. *Visitors:* weekdays only. *Society Meetings:* welcome weekdays, special packages available. Hon. Secretary: D. Britton (01274 833481).*

BRADFORD. **The Manor Golf Club,** Bradford Road, Drighlington, Bradford BD11 1AB (0113 2852644). *Location:* between Leeds and Bradford, just off M62 Junction 27. Undulating parkland/meadowland, features six lakes. 18 holes, 6564 yards. S.S.S 71, Par 72. 20 bay floodlit driving range, 6 hole Par 3 course. *Green Fees:* midweek £17.00 per round, weekend £21.00 per round - after 3.30pm £13.50. *Eating facilities:* clubhouse. *Visitors:* welcome at all times but prior enquiry advised. *Society Meetings:* welcome with reservation. Director of Golf/ Professional: Graham Thompson.

BRADFORD. **Northcliffe Golf Club,** High Bank Lane, Shipley BD18 4LJ (01274 584085). *Location:* three miles west of Bradford on A650; turn left at roundabout Junction of A650/A657. Undulating woodland parkland with feature holes. 18 holes, 6104 yards. S.S.S. 70. *Green Fees:* weekdays £25.00; weekends and Bank Holidays £30.00. *Eating facilities:* bars 11am to 11pm, food 11.30am to 9.00pm summer months. No catering or bar facilities on Mondays in winter, except Bank Holidays. *Visitors:* Monday to Friday, Saturday after 4.30pm, Sunday all day. Wide wheel/electric trolleys for hire. *Society Meetings:* welcome, packages available. Professional: M. Hillas (01274 587193). Hon. Secretary: I. Collins (01274 596731; Fax: 01274 584148).
website: www.northcliffegc.org.uk

BRADFORD. **Queensbury Golf Club,** Brighouse Road, Queensbury, Bradford BD13 1QF (01274 882155). *Location:* M62 Junction 25, A644 to Brighouse, Hipperholme and Queensbury. Wooded course. 9 holes, 5024 yards. S.S.S. 65. *Green Fees:* weekdays £15.00, weekends and Bank Holidays £30.00. *Eating facilities:* lunches, teas except Monday. Bar available. *Visitors:* welcome any day, must have Handicap. No parties at weekends. *Society Meetings:* by arrangement. Professional: G. Murray (01274 816864). Secretary: M . H . Heptinstall (01274 882155).

BRADFORD. **Shipley Golf Club,** Beckfoot Lane, Cottingley Bridge, Bingley BD16 1LX (01274 568652; Fax: 01274 567739). *Location:* off A650 at Cottingley Bridge, Bradford six miles, Bingley one mile. Flat parkland. 18 holes, 6220 yards. S.S.S. 70. Practice area and net putting green. *Green Fees:* Monday £29.00 per round, £35.00 per day; Tuesday-Sunday (excl. Saturday) £39.00 per round, £45.00 per day. Winter rates by arrangement. *Eating facilities:* available. *Visitors:* welcome by arrangement with Manager or Professional; not Tuesdays or Saturdays. *Society Meetings:* catered for by arrangement with Manager or Professional. Packages available. Professional: N. Stead (01274 563674; Fax: 01274 567739). Manager/ Secretary: Mrs M.J. Simpson (01274 568652; Fax: 01274 567739).
e-mail: office@shipleygc.co.uk
website: www.shipleygolfclub.com

BRADFORD. **South Bradford Golf Club,** Pearson Road, Odsal, Bradford BD6 1BH (01274 679195). *Location:* follow signs for Odsal Stadium, roundabout at Stadium turn left and first left again, road leads down to clubhouse. Parkland type course with some hilly sections. 9 holes, 6004 yards. S.S.S. 69. Practice ground. *Green Fees:* information not available. *Eating facilities:* bar meals available except Mondays. *Visitors:* welcome; not before 3.30pm on weekends and Bank Holidays. *Society Meetings:* welcome – must apply in writing.

BRADFORD. **West Bradford Golf Club Ltd,** Chellow Grange Road, Haworth Road, Bradford BD9 6NP. *Location:* 3 miles west of city centre off B6144 Haworth Road. Easy walking, undulating, wooded parkland course. 18 holes, 5723 yards. S.S.S. 68, Par 69. *Green Fees:* from £16.00. Package deals for parties and societies. Happy hour weekends after 4pm – reduced green fee. *Eating facilities:* available every day except Monday. *Visitors:* welcome, except Saturdays before 4pm. *Society Meetings:* welcome by arrangement. Professional: Warren Kemp (01274 542102). Secretary: N.S. Bey (01274 542767; Fax: 01274 482079).

BRIGHOUSE. **Castlefields Golf Club,** Rastrick Common, Rastrick, Brighouse HD6 3HL. *Location:* one mile out of Brighouse on A643. Parkland course, founded 1903. 6 holes, 2406 yards. S.S.S. 50, Par 54. *Green Fees:* information not provided. *Eating facilities:* Globe Inn 200 yards away. *Visitors:* welcome at all times but must be accompanied by a member. *Society Meetings:* contact Secretary for details at above address.

BRIGHOUSE. **Crow Nest Park Golf Club,** Coach Road, Hove Edge, Brighouse HD6 2LN (01484 401121). *Location:* Bradford Road out of Brighouse, left at Ritz Ballroom, right after one mile. Gently undulating parkland. 9 holes, 6020 yards. S.S.S. 69. Floodlit driving range with power tees and swingcam. *Green Fees:* weekdays 9 holes £10.00, 18 holes £16.00; weekends 9 holes £12.00, 18 holes £20.00. *Eating facilities:* food available from 11.30am till 2.30pm and then from 5.30pm till 9.30pm, bar open from 11am until 11pm. *Visitors:* welcome but tees must be booked in advance with Professional. *Society Meetings:* welcome by prior arrangement. Professional: Paul Everitt. Secretary: (01484 401121). Clubhouse: (01484 401152).
e-mail: info@crownestgolf.co.uk
website: www.crownestgolf.co.uk

BRIGHOUSE. **Willow Valley Golf,** Highmoor Lane, off Walton Lane, Clifton, Brighouse HD6 4JB (01274 878642). *Location:* Junction 25 off M62 to Brighouse A644, right at roundabout A643, two miles on right. American-style island greens, undulating fairway, water. Three courses. Willow Valley course: 18 holes, 7025 yards. S.S.S. 72. 18 hole Pine Valley course. 5032 yards. S.S.S. 64. 18-bay covered range. Fountain Ridge 9 hole course. *Green Fees:* Willow Valley - weekdays £26.00; weekends £38.00. Pine Valley - weekdays £15.00, weekends £17.00. 9-hole Fountain Ridge course from £7.50. 4 Ball & Buggy deal £99.00. Stay & Play deals. *Eating facilities:* fully licensed bar and catering. *Visitors:* always welcome. *Society Meetings:* society and group packages available, please contact Helen Newton.
website: www.wvgc.co.uk

CLECKHEATON. **Cleckheaton and District Golf Club Ltd,** Bradford Road, Cleckheaton BD19 6BU (01274 851266; Fax: 01274 871382). *Location:* four miles south of Bradford on A638, 200 yards from Junction 26 M62. Dr Alister MacKenzie designed parkland course. 18 holes, 5706 yards. Par 70, S.S.S. 68. Practice area. *Green Fees:* information not provided. *Eating facilities:* bar, lounge and diningroom. *Visitors:* welcome except Saturdays, suggest prior enquiry. *Society Meetings:* catered for by prior arrangement with Secretary except Saturdays. Professional: Warren Lockett. Secretary: Dick Guiver.
e-mail: info@cleckheatongolfclub.co.uk
website: www.cleckheatongolfclub.com

DEWSBURY. **Dewsbury District Golf Club,** The Pinnacle, Sands Lane, Mirfield WF14 8HJ (01924 492399). *Location:* turn off A644 opposite Swan Inn, two miles west of Dewsbury. Undulating moorland/parkland with panoramic views over surrounding countryside. 18 holes, 6360 yards. S.S.S. 71. Practice field, putting green. *Green Fees:* weekdays £25.00 per round, £30.00 per day; weekends £20.00 after 2pm. *Eating facilities:* bar and restaurant (catering every day). *Visitors:* welcome without reservation weekdays, weekends with member only before 2pm. *Society Meetings:* welcome by prior arrangement. Parties over 12: day £30.00 per person. Professional: N.P. Hirst (01924 496030). General Manager: Mick Thorpe (01924 492399).
e-mail: info@dewsburygolf.co.uk
website: www.dewsburygolf.co.uk

DEWSBURY. **Hanging Heaton Golf Club,** White Cross Road, Dewsbury WF12 7DT (01924 461606; Fax; 01924 430100). *Location:* one mile from town centre on main A653 Dewsbury to Leeds road. 9 holes, 5836 yards (for 18 holes). S.S.S. 68. *Green Fees:* Information not available. *Eating facilities:* available. *Visitors:* welcome without reservation, except weekends. *Society Meetings:* catered for by arrangement with Secretary. Professional: G. Moore (01924 467077). Secretary: Derek Atkinson (01924 430100).*

ELLAND. **Elland Golf Club,** Hammerstone Leach Lane, Elland HX5 0TA (01422 372505). *Location:* M62 Junction 24 exit off roundabout for Blackley, one mile. Parkland. 9 holes, 5498 yards. S.S.S. 67. *Green Fees:* weekdays £18.00; weekends £30.00. *Eating facilities:* meals/bar snacks except Mondays. *Visitors:* welcome weekdays except Thursdays. *Society Meetings:* by arrangement. Professional: N. Krzywicki (01422 374886). Secretary: P.A. Green (01422 251431).

GUISELEY. **The Bradford Golf Club,** Hawksworth Lane, Guiseley, Leeds LS20 8NP (01943 875570). *Location:* Shipley to Ilkley road, left at top of Hollins Hill, one mile up Hawksworth Lane. Moorland/parkland. 18 holes, 6259 yards. S.S.S. 71. *Green Fees:* £40.00 per round, £45.00 per day. Discounts available for parties over 20. *Eating facilities:* every day, preferably by prior arrangement. *Visitors:* welcome, phone Professional for availability, not on weekends without prior arrangement. *Society Meetings:* catered for on weekdays (except Tuesdays) by prior arrangement. Professional: Andrew Hall (01943 873719). Secretary: J. Washington (01943 875570).

HALIFAX. **Halifax Bradley Hall Golf Club,** Holywell Green, Halifax HX4 9AN (01422 374108). *Location:* three miles south of Halifax on B6112. Undulating moorland. 18 holes, 6138 yards. S.S.S. 70. Practice ground. *Green Fees:* information not available. *Visitors:* welcome. Snooker. *Society Meetings:* welcome with prior reservation weekdays. Handicap Certificate. Professional: P. Wood (01422 370231). Secretary: A. Berry (01422 374108).*

HALIFAX. **The Halifax Golf Club Ltd,** Union Lane, Ogden, Halifax HX2 8XR (01422 244171). *Location:* four miles out of Halifax, A629 towards Keighley. Moorland. 18 holes, 6037 yards. S.S.S. 70. *Green Fees:* information not available. *Eating facilities:* luncheons and dinners served. Good restaurant facilities. *Visitors:* welcome most days by arrangement (not Saturdays). *Society Meetings:* catered for by arrangement. Professional: David Delaney (01422 240047).*

HALIFAX. **Halifax West End Golf Club Ltd,** Paddock Lane, Highroad Well, Halifax HX2 0NT (01422 341878). *Location:* two miles west of town centre. Parkland. 18 holes, 5937 yards. S.S.S. 68 (White markers). *Green Fees:* information not available. *Eating facilities:* full bar and catering except Mondays. *Visitors:* welcome except Saturdays - please check with Professional. No visiting parties on Saturdays. *Society Meetings:* catered for by arrangement with Secretary. Professional: David Rishworth (01422 341878). Secretary: G. Gower (Tel & Fax: 01422 341878). e-mail: westendgc@btinternet.com

HALIFAX. **Lightcliffe Golf Club,** Knowle Top Road, Lightcliffe, Halifax HX3 8RG (01422 202459). *Location:* three miles east of Halifax on A58 (main Halifax to Leeds road). Parkland. 9 holes, 5388 metres. S.S.S. 68. *Green Fees:* information not available. *Eating facilities:* bar snacks and meals (except Mondays). *Visitors:* welcome without reservation but must confirm with Professional. Not Wednesdays. *Society Meetings:* catered for. Professional: Ron Tickle (01422 202459). Secretary: Rod Crampton (01484 384066). *

HALIFAX. **Ryburn Golf Club,** The Shaw, Norland, Sowerby Bridge, Near Halifax HX6 3QP (01422 831355). *Location:* Halifax to Sowerby Bridge, turn left on station road, turn right up hill, right towards Hobbit Inn (signposted), left after cottages. Demanding, hilly, windy course. 9 holes, 5127 yards. S.S.S. 65. *Green Fees:* see website. *Eating facilities:* good catering facilities and bar. *Visitors:* welcome weekdays, weekends by prior arrangement. *Society Meetings:* welcome by prior arrangement. Secretary: Raymond Attiwell (07904 834320). website: www.ryburngolfclub.co.uk

HEBDEN BRIDGE. **Hebden Bridge Golf Club,** Wadsworth, Hebden Bridge HX7 8PH (01422 842896). *Location:* one mile upwards past Birchcliffe Centre. Moorland with superb Pennine views. 9 holes, 5242 yards. S.S.S. 67. *Green Fees:* information not available. *Eating facilities:* bar and dining room facilities, private functions catered for. *Visitors:* welcome, please check first at weekends. *Society Meetings:* welcome midweek only except by special arrangement. Co-ordinator: Mark Blackwood (01422 842896; Mobile: 0777 908 9499).*

HUDDERSFIELD. **Bradley Park Municipal Golf Course,** Off Bradley Road, Huddersfield HD2 1PZ (01484 223772). *Location:* M62 Junction 25, follow Huddersfield signs then A6107. Parkland course, rolling hills with panoramic views. 18 holes, 6220 yards. S.S.S. 70. Floodlit driving range, 9 hole Par 3 course. *Green Fees:* information not provided. *Eating facilities:* full catering. *Visitors:* welcome, no restrictions. No block bookings for parties at weekends, only telephone bookings to the Professional for individuals. *Society Meetings:* all welcome, book through Professional. Professional: P.E. Reilly. Secretary: K. Blackwell (01484 223772; Fax: 01484 451613).

Set in peaceful and tranquil countryside near the picturesque village of Hawksworth, this undulating parkland course enjoys magnificent views over the Yorkshire moors. The spacious greens make this a fair test of golf which must be treated with respect. Traditional-style clubhouse with two well-stocked bars and excellent catering facilities. Special packages for individuals and golfing parties. No visitors on Saturdays; by prior arrangement on Sundays and Bank Holidays.

Bradford (Hawksworth)
GOLF CLUB
Hawksworth Lane, Guiseley LS20 8NP
Home of the Hawksworth Trophy

Enquiries to the Manager: 01943 875570
e-mail: bradford-golfclub@tiscali.co.uk

THE GOLF GUIDE 2011   NORTH REGION / West Yorkshire

HUDDERSFIELD. **Crosland Heath Golf Club Ltd,** Felks Stile Road, Crosland Heath, Huddersfield HD4 7AF (01484 653216). *Location:* 3 miles from town centre off A62 Oldham road. Flat heathland with extensive views. 18 holes, 6087 yards. Par 71. Practice facilities. *Green Fees:* £37.00 to £42.00. *Eating facilities:* full catering except Mondays. *Visitors:* welcome, suggest prior enquiry. *Society Meetings:* Tuesdays and Thursdays. Professional: (01484 653877). General Manager: (01484 653216). website: www.croslandheath.co.uk

HUDDERSFIELD. **Huddersfield Golf Club,** Fixby Hall, Lightridge Road, Fixby, Huddersfield HD2 2EP (01484 426203; Fax: 01484 424623). *Location:* M62 Junction 24; A643 from Cedar Court Hotel; turn right first traffic lights by Sun Inn. Parkland course. 18 holes, 6466 yards. S.S.S. 72. Practice ground. *Green Fees:* information not available. *Eating facilities:* available. *Visitors:* always welcome, reservation essential. Tuesday Ladies' Day; no visitors Saturdays. Snooker. *Society and Company Days:* catered for except weekends, well appointed private rooms. Catering to suit all occasions. Professional: P. Carman (01484 426463). Office Manager: Mrs D. Lockett (01484 426203). General Manager: T. Seaton (01484 426203).*
e-mail: secretary@huddersfield-golf.co.uk
website: www.huddersfield-golf.co.uk

HUDDERSFIELD. **Longley Park Golf Club,** Maple Street (off Somerset Road), Aspley, Huddersfield HD5 9AX (01484 426932). *Location:* one mile town centre, Wakefield side. 9 holes, 5212 yards. S.S.S. 66. *Green Fees:* £21.00 weekdays; £27.00 weekends and Bank Holidays. *Eating facilities:* available. *Visitors:* welcome Mondays, Tuesdays and Fridays, other times by previous arrangement only. *Society Meetings:* welcome by previous arrangement with Secretary. Professional: John Ambler (01484 422304). Secretary: (01484 431885)

HUDDERSFIELD. **Marsden Golf Club,** Hemplow, Marsden, Huddersfield HD7 6NN (01484 844253). *Location:* eight miles west of Huddersfield off A62 from Huddersfield to Manchester. Moorland. 9 holes, 5702 yards. S.S.S. 68. *Green Fees:* information not available. *Eating facilities:* lunches and snacks available except Tuesdays. *Visitors:* welcome weekdays, with a member only weekends. *Society Meetings:* catered for by arrangement. Society packages available. Professional: James Crompton (01484 844253). Secretary: R. O'Brien (01484 844678).*

HUDDERSFIELD. **Meltham Golf Club,** Thick Hollins Hall, Meltham, Huddersfield HD9 4DQ (Tel & Fax: 01484 850227). *Location:* half mile east of Meltham, six miles south west of Huddersfield (B6107). Gently sloping course in wooded valley. 18 holes, 6390 yards, 5832 metres. S.S.S. 70. Restricted practice area. *Green Fees:* Monday to Friday £28.00 per round, £33.00 per day; weekend £33.00 per round, £38.00 per day. 2-FORE!-1 vouchers accepted at day rate. *Eating facilities:* lunches, dinners (with reservation), bar meals available. *Visitors:* welcome weekdays and Sundays without reservation, not Saturdays. *Society Meetings:* catered for by arrangement. Professional: P. Davies (01484 851521). Secretary: J. Dixon.
website: www.meltham-golf.co.uk

HUDDERSFIELD. **Woodsome Hall Golf Club,** Woodsome Hall, Fenay Bridge, Huddersfield HD8 0LQ (01484 602739). *Location:* A629 five miles from Huddersfield. Parkland and wooded course. 18 holes, 6096 yards. S.S.S. 69. Practice ground. *Green Fees:* information not available. *Eating facilities:* bar snacks and dining available; new casual bar open. *Visitors:* welcome Mondays, Wednesdays, Thursdays and Fridays, limited on Sundays by application. *Society Meetings:* welcome by arrangement, jacket and tie in public rooms. Professional: J. Eyre (01484 602034). Hon Secretary: R.B. Shaw (01484 602739; Fax: 01484 608260). General Manager: Mrs T.J. Mee (01484 602739). *

ILKLEY. **Ben Rhydding Golf Club,** High Wood, Ben Rhydding, Ilkley LS29 8SB (01943 608759). *Location:* one mile south-east of Ilkley town centre via Ben Rhydding Road or Wheatley Lane. Turn up Wheatley Grove and keep going up and left.Moorside parkland course with fine panoramic views over Wharfedale and surrounding moors. 9 holes, 4611 yards (18 holes). S.S.S. 63. *Green Fees:* weekdays £18.00, with member £9.00; weekends £22.00, with member £11.00. *Society Meetings:* by prior arrangement. Secretary: John Watts (01943 608759/07751 092241).

ILKLEY. **Bracken Ghyll Golf Club,** Skipton Road, Addingham, Ilkley LS29 0SL (01943 831207; Fax: 01943 839453). *Location*: between Ilkley and Skipton on the A65, signposted just after roundabout indicating Silsden and Keighley. Parkland course in rolling dales countryside. 18 holes, 5600 yards, S.S.S. 68. Indoor nets, practice field and putting green. *Green Fees*: information not available. *Eating facilities*: fully licensed bar, lunches served seven days a week in season. *Visitors*: welcome at all times outside competitions weekends and Tuesday and Thursday mornings. Telephone bookings accepted. *Society Meetings*: welcome, brochure on application. Secretary: Patrick Lee.*
e-mail: office@brackenghyll.co.uk
website: www.brackenghyll.co.uk

ILKLEY. **Ilkley Golf Club,** Nesfield Road, Ilkley LS29 0BE (01943 607277). *Location:* 15 miles north of Bradford. Flat course. 18 holes, 6235 yards. S.S.S. 70. *Green Fees:* 1st April to 31st October - weekdays £50.00, weekends £55.00; 1st November to 31st March - £35.00. 2010 rates (subject to review. *Eating facilities:* by arrangement. *Visitors:* welcome by arrangement. *Society Meetings:* catered for by arrangement. Professional: J.L. Hammond (01943 607463). Secretary: Peter G. Richardson (01943 600214; Fax: 01943 816130).
e-mail: honsec@ilkleygolfclub.co.uk
website: www.ilkleygolfclub.co.uk

330 West Yorkshire / NORTH REGION　　　　　　　　　　　**THE GOLF GUIDE 2011**

KEIGHLEY. **Branshaw Golf Club,** Branshaw Moor, Oakworth, Keighley BD22 7ES (01535 643235). *Location:* on B6143, two miles from town centre. Moorland with extensive views. 18 holes, 5888 yards. S.S.S. 68. *Green Fees:* information not provided. *Eating facilities:* full catering except Mondays. *Visitors:* welcome anytime by prior arrangement. *Society Meetings:* catered for weekdays and weekends. Professional: Simon Jowitt (01535 647441). Secretary: Simon Jowitt (01535 643235).
e-mail: enquiries@branshawgolfclub.co.uk
website: www.branshawgolfclub.co.uk

KEIGHLEY. **Keighley Golf Club,** Howden Park, Utley, Keighley BD20 6DH (01535 604778). *Location:* one mile west of Keighley towards Utley on B6143. Parkland. 18 holes, 6141 yards. S.S.S. 70. Practice ground and green. *Green Fees:* £16.00-£40.00 dependent on day and time. Visit website for offers. *Eating facilities:* full catering and bar facilities available. *Visitors:* welcome by prior arrangement. *Society Meetings:* catered for by arrangement. Professional: Andy Rhodes. Secretary: Cameron Dawson (Fax: 01535 604778).
e-mail: manager@keighleygolfclub.com
website: www.keighleygolfclub.com

KEIGHLEY. **Riddlesden Golf Club,** Howden Rough, Riddlesden, Keighley BD20 5QN (01535 602148). *Location:* A650 Keighley-Bradford road, left into Bar Lane, left on Scott Lane, which leads on to Scott Lane West and Elam Wood Road, approximately two miles. Moorland, with spectacular 3 par 3s in "Best Extraordinary Golf Holes Book". 18 holes, 4295 yards. S.S.S. 61. *Green Fees:* information not available. *Eating facilities:* catering available during bar hours. *Visitors:* welcome except between 10am–2pm Saturdays and before 2pm Sundays. *Society Meetings:* catered for by prior arrangement. Secretary: S. Morton (01535 604450).*

KEIGHLEY. **Silsden Golf Club,** Brunthwaite Lane, Brunthwaite, Silsden, Near Keighley BD20 0ND (01535 652998). *Location:* five miles north of Keighley. Undulating downland with extensive views. 18 holes, 5062 yards. S.S.S. 64. Practice area and putting green. *Green Fees:* information not available. *Eating facilities:* licensed bar, full catering available except Mondays. *Visitors & Society Meetings:* Welcome anytime by prior arrangement with the office (01535 652998).*

KNOTTINGLEY. **Ferrybridge Golf Club,** PO Box 39, Stranglands Lane, Knottingley WF11 8SQ. *Location:* off the A1 at Ferrybridge and quarter of a mile towards Castleford on the B6136. Undulating land. 9 holes, 6047/6076 yards. S.S.S. 69. Architect: George Barton. Practice ground. *Green Fees:* information not available. *Visitors:* welcome by prior booking. *Society Meetings:* by prior arrangement with Secretary. Secretary: T.D. Ellis (01977 884165).*

LEEDS. **Alwoodley Golf Club,** Wigton Lane, Alwoodley, Leeds LS17 8SA (0113 2681680). *Location:* five miles north of Leeds on A61 (Leeds to Harrogate). 18 holes, 6673 yards. S.S.S. 72. *Green Fees:* £78.00 weekdays (summer); £55.00 weekdays (winter); £90.00 weekends, £40.00 Summer twilight. 2010 rates (subject to review). *Eating facilities:* available. *Visitors:* welcome by arrangement. *Society Meetings:* catered for by arrangement. Professional: J.R. Green (0113 2689603). Secretary: Mrs J. Slater.
website: www.alwoodley.co.uk

LEEDS. **Calverley Golf Club,** Woodhall Lane, Pudsey, Leeds LS28 5QY (0113 256 9244; Fax: 0113 256 4362). *Location:* off Leeds outer ring road, signposted Pudsey. Bradford turn off, turn right at next roundabout onto Woodhall Lane. Parkland course. 18 holes, 5649 yards. S.S.S. 67. Practice ground, putting green. *Green Fees:* weekdays £16.00, with a member £10.00; weekends £20.00, with a member £13.00. Juniors £7.00. *Eating facilities:* full bar and catering facilities available. *Visitors:* very welcome, booking advisable. Members only weekends till 1pm. Buggies. Tuition available. *Society Meetings:* welcome by prior arrangement. Professional: Neil Wendel-Jones (0113 256 9244; Fax: 0113 256 4362). Hon. Secretary: Bill Gall (0113 256 9244; Fax: 0113 256 4362).

LEEDS. **Cookridge Hall Golf Club,** Cookridge Lane, Leeds LS16 7NL (0113 2300641; Fax: 0113 2030198). **Location:** A mere five miles from Leeds and Bradford city centres, the golf course, American in design, nestles away beautifully offering spectacular views of the Yorkshire Dales. Home to a championship 6788 yard par 72 golf course, 22-bay floodlit driving range and sports bar. PGA credited golf academy with short game practice facilities. **Green Fees:** weekdays £25.00, weekends and Bank Holidays £30.00. Twilight golf also available. **Eating facilities:** 18th Century built clubhouse with fully licensed bar and restaurant offering an extensive homemade menu. Available to hire for private functions. **Visitors:** very welcome anytime Monday – Friday, after 1pm on weekends and Bank Holidays. Tee times can be reserved 7 days in advance subject to availability. **Society Meetings:** very welcome 7 days a week, after 1pm on weekends and Bank Holidays. Discounted rates, minimum number of golfers 8. For more information contact Gary Day.
e-mail: info@cookridgehall.co.uk
website: www.cookridgehall.co.uk

LEEDS. **Garforth Golf Club Ltd,** Long Lane, Garforth, Leeds LS25 2DS (0113 286 3308). *Location:* six miles east of Leeds on A63, then turn left on to A642. Flat parkland. 18 holes, 6373 yards. S.S.S. 71. Practice area. *Green Fees:* weekdays £36.00 per round, £42.00 per day. 2010 rates (subject to review). *Eating facilities:* available. *Visitors:* welcome, but not before 9.30am or between 12 noon and 1.30pm. Weekend as member's guest only. *Society Meetings:* catered for. Professional: K. Findlater (0113 286 2063). Managing Secretary: Dave Carlisle (Tel & Fax: 0113 286 3308).

LEEDS. Gotts Park Municipal Golf Club, Gotts House, Gotts Park, Armley Ridge Road, Leeds LS12 2QX (0113 231 0492). *Location:* two miles west of city centre off A647 Stanningley Road. Undulating parkland. 18 holes, 4319 yards. S.S.S. 64. Putting green and practice area. *Green Fees:* information not provided. *Eating facilities:* cafe, bar facilities evenings/weekends only. *Visitors:* welcome, tee reserved Sundays 7am to 10am for members. Secretary: Clive Walton (0113 368 5500; Mobile: 07843 689377).

LEEDS. Headingley Golf Club, Back Church Lane, Adel, Leeds LS16 8DW (0113 2679573). *Location:* leave Leeds/Otley road (A660) at Church Lane, Adel about five miles from city centre. 18 holes, 6608 yards. S.S.S. 72. *Green Fees:* £40.00 per round; £55.00 per day. *Eating facilities:* full catering and bar facilities. *Visitors:* members of other golf clubs welcome, preferably with prior reservation. Snooker room. *Society Meetings:* catered for by arrangement. Professional: N.M. Harvey (0113 2675100; Fax: 0113 2817334). Secretary: J.L. Hall (0113 2679573).

LEEDS. Horsforth Golf Club Ltd, Layton Rise, Horsforth, Leeds LS18 5EX (0113 258 6819; Fax: 0113 258 9336). *Location:* midway between Leeds and Bradford, close to the Leeds and Bradford Airport. Easily accessible from the Leeds outer ring road and the main Bradford to Harrogate road. White tees 6258 yards, Yellow tees 5976, Ladies' tees 5563 yards. Par 71. *Green Fees:* information not available. *Eating facilities:* Bar sevice available from 11.30am to 11pm. Catering ranges from coffees, breakfast, light or full lunches; buffet and formal evening meals. *Visitors:* welcome, must comply with dress code. *Society Meetings:* welcome. Professionals: Dean Stokes & Simon Booth (0113 258 5200) Steward: C. Taylor (0113 258 1703). Secretary: Mrs L. Harrison (0113 258 6819).*
e-mail: lesley@horsforthgolfclub.co.uk
            hosforthgolfclub@tiscali.co.uk
website: www.horsforthgolfclub.co.uk

Please mention THE GOLF GUIDE when you enquire about clubs or accommodation

Horsforth Golf Club

Enjoy a day's golf at this great Alister MacKenzie course situated in North Leeds. Excellent hospitality and catering. Society, corporate and visitors welcome. Contact the Secretary for details.
Tel: **0113 258 6819**
or e-mail
lesley@horsforthgolfclub.co.uk
www.horsforthgolfclub.co.uk

LEEDS. Howley Hall Golf Club, Scotchman Lane, Morley, Leeds LS27 0NX (01924 350107; Fax: 01924 350104). *Location:* turn off the A650 Bradford/ Wakefield road at the Halfway House Public House, take the B6123 towards Batley – the course is on the left. Parkland. 18 holes, 6454 yards, S.S.S. 71. Practice ground. *Green Fees:* weekdays £31.00 per round, £37.00 per day; weekends £41.00 per round/day. 2010 rates (subject to review). *Eating facilities:* dining room and bar snacks available. *Visitors:* welcome. *Society Meetings:* welcome by reservation. Professional: Gary Watkinson (01924 350102). Secretary/ Manager: David Jones (01924 350100; Fax: 01924 350104).
e-mail: office@howleyhall.co.uk

Recognised as the fastest growing golf facility in the North of England, Cookridge Hall is home to a championship 6788 yard par 72 golf course that was designed and built by the American design team who built the Emirates Club in Dubai.
The golf course rolls gently through the countryside of North Leeds, offering spectacular views of the Yorkshire Dales. Adding to its overall splendour is the 18th century clubhouse and patio adjacent to the 18th green. Golfers and their guests can relax over a drink, sample the extensive homemade menu, whilst watching fellow golfers try to negotiate the demanding approach shot over the water. It provides a perfect setting to complement a great day's golf. 22-bay floodlit driving range & sports bar • Open to the public 7 days a week.

www.cookridgehall.co.uk
for more information call **0113 230 0641**
COOKRIDGE HALL GOLF CLUB

LEEDS. Leeds Golf Club, Cobble Hall, Elmete Lane, Leeds LS8 2LJ (0113 2659203). *Location:* Leeds ring road to A58, turn left if from east, right if from west, fork right at dual carriageway, turn right after 250 yards. 18 holes, 6115 yards. S.S.S. 69. *Green Fees:* £50.00 per day, £40.00 per round weekdays only; weekends only with a member. 2010 rates on application. Golf packages available with restrictions. *Eating facilities:* full catering, all day bar. *Visitors:* welcome. *Society Meetings:* very welcome. Some limited society days available on Sundays. Professional: Simon Longster (0113 2658786). Secretary: Paul Mawman (0113 2659203; Fax: 0113 2323369).
e-mail: secretary@leedsgolfclub.co.uk
website: www.leedsgolfclub.co.uk

LEEDS. Leeds Golf Centre, Wike Ridge Lane, Shadwell, Leeds LS17 9JW (0113 288 6000; Fax: 0113 288 6185). *Location*: two miles north of Leeds between A61 and A58 at the village of Wike. Set in magnificent rolling Yorkshire countryside. Leeds Golf Centre is open to the public and members all year round. Wike Ridge course: 18 hole Championship Course. 18 holes, 6482 yards, Par 71. Oaks course: 12 holes, 1610 yards. Par 36. The centre offers the best practice facilities in the area which include 20-bay fully floodlit and covered driving range, chipping green, putting green and bunker facilities. *Green Fees:* information not available. *Eating facilities:* restaurant, bar and function room. *Visitors:* welcome any time. Resident teaching Professionals–tuition for individuals and groups. *Society Meetings:* welcome any time; society packages and special offers available throughout the year. General Manager: Mick Redmond.*
e-mail: info@leedsgolfcentre.com
website: www.leedsgolfcentre.com

LEEDS. Middleton Park (Municipal) Golf Club, Ring Road, Beeston, Middleton, Leeds LS10 3TN (0113 270 9506). *Location:* ring road to Middleton off A653 (Water Tower). Parkland, wooded course. 18 holes, 5036 yards. S.S.S. 66. Practice ground. *Green Fees:* information not available. *Visitors:* welcome any time, contact the Pro Shop for bookings. *Society Meetings:* contact the Pro Shop. Professional: (0113 270 9506).*

LEEDS. Moor Allerton Golf Club, Coal Road, Wike, Leeds LS17 9NH (0113 2661154; Fax: 0113 2371124). *Location:* off the A61, 6 miles from Leeds city centre. Undulating parkland, PGA European Tour championship course designed by Robert Trent Jones Senior. 27 holes - three loops of 9 holes. Any combination playable. 6 bay driving range, practice ground. *Green Fees:* information not available. *Eating facilities:* full restaurant facilities plus snack bar. *Visitors:* welcome but must pre-book via Professional Shop. No visitors Sundays. Banqueting facilities for 200 people; conference/room hire for groups of all sizes. *Society Meetings:* welcome by prior arrangement via club office. Professional: James Whitaker (0113 2665209). Office: (0113 2661154; Fax: 0113 2371124).
e-mail: info@magc.co.uk
website: www.magc.co.uk

LEEDS. Moortown Golf Club, Harrogate Road, Alwoodley, Leeds LS17 7DB (0113 2686521). *Location:* five miles north of Leeds centre, A61 Harrogate Road. 18 holes, 6767 yards. Par 71, S.S.S. 73 (from the white tees). Practice facilities including short game area, putting green, teaching area and large grass tee area. *Green Fees:* £45.00 to £80.00 per round/day. *Eating facilities:* full catering services available. *Visitors:* welcome Sunday - Friday all day and after 2.30pm on a Saturday (subject to some tee-off time restrictions). Professional Shop. *Society Meetings:* Societies and groups catered for, contact the Secretary. Secretary: P. Rishworth (0113 2686521).
e-mail: secretary@moortown-gc.co.uk
website: www.moortown-golf-club.co.uk

LEEDS. Oulton Park, Rothwell Lane, Rothwell, Leeds LS26 8EX (0113 282 3152; Fax: 0113 282 6290). *Location:* M62 - Rothwell turn off, Junction 30; left at second roundabout. Parkland course built by Dave Thomas, many bunkers. 27 holes, 22 bay driving range, putting green. *Green Fees:* information not available. *Eating facilities:* restaurant and bar. *Visitors:* welcome, no restrictions; advance booking (five days) available. Dress code on course. *Society Meetings:* welcome except weekends. Professional: Steve Gromett. Manager: Allan Cooper.*

THE GOLF GUIDE 2011   NORTH REGION / West Yorkshire   333

LEEDS. **Rawdon Golf and Lawn Tennis Club,** Buckstone Drive, Micklefield Lane, Rawdon, Leeds LS19 6BD (0113-250 6040). *Location:* eight miles north of Leeds on A65, left at Rawdon traffic lights on to Micklefield Lane. Undulating parkland, with trees a special feature. 9 holes (18 tees), 5842 yards. S.S.S. 68. *Green Fees:* information not available. *Eating facilities:* meals and bar snacks except Mondays. *Visitors:* welcome. Facilities for tennis, visitors welcome. *Society Meetings:* catered for on application to Secretary. Secretary: Ian Scuffins (01132 506050).*

LEEDS. **Roundhay Golf Club,** Park Lane, Leeds LS8 2EJ (0113 2662695). *Location:* four miles north of Leeds city centre, leave A58 to Wetherby at Oakwood. Wooded parkland. 9 holes, 5322 yards. S.S.S. 65. Practice ground. *Green Fees:* on application. *Eating facilities:* bar for members, guests, and anyone purchasing a green fee, restaurant in evenings. *Visitors:* welcome without reservation. *Society Meetings:* arrangements with Leeds City Council. Professional: A. Newboult (0113 2661686). Hon. Secretary: G.M. Hodgson.

LEEDS. **Sand Moor Golf Club,** Alwoodley Lane, Leeds LS17 7DJ (0113 2681685). *Location:* five miles north of Leeds off A61. Moorland, overlooking picturesque Wharfedale. 18 holes, 6446 yards, 5894 metres. S.S.S. 71. *Green Fees:* £50.00 per round, £60.00 per day. 2010 rates (subject to review). *Eating facilities:* lunches daily, evening meals by arrangement. *Visitors:* welcome most weekdays and Sundays by arrangement. *Society Meetings:* catered for by arrangement. Professional: Frank Houlgate (0113 2685180). Secretary: Jackie Hogan (0113 2685180; Fax: 0113 2661105).

LEEDS. **Scarcroft Golf Club,** Syke Lane, Leeds LS14 3BQ (0113 289 2311). *Location:* A58 Wetherby road; turn left at Bracken Fox Public House, Scarcroft village seven miles north of Leeds. Undulating parkland. 18 holes, 6426 yards. S.S.S. 71. Practice ground. *Green Fees:* information not provided. *Eating facilities:* bar and restaurant. *Visitors:* casuals after 9.30am. *Society Meetings:* accepted Mondays to Fridays April to October. Must have official Handicaps. Party rates for groups of 5 or more. Professional: David Hughes (0113 289 2780). General Manager: Mike Gallagher (0113 289 2311).

LEEDS. **South Leeds Golf Club,** Parkside Links, Gipsy Lane, Leeds LS11 5TU (0113 277 1676). *Location:* M62 and M1 within five minutes' drive, Leeds City Centre 5 minutes' drive. Parkland course with undulating fairways. 18 holes, 5865 yards. S.S.S. 69. Practice ground and net. *Green Fees:* information not available. *Eating facilities:* full catering except Mondays; bar. *Visitors:* welcome weekdays. *Society Meetings:* catered for by prior arrangement. Professional: Nick Sheard (0113 272 3757). Secretary: B. Clayton (0113 277 1676).*

LEEDS. **Temple Newsam Golf Club,** Temple Newsam, Leeds LS15 0LN (0113 264 5624). *Location:* easily reached by public transport from City (to Temple Newsam or Halton). Two 18 hole courses. No. 1 Course 6448 yards. S.S.S. 71. No. 2 Course 5731 yards. S.S.S. 70. *Green Fees:* information not provided. *Visitors:* welcome without reservation, except that parties must book in advance. *Society Meetings:* catered for. Professional: Adrian Newbould (0113 264 1464). Secretary: Christine Wood.
e-mail: secretary@tngolfclub.co.uk
website: www.tngolfclub.co.uk

OTLEY. **Otley Golf Club,** West Busk Lane, Otley LS21 3NG (01943 465329). *Location:* off main Bradford to Otley road. Parkland with magnificent views across Wharfedale. 18 holes, 6211 yards. S.S.S. 70. Large practice ground. *Green Fees:* weekdays £38.00 for 18 or 27 holes, £45.00 for two rounds; weekends £45.00 for 18 or 27 holes, £51.00 for two rounds. *Eating facilities:* large dining rooms. *Visitors:* welcome except Tuesday mornings and Saturdays. Trolleys and clubs for hire. *Society Meetings:* catered for by arrangement; special facilities for company days. Professional: Steven Tomkinson (01943 465329 ext. 3; Fax: 01943 463403). Secretary/Manager: Peter J. Clarke (01943 465329 ext 1; Fax: 01943 850387).

OUTLANE. **Outlane Golf Club,** Slack Lane, off New Hey Road, Outlane, Near Huddersfield HD3 3FQ (01422 374762; Fax: 01422 311789). *Location:* from Huddersfield (A640) through Outlane Village, entrance on left just after bus terminus. Semi-moorland course, part wooded. Offers panoramic views and is challenge to the amateur. 18 holes, 5872 yards. S.S.S. 69. Practice areas and nets available. *Green Fees:* £20.00 midweek; £25.00 weekends and Bank Holidays. Reduced rates playing with member and after 1pm Sundays. *Eating facilities:* full catering available except Mondays. *Visitors:* welcome except Saturdays; Sundays by arrangement. Carts available. *Society Meetings:* welcome with reservation. Professional: D.M. Chapman (01422 374762; Fax: 01422 311789). Secretary: P. Turner (Tel & Fax: 01422 311789). Stewardess: Mrs C.E. Hirst (01422 374762).
website: www.outlanegolfclub.ltd.uk

For full details of convenient accommodation near clubs and courses

www.holidayguides.com

334 West Yorkshire / NORTH REGION — THE GOLF GUIDE 2011

PONTEFRACT. **Mid Yorkshire Golf Club,** Havercroft Lane, Darrington, Pontefract WF8 3BP (01977 704522; Fax: 01977 600823). *Location*: 300 yards from A1 at Darrington half-mile south of A1/M62 interchange. Undulating with established woodland and lakes. 18 holes, 6308 yards. Par 70. Covered floodlit driving range, tee to green irrigation. *Green Fees:* from £12.50. *Eating facilities:* two bars; private functions catered for. *Visitors:* welcome weekdays, afternoons only at weekends. Buggies available. *Society Meetings:* welcome weekdays, afternoons only at weekends. Professional: Mike Hessay (01977 704522).
website: www.midyorkshiregolfclub.com

PONTEFRACT. **Pontefract and District Golf Club,** Park Lane, Pontefract WF8 4QS (01977 792241). *Location:* M62 Exit 32, one mile from Pontefract on B6134. Parkland. 18 holes, 6519 yards. S.S.S. 72. Practice ground. *Green Fees:* weekdays £30.00 per round, £35.00 per day; weekends £37.00. *Eating facilities:* available all week. *Visitors:* welcome. *Society Meetings:* catered for Mondays, Tuesdays, Thursdays and Fridays by arrangement. Professional: Ian Marshall (01977 792241). Manager: (01977 792241).
e-mail: manager@pdgc.co.uk
website: www.pdgc.co.uk

PUDSEY. **Fulneck Golf Club Ltd,** Fulneck, Pudsey LS28 8NT (0113 2565191). *Location:* between Leeds and Bradford. Undulating wooded parkland course. 9 holes, 5456 yards. S.S.S. 67. *Green Fees:* information not available. *Society Meetings:* catered for by arrangement. Secretary: S. Tempest.*
e-mail: fulneckgolf@aol.com

PUDSEY. **Woodhall Hills Golf Club Ltd,** Woodhall Road, Calverley, Pudsey, Leeds LS28 5UN (0113 256 4771). *Location:* signposted Calverley from A647 Leeds to Bradford Road, quarter of a mile beyond Calverley Golf Club. Parkland course. 18 holes, 6184 yards. S.S.S. 71. *Green Fees:* weekdays £25.00 per round, £30.00 per day; weekends £30.00 per round, £35.00 per day; Bank Holidays £20.00 per round. All fees negotiable depending on numbers. Please contact Club Professional. *Eating facilities:* available daily except Mondays. *Visitors:* welcome without reservation. *Society Meetings:* catered for by previous arrangement. Golf Manager/Professional: R. Hedley (0113 256 2857). Club Office: (0113 255 4594)

SHIPLEY. **Marriott Hollins Hall Hotel & Country Club,** Hollins Hill, Baildon, Shipley BD17 7QW (01274 534212). Home to the PGA European Professional Tour. *Location:* North/South Leeds Ring Road, take A65 Skipton Road, then A6038 (towards Shipley), entrance on right. Superb championship heathland course in the beautiful Yorkshire Dales. 18 holes. Par 71. *Green Fees:* information not available. *Eating facilities:* available all day. *Visitors:* welcome. Trolley, buggy and shoe hire.*
website: www.marriotthollinshall.co.uk

TODMORDEN. **Todmorden Golf Club,** Rive Rocks, Cross Stone Road, Todmorden OL14 8RD (01706 812986). *Location:* A646 Halifax Road, half a mile from centre, turn into Cross Stone Road, half a mile, bear left at top. Moorland. 9 holes, 5902 yards. S.S.S. 68. *Green Fees:* weekdays £15.00; weekends and Bank Holidays £20.00. Packages (18 or 27 holes) available. *Eating facilities:* available. *Visitors:* welcome without reservation, but advisable to contact beforehand. Thursday is Ladies' Day. *Society Meetings:* welcome, please phone for course availability.
e-mail: secretarytodgolfclub@msn.com
website: www.todmordengolfclub.co.uk

WAKEFIELD. **City of Wakefield Golf Club,** Lupset Park, Horbury Road, Wakefield WF2 8QS (01924 360282). *Location:* one mile from city centre, two miles from M1 Junctions 39/40. Undulating partially wooded parkland. 18 holes, 6319 yards, 5760 metres. S.S.S. 70. *Green Fees:* information not provided. *Eating facilities:* full or snack catering, bar available. *Visitors:* booked times only. *Society Meetings:* by arrangement with Steward: (01924 367442).

MID YORKSHIRE GOLF CLUB
Ideally situated where the Yorkshires meet

Easily accessible all routes. M62 J33 – A1 south ½ mile.
Established 1993, around existing mature woodland.
18 holes, Par 70, 6308 yards. Superb clubhouse with function room. Covered floodlit driving range. Buggies available.

Havercroft Lane, Darrington, Pontefract WF8 3BP
Telephone: 01977 704622 • Fax: 01977 600823
www.midyorkshiregolfclub.com

WAKEFIELD. Lofthouse Hill Golf Club, Leeds Road, Wakefield WF3 3LR (Tel & Fax: 01924 823703). *Location*: A61 between Leeds and Wakefield. Parkland course. 18 holes, 5933 yards, S.S.S. 68. *Green Fees*: information not available. *Eating facilities*: food available all day in bar. *Visitors*: welcome, please telephone. Teaching professional. *Society Meetings*: welcome, see website. Professional: Derek Johnson (Tel & Fax: 01924 823703). Secretary: Phill Moon.*
website: www.lofthousehillgolf.co.uk

WAKEFIELD. Low Laithes Golf Club Ltd, Parkmill Lane, Flushdyke, Ossett, Wakefield WF5 9AP (01924 266067). *Location:* one mile from Junction 40 M1, or along A638 Dewsbury to Wakefield road. Parkland, undulating. 18 holes, 6456 yards. S.S.S. 71. Practice area. *Green Fees:* Monday - Friday £25.00 per round, £30.00 per day. *Eating facilities:* bar and catering. *Visitors:* welcome weekdays after 9.30am to 12.30 and after 1.30pm. *Society Meetings:* by arrangement, not weekends or Bank Holidays - 27 holes and catering £39.00. Professional: Paul Browning (01924 274667). Secretary: Paul Browning (01924 266067; Fax: 01924 266266).

WAKEFIELD. Normanton Golf Club, Hatfeild Hall. Aberford Road, Stanley WF3 4JP (01924 377943; Fax: 01924 200777). *Location:* M62 Junction 30, A642 toward Wakefield. Parkland course. Practice area. 18 holes, 6191 yards, 5662 metres. S.S.S. 70. *Green Fees:* information not provided. *Society Meetings:* welcome during the week. Restricted at weekend. Professional: Gary Pritchard (01924 200900). General Manager (01924 377943).

WAKEFIELD. Wakefield Golf Club, Woodthorpe Lane, Sandal, Wakefield WF2 6JH (01924 258778; Fax: 01924 242752). *Location:* leave M1 at Junction 39, golf club off Barnsley Road. Parkland. 18 holes, 6663 yards. S.S.S. 72. *Green Fees:* information not available. *Eating facilities:* full catering available. *Visitors:* visiting parties by arrangement Mondays, Wednesdays, Thursdays, Fridays and Sunday (pm only). *Society Meetings:* welcome, catered for by arrangement. Professional: I.M. Wright. Secretary: Mrs E. Newton (01924 258778).

WAKEFIELD. Woolley Park Golf Club, New Road, Abbot Lane, Woolley, Wakefield WF4 2JJ (01226 380144). *Location*: half a mile from A61 half way between Barnsley and Wakefield. Parkland course. 18 holes, 6636 yards (white tees), S.S.S. 72. New 9 hole Par 3 course. Practice area, putting green. *Green Fees:* weekdays £21.00; weekends £29.00. 9-hole course: adults £7.50, Juniors £3.00. 2010 fees (subject to review). *Eating facilities*: food available all day every day, bar. *Visitors*: welcome all week, weekend bookings from Thursday only. Tuition available. *Society Meetings*: welcome, please telephone for details. Professional: Jon Baldwin (01226 380144). Secretary: Robert Stoffel (01226 380144).
e-mail: woolleyparkgolf@yahoo.co.uk
website: www.woolleyparkgolfclub.co.uk

WETHERBY. Wetherby Golf Club, Linton Lane, Linton, Wetherby LS22 4JF (01937 580089; Fax: 01937 581915). *Location:* three quarters of a mile west of A1 roundabout. Parkland course adjoining River Wharfe. 18 holes, 6288 yards. S.S.S. 71. Practice ground. *Green Fees:* information not available. *Eating facilities:* available seven days a week. *Visitors:* welcome, advisable to phone first. *Society Meetings:* catered for weekdays except Tuesday mornings. Professional: Mark Daubney (01937 580089 ext. 22). Golf Club Manager: Stan Owram (01937 580089 ext. 20).
e-mail: manager@wetherbygolfclub.co.uk
website: www.wetherbygolfclub.co.uk

> **THE APPEARANCE OF AN ASTERISK (*) AT THE END OF A CLUB OR COURSE ENTRY INDICATES THAT UP-TO-DATE INFORMATION HAS NOT BEEN SUPPLIED**

Wetherby Golf Club • Tel: 01937 580089

Linton Lane, Wetherby, West Yorkshire LS22 4JF
info@wetherbygolfclub.co.uk • www.wetherbygolfclub.co.uk

Beautiful parkland 18-hole course adjacent to the River Wharfe.
Casual visitors and Golf Societies welcome.
Please visit our website for current offers and booking details.

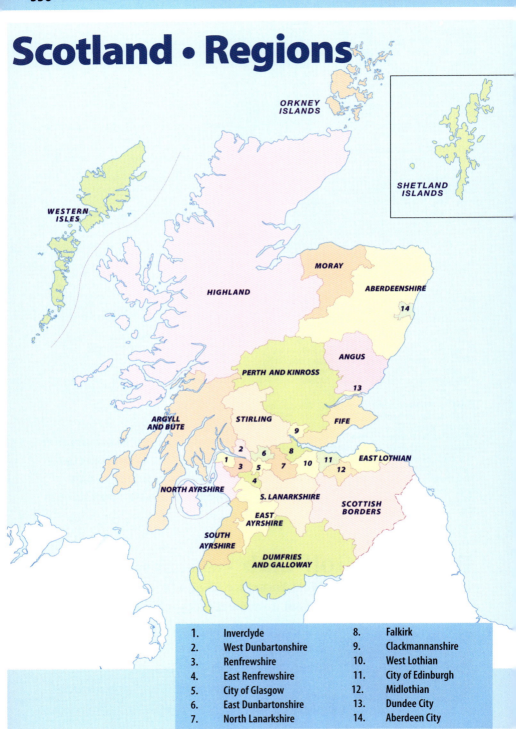

THE GOLF GUIDE 2011   SCOTLAND 337

Golf in Scotland

Nick Rodger

**Aberdeen, Banff & Moray • Angus & Dundee
Argyll & Bute • Ayrshire & Arran • Borders
Dumfries & Galloway • Dunbartonshire
Edinburgh & Lothians • Fife • Glasgow & District
Highlands • Lanarkshire • Perth & Kinross
Renfrewshire • Stirling & The Trossachs
Scottish Islands**

Fort Augustus Golf Club, Highlands (South)

While the number of options for a golfing trip in the UK and beyond appears to grow by the year, a visit to the cradle of the game in Scotland will never be far from the top of the destination leaderboard.

From the venerable Major venues to the hidden treasures that are dotted throughout the country, the lure of the home of golf remains strong, while the abundance of accommodation, from five-star hotels, to homely bed and breakfasts and family-run guesthouses, ensures there is something to cater for all budgets.

Playing opportunities may be in bountiful supply, but a golfing break in Scotland can be enhanced by the chance to take in a splendid

9th hole at Pitlochry Golf Club, Perthshire

variety of top-level amateur and professional competitions at some of the nation's most celebrated courses.

For a sneak preview of the stars of tomorrow, the Scottish Boys' Championship makes for excellent viewing, and in April of 2011 the prestigious matchplay event heads to Dunbar. Nestling in the invitingly compact golfing heartland of East Lothian, Dunbar sits at the end of an impressive 30-mile chain of notable courses that stretches from Scotland's capital city of Edinburgh through Musselburgh, Longniddry, Aberlady, Gullane and North Berwick.

The following month, an international field of amateurs will gather at Blairgowrie for the Scottish Open Strokeplay championship, the first of three major events to be staged in Perthshire during the 2011 campaign. With its central location and plethora of scenic courses, the Perthshire area is an ideal base for the avid golfer, and with the build-up to the 2014 Ryder Cup at Gleneagles gathering pace, the chance to see the leading lights of the European game competing over the luxurious resort's PGA Centenary course in the Johnnie Walker championship in the summer should not be missed. Later in the year, the domestic pros will get their chance to shine when the Tartan Tour's Scottish PGA championship takes place on the neighbouring King's course.

The A9 route north from Gleneagles opens up the majesty of the Highlands and, for the third year running, the Macdonald Spey Valley course in Aviemore, with the Cairngorms providing a spectacular backdrop, will host the Scottish Hydro Challenge in June. This is one of the most lucrative events on the second-tier European Challenge Tour.

With its enchanting scenery, historical sites and whisky trails, the north of Scotland has plenty to offer the visitor. The golf is equally alluring, with the likes of Nairn, Castle Stuart and Royal Dornoch among the big-hitters on an impressive list of courses.

As the campaign progresses, the focus of attention will switch to the west of the country with some of the world's finest players heading for the captivating beauty of Loch Lomond and the Barclays Scottish Open in July. A couple of weeks later, the Scottish Amateur championship will take place at Western Gailes,

The Queen's Course at Gleneagles, Auchterarder, Perthshire

one of the many great courses that are peppered around Ayrshire and the South West. While the Open trail, incorporating the redoubtable links of Prestwick, Royal Troon and Turnberry, grabs the limelight, a visit to this neck of the woods can offer a host of other golfing delights, such as a trip across the water to the Isle of Arran or a venture south to the Galloway coast where a host of gems abound.

July is always jam-packed with quality competitions and at the end of the month the elite from the female professional game will face up to the rigours of Carnoustie in the Ricoh British Women's Open. With a first-class golfing pedigree and a rich heritage, 'Carnoustie Country' encompasses the whole of the ancient county of Angus and surrounding area and boasts no fewer than 32 courses within a 40 minute drive of one another.

Journeying further up the coast, visitors to the north east of Scotland will have the chance to immerse themselves in the cut and thrust of team competition in September when the biennial Walker Cup, between Great Britain and Ireland and the USA, takes place at Royal Aberdeen. This is the sixth oldest course in the world and one of over 60 classic tracks that are all within easy travelling distance of the vibrant Granite City.

No trip to Scotland would be complete without a stop in St Andrews and, along with Kingsbarns and Carnoustie, the Auld Grey Toon will play host to a glittering array of professionals and celebrities in the Dunhill Links championship in October to bring the curtain down on another mouth-watering year of action north of the Border.

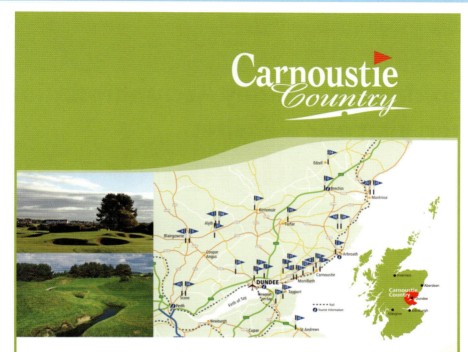

THE GOLF GUIDE 2011

Looking for Holiday Accommodation? then visit our website:
www.holidayguides.com

Search for holiday accommodation by region, location, type of accommodation (B&B, Self-Catering, Hotel etc)

Special requirements – Are you looking for accommodation where children and pets are welcome or maybe you want to be close to a golf course...

for details of hundreds of properties throughout the U

Aberdeen, Banff & Moray

ABERDEEN. **Aberdeen City Golf, Balnagask Golf Course,** St Fitticks Road, Aberdeen. (01224 876407). *Location:* on coast beside Girdleness Lighthouse between Aberdeen Harbour and Nigg Bay, south side of city. Seaside links. 18 holes, 5541 metres. 9-hole pitch and putt. *Green Fees:* information not available. *Visitors:* welcome. Starter: (01224 876407).*
website: www.aberdeencity.org.uk

ABERDEEN. **Aberdeen City Golf, Hazlehead Golf Course,** Hazlehead Avenue, Aberdeen AB9 1XJ (01224 321830). *Location:* situated on west edge of city, four miles from city centre. From A944 into Aberdeen turn off into Groats Road. Two courses - 18 holes, 5690 metres; 18 holes, 5270 metres. 9 hole course, 2531 metres. *Green Fees:* information not available. *Eating facilities:* restaurant adjoining park. *Visitors:* welcome. Professional: (01224 317336). Starter: (01224 321830).*
e-mail: golf@aberdeencity.org.uk
website: www.aberdeencity.org.uk/golf

ABERDEEN. **Aberdeen City Golf, King's Links Golf Course,** Golf Road, Aberdeen (01224 632269). *Location:* behind the Pittodrie Stadium, on the King's Links, by the beach. Seaside links. 6-hole, 1273 yards. 18-hole, 6296 yards, S.S.S 71. *Green Fees:* information not available. *Visitors:* welcome at all times. Starter: (01224 632269).*
website: www.aberdeencity.gov.uk

ABERDEEN. **Auchmill Golf Club,** Bonnyview Road, Aberdeen AB2 7FQ (01224 715214). *Location:* approximately four miles from city centre, at end of Provost Rust Drive. Parkland, wooded course. 18 holes, 5391 metres. Practice area. Putting area. *Green Fees*: day ticket £25.00; 18 holes £15.00; Seniors £10.00; Juniors £7.50. *Visitors*: welcome anytime. Starter: (01224 714577).
website: www.aberdeencity.gov.uk

ABERDEEN. **Bon Accord Golf Club,** 19 Golf Road, Aberdeen AB24 5QB (01224 633464). *Location*: next to Pittodrie Stadium at Aberdeen beach. Seaside links. 18 holes, 6300 yards. S.S.S. 69. *Green Fees:* information not available. *Eating facilities:* meals on request. *Visitors:* welcome; please call starters box (01224 632269) for information regarding booking of tee times and green fees. *Society Meetings:* bookings in advance. Secretary: J. A. Morrison.*

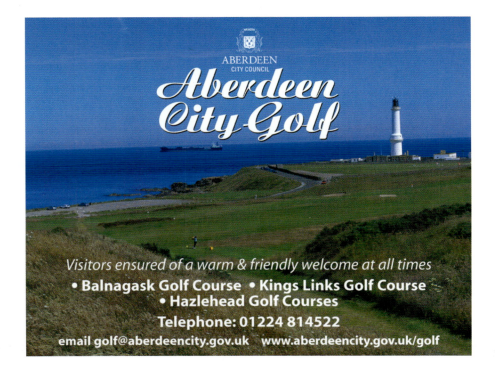

ABERDEEN. **Caledonian Golf Club,** 20 Golf Road, Aberdeen AB24 5QB (01224 632443). *Location:* 50 yards to right of Richard Donald Stand/Pittodrie Football Club. Seaside links. 18 holes, 6437 yards. S.S.S. 69. 6 hole course; driving range nearby. *Green Fees:* information not available. *Eating facilities:* clubhouse snacks and meals. *Visitors:* welcome. Entertainment is provided in clubrooms on Saturdays for members and their guests. Secretary: A. Sheldrick.*

ABERDEEN. **Deeside Golf Club,** Golf Road, Bieldside, Aberdeen AB15 9DL (01224 869457). *Location:* A93 from Aberdeen to Braemar. Wooded parkland. 18 holes, 6264 yards. S.S.S. 70. Also 9 hole course, 5042 yards. S.S.S. 68. Practice ground. *Green Fees:* information not available. *Eating facilities:* full catering and bar facilities. *Visitors:* welcome weekdays up to 4pm, weekends after 4pm. *Society Meetings:* by arrangement. Professional: F.J. Coutts (01224 861041). Managing Secretary: D. P. Pern (Tel & Fax: 01224 869457).*
e-mail: admin@deesidegolfclub.com
website: www.deesidegolfclub.com

ABERDEEN. **Murcar Links Golf Club,** Bridge of Don, Aberdeen AB23 8BD (01224 704354). *Location:* A90 Aberdeen - Fraserburgh Road, 5 miles north of Aberdeen city centre. Championship seaside links. 18 holes, 6303 yards. S.S.S. 72; Strabathie 9-hole course, 5364 yards. S.S.S 71. Practice ground, driving range. *Green Fees:* Murcar, weekdays £70.00 per round, £95.00 per day; weekends £90.00 per round. Strabathie, weekdays £15.00 per 9 holes, £38.00 per day; weekends £22.50 per 9 holes, £45.00 per 18 holes. *Eating facilities:* dining room/bars. *Visitors:* welcome by advance booking. Hand trolleys for hire. *Society Meetings:* catered for by advance booking. Professional: Gary Forbes (Tel & Fax: 01224 704370). Secretary: Carol O'Neill (Tel & Fax: 01224 704354).
e-mail: golf@murcarlinks.com
website: www.murcarlinks.com

ABERDEEN. **Nigg Bay Golf Club,** St Fitticks Road, Torry, Aberdeen AB1 3QT (01224 871286; Fax: 01224 873418). *Location:* junction of Victoria Road and St Fitticks Road. Seaside links, hills and hidden holes. 18 holes, 5986 yards, 5472 metres. S.S.S. 69. 9 hole pitch and putt. *Green Fees:* information not available. *Eating facilities:* full catering. *Visitors:* welcome anytime (Municipal course); golfers welcome in clubhouse after playing. Secretary: Alan Fraser.*

ABERDEEN. **Northern Golf Club** 22 Golf Road, Aberdeen AB24 5QB (01224 636440; Fax: 01224 622679). *Location:* Golf Road, opposite Pittodrie Stadium. 18 holes, 5731 metres. S.S.S. 70. 6 hole course, 1251 metres; driving range next door. *Green Fees:* information not available. *Visitors:* welcome, book in person on the day of play. Public bookings restricted on Saturdays for club matches. *Society Meetings:* all welcome by writing to Aberdeen District Council (14 days notice). Professional: B. Davidson (01224 641577). Secretary: Denis Sangster (Tel & Fax: 01224 622679). Steward: (01224 636440).*

ABERDEEN. **Royal Aberdeen Golf Club,** Links Road, Balgownie, Bridge of Don AB23 8AT (01224 702571; Fax: 01224 826591). *Location:* on A92 Aberdeen/Fraserburgh Road, cross Bridge of Don, second right. Seaside links. Two Courses - Championship (Balgownie): 18 holes, 6900 yards, 6309 metres. S.S.S. 72; Silverburn: 18 holes, 4021 yards, 3717 metres. S.S.S. 61. Practice putting green. *Green Fees:* weekdays £100.00 per person per round, £150.00 per day; weekends £120.00 per person per round. *Eating facilities:* Old Bar, main lounge and dining room - jacket and tie. *Visitors:* welcome weekdays 10am to 11.30am and 2pm to 3.30pm, weekends after 3.30pm. Letter of introduction or Handicap Certificate required. Hire carts. *Society Meetings:* welcome. Professional: David Ross (01224 702571). Director of Golf: Ronnie MacAskill (01224 702571; Fax: 01224 826591). Exe. Secretary: Sandra Nicolson.
e-mail: admin@royalaberdeengolf.com

ABERDEEN. **Tarland Golf Club,** Aberdeen Road, Tarland, Aboyne AB34 4TB (Tel & Fax: 013398 81000). *Location:* six miles north of Aboyne, 30 miles west of Aberdeen on B9119. Parkland, Tom Morris course in picturesque scenery. 9 holes, 5816 yards for 18 holes, S.S.S. 68. Small practice area. *Green Fees:* weekdays £18.00 per day; weekends £24.00. 2010 rates (subject to review). *Eating facilities:* snacks available. *Visitors:* welcome without reservation but phone call advisable due to club competitions at weekends. *Society Meetings:* catered for with prior reservation at all times.

ABOYNE. **Aboyne Golf Club,** Formaston Park, Aboyne AB34 5HP (013398 86328). *Location:* A93, 30 miles west of Aberdeen. Part parkland, part hilly with lovely views. 18 holes, 6009 yards. S.S.S. 69. Practice ground. *Green Fees:* weekdays £30.00 per round, £40.00 per day; weekends £35.00 per round, £50.00 per day. *Eating facilities:* full restaurant and bar facilities. *Visitors:* welcome without reservation. *Society Meetings:* by arrangement with Secretary. Professional: Steven Moir (013398 86328). Secretary: (013398 87078; Fax: 013398 87592).
e-mail: aboynegolfclub@btconnect.com
website: www.aboynegolfclub.co.uk

ABOYNE. **Aboyne Loch Golf Centre,** The Lodge on the Loch of Aboyne, Aboyne AB34 5BR (013398 86444 reservations). *Location*: 30 minutes' drive from Aberdeen. A scenic 9 hole course and driving range beside the Loch of Aboyne, with a combination of Par 3, 4 and 5s, together with water hazards, offering a challenge to golfers of any ability. *Green Fees:* weekdays 9 holes £10.00, 18 holes £14.00; weekends 9 holes £12.00, 18 holes £16.00. *Eating facilities:* restaurant and bar. *Visitors:* always welcome. Clubs, carts and golf car hire. Health and Beauty Spa. *Society Meetings:* golf outings, corporate and family fun days catered for.
e-mail: info@thelodgeontheloch.com
website: www.thelodgeontheloch.com

www.holidayguides.com

MURCAR LINKS GOLF CLUB

"A Century in the making and a venue used by the PGA European Tours"

Par 71 – SS 73 – USGA Rating 72.6 – USGA Slope 138

www.murcarlinks.com
Tel/Fax: +44 (0)1224 704354
www.links2links.info

Aberdeen, Scotland
(Airport Code ABZ)

Other useful guides to holidays in Britain from FHG Guides

PUBS & INNS
300 GREAT HOTELS
SHORT BREAK HOLIDAYS
The original PETS WELCOME!
500 GREAT PLACES TO STAY
SELF-CATERING HOLIDAYS
BED & BREAKFAST STOPS
CARAVAN & CAMPING HOLIDAYS
FAMILY BREAKS

Published annually: available in all good bookshops or direct from the publisher:
FHG Guides, Abbey Mill Business Centre, Seedhill, Paisley PA1 1TJ
Tel: 0141 887 0428 • Fax: 0141 889 7204
e-mail: admin@fhguides.co.uk
www.holidayguides.com

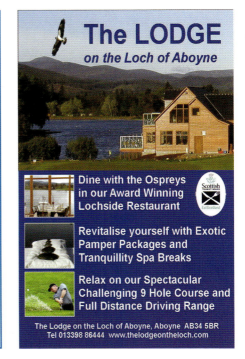

The LODGE on the Loch of Aboyne

Dine with the Ospreys in our Award Winning Lochside Restaurant

Revitalise yourself with Exotic Pamper Packages and Tranquillity Spa Breaks

Relax on our Spectacular Challenging 9 Hole Course and Full Distance Driving Range

The Lodge on the Loch of Aboyne, Aboyne AB34 5BR
Tel 013398 86444 www.thelodgeontheloch.com

ALFORD. **Alford Golf Club,** Montgarrie Road, Alford AB33 8AE (Tel & Fax: 019755 62178; Fax: 019755 64910). *Location:* A944, 26 miles west of Aberdeen. Flat, parkland course. 18 holes, 5481 yards. S.S.S. 66. Practice area. *Green Fees:* £20.00 per round, £25.00 per day weekdays; £25.00 per round, £30.00 per day weekends. 2010 rates (subject to review). *Eating facilities:* catering available; bar services. *Visitors:* always welcome; call club to book tee, weekends very busy. Changing rooms and showers. Buggy Hire available. *Society Meetings:* welcome by prior arrangement. Secretary: Julie Alexander.
e-mail: info@alford-golf-club.co.uk
website: www.alford-golf-club.co.uk

AUCHENBLAE. **Auchenblae Golf Course,** Auchenblae, Laurencekirk AB30 1TX (contact Auchenblae Parks Committee, Linwood, Auchenblae AB30 1WQ). *Location:* nine miles south of Stonehaven, off A90, two miles west of Fordoun. Parkland. 9 holes, 4434 yards SSS 61. *Green Fees:* weekdays £15.00; weekends £18.00; also concessionary rates. *Eating facilities:* shop open April to October. *Visitors:* welcome. Telephone Pavilion (01561 320002) for details of club nights and current information. Trolleys and clubs for hire. *Society Meetings:* welcome. Corr/Secretary: J.M. Thomson (01561 320245).
website: www.auchenblae.org.uk

BANCHORY. **Banchory Golf Club,** Kinneskie Road, Banchory AB31 5TA (01330 822365; Fax: 01330 822491). *Location:* 100 yards off the A93 Aberdeen to Braemar Road. Flat parkland course, several holes on the banks of the River Dee. 18 holes, 5801 yards. S.S.S. 68. Practice ground and putting green. *Green Fees:* £30.00 per round, £40.00 per day. 7 month season ticket £340.00, 12 monthly season ticket £380.00. *Eating facilities:* attractive lounge and dining room. *Visitors:* welcome any time, restrictions on Tuesdays and weekends. *Society Meetings:* welcome but restrictions on Tuesdays and at weekends. Professional: David Naylor (Tel & Fax: 01330 822447). Secretary: Ann Smart (01330 822365; Fax: 01330 822491).
e-mail: info@banchorygolfclub.co.uk
website: www.banchorygolfclub.co.uk

THE APPEARANCE OF AN ASTERISK (*) AT THE END OF A CLUB OR COURSE ENTRY INDICATES THAT UP-TO-DATE INFORMATION HAS NOT BEEN SUPPLIED

Alford Golf Club
Montgarrie Road, Alford AB33 8AE
Tel: **019755 62178**
e-mail: info@alford-golf-club.co.uk

VISITORS WELCOME
(Advance booking available)

**Corporate, Societies and Groups Welcome
Packages tailored to individual needs
Bar & Excellent Catering Facilities
Meals served all day
Buggy, Trolley & Club Hire available.**

www.alford-golf-club.co.uk

Kildrummy Castle Hotel
Kildrummy, Alford, Aberdeenshire AB33 8RA
Tel: 0197 557 1288 • Fax: 0197 557 1345
e-mail: kildrummy@btconnect.com • www.kildrummycastlehotel.co.uk

Set in the breathtaking Grampian Highlands in Aberdeenshire, the hotel enjoys an enviable location amongst some of the world's most beautiful scenery.
Managed by the proprietors, Frans and Jayne Faber. Their experienced, professional team will make your visit, however long or short, a truly memorable experience.
Kildrummy Castle Hotel is located only 35 miles from Aberdeen Airport and three and half hours' drive from Edinburgh, making it a perfect venue for a short break or a longer relaxing treat.

Built as a coaching inn in the 16th century and graduating into an elegant Georgian manor house, Banchory Lodge stands in lovely wooded surroundings beside the River Dee, world-famous for its salmon. It is natural therefore that angling enthusiasts are attracted by its hospitable atmosphere, to say nothing of its high standards of service, cuisine and accommodation.

Log fires, fresh flowers, traditional furnishings and original paintings add to the air of tranquillity. There is also ample scope nearby for golf, as well as numerous forest walks and nature trails. The best of fresh local produce features on the imaginative menus presented in the spacious dining room.

There are two 18 hole golf courses and a driving range within walking distance of the Hotel. There are almost 50 courses in the area and include a championship course, classic links, and hidden gems.

Banchory, Kincardineshire AB31 5HS
Tel: 01330 822625 • Fax: 01330 825019
www.banchorylodge.co.uk
e-mail: enquiries@banchorylodge.co.uk

BALLATER. Ballater Golf Club, Victoria Road, Ballater AB35 5QX (013397 55567). *Location*: A93, 42 miles west of Aberdeen and 62 miles from Perth. Flat picturesque parkland course close to Balmoral Castle. 18 holes, 5638 yards. S.S.S. 67. Practice ground, putting. *Green Fees:* weekdays £26.00, weekends £29.00. *Eating facilities:* full catering and refreshments April to October. *Visitors:* all welcome, booking well in advance is advisable. Tennis, bowling. *Society Meetings:* all welcome, book well in advance. Professional: Bill Yule (013397 55658). Secretary: Colin Smith (013397 55567).
e-mail: sec@ballatergolfclub.co.uk
website: www.ballatergolfclub.co.uk

BANCHORY. Inchmarlo Golf Club, Glassel Road, Inchmarlo AB31 4BQ (01330 826424). *Location*: half a mile from A93 Aberdeen-Braemar road, 25 minutes from Aberdeen city centre. Queen's Course (9-holes): beautiful but tricky parkland course, 4300 yards, Par 64, S.S.S. 62. Laird's Course (18 holes): tree-lined fairways, secluded greens and spectacular Royal Deeside scenery, 6063 yards, Par 70, S.S.S. 70. 25-bay floodlit driving range. *Green Fees:* weekdays – Queen's Course £13.00, £19.00 for 2x9 holes; Laird's Course £35.00. Weekends – Queen's Course £15.00, £23.00 for 2x9 holes; Laird's Course £40.00. *Eating facilities:* Inchmarlo Restaurant, function/conference room, choice of bars. *Visitors:* very welcome any time, advisable to book in advance. *Society Meetings*: welcome all year by prior arrangement. Luxury serviced apartments and villas on site. Secretary: Pat Prentice (01330 826427).
e-mail: secretary@inchmarlo.com (golf)
reception@inchmarlo.com (accommodation)
website: www.inchmarlo.com
www.inchmarlogolf.com

BANCHORY. Lumphanan Golf Club, Main Road, Lumphanan, Banchory AB31 4PW (01339 883480). *Location*: on the road between Torphins and Lumphanan about 10 miles from Banchory. Hilly, quiet, village course. 9 holes, 3718 yards, S.S.S 61. Course re-designed in 2000. *Green Fees:* information not available. *Eating facilities:* clubhouse/bar open weekends and some evenings; food weekends only. *Visitors:* welcome - no need to book. *Society Meetings*: outings welcome by arrangement with Secretary. Secretary: Yvonne Taite (01339 883696).*
e-mail: info@lumphanangolfclub.com
website: www.lumphanangolfclub.com

BANFF. Duff House Royal Golf Club, The Barnyards, Banff AB45 3SX (01261 812062; Fax: 01261 812224). *Location*: two minutes from town centre, A97, A98. Level parkland. Designed by Dr Alister MacKenzie. 18 holes, 6161 yards. S.S.S. 69. Practice putting area. *Green Fees:* weekdays £30.00 per round, £40.00 per day; weekends £36.00 per round, £50.00 per day. *Eating facilities:* lounge bar and full catering service. *Visitors:* welcome weekdays after 9.30am, restrictions at weekends but times available. Second round discount: weekdays £35.00, weekends £45.00. Pro shop. *Society Meetings:* catered for by prior arrangement. Professional: G. Holland (01261 812075). Manager: J. Cameron (01261 812062).
e-mail: info@duffhouseroyal.com

BRAEMAR. **Braemar Golf Club,** Cluniebank Road, Braemar AB35 5XX (013397 41618). *Location:* about one mile from centre of the village, signposted opposite Fife Arms Hotel. Flat parkland, highest 18 hole course in Scotland, course split in two by River Clunie. 18 holes, 5030 yards. S.S.S. 64. *Green Fees:* £25.00 per round, £30.00 per day. Weekly ticket £100.00. Special rates for parties of more than 10. *Eating facilities:* full bar and catering facilities. *Visitors:* No restrictions on visitors but advisable to phone in advance for weekends. *Society Meetings:* welcome - book through Secretary. Secretary: Colin McIntosh (013397 41595).
e-mail: info@braemargolfclub.co.uk
website: www.braemargolfclub.co.uk

CAMBUS O'MAY HOTEL

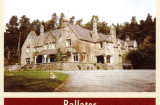

Ballater
Aberdeenshire AB35 5SE
Tel & Fax: 013397 55428
www.cambusomayhotel.co.uk

This family-run country house hotel is situated four miles east of Ballater overlooking the River Dee and its environs. The hotel prides itself on the old-fashioned standards of comfort and service it offers to its guests. Excellent food is available from the table d'hôte menu which changes daily and can be complemented by fine wines from the cellar. The 12 bedrooms have en suite facilities and the hotel is centrally heated throughout.

The hotel is ideally located to sample the many beautiful and varied golf courses on Deeside. For the non-golfer there is a myriad of other pursuits - hillwalking, fishing, shooting, gliding and the Whisky and Castle Trails.

3 nights DB&B £185pp from end of October to March, based on two sharing.

SCOTLAND / Aberdeen, Banff & Moray

www.holidayguides.com

For full details of convenient accommodation near clubs and courses

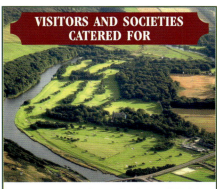

VISITORS AND SOCIETIES CATERED FOR

DUFF HOUSE ROYAL
GOLF CLUB

THE BARNYARDS, BANFF AB45 3SX
OFFICE: 01261 812062 • PRO SHOP: 01261 812075
e-mail: info@duffhouseroyal.com
www.duffhouseroyal.com

18-HOLE PARKLAND COURSE
PRACTICE PUTTING AREA • GOLF SHOP
PGA PROFESSIONAL • PUTTING GREEN
LOUNGE BAR • CATERING FACILITIES
OPEN DAYS • CHANGING FACILITIES

~ *The Royal British Legion Scotland* ~
RAVENSWOOD RESIDENTIAL CLUB
Ramsay Road, Banchory AB31 5TS
Secretary: 01330 822347
www.banchorylegion.com

Extends a warm welcome to Legion members and guests. Single and Double rooms available. Usual Club activities and entertainment.
Bed and Breakfast from £31.

sales@learneyarmshotel.com
www.learneyarmshotel.com
Tel: 013398 82202
Fax: 013398 82123

LEARNEY ARMS HOTEL
Torphins, Banchory AB31 4GP

Overlooking the peaceful village of Torphins, the Learney Arms lies within easy reach of two of Scotland's most famous salmon rivers and only 22 miles from Aberdeen. There are some excellent golf courses nearby.

There are 10 bedrooms with en suite facilities, all individually and comfortably furnished. Good food is served in the Craigmyle Dining Room, which enjoys views over the landscaped gardens, and also in the Golfer's Return lounge bar, along with real ales and a wide selection of whiskies.
Families welcome.

FHG Guides publish a large range of well-known accommodation guides. We will be happy to send you details or you can use the order form at the back of this book.

BUCKIE. **Buckpool Golf Club (Buckie),** Barhill Road, Buckie AB56 1DU (Tel & Fax: 01542 832236). *Location:* turn off A98 signposted Buckpool. Links course with superlative view over Moray Firth. 18 holes, 6149 yards. S.S.S. 69. Putting green and net area. *Green Fees:* £22.00 per round, £28.00 per day; Senior Citizens £18.00 per round, £24.00 per day. Juniors (up to 16 years) half price. 2010 rates (subject to review). *Eating facilities:* full catering daily (pre-arranged bookings), normal bar hours. *Visitors:* no restrictions except when there are scheduled competitions and visiting parties; advisable to telephone first. Two changing rooms with showers, etc; snooker, pool and squash. *Society Meetings:* welcome by prior arrangement. Club Administrator: Mrs Moira Robertson (Tel & Fax: 01542 832236).

BUCKIE. **Strathlene Golf Club,** Portessie, Buckie AB56 2DJ (01542 831798). *Location:* equidistant between Aberdeen and Inverness. Raised links course which follows the natural contours of the land. 18 holes, 5996 yards. S.S.S 69. Practice facilities. 3-hole pitch and putt, driving range. *Green Fees:* weekdays £20.00 per round, £24.00 per day; weekends £23.00 per round, £32.00 per day. 2010 rates (subject to review). *Eating facilities:* summer catering and all-day bar. *Visitors:* prior booking advised; avoid Saturday and Sunday mornings. Locker room. *Society Meetings:* booking required. Administrator: David Lyon (01542 831798).

BUCKSBURN. **Craibstone Golf Centre,** Craibstone Estate, Bucksburn AB21 9YA (01224 716777; Fax: 01224 711298). *Location*: on A96 5 miles north of Aberdeen turn left at Craibstone Roundabout (private access) through Estate to T-junction, left then first right. Parkland course. 18 holes S.S.S. 67. *Green Fees*: information not available. *Eating facilities*: available, also bar. *Visitors*: welcome. *Society Meetings*: welcome - please telephone for details. Professional: Iain Buchan (01224 716777) Secretary: Susan May (01224 711195).*
e-mail: ballumbie2000@yahoo.com

CRUDEN BAY. **Cruden Bay Golf Club,** Aulton Road, Cruden Bay, Peterhead AB42 0NN (01779 812285). *Location:* seven miles south of Peterhead, 23 miles north east of Aberdeen, just off A92. Traditional seaside links with magnificent views near Bay of Cruden. 18 holes, 6287 yards. S.S.S. 71; 9 holes, 2463 yards. S.S.S. 64. Covered driving range. *Green Fees:* weekdays – £70.00; weekends £75.00. *Eating facilities:* full bar and catering facilities. *Visitors:* welcome but restricted at weekends, telephone for details. *Society Meetings:* welcome weekdays only. Professional: Neil Murray (Tel & Fax: 01779 812414). Director of Golf: Robbie Stewart (01779 812285; Fax: 01779 812945).

CULLEN. **Cullen Golf Club,** The Links, Cullen AB56 4WB (01542 840685). *Location:* off A98 midway between Aberdeen and Inverness, on Moray Firth coast. Seaside links course designed by Old Tom Morris, with elevated section, natural rock landscaping and sandy beach coming into play at several holes. 18 holes, 4597 yards. S.S.S. 62. Putting green and net area. *Green Fees:* information not available. *Eating facilities:* catering and bar facilities. *Visitors:* welcome, check for club competitions. *Society Meetings:* welcome.*
e-mail: cullengolfclub@btinternet.com
website: www.cullengolfclub.co.uk

DUFFTOWN. **Dufftown Golf Club,** Tomintoul Road, Dufftown AB55 4BS (Tel & Fax: 01340 820325). *Location:* on B9009 Dufftown to Tomintoul Road, one mile from Dufftown. Moorland/ Parkland course, partially hilly. 18 holes, 5308 yards. S.S.S. 67. Practice and putting facilities. *Green Fees:* information not available. *Eating facilities:* available by arrangement. *Visitors:* welcome at all times. Tee reserved at some times Tuesdays, Wednesdays and Sundays . Please phone for details. Trolleys, clubs and buggies for hire, advance notice. *Society Meetings:* welcome by arrangement.*
e-mail: admin@dufftowngolfclub.com

This links course was designed by Old Tom Morris and upgraded by Charles Neaves.

The unbridled thrill of the course lies in its par 3s. A quartet of short holes from the 11th to the 14th is the highlight of the back nine holes and each features Cullen's signature landmark – 80ft Boarcrag.

Magnificent views over the Moray Firth can be appreciated even more from the 7th tee now that the descent has been dramatically improved allowing for ride-on buggies.

Full catering available.

Visiting parties most welcome.

Cullen Golf Club
The Links
The Royal Burgh of Cullen
Moray AB56 4WB
Tel: 01542 840685
e-mail: cullengolfclub@btinternet.com
www.cullengolfclub.co.uk

ELGIN. Elgin Golf Club, Hardhillock, Birnie Road, Elgin IV30 8SX (01343 542338; Fax: 01343 542341). *Location:* half a mile south of Elgin town centre just off A941 Rothes Road; on Birnie Road. Undulating parkland on sandy subsoil, many tree-lined fairways. 18 holes, 6411 yards. S.S.S. 71. Driving range, practice ground and net. *Green Fees:* £37.00 per round, £47.00 per day. *Eating facilities:* bar and catering every day. *Visitors:* welcome, arrangement through Professional is advisable. *Society Meetings:* by arrangement with Professional. Professional: Kevin Stables (Tel & Fax: 01343 542884). Secretary: Yvonne Forgan (01343 542338).
e-mail: secretary@elgingolfclub.com
website: www.elgingolfclub.com

ELGIN. Hopeman Golf Club, Hopeman, Elgin IV30 5YA (01343 830578). *Location:* 7 miles north-east of Elgin on B9012. Seaside links, with spectacular 12th hole. 18 holes, 5624 yards. S.S.S. 68. *Green Fees:* weekdays £23.00 per round, £29.00 per day; Saturdays £30.00 per round, £36.00 per day; Sundays £22.00 per round, £28.00 per day. Juniors half price. Senior Citizens reduced rates. Generous discounts for parties of ten or more. 2010 rates (subject to review). *Eating facilities:* bar, catering. *Visitors:* welcome, some restrictions on tee times at weekends. Trolleys and golf buggies for hire. *Society Meetings:* welcome by arrangement. Secretary: Jim Fraser (01343 835068; Fax: 01343 830152).
e-mail: hopemangc@aol.com
website: www.hopemangc.co.uk

Hay Street, Elgin IV30 1NH • Tel: 01343 547799
Imposing Victorian house standing in its own grounds.
Offering superb accommodation. Extensive menu with local produce.
The bar stocks local real ales and large selection of malt whiskies.
Most rooms have Wi-Fi and broadband.
Local golf courses: Elgin, Moray and Forres.
e-mail: wross@sunninghillhotel.com
www.sunninghillhotel.com

Hopeman Golf Club, Hopeman, Moray IV30 5YA • Tel: 01343 830578
Fax: 01343 830152 • e-mail: hopemangc@aol.com • www.hopemangc.co.uk
The course is a typical Scottish links and was only extended to 18 holes as recently as 1985. The signature hole at Hopeman is the par 3 12th known as 'The Prieshach', with its green spectacularly nestling adjacent to the Clashach Cove over 100ft below. Golfers are faced with panoramic views over the Moray Firth, plus, if they are lucky, they may see dolphins. Special rates for parties over 10, with catering packages to suit all. Visitors especially welcome, though booking at weekends is recommended.

Looking for accommodation near golf clubs?, then visit
www.holidayguides.com
for where to stay when playing golf around the regions

ELLON. **McDonald-Ellon Golf Club,** Hospital Road, Ellon AB41 9AW (01358 720576). *Location:* A90 from Aberdeen to Ellon. One mile down A948, on left. Flat parkland with trees and stream. 18 holes, 6012 yards. S.S.S. 70. Putting green and practice nets. *Green Fees:* on application. *Eating facilities:* full catering and bar facilities all week. *Visitors:* welcome at all times weekdays; after 10am and booking advisable at weekends. *Society Meetings:* must book in advance. Professional: Sandy Aird (01358 722891). Secretary: George Ironside (01358 720576).
e-mail: mcdonald.golf@virgin.net

FOCHABERS. **Garmouth & Kingston Golf Club,** Spey Street, Garmouth, Fochabers IV32 7NJ (Tel & Fax: 01343 870388). *Location:* three miles north from A96 at Mosstodloch crossroads. Flat parkland/part links. 18 holes, 5957 yards. S.S.S. 69. Practice net. *Green Fees:* weekdays £20.00 per round, £28.00 per day, half price for Senior Citizens; weekends £25.00 per round, £28.00 per day. Reductions for parties over 10. 2010 fees (subject to review). *Eating facilities:* catering available on request. *Visitors:* very welcome except 4pm to 7pm Tuesdays (Ladies) and during club competitions (evenings). *Society Meetings:* welcome by arrangement with Admin. Assistant: I. Fraser (01343 870388).
e-mail: garmouthgolfclub@aol.com
website: www.garmouthkingstongolfclub.com

FORRES. **Forres Golf Club,** Muiryshade, Forres IV36 2RD (Tel & Fax: 01309 672250). *Location:* one mile south from clock tower in town centre; 26 miles east of Inverness on A96. Parkland - feature hole 16th. 18 holes, 6236 yards. S.S.S. 70. Practice ground and putting green. *Green Fees:* information not available. *Eating facilities:* bar and catering all day every day. *Visitors:* welcome - booking system in operation by Professional. Buggies/Trolleys for hire. *Society Meetings:* welcome. Professional: S. Aird (Tel & Fax: 01309 672250). Secretary: (01309 672949; Fax: 01309 672261).*

FORRES. **Kinloss Country Golf Course,** Kinloss, Forres IV36 2UB (01343 850585). *Location*: 4 miles east of Forres on B9089. Parkland courses. Two 9 hole courses, Course 1 - 2535 yards, Course 2 - 2939 yards. Practice area, driving range. *Green Fees*: information not available. *Eating facilities*: cafe, bar. *Visitors*: welcome everyday, pay-as-you-play. Trolleys, clubs and buggies for hire. *Society Meetings*: discounts for large parties. Corporate outings catered for. Contact Karen or Tommy (01343 850585).*

McDONALD GOLF CLUB
**Hospital Road, Ellon
Aberdeenshire AB41 9AW
Tel: 01358 720576
E-mail: mcdonald.golf@virgin.net
www.ellongolfclub.co.uk**

**Scenic 18 Hole Parkland course only 16 miles from Aberdeen
Golf Shop • PGA Professional • Putting Green
Excellent Clubhouse and Catering Facilities
Visitors Welcome • Special Rates for Visiting Parties
MEMBERSHIPS AVAILABLE**

Other British holiday guides from FHG Guides

**PUBS & INNS • 300 GREAT HOTELS • SHORT BREAK HOLIDAYS
The bestselling and original PETS WELCOME! • 500 GREAT PLACES TO STAY
SELF-CATERING HOLIDAYS • BED & BREAKFAST STOPS
CARAVAN & CAMPING HOLIDAYS • FAMILY BREAKS**

Published annually: available in all good bookshops or direct from the publisher:
**FHG Guides, Abbey Mill Business Centre, Seedhill, Paisley PA1 1TJ
Tel: 0141 887 0428 • Fax: 0141 889 7204
e-mail: admin@fhguides.co.uk • www.holidayguides.com**

FRASERBURGH. **Fraserburgh Golf Club,** Philorth Links, Fraserburgh AB43 8TL (01346 516616). *Location:* turn right at roundabout on entry to town from Aberdeen then first right. Splendid true seaside links, reputedly the 7th oldest in the world, founded 1777. 18 holes, 6308 yards. S.S.S. 71. Additional 9 hole Rosehill Family Course 2400 yards. Practice area. *Green Fees:* information not available. *Eating facilities:* full bar and catering facilities. *Visitors:* welcome, some restrictions weekends. *Society Meetings:* welcome, book in advance. Tel (01346 516616).*

GRANTOWN-ON-SPEY. **Craggan Golf Course,** Grantown-on-Spey PH26 3NT (01479 873283). *Location:* beside the A95, one mile south of Grantown-on-Spey, en route from/to Aviemore. Parkland course set beside the River Spey with views to Cairngorms and Cromdales. 18-hole Par 3; holes from 51 yards to 209 yards; 2005 yards in total. Suitable for beginners through to more accomplished players. *Green Fees:* adults £17.50 per round or £25 for a day ticket; unders-16s £7.50. Club hire available, £7.50 per half set. *Eating Facilities:* licensed Clubhouse serves freshly prepared refreshments. *Visitors:* non-members welcome. Award-winning outdoor activity centre also on-site.
e-mail: fhglaing@btopenworld.com
website: www.cragganforleisure.co.uk
www.cragganoutdoors.co.uk

HUNTLY. **Huntly Golf Club,** Cooper Park, Huntly AB54 4SH (01466 792643). *Location:* north side of Huntly, 38 miles from Aberdeen on A96. Open parkland course between the Rivers Deveron and Bogie. 18 holes, 5399 yards. S.S.S. 66. Practice area. *Green Fees:* information not available. *Eating facilities:* full catering by arrangement, lounge bar. *Visitors:* welcome, no restriction except Wednesday and Thursday evenings. Carts for hire. *Society Meetings:* by arrangement with Secretary, maximum of 40. Special package deal Monday-Friday.*

INSCH. **Insch Golf Club,** Golf Terrace, Insch AB52 6JY (Tel & Fax: 01464 820363). *Location:* A96 27 miles from Aberdeen. Parkland; trees, water hazards. 18 holes, 5350 yards. S.S.S. 67. *Green Fees:* Summer: weekdays £19.00 per round, £24.00 for two rounds; weekends £26.00 per round, £32.00 for two rounds; guests £12.00 per round. Seniors £12.00 per round; Juniors (under 16) £7.50 per round. 2010 rates (subject to review). *Eating facilities:* bar and catering available. *Visitors:* welcome except Mondays from 4.30pm, Tuesdays from 5pm and Wednesdays from 3.30pm. *Society Meetings:* welcome.
website: www.inschgolfclub.co.uk

Please mention THE GOLF GUIDE when you enquire about clubs or accommodation

Fraserburgh Golf Club FOUNDED 1777
7th oldest in the world

Philorth, Fraserburgh AB43 8TL
01346 516616

Fraserburgh boasts a 27-hole complex with excellent practice facilities. **CORBIEHILL**, the 18-hole course is 6308 yards (Par 70) of largely unspoiled traditional Scottish links. Its main features are the tricky Par 3s together with a handful of short but very interesting Par 4s. When visiting Fraserburgh, take some time out at the third tee – the view itself is worth the trip.
ROSEHILL, the 2400 yard 9-hole course is essentially parkland. Although short in yards, it plays its length and has two superb finishing holes.

Gordon Arms Hotel

The Square, Huntly AB54 8AF
Tel: 01466 792288 • Fax: 01466 794556
e-mail: reservations@gordonarms.demon.co.uk
www.gordonarms.demon.co.uk

Set in the historic square of Huntly, the Gordon Arms is an attractive Grade B Listed building run under the personal supervision of the resident proprietors, David and Jennifer Sherriffs. The hotel is renowned for its good food, hospitality and the use of locally sourced produce. *('As well as quantity you definitely get quality' – Aberdeen Evening Express Pub Spy)*. *The Gordon Arms is ideally positioned for the many golf courses in the North East as well as being in the heart of the Castle and Whisky Trails.* All rooms are en suite and rates include a full hearty Scottish breakfast. Highlander Bunk House now open.

INVERALLOCHY. Inverallochy Golf Club, Whitelink, Inverallochy, Fraserburgh AB43 8XY (01346 582000). *Location:* three miles south of Fraserburgh. Seaside links course. 18 holes, 5431 yards. S.S.S. 67. *Green Fees:* weekdays £20.00 per round, £25.00 per day; weekends £25.00 per round, £30.00 per day. *Eating facilities:* full catering/ fully licensed, advance booking required. *Visitors:* welcome, apply in writing. *Society Meetings:* welcome, apply in writing. Secretary: George Young.

INVERURIE. Inverurie Golf Club, Davah Wood, Inverurie AB51 5JB (01467 624080; Fax: 01467 672869). *Location*: off A96 Blackhall roundabout, at next roundabout, approx. 300 yards, turn right. Parkland with three tree-lined (wood holes). 18 holes, 5483 yards. S.S.S. 67. Practice ground. *Green Fees*: information not provided. *Eating facilities*: full catering, bar and lounge area. *Visitors*: welcome, phone 01467 672863. *Society Meetings*: catered for. Professional: Steven McLean (01467 672863). Secretary: Eric Stevenson (01467 672860; Fax: 01467 672869).
e-mail: administrator@inveruriegc.co.uk
website: www.inveruriegc.fsbusiness.co.uk

KEITH. Keith Golf Club, Mar Court, Fife Park, Keith AB55 5GF (01542 882469). *Location:* leave A96 on B9014 take first right. Parkland, open, panoramic views. 18 holes, 5800 yards, 5300 metres. S.S.S. 68. Small practice area and putting green. *Green Fees:* £15.00 per round, £20.00 per day. *Eating facilities:* catering available by arrangement, normal bar hours. *Visitors:* welcome anytime, advisable to telephone in advance during playing season. Buggy hire available. *Society Meetings:* all welcome, applications to Outings Convener N. Wilson.
e-mail: Secretary@keithgolfclub.org.uk
website: www.keithgolfclub.org.uk

KEMNAY. Kemnay Golf Club, Monymusk Road, Kemnay AB51 5RA (01467 642225). *Location:* from A96 main Aberdeen/Inverness road. Take B994 signposted Kemnay and pass through village of Kemnay to find golf course on left hand side on leaving village. Flat wooded parkland. 18 holes, 6342 yards, 5398 metres. S.S.S. 71. *Green Fees:* weekdays £27.00 per round, £33.00 per day; weekends £33.00 per round, £39.00 per day. *Eating facilities:* bar and full catering. *Visitors:* welcome at all times except during club competitions/matches; phone club shop to book tee time. *Society Meetings:* welcome by arrangement. Professional: D. Brown (01467 642225). Secretary: F. Webster (Tel & Fax: 01467 643746). Club Shop: (01467 642225). Administrator: (Tel & Fax: 01467 643746).
e-mail: admininstrator@kemnaygolfclub.co.uk
website: www.kemnaygolfclub.co.uk

INVERURIE GOLF CLUB

An 18 hole parkland golf course with a varied layout providing an enjoyable challenge to all.

Spring Midweek Special Offers for Outings and Visiting Golfers.
Visitors always welcome!
Davah Wood, Inverurie AB51 5JB
Telephone: 01467 672860
administrator@inveruriegc.co.uk
www.inveruriegc.fsbusiness.co.uk

PLEASE NOTE

All the information regarding Golf Clubs in this guide is given in good faith in the belief that it is correct. However, the publishers cannot guarantee the facts given in these pages, neither are they responsible for changes in ownership or facilities, such as green fees, that may take place after the date of going to press. Readers should always satisfy themselves that the facilities they require are available and that the terms, if quoted, still apply.

KINTORE. **Kintore Golf Club,** Balbithan Road, Kintore, Inverurie AB51 0UR (01467 632631). *Location:* off A96 12 miles north of Aberdeen. Undulating moorland course. 18 holes, 5323 yards. S.S.S. 66. *Green Fees:* weekdays and weekends £25.00 per round. *Eating facilities:* available all day during the season, by arrangement at other times. *Visitors:* welcome daily except Tuesdays, Wednesdays and Fridays between 4pm and 7pm. Trolleys and buggies for hire during season. *Society Meetings:* welcome by appointment. Secretary: C. Lindsay.
e-mail: info@kintoregolfclub.net
website: www.kintoregolfclub.net

LOSSIEMOUTH. **Moray Golf Club,** Stotfield Road, Lossiemouth IV31 6QS (01343 812018; Fax: 01343 815102). *Location:* five miles from Elgin on A941, 40 miles from Inverness A96 Links course. Old Course 18 holes, 6697 yards. S.S.S. 73. New Course 18 holes, 6008 yards. S.S.S. 69. Practice ground, putting green. *Green Fees*: information not provided. Discounts through local hotel and for parties of 12 or more. *Eating facilities*: bar plus full catering. *Visitors*: welcome every day. Secretary will advise on availability. Buggies, carts, caddies. *Society Meetings*: welcome by arrangement with Secretary. Professional: John Murray (01343 813330). Secretary: S. Crane (01343 812018 Ext 2; Fax: 01343 815102).
e-mail: secretary@moraygolf.co.uk
website: www.moraygolf.co.uk

MACDUFF. **Royal Tarlair Golf Club,** Buchan Street, Macduff AB44 1TA (01261 832897). *Location:* A98 Fraserburgh to Inverness road. Seaside cliff top course, beautiful seascapes, 13th feature hole. 18 holes, 5866 yards, 5373 metres. S.S.S. 68. *Green Fees:* weekdays £20.00 per round, £25.00 per day; weekends £25.00 per round, £30.00 per day. £20.00 per round local public holidays, *Eating facilities:* full catering and bar available. *Visitors:* very welcome. *Society Meetings:* welcome, bookings through Secretary. Treasurer/Secretary: Mrs M. McMurray (01261 832897 weekdays 9-1pm).
e-mail: info@royaltarlair.co.uk
website: www.royaltarlair.co.uk

NAIRN. **The Nairn Golf Club,** Seabank Road, Nairn IV12 4HB (01667 453208; Fax: 01667 456328). *Location:* Nairn West Shore, on the southern shore of the Moray Firth, 16 miles east of Inverness on A96. Hosted "Amateur" Championship in 1994. Traditional Scottish links championship course, hosted 37th Walker Cup in 1999. Championship Course - 18 holes, 6705 yards. S.S.S. 73 (blue tees); Medal Course 18 holes, 6430 yards. S.S.S 72 (white tees); 9 holes (Newton Course), 1918 yards. Practice area. *Green Fees:* information not available. *Eating facilities:* full catering facilities and two bars available. *Visitors:* welcome subject to availability, restrictions at weekends - 8am to 11.00am and from 12 noon to 2.30pm for members only. Full size snooker table. *Society Meetings:* welcome subject to availability. Professional: Robin P. Fyfe (01667 452787). Secretary: David Corstorphine (01667 453208; Fax: 01667 456328). Catering Manager: (01667 452103).
e-mail: bookings@nairngolfclub.co.uk
website: www.nairngolfclub.co.uk

NEWBURGH. **Newburgh-on-Ythan Golf Club,** Beach Road, Newburgh AB41 6BY (01358 789058). *Location:* 10 miles north of Aberdeen. Championship links course, founded 1888. Past hosts of Paul Lawrie Golf Classic and North East District Amateur Championships, only 2 miles from Trump International. 18 holes, 6423 yards. S.S.S. 72. 6 hole practice course. Driving range. *Green Fees:* weekdays £35.00 per round, weekends £45.00 per round. *Eating facilities:* bar/restaurant. *Visitors:* welcome at all times. Tennis courts, wireless access, indoor swing studio. Corporate and meeting facility available; function suite for 120. Contact Professional Ian Bratton (01358 789058).
e-mail: secretary@newburghgolfclub.co.uk
website: www.newburghgolfclub.co.uk

THE APPEARANCE OF AN ASTERISK (*) AT THE END OF A CLUB OR COURSE ENTRY INDICATES THAT UP-TO-DATE INFORMATION HAS NOT BEEN SUPPLIED

The Moray Golf Club
founded 1889

There are 36 individual reasons to play golf at Moray - and every one is designed for enjoyment!

Moray Golf Club at Lossiemouth offers two traditional Scottish golf links 18-hole courses - Moray Old and Moray New. Like the Old Course at the "Home of Golf", St Andrews, the courses start and finish within the town boundaries.

Stotfield Road, Lossiemouth IV31 6QS
Tel: 01343 812018 • Fax: 01343 815102 • e-mail: secretary@moraygolf.com

NEWMACHAR. **Newmachar Golf Club,** Swailend, Newmachar AB21 7UU (01651 863002). *Location:* two and a half miles north of Dyce on A947. Two courses – Hawkshill: Championship standard wooded parkland course with ponds being main feature. 18 holes, 6700 yards. S.S.S. 74; Swailend: undulating parkland course. 18 holes, 6388 yards. S.S.S. 71. 12 bay driving range, practice bunker and putting green. *Green Fees:* information not provided. *Eating facilities:* fully licensed clubhouse with restaurant. *Visitors:* welcome by prior arrangement. Handicap Certificate required. *Society Meetings:* welcome by prior arrangement. Head Professional: Andrew Cooper (01651 863222). Secretary: Alasdair Macgregor (01651 863002; Fax: 01651 863055).

OLDMELDRUM. **Oldmeldrum Golf Club,** Kirk Brae, Oldmeldrum, Inverurie AB51 0DJ (01651 872648). *Location:* 17 miles north-west of Aberdeen on A947 to Banff. First on right entering from Aberdeen direction. Undulating parkland with tree-lined fairways and water features. 18 holes, 6123 yards. S.S.S. 70. Practice area. *Green Fees:* information not available. *Eating facilities:* fully licensed bar, full catering. *Visitors:* welcome, advisable to phone first. Professional's Shop: (01651 873555) for tee reservations. *Society Meetings:* catered for by arrangement. Professional: Hamish Love (01651 873555). Administrator: Hamish Dingwall (01651 872648).*

PETERCULTER. **Peterculter Golf Club,** Oldtown, Burnside Road, Peterculter, Aberdeen AB14 0LN (01224 735245; Fax: 01224 735580). *Location:* from North Deeside Road (A93) at west end of Peterculter travel southwards, following signs for club. Scenic, undulating course, bounded by River Dee, excellent views of hills to west. 18 holes, Medal 6219 yards, Forward Tees 6000 yards, S.S.S. Medal 69, Forward Tees 68. Small practice/teaching area. *Green Fees:* information not available. *Eating facilities:* dining room, lounge bar. *Visitors:* welcome except weekdays 3.30pm to 6pm. *Society Meetings:* welcome Tuesdays to Fridays. Not Public/local holidays. Professional: Dean Vannet (01224 734994). e-mail: info@petercultergolfclub.co.uk
website: www.petercultergolfclub.co.uk

PETERHEAD. **Peterhead Golf Club,** Riverside Drive, Peterhead AB42 1LT (01779 472149; Fax: 01779 480725). *Location:* north end of town off Blackhouse Terrace at mouth of River Ugie. Seaside links – can be affected by variable wind conditions. Old Course – 18 holes, 6173 yards. S.S.S. 71; New Course – 9 holes, 2228 yards. Par 62 for 4456 yards. Practice area. *Green Fees:* information not available. *Eating facilities:* snacks, meals, full bar facilities. *Visitors:* welcome anytime except some restrictions on a Saturday. Phone call advised. *Society Meetings:* welcome by arrangement. Handicap Certificate may be asked for. Secretary: D.G. Wood (Fax: 01779 480725).*

Meldrum House Country Hotel & Golf Course,
Oldmeldrum, Aberdeenshire AB51 0AE
T: 01651 872294 • E: enquiries@meldrumhouse.com
Golf Club: T: 01651 873553 • E: info@meldrumhousegolfclub.co.uk
www.meldrumhouse.com

Set amidst beautiful countryside, The Meldrum House Country Hotel & Golf Course offers unrivalled quality. Only a few miles from Aberdeen, this is one of the finest luxury hotels Scotland has to offer.

If golf is your passion, we offer a range of golf vacation packages and golf breaks at our spectacular and challenging course, including a world-class golf academy and teaching centre. Course open to hotel guests only.

An Unbeatable Hotel and Golfing Experience

Palace Hotel • Peterhead

Independent 3-Star Hotel with an excellent reputation for first class service • Ideal base for golfing on several renowned Aberdeenshire courses • 64 bedrooms with en suite facilities • Two restaurants and two bars
• Discounted green fees at several clubs
• Visit our website for details of golf packages.

Palace Hotel, Prince Street, Peterhead, Aberdeenshire AB42 1PL
Tel: 01779 474821 • www.palacehotel.co.uk • info@palacehotel.co.uk

PETERHEAD. **Longside Golf Club,** West End, Longside, Peterhead AB42 4XJ (01779 821558). *Location*: take A950 west from Peterhead towards Mintlaw. Wooded course with river. 18 holes, 5225 yards, S.S.S 66. *Green Fees*: £15.00 Monday to Saturday, £20.00 Sunday. *Eating facilities*: full bar and catering facilities. *Visitors*: always welcome - no visitors before 10.30am on Sunday. *Society Meetings*: welcome, £35.00 for two rounds including catering. £24.00 for one round including catering, booking forms available from club. Secretary: Mrs Kathleen Allan (01771 622424).

PORTLETHEN. **Portlethen Golf Club,** Badentoy Road, Portlethen, Aberdeen AB12 4YA (01224 781090). *Location:* five miles south of Aberdeen on main Stonehaven Road. Rolling parkland. 18 holes, 6670 yards. S.S.S. 72. Large practice area. *Green Fees:* information not available. *Eating facilities:* bar and restaurant. *Visitors:* welcome, no visitors Saturdays, Sundays also difficult in summer. Golf buggies for hire. Snooker. *Society Meetings:* welcome weekdays by arrangement. Professional: Muriel Thomson (01224 782571). Bar/catering: 01224 782575.*

ROSEHEARTY. **Rosehearty Golf Club,** C/o Masons Arms Hotel, 1 Castle Street, Rosehearty, Fraserburgh AB43 4JP (01346 571250). *Location:* east of Rosehearty on Fraserburgh Road. Seaside links. 9 holes, 2197 yards. S.S.S. 62. *Green Fees:* Gents and Ladies £15.00. Seniors and Juniors £8.00. *Eating facilities:* Masons Arms Hotel adjacent to course. *Visitors:* always welcome. *Society Meetings:* welcome by prior arrangement. Secretary: Alan Downie.

ROTHES. **Rothes Golf Club,** Blackhall, Rothes, Aberlour AB38 7AN (01340 831343). *Location:* south west of Rothes, off A941 Elgin to Craigellachie road. A parkland course with fine views over the River Spey. 9 holes, 2615 yards (5230 yards), 2391 metres (4782 metres). S.S.S. 65. Practice net. *Green Fees:* information not provided. *Eating facilities:* licensed bar open summer evenings and weekends, catering available; parties by arrangement. *Visitors:* always welcome, tee reserved for Ladies 5pm to 7.30pm Tuesdays, and 5pm to 6.30pm Mondays for Juniors. *Society Meetings:* welcome, contact Secretary. Secretary: K.J. MacPhee (01340 831676).

SPEY BAY. **Spey Bay Golf Club,** Spey Bay Golf Course, The Links, Tugnet, Fochabers IV32 7PJ Contact for Tee Bookings (078267 48071). *Location:* midway between Inverness and Aberdeen, at the mouth of River Spey. Traditional 18-hole championship links layout designed by Ben Sayers in 1907 with special characteristics of small fast greens and tight undulating gorse-lined fairways with superb scenic views over the Moray Firth to the mountains of Caithness and Sutherland. 6220 yards. S.S.S. 70. Par 70. Practice area. *Green Fees:* £20.00 (group discounts). Buggies available with prior notice. *Eating facilities:* no catering at present. Contact: Dave Barron (078267 48071).
e-mail: speybaygolf@freeuk.com

STONEHAVEN. **Stonehaven Golf Club,** Cowie, Stonehaven AB39 3RH (01569 762124; Fax: 01569 765973). *Location:* A92, one mile north of town signposted at mini roundabout near Leisure Centre. Parkland course on cliffs overlooking North Sea with some challenging holes over natural gullies. 18 holes, 5128 yards. S.S.S. 65. Limited practice area. *Green Fees:* £30.00 for one/two rounds. *Eating facilities:* full catering including bar lunches. *Visitors:* welcome, but advised to reserve tee time in advance, restricted Saturdays after 4pm. *Society Meetings:* catered for except for Saturday. Secretary/ Manager: Morag Duncan.
e-mail: info@stonehavengolfclub.com

TORPHINS. **Torphins Golf Club,** Bog Road, Torphins, Banchory AB31 4JU (013398 82115). *Location:* through village towards Lumphanan, club signposted to right. Parkland with lovely views to Highlands. 9 holes, 4724 yards (18 holes). S.S.S. 64. *Green Fees:* £15.00; £10.00 for 9 holes. Juniors half price. *Eating facilities:* light refreshments at weekends, unlicensed. *Visitors:* welcome at weekends; on medal days by arrangement. *Society Meetings:* welcome; at weekends by arrangement. Secretary: Stuart MacGregor (013398 82402).
e-mail: stuartmacgregor5@btinternet.com

TURRIFF. **Turriff Golf Club,** Rosehall, Turriff AB53 4HD (01888 562982; Fax: 01888 568050). *Location:* A947 signposted on south side of Turriff. Wooded parkland course. 18 holes, 6118 yards. S.S.S. 70. Practice area, putting green. *Green Fees:* weekdays £23.00 per round, £27.00 per day; weekends £27.00 per round, £33.00 per day. *Eating facilities:* bar and restaurant. *Visitors:* no visitors before 10am weekends, selected times on Medal days. Tee reservation by contacting Professional – during the week up to four days in advance, weekends up to two days in advance. Buggy and electric trolley hire. *Society Meetings:* by arrangement with Secretary. Professional: Gordon Dunn (01888 563025). Secretary: Mrs M. Smart (01888 562982; Fax: 01888 568050). Administrator: Grace Stephen.
e-mail: grace@turriffgolf.sol.co.uk
website: www.turriffgolfclub.com

WESTHILL. **Westhill Golf Club,** Westhill Heights, Westhill AB32 6RY (01224 742567; Fax: 01224 749124). *Location:* six miles from Aberdeen on A944. Parkland course. 18 holes, 5849 yards. S.S.S. 69. Practice ground. *Green Fees:* weekdays £20.00 per round, £25.00 per day; weekends and Public Holidays £25.00 per round, £30.00 per day. 2010 rates (subject to review). Special packages available on request. *Eating facilities:* lounge bar and dining area. *Visitors:* welcome any time. *Society Meetings:* welcome as visitors' times by arrangement. Professional: George Bruce (01224 740159).

Please mention THE GOLF GUIDE when you enquire about clubs or accommodation

Angus & Dundee

ARBROATH. **Arbroath Golf Course,** Elliot, By Arbroath DD11 2PE (Tel & Fax: 01241 875837). *Location*: off Dundee Road. Seaside links course. 18 holes, 6200 yards. S.S.S 70. Driving range, new putting green. *Green Fees*: weekdays £30.00 per round, weekends £35.00 per round. *Eating facilities*: full catering and bar facility. *Visitors*: welcome. *Society Meetings:* all welcome. Professional: L. Ewart (Tel & Fax: 01241 875837). Secretary: Scott Milne (01382 229111).
e-mail: lindsay.ewart@btconnect.com

ARBROATH near. **Letham Grange Golf Course,** Colliston, By Arbroath DD11 4RL (01241 890373; Fax: 01241 890725). *Location:* follow brown Scottish Tourist Board signs for Letham Grange from Arbroath. Two courses – Old Course is a blend of tree-lined parkland and open rolling fairways; water plays a major role which makes the course both scenic and dramatic. Glens Course is slightly shorter and without water hazards, offers golfers a more relaxed and less arduous round; however, it could be deceptive! 36 holes, Old 6968 yards, Glen's 5528 yards. S.S.S. Old 73, Glen's 68. Very large practice area, practice putting green, practice chipping green. *Green Fees:* information not available. *Eating facilities:* golfers' bar and restaurant. *Visitors:* welcome. Hotel on site. Trolley, club and buggy hire, PGA Professional group tuition available. *Society Meetings:* all most welcome. Golf shop (01241 890377 or 01241 890373).*
website: www.lethamgrangehotel.co.uk

BARRY. **Panmure Golf Club,** Burnside Road, Barry, By Carnoustie DD7 7RT (01241 855120). *Location:* two miles west of Carnoustie on A930, signposted from the Barry village bypass. Championship links. 18 holes, 6551 yards. S.S.S. 70. Driving range, practice area. *Green Fees:* £68.00 per round, £88.00 per day. *Eating facilities:* full catering seven days a week. *Visitors:* welcome daily except Tuesday and Saturday mornings. Buggy hire. Putting Simulator. *Society Meetings:* restricted but welcome. Professional: Andrew Crerar. Managing Secretary: Charles Philip (01241 855120).
e-mail: secretary@panmuregolfclub.co.uk
website: www.panmuregolfclub.co.uk

BRECHIN. **Brechin Golf and Squash Club**, Trinity, By Brechin DD9 7PD (01356 622383). *Location*: Trinity Village, one mile north of Brechin just off A90. Rolling parkland course with glorious views of Grampian Mountains. 18 holes, 6096 yards. S.S.S. 70. Practice ground. *Green Fees*: information not provided. Midweek special: 2 rounds, full catering only £40.00. Please contact Professional for tee bookings. *Eating facilities*: excellent catering available at all times; large bar. *Visitors*: very welcome seven days. Buggies, carts, club hire. Two squash courts. *Society Meetings*: catered for, reservations in advance. Professional: Stephen Rennie (01356 625270).
e-mail: brechingolfclub@tiscali.co.uk
website: www.brechingolfclub.co.uk

Panmure is one of the 20 oldest Golf Clubs in the world. Situated on the western edge of Carnoustie and less than an hour from St Andrews, the course has been used as a Final Qualifying venue for The Open on seven occasions, and has hosted a number of championships. Panmure provides a fine test of golf at 6551 yards with narrow fairways and undulating greens.

For bookings please telephone or e-mail the Secretary or the Professional.
Panmure Golf Club, Burnside Road, Barry, By Carnoustie, Angus DD7 7RT
Tel: 01241 855120 • Fax: 01241 859737 • www.panmuregolfclub.co.uk
e-mail: secretary@panmuregolfclub.co.uk or professional@panmuregolfclub.co.uk

---

**Visit www.holidayguides.com
for convenient accommodation
when playing golf around the regions**

lethamgrange
HOTEL, GOLF & COUNTRY ESTATE

Letham Grange is home to two of the finest inland golf courses in Scotland and is situated in an arc encompassing the world famous courses of Carnoustie, St. Andrews, Gleneagles and Rosemount.

The Old Course incorporates narrow tree lined holes and open, rolling, and undulating fairways and is a challenge to golfers of all levels, whilst The Glens Course offers a more relaxing round, with just a little sting in the tail to help keep you focused. Check out the golf packages for great savings.

The very friendly staff create a great atmosphere and are delighted to welcome visitors from near and far. There is a golf shop, changing rooms, showers, and trolley and buggy hire. Drinks and refreshments can be purchased and the adjoining Letham Grange Hotel provides spacious accommodation for visitors and golfers alike.

Letham Grange Hotel, Golf & Country Estate
Colliston, Arbroath, Angus DD11 4RL

Golf Tel: 01241 890373
Hotel Tel: 01241 890459

www.lethamgrangehotel.co.uk

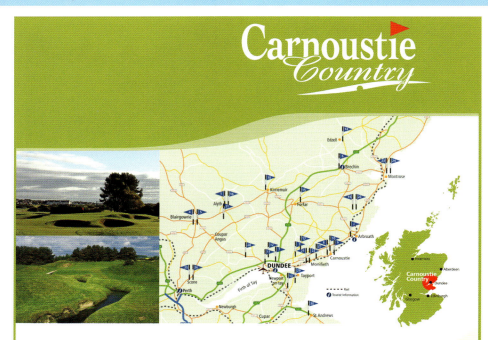

Follow in the Footsteps of Champions

Carnoustie Country's historic courses are every golfer's dream - over 30 classic links and parkland courses, all within a 40 minute drive of Carnoustie Championship, venue of The Open since 1931.

- Take part in the Carnoustie Country Classic, an annual tournament played on four Open Championship and Qualifying courses each May

- The Carnoustie Country Dream Ticket enables you to live the dream and play on four of the world's classic links courses, Montrose, Monifieth, Panmure and Carnoustie Championship

- We can arrange your ideal Stay & Play Golfing Break, including transfers, tee times and accommodation

Find out more at:
www.carnoustiecountry.com

CARNOUSTIE. **Carnoustie Golf Links,** 20 Links Parade, Carnoustie DD7 7JF (01241 802270; Fax: 01241 802271). *Location:* 12 miles east of Dundee. Three 18-hole courses. Championship Course 6941 yards. S.S.S. 75; Burnside Course 6028 yards. S.S.S. 70; Buddon Links 5420 yards. S.S.S. 66. Golf trolleys permitted. *Green Fees:* information not available. *Eating facilities:* catering facilities can be arranged with the local golf clubs. *Visitors:* welcome, times must be booked. Handicap Certificates required for play on Championship Course. *Society Meetings:* catered for by arrangement. Professional: Colin Sinclair. Course Manager: John Philp. General Manager: G. Duncan. Golf Services Manager: Colin McLeod.

DUNDEE. **Ballumbie Castle Golf Club,** 3 Old Quarry Road, Off Ballumbie Road, Dundee DD4 0SY (01382 770028). *Location*: one and a half miles north of Claypotts Junction, less than 2 miles from Dundee city centre. Parkland/heathland course. 18 holes, 6127 yards, S.S.S. 70. 22 bay driving range, putting green, chipping green. *Green Fees*: information not available. *Eating facilities*: clubhouse facilities with menu and full bar. Public house licence. *Visitors*: welcome. Tuition available at driving range. *Society Meetings*: welcome, please telephone for details. Professional: Lee Sutherland (01382 770028).*
e-mail: ballumbie2000@yahoo.com
website: www.ballumbiecastlegolfclub.com

DUNDEE. **Caird Park Golf Club,** Mains Loan, Dundee DD4 9BX (01382 453606). *Location:* northern edge of city, off Kingsway. Wooded parkland. 18 holes, 6273 yards, 5740 metres. S.S.S. 70. Practice range on course. *Green Fees:* information not available. *Eating facilities:* at clubhouse. *Visitors:* welcome, must book in advance to ensure game. *Society Meetings:* see Dundee District Council, Parks Department. Professional: Jackie Black (01382 459438). Secretary: Greg Martin (01382 461460).*

DUNDEE. **Camperdown Golf Club,** Camperdown House, Camperdown Park, Dundee DD2 4TF (01382 623398). *Location:* two miles north-west of city, enter at Kingsway/Coupar Angus road junction. Wooded parkland. 18 holes, 6561 yards. S.S.S. 72, Par 71. *Green Fees:* information not available. *Eating facilities:* must be booked in advance. *Visitors and Society Meetings:* please contact by e-mail: admin@camperdowngolfclub.co.uk. Professional: Roddy Brown (01382 623398). Secretary: Elaine Hendry (01382 884741).*
e-mail: jack.clinton@blueyonder.co.uk
jack.clinton@dundeecity.gov.uk

Please mention THE GOLF GUIDE when you enquire about clubs or accommodation

Coach House Bed & Breakfast

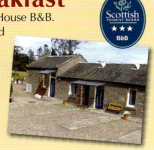

A warm welcome awaits you at Carnoustie Coach House B&B. Chalets set in a beautiful courtyard overlooking a secluded garden and patio. Golf at Monifieth, Panmure and Championship course of Carnoustie.
Prices from £32 pppn.

Carlogie Road, Carnoustie, Angus DD7 6LD
Tel: 01241 857319
E-mail: aevicks35@hotmail.co.uk

Seabraes Self Catering Flats • Dundee

Seabraes Self Catering Flats are available July and August for individuals or groups. Great value accommodation, close to city centre, ideally located within 30 minute drive of St Andrews and Carnoustie and surrounding courses, making it a perfect base for groups of golfers. All rooms en suite, flats sleep a max of 8 (one double, six singles). Fully furnished kitchen/dining area with TV. Free car parking. Minimum stay 3 nights for groups. For availability and prices please contact:

Heathfield Office, 75 Old Hawkhill, Dundee DD1 5EN
E-mail: enquiries-dundee@sanctuary-housing.co.uk
Tel: 01382 383111 • www.Scotland2000.com/Seabraes

DUNDEE. **Downfield Golf Club,** Turnberry Avenue, Dundee DD2 3QP (01382 825595; Fax: 01382 813111). *Location*: follow tourist signs from the main A90 Kingsway for Downfield Golf Course. Wooded, parkland course. 18 holes, 6802 yards, 6266 metres. S.S.S. 73. Large practice area. *Green Fees*: information not provided. *Eating facilities*: full catering and bar seven days. *Visitors*: welcome weekdays 9.30am to 3.30pm, Sunday after 2pm only, pre-booking essential. Carts for hire. Professional: Kenny Hutton (01382 889246). Secretary: Margaret Stewart (01382 825595; Fax: 01382 813111).

DUNDEE. **Piperdam Golf and Leisure Resort Osprey Club,** Fowlis, Dundee DD2 5LP (01382 581374; Fax: 01382 581102). *Location:* off A923 Coupar Angus road. If using sat nav type in "Piperdam Drive" for directions, not post code. Parkland course, Osprey 18 holes; Wee Piper Par 3 course, 6437 yards. S.S.S. 72.11 bay driving range, putting green, pitching green. *Green Fees:* visit web site for variable deals. *Eating facilities:* restaurant and bar. *Visitors:* welcome. No restrictions. 20 petrol buggies available for hire; £20 per round, £34 per day. Leisure Centre and Spa. Holiday lodges on site, visit web site for details. *Society Meetings:* welcome. Packages available.
e-mail: enquiries@piperdam.com
website: www.piperdam.com

EDZELL. **Edzell Golf Club,** High Street, Edzell DD9 7TF (01356 647283; Fax: 01356 648094). *Location:* travelling north from Dundee on A90, take B966 north of Brechin by-pass, continue 3.5 miles to village of Edzell. Parkland course with tree-lined fairways at the entrance to the Angus Glens and in the foothills of the Grampians. "Golfers who are visiting the Angus area cannot afford to miss what is one of Scotland's true hidden gems" Golf Monthly, 1999. 18 holes, 6445 yards. S.S.S. 71. 9-hole West Water Course 4114 yards, S.S.S. 61. 300 yard driving range, chipping area and putting green. *Green Fees:* weekdays £36.00 per round, £48.00 per day; weekends £42.00 per round, £60.00 per day. West Water Course; Monday to Sunday £12.00 per 9 holes, £16.00 per 18 holes. *Eating facilities:* dining room, lounge and bar. *Visitors:* welcome, apply to Secretary. Online booking available. *Society Meetings:* welcome apply to Secretary. Professional: Alistair J. Webster (01356 648462). Secretary: Ian G. Farquhar (01356 647283). Caterer: Louise Robertson (01356 648235).
e-mail: awebsterpro@aol.com
secretary@edzellgolfclub.net
website: www.edzellgolfclub.com

FORFAR. **Forfar Golf Club,** Cunninghill, Arbroath Road, Forfar DD8 2RL (01307 463773). *Location:* one mile from Forfar on A932 to Arbroath. Undulating wooded heathland Tom Morris/James Braid designed course. 18 holes, 6066 yards. S.S.S. 69. *Green Fees:* information not available. *Eating facilities:* available. *Visitors:* welcome. *Society Meetings:* catered for. Professional: Peter McNiven (01307 465683). Secretary: Stuart Wilson (01307 463773; Fax: 01307 468495).*

KIRRIEMUIR. **Kirriemuir Golf Club Ltd,** Northmuir, Kirriemuir DD8 4LN (01575 573317; Fax: 01575 574608). *Location:* 20 miles north-west of Carnoustie and six miles north-west of Forfar on A926 and A928, just on edge of Kirriemuir, north of town centre. Heathland course with stunning views of Angus Glens. 18 holes, 5510 yards, 5038 metres. S.S.S. 67. Putting green, practice ground. *Green Fees:* information not available. *Eating facilities:* full catering and bar facilities. *Visitors:* welcome weekdays and weekends. *Society Meetings:* Special golf/ catering packages available. Professional: Karyn Dallas (01575 573317; Fax: 01575 574608).*
e-mail: kirriemuirgolfclub@fsmail.net
website: www.kirriemuirgolfclub.co.uk

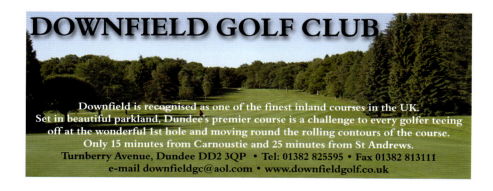

DOWNFIELD GOLF CLUB

Downfield is recognised as one of the finest inland courses in the UK.
Set in beautiful parkland, Dundee's premier course is a challenge to every golfer teeing off at the wonderful 1st hole and moving round the rolling contours of the course.
Only 15 minutes from Carnoustie and 25 minutes from St Andrews.
Turnberry Avenue, Dundee DD2 3QP • Tel: 01382 825595 • Fax 01382 813111
e-mail downfieldgc@aol.com • www.downfieldgolf.com

SCOTLAND / Angus & Dundee 363

Welcome to EDZELL GOLF CLUB

Midway between Dundee and Aberdeen, with the Grampian mountains forming a backdrop to this lovely heathland/parkland course.

"Golfers who are visiting the Angus area cannot afford to miss what is one of Scotland's true hidden gems" Golf Monthly. Online booking available.

**The Edzell Golf Club,
High Street, Edzell, Angus DD9 7TF**

Secretary: 01356 647283
Professional: 01356 648462
e-mail: secretary@edzellgolfclub.net
www.edzellgolfclub.com

Forfar Golf Club
Cunninghill, Arbroath Road,
Forfar DD8 2RL

Tel: 01307 463773 (Secretary)
Fax: 01307 468495

Only 12 miles from the 2007 Open Championship venue at Carnoustie, Forfar Golf Club is an undulating, wooded, heathland 18 hole course, combining a links type layout with generous grassy lies. In the heart of picturesque Angus, this compact course, laid out in 1871 by 'Old' Tom Morris, provides an ideal test for all abilities of golfer and an enjoyable and memorable day for anyone wishing to play golf in Scotland.

e-mail: info@forfargolfclub.com • www.forfargolfclub.com

Muirhouses Farm

Muirhouses is a livestock and arable farm set amidst beautiful Angus countryside, close to the Cairngorm National Park. The accommodation is very comfortable with en suite rooms and central heating. Every comfort is assured, from the homely welcome on arrival to the delicious breakfast. An excellent base for golf, walking and cycling.

**Cortachy, Kirriemuir, Angus DD8 4QG
Tel: 01575 573128 • *Mrs S. McLaren***
e-mail: susan@muirhouses.plus.com   www.muirhousesfarm.co.uk

MONIFIETH. **Broughty Golf Club,** 6 Princes Street, Monifieth, Dundee DD5 4AW (01382 532147). Starter (01382 532767). *Location:* eight miles east of Dundee, in village of Monifieth. Seaside links, some fairways fringed with trees. Medal Course: 18 holes, 6655 yards. S.S.S. 72. Ashludie Course: 18 holes, 5123 yards. S.S.S. 65. Practice area. *Green Fees:* information not available. *Eating facilities:* full catering; no catering Tuesdays or Thursdays. *Visitors:* no visitors before 2pm on Saturdays or before 10am Sundays. All tee times must be booked through Starter's Box. *Society Meetings:* by arrangement. Professional: Mr I. McLeod. Secretary: Peter Flynn.*

MONIFIETH. **Monifieth Golf Links,** Princes Street, Monifieth, Angus DD5 4AW (01382 532767). *Location:* seven miles east of Dundee, Monifieth High Street. Seaside links. Medal Course 18 holes, 6657 yards. S.S.S. 72; Ashludie Course 18 holes, 5123 yards. S.S.S. 64. Practice facilities. *Green Fees:* Medal Course - weekdays £49.00, weekends £59.00. Ashludie Course - weekdays £24.00, weekends £26.00. *Eating facilities:* clubs and Hotel. *Visitors:* welcome after 9.30am Monday to Friday; Saturdays after 2pm; Sundays after 10am. *Society Meetings:* parties over 12, must provide club Handicap Certificates. Buggies for hire. Packages available Monday-Friday only £69.00. Professional: Ian McLeod (01382 532945). Managing Secretary: J. Brodie (01382 535553); Fax: 01382 535816).
e-mail: monifiethgolf@freeuk.com
website: www.monifiethgolf.co.uk

THE APPEARANCE OF AN ASTERISK (*) AT THE END OF A CLUB OR COURSE ENTRY INDICATES THAT UP-TO-DATE INFORMATION HAS NOT BEEN SUPPLIED

MONTROSE. **Montrose Golf Links Ltd,** Traill Drive, Montrose DD10 8SW (01674 672932). *Location*: A92 runs from Aberdeen, through Montrose. Links Medal Course 6544 yards. Par 71. S.S.S. 72. Broomfield Course 4825 yards. Par 66. S.S.S. 63. *Green Fees*: Medal: Monday to Friday £50.00 per round, £65.00 per day, Juniors £20.00 per round, £32.00 per day; Saturday £55.00 per round, £75.00 per day; Sunday £45.00 per round, £60.00 per day; Juniors Saturday £25.00. per round, £35.00 per day; Sunday £20.00 per round, £30.00 per day. Broomfield: Monday to Friday £20.00 per round, £30.00 per day; Juniors £7.00 per round; Saturday £22.00 per round, £35.00 per day, Junior £7.00; Sunday £20.00 per round, £30.00 per day, Junior £7.00. Composite day fees and special rates on request. Group discounts available. 2010/2011 rates. *Eating facilities*: catering facilities available by arrangement in golf clubs. *Visitors:* very welcome; no restrictions midweek, visitors allowed on Medal Course between 2.44pm and 3.40pm on Saturdays and after 10am on Sundays. Handicap Certificates required on Medal Course. *Society Meetings*: welcome by arrangement. Temporary membership available at the following clubs: Caledonia Golf Club (01674 672313); Mercantile Golf Club (01674 672408); Royal Montrose (01674 672376). Professional: Jason J. Boyd. Secretary: Andrew D. Carcary (01674 672932; Fax: 01674 671800).
e-mail: secretary@montroselinks.co.uk
website: www.montroselinks.co.uk

MONTROSE. **Royal Montrose Golf Club,** Traill Drive, Montrose DD10 8SW (01674 672376). *Location:* A92 north from Dundee. Private club playing over the Montrose courses. 18 holes, 6533 yards. S.S.S. 72. *Green Fees:* information not available. *Eating facilities:* available. *Visitors:* apply Montrose Golf Links Ltd. *Society Meetings:* apply Montrose Golf Links Ltd. Professional: Jason Boyd. Secretary: M.J. Cummins (07811 200257).*

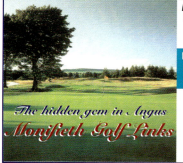

Located four miles from Carnoustie and ½ hour from St Andrews. Two courses offer golf for all levels with the Medal being used as an Open Championship Qualifier. These beautiful links courses also feature tree-lined fairways in many places.

Medal Course £49 Monday to Friday and £59 at weekends; Ashludie Course £24 Monday to Friday and £26 at weekends; a package includes a round of golf on each course, coffee, bacon rolls, soup and sandwiches, and high tea at the day's end **all for £69**

**For bookings call the Golf Manager on
01382 532767
The Starter's Box, Monifieth Links,
Princes Street, Monifieth DD5 4AW
monifiethgolf@freeuk.com**

Argyll & Bute

BALLACHULISH. **Ballachulish House Golf Course**, Ballachulish PH49 4JX (01885 811695). *Location*: near the village of Glencoe, two hours north of Glasgow and Edinburgh, 13 miles south of Fort William. Challenging course with spectacular views. 9 holes (18 tees), 5038 yards. Par 68/65. *Green Fees:* information not available. E*ating facilities:* clubhouse with bar and grill. *Visitors:* welcome. Golf packages available.*
e-mail: mclaughlins@btconnect.com

CAMPBELTOWN. **The Machrihanish Golf Club,** Machrihanish, by Campbeltown PA28 6PT (01586 810213). *Location:* five miles west of Campbeltown on B843 road. Championship standard natural links course. 18 holes, 6225 yards. S.S.S. 71. Also 9 holes, 2395 yards. Practice area. *Green Fees:* £60.00 per round, £90.00 per day. Advance booking necessary. *Eating facilities:* full catering and bar facilities. *Visitors:* welcome, some restrictions on competition days. Open competitions in summer. Special Flight/Golf packages available through Loganair, Glasgow Airport, Paisley. *Society Meetings:* as visitors. Professional: Ken Campbell (01586 810277; Fax: 01586 810221). Secretary: Mrs Anna Anderson (01586 810213).
e-mail: secretary@machgolf.com
website: www.machgolf.com

Lyn-Leven, a superior, award-winning licensed guest house overlooking Loch Leven, with every comfort, in the beautiful Highlands of Scotland, is situated one mile from historic Glencoe village.

Four double, two twin and two family bedrooms, all rooms en suite; sittingroom and diningroom. Central heating. Excellent and varied home cooking served daily. Children welcome at reduced rates. An ideal location for touring. Fishing, walking and climbing in the vicinity.
**Several Argyllshire golf courses in the area.
Dragon's Tooth Golf Club 2 miles.**
The house is open all year except Christmas. Car not essential but private car park provided.
Bed and Breakfast from £25 • Dinner, Bed and Breakfast from £235 to £255pp per week. Credit and debit cards accepted.
**Mr & Mrs J.A. MacLeod, Lyn-Leven Guest House, Ballachulish PH49 4JP
Tel: 01855 811392 • Fax: 01855 811600 • www.lynleven.co.uk**

The Machrihanish Golf Club
welcomes golfers from across the globe
This first-class natural links course is situated on the Kintyre Peninsula, approx. 3 hours' drive from Glasgow; packages including flights Glasgow-Campbeltown Airport available.
Pro Shop • Full catering facilities • 18-hole and 9-hole courses
Tel: 01586 810213 • Fax: 01586 810221 • www.machgolf.com • e-mail: secretary@machgolf.com

Other British holiday guides from FHG Guides
**PUBS & INNS · 300 GREAT HOTELS · SHORT BREAK HOLIDAYS
The bestselling and original PETS WELCOME! · 500 GREAT PLACES TO STAY
SELF-CATERING HOLIDAYS · BED & BREAKFAST STOPS
CARAVAN & CAMPING HOLIDAYS · FAMILY BREAKS**

Published annually: available in all good bookshops or direct from the publisher:
**FHG Guides, Abbey Mill Business Centre, Seedhill, Paisley PA1 1TJ
Tel: 0141 887 0428 • Fax: 0141 889 7204
e-mail: admin@fhguides.co.uk • www.holidayguides.com**

CARRADALE. **Carradale Golf Club,** Carradale, By Campbeltown PA28 6QT. *Location:* 15 miles north of Campbeltown on B842. Seaside course, short but demanding, unbelievable views. 9 holes. Medal Tees – 2358 yards out, 2336 yards in; Yellow Tees – 1999 yards. Par 65. S.S.S. 62 (18 holes). *Green Fees:* £16.00 per round, £20.00 per day; £75.00 per week, £95 two weeks. Country Membership £119.00 per annum (may take part in competitions). *Eating facilities:* Carradale Hotel at first tee, Ashbank Hotel 100 yards. Dunvalanree close by. Network centre one mile (open Easter to October for midday meals and snacks). Glen Bar and Restaurant 1½ miles. *Visitors:* all welcome, no restrictions. *Society Meetings:* welcome, would be advisable to book tee-off times. Secretary: Dr R.J. Abernethy (01583 431321).

DALMALLY. **Dalmally Golf Club,** c/o Old Sawmill, Dalmally PA33 1AE (Clubhouse 01838 200619). *Location:* alongside the A85, two miles west of Dalmally. Flat parkland course bounded by the River Orchy and surrounded by mountains. 9 holes, 2264 yards. S.S.S. 63. *Green Fees:* £15.00 per day. *Eating facilities:* bar and snacks by arrangement. *Visitors:* welcome at all times. Clubs and carts by arrangement. *Society Meetings:* all welcome by arrangement.

DUNOON. **Blairmore and Strone Golf Club,** High Road, Strone, by Dunoon PA23 8TH (01369 840676). *Location:* take A880, five miles north of Dunoon and first left after leaving Kilmun. Braid-designed course set above the Clyde with spectacular views, mixture of hill and flatter parkland. 9 holes, 2112 yards, 1933 metres. S.S.S. 62. *Green Fees:* weekdays and weekends, £12.00. *Eating facilities:* bar facilities Saturdays. *Visitors:* welcome but some restrictions on competition days. *Society Meetings:* welcome, apply through Secretary. Secretary: Graham Thompson (01369 840208).
e-mail: thompsongg@talk21.com

DUNOON. **Cowal Golf Club,** Ardenslate Road, Kirn, Dunoon PA23 8LT (01369 705673). *Location:* quarter mile off A815 at Kirn (north-east boundary of Dunoon). Rising wooded parkland with superb views over Firth of Clyde. 18 holes, 6063 yards. S.S.S. 70. Practice area. *Green Fees:* information not available. *Eating facilities:* full service available. *Visitors:* welcome weekdays, possible restrictions weekends. Separate visitor changing/shower facilities. Local hotels offer golf holidays – apply to Secretary for details. *Society Meetings:* welcome, special rates available. Professional: R.D. Weir (01369 702395). Secretary: Alan Douglas (Tel & Fax: 01369 705673).*
e-mail: secretary@cowalgolfclub.com
website: www.cowalgolfclub.com

DUNOON. **Innellan Golf Club,** Knockamillie Road, Innellan, By Dunoon PA23 7SG (01369 830242). *Location:* south of Dunoon to Innellan Pierhead, then follow signposts. Parkland course in elevated position overlooking Firth of Clyde. 9 holes, 2343 yards. S.S.S. 64. *Green Fees:* £13.00 per 9 holes, £15.00 per day. 25% discount for parties. *Eating facilities:* snack/bar; food by arrangement. *Visitors:* welcome, except Monday evenings, ladies welcome Thursday evenings. *Society Meetings:* welcome by arrangement.

INVERARAY. **Inveraray Golf Club,** North Cromalt, Inveraray PA32 8XT. *Location:* on the A83 Campbeltown road, one mile west of Inveraray, signposted. Testing course, wooded with natural trees, oak, birch, etc. Flat, some water hazards. 9 holes, 2814 yards. S.S.S. 69. *Green Fees:* £15.00 per day. *Eating facilities:* none at course but good choice locally. *Visitors:* very few restrictions weekdays, occasionally at weekends. *Society Meetings:* welcome by prior arrangement through George Morrison (01499 302116).
website: www.inveraraygolfclub.co.uk

ISLE OF BUTE. **Bute Golf Club,** c/o St. Ninians, 32 Marine Place, Ardbeg, Rothesay PA20 0LF (01700 503091). *Location:* six miles from Rothesay on the A845, situated on shores of Stravanan Bay. Flat seaside links in beautiful setting. 9 holes, 2497 yards, 2284 metres. S.S.S. 64 (18 holes). *Green Fees:* £12.00 adults, £5.00 Juniors. *Visitors:* welcome any day, Saturdays after 11.30am. *Society Meetings:* catered for by arrangement. Secretary: Frazer Robinson (01700 503091).
e-mail: administrator@butegolfclub.com
website: www.butegolfclub.com

LOCHGILPHEAD. **Lochgilphead Golf Club,** Blarbuie Road, Lochgilphead PA31 8LE (01546 602340). *Location:* close to Argyll and Bute Hospital, Lochgilphead. Signposted from town centre. Parkland. 9 holes, 4518 yards. S.S.S. 63. *Green Fees:* £20.00 weekdays, £25.00 weekends. *Eating facilities:* limited snacks available at weekends. *Visitors:* welcome but some restriction on competition days. *Society Meetings:* welcome by arrangement. Secretary: E. Hunter (01546 602381).

OBAN. **Glencruitten Golf Club,** Glencruitten Road, Oban PA34 4PU (01631 562868). *Location:* one mile from town centre. Hilly parkland. 18 holes, 4452 yards. S.S.S. 63. Practice area. Putting green. *Green Fees:* weekdays £25.00, weekends £30.00 per day. *Eating facilities:* full catering and bar facilities. *Visitors:* very welcome. *Society Meetings:* welcome. Shop: (01631 564115). Secretary: (01631 562868).
e-mail: enquiries@obangolf.com
website: www.obangolf.com

OBAN. **Isle of Seil Golf Club,** Balvicar, Isle of Seil, by Oban PA34 4TF. *Location*: turn off the A816 Oban-Lochgilphead Road at Kilninver onto the B844, follow B844, cross the Atlantic Bridge onto Seil, then on to Balvicar. Partly on shore of Balvicar Bay, partly on reclaimed quarry land. 9 holes, 2141 yards, Par 31. *Green Fees:* £12.00 per day; Juniors £5.00. 2010 rates (subject to review). *Visitors:* welcome all day, every day. *Society Meetings*: by arrangement. Secretary: J. Blackstock (01852 300347).

SCOTLAND / Argyll & Bute

COWAL GOLF CLUB DUNOON

A superb course overlooking the Firth of Clyde on the Cowal Peninsula in Argyll, with spacious clubhouse, catering, Pro Shop.

Ardenslate Road, Dunoon, Argyll PA23 8LT
Call the Secretary on 01369 705673 (Tel & Fax)
e-mail: secretary@cowalgolfclub.com
www.cowalgolfclub.com

Cairndow Stagecoach Inn

Cairndow, Argyll PA26 8BN
Tel: 01499 600286 • Fax: 01499 600220
www.cairndowinn.com

A Warm Scottish Welcome on the Shores of Loch Fyne

Discounted rates for golfers at Inveraray Golf Club.
Tee times available at Loch Lomond.

★ Historic Coaching Inn on Loch Fyne
★ 18 well-appointed en suite bedrooms
★ 7 de luxe bedrooms; 5 new Lochside rooms
★ Excellent cuisine in Stables Restaurant and lounge meals all day
★ Amenities include lochside beer garden, sauna, and solarium.

AA ★★★ Inn

Inchmurrin Island Self-Catering Holidays

Inchmurrin Island, Loch Lomond G63 0JY
Tel: 01389 850245 • Fax: 01389 850513

Inchmurrin is the largest island on Loch Lomond and offers a unique experience. Three self-catering apartments, sleeping from four to six persons, and a detached cedar clad cottage sleeping eight, are available. A ferry service is provided and jetties are available for customers with their own boats. Come and stay and have the freedom to roam and explore anywhere on the island. Ferry service available direct to Loch Lomond championship golf course - no need to queue in traffic. New public course at ferry terminal.

e-mail: scotts@inchmurrin-lochlomond.com • www.inchmurrin-lochlomond.com

---

Visit
www.holidayguides.com
for convenient accommodation
when playing golf around the regions

ROTHESAY. **Port Bannatyne Golf Club,** Bannatyne Mains Road, Port Bannatyne PA20 0PH (01700 504544). *Location:* two miles north of Rothesay (ferry terminal). Hill course overlooking bays and sea lochs. 13 holes, 5085 yards, S.S.S. 65. *Green Fees:* information not available. *Eating facilities:* can be arranged in new clubhouse. *Visitors:* welcome – almost unrestricted. *Society Meetings:* very welcome. Secretary: A. Stevenson (01700 504872).

ROTHESAY. **Rothesay Golf Club,** Canada Hill, Rothesay PA20 0PG. *Location:* Beautiful island in the Firth of Clyde, frequent ferries from Wemyss Bay, 35 miles south-west of Glasgow, and from Colintraive in mainland Argyll. One of Scotland's most scenic island courses, designed by James Braid and Ben Sayers. 18 holes, 5456 yards. S.S.S. 67. Practice area. *Green Fees:* information not available. *Eating facilities:* full catering and bar facilities. *Visitors:* welcome, but prior booking at weekends through Professional. *Society Meetings:* welcome by arrangement. PGA Professional: James M. Dougal (Tel & Fax: 01700 503554).*
website: www.rothesaygolfclub.co.uk

SOUTHEND. **Dunaverty Golf Club,** Southend, Campbeltown PA28 6RW (Tel & Fax: 01586 830677). *Location:* about 10 miles south of Campbeltown on B842. Scenic seaside course with great views to Ireland and Mull of Kintyre. 18 holes, 4799 yards. S.S.S. 63. Small practice ground. *Green Fees:* weekday £25.00 per round, £38.00 per day; weekend £28.00 per round, £40.00 per day; weekly ticket £85.00; two weeks £120.00. *Eating facilities:* snacks, teas/coffees, meals by arrangement; no bar. *Visitors:* welcome, phone if visiting at weekends. Clubs and trolleys for hire. *Society Meetings:* welcome, phone or write to N. Hind for bookings. Steward: J Cooper.
website: www.dunavertygolfclub.com

TARBERT. **Tarbert Golf Club,** Kilberry Road, Tarbert PA29 6XX (01880 820565). *Location:* approximately one mile south of Tarbert on B8024. Hilly wooded parkland. 9 holes, 4460 yards. S.S.S. 63. *Green Fees:* £15.00 per day. *Eating facilities:* licensed clubhouse, open weekends. *Visitors:* welcome at all times. *Society Meetings:* by arrangement. Secretary: Peter Cupples (01546 606896).

TAYNUILT. **Taynuilt Golf Club,** Taynuilt PA35 1JE (01866 822429). *Location:* 12 miles from Oban on A85, quarter of a mile through the village from the main road. Situated in a scenic and majestic location, surrounded by mountains and overlooking picturesque Loch Etive. The challenging 9 hole course of undulating parkland is dominated by Ben Cruachan. 9 Holes, 4510 yards. S.S.S.63 (men), 67 (ladies). *Green Fees:* £16.00. See green fee deals on website. *Eating facilities:* not available - two hotels and a tearoom nearby. *Visitors:* welcome every day, some restrictions Tuesdays and Sundays for club competitions. Toilet facilities available. *Society Meetings:* welcome. Secretary: Jeremy Church (01631 770633).
e-mail: jeremy.church@virgin.net
website: www.taynuiltgolfclub.co.uk

TIGHNABRUAICH. **Kyles Of Bute Golf Club,** The Moss, Kames, Tighnabruaich PA21 2AB. *Location:* access from Dunoon and Strachur. Clubhouse by Kames Farm, turn south off B8000 Kames to Millhouse road. Hillside course with magnificent views. 9 holes, 4778 yards. S.S.S. 64. *Green Fees:* 9 holes £10.00, £15.00 per day. *Eating facilities:* no bar. *Visitors:* welcome, except Sunday mornings. *Society Meetings:* by special arrangement. Secretary: Dr Jeremy Thomson (01700 811603).

TAYNUILT GOLF CLUB
TAYNUILT, ARGYLL PA35 1JE

Situated in a scenic and majestic location, Taynuilt Golf Course is surrounded by mountains and overlooks the picturesque Loch Etive. Dominated by Ben Cruachan at 3695 feet, the challenging 9-hole course of undulating parkland was founded in 1987 and officially opened by Michael Bonallack of the R&A in 1991.

Tel: 01866 822 429 • www.taynuiltgolfclub.co.uk

Ayrshire & Arran

AYR. **Belleisle Golf Course,** Doonfoot Road, Ayr KA7 4DU (01292 441258). *Location:* follow main road south through Ayr. Gently sloping parkland course with fine mature trees. 18 holes, 6477 yards. S.S.S. 72. Practice area. *Green Fees:* information not available. *Eating facilities:* hotel and bars with catering. *Visitors:* no restrictions but booking in advance advisable. Juniors under 17 must have handicap of 12 or under. *Society Meetings:* catered for, groups up to 40; groups over 40 by special application. Professional: David Gemmell (Tel & Fax: 01292 441314). Starter: Alan Thomson (01292 441258; Fax: 01292 442632).*

AYR. **Dalmilling Golf Course,** Westwood Avenue, Ayr KA8 0QR (01292 263893; Fax: 01292 610543). *Location:* A77, on north-east boundary, one mile from town centre. Parkland. 18 holes, 5724 yards. S.S.S. 68. Putting green. *Green Fees:* information not available. *Eating facilities:* snacks/lunches/high teas, table licence. *Visitors:* welcome, not before 9.30am weekends, telephone to ensure availability. *Society Meetings:* welcome by arrangement. Professional: Philip Cheyney. Secretary: George Campbell (01292 521351).*

e-mail: eglintonguesthouse@yahoo.co.uk
www.eglintonguesthouse.com

Situated within a part of Ayr steeped in history, within a few minutes' walk of the beach, town centre and many other amenities. Golf, swimming pool, cycling, tennis, sailing, windsurfing, walking, fishing all available nearby; Prestwick Airport only three miles away.
Family, double and single rooms, all with washbasins, colour TV and tea/coffee making facilities. En suite facilities and cots available on request. Open all year round. B&B from £27.

**Peter & Julia Clark, Eglinton Guest House,
23 Eglinton Terrace, Ayr KA7 1JJ • Tel/Fax: 01292 264623**

Largs Golf Club, Largs

AYR. **Seafield Golf Course,** Doonfoot Road, Ayr KA7 4DU (01292 441258). *Location:* follow main road south through Ayr. Parkland and links, gently sloping. 18 holes, 5498 yards. S.S.S. 66. *Green Fees:* information not available. *Eating facilities:* hotel and bars with catering. *Visitors:* welcome, no restrictions but booking in advance advisable. *Society Meetings:* catered for, groups up to 40; groups over 40 by special application. Professional: David Gemmell (Tel & Fax: 01292 441314). Starter: Alan Thomson (01292 441258; Fax: 01292 442632).*

BEITH. **Beith Golf Club,** Threepwood Road, Beith KA15 2JR (01505 503166). *Location:* first left off Beith bypass road travelling south. Hilly parkland course with trees and gorse. 18 holes, 5616 yards. S.S.S. 68. *Green Fees:* available on request. *Eating facilities:* snacks and meals available. *Visitors:* welcome. Restrictions as follows: Tuesday 4.30pm to 6.30pm. Saturday 7am to 2pm. Sunday 1pm to 2.30pm. *Society Meetings:* welcome by prior arrangement. Secretary: Margaret Murphy (Tel & Fax: 01505 506814).

DAILLY. **Brunston Castle Golf Course,** Dailly, Girvan KA26 9GD (01465 811471). *Location:* 18 hole championship course in most scenic part of Ayrshire, five miles north of Girvan on B471, five miles from Turnberry. *Green Fees*: information not available. *Eating facilities:* full bar and restaurant facilities. *Visitors:* welcome 7 days a week. 16-seater minibus and trailer available. On-line booking available. Professional: Stuart Smith (01465 811825).*
e-mail: golf@brunstoncastle.co.uk
        sjsgolfsales@aol.com
website: www.brunstoncastle.co.uk

GALSTON. **Loudoun Gowf Club,** Galston KA4 8PA (01563 821993). *Location*: five miles east of Kilmarnock on A71. Fairly flat wooded parkland. 18 holes, 6005 yards. S.S.S. 69. *Green Fees*: information not available. *Eating facilities*: full catering and bar. *Visitors*: welcome weekdays only. Trolleys and buggies available for hire. *Society Meetings*: welcome by arrangement. Secretary: (01563 821993; Fax: 01563 820011).*
e-mail: secy@loudoungowfclub.co.uk
website: www.loudoungowfclub.co.uk

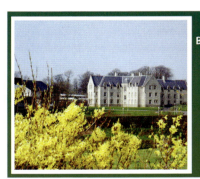

Golfing in Ayrshire?

Budget accommodation available July to September incl.
Choice of 40 golf courses, including three
Open Championship courses.
Single and twin rooms available
B&B with full Scottish breakfast £22pppn

Contact: Lorna Cunningham
SAC Auchincruive, AYR KA6 5HW
Tel: 01292 525203
Fax: 01292 525207
e-mail: lorna.Cunningham@sac.co.uk
www.sac.ac.uk/holidayletsayr

★ Abbotsford Hotel ★

A friendly, family-owned hotel situated 10 minutes from the town centre, close to Belleisle, Seafield, Turnberry, Troon and Prestwick golf courses. Tee-off times can be arranged. The hotel has been skilfully converted from a 19th century house and offers a pleasantly warm, relaxing and informal atmosphere. Open fires. The double, single and family rooms are all en suite and have satellite TV and tea/coffee makers. The fully licensed Scottish restaurant serves the best of local produce, and there is a conservatory and beer garden to the rear.
Open all year. Single from £39; Double/twin/family from £75.

www.abbotsfordhotel.co.uk
e-mail: info@abbotsfordhotel.co.uk

14 Corsehill Road, Ayr KA7 2ST
Tel: 01292 261506
Top Rating on tripadvisor.co.uk

GIRVAN. **Girvan Golf Course,** 40 Golf Course Road, Girvan, KA26 9HW (01465 714346). *Location:* A77 from Glasgow, through Ayr, on coast road to Stranraer, off A77 north of Harbour. 8 holes seaside, 10 holes parkland. 18 holes, 5064 yards. S.S.S. 64. Practice area. *Green Fees:* information not provided. *Eating facilities:* full catering available in clubhouse. *Visitors:* welcome, no restrictions except when course closed for local competitions (approximately 4 per year). *Society Meetings:* welcome, book through Starter. Secretary: W.B. Tait.

IRVINE. **Glasgow Golf Club,** Gailes Links, Irvine KA11 5AE (01294 311258; Fax: 01294 279366). *Location:* eight miles from Kilmarnock, two miles south of Irvine, four miles north of Troon. Championship links course with heather lined fairways. 18 holes, 6535 yards. S.S.S. 72, Par 71. Practice ground. *Green Fees:* information not available. *Eating facilities:* full catering and bar facilities. *Visitors:* welcome weekdays 8.30am-4.30pm, weekend afternoons. Prior booking recommended through the Secretary. Caddy cars/buggies for hire, caddies by arrangement. *Society Meetings:* by application to Managing Secretary. Professional: John Greaves (01294 311561). Managing Secretary: P. G. McMillan (0141-942 2011; Fax: 0141-942 0770).*
e-mail: secretary@glasgow-golf.com
website: www.glasgowgailes-golf.com

IRVINE. **The Irvine Golf Club,** Bogside, Irvine KA12 8SN (01294 275979). *Location:* through Irvine going towards Kilwinning, turn left at Ravenspark Academy. Flat links course. 18 holes, 6408 yards. S.S.S. 72. Practice ground. *Green Fees:* information not provided. *Eating facilities:* dining room and bars. *Visitors:* welcome, after 3pm weekends. *Society Meetings:* welcome. Professional: J. McKinnon (01294 275626). Secretary: W.J. McMahon (01294 275979).

Please mention THE GOLF GUIDE when you enquire about clubs or accommodation

IRVINE. **Irvine Ravenspark Golf Club,** 13 Kidsneuk Lane, Irvine KA12 8SR (01294 271293). *Location:* on A78 between Irvine and Kilwinning at Irvine Royal Academy. Flat parkland course. 18 holes, 6453 yards. S.S.S. 71. *Green Fees:* information not available. *Eating facilities:* diningroom, bar. *Visitors:* welcome, except on Saturdays before 2.30pm March to October. No jeans or training shoes allowed in the clubhouse. *Society Meetings:* welcome, by arrangement weekends. Professional: P. Bond (01294 276467). Secretary: S. Howie (01294 553904). Steward: J. McVay (01294 271293).*
e-mail: secretary@irgc.co.uk
website: www.irgc.co.uk

IRVINE. **Roseholm Golf Course**, 46 Annick Road, Irvine KA11 4LD (Menzies Irvine Hotel Tel: 01294 274272; Fax: 01294 277289). *Location:* course is situated on the grounds of the Menzies Irvine Hotel. Flat parkland. 9-hole Junior course, 1277 yards. *Green Fees:* information not available. Golf free to hotel guests. Club hire for hotel guests. *Eating facilities:* lunches, snacks, tea and coffee served in the hotel bar. *Visitors:* welcome all year.*
e-mail: irvine@menzieshotels.co.uk
website: www.menzieshotels.co.uk

IRVINE. **Western Gailes Golf Club,** Gailes, By Irvine KA11 5AE (01294 311649; Fax: 01294 312312). *Location:* three miles north of Troon. Seaside links. 18 holes, 6639 yards, 6179 (yellow tees). S.S.S. 74. Par 71. Limited practice facilities. *Green Fees:* weekdays £115.00 per round, £165.00 per day, both include lunch; Sunday after 2pm £125.00 per round (lunch not included). 2010 rates (subject to review). *Eating facilities:* full bar and catering facilities. *Visitors:* welcome Mondays, Wednesdays and Fridays and Sunday afternoons; limited availability Saturday twilight golf. Advance booking required, telephone Reservations Department, Lyn or Vicky (01294 311649). Caddies and trolleys available for hire. *Society Meetings:* welcome by arrangement with Secretary. Secretary: Barry J. Knowles.
e-mail: enquiries@westerngailes.com

LOUDOUN GOWF CLUB
"Gowfing" for over 400 years

**Loudoun Gowf Club (Founded 1909)
Newmilns Road, Galston, Ayrshire KA4 8PA**
This privately owned course is a fairly flat parkland course with picturesque tree-lined fairways set in the Irvine Valley midway between Newmilns and Galston.
Visiting parties welcome except at weekends.
Parties must pre-book. Course 6005 yards, Par: 68, S.S.S: 69
Club Secretary: W. Barry Buchanan
**Telephone: Secretary 01563 821993 • Clubhouse 01563 821993
e-mail: secy@loudoungowfclub.co.uk • www.loudoungowfclub.co.uk**

KILBIRNIE. Kilbirnie Place Golf Club, Largs Road, Kilbirnie KA25 7AT (01505 683398). *Location:* on main Kilbirnie to Largs Road, left hand side just outside town boundary. Parkland. 18 holes, 5116 yards. S.S.S. 67. *Green Fees:* information not available. *Eating facilities:* catering and bar. *Visitors:* welcome weekdays and Sundays only, no visiting parties Saturdays. Secretary: C. McGurk (01505 684444/ 683398).*

KILMARNOCK. Annanhill Golf Club, Irvine Road, Kilmarnock KA1 2RT (01563 521644). *Location:* between Kilmarnock and Crosshouse on road to Irvine. Parkland course with excellent views and tree-lined fairways. 18 holes, 6285 yards. S.S.S. 70. Practice area. *Green Fees:* prices on request to Starter on (01563 521512). *Eating facilities:* full catering available on application. *Visitors:* no parties Saturdays, but welcome Sundays and weekdays by reservation. *Society Meetings:* catered for. Secretary: Thomas C. Denham (01563 521644).

KILMARNOCK. Caprington Golf Club, Ayr Road, Kilmarnock (01563 523702). Parkland/wooded course. 18 holes, 5810 yards. S.S.S. 68. *Green Fees:* information not available. *Eating facilities:* available. *Visitors:* welcome except Saturdays. *Society Meetings:* all welcome. Secretary: Gordon Bray (01563 520566).*

LARGS. Largs Golf Club, Irvine Road, Largs KA30 8EU (01475 673594). *Location:* A78, one mile south of Largs town centre (opposite Marina). Parkland/ woodland with scenic views over Cumbraes and Isle of Arran. 18 holes, 6150 yards. S.S.S. 71. *Green Fees:* on request. *Eating facilities:* full catering and bar. *Visitors:* welcome, tee can be reserved one day ahead of play. *Society Meetings:* catered for by prior arrangement Tuesdays and Thursdays, Fridays between 9.30am and 11am and 2.30pm and 4pm. Professional: Andrew Fullen PGA (01475 686192). Secretary: Barry Streets (Tel & Fax: 01475 673594). e-mail: secretary@largsgolfclub.co.uk
website: www.largsgolfclub.co.uk

LARGS. Routenburn Golf Club, Routenburn Road, Largs KA30 8SQ (01475 686475). Hilly moorland course. 18 holes, 5765 yards. S.S.S. 67. *Green Fees:* information not available. *Eating facilities:* lunches at club except Thursdays, order in advance. *Visitors:* welcome. Parties welcome, contact Professional. Professional: Greig McQueen (01475 687240). Secretary: R.B. Connal.*

LARGS. sportscotland National Centre: Inverclyde, Bob Torrance School of Golf, Burnside Road, Largs KA30 8RW (01475 674666). *Location:* 40 minutes from Glasgow and Prestwick airports. Training bunkers, 4-hole practice area plus driving bays. *Green Fees:* information not provided. *Eating facilities:* cafeteria, dining room, accommodation and bar. *Visitors:* one and two day courses, booking essential. Professionals: Graham Ross, Gordon Sherry, Andrew MacPherson, Campbell Donaldson, Andy Fullan. Admin. Co-ordinator: Sandra Samuel. Manager: Angela Liddel.

LARGS GOLF CLUB
IRVINE ROAD, LARGS KA30 8EU

- Green fees on request.
- Package deals for 12 or more golfers
- Contact the Secretary for details

Largs Golf Club is a long-established private club with a superb 18 hole parkland course, situated in front of Kelburn Castle, one mile south of Largs town centre. From the clubhouse and course there are magnificent views of the Firth of Clyde towards the Cumbraes, Bute and the mountains of Arran.

The course is enduringly popular with visitors, who return regularly year after year. The well-balanced layout offers an interesting and challenging experience to golfers across the broad spectrum of enthusiasm and ability.

Tel/Fax: 01475 673594 • e-mail: secretary@largsgolfclub.co.uk • www.largsgolfclub.co.uk

Willowbank Hotel • Largs

A quality hotel offering excellent service.
All rooms en suite, with TV, phone and coffee facilities. Restaurant and lounge bar.
Ideally situated on Clyde coast, close to all amenities, golf, sailing etc. Open all year.

www.thewillowbankhotel.com

96 Greenock Road, Largs, Ayrshire KA30 8PG
Tel: 01475 672311 • Fax: 01475 689027
e-mail: iaincsmith@btconnect.com

Single £75
Double/Twin/Triple/Family £50-£60pp

THE GOLF GUIDE 2011   SCOTLAND / Ayrshire & Arran

MAUCHLINE. Ballochmyle Golf Club, Mauchline KA5 6LE (01290 550469; Fax: 01290 553657). *Location:* on B705 off A76, one mile south of Mauchline. Wooded parkland course. 18 holes, 5990 yards. S.S.S. 69. *Green Fees:* information not available. *Eating facilities:* all day bar opening from 1st April until 30th September, snacks and meals available during bar hours. *Visitors:* welcome every day except Saturdays. Dress regulations both on and off the course must be adhered to. Two full size snooker tables. *Society Meetings:* all welcome to a total of 30 per party. Secretary: R. Leslie Crawford (01290 550469).*
e-mail: secretary@ballochmylegolf.wanadoo.co.uk

MAYBOLE. Maybole Golf Course, Memorial Park, Kirkoswald Road, Maybole KA19 7DX (01292 612000). *Location:* A77 from Glasgow, on main Girvan road at Maybole. Hilly parkland. 9 holes, 2635 yards. S.S.S. 33. *Green Fees:* information not available. *Visitors:* welcome. *Society Meetings:* welcome. Secretary: A. Ferguson. Starter (01655 889770).*

MUIRKIRK. Muirkirk Golf Club, "Southside", Furnace Road, Muirkirk KA18 3RE. *Location:* 10 miles off A74 on A70 to Ayr. Picturesque country scenery, the course nestles amongst heather clad hills. 9 holes, 5380 yards. S.S.S. 67. *Green Fees:* £10.00 per day. *Eating facilities:* can be accommodated. Secretary: Robert Bradford (01290 660184 night; 01292 570728 day).

NEW CUMNOCK. New Cumnock Golf Club, 55 Pathhead, New Cumnock KA18 4DQ (01290 338000). *Location:* A76, one mile west of New Cumnock. Parkland, protected area for wildlife birds, next to loch. 9 holes, 5176 yards (18). S.S.S. 66. *Green Fees:* information not available. *Eating facilities:* Lochside House Hotel sits on the edge of the course. *Visitors:* welcome at all times except Sunday up to 4pm for competitions. Clubhouse. *Society Meetings:* welcome. Secretary: John McGinn (01290 338000).*

PATNA. Doon Valley Golf Club, Hillside, Patna KA6 7JT (01292 531607). *Location:* 10 miles south of Ayr on the A713 Ayr to Castle Douglas road. Undulating hillside parkland course. 9 holes, 5859 yards, 5402 metres. S.S.S. 70. *Green Fees:* weekdays £14.00 per round; weekends £16.00. *Eating facilities:* bar open weekdays 7pm to 11pm, weekends 12 noon to 12 midnight. *Visitors:* welcome anytime weekdays, weekends by arrangement. *Society Meetings:* welcome, groups of more than six must apply for tee off times. Secretary: Hugh Johnstone MBE (01292 550411).

PRESTWICK. Prestwick Golf Club, Links Road, Prestwick KA9 1QG (01292 477404). *Location:* one mile from Prestwick airport, 40 minutes by car from Turnberry Hotel, 10 minutes from Troon, 15 minutes from Ayr. 18 holes, 6544 yards. S.S.S. 73. *Green Fees:* information not available. *Eating facilities:* dining room (male only: prior booking required) open from 12.30pm to 2.30pm. Cardinal Room (light lunches) open to ladies and gentlemen from 10.00am until 3.30pm. *Visitors:* welcome with reservation. *Society Meetings:* catered for. Professional: D. A. Fleming. Secretary: I.T. Bunch (01292 477404; Fax: 01292 477255).*
e-mail: secretary@prestwickgc.co.uk
website: www.prestwickgc.co.uk

Enjoy a round of golf in the heart of Burns' Country

BALLOCHMYLE GOLF CLUB

- Visitors & Societies welcome
- 2 for 1 tee-off times
- Corporate Days available
- Catering and Bar with Games Room

Ballochmyle Golf Club, Mauchline, Ayrshire KA5 6LE
Tel: 01290 550469 • ballochmylegolf@btconnect.com
www.ballochmylegolfclub.co.uk

A terraced guest house in a conservation area, tastefully refurbished providing quality surroundings and a relaxed atmosphere.
Centrally located, close to the seafront, shops, restaurants and local amenities.
Near Prestwick Airport and easily accessible from both Glasgow and the south.
Single, twin, double and family rooms available with en suite or private facilities.
Relax with comfortable beds, TV/DVD, tea/coffee, hairdryers, ironing facilities and wireless internet connection in rooms. Enjoy a wide and varied choice on the breakfast menu.
Local attractions include Robert Burns' Cottage, Culzean Castle, Ayr Racecourse and over 30 golf courses, including Turnberry, Old Prestwick and Royal Troon. Esplanade and children's play area within a few yards. Amenities for all ages.
You are assured of a warm Scottish welcome and a pleasant stay.
A quality self-catering apartment is also available which sleeps 5 persons.

Burnside Guest House
14 Queens Terrace Ayr KA7 1DU
Tel: +44 (0)1292 263912
liz@theburnsideguesthouse.co.uk
www.theburnsideguesthouse.co.uk

The Carlton Hotel

187 Ayr Road, Prestwick KA9 1TP
(near to Prestwick Airport)

Ideally situated for Ayrshire's finest golf courses and only a five minute drive from Prestwick International Airport.

- Modern en suite bedrooms
- Restaurant and Bar facilities including Logan's Restaurant and Ayrshire's finest Carvery Restaurant
- Conference and Banqueting Facilities
- Free WiFi access throughout

Championship Courses on offer within the area include:

- Prestwick Old Course
- Royal Troon
- Turnberry

Tel: 01292 476811 • e-mail: reception@carlton-prestwick.com
www.carlton-prestwick.com

Prestwick St Cuthbert Golf Club

A warm welcome awaits you at Prestwick St Cuthbert Golf Club.

secretary@stcuthbert.co.uk
www.stcuthbert.co.uk

Visitors play the Yellow Course which has a Par of 70. With cunningly sloped greens and no fewer than nine doglegs, accuracy in positioning from the tee is as important as length. Full bar and restaurant facilities; buggies and caddy carts for hire.

"Top class provision for visitors, a great golfing experience"

East Road, Prestwick, Ayrshire KA9 2SX
Tel: 01292 477 101 • Fax: 01292 671 730

Prestwick St Nicholas Golf Club

Grangemuir Road
Prestwick KA9 1SN

This true links course, which counts 'Old' Tom Morris as a founder member, was described by Henry Cotton as "a smaller edition of the best championship courses we possess". The high quality of the course remains true today, evidenced by the Club having being invited to host various professional and amateur competitions, including in 2009 a Young Professionals' Tournament, and the final of the Scottish Club Championship.

Tel: 01292 477608
Fax: 01292 437900
e-mail: secretary@prestwickstnicholas.com
www.prestwickstnicholas.com

PRESTWICK. **Prestwick St Cuthbert Golf Club,** East Road, Prestwick KA9 2SX (01292 477101; Fax: 01292 671730). *Location:* south-east area of Prestwick near A77 Whitletts roundabout, follow signs for Heathfield and Prestwick Airport. Flat parkland. 18 holes, 6470 yards, 6063 metres. S.S.S. 71. Limited practice area. *Green Fees:* £35.00, day ticket £48.00. *Eating facilities:* bar and restaurant. *Visitors:* welcome except Saturdays unless introduced by and playing with member. Buggies and caddy carts for hire. *Society Meetings:* catered for. Secretary: Jim Jess (01292 477101).
e-mail: secretary@stcuthbert.co.uk
website: www.stcuthbert.co.uk

PRESTWICK. **Prestwick St Nicholas Golf Club,** Grangemuir Road, Prestwick KA9 1SN (01292 477608; Fax: 01292 473900). *Location:* Grangemuir Road is half a mile from town centre on Prestwick to Ayr Road. Traditional links course enjoying wonderful panoramic views across Firth of Clyde to island of Arran. 18 holes, 6044 yards, 5526 metres. S.S.S. 69. *Green Fees:* weekdays £55.00 per round, weekend £60.00 per round. Weekday day ticket £75.00. 2010 rates (subject to review). *Eating facilities:* full service. *Visitors:* welcome most weekdays and weekend afternoons. *Society Meetings:* welcome by arrangement. Secretary: Tom Hepburn (01292 477608; Fax: 01292 473900).
e-mail: secretary@prestwickstnicholas.com
website: www.prestwickstnicholas.com

SKELMORLIE. **Skelmorlie Golf Club,** Beithglass Road, Skelmorlie PA17 5ES (01475 520152). *Location:* two miles from Wemyss Bay Pier. Hillside, moorland course. 18 holes, 5030 yards. S.S.S. 65. *Green Fees:* weekdays £22.00 per round, £27.00 per day; weekends £27.00 per round, £32.00 per round. 2010 rates (subject to review). *Eating facilities:* bar 11am to 10 pm, catering by arrangement. *Visitors:* welcome except Saturdays before 3pm. *Society Meetings:* welcome by arrangement. Parties at discounted "all-in" rate. Secretary: Mrs E. Linton (01475 522626).

STEVENSTON. **Ardeer Golf Club,** Greenhead, Stevenston KA20 4JX (01294 464542). *Location:* north of Ayr, six miles from Irvine New Town, off A78. Parkland course lined with trees incorporating water on several holes. 18 holes, 6409 yards. S.S.S. 71. *Green Fees:* on application. *Eating facilities:* restaurant and bars. *Visitors:* welcome except Saturdays before 3pm, check for availability. *Society Meetings:* special rates available for groups of 12 or more. Secretary: Peter Watson (Tel & Fax: 01294 464542).

STEVENSTON. **Moorpark Golf Club,** Auchenharvie Golf Complex, Moorpark Road West, Stevenston KA20 3HU. *Location:* on the A738 Stevenston/ Saltcoats; five miles from Irvine, 20 miles from Glasgow. Flat parkland course with water feature incorporated into two holes. 18 holes, 5203 yards. S.S.S. 66. 18 bay floodlit driving range. *Green Fees:* information not available. *Eating facilities:* privately owned lounge bar within complex open to public, bar meals, functions, snacks available (01294 469051). *Visitors:* welcome, restrictions when there are club competitions. *Society Meetings:* all welcome. The course is situated right next door to Sandylands Caravan Park and there are plenty of other golf courses to play all within easy reach. Secretary: R. Paterson (01294 602493).*

TROON. **Kilmarnock (Barassie) Golf Club,** 29 Hillhouse Road, Barassie, Troon KA10 6SY (01292 313920; Fax: 01292 318300). *Location:* two miles north of Troon. Links course. 27 holes: Barassie Links 18 holes, 6484 yards. S.S.S. 74; Hillhouse 9 holes, 2888 yards, par 34. Practice ground. *Green Fees:* weekdays £57.00 per round, £82.00 per day; Sundays £67.00 per round. 2010 rates (subject to review). *Eating facilities:* coffee, lunches, snacks, high teas. *Visitors:* welcome Mondays, Tuesdays, Thursdays and Friday afternoons; limited visitors Wednesdays; Sundays after 2.30pm. Check website for details. All visitors must adhere to club dress code – no denim, trainers, etc. *Society Meetings:* catered for Tuesdays and Thursdays. Professional: Gregor Howie (Tel & Fax: 01292 311322). Secretary: Donald D. Wilson (01292 313920/311077).
e-mail: golfkbgc@lineone.net
website: www.kbgc.co.uk

TROON. **Troon Municipal Golf Courses,** Harling Drive, Troon (01292 312464). *Location:* adjacent to railway station, one mile off the Ayr-Glasgow road. Three 18 hole courses. Lochgreen 6820 yards. S.S.S. 73. Darley 6360 yards. S.S.S. 72. Fullarton 4870 yards. S.S.S. 63. *Green Fees:* information not available. *Eating facilities:* hot snacks, 8am - 6pm. Bar snacks and lunches, evening meals bookings only. *Visitors:* catered for. Broad wheeled trolleys only. *Society Meetings:* catered for. Caterer: John Darge. Professional: Gordon McKinley. Advance booking should be made in writing to Starter's Office, Troon Municipal Golf Courses, Harling Drive, Troon, Ayrshire (Fax: 01292 312578). Special short breaks and day tickets available, for details telephone 01292 616270.*

TROON. **Royal Troon Golf Club,** Craigend Road, Troon KA10 6EP (01292 311555; Fax: 01292 318204). *Location:* three miles from A77 (Glasgow/Ayr trunk road). Old Course (Championship) 18 holes, 6493 metres, 7101 yards. S.S.S. 74. Portland Course 18 holes, 5751 metres, 6289 yards. S.S.S. 71. *Green Fees:* on request. *Eating facilities:* full restaurant service available, including bar snacks. *Visitors:* Mondays, Tuesdays and Thursdays between 9.30 and 11.00am and 14.30 to 16.00pm. Limited availability also on Sundays. Handicap Certificate required (maximum: Gents 20; Ladies 30). Golfers under 16 years not allowed. *Society Meetings:* parties in excess of 24 by special arrangement. Professional: Kieron Stevenson (01292 313281). Manager: Niall Thompson (01292 311555; Fax: 01292 318204).
e-mail: bookings@royaltroon.com
website: www.royaltroon.com

TURNBERRY. **Turnberry, A Luxury Collection Resort, Scotland,** Maidens Road, Turnberry KA26 9LT (01655 331000; Fax: 01655 331706). *Location:* on main A77 between Maybole and Girvan. Two Championship Links Courses, The Ailsa (host to 4 British Opens) 18 holes, 6976 yards. S.S.S. 72; The Kintyre, 6376 yards. S.S.S. 72, and The Arran (9 holes). The Colin Montgomerie Links Golf Academy, putting greens. *Green Fees:* from £50.00. *Eating facilities:* clubhouse, restaurants and bars. *Visitors:* welcome every day. Accommodation at Turnberry, A Luxury Collection Resort, Scotland, 198 rooms. *Society Meetings:* contact Reservations. Director of Golf: Chris Card (01655 331000). Golf Reservations Team: (01655 334032).

WEST KILBRIDE. **The West Kilbride Golf Club,** 33-35 Fullerton Drive, Seamill, West Kilbride KA23 9HT (01294 823911; Fax: 01294 829573). *Location:* midway between Largs (to north) and Ardrossan (south) on A78. Seaside links course with magnificent views to Isle of Arran and Cumbraes across Firth of Clyde. 18 holes, 6452 yards, 5898 metres. S.S.S. 71. Practice area, putting greens. *Green Fees:* on application. *Eating facilities:* bar, lounge, dining room. *Visitors:* welcome weekdays only. Caddy cars for hire. *Society Meetings:* catered for Tuesdays and Thursdays. Handicap Certificates required. Professional: Iain Darroch (01294 823042). Secretary: John Campbell (01294 823911).
website: www.westkilbridegolfclub.com

South Beach Hotel
Troon, Ayrshire KA10 6EG
Tel: 01292 312033 • Fax: 01292 318438
e-mail: info@southbeach.co.uk
www.southbeach.co.uk

★ Privately-owned hotel, facing the sea.
★ Easy reach of 15 quality courses. ★ Golf club store and drying facilities. ★ Can arrange golf to suit your requirements. ★ 32 en suite bedrooms (suites available). ★ Enjoy your golf break in a happy, friendly atmosphere. ★ Phone for details.

West Kilbride Golf Club

The West Kilbride Golf Club 18 hole championship links course is set on the beautiful Ayrshire coast, with breathtaking views of the Isle of Arran and is only 30 minutes' drive from Royal Troon and Turnberry courses. Green fees on application. Visitors welcome Mondays-Fridays. Groups and Societies welcome Tuesdays and Thursdays. Excellent catering and well stocked bar.

The West Kilbride Golf Club, 33-35 Fullerton Drive, Seamill, West Kilbride, Ayrshire KA23 9HT
Tel: 01294 823911 • www.westkilbridegolfclub.com

Isle of Arran

BLACKWATERFOOT. **Shiskine Golf and Tennis Club,** Blackwaterfoot, Shiskine, Isle of Arran KA27 8HA (01770 860226. Fax: 01770 860205). *Location:* off B880 at Blackwaterfoot. Seaside links with outstanding views. 12 holes, 2990 yards. S.S.S. 42. Putting green, nets. *Green Fees:* weekdays £20.00 per round, £33.00 per day; weekends £25.00 per round, £38.00 per day. Special rates: Week £118.00, Fortnight £174.00. 2010 fees (subject to review). Maximum of two rounds per day. *Eating facilities:* new clubhouse, snacks, lunches, high teas, dinner. *Visitors:* welcome, preferably with Club Handicap. July and August are very busy so prefer visitors September to June. Tennis and bowls. Pro Shop and lessons, all year. *Society Meetings:* only if pre-booked with Match Secretary. Proof of Handicap required. Club Secretary: Pietre Johnston. Golf Manager/PGA Professional: Douglas Bell.
e-mail: info@shiskinegolf.com
website: www.shiskinegolf.com

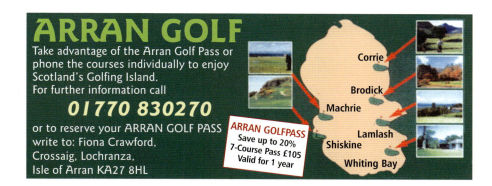

378 Ayrshire & Arran / SCOTLAND — THE GOLF GUIDE 2011

BRODICK. **Brodick Golf Club,** Brodick KA27 8DL (Tel & Fax: 01770 302349). *Location:* one mile north of pier. Flat seaside course. 18 holes, 4736 yards. S.S.S. 64. Practice area. *Green Fees:* information not available. *Eating facilities:* bar snacks available. *Visitors:* welcome without restriction. *Society Meetings:* welcome with reservation by letter. Professional: P.S. McCalla (01770 302513). Secretary: Douglas Robertson (Tel & Fax: 01770 302349).*

CORRIE. **Corrie Golf Club,** Sannox, Corrie KA27 8JD (01770 810223). *Location:* seven miles north of Brodick. Short 9 hole course, full of character and very picturesque with some magnificent views. 9 holes, 1948 yards. S.S.S. 61. *Green Fees:* £20.00 per day ticket; twilight ticket £10.00. *Eating facilities:* meals available 9am to 6pm April to October. *Visitors:* welcome, course closed Saturday afternoons. *Society Meetings:* catered for by arrangement (maximum number 12). Secretary: G. Murray (01770 810 652).

LAMLASH. **Lamlash Golf Club,** Lamlash KA27 8JU (Tel & Fax: 01770 600296). *Location:* A841, three miles south of Brodick Pier ferry terminal. Undulating heathland course. 18 holes, 4640 yards. S.S.S. 64. *Green Fees:* weekdays £22.00 per day; weekends £28.00. After 4pm any day £15.00 per round. Reductions for Senior Citizens. 2010 rates (subject to review). *Eating facilities:* catering, lounge bar. *Visitors:* welcome, no restrictions. Pro shop: (01770 600196). Carts/buggies for hire. *Society Meetings:* welcome, book in advance by letter. Secretary: J. Henderson (01770 600272). Starter: (01779 600196).website: www.lamlashgolfclub.co.uk

LOCHRANZA. **Lochranza Golf,** Isle of Arran KA27 8HL (01770 830273). *Location:* Lochranza village. A special 'pay & play' golf course in spectacular setting with extensive wildlife. Very interesting challenging layout, fun for everyone. All Handicaps may play medal tees. 18 holes from 18 tees to 12 greens (6 double, 6 single), 5470 yards, 5033 metres. Par 70. *Green Fees:* £18.00 per round. 4-ball £60.00 (£15.00 each). Season (May to October) £100.00. *Visitors:* welcome daily May to October incl. Proprietor: Nigel Wells.
e-mail: office@lochgolf.demon.co.uk
website: www.lochranzagolf.com

MACHRIE. **Machrie Bay Golf Course,** Machrie, Near Brodick KA27 8DZ (01770 840329). *Location:* on A841, three and a half miles north of Blackwaterfoot. Flat seaside course. 9 holes, 2200 yards. S.S.S. 32. Putting green and small practice area. *Green Fees:* £16.00 per day, under 17s £8.00. 2010 rates (subject to review). *Eating facilities:* tea room, snacks/meals; no licence. *Visitors:* welcome anytime. *Society Meetings:* by arrangement. Secretary: E. Ross. website: www.machriebay.com

WHITING BAY. **Whiting Bay Golf Club,** Golf Course Road, Whiting Bay, Brodick KA27 8QT (01770 700487). *Location:* eight miles south of Brodick. Undulating parkland. 18 holes, 4405 yards. S.S.S. 63. Practice net. *Green Fees:* information not provided. *Eating facilities:* catering and bar. *Visitors:* welcome anytime. Clubhouse, shower, snooker and pool rooms; buggies and caddy cars for hire. *Society Meetings:* by prior booking. Secretary: Margaret Auld (01770 820208).

This comfortable guest house is set in delightful gardens in beautiful countryside. Guests can relax in the lounge with its attractive garden views. There is one twin room, two double rooms, two family rooms (double and single bed with the possibility to add an extra bed or baby cot), and one triple room. All rooms have pleasing colour schemes and are en suite (the twin room has a private bathroom opposite). In a peaceful location, Allandale is convenient for the CalMac Ferry and Brodick centre.

Allandale House

Corriegills Road, Brodick, Isle of Arran KA27 8BJ
Telephone: 01770 302278
e-mail: info@allandalehouse.co.uk
www.allandalehouse.co.uk

Play golf at nearby Brodick Golf Club

Looking for accommodation near golf clubs?, then visit www.holidayguides.com for where to stay when playing golf around the regions

Borders

ASHKIRK. **Woll Golf Course,** New Woll Estate, Selkirk TD7 4PE (01750 32711). *Location:* through the village of Ashkirk, just off the A7 and only an hour from Edinburgh, Newcastle and Carlisle. Challenging course in natural parkland setting of outstanding beauty incorporating the Woll Burn and other water features. Flat course. 18 holes, 6051 yards, S.S.S. 70. *Green Fees:* £28.00. *Eating facilities:* full clubhouse facilities available; bar, restaurant and function suite all year round. *Visitors:* most welcome at all times. Luxury self-catering accommodation available on the course, including free golf.
e-mail: wollgolf@btinternet.com
website: www.wollgolf.co.uk

COLDSTREAM. **Hirsel Golf Club,** Kelso Road, Coldstream TD12 4NJ (01890 882678; Fax: 01890 882233). *Location:* A697 west end of Coldstream. Parkland. 18 holes, 6024 yards, 5570 metres. S.S.S. 70. Practice ground. *Green Fees:* information not available. *Eating facilities:* full catering all year. Snack catering November to mid-March. *Visitors:* welcome, no restrictions; groups of over 10 players must book in advance. Two person golf carts for hire (8). *Society Meetings:* catered for by arrangement.*
e-mail: bookings@hirselgc.co.uk
website: www.hirselgc.co.uk

DUNS. **Duns Golf Club,** Hardens Road, Duns TD11 3NR (01361 882194). *Location:* about one mile west of Duns just off A6105, signposted Longformacus. Upland, undulating course with view south to Cheviot Hills. A burn runs through the course and is the main hazard. 18 holes, 6298 yards. S.S.S. 70. Practice ground. New driving range 2 miles from golf course. *Green Fees:* information not available. *Eating facilities:* lounge bar open weekdays and weekends, light snacks and full catering available. *Visitors:* welcome at all times except during club competitions, visitors must tee off before 4pm Mondays, Tuesdays and Wednesdays. *Society Meetings:* welcome, booking through Clubhouse (01361 882194). Club Manager: Graham Clark (01361 883599).*

EYEMOUTH. **Eyemouth Golf Club,** Gunsgreenhill, Eyemouth TD14 5SF (018907 50004). *Location:* eight miles north of Berwick-on-Tweed, one mile off the A1. Superb cliff-top course with spectacular sea views. Play the Par 3 - 6th hole over a vast gully, with crashing waves below. Recently voted "Britain's most extraordinary Golf Hole'. 18 holes, 6520 yards, Par 72. Practice area. *Green Fees:* weekdays £28.00 per round, £38.00 per day; weekends £33.00 per round, £43.00 per day. Winter: £14.00 per round weekdays, £16.50 per round weekends. *Eating facilities:* full catering facilities with the `Bay View' restaurant specializing in local sea food. *Visitors:* very welcome, phone Professional for booking. Games room, changing rooms, showers. *Society Meetings:* golfing groups and society packages very welcome. Professional: Michael Hackett (018907 50004). Secretary: Mrs M. Gibson (018907 50551).

GALASHIELS. **Galashiels Golf Club,** Ladhope Recreation Ground, Galashiels TD1 2NJ (01896 753724). *Location*: north end of town, quarter of a mile off A7 on Ladhope Drive. New 9-hole undulating parkland course. 5424 yards. Par 68. *Green Fees*: 9 holes £10.00, 18 holes £20.00, 27 holes £25.00, 36 holes £30.00. Package deals available for parties on application. *Eating facilities*: catering by arrangement only. *Visitors*: welcome anytime, booking essential for weekends. Contact: (01896 753724 or 01896 755525 after 1pm).

THE APPEARANCE OF AN ASTERISK (*) AT THE END OF A CLUB OR COURSE ENTRY INDICATES THAT UP-TO-DATE INFORMATION HAS NOT BEEN SUPPLIED

Hirsel Golf Club — Coldstream

The First and Last course in Scotland. A parkland course of great natural beauty and breathtaking views of the Cheviot Hills and surrounding countryside. Nestling in the beautiful and historic Scottish Borders. 18 very different holes designed to make the most of the hills, valleys and natural hazards. Recently voted "The Friendliest Course in the Borders", you are assured of a warm welcome from our members. Excellent bar and restaurant facilities. Golf societies welcome.

Hirsel Golf Club, Kelso Road, Coldstream TD12 4NJ Tel: 01890 882678
e-mail: bookings@hirselgc.co.uk • www.hirselgc.co.uk

380 Borders / SCOTLAND

THE GOLF GUIDE 2011

18 holes, 6021 yards, par 69, SSS 70
- lunch • dinner • club bar • bar snacks
- tea and coffee • cart hire
- trolley hire • changing room

Situated just one mile north of Galashiels on the A7

Societies and visitors welcome • Contact Lorraine

"Freedom of the Fairways" Favourite Course

Torwoodlee GOLF CLUB

Edinburgh Road, Galashiels TD1 2NE • Tel: 01896 752260
e-mail: torwoodleegolfclub@btconnect.com • www.torwoodleegolfclub.org.uk

---

Situated at the gateway to the Scottish Borders, Jedburgh Golf Club is a must for any golfer visiting the area. The original 9-hole layout, established in 1892, was extended to 18 holes in 2006. The new layout has been well received by visitors and members alike. The parkland/moorland layout provides an enjoyable challenge to golfers of all abilities. Accuracy and course management will be rewarded, especially on the shorter par 4 holes. The golfing experience, allied to stunning views of the surrounding countryside, will ensure visitors have a memorable stay and will return year after year. Further details on the club's website **www.jedburghgolfclub.co.uk**

Jedburgh Golf Club

5819 yards ♦ Full catering facilities ♦ Green fees £25/£30 ♦ Buggy & trolley hire

Dunion Road, Jedburgh TD8 6TA • All enquiries please phone 01835 863587 •

GALASHIELS. **Torwoodlee Golf Club,** Edinburgh Road, Galashiels TD1 2NE (01896 752260). *Location:* leave Galashiels on A7 for Edinburgh. Entrance to course one mile on left. Parkland with wooded greens alongside river and splendid par 5. Designed by Willie Park/John Garner. 18 holes, 6021 yards. S.S.S. 70. *Green Fees:* weekdays £30.00 per round, £40.00 per day; weekends £35.00 per round, £45.00 per day. 2010 rates (subject to review). *Eating facilities:* bar, dining room. *Visitors:* welcome except 8.30 to 9.30, 12.00 to 13.30 weekdays or 07.30 to 10.15, 12.15 to 15.00 and 16.15 to 17.00 Saturdays. Showers available. *Society Meetings:* bookings required in advance, packages available. Administrator: L. Moffat (01896 752260).
e-mail: torwoodleegolfclub@btconnect.com
website: www.torwoodleegolfclub.org.uk

HAWICK. **Hawick Golf Club,** Vertish Hill, Hawick TD9 0NY (01450 372293). *Location:* north along A7 from Carlisle or south on A7 from Edinburgh. Course situated half a mile south-west of town. Hill course with spectacular views. 18 holes, 5929 yards, 5422 metres. S.S.S. 69. Restricted practice area. *Green Fees:* information not provided. *Eating facilities:* full bar and catering daily. *Visitors:* welcome Saturdays and after 10am Sundays. *Society Meetings:* catered for, advisable to book in advance. Secretary: J. Reilly (01450 375594).
e-mail: thesecretary@hawickgolfclub.com
website: www.hawickgolfclub.com

HAWICK. **Minto Golf Club,** Denholm, Hawick TD9 8SA (01450 870220). *Location:* five miles north-east of Hawick leaving A698 at Denholm village. Parkland, trees. 18 holes, 5542 yards, 4992 metres. S.S.S. 67. Practice area. *Green Fees:* £25.00 per round, £30.00 per day. *Eating facilities:* full facilities. *Visitors:* welcome, with prior booking. *Society Meetings:* accepted with Handicap Certificate (weekends difficult). Secretary: John Simpson.

INNERLEITHEN. **Innerleithen Golf Club,** Leithen Water, Leithen Road, Innerleithen EH44 6NL (01896 830951). *Location:* 25 miles south of Edinburgh, six miles south of Peebles, off A72 less than one mile from main street. Attractive 9 hole course set in valley with lovely views of surrounding hills, easy walking but challenging. 9 holes, 3033 yards, 2773 metres. S.S.S. 69. Practice ground. *Green Fees:* information not available. *Eating facilities:* by prior arrangement. *Visitors:* welcome without reservation, though parties should book. *Society Meetings:* catered for by arrangement, limit 40. Secretary: Norman Smith (01896 830050).*

THE APPEARANCE OF AN ASTERISK (*) AT THE END OF A CLUB OR COURSE ENTRY INDICATES THAT UP-TO-DATE INFORMATION HAS NOT BEEN SUPPLIED

JEDBURGH. **Jedburgh Golf Club,** Dunion Road, Jedburgh TD8 6TA (01835 863587). *Location:* one mile south of Jedburgh on Dunion Road to Hawick. Undulating course with trees. New 18 hole course. Parkland style with natural areas of gorse and broom. An undulating course with trees and water features. 5819 yards, S.S.S. 69. *Green Fees:* weekdays £20.00 per round, £30.00 per day; weekends £25.00 per round, £35.00 per day. *Eating facilities:* bar and catering facilities available 11am to 11pm Wednesday to Sunday or by prior arrangement. *Visitors:* welcome. Buggy, trolley hire. *Society Meetings:* group discount on application. All enquiries please telephone 01835 863587.
e-mail: info@jedburghgolfclub.co.uk

KELSO. **Kelso Golf Club,** Golf Course Road, Kelso TD5 7SL (01573 223009). *Location:* one mile north-east of town within Kelso Racecourse. Flat parkland course. 18 holes, 6032 yards. S.S.S. 70. Practice ground. *Green Fees:* information not available. *Eating facilities:* snacks available daily from 11.30am until 2pm. Special packages available to groups of 8 or more. *Visitors:* daily bookings through Starter. *Society Meetings:* bookings through Office Administrator, 9.30am to 12.30pm weekdays.

KELSO. **The Roxburghe Golf Club,** The Roxburghe Hotel, Heiton, by Kelso TD5 8JZ (01573 450333); Fax: 01573 450611). *Location:* eight miles east of Jedburgh on the A698, three miles south of Kelso. Parkland, woodland course with water set in 200 acres alongside the River Teviot; designed by Dave Thomas to USPGA specifications. The Championship Course is home to the Scottish Seniors Open. 18 holes, 7111 yards. Chipping area, putting green, practice ground. *Green Fees:* information not provided. *Eating facilities:* spike bar, fine dining. *Visitors:* welcome at all times, Handicap Certificate required. *Society Meetings:* welcome by prior arrangement. Accommodation available; tuition, clay pigeon shooting. The course is owned by the Duke and Duchess of Roxburghe. Professional: Craig Montgomerie. General Manager: George Mack.
e-mail: hotel@roxburghe.net
website: www.roxburghegolfclub.co.uk

LAUDER. **Lauder Golf Club,** Galashiels Road, Lauder TD2 6RS (01578 722240). *Location*: off A68, 28 miles south of Edinburgh. Undulating course, originally designed by W. Park of Musselburgh, on Lauder Hill. 9 holes, 6030 yards. S.S.S. 69. Practice ground. *Green Fees:* £15.00 all day, anyday. *Eating facilities*: none; good hotels in Lauder. *Visitors*: individuals, groups and parties welcome. Telephone to book your tee time. Secretary: R. Dick (01578 722398).
website: www.laudergolfclub.co.uk

MELROSE. **Melrose Golf Club,** Dingleton Road, Melrose TD6 9HS (01896 822855). *Location:* 4 miles south of Galashiels, less than one hour from Edinburgh. Tree-lined parkland course situated beneath Eildon Hills. 9 holes, 5562 yards, 5075

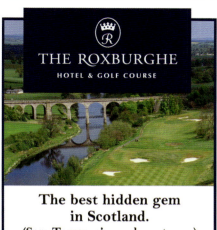

The best hidden gem in Scotland.
(Sam Torrance's words, not ours)

The Roxburghe Hotel & Golf Course, Kelso.
Just one hour from Edinburgh & Newcastle.

**Individual and group packages available.
Tee off times now bookable online.
For more information, call 01573 450 333**

www.roxburghe.net

metres. S.S.S. 68. *Green Fees:* £25.00 per round/day. £15.00 9 holes. Juniors £10.00. *Eating facilities:* bar open at given times, catering on request for larger parties. *Visitors:* welcome anytime when no competitions taking place, Ladies have priority on Tuesdays; Juniors have priority on Wednesday mornings during school holidays. Locker room, shower. *Society Meetings:* welcome by arrangement. Contact: D.F. Campbell (01896 822957).

NEWCASTLETON. **Newcastleton Golf Club,** C/o 5 Union Street, Newcastleton TD9 0QS. *Location:* midway between Carlisle 25 miles and Hawick 21 miles; off A7 at Canonbie. Hilly course with picturesque views, first three holes uphill. 9 holes, 5483 yards. S.S.S. 70. *Green Fees:* 18 holes £12.00, 9 holes £8.00. 2-day ticket £20.00, 3-day ticket £30.00, 5-day ticket £40.00. 2010 rates (subject to review). *Eating facilities:* can be arranged. *Visitors:* welcome, no restrictions except competition days. *Society Meetings:* welcome. Secretary: G.A. Wilson (013873 75608).

Borders / SCOTLAND

PEEBLES. **Macdonald Cardrona Hotel, Golf and Country Club,** Cardrona, Peebles EH45 6LZ (01896 831971; Fax: 01896 831166). *Location:* from Edinburgh take 'Bridges' road to Cameron Toll; turn right at roundabout; heading to Penicuik take A703 to Peebles, turn left to Innerleithen. Club situated 3 miles out of Peebles. Flat parkland/woodland championship standard course. 18 holes, 6856 yards. S.S.S. 72. Putting/practice area. *Green Fees:* information not provided. *Eating facilities:* Spikes Bar. *Visitors:* welcome at any time. *Society Meetings:* welcome at any time, special rates on request. 100-bedroom de luxe hotel on site. Director of Golf: Ross Harrower (01896 833701; Fax: 01896 831166).
e-mail: cardrona@macdonald-hotels.co.uk
website: www.macdonald-hotels.co.uk

PEEBLES. **Peebles Golf Club,** Kirkland Street, Peebles EH45 8EU (01721 720197). *Location:* 51 miles from Glasgow, off A72 at west side of town, 23 miles from Edinburgh. Undulating parkland with panoramic views. 18 holes, 6137 yards. S.S.S. 70. *Green Fees:* weekdays £40.00 per round. Generous discounts for society bookings. *Eating facilities:* full catering daily. *Visitors:* welcome subject to tee availability. Golf buggy hire April to October. *Society Meetings:* catered for subject to prior booking, groups of up to 40 persons catered for. Secretary: Mark McGorum.

ST BOSWELLS. **St Boswells Golf Club,** Braeheads, St Boswells, Melrose TD6 0DE (01835 823527). *Location:* quarter of a mile off trunk route A68 at St. Boswells Green. Flat attractive scenery along the banks of the River Tweed. 9 holes, 5250 yards. S.S.S. 66. *Green Fees:* information not available. *Visitors:* no visitors after 4pm on a weekday and when competitions are being held. Secretary: Linda Cessford (01835 823527).*

SELKIRK. **Selkirk Golf Club,** The Hill, Selkirk TD7 4NW (01750 20621). *Location:* one mile south of Selkirk on A7 road. Heather covered hill course, superb views of Border valleys. 9 holes, 5620 yards. S.S.S. 68. *Green Fees:* weekdays only - £12.00 for 9 holes, £20.00 for 18 holes. *Eating facilities:* bar, open evenings. Cafe 200 yards. *Visitors:* welcome morning and afternoon weekdays, weekends booking needed. Secretary: A. Robertson (01750 20621; 01750 20519 pm).
e-mail: secretary@selkirkgolfclub.co.uk
website: www.selkirkgolfclub.co.uk

WEST LINTON. **Rutherford Castle Golf Club,** West Linton EH46 7AS (Tel & Fax: 01968 661233). *Location:* A702 ten miles south of Edinburgh City Bypass. Undulating parkland course at the foot of the Pentland Hills. 18 holes, 6525 yards, 5872 metres. S.S.S. 71. *Green Fees:* £15.00 weekdays, £25.00 weekends. *Visitors:* no restrictions. Buggy and trolley hire. Contact: (01968 661233).
e-mail: clubhouse@rutherfordcastle.org.uk

WEST LINTON. **West Linton Golf Club,** West Linton EH46 7HN (01968 660970). *Location:* A702 road 17 miles south west of Edinburgh. Scenic moorland course. 18 holes, 6161yards, 5633 metres. S.S.S. 70. Two practice areas. *Green Fees:* weekdays £30.00 per round, £40.00 per day; weekends £40.00 per round (group discounts available). Weekly ticket (Mon-Fri) £100.00. Season ticket (10 rounds) £150.00. *Eating facilities:* lunches, bar snacks, high teas, morning coffee, bar. *Visitors:* welcome at all times except on Medal days and weekends before 1pm. Buggy and carts for hire. *Society Meetings:* catered for weekdays. Professional: I. Wright (01968 660256). Secretary: John Johnson (01968 660970).

Jedburgh Golf Club, Scottish Borders

Dumfries & Galloway

ANNAN. **Powfoot Golf Club,** Cummertrees, Annan DG12 5QE (01461 204100; Fax: 01461 204111). *Location*: three miles from Annan on the B724, turnoff in the village of Cummertrees. Semi-links course on Solway shore with outstanding views. 18 holes, 6255 yards (white). S.S.S. 71. Two practice grounds. *Green Fees*: information not available. *Eating facilities*: morning coffee, lunches and teas in clubhouse - ordering in advance essential for large parties. Steward (01461 207521). *Visitors*: welcome weekdays 9am till 11am, 1pm till 3.30pm. Saturday 2.30pm to 3.30pm. Sundays 10.30am to 11.15am, 1pm to 3.30pm. All bookings through the office. *Society Meetings*: as per visitors. Office Manager: Steven Gardner.
e-mail: info@powfootgolfclub.com
website: www.powfootgolfclub.com

CASTLE DOUGLAS. **Castle Douglas Golf Club,** Abercromby Road, Castle Douglas DG7 1BA (01556 502801). *Location:* half a mile from town centre on A713 Castle Douglas to Ayr Road. Parkland course, a challenge for golfers of all standards. 9 holes, 5390 yards. S.S.S. 71. *Green Fees:* £20.00 per day; 9 holes £12.00; Juniors (under 16 years) half price. *Eating facilities:* bar and catering facilities available all day April through September. *Visitors:* welcome without reservation April through September. Tuesdays and Thursdays club competitions. Buggies £12.00 per hire. *Society Meetings:* welcome by arrangement with the Secretary; special packages for groups of 8 or more. Secretary: J. Duguid (01556 503527).
e-mail: cdgolfclub@aol.com
website: www.cdgolfclub.com

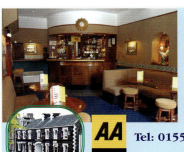

The Imperial Hotel
35 King Street, Castle Douglas DG7 1AA
- Golf itineraries arranged, enjoy the golf 'craic'.
- Good choice of beer and malts.
- A hearty breakfast to tee off.
- Special rates for golfers.

Accommodation, good food and plenty of it. Private car park. Drying room. Club storage. Three bars, pool room. Live sport on TV. All rooms en suite, with TV, tea/coffee etc.
Tel: 01556 502086 • e-mail: info@theimperialgolfhotel.com
www.theimperialgolfhotel.com
The Golfers' Hotel in Galloway - run by Golfers for Golfers

Other British holiday guides from **FHG Guides**
PUBS & INNS · 300 GREAT HOTELS · SHORT BREAK HOLIDAYS
The bestselling and original **PETS WELCOME!** · **500 GREAT PLACES TO STAY**
SELF-CATERING HOLIDAYS · BED & BREAKFAST STOPS
CARAVAN & CAMPING HOLIDAYS · FAMILY BREAKS

Published annually: available in all good bookshops or direct from the publisher:
FHG Guides, Abbey Mill Business Centre, Seedhill, Paisley PA1 1TJ
Tel: 0141 887 0428 • Fax: 0141 889 7204
e-mail: admin@fhguides.co.uk • www.holidayguides.com

DALBEATTIE. **Colvend Golf Club,** Sandyhills, Colvend, By Dalbeattie DG5 4PY (01556 630398). *Location:* six miles from Dalbeattie on the A710, Solway Coast road, between Dalbeattie and Dumfries. Picturesque course on the Solway Coast with superb views over Galloway Hills and the Solway Firth. 18 holes visitors' tees,5035 yards, 4616 metres. S.S.S. 66; medal tees 5297 yards 4856 metres, S.S.S. 67. *Green Fees:* £25.00. Juniors £10.00. *Eating facilities:* modern clubhouse with full changing, catering and bar facilities. *Visitors:* all welcome. Buggies available. *Society Meetings:* welcome by booking through the club. Secretary: (01556 630398).

DALBEATTIE. **Dalbeattie Golf Club,** c/o The Secretary, Dalbeattie DG5 4LR (01556 650616). Clubhouse (01556 611421 – not always manned). *Location*: signposted off the B794 Haugh of Urr Road on the outskirts of Dalbeattie. Slightly undulating parkland course. 9 holes, 5710 yards (18 holes). S.S.S. 68. *Green Fees*: £18.00 for 18 holes. *Eating facilities*: bar available. *Visitors*: very welcome anytime and should club competitions be in progress, every effort will be made to accommodate them. *Society Meetings*: all welcome. Contact clubhouse for further information regarding tee times, accommodation, restaurants, etc.
website: www.dalbeattiegc.co.uk

DUMFRIES. **Crichton Golf Club,** Bankend Road, Dumfries DG1 4TH (01387 247894). *Location:* directly opposite Dumfries and Galloway Royal Infirmary, one mile outside Dumfries on Bankend Road. Wooded parkland. Views overlooking the town of Dumfries. 9 holes, 5952 yards. S.S.S. 69. *Green Fees:* 9 holes £10.00, 18 holes £20.00. *Visitors:* welcome, restrictions depending on club competitions, Thursdays last tee off time 1pm. *Society Meetings:* on application to the Administrator. Match Secretary: Lee Sterritt (07770 553320).

DUMFRIES. **Dumfries and County Golf Club,** Nunfield, Edinburgh Road, Dumfries DG1 1JX (01387 253585). *Location:* one mile north-east town centre on A701. 18 holes, 5918 yards. S.S.S. 69. Limited practice facilities. *Green Fees:* on application. *Eating facilities:* restaurant and bar snacks. *Visitors:* welcome except on competition days. *Society Meetings:* by arrangement with Club Professional. Professional: S.J. Syme (Tel & Fax: 01387 268918). Secretary: B.R.M. Duguid (Tel & Fax: 01387 253585).
e-mail: admin@thecounty.co.uk
website: www.thecounty.org.uk

DUMFRIES. **The Dumfriesshire,** Lockerbie Road, Dumfries DG1 3PF (Tel & Fax: 01387 247444). *Location:* beside A75 Dumfries bypass off Lockerbie Road roundabout. Mixed park and heathland with mature trees and water features. 18 holes, 5940 yards. S.S.S. 68. 20-bay driving range with video teaching facility. Short game practice area and large undulating putting green. *Green Fees:* from £16.00 to £26.00. *Eating facilities:* bar with meals. *Visitors:* welcome. *Society Meetings:* welcome. Professional: Gareth Dick.

DUMFRIES. **Dumfries and Galloway Golf Club,** 2 Laurieston Avenue, Dumfries DG2 7NY (01387 253582). *Location:* one mile from Dumfries on Castle Douglas road, A780. Parkland course. 18 holes, 6222 yards. S.S.S. 71. Practice area. Putting green. *Green Fees:* weekdays £30.00 per round, £38.00 per day; weekends £35.00 per round, £45.00 per day. *Eating facilities:* full catering during bar hours. *Visitors:* welcome, except on competition days. Ladies' Day Tuesday. *Society Meetings:* catered for weekdays, except Tuesdays or Saturdays. Buggies available. Professional: Joe Fergusson (01387 256902; Fax: 01387 276297). Secretary: Alasdair T. Miller (Tel & Fax: 01387 263848).
e-mail: info@dandggolfclub.co.uk
website: www.dandggolfclub.co.uk

The Aston Hotel is located on the Crichton Estate, which extends to over 100 acres. With 71 deluxe bedrooms, we offer Scottish hospitality in an atmosphere of luxurious simplicity. The Crichton Golf Course is directly opposite the hotel and transport to and from courses can be arranged.

www.astonhotels.co.uk

Aston Hotel

The Crichton, Bankend Road, Dumfries DG1 4ZZ
Tel: 01387 272410 • Fax: 01387 267303
e-mail: enquiries@astonhoteldumfries.co.uk

The Summerhill Course, Dumfries & Galloway Golf Club's championship 18-hole layout (6222 yards, Par 70) has magnificent views over the hills to the north of Dumfries. The course is maintained in excellent condition, and is a very good test of golf. Visitors are welcome on most days (limited times on competition days), and an on-line booking system is available.

SGU Sutherland Chalice Counting Competition held annually.

Well-stocked Pro Shop • Practice facilities • Full catering service • Dining Room • Bar • Visitor Locker Room

Secretary: Alasdair T. Miller (Tel/Fax: 01387 263848)

Dumfries & Galloway Golf Club, Laurieston Avenue, Dumfries DG2 7NY
info@dandggolfclub.co.uk • www.dandggolfclub.co.uk

---

the Aberdour

www.aberdour-hotel.co.uk

We are a small friendly Hotel offering B&B accommodation in twelve tastefully decorated bedrooms, all with en suite or private facilities. Bar lunches and suppers served daily.

Dumfries and Galloway is home to some of the finest golfing facilities in the world, where stunning scenery and excellent courses make for a fantastic golfing break.

With 32 courses to choose from in the region, you'll find yourself spoilt for choice, whether you are wanting to work on your technique on a professional course, or just play a little relaxing holiday golf.

The Aberdour Hotel, 16-20 Newall Terrace, Dumfries DG1 1LW
Tel: 01387 252060 • e-mail: info@aberdour-hotel.co.uk

"Where Quality and Tradition meet"

The Galloway Arms Hotel

The Galloway Arms is a traditional hotel situated midway between Dumfries and Castle Douglas. Retaining all the charm and character of a village setting, this heritage listed, family-run hotel offers friendly service, fabulous food and a warm and welcoming atmosphere. All bedrooms are en suite and attractively furnished, with digital television and a tea/coffee hospitality tray. The hotel is situated near a wide variety of golf courses and caters for golfing parties of up to 20 people on a room share basis, with bed and breakfast or dinner, bed and breakfast packages available.

Crocketford – Nine Mile Bar, near Dumfries DG2 8RA
Tel: 01556 690 248 • Fax: 01556 690 266
e-mail: info@gallowayarmshotel.co.uk
www.gallowayarmshotel.co.uk

DUMFRIES. **Southerness Golf Club,** Southerness, Kirkbean, Dumfries DG2 8AZ (01387 880677; Fax: 01387 880471). *Location:* 16 miles south west of Dumfries on A710 (Solway Coast Road). Natural challenging Championship links, designed by MacKenzie Ross, with panoramic views of Solway Firth and Galloway hills. Hosted British Ladies' Amateur 1989 and British Youths' 1990. Scottish Amateur 1995. Scottish Amateur Stroke-play 2002. 18 holes, 6566 yards. S.S.S. 73. Practice ground. *Green Fees:* information not available. *Eating facilities:* full bar and catering facilities. *Visitors:* welcome every day other than 9 days when there are Open Competitions, other golf club members only with Handicap Certificates. Trolley hire. *Society Meetings:* welcome by prior arrangement. Secretary: J.R. Handley.

GATEHOUSE OF FLEET. **Cally Palace Hotel,** Gatehouse of Fleet DG7 2DL. (01557 814341; Fax: 01557 814522). *Location*: one and a half hours drive from M6 and A74, nearest large town - Dumfries. Parkland. 18 holes, 6062 yards. Par 70. Course is restricted to hotel residents and those of sister hotels. *Visitors/Society Meetings*: course open only to hotel residents and those of sister hotels. Eating facilities: conservatory bar for snacks and dining room lunch.*

GATEHOUSE OF FLEET. **Gatehouse of Fleet Golf Club,** Laurieston Road, Gatehouse of Fleet, Castle Douglas DG7 2BE (01557 814766). *Location:* quarter of a mile north of Gatehouse – Laurieston road. Sloping and wooded course with magnificent views of hills and over Fleet Bay. Very well drained; rarely closed. 9 holes, 2521 yards. S.S.S. 66. Practice net. *Green Fees:* £15.00 per round/day. *Visitors:* welcome at all times except Sunday mornings before 11.30am.

KIPPFORD. **Craigieknowes Golf Club,** Barnbarroch Farm, Kippford, Dalbeattie DG5 4QS (01556 620244; mobile: 07760 230959). *Location:* half a mile from Kippford on side road from A710, three miles from Dalbeattie. Parkland course with lots of rocks. 9 holes, Par 3, 1391 yards. S.S.S. 54. Putting green. *Green Fees:* Adult 9 holes £7.00, 18 holes £12.00; Junior 9 holes £5.00, 18 holes £8.00. Weekly ticket Adult £35.00, Junior £20.00. *Eating facilities:* tearoom. *Visitors:* welcome, no restrictions on times of play. Car park, club hire. *Society Meetings:* welcome by arrangement. Secretary: D. Roan.

KIRKCUDBRIGHT. **Brighouse Bay Golf Club and Driving Range,** Borgue, Kirkcudbright DG6 4TS (Tel & Fax: 01557 870509). *Location:* 6 miles south-west of Kirkcudbright off the B727. Come and play one of Scotland's finest new 18 hole courses in the south west of Scotland, with natural coastal undulations and water feautres it is an exceptional experience for golfers of all levels, with four tees on each hole. 18 holes, 6501 yards, par 72, S.S.S.72 (white tees); 5664 yards, par 70, S.S.S. 68 (yellow tees). Carts, club and trolley hire, driving range, short game area, changing and shower facilities. 9 hole course. *Green Fees:* information not provided. *Eating facilities:* full range of bar and catering facilities in bistro, lounge bar and function suite. *Visitors:* welcome at all times by prior arrangement, sensible dress at all times. Award-winning holiday park adjacent with accommodation and leisure facilities available all year. *Society Meetings:* welcome, inclusive golf packages now available, book in advance.
website: www.brighousebay-golfclub.co.uk

KIRKCUDBRIGHT. **Kirkcudbright Golf Club,** Stirling Crescent, Kirkcudbright DG6 4EZ (01557 330314). *Location*: signposted near centre of town. Hilly parkland. 18 holes, 5896 yards. S.S.S. 69. Carts available. *Green Fees*: £25.00 per round, £30.00 per day, £80.00 per week. Buggies £16.00. *Eating facilities:* coffee, lunch, evening meal, usual bar hours. *Visitors:* welcome most days with phone call for availability; Tuesday Ladies' Day, Wednesday Men's. *Society Meetings*: welcome, advance bookings.
website: www.kirkcudbrightgolf.co.uk

LANGHOLM. **Langholm Golf Club,** Whitaside, Langholm DG13 0JR *Location:* on A7 Carlisle-Edinburgh road. Turn off at market place in centre of town. Hillside course with stunning views over the town and down towards the "Lakes". 9 holes, 6180 yards. S.S.S. 69. Practice ground. *Green Fees:* £20.00; £10.00 playing with a member. *Eating facilities:* on request, bar open weekends. *Visitors:* welcome without reservation; restrictions Saturdays 1pm to 2pm (competition times). *Society Meetings:* apply in writing to Secretary. Secretary: W. Goodfellow (013873 81408/07724 875151).

English St, Dumfries DG1 2DF
Tel: 01387 254111

For details of all breaks including golf passes contact our golf co-ordinator Michael Dickie on 01387 240286 or by e-mail golf@cairndalehotel.co.uk

The Cairndale Hotel & Leisure Club

Golf Breaks include "Play the Best in the South West"

Two nights DBB and one round of golf at Powfoot, Southerness and Dumfries & County from £236.

www.cairndalehotel.co.uk

SCOTLAND / Dumfries & Galloway

LOCHMABEN. Lochmaben Golf Club, Castlehillgate, Lochmaben, Lockerbie DG11 1NT (01387 810552). *Location:* Lockerbie four miles, Dumfries eight miles on A709 road. Attractive parkland course surrounding the Kirk Loch, excellent views on this well-maintained course. 18 holes, 5933 yards. S.S.S. 70. Practice area. *Green Fees:* weekdays £32.00; weekends £35.00. *Eating facilities:* full catering and bar. *Visitors:* welcome, bookings advisable (01387 810552). Caddy car and buggy hire. *Society Meetings:* welcome. Secretary: J.M. Dickie (01387 810552).
e-mail: enquiries@lochmabengolf.co.uk
website: www.lochmabengolf.co.uk

LOCKERBIE. Hoddom Castle Golf Course, Hoddom, Lockerbie DG11 1AS (01576 300251). *Location:* A74, Junction 19 Ecclefechan. Follow signs to Hoddon Castle or A75 Annan, B723 and follow signs to Hoddon Castle. Parkland, partially wooded, bounded on two sides by River Annan. 9 holes, 2274 metres. S.S.S. 33. *Green Fees:* information not available. *Eating facilities:* bar. *Visitors:* welcome anytime.*
website: www.hoddomcastle.co.uk

LOCKERBIE. Lockerbie Golf Club, Corrie Road, Lockerbie DG11 2ND (Tel & Fax: 01576 203363). *Location:* leave M74, proceed to town centre and follow signs. Parkland featuring pond which is in play on three holes – fair test of golf for all standards of golfers. 18 holes, 5614 yards. S.S.S. 67. Small practice area. *Green Fees:* information not provided. *Eating facilities:* catering available 8am–8pm, bar 11am–11pm. *Visitors:* welcome, restricted on Sundays. Caddy cars and buggies available. *Society Meetings:* welcome by arrangement. Secretary: R. Barclay (Tel & Fax: 01576 203363).
e-mail: enquiries@lockerbiegolf.com

MOFFAT. The Moffat Golf Club, Coatshill, Moffat DG10 9SB (01683 220020). *Location:* leave M74 at Beattock. Take A701 for Moffat, club signposted one mile on left. Scenic moorland course with tree plantations. 18 holes, 4866 yards. S.S.S. 67. Putting green and practice net. *Green Fees:* weekdays £25.00 per round, £30.00 per day; weekends and Bank Holidays £30.00 per round, £36.00 per day. Juniors (up to 18) half price. Special Packages available to parties of 8 or more: £35.00 to £42.00 weekdays; £42.00 to £49.95 weekends – two rounds of golf, coffee/biscuits on arrival, soup and rolls lunchtime, and evening meal. 2010 rates (subject to review). *Eating facilities:* bar meals served, bar open 11am to 10pm; dining room. *Visitors:* welcome daily including weekends. Booking advisable. Games room (two full-size snooker tables, pool table, darts, table tennis). Motorised buggies, pull trolleys and clubs for hire. *Society Meetings:* welcome, make reservations with Club Manager: Jeff Rogers (01683 220020).
e-mail: bookings@moffatgolfclub.co.uk
website: www.moffatgolfclub.co.uk

BRIGHOUSE BAY GOLF & LEISURE COMPLEX
BORGUE, KIRKCUDBRIGHT, DUMFRIES AND GALLOWAY DG6 4TS

ALSO... AWARD WINNING

Come and play one of the finest new 18 hole courses in the south west of Scotland, with natural coastal undulations and water features it is an exceptional experience for golfers of all levels.

White tees 6501 yards
par 72, SSS 72
Yellow tees 5664 yards
par 70, SSS 68

Club, cart, trolley hire – visitors welcome. Packages available.

www.brighousebay-golfclub.co.uk

LEISURE FACILITIES
Heated indoor pool, jacuzzi, steam room, sunbed, fitness room, games room with 10 pin bowling and pony trekking, nature trails

ACCOMMODATION
Luxury self-catering lodges, cottages and caravans.
Short breaks on request

Golf & Leisure facilities – 01557 870509   Accommodation – 01557 870267
HIDDEN AWAY WITHIN 1200 ACRES ON QUIET, UNSPOILED PENINSULA

388 Dumfries & Galloway / SCOTLAND — THE GOLF GUIDE 2011

NEW GALLOWAY. New Galloway Golf Club, New Galloway, Castle Douglas DG7 3RN (Tel & Fax: 01644 450685). *Location:* one mile off A713 Castle Douglas to Ayr road. Scenic with fine turf. 9 holes, 5006 yards. S.S.S. 67. *Green Fees:* information not available. *Eating facilities:* bar. *Visitors:* very welcome without reservation. Accommodation and meals available in village. *Society Meetings:* by arrangement with Secretary. Secretary: N.E. White (Tel & Fax: 01644 450685).*

NEWTON STEWART. Newton Stewart Golf Club, Kirroughtree Avenue, Newton Stewart DG8 6PF (01671 402172). *Location:* outskirts of Newton Stewart off the A75, Euroroute to Ireland. Parkland course set amidst Galloway Hills with pine forest backdrop, views from most tees have to be seen to be believed. 18 holes, 5806 yards. S.S.S. 69. Practice area. *Green Fees:* information not available. *Eating facilities:* bar meals, lunches and high teas. *Visitors:* welcome all year round after 9.45am. Phone call in advance advisable. Caddy cars and buggies available. *Society Meetings:* all welcome, booking required.*

NEWTON STEWART. Wigtownshire County Golf Club, Mains of Park, Glenluce, Newton Stewart DG8 0NN (Tel & Fax: 01581 300420). *Location:* A75 two miles west Glenluce, eight miles east Stranraer. Seaside links. 18 holes, 6104 yards, 5581 metres. S.S.S. 70. 4.5-acre practice area. *Green Fees:* weekdays £28.00 per round, £36.00 per day; weekends £30.00 per round, £38.00 per day. Half price for under 18s. Discounts for parties of 10 and over. *Eating facilities:* available all year round. *Visitors:* unrestricted except Wednesday evenings and competitions. Hand trolleys. *Society Meetings:* catered for but should pre-book. Secretary: R. McKnight (01581 300420).
e-mail: enquiries@wigtownshirecountygolfclub.com
website: www.wigtownshirecountygolfclub.com

PORTPATRICK. Lagganmore Golf Club & Hotel, Lagganmore, Portpatrick DG9 9AB (Tel & Fax: 01776 810499). Two miles outside Portpatrick, six miles from Stranraer. 18 holes parkland heath course, 5698 yards. S.S.S. 68. Par 69. *Green Fees:* information not available. *Eating facilities:* bar food and beverages served all day. *Visitors:* welcome, packages available for parties, to include dinner, bed and breakfast and unlimited golf. Hotel on site, all rooms en suite. Buggy hire available. *Society Meetings:* welcome, telephone (01776 810499).*
e-mail: info@lagganmoregolf.co.uk
website: www.lagganmoregolf.co.uk

PORTPATRICK. Portpatrick Golf Club, Clubhouse, Golf Course Road, Portpatrick DG9 8TB (01776 810273; Fax: 01776 810811). *Location:* A77 to Stranraer, follow signs to Portpatrick; A75 fork left one and a half miles after Glenluce bypass, follow signs to Portpatrick. Enter village, fork right at war memorial, then 400 yards on right. Cliff top links-type course. "Dunskey" 18 holes, 5913 yards. S.S.S. 69; "Dinvin" 9 holes, 1346 yards. S.S.S. 27. Practice ground. *Green Fees:* see website. *Eating facilities:* bar and catering available all year round. *Visitors:* advisable to book in advance (members times). Handicap Certificate required for Dunskey Course. *Society Meetings:* catered for by prior arrangement. Secretary: Robin Murdoch (01776 810273; Fax: 01776 810811).
e-mail: enquiries@portpatrickgolfclub.com
website: www.portpatrickgolfclub.com

PORT WILLIAM. St Medan Golf Club, Monreith, Port William, Newton Stewart DG8 8NJ (01988 700358). *Location:* on A747, three miles south of Port William. Seaside links course with panoramic views of Mull of Galloway and Isle of Man - Scotland's most southerly course. 9 holes, 18 tees 4520 yards. S.S.S. 63. Practice driving net and green. *Green Fees:* 9 holes £12.00, 18 holes £18.00; day ticket £30.00, weekly ticket £60.00. 2010 rates (subject to review). *Eating facilities:* available (also bar), summer only. *Visitors:* welcome without reservation. Telephone clubhouse for further information.

SANQUHAR. Sanquhar Golf Club, Euchan Course, Barr Road, Sanquhar DG4 6JZ (01659 50577). *Location*: situated quarter-of-a-mile from A76 Dumfries-Kilmarnock trunk road. Undulating parkland with views across the town. Practice areas/ net. 9 holes, 5144 metres. S.S.S. 68. *Green Fees*: £15.00 per day. Senior Citizens and Juniors £10.00. 2010 rates (subject to review). *Eating facilities*: bar available if requested in advance. *Visitors*: welcome without reservation. Licensed clubhouse with full-size snooker table. *Society Meetings*: Golf package including catering for parties of 12 and over £30.00 per person.

One of the most popular holiday golf courses in South West Scotland

WIGTOWNSHIRE COUNTY GOLF CLUB

18 hole true links course situated on the shores of Luce Bay, eight miles from Stranraer.

Mains of Park, Glenluce, Newton Stewart
Dumfries and Galloway DG8 0AG
Tel/Fax: 01581 300420
www.wigtownshirecountygolfclub.com
E-mail: enquiries@wigtownshirecountygolfclub.com

SCOTLAND / Dumfries & Galloway

SOUTHERNESS. Solway Links Golf Club, Southerness, Kirkbean, Dumfries DG2 8BE (01387 880323; Fax: 01387 880555). *Location*: 12 miles south-west of Dumfries on A710 (500 yards from Southerness Golf Course). Built on an ancient raised beach, in a stunning location overlooking the Solway Firth and Lake District hills. The fairways have received lots of praise for their spongy grass and generous width. 18 holes, 5037 yards. Par 67. 9-hole option and 9 holes of GolfCross Game (1st in UK). *Green Fees:* information not available. *Visitors*: welcome. Buggy and club hire available.*
e-mail: info@solwaylinks.co.uk
website: www.solwaylinks.co.uk

STRANRAER. Stranraer Golf Club, Creachmore, Leswalt, Stranraer DG9 0LF (01776 870245; Fax: 01776 870445). *Location*: three miles from Stranraer on the Kirkcolm Road (A718). Parkland, seaside – the last course James Braid designed. 18 holes, 6308 yards. S.S.S. 72. Practice area and putting green. *Green Fees*: information not provided. *Eating facilities*: full catering all day, lounge bar overlooks course. *Visitors*: weekdays 9.15am to 12.30pm then 1.30 to 5pm; weekends 9.30am to 11.45am then 1.45pm to 5pm. Pull trolleys and golf carts available for hire. *Society Meetings*: all welcome with prior arrangement. Secretary: James Burns (01776 870245; Fax: 01776 870445).
e-mail: stranraergolf@btclick.com
website: www.stranraergolfclub.net

THORNHILL. Thornhill Golf Club, Blacknest, Thornhill DG3 5DW (01848 330546) *Location:* 14 miles north of Dumfries on A76, one mile east of village. Parkland/open moorland. 18 holes, 6085 yards. S.S.S. 70. Practice ground (two areas). *Green Fees:* information not available. *Eating facilities:* catering available, bar facility. *Visitors:* welcome without reservation, but please contact the club steward to ensure tee times are available. Buggies. *Society Meetings:* welcome, contact Alex Hillier (01848 331779).*
e-mail: info@thornhillgolfclub.co.uk
website: www.thornhillgolfclub.co.uk

WIGTOWN. **Wigtown and Bladnoch Golf Club,** Lightlands Terrace, Wigtown, Newton Stewart DG8 9DY (01988 403354). *Location:* 200 yards from square in Wigtown. Parkland course. 9 holes, 5400 yards. S.S.S. 67. Practice bays. *Green Fees:* £20.00 for 18 holes, £12.00 for 9 holes; Senior Citizens £15.00 (9 or 18 holes), £25.00 per day; Juniors £10.00 (9 or 18 holes). Five day ticket £52.00. *Visitors:* welcome most days, tee reserved for open competitions occasional weekends. No prior booking necessary. *Society Meetings:* welcome by arrangement.

GolfCross in Scotland • Solway Links Golf Club
Southerness • Pay & Play
Tel: 01387 880323 • www.solwaygolf.co.uk

This stunning location overlooking the Solway Firth and Lake District Hills, is an 18 hole course with a 9 hole option and 9 holes of the new and exciting GolfCross Game (1st in UK).

Southerness, Kirkbean, Dumfries DG2 8BE

The 18-hole course is a mixture of park and heathland with magnificent panoramic views. It has often been described as a 'hidden jewel'. The course is easy on the high handicapper, but offers a real challenge to the scratch golfer.
The fully licensed clubhouse offers snacks and excellent quality meals throughout the day. Situated one mile from the village cross in Thornhill which is on the main A76 Dumfries to Kilmarnock road.

**Blacknest, Thornhill DG3 5DW
Tel: 01848 330546**

Dunbartonshire

ALEXANDRIA. **Vale of Leven Golf Club,** Northfield Road, Bonhill, Alexandria G83 9ET (01389 752351). *Location:* A82 to Dumbarton, follow signs at roundabout at Dumbarton for Bonhill then club signs. Parkland with splendid views of Loch Lomond. 18 holes, 5330 yards. S.S.S. 67. *Green Fees:* weekdays £22.00 per round, £32.00 per day; weekends £27.00 per round, £40.00 per day. Weekly ticket (Monday to Friday) £90.00. *Eating facilities:* catering and bar available. *Visitors:* welcome all year round. Full changing and locker facilities. Shop: Barry Campbell. *Society Meetings:* on application. Club Administrator: Richard Barclay (01389 752351).
e-mail: rbarclay@volgc.com
website: www.volgc.org

CARDROSS. **Cardross Golf Club,** Main Road, Cardross G82 5LB (01389 841213). *Location:* on A814 west of Dumbarton. Championship parkland course. 18 holes, 6447 yards. S.S.S. 72. Practice ground. *Green Fees:* visit website. *Eating facilities:* lunches/bar snacks available. *Visitors:* weekdays only (by phoning Professional to book time). *Society Meetings:* catered for weekdays by arrangement. Professional: Robert Farrell (01389 841350). Secretary: Iain T. Waugh (01389 841754; Fax: 01389 842162).
e-mail: golf@cardross.com
website: www.cardross.com

CLYDEBANK. **Clydebank and District Golf Club,** Glasgow Road, Hardgate, Clydebank G81 5QY (01389 383831). *Location:* Hardgate village. Off A82 10 miles west of Glasgow (off Great Western Road). 18 holes, 5832 yards, 5325 metres. S.S.S. 69. *Green Fees:* information not available. *Eating facilities:* catering as required. *Visitors:* welcome weekdays only. Professional: Alan Waugh (01389 383835). Secretary: Mrs K. Stoddart (01389 383831; Fax: 01389 383831 by request).*

CLYDEBANK. **Clydebank Municipal Golf Course,** Overtoun Road, Clydebank G81 3RE (0141-952 6372). *Location:* one mile west of Clydebank centre off Duntocher Road. Parkland course - one of the best Par 3s in Scotland. 18 holes, 5349 yards. S.S.S. 66. *Green Fees:* information not available. *Eating facilities:* tearoom. *Visitors:* municipal course, tee closed Saturdays 7.30am till 10.00am and 11.00am to 3.00pm. *Society Meetings:* contact District Council. Secretary: District Council (01389 738762).*

DUMBARTON. **Dumbarton Golf Club,** Broadmeadow, Dumbarton G82 2BQ (01389 765995). *Location:* off A82, one mile from town centre. Flat parkland. 18 holes, 5905 yards. S.S.S. 69. Practice area. *Green Fees:* weekdays £20.00 per round, £30.00 per day. Packages available; check website. *Eating facilities:* catering and bar available. *Visitors:* welcome weekdays; not Saturdays, limited availablity on Sundays/Bank Holidays. No jeans or shellsuits on course or in clubhouse. *Society Meetings:* all welcome with prior bookings through Secretary. Secretary: Mo Buchanan.
website: www.dumbartongolfclub.co.uk

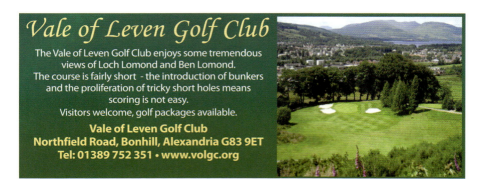

HELENSBURGH. Helensburgh Golf Club, 25 East Abercromby Street, Helensburgh G84 9HZ (01436 674173; Fax: 01436 671170). *Location*: A82 from Dumbarton, then A818 to Helensburgh; signposted from A818 on entering town. Moorland course with panoramic views across Loch Lomond and the Clyde Estuary. 18 holes, 5942 yards. S.S.S. 69 Practice area and putting green. *Green Fees*: £35.00 per round, £45.00 per day weekdays. Winter conditions £15.00 per day. *Eating facilities*: full catering and bar. *Visitors*: welcome weekdays only, dress in recognised golfing attire, no denims or trainers. Clubs for hire. *Society Meetings*: welcome by arrangement. Professional: Fraser Hall (Tel & Fax: 01436 675505). Secretary: Howard Mercer (01436 674173; Fax: 01436 671170).
e-mail: thesecretary@helensburghgolfclub.co.uk
website: www.helensburghgolfclub.co.uk

KIRKINTILLOCH. **Kirkintilloch Golf Club,** Todhill, Campsie Road, Kirkintilloch G66 1RN (0141-776 1256). *Location:* from Glasgow to Bishopbriggs, then straight on to Kirkintilloch. Undulating, parkland course. 18 holes, 5860 yards. S.S.S. 69. Par 70. Putting green and practice areas. *Green Fees:* information not available. *Eating facilities:* dining room and bar. *Visitors:* phone Secretary for tee times. *Society Meetings:* catered for Monday to Friday, information from Secretary including catering. Secretary: T. Cummins (0141-775 2387).*

LENZIE. **Lenzie Golf Club,** 19 Crosshill Road, Lenzie, Glasgow G66 5DA (0141-776 1535; Fax: 0141-578 0142). *Location:* two miles from M80/A80 Junction to Kirkintilloch. Parkland. 18 holes, 5982 yards. S.S.S. 69. Practice ground. *Green Fees:* information not available. *Eating facilities:* bar and catering facilities available. *Visitors:* welcome any day except weekends. Carts for hire. Private room available for meetings or dinners. *Society Meetings:* welcome. Professional: James McCallum (Tel & Fax: 0141-777 7748). Club Manager: Roy R. McKee (0141-776 1535 9am-1pm).*
website: www.lenziegolfclub.co.uk

THE APPEARANCE OF AN ASTERISK (*) AT THE END OF A CLUB OR COURSE ENTRY INDICATES THAT UP-TO-DATE INFORMATION HAS NOT BEEN SUPPLIED

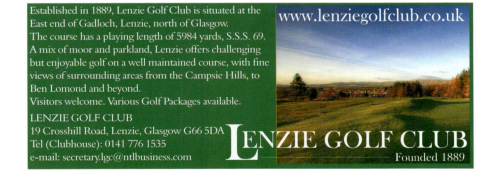

Visit www.holidayguides.com for convenient accommodation when playing golf around the regions

Edinburgh & Lothians

ABERLADY. **Craigielaw Golf Club,** Aberlady EH32 0PY (01875 870800; Fax: 01875 870620). *Location:* half mile west of Aberlady on A198. Links course. 18 holes, 6601 yards, S.S.S. 71, Par 71. Golf Academy and short course. *Green Fees:* information not available. *Eating facilities:* full catering all day; restaurant open to public. *Visitors:* welcome anytime except competition days; advisable to book in advance. Club and buggy hire. *Society Meetings:* society and group bookings welcome.*
website: www.craigielawgolfclub.com

ABERLADY. **Kilspindie Golf Club,** The Clubhouse, Aberlady, East Lothian EH32 0QD (01875 870358). *Location:* A198 North Berwick Road (off A1 East of Edinburgh). Club's access road signposted at east end of Aberlady, overlooking nature reserve and Aberlady Bay. Traditional Scottish links course. 18 holes, 5502 yards, S.S.S. 66, Par 69. *Green Fees:* weekdays £39.00 per round, £59.50 per day; Saturdays and Sundays £49.50 per round, £69.50 per day. *Eating facilities:* dining room with full catering and licensed bar. *Visitors:* welcome, booking advisable. *Society Meetings:* welcome, prior booking essential (01875 870358 or e-mail). Professional: Graham Sked (Tel & Fax: 01875 870695). General Manager: P. B. Casely (01875 870358).
e-mail: kilspindie@btconnect.com
website: www.kilspindiegolfclub.com

ABERLADY. **Luffness New Golf Club,** Aberlady EH32 0QA (01620 843336; Fax: 01620 842933). *Location:* A198 - 17 miles east of Edinburgh. One mile from Gullane. Links course, 18 holes, 6328 yards. S.S.S. 71. *Green Fees:* £75.00 per round, £95.00 per day. *Eating facilities:* dining room except Mondays. *Visitors:* weekdays only. *Society Meetings:* by prior arrangement. Secretary: Group Captain A.G. Yeates (01620 843336; Fax: 01620 842933).
e-mail: secretary@luffnessnew.com
website: www.luffnessgolf.com

BATHGATE. **Bathgate Golf Club,** Edinburgh Road, Bathgate EH48 1BA (01506 652232). *Location:* three miles from M8, 400 yards east of George Square, the town centre and railway station. Flat course. 18 holes, 6328 yards. S.S.S. 71. Practice area. *Green Fees:* weekdays £30.00 per round, £35.00 per day; weekends £35.00 per round, £45.00 per day. *Eating facilities:* dining room facilities open all week. *Visitors:* welcome without reservation except on Competition days at weekends. Handicap Certificates preferred. Electric buggies available. *Society Meetings:* welcome, numbers limited at weekends. Professional: Stuart Callan (01506 630553). Secretary: W. Allan Osborne (01506 630505).

BO'NESS. **West Lothian Golf Club,** Airngath Hill, Bo'ness EH49 7RH (01506 825060; Fax: 01506 826030). *Location:* situated midway between Linlithgow and Bo'ness. Undulating parkland course with panoramic views over River Forth beyond Stirling to below the Bridges. 18 holes, 6249 yards. S.S.S. 71. Practice ground. *Green Fees:* 18 holes weekdays £30.00; 36 holes weekdays £40.00. Packages available. *Eating facilities:* bar and catering service. *Visitors:* welcome, advisable to phone weekends. Trolleys and buggies. *Society Meetings:* welcome by arrangement. Professional: Alan Reid (01506 825060). Secretary: Alan Gibson.

BONNYRIGG. **Broomieknowe Golf Club Ltd,** 36 Golf Course Road, Bonnyrigg EH19 2HZ (0131-663 9317; Fax: 0131-663 2152). *Location:* south of Edinburgh, A6094 from Dalkeith. Flat parkland course. 18 holes, 6150 yards. S.S.S. 70. Practice ground. *Green Fees:* weekdays £30.00 per round, £45.00 per day; £34.00 per round at weekends. *Eating facilities:* meals and snacks. *Visitors:* welcome Monday to Friday 9.30am to 4pm, weekends by prior arrangement. *Society Meetings:* welcome weekdays by arrangement. Professional: Mark Patchett (0131-663 9317). Secretary: Robert H. Beattie (0131-663 9317; Fax: 0131-663 2152).
e-mail: administrator@broomieknowe.com
website: www.broomieknowe.com

DALKEITH. **Newbattle Golf Club Ltd,** Abbey Road, Dalkeith EH22 3AD (0131-663 2123). *Location:* approximately seven miles south-east of Edinburgh A7 to Eskbank Toll (Newbattle exit). Parkland, wooded course. 18 holes, 6012 yards, 5498 metres. S.S.S. 69. Small practice area. *Green Fees:* £30.00 per round, £40.00 per day. Package deals available. *Eating facilities:* full catering available on request. *Visitors:* weekdays 9.30am to 4pm. Limited numbers Sunday afternoons. No jeans/trainers on course or in clubhouse. *Society Meetings:* welcome. Professional: S. McDonald (0131-660 1631). Secretary: H.G. Stanners (0131-663 1819).
e-mail: mail@newbattlegolfclub.com
website: www.newbattlegolfclub.com

DUNBAR. **Dunbar Golf Club,** East Links, Dunbar EH42 1LL (01368 862317; Fax: 01368 865202). *Location:* on coast half a mile east of Dunbar. Seaside links, used for final qualifying 1992 and 2002 Open Championship. 18 holes, 6597 yards. S.S.S. 72. *Green Fees:* weekdays £57.00 per round, £73.00 per day; weekends £75.00 per round, £105.00 per day. Twilight golf (after 3pm) weekdays £37.00, weekends £48.00; Shoulder rate (March and October) weekdays £44.00 per round, £55.00 per day; weekends £56.00 per round, £85.00 per day; winter weekdays only £32.00 (November to February). 2010 rates (subject to review). *Eating facilities:* full catering facilities. *Visitors:* no visitors on Thursdays or before 9.30am and between 12.30pm and 2pm weekdays; or before 10am and between 12 noon and 2pm weekends. *Society Meetings:* welcome. Professional: Jacky Montgomery (01368 862086). Manager: John I. Archibald (01368 862317; Fax: 01368 865202).
e-mail: manager@dunbargolfclub.com
website: www.dunbargolfclub.com

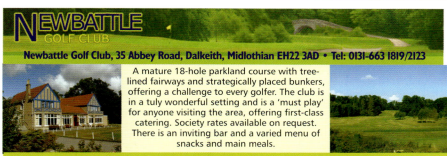

Newbattle Golf Club, 35 Abbey Road, Dalkeith, Midlothian EH22 3AD • Tel: 0131-663 1819/2123

A mature 18-hole parkland course with tree-lined fairways and strategically placed bunkers, offering a challenge to every golfer. The club is in a tuly wonderful setting and is a 'must play' for anyone visiting the area, offering first-class catering. Society rates available on request. There is an inviting bar and a varied menu of snacks and main meals.

e-mail: mail@newbattlegolfclub.com • www.newbattlegolfclub.com

The Rossborough Hotel

Some of the finest Scottish Golf Courses are in East Lothian, all between two and twenty minutes from the Hotel. The Rossborough boasts nineteen fully en suite rooms complete with colour TV and telephone. Edinburgh's Airport and nightlife are only 28 miles away.

1 night B/B+1 round of golf from £76pp

Queens Road, Dunbar, East Lothian EH42 1LG
Tel: 01368 862356 • Fax: 01368 865644
e-mail: info@therossborough.com • www.therossborough.com

Proprietors: Robin & Ann Rossborough BA (Hons) MHCIMA

LOUNGE | BAR | FUNCTION ROOM | RESTAURANT

E-mail: secretary@dunbargolfclub.com
www.dunbargolfclub.com

East Links, Dunbar EH42 1LL
Tel: 01368 862 317

Welcome to Dunbar Golf Club

You are sure to enjoy a wonderful experience on this traditional links course and in the warm atmosphere of the clubhouse and restaurant. Golf has been played here for over 150 years and the course is used as an Open Championship qualifying venue. We have practice facilities, and a Pro Shop; caddies are available to guide you round the course.

PLEASE NOTE

All the information regarding Golf Clubs in this guide is given in good faith in the belief that it is correct. However, the publishers cannot guarantee the facts given in these pages, neither are they responsible for changes in ownership or facilities, such as green fees, that may take place after the date of going to press. Readers should always satisfy themselves that the facilities they require are available and that the terms, if quoted, still apply.

DUNBAR. **Winterfield Golf Club,** St. Margarets, North Road, Dunbar EH42 1AU (01368 862280). Seaside course. 18 holes, 4686 metres. S.S.S. 65. *Green Fees:* information not available. *Eating facilities:* Full catering and bar facilities. *Visitors:* welcome without reservation or restriction. Secure changing facilities. *Society Meetings*: welcome without reservation. Pro Shop: (01368 863562). Professional: Kevin Phillips (01368 863562) Vice Captain: E. Coulter; Captain: W. G. Kerr (01368 862280).*

EDINBURGH. **Baberton Golf Club,** 50 Baberton Avenue, Juniper Green, Edinburgh EH14 5DU (0131-453 4911). *Location:* five miles west of Edinburgh on the A70. 18 holes, 6134 yards. S.S.S. 70. *Green Fees:* weekdays £32.00 per round, £42.00 per day; weekends £35.00 per round. *Eating facilities:* by arrangement (phone Andrew Grieve (0131-453 4911). *Visitors:* welcome by arrangement with Secretary. *Society Meetings:* catered for. Professional: K. Kelly Tel & Fax: 0131-453 3555). Club Manager: K. Nicholson (0131-453 4911; Fax: 0131-453 4678).
e-mail: manager@baberton.co.uk
website: www.baberton.co.uk

EDINBURGH. **Braid Hills Golf Course,** Braid Hills Approach, Morningside, Edinburgh EH10 6JY (0131-447 6666). *Location:* Braid Hills on south side of Edinburgh. Established 1889. 18 holes, 5865 yards. S.S.S. 68. *Green Fees:* information not available. *Visitors:* welcome; pay and play course; season tickets and club membership available. Clubs for hire. Braids United Golf Club, Edinburgh Thistle Golf Club, Edinburgh Western Golf Club and Harrison Golf Club all have clubhouses at Braid Hills and welcome visitors. Catering available on request. Managed by Edinburgh Leisure.*

EDINBURGH. **Bruntsfield Links Golfing Society Ltd,** The Clubhouse, 32 Barnton Avenue, Edinburgh EH4 6JH (0131-336 2006). *Location:* off A90 at Davidson's Mains. Mature parkland course with magnificent views to north over Firth of Forth and to the west. 18 holes, 6446 yards. S.S.S. 71. Excellent practice facilities. *Green Fees:* weekdays £60.00 per round, £80.00 per day; weekends £65.00 per round, £85.00 per day. 2010 rates (subject to review). *Eating facilities:* morning coffee, lunches, dinner by arrangement. *Visitors:* welcome - telephone Professional to arrange times. *Society Meetings:* catered for by arrangement. Professional: Richard Brian (0131-336 4050). Secretary: Cdr D.M. Sandford (0131-336 1479; Fax: 0131-336 5538).
e-mail: secretary@bruntsfield.sol.co.uk
blgsproshop@hotmail.co.uk
website: www.bruntsfieldlinks.co.uk

EDINBURGH. **Carrick Knowe Golf Course.** *Location:* situated on the west side of the city on Glendevon Park. Undulating parkland course which has recently undergone a major remodelling. 18 holes, 6150 yards. S.S.S. 69. *Green Fees:* information not available. *Visitors*: welcome. Managed by Edinburgh Leisure.*

EDINBURGH. **City of Edinburgh Golf Club,** Craigentinny Golf Course, Fillyside Road, Edinburgh EH7 6RG. *Location:* Club plays over the following pay and play courses - Carrick Knowe: 18 holes, 6150 yards. S.S.S. 69; Braid Hills: 18 holes, 5692 yards. S.S.S. 67; Silverknowes: 18 holes, 6198 yards. S.S.S. 69; Craigentinny: 18 holes, 5413 yards. S.S.S. 66; Portobello: 9 holes, 4816 yards. S.S.S. 64; Princes: 9 holes, 3800 yards. Par 60. *Green Fees:* information not available. *Visitors:* welcome all year round. Secretary: Peter Long (0131-554 7501).*
website: www.edinburghleisure.co.uk

EDINBURGH. **Craigentinny Golf Course.** *Location*: Situated on the east side of the city on Fillyside Road. Undulating parkland course. 18 holes, 5511 yards. S.S.S. 66. *Green Fees*: information not available. *Visitors*: welcome. Managed by Edinburgh Leisure.*

EDINBURGH. **Craigmillar Park Golf Club,** 1 Observatory Road, Edinburgh EH9 3HG (0131-667 2837). *Location:* A702 from City Centre on Mayfield Road, right at King's Buildings. Parkland. 18 holes, 5825 yards, 5350 metres. S.S.S. 68. *Green Fees:* information not provided. *Eating facilities:* lunches, snacks, high teas and dinners. *Visitors:* welcome weekdays and on weekends after 3pm. *Society Meetings:* catered for by previous arrangement. Professional: S. Gourlay (0131-667 2850). Club Manager: Mrs D. Nichol (0131-667 0047).
e-mail: secretary@craigmillarpark.co.uk

Craigmillar Park Golf Club

1 Observatory Road, Edinburgh EH9 3HG
Secretary@craigmillarpark.co.uk
www.craigmillarpark.co.uk

Situated in Edinburgh, near the Royal Observatory on Blackford Hill, Craigmillar Park Golf Club is a parkland course with panoramic views over the city of Edinburgh, to East Lothian and north towards central Fife and the Perthshire Hills.

Club Manager Diane Nichol - 0131 667 0047 Professional Scott Gourlay - 0131 667 2850
Club Steward Annie Vallance - 0131 667 2837

EDINBURGH. Duddingston Golf Club Ltd, Duddingston Road West, Edinburgh EH15 3QD (0131-661 1005). *Location:* adjacent to A1 Willowbrae Road, turn right at Duddingston crossroads then one mile on Duddingston Road West. Undulating parkland with stream. 18 holes, 6487 yards. S.S.S. 72. *Green Fees:* £32.00 per round, £45.00 per day. *Eating facilities:* full catering and bar facilities. *Visitors:* welcome weekdays only. *Society Meetings:* by arrangement (rates on request). Professional: Alistair McLean (0131-661 4301). Secretary: Duncan Ireland (0131-661 7688).
e-mail: secretary@duddingstongolf.co.uk

EDINBURGH. The Edinburgh Golf Club, Craigentinny Golf Course, Fillyside Road, Edinburgh EH7 6RG. *Location:* club plays over the following pay and play courses - Carrick Knowe: 18 holes, 6150 yards. S.S.S. 69; Braid Hills: 18 holes, 5692 yards. S.S.S. 67; Silverknowes: 18 holes, 6198 yards. S.S.S. 69; Craigentinny: 18 holes, 5413 yards. S.S.S. 66; Portobello: 9 holes, 4816 yards. S.S.S. 64; Princes: 9 holes, 3800 yards. Par 60. *Green Fees:* information not available. *Visitors:* welcome all year round. Secretary: C. Hutchison (0131 652 4348).*
website: www.edinburghleisure.co.uk

EDINBURGH. Kingsknowe Golf Club, 326 Lanark Road, Edinburgh EH14 2JD (0131 4411144). *Location:* on the western boundary of Edinburgh with easy access from the City Bypass (Calder Junction). The Clubhouse is located on the A70 Lanark Road. Designed by 1902 Open Champion Alec Herd, Kingsknowe offers a picturesque challenge for all players. The clubhouse offers excellent facilities, including a warm welcome upon completion of your round. Parkland course. 18 holes, 5938 yards. Par 69. Practice area. *Green Fees:* information not available. *Eating facilities:* full catering and bar services available. *Visitors:* welcome Monday to Friday, also weekends subject to availability. *Society Meetings:* prices available on request. Professional: Chris Morris (0131-441 4030). Secretary/Manager: L.I. Fairlie (0131-441 1145).*
website: www.kingsknowe.com

EDINBURGH. Liberton Golf Club, 297 Gilmerton Road, Edinburgh EH16 5UJ (0131-664 3009). *Location:* Corporation transport to Lodge Gate, buses 3 and 8 from Edinburgh. By car on A7 (visitors' car park). Parkland, rolling. 18 holes, 5344 yards, 4888 metres. S.S.S. 66. *Green Fees:* £32.00 weekdays, £37.00 weekends. *Eating facilities:* full catering and bar service. *Visitors:* phone Professional. *Society Meetings:* catered for by arrangement. Professional: I. Seath (0131-664 3009). Secretary: John L. Masterton (0131-664 3009).
e-mail: info@libertongc.co.uk
website: www.libertongc.co.uk

Kingsknowe Golf Club

Originally designed by 1902 Open Champion, Alec Herd, and later redesigned by James Braid, this parkland course, with tree-lined fairways and relatively small greens, offers an interesting and varied challenge to golfers of all abilities, whilst the clubhouse offers excellent facilities, including a warm welcome upon completion of your round.

The clubhouse is located on the A70 Lanark Road, easily accessible from the Edinburgh City Bypass, yet only 15 minutes from the city centre.

For more information please contact the Club Secretary on 0131 441 1145

**Kingsknowe Golf Course, 326 Lanark Road, Edinburgh EH14 2JD
Telephone: Secretary/Clubhouse 0131 441 1145 • Professional 0131 441 4030
www.kingsknowe.com**

EDINBURGH. **Lothianburn Golf Club,** 106a Biggar Road, Edinburgh EH10 7DU (0131 445 2206). *Location*: south on the A702 approximately four miles from city centre or easily reached from Edinburgh bypass road coming off at Lothianburn junction. Hill course close to Pentland Hills. 18 holes, 5662 yards. S.S.S. 69. Practice ground. *Green Fees*: £25.00 per round weekdays; £30.00 weekends. 2010 rates (subject to review). *Eating facilities*: normal bar hours, no hot food on weekdays. *Visitors*: welcome mid-week, weekends restricted. *Society Meetings*: catered for by prior arrangement with the Secretary. Professional: Kurt Mungall (0131-445 2288). Secretary: John Melrose (0131-445 5067).
website: www.lothianburngc.co.uk

EDINBURGH. **Melville Golf Centre, Golf Course, Range and Shop,** Lasswade, Near Edinburgh EH18 1AN (0131-663 8038; Fax: 0131-654 0814). *Location:* three minutes from Edinburgh City Bypass (signposted), on A7. Short but challenging parkland course with large tees and greens, lying in the Esk Valley with panoramic views. 9 holes, 2265 yards, 2070 metres. Par 66. S.S.S. 62. Built to USPGA standard. Floodlit range, 9-hole pay and play course, 4-hole practice/short game area, bunker and putting green. Golf range with automatic pop-up Powertees. *Green Fees:* weekdays 9 holes £12.00, 18 holes £20.00; weekends 9 holes £14.00, 18 holes £25.00. Concessions available. *Eating facilities:* hot/ cold drinks and confectionery. *Visitors:* welcome at all times. Full club equipment and shoe hire, PGA tuition. Golf shop; fully stocked ladies, gents, and juniors. Junior Golf Academy. *Society Meetings:* welcome, advance bookings arranged. Contact Mr & Mrs MacFarlane (0131-663 8038; Fax: 0131-654 0814; Course 0131-654 0224).
e-mail: golf@melvillegolf.co.uk
website: www.melvillegolf.co.uk

EDINBURGH. **Merchants Of Edinburgh Golf Club,** 10 Craighill Gardens, Edinburgh EH10 5PY (0131-447 1219; Fax: 0131-446 9833). *Location:* car park Glenlockhart Road, Edinburgh EH10. Hilly, parkland. 18 holes, 4889 yards. S.S.S. 64. *Green Fees:* weekdays £25.00, weekends £30.00. *Eating facilities:* full catering available daily. *Visitors:* welcome weekdays, weekends by arrangement. *Society Meetings:* catered for except weekends. Professional: N.E.M. Colquhoun (0131 447 8709). Administrator: John Leslie (0131 447 1219).
e-mail: admin@merchantsgolf.com
website: www.merchantsgolf.com

EDINBURGH. **Mortonhall Golf Club,** 231 Braid Road, Edinburgh EH10 6PB. *Location:* take A702 south from City to Morningside traffic lights, up Braid Road one mile, course on left. Moorland course with scenic views. 18 holes, 6530 yards. S.S.S. 72. *Green Fees:* weekdays £45.00 per round, £65.00 per day; weekends £55.00 per round. 2010 rates (subject to review). *Eating facilities:* lunch and bar snacks available. *Visitors:* welcome. *Society Meetings:* catered for (not at weekends). Professional: Malcolm Leighton. Club Manager: Bernadette M. Giefer (0131-447 6974).
e-mail: clubhouse@mortonhallgc.co.uk
website: www.mortonhallgc.co.uk

Mortonhall Golf Club

Founded in 1892, this is the oldest course on which golf is still played in the city of Edinburgh. It is one of outstanding scenic beauty, emerging from a narrow valley to an open area bounded by a wood on the south and the Braid Hills in the north. At 6523 yards, it is the longest course in the city, and at 600ft above sea level, the wind can make it a formidable challenge.

The well appointed clubhouse contains many interesting photographs and golfing memorabilia.
Bar and catering facilities available.

Vistors are welcome to play this picturesque and challenging course.

231 Braid Road, Edinburgh EH10 6PB
Tel: 0131 447 6974 • Fax: 0131 447 8712
www.mortonhallgc.co.uk • clubhouse@mortonhallgc.co.uk

EDINBURGH. **Murrayfield Golf Club Ltd,** 43 Murrayfield Road, Edinburgh EH12 6EU (0131-337 3478). *Location:* Corstorphine Road, two miles west of city centre. Parkland on east side of Corstorphine Hill. 18 holes, 5799 yards. S.S.S. 69. Practice area, net and putting green. *Green Fees:* weekdays £40.00 per round, £50.00 per day. *Eating facilities:* lunch each day, snacks in casual bar, also full bar facilities. *Visitors:* welcome playing with member or by prior arrangement only. No visitors weekends. *Society Meetings:* catered for by prior arrangement. Professional: J. Cliff. Club Manager: J.A. Fraser (0131-337 3478).
e-mail: info@murrayfieldgolfclub.co.uk

EDINBURGH. **Portobello Golf Course,** Stanley Street, Portobello, Edinburgh EH15 1JJ (0131-669 4361). *Location:* on A1 at Milton Road East. Parkland course. 9 holes, 2400 yards, 2167 metres. S.S.S. 32. *Green Fees:* information not available. *Visitors:* welcome. *Society Meetings:* not catered for. Managed by Edinburgh Leisure.*

EDINBURGH. **Prestonfield Golf Club,** 6 Priestfield Road North, Edinburgh EH16 5HS (0131-667 9665; Fax: 0131-777 2727). *Location:* off Dalkeith Road, near Royal Commonwealth Pool on A7. Parkland. 18 holes, 6207 yards. S.S.S. 70, Par 70. Practice area. *Green Fees:* information not available. *Eating facilities:* full catering. *Visitors:* welcome all day weekdays; weekends only after 3pm. Petrol buggies available. *Society Meetings:* welcome all day weekdays; weekends only after 3pm. Professional: Gavin Cook (0131-667 8597). General Manager: John I. Archibald.*
e-mail: generalmanager@prestonfieldgolf.com
website: www.prestonfieldgolf.com

EDINBURGH. **Princes Golf Course,** Braid Hills Road, Edinburgh EH16 6NS (0131-447 3568). *Location:* Braid Hills on south side of Edinburgh. 9-hole course, ideal for beginners, children and families. Managed by Edinburgh Leisure. *Green Fees:* information not available.*

EDINBURGH. **Ratho Park Golf Club Ltd,** Ratho, Edinburgh EH28 8NX (0131-335 0069). *Location:* west side of Edinburgh near Airport, access from A71 or A8. Flat parkland course of outstanding natural beauty. 18 holes, 5960 yards. S.S.S. 68. *Green Fees:* weekdays £33.00 per round, £46.00 per day; weekends £46.00 per round. *Eating facilities:* full catering available. *Visitors:* very welcome, please telephone Professional in advance. *Society Meetings:* welcome Monday-Friday, up to 40, subject to availability. Professional: Alan Pate (0131-333 1406). Secretary/Manager: Craig R Innes (0131-335 0068).
e-mail: secretary@rathoparkgolfclub.co.uk
website: www.rathoparkgolfclub.co.uk

EDINBURGH. **Ravelston Golf Club Ltd,** 24 Ravelston Dykes Road, Blackhall, Edinburgh EH4 3NZ (Tel & Fax: 0131-315 2486). *Location:* A90 Queensferry Road (leading to Forth Road Bridge). Left at traffic lights by Blackhall junction to Strachan Road, cross Craigcrook Road, clubhouse on right. Parkland course. 9 holes, 2615 yards. S.S.S. 66. *Green Fees:* £30.00 weekdays. 2010 rates (subject to review). Eating facilities; tea, coffee, soft drinks and light snacks. *Visitors:* welcome during quiet periods weekdays only. *Society Meetings:* permitted by special application only. Secretary: Jim Lowrie.

EDINBURGH. **Royal Burgess Golfing Society of Edinburgh,** 181 Whitehouse Road, Barnton, Edinburgh EH4 6BU. *Location:* A90 to Forth Road Bridge, behind Barnton Hotel. Parkland. 18 holes, 6511yards. S.S.S. 71. *Green Fees:* weekdays £55.00 per day/round, weekends £75.00 per round. *Eating facilities:* snacks and lunches available. *Visitors:* welcome all week; Saturdays after 2.30pm, Sundays after 12 noon. *Society Meetings:* catered for Tuesdays, Thursdays and Fridays. Professional: Steven Brian (0131-339 6474). General Manager: Graham Callander (0131-339 2075; Fax: 0131-339 3712).
e-mail: generalmanager@royalburgess.co.uk
website: www.royalburgess.co.uk

Prestonfield Golf Club

6 Priestfield Road North, Edinburgh EH16 5HS

A testing par 70 course of 6207 yards, set in beautiful parkland within the heart of Edinburgh, beneath Arthur's Seat, next to Holyrood Park and Duddingston Loch. This easy to walk golf course, created by James Braid, is playable all year round. Visitors, Societies and Corporate Parties always welcome. Catered packages available, contact General Manager for details.

Tel: 0131 667 9665 • Fax: 0131 777 2727 • e-mail: generalmanager@prestonfieldgolf.com
www.prestonfieldgolf.com

EDINBURGH: Silverknowes Golf Course, Silverknowes, Parkway, Edinburgh EH4 5ET (0131-336 5359). *Location:* nearest main road Queensferry Road; signs Davidson Mains, Silverknowes. Parkland, flat. 18 holes, 6216 yards. S.S.S. 71. *Green Fees:* information not available. *Eating facilities:* catering available on request. Managed by Edinburgh Leisure.*

EDINBURGH. **Swanston Golf Course,** 111 Swanston Road, Edinburgh EH10 7DS (0131-445 2239). *Location:* five miles south of Edinburgh city centre, west of Biggar Road (A702) in the foothills of the Pentland Hills. Spectacular views to the north across Edinburgh; a great place for golfers of all abilities and ages. Parkland course. Remodelled facility including the 18-hole Swanston Course - 5544 yards, Par 68, S.S.S. 67 - with the replacement of 6 holes on the steeper part of the old course, with 6 new holes on the lower level (parallel with City Bypass). 9-hole (Par 3s) Templar Course - 1028 yards, Par 27. Driving range, practice pitching facilities and putting green. *Green Fees:* information not available. *Eating facilities:* new clubhouse; modern bar/restaurant. *Visitors:* welcome weekdays only (phone for reservation). Golf carts available. Changing rooms, showers, lockers, fitness suite. *Society Meetings:* catered for on application.*
e-mail: golf@swanston.co.uk
website: www.swanstongolf.co.uk

EDINBURGH. **Torphin Hill Golf Club,** Torphin Road, Edinburgh EH13 0PG (0131-441 4061). *Location:* south west of Colinton Village at terminus of No. 10 bus. Holes 5 to 15 on plateau with outstanding views of Edinburgh. 18 holes, 5285 yards. Par 68. Practice area. *Green Fees:* weekdays £18.00; weekends £25.00. *Eating facilities:* dining room and bar snacks. *Visitors:* welcome without reservation except on Competition Days. *Society Meetings:* catered for except Tuesday. Reduced rates for parties over 20. Professional: (0131-441 4061). Secretary: Bill Ramsay (0131-441 1100; Fax: 0131 441 7166).
e-mail: torphinhillgc@btconnect.com
website: www.torphinhillgolfclub.co.uk

EDINBURGH. **Turnhouse Golf Club,** Lennie Park, 154 Turnhouse Road, Edinburgh EH12 0AD (0131-339 1014). *Location:* west side of Edinburgh, close to Edinburgh International Airport and Edinburgh Park. James Braid designed course. 18 holes, 6060 yards. S.S.S. 71. Par 69. *Green Fees:* weekdays £30.00 per round, £40.00 day ticket; weekends £40.00 per round. *Eating facilities:* full service. *Visitors:* welcome, contact Professional. *Society Meetings:* welcome by prior arrangement with Professional (0131-339 7701). Secretary: Lindsay Gordon.
e-mail: info@turnhousegc.com
website: www.turnhousegolfclub.com

EDINBURGH (SOUTH). **Whitehill House Golf Club,** Rosewell EH24 9EG (0131-220 2440; Fax: 0131-220 2665). *Location:* 20 minutes south of central Edinburgh; may be reached by a short trip through Lasswade from A720 bypass to Rosewell. Parkland course in mature woodland setting. Located in the grounds of Whitehill House, one of Scotland's most historic houses. 9/18 holes, 6324 yards. SGU standard scratch 71. Par 70. Practice holes and driving area, tuition available from Professional. *Green Fees:* weekdays 9 holes £13.00, 18 holes £18.00; weekends 9 holes £14.00, 18 holes £20.00. Annual memberships, no waiting lists. Concessions available. *Eating facilities:* hot and cold drinks. *Visitors:* welcome at all times, no restrictions. Club and trolley hire. Lockers and Pro Shop. *Society Meetings:* by prior arrangement.
e-mail: mail@businessparcs.com
website: www.whitehillhousegolf.com

FAULDHOUSE. **Greenburn Golf Club,** 6 Greenburn Road, Fauldhouse EH47 9HJ (01501 770292). *Location:* four miles south of Junctions 4 and 5 of M8 motorway. Undulating course, a mixture of moorland and parkland settings. 18 holes, 6055 yards. S.S.S. 70. Practice area. *Green Fees:* information not available. *Eating facilities:* catering available all week. *Visitors:* welcome. *Society Meetings:* welcome by arrangement with Administrator. Professional: Scott Catlin (01501 771187). Club Administrator: Adrian McGowan.*

GULLANE. **Gullane Golf Club,** West Links Road, Gullane EH31 2BB (01620 842255; Fax: 01620 842327). *Location:* 18 miles east of Edinburgh on A198 Edinburgh to North Berwick Road. Links. Three 18 hole courses. No. 1 - (Medal) 6466 yards, 5913 metres. S.S.S. 72; (FWD) 6077 yards, 5557 metres. S.S.S 70. No. 2 - 6385 yards, 5838 metres. S.S.S. 71. No. 3 - 5259 yards, 4809 metres. S.S.S. 66. Practice, driving range. *Green Fees:* please visit website for information. *Visitors:* welcome. Call Office for bookings. *Society Meetings:* catered for. Professional: Alasdair Good (01620 843111; Fax: 01620 843090). Office: (01620 842255; Fax: 01620 842327).
e-mail: bookings@gullanegolfclub.com
website: www.gullanegolfclub.com

GULLANE. **The Honourable Company Of Edinburgh Golfers,** Muirfield, Gullane EH31 2EG (01620 842123; Fax: 01620 842977). *Location:* 20 miles from Edinburgh along the coast road to North Berwick. Championship links course. 18 holes, 6601 yards. S.S.S. 73. *Green Fees:* £185.00 18 holes, £230.00 36 holes. 2010 rates (subject to review). *Eating facilities:* morning coffee, lunches and afternoon teas if ordered in advance. *Visitors:* welcome Tuesdays and Thursdays, max. Handicap 18 for men, 20 for ladies. Secretary: A.N.G. Brown.
e-mail: hceg@muirfield.org.uk

HADDINGTON. **Castle Park Golf Club,** Gifford EH41 4PL (01620 810733). *Location:* B6369 from Haddington to Gifford, Castle Park is 2 miles south of Gifford, well signposted. Originally 9 holes, now extended to 18 (opened in 2002) combines a unique test of golf with stunning views. 6443 yards (blue), 6202 yards (white), 5851 yards (yellow), S.S.S. 71. 7 bay driving range, 6 hole putting green and practice bunker. *Green Fees:* from £24.00. *Eating facilities:* bar with full catering available. *Visitors:* welcome. Buggies available for hire. *Society Meetings:* welcome. Professional: Derek Small (01368 862872; mobile: 07968 209167). Secretary: Jim Wilson.
e-mail: castleparkgolf@hotmail.com
website: www.castleparkgolfclub.co.uk

HADDINGTON. Haddington Golf Club, Amisfield Park, Haddington EH41 4PT (01620 822727). *Location:* three-quarters of a mile from A1, 17 miles east of Edinburgh. Wooded parkland, slightly undulating. 18 holes, 6335 yards. S.S.S. 71, Par 71. Practice area. *Green Fees:* information not available. *Eating facilities:* two bars and dining room. *Visitors:* welcome, midweek no restrictions, weekends permitted 10am-12 noon, 2-4pm. *Society Meetings:* packages available on request. Professional: J. Sandilands (01620 822727). Office (01620 823627; Fax: 01620 826580).
e-mail: info@haddingtongolf.co.uk
proshop@haddingtongolf.co.uk (for bookings)
website: www.haddingtongolf.com

HADDINGTON near. Gifford Golf Club, Edinburgh Road, Gifford, Near Haddington EH41 4JE (0162-810 591). *Location:* quarter of a mile west of village. Undulating parkland with burn crossing the course. 9 holes, 6050 yards. S.S.S. 69. *Green Fees:* £22.00 18 holes, £14.00 9 holes; day ticket £35.00; Juniors (under 18s) £3.00. *Visitors:* closed all day first Sunday in the month. Secretary: R. Stewart (01620 810267). Starter (01620 810 591).
e-mail: secretary@giffordgolfclub.com
website: www.giffordgolfclub.com

Aaran Luxury Apartments
COOL • CONTEMPORARY • STYLISH

5 Star Luxury Apartments. Ideally located near some of Scotland's finest golf courses.
Please see our website for full details.

www.aaranluxuryapartments.co.uk
Muirfield Apartments, Gullane EH31 2HZ
Tel: 0131-665 4608 or 07789 485022
e-mail: evelynaleigh@hotmail.com

Local golf courses: Muirfield • Gullane • North Berwick

HADDINGTON GOLF CLUB Est 1865

A superb parkland course set in a quiet country estate. Mature trees line most holes, and three new ponds provide an excellent challenge on the closing stretch for golfers of all standards. Excellent value for both groups and individuals.

**For details on packages and memberships call
Pro Shop: 01620 822727 • Tel: 01620 823627
e-mail: info@haddingtongolf.co.uk
www.haddingtongolf.com**

Gifford Golf Club

A beautiful 9-hole parkland course with the Lammermuir Hills as a backdrop, only 30 minutes from Edinburgh.
• Bar, snacks and light meals
• Changing room and showers
• Trolley and buggy hire
• Booking advisable

**01620 810591 • 01620 810267
secretary@giffordgolfclub.com • www.giffordgolfclub.com
Edinburgh Road, Gifford, East Lothian EH41 4JE**

KIRKNEWTON. Marriott Dalmahoy Hotel and Country Club, Kirknewton, Midlothian EH27 8EB (Hotel 0131-333 1845; Fax: 0131-333 1433). *Location:* seven miles west of Edinburgh on A71. Parkland courses. East Course: (Championship) host to many major tournaments, 18 holes, 7055 yards. S.S.S. 74. West Course: with a finish around the Gogar Burn that will test your nerve. 18 holes, 5168 yards. S.S.S. 65. Driving range, extensive practice area. *Green Fees:* from £30.00 per person. *Eating facilities:* The Long Weekend Restaurant and Club Bar in Country Club, restaurant and bars in Hotel also. *Visitors:* welcome 7 days. Hotel accommodation. Golf buggies, trolleys and clubs for hire. Country Club facilities include swimming pool, two outdoor tennis courts, sauna, steam room, spa, gymnasium, fitness and aerobics studio. *Society Meetings:* welcome weekdays only. Director of Golf: Alan Tait (0131-335 8010). Secretary: Gordon Watt (0131-335 8010).

LASSWADE. Kings Acre Golf Course and Academy, Lasswade EH18 1AU (0131 663 3456; Fax: 0131 663 7076). *Location:* A720 Edinburgh City Bypass. Lasswade is two minutes from City Bypass. Parkland course with matured woodland and large contoured greens, set in picturesque countryside close to Edinburgh City Bypass.18 holes (pay and play), 6031 yards. S.S.S. 69. State of the art practice facility. *Green Fees*: weekdays £28.00 per round, £38.00 per day; weekends £38.00 per round, £49.00 per day. 2010 rates (subject to review). *Eating facilities*: spike bar, fully licensed restaurant. *Visitors*: all visitors welcome all year (no restrictions), accommodation available on site. PGA tuition, buggy and club hire. *Society Meetings:* all welcome. Director of Golf/Secretary: Alan Murdoch.
e-mail: info@kings-acregolf.com
website: www.kings-acregolf.com

LINLITHGOW. Bridgend & District Golf Club, Willowdean, Bridgend, Linlithgow EH49 6NW (01506 834140; Fax: 01506 834706). *Location*: between Winchburgh and Linlithgow, signposted on main road. 9 holes, 5451 yards, S.S.S. 66. *Green Fees*: information not available. *Eating facilities*: no catering on Tuesdays, bar facilities all week. *Visitors*: welcome any time. Buggies for hire. Secretary: George Green.*

LINLITHGOW. Linlithgow Golf Club, Braehead, Linlithgow EH49 6QF (01506 844356; Fax: 01506 842764). *Location:* M8, M9, 20 miles west of Edinburgh, west end of Linlithgow - fork left. Parkland and wooded course with panoramic views. 18 holes, 5851 yards, 5239 metres. S.S.S. 68. Practice area. *Green Fees:* information not provided. *Eating facilities:* full catering available, bar open every day. *Visitors:* welcome except Saturdays. *Society Meetings:* welcome by arrangement with Secretary. Professional: Graeme Bell (01506 844356). Secretary: T.I. Adams (01506 842585).

LIVINGSTON. Deer Park Golf & Country Club, Golf Course Road, Carmondeans, Livingston EH54 8AB (01506 446699; Fax: 01506 435608). *Location:* off M8 Junction 3 onto Deer Park roundabout. Parkland course, first 9 holes flat, back 9 holes hilly. 18 holes, 6688 yards. S.S.S. 72. *Green Fees:* information not available. *Eating facilities:* four bars, catering seven days. *Visitors:* welcome. Snooker, ten pin bowling, squash courts, gym, pool, sauna, steam room. *Society Meetings:* catered for. Professional: Sandy Strachan.*
website: www.deer-park.co.uk

LIVINGSTON. Pumpherston Golf Club, Drumshoreland Road, Pumpherston, Livingston EH53 0LQ (01506 432869). *Location:* one mile east of Livingston, one and a half miles south of M8. Challenging parkland course, recently redeveloped. 18 holes, 6006 yards, 5492 metres. Par 70, S.S.S. 69. Practice area with pitching and bunker facilities, putting green, designed particularly for juniors. *Green Fees:* information not provided. *Eating facilities:* new clubhouse with bar, dining room and entertainment facilities; junior lounge. *Visitors:* welcome. *Society Meetings:* Mondays to Thursdays, maximum number 30. Professional: R. Fyvie (01506 433337). Secretary: J.F. Taylor (01506 432869).
website: www.pumpherstongolfclub.co.uk

Ideally situated just off J3 on the M8, we specialise in excellent value Corporate, Society and Visitor golf packages. With our superb Country Club, Ten-Pin Bowling Centre, Leisure Facilities, Golfers' Bar and Monarch Restaurant, there's something for everyone at West Lothian's home of golf.
Deer Park Golf & Country Club, Golf Course Road, Livingston, West Lothian EH54 8AB
Tel: 01506 446699 • Pro Shop: 01506 446688 • book online

www.deer-park.co.uk

LONGNIDDRY. **Longniddry Golf Club Ltd,** Links Road, Longniddry EH32 0NL (01875 852141; Fax: 01875 853371). *Location:* at the foot of Links Road in Longniddry village. Unique combination of woodland and links. Superb views over the Firth to Edinburgh and Fife. 18 holes, 6260 yards, 5690 metres. S.S.S. 71. Practice area, putting green, nets. *Green Fees:* weekdays £45.00 per round, £70.00 per day; weekends £65.00 per round. *Eating facilities:* catering available seven days, two bars and dining room. *Visitors:* welcome daily, though limited availability at weekends; advance booking recommended. *Society Meetings:* welcome Monday to Friday with Handicap Certificates. Professional: John Gray (01875 852228). Secretary: Bob Gunning (01875 852141).
e-mail: secretary@longniddrygolfclub.co.uk
website: www.longniddrygolfclub.co.uk

MUSSELBURGH. **Musselburgh Golf Club,** Monktonhall, Musselburgh EH21 6SA (0131-665 2005). *Location:* from the A1 end of the Edinburgh City bypass, on B6415 to Musselburgh. Wooded parkland, rivers. 18 holes, 6725 yards. S.S.S. 72. *Green Fees:* on application. *Eating facilities:* catering available. *Visitors:* welcome with reservation. *Society Meetings:* catered for. Professional: F. Mann (0131-665 7055).
e-mail: secretary@themusselburghgolfclub.com

MUSSELBURGH. **Musselburgh Old Course Golf Club,** 10 Balcarres Road, Musselburgh EH21 7SD (0131-665 6981). *Location*: A199 road at Musselburgh racecourse half a mile east of town centre. Seaside links course. 9 holes, 2887 yards. S.S.S. 69. Large practice area. *Green Fees*: information not available. *Eating facilities*: available. *Visitors*: welcome. Starter (0131-665 5438). Secretary: R. McGregor (0131 665 6981).
e-mail: secretary@mocgc.com
website: www.mocgc.com

NORTH BERWICK. **Glen Golf Club,** East Links, Tantallon Terrace, North Berwick EH39 4LE (01620 892726; Fax: 01620 895447). *Location:* one mile east of town centre, off A198. Seaside links with magnificent panoramic views. 18 holes, 6275 yards. S.S.S. 70. Practice ground, putting green. *Green Fees:* midweek £37.00, weekends £49.00. *Eating facilities:* full facilities available. *Visitors:* welcome anytime, no restrictions. Pro Shop. Trolleys, electric buggies and caddies available. *Society Meetings:* welcome, advance booking required. Office Manager: Rita Wilson (01620 892726; Fax: 01620 895447). Starter: (01620 892726).
e-mail: secretary@glengolfclub.co.uk
website: www.glengolfclub.co.uk

Overlooking the Almond Valley and the Pentland Hills beyond, Pumpherston Golf Club has a challenging 6000 yard, par 70, 18 hole course, and an excellent 280 yard practice area. Pumpherston Golf Club can cater for all your golfing requirements. Restaurant open 7 days Situated 15 minutes from Edinburgh/40 minutes from Glasgow and just 5 minutes off Junction 3 on the M8

Contact Richard Fyvie, Club Professional: 01506 433337
or Sheena Corner, Club Manager: 01506 432869
www.pumpherstongolfclub.co.uk

Pumpherston Golf Club
Drumshoreland Road
Pumpherston
Livingston EH53 0LQ

Tel: 01620 892726
Glen Golf Club
North Berwick
www.glengolfclub.co.uk

The Glen is one of the finest courses on the East Lothian Golf Coast.

Designed by James Braid and Ben Sayers, it is the most scenic course in Scotland. Every hole has a view of the sea and the spectacular Bass Rock.

Visitors and societies welcome seven days a week.
Green fees from £30.

402 Edinburgh & Lothians / SCOTLAND — THE GOLF GUIDE 2011

NORTH BERWICK. **The North Berwick Golf Club,** New Clubhouse, Beach Road, North Berwick EH39 4BB (01620 895040; Fax: 01620 890312). *Location*: 24 miles east of Edinburgh, A1 to Meadowmill roundabout then A198 to North Berwick. Seaside links. 18 holes, 6420 yards. S.S.S. 72. Practice ground. *Green Fees:* 2010 rates (subject to review). *Eating facilities:* diningroom and bar. *Visitors:* welcome from 10am, advance bookings (01620 892135) Saturdays – restricted when there are club fixtures. Lounge and changing rooms available. *Society Meetings:* catered for by arrangement. Professional: Martyn Huish (01620 893233); Secretary: C. J. Spencer (01620 895040). Advance Bookings: (01620 892135).
e-mail: secretary@northberwickgolfclub.com
website: www.northberwickgolfclub.com

PENICUIK. **Glencorse Golf Club,** Milton Bridge, Penicuik EH26 0RD (01968 677177). *Location:* A701 nine miles south of Edinburgh on Peebles Road. Voted one of Scotland's hidden gems by U.S. Sports Illustrated magazine. Parkland course with stream affecting 10 holes. 18 holes, 5217 yards. S.S.S. 66. *Green Fees:* weekdays £25.00 per round, £32.00 per day; weekends £32.00 per round. Package deals available. *Eating facilities:* all day catering and bar. *Visitors:* welcome at all times subject to Club Competitions. *Society Meetings:* catered for Mondays to Fridays and Sunday afternoons. Professional: Cliffe Jones (01968 676481). Secretary: Bill Oliver (01968 677189; Fax: 01968 674399).

PRESTONPANS. **Royal Musselburgh Golf Club,** Prestongrange House, Prestonpans EH32 9RP (Tel & Fax: 01875 810216). *Location*: B1361 North Berwick Road, Prestonpans. Fairly flat parkland, wooded course. 18 holes, 6254 yards. S.S.S. 70. *Green Fees*: weekday £35.00 per round, £45.00 per day; weekend round £40.00 (by appointment only). *Visitors*: welcome. *Society Meetings*: welcome by arrangement with the Management Secretary. Professional: John Henderson (Tel & Fax: 01875 810139). Management Secretary: D. Thomson (Tel & Fax: 01875 810276). Competition Secretary: David Sinclair (01875 819000).
e-mail: royalmusselburgh@btinternet.com
website: www.royalmusselburgh.co.uk

SOUTH QUEENSFERRY. **Dundas Parks Golf Club,** Dundas Estate, South Queensferry, West Lothian EH30 9SS. *Location:* five miles west of Edinburgh, on South Queensferry to Kirkliston road on right of A8000. Parkland course in open countryside. 9 holes (x 2), 6024 yards, 5510 metres. S.S.S. 70. Small practice area. *Eating facilities:* no bar or food facilities. *Visitors:* welcome with member, or by prior arrangement with Club Administrator. *Society Meetings:* by prior arrangement with Club Administrator. Club Administrator: Christine Wood (07747 854802).

UPHALL. **Uphall Golf Club,** Uphall, West Lothian EH52 6JT (01506 856404; Fax: 01506 855358). *Location:* eight miles west of Edinburgh Airport on the A89 Edinburgh to Glasgow road. Established parkland course. 18 holes, S.S.S. 67. *Green Fees:* information not available. *Eating facilities:* hot and cold snacks, lunches, high teas and bars, à la carte available Saturday evenings. *Visitors:* welcome weekdays without reservation. A booking through the Professional is required at weekends. *Society Meetings:* catered for. Professional: Gordon Law (01506 855553). Club Administrator Manager: Mima O'Connor (01506 856404; Fax: 01506 855358).*
e-mail: uphallgolfclub@btconnect.com

WEST CALDER. **Harburn Golf Club,** Harburn, West Calder EH55 8RS (01506 871256). *Location:* two miles south of West Calder on B7008. Parkland course. 18 holes, 6125 yards. S.S.S. 70. Practice ground. *Green Fees:* information not provided. *Eating facilities:* full catering and bar service available. *Visitors:* welcome any time, no restrictions. *Society Meetings:* special terms on request. Professional: S.J. Mills (01506 871582). Secretary: Mrs H. Warnock (01506 871131; Fax: 01506 870286).
e-mail: info@harburngolfclub.co.uk
website: www.harburngolfclub.co.uk

WHITBURN. **Polkemmet Golf Course,** Polkemmet Country Park, Whitburn, West Lothian (01501 743905). *Location:* off B7066, one mile west of Whitburn. Inland course set within old private estate, mature varied woodland with belts of rhododendrons. 9 holes, 2946 metres. Par 37. 15 bay floodlit driving range. *Green Fees:* information not available. *Eating facilities:* not functioning at present. *Visitors:* welcome. Public course. Facilities include bowling green, picnic areas, etc. Caddy cart available for hire. Secretary: West Lothian Council, Countryside Section, Property Services, Development and Environmental Services, Lammermuir House, Livingston.*

WHITEKIRK. **Whitekirk Golf & Country Club,** Whitekirk, Near North Berwick EH39 5PR (01620 870300; Fax: 01620 870330). *Location*: east of North Berwick, off the main A1 Edinburgh - Berwick upon Tweed road, on the A198. Heathland, wooded, lakes, commanding views over East Lothian. 18 holes, 6526 yards. S.S.S. 72. *Green Fees:* information not provided. *Eating facilities*: lunches, dinners, bar snacks. *Visitors*: welcome, no restrictions. Golf academy; buggies and carts available. *Society Meetings:* welcome seven days, special rates available. Professional: Paul Wardell (01620 870300; Fax: 01620 870330). Secretary: David Brodie (01620 870300; Fax: 01620 870330).
e-mail: countryclub@whitekirk.com
website: www.whitekirk.com

WINCHBURGH. **Niddry Castle Golf Club,** Castle Road, Winchburgh, Broxburn EH52 6RQ (01506 891097). *Location:* 10 miles west of Edinburgh on B9080 between Kirkliston and Linlithgow. Wooded, natural parkland. 18 holes, 5914 yards. S.S.S. 69. Practice net. *Green Fees:* weekday £22.00 per round, £29.00 per day; weekend £29.00 per round, £35.00 per day; member's guest £8.00 per round. *Eating facilities:* full catering; bar. *Visitors:* welcome weekdays before 4.30pm, weekends on competition days after 2.30pm. *Society Meetings:* by arrangement. Secretary: Brian Brooks.
website: www.niddrycastlegc.co.uk

The North Berwick Golf Club

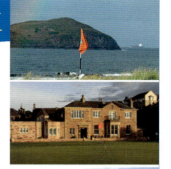

This is golfing heaven – a pure links course which has hosted final Qualifying for The Open at Muirfield since 1992 and hosted the Amateur Championship in 2010. It is a true Championship course

The Club is over 175 years old and still playing over the same piece of land as when it was formed. It has breathtaking views of the islands in the Forth and towards Fife.

The course is sprinkled with classic holes, including the 15th – Redan – a tricky par 3 with a severely sloping green. A must for lovers of links!

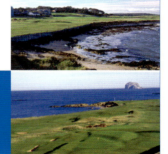

Tel: 01620 892135 • Fax: 01620 893274
e-mail: bookings@northberwickgolfclub.com
New Clubhouse, Beach Road,
North Berwick, East Lothian EH39 4BB
www.northberwickgolfclub.com

WEST FENTON Court

Luxury self-catering holiday cottages near North Berwick

www.westfenton.co.uk

perfect for families, golf, walking, beaches and relaxation

Kitchen & dining areas for enjoying long, relaxed meals.
Lounge rooms with hardwood floors and sumptuous sofas for relaxing after a day's golf or sightseeing.
Bathrooms - beautifully tiled and equipped.
Bedrooms - tastefully furnished for a comfortable sleep in the quiet of the country.
Patio gardens - lawned and fenced, ideal for barbecues, alfresco dining or an evening drink.

West Fenton Court is located in a conservation area, adjacent to a nature reserve, just one mile south of Gullane and close to North Berwick, ideal for golf, beaches and coastal walks. Edinburgh is just 35 minutes by car or train.

West Fenton, North Berwick, East Lothian EH39 5AL • 01620 842154 • e-mail: info@westfenton.co.uk

---

Other British holiday guides from FHG Guides

**PUBS & INNS • 300 GREAT HOTELS • SHORT BREAK HOLIDAYS
The bestselling and original PETS WELCOME! • 500 GREAT PLACES TO STAY
SELF-CATERING HOLIDAYS • BED & BREAKFAST STOPS
CARAVAN & CAMPING HOLIDAYS • FAMILY BREAKS**

Published annually: available in all good bookshops or direct from the publisher:
**FHG Guides, Abbey Mill Business Centre, Seedhill, Paisley PA1 1TJ
Tel: 0141 887 0428 • Fax: 0141 889 7204**
e-mail: admin@fhguides.co.uk • www.holidayguides.com

Fife

ABERDOUR. **Aberdour Golf Club,** Seaside Place, Aberdour KY3 0TX (01383 860080; Fax: 01383 860050). *Location:* take Shore Road from centre of village. Parkland course situated along the shoreline of the River Forth. 18 holes, 5460 yards. S.S.S. 67. *Green Fees:* Monday to Thursday £32.00 per round, £42.00 per day; Fridays £35.00 per round, £45.00 per day; weekends £42.00 per round, £52.00 per day. 2010 rates (subject to review). *Eating facilities:* full catering. *Visitors:* welcome. *Society Meetings:* catered for on weekdays and Sundays. On Sundays, maximum size of group 24. Professional: David Gemmell (01383 860256). Manager (01383 860080; Fax: 01383 860050).
e-mail: info@aberdourgolfclub.co.uk
website: www.aberdourgolfclub.co.uk

ANSTRUTHER. **Anstruther Golf Club,** Marsfield, Shore Road, Anstruther KY10 3DZ (01333 310956). *Location:* nine miles south of St Andrews, west side of Anstruther. Seaside links course. 9 holes, 4690 yards. S.S.S. 63. Hardest Par 3 in UK. *Green Fees:* 9 holes £15.00. 18 holes £25.00. *Eating facilities:* bar meals, high tea, lunches, dinner. Rockies Restaurant (01333 310981). *Visitors:* welcome except during club competitions. *Society Meetings:* welcome except Saturdays and competition days. Secretary: Malcolm MacDonald.
e-mail: captain@anstruthergolf.co.uk

BURNTISLAND. **Burntisland Golf House Club,** Dodhead, Burntisland KY3 9LQ (01592 874093). *Location*: Burntisland, Fife. Parkland with some hills. 18 holes, 5965 yards. S.S.S. 70. Practice ground and net. *Green Fees:* information not available. *Eating facilities:* all day bar and catering. *Visitors*: all parties catered for. Changing room. *Society Meetings*: welcome with advance bookings. Professional: P. Wytrazek (01592 872116).*
website: www.burntislandgolfhouseclub.co.uk

CARDENDEN. **Auchterderran Golf Club,** Woodend Road, Cardenden KY5 0NH (01592 721579). *Location:* six miles north of Kirkcaldy. Flat course. 9 holes, 5252 yards. S.S.S. 66. *Green Fees*: information not available. *Eating facilities:* clubhouse bar facilities, meals available on request, snacks available most times. *Visitors*: all welcome, Saturdays and some Sundays members' competitions held from 7am to 11am and 1pm to 3pm. *Society Meetings:* welcome. Secretary: Charles Taylor (01592 720080).*

COLINSBURGH. **Charleton Golf Club,** Colinsburgh Golf Ltd, Charleton, Colinsburgh KY9 1HG (01333 340505; Fax: 01333 340583). *Location:* B942, Colinsburgh (near Elie). Parkland course. 18 holes, 6446 yards, 5684 metres. S.S.S. 72. Driving range, bunker practice area, putting green. *Green Fees:* weekday £27.00 per round, £44.00 day ticket; weekend £32.00 per round, £64.00 day ticket. *Eating facilities:* fully licensed clubhouse with restaurant. *Visitors:* all welcome, pay as you play, no restrictions, please book. Carts, buggies. *Society Meetings:* all welcome. Professional: George Finlayson. General Manager: Laura Paterson.

THE APPEARANCE OF AN ASTERISK (*) AT THE END OF A CLUB OR COURSE ENTRY INDICATES THAT UP-TO-DATE INFORMATION HAS NOT BEEN SUPPLIED

Cottage to let in a conservation village in the attractive East Neuk of Fife, 3 miles from Elie and 11 from St Andrews.
Easy reach of sandy beaches, coastal walks and numerous golf courses.
Two bedrooms, lounge, kitchen/diner and a walled rear garden. Sleeps 4/5, pets welcome. Prices from £275 per week.

For further details, telephone
01788 890942 or see
www.eastneukcottage.co.uk

SCOTLAND / Fife

COWDENBEATH. **Cowdenbeath Golf Club,** Seco Place, Cowdenbeath KY4 8PD (01383 511918). *Location:* just off the A92 after Dunfermline. Parkland course. 18 holes, 6212 yards. S.S.S. 71. Practice ground and putting green. *Green Fees:* information not available. *Visitors:* welcome at any time. *Society Meetings:* booking available by telephone (01383 513079/01383 511918). Secretary: L. Connelly.*

COWDENBEATH. **Dora Golf Course,** Seco Place, Cowdenbeath KY4 8PF (01383 513079). Parkland course, 18 holes. Par 71. *Green Fees:* information not available. *Eating facilities:* bar available, catering by arrangement. *Society Meetings*: please telephone for details.*
website: www.cowdenbeath-golf.com

CRAIL. **Crail Golfing Society,** Balcomie Clubhouse, Fifeness, Crail KY10 3XN (01333 450686; Fax: 01333 450416). Instituted 1786. *Location:* eleven miles south-east of St Andrews on A917. Traditional links courses. Balcomie Links: 18 holes, 5861 yards. S.S.S. 70. Par 69. Craighead Links: 18 holes, 6722 yards. S.S.S. 74. Par 72. Practice ground. *Green Fees:* weekdays £52.00 per round, £72.00 per day; weekends and Public Holidays £65.00 per round, £92.00 per day. *Eating facilities:* quality catering and bar. *Visitors:* welcome. *Society Meetings:* advance booking available for parties. Professional: Graeme Lennie (01333 450960). Secretary: (01333 450686; Fax: 01333 450416).
e-mail: info@crailgolfingsociety.co.uk
website: www.crailgolfingsociety.co.uk

CUPAR. **Cupar Golf Club,** Hilltarvit, Cupar KY15 5JT (01334 653549). *Location:* near cemetery on Ceres Road. Hillside/parkland course. 9 holes, 5153 yards. S.S.S. 66. Practice putting green. *Green Fees:* 9 holes £15.00, 18 holes £20.00. *Eating facilities:* full catering/bar. *Visitors:* welcome, except Saturdays. *Society Meetings:* by arrangement with Secretary. Secretary: (01334 653549).
e-mail: cupargc@fsmail.net
website: www.cupargolfclub.co.uk

CUPAR. **Elmwood,** Stratheden, Near Cupar KY15 5RS (01334 658780; Fax: 01334 658781). *Location:* signposted from both A91 and A914, one mile west of Cupar, nine miles from St Andrews. Gently undulating parkland. 18 holes, 6300 yards. S.S.S 70. *Green Fees:* weekdays: £24.00 per round, £34.00 per day; weekends £26.00 per round, £36.00 per day. 2010 rates (subject to review). *Eating facilities:* full catering and bar. New lounge. *Visitors:* welcome anytime. Trolleys and buggies available. New indoor Golf Swing Analysis Studio. *Society Meetings:* welcome, advance bookings and special rates. Golf Administrator: Sharif Sulaiman
e-mail: clubhouse@elmwood.ac.uk
website: www.elmwoodgc.co.uk

DUNFERMLINE. **Canmore Golf Club,** Venture Fair Avenue, Dunfermline KY12 0PE (01383 724969). *Location:* one mile north of town centre on A823. Parkland, undulating. 18 holes, 5347 yards. S.S.S. 66. *Green Fees:* information not available. *Eating facilities:* full catering and bar. *Visitors:* welcome weekdays, limited Sundays. *Society Meetings:* we welcome visiting societies with prior reservation (not on Saturdays). Professional: David Gemmell (01383 728416). Secretary: Andrew Watson (01383 724969).*
e-mail: canmoregolfclub@btconnect.com
website: www.canmoregolfclub.co.uk

www.holidayguides.com

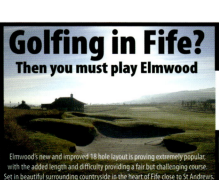

406 Fife / SCOTLAND

DUNFERMLINE. Dunfermline Golf Club, Pitfirrane, Crossford, By Dunfermline KY12 8QW (01383 723534). *Location:* two miles west of Dunfermline on A994 to Kincardine Bridge. Undulating parkland. 18 holes, 6121 yards, 5597 metres. S.S.S. 70. Practice area. *Green Fees:* £35.00 per round, £50.00 per day weekdays; £40.00 per round Sundays. *Eating facilities:* full catering, bar snacks available. *Visitors:* welcome 9.30am to 4pm weekdays and Sunday. Must have official Club Handicap. *Society Meetings:* accepted weekdays and Sunday by prior arrangement. Professional: Chris Nugent (01383 729061). Secretary: Robert De Rose (01383 723534). e-mail: secretary@dunfermlinegolfclub.com

DUNFERMLINE. Forrester Park Resort, Pitdinnie, Cairneyhill KY12 8RF (01383 880505; Fax: 01383 882430). Parkland course with gentle undulations and lots of water features. 300m driving range, practice bunkers. *Green Fees:* Winter, £25.00 weekday, £35.00 weekend; Summer, £35.00 weekday, £45.00 weekend. Open all year, no mats, no winter tees or greens. *Eating facilities:* Acanthus 5 star à la carte restaurant and bar/bistro. New members area, sports bar. *Visitors:* welcome, no restrictions. *Society Meetings:* always welcome. Tuition, golfshop, showers available. Professional: Paul Edgcombe. Secretary: Robert Forrester.
e-mail: forresterpark@aol.com
website: www.forresterparkresort.com

DUNFERMLINE. Pitreavie (Dunfermline) Golf Club, Queensferry Road, Dunfermline KY11 8PR (01383 722591; Fax: 01383 722592). *Location*: M90 Edinburgh/Perth, leave at Junction 2 for Dunfermline. Undulating parkland with views across Firth of Forth. 18 holes, 6032 yards. S.S.S. 69. Practice ground. *Green Fees:* weekdays £25.00, weekends £30.00. 2010 rate (subject to review). *Eating facilities*: full catering and bar facilities. *Visitors*: welcome. Please phone the Professional in advance. Pull trolleys available. No overnight accommodation. *Society Meetings*: catered for, must be booked through Secretary. Professional: Paul Brookes (01383 723151). Secretary: Malcolm Brown (01383 722591).
website: www.pitreaviegolfclub.co.uk

DUNFERMLINE. Saline Golf Club, Kinneddar Hill, Saline KY12 9LT (01383 852591). *Location:* turn off M90 at Junction 4, 7 miles along B914 to Dollar. Hillside parkland course. 9 holes, 5302 yards. S.S.S. 66. Practice net, putting green. *Green Fees:* Adult, Monday to Saturday £12.00 18 holes, Sunday £14.00 18 holes; Adult, Monday to Friday £9.00 9 holes, Sunday £9.00 9 holes; Monday to Friday £6.00 per day, Sunday £6.00 per day; Junior and Senior Citizens, Monday to Friday £6.00 per day, Sunday £6.00 per day. Two for One vouchers accepted. *Eating facilities:* bar snacks; meals by prior arrangement. *Visitors:* welcome, restricted Saturdays and Thursdays. *Society Meetings:* catered for midweek or Sundays; maximum 24. Secretary: Mrs Adrienne Lyon.
e-mail: saline-golf-club@supanet.com
website: www.saline-golf-club.co.uk

THE GOLF GUIDE 2011

ELIE. Earlsferry Thistle Golf Club, Melon Park, Elie (01333 330301). *Location:* A917 golf course signs in Elie. Seaside links. 18 holes, 6250 yards. S.S.S. 70. *Green Fees:* information not available. *Visitors:* welcome weekdays. The course belongs to Elie Golf House Club, also played by Earlsferry Thistle.*

ELIE. Golf House Club, Elie KY9 1AS (01333 330301; Fax: 01333 330895). *Location:* 10 miles south of St Andrews on A917. Links course. 18 holes, 6273 yards. S.S.S. 70. *Green Fees:* weekdays £70.00 per round, £90.00 per day; weekends £80.00 per round, £100.00 per day. *Eating facilities:* lunches, teas, etc. *Visitors:* welcome with reservation. Elie Sports Centre nearby with leisure facilities and cafeteria. *Society Meetings:* catered for except at weekends. Professional: Ian Muir (01333 330955). Secretary: Graham Scott (01333 330301; Fax: 01333 330895).
website: www.golfhouseclub.org

FALKLAND. Falkland Golf Club, The Myre, Falkland KY15 7AA (01337 857404). *Location:* entrance on A912, 12 miles from Kirkcaldy – approximately 20 minutes from St. Andrews. Lies at the foot of East Lomond Hills. Flat meadowland, beautiful views. 9 holes, 4988 yards, 4560 metres. S.S.S. 65 for 18 holes. *Green Fees:* contact clubhouse. *Eating facilities:* by arrangement. *Visitors:* welcome.

GLENROTHES. Glenrothes Golf Club, Golf Course Road, Glenrothes KY6 2LA (01592 758686). *Location:* at the western end of town, near airfield. Parkland, wide fairways, with burn crossing four fairways on back nine holes. 18 holes, 6444 yards, 5984 metres. S.S.S. 71. *Green Fees:* information not available. *Eating facilities:* full catering service and bar. Temporary day membership of club available to visitors. *Visitors:* welcome, some restrictions weekends. *Society Meetings:* welcome, advance booking, numbers 12-40. Hon. Secretary: Claire Dawson (01592 754561).*
e-mail: secretary@glenrothesgolf.org.uk
website: www.glenrothesgolf.org.uk

KINCARDINE. Tulliallan Golf Club, Alloa Road, Kincardine on Forth, by Alloa FK10 4BB (01259 730396; Fax: 01259 731395). *Location:* on A908 five miles east of Alloa, one mile north of Kincardine Bridge. Parkland, slightly wooded, burn winds through the course. 18 holes, 6000 yards. S.S.S. 69. Practice ground. *Green Fees:* £22.00 per round, £36.00 per day; Sunday £26.00 per round, £43.00 per day, with catering £46.00 weekday, £57.75 weekends. *Eating facilities:* dining room, bar 11am to 11pm. *Society Meetings:* catered for by phoning Pro shop. Professional: Steve Kelly (Tel & Fax: 01259 730798). Secretary: Amanda Maley (01259 730396).
e-mail: tulliallangolf@btconnect.com
website: www.tulliallangolf.com

KINGHORN. Kinghorn Municipal Golf Club, Burntisland Road, Kinghorn KY3 9RE (01592 890345). *Location:* bus stop at course, railway station three minutes away. Semi links course with hills. 18 holes, 5166 yards, S.S.S. 66. *Green Fees:* weeekday £15.00, weekend £20.00; Junior weekeday £5.00, weekend £8.00. *Eating facilities:* meals at clubhouse on request, local hotels. *Visitors:* welcome at any time; no large parties on Saturdays. *Society Meetings:* catered for by arrangement. Secretary: Gordon Tulloch (01592 891008). Starter: (01592 890978).

KINGSBARNS. Kingsbarns Golf Links, Kingsbarns, St Andrews KY16 8QD (01334 460860; Fax: 01334 460877). *Location*: on the coast near the village of Kingsbarns, 10 miles south-east of St Andrews. 18 holes, 6174 yards, Par 72. Driving range. *Green Fees:* information not available. *Eating facilities:* bar; light meals available. *Visitors*: welcome. Maximum handicap 28 (Men), 36 (Ladies). Fully stocked Pro Shop; locker lounges with showers and changing facilities.*
website: www.kingsbarns.com

KIRKCALDY. Dunnikier Park Golf Club, Dunnikier Way, Kirkcaldy KY1 3LP (01592 261599 (Clubhouse). *Location:* one mile off A92 on the B981 north side of Kirkcaldy. Municipal parkland course, not hilly. 18 holes, 6601 yards, 6036 metres. S.S.S. 72. Practice ground. *Green Fees:* information not provided. *Eating facilities:* full bar and catering facilities. *Visitors:* welcome, no restrictions. *Society Meetings:* welcome by arrangement with Secretary (min. 12, max. 30). Professional: (01592 642121). Secretary: Raymond Johnston (01592 261599).
e-mail: dunnikierparkgolfclub@btinternet.com
website: www.dunnikierparkgolfclub.com

KIRKCALDY. Kirkcaldy Golf Club, Balwearie Road, Kirkcaldy KY2 5LT (01592 205240). *Location*: west end of town adjacent to Beveridge Park. Challenging parkland layout in rural setting with views across Firth of Forth. 18 holes, 6086 yards. S.S.S. 70, Par 71. Practice ground. *Green Fees*: information not available. *Eating facilities*: bar and full catering facilities. Magnificent clubhouse. *Visitors*: welcome, restricted Tuesdays and Saturdays. Pro Shop. Trolleys for hire. *Society Meetings*: welcome but please phone or write in advance. Professional: Anthony Caira (01592 203258). Secretary: Mike Langstaff (01592 205240).*

LADYBANK. Ladybank Golf Club, Annsmuir, Ladybank KY15 7RA (01337 830814). *Location:* on A92 off A91, 15 miles St. Andrews. Wooded heathland. 18 holes, 6641 yards. S.S.S. 72. Practice ground. *Green Fees:* information not provided. *Eating facilities:* full catering facilities and bar. *Visitors:* welcome without reservation. Party bookings by arrangement with Secretary. *Society Meetings:* by arrangement. Professional: Sandy Smith (Tel & Fax: 01337 830725). Secretary: Fraser McCluskey (01337 830814; Fax: 01337 831505).

Best Western Keavil House Hotel is a relaxed 73-bedroom country house hotel, with beautifully appointed bedrooms, an award-winning restaurant, and health and leisure spa. The hotel is centrally located in the Kingdom of Fife, the home of golf, offering the perfect place to enjoy golf breaks on the best links and parkland courses. Between St Andrews in the east and Scotland's ancient capital of Dunfermline in the west there is an abundance of great golf courses to choose from, one of which is adjacent to the hotel.

Best Western Keavil House Hotel, Crossford, Dunfermline KY12 8NN
Tel: 01383 736258 • Fax: 01383 621600
e-mail: reservations@keavilhouse.co.uk •
www.keavilhouse.co.uk

AA Rosette Cardoon Restaurant • Picture of Health spa
FREE high speed internet access • Ample free car parking
Classic, Superior and Master bedrooms • Family rooms

TULLIALLAN GOLF CLUB
Alloa Road, Kincardine FK10 4BB

An outstanding parkland course renowned for its true greens.
Golf and catering packages available at very competitive rates.
Centrally located in Fife with easy access from the motorway.

Contact Steve Kelly on **01259 730798**

e-mail: tulliallangolf@btconnect.com

www.tulliallangolf.co.uk

LESLIE. Leslie Golf Club, Balsillie Laws, Leslie, Glenrothes KY6 3EZ (01592 620040). Parkland with small stream running through some fairways. 9 holes, 4940 yards. S.S.S. 65. *Green Fees:* information not provided. *Eating facilities:* bar open all day. *Visitors:* always welcome, some restrictions on competition days.

LEUCHARS. St Michaels Golf Club, Gallowhill, Leuchars KY16 0DX (01334 839365; Fax: 01334 838789). *Location:* quarter of a mile outside Leuchars on A919 towards Dundee. Undulating parkland course surrounded by plantations. 18 holes, 5802 yards. S.S.S. 68. *Green Fees:* information not provided. *Eating facilities:* bar and catering available. *Visitors:* welcome anytime but not before 12 noon Sundays. Changing rooms and showers. Trolley hire and electric carts. *Society Meetings:* by prior arrangement. A booking fee is payable before confirmation of reservation. Secretary: G. Dignan (01334 838666; Fax: 01334 838789).

LEVEN. Leven Golfing Society, PO Box 14609, Links Road, Leven KY8 4HS (01333 426096; Fax: 01333 424229). *Location:* 14 miles south west of St Andrews. Championship Links course used for national and international events. 18 holes, 6506 yards. S.S.S. 72. *Green Fees:* weekdays £50.00 per round, £65.00 per day; weekends £55.00 per round, £70.00 per day. Juniors (under 18) £10.00. Family ticket (2 adults + 2 Juniors) £90.00. 3-day ticket £110.00, 7-day ticket £200.00. Details of special rates from Link Secretary. *Eating facilities:* full catering available. *Visitors:* welcome except Saturdays. *Society Meetings:* by arrangement, please contact the Secretary, Links Joint Committee, Promenade, Leven KY8 4HS (01333 428859). Secretary: Verne Greger (Tel & Fax: 01333 424229).

LEVEN. Leven Thistle Golf Club, Balfour Street, Leven KY8 4JF (01333 426333; Fax: 01333 439910). *Location:* 10 miles south west of St. Andrews. Top championship links used for national and international events including Open qualifying. 18 holes, 6506 yards. S.S.S. 72. *Green Fees:* information not available. *Eating facilities:* full catering available, two bars, function hall. *Visitors:* welcome without reservation, except Saturdays. *Society Meetings:* for group bookings contact Leven Links Joint Committee, Promenade, Leven, Fife KY8 4HS (01333 428859). Secretary: I. Winn. Links Secretary: Ms J. Clark.*
e-mail: secretary@leventhistlegolf.org.uk

LEVEN. Scoonie Golf Club, North Links, Leven KY8 4SP (01333 307007). *Location:* nearest town Leven on coastal road to St Andrews. Flat, typical seaside bunkers. 18 holes, 5476 yards. S.S.S. 66. *Green Fees:* information not available. *Eating facilities:* full catering available, bar open normal hours. *Visitors:* welcome anytime. *Society Meetings:* welcome by bookings except Saturdays. Secretary: J. Divers (01333 307007; Fax: 01333 307008).*

LOCHGELLY. Lochgelly Golf Club, Cartmore Road, Lochgelly KY5 9PB (01592 780174). *Location:* take M90 to Junction 3A Halbeath Interchange, follow signs. Parkland. 18 holes, 5491 yards, 5063 metres. S.S.S. 67. *Green Fees:* weekdays £10.00 per round, £18.00 per day; weekends £18.00 per round, £25.00 per day. *Eating facilities:* catering available. *Visitors:* welcome, no restrictions weekdays, weekends parties limited to 24. Professional: Martin Goldie (01592 782589). Secretary: A. Robertson (01592 782589).

LUNDIN LINKS. Lundin Golf Club, Golf Road, Lundin Links KY8 6BA (01333 320202). *Location:* three miles east of Leven, 12 miles SW of St Andrews. Seaside links. 18 holes, 6371 yards. S.S.S. 71. Practice ground. *Green Fees:* £55.00 per round, £75.00 per day weekdays; Saturdays and Sundays after 2.30pm £60.00 per round. 2010 rates (subject to review). *Eating facilities:* bar and dining room. *Visitors:* welcome Monday/Thursday 9am to 3.30pm; Friday 9am to 3pm; Saturdays no visitors before 2.30pm; limited Sunday golf available. Professional: Ron Walker (01333 320051). Secretary: A.J. McDonald (01333 320202).
e-mail: secretary@lundingolfclub.co.uk
website: www.lundingolfclub.co.uk

LUNDIN LINKS. Lundin Ladies Golf Club, Woodielea Road, Lundin Links KY8 6AR. *Location:* at Lundin Links on A915, turn into road opposite Royal Bank of Scotland. Excellent parkland course, with famous standing stones. 9 holes, 2365 yards. S.S.S. 68. *Green Fees:* information not available. *Eating facilities:* none available, but local hotels within walking distance. *Visitors:* welcome, restricted tee times on Wednesdays during season. Starter (01333 320022). Clubhouse: (01333 320832).*

Looking for accommodation near golf clubs?, then visit www.holidayguides.com for where to stay when playing golf around the regions

The Promenade, Leven, Fife KY8 4HS
Tel/Fax: 01333 428859
e-mail: secretary@leven-links.com
www.leven-links.com

Leven Links, in part one of the oldest pieces of golfing ground in the world, is a true seaside links course. It has hosted many national and international events and is used as a final qualifying course for the Open Championship when it is held at St Andrews. The strength of Leven Links lies in its fine variety of links-type holes combined with large greens; turning into the prevailing west wind at the 13th leaves the golfer with a lot of work to do before reaching one of the finest finishing holes in golf.

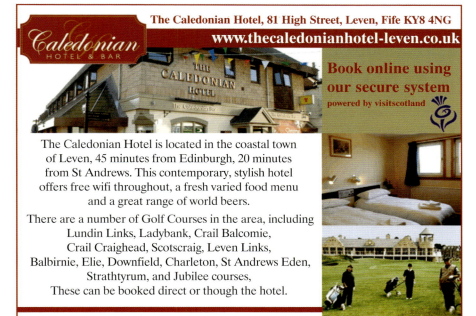

The Caledonian Hotel, 81 High Street, Leven, Fife KY8 4NG
www.thecaledonianhotel-leven.co.uk

Book online using our secure system
powered by visitscotland

The Caledonian Hotel is located in the coastal town of Leven, 45 minutes from Edinburgh, 20 minutes from St Andrews. This contemporary, stylish hotel offers free wifi throughout, a fresh varied food menu and a great range of world beers.

There are a number of Golf Courses in the area, including Lundin Links, Ladybank, Crail Balcomie, Crail Craighead, Scotscraig, Leven Links, Balbirnie, Elie, Downfield, Charleton, St Andrews Eden, Strathtyrum, and Jubilee courses, These can be booked direct or though the hotel.

Tel: 01333 424 101 • E-mail: caledonianhotel.leven@belhavenpubs.net

Situated in the East Neuk of Fife only 12 miles from St Andrews with panoramic views over the Firth of Forth.
Voted among the top links courses in Britain and has hosted the British Open Final Qualifying. Members and staff at Lundin take great pride in ensuring their many visitors and guests enjoy the magnificent links and renowned hospitality.

**Lundin Golf Club, Golf Road,
Lundin Links (By St Andrews), Fife KY8 6BA**
Tel: Secretary/Steward (01333) 320202
Professional: (01333) 320051
e-mail: secretary@lundingolfclub.co.uk

MARKINCH. **Balbirnie Park Golf Club,** The Clubhouse, Balbirnie Park, Markinch, Glenrothes KY7 6NR (01592 612095; Fax: 01592 612383). *Location:* outside Markinch near the A92. Wooded parkland course. 18 holes, 6334 yards. S.S.S. 71. *Green Fees:* information not available. *Eating facilities:* snacks, lunch, high tea and full meals available during clubhouse hours. *Visitors:* no restrictions at present other than maximum number of 24 at weekends and no visitors before 10am weekends. *Society Meetings:* welcome. Professional: Craig Donnelly (Tel & Fax: 01592 752006). Club Administrator: Steve Oliver (01592 612095; Fax: 01592 612383). Starter: (01592 752006).*
e-mail: craigfdonnelly@aol.com
website: www.balbirniegolf.com

THE APPEARANCE OF AN ASTERISK (*) AT THE END OF A CLUB OR COURSE ENTRY INDICATES THAT UP-TO-DATE INFORMATION HAS NOT BEEN SUPPLIED

One of the finest golf courses in the home of golf...

Balbirnie Park Golf Club

Balbirnie Park, Markinch,
Glenrothes KY7 6NR
Tel & Fax: 01592 752006
e-mail: craigfdonnelly@aol.com
www.balbirniegolf.com

Situated in Markinch near Glenrothes and set within 140 acres of superb woodland, this beautiful layout is a fine example of parkland golf – with the natural contours being the inspiration behind the course.
Visitors most welcome. Full clubhouse facilities available including licensed restaurant.
Only 20 miles from the Old Course at St Andrews.

The Crusoe Hotel

Main Street, Lower Largo, Fife KY8 6BT
Tel: 01333 320759 • Fax: 01333 320865
email: relax@crusoehotel.co.uk
www.crusoehotel.co.uk

*Old-world ambience with fine harbour views. En suite accommodation, outstanding cuisine, free house.
Only 15 minutes from St Andrews.
3 courses, including The Old Course from £120*

BEST WESTERN SCORES HOTEL ST ANDREWS

The closest hotel to the first tee of the Old Course and the Royal and Ancient Clubhouse with stunning views over St Andrews West Sands beach.

3 DAY UNLIMITED GOLF PACKAGES
On the New, Jubilee, Eden and Strathtyrum Courses
3 nights Dinner, Bed and Breakfast
From £247 per person *

EXCELLENT FACILITIES FOR GOLFERS PROVIDED
Single and Twin Accommodation
Golf Bag Store and Drying Facilities
Golf Manager and Concierge

3 DINING OPTIONS
19th Hole Bar
Champions Coffee Shop and Grill
Alexander's Restaurant and Scorecards Bar

76 The Scores, St Andrews, KY16 9BB
Email: reception@scoreshotel.co.uk
Website: www.scoreshotel.co.uk
Tel: 01334 472451   Fax: 01334 473947

* Sharing Traditional Double/Twin, subject to availability. Terms and Conditions apply.

ST ANDREWS. Old Course, St Andrews KY16 9SF (01334 466666; Fax: 01334 466664). *Location:* go into St Andrews on the A91, follow signs to West Sands. Approximately 50 miles from Edinburgh. Public links. 18 holes, 6721 yards. S.S.S. 73. 60 bay driving range, practice facilities. *Green Fees:* information not provided. *Eating facilities:* Links Clubhouse with full facilities; there is a buggy shuttle run from the clubhouse to the Old Course. *Visitors:* Handicap Certificate required. Handicap limit 24 or less (Men), 36 or less (Ladies). Trolleys allowed after 12 noon from May to September.
website: www.standrews.org.uk

Visit
www.holidayguides.com
for convenient accommodation when playing golf around the regions

PITCAIRLIE HOUSE — Hidden Secret of Fife

Set within a 120 acre estate of woods, streams, parklands and two ornamental lakes, Pitcairlie is a 16th century castle offering luxury self catering holiday cottage accommodation. All of our properties have been newly refurbished to a very high standard, including fully fitted kitchens and gas central heating. Our guests are welcome to enjoy our indoor heated swimming pool and sauna. Free WiFi. All linen and heating provided. For golfers, there are many excellent golf courses within easy reach, including the Old Course in St Andrews and Carnoustie in Tayside.

Pitcairlie House, Auchtermuchty, Fife KY14 6EU
Tel: 01337 827418 • Mobile: 07831 646157
e-mail: reservations@pitcairlie-leisure.co.uk • www.pitcairlie-leisure.co.uk

Big Sky & Room to Breathe

We are a locally run family business who take pride in giving individual attention. Our superb and exciting range of hand-picked quality accommodation will offer inspiration for all needs and tastes. The East Coast of Fife is an area of outstanding natural beauty boasting long sandy beaches, rolling seas, picture postcard fishing villages, a truly stunning coastline shared by seals, whales and dolphins, and an abundance of historic golf courses, spectacular sunrises and sunsets and much much more!!

Peter & Sue Griffiths

The **East Fife** Letting Company
Craigforth Cottage, Earlsferry, Elie, Fife KY9 1AD • Tel: 01333 330 241
e-mail: info@eastfifeletting.co.uk • www.eastfifeletting.co.uk

412 Fife / SCOTLAND — THE GOLF GUIDE 2011

DRUMOIG – GOLF HOTEL –

Drumoig, Leuchars, St Andrews KY16 0DS

Hotel Bookings:
Tel: +44 (0) 1382 541800 • Fax: +44 (0) 1382 542211
e-mail: drumoig@sol.co.uk
Golf Bookings Tel: +44 (0) 1382 541898
e-mail: DrumoigGolf@btconnect.com

The resort, located near St Andrews in Fife, includes a par 72-championship golf course, golf practice centre and hotel.

Set amongst 250 acres, the on-site hotel offers a superb vantage point overlooking the golf course's 18th fairway and lochs. The 18-hole golf course is exciting and varied and has its own driving range, allowing you to polish your golf skills before your round.

Visiting golfers to Drumoig and the St Andrews area will enjoy the spectacular views of St Andrews Bay, the River Tay and of the stunning Fife countryside that are available from Drumoig Golf Course, before enjoying an evening dining in the hotel restaurant or a relaxed drink in the hotel bar.

So for a memorable experience, true enjoyment and real relaxation, join us in Fife at Drumoig.

www.drumoigleisure.com

ST ANDREWS. Balgove Course, St Andrews Links Trust, St Andrews KY16 9SF (01334 466666; Fax: 01334 466664). *Location:* A91 to St Andrews, turning is on the left just before the town. Public nine hole beginners' course, 1520 yards. S.S.S. 60 (18 holes). *Green Fees:* £8.00-£12.00. 2010 rates (subject to review). *Eating facilities:* adjacent Eden Clubhouse with full facilities. Children's room. *Visitors:* welcome with or without reservation. Trolleys £4.00 per round; battery-powered trolleys £12.00 per round. *Society Meetings:* welcome.
website: www.standrews.org.uk

ST ANDREWS. The Castle Course, St Andrews Links Trust, Kinkell, By St Andrews KY16 9PL (01334 466666; Fax: 01334 466664). Open 1st April to 30th November. *Location:* from St Andrews take the A917, the course is on the left. Public clifftop course. 18 holes, 6759 yards. Par 71. *Green Fees:* to be confirmed. *Eating facilities:* The Castle Clubhouse with full facilities. *Visitors:* welcome. Trolleys £4.00 per round; battery-powered trolleys £12.00 per round. *Society Meetings:* welcome.
website: www.standrews.org.uk

ST ANDREWS. Drumoig Golf Hotel, Drumoig, Leuchars, St Andrews KY16 0DS (Tel & Fax: 01382 541898). *Location*: on A92 (St Andrews to Dundee), four miles south of Dundee. Natural free draining, rolling countryside over sandy based ground featuring spectacular water holes. Unusual quarry greens and views of St Andrews Bay and Carnoustie. 18 holes, 6835 yards. S.S.S 72. Driving range. *Green Fees*: weekdays £25.00 per round, £35.00 per day; weekends £33.00 per round, £45.00 per day. Special offers throughout the season. *Eating facilities*: bar and restaurants. *Visitors*: welcome. *Society Meetings*: welcome.
website: www.drumoigleisure.com

ST ANDREWS. The Duke's, Craigtoun, St Andrews KY16 8NS (01334 470214; Fax: 01334 479456). *Location*: two miles from St Andrews, signposted on A91. Heathland championship tree-lined course with undulating fairways, spectacular bunkers and panoramic views over surrounding countryside to the sea. Multiple tees to suit all golfers. 18 holes, 7500+ yards. Par 71. Grassed practice range and short game area. *Green Fees*: information not provided. *Eating facilities*: restaurant and bar; private dining/meeting facilities. *Visitors*: all welcome, no restrictions. Cart, trolley, club and shoe hire available from the comprehensively stocked Pro Shop. *Society Meetings*: please call for details of packages. Professional: Ayden Roberts-Jones. Events and Membership Co-ordinator: Alan McColm.
e-mail: reservations@oldcoursehotel.co.uk
website: www.playthedukes.com

ST ANDREWS. Eden Course, St Andrews Links Trust, Pilmour House, St Andrews KY16 9SF (01334 466666; Fax: 01334 466664). *Location*: A91 main road into St Andrews, turning is left just before the town; approximately 50 miles from Edinburgh. Public links. 18 holes, 6250 yards. S.S.S. 70. 60 bay driving range. Practice facilities. *Green Fees:* information not provided. *Eating facilities:* Eden Clubhouse, lounge bar, dining room children's room. *Visitors:* welcome with or without reservation. Trolleys £4.00 per round; battery-powered trolleys

---

Woodland Holiday Lodges

Kincaple, St Andrews, Fife KY16 9SH
Tel: 01334 850217

Fifteen lodges in rolling countryside with panoramic views to the sea, St Andrews golf courses, and the town. The comfortable lodges provide the ideal base for golf, birdwatching, touring, or just to relax. Sorry, no pets.

stay@woodlandholidays.co.uk • www.woodlandholidays.co.uk

THE GOLF GUIDE 2011 — SCOTLAND / Fife

£12.00 per round. *Society Meetings:* welcome. website: www.standrews.org.uk

ST ANDREWS. **Jubilee Course,** St Andrews Links Trust, Pilmour House, St Andrews KY16 9SF (01334 466666; Fax: 01334 466664). *Location:* go into St Andrews on the A91, follow signs to West Sands; approximately 50 miles from Edinburgh. Public links. 18 holes, 6742 yards. S.S.S. 73. 60 bay driving range, practice facilities available. *Green Fees:* information not provided. *Eating facilities:* Links Clubhouse, dining room. *Visitors:* always welcome. Trolleys £4.00 per round; battery-powered trolleys £12.00 per round. *Society Meetings:* welcome.
website: www.standrews.org.uk

ST ANDREWS. **New Course,** St Andrews Links Trust, Pilmour House, St Andrews KY16 9SF (01334 466666; Fax: 01334 466664). *Location:* go into St Andrews on the A91, follow signs to West Sands; approximately 50 miles from Edinburgh. Public links course. 18 holes, 6625 yards. S.S.S. 73. 60 bay driving range, practice ground. *Green Fees:* information not provided. *Eating facilities:* Links Clubhouse, dining room. *Visitors:* welcome. Buggies may be hired, trolleys are £4.00 per round; battery-powered trolleys £12.00 per round. *Society Meetings:* welcome.
website: www.standrews.org.uk

ST ANDREWS. **Strathtyrum Course,** St Andrews Links Trust, Pilmour House, St Andrews KY16 9SF (01334 466666; Fax: 01334 466664). *Location:* A91 main road into St Andrews, turning is on the left just before the town. Approximately 50 miles from Edinburgh. Public links course, 18 holes, 5620 yards. S.S.S. 67. 60 bay driving range, practice ground.

Green Fees: information not provided. *Eating facilities:* Eden Clubhouse with full facilities. Children's room. *Visitors:* welcome. Buggies may be hired, trolleys are £4.00 per round; battery-powered trolleys £12.00 per round. *Society Meetings:* welcome.
website: www.standrews.org.uk

TAYPORT. **Scotscraig Golf Club,** Golf Road, Tayport DD6 9DZ (01382 552515; Fax: 01382 553130). *Location:* ten miles north of St Andrews. Links/parkland. 18 holes, 6550 yards. S.S.S. 72. *Green Fees:* information not available. *Eating facilities:* lunches and high teas. *Visitors:* welcome on weekdays or weekends by prior arrangement. *Society Meetings:* catered for subject to approval. Company Days available. Professional: Craig Mackie (01382 552855). Secretary: B.D. Liddle (01382 552515).
e-mail: scotscraig@scotscraiggolfclub.com
website: www.scotscraiggolfclub.com

THORNTON. **Thornton Golf Club,** Station Road, Thornton KY1 4DW (01592 771111 office, 771173 starter). *Location:* southeast Fife located off A92, midway between Glenrothes and Kirkcaldy. Easily walked parkland course bounded by River Ore. Renowned for condition of greens. 18 holes, 6210 yards. S.S.S. 70. Practice area, chipping and putting areas. *Green Fees:* Monday to Friday £25.00 per round, £35.00 per day; Saturday/Sunday £35.00 per round, £50.00 per day. Parties of 8 or more get one free place. *Eating facilities:* full catering service and bar. *Visitors:* very welcome, restricted weekends before 10am and between 12 noon and 2.30pm. Recently built clubhouse; buggies for hire. *Society Meetings:* catered for. Secretary: W.D. Rae.

OPEN QUALIFYING COURSE

Situated on the Tay Estuary, 10 miles north of St Andrews. With fine links turf, smooth fast greens, whin bushes and rolling fairways, this is a demanding and interesting test of golf for all levels of player.

Special Golf Packages for parties of 12+.
Meals, snacks and refreshments served daily.
Well-stocked Shop with resident PGA Professional.

Golf Road, Tayport DD6 9DZ
Tel: 01382 552515 • Pro Shop 01382 552855
e-mail: scotscraig@scotscraiggolfclub.com
www.scotscraiggolfclub.com

Scotscraig Golf Club

Thornton Golf Club — Simply a welcome

Our philosophy is that we treat all of our guests as members. A truly warm Thornton welcome awaits everyone, including casual visitors, visiting parties, and experienced golfers alike. We are proud of our well kept parkland course with its legendary excellent greens. So why not arrive early and enjoy a light bite, tea or coffee, and after your game join us for a drink and choose from a range of tasty meals to finish your visit in style. Simply call the number below and our General Manager will be happy to discuss your requirements with you.

THORNTON awaits your company.

Thornton Golf Club, Station Road, Thornton, Fife KY1 4DW
Tel: 01592 771111 • e-mail: thorntongolf@btconnect.com

Glasgow & District

BISHOPBRIGGS. The Bishopbriggs Golf Club, Brackenbrae Road, Bishopbriggs G64 2DX (0141-772 1810). *Location:* quarter mile from Bishopbriggs Cross off Glasgow-Kirkintilloch road. Fairly flat parkland course. 18 holes, 6262 yards. S.S.S. 70. *Green Fees:* £30.00 per round, day ticket £40.00. *Eating facilities:* full service always available. *Visitors:* weekends/Public Holidays with member only, other times apply to Secretary. *Society Meetings:* catered for Monday to Friday, application to committee at least one month in advance. Secretary: Andrew Smith (0141-772 8938).

CUMBERNAULD. Palacerigg Golf Club, Palacerigg Country Park, Cumbernauld, Near Glasgow G67 3HU (01236 734969). *Location:* Cumbernauld off A80 between Glasgow and Stirling, Palacerigg Road, three miles south of Cumbernauld. Wooded parkland with good views to Campsie Hills, designed by Henry Cotton. 18 holes, 6444 yards, 5894 metres. S.S.S. 72. Practice area. *Green Fees:* weekdays £8.00, weekends £10.00. *Eating facilities:* full catering facilities. *Visitors:* welcome, advance booking recommended for individual rounds. *Society Meetings:* welcome weekdays. Packages available contact Secretary or club steward. Starter: John Murphy (Tel & Fax: 01236 721461). Secretary: David S.A. Cooper (01236 734969; Fax: 01236 721461).
e-mail: palacerigg-golfclub@lineone.net
website: www.palaceriggolfclub.co.uk

CUMBERNAULD. The Westerwood Hotel, Golf and Country Club, Westerwood, Cumbernauld G68 0EW (01236 457171; Fax: 01236 738478). *Location:* between Glasgow and Stirling, off A80 towards Dullatur. Parkland, rolling American style; designed by Seve Ballesteros and Dave Thomas. 18 holes, 6616 yards. S.S.S. 72. *Green Fees*: £35.00. 2-Fore-1 vouchers accepted. *Eating facilities*: full catering facilities. *Visitors*: welcome at all times, no restrictions. Advance booking of tee times recommended. 150-bedroom Hotel, full leisure facilities and indoor pool. *Society Meetings*: welcome by arrangement, packages available, including corporate membership. Head Golf Professional: Vincent Brown (01236 725281; Fax: 01236 738478).
e-mail: westerwoodgolf@qhotels.co.uk
website: www.qhotels.co.uk

Glasgow's premier boutique hotel, the welcoming Carlton George is the ideal base for any discerning business or leisure traveller. Based in the heart of the city of Glasgow, the Carlton George Hotel is within walking distance of the business district, fabulous shopping, and numerous cultural attractions.
With 64 beautifully decorated bedrooms, a rooftop Restaurant and an exclusive Executive Lounge, the Carlton George is the epitome of sophistication and style.
Within easy travelling distance of many fine golf courses in Central and Southern Scotland.

Tel. 0141 353 6373
Fax 0141 353 6263

Carlton George Hotel, 44 West George St, Glasgow G2 1DH
reservations@george.carltonhotels.co.uk • www.carltonhotels.co.uk

The Bishopbriggs Golf Club
The Bishopbriggs Golf Club is situated just north of Glasgow. This tree-lined scenic park, established in 1906, measures 6262 yards with S.S.S. of 71. The Bishopbriggs Burn, which meanders through the course, adds to an enjoyable and challenging golfing experience.
Tel: 0141 772 8938   www.thebishopbriggsgolfclub.com

GLASGOW. **Alexandra Golf Club,** Alexandra Park, Alexandra Parade, Glasgow G31 8SE (0141-556 1294). *Location:* M8 off ramp to Alexandra Parade. Wooded Parkland, very hilly. 9 holes, 1965 yards, S.S.S. 35. Practice area. *Green Fees:* information not available. *Visitors:* welcome at all times. Blind Club and Unemployed Club use this course. Bowling greens are available from Easter to September. Professional: G. McArthur (0141-556 1294). Secretary: F. Derwin (0141-556 1294).*

GLASGOW. **Balmore Golf Club,** Balmore, Torrance G64 4AW (01360 620284; Fax: 01360 622742). *Location:* A803 then A807 from Glasgow. Parkland. 18 holes, 5530 yards. S.S.S. 67. Practice area. *Green Fees:* weekdays £30.00 per round, £40.00 day ticket. *Eating facilities:* catering and bar facilities. *Visitors:* welcome. *Society Meetings:* welcome Monday to Friday only. Professional: Paul Morrison (01360 620123). Secretary: C. Campbell (01360 620284).
e-mail: balmoregolf@btconnect.com
website: www.balmoregolfclub.co.uk

GLASGOW. **Bearsden Golf Club,** Thorn Road, Bearsden G61 4BP. *Location:* seven miles north-west of Glasgow. Parkland. 9 holes, 6014 yards. S.S.S. 69. *Green Fees:* information not provided. *Visitors:* welcome, but must be accompanied by member. Secretary: Alan Harris (0141 586 5300).

GLASGOW. **Blairbeth Golf Club,** Fernbrae Avenue, Rutherglen, Glasgow G73 4SF (0141-634 3355). *Location:* two miles south of Rutherglen off Burnside Road. Parkland. 18 holes, 5518 yards. S.S.S. 68. *Green Fees:* visit website for special offers on fees. *Eating Facilities:* available. *Visitors:* welcome weekdays. Captain: Stuart McPhail. Administrator: Pamela McGregor (0141-634 3325).
e-mail: bgc1910@yahoo.co.uk
website: www.blairbeth.com

GLASGOW. **Bonnyton Golf Club,** Kirktonmoor Road, Eaglesham, Glasgow G76 0QA (01355 303030; Fax: 01355 303151). *Location:* B764. Moorland course. 18 holes, 6252 yards. S.S.S. 71. *Green Fees:* £45.00 per day. *Eating facilities:* full diningroom and snack facilities. *Visitors:* welcome except weekends. Professional: D. Andrews (01355 303030 Option 2). Secretary: Mags Crichton (01355 303030 Option 1).

GLASGOW. **Bothwell Castle Golf Club,** Uddingston Road, Bothwell G71 8TD (Tel & Fax: 01698 801971). *Location:* adjacent to M74, three miles north of Hamilton. Flat parkland course. 18 holes, 6230 yards. S.S.S. 70. Golf clubs and caddy cars for hire. Practice ground. *Green Fees:* weekdays £35.00 per round. *Eating facilities:* full catering and bar. *Visitors:* welcome Monday to Friday only between 10am and 12 noon. *Society Meetings:* catered for, courtesy granted by application. Professional: A. McCloskey (01698 801969). General Manager: Jim Callaghan (Tel & Fax: 01698 801971).

GLASGOW. **Buchanan Castle Golf Club,** Buchanan Estate, Drymen, Glasgow G63 0HY (01360 660307). *Location:* A811, one mile beyond Croftamie village. Flat parkland course. 18 holes, 6131 yards. S.S.S. 69. 6 hole putting green. 8 bay open air driving range. 8 bay covered and floodlit driving range. 9 hole Par 3 course. Newly refurbished Clubhouse. *Green Fees:* weekday £40.00; weekend £45.00. 9-hole course £10.00. *Eating facilities:* full catering and bar available. *Visitors:* welcome except Tuesday and Saturday mornings. *Society Meetings:* welcome, except Tuesday and Saturday mornings. Professional: Keith Baxter (01360 660330). Secretary: Janet Dawson (01360 660307; Fax: 01360 870382).
e-mail: buchanancastle@sol.co.uk
website: www.buchanancastlegolfclub.com

GLASGOW. **Cambuslang Golf Club,** 30 Westburn Drive, Cambuslang (0141-641 3130). *Location:* half a mile north of Cambuslang main street. Parkland. 9 holes, 6146 yards. S.S.S. 69. *Green Fees:* information not available. *Eating facilities:* bar snacks, lunches, evening meals. *Visitors:* welcome if introduced by a member. *Society Meetings:* by arrangement. Secretary: R.M. Dunlop.*

GLASGOW. **Cathcart Castle Golf Club,** Mearns Road, Clarkston, Glasgow G76 7YL (0141-638 9449). *Location:* one and a half miles from Clarkston Toll. Undulating parkland course. 18 holes, 5832 yards. S.S.S. 69. *Green Fees:* information not available. *Eating facilities:* full catering available, lounge bar. *Visitors:* welcome weekdays by prior arrangement. *Society Meetings:* weekdays by application. Professional: Stephen Duncan (0141-638 3436). Secretary: I.G. Sutherland (0141-638 9449).*

GLASGOW. **Cathkin Braes Golf Club,** Cathkin Road, Rutherglen, Glasgow G73 4SE (0141-634 6605). Moorland course. 18 holes, 6208 yards. S.S.S. 71. Practice ground. *Green Fees:* £35.00 per round. *Eating facilities:* available. *Visitors:* welcome Monday to Friday by prior arrangement. *Society Meetings:* catered for. Professional: Stephen Bree (0141-634 0650). Secretary/Treasurer: David Moir.
e-mail: secretary@cathkinbraesgolfclub.co.uk
website: www.cathkinbraesgolfclub.co.uk

GLASGOW. **Cawder Golf Club,** Cadder Road, Bishopbriggs, Glasgow G64 3QD (0141-761 1281; Fax: 0141-761 1285). *Location:* A803 north of city. Parkland. Cawder: 18 holes, 6279 yards, 5741 metres. S.S.S. 70. Keir: 18 holes, 5878 yards, 5374 metres. S.S.S. 68. Practice area. *Green Fees:* £35.00 per round, £45.00 per day. *Eating facilities:* lunches, high teas, dinners available. *Visitors:* welcome weekdays. *Society Meetings:* welcome weekdays. Professional: Gordon Stewart (0141-772 7102). Secretary: (0141-761 1281).
e-mail: secretary@cawdergolfclub.com
website: www.cawdergolfclub.com

GLASGOW. **Clober Golf Club,** Craigton Road, Milngavie G62 7HP (0141-956 1685). *Location:* five minutes from Milngavie centre, seven miles from Glasgow city centre. Parkland course. 18 holes, 4963 yards. S.S.S. 65. *Green Fees:* information not available. *Eating facilities:* morning coffee, lunches, high teas. *Visitors:* welcome Monday to Thursday before 4pm, some Fridays also before 4pm; not at weekends unless introduced by a member. *Society Meetings:* catered for. Professional: Gary McFarlane. (0141-956 6963). Secretary: Brian Davidson (0141-956 1685).*
e-mail: clobergolfclub@btopenworld.com
website: www.clober.co.uk

GLASGOW. **Cowglen Golf Club,** 301 Barrhead Road, Glasgow G43 1AU (0141-632 0556). *Location:* south-west Glasgow, follow M77 from Glasgow taking Pollok turnoff, turn left at traffic lights. Course half mile on right. Undulating parkland course. 18 holes, 6079 yards, 5559 metres. S.S.S. 70. Extensive practice facilities available. *Green Fees:* £35.00 per round, £45.00 per day. *Eating facilities:* full catering facilities available. *Visitors:* welcome if arranged beforehand with Secretary. Lockers and showers available. *Society Meetings:* restricted numbers, apply to Secretary. Professional: Simon Payne (0141-649 9401). Secretary: James A. Herald (Tel & Fax: 0141 632 7463).
e-mail: secretary@cowglengolfclub.co.uk
website: www.cowglengolfclub.co.uk

GLASGOW. **Crow Wood Golf Club,** Garnkirk House, Cumbernauld Road, Muirhead G69 9JF (0141-779 2011). *Location:* on A80 on Stirling Road, 6 miles north east of Glasgow. Wooded parkland. 18 holes, 6160 yards. S.S.S. 70. Practice area. *Green Fees:* information not provided. *Eating facilities:* fully licensed, snacks or full meals served all day. *Visitors:* welcome Monday to Friday except Bank Holidays and only by arrangement with Secretary. *Society Meetings:* catered for as visitors. Professional: Ian Graham (0141-779 1943). Secretary: G. Blyth (0141-779 4954).

GLASGOW. **Douglas Park Golf Club,** Hillfoot, Bearsden, Glasgow G61 2TJ (0141-942 0985). *Location:* adjacent to railway station, Hillfoot, Bearsden, off Milngavie Road. Undulating parkland course. 18 holes, 5962 yards. S.S.S. 69. *Green Fees:* weekdays £30.00; weekends £40.00. *Eating facilities:* full service available, usual licensing hours. *Visitors:* welcome. *Society Meetings:* on application to Secretary. Professional: Robert Irvine (0141-942 1482). Secretary: (Tel & Fax: 0141-942 0985)

GLASGOW. **Dullatur Golf Club,** 1A Glen Douglas Drive, Cumbernauld G68 0DW (01236 723230; Fax: 01236 727171). *Location:* 12 miles east of Glasgow - leave A80 for Dullatur then off third roundabout (Craigmarloch). Moorland, rolling courses. Two courses Antonine, 5205 yards and Carrickstone, 5673 yards. 36 holes, S.S.S. 70. *Green Fees:* telephone for latest offers. *Eating facilities:* full catering facilities. *Visitors:* welcome. Smart casual dress required in clubhouse. Full leisure centre. *Society Meetings:* welcome, book through Secretary. Professional: Duncan Sinclair (01236 723230; Fax: 01236 727271). Secretary: Karen Dyer.

GLASGOW. **East Kilbride Golf Club,** Chapelside Road, Nerston, East Kilbride G74 4PH (01355 247728). *Location:* Glasgow Road exit from East Kilbride. Parkland course with variable topography. 18 holes, 6419 yards. S.S.S. 71. *Green Fees:* information not available. *Eating facilities:* full bar and catering facilities seven days per week. *Visitors:* welcome weekdays only. *Society Meetings:* catered for weekdays only. Professional: Paul McKay (01355 222192). Secretary: W.G. Gray (01355 247728).*

GLASGOW. **The East Renfrewshire Golf Club,** Pilmuir, Newton Mearns, Glasgow G77 6RT (01355 500256). *Location:* off M77 Junction 5; on A77, one and a half miles south of Newton Mearns. Moorland course with plantations of evergreen trees. 18 holes, 6107 yards, 5584 metres. S.S.S. 70. Practice ground. *Green Fees:* weekdays £45.00 per round, £60.00 per day. *Eating facilities:* catering available. *Visitors:* welcome except Saturdays but always by prior arrangement with Professional. *Society Meetings:* welcomed weekdays on prior application. Professional: Stewart Russell (01355 500206). Secretary: Graham Tennant (01355 500256; Fax: 01355 500323).
e-mail: secretary@eastrengolfclub.co.uk
website: www.eastrengolfclub.co.uk

GLASGOW. **Eastwood Golf Club,** Muirshield, Loganswell, Newton Mearns, Glasgow G77 6RX (01355 500261). *Location:* on A77 road to Kilmarnock two miles south of Newton Mearns. Moorland course. 18 holes, 6071 yards. S.S.S. 70. Par 70. Practice area. *Green Fees:* weekdays £30.00 per round, £40.00 per day. *Eating facilities:* snacks or full meals available. *Visitors:* welcome on application to Secretary. *Visiting parties:* welcome weekdays on prior application. Professional: S. Wilson (01355 500285). Secretary: I.M. Brown (01355 500280).

GLASGOW. **Esporta (Dougalston Golf Club),** Strathblane Road, Milngavie, Glasgow G62 8HA (0141-955 2404; Fax: 0141-955 2406). *Location:* A81 half a mile from Milngavie. Parkland course set in woodland estate. 18 holes, 6040 yards. S.S.S. 71, Par 70. Putting green, practice nets. *Green Fees:* weekdays £30.00, weekends £40.00. 2010 rates (subject to review). *Eating facilities:* restaurant, sports bar and leisure facilities. *Visitors:* welcome 7 days a week. *Society Meetings:* welcome weekdays. Weekends subject to availability. Other facilities include 25 metre swimming pool, along with a health suite, aerobic studios, air-conditioning fitness area, gymnasium, indoor - outdoor tennis, Sports Bar and banqueting facilities. Golf Shop (0141-955 2404; Fax: 0141-955 2406). Secretary: Stephen Gilbey (0141-955 2404; Fax: 0141-955 2406).

GLASGOW. **Glasgow Golf Club,** Killermont, Bearsden, Glasgow G61 2TW (0141-942 1713). *Location:* taking Maryhill Road out of Glasgow turn right at Killermont Avenue, half a mile before Canniesburn Toll and then turn immediately right again. Tree-lined parkland. 18 holes, 5977 yards. S.S.S. 69, Par 70. *Green Fees:* on application. *Eating facilities:* bar and dining room. *Visitors:* only if introduced by member; no visitors at weekends. *Society Meetings:* by application to Managing Secretary. Professional: John Greaves (0141-942 8507). Managing Secretary: A.G. McMillan (0141-942 2011; Fax: 0141-942 0770).
e-mail: secretary@glasgowgolfclub.com

GLASGOW: **Haggs Castle Golf Club,** 70 Dumbreck Road, Glasgow G41 4SN (0141-427 0480). *Location:* off Junction 1 of M77 from Glasgow. Flat, tree-lined course. 18 holes, 6426 yards. S.S.S. 72. Practice area and putting green. *Green Fees:* weekdays £40.00 per round, £60.00 per day. Weekends, members only. *Eating facilities:* full catering available. *Visitors:* welcome except weekends; must book through Professional. Handicap Certificate required. Golf shoes must be worn. *Society Meetings:* by arrangement through General Manager. Professional: C. Elliott (0141-427 3355). General Manager: Alan Williams (Tel & Fax: 0141-427 1157).

GLASGOW. **Hayston Golf Club,** Campsie Road, Kirkintilloch, Glasgow G66 1RN (0141-776 1244). *Location:* 10 miles north-east of Glasgow and one mile north of Kirkintilloch. Parkland course with tree-lined fairways. 18 holes, 6042 yards. S.S.S. 70. Practice area. *Green Fees:* information not provided. *Eating facilities:* lunches, dinners, bar snacks. *Society Meetings:* Tuesdays, Wednesdays and Thursdays on application to Secretary, max 24. Professional: Steve Barnett (0141-775 0882). Secretary: T. Cowan (0141-775 0723; Fax: 0141-776 9030).
e-mail: secretary@haystongolf.com
website: www.haystongolf.com

GLASGOW. **Hilton Park Golf Club,** Stockiemuir Road, Milngavie, Glasgow G62 7HB (0141-956 4657). *Location:* on A809. Moorland courses. Allander course: 18 holes, 5487 yards. S.S.S. 67. Hilton course: 18 holes, 6054 yards. S.S.S. 70. Practice area. *Green Fees:* information not available. *Eating facilities:* full catering and bar. *Visitors:* on application to the Secretary (not at weekends). *Society Meetings:* as visitors. Professional: W. McCondichie (0141-956 5125). Secretary: Mrs J.A. Dawson (0141-956 4657/5124).*

THE APPEARANCE OF AN ASTERISK (*) AT THE END OF A CLUB OR COURSE ENTRY INDICATES THAT UP-TO-DATE INFORMATION HAS NOT BEEN SUPPLIED

GLASGOW. **Kirkhill Golf Club,** Greenlees Road, Cambuslang, Glasgow G72 8YN (0141-641 3083). *Location:* between Rutherglen and East Kilbride adjacent to A749, three miles from East Kilbride. Slightly hilly parkland course. 18 holes, 6030 yards. S.S.S. 70. Practice area. *Green Fees:* information not provided. *Eating facilities:* dining room and bar. *Visitors:* welcome weekdays only. *Society Meetings:* welcome weekdays only. Professional: D. Williamson (0141-641 7972). Hon. Secretary: Carol Downes (Tel & Fax: 0141-641 8499).
e-mail: secretary@kirkhillgolfclub.org.uk
website: www.kirkhillgolfclub.org.uk

GLASGOW. **Knightswood Golf Club,** Lincoln Avenue, Glasgow G13 3DN (0141-959 6358). *Location:* west along Great Western Road, turn left into Lincoln Avenue. Flat parkland course. 9 holes, 2792 yards. S.S.S. 67. *Green Fees:* information not available. *Visitors:* tee reserved for Club Wednesdays and Fridays 8am to 9am and 10am to 11am, otherwise no restrictions. 24 hours' notice required. Ladies' and gents' changing areas. *Society Meetings:* welcome, as for visitors. Secretary: James Lavery (0141-954 8614).*

GLASGOW. **Lethamhill Golf Course,** 1240 Cumbernauld Road, Glasgow G33 1AH (0141-770 6220; Fax: 0141-770 0520). *Location:* 100 yards off M8 Junction 12. Parkland, many holes with views of Hogganfield Loch. 18 holes, 5836 yards. S.S.S. 68. 18 holes pitch and putt course. *Green Fees:* information not provided. *Visitors:* welcome at all times - this is a public course, 24 hour in advance booking system. Ladies and gents changing. *Society Meetings:* contact Golf Professional G. Taggart (0141-770 7135).

GLASGOW. **Linn Park Golf Club,** Simshill Road, Glasgow G44 9DT (0141 276 0702). *Location:* five miles south of city centre near Carmunnock Road, near Croftfoot roundabout. Parkland. 18 holes, 5005 yards. S.S.S. 66. *Green Fees:* information not available. *Visitors:* welcome, 24 hours notice required. *Society Meetings:* all welcome. Secretary: J. Welsh (0141 276 0702).*

GLASGOW. **Littlehill Golf Club,** Auchinairn Road, Bishopbriggs, Glasgow G64 1UT. *Location:* from Glasgow on A803, turn off for Stobhill Hospital. Flat, parkland. 18 holes, 6364 yards. S.S.S. 70. Small practice area. *Green Fees:* information not available. *Eating facilities:* canteen open five days weekly in season, three outwith. *Visitors:* welcome without reservation - pay and play. *Society Meetings:* no restrictions. Professional: Kevin Hughes (0141-762 3998). Secretary: W. Burke.*

GLASGOW. **Milngavie Golf Club,** Laighpark, Milngavie, Glasgow G62 8EP (0141-956 1619; Fax: 0141-956 4252). *Location:* situated off Glasgow to Drymen road approximately one mile past Stockiemuir Service Station, turn right at signpost. Moorland course. 18 holes, 5818 yards. S.S.S. 68. *Green Fees:* information not available. *Eating facilities:* catering available. *Visitors:* welcome when introduced by member or by prior arrangement with the Secretary. *Society Meetings:* catered for. Secretary: S. Woods.*

Glasgow & District / SCOTLAND

GLASGOW. **Pollok Golf Club,** 90 Barrhead Road, Glasgow G43 1BG (0141-632 1080; Fax: 0141-649 1398). *Location:* Junction 2 M77. Wooded parkland. 18 holes, 6358 yards. S.S.S. 70. *Green Fees:* information not available. *Eating facilities:* dining room and bar. *Visitors:* welcome with reservation by letter or telephone to Secretary. No visitors Saturday or Sunday. *Society Meetings:* catered for by letter. Secretary: David Morgan (0141-632 4351; Fax: 0141-649 1398).*

GLASGOW. **Rouken Glen Golf Centre,** Stewarton Road, Thornliebank, Glasgow G46 7UZ (0141-638 7044 or 0141-620 0826). *Location:* on Stewarton Road at Rouken Glen Park, only 250 yards from the A726. Parkland with wooded features, designed by James Braid. 18 holes, 4800 yards. S.S.S. 63 (Par 64). 15-bay floodlit driving range. *Green Fees:* information not available. *Eating facilities:* catering and bar facilities available. *Visitors:* welcome all week. Shop, club hire, etc. *Society Meetings:* bookings taken. Professional: (0141-638 7044). Secretary: Christine Cosh (0141-632 6816).*

GLASGOW. **Sandyhills Golf Club,** 223 Sandyhills Road, Glasgow G32 9NA (0141-763 1099). *Location:* three miles east from centre of Glasgow. Parkland. 18 holes, 6253 yards. S.S.S. 71. *Green Fees:* information not available. *Eating facilities:* full catering facilities available. *Visitors:* welcome when introduced by a member. *Society Meetings:* welcome by prior arrangement. General Manager (0141-763 0787).*
e-mail: generalmanager@sandyhillsgolfclub.co.uk

GLASGOW. **Whitecraigs Golf Club,** 72 Ayr Road, Giffnock, Glasgow G46 6SW (0141-639 4530; Fax: 0141-616 3648). *Location:* on A77 south of city, two miles from Eastwoodmains roundabout. Parkland course. 18 holes, 6013 yards. S.S.S. 69. *Green Fees:* £40.00 per round, £50.00 per day. *Eating facilities:* restaurant and lounge bar. *Visitors:* welcome midweek, letter of introduction required. *Society Meetings:* catered for Wednesday only. Professional: Alastair Forrow (0141-639 2140). Secretary: Alan Keith (0141-639 4530).

GLASGOW. **Williamwood Golf Club,** Clarkston Road, Glasgow G44 3YR (0141-637 1783; Fax: 0141-571 0166). *Location:* behind service station on Clarkston Road. Attractive parkland course designed by James Braid. 18 holes, 6045 yards. S.S.S. 69. Practice area and putting. *Green Fees:* information not available. *Eating facilities:* meals must be ordered. *Visitors:* welcome by arrangement with Secretary or Professional. *Society Meetings:* weekdays only by arrangement. Professional: Stewart G. Marshall (0141-637 2715; Fax: 0141-637 2600). Managing Secretary: L. W. Conn (0141-637 1783; Fax: 0141-571 0166).
e-mail: secretary@williamwoodgc.co.uk
website: www.williamwoodgc.co.uk

GLASGOW. **Windyhill Golf Club,** Baljaffray Road, Bearsden, Glasgow G61 4QQ (0141-942 2349; Fax: 0141-942 5874). *Location:* one mile north from Bearsden Cross. Undulating parkland course. 18 holes, 6254 yards. S.S.S. 70. Practice area. *Green Fees:* information not provided. *Eating facilities:* full catering and bar. *Visitors:* welcome weekdays only, £35.00; weekends £6.00 with member only. *Society Meetings:* welcome weekdays by arrangement. Professional: Christopher Duffy (0141-942 7157; Fax: 0141-942 5874). Secretary: James M. Young (0141-942 2349; Fax: 0141-942 5874).

KILSYTH. **Kilsyth Lennox Golf Club,** Tak-Ma-Doon Road, Kilsyth, Glasgow G65 0RS (01236 824115). *Location:* 12 miles from Glasgow on A80. Parkland/moorland, undulating ground with superb views across central Scotland. 18 holes, 6225 yards. S.S.S. 71. *Green Fees:* information not available. *Eating facilities:* new clubhouse. *Visitors:* welcome weekdays up to 5.00pm, Saturdays after 3.00pm and Sundays. *Society Meetings:* welcome, details on website. Secretary: Louise Reed.*
e-mail: admin@kilsythlennox.com
website: www.kilsythlennox.com

Other British holiday guides from FHG Guides

PUBS & INNS · 300 GREAT HOTELS · SHORT BREAK HOLIDAYS
The bestselling and original PETS WELCOME! · 500 GREAT PLACES TO STAY
SELF-CATERING HOLIDAYS · BED & BREAKFAST STOPS
CARAVAN & CAMPING HOLIDAYS · FAMILY BREAKS

Published annually: available in all good bookshops or direct from the publisher:
FHG Guides, Abbey Mill Business Centre, Seedhill, Paisley PA1 1TJ
Tel: 0141 887 0428 · Fax: 0141 889 7204
e-mail: admin@fhguides.co.uk · www.holidayguides.com

Highlands (North)

BRORA. Brora Golf Club, 43 Golf Road, Brora KW9 6QS (+44 (0)1408 621417; Fax: +44 (0)1408 622157). *Location:* 52 miles north of Inverness on A9 trunk road. Traditional links course designed by James Braid. 18 holes, 6110 yards. S.S.S. 70. Practice ground available. *Green Fees:* information not available. *Eating facilities:* full catering, bar facilities April to October. *Visitors:* welcome anytime except on tournament days, advisable to book tee times in season. Welcome to participate in open events (Certificate of Handicap required). Carts, caddies, etc available. *Society Meetings:* by arrangement with Secretary. Secretary: Tony Gill (01408 621417; Fax: 01408 622157).*
e-mail: secretary@broragolf.co.uk
website: www.broragolf.co.uk

Royal Marine Hotel, Restaurant & Spa

Golf Road, Brora, Sutherland KW9 6QS
Telephone: 01408 621252
Fax: 01408 621181

info@royalmarinebrora.com
www.royalmarinebrora.com

Built in the early 1900s by renowned Scottish architect Sir Robert Lorimer, this 21-bedroom hotel has undergone extensive bedroom refurbishment in 2008, with further development planned in the future for the Spa complex. One hour's drive north of Inverness, the hotel is situated in the small village of Brora, one minute from the Brora Golf Links Course and a 20 minute drive from the World Championship Course Royal Dornoch.

Two bedroom luxury self-catering apartments overlooking Brora Golf Course are also available.

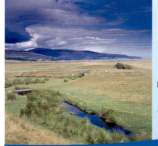

BRORA GOLF CLUB
Est. 1891
A James Braid Traditional Links Course
Warm, Friendly & Welcoming

Welcome to Brora Golf Club, a traditional Links course, the most northerly designed by James Braid and ranked in the top hundred in Britain and Ireland.
Here the visitor will enjoy the mixture of bent grass and beach sand, burn water and gorse in glorious yellow bloom, even a railway which comes into play from the tenth tee.

• Buggy and Electronic Trolley Hire • Well stocked shop • Putting Green • Practice area
• Club Hire • Lockers, changing area • Friendly clubhouse with bar and catering.

Brora Golf Course, Golf Road, Brora, Sutherland KW9 6QS
Tel: 01408 621417 • Fax: 01408 622157 • e-mail: secretary@broragolf.co.uk • www.broragolf.co.uk

Highlands (North) / SCOTLAND

BONAR BRIDGE. Bonar Bridge-Ardgay Golf Club, Market Stance, Migdale Road, Bonar Bridge IV24 3EJ (01863 766199). *Location:* off the A9, driving north cross Bonar Bridge, straight up hill for half a mile. Wooded heathland. 9 holes, 5284 yards. S.S.S. 65. *Green Fees:* information not provided. *Eating facilities:* limited catering available May to September. *Visitors:* always welcome. *Society Meetings:* limited to weekdays. Joint Secretary: Jeani Hunter (01549 421282).
e-mail: bonarbridgeardgay-golf@bigfoot.com

DORNOCH. Royal Dornoch Golf Club, Golf Road, Dornoch IV25 3LW (01862 810219; Fax: 01862 810792). *Location:* one mile from A9 between Tain and Golspie. Seaside links. Championship Course and Struie Course. Championship: 18 holes, 6595 yards, 6087 metres. S.S.S. 73; Struie: 18 holes, 6276 yards, 5793 metres. S.S.S. 70. Practice area. *Green Fees:* Championship Course: weekdays £85.00 per round, weekends £95.00 per round. Struie Course: £35.00 per round, £45.00 day ticket. Combination Day Ticket (one round each course) £100.00 weekdays, £110.00 weekends. All green fees discounted £10.00 in April and October and are subject to alteration. *Eating facilities:* available to visiting golfers. *Visitors:* welcome, no major restrictions other than competitions – bookings can be heavy. Saturdays: members only until late afternoon with limited morning availablity. *Society Meetings:* must be arranged through the Secretary. (01862 811923; Fax: 01862 810792). Professional: A. Skinner (01862 810902).
e-mail: bookings@royaldornoch.com
website: www.royaldornoch.com

DORNOCH. The Carnegie Golf Club at Skibo Castle, Skibo Castle, Dornoch (01862 894600; Fax: 01862 894601). *Location*: off A9 between Tain and Dornoch. Links course, built on peninsula, naturally contoured; Donald Steel designed. 18 holes, 6671 yards. S.S.S. 72. Practice facilities. *Green Fees*: information not available. *Eating facilities*: bar, luncheon table. *Visitors*: by prior arrangement, write or telephone only. Private members club, daily golf membership available, must be booked in advance. *Society Meetings*: welcome. Accommodation available, charges on request. Golf Secretary: Sharon Stewart. Professional: David Thomson (01862 881260).*
e-mail: sharon.stewart@carnegieclubs.com

DURNESS. Durness Golf Club, Balnakiel, Durness IV27 4PN. *Location:* 57 miles northwest of Lairg on A838. Links course with final hole played over deep gully. 9 greens, 18 tees, 5555 yards. S.S.S 69. *Green Fees:* £20.00 per day. Weekly ticket £50.00. *Eating facilities:* snacks available 12-5pm June to September. *Visitors:* welcome, restriction on Sunday mornings and other competition days. Check website for details. *Society Meetings:* by arrangement. Secretary: Lucy MacKay (01971 511364).
e-mail: lucy@durnessgolfclub.org
website: www.durnessgolfclub.org

DORNOCH CASTLE
An idyllic retreat in the Scottish Highlands

Dornoch Castle is set in the beautiful, historic town of Dornoch, directly opposite the inspiring 12th century Dornoch Cathedral in the quaint Market Square, a dramatic backdrop for an overnight stay. This impressive Castle offers a cosy and comfortable stay, and is renowned for the best in Scottish hospitality. Dornoch Castle makes an ideal base for touring in the area, providing information such as local maps, walks, heritage trails and visitor attractions. As a family-run Castle, Dornoch offers a friendly and relaxed atmosphere for guests to soak in the tranquillity and delight of the Highlands.
Pets welcome by arrangement.

**Dornoch Castle Hotel, Castle Street, Dornoch, Sutherland IV25 3SD
Tel: 01862 810216 • Fax: 01862 810981
e-mail: enquiries@dornochcastlehotel.com • www.dornochcastlehotel.com**

FHG Guides publish a large range of well-known accommodation guides. We will be happy to send you details or you can use the order form at the back of this book.

Royal Dornoch Golf Club

Formed in 1877, Dornoch has been a Royal club for over 100 years! We always aim to exceed the expectations of our frequent visitors in a relaxed, informal environment, with an emphasis on traditional Highland hospitality.

Royal Dornoch has a modern clubhouse with well stocked bar and comfortable restaurant. Only 45 miles from Inverness, but a true haven of peace, tranquillity and world-class golf.

The Championship Course is ranked No 16 in the World Top 20 (No 11 in Britain & Ireland) and is ranked No 3 in Scotland.

It is a classic links, providing both pleasure to the eye and a challenge to the golfer's skills. Royal Dornoch is considered the finest northerly course in the world, and offers a delicious feeling of getting away from it all.

Royal Dornoch aims to provide traditional links golf of the highest quality. Golfers and their friends will be made welcome to enjoy Highland hospitality in an informal relaxed style.

Royal Dornoch Golf Club
Golf Road, Dornoch, Sutherland IV25 3LW

Tel Reservations: 01862 810219 Ext 1
Fax: 01862 810792
e-mail: bookings@royaldornoch.com
www.royaldornoch.com

Highlands (North) / SCOTLAND

GOLSPIE. Golspie Golf Club, Ferry Road, Golspie KW10 6ST (01408 633266). *Location*: 53 miles on A9 north of Inverness. Fairly flat course, seaside links and wooded. 18 holes, 6021 yards. S.S.S. 69. Par 70. Practice area available. *Green Fees*: £40.00 per round, £50.00 per day (7 days). *Eating facilities*: bar and catering service, available during season. *Visitors*: welcome, no restrictions except on competition days. Carts, caddies must be booked in advance. Self-catering holiday apartment adjacent to clubhouse, sleeps four, golf-package available. *Society Meetings*: welcome by prior arrangement, packages available. Golf Shop.
e-mail: info@golspie-golf-club.co.uk
website: www.golspie-golf-club.co.uk

GRANTOWN-ON-SPEY. **Grantown-on-Spey Golf Club,** The Clubhouse, Golf Course Road, Grantown-on-Spey PH26 3HY (01479 872079; Fax: 01479 873725). *Location:* turn off main road opposite police station. Parkland and woodland. 18 holes, 5710 yards, S.S.S. 68, Par 70. Practice ground and putting green. *Green Fees:* weekdays £29.00, weekends £34.00. Group disconts available. *Eating facilities:* full bar and catering facilities. *Visitors:* welcome, members have priority before 10am weekends. Shop. *Society Meetings:* welcome except before 10am weekends. Secretary: Paul Mackay (01479 872079/ 873154; Fax: 01479 873725).
e-mail: secretary@grantownonspeygolfclub.co.uk
website: www.grantownonspeygolfclub.co.uk

HELMSDALE. **Helmsdale Golf Club,** Golf Road, Helmsdale KW8 6JA. *Location:* on A9, 28 miles north of Dornoch, follow signs for Melvich. undulating parkland/moorland course. 9 holes, 3720 yards. S.S.S. 61 (2 x 9 holes). *Green Fees:* 9 holes £10.00 per round; 18 holes £15.00 per round. *Visitors:* welcome at all times. *Society Meetings:* welcome by appointment. Secretary: Ronald Sutherland (01431 821063).

LYBSTER. **Lybster Golf Club,** Main Street, Lybster KW3 6BJ *Location:* 14 miles south from Wick on A9, half-way down village street. One of smallest courses in Scotland, heathland/parkland. 9 holes, 2002 yards. S.S.S. 61. *Green Fees:* £10.00 per round/day (adults); £5.00 per round/day (juniors). *Eating facilities:* at nearby hotels in village. *Visitors:* welcome anytime. *Society Meetings:* welcome anytime. Full membership available. Secretary: Alex Calder.
website: www.lybstergolfclub.co.uk

REAY. **Reay Golf Club,** Clubhouse, Reay, By Thurso KW14 7RE (01847 811288). *Location:* 12 miles west of nearest main town of Thurso. Most northerly 18 hole seaside links. 18 holes, 5831 yards. S.S.S. 69. *Green Fees:* information not available. *Eating facilities:* restricted: bar open 12-3pm, 8-11pm daily July/August. *Visitors:* welcome anytime, restricted during competitions. *Society Meetings:* welcome, advance bookings via Secretary. Captain: Bob Earnshaw. Secretary: John Disbury (01847 895277).
e-mail: info@reaygolfclub.co.uk
website: www.reaygolfclub.co.uk
www.caithnessgolfweek.co.uk
www.scottishopengolf.co.uk

THURSO. **Thurso Golf Club,** Newlands of Geise, By Thurso KW14 7XD (01847 893807). *Location:* two miles from Railway Station, on road to Reay. Flat parkland with newly planted trees. 18 holes, 5828 yards, 5290 metres. S.S.S. 69. *Green Fees:* £25.00 per day; Juniors £15.00 per day. *Eating facilities:* bar only during the day June to August. *Visitors:* welcome, no restrictions. *Society Meetings:* welcome, notice required. Secretary: R.M. Black (01847 892575).

WICK. **Wick Golf Club,** Reiss, By Wick KW1 4RW (01955 602726). *Location:* three miles north of Wick on A9. Seaside links course. 18 holes, 6123 yards. S.S.S. 71. Practice area. *Green Fees:* information not available. *Eating facilities:* licensed; snacks available. *Visitors:* welcome. *Society Meetings:* catered for. Secretary: I. Miller (01955 605680).*

PLEASE MENTION THIS GUIDE WHEN YOU ENQUIRE ABOUT CLUBS OR ACCOMMODATION

THE GOLF GUIDE 2011   SCOTLAND / Highlands (North)   423

Golspie Golf Club
Ferry Road, Golspie, Sutherland KW10 6ST
Tel: 01408 633266 • www.golspie-golf-club.co.uk

Situated at the foot of Ben Bhragghie, Golspie Golf Course, founded in 1889 and designed by the legendary James Braid, offers one of the finest settings for a round of golf. The course offers a variety of sea-side links, parkland, heath and woodland. The clubhouse offers snacks, meals and drinks. Societies welcome.
Round Ticket: £40   (all week)   Day Ticket: £50.
SELF-CATERING COTTAGE/GOLF PACKAGE AVAILABLE

GRANTOWN-ON-SPEY GOLF CLUB
ESTABLISHED 1890

Scenic 5710 yard parkland and woodland course, situated in the Cairngorms National Park.
Lounge bar, catering facilities, well stocked golf shop.
Par 70 SSS 68. Practice facilities.
Buggies, trolleys and clubs for hire.
Visitors and societies welcome.

Golf Course Road, Grantown-on-Spey, Morayshire PH26 3HY
Tel: 01479 872 079 • Fax: 01479 873 725
www.grantownonspeygolfclub.co.uk • E-mail: secretary@grantownonspeygolfclub.co.uk

10th hole at Royal Dornoch Golf Club, Sutherland

Highlands (Mid)

ALNESS. **Alness Golf Club,** Ardross Road, Alness IV17 0QA (01349 883877). *Location:* 20 miles from Inverness; turn into Alness from A9 (north). Beautiful surroundings with views over Cromarty Firth and Alness River. 18 holes, 4886 yards. S.S.S. 64. Practice green available. *Green Fees:* information not available. *Eating facilities:* licensed bar. *Visitors:* welcome all week. Changing rooms, hot showers; clubs and trolleys for hire. PGA Pro Shop, lessons available. *Society Meetings:* welcome with advance notice. Secretary: Dawn Fraser.*
website: www.alness-golfclub.co.uk

FORTROSE. **Fortrose and Rosemarkie Golf Club,** Ness Road East, Fortrose IV10 8SE (Office: 01381 620529, Shop: 01381 620733; Fax: 01381 621328). *Location:* on the Black Isle. A9 north from Inverness, across Kessock Bridge, through Munlochy, follow signs to Fortrose. James Braid designed links course, sea both sides, founded 1888. 18 holes, 5890 yards. Par 71, S.S.S. 69. Practice area, outting green. Golf shop. *Green Fees:* weekdays £36.00 per round, weekends £43.00 per round; day ticket weekdays £54.00, weekends £55.00. *Eating facilities:* catering available. *Visitors:* welcome without reservation. Buggy hire. *Society Meetings:* catered for.
e-mail: secretary@fortrosegolfclub.co.uk
website: www.fortrosegolfclub.co.uk

GAIRLOCH. **Gairloch Golf Club,** Gairloch IV21 2BE (01445 712 407). *Location:* 75 miles west of Inverness on the A832. Seaside links with superb views. 9 holes, 4108 yards. S.S.S. 62 over 18 holes. *Green Fees:* £18.00 per round, £25.00 per day, £70.00 per week. Juniors £10.00 per day, £35.00 per week. 2010 rates (subject to review). *Eating facilities:* licensed bar and light refreshments available. *Visitors:* welcome anytime but must be regular golfers. Tee times must be booked during the summer season – call clubhouse for details. *Society Meetings:* welcome, no restrictions. Secretary: Joanna Powell (01445 712407).
e-mail: gairlochgolfclub@hotmail.co.uk
website: www.gairlochgolfclub.co.uk

THE APPEARANCE OF AN ASTERISK (*) AT THE END OF A CLUB OR COURSE ENTRY INDICATES THAT UP-TO-DATE INFORMATION HAS NOT BEEN SUPPLIED

Tarbat Golf Club, Portmahomack, Tain

FORTROSE & ROSEMARKIE GOLF CLUB
NESS ROAD EAST, FORTROSE, ROSS-SHIRE IV10 8SE

Tel: 01381 620529/620733 • Fax: 01381 621328
e-mail: secretary@fortrosegolfclub.co.uk • www.fortrosegolfclub.co.uk

This James Braid designed links has been acclaimed by golf writers as "a gem of a course" and "perhaps the brightest jewel in the Highlands' golfing crown". Small deceptive greens and strategically placed bunkers, as well as sea alongside eight holes and gorse waiting to devour the wayward shot inland, all add up to a greater golfing experience than many a longer course. This private club, established in 1888, gives a warm welcome to visitors in the knowledge that they will almost certainly wish to come back. A big off-course attraction is the bottle-nosed dolphins in the Firth in the view of the golfers. 15 miles north of Inverness – take the A832 off A9 North. Green fees £36 per round weekdays, £43 per round weekends. Day ticket (7 days) £54 weekdays and £55 weekends. Buggy hire, practice area, putting green, golf shop, catering and bar.

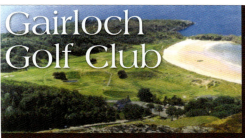

9-hole seaside links course, set in spectacular scenery with the backdrop of mountains and views to Skye and the Western Isles. Clubhouse by the beach, overlooking the 8th and 9th greens. New putting green, practice bunker and nets. Licensed bar and shop.
Visitors always welcome.

Gairloch Golf Club
Gairloch, Ross-shire IV21 2BE
Tel: 01445 712407
e-mail: gairlochgolfclub@hotmail.co.uk
www.gairlochgolfclub.co.uk

Possibly the best wee golf course in the Highlands

A warm welcome awaits at Heatherdale, situated on the outskirts of Gairloch, overlooking the harbour and bay beyond. Within easy walking distance of the golf course and sandy beaches. Ideal base for hill walking. All rooms have en suite facilities, some with sea view. Excellent eating out facilities nearby. Ample parking. Residents' lounge with open fire.

Bed and Breakfast prices from £28 per person per night.

Mrs A. MacIver, Heatherdale, Charleston, Gairloch IV21 2AH
Tel: 01445 712388 • e-mail: BrochoD1@aol.com
www.heatherdalebandb.co.uk

PLEASE NOTE

All the information regarding Golf Clubs in this guide is given in good faith in the belief that it is correct. However, the publishers cannot guarantee the facts given in these pages, neither are they responsible for changes in ownership or facilities, such as green fees, that may take place after the date of going to press. Readers should always satisfy themselves that the facilities they require are available and that the terms, if quoted, still apply.

Highlands (Mid) / SCOTLAND

INVERGORDON. Invergordon Golf Club, King George Street, Invergordon IV18 0BD (01349 852715). *Location:* A9 (B817), two miles, west side of town. Relatively flat, parkland. 18 holes, 6030 yards. S.S.S. 69. *Green Fees:* information not available. *Eating facilities:* bar, bar snacks - normal licensing hours. *Visitors:* welcome without restrictions other than club competition times. Locker rooms. Club/caddy carts for hire. *Society Meetings:* welcome by prior arrangement.*
e-mail: invergordongolf@tiscali.co.uk

LOCHCARRON. Lochcarron Golf Club, Lochcarron IV54 8YS. *Location:* one mile east of Lochcarron village by A896. Seaside course, combined parkland and shore. Interesting opening hole. A short course but great accuracy required. 9 holes with some alternative tees for second nine. 3575 yards (18 holes). S.S.S. 60. *Green Fees:* £15.00 per day; £60.00 per week. Juniors (under 16 years old) half price. 2010 rates (subject to review). *Eating facilities:* snacks and refreshments available in clubhouse. *Visitors:* welcome anytime except Saturdays between 2pm and 5pm. Bookings not required. Clubs for hire. *Society Meetings:* welcome. Secretary: Gerald Arscott (01599 577219).

MUIR OF ORD. The Muir of Ord Golf Club, Great North Road, Muir of Ord IV6 7SX (01463 870825; Fax: 01463 871867). *Location:* 15 miles north of Inverness beside A862, 12 miles north of Inverness on A832. Heathland, moorland course, excellent greens. 18 holes, 5559 yards. S.S.S. 68. Practice area. *Green Fees:* weekdays £28.00 per round, £32.00 per day; weekends £40.00 per round, £44.00 per day. 2010 rates (subject to review). *Eating facilities:* lounge bar (snacks all day), meals weekends or by appointment. *Visitors:* welcome weekdays outwith competition times, weekends by appointment. Trolleys available; buggy hire. *Society Meetings:* welcome. Shop (01463 871311). Club Secretary: A. Pollock (01463 870825).
e-mail: muir.golf@btconnect.com
website: www.muirofordgolfclub.com

PORTMAHOMACK. Tarbat Golf Club, Tarbatness Road, Portmahomack, Tain IV20 1YJ. *Location:* 10 miles east of Tain. B9165 off A9. Seaside links course with scenic views. 9 holes, 5082 yards. S.S.S. 65. Practice area. *Green Fees:* £20.00 per day. *Eating facilities:* catering April-October, light snacks; local hotels. *Visitors:* welcome, some restrictions Saturdays. *Society Meetings:* welcome, please telephone Secretary. Secretary: John Mackay (07849 177353; 07840 773834).

STRATHPEFFER. **Strathpeffer Spa Golf Club,** Golf Course Road, Strathpeffer IV14 9AS (01997 421219 or 01997 421011). *Location:* 20 minutes north of Inverness by A9, 5 miles west of Dingwall, quarter of a mile north of Strathpeffer Square (signposted). Upland course, panoramic views of moorland and mountain; water hazards at 3rd, 6th, 10th and 11th. 18 holes, 5001 yards. S.S.S. 65. Par 67. Small practice area and putting green. *Green Fees:* weekdays £26.00; weekends £30.00. *Eating facilities:* bar and catering available seven days a week. *Visitors:* welcome without reservation, but check weekends and competition days. Club, buggy and trolley hire. *Society Meetings:* catered for by arrangement. Clubhouse (Bookings): 01997 421219.
e-mail: mail@strathpeffergolf.com
website: www.strathpeffergolf.co.uk

TAIN. **Tain Golf Club,** Chapel Road, Tain IV19 1JE (01862 892314; Fax: 01862 892099). *Location*: off A9, 34 miles north of Inverness. Travelling north, turn right in middle of High Street - Golf Club one mile. Traditional links course designed by Old Tom Morris. 18 holes, 6404 yards. S.S.S. 72. All practice facilities available. *Green Fees:* peak season: weekdays £45.00 per round, £65.00 per day; weekends £50.00 per round, £70.00 per day. *Eating facilities*: full catering, licensed. *Visitors*: welcome anytime except when competitions are being held. Electric buggy, trolley, club hire. Pro Shop: 01862 893313. *Society Meetings*: catered for. Secretary: Mrs Joanna Bell.
e-mail: info@tain-golfclub.co.uk
website: www.tain-golfclub.co.uk

ULLAPOOL. **Ullapool Golf Club,** North Road, Ullapool IV26 2TH (01854 613323; Fax: 01854 613133). *Location*: situated at the northern outskirts of the village. Parkland seaside course. 18 tees, 9 holes, 5338 yards, S.S.S. 67. Practice area, bunker. *Green Fees*: £20.00 per day adults, £10.00 per day juniors. *Eating facilities*: catering/bar available at open competitions and summer weekdays. *Visitors*: welcome except during competitions. *Society Meetings*: welcome, group rates by negotiation. Secretary: A. Paterson.
website: www.ullapool-golf.co.uk

Muir of Ord Golf Club
Great North Road, Muir of Ord IV6 7SX
Contact Secretary: 01463 870825
For tee reservations: Shop 01463 871311
e-mail: muir.golf@btconnect.com
www.muirofordgolfclub.com

Established in 1875 and partly designed by James Braid, with 3 new holes laid out in 1996, Muir of Ord Golf Club is a heathland/moorland course situated on the outskirts of the village of Muir of Ord. The clubhouse offers a friendly atmosphere, and visitors and societies are guaranteed a warm Highland welcome.

Located on the Tarbat peninsula, Tarbat is a friendly nine-hole golf course with stunning, all-round views. It sits beside the village of Portmahomack, which has a wonderful beach and harbour, and Tarbatness lighthouse is only 3 miles away at the end of the peninsula. Enjoying below-average rainfall, the course is usually very dry and playable most of the winter. And it may only be 9 holes but, to score well, you have to play well.

To learn more about the course and surrounding area, and to find out what there is to do and see, visit our website at

www.tarbatgolf.com

Tarbat Golf Club
Tarbatness Road, Portmahomack
Tain, Ross-shire IV20 1YB

Better still, come and see us in person. You'll get a warm welcome.

Highlands (South)

ARISAIG. **Traigh Golf Course,** Traigh, Arisaig PH39 4NT (01687 450 337). *Location:* one mile off A830 Fort William to Mallaig road, 2 miles north of Arisaig on the B8008 coast road. Seaside links, close to sandy beaches on the beautiful Morar coast. 9 holes, 2456 yards. S.S.S 65. Practice green. *Green Fees:* £20.00 per day. *Eating facilities:* unlicensed; soft drinks and confectionery only. *Visitors:* welcome at all times. Clubs may be hired. *Society Meetings:* by arrangement. Manager: Bill Henderson (01687 450337/450645).
website: www.traighgolf.co.uk

BEAULY. **Aigas Golf Course,** By Beauly IV4 7AD (01463 782942 or 782423). *Location:* A831, five miles from Beauly village. Aigas nestles spectacularly between the River Beauly and Aigas Forest in beautiful Strathglass. Challenging parkland course. 9 holes, 2439 yards, S.S.S. 63 (2 x 9 holes). Practice area. *Green Fees:* information not available. *Eating facilities:* coffee shop for light refreshments. *Visitors:* welcome almost anytime, booking at weekends advisable. Club and trolley hire.*
e-mail: info@aigas-holidays.co.uk
website: www.aigas-holidays.co.uk

BOAT OF GARTEN. **Boat of Garten Golf and Tennis Club,** Boat of Garten PH24 3BQ (01479 831282; Fax: 01479 831523). *Location:* A9, A95 Turnoff. 6 miles from Aviemore. Highly rated, beautiful, challenging course, designed by James Braid, cut through moorland and birch forest and set amid stunning scenery of Cairngorms National Park. 18 holes, 5876 yards, 5373 metres. S.S.S. 69. Practice net. *Green Fees:* weekdays £36.00 per round, £41.00 per day; weekends £46.00 per round, £51.00 per day. 2010 rates (subject to review). *Eating facilities:* catering facilities open 9am to 8pm, bar open from 11am daily. *Visitors:* welcome 9.30am to 5.30pm. Two tennis courts. *Society Meetings:* catered for. Professional: Ross Harrower (01479 831282; Fax: 01479 831523). Secretary: (01479 831282; Fax: 01479 831523).
e-mail: office@boatgolf.com
website: www.boatgolf.com

CARRBRIDGE. **Carrbridge Golf Club,** Inverness Road, Carrbridge PH23 3AU (01479 841623). *Location:* off A9, 27 miles south of Inverness. Moorland/parkland. 9 holes, 5402 yards. S.S.S. 68, Par 71. *Green Fees:* April-September £23.00. 9-hole ticket £15.00; reduced rates for Juniors. *Eating facilities:* breakfast, morning coffee, lunch, afternoon tea and dinner by arrangement. Clubhouse open April to October only. *Visitors:* always welcome. Tee booking system in operation, call first to avoid delay. *Society Meetings:* group bookings very welcome.
e-mail: secretary@carrbridgegolf.co.uk
website: www.carrbridgegolf.co.uk

CAWDOR CASTLE. **Cawdor Castle Golf Course,** Cawdor Castle, Nairn IV12 5RD (01667 404401; Fax: 01667 404674). *Location:* situated between Inverness and Nairn on the B9090 off A96. Parkland. 9 holes, 1303 yards. S.S.S. 32. *Green Fees:* day ticket £10.00. 2010 rates (subject to review). *Eating facilities:* licensed Courtyard Restaurant in Castle, snack bar in grounds. *Visitors:* welcome every day from 1st May to first Sunday in October, 10am to 5pm.
e-mail: info@cawdorcastle.com
website: www.cawdorcastle.com

FORT AUGUSTUS. **Fort Augustus Golf Club,** Markethill, Fort Augustus PH32 4DS (01320 366660). *Location:* half-a-mile south of village on A82. Moorland course, tree lined to north, heather covered hills to the south. 9 holes (18 tees), 5379 yards. S.S.S. 67. *Green Fees:* £18.00 per round, £25.00 per day. *Eating facilities:* hot and cold snacks, lounge bar. *Visitors:* welcome anytime except Saturday afternoons from 12 noon to 4.30pm. Clubs and trolleys for hire. *Society Meetings:* welcome, please book in advance. Secretary: Karen Callow (07824 785003).
e-mail: fortaugustusgc@aol.com .
website: www.fortaugustusgc.webeden.co.uk

FORT WILLIAM. **Fort William Golf Club,** Torlundy, Fort William PH33 6SN (01397 704464). *Location*: north from Fort William, approx. 3 miles through town. Parkland course. 18 holes, 6217 yards, S.S.S 71. Practice area. *Green Fees*: £25.00 per round, £30.00 per day. *Eating facilities*: snacks available from the bar. *Visitors*: welcome all week except Saturday and Sunday between 8am and 11am. *Society Meetings*: welcome, discount available for parties of more than 15.

INVERNESS. **Castle Stuart Golf Links,** Balnaglack Farmhouse, Inverness IV2 7JL (01463 795440). *Location*: two miles from Inverness Airport and 7 miles from Inverness city centre. Links Course. 18 holes, 7009 yards. *Green Fees*: on application. General Manager: Stuart McColm (01463 796111).
e-mail: info@castlestuartgolf.com
website: www.castlestuartgolf.com

INVERNESS. **Torvean Golf Club,** Glenurquhart Road, Inverness IV3 8JN (Starter: 01463 711434). *Location*: A82 towards Fort William, approximately one mile from town centre. Parkland course. 18 holes, 5799 yards. S.S.S. 69. *Green Fees:* information not available. *Eating facilities:* all day catering provided year round. *Visitors:* booking preferred, especially at weekends (01463 711434). Clubs and trolleys for hire. *Society Meetings:* discounts for parties over 10. Club Manager: Susan Downer.*
e-mail: sarah@torveangolfclub.co.uk

Boat of Garten Golf Club

Boat of Garten, Inverness-shire PH24 3BQ

James Braid's masterpiece in the magnificent setting of the Cairngorms National Park.

Tel: 01479 831282
www.boatgolf.com

Tyndrum, Boat of Garten

Tel: 01479 831242

Completely renovated, well furnished and equipped self-catering accommodation, sleeps 5. In beautiful Strathspey, six miles from Aviemore, an ideal base for touring. Fishing available on the River Spey, just two minutes away, with attractive riverside picnic spots. The famous Osprey nest is nearby. Local steam train journeys, good golf and water sports; skiing at Cairngorm.

Shop and pub half a mile • Parking • Garden

Contact: Mrs N.C. Clark, Dochlaggie, Boat of Garten PH24 3BU • e-mail: dochlaggie99@aol.com

Fort Augustus Golf Club
Market Hill, Fort Augustus, PH32 4DS

Traditional heathland course, widely regarded as the most challenging 9-hole course in Scotland. Dual tee positions give a true 18-hole feel. Cosy welcoming clubhouse. Clubs and trolleys available for hire. Green Fees £18 per 18 holes, £25 per day. Visitors and Societies welcome, just call Secretary Karen Callow for details: Tel: 01320 366660
Contact: E-mail: fortaugustusgc@aol.com • www.fortaugustusgc.webeden.co.uk

Fort William Golf Club

Fort William Golf Club sits right at the foot of Ben Nevis, Britain's highest mountain. It is an 18-hole heathland course with a fine mix of challenging and varied holes with excellent views of the surrounding mountains from its fairways and greens. Club and trolley rentals are available, and tees, balls and gloves are for sale.

Fort William Golf Club
North Road, Torlundy
Fort William PH33 6SN
Tel: 01397 704464
www.fortwilliamgolf.co.uk

430 Highlands (South) / SCOTLAND — THE GOLF GUIDE 2011

INVERNESS. **Inverness Golf Club,** The Clubhouse, Culcabock Road, Inverness IV2 3XQ (01463 239882). *Location:* one mile south of town centre. Parkland course with tree-lined fairways, an excellent test of golf for all levels of player and a great alternative to traditional links courses. The Mill Burn poses a challenge at several holes. 18 holes, 6256 yards. S.S.S. 70. *Green Fees:* £38.00 per round, £52.00 per day. Group discounts available. 2010 rates (subject to review). *Eating facilities:* the impressive clubhouse is a first-class venue for relaxation; sandwiches, lunches, high teas and dinners served. *Visitors:* welcome. Club Secretary/Manager: (01463 239882/ 231989; Fax: 01463 240616).
e-mail: manager@invernessgolfclub.co.uk
website: www.invernessgolfclub.co.uk

INVERNESS. **Loch Ness Golf Course,** Fairways, Castle Heather, Inverness IV2 6AA (01463 713335; Fax: 01463 712695). *Location:* on the southern outskirts of Inverness, heading west along new Ring Road. Parkland course with panoramic views over Inverness and Moray Firth. 27 holes. New Course 5631 yards (yellow), 5948 yards (white); 9-hole family course 1412 yards. *Green Fees:* New Course - weekdays £30.00 per round; weekends £35.00 per round. 9-hole course £10.00 per round at all times. *Eating facilities:* lounge bar, sports bar, full catering facilities. *Visitors:* welcome. Buggies and carts available. *Society Meetings:* most welcome by prior arrangement. Professional: Martin Piggot (01463 713334). Manager: Neil D. Hampton (01463 713335; Fax: 01463 712695).
e-mail: info@golflochness.com
website: www.golflochness.com

KINGUSSIE. **Kingussie Golf Club,** Gynack Road, Kingussie PH21 1LR (01540 661600). *Location:* half a mile from Kingussie High Street, turning at Duke of Gordon. 18 holes, 5501 yards. S.S.S. 68. *Green Fees:* weekdays £28.00 per round, £36.00 per day; weekends £32.00 per round, £38.00 per day. Juniors £12.00. Weekly (7 days) £100.00. 2010 rates (subject to review). *Eating facilities:* bar and excellent catering. *Visitors:* welcome. *Society Meetings:* welcome at all times, book in advance. Secretary: Ian Chadburn (01540 661600).
e-mail: sec@kingussie-golf.co.uk
website: www.kingussie-golf.co.uk

NAIRN. **Nairn Dunbar Golf Club,** Lochloy Road, Nairn IV12 5AE (01667 452741; Fax: 01667 456897). *Location:* off A96, at east end of town. Championship links. 18 holes, 6765 yards. S.S.S. 74. *Green Fees:* information not provided *Eating facilities:* new spacious clubhouse with full catering and visitors facilities. *Visitors:* welcome, also groups. Professional: David Torrance (01667 453964). Secretary: Jim Gibson (01667 452741; Fax: 01667 456897).
e-mail: secretary@nairndunbar.com
website: www.nairndunbar.com

NETHY BRIDGE. **Abernethy Golf Club,** Nethy Bridge PH25 3EB (01479 821305). *Location:* 10 miles from Aviemore lying on the B970 between Boat of Garten and Grantown-on-Spey. Delightful nine hole course close to pine woods and with commanding view of the valley of the River Spey. 9 holes, 5068 yards. S.S.S. 66. *Green Fees:* weekdays £20.00, weekend £22.00. Late weekdays £10.00, late weekend £12.00. Juniors half price. 2010 rates (subject to review). *Eating facilities:* clubhouse is unlicensed but there are full catering facilities available. *Visitors:* welcome subject to short restrictions when club competitions being held.
e-mail: info@abernethygolfclub.com
website: www.abernethygolfclub.com

NEWTONMORE. **Newtonmore Golf Club,** Golf Course Road, Newtonmore PH20 1AT (01540 673878). *Location:* turn off A9 at Newtonmore, course in centre of village, 45 miles south of Inverness. Mainly flat course set by River Spey amidst beautiful scenery. 18 holes, 6029 yards. S.S.S. 69. Practice green. *Green Fees:* midweek £28.00 per round, £33.00 per day; weekends £30.00 per round, £38.00 per day. *Eating facilities:* full catering (except Tuesdays) and bar facilities. Locker and shower facilities. *Visitors:* welcome. *Society Meetings:* all welcome. Professional: Robert Henderson (01540 673611). Secretary: Roy Alexander (01540 673878).
e-mail: secretary@newtonmoregolf.com
website: www.newtonmoregolf.com

SPEAN BRIDGE. **Spean Bridge Golf Club,** Station Road, Spean Bridge PH34 4EU. *Location:* on main A82, eight miles north of Fort William. Wooded course set on the hillside, full view of Nevis Range ski slopes and Ben Nevis. 9 holes, 2271 yards. S.S.S. 63. *Green Fees:* day ticket £18.00; 9 hole ticket £10.00. *Eating facilities:* Hotel nearby. *Visitors:* welcome. Tees reserved Saturday 10am to 11am; Sunday 11am to 3pm; Tuesday 9.30am to 11am. *Society Meetings:* all welcome. Secretary: K. Dalziel (07710 105478).

Abernethy Golf Club, established in 1893, is a traditional, Highland course of nine challenging holes built on natural moorland bordered by the ancient pines of the Abernethy Forest. The clubhouse (unlicensed) offers traditional Highland catering and a warm welcome. We welcome families and a Handicap Certificate is not required.
• Changing facilities • Club and trolley hire • Green Fees: £20 weekdays, £22 weekends – 30% discount using Aviemore and Cairngorms Golf Pass (on sale in Clubhouse)
• Special terms for groups. Further details from:
Secretary, Abernethy Golf Club
Nethy Bridge, Inverness-shire PH25 3EB
info@abernethygolfclub.com
www.abernethygolfclub.com
Telephone: **01479 821305**

Bunchrew House
'the romantic hotel on the shore'

Set within 20 acres of beautiful landscaped gardens and woodland on the shores of the Beauly Firth near Inverness, Bunchrew House is a 17th century Scottish mansion steeped in tradition and history, offering quality accommodation, award-winning cuisine and a Highland welcome second to none.

Within 90 minutes' drive of Bunchrew you will find 25 golf courses – to suit all standards of player from the deadly serious whose desire is to pit their skills against the toughest courses, to the occasional golfer who just enjoys getting out in the fresh air. They include • Royal Dornoch Championship (50 mins) • Castle Stuart Golf Links (15 mins) • Nairn Golf Club & Nairn Dunbar Golf Club (20 mins)

Bunchrew House Hotel, Inverness IV3 8TA
Tel: 01463 234917 • Fax: 01463 710720
e-mail: welcome@bunchrewhousehotel.com • www.bunchrewhousehotel.com

CULLODEN HOUSE HOTEL
Culloden • Inverness

Once used as Bonnie Prince Charlie's battle headquarters prior to the fateful Battle of Culloden in 1746, today this Palladian country house stands in nearly 40 acres of parkland where guests are free to wander and enjoy the peace and tranquillity. Wonderfully comfortable drawing-room and dining room, both with magnificent Adam plasterwork and log fires; uniquely decorated luxury bedrooms.

Tel: 01463 790461 • Fax: 01463 792181
e-mail: info@cullodenhouse.co.uk
www.cullodenhouse.co.uk

• Condé Nast "Gold List" 2010 • Condé Nast Traveller "Best Hotel In Scotland 2006
• Golf Tourism Scotland "Most Outstanding Scottish Country House Hotel" 2005 • Johansens Recommended
• STB and AA ★★★★ AA Two Rosettes for Food • A Taste of Scotland • "Best Loved Hotel of the World"

Loch Ness Golf Course
Home of Loch Ness Golf Club
FAIRWAYS • CASTLE HEATHER • INVERNESS IV2 6AR
Phone: (01463) 713335 • Fax: (01463) 712695
e-mail: info@golflochness.com • www.golflochness.com

"Everything for the Golfer in the Highland Capital"

LOCH NESS GOLF COURSE

19-bay floodlight driving range – quality mats and 2-piece balls. Lounge bar, restaurant, sports bar. Children welcome. Petanque, Forest Walks, Indoor Bowls. Travelodge.

18-hole course 5900 yards
9-hole family course
Practice Putting Green
Pitching and Bunker area

Open all day, every day for EVERYONE!

NAIRN DUNBAR GOLF CLUB
Championship Links Course

❖ 10 minutes from Inverness Airport
❖ Some weekend availability
❖ Attractive Visitor rates
❖ Full catering and bar service from our modern clubhouse overlooking the Moray Firth

Lochloy Road, Nairn IV12 5AE • Tel 01667 452741
secretary@nairndunbar.com • www.nairndunbar.com

Lanarkshire

AIRDRIE. **Airdrie Golf Club,** Glenmavis Road, Airdrie ML6 0PQ (01236 762195). *Location:* one mile north of Airdrie Cross. 18 holes, 5772 yards. S.S.S. 68. *Green Fees:* information not available. *Eating facilities:* available. *Visitors:* welcome only on application to the Secretary. Professional: S. McLean (01236 754360). Secretary: W. Campbell.*

AIRDRIE. **Easter Moffat Golf Club,** Plains, Airdrie ML6 8NP (01236 842878; Fax: 01236 842904). *Location:* three miles east of Airdrie on old Edinburgh Road. 18 holes, 6221 yards. S.S.S. 70. Practice ground. *Green Fees:* information not provided. *Eating facilities:* bar and dining room. *Visitors:* welcome except weekends. *Society Meetings:* welcome. Professional: Graham King (01236 843015). Secretary: Gordon Miller (01236 620972).

BELLSHILL. **Bellshill Golf Club,** Community Road, Orbiston, Bellshill ML4 2RZ (01698 745124). *Location:* Bellshill to Motherwell road, turn right. Parkland course. 18 holes, 5852 yards. S.S.S. 69. *Green Fees:* May to October, midweek £20.00 per round, £25.00 per day, Juniors (accompanied by adult) £5.00 per round; weekends and Public Holidays £30.00 per round, £35.00 per day, Juniors (with adult) £10.00. November to March £10.00 per round. Half price rates for students. Midweek packages for visiting parties of 8 or more: two rounds of golf plus coffee, soup and rolls, and high tea from £40.00; one round of golf plus coffee/roll and a meal from £30.00. All prices subject to review. *Eating facilities:* by prior arrangement with Clubmaster. *Visitors:* welcome, Sundays by prior arrangement, parties by prior application (not competition days). *Society Meetings:* by prior arrangement with Administrator: J. McNeil or Secretary: Anthony Deerin.
e-mail: info@bellshillgolfclub.com

BIGGAR. **Biggar Golf Club,** Broughton Road, Biggar ML12 6HA (01899 220618 (Clubhouse)). *Location:* from Edinburgh A702, from Glasgow A74 or M8, turn off at Newhouse. Flat, scenic parkland course. 18 holes, 5416 yards. S.S.S. 66. *Green Fees:* information not available. *Eating facilities:* all day licence, full catering, snacks only on Tuesdays. *Visitors:* unrestricted, casual dress – no jeans. All weather tennis courts and caravan park. Buggies and carts available. *Society Meetings:* welcome, early reservation essential. Secretary: Tom Rodger. Tee Reservations: (01899 220319). *

CARLUKE. **Carluke Golf Club,** Mauldslie Road, Hallcraig, Carluke ML8 5HG (01555 771070). *Location:* Carluke Cross, go west along Clyde Street for two miles. Parkland course. 18 holes, 5800 yards. S.S.S. 69. Practice area. *Green Fees:* information not provided. *Eating facilities:* available. *Visitors:* till 4pm weekdays, no visitors weekends. Tuition. *Society Meetings:* by written application to the Secretary, restriction on numbers. Professional: Craig Ronald (01555 751053). Administration: Tom Fraser (01555 770574).
e-mail: carlukegolfsecy@tiscali.co.uk
website: www.carlukegolfclub.com

CARNWATH. **Carnwath Golf Club,** 1 Main Street, Carnwath ML11 8JX (01555 840251; Fax: 01555 841070). *Location:* on main Ayr/Edinburgh Road. Fairly hilly inland course. 18 holes, 5953 yards. S.S.S. 69. *Green Fees:* weekdays £25.00 per round, £35.00 per two rounds; Sundays £30.00 per round, £40.00 per two rounds. *Eating facilities:* lounge bar and dining room daily. *Visitors:* welcome. Not Saturdays or after 4pm weekdays. Sunday with prior booking. *Society Meetings:* catered for by prior arrangement. Secretary: Mrs L. McPate (01555 840251).
e-mail: carnwathgc@hotmail.co.uk

COATBRIDGE. **Drumpellier Golf Club,** Drumpellier Avenue, Coatbridge ML5 1RX (01236 424139). *Location:* one mile from town centre. Parkland, wooded. 18 holes, 6227 yards. S.S.S. 70. Practice area. *Green Fees:* £35.00 per round, £50.00 per day weekdays. *Eating facilities:* available seven days. *Visitors:* welcome daily except weekends. *Society Meetings:* catered for by arrangement. Professional: I. Taylor. Secretary: J.M. Craig (01236 424139; Fax: 01236 428723).
e-mail: administrator@drumpelliergolfclub.com

DOUGLAS WATER. **Douglas Water Golf Club,** Ayr Road, Rigside, Lanark ML11 9NP (01555 880361). *Location:* five miles south of Lanark on A70, Junction 11 from M74. Hilly course, small greens, undulating fairways. 9 holes, 2947 yards, 2694 metres. S.S.S. 69. *Green Fees:* information not provided. *Visitors:* welcome any time, except Saturdays because of competitions. *Society Meetings:* contact Secretary. Secretary: D. Hogg (01698 882432).

THE APPEARANCE OF AN ASTERISK (*) AT THE END OF A CLUB OR COURSE ENTRY INDICATES THAT UP-TO-DATE INFORMATION HAS NOT BEEN SUPPLIED

EAST KILBRIDE. Torrance House Golf Club, Calderglen Country Park, Strathaven Road, East Kilbride G75 0QZ (013552 49720). *Location:* East Kilbride boundary on main Strathaven road. Parkland. 18 holes, 6423 yards. S.S.S. 71. Practice area. *Green Fees:* information not available. *Eating facilities:* private clubhouse. *Visitors:* welcome mid-week only. *Society Meetings:* details on request. Secretary: M.D. McKerlie (013552 49720). Booking Office: (01355 248638).*

GARTCOSH. Mount Ellen Golf Club, Lochend Road, Gartcosh, Glasgow G69 8BD (Tel & Fax: 01236 872277). *Location:* approximately six miles north-east of Glasgow, near old Gartcosh steelworks. Parkland. 18 holes, 5525 yards. S.S.S. 67. *Green Fees:* information not provided. *Eating facilities:* bar and full catering service. *Visitors:* welcome weekdays from 9am to 4pm, no weekend visitors. Carts available for hire. *Society Meetings:* weekdays by arrangement with Secretary. Professional: I. Bilsborough (01236 872277). Secretary: R. Watt.

HAMILTON. Hamilton Golf Club, Carlisle Road, Ferniegair, Hamilton ML3 7UE (01698 282872). *Location:* off M74 Hamilton turnoff, 1½ miles up Larkhall road. Parkland course. 18 holes, 6444 yards. S.S.S. 71. *Green Fees:* £35.00 per round, day ticket £45.00. 1 x 4 ball £100.00 twice daily. *Eating facilities:* meals must be ordered. *Visitors:* by arrangement, please contact Secretary. *Society Meetings:* visitors by arrangement, contact Secretary. Professional: Derek Wright (01698 282872). Secretary: Graham Mackenzie (01698 282872; Fax: 01698 204650).

HAMILTON. Strathclyde Park Golf Club, Motehill, Hamilton ML3 6BY (01698 429370). *Location:* Hamilton/Motherwell exit off M74 to roundabout second exit East Kilbride, to new roundabout second exit, to third roundabout third exit straight ahead, to golf course passing ice rink on left hand side. Wooded parkland course surrounded by race course on one side and nature reserve on other. 9 holes, 3128 yards. S.S.S. 70. Large practice area, putting green and driving range (24 bays). *Green Fees:* weekdays £4.20, Juniors/Senior Citizens £2.10; weekends and public holidays £4.85, Juniors/Senior Citizens £2.45. 2010 rates (subject to review). *Eating facilities:* bar within complex. *Visitors:* welcome, same day booking system in operation. Course opens 7am Summer, 8am Winter. *Society Meetings:* welcome by arrangement through management (01698 429370). Professional: W. Walker. Secretary: K. Will (01698 429370).

LANARK. Kames Golf Club, Eastend, Cleghorn ML11 8NR (01555 870015; Fax: 01555 870022). *Location:* situated on the A721 between Carluke and Carnwath. Home of the championship Mouse Valley Golf Course, 18 holes, 6300 yards. S.S.S. 72, and the delightful Kames Course, 18 holes, 3600 yards. *Green Fees:* information not provided. *Eating facilities:* full bar and catering. *Visitors:* welcome. *Society Meetings:* all welcome, weekend bookings taken.
e-mail: info@kames-golf-club.com
website: www.kames-golf-club.com

Visit www.holidayguides.com
for convenient accommodation
when playing golf around the regions

434 Lanarkshire / SCOTLAND — THE GOLF GUIDE 2011

LANARK **Lanark Golf Club,** The Moor, Whitelees Road, Lanark ML11 7RX (01555 663219). *Location:* off A73. Tough moorland course. 18 holes, 6306 yards. S.S.S. 71. Also 9-hole course. Two practice grounds. *Green Fees:* weekdays £40.00 per round, £50.00 per day. 2010 rates (subject to review). *Eating facilities:* full catering and bar. *Visitors:* welcome daily until 4pm, no visitors weekends. *Society Meetings:* groups of 8/40 and over catered for Monday to Friday. Professional: Alan White (01555 661456). Secretary: G.H. Cuthill.

LANARK. **Mouse Valley Golf Course,** Eastend, Cleghorn, Lanark ML11 8NR (01555 870015; Fax: 01555 870022). *Location:* 5 miles from Carluke on A721 Peebles Road. Pay as you play. Links style course, inland undulating terrain. Mouse Water (river) runs through the course. Two courses - Mouse Valley 18 holes, 6376 yards, Par 70 and Kames course - 18 holes, 3617 yards, Par 62. Practice ground. *Green Fees:* information not provided. *Eating facilities:* full bar and catering. *Visitors:* welcome, no restrictions. *Society Meetings:* welcome at all times. Company days. Contact: (01555 870015).

LARKHALL. **Larkhall Golf Club,** Burnhead Road, Larkhall ML9 2AA (01698 889597). *Location:* on A74, close to M74. Parkland. 9 holes, 6432 yards. S.S.S. 70. *Green Fees:* information not available. *Eating facilities:* bar, lunch only on Saturdays. *Visitors:* welcome, but check beforehand; not Saturdays. Secretary: Malcolm Mallinson; Booking Office (01698 881113).*

LEADHILLS. **Leadhills Golf Club,** The Lowthers, Horners Place, Leadhills, Biggar ML12 6AR (01659 74633). *Location:* seven miles south of Abington on B797. This short but testing course is the highest in Scotland. 9 holes, 4578 yards. Par 34. S.S.S. 68. *Green Fees:* per round/day – adults £10.00, Juniors £3.00. *Eating facilities:* hotel nearby. *Visitors:* welcome any time. *Society Meetings:* welcome. Secretary: Stuart Lang (07768 225890). e-mail: leadhillsgolfclub@hotmail.co.uk

LESMAHAGOW. **Hollandbush Golf Club,** Acretophead, Lesmahagow ML11 0JS (01555 893484). *Location:* off M74 (Junction 9). Golf course is between Lesmahagow and Coalburn. 18 holes, 6246 yards. S.S.S. 70. Practice area. *Green Fees:* information not provided. *Eating facilities:* meals at club. *Visitors:* welcome without restriction. *Society Meetings:* catered for. Starter's Office (01555 893646). Secretary: James Hamilton (01555 893484). Administrator: Loraine Affleck.

MOTHERWELL. **Colville Park Golf Club,** Jerviston Estate, Merry Street, Motherwell ML1 4UG (01698 263017; Fax: 01698 230418). *Location:* one mile from town centre and train station (Merry Street, Motherwell). Parkland, wooded first six holes. 18 holes, 6301 yards. S.S.S. 71. *Green Fees:* information not available. *Eating facilities:* full facilities. *Visitors:* welcome between 11am and 3pm Mondays to Thursdays only. Advance booking not required. *Society Meetings:* by prior written arrangement, weekdays only. Professional Shop: (01698 265779). Secretary: Leslie Innes (01698 262808).*

Ideally situated halfway between Edinburgh and Glasgow, with easy access from the M8, this 18-hole moorland course provides a challenge for all standards of golfers. Visitors should beware the notorious 4th hole, 'The Devil's Elbow', which has ruined the cards of many aspiring hopefuls. A refurbished clubhouse provides a warm and friendly welcome, with catering and bar facilities.

Shotts Golf Club
Blairhead, Shotts ML7 5BJ

Clubhouse: 01501 820431
Pro Shop: 01501 822658
Office: 01501 825868
e-mail: info@shottsgolfclub.co.uk
www.shottsgolfclub.co.uk

SCOTLAND / Lanarkshire

MOTHERWELL. Dalziel Park Golf & Country Club, 100 Hagen Drive, Motherwell ML1 5RZ (01698 862862; Fax: 01698 862863). *Location*: four miles from Motherwell with good access to M74 and M8 at Junction 6. Midway between Glasgow and Edinburgh. Wooded Parkland. 18 holes, 6300 yards, S.S.S. 70. 15 bay floodlit driving range and extensive dry and outdoor sports facilities. *Green Fees*: information not available. *Eating facilities*: Italiam and Scottish restaurants, bars and lounges. 10 bedrooms, conference facilities and all functions catered for in Country Club. *Visitors*: all welcome, only restricted on Saturday morning (during Men's medal day). *Society Meetings*: welcome at all times. Secretary: Russell Weir (01698 862862; Fax: 01698 862863).*

SHOTTS. **Shotts Golf Club,** Blairhead, Benhar Road, Shotts ML7 5BJ (01501 822658). *Location:* off M8 at Junction 5, one and a half miles south. Semi-flat moorland/wooded course. 18 holes, 6204 yards. S.S.S. 70. Practice area, professional tuition. *Green Fees:* weekday £22.00 per round, day ticket £30.00. *Eating facilities:* full catering and bar service. *Visitors:* welcome anytime except Saturdays, Sundays (prior booking needed) or Public Holidays. *Society Meetings:* weekdays only (not Public Holidays) by arrangement. Professional: John Strachan (01501 822658). Secretary: George Stoddart (01501 825868).
e-mail: info@shottsgolfclub.co.uk
website: www.shottsgolfclub.co.uk

STRATHAVEN. **Strathaven Golf Club,** Overton Avenue, Glasgow Road, Strathaven ML10 6NL. *Location:* on A726 on outskirts of town. 18 holes, 6250 yards. S.S.S. 71. *Green Fees:* please contact Secretary for information. *Eating facilities:* full catering and bar. *Visitors:* welcome weekdays, casual visitors before 4pm; party bookings Tuesdays only by prior arrangement. Professional: Stuart Kerr (01357 520421). General Manager: I.F. Neil (01357 520421).

UDDINGSTON. **Calderbraes Golf Club,** 57 Roundknowe Road, Uddingston G71 7TS (01698 813425). *Location:* at end of M74, overlooking Calderpark Zoo. 9 holes, 3425 yards. S.S.S. 67. *Green Fees:* day ticket £15.00. *Visitors:* welcome. *Society Meetings:* welcome, contact Secretary. Secretary: S. McGuigan.

WISHAW. **Wishaw Golf Club,** 55 Cleland Road, Wishaw ML2 7PH (01698 372869). *Location:* 400 yards from Wishaw Main Street at West Cross. Tree-lined parkland course. 18 holes, 5999 yards. S.S.S 69. Practice area. *Green Fees:* Monday to Friday £26.00 per round, £36.00 per day; Sunday £30.00 per round, £40.00 per day. *Eating facilities:* full catering, two bars, and dining room. *Visitors:* welcome before 4pm weekdays, after 10.30am Sundays, no visitors Saturdays. *Society Meetings:* by application. Professional: Stuart Adair (01698 358247). General Manager: James W. Douglas (01698 357480).
e-mail: jwdouglas@btconnect.com

Wishaw Golf Club (est.1897) 18-hole parkland course designed by James Braid.
• Tree-lined fairways, tricky par 3s and a testing last 5 holes require concentration and a strong finish to test the 69 SSS. • The clubhouse has been totally refurbished with new bar, lounge, dining room, locker room and Pro Shop. • Catering is to a very high standard, and includes an à la carte menu, all at very favourable prices. • **55 Cleland Road, Wishaw ML2 7PH**
Tel: Pro Shop 01698 358247 or 357480 for society bookings.

Wishaw Golf Club

Perth & Kinross

ABERFELDY. **Aberfeldy Golf Club,** Taybridge Road, Aberfeldy PH15 2BH (01887 820535). *Location:* A9 from Ballinluig. Scenic riverside course. 18 holes, 5283 yards. S.S.S. 66, Par 68. *Green Fees:* information not provided. *Eating facilities:* high teas, lunches, etc. *Visitors:* welcome anytime. Buggy and trolley hire. *Society Meetings:* catered for. Secretary: (01887 820535).

ALYTH. **Glenisla Golf Centre,** Pitcrocknie, Alyth PH11 8JJ (01828 632445; Fax: 01828 633749). *Location:* five miles east of Blairgowrie on the B954. Parkland, with undulating, rolling fairways, and featuring over 40 bunkers and 5 water hazards. 'One of Scotland's favourite courses' (Insider Business Magazine Top 500 Survey, March 2001). 18 holes, 6402 yards. S.S.S. 71. *Green Fees:* information not available. *Eating facilities:* superbly appointed, fully licensed clubhouse with panoramic bar and restaurant overlooking the course. *Visitors:* always welcome. Conference and Function facilities and on site B&B and self-catering cottages available. *Society Meetings:* always welcome. Golf Administrator: Ewan Wilson.*
e-mail: info@golf-glenisla.co.uk
website: www.golf-glenisla.co.uk

AUCHTERARDER. **Auchterarder Golf Club,** Orchil Road, Auchterarder PH3 1LS (01764 662804). *Location:* off A9 to southwest of town, next to Gleneagles. Flat parkland, part wooded. 18 holes, 5750 yards. S.S.S. 69. Small practice area. *Green Fees:* Monday to Thursday £30.00 per round, £42.00 per day; Friday to Sunday £35.00 per round, £50.00 per day. *Eating facilities:* lounge, dining room, bar. *Visitors:* welcome without reservation except major competition days. *Society Meetings:* welcome. Professional: Gavin Baxter. Secretary: D.D. Smith (01764 662804; Fax: 01764 664423).
e-mail: secretary@auchterardergolf.co.uk
website: www.auchterardergolf.co.uk

AUCHTERARDER. **Gleneagles Hotel Golf Courses,** Auchterarder PH3 1NF (Golf Office: 01764 694469; Fax: 01764 694383). *Location:* 20 miles south of Perth, 20 miles north of Stirling. Gleneagles offers two moorland 18 hole courses and a third parkland/moorland course. King's Course: 6125 yards par 68; Queen's Course: 5660 yards par 68; PGA Centenary Course: 18 holes, 6141 yards S.S.S. 72 and a 9 hole course, The Wee Course: 1481 yards par 27. *Green Fees:* information not available. *Eating facilities:* at The Dormy Clubhouse (Bar & Restaurant) and The Gleneagles Hotel. *Visitors:* welcome. Professional: Russell Smith. Hotel General Manager:Bernard Murphy (01764 662231). Golf Bookings: (01764 694469; Fax: 01764 662134).*
website: www.gleneagles.com

BLAIR ATHOLL. **Blair Atholl Golf Club,** Blair Atholl, Pitlochry PH18 5TG (01796 481407). *Location:* off A9 Perth/Inverness Road, down Invertilt Road. Flat parkland. 9 holes, 5816 yards, 5322 metres. S.S.S. 68. *Green Fees:* information not available. *Eating facilities:* meals/bar. *Visitors:* welcome at all times. Carts and clubs available. *Society Meetings:* by arrangement with Secretary. Secretary: D.A. Boon.*

BLAIRGOWRIE. **The Alyth Golf Club,** Pitcrocknie, Alyth, Blairgowrie PH11 8HF (01828 632268; Fax: 01828 633491). *Location:* five miles from Blairgowrie on B954. Parkland/heathland course with interesting dog leg Par 4 5th played to a plateau green with out-of-bounds on right. 18 holes, 6205 yards, 5676 metres. S.S.S. 71. Large practice area. *Green Fees:* information not provided. *Eating facilities:* all day catering and bar. *Visitors:* welcome, phone 01828 632411 six days ahead. *Society Meetings:* welcome, prior booking essential. Professional: Tom Melville (01828 632411). Secretary: Jim Docherty (01828 632268; Fax: 01828 633491).
e-mail: enquiries@alythgolf.co.uk
website: www.alythgolfclub.co.uk

Acharn, By Aberfeldy

Escape the rat race in comfort, peace and tranquillity. Self-catering by loch, woodlands and mountains. With the 18 hole Taymouth Castle and Kenmore courses on the doorstep. Highland Perthshire has half a dozen golf courses. Gleneagles and Rosemount one hour's drive. £235-£630 per house per week.

Tel: 01887 830209
Fax: 01887 830802
e-mail: remony@btinternet.com
www.lochtaylodges.co.uk

LOCH TAY LODGES

THE GOLF GUIDE 2011 — SCOTLAND / Perth & Kinross 437

For a peaceful break in the Perthshire countryside, Five Roads is the perfect location. It is situated on the outskirts of Alyth, a small, historic town offering a wide variety of attractions in close proximity. The park is open all year and welcomes tourers and tents. Each pitch has an electric hook-up. There are two Thistle Award holiday homes for hire; each has central heating, double glazing, shower, microwave, TV and is fully furnished. WiFi available. Bed linen is provided. Play area for small children. Pets not permitted in holiday homes. There are three golf courses within a one mile radius.

FIVE ROADS CARAVAN PARK, Alyth, Blairgowrie PH11 8NB
Tel: 01828 632255
steven.ewart@btopenworld.com • www.fiveroads-caravan-park.co.uk

---

AUCHTERARDER GOLF CLUB

The Clubhouse, Orchil Road, Auchterarder PH3 1LS
Managing Secretary, Mr D.D. Smith: Tel 01764 662804 • Fax: 01764 664423
e-mail: secretary@auchterardergolf.co.uk • www.auchterardergolf.co.uk

Monday - Thursday Round £30, Day £42
Friday - Sunday Round £35, Day £50

This is a flat parkland course that is part woodland, with fine examples of pine, larch and birch. Just a few minutes from its famous neighbour Gleneagles, but with a character of its own. At just 5,750 yards, it is relatively short, although a mix of tricky doglegs and heavily guarded greens make it a course to remember.

The Alyth Hotel
6 Commercial Street, Alyth, Perthshire PH11 8AF

A warm welcome

The Alyth Hotel is situated in the heart of rural Perthshire, with around 70 superb golf courses within reasonable travelling distance, and many classic courses on our doorstep. We look forward to welcoming you • 12 en suite bedrooms • Friendly licensed restaurant • Lounge Bar

Tel: (01828) 632447 • Fax: (01828) 632355 • e-mail: info@alythhotel.com • www.alythhotel.com

---

The Red House Hotel

Relax and enjoy a meal after your round of golf. The Red House Hotel menu is served in our Restaurant & Conservatory from 12 noon to 9pm. Stay in one of our 20 en suite rooms, and play some of the finest golf courses in Scotland which are only a 15-minute drive away. Also within the Red House Hotel we can provide Snooker, Squash, Sauna and Gymnasium.

STATION ROAD, COUPAR ANGUS, PERTHSHIRE PH13 9AL
Tel: 01828 628500 • Fax: 01828 628574
e-mail: stay@red-house-hotel.co.uk • www.red-house-hotel.co.uk

BLAIRGOWRIE. **Blairgowrie Golf Club,** Golf Course Road, Rosemount, Blairgowrie PH10 6LG (01250 872622; Fax: 01250 875451). *Location:* take A923 out of Perth, turn right at "Rosemount" sign. Gently undulating heathland. Rosemount Course: 18 holes, 6689 yards. S.S.S. 72. Lansdowne Course: 18 holes, 7007 yards. S.S.S. 74. Wee Course: 9 holes, 4704 yards. S.S.S. 63. Two practice grounds. *Green Fees:* information not available. *Eating facilities:* full catering available. *Visitors:* welcome by appointment. *Society Meetings:* catered for by application to Office. Professional: Charles Dernie (01250 873116). Secretary/Manager: Ron Mclaren (01250 872622).*
e-mail: office@theblairgowriegolfclub.co.uk
website: www.theblairgowriegolfclub.co.uk

BLAIRGOWRIE. **Dalmunzie Golf Course,** Spittal O' Glenshee, Blairgowrie PH10 7QE (01250 885226). *Location:* A93 Blairgowrie to Braemar road, left at Spittal O' Glenshee. A small well-kept hill course amid glorious scenery. 9 holes, 2099 yards. *Green Fees:* £15.00 per day. Under 8 free, 8–17 half price (we like young golfers). *Eating facilities:* restaurant facilities at Dalmunzie Hotel. Bar. *Visitors:* welcome without reservation. Self-catering cottages available. *Society Meetings:* catered for. Secretary: Simon Winton.
e-mail: enquiries@dalmunziecottages.com
website: www.dalmunziecottages.com

BLAIRGOWRIE. **Strathmore Golf Centre,** Leroch, Alyth, Blairgowrie PH11 8NZ (01828 633322; Fax: 01828 633533). *Location:* one mile south of Alyth off A926 Blairgowrie to Kirriemuir road. Rolling parkland course with magnificent views over the valley of Strathmore. Two courses - Rannaleroch Course: 18 holes, 6454 yards, 5901 metres. Par 72. S.S.S. 72; Leitfie Links Course: 9 holes, 1719 yards, 1572 metres. Par 29. S.S.S. 29. Driving range adjacent. *Green Fees:* from £30.00 per round weekdays, £36.00 weekends. *Eating facilities:* friendly clubhouse with bar and restaurant. *Visitors:* always welcome. *Society Meetings:* always welcome.
e-mail: enquiries@strathmoregolf.com
website: www.strathmoregolf.com

CRIEFF. **Crieff Golf Club,** Ferntower, Perth Road, Crieff PH7 3LR (01764 652397; Fax: 01764 655096). *Location*: A85 north-east outskirts of Crieff. Ferntower Course - 18 holes, 6493 yards. S.S.S. 72. Dornock Course - 9 holes, 4540 yards. S.S.S. 63. Two practice areas. *Green Fees*: visit website for information. *Eating facilities*: full restaurant facilities by arrangement (phone 01764 652397) and bar snacks. *Visitors*: welcome with reservation, prior arrangement advisable by phone. *Society Meetings*: book by phone (01764 652909) and confirm in writing. Professional: David Murchie (01764 652909; Fax: 01764 655096). Managing Secretary: D.S. Ramsay.
website: www.crieffgolf.co.uk

DALMUNZIE GOLF COURSE

Nine challenging holes set on a privately owned 6000-acre estate in spectacular and beautiful scenery. The course has been owned and maintained by the Winton Family for over 50 years, alongside Dalmunzie Highland Cottages. Why not come to stay, and enjoy carefree golf in spectacular surroundings? Send for details to Simon Winton.

SPITTAL OF GLENSHEE, BLAIRGOWRIE, PERTHSHIRE PH10 7QE
TEL: 01250 885226
enquiries@dalmunziecottages.com
www.dalmunziecottages.com

STRATHMORE GOLF CENTRE
The Friendly Place to Play Golf

An impressive Golf Centre comprising the magnificent 18 hole Rannaleroch Course, 9 hole Leitfie Links Course, a floodlit driving range and a well-appointed Clubhouse in a beautiful Perthshire setting.
Green Fee Rates from £30 per round weekdays, £36 weekends.

Alyth, Perthshire PH11 8NZ • Tel: 01828 633322
enquiries@strathmoregolf.com
www.strathmoregolf.com

The Blairgowrie Golf Club

The Blairgowrie Golf Club was founded as a private members' club in 1889 and is situated in the heart of the magnificent Perthshire countryside. The Club features the renowned Rosemount and Lansdowne championship courses plus a very attractive 9-hole course set in heather-lined avenues of pine and silver birch.

The magnificent clubhouse is synonymous with Blairgowrie Golf Club and is rightly acclaimed in all four corners of the golfing world. It offers visitors a warm welcome at the bar and good food in fitting surroundings. A mouth-watering selection of appetizing dishes is available, with special menus for visiting parties available on request. Our club steward and his staff are on hand to dispense drinks from our well stocked gantry.

The courses of The Blairgowrie Golf Club are virtually unique and have that wonderful charm found at very few courses, where each hole is unaffected and untouched by another. The combination of heathland and woodland provides each hole with a peace and tranquillity completely unspoilt by preceding or following games.

The Rosemount Course, described by Tom Morris as, "The most beautiful inland green I have ever seen", certainly lives up to its reputation. Rosemount has played host to a number of prestigious professional and amateur tournaments. Rosemount was voted 11th best course to play in Scotland by the readers of Scotland's premier golf magazine.

The Lansdowne Course is more modern than the Rosemount course in layout, and offers a more challenging test. It was designed by the respected partnership of Peter Allis and Dave Thomas and officially opened in 1979. The course provides a challenging but pleasurable test for all levels of golfer.

The Wee Course formed part of the original layout designed by Dr Alister MacKenzie of Augusta National and Cypress Point fame. The nine-hole layout is heathland in character, comprising four par 3s and five par 4s, and provides a delightful and charming contrast to Rosemount and Lansdowne.

The Blairgowrie Golf Club

Golf Course Road, Rosemount,
Blairgowrie, Perthshire PH10 6LG
Tel: 01250 872622 • Fax: 01250 875451
e-mail: office@theblairgowriegolfclub.co.uk • www.theblairgowriegolfclub.co.uk

CRIEFF. **Comrie Golf Club,** Laggan Braes, Comrie PH6 2LR (01764 670055). *Location:* six miles west of Crieff on A85 at east end of village. Parkland, wooded course with two long and tricky Par 3 holes (3rd and 5th) and well guarded Par 5 (6th). 9 holes, 6016 yards. S.S.S. 70. *Green Fees:* information not provided. *Eating facilities:* light refreshments and meals during summer months. *Visitors:* welcome at all times. Club Medals - Monday 1pm and 4.30pm, Ladies Tuesdays 1pm. *Society Meetings:* always welcome. e-mail: enquiries@comriegolf.co.uk
website: www.comriegolf.co.uk

CRIEFF. **Culcrieff Golf Club,** Ferntower Road, Crieff PH7 3LQ (01764 651615; Fax: 01764 653087). *Location:* set high in the Strathearn Valley. A85 from Perth, A822 from Stirling. Parkland course. 18 holes, 4876 yards, S.S.S. 64, Par 66. 8-bay driving range, practice green, 6-hole pitch and putt course. *Green Fees:* information not available. *Eating facilities:* licensed clubhouse with restaurant. *Visitors:* welcome. *Society Meetings:* welcome with advance reservation. Contact Andrew Devine for details.*
e-mail: enquiries@crieffhydro.com
website: www.crieffhydro.com.

CRIEFF. **Foulford Inn Golf Course,** Foulford Inn, Sma' Glen, Crieff PH7 3LN (Tel & Fax: 01764 652407). *Location*: 5 miles north of Crieff on the A822 in the direction of Dunkeld. Upland course with water hazards. 9 holes, 916 yards, S.S.S. 27. *Green Fees*: £6.00 per round, £9.00 per day. *Visitors*: welcome anytime. Self catering unit available (sleeps 8). Golf free to guests. *Society Meetings*: welcome, on application. Secretary: B.A. Beaumont.
e-mail: foulford@btconnect.com
website: www.foulfordinn.co.uk

CRIEFF. **Muthill Golf Club,** Peat Road, Muthill, Crieff PH5 2DA (01764 681523; Fax: 01764 681557). *Location:* two miles from Crieff at entrance to Muthill. Parkland course with magnificent views. 9 holes, 4700 yards. S.S.S. 63. *Green Fees:* weekdays 9 holes £12.50, £18.00 per day; weekends 9 holes £14.00, £20.00 per day. *Eating facilities:* full meals service available. *Visitors:* no restrictions except after 5pm Wednesdays and Thursdays (club competitions). Trolleys available. *Society Meetings:* welcome. Secretary: Nan Shaw (01764 681523; Fax: 01764 681557).
e-mail: muthillgolfclub@btconnect.com

DUNBLANE. **Dunblane New Golf Club,** Perth Road, Dunblane FK15 0LJ (01786 821521; Fax: 01786 821522). *Location:* two miles off main road M9 at Fourways Roundabout. Parkland/undulating. 18 holes, 5936 yards. S.S.S. 69. *Green Fees:* £32.00 per round, £45.00 per day. Online booking available. *Eating facilities:* available seven days a week. *Visitors:* welcome, 9.30am-12 noon, 2.30pm-4pm. *Society Meetings:* catered for Mondays, Wednesdays, Thursdays, Fridays and Sundays. Professional: R.M. Jamieson (01786 821521; Fax: 01786 821522). Secretary: Roddy Morrison (01786 821527; Fax: 01786 825066).
e-mail: secretary@dngc.co.uk
website: www.dngc.co.uk

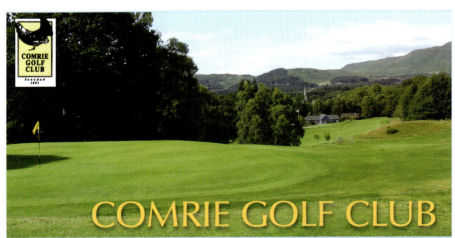

COMRIE GOLF CLUB is a 9-hole golf course providing a test for all standards of golfers, maintained to the very highest standard, and with beautiful views of the surrounding countryside. Visitors are welcome, especially at weekends, and catering is available in our clubhouse. We offer special rates to golfing parties. 6 miles from Crieff; half an hour's drive from Gleneagles.

Turn up and play, or telephone for a booking
Laggan Braes, Comrie, Perthshire PH6 2LR
Tel: 01764 670055 • enquiries@comriegolf.co.uk • www.comriegolf.co.uk

DUNKELD. Dunkeld and Birnam Golf Club, Fungarth, Dunkeld PH8 0ES (01350 727524; Fax: 01350 728660). *Location:* one mile north of Dunkeld on the A923. Heathland course with panoramic views. 18 holes, 5508 yards. S.S.S. 67. Practice area. *Green Fees:* on application. *Eating facilities:* bar and full catering facilities. *Visitors:* welcome; buggies available. *Society Meetings:* catered for. Secretary: (01350 727524; Fax: 01350 728660).
e-mail: secretary-dunkeld@tiscali.co.uk
website: www.dunkeldandbirnamgolfclub.co.uk

DUNNING. Dunning Golf Club, Rollo Park, Station Road, Dunning PH2 0QX (01764 684747). *Location:* 10 miles south-west of Perth, two miles from A9. Parkland, gently undulating. 9 holes, 4894 yards. S.S.S. 64. Small practice area. *Green Fees:* £20.00 per round. *Eating facilities:* tea/ coffee, soft drinks, snacks. Meals can be arranged with the Kirkstyle Inn at a 10% discount on production of a visitor's ticket. *Visitors:* welcome, Handicap restrictions apply. *Society Meetings:* welcome weekdays and most Sundays. Secretary: N.C. Morton (01738 626701).

Dunblane New Golf Club

has been welcoming members and visitors alike since 1923.
This quality parkland course provides an enjoyable and testing challenge for golfers of all abilities. Its lush fairways and manicured greens, together with wonderful views in all directions, ensure a golfing experience not quickly forgotten.

Perth Road, Dunblane, Perthshire FK15 0LJ
Telephone: 01786 821527
Fax: 01786 825066

e-mail: secretary@dngc.co.uk
www.dngc.co.uk

The Munro Inn
Strathyre, Perthshire FK18 8NA
Tel: 01877 384333

Traditional Highlands Inn set in beautiful Perthshire. Only an hour fron Edinburgh, Glasgow and Loch Lomond. Perfect base for walking, cycling, climbing, water sports, fishing or relaxing! Five different golf courses nearby. Great home cooking, lively bar, luxurious en suite bedrooms, drying room, broadband internet.

enquiries@munro-inn.com • www.munro-inn.com

Royal Dunkeld Hotel

The Royal Dunkeld, a former coaching inn, is now a modern, comfortable hotel. All bedrooms have en suite facilities, colour TV, radio, hospitality tray, hairdryer, trouser press and direct-dial telephone. Located in some of the most beautiful countryside in Britain, Dunkeld is an ideal base for touring and for sporting activities such as golf, salmon fishing and trout fishing. Bed & Breakfast from £34 pppn, based on two sharing.

Atholl Street, Dunkeld, Perthshire PH8 0AR
Tel: 01350 727322 • Fax: 01350 728989 • www.royaldunkeld.co.uk

442 Perth & Kinross / SCOTLAND

DUNNING. **Whitemoss Golf Club,** Whitemoss Road, Dunning PH2 0GX (01738 730300; Fax: 01738 730490). *Location*: 10 miles south-west of Perth, two miles from A9. Parkland course. 18 holes, 5968 yards, S.S.S. 69. Practice range, chipping bunkers, practice net and putting green. *Green Fees:* information not provided. *Eating facilities*: New clubhouse with restaurant and bar. *Visitors:* welcome all the time, on medal days after 10am. *Society Meetings:* Welcome, after 10am on medal days. Tuition on request. Shower facilities. Secretary: Victor Westwood (01738 730300).

KENMORE. **Kenmore Golf Course,** Mains of Taymouth, Kenmore, Aberfeldy PH15 2HN (01887 830226; Fax: 01887 830775). *Location:* west off A9 at Ballinluig on A827, six and a half miles west of Aberfeldy through village of Kenmore on RHS. Testing well kept course on natural undulating terrain, lovely scenery and first class facilities. 9 holes, 6052 yards, 5600 metres. S.S.S. 70. Practice facilities, putting green. *Green Fees:* weekdays 9 holes £15.00, 18 holes £20.00; weekends 9 holes £17.00, 18 holes £25.00. Weekly Ticket £75.00. *Eating facilities:* full bar and restaurant facilities in pleasant surroundings. *Visitors:* welcome anytime. Cottages to let (self-catering included). Pro shop; club and trolley hire; changing and shower facilities. *Society Meetings:* all welcome, please book. Secretary: Robin Menzies.
e-mail: info@taymouth.co.uk
website: www.kenmoregolfcourse.co.uk

KENMORE. **Taymouth Castle Golf Course,** Kenmore, by Aberfeldy PH15 2NT (01887 830228). *Location:* six miles west of Aberfeldy. Parkland set in scenic mountain terrain. 18 holes, 6066 yards. S.S.S. 69. Practice area. *Green Fees:* information not available. *Eating facilities:* restaurant and bar. *Visitors:* welcome, tee reservations necessary (phone or letter). Tuition available, motorised buggies. *Society Meetings:* parties welcome; catered for by previous arrangement only. PGA Professional: Gavin Dott (01887 830228).*
e-mail: taymouthcastlegolf@hotmail.com

KILLIN. **Killin Golf Club,** Killin FK21 8TX (01567 820312). *Location:* west end of Loch Tay. Hilly parkland amongst beautiful scenery. 9 holes, 2510 yards. S.S.S. 65. Small practice area includes bunker and net. *Green Fees:* information not provided. *Eating facilities:* available all day. *Visitors:* welcome. *Society Meetings:* catered for by arrangement. Secretary: Peter Stallard.
e-mail: bookings@killingolfclub.co.uk
website: www.killingolfclub.co.uk

KINNESSWOOD. **Bishopshire Golf Club,** Kinnesswood, By Kinross KY13 9HX. *Location:* take road to Glenrothes from M90, three miles. Course has panoramic views overlooking Loch Leven. 10 holes, 4830 yards, 2268 metres. S.S.S. 63. *Green Fees:* information not available. *Eating facilities:* by arrangement or available at the hotel 400 yards away. *Visitors:* welcome, no restrictions. *Society Meetings:* by arrangement. Secretary: Ian Davidson (01592 773224).*

KINROSS. **Kinross Golf Courses,** owned and operated in conjunction with The Green Hotel and The Windlestrae, The Muirs, Kinross KY13 8AS (01577 863407). *Location:* turn left in Kinross off M90 Junction 6, courses 500 yards on right. Set in beautiful unspoilt parkland bordering Loch Leven. Two courses: Montgomery 18 holes, 6508 yards, 5951 metres. S.S.S. 72. Bruce 18 holes, 6231 yards, 5698 metres. S.S.S. 71. Practice ground. *Green Fees:* information not available. *Eating facilities:* in clubhouse, Green Hotel or The Windlestrae. *Visitors:* welcome any time. Accommodation and leisure facilities available. *Society Meetings:* welcome by prior arrangement. Professional: Greg McSporran (01577 865125). Secretary: Eileen Gray (01577 863407; Fax: 01577 863180).*
e-mail: bookings@golfkinross.com
website: www.golfkinross.com

MILNATHORT. **Milnathort Golf Club Ltd,** South Street, Milnathort KY13 9XA (01577 864069). *Location:* one mile north of Kinross, M90 Junction 6 (north) or Junction 7 (south). Undulating inland course with lush fairways and excellent greens, with the addition of extra trees around the margins along with current plantations. Strategically placed copses of trees require acurate tee shots. The course is being made more interesting by the addition of extra tees/greens for some holes. 9 holes, 5973 yards. S.S.S. 69. Practice ground/green. *Green Fees*: weekdays £15.00 per round, £22.00 per day; weekends £17.00 per round, £25.00 per day. 9 hole sundowner ticket £8.00 weekends, £7.00 weekdays.

Why would you want to stay and play anywhere else

Just a short iron from our 46 bedroom hotel you'll find the first tees of our two scenic golf courses. **The Montgomery,** Par 72, 6508 yards and **The Bruce,** Par 73, 6231 yards. Both offer an enjoyable and stimulating challenge, whether you are a holiday golfer or low handicap player. And situated in Kinross we are well placed to reach some of Scotland's leading championship courses including: St Andrews, Gleneagles and Carnoustie. Call or email us today for a brochure and further details.

2 The Muirs, Kinross KY13 8AS, Scotland, Tel: +44 (0) 1577 863547, Email: reservations@green-hotel.com
www.green-hotel.com

SCOTLAND / Perth & Kinross

2010 rates (subject to review). *Eating facilities*: full bar available, catering by arrangement. *Visitors*: welcome but suggest you phone. Dress code. *Society Meetings:* must be booked in advance. Secretary: via Club House.
e-mail: milnathort.gc@btconnect.com

PERTH. Craigie Hill Golf Club (1982) Ltd, Cherrybank, Perth PH2 0NE (01738 620429). *Location:* at west end of town, easy access from M90 and A9. Parkland course with stunning view of Perth and surrounding hills. 18 holes, 5386 yards. S.S.S. 67. Practice ground and putting green. *Green Fees:* weekday £24.00; weekend £29.00. *Eating facilities:* dining room, full catering facilities and lounge bar. *Visitors:* welcome 7 days. *Society Meetings:* catered for 7 days, contact Professional. Car park. Professional: Niall McGill (01738 622464). Administration: (01738 620829).
e-mail: professional@craigiehill.co.uk

PERTH. King James VI Golf Club, Moncreiffe Island, Perth PH2 8NR (01738 625170). *Location:* situated on Island in River Tay, access by Footbridge alongside railway from Tay Street, Perth. Flat parkland course, surrounded by River Tay. 18 holes, 6038 yards. S.S.S. 69. Practice nets. *Green Fees:* weekdays £24.00 per round, £32.00 per day; weekends £26.00 per round, £34.00 per day. April/July/October £15.00 per round, £20.00 per day. *Eating facilities:* full catering. *Visitors:* welcome, phone for reservation, no visitors on Saturday mornings. Carts available. *Society Meetings:* catered for by prior booking. Fully stocked golf shop. Professional: Allan Knox (01738 632460). Secretary: (Tel & Fax: 01738 445132).
e-mail: mansec@kingjamesvi.com
website: www.kingjamesvi.com

PERTH. North Inch Golf Course. Hay Street, Perth PH1 5HS (01738 636481). *Location:* on the historic North Inch, beside the River Tay. A9 entering Perth, follow signs for Bell's Sports Centre, Hay Street. Parkland course with tight greens guarded by well placed bunkers. A truly lovely setting well suited to beginners and high handicap players, although there is something testing for the expert. 18 holes, 5154 yards. S.S.S. 66. *Green Fees:* weekdays £15.00, weekends £18.00. 2010 rates (subject to review). *Eating facilities:* Sport Active Restaurant, Bell's Sports Centre. *Visitors*: welcome. *Society Meetings*: by prior arrangement, excellent rates. Professional: Colin Roberts (07933 704447). Starter: (01738 636481).
website: www.pkc.gov.uk/northinchgolf

PITLOCHRY. Pitlochry Golf Ltd, Golf Course Road, Pitlochry PH16 5QY (01796 472792). *Location:* half mile from centre of Pitlochry on A9. 18 holes, 5681 yards, S.S.S. 69. *Green Fees:* information not available. *Eating facilities:* licensed clubhouse. *Visitors:* welcome. Caddy cars available for hire, fully refurbished clubhouse facilities. *Society Meetings:* catered for. Phone Professional for all bookings. Professional: Mark Pirie (01796 472792). Golf Club Secretary: T.C. Leadbetter (01796 472314; Fax: 01796 473947).
e-mail: pro@pitlochrygolf.co.uk
website: www.pitlochrygolf.co.uk

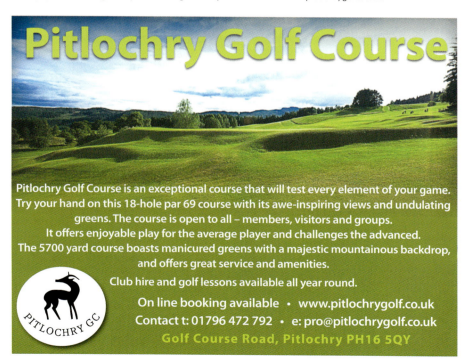

Pitlochry Golf Course is an exceptional course that will test every element of your game. Try your hand on this 18-hole par 69 course with its awe-inspiring views and undulating greens. The course is open to all – members, visitors and groups.
It offers enjoyable play for the average player and challenges the advanced.
The 5700 yard course boasts manicured greens with a majestic mountainous backdrop, and offers great service and amenities.

Club hire and golf lessons available all year round.

On line booking available • www.pitlochrygolf.co.uk
Contact t: 01796 472 792 • e: pro@pitlochrygolf.co.uk
Golf Course Road, Pitlochry PH16 5QY

ST FILLANS. **St Fillans Golf Club,** South Loch Earn Road, St Fillans, Loch Earn PH6 2NJ (01764 685312). *Location:* 13 miles west of Crieff on A85; turn off at east end of village, club 300 yards on left. A testing parkland course nestling between magnificent Perthshire mountains with one elevated tee and green. 9 holes length (18 holes), 6054 yards. S.S.S. 69. Practice facilities and putting green. *Green Fees:* information not available. *Eating facilities:* full meals and snacks available throughout the day; licensed restaurant. Golf trolleys, powered trolleys, buggies and clubs for hire. *Visitors:* welcome at all times except when matches on. *Society Meetings:* welcome with advance booking. Managing Secretary: Gordon Hibbert.*

SCONE. **Murrayshall Golf Course,** Murrayshall, Scone, By Perth PH2 7PH (01738 551171). *Location:* three miles north of Perth on A94 Coupar Angus Road. Undulating wooded parkland. Murrayshall Course - 6441 yards, Par 73. Lynedoch Course - 5400 yards, Par 69. 18-bay driving range. *Green Fees:* information not provided. *Eating facilities:* clubhouse open all day. *Visitors:* welcome, no restrictions - advance booking essential. *Society Meetings:* welcome - must pre-book. Professional: Alan Reid (01738 552784).
website: www.murrayshall.com

STRATHTAY. **Strathtay Golf Club,** c/o Secretary, Donfield, Strathtay, Pitlochry PH9 0PJ. *Location:* on the right, three-quarters of a mile westwards on the minor road to Weem off the A827 Ballinluig to Grandtully. Wooded, mainly hilly course with beautiful panoramic views. 9 holes, 1887 yards. S.S.S. 61. *Green Fees:* £15.00 per day, £20.00 weekends and public holidays. *Visitors:* welcome at any time without restrictions. Changing room, toilets. *Society Meetings:* must be arranged in advance. Secretary: Jim Wilson (01887 840493).

For full details of convenient accommodation near clubs and courses
www.holidayguides.com

Warm hospitality and delicious home cooked cuisine: A wonderful short break destination as well as a home from home for an extended Scottish vacation

40 Perthshire Golf Courses within 45 minutes

Reduced Green Fees with the Perthshire Green Card, Perthshire Highlands Golf Ticket or First in Fife Golf Pass

Stay & Play on the Green Card
(4 or 6 Nights Half Board Breaks Available including 3 or 5 Rounds of Golf - prices based on 2 sharing)

Mill St, Stanley, Perthshire PH1 4NL
www.taysidehotel.co.uk
reception@taysidehotel.co.uk   01738 82 82 49

Other British holiday guides from FHG Guides

PUBS & INNS · 300 GREAT HOTELS · SHORT BREAK HOLIDAYS
The bestselling and original PETS WELCOME! · 500 GREAT PLACES TO STAY
SELF-CATERING HOLIDAYS · BED & BREAKFAST STOPS
CARAVAN & CAMPING HOLIDAYS · FAMILY BREAKS

Published annually: available in all good bookshops or direct from the publisher:
FHG Guides, Abbey Mill Business Centre, Seedhill, Paisley PA1 1TJ
Tel: 0141 887 0428 • Fax: 0141 889 7204
e-mail: admin@fhguides.co.uk • www.holidayguides.com

Renfrewshire

BARRHEAD. **Fereneze Golf Club,** Fereneze Avenue, Barrhead, Glasgow G78 1HJ (0141-881 1519). *Location:* nine miles south west of Glasgow. Hilly moorland. 18 holes, 5962 yards. S.S.S. 70. *Green Fees:* information not available. *Eating facilities:* full catering/lounges. *Visitors:* welcome by arrangement. *Society Meetings:* welcome, bookings arranged in advance. Professional: James Smallwood (0141-880 7058). Secretary: Graham McCreadie (Tel & Fax: 0141-881 7149).*

BISHOPTON. **Erskine Golf Club,** Bishopton PA7 5PH (01505 862302). *Location:* club situated on south bank of the River Clyde. Leave M8 at Junction 30 onto M898 then left onto B815 (before bridge toll barriers), follow sign for Bishopton, Club approx. one mile on right. Parkland course, with breathtaking views over the river to the hills beyond. 18 holes, 6371 yards. S.S.S. 71. Putting green and practice area. *Green Fees:* £35.00 per round, £45.00 per day ticket. 2010 rates (subject to review). *Eating facilities:* restaurant and bar, lunches, teas and dinners served at club. *Visitors:* welcome Monday to Friday. Professional: Peter Thomson. Secretary: Donald F. McKellar.
website: www.erskinegolfclublimited.co.uk

BRIDGE OF WEIR. **Old Course Ranfurly Golf Club Ltd,** Ranfurly Place, Bridge of Weir PA11 3DE (01505 613612). *Location:* five miles west of Glasgow Airport. Moorland course. 18 holes, 6089 yards. S.S.S. 70. *Green Fees:* weekends only if introduced by and playing with a member. *Eating facilities:* dining room, lounge. *Visitors:* welcome weekdays, should contact club beforehand. Must be members of recognised golf clubs with Handicap Certificates. *Society Meetings:* on written application only. Managing Secretary: (Tel & Fax: 01505 613214).
e-mail: secretary@oldranfurly.com
website: www.oldranfurly.com

BRIDGE OF WEIR. **Ranfurly Castle Golf Club Ltd,** Golf Road, Bridge of Weir PA11 3HN (01505 612609). *Location:* M8 from Glasgow exit Junction 29, A240 and A761 to Bridge of Weir. Moorland. 18 holes, 6284 yards. S.S.S. 71. Practice ground. *Green Fees:* weekdays £35.00 per round, £45.00 day ticket. *Eating facilities:* bar snacks all day; lunches, high teas, etc by arrangement. *Visitors:* welcome weekdays, limited availability at weekends. *Society Meetings:* catered for weekdays only. Professional: Tom Eckford (01505 614795; Fax: 01505 612609). Secretary: J. King (01505 612609).
e-mail: secretary@ranfurlycastlegolfclub.co.uk
website: www.ranfurlycastlegolfclub.co.uk

Erskine Golf Club

One of the finest courses in the West of Scotland, this is a club steeped in history and tradition, offering the opportunity for golfers of all skill levels to test their ability. With commanding views of the Kilpatrick Hills and the Clyde Estuary, to play golf here is an experience not to be forgotten. Within minutes of Glasgow Airport, the club is easily accessible from the M8.

• spacious changing rooms • practice area
• chipping area • putting green • fully stocked Pro Shop • catering available 7 days a week

Golf Road, Bishopton PA7 5PH
Tel: 01505 862302
www.erskinegolfclublimited.co.uk

ELDERSLIE. **Elderslie Golf Club,** 63 Main Road, Elderslie PA5 9AZ (01505 322835). *Location:* off M8 at Linwood turn-off, continue to roundabout, follow Elderslie signs A737. Club on main road. Parkland course. 18 holes, 6175 yards. S.S.S. 70. Practice area. *Green Fees:* £30.00 per round, £40 per day (golf only). *Eating facilities:* full meals and bar meals. *Visitors:* welcome weekdays, no visitors weekends. Caddy hire. *Society Meetings:* welcome weekdays, book through Secretary. Professional: R. Bowman (01505 320032). Secretary: Mrs A. Anderson (01505 323956; Fax: 01505 340546).
e-mail: eldersliegolfclub@btconnect.com
website: www.eldersliegolfclub.net

THE APPEARANCE OF AN ASTERISK (*) AT THE END OF A CLUB OR COURSE ENTRY INDICATES THAT UP-TO-DATE INFORMATION HAS NOT BEEN SUPPLIED

GOUROCK. **Gourock Golf Club,** Cowal View, Gourock PA19 1HD (01475 631001; Fax: 01475 631001). *Location:* two miles west of Gourock Station above Yacht Club. Heathland/parkland with spectacular views. 18 holes, 6408 yards. S.S.S. 72. *Green Fees:* information not available. *Eating facilities:* restaurant, full meals also bar snacks. *Visitors:* welcome; Saturdays not before 4 pm. *Society Meetings:* catered for on application. Professional: Derek Watters (01475 636834). Secretary: Margaret Paterson (01475 631001).*
e-mail: pro@gourockgolfclub.com

GREENOCK. **Greenock Golf Club,** Forsyth Street, Greenock PA16 8RE (01475 720793). *Location:* one mile from town centre. Moorland course. 18 holes, 5835 yards. S.S.S. 68. Golf shop. Lessons available. *Green Fees:* weekdays £30.00 per round; weekends £35.00 per round. *Eating facilities:* available. *Visitors:* welcome weekdays, not Saturdays. *Society Meetings:* advance booking required. Professional: Kevin Campbell (01475 787236). Secretary: Mrs Heather Sinclair (01475 720793).

GREENOCK. **Greenock Whinhill Golf Club,** Beith Road, Greenock PA16 9LN (01475 724694). *Location:* off Old Largs Road from Drumfrochar Road, Upper Greenock. Municipal course. Situated in hills high above Greenock, panoramic views of River Clyde and the surrounding area. 18 holes, 5504 yards. S.S.S. 67. *Green Fees:* information not available. *Visitors:* welcome except Saturdays. Secretary: Joe Blyth.*

JOHNSTONE. **Cochrane Castle Golf Club,** Scott Avenue, Craigston, Johnstone PA5 0HF (01505 320146; Fax: 01505 325338). *Location:* turn left off Beith Road at Rannoch Road, second on right to end of Scott Avenue. Parkland course, fairly hilly wth excellent views to north. 18 holes, 6194 yards. S.S.S. 71. Practice area and green. *Green Fees:* weekdays £25.00 per round, £35.00 per day; weekends by introduction only. *Eating facilities:* full catering and bar. *Visitors:* welcome Monday to Friday, limited to 24. Arrangement by letter to Secretary. Trolleys. *Society Meetings:* catered for by arrangement, weekdays only. Professional: Alan J. Logan (01505 328465). Secretary: Mrs P. I. J. Quin (01505 320146).

KILMACOLM. **Kilmacolm Golf Club,** Porterfield Road, Kilmacolm PA13 4PD (01505 872139). *Location:* Take M8 from Glasgow heading for airport. At junction 28a, exit on to A737 towards Irvine. Take the B789 exit and turn right. Pick up the A761 and follow it to Kilmacolm. Moorland course. 18 holes, 5964 yards. S.S.S. 69. Excellent practice area. *Green Fees:* information not available. *Eating facilities:* Bar menu and dining room, excellent catering. *Visitors:* welcome on weekdays and Sunday afternoon. *Society Meetings:* welcome by arrangement. Contact Secretary: Mr Vic Weldin. Professional: Iain Nicholson (01505 872695).*

LANGBANK. **Gleddoch Golf Club,** Langbank PA14 6YE (01475 540304; Fax: 01475 540201). *Location:* M8 west to Greenock/Langbank, exit B789 signposted Langbank/Houston. Parkland/moorland. 18 holes, 6357 yards. S.S.S. 71. Practice area, putting green. *Green Fees:* information not available. *Eating facilities:* bar, lounge and restaurant open all day. *Visitors:* welcome weekdays, restrictions only when competitions. Gleddoch House Hotel, 39 bedrooms plus self catering lodges. *Society Meetings:* welcome weekdays only excluding Bank Holidays. Professional: Keith Campbell (01475 540704; Fax: 01475 540201). Secretary: D.W. Tierney (01475 540304; Fax: 01475 540201).*

LOCHWINNOCH. **Lochwinnoch Golf Club,** Burnfoot Road, Lochwinnoch PA12 4AN (01505 842153; Fax: 01505 843668). *Location:* between Johnstone and Beith, off A737 on Largs road A760. Parkland, extremely scenic, set in quiet country village. 18 holes, 6243 yards. S.S.S. 71. Practice area. *Green Fees:* information not available. *Eating facilities:* licensed bar and catering every day. *Visitors:* welcome weekdays, weekends restricted. *Society Meetings;* welcome weekdays. Professional: Gerry Reilly (01505 843029). Administrator: R.J.G. Jamieson. *
e-mail: enquiries@lochwinnochgolf.co.uk
website: www.lochwinnochgolf.co.uk

PAISLEY. **Barshaw Golf Club,** Barshaw Park, Glasgow Road, Paisley (0141-889 2908). *Location:* one mile from Paisley Cross travelling east towards Glasgow (Glasgow Road). Parkland course, flat/hilly. 18 holes, 5703 yards. S.S.S. 67. Putting green. *Green Fees:* information not available. *Eating facilities:* mobile van rear of clubhouse. *Visitors:* welcome anytime, must have a bag of clubs. *Society Meetings:* apply to Director of Environmental Services, Paisley. Secretary: W. Collins (0141-884 2533).*

PAISLEY. **Paisley Golf Club,** Braehead Road, Paisley PA2 8TZ (0141-884 3903). *Location:* up Causeyside Street, Neilston Road, turn right into Glenburn, left at roundabout. Moorland course. 18 holes, 6466 yards. S.S.S. 72. Practice area. *Green Fees:* weekdays £40.00 per round, £50.00 per day for individuals. Full day golf package available for large and small groups. *Eating facilities:* bar snacks and full meals. *Visitors:* welcome by prior arrangement with Handicap Certificate, midweek not after 4pm and not at weekends or Public Holidays. *Society Meetings:* by arrangement with Secretary. Professional: Andy Carlton (0141-884 4114). Club Manager: John Hillis (0141-884 3903).

PAISLEY. **Ralston Golf Club,** Strathmore Avenue, Ralston, Paisley PA1 3DT (0141-882 1349; Fax: 0141 883 9837). *Location:* Glasgow Road, two miles east of Paisley Cross. Parkland course. 18 holes, 6091 yards. S.S.S. 69. *Green Fees:* information not available. *Eating facilities:* dining room, bar. *Visitors:* welcome subject to course availability. *Society Meetings:* catered for on application subject to course availability. Professional: Colin Munro (0141-810 4925). Secretary: B.W. Hanson (0141-882 1349; Fax: 0141-883 9837).*
e-mail: thesecretary@ralstongolf.co.uk

PORT GLASGOW. **Port Glasgow Golf Club,** Devol Road, Port Glasgow PA14 5XE (01475 704181). *Location:* M8 to Newark Castle to roundabout, follow signs for Industrial Estate. Heathland with panoramic views of the Clyde and Argyll Hills. 18 holes, 5712 yards, 5224 metres. S.S.S. 68. *Green Fees:* information not available. *Eating facilities:* full catering service. *Visitors:* welcome, only by prior arrangement. *Society Meetings:* welcome by prior arrangement with Hon. Secretary (36 maximum), full catering available. Hon. Secretary: Tommy Rodger (01475 704181).*

RENFREW. **Renfrew Golf Club,** Blythswood Estate, Inchinnan Road, Renfrew PA4 9EG (0141-886 6692). *Location:* A8 Renfrew, turn in at Normandy Hotel. Flat parkland, wooded. 18 holes, 6818 yards, 6231 metres. S.S.S. 72. *Green Fees:* £35.00 per round, £45.00 per day. *Eating facilities:* daily restaurant facilities and bar. *Visitors:* welcome on introduction by members. Visiting parties by arrangement. *Society Meetings:* catered for on Mondays, Tuesdays, Thursdays and Fridays only by written application to Secretary. Managing Secretary: Andy McLaughlin (0141-886 6692).
e-mail: andy.mclaughlin@renfrewgolfclub.net

UPLAWMOOR. **Caldwell Golf Club Ltd,** Uplawmoor, Glasgow G78 4AU (01505 850329; Fax: 01505 850604). *Location:* five miles south of Barrhead, Glasgow on A736 Irvine Road. Parkland bounded by mature trees and a natural water hazard. 18 holes, 6335 yards, 5793 metres. S.S.S. 71. Practice area. *Green Fees:* information not provided. *Eating facilities:* every day bar menu; filled rolls on Thursdays. *Visitors:* welcome weekdays only before 4.30pm, not weekends and Public Holidays (local and national). *Society Meetings:* weekdays only by prior arrangement. Professional: Craig Everett (Tel & Fax: 01505 850616). Secretary: K. Morrison (01505 850366; Fax: 01505 850604).
e-mail: secretary@caldwellgolfclub.co.uk
website: www.caldwellgolfclub.co.uk

Please mention THE GOLF GUIDE when you enquire about clubs or accommodation

Stirling & The Trossachs

ABERFOYLE. **Aberfoyle Golf Club,** Braeval, Aberfoyle, By Stirling FK8 3UY (01877 382493). *Location:* A81 Glasgow–Stirling. Parkland. 18 holes, 5204 yards. S.S.S. 66. *Green Fees:* available on request. *Eating facilities:* bar and catering available all day April to October; restricted service October to March. *Visitors:* welcome anytime but restrictions at weekends. Club Steward: Duncan Brown.

ALLOA. **Alloa Golf Club,** Schawpark Golf Course, Sauchie, Alloa FK10 3AX (01259 722745 Fax: 01259 218796). *Location:* on A908 between Alloa and Tillicoultry. Parkland, tree lined fairways with spectacular views of Ochil Hills and beyond. 18 holes, 6229 yards, 5695 metres. S.S.S. 70. *Green Fees:* information not available. *Eating facilities:* restaurant and lounge bar. *Visitors:* welcome. Phone to confirm booking. Guaranteed tee times can be booked. Ladies and gents changing rooms. *Society Meetings:* welcome weekdays only. Packages available. Professional/Bookings: David Herd (Tel & Fax: 01259 724476). Secretary: R. McMillan (01259 722745; Fax: 01259 218796).*

ALLOA. **Braehead Golf Club,** Cambus, By Alloa FK10 2NT (01259 725766). *Location:* one mile west of Alloa on A907. Gently undulating parkland course with scenic views and a variety of challenging holes. 18 holes, 6053 yards. S.S.S. 69. Practice area. *Green Fees:* weekdays £24.00 per round, £32.00 per day; weekends £32.00 per round, £40.00 per day. *Eating facilities:* bar/full catering available all day during Summer months; slightly restricted during Autumn/Spring. *Visitors:* no restrictions but advisable to telephone in advance. Buggy and cart hire. *Society Meetings:* catered for with prior booking. Professional: Jamie Stevenson. Starter's Shop (01259 722078). Secretary: Ron Murray.

ALVA. **Alva Golf Club,** Beauclerc Street, Alva FK12 5LH (01259 760431). *Location:* seven miles from Stirling on A91 Stirling to St Andrews Road - course lies at foot of Ochil Hills. Inland wooded hillside course with fast greens. 9 holes, 2423 yards, 2213 metres. S.S.S. 63. *Green Fees:* information not provided. *Visitors:* welcome at all times. Secretary: P. MacFarlane.

BALFRON. **Balfron Golf Society,** Kepculloch Road, Balfron, By Glasgow G63 0PZ. *Location*: situated at the north end of the village on the A875, 18 miles from Glasgow and 18 miles from Stirling. Interesting, undulating upland course with splendid views. 18 holes, 6094 yards, S.S.S. 70. *Green Fees*: weekday £20.00; weekend £25.00. *Visitors*: welcome weekdays until 4pm, and at weekends, restrictions during competition days. *Society Meetings*: welcome subject to prior booking. Secretary: Brian Davidson (01360 550613).
website: www.balfrongolfsociety.org.uk

CALLANDER. **Callander Golf Club,** Aveland Road, Callander FK17 8EN (01877 330090; Fax: 01877 330062). *Location*: M9 Stirling, Junction 10 Crianlarich exit to A84 to Callander. Parkland, partly wooded, with panoramic views. 18 holes, 5185 yards. S.S.S. 65. Small practice ground and putting green. *Green Fees*: from £25.00. *Eating facilities*: bar snacks, lunches, high teas, dinners by arrangement. *Visitors*: welcome, no restrictions. Handicap Certificate required Sundays. *Society Meetings*: welcome, book in advance. Professional: A. Martin (01877 330975). Secretary: Miss E. MacDonald (01877 330090; Fax: 01877 330062).
e-mail: callandergolf@btconnect.com
website: www.callandergolfclub.co.uk

"... a fantastically secluded location, diverse holes with great greens and stunning views of Ben Ledi and the Trossachs all combine to create a memorable experience." **National Club Golfer**
Add to this a welcoming atmosphere, great support staff and golf at reasonable prices. Come and try it for yourself.
Tel: **01877 330975** to book a tee-time or
01877 330090 for a Membership application form.

Callander Golf Club
Aveland Road, Callander FK17 8EN
e-mail: callandergolf@btconnect.com
www.callandergolfclub.co.uk

SCOTLAND / Stirling & The Trossachs

DOLLAR. Dollar Golf Club, Brewlands House, 2 Back Road, Dollar FK14 7EA (01259 742400). *Location:* off A91 in Dollar, signposted. Hillside course without bunkers as designed by Ben Sayers in 1908. 18 holes, 5242 yards, 4796 metres. S.S.S. 66. *Green Fees:* information not available. *Eating facilities:* full catering (except Tuesdays) and bar. *Visitors:* welcome, booking in advance advisable weekends. Snooker table available. *Society Meetings:* welcome (maximum 30). Secretary: J. McMillan.*

DRYMEN. Strathendrick Golf Club, Glasgow Road, Drymen, Glasgow G63 0HU (01360 660695). *Location:* one mile south of Drymen on A811. Undulating course, designed by Willie Fernie in 1901. 9 holes, 5116 yards. S.S.S. 64. *Green Fees:* weekdays £15.00 per 18 holes, £10.00 per 9 holes. *Visitors:* welcome 8.30am to 3.30pm weekdays only. *Society Meetings:* by arrangement with Secretary. Visitors' Convener: John Greig (01389 830622).

FALKIRK. Bonnybridge Golf Club, Larbert Road, Bonnybridge FK4 1NY (01324 812822). *Location*: five miles west of Falkirk. Parkland. 9 holes, 6132 yards. S.S.S. 70 Par 72. Practice area. *Green Fees:* information not available. *Eating facilities:* bar open lunchtimes and evenings; all day Saturday and Sunday. *Visitors:* welcome with prior permission, or accompanied by a member. *Society Meetings*: by arrangement with Hon. Secretary. Secretary: J. Mullen (01324 812323).*

FALKIRK. Falkirk Golf Club, Carmuirs, 136 Stirling Road, Camelon, Falkirk FK2 7YP (01324 611061; Fax: 01324 639573). *Location*: one and a half miles west of town centre on A9. Parkland with streams. 18 holes, 6282 yards. S.S.S. 70. Large practice area. *Green Fees*: information not available. *Eating facilities*: full catering and bar facilities. *Visitors*: welcome Monday to Friday up to 4pm unaccompanied; with member only at weekends. *Society Meetings*: weekdays except Saturdays. Make arrangements with Starter (01324 612219). Professional: Stewart Craig. Secretary: Mrs Aileen Jenkins (01324 634118).
e-mail: falkirkgolfclub@btconnect.com

FALKIRK. Polmont Golf Club, Manuelrigg, Maddiston, Falkirk FK2 0LS (01324 711277; Fax: 01324 712504). *Location:* first turn to the right past Fire Brigade HQ in Maddiston. Undulating course. 9 holes, 6603 yards. S.S.S. 70. *Green Fees:* weekdays £10.00, Saturdays after 6pm, and Sundays £15.00. *Eating facilities:* none. *Visitors:* welcome without reservation, no visitors after 5pm weekdays or all day Saturday, and Sunday between 10am and 11am. *Society Meetings:* catered for. Secretary: Mrs Margaret Fellows (01324 711277).

LARBERT. Falkirk Tryst Golf Club, 86 Burnhead Road, Stenhousemuir, Larbert FK5 4BD (01324 562415). *Location:* three miles from Falkirk (A9/A88), one mile from Larbert Station. Flat/seaside links style surface. 18 holes, 6053 yards, 5533 metres. S.S.S. 69. Practice area. *Green Fees:* information not available. *Eating facilities:* full catering - lunches, high teas, bar service. *Visitors:* welcome weekdays only except Bank and local Holidays. *Society Meetings:* catered for weekdays only except Bank and local Holidays. Professional: Mr Steven Dunsmore (01324 562091). Secretary: Mr R.C. Chalmers (01324 562054).*

LARBERT. Glenbervie Golf Club Ltd, Stirling Road, Larbert FK5 4SJ (01324 562725). *Location:* one mile north of Larbert on A9 Falkirk to Stirling road. Parkland course. 18 holes, 6438 yards. S.S.S. 71. Two practice areas. *Green Fees:* £35.00 per round, £50.00 per day. *Eating facilities:* lunches and high teas, bar snacks. *Visitors:* welcome weekdays until 4pm. Weekends as members' guests only. *Society Meetings:* up to 50 competitors catered for, Tuesdays, Thursdays and Friday (pm) only. Professional: Steven Rosie (01324 562725). Secretary: Ian R. Webster CA (01324 562605; Fax: 01324 551054).
e-mail: secretary@glenberviegolfclub.com

LENNOXTOWN. Campsie Golf Club, Crow Road, Lennoxtown, Glasgow G66 7HX (01360 310244). *Location:* on B822 Lennoxtown to Fintry. Hillside course with panoramic views. 18 holes, 5509 yards. S.S.S. 68. Practice fairway, bunker and putting green. *Green Fees:* information not available. *Eating facilities:* full catering available. *Visitors:* welcome, weekdays unrestricted, weekends by prior arrangement. *Society Meetings:* catered for by arrangement. Professional: Mark Brennan (01360 310920). Club Manager: H.B. Weston.*

PLEASE NOTE

All the information regarding Golf Clubs in this guide is given in good faith in the belief that it is correct. However, the publishers cannot guarantee the facts given in these pages, neither are they responsible for changes in ownership or facilities, such as green fees, that may take place after the date of going to press. Readers should always satisfy themselves that the facilities they require are available and that the terms, if quoted, still apply.

MUCKHART. **Muckhart Golf Club,** Muckhart, By Dollar FK14 7JH (01259 781323). *Location:* off A91 east from Stirling, three miles north of Dollar. Undulating heathland. 27 holes played as 3 x 18 holes in rotation. 6069 yards, 6086 yards and 6485 yards; the other 9 hole course is always available. Practice ground. *Green Fees:* 18 holes weekday £30.00, day ticket £40.00, 18 holes weekend £35.00, day ticket £45.00. *Eating facilities:* 11am until 8.45pm (except Monday), bar available. *Visitors:* welcome. Trolley hire. *Society Meetings:* catered for. Professional: Keith Salmoni (Tel & Fax: 01259 781493). Club Secretary: Alison Houston.
e-mail: enquiries@muckhartgolf.com
website: www.muckhartgolf.com

POLMONT. **Grangemouth Golf Club,** Polmonthill, Polmont, Falkirk FK2 0YA (01324 711500). *Location:* quarter of a mile north of Junction 4 M9 motorway. Parkland course. 18 holes, 6314 yards. S.S.S. 70. Practice area. *Green Fees:* information not available. *Eating facilities:* catering and bar facilities available, open all day during season. *Visitors:* welcome, no restrictions. *Society Meetings:* welcome any day except Saturday. Professional: Greg McFarlane (01324 503840). Secretary: Jim McNairney (01324 713612).*
e-mail: jim.mcnairney@btinternet.com

STIRLING. **Bridge Of Allan Golf Club,** Sunnylaw, Bridge of Allan FK9 4LY (Tel & Fax: 01786 832332). *Location*: from Stirling, three miles, turn right at Bridge, keep taking the high road. Hilly course, spectacular views. 9 holes, 4932 yards, 4508 metres. S.S.S. 66. *Green Fees:* weekdays £15.00, weekends £20.00. *Eating facilities*: catering available during season or by arrangement outwith season. Licensed bar. *Visitors*: welcome without reservation, Saturdays after 4pm. *Society Meetings:* catered for by arrangement, phone in advance.
e-mail: secretary@bofagc.com
website: www.bofagc.com

STIRLING. **Brucefields Family Golf Centre,** Pirnhall Road, Bannockburn, Stirling FK9 8EH (01786 818184; Fax: 01786 817770). *Location:* half-a-mile from M9 and M80 interchange on A91. Parkland. 9 holes, 5025 yards. S.S.S. 66, Par 68; 9 hole par 3 course; driving range; putting green. *Green Fees:* weekdays; 9 holes £11.00, 18 holes £18.00, weekends, 9 holes £12.00, 18 holes £20.00. *Eating facilities:* Clive Ramsay Cafe Bar. *Visitors:* welcome. *Society Meetings:* welcome. Corporate Membership and packages available. Managing Director: Kirsty Burge. Secretary: Christine Frost.

STIRLING. **Stirling Golf Club,** Queen's Road, Stirling FK8 3AA (01786 464098; Fax: 01786 460090). *Location:* one mile from town centre, rail and bus stations; two miles from Junction 10 M9. Rolling parkland course. 18 holes, 6400 yards. S.S.S. 71. Practice area. *Green Fees:* £30.00 per round; £45.00 per day. *Eating facilities:* full bar and catering. *Visitors:* visiting parties welcome midweek. Casual visitors may reserve tee times only at weekends. *Society Meetings:* welcome. Professional: Ian Collins (01786 471490). Secretary: Alan Rankin (01786 464098; Fax: 01786 460090).
e-mail: enquiries@stirlinggolfclub.tv
website: www.stirlinggolfclub.com

STIRLING. **Tillicoultry Golf Club,** Alva Road, Tillicoultry FK13 6BL (01259 750124). *Location:* on A91, nine miles east of Stirling. Parkland at foot of Ochil Hills. 9 holes, 5358 yards, 4904 metres. S.S.S. 67. *Green Fees:* weekdays £12.00 per round; weekends £18.00 per round. *Eating facilities:* clubhouse bar. *Visitors:* welcome at all times outwith competitions. No children under 15 weekends until 4pm. *Society Meetings:* welcome by booking through Club Manager. Club Manager: (01259 750124).

Callander Golf Club

Scottish Islands

COLONSAY

ISLE OF COLONSAY. **Colonsay Golf Club,** Machrins, Isle of Colonsay PA61 7YP. *Location:* two miles from ferry terminal. Traditional links course, reputedly 200 years old, natural, challenging and fun course. The 10th green has one of the best views in golf. 18 holes, 4775 yards. S.S.S. 72. *Green Fees:* information not available. *Eating facilities:* none on course, bar/ cafe/shop two miles away. *Visitors:* always welcome. *Society Meetings:* always welcome. Secretary: Donald MacAllister (01951 200307; Fax: 01951 200232).*
e-mail: donald@macallister4666.fslife.co.uk

CUMBRAE

MILLPORT. **Millport Golf Club,** Golf Road, Millport KA28 0HB (Tel & Fax: 01475 530306). *Location:* Caledonian McBrayne car ferry Largs slip to Cumbrae slip (seven minutes). Millport town four miles. On hill overlooking Firth of Clyde over Bute and Arran to Mull of Kintyre. Heathland with panoramic views. 18 holes, 5828 yards. S.S.S. 69. Large practice area. *Green Fees:* weekdays from £22.00 ; weekends and Bank Holidays from £30.00. *Eating facilities:* full à la carte and bar menu. *Visitors:* welcome without reservation. Tee reservations available for parties. Well stocked Professional's shop. Starter's telephone (01475 530305). *Society Meetings:* catered for. Special open amateur competition, Cumbrae Cup. Professional: (01475 530305). Secretary: William Reid (Tel & Fax: 01475 530306).
e-mail: secretary@millportgolfclub.co.uk
website: www.millportgolfclub.co.uk

GIGHA

ISLE OF GIGHA. **Isle of Gigha Golf Club,** The Croft, Isle of Gigha PA41 7AA (01583 505287). *Location:* by ferry from Tayinloan to Gigha, course half a mile north from Post Office. Seaside course with scenic views looking over the Sound of Gigha and the Kintyre coast. 9 holes, 5042 yards (18 holes). S.S.S. 65. *Green Fees:* £12.50 per round. Phone for special rates. *Eating facilities:* available at Gigha Hotel. *Visitors:* always welcome. *Society Meetings:* welcome. Secretary: John Bannatyne (01583 505242).

HARRIS

SCARISTA. **Isle of Harris Golf Club,** Scarista, Isle of Harris HS3 3HX. *Location:* 10 miles south of Tarbert, 50 miles south of Stornoway. Seaside links course on machair land, in an Area of Outstanding Natural Beauty. 9 holes, 2452 yards. S.S.S. 64 (18 holes). *Green Fees:* day ticket £20.00. Life membership £295.00 *Visitors:* welcome, no restrictions. Secretary: Roddy MacDonald (01859 550226).

ISLAY

PORT ELLEN. **Islay Golf Club,** 25 Charlotte Street, Port Ellen PA42 7DQ (01496 300094; Fax: 01496 302117). *Location:* five miles north of Port Ellen. Championship course. 18 holes, 6235 yards, 5695 metres. S.S.S. 70. Practice area. *Green Fees:* information not available. *Eating facilities:* full range at adjoining Machrie Hotel. *Visitors:* welcome anytime. Trolleys, caddies by arrangement. *Society Meetings:* all welcome.*

PORT ELLEN. **Machrie Golf Links,** The Machrie Hotel and Golf Links, Port Ellen PA42 7AN (01496 302310; Fax: 01496 302404). *Location:* adjacent Airport. Classic links. 18 holes, 6324 yards. S.S.S. 71. *Green Fees:* information not available. *Eating facilities:* full service in hotel. *Visitors:* welcome any day without reservation. *Society Meetings:* any number catered for. Golf packages available. Manager: Ian Brown.*
e-mail: machrie@machrie.com
website: www.machrie.com

LEWIS

STORNOWAY. **Stornoway Golf Club,** Lady Lever Park, Stornoway, Isle of Lewis HS2 0XP (01851 70 2240). *Location:* close proximity to town of Stornoway, in grounds of Lews Castle. Hilly parkland course with good views. 18 holes, 5252 yards. S.S.S. 67. *Green Fees:* £25.00 per round, £30.00 per day. Weekly tickets available - no Sunday golf. *Eating facilities:* light bar snacks available. *Visitors:* welcome. Car ferry daily (except Sunday) from Ullapool. Air services daily from Glasgow, Inverness, Aberdeen and Edinburgh. *Society Meetings:* welcome, book through Secretary. Secretary: K.W. Galloway (01851 702240).
e-mail: admin@stornowaygolfclub.co.uk
website: www.stornowaygolfclub.co.uk

MULL

CRAIGNURE. **Craignure Golf Club,** Scallastle, Craignure PA65 6AY. *Location:* one mile from Oban/Mull main ferry terminal. Links course - first layout 1895, superb natural setting. 9 holes, 18 tees, 5351 yards. S.S.S. 66. Small practice area. *Green Fees:* information not provided. *Eating facilities:* ¾ mile from MacGregor's Road House and Craignure Inn. *Visitors:* always welcome, except for Club inter-match days - please phone for details. Clubs, trolleys for hire, balls for sale. *Society Meetings:* welcome, discounts available. Secretary: Sheila Weir (01680 812370).

TOBERMORY. **Tobermory Golf Club,** Erray Road, Tobermory PA75 6PS. *Location:* situated on the cliffs above the town to the north west. Panoramic views of Sound of Mull; beautifully maintained and challenging course. 9 holes, 4921 yards, 4362 metres. S.S.S. 64. Practice ground. *Green Fees:* £20.00 per day, Juniors (under 18) £10.00 per day. *Eating facilities:* Club licence. Catering April to October by arrangement. Green Fee ticket includes temporary membership. *Visitors:* unrestricted except for some competition days. Membership available, contact Secretary. Club and trolley hire available. *Society Meetings:* welcome. Secretary: Gordon Chalmers (Tel/Fax: 01688 302741).
e-mail: secretary@tobermorygolfclub.com
website: www.tobermorygolfclub.com

ORKNEY

KIRKWALL. **Orkney Golf Club,** Grainbank, Kirkwall KW15 1RD (01856 872457). *Location:* half-a-mile west of Kirkwall. Parkland with good views over Kirkwall Bay and North Isles. 18 holes, 5411 yards, 4964 metres. S.S.S. 67. Practice area. *Green Fees:* information not available. *Eating facilities:* bar lunches during summer months. *Visitors:* welcome at all times, restrictions only during competitions. *Society Meetings:* welcome, booking advised. Secretary: Andrew Bonner (01856 741317).*
website: www.orkneygolfclub.co.uk

STROMNESS. **Stromness Golf Club Ltd,** Ness, Stromness KW16 3DW (01856 850772). *Location:* situated at south end of town. Seaside course bordering Hoy Sound. 18 holes, 4804 yards. S.S.S 64. *Green Fees:* £25.00 per day. *Visitors:* welcome. Bowling. *Society Meetings*: welcome by arrangement through Secretary. Secretary: Colin Mac Leod (01856 850079).
e-mail: colin_john_macleod@btopenworld.com
website: www.stromnessgc.co.uk

WESTRAY. **Westray Golf Club,** Westray, Orkney Islands KW17 2DH (01857 677373). *Location:* half a mile from Pierowall Village. Seaside links course. 9 holes, 2316 yards, 2084 metres. S.S.S. 33. *Green Fees:* information not available. *Visitors:* welcome anytime. Secretary: Mr John Cable (01857 677287).*

SHETLAND

LERWICK. **Shetland Golf Club,** Dale, Gott, Shetland ZE2 9SB (01595 840369). *Location:* four miles north of Lerwick on the A970. Parkland. 18 holes, 5562 yards. Par 68. S.S.S 68. Practice nets, chipping green and putting green. Driving range three miles away. *Green Fees:* information not available. *Eating facilities:* bar with sandwiches and snacks at lunchtimes, evenings and weekends. *Visitors:* welcome, no restrictions except on club competition days. Club and trolley hire available. Changing rooms, showers. *Society Meetings:* in writing by letter or e-mail. Secretary: Mrs J. Wishart.*
e-mail: info@shetlandgolfclub.co.uk
website: www.shetlandgolfclub.co.uk

WHALSAY. **Whalsay Golf Club,** Skaw Taing, Whalsay ZE2 9AL (01806 566259). *Location:* five miles from Symbister ferry terminal - ferries run from Laxo to Symbister. Seaside course with wonderful scenery and birdlife in abundance - Britain's most northerly 18 holes. 18 holes, 6140 yards. S.S.S. 69. Changing rooms. *Green Fees:* information not available. *Eating facilities:* lunch/dinner available by arrangement. *Visitors:* welcome. Trolleys for hire. Saturday/Sunday competitions, check before travelling. Secretary: Charles Hutchison (01806 566450) and Harry Sandison (01806 566481).*

SKYE

SCONSER. **Isle of Skye Golf Club,** Sconser IV48 8TD (01478 650414). *Location:* on A87 halfway between Broadford and Portree, 20 miles from Skye Bridge. Seaside course with spectacular views to Isle of Raasay and North Skye. 9 holes (with different tee settings on back 9), 4775 yards. S.S.S. 65. *Green Fees:* 9 holes £14.00, 18 holes £21.00. 2010 rates (subject to review). *Eating facilities*: tearoom serving light snacks. *Visitors:* welcome at all times. Changing and toilet facilities, trolleys and clubs for hire, small shop. *Society Meetings:* welcome. Secretary: R. Davison (01478 650414).
e-mail: info@isleofskyegolfclub.co.uk
website: www.isleofskyegolfclub.co.uk

SKEABOST BRIDGE. **Skeabost Golf Club,** Skeabost House Hotel, Skeabost Bridge IV51 9NP (01470 532202; Fax: 01470 532454). *Location:* A850 Portree to Dunvegan Road. Woodland course. 9 holes, 3114 yards. S.S.S. 59 (for 18 holes). *Green Fees:* information not available. *Eating facilities:* lunch, evening meals in hotel; bar food in public bar. *Visitors:* welcome, under 13s must be accompanied by an adult. *Society Meetings:* accepted. Club Captain: D. Sutherland. Secretary: D.J. Matheson.*
e-mail: reception@skeabostcountryhouse.com

SOUTH UIST

LOCHBOISDALE. **Askernish Golf Club,** Askernish, Lochboisdale. *Location:* off South Uist main road B888. Seaside, undulating, designed by Tom Morris Senior 1891. 9 holes, 18 tees, 5042 yards. S.S.S. 68. *Green Fees:* information not available. *Visitors:* welcome. Secretary: Neil Elliot (01878 700298).*
e-mail: askernish.golf.club@cwcom.net

TIREE

SCARINISH. **Vaul Golf Club,** Scarinish, Isle of Tiree PA77 6XH. *Location:* two miles from Scarinish and half a mile from Lodge Hotel, ferry from Oban four hours and plane from Glasgow 45 minutes. Links course with crystal white beaches to north and south with beautiful views on all sides. 9 holes, 5674 yards (18 holes). S.S.S. 68 (18 holes). *Green Fees:* information not provided. *Visitors:* welcome, no restrictions. Enquiries and fees to R. Omand, Royal Bank of Scotland, Scarinish. Secretary: Mrs S. Sweeney (01879 220729).

Looking for Accommodation near Golf Clubs and Courses? then visit our website:

www.holidayguides.com

for details of hundreds of properties throughout the UK

Golf in Wales

Chris Smart

Anglesey & Gwynedd • North Wales
Carmarthenshire • Ceredigion
Pembrokeshire • Powys • South Wales

For six years the main topic of conversation around the clubs of Wales has been the Ryder Cup at Celtic Manor, and with that momentous event now behind us its legacy is all-important and no doubt future generations will benefit from its great success.

Celtic Manor's millionaire owner Sir Terry Matthews left no stone unturned to ensure that the showpiece transatlantic clash was an outstanding occasion.

In the aftermath of the battle the Manor, with its three top-class courses -Twenty Ten, Montgomerie and Roman Road - will attract thousands of visitors, all keen to sample this splendid complex which boasts a five-star hotel, various restaurants, spa and conference facilities.

While the famous Celtic Manor Resort, sprawling above the M4 motorway on the edge of Wales's newest city, Newport, has grabbed the limelight for some time it would of course be totally wrong to believe that golf in Wales begins and ends there.

Until the announcement that the 2010 Ryder Cup would be staged at the Manor the course that every golf enthusiast in Wales recognised was the renowned Royal Porthcawl, the venue for the 1995 Walker Cup match in which Tiger Woods played his last competitive game as an amateur.

Porthcawl has over the years staged numerous top championships, including six Amateurs, stretching back to 1951, and professional events including the old Dunlop Masters. This a must for the serious golfer – a very challenging links - unique in that there is a view of the sea from every hole and four finishing holes that have undone many promising medal cards.

In 2011 the bi-ennial Vagliano Trophy match between the ladies of Great Britain and Ireland and the Continent of Europe will be contested at "The Royal" with a Welsh captain, Tegwen Matthews.

Porthcawl, with a clubhouse closer to the sea than all but one in Britain – Dunbar in Scotland is nearer – forms part of what is known as the South Wales triangle of courses. The others are Southerndown and Pyle and Kenfig, which also have championship layouts. Southerndown is 500 feet above sea level with superb views over the River Ogmore. It has a

18th hole, Mackintosh Course, Cottrell Park Golf Course, Cardiff, South Wales

very tough uphill opening hole and a fascinating short fifth, known affectionately as Carter's Folly. Pyle and Kenfig, with a particularly challenging second nine-hole layout, is a real test. Very few people take Pyle and Kenfig to pieces, the exception being Richard Finch, who fired a 62 in the 2003 British Amateur qualifying phase.

Moving west there is a pleasant cluster of courses around Swansea with Clyne, Langland Bay, Swansea Bay, Pennard and Neath all well worth a visit. In Carmarthenshire the famous Ashburnham links provides a very stern Test, with one of the trickiest opening holes - a par three with out of bounds on the right and bunkers on the left, difficult particularly for the nervous golfer. A few miles from the "Ash" the five-year-old Jack Nicklaus-designed Machynys Peninsula is already attracting championship golf, and with a new course built on a disused coal tip having been opened at Trimsaran and Allt-Yr-Graban this really is an area well worth a visit.

Tenby is Wales's oldest course and has some truly delightful but demanding holes and the high quality of the course was recognised by the Ladies' Golf Union who staged their stroke-play championship on the superb layout.

Newport Links, Milford Haven and Haverfordwest are all interesting courses and the golfing tourist would be well advised to check them out.

Moving back eastwards there are some splendid courses within a short radius of Cardiff City centre – Whitchurch, Radyr, Wenvoe Castle, Cardiff and Llanishen are particularly noteworthy – while a little further out St Mellons is a pleasing inland course.

It would be totally wrong to believe that Celtic Manor is the only course of substance in Monmouthshire as there are a whole host of other attractive layouts for the discerning golfer. The tree-lined Newport course at Rogerstone, the permanent home of the Great Oaks competition, is one of the finest inland courses in Wales. It has hosted a number of major tournaments, including the British Ladies' Amateur title event. The Monmouthshire course at Abergavenny, together with Llanwern and the proprietory Bryn Meadows to name just a few, have plenty of appeal, while St Pierre, which used to stage the old Dunlop Masters, is a fantastic complex with top-class accommodation as well as the golf.

Mid and North Wales also possess some marvellous courses, some of which are little treasures about which not so much is known. Cradoc, situated alongside the spectacularly beautiful Brecon Beacons National Park, is a must for any visitor to Wales. The 18-hole parkland course is superb and the hospitality second to none. On the way there from the south it would be wise to call in at Builth Wells and Llandrindod Wells.

Along the Mid-Wales coast are Borth and Ynyslas and Aberystwyth, both ideal for holiday golf. Slightly to the north is the breathtaking championship course of Aberdovey, a links layout revered by the distinguished golfing journalist Bernard Darwin and more recently regularly visited by Ian Woosnam. The favourite course of many is Royal St David's, Harlech, situated beneath Harlech Castle within sight of Mount Snowdon – it has been the venue for numerous top events down the years. Porthmadog nearby and Nefyn on the Llyn Peninsula should not be missed on a tour of the north.

One is spoilt for choice along the North Wales coast, with the two Llandudno courses, Maesdu and North Wales, and Conwy all within five miles of one another and Old Colwyn and Rhos-on-Sea. Further to the east there is the long seaside links of Prestatyn and the inland Wrexham course, both appealing in contrasting ways.

Finally we must not forget Anglesey where there are several challenging courses. Trearddur Bay on the outskirts of Holyhead is the best known, but on the tip of the Island Bull Bay has some of the most magnificent views imaginable and on a day when the wind blows it is a severe test - but the visitor will be warmly greeted in the clubhouse afterwards.

Wales is certainly no longer merely a country of heavy industry- there are golf courses to suit all tastes and abilities with plenty of high-class accommodation.

Newport Links Golf Club, Newport, Pembrokeshire

Glyn Abbey Golf Club
Trimsaran • Carmarthenshire
"Welsh Golf Club of the Year"

Recently awarded the prestigious title of "Welsh Golf Club of the Year" by the Golf Union of Wales, Glyn Abbey Golf Club offers the full package: Amazing views over the Gwendraeth Valley; Beautiful wooded surroundings; Arguably the best layout in South Wales. Add to that a friendly, relaxed atmosphere and the warmest welcome anywhere and Glyn Abbey needs to be top of your list for enjoyable golf.

The Abbey Course is a challenging par 70 of 6202 yards, whilst the Mission Course is a fun 9 hole par 3 course for beginners and families to enjoy. Practice facilities on-site include a fantastic 6 bay covered driving range as well as a fully equipped gymnasium. The newly extended Clubhouse now has a superb new dining room, a panoramic lounge and balconies with views over the Course and the Valley.

Call us now to arrange your special golf experience.

Right opposite the award winning Ffos Las Racecourse!

Ask us about our "putter and flutter" deals.

**Glyn Abbey Golf Club
Trimsaran, Kidwelly
Carmarthenshire SA17 4LB
Telephone: 01554 810278
Fax: 01554 810889
www.glynabbey.co.uk**

"Come for the golf, stay for the welcome"

Anglesey & Gwynedd

ABERDOVEY. **Aberdovey Golf Club,** Aberdovey LL35 0RT (01654 767493; Fax: 01654 767027). *Location*: west end of Aberdovey on A493, adjacent to railway station. Seaside links, easy walking. 18 holes, 6655 yards. S.S.S. 71. Practice ground, limited. *Green Fees*: information available on website. *Eating facilities*: restaurant, bar and lounge. *Visitors*: welcome on production of Handicap Certificate, restrictions some weekends. *Society Meetings*: catered for by prior arrangement. Professional: John Davies (01654 767493, Option 2). Manager: G. Pritchard (01654 767493; Fax: 01654 767027). website: www.aberdoveygolf.co.uk

ABERSOCH. **Clwb Golff Abersoch,** Golf Road, Abersoch LL53 7EY (01758 712622; Fax: 01758 712777). *Location:* A55 to Bangor, coast road to Abersoch. Parkland and seaside links course. 18 holes, 5671 yards. S.S.S. 68, Par 69. Practice area, putting green. *Green Fees:* information not available. *Eating facilities:* full catering and bar service. *Visitors:* welcome, Ladies' day Thursdays, Gents' competition day Sundays. Handicap Certificate required. Shop. Buggies, carts. *Society Meetings:* welcome by prior arrangement. Professional/Manager: Alan Drosinos Jones (01758 712622; Fax: 01758 712777).*
e-mail: pro@abersochgolf.co.uk
website: www.abersochgolf.co.uk

ANGLESEY. **Baron Hill Golf Club Ltd,** Beaumaris, Anglesey LL58 8YW (01248 810231). *Location:* turn left on approach to Beaumaris from Menai Bridge on A545. Moorland course with panoramic view of Snowdonia and Menai Straits. 9 holes, 5570 metres. S.S.S. 69. *Green Fees:* £20.00, £15.00 with a member. *Eating facilities:* comprehensive menu (closed Mondays). *Visitors:* welcome, competitions most Sundays, Ladies' Day on Tuesday mornings. *Society Meetings:* welcome by prior arrangement - special rates and packages available. Secretary: John Williams.

ANGLESEY. **Bull Bay Golf Club Ltd,** Bull Bay, Amlwch, Isle of Anglesey LL68 9RY (01407 830213). *Location:* one mile west of Amlwch on A5025 coastal road towards Cemaes Bay and Holyhead. Coastal heathland championship course; Wales' northernmost golf course. 18 holes, 6217 yards. S.S.S. 70. Practice ground and putting green. *Green Fees:* information not available. *Eating facilities:* bar snacks, dining room; limited facilities on Mondays. *Visitors:* welcome, competitions permitting; advance bookings advised. Snooker and pool. *Society Meetings:* welcome, booking essential. Professional: John Burns (01407 831188). Manager: (01407 830960; Fax: 01407 832612).*
website: www.bullbaygc.co.uk

ANGLESEY. **Penrhyn Golf Complex,** Llanddaniel - Fâb LL60 6NN (01248 421150). *Location:* A5 turn off at Star Crossroads taking Llanddaniel road. Follow Brown Tourism signs from the village. Parkland with some small hills. 9 holes, Par 3. 14-bay covered and floodlit driving range and putting area. *Green Fees:* information not provided. *Visitors*: no restrictions. Owner: W.R. Carter.

BALA. **Bala Golf Club,** Penlan, Bala LL23 7YD (01678 520359; Fax: 01678 521361). *Location:* turn right before coming to Bala Lake on the main Bala-Dolgellau road. Upland course with superb views in the Snowdonia National Park. 10 holes, 4970 yards, 4512 metres. S.S.S. 64. *Green Fees:* £15.00 weekdays, £20.00 weekends; weekly tickets £50.00. *Eating facilities:* bar with snacks available. *Visitors:* welcome all year, some restrictions Bank Holidays and weekends. Snooker table and small golf shop. *Society Meetings:* very welcome by prior arrangement. Secretary: G. Rhys Jones.
e-mail: balagolfclub@onetel.com
website: www.golffbala.co.uk

Henllys Hall Apartments
Beaumaris • Anglesey LL58 8HU
Tel: 01248 811303
enq@henllyshallapartments.co.uk
www.henllyshallapartments.co.uk

Set between 120 acres of dedicated woodland walks and the on-site Prince's golf course, within the courtyard of the ancient Henllys Hall Country Manor House, 4-Star Self-catering cottage-style apartments, each offering two bedrooms and centrally heated accommodation. Secluded, but just one mile from the beautiful conservation town of Beaumaris.

The Prince's Golf Course – 18-hole parkland, championship golf course with dramatic views over the sea to the Snowdonia mountain range. Spectacular. Golf clubhouse serving food and drinks all day. Separate gourmet restaurant. Caddy car hire. Extensive practice area. Tuition packages. Professional golf shop. Three resident PGA golf professionals. Tennis Court. Short Breaks and Golf Weekends available.

BANGOR. **St Deiniol Golf Club,** Penybryn, Bangor LL57 1PX (01248 353098; Fax: 01248 370792). *Location:* at A5/A55 Junction 11 intersection, follow A5122 for one mile to eastern outskirts of Bangor. Parkland course with magnificent views. 18 holes, 5652 yards, 5168 metres. S.S.S. 68. *Green Fees:* weekdays £20.00, weekends and Bank Holidays £25.00. *Eating facilities:* two bars; full catering Mondays excepted. *Visitors:* welcome without reservation, restrictions at weekends. Golf buggies available for hire. *Society Meetings:* welcome by prior arrangement. Secretary: Bob Thomas M.B.E.
e-mail: secretary@st-deiniol.co.uk
website: www.st-deiniol.co.uk

BEAUMARIS. **Henllys Golf Course,** Henllys Hall, Beaumaris, Anglesey LL58 8HU (01248 811717; Fax: 01248 811511). *Location*: quarter of a mile through Beaumaris town centre. Parkland course. 18 holes, 6062 yards, S.S.S. 70. Practice ground. *Green Fees:* information not provided. *Visitors*: welcome, please telephone before. Tuition from PGA Professionals available. Professionals: Peter Maton/ David Gadsby (01248 811717; Fax: 01248 811511). Director of Golf: Peter Maton.
e-mail: HG@HPB.co.uk

BRYNTEG. **Storws Wen Golf Club,** Brynteg LL78 8JY (01248 852673). *Location*: one-and-three-quarter miles along the B5108 from Benllech to Brynteg. Parkland course with a stream, three lakes and spectacular views. 9 holes, 5589 yards. Par 70. S.S.S. 68. *Green Fees:* information not available. *Eating facilities*: clubhouse with full facilities. *Visitors*: always welcome. Accommodation available. *Society Meeting*s: welcome, terms on request. General Manager: Emyr Rowlands.*

CAERNARFON. **Royal Town of Caernarfon Golf Club,** Aberforeshore, Llanfaglan, Caernarfon LL54 5RP (Tel & Fax: 01286 673783). *Location:* less than a mile from the historic Royal town of Caernarfon. Parkland course in superb sea and mountain setting. 18 holes, 5941 yards. S.S.S. 68. *Green Fees:* weekdays £27.00, weekends £30.00. *Eating facilities:* excellent catering and bar facilities, except Mondays. *Visitors:* welcome with no restrictions except Saturdays, please contact Professional to reserve tee time. Tuition, shop. *Society Meetings:* welcome, subject to pre-arranged bookings. Professional: Aled Owen (01286 673783). Secretary/Manager: E.G. Angel.
e-mail: secretary@caernarfongolfclub.co.uk
website: www.caernarfongolfclub.co.uk

CRICCIETH. **Criccieth Golf Club,** Ednyfed Hill, Criccieth LL52 0PH (01766 522154). *Location:* in High Street (A497) turn right past Memorial Hall, keep going up lane to Club. 18 holes, 5535 yards. S.S.S. 68. *Green Fees:* information not available. *Eating facilities:* light meals available. *Visitors:* welcome without reservation. *Society Meetings:* catered for with prior reservation. Secretary: T. Williams.
e-mail: tonywills7@btinternet.com

DOLGELLAU. **Dolgellau Golf Club,** Pencefn Road, Dolgellau LL40 2ES (01341 422603). *Location:* half-a-mile from town centre. Parkland with panoramic views of Mawddach estuary and Cader Idris mountain. 9 holes and alternate tees, 4671 yards. Par 66. Practice facility. *Green Fees:* 9 holes from £10.00; 18 holes from £18.00. *Eating facilities:* catering facilities available. All day bar menu. *Visitors:* welcome, please telephone before arrival. *Society Meetings:* catered for. Special packages available. Secretary: Mark White (01341 422603).
website: www.dolgellaugolfclub.com

Beach Bank, Criccieth
Gwynedd, North Wales LL52 0HW

Caerwylan Hotel
The Hotel by the Sea

The Caerwylan is a friendly, privately owned 3 star hotel, situated in a unique location on the East shore of Criccieth's Esplanade. A landmark Victorian building which faces south with stunning views over the main beach, Cardigan Bay and towards the ruins of Criccieth Castle. Championship golf courses only a short drive from hotel.
phone: 01766 522547 • fax: 01248 800100 • e-mail: info@caerwylan.com • www.caerwylan.com

Anglesey & Gwynedd / WALES

FFESTINIOG. **Clwb Golff Ffestiniog,** Y Cefn, Ffestiniog LL41 4PS (01766 762637). *Location:* located on B4391, one mile from Ffestiniog village. Upland course. 9 holes, 4570 yards. S.S.S. 66. *Green Fees:* £10.00. *Visitors:* welcome at any time, some restrictions mainly at weekends during club competitions. *Society Meetings:* by prior arrangement. Secretary: Andrew Roberts.
e-mail: info@ffestinioggolf.org

HARLECH. **Royal St David's Golf Club,** Harlech LL46 2UB (01766 780361). *Location:* A496 lower Harlech road. Championship links course. 18 holes, 6629 yards. S.S.S. 73. Large practice ground. *Green Fees:* information not provided. *Eating facilities:* full catering and bar facilities available. *Visitors:* must be members of bona fide golf clubs with Handicap - booking essential. *Society Meetings:* catered for by prior arrangement. Professional: John Barnett (01766 780857). Secretary: T. Davies (01766 780361).
e-mail: secretary@royalstdavids.co.uk
website: www.royalstdavids.co.uk

LLANGEFNI. **Llangefni Public Golf Course,** Clai Road (B5111), Llangefni, Isle of Anglesey LL77 8YQ. Parkland course, six Par 3s, three Par 4s. 9 holes, 1781 yards, 1628 metres. Practice net. 16-bay floodlit driving range. *Green Fees:* information not available. *Eating facilities:* light refreshments only. *Visitors:* welcome at all times, no restrictions. Fully stocked Discount Golf Shop. Professional: Paul Lovell (01248 722193).*

MORFA BYCHAN. **Porthmadog Golf Club,** Morfa Bychan, Porthmadog LL49 9UU (Tel & Fax: 01766 514124). *Location:* turn in Porthmadog High Street towards Black Rock Sands, club on left hand side of road one mile west. Part heathland, part seaside links. 18 holes, 6322 yards. S.S.S. 71. Two practice grounds. *Green Fees:* per round £35.00 weekdays, £40.00 weekends and Bank Holidays; £45.00 and £50.00 for day tickets. Discounts available for larger parties. 2010 rates (subject to review). *Eating facilities:* lounge bar, golfers' bar and large restaurant. *Visitors:* welcome, no restrictions except for competition days. Snooker room. *Society Meetings:* catered for by prior arrangement. Bookings via Office Manager: Åse Richardson (01766 514124). Professional: Peter L. Bright (01766 513828). Club Manager: Gwilym Jones.
e-mail: secretary@porthmadog-golf-club.co.uk
website: www.porthmadog-golf-club.co.uk

NEFYN. **Nefyn and District Golf Club,** Golf Road, Morfa Nefyn, Pwllheli LL53 6DA (Fax: 01758 720476). *Location:* north coast of Lleyn Peninsula, two miles west of Nefyn. Seaside course. 27 holes. Main Course - 18 holes, 6548 yards. S.S.S. 71. Practice area. *Green Fees:* information not available. *Eating facilities:* full restaurant facilities and two bars. *Visitors:* welcome without reservation, except club competition days. Snooker. *Society Meetings:* catered for by arrangement with Secretary. Professional: John Froom (01758 720102). Secretary: S. Dennis (01758 720966).*
website: www.nefyn-golf-club.co.uk

Royal St David's Golf Club
Harlech, Gwynedd LL46 2UB
Tel: 01766 780361
email: secretary@royalstdavids.co.uk
www.royalstdavids.co.uk

Nationally and internationally renowned, Royal St David's is one of Wales' premier golf courses. It provides a challenging test of golf in a breathtaking setting in the most beautiful and scenic part of the Principality, dominated by the brooding presence of Harlech Castle.
The undulating fairways and fast true greens are all that would be expected of a championship links course.
The course is rated 73rd in the Golf Digest Best 100 courses outside the USA, 42nd in Golf World's Top 100 courses in Britain & Ireland and 45th in Golf Monthly's Top 100 in the UK & Ireland.

Porthmadog Golf Club
Morfa Bychan, Porthmadog, Gwynedd LL49 9UU

Situated in the seaside village of Morfa Bychan, renowned for its Black Rock Sands, the course offers an intriguing mixture of heathland and links for the discerning golfer. The front nine are away from the coast with the back nine heading for the sea, where the course is transformed into pure links, often claimed to be the most natural nine holes in Wales.
Special deals available for societies and visiting clubs.

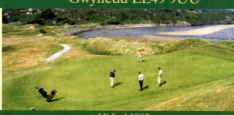

Tel: 01766 514124 • Fax: 01766 514124
e-mail: secretary@porthmadog-golf-club.co.uk • www.porthmadog-golf-club.co.uk
• *established 1905* •

PWLLHELI. **Llyn Golf**, Pen-y-Berth, Penrhos, Pwllheli LL53 7HG (01758 701200). *Location*: off A499 between Pwllheli and Abersoch. New 9-hole pay and play course. 1782 yards, Par 3 and 4. 14-bay driving range, bunker practice area. *Green Fees:* information not available. *Eating facilities:* refreshments available. *Visitors*: welcome. Open daily. Clubs for hire. *Society Meetings:* welcome.*
website: www.pen-y-berth.co.uk

PWLLHELI. **Pwllheli Golf Club,** Golf Road, Pwllheli L53 5PS (01758 701644). *Location:* A499 from Caernarvon (20 miles). Parkland/seaside links. 18 holes, 6108 yards. S.S.S. 70. Two practice areas and putting green. *Green Fees:* weekday £34.00, weekend £37.00; twilight after 4pm £20.00. *Eating facilities:* two large lounge bars and diningroom. Steward: (01758 701644). *Visitors:* welcome without reservation. Pro shop. *Society Meetings:* welcome. Professional: S. Pilkington (01758 701644). General Manager: Dennis Moore (01758 701644).
e-mail: admin@pwllheligolfclub.co.uk
website: www.pwllheligolfclub.co.uk

Clwb Golff Pwllheli • Pwllheli Golf Club

Heaven can wait

e-mail: admin@pwllheligolfclub.co.uk • www.pwllheligolfclub.co.uk

Golf Road, Pwllheli, Gwynedd LL53 5PS
Office: 01758 701644 • Professional: 01758 701644

Excellent 18-hole course combining both parkland and links, with superb views of the Snowdonia and Cambrian mountain ranges, and across Cardigan Bay.
Green Fees: on request
Societies welcome and special rates are available for parties of 8 or more players.

PLEASE NOTE

All the information regarding Golf Clubs in this guide is given in good faith in the belief that it is correct. However, the publishers cannot guarantee the facts given in these pages, neither are they responsible for changes in ownership or facilities, such as green fees, that may take place after the date of going to press. Readers should always satisfy themselves that the facilities they require are available and that the terms, if quoted, still apply.

RHOSNEIGR. The Anglesey Golf Club Ltd, Station Road, Rhosneigr, Anglesey LL64 5QX (Tel & Fax: 01407 811202; Club House 01407 810219). *Location*: turn south off A55 Junction 5 signposted Rhosneigr, Aberffraw. In about three miles turn right at Llanfaelog church about one mile from course. Flat links course with sand dunes and heathland. 18 holes, 6300 yards. S.S.S. 71. *Green Fees*: information not available. *Eating facilities*: catering facilities available all day. *Visitors*: welcome, advanced booking advisable. Dress smart casual. *Society Meetings*: club societies welcome. Professional tuition. Contact Matthew Parry for further details (01407 811202).*
e-mail: info@theangleseygolfclub.com
website: www.angleseygolfclub.co.uk

TREARDDUR BAY. Holyhead Golf Club, Trearddur Bay, Anglesey LL62 2YL (Tel & Fax: 01407 763279). *Location*: A55 to Holyhead, turn left at roundabout on B4545 for 1 mile, left for Trearddur Bay. Heathland, heavy gorse cover, superb sea views. Course designed by James Braid. 18 holes, 6058 yards. S.S.S. 70. *Green Fees*: information not provided. *Eating facilities*: restaurant/bar. *Visitors*: welcome. *Society Meetings*: catered for weekdays. Dormy House accommodation available for up to 14. Director of Golf: Steve Elliott
website: www.holyheadgolfclub.co.uk

www.holidayguides.com

For full details of convenient accommodation near clubs and courses

Anglesey Golf Club

- Society Packages available from £14.50, excellent links all year round.
- Bar Meals • Professional tuition
- Membership available, no joining fee.
- Fully-stocked Pro Shop
- Ideal stopover for parties going to or coming over from Ireland.

Contact Matthew Parry for further details
Tel: 01407 811202
www.angleseygolfclub.co.uk • info@theangleseygolfclub.com

North Wales

ABERGELE. **Abergele Golf Club,** Tan-y-Gopa Road, Abergele, Conwy LL22 8DS (01745 824034; Fax: 01745 824772). *Location:* A55 from Chester. Below Gwrych Castle, Abergele. Parkland in scenic setting. 18 holes, 6256 yards. S.S.S. 70. USGA greens. Practice ground and indoor practice nets. *Green Fees:* information not available. *Eating facilities:* restaurant and bar. *Visitors:* welcome, avoid Tuesdays (Ladies' Day) and Saturdays difficult due to club competitions. Buggy hire available, trolleys. *Society Meetings:* visiting party packages available. Professional: Iain R. Runcie (Tel & Fax: 01745 823813). Secretary: Chris Langdon (01745 824034; Fax: 01745 824772).*
website: www.abergelegolfclub.co.uk

BETWS-Y-COED. **Betws-y-Coed Golf Club,** The Clubhouse, Betws-y-Coed LL24 0AL (01690 710556). *Location:* take Railway Museum Road in centre of the village. Parkland, flat scenic course on valley floor of River Conwy. 9 holes, 18 tees, 4998 yards. S.S.S. 63. *Green Fees*: information not available. *Eating facilities*: bar open from 12 noon onwards. *Visitors*: no restrictions provided there are no club competitions. *Society Meetings*: welcome. Secretary: Dafydd Hughes.*
e-mail: info@golf-betws-y-coed.co.uk
website: www.betws-y-coedgolfclub.co.uk

BODELWYDDAN. **Kinmel Park Golf Complex,** Abergele Road, Bodelwyddan LL18 5SR (01745 833548). *Location:* Junction 25 off A55 Expressway at the famous White Marble church. Flat parkland course. 9 holes, 1550 yards. S.S.S. 58. 25 bay undercover and floodlit driving range. Practice chipping and putting green. *Green Fees:* Pay and Play course £5.00 weekdays, £6.00 weekends. *Visitors:* welcome. Golf lessons available. *Society Meetings:* welcome, special rates. Professional: Rhodri Lloyd Jones. Director: Mrs Fetherstonhaugh. website: www.kinmelgolf.co.uk

CHESTER near. **Northop Country Park Golf Club,** Northop, Near Chester CH7 6WA (01352 840440; Fax: 01352 840445). *Location:* travel west on M56, follow signs for North Wales. A494/A55 for Northop. Parkland course set amongst 300-year-old oak trees, designed by John Jacobs. 18 holes, 6735 yards, 6128 metres. S.S.S. 72. Practice range and academy. *Green Fees:* information not provided. *Eating facilities:* clubroom for snacks, club restaurant for full meals. *Visitors:* welcome. St David's Park Hotel only five minutes away for accommodation. *Society Meetings:* welcome depending on availability. Professional/Director of Golf: John Nolan.

CHIRK. **Chirk Golf Club,** Chirk, Near Wrexham LL14 5AD (01691 774407; Fax: 01691 773878). *Location*: just off A5 towards Llangollen. Generally flat course. 18 holes, 6541 yards. S.S.S. 72. 9 hole Par 3 course, 15 bay driving range. *Green Fees:* weekdays £20.00, weekends £25.00. *Eating facilities*: bar and restaurant. *Visitors*: welcome seven days a week. *Society Meetings*: all welcome. Professional: C.J. Hodges (01691 774407).

CLWB GOLFF BETWS-Y-COED GOLF CLUB

"The Jewel of the Nines"

Situated in the heart of the Snowdonia National Park you will find something special. Visitors and societies always welcome. Packages available.

Contact Secretary: Mr Lionel Phillips
01690 710556
e-mail: info@golf-betws-y-coed.co.uk • www.golf-betws-y-coed.co.uk

THE APPEARANCE OF AN ASTERISK (*) AT THE END OF A CLUB OR COURSE ENTRY INDICATES THAT UP-TO-DATE INFORMATION HAS NOT BEEN SUPPLIED

COLWYN. **Old Colwyn Golf Club,** The Clubhouse, Woodland Avenue, Old Colwyn LL29 9NL (01492 515581). *Location:* signposted at main Abergele road, Old Colwyn. Parkland. 9 holes (x 2), 5263 yards. S.S.S. 68. Practice area. *Green Fees:* weekday £12.00, weekend £16.00, twilight (after 5pm) £6.00. *Eating facilities:* bar and meals by arrangement. *Visitors:* welcome except Saturday afternoons and Wednesday evenings. *Society Meetings:* welcome by arrangement with Secretary. Manager/Secretary: Mike Eccles (07799 575369).

CONWY. **Conwy (Caernarfonshire) Golf Club,** Morfa, Conwy LL32 8ER (01492 592423). *Location:* follow signs for Conwy Marina off A55 Junction 17. Seaside links. 18 holes, 6647 yards. S.S.S. 74. Practice facilities. *Green Fees:* Summer (April to October) - weekdays £45.00 per round, £50.00 per day; weekends £50.00 per round. *Eating facilities:* available. *Visitors:* welcome with reservation, restrictions at weekends. On-line bookings available. *Society Meetings:* catered for on application to Secretary. Professional: Peter Lees (Tel & Fax: 01492 593225). Secretary: A. Jones (01492 592423; Fax: 01492 593363).
e-mail: secretary@conwygolfclub.com
website: www.conwygolfclub.com

DENBIGH. **Denbigh Golf Club,** Henllan Road, Denbigh LL16 5AA (01745 816669. Fax: 01745 814888). *Location:* one mile from Denbigh town centre on the B5382 road. Parkland with excellent views. 18 holes, 5828 yards. S.S.S. 68. *Green Fees:* weekdays £26.00, weekends £32.00. *Eating facilities:* catering daily, bar. *Visitors:* welcome. *Society Meetings:* by arrangement. Professional: M.D. Jones (01745 814159). Manager: John Williams.
e-mail: denbighgolfclub@aol.com
website: www.denbighgolfclub.co.uk

DENBIGH near. **Bryn Morfydd Hotel Golf Club,** Llanrhaeadr, Near Denbigh LL16 4NP (01745 589090; Fax: 01745 589093). *Location:* off A525 between Denbigh and Ruthin. Mature parkland course overlooking Vale of Clwyd. The Duchess Course: 9 holes, 1146 yards. Par 27. The Duke's Course: 18 holes, 5685 yards. S.S.S. 67, Par 70. Practice area. *Green Fees:* information not available. *Eating facilities:* courses attached to three star Hotel, two restaurants, two bars, clubhouse. *Visitors:* welcome by arrangement. Hotel with 25 rooms en suite. *Society Meetings:* welcome by arrangement all year. Secretary/ Director of Golf: C. Henderson. Proprietors: D. & S. Frith.*

CONWY CAERNARFONSHIRE GOLF CLUB

Welcome to Conwy Golf Club

... Home for the S$C Wales Ladies' Championship of Europe 2010, the Ryder Cup Wales Seniors Open for 2007/2008 and the venue for the prestigious European Amateur Team Championship in July 2009.

Set in a spectacular location along the North Wales coast, our links provide a great test of golf all year round, as one would expect of an Open Qualifying course and whilst we strive to maintain these high standards, our objective is also to ensure that our members, visitors and societies enjoy their golf here.

And once you have completed your round, come and enjoy the magnificent views of the course from our modern clubhouse, with a drink or two and a bite to eat from our wide-ranging bar & restaurant menu.

Because of the Ryder Cup in 2010, we anticipate that many golfers are coming to Wales for the very first time and believe that Conwy Golf Club is a must on your itinerary! We look forward to welcoming you. Tee booking is available online or contact admin@conwygolfclub.com in order for us to arrange your golf at Conwy.

Societies are very welcome and Corporate Days are also available – we can tailor a day to suit your requirements.

Morfa, Conwy LL32 8ER
Tel: (Secretary): 01492 592423 • Fax: 01492 593363
e-mail: secretary@conwygolfclub.com
www.conwygolfclub.com

FLINT. **Flint Golf Club,** Cornist Park, Flint CH6 5HJ (01352 732327). *Location:* A548 coast road, one mile from town centre. Hilly parkland. 9 holes, 5927 yards. S.S.S. 69. Practice area. *Green Fees:* information not available. *Eating facilities:* full bar and catering 11am to 11pm. *Visitors:* welcome except Sundays. *Society Meetings:* welcome by arrangement. Secretary: D. Lerston (01352 732327).*
e-mail: secretary@flintgolfclub.co.uk

HAWARDEN. **Hawarden Golf Club,** Groomsdale Lane, Hawarden CH5 3EH (01244 531447). *Location:* A55, left at Ewloe interchange, follow Hawarden signs. Undulating parkland. 18 holes, 5842 yards, 5340 metres. S.S.S. 69, Par 69. *Green Fees:* Monday to Friday £25.00, Sunday and Bank Holidays £30.00. *Eating facilities:* full bar and catering. *Visitors:* welcome by arrangement. Some restrictions Wednesday (Ladies' Day). *Society Meetings:* catered for by prior arrangement. Summer and Winter packages available. Professional/Secretary: Alex Rowland (01244 520809).
e-mail: secretary@hawardengolfclub.co.uk

HOLYWELL. **Holywell Golf Club,** Brynford, Near Holywell CH8 8LQ (01352 713937). *Location:* turn off A55 at Junction 32 onto A5026, turn left at traffic lights, signed for Brynford, up hill for half mile, turn right at crossroads. Flat natural terrain, links type course, a good test of golf. 18 holes, 6100 yards. S.S.S. 70. *Green Fees:* information not available. *Eating facilities:* full bar facilities and catering. *Visitors:* welcome weekdays without reservation; Bank Holidays and weekends by prior arrangement with Secretary. Snooker table. *Society Meetings:* by prior arrangement with Secretary. Professional/ Secretary: Matthew J. Parsley (01352 710040 opt. 2).*
e-mail: holywell_golf_club@lineone.net

HOLYWELL. **Kinsale Golf Course,** Llanerchymor, Holywell CH8 9DX (01745 561080). *Location:* A55 expressway, Holywell to A548; opposite White Ship Abakham Textiles. Magnificent view over Dee Estuary towards the Wirral. 9 holes, 5944 yards. S.S.S. 69. Driving range. *Green Fees:* 9 holes £10.00, 18 holes £15.00. *Eating facilities:* snacks in clubhouse. *Visitors:* always welcome; pay as you play course.

LLANDUDNO. **Llandudno Golf Club (Maesdu) Ltd,** Hospital Road, Llandudno LL30 1HU (Tel & Fax: 01492 876450). *Location:* Llandudno General Hospital. A55 and then A470. Parkland. 18 holes, 6545 yards. S.S.S. 72. Practice ground. *Green Fees*: weekdays £29.00 per round, £36.00 per day; weekends and Bank Holidays £34.00 per round, £41.00 per day. *Eating facilities*: full catering, bar (large) available. *Visitors*: welcome, must book. Buggies, electric trolleys for hire. *Society Meetings*: must be booked. Professional: S. Boulden (01492 875195). Secretary: George Dean (01492 876450)
e-mail: secretary@maesdugolfclub.co.uk
website: www.maesdugolfclub.co.uk

LLANDUDNO. **North Wales Golf Club Ltd,** 72 Bryniau Road, West Shore, Llandudno LL30 2DZ. *Location*: two miles off the A55 expressway on the A470 Junction. Seaside links with wonderful views of Conwy estuary and mountains. 18 holes, 6287 yards, S.S.S. 71. Practice ground. *Green Fees:* information not available. *Eating facilities:* full bar and catering facilities. *Visitors:* welcome after 9.30am weekdays, 10.30am weekends. Buggies, carts and clubs for hire. *Society Meetings:* catered for by arrangement. Professional: R.A. Bradbury (01492 876878; Fax: 01492 872420).Secretary: Nick Kitchen (01492 875325; Fax: 01492 873355).*
e-mail: enquiries@northwalesgolfclub.co.uk
website: www.northwalesgolfclub.co.uk

LLANDUDNO. **Rhos-on-Sea Residential Golf Club,** Penrhyn Bay, Llandudno LL30 3PU (01492 549641; Fax: 01492 549100). *Location:* A55 to Colwyn Bay follow signs to Rhos-on-Sea, one mile past Rhos-on-Sea on coast road in Penrhyn Bay. Flat seaside parkland course. 18 holes, 6064 yards. S.S.S. 69. *Green Fees:* information not available. *Eating facilities:* full catering available 8.30am tp 9pm, 7 days a week. Licensed bar with new licensing hours available. *Visitors:* welcome 7 days a week, prior booking required. Dormy house hotel with 12 bedrooms, sleeping up to 24 all ensuite with televisions. Licensed for weddings. Snooker tables, TV lounge. Trolley and buggy hire available. *Society Meetings:* all welcome. Professional: Jonathan Kelly (01492 548115). Secretary: Gordon Downs.*

Vine House Bed & Breakfast
23 Church Walks, Llandudno LL30 2HG
Tel: 01492 876493 • www.vinehouse-llandudno.co.uk

Molly (our Cocker Spaniel) will welcome you with a happy bark to our comfortable family-run guest house.

We are situated opposite the Great Orme Tramway, as well as being close to the town centre, Promenade and beach. There are views to the Great Orme or the sea from all rooms.

LLANFAIRFECHAN. Llanfairfechan Golf Club, Llannerch Road, Llanfairfechan LL33 0EB (01248 680144 evenings and after 11am at weekends, 07737385070 anytime). *Location:* signposted off old A55, 300 yards west of traffic lights. Hillside parkland. 9 holes (14 tees & 12 greens), 3103 yards. Par 54, S.S.S. 57. *Green Fees:* information not available. *Eating facilities:* no eating facilities at club without prior arrangement, (available in village); bar opens weekday evenings (afternoons June-August) and from 11am weekends. *Visitors:* welcome anytime except Sundays and most Saturdays from May to September. *Society Meetings:* by arrangement, weekdays only in Summer. Secretary: Mrs S. Kendall.*
e-mail: hon.sec.llgc@btconnect.com

LLANGOLLEN. Vale of Llangollen Golf Club Ltd., The Clubhouse, Llangollen LL20 7PR (01978 860906; Fax: 01987 869165). *Location:* one and a half miles east of town on the A5. Course is set on the valley floor bordered by the River Dee. 18 holes, 6656 yards, 6086 metres. S.S.S. 73. Practice ground. *Green Fees:* information not available. *Eating facilities:* full catering service. *Visitors:* welcome any day subject to availability, Handicap Certificate essential. *Society Meetings:* welcome. Professional: David Vaughan (01978 860906). Secretary: Bob Hardy (01978 860906; Fax: 01987 869165).*
e-mail: info@vlgc.co.uk

MOLD. Mold Golf Club, Cilcain Road, Pantymwyn, Mold CH7 5EH (01352 741513; Fax: 01352 741517). *Location:* 14 miles west of Chester. Take A55 from Chester for Mold. Follow Pantymwyn signs from Mold. Uplands course offering extensive views of Cheshire, Liverpool, Peak District. 18 holes, 5628 yards. S.S.S. 67. Practice ground and practice green. *Green Fees:* information not provided. *Eating facilities:* extensive restaurant and bar facilities. *Visitors:* welcome by prior arrangement. Tee bookings advised at weekends. Trolley hire. *Society Meetings:* welcome, subject to tee availability. Professional: (01352 740318) (Lessons by appointment). Secretary: C. Mills (01352 741513; Fax: 01352 741517).
e-mail: info@moldgolfclub.co.uk

MOLD. Padeswood and Buckley Golf Club, The Caia, Station Lane, Padeswood, Near Mold CH7 4JD (01244 550537). *Location:* A5118 Chester - Mold, one mile west of Castle Cement Works, half a mile off main road. Flat parkland; river, lakes. 18 holes, 6078 yards. S.S.S. 70. Practice ground. *Green Fees:* weekdays £30.00 per round. £35.00 per day. Saturdays/Sundays £35.00 per round, contact Professional for availablity. *Eating facilities:* bar all day every day, catering daily. *Visitors:* welcome subject to availability. Buggies, carts for hire. Two snooker tables and pool table. *Society Meetings:* welcome, enquiries through Secretary; packages available. Professional: David Ashton (01244 543636). Secretary: Mrs S.A. Davies (01244 550537).
e-mail: admin@padeswoodgolf.plus.com
padeswoodgolfclub@googlemail.com
website: www.padeswoodgolfclub.com

PADESWOOD. Old Padeswood Golf Club Ltd, Station Road, Padeswood, Near Mold CH7 4JD (01244 547701). *Location:* off A5118 Chester to Mold road, eight miles from Chester and three miles from Mold. Situated in the beautiful Alyn Valley - nine holes flat parkland, nine holes slightly undulating. 18 holes, 6668 yards, 6079 metres. S.S.S. 72/Ladies 73. Practice ground. *Green Fees:* weekdays £27.00, with member £15.00; weekends £35.00, with member £20.00. *Eating facilities:* diningroom, bar meals - two bars. *Visitors:* welcome anytime subject to tee availability. *Society Meetings:* welcome, written applications or telephone Rob Jones (01244 550414; Mobile: 07973 864522). Professional: Tony Davies (01244 547401). Co-Secretary: Mrs B. Jones (01244 550414; Fax: 01244 545082). Hon. Secretary: B. Slater (01244 816573; Fax: 01244 545082).
e-mail: sec@oldpadeswoodgolfclub.co.uk
website: www.oldpadeswoodgolfclub.co.uk

Penmaenmawr Golf Club

North Wales / WALES

PENMAENMAWR. Penmaenmawr Golf Club, Conwy Old Road, Penmaenmawr LL34 6RD (01492 623330). *Location:* A55 expressway three miles west of Conwy. Parkland with panoramic views. 9 holes (18 tees), 5372 yards. S.S.S. 67. Two practice areas. *Green Fees:* £18.00 weekdays and weekends. *Eating facilities:* bar and bar snacks, meals available. *Visitors:* welcome (phone or book online). *Society Meetings:* welcome by arrangement. Secretary: Mrs A. Greenwood.
e-mail: clubhouse@pengolf.co.uk
website: www.pengolf.co.uk

PRESTATYN. Prestatyn Golf Club, Marine Road East, Prestatyn LL19 7HS (01745 854320). Location: A548, on approaching Prestatyn from Chester direction turn right at sign for Pontins Holiday Village and follow club sign. Seaside links Championship course. 18 holes, 6564 yards, 5959 metres. S.S.S. 72. Practice areas. Green Fees: information not available. Eating facilities: full catering available, bar. Visitors: welcome. Society Meetings: special "all-in" arrangement for 27 holes. Professional: D. Ames (01745 854320). Manager: S.L. Owen (Tel & Fax: 01745 854320).*
e-mail: prestatyngcmanager@freenet.co.uk
website: www.prestatyngolfclub.co.uk
         www.ukgolfer.org

PRESTATYN. St Melyd Golf Club, The Paddock, Meliden Road, Prestatyn LL19 8NB (01745 854405; Fax: 01745 856908). *Location:* on main Prestatyn to Rhuddlan road, just outside Meliden. Parkland course with tight fairways and varied greens, set twixt the hills and the sea. 9 holes, 5811 yards. S.S.S. 68. *Green Fees:* information not provided. *Eating facilities:* full range of catering facilities except Tuesdays which is by arrangement. *Visitors:* welcome without reservation but advise phone call first in summer season. Restriction Saturdays Competition Day; Thursdays Ladies' Day. Snooker room. *Society Meetings:* catered for by arrangement with Secretary (various golf packages).
e-mail: enquiries@stmelydgolfltd.co.uk
website: www.stmelydgolf.co.uk

RHUDDLAN. Rhuddlan Golf Club, Meliden Road, Rhuddlan LL18 6LB (01745 590217). *Location*: leave A55 at St Asaph for Rhuddlan, clubhouse 100m from roundabout at Prestatyn end of Rhuddlan. Gently undulating, parkland course with natural hazards; set amid splendid scenery with fine views of the Clwydian Hills. 18 holes, White 6473 yards. S.S.S. 71; Yellow 6291 yards, S.S.S. 70; Ladies 5768 yards, Par 70. Extensive practice ground. *Green Fees*: from £27.50. *Eating facilities*: full restaurant facilities daily. *Visitors*: welcome at all times when course demand permits. Sundays with member only. No denim. Snooker table. *Society Meetings*: weekdays only, maximum 50. Professional: A.Carr (01745 590898). Secretary: Jill Roberts (01745 590217; Fax: 01745 590472).
e-mail: secretary@rhuddlangolfclub.co.uk
website: www.rhuddlangolfclub.co.uk

RHYL. Rhyl Golf Club, Coast Road, Rhyl LL18 3RE (01745 353171). *Location:* situated alongside A548, the Rhyl/ Prestatyn coast road. Flat links. 9/18 holes, 6220 yards. S.S.S. 71. Practice ground. *Green Fees:* information not provided. *Eating facilities:* dining room, catering and bar snacks available. *Visitors:* always welcome; some restrictions when club competitions in play. Trolleys for hire. *Society Meetings:* society specials available, maximum 60; discounts for 10 or more. Professional: Robert Dunbar. Secretary: Mrs Gill Davies (01745 353171).
e-mail: rhylgolfclub@btconnect.com
website: www.rhylgolfclub.co.uk

Penmaenmawr Golf Club
Est. 1910

Celebrating 100 years of golf

- 9 Hole Course (18 tee positions)
- Scenic, Challenging but Forgiving, "A Hidden Treasure"
- Green fees £18 per any day of the week
- Societies welcomed

To book or for further information call
01492 623330
e-mail: **clubhouse@pengolf.co.uk**
www.pengolf.co.uk

Penmaenmawr Golf Club
Conwy Old Road,
Penmaenmawr, Conwy LL34 6RD

Prestatyn Golf Club

♦ Seaside links Championship course, host to WGU Championships and many other national events. ♦ 18 holes, 6564 yards, 5959 metres. S.S.S. 72.
♦ Visitors and societies welcome. ♦ Quote ref GG8 and get £1 off your green fee.
♦ Full bar and catering service. ♦ Hire of buggy, trolley and clubs available.

Marine Road East, Prestatyn LL19 7HS ♦ Tel: 01745 854320
www.prestatyngolfclub.co.uk ♦ e-mail: prestatyngcmanager@freenet.co.uk

RUTHIN. **Ruthin-Pwllglas Golf Club,** Pwllglas, Ruthin LL15 2PE (01824 702296). *Location:* Corwen Road (A494), two miles south of Ruthin. Parkland. 10 holes, 5354 yards. S.S.S. 66. Practice area. *Green Fees:* weekdays £16.00, weekends and Bank Holidays £22.00 2010 rates (subject to review). *Catering facilities:* Secretary can arrange catering and bar service for visiting parties. *Visitors:* welcome without reservation, phone call advisable in high season and at weekends. *Societies & Groups:* catered for. Hon. Secretary: Neil Roberts (07881 426178).
e-mail: secretary@ruthinpwllglasgc.co.uk
website: www.ruthinpwllglasgc.co.uk

WREXHAM. **Moss Valley Golf Course,** Moss Road, Wrexham LL11 6HA (Tel & Fax: 01978 720518). Proprietary club. *Location:* off A541 from Wrexham roundabout. Parkland course meandering through wooded valley. 18 holes, 5313 yards. S.S.S. 68. *Green Fees:* £11.00 9 holes; £15.00 18 holes; telephone for 2 for 1 deals. *Visitors:* welcome, booking required at weekend. *Society Meetings:* contact in advance. Manager/Secretary: John Nolan.
e-mail: info@mossvalleygolf.co.uk
website: www.mossvalleygolf.co.uk

WREXHAM. **Plassey Oaks Golf Complex,** Eyton, Wrexham LL13 0SP (01978 780020; Fax: 01978 781397). *Location:* 4 miles south-east of Wrexham. Take B5426 and follow brown "Tourist Attraction" signs to "Plassey" from A483 Wrexham by-pass. Undulating parkland course. 9 holes, 4961 yards, Par 66. Driving range and Par 3 course. *Green Fees:* information not available. *Visitors:* welcome. Please book start times at weekends. Full bar and catering facilities. Golf course is part of Plassey Leisure Park which includes shops, boutiques, craft centre, brewery, garden centre, blacksmith and award-winning Caravan & Campsite. *Society Meetings:* most welcome (please book start times at weekends). Professional: Richard Stockdale. Proprietor: Stuart Kirkham.*
website: www.plasseygolf.co.uk

WREXHAM. **Wrexham Golf Club,** Holt Road, Wrexham LL13 9SB (01978 364268; Fax: 01978 362168). *Location*: A543 north east of Wrexham. 18 holes, 6148 yards. S.S.S. 70. Practice facilities. *Green Fees*: weekdays £35.00, weekends and Bank Holidays £40.00. *Eating facilities*: daily. *Visitors*: welcome, subject to competitions and Society bookings. *Society Meetings*: catered for Monday, Wednesday, Thursday and Fridays only. Professional: P. Williams (01978 351476). Secretary: Richard West (01978 364268).

RHUDDLAN GOLF CLUB

Our gently undulating and scenic parkland course is only 25 miles from Chester and less than an hour's drive from Holyhead. We offer a warm welcome, a championship quality course, and full bar and restaurant facilities. Please telephone the Secretary for details of golfing breaks, our many open competitions and good local hotels. Societies must book.

Tel: 01745 590217 (Secretary) • 01745 590898 (Pro)
Fax: 01745 590472
e-mail: secretary@rhuddlangolfclub.co.uk
www.rhuddlangolfclub.co.uk
Meliden Road, Rhuddlan, Denbighshire LL18 6LB

Visit the FHG website
www.holidayguides.com
for details of the wide choice of accommodation featured in the full range of FHG titles

Carmarthenshire

A charming four-star boutique hotel and AA rosette award-winning restaurant set in the beautiful Towy Valley at the foot of the Brecon Beacons. A traditional Welsh welcome, in a warm and relaxed atmosphere with that all important personal touch. En suite rooms equipped with queen sized beds, wireless broadband, sofas and disabled facilities. Gymnasium with the latest state-of-the-art equipment, plus sauna and Jacuzzi.

Visit website to see all our special offers

Rhosmaen, Llandeilo, Carmarthenshire SA19 6NP
Tel: 01558 823 431 • Fax: 01558 823 969
www.ploughrhosmaen.com

THE APPEARANCE OF AN ASTERISK (*) AT THE END OF A CLUB OR COURSE ENTRY INDICATES THAT UP-TO-DATE INFORMATION HAS NOT BEEN SUPPLIED

AMMANFORD. **Glynhir Golf Club,** Glynhir Road, Llandybie, Ammanford SA18 2TF (Tel & Fax: 01269 851365). *Location:* seven miles from end of M4, between Ammanford and Llandybie on the A483. Turn right up Glynhir Road and proceed for about two miles. Undulating wooded parkland course. 18 holes, 6010 yards. S.S.S. 70. *Green Fees:* weekdays £18.00; weekends £23.00. *Eating facilities:* full catering available. *Visitors:* welcome. *Society Meetings:* welcome anytime by prior arrangement with the Secretary (special rates available). Professional: Richard Herbert (01269 851010). Secretary: Mrs Sonia Davis (01269 851365).
e-mail: glynhirgolfclub@tiscali.co.uk
website: www.glynhirgolfclub.co.uk

CARMARTHEN. **Carmarthen Golf Club,** Blaenycoed Road, Carmarthen SA33 6EH (01267 281588). *Location:* four miles north-west of town. Undulating heathland - a good test of golf. 18 holes, 6210 yards. S.S.S. 71. Floodlit covered 8 bay driving range. Venue for the 2007 Welsh Team Championships. *Green Fees:* weekdays £27.50; weekends £32.50. *Eating facilities:* catering available every day. Also for weddings, conferences and parties. *Visitors:* welcome, telephone call advisable at weekends. *Society Meetings:* by arrangement. Professional: Darren Griffiths (Welsh PGA Professional of the Year 2008) (01267 281493). Secretary: Gemma Voaden (01267 281588).
e-mail: info@carmarthengolfclub.co.uk
website: www.carmarthengolfclub.co.uk

CARMARTHEN. **Derllys Court Golf Club,** Llysonnen Road, Bancyfelin, Carmarthen SA33 5DT (Tel & Fax: 01267 211575). *Location:* three miles west of Carmarthen on A40, signposted. Gently undulating parkland. 18 holes, 5650 yards. Practice area. Contact Professional for coaching. *Green Fees*: information not provided. *Eating facilities:* bar/lounge and restaurant. *Visitors:* welcome at all times. *Society Meetings:* welcome by prior arrangement. PGA Professional: Robert Ryder: (07771 902604). Secretary: Rhian Walters.
e-mail: derllys@hotmail.com
website: www.derllyscourtgolfclub.com

THE GOLF GUIDE 2011 — WALES / Carmarthenshire

LLANDYSUL. Saron Golf Course, Penwern, Saron, Llandysul SA44 5EL (01559 370705). *Location*: midway between Carmarthen and Newcastle Emlyn on the A484. Parkland course in the Teifi Valley set in 50 acres. 9 holes (18 tees). 9 holes 2091 yards, 18 holes 4412 yards. *Green Fees*: 9 holes £9.00, under 16s £6.00; 18 holes £12.00, under 16s £8.00. *Visitors*: welcome at all times. Three cottages on course, sleeping six/four/two. *Society Meetings*: welcome. Secretary: C. Searle (01559 370705).
e-mail: c9mbl@sarongolf.freeserve.co.uk
website: www.saron-golf.com

LLANELLI. Ashburnham Golf Club, Cliffe Terrace, Burry Port SA16 0HN (01554 833846). *Location:* south side of A484, four miles west of Llanelli. Seaside links with Championship status. 18 holes. S.S.S. 73. Practice area. *Green Fees:* information not available. *Eating facilities:* catering except Mondays, two bars. *Visitors:* welcome, up to seven days in advance; starting times available from the Pro Shop. Handicap Certificates required. Carts available. *Society Meetings:* by arrangement with Secretary. Professional: Martin Stimson (01554 833846). Secretary: Mr Pritchard (01554 832269).*
e-mail: golf@ashburnhamgolfclub.co.uk
website: www.ashburnhamgolfclub.co.uk

Saron Golf Course
Llandysul, Carmarthenshire

Saron Golf Course is a family-owned pay-and-play parkland course set in 50 acres - 9 holes (18 tees).

Accommodation is available in three barn conversion cottages (sleep 6/4/2) and guests can enjoy a free round of golf. Coarse fishing lake in grounds.

Peaceful location within walking distance of village, with many beaches and coves within a 20 minute drive.

Contact: 01559 370 705 for more details
Penwern, Saron, Llandysul SA44 5EL
www.saron-golf.com

The Ashburnham Hotel, a super convenient base to stay while you play golf at either of the two near 18-hole golf clubs.
- Twelve en suite bedrooms • Restaurant & Bar
- Set in own grounds overlooking the championship Ashburnham golf links (special green fees for residents).
- Jack Nicklaus 18-hole championship golf course at Machynys is only a short distance away.
- Located on the edge of the Millennium Coastal Park.
- Four miles from Ffos Las Racecourse.
- Views of the Gower Peninsula.

Ashburnham Hotel, Ashburnham Road, Pembrey,
Llanelli, Carmarthenshire, South West Wales SA16 0TH
Telephone: 01554 834343 / 834455 • Fax: 01554 834483
e-mail: info@ashburnham-hotel.co.uk • www.ashburnham-hotel.co.uk

Ashburnham Hotel

Other British holiday guides from FHG Guides

PUBS & INNS • 300 GREAT HOTELS • SHORT BREAK HOLIDAYS
The bestselling and original PETS WELCOME! • 500 GREAT PLACES TO STAY
SELF-CATERING HOLIDAYS • BED & BREAKFAST STOPS
CARAVAN & CAMPING HOLIDAYS • FAMILY BREAKS

Published annually: available in all good bookshops or direct from the publisher:
FHG Guides, Abbey Mill Business Centre, Seedhill, Paisley PA1 1TJ
Tel: 0141 887 0428 • Fax: 0141 889 7204
e-mail: admin@fhguides.co.uk • www.holidayguides.com

472 Carmarthenshire / WALES — THE GOLF GUIDE 2011

LLANELLI. Machynys Peninsula Golf and Country Club, Nicklaus Avenue, Machynys, Llanelli SA15 2DG (01554 744888; Fax: 01554 744680). *Location*: M4 J47, take A484, then B4304. 20 minutes from Swansea. Modern links course. 18 holes, 7051 yards, Par 72. Welsh Centre of Excellence. 300m driving range, large chipping green, greenside bunkers and putting green. Tuition packages available. *Green Fees:* information not available. *Eating facilities:* bar and brasserie. *Visitors:* welcome at all times. *Society Meetings:* welcome. Corporate days can be tailored to your needs. Professional: John Peters (01554 744666; Fax: 01554 744680). Golf Operations Manager: Andrew Minty (01554 744666).*
e-mail: golf.pro@machynys.com
andrew.minty@machynys.com

TRIMSARAN. Glyn Abbey Golf Club, Trimsaren SA17 4LB (01554 810278; Fax: 01554 810889). *Location*: five miles north west of Llanelli on the B4317 between Trimsaran and Carway. Parkland course with spectacular views, Hawtree design, mature woodland. 18 holes, 6173 yards, Par 70. S.S.S. 70. *Green Fees*: £20.00 midweek, £25.00 weekends. *Eating facilities*: fully licensed clubhouse and restaurant. *Visitors*: welcome at all times with no restrictions. Advisable to phone ahead and book. *Society Meetings*: always very welcome by prior arrangement. Professional: Mike Davies. Managing Director: Martin Lane
e-mail: info@glynabbey.co.uk
website: www.glynabbey.co.uk
website: www.machynys.com

Best Western Diplomat Hotel
Felinfoel, Llanelli SA15 3PJ
Tel: 01554 756156 • Fax: 01554 751649
AA/WTB ★★★

The Diplomat Hotel offers a rare combination of charm and character, with excellent well appointed facilities to ensure your comfort. Explore the Gower Peninsula and the breathtaking West Wales coastline. Salmon & trout fishing, horse riding, golf, and motor racing at Pembrey are all within reach.
e-mail: reservations@diplomat-hotel-wales.com
www.bw-diplomathotel.co.uk

Glyn Abbey Golf Club
Once regarded as "The Best Kept Secret in Wales", now The Golf Union of Wales' "Welsh Golf Club of the Year". Come and visit us to see why
Societies welcome on Weekends.
Trimsaran, Carmarthenshire SA17 4LB
Tel: 01554 810278 • Fax: 01554 810889 • www.glynabbey.co.uk

PLEASE MENTION THIS GUIDE WHEN YOU ENQUIRE ABOUT CLUBS OR ACCOMMODATION

Ceredigion

ABERYSTWYTH. **Aberystwyth Golf Club,** Brynymor Road, Aberystwyth SY23 2HY (01970 615104; Fax: 01970 626622). *Location:* north end of Promenade, access near to cliff railway. Undulating meadowland designed by Harry Vardon. 18 holes, white - 6119 yards. S.S.S. 71. Par 3. Pay and Play course. Driving range, practice nets. *Green Fees:* information not provided. *Eating facilities:* restaurant and bar. *Visitors:* welcome at all times, pre-booking helpful. *Society Meetings:* welcome, Special Deals available. Professional: (01970 615104). Secretary: (01970 615104).
e-mail: aberystwythgolf@talk21.com
website: www.aberystwythgolfclub.com

THE APPEARANCE OF AN ASTERISK (*) AT THE END OF A CLUB OR COURSE ENTRY INDICATES THAT UP-TO-DATE INFORMATION HAS NOT BEEN SUPPLIED

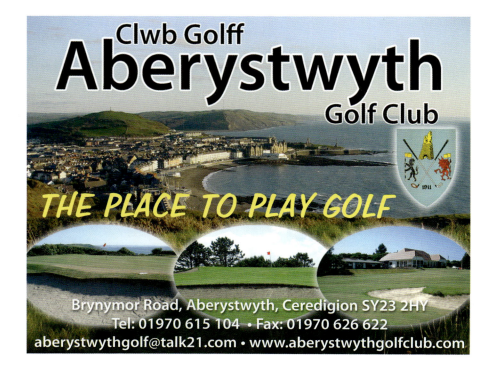

BORTH. Borth and Ynyslas Golf Club Ltd, Borth, Ceredigion SY24 5JS (Tel & Fax: 01970 871202). *Location:* A487 Machynlleth to Aberystwyth, turn off to Borth. Gently undulating links. 18 holes, 6116 yards. S.S.S. 70 men, 72 ladies. Practice ground. *Green Fees:* information not available. *Eating facilities:* clubhouse with full catering and bar. *Visitors:* welcome at all times. *Society Meetings:* by prior arrangement with the Secretary, special rates available. Professional: J.G. Lewis (01970 871557). Secretary: Den York (01970 871202).*
e-mail: secretary@borthgolf.co.uk

CARDIGAN. Cardigan Golf Club, Gwbert-on-Sea, Cardigan SA43 1PR (01239 612035). *Location*: three miles from Cardigan. Seaside links course. 18 holes, 6455 yards. S.S.S. 73. *Green Fees*: information not provided. *Eating facilities*: catering and bar facilities available. *Visitors*: welcome. Tee reserved for members 1pm–2pm. *Society Meetings*: very welcome. Reductions on application. Professional: S. Parsons (01239 615359). Secretary: Mr C. Day (Tel & Fax: 01239 621775).
e-mail: cgc@btconnect.com
website: www.cardigangolf.co.uk

LAMPETER. Cilgwyn Golf Club, Llangybi, Lampeter SA48 8NN (01570 493286). *Location:* five miles north-east of Lampeter, off A485 Tregaron Road at Llangybi. Flat parkland course with natural hazards. 9 holes, 5309 yards, S.S.S. 66. Large practice ground and putting green. *Green Fees:* weekdays £12.00, weekends £17.00. *Eating facilities:* full bar and snacks. *Visitors:* welcome without restrictions – please telephone at weekends April to September. Trolley hire, pool table, TV. Caravan parking and golf for Caravan Club members. *Society Meetings:* welcome Wednesdays and Fridays by prior arrangement. Package deals for parties of six or more. Secretary: J.M. Jones (01570 423226).

LLANDYSUL. Cwmrhydneuadd Golf Club, Pentregat, Plwmp, Llandysul SA44 6HD (01239 654933). *Location:* follow the Aberystwyth to Cardigan A487 trunk road to the village of Pentregat, then follow signs to golf club. Parkland course set in picturesque, secluded valley, surrounded by wooded hills. Includes three small lakes. 9 holes, 4061 yards. S.S.S. 62. *Green Fees*: information not provided. *Eating facilities:* club house; home-made snacks, meals. *Visitors:* welcome, no restrictions. *Society Meetings*: welcome. Secretary: J. Curry (01559 362253).

LLANRHYSTYD. Penrhos Golf and Country Club, Llanrhystyd SY23 5AY (01974 202999; Fax: 01974 202100). *Location:* nine miles south of Aberystwyth on A487. Parkland and meadowland with lakes and panoramic views of the Welsh countryside and Cardiagan Bay. 18 holes, 6641 yards. S.S.S. 73. Floodlit driving range, practice ground, 9 holes Par 3, Par 4. *Green Fees:* from £15.00. *Eating facilities:* bar meals and table d'hôte restaurant. *Visitors:* welcome at all times. Accommodation in en suite hotel on site with full leisure facilities. *Society Meetings:* welcome all week by appointment. Professional: Paul Diamond. Secretary: R. Rees-Evans.
e-mail: info@penrhosgolf.co.uk
website: www.penrhosgolf.co.uk

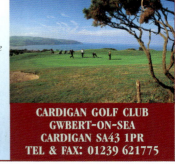

Cardigan Golf Club

One of the finest golf complexes in West Wales, this is a fine championship course, with outstanding views from every hole. It is a mixture of links and meadowland, with exceptional drainage making it playable all year round.

♦ Relaxed, friendly atmosphere
♦ Clubhouse with well-equipped changing rooms
♦ Three squash courts with spectator gallery
♦ Restaurant and comprehensive bar snack menu

Visitors and societies welcome every day by prior arrangement
cgc@btconnect.com • www.cardigangolf.co.uk

**CARDIGAN GOLF CLUB
GWBERT-ON-SEA
CARDIGAN SA43 1PR
TEL & FAX: 01239 621775**

Pembrokeshire

FISHGUARD/HAVERFORDWEST. **Priskilly Forest Golf Club,** Castlemorris, Haverfordwest SA62 5EH (Tel & Fax: 01348 840276). *Location*: A40 Haverfordwest to Fishguard road, left turn at Letterston B4331 towards Mathry. Picturesque undulating parkland surrounded by rhododendrons, etc – a challenging course. 9 holes, 5874 yards. S.S.S. 69. Practice net and ground, trolleys and buggy for hire. *Green Fees*: £14.00 for 9 holes, £20.00 for 18 holes, £24.00 per day. Special winter rates/packages available. *Eating facilities*: licensed bar, catering in restaurant. *Visitors*: a warm welcome is assured. Accommodation with golf inclusive packages on site in 5-Star country house. Buggies for hire £18.00 for 18 holes. *Society Meetings*: welcome. Secretary: P. Evans.
e-mail: jevans@priskilly-forest.co.uk
website: www.priskilly-forest.co.uk

HAVERFORDWEST. **Haverfordwest Golf Club,** Arnolds Down, Haverfordwest SA61 2XQ (01437 763565). *Location:* one mile east of town on A40 trunk road. A parkland course set in Pembrokeshire National Park – challenging but easy walking. 18 holes, 6002 yards. S.S.S. 69. Practice area and putting green. *Green Fees:* contact for current rate. *Eating facilities:* dining room, bar snacks. *Visitors:* welcome. *Society Meetings:* welcome by arrangement. Professional: Alex Pile (01437 768409). Secretary: Mike Foley (01437 764523; Fax: 01437 764143). Full details on our website.
e-mail: haverfordwestgc@btconnect.com
website: www.haverfordwestgolfclub.co.uk

MILFORD HAVEN. **Dawn till Dusk Golf Club**, Furze Hill Farm, Rosemarket, Milford Haven SA73 1JY (01437 890281). *Location*: from Haverfordwest Bypass take A4076 as far as Johnston, turn left, signposted Rosemarket, 1¼ miles to crossroads, turn right, one mile on left side of road. Flat parkland course. 9 holes (18 tees), 6373 yards. S.S.S. 71. Putting green, bunkers. *Green Fees*: information not available. *Visitors*: welcome at all times. *Society Meetings*: welcome, rates negotiable for larger groups. Grass airstrip available, by prior arrangement.*
website: www.dawntilldusk.co.uk

MILFORD HAVEN. **Milford Haven Golf Club Ltd,** Woodbine House, Clay Lane, Hubberston, Milford Haven SA72 3RX (01646 697762). *Location:* one mile west of Milford Haven on Dale Road. Parkland overlooking magnificent harbour. 18 holes, 6035 yards. S.S.S. 70. Practice area. *Green Fees:* information not available. *Eating facilities:* bar and restaurant facilities. *Visitors:* welcome at all times, please ring Pro shop to check availability. *Society Meetings:* welcome, special rates available. Professional: Martin Stimson (01646 697762). Secretary/Administrator: C. Pugh (01646 697822; Fax: 01646 697870).*
e-mail: cerithmhgc@aol.com
website: www.mhgc.co.uk

PEMBROKE DOCK. **South Pembrokeshire Golf Club,** Military Road, Pennar, Pembroke Dock SA72 6SE (01646 621453). *Location*: on headland overlooking Pembroke Dock and The Haven. 18 holes, 6100 yards. S.S.S. 69. Practice facilities. *Green Fees*: information not available. *Eating facilities*: bar, please book for food. *Visitors*: welcome except during club competitions, please telephone. *Society Meetings*: welcome by arrangement.*
e-mail: spgc06@tiscali.co.uk
website: www.southpembsgolf.co.uk

For full details of convenient accommodation near clubs and courses
www.holidayguides.com

Haverfordwest Golf Club
Arnolds Down, Haverfordwest, Pembrokeshire SA61 2XQ

Set near the Pembrokeshire National Park and boasting magnificent views of the Preseli Hills, Haverfordwest Golf Club offers a real challenge to golfers of all abilities. Easily reachable on the A40 one mile east of Haverfordwest, this course is located in majestic parkland, and despite being an easy walk, there are a few holes that test the golfer's skill. The clubhouse, built in 1994, has excellent facilities including pro shop, locker rooms, lounge, bars and full catering facilities.
Full details on our website: www.haverfordwestgolfclub.co.uk

- **Club founded 1904 • 18 holes • Parkland • 6002 yards • Par 70**
  - Societies welcome by arrangement • Green Fee Visitors Welcome • Special Winter Rate Packages
  - Contact: Alex Pile or Mike Foley on 01437 768409 or 01437 764523 • Fax: 01437 764143

TENBY GOLF CLUB
Est 1888

The Burrows, Tenby, Pembrokeshire SA70 7NP

Telephone/Fax: 01834 842978/844447
e-mail: tenbygolfclub@uku.co.uk
website: www.tenbygolf.co.uk

Visiting Golfers and Societies are welcome to play the oldest affiliated course in Wales

Ranked 84th in Golf Monthly Magazine's UK Top 120 Courses

NEWPORT. **Newport Links Golf Club Ltd,** The Golf Club, Golf Course Road, Newport SA42 0NR (01239 820244; Fax: 01239 821338). *Location:* two miles off A487 Cardigan-Fishguard at Newport, Pembrokeshire. Undulating seaside links course with breathtaking views over the mountains and bay. 18 holes, 6110 yards. S.S.S. 69. Driving range. *Green Fees:* £35.00. *Eating facilities:* full catering and bar facilities available. *Visitors:* welcome, tee times must be booked and Handicap Certificate may be required; Pro shop and buggy hire. 12 fabulous twin bedrooms and 3 luxury suites. *Society Meetings:* welcome, please phone Operations Manager (01239 820244). Professional: Alun Evans (01239 820244). Operations Manager: Amanda Payne (01239 820244).
e-mail: newportgc@lineone.net
website: www.newportlinks.co.uk

ST DAVIDS. **St Davids City Golf Club,** Whitesands Bay, St Davids SA62 6PT (01437 721751). *Location:* follow signs to Whitesands Bay, on Fishguard Road out of St Davids, for two miles. Car park is situated on crossroads with club sign at entrance. If you reach the beach you've gone too far! Seaside links course with spectacular panoramic views over Whitesands Bay and St David's Head. 9 holes, 6117 yards. S.S.S. 70. *Green Fees:* £18.00 for 18 holes. *Visitors:* welcome at all times but please check at weekends and Bank Holidays; Ladies' Day Friday afternoons, Seniors' Day Thursday afternoon. *Society Meetings:* welcome, book with Secretary (01437 721751).

TENBY. **Tenby Golf Club,** The Burrows, Tenby SA70 7NP. *Location:* on A478, near Tenby Railway Station. Seaside links, Championship course, oldest affiliated club in Wales. 18 holes, 6224 yards. S.S.S. 71. Practice ground. *Green Fees:* midweek £25.00-£45.00, weekends £26.00-£50.00. *Eating facilities:* complete dining facilities; licensed bar. *Visitors:* always welcome, subject to club competitions. Handicap Certificate required. Billiards rooms. *Society Meetings:* catered for by advance booking. Professional: Rhys Harry PGA (01834 844447). Secretary: D. Hancock (Tel & Fax: 01834 842978).
e-mail: tenbygolfclub@uku.co.uk
website: www.tenbygolf.co.uk

TENBY. **Trefloyne Golf Club,** Trefloyne Park, Penally, Tenby SA70 7RG (01834 842165). *Location:* on edge of village of Penally, just off A4139 Tenby/Pembroke road, about one mile from Tenby. Stunnng parkland course. Men's course - 18 holes, 6398 yards, S.S.S. yellow tees 72, white 73, Par 72. Ladies' course - 18 holes, 5754 yards, S.S.S. 74, Par 74. Practice ground. *Green Fees:* information not provided. *Eating facilities:* full restaurant and bar service, with breakfast and snack menu. *Visitors:* always welcome. *Society Meetings:* all welcome. Full equipment hire, clubs, trolleys and motorised buggies. Accommodation (5 en suite twin/double rooms on site in 4 star Manor house. Club Professional: Oliver Duckett (01834 845639). Manager/Secretary: Sarah Knight (01834 842165).
e-mail: sarah@trefloyne,com
website: www.trefloyne.com

A traditional links course located on the beautiful Pembrokeshire coast, overlooking Newport Bay and the Preseli Hills.

The 18-hole course was founded in 1925 by five times Open Champion, James Braid. Accommodation available in 12 fabulous twin bedrooms and three luxury suites.

Visitors and societies always receive a warm welcome.

Stunning **parkland** golf near Tenby

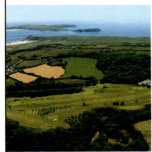

Tenby's Trefloyne golf course hides behind the resort in quiet countryside and gives you
18 holes of breathtaking views and challenging golf
with the warmest of welcomes at the 19th
in a bar and restaurant serving lunch and a very special la carte dinner menu

**Golf breaks in luxury accommodation
from just £50 per person per night *including* the golf!**

www.trefloyne.com

Pro-shop: 01834 845639   open daily from 9.00am   Accommodation: 01834 842165
Trefloyne Lane, Penally, Tenby, Pembrokeshire SA70 7RG

Powys

BRECON. **Brecon Golf Club,** Newton Park, Brecon LD3 8PA (01874 622004). *Location:* A40 west of town, half a mile from town centre. Flat parkland course. 9 holes, 6068 yards. S.S.S. 70, Par 70. *Green Fees:* information not provided. *Eating facilities:* bars and catering available. *Visitors:* welcome, some restriction Sundays when prior arrangement advisable. *Society Meetings:* by arrangement. Secretary: I. Chambers (01874 622004).
e-mail: info@brecongolfclub.co.uk
website: www.brecongolfclub.co.uk

BUILTH WELLS. **Builth Wells Golf Club,** Golf Links Road, Builth Wells LD2 3NF (01982 553296). *Location:* off A483, on outskirts of town on Llandovery Road. Parkland, easy walking. 18 holes. S.S.S. 66. Practice area. Host to the 2005 PGA Welsh Young Professionals Championship. *Green Fees:* £24.00 per round, £32.00 per day weekdays; £27.00 per round, £34.00 per day weekends and Bank Holidays. Three-day ticket £60.00, Five-day ticket £110.00. 2010 rates (subject to review). *Eating facilities:* catering all day. *Visitors:* welcome. *Society Meetings:* welcome, Handicap Certificate required. Professional/Secretary: Simon Edwards (01982 553296).
e-mail: info@builthwellsgolf.co.uk
website: www.builthwellsgolf.co.uk

CRADOC. **Cradoc Golf Club,** Penoyre Park, Cradoc, Brecon LD3 9LP (01874 623658; Fax: 01874 611711). *Location:* about two miles north of the market town of Brecon, off B4520 Upper Chapel Road (signposted) past Brecon Cathedral. Attractive parkland course adjoining the Brecon Beacons National Park, scenic views. 18 holes, 6188 yards. S.S.S. 71. (off back tees) 10-bay floodlit driving range. Welsh Golf Club of the Year 2005. Home of the Coors Champion of Champions Tournament. *Green Fees:* weekdays £28.00 per day, weekends and Bank Holidays £34.00 per day. *Eating facilities:* full catering facilities daily. *Visitors:* welcome daily but restricted on Sundays. Electric trolley/buggy hire. *Society Meetings:* welcome any day; prior arrangement advised especially for Sundays. Special packages available. Professional: R.W. Davies (01874 625524). Club Manager: Robert Southcott (01874 623658).
e-mail: secretary@cradoc.co.uk
manager@cradoc.co.uk
website: www.cradoc.co.uk

CRICKHOWELL. **Old Rectory Hotel and Golf Club,** Llangattock, Crickhowell NP8 1PH (01873 810373). *Location:* A40 to Crickhowell. Course is on a hill with spectacular views. 9 holes, 2878 yards. S.S.S. 54. *Green Fees:* information not available. *Eating facilities:* restaurant, bar meals, two bars. *Visitors:* welcome at all times, no restrictions. Accommodation available in 20 en suite bedrooms. *Society Meetings:* welcome. Secretary: G. Crawford.*

KNIGHTON. **Knighton Golf Club,** The Ffrydd, Knighton LD7 1DL (01547 528646). *Location:* on the A488 to Llandrindod Wells, signposted. Undulating wooded hill course with spectacular views. 9 holes, 5362 yards. S.S.S. 66. *Green Fees:* weekdays £10.00; weekends £15.00, discounts of £5.00 off day rate if playing with a member. *Eating facilities:* bar, meals available; contact Steward (01547 528646). *Visitors:* welcome, no visitors before 4.30pm on Sundays. *Society Meetings:* catered for by prior arrangement. Secretary: D. B. Williams (01547 528046).

LLANDRINDOD WELLS. **Llandrindod Wells Golf Club,** The Clubhouse, Llandrindod Wells LD1 5NY (01597 823873). *Location:* signposted off A483 at south east of town. An 'Inland Links' course set in the rolling hills of mid Wales and patrolled by Red Kites and Buzzards. 18 holes, Men 5759 yards white, 5543 yards yellow, Par 69. Ladies 5143 yards, Par 72. Floodlit driving range. *Green Fees:* information not available. *Eating facilities:* full catering daily except Tuesdays when bar snacks only available, two bars. *Visitors:* welcome at all times, no restrictions. Buggy, trolley hire. *Society Meetings:* welcome any day, booking essential. Golf Shop: (01597 822247). Secretary: (Tel & Fax: 01597 823873).*
e-mail: secretary@lwgc.co.uk
website: www.lwgc.co.uk

LLANIDLOES. **St Idloes Golf Club,** Penrallt, Llanidloes SY18 6LG (01686 412559). *Location:* signposted from the town. Take road to Trefeglwys from Llanidloes for one mile, turn left at sharp bend before house. Heathland and elevated course. 9 holes, 5510 yards. S.S.S. 66. Practice putting area. *Green Fees:* information not available. *Eating facilities:* Bar snacks available during opening hours, full meals by arrangement for large group, please phone first. *Visitors:* welcome anytime except Sunday mornings or special competitions. *Society Meetings:* welcome, packages available. Please ring the clubhouse.*

MACHYNLLETH. **Machynlleth Golf Club,** Felingerrig, Machynlleth SY20 8UH (01654 702000). *Location:* A489 from Newtown, left hand turn before the speed restriction sign on entering Machynlleth. Undulating moorland course. 9 holes, 5726 yards, 5285 metres. S.S.S. 68. Small practice area. *Green Fees:* £15.00 per day. *Eating facilities:* bar. *Visitors:* welcome except during competition days. *Society Meetings:* welcome.
e-mail: machgolf2@tiscali.co.uk
website: www.machynllethgolf.co.uk

Builth Wells Golf Club

The Club House
Golf Club Road, Builth Wells, Powys LD2 3NF
Tel: 01982 553296
www.builthwellsgolf.co.uk
e-mail: info@builthwellsgolf.co.uk

2010 GREEN FEES
- £24.00 per round, £32.00 per day weekdays • £27.00 per round, £34.00 per day weekends and Bank Holidays • Three-day ticket £60.00 • Five-day ticket £110.00
Prices are subject to increase

Cradoc Golf Club
Penoyre Park, Cradoc,
Brecon, Powys LD3 9LP
Tel: (01874) 623658
Fax: (01874) 611711
secretary@cradoc.co.uk

www.cradoc.co.uk

Cradoc Golf Club is situated alongside the spectacularly beautiful scenery of the Brecon Beacons National Park, just 2 miles outside Brecon and just a 45 minute drive from Celtic Manor, the venue of the 2010 Ryder Cup. It is an 18 hole parkland course, 6188 yards, Par 71.

In addition to providing a very enjoyable test of golf, Cradoc also offers excellent practice facilities including a 10 bay floodlit covered driving range, a double teaching bay, and an adjacent two-acre chipping and bunker practice area. The Clubhouse provides well appointed changing and shower facilities. There is a comfortable lounge area with a well stocked bar and a restaurant offering an extensive menu.

Cradoc offers a warm and friendly welcome to all visitors and societies, and the experienced staff will do everything possible to make your visit a truly enjoyable event.

BRECON CASTLE

In the heart of the Brecon Beacons National Park and ideal for a wide range of outdoor activities.

Brecon Castle is an historic coaching inn of great charm and character with the tower and Great Hall of the Medieval Castle located within its grounds. There are 37 bedrooms all en suite, with LCD TV, WiFi and tea/coffee facilities. There is an excellent bar and restaurant serving modern and traditional dishes all freshly prepared using the best of locally sourced meat, fish and Welsh cheeses.

Holistic and Beauty treatments are available within the hotel. Concession rates can be arranged for Cradoc Golf Club, one of the finest parkland courses in Mid Wales, and there is an array of other courses in the vicinity.

Brecon Castle Hotel, Castle Square, Brecon, Powys LD3 9DB
Tel : 01874 624611 • Fax : 01874 623737
www . breconcastle . co . uk

Llandrindod Wells Golf Club
Established 1905   Designed by Harry Vardon

The Clubhouse
Llandrindod Wells,
Powys LD1 5NY

Golf with a view...

Offering breathtaking views over the beautiful Mid Wales mountains. Every one of the 18 holes has a different character, with natural undulating fairways that offer a 'links type' golfing experience. Please contact us for details of our golfing breaks, open competitions and local hotels.
Full Bar and Catering • Floodlit Driving Range • Buggies Available • Society Packages
Tel/Fax 01597 823873 • e-mail: secretary@lwgc.co.uk • www.lwgc.co.uk

MACHYNLLETH GOLF CLUB

- Undulating heathland course   • 9 holes, 5726 yards, 5285 metres. S.S.S. 68.
- 3-hole Par 3 course   • Visitors welcome   • Societies & Groups welcome
- Bar meals available in clubhouse all year round.

Newtown Road, Machynlleth SY20 8UH • Tel: 01654 702000

e-mail: machgolf2@tiscali.co.uk
www.machynllethgolf.co.uk

Welshpool Golf Club

Welshpool Golf Club is a James Braid designed mountain top golf course located on the Golfa hilltops outside Welshpool, with breathtaking scenery like no other. With its stunning views and 18 full holes, the club is sure to be both a treat and a test for all abilities of golfer, providing year round play with no temporary greens during the winter months.
The clubhouse offers both a relaxing atmosphere and quality food.
Group packages including golf and food from £23.50 (min. 4 players).
2010 green fees: £20.00 weekday and winter weekend; £30.00 summer weekend.

Y Golfa, Welshpool SY21 9AQ
Tel: 01938 850249
e-mail: welshpool.golfclub@btconnect.com
www.welshpoolgolfclub.co.uk

NEWTOWN. **St Giles Golf Club,** Pool Road, Newtown SY16 3AJ (01686 625844). *Location:* convenient to town centre, quarter-of-a-mile north east on A483 from Newtown. Challenging riverside course. 9 holes, 6012 yards. S.S.S. 70. *Green Fees:* information not available. *Visitors:* welcome, with reservation Saturday afternoons and Sunday mornings. *Society Meetings:* catered for.*

RHOSGOCH. **Rhosgoch Golf Club,** Rhosgoch, Near Hay-on-Wye, Builth Wells LD2 3JY (01497 851251). *Location:* 6 miles north west of Hay-on-Wye, half-a-mile south east of the B4594. Parkland course in beautiful picturesque valley. 9 holes, 4955 yards, Par 68. S.S.S. 66. *Green Fees:* information not available. *Eating facilities:* bar /restaurant meals. *Visitors:* welcome anytime. *Society Meetings:* welcome weekdays and Saturdays. Club Steward: Norman Lloyd. Secretary: Chris Dance.*
website: www.rhosgoch-golf.co.uk

WELSHPOOL. **Welsh Border Golf Club,** Bulthy Farm, Middletown, Welshpool SY21 8ER (01743 884247). *Location:* situated off the A458. Parkland course. 9 holes (x2), 6114 yards. S.S.S. 68. Driving range. *Green Fees:* £10.00 for 9 holes, £16.00 for 18 holes on our Long Course. *Eating facilities:* lunchtime only unless otherwise arranged. *Visitors:* welcome, tee times must be booked. *Society Meetings:* welcome by prior arrangement. Secretary: Keith Farr (0796 653 0042).

WELSHPOOL. **Welshpool Golf Club,** Y Golfa, Golfa Hill, Welshpool SY21 9AQ (01938 850249). *Location:* A458 out of Welshpool, approximately three and a half to four miles on right. Mountain top golf course with spectacular views. 18 holes, 5708 yards. S.S.S. 69. *Green Fees:* £20.00 weekday and winter weekend; £30.00 summer weekend. *Eating facilities:* open most of the day for food and drink. *Visitors:* welcome, some weekend restrictions. Buggies available. *Society Meetings:* welcome by arrangement. Contact Secretary: Teresa Wright.

Builth Wells Golf Club, Powys

South Wales

ABERDARE. **Aberdare Golf Club,** Abernant, Aberdare CF44 0RY (01685 871188; Fax: 01685 872797). *Location:* half a mile from town centre. Mountain course with parkland features and view of whole Cynon Valley. 18 holes, 5875 yards. S.S.S. 69. *Green Fees:* weekdays £17.00, (with member £10.00); weekends and Bank Holidays £21.00, (with member £12.00). *Eating facilities:* bar, lounge and dining room. *Visitors:* welcome without reservation weekdays (see Professional). Saturdays and Sundays by prior arrangement with Secretary. Handicap Certificates required. Snooker room, and changing room. *Society Meetings:* catered for by prior arrangement with Secretary. Secretary: Tony Mears (01685 872797).

ABERGAVENNY. **Monmouthshire Golf Club,** Llanfoist, Abergavenny NP7 9HE. *Location*: two miles from A465 on Llanfoist-Llanellen Road (B4269). Parkland with scenic mountain views. 18 holes, 5747 yards. S.S.S. 70. Practice ground. *Green Fees:* weekdays £30.00, weekends £35.00 per 18 holes. *Eating facilities:* bar snacks available, evening meals by arrangement. *Visitors*: welcome. *Society Meetings:* catered for by arrangement. Professional: Brian Edwards (Tel & Fax: 01873 852532). Secretary: H.C. Sobik (01873 852606; Fax: 01873 850470).
e-mail: monmouthshiregc@btconnect.com
website: www.monmouthshiregolfclub.co.uk

ABERGAVENNY. **Wernddu Golf Club,** Old Ross Road, Abergavenny NP7 8NG (01873 856223; Fax: 01873 852177). *Location:* one and a half miles east of Abergavenny on B4521 (off A465). Sloping, well drained site with pond hazards on four holes and magnificent views. 18 holes, 5215 yards off yellow. S.S.S. 68. 22- bay covered floodlit driving range, 9 hole pitch and putt, practice putting and bunker area. *Green Fees:* £18.00 per 18 holes. *Eating facilities:* lounge bar, light snacks. *Visitors:* welcome. *Societies:* welcome. Professional: Tina Tetley (Ladies European Tour) (01873 856223; Fax: 01873 852177). Secretary: Lyn Turvey (01495 308161).
e-mail: info@wernddu-golf-club.co.uk
website: www.wernddu-golf-club.co.uk

BARGOED. **Bargoed Golf Club,** Heolddu, Bargoed CF81 9GF (01443 830143). *Location:* A469 to Bargoed town centre - Moorland Road. Flat mountain top course. 18 holes, 6210 yards. S.S.S. 70. Practice area, nets, etc. *Green Fees:* information not available. *Eating facilities:* full catering and bar. *Visitors:* welcome, only with member at weekends, no other restrictions. *Society Meetings:* catered for weekdays only by prior arrangement. Professional: C Easton (01443 836179).*

The Monmouthshire Golf Club
Founded 1892
A superb example of a mature parkland course, popular with golfers of all ages and abilities.
♦ Comfortable lounge and dining area ♦ Friendly clubhouse
♦ Pro Shop with top-brand equipment
♦ Expert tuition: practice area and indoor academy
♦ Societies and visitors welcome by prior arrangement.

Please telephone C. Sobik 01873 852606 • Fax: 01873 850470
Llanfoist, Abergavenny, Monmouthshire NP7 9HE
www.monmouthshiregolfclub.co.uk

Wernddu Golf Club
Open to all visitors
18 Hole Golf Course • Driving Range
Adults only Caravan Park • Snacks • Bar
Ring for Special Society Packages

Old Ross Road, Abergavenny, Monmouthshire NP7 8NG
Tel: 01873 856223 • Fax: 01873 852177
e-mail: info@wernddu-golf-club.co.uk
www.wernddu-golf-club.co.uk

BARRY. Brynhill (Barry) Golf Club, Port Road East, Colcot, Barry CF62 8PN (01446 720377). *Location:* leave M4 at Junction 33 (A4232), follow signs for Barry and Cardiff (Wales) Airport onto the A4050. Club on right of road, just before a roundabout. Challenging, undulating meadowland course. 18 holes, 6352 yards. S.S.S. 71. Par 72. *Green Fees:* information not provided. *Eating facilities:* Dean, our caterer, extends a warm welcome, and will provide lunches between 12 noon and 2pm, and dinner from 5pm. Your order prior to playing is requested. *Visitors:* welcome, except Sundays; must produce membership card and Handicap Certificate. *Society Meetings:* by arrangement with Secretary – no Sundays, must be members of a golf club. Competitive rates available. Professional: Duncan Prior (01446 720277). Secretary: Rita Cook (01446 720277; Fax: 01446 740422).
e-mail: postbox@brynhillgolfclub.co.uk
website: www.brynhillgolfclub.co.uk

BARRY. RAF St Athan Golf Club, Clive Road, St Athan CF62 4JD (01446 751043). *Location:* eight miles from Barry, turn right through St. Athan Village. Parkland. 9 holes, 6452 yards. S.S.S. 72. Practice area and nets. *Green Fees:* information not available. *Eating facilities:* available. *Visitors:* welcome except Sundays, telephone for information. *Society Meetings:* apply through the Secretary. Secretary: P.F. Woodhouse (01446 751043; Fax: 01446 751862).*

BARRY. St Andrews Major Golf Club, Coldbrook Road East, Near Cadoxton, Barry CF63 1BL (01446 722227; Fax: 01446 748953). *Location:* off Barry Docks Link Road, Junction 33 M4. Flat parkland course with excellent greens, full 18 holes, 5500 yards, Par 69. 12-bay floodlit driving range open 7.30am to 9.30am. *Green Fees:* £18.00 weekdays, £20.00 weekends. Full membership packages available to cater for all needs. *Eating facilities:* restaurant and snacks; full bar facilities, specialise in large functions up to 150 people, weddings, birthdays etc. *Visitors:* welcome anytime, but advisable to ring for bookings (especially at weekends). *Society Meetings:* we specialise in society meetings, special packages available on request. Contact Andrew Edmunds.
e-mail: info@standrewsmajorgolfclub.com
website: www.standrewsmajorgolfclub.com

BLACKWOOD. Blackwood Golf Club, Cwmgelli, Blackwood NP12 1BR (01495 222121/223152). *Location:* quarter of a mile north of Blackwood on A4048. 9 holes, 5350 yards. S.S.S. 67. *Green Fees:* £20.00 weekday; £15.00 with member; £15.00 with County Card. *Visitors:* welcome weekdays only. *Society Meetings:* by arrangement. Secretary: J. Bills (01495 222121 or 223152).

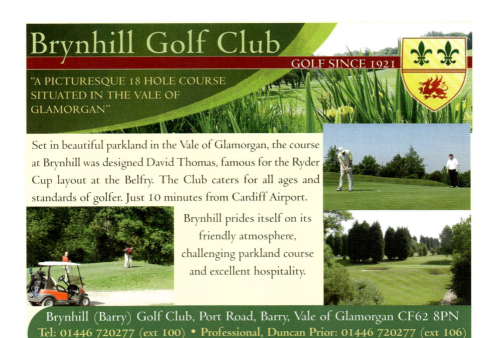

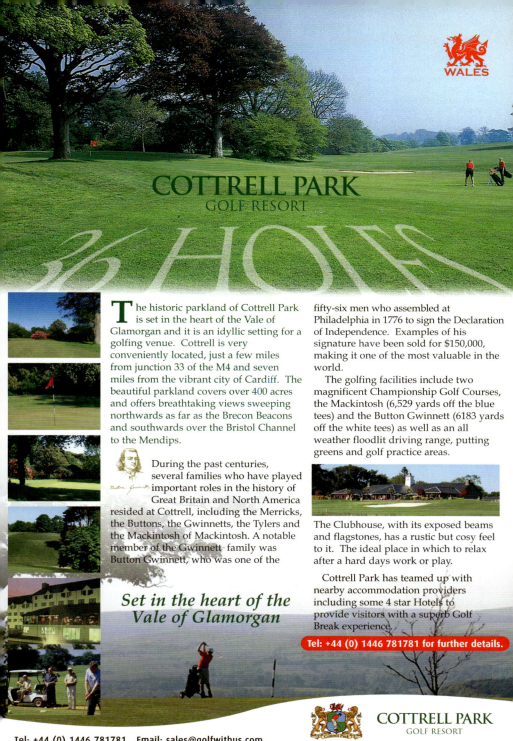

BRIDGEND. Coed-y-Mwstwr Golf Club, The Clubhouse, Coychurch, Bridgend CF31 6AF (01656 862121; Fax: 01656 864934). *Location:* Junction 35 M4, A473 towards Bridgend. Turn right into Coychurch. Parkland, south facing. 18 holes, 5703 yards. Par 69. Practice nets, putting green and chipping area. *Green Fees:* from £20.00. *Eating facilities:* bar meals and snacks. *Visitors:* members' guests only on Saturdays. *Society Meetings:* by prior arrangement. Secretary: (Tel & Fax: 01656 864934).
website: www.coed-y-mwstwr.co.uk

CAERLEON. **Caerleon Public Golf Course,** The Broadway, Caerleon, Newport NP18 1AY (01633 420342). *Location:* three miles off M4 at turnoff for Caerleon. Flat parkland. 9 holes, 3000 yards. S.S.S. 34 yellow, 35 white. Driving range, putting green, new Junior Academy course. *Green Fees:* information not available. *Eating facilities:* bar, light meals (kitchen facilities) available all day. *Visitors:* welcome. *Society Meetings:* welcome. PGA Teaching Professional: Joe Pritchard. Secretary: S. Dennis (01633 420342).*

CAERPHILLY. **Caerphilly Golf Club,** Pencapel, Mountain Road, Caerphilly CF83 1HJ (029 2088 3481). *Location:* seven miles north of Cardiff on A469, 250 yards south of both railway and bus stations. Situated opposite Magistrates' Court. Mountainside course with undulating features and wooded areas. 18 holes, 5728 yards (white tees). S.S.S. 69. Limited practice facilities. *Green Fees:* information not available. *Eating facilities:* member' and guests' bar, ladies' lounge, mixed lounge and dining room. *Visitors:* welcome weekdays (not Bank Holidays); weekends with member only. *Society Meetings:* most welcome; society packages on request. Professional: James Lee (029 2086 9104). Secretary: Roger Chaffey (029 2086 3441).*
e-mail: secretary@caerphillygolfclub.com
website: www.caerphillygolfclub.com

CAERPHILLY. **Castell Heights Golf Club,** Blaengwynlais, Caerphilly CF83 1NG (029 2088 6686). *Location:* 5 minutes from Junction 32 on M4. Flat parkland, many trees. 9 holes, 2688 yards. *Green Fees:* information not available. *Eating facilities:* snacks, lunches and afternoon tea available. *Visitors:* welcome anytime, only members can book times. Secretary: Gareth Richards (029 2086 1128; Fax: 029 2086 9030).*

CAERPHILLY. **Mountain Lakes Golf Club,** Blaengwynlais, Caerphilly CF83 1NG (029 2086 1128). *Location:* take exit 32, M4. Last exit of roundabout "Tongwynlais", right at Lewis Arms, past Castell Coch, three miles up road on left. Part parkland, part wooded, undulating. 20 water hazards, large penncross greens. 18 holes, 6500 yards. S.S.S. 73. *Green Fees:* information not available. *Visitors:* welcome at all times but must have registered Handicap. *Society Meetings:* welcome at all times but must book. Professional: Sion Bebb (029 2088 6666). Director of Golf: P. Page (029 2086 1128; Fax 029 2086 9030).*

CAERPHILLY. **Ridgeway Golf Club,** Thornhill, Caerphilly CF83 1LY (029 2088 2255). *Location:* driving out of Cardiff towards Caerphilly over Caerphilly mountains, take first left after Traveller's Pub. Mountain course but not too steep. 9 holes, 2314 yards. S.S.S. 65. Driving range. *Green Fees:* information not provided. *Eating facilities:* bar with snacks available. *Visitors:* welcome. *Society Meetings:* weekdays only by arrangement. Professionals: P. Johnson/R. Johnson. Secretary: Tim James.
e-mail: petethepro@tiscali.co.uk

CAERPHILLY. **Virginia Park Golf Club,** Virginia Park, Caerphilly CF83 3SW (029 2086 3919). *Location:* off Pontygwindy Road, near Caerphilly recreation centre. Flat parkland, Easy walking but challenging. 9 holes, 4661 yards, S.S.S. 63. 20 bay covered, floodlit, driving range. Practice putting green. *Green Fees*: information not available. *Eating facilities:* catering available every day. *Visitors:* welcome but must observe dress code. Function room. *Society Meetings:* telephone bookings. Members' Secretary: Graham Taylor (02920 863919).*

CARDIFF. **Cardiff Golf Club,** Sherborne Avenue, Cyncoed, Cardiff CF23 6SJ (029 2075 3320). *Location:* two miles north of city centre or M4, A48 or A48M from east to Pentwyn exit on Eastern Avenue, and take Pentwyn Industrial Road to top of hill at Cyncoed Village, turn left at Spar shop into Sherborne Avenue. Undulating parkland, all greens bunkered. 18 holes. S.S.S. 70. *Green Fees:* £50.00. *Eating facilities:* catering and bars available from 11am every day. *Visitors:* welcome; Saturdays must play with a member. *Society Meetings*: by arrangement - dining facility for up to 130 people. Professional: Terry Hanson (029 2075 4772). Secretary: Kenvyn Newling (029 2075 3320; Fax: 029 2068 0011).

Mike and Sue welcome you to their 17 bedroom motel, with all rooms en suite and non-smoking. Facilities include squash court, Sky TV in all rooms, and bar meals served 12-2pm and 6-9pm, à la carte from 6-9pm; Sunday lunch available.

**From £39 single room per night,
from £49 double room per night.
All prices inclusive of breakfast and VAT.**
(subject to slight increase). All bedrooms non-smoking.

111 Heol Fach, North Cornelly, Near Bridgend, South Wales CF33 4LH
Tel: 01656 743041/744707 • Fax: 01656 744208

CARDIFF. **Cottrell Park Golf Resort,** St Nicholas, Cardiff CF5 6SJ (01446 781781; Fax: 01446 781187). *Location*: four miles west of Cardiff on A48 main road. Two parkland courses. Driving range (20 bays) - Clubhouse. Two courses: Mackintosh – 18 holes, 6313 yards off white tees. S.S.S. 70; Button – 18 holes, 6183 yards off white tees. S.S.S. 70. *Green Fees*: on application. *Eating facilities*: all day. *Visitors*: welcome anytime. Professionals: various PGA Qualified Professionals.
e-mail: sales@golfwithus.com
website: www.golfwithus.com

CARDIFF. **Creigiau Golf Club,** Llantwit Road, Creigiau, Cardiff CF15 9NN (029 2089 0263). *Location:* seven miles north-west of Cardiff, two miles off A4199, M4 Junction 34 two miles. 18 holes, 6063 yards. S.S.S. 70 (Par 71). Limited practice facilities. *Green Fees:* information not provided. *Eating facilities:* bars and full catering available. *Visitors:* welcome weekdays except Tuesdays, prior phone call requested; weekends with members only. Must hold Handicap Certificate. *Society Meetings:* catered for by prior arrangement (maximum 40). Professional: Ian Luntz (029 2089 0263). Secretary: (029 2089 0263; Fax: 029 2089 0706). Caterer: (029 2089 0263).
e-mail: creigiaugolfclub@btconnect.com
website: www.creigiaugolfclub.co.uk

CARDIFF. **Llanishen Golf Club,** Heol Hir, Cardiff CF14 9UD (029 2075 5078). *Location*: five miles north of Cardiff city centre. Established in 1905, a parkland course situated on the hillside with panoramic views of the city, the Bristol Channel and Somerset coastline. The course is not long, but presents a challenge to all Handicap players. Following an extensive 3 year drainage project, all 18 greens have been drained and provide a much drier golfing experience in wet conditions. Fully stocked Professional shop. 18 holes, 5301 yards, 4847 metres. S.S.S. 67, Par 68. *Green Fees:* £25.00 weekday; £30.00 weekend. Handicap Certificate required. *Eating facilities:* club bar, lounge bar, restaurant with magnificent views. *Visitors:* welcome. S*ociety Meetings:* welcome most weekdays, and Sundays. Full sized snooker table. Professional: Adrian Jones (029 2075 5076). Manager: Colin Duffield.
e-mail: secretary.llanishengc@virgin.net
website: www.llanishengc.co.uk

CARDIFF. **St Mellons Golf Club,** St Mellons, Cardiff CF3 2XS (01633 680408; Fax: 01633 681219). *Location*: Junctions 28 and 30 of M4 to A48 between Cardiff and Newport. 70-year-old parkland course. 18 holes, 6225 yards. S.S.S. 70. *Green Fees*: telephone for special rates. *Visitors*: welcome by arrangement. *Society Meetings*: catered for on written or telephone application. Professional: Barry Thomas (01633 680101). Office: (01633 680408; Fax: 01633 681219).*
website: www.stmellonsgolfclub.co.uk

St Mellons Golf Club (1964) Ltd
St Mellons, Cardiff CF3 2XS

Tel: 01633 680408
www.stmellonsgolfclub.co.uk

Opened in 1937, designed by H.S. Colt, St Mellons Golf Club became a members' club in 1964 and is a lovely parkland course situated on the eastern edge of Cardiff.
The course provides a pleasant walk with occasional views of the Bristol Channel.
The course is very well laid out and provides one of the best tests of golf in South Wales.

486 South Wales / WALES — THE GOLF GUIDE 2011

CARDIFF. **Peterstone Lakes Golf Club,** Peterstone, Wentloog, Cardiff CF3 2TN (01633 680009; Fax: 01633 680563). *Location:* in between Newport and Cardiff off the A48 at Castleton. Parkland/links course bordering the Bristol Channel. 18 holes, 6555 yards. S.S.S. 72. Indoor teaching academy. *Green Fees*: from £12.00. *Eating facilities:* lounge bar, Crystal Suite. *Visitors:* welcome, strongly recommend telephone enquiry for a tee time. *Society Meetings:* welcome. Professional: Paul Glynn (01633 680075; Fax: 01633 680563).

CARDIFF. **Radyr Golf Club,** Drysgol Road, Radyr, Cardiff CF15 8BS (029 2084 2408). *Location:* Junction 32 M4, A470 to Merthyr Tydfil, first exit. Parkland course. 18 holes, 6015 yards. S.S.S. 70. *Green Fees:* information not available. *Eating facilities:* snacks, lunches and evening meals. *Visitors:* welcome. *Society Meetings:* catered for Mondays, Wednesdays and Thursdays only. Professional: Simon Swales (029 2084 2476; Fax: 029 2084 3914). Club Manager: Sarah Rodgers (029 2084 2408; Fax: 029 2084 3914).*
e-mail: manager@radyrgolf.co.uk

CARDIFF. **Wenvoe Castle Golf Club,** Wenvoe, Near Cardiff CF5 6BE (029 2059 1094; Fax: 029 2059 4371). *Location*: exit Junction 33 M4, follow signs for Cardiff Airport. Parkland course founded in 1936, hosted first PGA Welsh Classic. 18 holes, 6544 yards. S.S.S. 72. Practice areas. *Green Fees:* information not provided. *Eating facilities:* bar snacks and restaurant meals. *Visitors:* welcome weekdays and weekends. *Society Meetings:* catered for weekdays only, parties of 16 or more. Professional: Jason D. Harris (029 2059 3649). Secretary: Nicola Sims (Tel & Fax: 029 2059 4371).
e-mail: wenvoecastle@btconnect.com
website: www.wenvoecastlegolfclub.co.uk

CARDIFF. **Whitchurch (Cardiff) Golf Club,** Pantmawr Road, Whitchurch, Cardiff CF14 7TD (029 2062 0985). *Location*: three miles north west of Cardiff on A470, 600 metres Junction 32 M4. Parkland, undulating and easy walking with panoramic views of Cardiff. A championship course with Ian Woosnam holding course record of 62. 18 holes - white tees 6278 yards. S.S.S. 71. Practice facilities. *Green Fees*: £50.00 per day weekdays; £60.00 per day weekends and Bank Holidays (limited availability). *Eating facilities*: restaurant and bars. *Visitors*: welcome, please phone first. Trolleys for hire. *Society Meetings*: catered for by arrangement with Club Manager. Professional: Rhys Davies (029 2061 4660). Club Manager: Graham Perrott (029 2062 0985; Fax: 029 2052 9890).
e-mail: secretary@whitchurchcardiffgolfclub.com
website: www.whitchurchcardiffgolfclub.com

Please mention THE GOLF GUIDE when you enquire about clubs or accommodation

CHEPSTOW. **Dewstow Golf Club,** Caerwent, Monmouthshire NP26 5AH (01291 430444; Fax: 01291 425816). *Location*: off A48 at Caerwent, between Chepstow and Newport, five miles from the Old Severn Bridge. Two 18-hole parkland courses, special features include Totem pole, Ekki bridge, 26-bay golf range. The Valley Course–Par 72, 6100 yards, The Park Course–6200 yards. *Green Fees*: information not available. *Eating facilities*: restaurant, function rooms and bar snacks available all day. *Visitors*: welcome at all times. Trolley and buggy hire in season. *Society Meetings*: Society and corporate days are our speciality. Bookings and information: Emma Corner (01291 430444). Professional: Steve Truman. Golf Secretary: Dave Bradbury.*
e-mail: info@dewstow.com
website: www.dewstow.com

CHEPSTOW. **Marriott St Pierre Hotel and Country Club,** St Pierre Park, Chepstow, Monmouthshire NP16 6YA (01291 635205; Fax: 01291 629975). *Location*: Junction 2 of M48, A466 Chepstow, A48 Caerwent. 400 acres of beautiful parkland, some of the rarest and oldest trees in Britain. Old Course: 18 holes, 6818 yards. S.S.S. 73 off white, 71 off yellow, 75 Ladies. Mathern Course: 18 holes, 5762 yards, S.S.S. 68. 13-bay driving range with computerised tuition facilities. *Green Fees*: information not available. *Eating facilities:* Trophy Bar serves light bites during day, Long Weekend Cafe Bar, private suites for groups. *Visitors*: welcome, book 10 days in advance for weekdays and 48 hours in advance for weekends. *Society Meetings*: weekdays only except when resident in hotel which has 148 bedrooms all en suite, conference rooms and extensive leisure facilities. Director of Golf: Ben Laing.*

CWMBRAN. **Greenmeadow Golf and Country Club,** Treherbert Road, Croesyceiliog, Cwmbran NP44 2BZ (01633 869321; Fax: 01633 868430). *Location:* M4 Junction 26 north on A4042, turn right at brown tourist sign for Golf Course and Driving Range. Next to Gwent Crematorium. Parkland course with undulating fairways, mature woodlands, strategically positioned lakes and bunkers. 18 holes, 6200 yards. S.S.S. 71. 26 bay floodlit driving range (9am to 9.30pm), putting green. *Green Fees:* information not available. *Eating facilities:* lounge bar, patio coffee lounge and restaurant. Private function room available if required. *Visitors:* welcome, telephone golf shop for tee time. *Society Meetings:* always welcome, bookings via our golf shop. Package deals with meals available. Professional: Dave Woodman (01633 862626). Secretary: P.J. Richardson (Fax: 01633 868430).*

CWMBRAN. **Llanyrafon Golf Course,** Llanfrechfa Way, Cwmbran NP44 8HT (01633 874636). *Location*: M4 Junction 26, A4042 to Cwmbran. Flat, parkland, wooded, river enclosed course. 9 holes, 1283 yards. Practice nets, putting green. *Green Fees*: information not available. *Visitors*: always welcome. Tuition available. Professional Golf Shop. Professional: David Woodman (01633 874636).*

Wenvoe Castle Golf Club
Founded 1936
**Wenvoe
Cardiff CF5 6BE
Tel/Fax: 029 2059 4371**
wenvoecastle@btconnect.com
www.wenvoecastlegolfclub.co.uk

- Exit Junction 33 M4, follow signs for Cardiff Airport.
- Parkland course founded in 1936, fairly open layout with hilly front 9, hosted first PGA Welsh Classic. Practice areas.
- 18 holes, 6544 yards. S.S.S. 72.
- Bar snacks and restaurant meals.
- Visitors welcome.
- Society Meetings catered for weekdays only.

Whitchurch (Cardiff) Golf Club
18 holes Par 71 SSS 71 Est. 1914

A parkland golf course in an urban setting with panoramic views of Cardiff.
4 miles from City Centre and 600 metres from Junction 32 of M4.
Green Fees: £50 weekdays, £60 Sundays • Visitors and Societies: welcome.
Full catering facilities available.
Club Professional: 029 2061 4660 • Club Manager: 029 2062 0985
secretary@whitchurchcardiffgolfclub.com • www.whitchurchcardiffgolfclub.com

DEWSTOW GOLF • CLUB

Golf at its best, supported by facilities designed for your sheer enjoyment

- Two golf courses – Valley Course and Park Course
- Golf Academy with 26-bay floodlit covered driving range, coffee shop and golf shop.
- Clubhouse with lounge, bars and restaurant open every day
- Function rooms for meetings, conferences and training.
- Societies welcome weekdays; weekends by arrangement
- Please ring Emma for a brochure or more information.

**Dewstow Golf Club, Caerwent, Monmouthshire NP26 5AH
Tel: 01291 430444 • Fax: 01291 425816
e-mail: info@dewstow.com
www.dewstow.com**

MARRIOTT ST. PIERRE HOTEL & COUNTRY CLUB
CHEPSTOW, MONMOUTHSHIRE

Nestled among ancient trees and peaceful hills, this is a top destination for professional and amateur golfers alike, with two 18-hole courses. Sharing these beautiful grounds is the Marriott St Pierre Hotel & Country Club, a classic and elegant retreat with all contemporary comforts including a swimming pool and health spa.

Visitors and Societies welcome,
call **01291 635205** to book a tee time.

St. Pierre Park, Chepstow,
Monmouthshire NP16 6YA
www.stpierregolf.com • www.marriottgolf.co.uk

DINAS POWIS. **Dinas Powis Golf Club,** Golf House, Highwalls Road, Dinas Powis CF64 4AJ *Location:* M4 Cardiff, Junction Cardiff West, thereafter signposted Dinas Powis, Penarth and Barry. Mostly parkland, a challenging course. Superb natural drainage offers all year golf. 18 holes, 5532 yards. S.S.S. 67. *Green Fees:* weekdays £25.00, £15.00 with member.; weekends and Bank Holidays £35.00, £20.00 with member. *Eating facilities:* dining room/bar snacks. *Visitors:* welcome weekdays, weekends by arrangement. Buggies available. Separate function room with bar available for hire. *Society Meetings:* call for details. Professional: G. Bennett (029 2051 3682). Secretary: S. Phelps (Tel & Fax: 029 2051 2727); Club (029 2051 2157).

GLYNNEATH. **Glynneath Golf Club,** 'Penygraig', Pontneddfechan, Near Glynneath SA11 5UH (01639 720452). *Location*: A465 trunk road to Glynneath onto B4242 to Pontneathvaughan, one and a half miles. Picturesque course overlooking Vale of Neath, in Brecon Beacons National Park, reasonably flat, half woodland, half parkland. 18 holes - white tees 6122 yards. S.S.S. 71. *Green Fees*: Monday £10.00, Tuesday to Friday £18.00; Saturday, Sunday £25.00. 2010 rates (subject to review). *Visitors*: welcome, trolleys and buggies available; catering; snooker. *Society Meetings*: welcome weekdays and weekends, only by arrangement. Professional: Shane McMenamin (01639 720452). Secretary: T.A. Roberts (01639 720452).
website: www.glynneathgolfclub.co.uk

HENGOED. **Bryn Meadows Golf Club,** Maesycwmmer, Near Hengoed CF82 7SN (01495 225590; Fax: 01495 228272). *Location:* just off A472 near Blackwood, 15 minutes to M4 Junction 28. Parkland course, spectacular views, new challenge from every tee. 18 holes, 6100 yards. Par 72. *Green Fees:* information not available. *Eating facilities:* à la carte restaurant, bar snacks, etc. *Visitors:* welcome weekdays, weekends by prior arrangement only. Award-winning hotel and leisure club. Buggy hire. *Society Meetings:* welcome weekdays, weekends by prior arrangement. For all golf enquiries please contact: Bruce Hunter (01495 221905/225590).*
website: www.brynmeadows.com

HENSOL. **The Vale Hotel, Golf and Spa Resort,** Hensol Park, Hensol, Near Cardiff CF72 8JY (01443 667800). *Location:* set in over 650 acres of beautiful countryside yet only three minutes from Junction 34 of M4, 15 minutes from Cardiff city centre and International airport. Home to the Welsh PGA. 2 Championship standard courses - Lake Course, 6436 yards, and Wales National Course, 7433 yards, Par 72, water features, greens to USGA standard. 16 bay driving range, short play area. *Green Fees:* information not available. *Eating facilities:* superb eating facilities in the clubhouse and AA Rosette Mediterranean restaurant. *Visitors:* welcome – Handicap Certificate required. Coaching available using latest video technology; Pro shop. spike and lounge bar. Buggy and trolley hire. *Society Meetings:* welcome, corporate days with full management service. Accommodation available in four-star hotel.*
website: www.vale-hotel.com

LLANWERN. **Llanwern Golf Club (Est 1929),** Llanwern Village, Newport NP18 2DW (01633 412029; Fax: 01633 412260). *Location:* four miles east of Newport city centre, one mile from M4 Junction 24. Mature parkland course in a picturesque village setting, established in 1928. 18 holes, 6177 yards, S.S.S. 70 Men; 5214 yards, S.S.S. 71 Ladies. Extensive practice facilities. *Green Fees:* on application; various summer and winter packages. *Eating facilities:* full catering and bar. *Visitors:* welcome Monday to Friday and by arrangement on Saturday (no Sundays). Bookings: (01633 412029). Professional: (01633 413233).
e-mail: llanwerngolfclub@btconnect.com
website: www.llanwerngolfclub.co.uk

MAESTEG. **Maesteg Golf Club,** Mount Pleasant, Neath Road, Maesteg CF34 9PR (01656 732037). *Location:* half a mile out of Maesteg town centre on the Port Talbot road (B4282). Reasonably flat hilltop course with scenic views over wooded hills and valleys down to Swansea Bay. 18 holes, 5929 yards. S.S.S. 69. Practice area and putting green. *Green Fees:* information not available. *Eating facilities:* meals available in restaurant overlooking the course, bar meals and snacks throughout the day. *Visitors:* welcome without reservation, groups of more than 12 by arrangement. *Society Meetings:* catered for weekdays only by arrangement. Secretary: (01656 734106).*

MERTHYR TYDFIL. **Merthyr Tydfil Golf Club,** Cloth Hall Lane, Cefn Coed, Merthyr Tydfil CF48 2NU (01685 723308). *Location:* off A470 Merthyr Tydfil to Brecon Road. Mountain top course in Brecon Beacons National Park area with outstanding views. 18 holes, 5625 yards. S.S.S. 68. *Green Fees:* information not available. *Eating facilities:* available by prior arrangement. *Visitors:* welcome anytime except competition days (usually Sundays). *Society Meetings:* catered for by prior arrangement. Secretary: Keith Anderson.*

MERTHYR TYDFIL. **Morlais Castle Golf Club,** Pant, Dowlais, Merthyr Tydfil CF48 2UY (01685 722822). *Location:* near "Heads of Valley Road", Dowlais roundabout, follow signs for Brecon Mountain Railway. Very pleasant moorland course with excellent views. 18 holes, 6320 yards, 5744 metres. S.S.S. 71. Practice area. *Green Fees:* information not available. *Eating facilities:* clubhouse offers excellent eating facilities; lounge, bars and restaurant. *Visitors:* welcome, weekends by prior arrangement with/or by application to the Secretary. *Society Meetings:* please contact Secretary. Professional: H. Jarrett (01685 388700). Secretary: Steven Jones.*
website: www.morlaiscastlegolf.co.uk

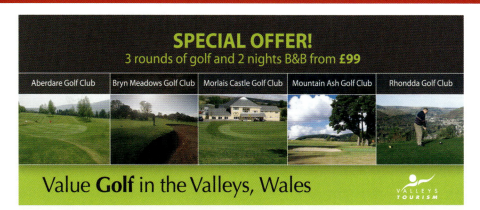

SPECIAL OFFER!
3 rounds of golf and 2 nights B&B from **£99**

Aberdare Golf Club | Bryn Meadows Golf Club | Morlais Castle Golf Club | Mountain Ash Golf Club | Rhondda Golf Club

Value **Golf** in the Valleys, Wales

VALLEYS TOURISM

Our Golf break deal offers unbeatable value and exceptional golf in the Valleys of Wales. You have the choice of five courses to play within the area, each offering something different, so you can tailor your golf holiday to your exact requirements and playing ability.

3 rounds of golf at the following venues:
- Aberdare Golf Club
- Mountain Ash Golf Club
- Morlais Castle Golf Club
- Rhondda Golf Club
- Bryn Meadows Golf Hotel & Spa

... and select from one of the following hotels:
- Bryn Meadows Golf Hotel and Spa
- Dare Valley Country Park
- The Dunravan Hotel
- Ty Newydd Country Hotel

from only **£99** per person

For more information and to book, visit: www.valleysgolfbreaks.co.uk or telephone 01685 722822

Monmouth Golf Club, Monmouth

The Rolls of Monmouth Golf Club
The Hendre, Monmouth NP25 5HG
Phone: 01600 715353 • Fax: 01600 713115
E-mail: enquiries@therollsgolfclub.co.uk
www.therollsgolfclub.co.uk

The Rolls of Monmouth Golf Club, with its championship 6,733 yard golf course, is set in superb countryside with spectacular views of the Welsh hills.

It is one of the most outstanding golf courses, not just in Wales, but in the whole of the UK.

We can offer two superb self-catering cottages for short or week-long breaks, both situated within the club grounds. Sleep 4-8

Stay to Play with Us

THE APPEARANCE OF AN ASTERISK (*) AT THE END OF A CLUB OR COURSE ENTRY INDICATES THAT UP-TO-DATE INFORMATION HAS NOT BEEN SUPPLIED

MONMOUTH. **Monmouth Golf Club,** Leasbrook Lane, Monmouth NP25 3SN (01600 712212). *Location*: outskirts of town on Monmouth - Ross-on-Wye dual carriageway, left turn 100 yards from roundabout; signposted. Undulating parkland, very scenic. 18 holes, 5700 yards. S.S.S. 69. Practice area, putting green. *Green Fees*: weekdays £20.00 per round, £30.00 per day; £10.00 per round with member; weekends and Bank Holidays £25.00 per round. £35.00 per day, £14.00 per round with member; Juniors £10.00 at all times. *Eating facilities*: bar snacks, dining room facilities daily. *Visitors*: welcome at all times. Trolley and buggy hire. *Society Meetings*: contact the Secretary or Professional in advance. Professional: Richard Ballard (01600 712212/07779 712323). Secretary: Peter Tully (01600 712212; Fax: 01600 772399).
e-mail: sec@monmouthgolfclub.co.uk
website: www.monmouthgolfclub.co.uk

MONMOUTH. **The Rolls of Monmouth Golf Club,** The Hendre, Monmouth NP25 5HG (01600 715353; Fax: 01600 713115). *Location*: B4233 old Monmouth/ Abergavenny road. Arboretum wooded, hilly parkland course on private estate. 18 holes, 6283 yards. S.S.S. 71. Practice area, putting green. *Green Fees:* information not available. *Eating facilities:* bar and catering facilities seven days a week. *Visitors:* welcome any day. Buggies and trolleys for hire. *Society Meetings:* welcome on any day including weekends. Secretary: Mrs Sandra Orton.*
e-mail: sandra@therollsgolfclub.co.uk

MOUNTAIN ASH. **Mountain Ash Golf Club,** Cefn Pennar, Mountain Ash CF45 4DT (01443 479459). *Location:* A470 Pontypridd to Aberdare road, approximately 10 miles from Pontypridd, four miles north of Abercynon. Picturesque heathland course. 18 holes, 5553 yards. S.S.S. 67. *Green Fees:* information not available. *Eating facilities:* catering at club. *Visitors:* welcome anytime without reservation. *Society Meetings:* catered for, special rates by arrangement. Secretary: Sharon Rees (01443 479459).*

NANTYGLO. **West Monmouthshire Golf Club,** Pond Road, Nantyglo, Brynmawr NP23 4QT (01495 310233). *Location:* Heads of the Valleys Road to Brynmawr, roundabout to Nantyglo, signposted. Mountain and heathland course. Now recognised as

Monmouth Golf Club
Leasbrook Lane, Monmouth NP25 3SN
Tel: 01600 712212 • Fax: 01600 772399
sec@monmouthgolfclub.co.uk
www.monmouthgolfclub.co.uk

Monmouth Golf Club is situated on the A40, half a mile north of the town. It was extended to an 18-hole course in 1992, when a new clubhouse was opened, offering a most comfortable location for a drink or a meal, with magnificent views of the course and the surrounding countryside. Monmouth certainly has every justification for its claim to be one of the prettiest courses in Wales, and is renowned for the warm welcome offered to its guests.

Standing on high ground above the town, the undulating parkland course plays 5698 yards off white tees, 5507 off yellow, and 5118 off red (ladies). Each aptly named hole offers a different challenge. The 8th (Cresta Run) was recently included in "Britain's 100 most extraordinary golf holes" which also nominated Monmouth as having the best value green fees in the country.

As you leave the clubhouse you become aware of the tranquillity of the verdant surroundings, mature trees, wild flowers and an abundance of wildlife.

Visit the Monmouth Golf Club - you will not be disappointed.

THE GOLF GUIDE 2011 — WALES / South Wales 491

the highest golf course in Great Britain. 18 holes, 6118 yards. S.S.S. 69. *Green Fees:* information not available. *Eating facilities:* 24 hours notice required. *Visitors:* welcome. *Society Meetings:* welcome. Special package for parties – details on request. Secretary: S.E. Williams (01495 310233).*

NEATH. **Earlswood Golf Club,** Jersey Marine, Neath SA10 6JP (01792 321578). *Location:* half a mile southeast of Jersey Marine village, take B4290 turning off A483 then first right. Scenic, gently undulating course. 18 holes, 5174 yards. S.S.S. 68. *Green Fees:* £8.00 to £12.00. *Visitors:* pay as you play course, all visitors welcome. *Society Meetings:* by arrangement.

NEATH. **Neath Golf Club,** Cadoxton, Neath SA10 8AH (01639 643615). *Location:* two miles from Neath town centre. James Braid designed (1934) heathland course – gentle slopes, magnificent views of Brecon Beacons and Bristol Channel. 18 holes, 6490 yards. S.S.S. 72, Par 72. *Green Fees:* Summer: weekdays £25.00, weekends £30.00; Winter: £15.00 all week. *Eating facilities:* full catering facilities Tuesday to Sunday. *Visitors:* welcome at any time; phone Secretary in advance. Buggy (£20.00) and trolley hire available. *Society Meetings:* welcome at any time by prior arrangement with Secretary. Professional: R.M. Bennett (01639 633693). Secretary: D.M. Gee (01639 632759).
e-mail: neathgolf@btconnect.com
website: www.neathgolfclub.co.uk

NEATH. **Swansea Bay Golf Club,** Jersey Marine, Neath SA10 6JP (01792 812198). *Location:* exit 42 off M4. At 1st roundabout, take B4290 turning off A483 then first right. Seaside links. 18 holes, 6459 yards. S.S.S. 72. *Green Fees:* information not provided. *Eating facilities:* bar/ catering available every day from 11.00am; dinners by arrangement. *Visitors:* welcome without reservation. *Society Meetings:* by arrangement. Professional: M. Day (01792 816159). Secretary: (01792 812198).
e-mail: swanseabaygolfclub@hotmail.co.uk

NELSON. **Whitehall Golf Club,** The Pavilion, Nelson, Treharris CF46 6ST (01443 740245). *Location*: 15 miles north of Cardiff, take A4054 off A470. Hillside course with pleasant views. 9 holes (x2), 5666 yards. S.S.S. 68. *Green Fees*: Monday to Friday £10.00, with or without a member. Saturdays £10.00 with or without a member, but Captain's permission must be requested. Sundays/Bank Holidays by arrangement with Hon. Secretary. *Eating facilities*: available, contact Stewardess for cooked meals. *Visitors*: welcome weekdays, weekends with members. *Society Meetings*: by prior arrangement with Secretary. Secretary: P.M. Wilde (01443 451357).

NEWPORT. **The Celtic Manor Resort,** Coldra Woods, The Usk Valley, South Wales NP18 1HQ (Resort Enquiries 01633 413000; Fax: 01633 410269). *Location:* 90 minutes from London, off Junction 24 of the M4 motorway, five minutes from new Severn Bridge. The Resort is the home of The Celtic Manor Wales Open and the venue for the 2010 Ryder Cup. It features three very different and challenging championship courses. The new Ryder Cup course is the world's first-ever course designed specifically for golf's most prestigious tournament. Roman Road has played host to The Celtic Manor Wales Open and the celebrity All*Star Cup. The newly designed Montgomerie Course is the latest addition to the Resort's world class golf facilities. The Golf Academy offers comprehensive practice and coaching facilities, a two-tier floodlit driving range, 3 coaching bays with A-star video graphics, practice range, Pro Shop and short play areas. *Green Fees:* information not available. *Eating facilities:* superb dining facilities at The Lodge and hotels. *Visitors:* welcome. Meeting and banqueting rooms available. *Society Meetings:* welcome. Full event management service for Corporate Golf Days. Accommodation available at 330 room Resort Hotel or 70 room Manor House. Director of Golf Courses and Estates: Jim McKenzie. For tee times, call reservations (01633 410262).*

NEWPORT. **Newport Golf Club,** Great Oak, Rogerstone, Newport NP10 9FX (01633 892643; Fax: 01633 896676). *Location:* M4 Junction 27, take B4591 to RISCA, one and a half miles on right. Rolling parkland. 18 holes, white tees 6500 yards, S.S.S. 72 yellow tees 6273 yards. S.S.S. 71. Two practice areas. *Green Fees:* information not available. *Eating facilities:* full dining facilities at club. *Visitors:* welcome Sunday-Friday, advisable to ring in advance. *Society Meetings:* welcome most days, book through Secretary. Professional: Paul Mayo (01633 893271). Secretary: Russell Thomas (01633 892643; Fax: 01633 896676).*
website: www.newportgolfclub.org.uk

NEWPORT. **Parc Golf Club,** Church Lane, Coedkernew, Newport NP10 8TU (01633 680933; Fax: 01633 681011). *Location:* Junction 28 M4, then A48 three miles from Newport. Flat parkland course. 18 holes, 5884 yards, S.S.S. 68. Golf range 38 bays, 9 hole short course, practice putting greens (grass and astro turf). *Green Fees:* April/May £15.00 weekdays, £18.00 weekends; after May ring for prices. *Eating facilities:* bar, conservatory, function room (can cater for 120 plus). *Visitors:* always welcome, must pre-book. Golf days arranged, weddings, conference facilities, exhibitions etc. *Society Meetings:* minimum 10 persons. Professionals: Richard Dinsdale, N. Humphries and Brian Lee. Secretary: M.V. Cleary. Manager: Carl Hicks.
e-mail: parc.golf@btconnect.co.uk
website: www.parcgolf.co.uk

FHG Guides publish a large range of well-known accommodation guides. We will be happy to send you details or you can use the order form at the back of this book.

NEWPORT. **Tredegar Park Golf Club Ltd,** Parc-Y-Bryn, Rogerstone, Newport NP10 9TG (01633 894433). *Location:* north of M4 between Junctions 26 and 27. Parkland course. 18 holes, 6400 yards, 5850 metres. S.S.S. 72. Practice area. *Green Fees:* information not provided. *Eating facilities:* restaurant and bar. *Visitors:* welcome, must be member of affiliated club. *Society Meetings:* groups of 16 and over catered for. Professional: Mark Phillips. General Manager: Stuart Salway (01633 894433; Fax: 01633 897152).

OAKDALE. **Oakdale Golf Course,** Llwynon Lane, Oakdale NP12 0NF (01495 220044). Parkland course, 9 holes. Pay & Play course. 18 bay floodlit driving range. *Green Fees:* information not available. *Eating facilities*: licensed bar, snacks. Full-sized snooker tables. *Visitors*: welcome. *Society Meetings*: welcome.*

PENARTH. **Glamorganshire Golf Club,** Lavernock Road, Penarth CF64 5UP (Tel & Fax: 029 2070 1185). *Location:* five miles west Cardiff, one mile west Penarth Centre. Parkland course overlooking Bristol Channel. 18 holes, 6150 yards. S.S.S. 70. Practice area. *Green Fees:* information not available. *Eating facilities:* full restaurant and bar snacks, Men's bar and mixed lounge bar. *Visitors:* welcome providing no competitions in progress and/or Societies on course. Telephone call recommended. All visitors must possess current Handicap Certificate. *Society Meetings:* applications to Secretary/Manager. Reductions for parties exceeding 20. Professional: Mr A.K. Smith (029 2070 7401). Secretary/Manager: B.M. Williams (029 2070 1185).*

PENCOED. **St Mary's Golf Club,** St Mary's Hill, Pencoed CF35 5EA (01656 861100; Fax: 01656 863400). *Location*: Junction 35 of M4 and take third exit at roundabout, follow A473, take road signposted Felindre for about 300 yards, we are on left. Parkland course. 18 holes, 5291 yards. S.S.S. 66. Kingfisher 12 hole Public Course, practice area, driving range. *Green Fees:* information not available. *Eating facilities:* restaurant, three bars. *Visitors*: welcome weekdays 9am to 4pm; weekends 1pm to 4pm. 24 bedroom hotel. *Society Meetings*: welcome weekdays, restricted times at weekends. Society Secretary: Leighton Janes (01656 860280).*

PONTYPOOL. **Pontypool Golf Club,** Lasgarn Lane, Trevethin, Pontypool NP4 8TR (01495 763655). *Location:* Pontypool A4042 to St. Cadoc's Church, Trevethin. Undulating hillside course, with mountain turf and fine views. 18 holes, yellow tees 5838 yards. S.S.S. 69. Practice area, Indoor teaching academy. *Green Fees:* £30.00; £10.00 from 2-4pm Monday to Friday and Sunday. *Eating facilities:* diningroom and bar snacks. *Visitors:* welcome, must have Handicap Certificates. *Society Meetings:* special packages available. Professional: Kyle Smith (01495 755444). Secretary: Les Dodd (01495 763655).
e-mail: pontypoolgolf@btconnect.com
website: www.pontypoolgolf.co.uk

PONTYPOOL. **Woodlake Park Golf and Country Club,** Glascoed, Pontypool NP4 0TE (01291 673933; Fax: 01291 673811). *Location:* three miles from Usk overlooking Llandegfedd Reservoir. Undulating parkland with superb greens built to USGA specification. 18 holes, 6400 yards. S.S.S. 72. *Green Fees:* weekdays £25.00; weekends £32.00 (summer); weekdays £15.00, weekends £18.00 (winter). *Eating facilities:* spikes bar, lounge bar. *Visitors:* welcome, no restrictions. Function room for 130, private diningroom for up to 36 adjacent to Spikes Bar. *Society Meetings:* welcome, must pre-book, can cater for up to 100. Professional: Leon Lancey. Secretary: M.J. Wood BSc.

PONTYPRIDD. **Pontypridd Golf Club,** Ty Gwyn Road, Pontypridd CF37 4DJ (01443 402359). *Location:* east side of town, off A470, 12 miles from Cardiff. Wooded mountain course. 18 holes, 5881 yards, 5378 metres. S.S.S. 68. *Green Fees:* contact Professional for information. *Eating facilities:* bar, restaurant, snacks available. *Visitors:* welcome weekdays, Ladies' Day Tuesdays; weekends with member only. Must be member of recognised golf club in possession of Handicap Certificate. *Society Meetings:* catered for weekdays with prior reservation. Professional: (01443 409904). Secretary: Sonja Mcfadden (01443 409904)
e-mail: sonja.mcfadden@pontypriddgolfclub.co.uk

PORTHCAWL. **Grove Golf Club Ltd.,** South Cornelly, Porthcawl, Mid Glamorgan CF33 4RP (01656 788771; Fax: 01656 788414). *Location:* near Porthcawl on A4229 two minutes from Junction 37 off M4. Parkland course with spectacular views. 18 holes, 6128 yards, S.S.S. 69. *Green Fees:* information not available. *Eating facilities:* full restaurant and bar snacks from 8am daily. *Visitors:* welcome every day, bookings advisable. *Society Meetings:* welcome by arrangement. A variety of packages available. Secretary: Mike Thomas (01656 788771).*
e-mail: enquiries@grovegolf.com
website: www.grovegolf.com

PORTHCAWL. **Pyle and Kenfig Golf Club,** Waun-y-Mer, Kenfig, Bridgend CF33 4PU (01656 783093; Fax: 01656 772822). *Location:* one mile off M4 at Junction 37, follow Porthcawl signs. Undulating dune and downland course. 18 holes, 6588 yards (white tees). S.S.S. 73. Five practice holes, practice range. *Green Fees:* £50.00, £70.00 Sundays. *Eating facilities:* full catering facilities. *Visitors:* welcome weekdays and Sundays. *Society Meetings:* welcome by arrangement. Professional: Dylan Williams (Tel & Fax: 01656 772446). Secretary: Mrs Bev Cronin (01656 783093; Fax: 01656 772822).
e-mail: secretary@pandkgolfclub.co.uk
website: www.pandkgolfclub.co.uk

PORTHCAWL. **Royal Porthcawl Golf Club,** Rest Bay, Porthcawl CF36 3UW (01656 782251; Fax: 01656 771687). *Location:* Junction 37 M4, head towards Porthcawl (three miles), club located at Rest Bay. Links course. 18 holes, 7065 yards. S.S.S. 76. 27-acre practice area. *Green Fees:* weekdays 18 holes £98.00 36 holes £143.00; weekends 18 holes £120.00, 36

holes £175.00. Weekday fee includes two course lunch, weekend fee is golf only. *Eating facilities:* full catering and bars. *Visitors:* accepted Monday afternoons, Tuesdays, Thursdays and Fridays; limited weekend availability. Dormy House – six single rooms (£45.00 B&B), three twin rooms (£80.00 B&B). *Society Meetings:* welcome. Professional: Peter Evans (01656 773702). Secretary: Martin Bond. e-mail: office@royalporthcawl.com
website: www.royalporthcawl.com

PORT TALBOT. **Corus (Port Talbot),** Groes Fields, Margam, Port Talbot SA13 2NF (01639 871111 Ext. 3368). *Location*: Margam Park exit from M4. Flat course. 12 holes, 5020 yards. S.S.S. 64. *Green Fees*: information not available. *Eating facilities*: bar meals available if ordered in advance. *Visitors*: welcome midweek, weekends by arrangement with Secretary. Secretary: David Wilkinson (01639 793194).*

PORT TALBOT. **Lakeside Golf Club,** Water Street, Margam, Port Talbot SA13 2PA (01639 899959). *Location:* Junction 38 of M4 Port Talbot, Margam Country Park. Flat parkland course. 18 holes, 4390 yards, S.S.S. 63. 20 bay driving range. *Green Fees:* information not available. *Eating facilities:* bar meals, restaurant. *Visitors:* welcome. *Society Meetings:* welcome. Professional: Matthew Wootton (07940 167202). Secretary: Brian Channell.*

Other useful guides to holidays in Britain from

FHG Guides

**PUBS & INNS
300 GREAT HOTELS
SHORT BREAK HOLIDAYS
The original PETS WELCOME!
500 GREAT PLACES TO STAY
SELF-CATERING HOLIDAYS
BED & BREAKFAST STOPS
CARAVAN & CAMPING HOLIDAYS
FAMILY BREAKS**

Published annually: available in all good bookshops or direct from the publisher:
**FHG Guides, Abbey Mill Business Centre, Seedhill, Paisley PA1 1TJ
Tel: 0141 887 0428 • Fax: 0141 889 7204
e-mail: admin@fhguides.co.uk
www.holidayguides.com**

PONTYPOOL GOLF CLUB
LASGARN LANE, TREVETHIN, PONTYPOOL NP4 8TR

Situated above the town of Pontypool, with excellent views of the Eastern Valley, and across the Bristol Channel. The course has lots of character and provides a good challenge to all golfers.

• indoor teaching academy • putting green • practice ground • trolley hire
• buggy hire • bar • restaurant • 18 holes, 5838 yards, Par 69, SSS 69.

pontypoolgolf@btconnect.com • www.pontypoolgolf.co.uk
Tel: 01495 763655 • Fax: 01495 755564

The Grove Golf Club
South Cornelly, Near Porthcawl, Bridgend CF33 4RP

A parkland course with stunning views across the Bristol Channel and along towards Swansea Bay. The 18-hole course provides a good challenge for all levels, with water as a feature on several holes.

Splendid clubhouse • Excellent restaurant/bar • Function and conference rooms • Terrace for relaxing

Tel: 01656 788771
Fax: 01656 788414
e-mail: enquiries@grovegolf.com
www.grovegolf.com

RAGLAN. **Raglan Parc Golf Club,** Parc Lodge, Raglan NP15 2ER (01291 690077; Fax: 01291 690075). *Location:* near junction A40 and A449. 18 holes, 6604 yards, Par 73. *Green Fees:* information not available. *Visitors:* welcome. *Society Meetings:* welcome; packages available. Professional: Chris Murphy.*
e-mail: info@raglanparc.co.uk
website: www.raglanparc.co.uk

RHONDDA. **Rhondda Golf Club,** Golf House, Penrhys, Ferndale, Rhondda CF43 3PW (01443 441384). *Location:* on the Penrhys road joining Rhondda Fach and Rhondda Fawr. Mountain course. 18 holes, 6206 yards. S.S.S. 70. *Green Fees:* information not available. *Eating facilities:* all facilities daily except Mondays during winter months. *Visitors:* welcome. please telephone regarding availablilty. Handicap Certificate required. *Society Meetings:* welcome, please telephone for availability. Handicap Certificate required. Golf Shop: (01443 441384). Secretary: Ian Ellis (01443 441384).*
e-mail: rhonddagolf@aol.com
website: www.rhonddagolf.co.uk

RHYMNEY. **Tredegar and Rhymney Golf Club,** Cwmtysswg, Rhymney NP22 5HA (01685 840743). *Location:* A4048 Rhymney, Heads of the Valley road. Very scenic mountain course, lots of hazards. 18 holes, 6120 yards. S.S.S. 67. *Green Fees:* information not available. *Eating facilities:* bar snacks, meals by prior arrangement. *Visitors:* welcome at all times except Sunday mornings. Pro Shop on site, lessons available. Bookings taken on club tel. no. or 07859 934059 (ask for Elwyn Eddington). *Society Meetings:* welcome at all times except Sunday mornings. Special rates. Secretary: Will Price (07761 005184).*
e-mail: tandrgc@googlemail.com
website: www.tandrgc@gmail.com

SOUTHERNDOWN. **Southerndown Golf Club,** Ogmore by Sea, Bridgend CF32 0QP (01656 880476; Fax: 01656 880317). *Location:* three miles from Bridgend on the Ogmore Road. Downland links overlooking Bristol Channel. 18 holes, 6449 yards. S.S.S. 72. Practice area. *Green Fees:* weekdays £55.00 am, £45.00 pm; weekends £75.00 am, £65.00 pm. *Eating facilities:* full dining room and bar facilities. *Visitors:* welcome any time except competition days (check with Secretary). Handicap Certificate required. *Society Meetings:* catered for by arrangement with Secretary. Special rates dependent on number. Professional: D. McMonagle (01656 881112). Secretary: (01656 881111).
e-mail: admin@southerndowngolfclub.com
website: www.southerndowngolfclub.com

SWANSEA. **Allt-y-Graban Golf Club,** Allt-y-Graban Road, Pontlliw, Swansea SA4 1DT (01792 885757). *Location:* two miles from Junction 47 M4 turn left off A48 towards Pontarddulais, half mile past Glamorgan Arms. Parkland course. 9 holes, 4486 yards. S.S.S. 63. *Green Fees:* information not available. *Eating facilities:* full club house facilities including licensed bar and meals. *Visitors:* welcome. Secretary: S. Holston.*

Langland Bay Golf Club, Swansea

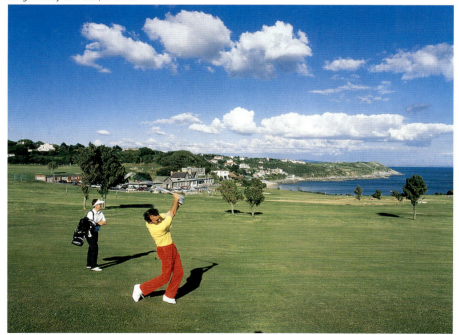

RAGLAN PARC GOLF CLUB

Parc Lodge, Raglan, Monmouthshire NP15 2ER

A superb rolling parkland course suitable for all standards of golfer, with a warm and friendly club atmosphere.

For further details, contact us on
Tel: 01291 690077 • Fax: 01291 690075
e-mail: info@raglanparc.co.uk
www.raglanparc.co.uk

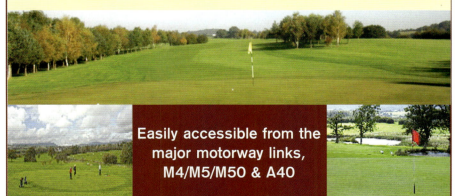

Easily accessible from the major motorway links, M4/M5/M50 & A40

SWANSEA. **Clyne Golf Club,** 120 Owls Lodge Lane, Mayals, Swansea SA3 5DP (01792 401989; Fax: 01792 401078). *Location:* west of Swansea, right off Mumbles Road, signposted. Moorland course with extensive sea views. 18 holes, 6334 yards. S.S.S. 72. Large practice area, indoor and outdoor driving nets and chipping and putting green. 6 electric buggies available for hire: £20.00 per buggy per round. *Green Fees:* weekdays £35.00; weekends £40.00. Winter offer - £20.00 including two course meal. *Eating facilities:* full catering facilities, fully licensed. *Visitors:* welcome except during competition days - check with Secretary. *Society Meetings:* welcome by application, reduction in fees for societies of 20 or more. Professional: Jonathan Clewett (01792 402094). Manager: Dave Thomas.
e-mail: clynegolfclub@supanet.com
clewett3@aol.com
website: www.swanseagolf.co.uk

SWANSEA. **Fairwood Park Golf Club Ltd,** Blackhills Lane, Upper Killay, Swansea SA2 7JN (01792 297849). *Location:* A4118 road - follow signs to "Sketty" and "Killay"; road to club opposite Swansea Airport. Parkland Championship course twice hosted the Welsh PGA. 18 holes, 6650 yards. S.S.S. 73. Practice facilities available. *Green Fees:* £27.00 weekdays; £34.00 Fridays and weekends. *Eating facilities:* every day all day full range, from bar snacks to three-course meals in restaurant, two licensed bars. *Visitors:* always welcome. *Society Meetings:* always welcome. Professional: Gary Hughes (Tel & Fax: 01792 299194). Secretary: Mrs C.J. Beer (01792 297849).
e-mail: info@fairwoodpark.com
website: www.fairwoodpark.com

SWANSEA. **Gower Golf Club,** Cefn Goleu, Three Crosses, Swansea (01792 872480). *Location:* Junction 47 follow signs to Gowerton. Signposted in Gowerton and Three Crosses. Rolling parkland course. 18 holes, 6441 yards. S.S.S. 72. Practice facilities. *Green Fees:* information not available. *Eating facilities:* licensed bar, full catering facilities. *Visitors:* welcome, members start times 10am to 11am. 4 star Wales Tourist Board accommodation available for visitors. Bookings via Pro Shop (01792 879905). Tuition area. *Society Meetings:* welcome, packages arranged. Professional: Alan Williamson.*

SWANSEA. **Gowerton Golf Range,** Victoria Road, Gowerton, Swansea SA4 3AB (01792 875188; Fax: 01792 874288). Flat wooded course with rivers and bunkers. 9 holes, 1000 yards, S.S.S. 27. *Green Fees:* 9 holes £5.00, 18 holes £7.00. *Eating facilities*: Diner, hot and cold meals provided. *Visitors:* open to the public. Lessons available. *Society Meetings*: welcome, group discounts. Professional: Mike Hobbs.
e-mail: waynebattye@yahoo.com
website: www.gowertongolfrange.co.uk

SWANSEA. **Langland Bay Golf Club,** Langland Bay Road, Langland, Swansea SA3 4QR (01792 361721). *Location:* M4 Junction 42, A483 Swansea, A4067 to Mumbles, followed by Langland Bay. Parkland/seaside course. 18 holes, 5857 yards. S.S.S. 70. *Green Fees:* available on request. *Eating facilities:* full catering and refreshment service provided; limited on Mondays. *Visitors:* welcome; book online. *Society Meetings:* welcome; book

Clyne Golf Club

At the entrance to the beautiful Gower Peninsula lies Clyne Golf Club, 300-400ft above sea level, and commanding wonderful views in all directions.

The course offers a challenging test of golf to all handicap levels.
There are 2 separate 9-hole loops: 18 holes, 6323 yards, SSS 72. Par 70.

Visitors are welcome – check with Secretary for competition days.

**120 Owls Lodge Lane, The Mayals, Swansea SA3 5DP
Tel: 01792 401989 • Fax: 01792 401078
e-mail: clynegolfclub@supanet.com • www.clynegolfclub.com
Professional: Jonathan Clewett • Tel: 01792 402094
e-mail: clewett3@aol.com • www.swanseagolf.co.uk**

online. Professional: Mark Evans. Director of Golf: Andrew Minty (01792 361721; Fax: 01792 361082). e-mail: info@langlandbaygolfclub.com website: www.langlandbaygolfclub.com

SWANSEA. **Morriston Golf Club,** 160 Clasemont Road, Morriston, Swansea SA6 6AJ (01792 796528). *Location:* off Junction 46 M4, turn first left and follow road for one mile, clubhouse on left hand side of road. Parkland course, rather difficult. 18 holes, 5708 yards. S.S.S. 68 (white tees). Practice area. *Green Fees:* see website for information. *Eating facilities:* restaurant and three bars. *Visitors:* welcome on application. Trolleys and buggies for hire. *Society Meetings:* welcome. Professional: Mark Govier (01792 772335). Secretary: David Fellowes (Tel & Fax: 01792 796528).
e-mail: morristongolf@btconnect.com
website: www.morristongolfclub.co.uk

SWANSEA. **Palleg and Swansea Valley Golf Course,** Palleg Road, Lower Cwmtwrch, Swansea SA9 2QQ (01639 842193). *Location:* off A4067 (A4068) north of Swansea 14 miles, 25 miles Brecon. Parkland course, open to the public 7 days a week. 18 holes, 5902 yards. S.S.S. 70. *Green Fees:* £18.00. *Eating facilities:* to be arranged with Steward. *Visitors:* welcome through week, check Pro Shop for weekends. *Society Meetings:* welcome if arranged. PGA Professional/ Director: Graham Coombe.

WINSTON HOTEL

Church Lane, Bishopston, Gower
Swansea SA3 3JT
Tel: 01792 232074
Fax: 01792 234902

We specialise in golfing breaks for groups, with 5 spectacular golf courses within 2 miles radius of the hotel...

The Winston Hotel is a comfortable, family run hotel where you are always assured of the warmest of welcomes. Situated in the Bishopston valley on the famous Gower peninsula, the hotel is within a mile of spectacular walks, and two miles of sandy beaches. Whether your visit is business or pleasure, to celebrate a special occasion or just to get away from it all, you are guaranteed a relaxing stay.

Langland Bay Golf Club, Gower

e-mail: enquiries@winstonhotel.com • www.winstonhotel.com

SWANSEA. Pennard Golf Club, 2 Southgate Road, Southgate, Swansea SA3 2BT (01792 233131; Fax: 01792 234797). *Location:* eight miles west of Swansea A4067, B4436. Seaside links. 18 holes, 6267 yards. S.S.S. 72, Par 71. Practice areas. *Green Fees:* weekdays £50.00, weekends and Bank Holidays £60.00. *Eating facilities:* dining room and two bars. *Visitors:* welcome. Snooker room. *Society Meetings:* by arrangement. Professional: M.V. Bennett (01792 233451). Secretary: Mrs S. Crowley (01792 233131).
e-mail: sec@pennardgolfclub.com
website: www.pennardgolfclub.com

SWANSEA. Pontardawe Golf Club, Cefn Llan, Pontardawe, Swansea SA8 4SH (01792 863118). *Location:* four miles north of M4 Junction 45 on A4067 Swansea-Brecon road. Wooded course. 18 holes, 6038 yards. S.S.S. 70. *Green Fees:* £25.00. *Eating facilities:* restaurant open daily except Mondays. *Visitors:* welcome, weekends by prior arrangement only. Handicap Certificate required. *Society Meetings:* catered for by application/appointment. Professional: Danny Evans (01792 830977). Secretary: Nigel Bowden. Administrator: Mrs M. Griffiths (01792 863118).
e-mail: enquiries@pontardawegolfclub.co.uk
website: www.pontardawegolfclub.co.uk

SWANSEA. Tawe Vale Golf Club, Clydach, Swansea SA6 5QR (01792 841257). *Location:* easily accessible from M4. Two minutes from Junction 45 on A4067 towards Pontardawe. A flat easy-walking parkland course bordered by the meandering River Tawe. 18 holes, 6064 yards. S.S.S 69. *Green Fees:* weekdays £20.00, weekends £25.00. *Eating facilities:* full catering facilities. *Visitors:* welcome at all times. *Society Meetings:* welcome, group discounts. Secretary: D.E. Jones (01792 842929).

TALBOT GREEN. Llantrisant and Pontyclun Golf Club, Talbot Green, Pontyclun CF72 8AL (01443 222148). *Location:* 10 miles north of Cardiff, two miles north of Junction 34 M4. Parkland. 18 holes, 5418 yards. S.S.S. 66. *Green Fees:* information not available. *Eating facilities:* available. *Visitors:* welcome weekdays. *Society Meetings:* catered for by arrangement. Professional: Andrew Bowen (01443 228169). Office: Theresa Morgan (01443 224601).*
e-mail: golf@lpgc.wanadoo.co.uk

USK. Alice Springs Golf Club, Kemeys Commander, Usk NP15 1PP (Fax: 01873 881381). *Location*: three miles north of Usk on B4598. Undulating parkland course with beautiful views across the Usk Valley. Usk Course: 18 holes, 6185 yards. S.S.S. 72. Monnow Course: 18 holes, 6041 yards. S.S.S. 69. Driving range. *Green Fees*: information not provided. *Eating facilities*: restaurant facilities all day; function room. *Visitors:* welcome at all times; telephone for tee time. *Society Meetings:* catered for, special packages available. Professional: (01873 880914). Managing Directors: J. & B. Morgan (01873 880708; Fax: 01873 881381).
e-mail: golf@alicespringsgolfclub.co.uk
website: www.alicespringsgolfclub.co.uk

THE GOLF GUIDE 2011 — IRELAND 499

Golf in Ireland

Tony McGee

Northern Ireland
Antrim • Armagh • Co.Down • Fermanagh Londonderry • Tyrone

The K Club, Straffan, Co Kildare

Republic of Ireland
Carlow • Cavan • Clare • Cork • Donegal Dublin • Galway • Kerry • Kildare • Kilkenny Laois • Leitrim • Limerick • Longford • Louth Mayo • Meath • Monaghan • Offaly Roscommon • Sligo • Tipperary • Waterford Westmeath • Wexford • Wicklow

Wicklow Golf Club

Wicklow Golf Club is a picturesque parkland course which follows the coastline of Wicklow Bay and is situated just outside the historic town of Wicklow. Each of the 18 holes make full use of the contours and natural features of the clifftop terrain, providing a challenging test for even the most ardent golfer. Our New Clubhouse facilities will complete the perfect golfing experience. Panoramic views, excellent golf, bar and dining facilities and a welcome which will make you feel right at home.

*But don't take our word for it.
So go on...treat yourself, you've no reason not to.*
**Dunbur Road, Wicklow Town, Co Wicklow
Tel: 00353 (0) 404 67379 • www.wicklowgolfclub.ie
e-mail: info@wicklowgolfclub.ie**

It is a huge tribute to Irish golf that nine courses on the Emerald Isle appear in the top 100 depicting the 'Very best golf courses on Earth'. This means that Ireland is joint fourth, quite an achievement for the little isle in the Atlantic Ocean.

Leading the way is Royal County Down in sixth place, the others being Royal Portrush (18), Ballybunion (37), Old Portmarnock (42), The European Club (43), Co Louth (68), Lahinch (73) and Doonbeg (99). Doonbeg in Co Clare is the youngest of the Irish clubs, having opened for play as late as 2002.

These are all links courses and it is rather difficult to give the reader a blanket picture of what is on offer to the visitor when they reach Ireland's shores. There is so much on the Emerald Isle to interest the golfer as well as friends who may not be all that keen on the game, that it is impossible to give anything beyond a thumbnail image of the delights in store.

Ireland has a greater percentage of links courses than any other country in the world, but many people prefer parkland tracks and there are plenty of them as well. Around 500 courses are dotted throughout the 32 counties, stretching from Fair Head in Antrim to Mizen Head in Cork, and from Malin Head in Donegal to Hook Head in Waterford.

There are clubs with two courses attached, clubs with 27 holes available and many little nine-holers plus driving ranges, so there is always something to satisfy the golfer who visits Europe's most westerly country.

If golf is not your game but you just tag along to keep the peace then you can indulge yourself in the many delights of the various restaurants, bars, etc that are available. Many of these provide excellent entertainment, some throughout the day, so that you can sit inside and put your feet up while your comrade(s) are sweating on that tricky putt on which fifty pence or a pound is riding.

Like everywhere else, the credit crunch has certainly affected Ireland but, in a strange way, it may have helped visiting golfers. Some clubs have reduced their fees to visitors, which can only be good news. No club, naturally, reduced its

16th at Lough Erne Resort, Co Fermanagh

welcome to visitors, with that traditional 'Welcome on the Mat' still very much the norm. *"Failte"* (welcome) is a word very familiar in Ireland and you should find it no matter where you go, north or south. (The English meaning would, of course, be much more common in some parts up north!).

Golf and entertainment go hand-in-hand and the visitor will never be stuck for a good night's *craic* (fun) after a day on the fairways and, particularly down south, *seisiúns* (Irish music, song and dance) can be found in most tourist areas. The *seisiúns* may be held in pubs, hotels or even by the fireside in a *Teach* (pronounced 'chalk') *Ceol,* a music house.

Accommodation is no problem either as the country is full of hotels, from the five-star and beyond to more modest family-run establishments. Scattered through the countryside, too, are hundreds of B&Bs which are moderately priced and where the *Beán A Tí* (woman of the house) looks after everyone as if they were a member of the family.

Often the visitor can just pull up at a B&B and be accommodated but, in the high season, it is much better to telephone, e-mail or fax ahead to make sure that there is available space. Regulated by the Tourist Boards, north and south, the standards have to be of the best. Many B&Bs are situated in farmhouses, which can be of great interest to foreigners. B&Bs don't normally provide an evening meal.

This gives you a picture of the *craic* and the accommodation that you can expect, and after a long, or even short, day on the course it adds to the enjoyment of the holiday to have a good relaxing evening.

Car hire is available everywhere and a car is necessary for the holidaymaker to get around the island, although a cruiser golf holiday is an alternative. Nowadays one can cruise from Enniskillen, up north in Co Fermanagh, to the Shannon Estuary in Co Clare. A cruiser can be hired at either end of the journey.

Right along this waterway there are dozens of nearby golf clubs. Tie up at one of the jetties, visit even more than one club, then, afterwards, have an evening meal and a night's entertainment in a nearby hostelry.

Start the journey up north after a visit to the magnificent Lough Erne Resort and its sister club, Castle Hume, just over three miles south of Enniskillen, followed by the trip down the Shannon.

The Lough Erne Resort, designed by Nick Faldo, was officially opened in 2009 with a challenge match between world tour pros Pádraig Harrington and Rory McIlroy. In the head-to-head battle McIlroy, who represents the club on tour, won on the last green.

Weaving around the shores of Lough Erne, the scenery is breathtaking. Fourteen holes are built around the lough, with a fantastic view across the water and some of its 365 islands from the elevated 16th green. Legend has it that a 366th island appears every leap year.

Designer Faldo gazed across the water from the 16th and was inspired by its tranquillity, remarking "This is one of the greatest courses in these islands and fit to host any tournament. It's the Loch Lomond of Ireland." This jewel in the north must surely be one of the most scenic golf courses in the world and golf agent Chubby Chandler agrees with Faldo that Lough Erne Resort could stage any tournament. Chandler wants to see a European Tour event played there.

A 75- room five-star hotel adjacent to the course opened in 2007 and there are 25 lodges and 60 chalets nestling among the trees that divide Castle Hume and the Lough Erne Resort. Not a course for the high handicapper, but worth a visit just the same. Take in a round on Castle Hume where Shaun Donnelly is the professional, although last year Lough Erne Resort appointed its own pro.

Moving up from The K Club to take charge was Lynn McCool, half of the Lynn and Liam McCool brother-sister pro act. Lynn, who is a member of the Ladies' European Tour, now channels all her energies into her new post of club professional and Golf Director.

Lough Erne Resort now proudly takes its place among the elite of Irish clubs, along with the likes of Royal Portrush and Royal County Down in the north; Co Sligo and Lahinch on the western seaboard; Ballybunion, Killarney, Fota Island, Adare Manor, Hangman's Point in Kerry (a reminder of the Stagecoach days) and Old Head in the deep south; Mount Juliet, Carton House,

14th at Galgorm Castle Golf Club, Ballymena, Co Antrim

The European Club, Druid's Glen and Druid's Heath, The Heritage, The K Club, Hermitage, Royal Dublin, Portmarnock and Portmarnock Links.

The 'big boys' are all well documented as they appear in many of the world's top course lists. Dromoland Castle and Doonbeg, with its on-site 'village', are among the elite as well, but some of these clubs, such as Hangman's Point and Old Head, are not really visitor country.

These upmarket clubs are for the more serious golfer who has a game equal to many professionals and who may have a few extra pounds to spend. They are not for the high handicap players who don't want to be frustrated during their holiday.

The good thing is that Ireland offers many, many more courses, among the near 500 that are doted all over the 'green isle'.

Slieve Russell Hotel & Country Club in Co Cavan is only a short drive from Enniskillen and the attached golf course is of the in-between category, not too difficult but challenging enough to interest the mid-handicap golfer. The Sean Quinn Complex – Sean also owns The Belfry – was created out of the Breffni Drumlin countryside. PGA events are staged annually at Slieve Russell, where secretary/manager Áine McCluskey will make you very welcome. Slieve Russell is the home club of record-breaking twin sisters Leona and Lisa Maguire who made history last year when, at the age of 14, they became the youngest ever to be selected on the GB&I Curtis Cup team.

Along the north coast of Ireland there is a chain of golf courses from Ballycastle to Ballyliffin, with the avid ball striker able to play up to three tracks in one day if he or she has the stamina. Some are tough, some are normal and others are for the less experienced golfer.

Royal Portrush is one of the most famous, with jumbo Dunluce Course and its tricky Calamity Corner one of the world's toughest par three holes, and the annual host to the North of Ireland Amateur Open Championship.

Along the coast also is the famed Bushmills brewery, just a few miles from Portrush, and the equally famous Giant's Causeway from where Finn McCumhaill (McCool) was supposed to have scooped up an armful of land and thrown it at the King of Scotland but it fell short and formed the Isle of Man. Looking at Lough Neagh and the Isle of Man the areas and shapes are very similar!

Of special interest to Scottish people is surely the Roe Park Resort at Limavady in Co Derry. The place is steeped in history and a spot on the course is unique. That's the mound – Mullagh Hill - where St Columba addressed the High Kings of Ireland at the Convention of Drumceatt in 575AD. He arrived by boat from Scotland to sort out a tax argument between the Irish and Scots and a special room in the Radisson Roe Hotel is named after him.

Roe Park Resort has a lot to offer to the touring golfer. Parkland with links views, for years Norman Wisdom stayed at the hotel and enjoyed his round of golf.

This web of courses, allied to the wide range of accommodation, from the likes of the Radisson Roe Hotel with its leisure centre, beauty salon, restaurants and golf academy to the popular B&B Guest Houses, offer the holidaymaker plenty to see and do.

With the north coast reasonably close to Belfast International and Belfast City (George Best) and City of Derry airports and Belfast docks, it is obvious that these courses are busy during the height of the tourist season, but on the way north there are many other pleasant courses to visit.

Belfast has 14 clubs, with Shandon Park, Malone and Belvoir Park, which in 2008 had a £3m facelift, among the most famous. Trees play a big part on these three courses and from the elevated Belvoir Park clubhouse there is a superb view over the city to the Black Mountain, with the shipyard and many high rise buildings, like the City Hospital and St Peter's Cathedral, nestling in between.

On leaving Belfast and heading north, the tree-lined Hilton Golf Club and Hotel at Templepatrick is quite a tough track, where the Northern Ireland Ladies' Professional Open Tournament was played in June 2008 and won by England's Lisa Hall after an eight-hole play-off with Gwladys Nocera (France) in lashing June rain!

Donegal is a haven of golf clubs – 17 of them – from Ireland's most northerly Ballyliffin to

Bundoran in the south of the county. Ballyliffin was another Nick Faldo conquest and so pleased was he with his work that he wanted to buy the place but the members wouldn't sell. The natural terrain has been expertly used on both tracks there, the Old Course and Glashedy, poised high on the edge of the Atlantic. From Ballyliffin the Alisa Craig rock looks a mere few yards away.

A European 'Double Badge' event, a Ladies' European Tour championship and the AIB Irish Seniors' Championship have all been held at Ballyliffin with the competitors experiencing what can be card-destroying winds.

Knightsbrook and Killeen Castle in Co Meath, where the Solheim Cup will be played this year, Moyvalley in Westmeath, Blarney Golf Resort in Cork and Castle Dargan, designed by Darren Clarke, in Co Sligo are some of the newer courses that have come on-stream, each a golfing paradise.

Another is surely Concra Wood Golf and Country Club at Castleblayney in Co Monaghan. Christy O'Connor Snr and Jnr, described as 'The Dream Team', jointly designed this 240-acre spectacle on the shores of Lough Mucknoo. The par 72, 6,824 metres course has a number of risk reward shot choices with eight holes close to the lake. The elevated clubhouse has all mod cons included. Designed by former Irish senior amateur international Brendan Cashell, it is certainly well worth a visit for the scenery alone.

Ulster certainly has its share of spectacular courses and of both top range, middle-of-the-road tracks and the easy courses that even a beginner could handle.

The eastern province of Leinster is no different. The coastline from Greenore in Co Louth to Tramore in Waterford has a long line of clubs that will often challenge but always delight players. Most of these are friendly to the player on holiday – friendly in the sense that they don't make play so difficult that it is not enjoyable.

Co Louth Club, at the sleepy little village of Baltray a few miles from Drogheda hosts the East of Ireland Open Amateur Championship annually and in 2009 staged The 3 Irish Open, ironically won by Irish amateur international Shane Lowry who outshot the top European pros. Four days later he turned professional.

This is Des Smyth country and just across the hedge from Co Louth is Seapoint, designed by Des and another local, amateur international Declan Brannigan. Opened in 1993, the course has hosted many top amateur events, as well as the once-off Glen Dimplex PGA International Tournament – ironically won by deadly Des – in 1995.

In 2009, it was voted No.27 in Golf Digest's Top 100 courses in Ireland and just last year hosted the 100th staging of the Ladbrokes.com PGA Irish Championship.

One club that falls just a little short of the really difficult is The European Club at Brittas Bay, a famed holiday resort in Co Wicklow. This Pat Ruddy-designed and owned jumbo has to be visited and you will get a very warm welcome from Pat and his entire family who run the business as a real friendly family affair.

The PGA Irish Championship was won there in July 2007, 2008 and 2009 by Pádraig Harrington on the weeks prior to the Dubliner winning back-to-back British Open titles. It is a massive 7,355 yards off the Blue tees with some card-wrecking holes included but still an enjoyable trip along the shore for the holiday golfer. Better to play matchplay on this superb, scenic track and enjoy the experience of the idyllic seaside journey.

"It is the first links I have played with 10 par fives (there are only two)!" joked 1976 British Open winner Johnny Miller. "I would love to see The Open played at The European Club."

Bunclody Golf and Fishing Club is one of Ireland's best-kept secrets. It is right in the heart of Bunclody on the Carlow-Wexford border. Designed by Canadian Jeff Howes, this exceptional course is crafted to a five-star finish. A luxurious location with a perfect balance of both rural and state-of-the-art amenities, featuring a traditional large and perfectly situated traditional thatched clubhouse and Ireland's first on-course elevator which links the 17th green to the 18th tee.

Surely the unusual clubhouse and the elevator set Bunclody apart. It covers 300 acres of parkland on the Carlow side of the River Slaney.

If one was to diagonally cross the country from Waterford in a north-west direction many neat parkland courses will be encountered, courses

18th fairway at Seapoint Golf Club, Drogheda, Co Louth

like the one at Dundrum House where mine host Willie Crowe gratefully entertains all-comers. The club is actually called County Tipperary Golf Club and is one mile from Thurles town (the club is sometimes called Thurles) where the GAA was born. This is a hotbed of hurling and the course is unusual in that it starts with two par fives.

Just short of Thurles is Cahir Park where David Ryan, husband of Ladies' European Tour player Claire Coughlan, is the professional, and further on is Cashel which combines golf with the famous Rock of Cashel.

Co Sligo, at Rosses Point, hosts the West of Ireland Amateur Open Championship every Easter. Set among sand dunes on cliffs overlooking three beaches, the wind factor plays a big part, while a burn meanders through the course and comes into play at a number of holes. The famous Benbulben Mountain, close to the grave of William B Yeats at Drumcliffe, towers in the distance to the north, with the Ox Mountains to the west giving a panoramic view to relax golfers who may be having a bad day.

Westport Town and the local golf club are among the busiest and friendliest in the country. This is a tourists' paradise, where sport and entertainment mingle daily. Traditional music pumps out from Matt Molloy's pub on the main street – Matt is the celebrated flute player with the Chieftains, in case you didn't know.

The Westport course commands a superb view of Clew Bay and is overshadowed by famous Croagh Patrick, the holy mountain to which pilgrims and visitors alike flock in their thousands throughout the year. The 15th hole, a jumbo par five of 580 yards, is played over an inlet of Clew Bay.

Christy O'Connor Jnr was the architect of the Galway Bay course on the Renville Peninsula where one needs to ignore the beautiful scenery if a good score is to be carded.

When visiting this rugged area of Ireland, no self-respecting tourist could miss out on playing Connemara, a remote course on the western seaboard, nine miles from Clifden, famous for its Pony Show, and past the old Marconi Wireless Station where Alcock and Brown landed after their trans-Atlantic flight in 1919. Big hitters will enjoy the long, flat meandering fairways of the Connemara Course at Ballyconeely.

The south-west corner of the country has a number of famous clubs and courses but one that most visitors like to play is Lahinch. Nestling on the Co Clare coast beside the Shannon, as with many clubs, there are two courses to choose from. It's the home of the South of Ireland Amateur Open Championship where sand dunes are the norm. A superb hole on the Old Course is 'The Dell', a great par three with the hidden cup in a basin well below the tee. 'The Klondyke' is another aptly named hole.

Doonbeg, where there is something of a holiday village with a luxurious hotel and self-catering cottages, has what has been judged as having one of the best first holes anywhere in the world. There are also a number of other holes, like the signature 14th and the 15th, which come in for special mention.

Fota Island, adjacent to the Wildlife Park on the outskirts of Cork City, and nearby Little Island – alias Cork Golf Club – should also be visited.

In the Kingdom of Kerry are the famed Killarney where the 2010 Irish Open was played, Ballybunion and Waterville courses, backed up by many lesser lights such as Tralee and Kilorglin, while across in Waterford are Tramore and Faithlegg courses, both suited to the traveller.

Nowadays, it takes only five to six hours to drive from Belfast to Limerick or Cork either via Dublin or through the centre of Ireland, where the scenery is more pleasing but the roads of a lesser standard. From Dublin to Galway is also a fast drive. Car hire is, of course, available all over the island, or if travelling by ferry visitors can bring their own transport.

There are a number of open tournaments in which holidaymakers are very welcome to take part. One such event is the West Coast Challenge, a four-day competition on the Bundoran, Donegal, Enniscrone and Strandhill links, with players switching courses each day. Players enter for this first week in September event from all over, including America, France and Germany.

There are many other such competitions for players of high and low handicaps, men's and women's, all over Ireland. Entry fees are not expensive, with generous prizes on offer. Of course, getting your name into the draw means filing an entry by the closing date and information can be obtained from the various tourist boards.

Waterville Golf Links, Waterville, Co Kerry

NORTHERN IRELAND

Antrim

ANTRIM. **Massereene Golf Club,** 51 Lough Road, Antrim BT41 4DQ (028 9442 9293). *Location:* one mile S.W. of town, 3 miles from Aldergrove Airport, situated alongside the shores of Lough Neagh. 18 holes, 6602 yards. S.S.S. 72. *Green Fees:* information not available. *Eating facilities:* full catering facilities 12 noon till 9pm. *Visitors:* welcome. Buggies for hire. *Society Meetings:* catered for. Professional: Jim Smyth (028 9446 4074). Secretary/Manager: Mr Gary Henry (028 9442 8096).*

BALLYCASTLE. **Ballycastle Golf Club,** Cushendall Road, Ballycastle BT64 6QP (028 2076 2536; Fax 028 2076 9909). *Location:* approximately 40 miles along the coast road west of Larne Harbour. Seaside links/undulating. 18 holes, 5876 yards, 5373 metres. S.S.S. 70. *Green Fees:* weekdays £26.00 (with member £12.50); weekends and Public Holidays £36.00, (with member £17.50). 2010 rates (subject to review). On-line booking available. *Eating facilities:* catering available (028 2076 2536). *Visitors:* welcome weekdays and afternoons at weekends by arrangement. *Society Meetings:* welcome weekdays and afternoons at weekends by arrangement. Professional: (028 2076 2506). General Manager: T. Peacock (028 2076 2536; Fax: 028 2076 9909). Hon. Secretary: D. Douglas (028 2076 2536; Fax: 028 2076 9909).
e-mail: info@ballycastlegolfclub.com
website: www.ballycastlegolfclub.com

BALLYCLARE. **Ballyclare Golf Club,** 25 Springvale Road, Ballyclare BT39 9JW (028 9332 2696/9334 2352). *Location:* one and a half miles north of Ballyclare. Parkland, lakes and river. 18 holes, 6339 yards. S.S.S. 71. Practice ground. *Green Fees:* information not available. *Eating facilities:* catering available. *Visitors:* welcome weekdays except Thursday. *Society Meetings:* catered for. Special rates for 15 plus. Professional: Colin Lyttle (028 9332 4541). Secretary Manager: Michael Stone (028 9332 2696).*

BALLYCLARE. **Greenacres Golf Club,** 153 Ballyrobert Road, Ballyclare BT39 9RT (028 9335 4111; Fax: 028 9335 4166). *Location:* three miles from Corrs Corner on B56. Parkland course, 18 holes. Par 71. S.S.S. 68. Floodlit driving range. *Green Fees:* weekdays £16.00, weekends and Public Holidays £24.00. 2010 rates (subject to review). *Eating facilities:* bar and catering available.

BALLYMENA. **Ballymena Golf Club,** 128 Raceview Road, Ballymena BT42 4HY (028 2586 1207). *Location:* two miles north east of town on A42. Flat/parkland/heathland. 18 holes, 5299 metres. S.S.S. 67. *Green Fees:* information not available. *Eating facilities:* restaurant and bar snacks. *Visitors:* welcome at all times, except Tuesdays and Saturdays. *Society Meetings:* catered for except Tuesdays and Saturdays.. Professional: Ken Revie (028 2586 1652). Secretary: George Small (Tel & Fax: 028 2586 1487).*

BALLYMENA. **Galgorm Castle Golf Club,** Galgorm Castle, Ballymena BT42 1HL (028 2564 6161; Fax: 028 2565 1151). *Location*: one mile south of Ballymena on A42 to Galgorm village. Mature parkland course in the grounds of one of Ireland's most historic castles. 18 holes, 6736 yards, S.S.S. 73. Driving range, practice area. *Green Fees:* weekdays £40.00; weekends £50.00. *Eating facilities:* full restaurant and bar. *Visitors*: welcome. Accommodation and tuition available. Fully equipped golf shop, hire facilities including buggies with GPS satellite navigation. *Society Meetings*: welcome, special rates available. Professional: Phil Collins (028 2564 6161; Fax: 028 2565 1151). General Manager: Gary Henry (028 2565 0210).
e-mail: golf@galgormcastle.com
website: www.galgormcastle.com

BALLYMONEY. **Gracehill Golf Club,** 141 Ballinlea Road, Stranocum, Ballymoney BT53 8PX (028 2075 1209; Fax: 028 2075 1074). *Location*: Ballymoney; International Airport (40 minutes). Parkland. Opened May 1995 with American-style water hazards. 18 holes, 6525 yards. S.S.S. 73. Practice area. Driving range adjacent to course. *Green Fees:* contact clubhouse for details. *Eating facilities*: seasonal, April to September; weekend only October to March. *Visitors:* telephone for tee time. *Society Meetings:* all welcome. Secretary/ Manager: M. McClure.
website: www.gracehillgolfclub.co.uk

BELFAST. **Castlereagh Hills Golf Club,** Upper Braniel Road, Castlereagh, Belfast BT5 7TX (028 9044 8477). *Location:* two miles from city centre, east Belfast. Parkland. 18 holes. 5398 metres. S.S.S. 67. Practice area and putting green. *Green Fees:* information not available. *Eating facilities:* every day. *Visitors:* welcome, no restrictions. Club hire *Society Meetings:* all welcome. Professional: R. Skillen (028 9044 8477). Secretary: L. Booth (028 9065 9653).*

BELFAST. **Cliftonville Golf Club,** 44 Westland Road, Belfast BT14 6NH (028 9074 4158). Parkland with rivers bisecting three fairways. 9 holes, 6210 yards, 5672 metres. S.S.S. 70. Practice fairway and nets. *Green Fees:* information not available. *Eating facilities:* bars, catering on request. *Visitors:* no visitors after 5pm weekdays, until 6pm on Saturdays, and until 1.30pm Sundays. *Society Meetings:* very welcome, especially by arrangement. Professional: Shaun Skeldon. Secretary: Victor Thompson (028 9074 6595).*
website: www.cliftonvillegolfclub.com

BELFAST. **Dunmurry Golf Club,** 91 Dunmurry Lane, Dunmurry, Belfast BT17 9JS (028 9061 0834; Fax: 028 9060 2540). *Location:* off M1 at Dunmurry, to village, turn left past Tesco, 1½ miles on right. Parkland, partially wooded. 18 holes, 6080 yards. S.S.S. 69. Practice area. *Green Fees:* information not available. *Eating facilities:* restaurant (not Mondays) and bar. *Visitors:* welcome by arrangement; not Fridays (Ladies' Day) and not Saturdays. Trolleys available. *Society Meetings:* welcome by written application. Professional: John Dolan (028 9062 1314; Fax: 028 9060 2540). Golf Manager: Tony Cassidy (028 9061 0834; Fax: 028 9060 2540).*

BELFAST. **Fortwilliam Golf Club,** Downview Avenue, Belfast BT15 4EZ (028 9037 0770). *Location:* one mile Fortwilliam Junction M2. Parkland. 18 holes, 6030 yards. S.S.S. 69. *Green Fees:* £30.00. *Eating facilities:* excellent catering and bar. *Visitors:* welcome every day except Saturdays. *Society Meetings:* catered for Tuesdays, Thursdays and Sundays; special rates available. Golf cart available, £20.00 per round. Professional: Peter Hanna (Tel & Fax: 028 9077 0980). Secretary: Pat Toal CB (028 9037 0770; Fax: 028 9078 1891).
website: www.fortwilliam.co.uk

BELFAST. **Malone Golf Club,** 240 Upper Malone Road, Dunmurry, Belfast BT17 9LB (028 9061 2758; Fax: 028 9043 1394). *Location:* five miles south of Belfast city centre, opposite Lady Dixon Park. Parkland, wooded course with large lake. 18 holes, 6706 yards. S.S.S. 72. 9 holes, 6320 yards. S.S.S. 70 (9 holes x 2). Practice ground, putting green. *Green Fees:* weekdays £75.00 per day, weekends £85.00 per day. *Eating facilities:* bar, bar snacks and restaurant. *Visitors:* welcome weekdays except Tuesdays (Ladies' Day) and Wednesday pm; time sheet on weekends. Dress code observed on course and in clubhouse. Golf carts for hire. *Society Meetings:* welcome by arrangement Mondays and Thursdays. Professional: Michael McGee (Tel & Fax: 028 9061 4917). Manager: J.N.S. Agate (028 9061 2758; Fax: 028 9043 1394).
website: www.malonegolfclub.co.uk

CARRICKFERGUS. **Carrickfergus Golf Club,** 35 North Road, Carrickfergus BT38 8LP (028 9336 3713; Fax: 028 9336 3023). *Location:* North Road, one mile from main shore road. Fairly flat parkland course, partially wooded. 18 holes, 5768 yards. S.S.S. 68. *Green Fees:* weekdays £19.00, weekends and Bank Holidays £25.00. *Eating facilities:* full catering and bar facilities. *Visitors:* welcome except on Saturdays. *Society Meetings:* catered for. PGA Professional: C.T. Farr PGA (028 9336 3713; Fax: 028 9336 3023). Secretary: I. McLean (028 9336 3713; Fax: 028 9336 3023).

CARRICKFERGUS. **Greenisland Golf Club,** 156 Upper Road, Greenisland, Carrickfergus BT38 8RW (028 9086 2236). *Location:* situated at the foot of Knockagh Hill and on the edge of Carrickfergus town; one of the best features is the scenic view over Belfast Lough. Mature tree-lined parkland course. 9 holes, 6090 yards. S.S.S. 69. *Green Fees:* weekdays £15.00, weekends £20.00. *Eating facilities:* lunch and evening meals available, bar snacks. *Visitors:* welcome; Saturdays after 4.30pm. *Society Meetings:* welcome by prior arrangement. Hon. Secretary: F.F. Trotter.

CARRICKFERGUS. **Whitehead Golf Club,** McCrea's Brae, Whitehead, Carrickfergus BT38 9NZ (028 9337 0822). *Location:* Whitehead, 15 miles from Belfast, 10 miles from Larne. 18 holes, 6050 yards. S.S.S. 69, par 70. *Green Fees:* information not provided. *Eating facilities:* by arrangement with Caterer. *Visitors:* welcome Monday to Friday, and Sunday. *Society Meetings:* by prior arrangement. Professional: C. Farr (028 9337 0821). Secretary/Manager: (028 9337 0820 9am-5pm; Fax: 028 9337 0825). Caterer (028 9337 0823).

CUSHENDALL. **Cushendall Golf Club,** 21 Shore Road, Cushendall BT44 0NG (028 2177 1318). *Location:* 25 miles north on Antrim coast road from Larne Harbour. Seaside wooded course; river comes into play in seven out of nine holes. 9 holes, 4384 metres. S.S.S. 63. *Green Fees:* weekdays £15.00 per day, weekends and Bank Holidays £20.00; £5.00 concession if playing with member. *Eating facilities:* normal bar hours, bar snacks, full catering by arrangement. *Visitors:* welcome without reservation, avoid Wednesday afternoons, Thursday Ladies' Day, time sheet in operation at weekends. *Society Meetings:* welcome. Hon. Secretary: Shaun McLaughlin (028 2175 8366).

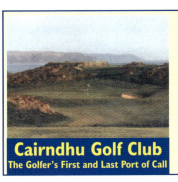

The Gem on the Coast

- Half an hour drive from Belfast and eight minutes from the ferry terminal.
- Famed for its manicured conditions and stunning views of the Antrim and Scottish coasts.
- This 18-hole Championship course is a must, and visitors are most welcome.
- Party bookings by prior arrangement with the Professional Shop.
- Monday-Friday Green Fees: £20.00 • Sunday Green Fees: £25.00

Cairndhu Golf Club
The Golfer's First and Last Port of Call

Tel: 028 2858 3954
192 Coast Road, Ballygally, Larne, Co Antrim

LARNE. **Cairndhu Golf Club Ltd,** 192 Coast Road, Ballygally, Larne BT40 2QG (028 2858 3954); Fax: 028 2858 3324). *Location:* three miles north of Larne on the famous Antrim Coast road leading to the Glens of Antrim. Parkland course with stunning views. 18 holes, 6150 yards. Par 70. Practice area, driving range. New buggies for hire. *Green Fees:* information not available. *Eating facilities:* restaurant and bar. *Visitors:* welcome except Saturdays. *Society Meetings:* welcome. Professional: Stephen Hood (Tel & Fax: 028 2858 3954). General Manager: Michael Keown.*

LARNE. **Larne Golf Club,** 54 Ferris Bay Road, Islandmagee, Larne BT40 3RT (028 9338 2228; Fax: 028 9338 2088). *Location:* six miles north of Whitehead on Browns Bay Road. Part links, part parkland. 9 holes, 18 tee boxes, 6288 yards. S.S.S. 70. Practice ground. *Green Fees:* information not provided. *Eating facilities:* bar, restaurant. *Visitors:* welcome Mondays to Thursdays, and Sundays. Snooker table. *Society Meetings:* welcome on application (not Friday or Saturday). 10% reduction for societies of 20 or more. Hon. Secretary: R.F. Niblock. Club Manager: L.I. Oldfield.

LISBURN. **Lisburn Golf Club,** Blaris Lodge, 68 Eglantine Road, Lisburn BT27 5RQ (028 9267 7216; Fax: 028 9260 3608). *Location:* three miles south of Lisburn on A1. Parkland. 18 holes, 6647 yards. S.S.S. 72. Practice area. *Green Fees:* information not available. *Eating facilities:* bar and restaurant. *Visitors:* welcome weekdays, Tuesdays Ladies have preference. Saturday after 5.30pm only, Sundays with member only. Snooker room. *Society Meetings:* Mondays and Thursdays only. Professional: S. Hamill (028 9267 7217). Manager: G.E. McVeigh (028 9267 7216).*
e-mail: lisburngolfclub@aol.com

MAZE. **Down Royal Park Golf Course,** 6 Dunygarton Road, Maze BT27 5RT (Tel & Fax: 028 9262 1339). *Location:* Belfast–Hillsborough road. Lisburn–Moira road. Heathland. 27 holes, 6940metres. S.S.S. 72. *Green Fees*: information not available. *Eating facilities*: available. Open to public. Special offers on regular basis. *Visitors*: G.U.I. dress code applies. Trolleys for hire. Golf Professional. *Society Meetings*: all welcome.*

NEWTOWNABBEY. **Ballyearl Golf and Leisure Centre,** 585 Doagh Road, Newtownabbey BT36 8RZ (028 9084 8287). *Location:* eight miles north of Belfast, 15 miles south of Larne. From Belfast follow signs to Larne via M2 (A8), turn right to Mossley approximately one miles from Corrs Corner Pub. Ballyearl is one mile on left. Parkland. 9 holes, 2402 yards, 2196 metres. Par 3. 24-bay covered floodlit driving range, outdoor grass teeing area. *Green Fees:* weekdays £6.80 adults, £3.80 concessions; weekends and Bank Holidays £8.90 adults, £5.00 concessions. *Eating facilities:* snacks available in Squash Club bar. *Visitors:* no restrictions – pay and play. Squash courts, hi-tech fitness suite and arts theatre. Golf lessons available by appointment, golf equipment tailored to individual requirements and can be tested on driving range. Professional: Richard Johnston (028 9084 0899).

PORTBALLINTRAE. **Bushfoot Golf Club,** 50 Bushfoot Road, Portballintrae BT57 8RR (028 2073 1317; Fax: 028 2073 1852). *Location:* off Ballaghmore Road, Portballintrae. Seaside links course. 9 holes, 6075 yards. S.S.S 67. *Green Fees:* weekdays £16.00; weekends £20.00. *Eating facilities:* full dining room, bars. *Visitors:* welcome, restrictions weekends July to September. *Society Meetings:* all welcome weekdays. Secretary/ Manager: J. Knox Thompson.

PORTRUSH. **Rathmore Golf Club,** Bushmills Road, Portrush BT56 8JG (028 7082 2285). *Location:* north east coast - six miles from Coleraine, beside roundabout on road to Bushmills. Royal Portrush Golf Club (valley links). Flat seaside links. 18 holes, 6304 yards. S.S.S. 70. *Green Fees:* information not provided. *Eating facilities:* bar but no eating facilities. *Visitors:* Saturday and Sunday 1.30 to 2.30pm, Monday to Friday no restrictions except Tuesday after 11am September to March and Thursday from 4-6pm May to August. *Society Meetings:* must register at Royal Portrush Golf Club and pay green fees before commencement of play. Professional: Gary McNeill (R.P.G.C.) (028 7082 2311). Club Administrator: Willie McIntyre (Tel & Fax: 028 7082 2996).

Ballyearl
ARTS & LEISURE CENTRE
Doagh Road
Newtownabbey

EXCELLENT 9 HOLE PAR 3 COURSE. A CHALLENGE TO BEGINNERS AND SEASONED GOLFERS

Also 27 Bay, floodlit Driving Range.
Now featuring 7 Automated Tees!
Opening times
Mon-Fri 9am-9.30pm,
Sat-Sun 9am-5pm.
All welcome
no booking required

Newtownabbey
BOROUGH COUNCIL

For further information contact
028 9084 8287

PORTRUSH. Royal Portrush Golf Club, Dunluce Road, Portrush BT56 8JQ (028 7082 2311). *Location:* one mile from Portrush on the main Portrush/Bushmills Road. Dunluce Course-natural seaside links. 18 holes, 7341 yards. S.S.S. 74. Valley Course - flat seaside links. 18 holes, 6304 yards. S.S.S 69. Two practice grounds. *Green Fees:* information not provided. *Eating facilities:* three bars, restaurant with snacks and à la carte. *Visitors:* Dunluce Course: must contact Secretary prior to visit. Restrictions Monday, Wednesday and Friday afternoons and Saturday and Sunday mornings. Valley Course: welcome weekdays, plus limited tee times at weekends. *Society Meetings:* accepted with prior bookings. Professional: Gary McNeill (028 7082 3335). Secretary: Miss W. Erskine (028 7082 2311; Fax: 028 7082 3139).
e-mail: info@royalportrushgolfclub.com
website: www.royalportrushgolfclub.com

TEMPLEPATRICK. Hilton Templepatrick Golf Club, Paradise Walk, Castle Upton Estate, Templepatrick BT39 0DD (02894 435542; Fax: 02894 435511). *Location*: 5 miles from Belfast International Airport, 15 miles from Belfast city centre. Parkland course - USGA greens. 18 holes, 7010 yards. S.S.S. 71. Driving range and putting green. *Green Fees*: information not available. *Eating facilities*: à la carte Restaurant and Bar Brasserie in 4 star hotel. *Visitors*: welcome. 129 bedroomed hotel, Livingwell Health Club, Tuition package. *Society Meetings*: welcome, no restrictions. Professionals: Eamonn Logue (02894 435542; Fax: 02894 435511). Director of Golf: Eamonn Logue (02894 435510).*
e-mail: eamonn.logue@hilton.com

4th hole at Galgorm Castle Golf Club, Ballymena, Co.Antrim

Armagh

ARMAGH. **County Armagh Golf Club,** 7 Newry Road, Armagh BT60 1EN (028 3752 2501). *Location:* Armagh/Newry road. Parkland course. 18 holes, 6212 yards. S.S.S. 69. Practice area available. *Green Fees:* £17.00 weekdays, £22.00 weekends. November to February (incl.) reduction of £1.00. *Eating facilities:* diningroom/bar meals Tuesdays to Sundays, bar facilities daily. *Visitors:* welcome by arrangement. Not Saturdays or Thursdays. Carts and buggies. *Society Meetings:* welcome by arrangement except Saturdays or Thursdays. Professional: Alan Rankin (Tel & Fax: 028 3752 5864). Secretary: Lynne Fleming (Tel & Fax: 028 3752 5861).

CRAIGAVON. **Craigavon Golf and Ski Club,** Turmoyra Lane, Lurgan, Craigavon (028 3832 6606; Fax: 028 3834 7272). *Location:* half a mile from motorway, one mile from town centre, adjacent to ski slope. Parkland/wooded. 18 holes, 5901 metres. S.S.S. 72. 9 hole Par 3. 12 hole pitch and putt. Driving range. *Green Fees:* information not available. *Eating facilities:* full restaurant facilities. *Visitors:* always welcome. Modern clubhouse, showers and lockers. *Society Meetings:* welcome - book beforehand. Professional: S.Dickson.*

CRAIGAVON. **Edenmore Golf and Country Club,** Edenmore House, 70 Drumnabreeze Road, Magheralin, Craigavon BT67 0RH (028 9261 9241; Fax: 028 9261 3310). *Location:* take main road for Lurgan, coming off M1 at Moira Exit. Signposted from village of Magheralin on main Moira – Lurgan Road. Undulating, parkland course with panoramic views. Well drained. 18 holes, 6244 yards. S.S.S. 70. Practice facilities, putting green. *Green Fees*: information not available. *Eating facilities:* Bailies restaurant. *Visitors*: Edenmore is a friendly, welcoming club. Visitors at all times except Saturdays before 3pm. Well stocked Pro Shop, lessons available. *Society Meetings:* welcome. Ring to book. PGA Professional: Andrew Manson. Secretary: Kenneth Logan (028 9261 1310; Fax: 028 9261 3310).*
e-mail: info@edenmore.com
website: www.edenmore.com

CULLYHANNA. **Ashfield Golf Club,** Freeduff Road, Cullyhanna, Newry BT35 0NA (028 3086 8180; Fax: 028 3086 8611). *Location:* A29 road, from Newry to Crossmaglen, 15 miles distance. Parkland course, lake, water hazard, bunkers. 18 holes, 5616 yards. S.S.S. 67. Par 69. Driving range. *Green Fees:* information not available. *Eating facilities:* licensed restaurant. *Visitors:* welcome at all times except before 11am on Sundays. *Society Meetings:* welcome, special rates available. Secretary: Seamus McNulty.*

LURGAN. **Lurgan Golf Club,** The Demesne, Lurgan, Craigavon BT67 9BN (028 3832 2087; Fax: 028 3831 6166). *Location:* one mile from motorway, half a mile from town centre. Parkland. 18 holes, 5895 metres. S.S.S. 69. Small practice area, putting green. *Green Fees:* weekdays £20.00; weekends £25.00. Reductions if playing with a member. Students £14.00, under 18s £10.00. *Eating facilities:* restaurant and lounge bar. Caterer: (028 3832 2087). *Visitors:* welcome Monday to Friday, and Sundays after 3pm. *Society Meetings:* welcome as per visitors. Professional: Des Paul (028 3832 1068). Secretary: Muriel Sharpe (028 3832 2087; Fax: 028 3831 6166).

PORTADOWN. **Portadown Golf Club,** 192 Gilford Road, Portadown BT63 5LF (028 3835 5356). *Location:* on main Gilford Road out of Portadown. Parkland. 18 holes, 6118 metres. S.S.S. 69 off white tees; 67 off green tees, 72 off red tees. *Green Fees:* weekday £18.00; weekend an Bank Holidays £22.00. *Eating facilities:* Contact caterer on 028 3835 2214. *Visitors:* welcome at all times except Tuesdays and Saturdays. Squash, indoor bowling and snooker. *Society Meetings:* catered for by booking. Professional: Paul Stevenson (028 3833 4655). Secretary: Ms Barbara Currie (028 3835 5356).
e-mail: info@portadowngolfclub.co.uk
website: www.portadowngolfclub.co.uk

TANDRAGEE. **Tandragee Golf Club,** Markethill Road, Tandragee, Craigavon BT62 2ER (028 3884 1272; Fax: 028 3884 0664). *Location*: approximately five miles from Portadown on road to Newry and Dublin. Hilly parkland and wooded. 18 holes, 5754 metres. S.S.S. 70, Par 71. Practice ground and net. *Green Fees*: weekday £20.00; weekend £25.00. *Eating facilities:* full catering except Mondays; two lounges. *Visitors*: welcome all days except Thursdays (Ladies' Day) and Saturdays (competition day). Carts and buggies available. *Society Meetings*: welcome by arrangement. Professional: D. Keenan (028 3884 1761). Mrs Ashley Stewart.
e-mail: office@tandragee.co.uk
website: www.tandragee.co.uk

For full details of convenient accommodation near clubs and courses

www.holidayguides.com

Co. Down

ARDGLASS. **Ardglass Golf Club,** 4 Castle Place, Ardglass BT30 7TP (028 4484 1219; Fax: 028 4484 1841). *Location:* nearest town – Downpatrick. Situated on the coast 30 miles due south of Belfast. Seaside links. 18 holes, White markers - 6268 yards. S.S.S. 70, Par 70. *Green Fees:* information not available. *Eating facilities:* bar and dining room. *Visitors:* welcome all week. *Society Meetings:* welcome except Saturdays, advance booking necessary. Professional: Philip Farrell (028 4484 1022). Club Manager: Mrs Deborah Turley (028 4484 1219; Fax: 028 4484 1841).*
e-mail: info@ardglassgolfclub.com
website: www.ardglassgolfclub.com

BALLYNAHINCH. **Spa Golf Club,** 20 Grove Road, Ballynahinch BT24 8PN (028 9756 2365; Fax: 028 9756 4158). *Location:* Ballynahinch half mile, 11 miles south of Belfast. Parkland, wooded course with panoramic views. 18 holes, 6469 yards. S.S.S. 72. Practice area. *Green Fees:* information not available. *Eating facilities:* bar snacks/ restaurant service. *Visitors:* welcome except Saturdays. *Society Meetings:* welcome, discount for large parties. Secretary: T.G. Magee (028 9756 2365).
e-mail: spagolfclub@btconnect.com
website: www.spagolfclub.net

BANBRIDGE. **Banbridge Golf Club,** Huntly Road, Banbridge BT32 3UR. *Location:* half-a-mile from town centre on the Huntly Road. Parkland. 18 holes, 5590 yards. S.S.S. 67. Practice ground. *Green Fees:* information not provided. *Eating facilities:* full catering and bar facilities. *Visitors:* welcome, restrictions on Ladies' Day (Tuesdays) and Men's competition day (Saturdays). *Society Meetings:* catered for. Club Professional: Jason Greenaway (028 4062 6189).
e-mail: info@banbridgegolfclub.net

BANGOR. **Bangor Golf Club,** Broadway, Bangor BT20 4RH (028 9127 0922; Fax: 028 9145 3394). *Location:* one mile from town centre off Donaghadee Road. Parkland. 18 holes, 6424 yards. S.S.S. 71. Practice facilities. *Green Fees:* information not available. *Eating facilities:* lunches and evening meals. *Visitors:* welcome except Saturdays; Tuesday is Ladies' Day. Trolleys and buggies available. *Society Meetings:* advance booking necessary. Professional: Michael Bannon (028 9146 2164).*
e-mail: office@bangorgolfclubni.co.uk
website: www.bangorgolfclubni.co.uk

BANGOR. **Blackwood Golf Centre,** 150 Crawfordsburn Road, Bangor BT19 1GB (028 9185 2706). *Location:* west of Bangor. Two 18-hole courses. Driving range. *Green Fees:* information not available. *Visitors:* welcome.*

BANGOR. **Carnalea Golf Club,** Station Road, Bangor BT19 1EZ (028 9127 0368). *Location:* one minute walk from Carnalea Railway Station. Seaside parkland. 18 holes, 5574 yards. S.S.S. 67. *Green Fees:* weekday £17.50; weekend and Bank Holidays £22.00. *Eating facilities:* full restaurant and two bars. *Visitors:* welcome without reservation. *Society Meetings:* catered for. Golf Shop (028 9127 0122). Professional: Tom Loughran (028 9127 0122). Secretary/Manager: N. Greene (028 9127 0368; Fax: 028 9127 3989).
e-mail: nicola@carnaleagolfclub.co.uk

BANGOR. **Helen's Bay Golf Club,** Golf Road, Helen's Bay, Bangor BT19 1TL (028 9185 2815). *Location:* A2 from Belfast - 9 miles. Parkland. 9 holes, 5383 yards. S.S.S. 67. *Green Fees:* information not provided. *Eating facilities:* available - full restaurant, bar and lounge bar (028 9185 2816). *Visitors:* welcome Sunday, Monday, Wednesday and Friday; Tuesday is Ladies' Day. *Society Meetings:* catered for by prior booking (maximum 40). (028 9185 2815; Fax: 028 9185 2660).

BELFAST. **Balmoral Golf Club Ltd,** 518 Lisburn Road, Belfast BT9 6GX (028 9038 1514). *Location:* M1 from Belfast exit Balmoral, turn right at lights Lisburn Road, quarter mile on left beside Kings Hall or two/three miles south of Belfast on main Lisburn Road next to Kings Hall. A flat undulating course with 44 plus bunkers and a stream to contend with. Excellent greens, approached by tree-lined fairways. 18 holes, 6034 metres. S.S.S. 70 Medal, 69 regular. Practice ground and nets. *Green Fees:* information not available. *Eating facilities:* restaurant, lunch, dinner, snacks à la carte, two bars. *Visitors:* welcome except Saturdays; restricted on Sundays. *Society Meetings:* Mondays, Thursdays and Sunday afternoons. Professional: Geoff Bleakley (028 9066 7747). Chief Executive: Terry Graham (028 9038 1514; Fax: 028 9066 6759).*
website: www.balmoralgolf.com

BELFAST. **Belvoir Park Golf Club,** 73/75 Church Road, Newtownbreda, Belfast BT8 7AN (028 9049 1693; Fax: 028 9064 6113). *Location:* two miles from city centre, Saintfield Road. Parkland, well wooded. 18 holes, 6597 yards. S.S.S. 71. Practice area. *Green Fees:* weekdays £65.00; weekends £75.00. *Eating facilities:* full catering and bar. *Visitors:* welcome except Saturday. *Society Meetings:* by prior booking only. Professional: Michael McGivern (028 9064 6714). Secretary: Ann Vaughan (028 9049 1693).

BELFAST. **Knock Golf Club,** Summerfield, Dundonald, Belfast BT16 2QX (028 9048 2249; Fax: 028 9048 7277). *Location:* Upper Newtownards Road in east of the city of Belfast. Parkland with huge trees, large bunkers and a stream running through the course. 18 holes, 6435 yards. S.S.S. 71. Practice ground. *Green Fees:* information not available. *Eating facilities:* full catering and bar facilities available. *Visitors:* welcome except Saturday but it is advisable to ring Professional first. Trolleys available. *Society Meetings:* catered for Mondays and Thursdays. Advance booking required. Professional: R. Whitford (028 9048 3825). Secretary/Manager: Mrs A. Armstrong (028 9048 3251).*

BELFAST. **Ormeau Golf Club,** 50 Park Road, Belfast BT7 2FX (028 9064 0700; Fax: 028 9064 6250). *Location:* Belfast south/east; Ravenhill Road. Flat, parkland wooded course. 9 holes, 2783 yards, 2542 metres. S.S.S. 67. *Green Fees:* information not available. *Eating facilities:* bars and restaurant. *Visitors:* welcome, restrictions on Tuesdays and Saturdays. Snooker. *Society Meetings:* welcome most days. Shop Manager: S. Rourke (028 90 640999). Manager: W. Lynn (028 9064 0700). Caterer: (028 9064 1999).*

BELFAST. **Shandon Park Golf Club,** 73 Shandon Park, Belfast BT5 6NY (028 9080 5030). Parkland. 18 holes, 6460 metres. S.S.S. 70. *Green Fees:* information not provided. *Eating facilities:* restaurant facilities, bar snacks. *Visitors:* welcome except Saturdays subject to advance clearance by Professional. *Society Meetings:* Mondays, Thursdays, Fridays and Sundays. Professional: Barry Wilson (028 9080 5031). Secretary/Manager: Greg Bailie (028 9080 5030; Fax: 028 9080 5999).

DONAGHADEE. **Donaghadee Golf Club,** 84 Warren Road, Donaghadee BT21 0PQ (028 9188 8697). *Location:* five miles south of Bangor on main coast road. Part links and inland park with scenic views over Copeland Islands and Scottish coast. 18 holes, 6000 yards, 5561 metres. Par 71, S.S.S. 69. Practice ground and putting green. *Green Fees:* information not provided. *Eating facilities:* full catering available, seven days in summer, Tuesday to Sunday in winter. *Visitors:* welcome on any weekday and Sundays; Members only on Saturdays. Ladies welcome on Tuesdays. Juveniles must be accompanied by an adult. Pro shop. Club and trolley hire. Lessons available by prior arrangement. *Society Meetings:* welcome any day except Saturday. Special rates available. Professional: Gordon Drew (028 9188 2392). General Manager: (028 9188 3624; Fax: 028 9188 8891).
e-mail: office@donaghadeegolfclub.net.

DOWNPATRICK. **Bright Castle Golf Club,** 14 Coniamstown Road, Bright, Downpatrick BT30 8LU (028 4484 1319). *Location:* turn right off the main B176, signposted to Bright/Minerstown. Bright Castle is an 18 hole mature woodland course featuring four formidable par 5s - your driving accuracy will be tested to the limit on the sloping, densely tree-lined fairways. 6645 yards. SSS 73. *Green Fees:* information not available. *Eating facilities:* Restaurant and bar available. *Visitors:* Welcome. *Society Meetings:* Welcome, must book in advance. Secretary: Thomas Johnston (028 4482 8428).*
e-mail: bright.castle@virgin.net

DOWNPATRICK. **Downpatrick Golf Club,** 43 Saul Road, Downpatrick BT30 6PA (028 4461 5947; Fax: 028 4461 7502). *Location:* one and a half miles from town centre, south-east direction. Parkland, challenging upland course. 18 holes, 6120 yards. S.S.S. 69. Practice area and putting area. *Green Fees:* information not available. *Eating facilities:* two lounges and diningroom. Catering: (028 4461 5244). *Visitors:* welcome, but advisable to make arrangements in advance for weekends. Snooker room. *Society Meetings:* welcome by prior arrangement. Professional: Robert Hutton (028 4461 5167). Office Manager: Elaine Carson.*

HOLYWOOD. **Holywood Golf Club,** Nuns Walk, Demesne Road, Holywood BT18 9LE (028 9042 3135/2138; Fax: 028 9042 5040). Parkland. 18 holes, 6078 yards. S.S.S. 68. *Green Fees:* visit website. *Eating facilities:* bars and restaurant. *Visitors:* welcome. *Society Meetings:* welcome Sundays. Professional: (028 9042 5503; Fax: 028 9042 5040). Secretary: (028 9042 3135; Fax: 028 9042 5040). website: www.holywoodgolfclub.co.uk

HOLYWOOD. **The Royal Belfast Golf Club,** Station Road, Craigavad BT18 0BP (028 9042 8165; Fax: 028 9042 1404). *Location:* two miles past Holywood, off main Belfast to Bangor Road. Mainly parkland, bordering shores of Belfast Lough. 18 holes, 5961 yards. S.S.S. 69. Practice ground. *Green Fees:* weekdays £60.00 (parties over 16 persons £50.00 each); weekends £70.00. *Eating facilities:* full catering and bar facilities. *Visitors:* with letter of introduction and by arrangement only. *Society Meetings:* by arrangement. Professional: A. Ferguson (028 9042 8586). Secretary/Manager: Mrs S.H. Morrison (028 9042 8165).

DONAGHADEE GOLF CLUB • 028 9188 3624
84 Warren Road, Donaghadee, Co. Down BT21 0PQ

Located 5 miles south of Bangor on A2 on coast road. A part links and part inland course with lovely views to the Scottish coast. Well-appointed clubhouse. Visitors welcome weekdays and Sundays. Club hire and trolleys available. Special rates for Societies. Limited memberships currently available.
18 holes, 5561 metres, Par 71, S.S.S. 69
e-mail: office@donaghadeegolfclub.net
General Manager: 028 9188 3624
Professional: Gordon Drew 028 9188 2392

KILKEEL. Kilkeel Golf Club, Mourne Park, Kilkeel BT34 4LB (028 4176 5095; Fax: 028 4176 5579). *Location:* Kilkeel to Newry road approximately three miles from Kilkeel. Parkland situated at the foot of Mourne Mountains. 18 holes, 6579 yards. S.S.S. 72. Practice area available. *Green Fees:* information not available. *Eating facilities:* restaurant and bar. *Visitors:* welcome, club competitions on Tuesday, Thursday and Saturday. Booking for Saturday late afternoons and Sundays. *Society Meetings:* catered for by prior arrangement.*

KNOCKBRACKEN. **Mount Ober Golf and Country Club,** 24 Ballymaconaghy Road, Knockbracken, Belfast BT8 6SB (028 9079 5666; Fax: 028 9070 5862). *Location:* 15 minutes from centre of Belfast; Saintfield Road, Cairnshill Road, Four Winds Roundabout. Parkland on undulating ground. 18 holes, 5203 yards, S.S.S. 66. Golf academy, floodlit driving range. *Green Fees:* Monday to Friday £18.00, Sunday and Bank Holidays £20.00. *Eating facilities:* full catering and bar service at all times; excellent restaurant. *Visitors:* welcome anytime, except Saturdays before 3pm. *Society Meetings:* welcome except Saturdays before 3pm. Professional: Wesley Ramsay (028 9070 1648; Fax: 028 9070 5862). Secretary: Ena Williams (028 9040 1811; Fax: 028 9070 5862).
e-mail: mt.ober@ukonline.co.uk
website: www.mountober.com

NEWCASTLE. **Royal County Down Golf Club,** Newcastle BT33 0AN. *Location:* adjacent to north side of Newcastle, approach from town centre. Championship Course: 18 holes, 7204 yards, S.S.S. 74. Annesley Links Course: 18 holes, 4681 yards. S.S.S. 66. *Green Fees:* information not provided. *Eating facilities:* light lunches and bar, weekdays only. *Visitors:* welcome with prior reservation. *Society Meetings:* catered for. Professional: Kevan J. Whitson (028 4372 2419). Secretary: David Wilson (028 4372 3314; Fax: 028 4372 6281).
website: www.royalcountydown.org

NEWTOWNARDS. **Clandeboye Golf Club,** Tower Road, Conlig, Newtownards BT23 7PN (028 9127 1767). *Location:* Conlig village off A21 between Bangor and Newtownards. Wooded, undulating parkland/heathland. Two courses: Dufferin – 18 holes, 6559 yards, S.S.S. 71; blue tees - 6742 yards, S.S.S. 72. Ava – 18 holes, 5755 yards, S.S.S. 68. Practice ground. Host to the Irish Seniors 2001; N.I. Masters, won by Darren Clarke. *Green Fees:* Dufferin Course - weekdays £35.00, weekends and Public Holidays £40.00; Ava Course - weekdays £30.00, weekends and Public Holidays £35.00. 2010 rates (subject to review). *Eating facilities:* full catering and bar. *Visitors:* welcome weekdays; no play before 2.30pm Saturdays, before 10am Sundays. Visitors changing facility. *Society Meetings:* welcome weekdays except Thursdays. Professional: Peter Gregory (028 9127 1750). General Manager: (028 9127 1767; Fax: 028 9147 3711).

NEWTOWNARDS. **Kirkistown Castle Golf Club,** 142 Main Road, Cloughey, Newtownards BT22 1JA (028 4277 1233). *Location:* approximately 45 minutes from Belfast, 16 miles from Newtownards on the A2. 18 holes, Par 69, S.S.S. 70. *Green Fees:* £25.00 weekdays; £30.00 weekends and Public Holidays. Tourists 10% discount in approved accommodation. *Eating facilities:* full catering and snacks. *Visitors:* welcome. *Society Meetings:* outings welcome by arrangement. Secretary/Manager: Rosemary Coulter (028 4277 1233). Professional: Neil Graham (028 9177 1004). Caterer: Marion Smyth (028 4277 2395; Fax: 028 4277 1699).
e-mail: kirkistown@supanet.com
website: www.linksgolfkirkistown.com

NEWTOWNARDS. **Mahee Island Golf Club,** Mahee Island, Comber, Newtownards BT23 6EP (028 9754 1234). *Location:* Comber/Killyleagh Road. After half a mile turn left signposted Ardmillan/Mahee Island. Keep left for six miles to course. Parkland course set on an island with magnificent views over Strangford Lough. 9 holes, 5822 yards, 5108 metres. S.S.S. 68. Par 71 over 18 holes. Putting green and pitching area. *Green Fees:* weekdays £13.00; weekends £18.00. *Eating facilities:* Sunday, Monday, Wednesday and Saturday, other times by arrangement with caterer (07968 449932). *Visitors:* welcome, restricted Saturdays until 5pm. *Society Meetings:* welcome, by prior arrangement. Professional: (Shop) Colin Macaw (028 9754 1234). Secretary: Mervyn Marshall (028 9754 1234).

NEWTOWNARDS. **Scrabo Golf Club,** 233 Scrabo Road, Newtownards BT23 4SL (028 9181 2355). *Location:* approximately 10 miles from Belfast off main Belfast to Newtownards dual carriageway, follow signs to Scrabo Country Park. Upland course. 18 holes, 5699 metres. S.S.S. 71. Practice area. *Green Fees:* call for details. *Eating facilities:* full catering (closed Mondays). *Visitors:* welcome except Saturdays and avoid Wednesdays 4.30pm to 6.30pm. *Society Meetings:* over 12 players, welcome.

WARRENPOINT. **Warrenpoint Golf Club,** Lower Dromore Road, Warrenpoint BT34 3LN (028 4175 3695; Fax: 028 4175 2918). *Location:* five miles south of Newry on coast road. Parkland. 18 holes, 5700 metres. S.S.S. 70. Practice ground. *Green Fees:* £30.00 weekdays, £34.00 weekends. *Eating facilities:* full catering and bar facilities. *Visitors:* welcome Sunday, Monday, Thursday, Friday. Snooker facilities available. *Society Meetings:* catered for by prior arrangement. Professional: Nigel Shaw (Tel & Fax: 028 4175 2371). Secretary: Marian Trainor.
e-mail: office@warrenpointgolf.com

www.holidayguides.com for accommodation near golf clubs

Fermanagh

ENNISKILLEN. **Castle Hume Golf Club,** Belleek Road, Enniskillen BT93 7ED (028 6632 7077; Fax: 028 6632 7076). *Location:* on A46 Belleek/Donegal Road, just a few minutes' drive from Enniskillen. Fast emerging as one of the best golfing facilities the North has to offer, this Championship Course provides golfers of all skill levels with a very enjoyable yet testing challenge. Hosted the Ulster PGA Championship 1996-2008. 18 holes, 5932 metres. Floodlit driving range. *Green Fees:* information not provided. *Eating facilities:* excellent hospitality in the bar and restaurant. *Visitors:* welcome. Fully stocked Pro Shop. Open Days every Wednesday April to September. *Society Meetings:* welcome. Resident PGA Professional: Shaun Donnelly.
e-mail: info@castlehumegolf.com
website: www.castlehumegolf.com
www.lougherneogolfresort.com

ENNISKILLEN. **Enniskillen Golf Club,** Castlecoole, Enniskillen BT74 6HZ (028 6632 5250). *Location:* off Enniskillen to Tempo Road on outskirts of town. Scenic parkland course with views of market town of Enniskillen on front nine, many mature trees on back nine. 18 holes, 6189 yards. S.S.S. 69. *Green Fees:* information not available. *Eating facilities:* catering by arrangement. *Visitors:* welcome at all times; some restriction on Tuesdays (Ladies' Day) and weekends. *Society Meetings:* welcome at all times, special rates available. Hon. Secretary: David McKechnie. Club Steward Daryll Robinson (028 6632 5250).*

Londonderry

CASTLEROCK. **Castlerock Golf Club,** 65 Circular Road, Castlerock, Coleraine BT51 4TJ (028 7084 8314). *Location:* A2, six miles west of Coleraine. Seaside links, stream in play at four holes. 18 holes, 6687 yards, S.S.S. 72. 9 holes, 2457 metres. S.S.S. 67. Practice area. *Green Fees:* weekdays £65.00 per round, weekends and Bank Holidays £80.00. 2010 rates (subject to review). *Eating facilities:* full restaurant facilities, two bars. *Visitors:* welcome weekdays Monday to Friday and weekends by arrangement. *Society Meetings:* welcome Monday to Friday. Professional: Tom Johnston (028 7084 9424). Secretary: Mark Steen (028 7084 8314; Fax: 028 7084 9440).

COLERAINE. **Brown Trout Golf and Country Club,** 209 Agivey Road, Aghadowey, Near Coleraine BT51 4AD (028 7086 8209; Fax: 028 7086 8878). *Location:* on A54 between Kilrea and Coleraine. Parkland course, heavily wooded, crossing water seven times in nine holes. 9 holes, 2755 metres. S.S.S. 68. *Green Fees:* information not provided. *Eating facilities:* à la carte restaurant, bar snacks, barbecues. *Visitors:* always welcome. 15 luxurious en suite bedrooms and four five-star cottages available. *Society Meetings:* welcome. Professional: Ken Revie. Secretary/ Manager: Bill O'Hara.
e-mail: bill@browntroutinn.com
website: www.browntroutinn.com

LIMAVADY. **Benone Golf Course,** Benone Tourist Complex, 53 Benone Avenue, Benone, Limavady BT49 0LQ (028 7775 0555). *Location:* situated on the A2 coast road, 12 miles from Limavady. Parkland course. 9 holes, 1458 yards, 1334 metres. S.S.S. 27. Practice range, putting green. *Green Fees:* information not available. *Eating facilities:* coffee shop open July/August, restaurant and bars within one mile. *Visitors:* welcome. Club hire available. *Society Meetings:* welcome. Secretary: M. Clark (028 7775 0555; Fax: 028 7775 0919).*

LIMAVADY. **Roe Park Golf Club,** Radisson SAS Roe Park Resort, Roe Park, Limavady BT49 9LB (028 7772 2222; Fax: 028 7772 2313). *Location:* on main A2 Londonderry-Limavady road, 16 miles from Londonderry and one mile from Limavady. (028 777 60105). Parkland. 18 holes, 6318 yards. S.S.S. 69. Floodlit driving range; putting green; equipment hire. *Green Fees:* information not available. *Eating facilities:* Coach House Brasserie. *Visitors:* welcome with some restrictions at weekend. *Society Meetings:* welcome; society packages available. Accommodation on site. Professional: Shaun Devenney. Golf Manager: Terry Kelly.*

LONDONDERRY. **Foyle International Golf Centre,** 12 Alder Road, Londonderry BT48 8DB (028 7135 2222; Fax: 028 7135 3967). *Location:* one-and-a-half miles from Foyle Bridge heading towards Moville, Co Donegal. Parkland Championship standard Par 71, notable holes with water coming into play are third Par 3, 10th and 11th. 18 holes, 6678 yard, 6164 metres. S.S.S. 71, Par 71. 9 hole course, Par 3. Indoor floodlit driving range with automated tees, putting greens. *Green Fees:* weekdays £17.00; weekends £20.00. 10% discount for groups over 12. *Eating facilities:* Pitchers Wine Bar and Restaurant within club house. *Visitors:* welcome anyday, anytime. Carts, caddies available. Golf academy with video analysis teaching system. *Society Meetings:* welcome. Professionals: Derek Morrison and Sean Young. Secretary: Margaret Lapsley.
e-mail: mail@foylegolf.club24.co.uk
website: www.foylegolfcentre.co.uk

MAGHERAFELT. **Moyola Park Golf Club,** 15 Curran Road, Castledawson, Magherafelt BT45 8DG (028 7946 8468; Fax: 028 7946 8626). *Location:* 35 miles north of Belfast on M2; off middle of Main Street, Castledawson. Attractive, spacious mature parkland. 18 holes, 6519 yards. S.S.S. 71. Practice ground, putting green. *Green Fees:* information not provided. *Eating facilities*: bars and restaurant. *Visitors:* welcome with prior notice. *Society Meetings:* welcome with prior notice. Professional: Bob Cockcroft (028 7946 8830). Secretary/ Manager: Michael Gribbin.

PORTSTEWART. **Portstewart Golf Club,** Strand Road, Portstewart, BT55 7PG (028 7083 2015; Fax: 028 7083 4097). *Location:* north from Coleraine. Coastal links. No 1 Strand - 18 holes, 6784 yards, S.S.S. 73. No 2 Riverside - 9 holes, 2622 yards. No 3 Old - 18 holes, 4733 yards, S.S.S. 64. Practice area. *Green Fees:* information not available. *Eating facilities:* meals available - advance orders; no catering on Mondays. *Visitors:* welcome Mondays to Fridays; limited Wednesdays. Prior booking essential on Strand. Enquire about special rates for parties. *Society Meetings:* catered for by arrangement. Professional: Alan Hunter (Tel & Fax: 028 7083 2601). Secretary: Michael Moss (028 7083 2015; Fax: 028 7083 4097).*
e-mail: michael@portstewartgc.co.uk.*

PREHEN. **City of Derry Golf Club,** 49 Victoria Road, Prehen BT47 2PU (028 7134 6369). *Location:* three miles from city centre on the road to Strabane - follow the River Foyle. Parkland, wooded. 18 holes, 5877 metres. S.S.S. 71, Par 71. Also 9 hole (Dunhugh) course, 4305 metres. Par 66. Practice area. *Green Fees:* information not available. *Eating facilities:* catering and bar facilities available. *Visitors:* welcome on weekdays up to 4.30pm, weekends please contact Professional. Convenient for hotels and guest houses. *Society Meetings:* rates by arrangement; discounts available for parties over 20 players. Professional: Sam Smallwoods (028 7131 1496). Hon. Secretary: Tony McCann (028 7134 6369). Admin: (028 7134 6369).*
e-mail: info@cityofderrygolfclub.com
website: www.cityofderrygolfclub.com

17th hole, Moyola Park Golf Club, Magherafelt

Tyrone

COOKSTOWN. Killymoon Golf Club, 200 Killymoon Road, Cookstown BT80 8TW (Tel & Fax: 028 8676 3762). *Location:* private road off A29. Signposted at Dungannon end of town opposite Drum Road. Mainly flat parkland. 18 holes, 6202 yards. S.S.S. 70. Practice ground. *Green Fees:* Mondays £16.00 (excluding Bank Holidays); Tuesdays to Fridays £22.00; weekends and Bank Holidays £28.00. *Eating facilities:* full catering at club (large groups please book). *Visitors:* welcome, after 4pm Saturdays, Thursday is Ladies' Day. Booking essential. *Society Meetings:* welcome. Booking essential. Professional: Gary Chambers (Tel & Fax: 028 8676 3460); Secretary: Brian Rouse (Tel & Fax: 028 8676 3762). General Manager: Norman Weir (028 8676 3762).

DUNGANNON. **Dungannon Golf Club,** 34 Springfield Lane, Dungannon BT70 1QX (028 8772 2098; Fax: 028 8772 7338). *Location:* a short distance from Dungannon along Donaghmore Road. Flat first 9, hilly second 9. Parkland course with some water hazards newly positioned. 18 holes, 6155 yards (white markers.) S.S.S. 69. *Green Fees:* weekdays £20.00; weekends and Bank Holidays £25.00. *Eating facilities:* bar snacks and licensed restaurant. *Visitors:* always welcome but please telephone first; precluded by timesheets at weekends, Ladies' Day Tuesdays. *Society Meetings:* welcome by prior arrangement; apply in writing. Professional: Christopher Jelly. Secretary: S.T. Hughes.

FINTONA. **Fintona Golf Club,** 1 Kiln Street, Ecclesville Demesne, Fintona BT78 2BJ (Tel & Fax: 028 8284 1480). *Location:* eight miles south of Omagh, county town of Tyrone. An attractive parkland course, its main features being a trout stream; rated one of the top nine hole courses in the Province. 9 holes, 5765 metres. S.S.S. 70. Putting green. *Green Fees:* information not available. *Eating facilities:* bar snacks, meals on request. *Visitors:* welcome weekdays, weekends by arrangement. *Society Meetings:* welcome weekdays, book in advance.*

NEWTOWNSTEWART. **Newtownstewart Golf Club,** 38 Golf Course Road, Newtownstewart, Omagh BT78 4HU (028 8166 1466; Fax: 028 8166 2506). *Location:* signposted from Strabane Road (A57) at Newtownstewart, two miles west of Newtownstewart on B84. Parkland and wooded course. 18 holes, 5320 metres. S.S.S. 69. Practice ground. *Green Fees:* information not provided. *Eating facilities:* available. *Visitors:* welcome at all times. Accommodation available in chalets beside clubhouse. Buggies available. *Society Meetings:* all welcome. Special packages available. Golf Shop: (028 8166 2242; Fax: 028 8166 2506). Club Administrator/Secretary: Mrs Lorraine Donnell (028 8166 1466; Fax: 028 8166 2506).
e-mail: newtown.stewart@lineone.net
website: www.newtownstewartgolfclub.com

OMAGH. **Omagh Golf Club,** 83a Dublin Road, Omagh BT78 1HQ (Tel & Fax: 028 8224 3160). *Location:* one mile from Omagh town centre on Belfast/Dublin Road. Parkland. 18 holes, 5638 metres. S.S.S. 70. *Green Fees:* information not available. *Eating facilities:* snacks and bar facilities. *Visitors:* welcome any day except Tuesday and Saturday. *Society Meetings:* welcome. Hon. Secretary: Joseph A. McElholm. Secretary: Florence E.A. Caldwell (Tel & Fax: 028 8224 3160).*

STRABANE. **Strabane Golf Club,** 33 Ballycolman Road, Strabane BT82 9PH (028 7138 2271/2007; Fax: 028 7188 6471). *Location:* A5 half mile from Strabane towards Omagh. Parkland. 18 holes, 5610 metres. S.S.S. 69. *Green Fees:* information not available. *Eating facilities:* two bars, catering by arrangement. *Visitors:* welcome, except Saturdays. Practice putting green and chipping area. *Society Meetings:* by arrangement. Secretary: Brian O'Kane (028 7138 2007).*

Other British holiday guides from FHG Guides

**PUBS & INNS · 300 GREAT HOTELS · SHORT BREAK HOLIDAYS
The bestselling and original PETS WELCOME! · 500 GREAT PLACES TO STAY
SELF-CATERING HOLIDAYS · BED & BREAKFAST STOPS
CARAVAN & CAMPING HOLIDAYS · FAMILY BREAKS**

Published annually: available in all good bookshops or direct from the publisher:

**FHG Guides, Abbey Mill Business Centre, Seedhill, Paisley PA1 1TJ
Tel: 0141 887 0428 • Fax: 0141 889 7204
e-mail: admin@fhguides.co.uk • www.holidayguides.com**

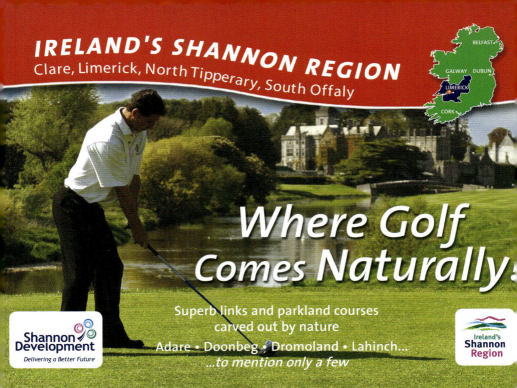

Ireland's Shannon Region

Ireland's Shannon Region – Counties of Clare, Limerick, North Tipperary and South Offaly – been carved by nature itself and its dramatic Atlantic coastline and unspoiled greenery is the per[fect] setting for superb golf courses. Golfers can test their skills on the windswept dunes of a champions[hip] links, challenge the water-traps and other hazards of courses created by some of the world's m[ost] famous designers, or just play a relaxing eighteen holes on a parkland course of tree-lined fairwa[ys].

There are five courses to choose from in the Shannon Region. Established in 1892, the Lahinch li[nks] course in Co. Clare is often referred to as 'the St. Andrews of Ireland', with its famous holes such 'The Dell'. A little further south along the Clare coast is another links gem, Doonbeg, with its mass[ive] dunes designed by Australian legend Greg Norman. When you travel inland, the choices are equ[ally] impressive. There are superb courses on the estates of the luxurious hotels, Dromoland Cas[tle] Co. Clare and Adare Manor, Co. Limerick. Other options include Birr, Co. Offaly with magnificent vie[ws] of the Slieve Bloom Mountains, Nenagh, North Tipperary with some fine panoramic views, and E[ast] Clare, Co. Clare. You have four excellent choices close to Limerick City, including Limerick County G[olf] & Country Club with its own indoor teaching facility.

Fly from the UK to Shannon Airport in less than 60 minutes, with a choice of direct flights fr[om] Birmingham, Bristol, Edinburgh, Glasgow (Prestwick), Liverpool, and from London Heathrow, Gatw[ick,] Luton, Stansted and Manchester.

For further information visit: www.DiscoverIreland.ie/ShannonRegion or request a brochure
from Tourism Marketing, Shannon Development, Shannon, Co.Clare, Ireland.
Tel: +353 61 317522; Fax: +353 61 363180

www.DiscoverIreland.ie/ShannonRegion
www.shortbreaksireland.ie

REPUBLIC OF IRELAND

County Carlow

BORRIS. **Borris Golf Club,** Deer Park, Carlow (059 9773310; Fax: 059 9773750). Scenic parkland course with tree-lined fairways and modern sandbased greens. 10 holes, 5680 yards, S.S.S. 69. Practice area and putting green. *Green Fees*: information not available. *Eating facilities*: bar meals available. *Visitors*: welcome weekdays by prior arrangement, restrictions Thursdays and weekends. *Society Meetings*: welcome by prior arrangement. Secretary: Nollaig Lucas (059 9773310; Fax: 059 9773750).*

CARLOW. **Carlow Golf Club**, Deer Park, Carlow (0503 31695; Fax: 0503 40065). *Location*: N9 2.5 miles north of Carlow town. Parkland, undulating, sandy sub-soil. 18 holes, 5974 metres. S.S.S. 71. Practice ground. New 9 hole golf course. *Green Fees*: information not provided. *Eating facilities:* bar and restaurant. *Visitors*: always welcome, weekends difficult, pre-booking advisable. Carts, caddies and club hire. *Society Meetings*: must be pre-booked with Secretary. Professional: Andrew Gilbert (059 9141745; Fax: 059 9140065). General Manager: Donard MacSweeney (059 9131695; Fax: 059 9140065).
e-mail: carlowgolfclub@eircom.net
website: www.carlowgolfclub.com

KILLERIG. **Killerig Golf Club**, Killerig, Carlow (059 91 63000; Fax: 059 91 63051). *Location:* from Dublin, on to Naas, straight through to Castledermot. At end of town take left for Tullow, through Killerig Crossroads (Walshes Pub). Golf club located on right hand side. Very challenging parkland course, designed by Des Smyth and Declan Brannigan. Water in play on 6/18 holes. 18 holes. 6165 metres. S.S.S. 72. Practice facilities available. *Green Fees:* from €20. *Eating facilities:* Brannigan's Bar - food served all day 8am-8pm. *Visitors:* welcome all year. Hotel accommodation available on site. Buggies, trolleys and clubs for hire. *Society Meetings:* welcome all year. Discounts available. Golf Administrator: Sarah O'Keeffe.
e-mail: golf@killerigresort.com
website: www.killerig-golf.ie

THE APPEARANCE OF AN ASTERISK (*) AT THE END OF A CLUB OR COURSE ENTRY INDICATES THAT UP-TO-DATE INFORMATION HAS NOT BEEN SUPPLIED

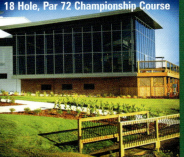

KILLERIG GOLF RESORT

KILLERIG GOLF CLUB
CO. CARLOW

18 Hole, Par 72 Championship Course

Design by Des Smyth and Declan Brannigan

Green Fees available
7 Days from €20 pp

★★★★ Accommodation
50 minutes from Dublin

Tel: 059 91 63000
www.killerig-golf.ie
golf@killerigresort.com

Visit **www.holidayguides.com**
for convenient accommodation
when playing golf around the regions

TULLOW. **Mount Wolseley Golf Club,** Tullow (00353 (0)59 918 0100; Fax: 00353 (0)59 915 2123). Mature parkland course, stunning views, immaculate playing surfaces. 18 holes, 7198 metres. S.S.S.74. Putting green. *Green Fees:* information not available. *Eating facilities:* clubhouse, bar and restaurant. *Visitors:* welcome at all times. Hotel accommodation available. *Society Meetings:* welcome, reduced packages available. Director of Golf: John Lawler.*

THE APPEARANCE OF AN ASTERISK (*) AT THE END OF A CLUB OR COURSE ENTRY INDICATES THAT UP-TO-DATE INFORMATION HAS NOT BEEN SUPPLIED

Other British holiday guides from FHG Guides

**PUBS & INNS · 300 GREAT HOTELS · SHORT BREAK HOLIDAYS
The bestselling and original PETS WELCOME! · 500 GREAT PLACES TO STAY
SELF-CATERING HOLIDAYS · BED & BREAKFAST STOPS
CARAVAN & CAMPING HOLIDAYS · FAMILY BREAKS**

Published annually: available in all good bookshops or direct from the publisher:
**FHG Guides, Abbey Mill Business Centre, Seedhill, Paisley PA1 1TJ
Tel: 0141 887 0428 • Fax: 0141 889 7204
e-mail: admin@fhguides.co.uk • www.holidayguides.com**

County Cavan

BALLYCONNELL. **Slieve Russell Hotel, Golf and Country Club,** Ballyconnel (049 952 5090; Fax: 049 952 6640). Mature parkland European Tour Championship course on 350 acres. 18 holes, 7001 yards, 6402 metres. Driving range and practice ground. *Green Fees*: information not provided. *Eating facilities*: Summit Bar and restaurant. *Visitors*: welcome everyday, pre-booking essential. Limited availablity on Saturdays. 4 Star Hotel on site. *Society Meetings*: welcome, please contact for details. Golf Director: Paul Crowe (049 952 5090).
e-mail: mccluskey@quinn-hotels.com

BELTURBET. **Belturbet Golf Club,** Erne Hill, Belturbet (00 353 49 9522287). *Location:* quarter-of-a-mile from Belturbet town centre on main N3 Cavan-Dublin road. Parkland with elevated greens. 9 holes, 5204 yards. S.S.S. 64. Practice area and putting green. *Green Fees:* €15.00; €10.00 with a member. *Eating facilities:* clubhouse and bar; catering available. *Visitors:* welcome at all times. *Society Meetings:* welcome at all times. Club/trolley hire. Various classes of membership available, including distance/overseas. All enquiries to 00 353 49 9522287.

BLACKLION. **Blacklion Golf Club,** Toam, Blacklion, via Sligo (071 985 3024). *Location:* Blacklion/Belcoo on Enniskillen to Sligo Road. Flat parkland, wooded copses, lake partially in play, scenic. 9 holes, 6175 yards, 5614 metres. S.S.S. 69. *Green Fees:* information not available. *Eating facilities:* full catering available. *Visitors:* welcome. Course surrounded on four holes by Loch McNean. Safe swimming in lake. Scenic hill walks. *Society Meetings:* by arrangement. Hon. Secretary: Pat Gallery.*

CAVAN. **County Cavan Golf Club,** Arnmore House, Drumelis, Cavan (049 4331541). *Location:* on Killeshandra road from Cavan. Parkland course. 18 holes, 5634 metres. S.S.S 69. Practice area, driving range. *Green Fees:* information not available. *Eating facilities:* full catering facilities including bar snacks. *Visitors:* welcome; limited availablility on Wednesdays and weekends. *Society Meetings:* on application to Professional. Professional: Bill Noble (049 4331388). Club Secretary: James Fraher (Tel & Fax: 049 4331541).*
e-mail: cavangc@iol.ie
website: www.cavangolf.ie

CAVAN. **Farnham Estate**, Cavan (+353 (0)49 437 7700). *Location:* 4km from Cavan, within 90 minutes' drive from Dublin and two hours from Belfast. 18 holes, 7047 yards, 6442 metres, Par 72. Designed by Jeff Howes, a parkland course over 500 acres of rolling countryside and dense woodland.*
website: www.farnhamestate.ie

Please mention this guide when enquiring about clubs or accommodation

Slieve Russell Hotel, Golf and Country Club, Ballyconnell

County Clare

CLONLARA. **Clonlara Golf and Leisure,** Clonlara (061 354141; Fax: 061 354143). *Location:* 7 miles from Limerick on Corbally to Killaloe road. Parkland. 12 holes. S.S.S.67. *Green Fees:* information not available. *Eating facilities:* fully licensed bar with bar food. *Visitors:* welcome. *Society Meetings:* welcome. No walkers, caddies, or children under 14 allowed on the course. Tennis courts, sauna, children's play area, crazy golf. Self-catering apartments available. Secretary: Ms A. O'Grady (061 354141; Fax: 061 354143).*
e-mail: tmcmahon@circom.net

DOONBEG. **Doonbeg Golf Club,** Doonbeg (353 65 9055246; Fax: 353 65 9055247). *Location*: The highly acclaimed Doonbeg Golf Club is situated between two of Ireland's greatest Links courses - Ballybunion and Lahinch. Designed by Greg Norman and host of the 2002 Palmer Cup matches, it is set along 1.5 miles of crescent-shaped beach encircling Doughmore Bay, providing magnificent views. Links course. 18 holes, 6885 yards, par 72. Practice green, putting green. *Green Fees:* information not available. *Eating facilities:* restaurant. *Visitors:* welcome.*
e-mail: links@doonbeggolfclub.com

ENNIS. **Ennis Golf Club,** Drumbiggle, Ennis (065 6824074; Fax: 065 6841848). *Location:* half a mile from Ennis town centre. Parkland course set in rolling hills with five challenging Par 3s. 18 holes, 6240 yards, 5706 metres. Par 70. *Green Fees:* €35 weekdays, €40 weekends. *Eating facilities:* full catering facilities and bar. *Visitors:* Monday, Thursday, Saturday, with some restrictions Tuesday and Wednesday. New club house. Carts, clubs and caddies available. *Society Meetings:* welcome. Club Manager: Pat McCarthy (065 6824074; Fax: 065 6841848).
e-mail: info@ennisgolfclub.com
website: www.ennisgolfclub.com

ENNIS. **Woodstock Golf and Country Club,** Shanaway Road, Ennis (00353 656 829463; Fax: 00353 656 820304). *Location:* from Ennis town take Lahinch Road, 18 miles Shannon Airport. Parkland course. 18 holes, 5879 metres. S.S.S. 71. *Green Fees:* information not available. *Eating facilities:* bar food served daily, The Bunker Bar (065 682 9463). *Visitors:* welcome at all times, telephone in advance advisable at weekends. Hotel on site. *Society Meetings:* all welcome, special rates available. Contact: Anne Marie Russell (+ 353 65 682 9463; Fax: + 353 65 682 0304).*
e-mail: proshopwoodstock@eircom.net
website: www.woodstockgolfclub.com

KILKEE. **Kilkee Golf Club,** East End, Kilkee (065 9056048; Fax: 065 9056977). *Location:* right on seafront at end of promenade. Seaside course with many cliff top tees and greens. 18 holes, 5960 metres. S.S.S. 71. *Green Fees:* information not available. *Eating facilities:* fully licensed restaurant and bar. *Visitors:* very welcome every day. Golf shop. *Society Meetings:* Society outings welcome, special reduced rates. Secretary/ Manager: Jim Leyden (065 9056048; Fax: 065 9056977).*
e-mail: kilkeegolfclub@eircom.net
website: www.kilkeegolfclub.ie

KILRUSH. **Kilrush Golf Club,** Kilrush (065 905 1138; Fax: 065 905 2633). *Location:* On main Ennis/Kilrush Road - 1km from Kilrush. Parkland course. 18 holes, 5960 yards. S.S.S. 70. *Green Fees:* information not available. *Eating facilities:* full bar and catering facilities. *Visitors:* always welcome - please book in advance. *Society Meetings:* welcome. Secretary/ Manager: Denis F. Nagle (087 623 7557).*
website: www.kilrushgolfclub.com

LAHINCH. **Lahinch Golf Club,** Lahinch (065 7081003). *Location:* 32 miles west of Shannon Airport, 200 yards from Lahinch Village on Lisconner Road. Links course. Old Course - 18 holes, 6950 yards. S.S.S. 74; Castle Course - 18 holes, 5594 yards. S.S.S. 67. *Green Fees:* information not available. *Eating facilities:* bar and restaurant. *Visitors:* welcome. *Society Meetings:* catered for by arrangement. Professional: Robert McCavery (065 7081003). Secretary: Alan Reardon (065 7081003; Fax: 065 7081592). *
e-mail: info@lahinchgolf.com

MILTOWN MALBAY. **Spanish Point Golf Club,** Spanish Point, Miltown Malbay (065-708 4198). *Location*: two miles south of Miltown Malbay at Spanish Point Beach. Links course. 9 holes, 2312 metres, S.S.S. 63. Practice facilities. *Green Fees*: information not available. *Eating facilities*: bar snacks. *Visitors*: welcome at all times, not before noon on Sundays. *Society Meetings*: welcome weekdays excluding July and August. Secretary: David Fitzgerald (086-812 5742).*
e-mail: david@spanish-point.com
e-mail: dkfitzgerald@tinet.ie
website: www.spanishpointgolf.com

NEWMARKET-ON-FERGUS. **Dromoland Castle Golf & Country Club,** Newmarket-on-Fergus (061 368444; Fax: 061 368498). *Location:* part of the Dromoland Castle Estate, 10 minutes' drive from Shannon Airport. 400 acres of wooded parkland, with the River Rine flowing through. Course designed by Ron Kirby and Joe Carr. 18 holes, 6824 yards. *Green Fees:* information not available. *Eating facilities:* available. *Visitors*: welcome. *Society Meetings:* welcome.*
e-mail: golf@dromoland.ie
website: www.dromoland.ie

SHANNON. **Shannon Golf Club,** Shannon (061 471849; Fax: 061 471507). *Location:* from Limerick take Airport road, course is 200 yards past Airport. Parkland. 18 holes, 6271 yards. S.S.S. 72. Practice area, club hire, buggy hire. *Green Fees:* information not available. *Eating facilities:* full bar and catering services. *Visitors:* welcome with prior booking. *Society Meetings:* welcome. Professional: Artie Pyke (061 471551). General Manager: Michael Corry.*

County Cork

BANDON. **Bandon Golf Club,** Castlebernard, Bandon (023 8841111; Fax: 023 8844690). *Location:* one mile west of Bandon town centre. Undulating parkland course with scenic views of West Cork. 18 holes, 6421 yards, 5780 metres. S.S.S. 70. Practice ground. *Green Fees:* information not available. *Eating facilities:* available, menu at bar. *Visitors:* welcome, restriction at weekends. Clubs, buggies and carts for hire. *Society Meetings:* welcome except Wednesdays and Sundays. Professional: Paddy O'Boyle (023 8842224; Fax: 023 8844690).*
e-mail: enquiries@bandongolfclub.com

BANTRY. **Bantry Bay Golf Club,** Bantry, West Cork (353 (0) 27 50579/53773; Fax: 353 (0) 27 53790). *Location:* approximately 1 mile from Bantry on N71 Killarney road. Clifftop parkland championship course to USGA standards. 18 holes, 6700 yards, 6100 metres. S.S.S. 72. *Green Fees:* information not available. *Eating facilities:* full bar and restaurant open all year. *Visitors:* welcome, with restrictions at weekend. Trolley, buggy and club hire. *Society Meetings:* rates on request. Secretary: John O'Sullivan.*
e-mail: info@bantrygolf.com
website: www.bantrygolf.com

BLARNEY. **Blarney Golf Resort**, Tower, Blarney (00353 21 438 4477; Fax: 00353 21 451 6453). *Location:* close to the town of Blarney, and only 8 miles from Cork. A challenging course with some of the best greens in Ireland. 18 holes, 6712 yards. Par 71. *Green Fees:* information not available. Fully equipped clubhouse. Accommodation in 56 two-bedroom Club Lodges or 62-bedroom hotel.*
e-mail: reservations@blarneygolfresort.com
website: www.blarneygolfresort.com

CARRIGALINE. **Fernhill Golf & Country Club,** Carrigaline (00 353 (0)21 4372226; Fax: 00 353 (0)21 437 1011). *Location*: 20 minutes from Cork city and Airport, 10 minutes from Ringaskiddy Ferry Port. From city/airport follow sign to Ringaskiddy Ferry Port until roundabout with sign for Carrigaline - take Ringaskiddy exit, 2nd right, club is on left on this road. Parkland course. 18 holes, 6340 yards, S.S.S. 67. *Green Fees*: information not available. *Eating facilities*: fully licensed clubhouse, bar and restaurant, barbecue area. *Visitors*: always welcome. Booking advised at weekends. 40 bedroom hotel on site, plus 10 holiday homes, tennis court, indoor pool and sauna. Pro shop. Golf packages available. *Society Meetings*: always welcome. Booking advised at weekends. General Manager: Alan Bowes.*
e-mail: info@fernhillgolfhotel.com
website: www.fernhillcountryclub.com

CASTLETOWNBERE. **Berehaven Golf Club and Amenity Park,** Filane, Castletownbere, Beara (027 70700). *Location:* on main Castletownbere - Glengarriff Road, three miles from Castletownbere. Scenic course overlooking Bantry Bay. 9 holes, 2598 metres, S.S.S. 65. *Green Fees:* information not available. *Eating facilities:* bar and restaurant. *Visitors:* welcome at all times. Tennis, crazy golf, sauna, caravan park. Club hire available. *Society Meetings:* welcome by appointment, special rates. Hon. Secretary: Chris Downey (027 70700).*
e-mail: info@berehavengolf.com
website: www.berehavengolf.com

CHARLEVILLE. **Charleville Golf Club,** Charleville (063 81257; Fax: 063 81274). *Location:* Two kilometres west of Charleville town which is on main Cork/Limerick road. Parkland, heavily wooded. 27 holes. 18 holes 6430 yards. S.S.S. 70. 9 holes 3451 yards. Driving range. *Green Fees:* from €20 per person. *Eating facilities:* full bar and restaurant facilities. *Visitors:* welcome, weekends by appointment. *Society Meetings:* welcome. Special rates apply. Professional: Jamie O'Sullivan (063 81257). Secretary/Manager: Patrick Nagle.
e-mail: info@charlevillegolf.com
website: www.charlevillegolf.com

CHARLEVILLE GOLF CLUB
Charleville, Co. Cork
Tel: 00353 063 81257/81515 • Fax: 00353 063 81274
e-mail: info@charlevillegolf.com • www.charlevillegolf.com

Charleville Golf Club, established in 1941 and famous for its lush fairways and beautiful greens, now offers an extended 27-hole wooded course. Situated at the foothills of the Ballyhoura Mountains and only 40 minutes from Cork and Limerick cities, it is an ideal centre for golf. One can relax in the luxuriously appointed and tastefully designed clubhouse, and avail oneself of the excellent catering and bar facilities.

A warm welcome is extended to Irish and overseas visitors alike.

COBH. **Cobh Golf Club,** Marino, Cobh (021 481 2399). A Hawtree-designed 18 hole parkland course with panoramic views of Cork's inner harbour. 6894 yards, S.S.S. 73, Par 72. Practice area with putting and chipping greens. Try our Par 3 10th hole to an island green!! *Green Fees*: €30 to €40. *Societies*: welcome but booking is advisable. Professional: Morgan O'Donovan (086 603 0318).
e-mail: info@cobhgolfclub.ie
website: www.cobhgolfclub.ie

DONERAILE. **Doneraile Golf Club,** Doneraile (022 24137). *Location*: three-and-a-half miles off main Cork/Limerick Road. Parkland, mature trees. 9 holes, 5768 yards. S.S.S.67. *Green Fees*: information not available. *Eating facilities:* by request. *Visitors:* welcome weekdays. *Society Meetings*: welcome Saturdays and weekdays. Secretary: Jimmy O'Leary (022 24379).*

DOUGLAS. **Douglas Golf Club,** Maryborough, Douglas (021 4891086; Fax: 021 4367200). *Location:* Douglas is on the main road from Cork to ferry port at Ringaskiddy, three miles south of Cork City. Beautifully maintained flat parkland course, greens and tees to full USGA spec – the views from the Clubhouse are some of the most panoramic in the country. 18 holes, 6669 yards, 5972 metres. S.S.S. 71. Practice ground. *Green Fees:* €40 all week. Groups of 20 or more €37. 2010 rates (subject to review). *Eating facilities:* full restaurant and bar available from 11am. *Visitors:* Monday, Thursday, Friday (mornings preferably); Saturday and Sunday after 2pm. Advisable to check in advance. *Society Meetings*: welcome but bookings should be made by end of April each year. Professional: Stephen Hayes (021 4362055). Secretary/Manager: Ronan Burke (021 4895297; Fax:021 4367200).*

FERMOY. **Fermoy Golf Club,** Corrin, Fermoy (025 32694; Fax: 025 33072). *Location*: 2km from Dublin to Cork main route. Parkland, wooded course. 18 holes, 5847 metres. S.S.S. 68. Practice ground. *Green Fees*: information not available. *Eating facilities*: full bar and restaurant. *Visitors*: welcome, Mondays very limited, weekends by reservation. Caddies. *Society Meetings*: welcome, booking essential. Professional: Brian Moriarty (025 31472; Fax: 025 33072). Secretary: Kathleen Murphy.
e-mail: fermoygolfclub@eircom.net

FOTA ISLAND. **Fota Island Resort,** Cork (021 4883700; Fax: 021 4883713). *Location*: take N25 east from Cork City (9 miles), turn off for Fota and Cobh. Gently undulating parkland bordered by mature woodland, very traditional in design. Championship courses, venue for the 2001 and 2002 Murphy's Irish Open. Voted 'Golf Course of the Year' 2002 by the Irish Golf Tour Operators. 27 holes, Deerpark course, 6927 yards, Par 72; Barryscourt course, 7362 yards, Par 74; Belvelly course, 7121 yards, Par 72. Practice range and putting green. *Green Fees*: information not available. *Eating facilities*: restaurant and bar. *Visitors*: welcome everyday, telephone or e-mail for tee times. Metal spikes not allowed. Buggies, carts and caddies available. *Society Meetings*: welcome everyday, but limited availability on weekends. 5 star Hotel and Spa plus Self-Catering Lodges all available on the Resort.Package deals available.Professional: Kevin Morris (021 4883700; Fax: 021 4883713).*
e-mail: reservations@fotaisland.ie
website: www.fotaisland.ie

GLENGARRIFF. **Glengarriff Golf Club,** Glengarriff (027 63150). Parkland course. 9 holes, Par 33. *Green Fees*: information not available. *Eating facilities*: light snacks available in the clubhouse. *Visitors*: welcome at all times. *Society Meetings*: welcome. Secretary: Noreen Deasy (027 50315). *

KINSALE. **Kinsale Golf Club,** Farrangalway, Kinsale (021 4774722; Fax: 021 4773114). *Location*: beautifully situated in meadowland and parkland. Two courses. 18 holes and 9 holes. *Green Fees:* information not available. *Eating facilities:* full bar and catering. *Visitors:* welcome.*
e-mail: office@kinsalegolf.com
website: www.kinsalegolf.com

KINSALE. **Old Head Golf Links,** Kinsale (+353 (0) 21 4778444; Fax: +353 (0) 214778022). *Location*: from Cork Airport follow R600 from Cork to Kinsale on to Old Head. 15 minutes south, signposted. Spectacular links course at an elevation of 200-300 ft. Practice ground, putting green, chipping green. 18 holes, 7200 yards. S.S.S. 72. *Green Fees:* 18 holes €200. 2010 rates (subject to review). *Eating facilities:* full bar and restaurant facilities. *Visitors:* Members' Club with outside play. Buggy hire and caddies available.Pro shop, shower and changing facilities. 15 members' suites, Old Head Spa and Fitness Suite. *Society Meetings:* welcome subject to availability, Special rates available for groups over 24. Course closed November to April. Golf Operations: Danny Brassil. General Manager: Jim O'Brien.
e-mail: info@oldhead.com
website: www.oldhead.com

LITTLE ISLAND. **Cork Golf Club,** Little Island (021 4353451; Fax: 021 4353410). *Location:* five miles east of Cork City N25, signposted. Parkland, very scenic championship course. 18 holes, 6065 metres. S.S.S. 72, 70. Practice ground. *Green Fees:* weekdays €85, weekends €95, earlybird €50, society weekdays €70, weekends €65. *Eating facilities:* full catering facilities, bar. *Visitors:* welcome Mondays, Tuesdays, Wednesdays and Fridays except 12.30 to 2pm; Thursdays, weekends ring in advance. *Society Meetings:* catered for, arrange with General Manager. Professional: Peter Hickey (021 4353421). General Manager: Matt Sands (021 4353451; Fax: 021 4353410).
e-mail: info@corkgolfclub.ie
website: www.corkgolfclub.ie

LITTLE ISLAND. **Harbour Point Golf Club,** Clash Road, Little Island (021 4353094; Fax: 021 4354408). *Location:* follow signs for Rosslare from Cork City and then take exit for Little Island (approx 6 miles from city). Parkland course by banks of River Lee. 18 holes, 6163 metres. S.S.S. 72. 21 bay floodlit driving range. *Green Fees:* information not available. *Eating facilities:* full bar and catering facilities. *Visitors:* welcome anytime, please book tee times. Carts, buggies and caddies for hire. Fully stocked golf store. *Society Meetings:* very welcome, special rates available. Professional: Morgan O'Donovan. General Manager: Aylmer Barrett (021 4353094; Fax: 021 4354408). *
e-mail: info@harbourpointgolfclub.com
website: www.harbourpointgolfclub.com

MACROOM. **Macroom Golf Club,** Lackaduve, Macroom (026 41072; Fax: 026 41391). *Location:* through castle gates at town centre. Parkland. 18 holes, 5574 metres. S.S.S. 69. *Green Fees:* weekdays €35, weekends €40, Early Bird €20. *Eating facilities:* full catering with restaurant and bar. *Visitors:* welcome, booking essential. *Society Meetings:* welcome March to October, booking essential. Manager: Cathal O'Sullivan.
e-mail: mcroomgc@iol.ie
website: www.macroomgolfclub.com

MALLOW. **Mallow Golf Club,** Ballyellis, Mallow (022 21145; Fax: 022 42501). *Location*: one mile from town, east, on the Killavullen road. Parkland course. 18 holes, 5960 metres. S.S.S.72. *Green Fees*: weekdays €30, weekends and Public Holidays €40. *Eating facilities*: available. *Visitors*: welcome Monday to Friday, restrictions on weekends and Public Holidays, please check for details. *Society Meetings*: welcome, please telephone for details. Professional: Sean Conway (022 43424). Secretary/Manager: David Curtin (022 21145; Fax: 022 42501).
e-mail: mallowgolfclubmanager@eircom.net
website: www.mallowgolfclub.net

MIDLETON. **East Cork Golf Club,** Gortacrue, Midleton (021 463 1687; Fax: 021 461 3695). *Location:* two miles off main Waterford to Cork road. Exit at Midleton 13 miles east of Cork city. Parkland course. 18 hole, 5491 yards. S.S.S. 67. Driving range. *Green Fees:* information not available. *Visitors:* welcome all year round. *Society Meetings:* special rates available. Professional: Don MacFarlane (021 463 3667). Secretary: Maurice Moloney.*

MITCHELSTOWN. **Mitchelstown Golf Club,** Limerick Road, Gurrane, Mitchelstown (025 24072). *Location:* one kilometre from Mitchelstown (main Dublin/Cork route). Flat parkland. 18 holes, 6008 metres. S.S.S. 70. Practice area. *Green Fees:* information not available. *Eating facilities:* bar food evenings/weekends. *Visitors:* welcome. Caddie car hire. *Society Meetings:* welcome. Secretary: D. Stapleton. (025 24072).*

MONKSTOWN. **Monkstown Golf Club,** Parkgarriff, Monkstown (021 4841376; Fax: 021 4863452). *Location:* 7 miles from Cork city, just 10 minutes' drive from the Cork/Swansea Ferry. Demanding parkland course for golfers of all levels and the greens have been noted for being amongst the best in the country. 18 holes, 5640 metres. S.S.S. 69. Practice ground. *Green Fees:* from €37 to €50. *Eating facilities:* full bar and restaurant available. *Visitors:* welcome, avoid Tuesday (Ladies' Day) and Bank Holiday Mondays. Phone at weekends. *Society Meetings:* welcome with restrictions. General Manager/Secretary: Hilary Madden.
e-mail: office@monkstowngolfclub.com
website: www.monkstowngolfclub.com

MUSKERRY. **Muskerry Golf Club,** Carrigrohane (021 4385297; Fax: 021 4516860). *Location:* seven and a half miles north west of Cork City, two and a half miles from Blarney. Parkland/wooded, two rivers. 18 holes, 5785 metres. S.S.S. 71. *Green Fees:* weekdays €30, weekends €35. *Eating facilities:* available. *Visitors:* welcome, online booking available. *Society Meetings:* welcome, contact office for details. Professional: W.M. Lehane (021 4381445). Manager: Hugo Gallagher (021 4385297; Fax: 021 4516860).
website: www.muskerrygolfclub.ie

OVENS. **Lee Valley Golf & Country Club,** Clashanure, Ovens (Tel & Fax: 00 353 (0)21 7331721). *Location:* eight miles from Cork on N22, turn right at Dan Sheehans. Parkland. 18 hole championship golf course designed by Ryder Cup star Christy O'Connor Jnr. 6725 yards. Par 72. *Green Fees:* information not available. *Eating facilities:* bar and full restaurant. *Visitors:* welcome. Club shop; club hire, caddy car hire and caddies and buggies available. *Society Meetings:* welcome. Corporate days. Lee Valley Bus available to cater for all your transport needs. 20 x 4 Star Self catering cottages on site overlooking the golf course, available for long and short breaks. Proprietor: Jerry Keohane.*
e-mail: reservations@leevalleygcc.ie
website: www.leevalleygcc.ie

SCHULL. **Coosheen Golf Club,** Coosheen, Schull (028 28182). *Location:* one mile from Schull. Seaside parkland. 9 holes, 2023 metres. S.S.S. 58. Club hire, trolley hire. *Green Fees:* information not available. *Eating facilities:* seasonal bar and daily lunches. *Visitors:* welcome. *Society Meetings:* welcome. Secretary: A. Good or Donal Morgan.*

YOUGHAL. **Youghal Golf Club,** Knockaverry, Youghal (024 92787; Fax: 024 92641). *Location:* N25 main road from Rosslare to Cork. Seaside course with panoramic views of Youghal Bay/Blackwater Estuary. 18 holes, 6102 metres. S.S.S. 70. *Green Fees:* information not available. *Eating facilities:* full bar and restaurant facilities. *Visitors:* welcome mid-week, phone re weekends and Wednesdays (Ladies' Day). *Society Meetings:* welcome, please phone. Special rates available. Professional: Liam Burns (024 92590). Secretary: Margaret O'Sullivan.*

County Donegal

BALLYLIFFIN. **Ballyliffin Golf Club,** Ballyliffin, Inishowen (00 353 74 93 76119; Fax: 00 353 74 93 76672). *Location:* Carndonagh from Derry, Buncrana from Letterkenny. 2 Championship Links. Glashedy; 18 holes, 7250 yards. S.S.S. 72. Old Links; 18 holes, 6910 yards. S.S.S. 71. Practice ground and three practice holes. *Green Fees:* €60-€70, or check website. *Eating facilities:* bar and restaurant. *Visitors:* welcome, booking advisable. *Society Meetings:* concessions for groups of 16 and over. Manager: John Farren (00 353 74 93 76119; Fax: 00 353 74 93 76672).
e-mail: info@ballyliffingolfclub.com
website: www.ballyliffingolfclub.com

BUNCRANA. **Buncrana Golf Club,** Ballymacarry, Buncrana (07493 20749). *Location*: on entry to Buncrana town take first left after Inishowen Gateway Hotel. Links course. 9 holes, 4310 yards, S.S.S. 62. *Green Fees*: all week 18 holes: male €15; lady €10; juvenile €8. *Visitors*: welcome Monday to Friday, weekends by prior arrangement. *Society Meetings*: welcome. Professional: J. Doherty (07493 62279). Secretary: Francis McGrory (07493 20749).

BUNCRANA. **North West Golf Club,** Lisfannon, Buncrana (07493 61027; Fax: 07493 63284). *Location:* eight miles north west of Derry, one mile Buncrana - main Derry/Buncrana Road. Traditional links course, established 1891 founder member of G.U.I. 18 holes, 5968 yards. S.S.S. 70. Putting green. *Green Fees:* information not available. *Eating facilities:* full bar and restaurant; bar snacks. *Visitors:* welcome anytime, phone in advance for weekends and Wednesdays. Caddies, carts available. *Society Meetings:* all welcome, booking essential. Professional: (07493 61715). Hon. Secretary: Eddie Curran (0866 047299).
e-mail: secretary@northwestgolfclub.com
website: www.northwestgolfclub.com

BUNDORAN. **Bundoran Golf Club,** Bundoran (071 9841302; Fax: 071 9842014). *Location:* 22 miles north of Sligo on edge of Bundoran Town. Parkland, seaside; not wooded. 18 holes, 5688 metres. S.S.S. 70. Practice ground. *Green Fees:* information not available. *Eating facilities:* tea, coffee and sandwiches in bar. *Visitors:* anytime with due notice but preferably Monday to Thursday. Buggies and carts. *Society Meetings:* very welcome with due notice. Professional: David T. Robinson (071 9841302). Secretary: John McGagh.*

DONEGAL. **Donegal Golf Club,** Murvagh, Laghey (074 9734054; Fax: 074 9734377). *Location:* N15 off main Donegal/Ballyshannon Road. Seaside links course, Murvagh Peninsula. 18 holes, 6874 yards, 6249 metres. S.S.S. 73. Practice area. *Green Fees:* weekdays €50, weekends €65. *Eating facilities:* restaurant and bar. *Visitors:* welcome. Buggies, carts available, caddies on request. Administrator: (074 9734054; Fax: 074 9734377).
e-mail: info@donegal-golfclub.ie
website: www.donegalgolfclub.ie

DOWNINGS **Rosapenna Hotel & Golf Links,** Rosapenna, Downings (074 915 5301; Fax: 074 915 5128). *Location:* 25 miles from Letterkenny. Links course, designed by Old Tom Morris. 18 holes, 6271 yards, 5735 metres. S.S.S. 71. New 18 holes opened June 2003. *Green Fees:* telephone Golf Pavilion on 074 915 5000, contact Frank Casey Jnr. *Eating facilities:* available at hotel. *Visitors:* welcome all times. Four star Hotel on course. *Society Meetings:* welcome, must have Club Handicap. Secretary: Michael Bonner. Hotel and Course Manager: Frank T. Casey.

DUNFANAGHY. **Dunfanaghy Golf Club,** Kill, Dunfanaghy, Letterkenny (074 9136335; Fax: 074 9136684). *Location:* on main Letterkenny-Dunfanaghy Road N56. Seaside links course overlooking Sheephaven Bay and overshadowed by Horn Head. 18 holes, 5000 metres. S.S.S. 66. *Green Fees:* information not available. *Eating facilities:* bar snacks - soup, tea and sandwiches. *Visitors:* welcome most days. Time sheet in operation at weekends, Bank Holidays (North & South) and Summer months. Buggies, carts and caddies by request. *Society Meetings:* all welcome. Club Secretary: Sandra McGinley (074 9136335). Hon. Secretary: Cairns Witherow.*
e-mail: dunfanaghygolf@eircom.net

KINCASSLAGH. **Cruit Island Golf Club,** Cruit Island, Kincasslagh (074 9543296). *Location:* five miles north of Dunglue, turn off opposite Daniel O'Donnell's Viking House Hotel, three miles to the clubhouse. Seaside links with 9 holes, spectacular views hugging ragged coastline. 9 holes, 4860 metres. S.S.S. 66. Practice green. *Green Fees:* information not available. *Eating facilities:* full menu available if pre-booked. *Visitors:* welcome all year. Secretary: Dermot Devenney (074 9548872).*

THE APPEARANCE OF AN ASTERISK (*) AT THE END OF A CLUB OR COURSE ENTRY INDICATES THAT UP-TO-DATE INFORMATION HAS NOT BEEN SUPPLIED

LETTERKENNY. Letterkenny Golf Club, Barnhill, Letterkenny (0749 121150). *Location:* off Ramelton Road, approx. 2.5km out of Letterkenny. Recently redeveloped/redesigned championship parkland course by the River Swilly. Practice area, putting green, golf academy and Pro Shop. 18 holes, 6259 yards. S.S.S. 71. *Green Fees:* €25 weekdays, €35 Saturday/Sunday. *Eating facilities:* award-winning restaurant; bar food served; à la carte menu available. *Visitors:* always welcome. *Society Meetings:* special reduced rates available, phone for details (00353 74 9121150). Hon. Secretary: Cynthia Fuery.
e-mail: info@letterkennygolfclub.com
website: www.letterkennygolfclub.com

NARIN/PORTNOO. Narin and Portnoo Golf Club, Narin, Portnoo (074 9545107; Fax: 074 9545994). *Location:* 6 miles north of Ardara adjacent to Blue Flag beach. Links course. 18 holes, 6269 metres. *Green Fees:* information not available. *Eating facilities:* full catering. *Visitors:* welcome seven days a week, please ring or e-mail for a tee time. *Society Meetings:* very welcome with special rates. Secretary: Willie Quinn.*
e-mail: narinportnoo@eircom.net
website: www.narinportnoogolfclub.ie

PORTSALON. Portsalon Golf Club, Portsalon, Fanad (074 9159459; Fax: 074 9159919). *Location:* 22 miles north of Letterkenny via Ramelton. Milford, Kerrykeel to Portsalon. Seaside links. 18 holes, white markers 6185 metres. S.S.S. 72, par 72. *Green Fees:* information not available. *Eating facilities:* diningroom and bar in clubhouse. *Visitors:* phone in advance. *Society Meetings:* welcome weekdays and some weekends, must book in advance - contact Cathal. Secretary: Peter Doherty (074 9159459; Fax: 074 9159919).*

RATHMULLAN. Otway Golf Club, Saltpans, Rathmullan (074 9158319). *Location*: from Rathmullan take road to Portsalon, course is two miles out on right. Seaside links course. 9 holes, 4234 yards. S.S.S. 64. *Green Fees*: €15. *Eating facilities*: bar. *Visitors:* always welcome. *Society Meetings*: by arrangement. Secretary: Kevin Toland (074 9151665).
e-mail: tolandkevin@eircom.net.

REDCASTLE. Redcastle Golf Club, Redcastle (074 9382073; Fax: 074 9382214). *Location:* 4 miles from Moville on Londonderry Road. Parkland. 9 holes, 6152 yards, 5700 metres. S.S.S. 69. *Green Fees:* information not available. *Eating facilities:* Redcastle Hotel. *Visitors:* Always welcome. *Society Meetings:* special group rates if pre-booked. 35 bedroom 3 star hotel. Secretary: Mark Wilson.*

Ballyliffin Golf Club

County Dublin

BALBRIGGAN. **Balbriggan Golf Club,** Blackhall, Balbriggan (8412173; Fax: 8413927). *Location:* quarter of a mile south of Balbriggan on main Belfast/Dublin Road. Parkland course with fine views of Cooley Peninsula and Mourne Mountains. 18 holes, 5922 metres. S.S.S. 71. *Green Fees:* information not available. *Eating facilities:* full restaurant facilities and bar. *Visitors:* welcome, Tuesday Ladies' Day, Saturdays and Sundays not good as club competitions take place. *Society Meetings:* catered for Mondays, Wednesdays, Thursdays and Fridays. Secretary: Michael O'Halloran (8412229).*

BALCARRICK. **Donabate Golf Club,** Balcarrick, Dublin (8434346; Fax: 8434488). *Location*: 5 miles north of Dublin Airport. Tree-lined parkland course, water in 9 holes. All sand based greens. 27 holes, 6085 metres. S.S.S. 73. Practice area including pitching and putting green. *Green Fees*: information not available. *Eating facilities*: full catering and bar facilities. *Visitors*: welcome every day. Must book in advance. Tuition available. Buggy hire. New ultra-modern clubhouse opened in 2003, with panoramic views of the course. *Society Meetings*: welcome every day, some restrictions at weekends. Professional: Hugh Jackson (8436346; Fax: 8434488).*
e-mail: info@donabategolfclub.com
website: www.donabategolfclub.com

BALLYBOUGHAL. **Hollywood Lakes Golf Club,** Ballyboughal (8433407; Fax: 8433002). *Location*: 15 minutes north of Dublin Airport via N1 and the R129 to Ballyboughal, right at 'T' junction then two miles on right. Parkland course with water features on 11 holes. 18 holes, 5763 metres, S.S.S. 71. Practice ground, putting greens. *Green Fees:* information not available. *Eating facilities*: bar and restaurant. *Visitors*: welcome, not before 1pm at weekends, not after 4pm Wednesdays. *Society Meetings*: welcome, rates negotiable. Secretary: Sid Baldwin PGA (8433407; Fax: 8433002).*

BRITTAS. **Slade Valley Golf Club,** Lynch Park, Brittas (01-458 2183; Fax: 01-458 2784). *Location*: signposted from Saggart Village (approx. 4 miles). Parkland course with spectacular views over Dublin City. 18 holes, 6195 yards, 5672 metres, Par 70, S.S.S. 70. Putting green, driving net. *Green Fees*: information not available. *Eating facilities*: bar/ restaurant. *Visitors*: welcome weekdays. Professional available for lessons. *Society Meetings*: welcome weekdays - rates negotiable. Professional: John Dignam. Secretary: Dermot Clancy.

BRITTAS. **South County Golf Club,** Lisheen Road, Brittas (01 458 2965; Fax: 01 458 2842). *Location*: on the Blessington road - N81, 7 miles from the M50 and 30 minutes from Dublin city centre. Parkland course. 18 holes, 7007 yards. S.S.S. 72. *Green Fees:* visit website. *Eating facilities:* clubhouse with catering. *Visitors:* welcome. Fully stocked Pro shop. *Society Meetings:* welcome.
e-mail: info@southcountygolf.ie
website: www.southcountygolf.com

CASTLEKNOCK. **Luttrellstown Castle Golf and Country Club,** Castleknock, Dublin 15 (353 1 8089988; Fax: 353 1 8089989). *Location:* six miles from Dublin City. 18 holes Championship parkland course with magnificent lakes and well manicured greens. 18 holes, 7091 yards, 6384 metres. S.S.S. 72. Practice ground. *Green Fees:* information not available. *Eating facilities:* restaurant and bar. *Visitors:* some tee times reserved for members, please phone in advance. Accommodation available at Luttrellston Castle and in stable yard apartments. *Society Meetings:* welcome subject to availability. Professional: Edward Doyle.*

DONABATE. **Balcarrick Golf Club,** Corballis, Donabate (8436957; Fax: 8436228). *Location:* from Dublin take the M1 motorway north past Dublin Airport and Swords and take the first exit signposted Donabate/Skerries/Lusk; turn right in the village of Donabate, travel 1.5km and turn right again, Balcarrick is 1km on the right hand side. Estuary style course. Recently placed in the Top 5 Golf Inc. Renovated Courses. 18 holes, 6191 metres. Par 73. *Green Fees:* from €18; visit website for details. *Eating facilities:* full catering and bar facilities available. *Visitors:* welcome, please telephone Professional for time sheet details. *Society Meetings*: welcome. Professional: Stephen Rayfus (8434034).*

DONABATE. **Beaverstown Golf Club,** Beaverstown Road, Donabate (00 353 1 843 6439 /843 6721; Fax: 00 353 1 843 5059). *Location*: on the shores of Rogerstown Estuary in North Dublin, 6km north of Dublin Airport. Attractive course set in 140 acres of lush parkland, with orchards bordering the tees and fairways. Water comes into play on 12 holes. 18 holes, 5972 metres. S.S.S. 72, Par 72. Practice facilities. *Green Fees*: contact Reservations for information. *Eating facilities*: bar, catering. *Visitors*: welcome. Please contact Club Manager in advance. Ladies' Day Tuesday. *Society Meetings:* welcome most Saturdays.
e-mail: office@beaverstown.com
website: www.beaverstown.com

DONABATE. **Corballis Golf Links,** Donabate (8436583). *Location:* main Dublin to Belfast Road. Links course. 18 holes, 4971 yards. S.S.S. 64. Putting green. *Green Fees:* information not available. *Eating facilities:* snack food. *Visitors:* welcome anytime. Carts available. *Society Meetings:* welcome. Manager: Austin Levins.*

THE GOLF GUIDE 2011 — IRELAND / Dublin

DONABATE. **The Island Golf Club,** Corballis, Donabate (00 353 (01)1 8436205; Fax: 00 353 (01)1 8436860). *Location:* 15 minute drive from Dublin Airport, across the estuary from the village of Malahide. Links course with challenging greens. Ranked 26th in World by *Golf Weekly* (Nov. 05 issue). 18 holes, 6236 metres, S.S.S. 73, Par 71. *Green Fees:* information not available. *Visitors:* warmly welcomed.*
e-mail: info@theislandgolfclub.com
website: www.theislandgolfclub.com

DUBLIN. **Deer Park Golf Hotel & Spa,** Howth, Co. Dublin (832 2624; Fax: 839 2405). *Location:* Deer Park Hotel, 9 miles east of the city centre. Parkland with panoramic sea views. 18 holes, 6830 yards, Par 72; two 9 hole courses (3100 yards and 3370 yards) each Par 3, and 12-hole Par 36. Pitch and putt. *Green Fees:* information not available. *Eating facilities:* full à la carte restaurant, bistro and bar; meal bookings required at weekends. *Visitors:* welcome at all times, Sunday mornings expect delays. 78-bedroom hotel, swimming pool, new spa. Special golf holidays available. Clubs and carts for hire. *Society Meetings:* welcome. Hotel: (832 2624; Fax: 839 2405). Golf Shop: (839 8777).*
e-mail: sales@deerpark.iol.ie
website: www.deerpark-hotel.ie

DUBLIN. **Dublin City Golf Club,** Ballinascorney (01451 6430/2082; 01459 8445). *Location:* take Exit 12 off M50, head west and turn left along R114 at The Old Mill pub, course is two miles further on. Gently sloping parkland. 18 holes, 5800 yards. S.S.S. 69. *Green Fees:* information not available. *Eating facilities:* excellent clubhouse facilities. *Visitors:* welcome, phone in advance. *Society Meetings:* welcome 7 days. Buggy, club and trolley hire. Secretary: Francis Bagnall.*
e-mail: info@dublincitygolf.com
website: www.dublincitygolf.com

DUBLIN. **Edmondstown Golf Club**, Edmondstown Road, Rathfarnham, Dublin 16 (493 2461; Fax: 493 3152). *Location*: south west suburbs of Dublin city. Parkland. 18 holes, 6011 metres. S.S.S. 73 Par 71. Practice facilities available. *Green Fees:* information not available. *Eating facilities*: bar and restaurant. *Society Meetings:* welcome. Professional: Gareth McShea (494 1049). Secretary: Selwyn S. Davies (493 1082).*
e-mail: info@edmondstowngolfclub.ie
website: www.edmondstowngolfclub.ie

DUBLIN. **Elm Park Golf and Sports Club,** Nutley House, Donnybrook, Dublin 4 (2693438; Fax: 2694505). *Location:* between R.T.E. and St. Vincent's Hospital. Flat parkland course. 18 holes, 5929 yards, 5422 metres. S.S.S. 68. *Green Fees:* €70. 2010 rates (subject to review). *Eating facilities:* full bar and dining facilities. *Visitors:* welcome but must telephone to arrange times with Professional. *Society Meetings:* by special arrangement. Professional: S. Green (2692650). Secretary: A. McCormack.
e-mail: office@elmparkgolfclub.ie
website: www.elmparkgolfclub.ie

DUBLIN. **Lucan Golf Club,** Cellbridge Road, Lucan (01 628 2106 ; Fax: 01 628 2929). *Location:* exit M50 at J7, head west on N4 for approx. 4 miles, head for Cellbridge off dual carriageway. 8 miles from Dublin and within easy reach of Dublin Airport. Beautifully maintained and challenging parkland course, with many elevated greens and water features. 18 holes, 5969 metres, Par 71. *Green Fees:* information not available. *Eating facilities:* clubhouse bar and restaurant. *Visitors:* welcome weekdays; weekends and Bank Holidays with member only. *Society Meetings:* welcome Mondays, Tuesdays and Fridays. Secretary/ Manager: Francis Duffy.*
e-mail: lucangolf@eircom.net
website: www.lucangolfclub.ie

DUBLIN. **The Royal Dublin Golf Club,** North Bull Island Nature Reserve, Dollymount, Dublin 3. *Location:* three and a half miles north east of city centre on coast road to Howth. Seaside links. Championship course. 18 holes, 7269 yards. S.S.S. 76. Medal course. 18 holes, 6888 yards, S.S.S. 74. Par 72. Large practice ground. *Green Fees:* €125. Early bird rate before 9.20am €75. *Eating facilities:* grill room, restaurant, two bars. *Visitors:* welcome. Trolleys, buggies and caddies by arrangement. *Society Meetings:* welcome by arrangement. Senior Professional: Leonard Owens (+353 1 8336477). Manager: Eoin O'Sullivan (+353 1 8336346; Fax: +353 1 8336504).
e-mail: info@theroyaldublingolfclub.com
website: www.theroyaldublingolfclub.com

Deer Park Spa Hotel & Golf

Deer Park Hotel incorporates Ireland's largest golf complex, with four courses to choose from, ranging from a testing 12-hole par 36 course to a par 72, 6830 yard 18 hole course.

Deer Park is just 9 miles from Dublin City and Airport. The hillside location offers spectacular views of Dublin Bay and the Northeastern coastline. 78 superb en suite rooms, new Spa, 17m swimming pool complex and all weather tennis courts, bar, bistro and the elegant "Four Earls" Restaurant.

Deer Park Spa Hotel & Golf, Howth, Co. Dublin
Tel: (01) 832 2624 • Fax: (01) 839 2405
e-mail: sales@deerpark.iol.ie • www.deerpark-hotel.ie

★★★

AA / Bord Failte

Dublin / IRELAND

DUN LAOGHAIRE. **Dun Laoghaire Golf Club,** Eglinton Park, Tivoli Road, Dun Laoghaire (280 3916; Fax: 280 4868). *Location:* half a mile from town centre and ferry port. Parkland. 18 holes, 5313 metres. S.S.S. 68. *Green Fees:* information not available. *Eating facilities:* full bar and restaurant facilities. *Visitors:* welcome by prior arrangment Saturdays. Local accommodation available. *Society Meetings:* welcome by prior arrangement. Professional: Vincent Carey (280 1694). General Manager: Dermot Murphy (280 3916; Fax: 280 4868).*
e-mail: dlgc@iol.ie

HOLLYSTOWN. **Hollystown Golf Club,** Hollystown, Dublin 15 (01 820 7444; Fax: 01 820 7447). *Location*: N2 Dublin to Derry Road, 7 minutes from M50 (Dublin City ring road), 10 minutes from Dublin Airport. Parkland course. 27 holes. 5-bay driving range, two 6-hole putting greens. *Green Fees:* information not available. *Eating facilities:* restaurant/bar. *Visitors:* welcome. Changing rooms and showers available. *Society Meetings:* welcome, call for rates (Ray O'Brien 00353 86 3808812). Professional: Joe Murray (087 2734993). Secretary: Joe Bedford (01 820 7444).*
e-mail: info@hollystown.com
website: www.hollystown.com

KILLINEY. **Killiney Golf Club,** Ballinclea Road, Killiney (Tel. & Fax: 01 2852823). *Location:* south Dunlaoghaire. Parkland. 9 holes, 5655 metres. S.S.S. 70. *Green Fees:* information not available. *Eating facilities:* snacks available. *Visitors:* welcome with restrictions. Professional: P. O'Boyle. Secretary: M.F. Walsh.*

KILSALLAGHAN. **Corrstown Golf Club,** Kilsallaghan, Co. Dublin (01 864 0533; Fax: 01 864 0537). *Location*: 10 minutes north of Dublin Airport. Parkland course. 27 holes. Practice green and nets. *Green Fees*: weekdays €40, weekends €50. Check our website for special offers. *Eating facilities*: full bar and restaurant. *Visitors*: welcome Monday to Friday; Saturday and Sunday when available. *Society Meetings*: outings welcome. Professional: Pat Gittens (01 864 3322).
e-mail: info@corrstowngolfclub.com
website: www.corrstowngolfclub.com

MALAHIDE. **Malahide Golf Club,** Beechwood, The Grange, Malahide (8461611; Fax: 8461270) *Location:* 15 minutes from Dublin city, 7 miles from Dublin Airport. Parkland. 27 holes, 6066 metres. S.S.S. 71. Practice area, Proshop. *Green Fees:* information not available. *Eating facilities*: full bar and restaurant available. *Visitors:* welcome, must book in advance. *Society Meetings*: society outings welcome. Professional: John Murray (8460002; Fax: 8461270). General Manager: Mark Gannon.*
e-mail: manager@malahidegolfclub.ie
website: www.malahidegolfclub.ie

PORTMARNOCK. **Portmarnock Hotel and Golf Links,** Strand Road, Portmarnock (8461800). *Location:* 8 miles north east of Dublin, 15 minutes from Dublin Airport. Seaside links designed by Bernhard Langer. 18 holes, 6422 metres. S.S.S. 74. Pitching area with bunker and putting green. *Green Fees:* €50. *Eating facilities:* restaurant and three bars. *Visitors:* no restrictions. Four star de luxe hotel, 138 bedrooms and conference facilities. *Society Meetings:* group rates and corporate packages available on request. Director of Golf: Moira Cassidy.
e-mail: golfres@portmarnock.com
website: www.portmarnock.com

RATHCOOLE. **Beech Park Golf Club,** Johnstown, Rathcoole (4580522; Fax: 4588365). Gently undulating parkland course. 18 holes, 5774 metres. S.S.S. 70. *Green Fees:* information not available. *Eating facilities:* bar and restaurant. *Visitors:* welcome Monday-Friday. *Society Meetings:* welcome Monday, Thursday, Friday. General Manager: Karl Young.*
e-mail: info@beechpark.ie
website: www.beechpark.ie

RATHFARNHAM. **Stackstown Golf Club,** Kellystown Road, Rathfarnham, Dublin 16 (01-494 1993; Fax: 01-493 3934). *Location*: one mile from Exit 13 on M50 towards Rathfarnham. Parkland course situated on slopes of Dublin mountains. Home club of Padraig Harrington. 18 holes, 6152 yards, S.S.S. 70. Practice fairway, putting green, driving nets. *Green Fees*: information not available. *Eating facilities*: full catering and bar facilities. *Visitors*: welcome everyday except Tuesday (Ladies' Day), Wednesday afternoons,

Saturday, Sunday subject to availability. Professional tuition available. Fully stocked shop, buggies, clubs, trolley for hire. *Society Meetings*: welcome Monday, Thursday, Friday and Sunday, special rates available. Professional: Michael Kavanagh (01-494 4561; Fax: 01-493 3934). General Manager: Larry Clarke (01 494 1993; Fax: 01-493 3934).*
e-mail: stackstowngc@eircom.net
website: www.stackstowngolfclub.com

ST MARGARET'S. **St Margaret's Golf and Country Club,** St Margaret's, Dublin (8640400; Fax: 8640289). *Location:* 10 minutes from Dublin Airport and 25 minutes from Dublin city centre. Parkland, championship course. 18 holes, 6917 yards. S.S.S. 73. Putting and practice areas. *Green Fees:* information not available. *Eating facilities:* full bar and restaurant facilities. *Visitors:* welcome 7 days a week. *Society Meetings:* welcome 7 days a week. Professionals: Gary Kearney, John Kelly.*
e-mail: reservations@stmargaretsgolf.com
website: www.stmargaretsgolf.com

ST MARGARET'S. **The Open Golf Centre,** Newtown House, St Margarets (8640324; Fax: 8341400). *Location:* 2km from Dublin Airport, adjacent to N2 (Derry road). Inviting parkland course, three lakes feature prominently. 27 holes, 9500 yards. S.S.S. 69/31. 20 bay driving range. *Green Fees:* information not available. *Eating facilities*: coffee shop. *Visitors:* welcome everyday. Teaching auditorium. *Society Meetings*: welcome. Professional: R. Machin (8640324; Fax: 8341400). Secretary: R. Yates (8640324 Fax: 8341400).*

SKERRIES. **Skerries Golf Club,** Hacketstown, Skerries (01 8491567; Fax: 01 8491591). *Location:* east of Dublin/Belfast road, approximately six miles. Parkland course close to sea with undulating fairways. 18 holes, 6081 metres. Par 73. Practice ground. *Green Fees:* contact Professional for daily specials. *Eating facilities:* restaurant, snack bar, bar, lounge. *Visitors:* welcome Mondays, Thursdays, Fridays; weekends by arrangement. *Society Meetings:* welcome. Professional: Bobby Kinsella (01 8491567). General Manager: Padraig Faughnan (01 8491567; Fax: 01 8491591).

SUTTON. **Howth Golf Club,** St. Fintan's, Carrickbrack Road, Sutton, Dublin 13 (8323055; Fax: 8321793). *Location:* one and a half miles from Sutton Cross on city side of Hill of Howth. Moorland course with scenic views of Dublin Bay. 18 holes, 5672 metres. S.S.S. 71. Practice ground. *Green Fees:* Monday to Sunday €60. On-line booking available. *Eating facilities:* restaurant facilities every day from midday. *Visitors:* welcome at all times, subject to availability. Carts. *Society Meetings:* Corporate/Society groups welcome at reduced rates. Professional: John McGuirk (8392617). Club Manager: Darragh Tighe.
e-mail: secretary@howthgolfclub.ie
website: www.howthgolfclub.ie

SWORDS. **Swords Open Golf Course,** Balheary Avenue, Swords (Tel & Fax: 01 8409819). *Location*: three miles west of Swords. Parkland. Broadmeadow river divides course. No climbing, flat course. 18 holes, 5631 metres. S.S.S. 69. Putting green. *Green Fees:* weekdays €20, weekends €25. *Eating facilities:* coffee shop. *Visitors:* any time, very welcome. *Society Meetings:* very welcome. Secretary: Orla McGuinness.
e-mail: info@swordsopengolfcourse.com
website: www.swordsopengolfcourse.com

St Margaret's, Co. Dublin, Ireland
Tel: +353 1 864 0400 • Fax: +353 1 864 0289
e-mail: reservations@stmargaretsgolf.com • www.stmargaretsgolf.com

St Margaret's is proud to have hosted the
**IRISH PGA CHAMPIONSHIP,
LADIES' IRISH OPEN, & IRISH SENIORS' OPEN**

Visitors are always most welcome

*St Margaret's is one of Ireland's top championship venues.
Located only 10 minutes from Dublin Airport and some 25 minutes
from Dublin city centre, we offer great golf at affordable rates!!!*

**Green fees from €40 Low Season
and from €50 High Season**

Visit www.holidayguides.com
for convenient accommodation
when playing golf around the regions

County Galway

ANNAGHVANE. **Connemara Isles Golf Club,** Annaghvane, Lettermore (091 572498). *Location:* Take the coast road from Galway City, at Casla (Costello) take the first right after the Texaco Station. Continue on that road for four and a half miles until you pass "An Hooker Bar" (on a bend). The golf course is 500 metres ahead. Seaside links Championship course. *Green Fees:* information not available. *Visitors:* always welcome. *Society Meetings:* welcome. Manager Anthony Lynch.*

ATHENRY. **Athenry Golf Club,** Palmerstown, Oran More (091 794466; Fax: 091 794971). *Location:* 8 miles from Galway city. Parkland. 18 holes, 5687 metres. Par 70, S.S.S. 70. Practice ground. *Green Fees:* information not available. *Eating facilities:* full bar and catering. *Visitors:* welcome except Sunday. Deals available with local hotels. Club hire and tuition. *Society Meetings:* welcome. Pro shop (091 790599). Professional: R. Ryan. Secretary/Manager: Padraig Flattery.*
e-mail: athenrygc@eircom.net
website: www.athenrygolfclub.net

BALLINASLOE. **Ballinasloe Golf Club,** Rossgloss, Ballinasloe (0905 42126; Fax: 0905 42538). *Location*: 2 miles from Ballinasloe town on Portumna side. Ballinasloe on main Dublin-Galway Road, two hours from Dublin. Mature parkland course. 18 holes, 5865 metres, Par 72. Practice area, putting green. *Green Fees:* information not available. *Eating facilities:* full bar and catering facilities. Buggy and cart hire. *Society Meetings*: welcome Monday-Saturday. Secretary: Dr Conor Corr (0905 42126).*
e-mail: ballinasloegolfclub@eircom.net
website: www.ballinasloegolfclub.com

CLIFDEN. **Connemara Golf Club,** Ballyconneely, Near Clifden (095 23502/23602; Fax: 095 23662). *Location:* from Clifden to Ballyconneely, 4 miles on the right. Seaside links Championship course. 27 holes, 6611 metres. S.S.S. 73. 220 yard Par 3 13th is feature hole. Practice fairway, putting green and driving net. *Green Fees:* €70, October €45. November-March €35. *Eating facilities:* full restaurant and bar facilities. *Visitors:* always welcome. Fully equipped Pro Shop. *Society Meetings:* groups of 20 or more welcome. Professional: Hugh O'Neill. Secretary: Kathleen Burke.*
e-mail: info@connemaragolflinks.net
website: www.connemaragolflinks.com

GORT. **Gort Golf Club,** Castlequarter (091 632244; Fax: 091 632387). *Location*: 20 minutes Galway Airport, 40 minutes Shannon Airport, 60 minutes Knock Airport, on edge of the world-famous Burren, overlooking Coole Lake. Undulating parkland. 18 holes, 5974 metres. S.S.S.71. *Green Fees:* summer - weekdays €30, weekends €35; winter - weekdays €25, weekends €30. *Eating facilities:* full bar and restaurant. *Visitors:* welcome all year, restrictions on Sundays. *Society Meetings:* welcome with prior booking. Time Sheet in operation weekends and Open Mondays. Administrator: Pauline Faithfull (091 632244). Designer: Christy O'Connor Jnr.
e-mail: info@gortgolf.com
website: www.gortgolf.com

LOUGHREA. **Loughrea Golf Club,** Craigue, Loughrea (091 841049). *Location:* one and a half miles north east of town, on New Inn Road. Parkland, undulating, with beautiful views of town and Slieve Aughty Mountains in background. 18 holes, 5261 yards. Par 67. Practice area. *Green Fees:* information not available. *Eating facilities:* tea, coffee, sandwiches at bar. New clubhouse with full catering under construction. *Visitors:* welcome weekdays and weekends with advance booking. *Society Meetings:* welcome, please telephone. Secretary: Vinny Ryan.*

ORANMORE **Galway Bay Golf Resort,** Renville, Oranmore (353 91 790711; Fax: 353 91 792510). *Location:* seven miles from Galway City, through Oranmore Village. Parkland by the sea, many water hazards with the Atlantic Ocean surrounding on three sides. Recently re-designed as 5-Star. 18 holes, 7308 yards. S.S.S. 72. Putting greens, chipping green, practice areas, indoor practice bays, academy of golf. *Green Fees:* information not available. *Eating facilities:* restaurant, spike bar, cocktail bar. *Visitors:* welcome daily. Wellness Centre. *Society Meetings:* welcome daily, reduced rates for groups. Director of Golf: Anne Hanley (353 91 790711). Director: John Cassidy.*
e-mail: info@galwaybaygolfresort.com
website: www.galwaybaygolfresort.com

OUGHTERARD. **Oughterard Golf Club,** Gortreevagh, Oughterard (091 552131; Fax: 091 552733). *Location:* 15 miles west of Galway City on N59 to Connemara. Parkland, newly re-modelled with Greens to USPGA Standards. 18 holes, 5876 metres. S.S.S. 70. Practice area and putting green. *Green Fees:* information not available. *Eating facilities:* full dining facilities during daylight hours. *Visitors:* welcome. *Society Meetings:* welcome, for further information contact Pro Shop. (091 557352). Administration Office (091 557354).*
e-mail: oughterardgc@eircom.net
website: www.oughterardgolf.com

SALTHILL. **Galway Golf Club,** Blackrock, Salthill (091 522033; Fax: 091 529783) *Location*: three miles west of Galway city. Parkland. 18 holes, 5832 metres. S.S.S. 71. *Green Fees:* €30. *Eating facilities*: full bar and catering facilities. *Visitors:* welcome, avoid Tuesdays and weekends. *Society Meetings:* all welcome. Professional: Don Wallace (091 523038) Secretary: Padraic Fahy (091 522033; Fax: 091 529783).

Connemara Golf Club
Ballyconneely, Clifden, Co. Galway
Tel: 095 23502/23602 • Fax: 095 23662

Opened in 1973, the links course is bounded on three sides by the Atlantic Ocean, with, on the inland side, superb views of the Twelve Bens. *Clubs, caddie cars, golf carts and caddies for hire.*
27 holes • practice range • pitching green • putting green
Green Fees: weekdays €65 , weekends €70.

e-mail: info@connemaragolflinks.net • www.connemaragolflinks.com

---

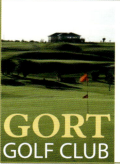

GORT GOLF CLUB

Designed by Ryder Cup star, Christy O'Connor Jnr and set in 160 acres of picturesque, undulating parkland on the edge of the world-famous Burren, overlooking Coole Lake.
20 minutes Galway Airport, 40 minutes Shannon Airport, 60 minutes Knock Airport.
18 holes, 5974 metres. S.S.S.71
Full bar and restaurant. Visitors welcome all year

Castlequarter, Gort, Co Galway
Tel: +353 91 632244 • Fax: +353 91 632387
e-mail: info@gortgolf.com • www.gortgolf.com

15th green at Connemara Golf Club

County Kerry

BALLYBUNION. **Ballybunion Golf Club,** Sandhill Road, Ballybunion (068 27146; Fax: 068 27387). *Location:* 20 miles from Tralee, 10 miles from Listowel. Links course established 1893, ranked in top ten in world. Two courses - Old and Cashen. 36 holes, 6800 yards. S.S.S. 71. *Green Fees:* from €75 to €180. *Eating facilities:* full bar and catering facilities. *Visitors:* welcome weekdays, some weekends; telephone bookings in advance. Carts and caddies for hire. *Society Meetings:* catered for. Professional: Brian O'Callaghan. Secretary: Vari McGreevy.

BALLYFERRITER. **Dingle Golf Links/Ceann Sibeal,** Ballyferriter (066 915 6255; Fax: 066 915 6409). *Location:* turn right quarter of a mile after Ballyferriter, 40 miles Tralee, 10 miles Dingle. Traditional links, most westerly golf course in Europe. 18 holes, 6696 yards. S.S.S. 71. Practice ground. *Green Fees:* information not available. *Eating facilities:* full bar and dining room. *Visitors:* welcome at all times, book in advance. *Society Meetings:* all welcome. Secretary: Steve Fahy (066 9156255; Fax: 066 9156409).*
e-mail: dinglegc@iol.ie
website: www.dinglelinks.com

CASTLEGREGORY. **Castlegregory Golf Club,** Stradbally, Castlegregory (066 7139444). *Location:* from Tralee N86 to Dingle; Conor Pass Road. Scenic links course with water features. 9 holes, 5264 metres, S.S.S. 67. Putting green. *Green Fees:* information not provided. *Eating facilities:* tea and snacks available. *Visitors:* welcome at all times. *Society Meetings:* welcome.

GLENBEIGH. **Dooks Golf Links,** Glenbeigh (066 9768205; Fax: 066 9768476). *Location:* on the N70 between Killorglin and Glenbeigh. Links course. 18 holes, 6586 yards. Par 71, S.S.S. 70. Putting green. *Green Fees:* information not available. *Eating facilities:* bar and restaurant. *Visitors:* welcome Monday to Saturday. *Society Meetings:* welcome with advance booking. Secretary/Manager: Brian Hurley.*
e-mail: office@dooks.com
website: www.dooks.com

KENMARE. **Ring of Kerry Golf and Country Club,** Templenoe, Kenmare (00 353 646642000; Fax: 00 353 646642533). *Location:* take the N70 Ring of Kerry road from Kenmare. Club is three miles on right. Parkland/ links course. 18 holes, 6820 yards. S.S.S. 73. Driving range, putting green. *Green Fees:* information not provided. *Eating facilities:* full bar and à la carte restaurant with terrace overlooking 17th/18th holes and bay. *Visitors:* welcome anytime. Pre-booking at weekends advisable. Some restrictions throughout the year. Tuition available. Clubhouse can be hired for private and corporate functions. On-course holiday homes. *Society Meetings:* welcome anytime with advance notice, contact club for details. Professional Adrian Whitehead. Manager: James Mitchell.
e-mail: reservations@ringofkerrygolf.com
        marketing@ringofkerrygolf.com
website: www.ringofkerrygolf.com

KENMARE. **Kenmare Golf Club,** Kenmare (064 6641291; Fax: 064 6642061). *Location:* on R569; just off main street in Kenmare. Partly links, partly parkland surrounded by some breathtaking views. 18 holes, 6083 yards. S.S.S. 69. Putting green, driving net. *Green Fees:* information not available. *Eating facilities:* snacks available. *Visitors:* welcome at all times, enquire for weekends. Booking in advance is advisable. Club hire, pull-cart hire. *Society Meetings:* welcome, booking in advance is advisable. Secretary: Donna Harrington.*
e-mail: info@kenmaregolfclub.com
website: www.kenmaregolfclub.com

Please mention THE GOLF GUIDE when you enquire about clubs or accommodation

DINGLE GOLF LINKS
CEANN SIBÉAL

Experience the Magic! 6,696 yards, Par 72 Traditional Championship Links. Each hole on this magnificent links is carved from the natural landscape of one of the most unspoiled parts of Europe, with hazards laid down long before the game of golf was dreamt of, including a winding "burn" that twists and turns through the entire course. As you play, the whole panorama of the Dingle Peninsula is revealed - hidden bays with small fishing villages, glorious hills and mountains and the Blasket Islands out in the wild Atlantic. This area abounds in archaeological treasures, wild flora and fauna, arts and crafts and ancient Gaelic culture. The Irish language is still spoken here. Thank you for visiting us!

Dingle Golf Club, Ceann Sibéal, Ballyferriter, Dingle, Co Kerry, Ireland
Tel +353 66 915 62 55 • mobile 085 8030774• Fax +353 66 915 64 09
e-mail: dinglegc@iol.ie • www.dinglelinks.com

KILLARNEY. **Beaufort Golf Club,** Churchtown, Beaufort, Killarney (064 44440; Fax: 064 44752). *Location:* seven miles west of Killarney town, just off the N72. Parkland course in unique setting surrounded by the Kerry Mountains. 18 holes, 6587 yards, 6023 metres. Par 71, S.S.S. 72. Practice facilities. *Green Fees:* information not available. *Eating facilities:* large bar and full food menu. *Visitors:* welcome seven days, but please pre-book. Electric buggies and carts. *Society Meetings:* welcome. Special rates available on request. Secretary: Colm Kelly (064 4440).*
e-mail: info@beaufortgolfresort.com
website: www.beaufortgolfclub.com

KILLARNEY. **Dunloe Golf Club,** Gap of Dunloe, Kilarney (00353 64 44578). *Location:* 10 minutes from Killarney town. Take N72 (main Killarney/Killorglin Road); first left after passing Hotel Europe. Outstanding parkland layout with spectacular views of Killarney's lakes and mountains. 9 holes. Par 34. *Green Fees:* information not available. *Eating facilities:* snack bar from 8am to 9pm (from 10am in winter). Professional: Kieran P. Crehan.*
e-mail: enquiries@dunloegc.com

KILLARNEY. **Killarney Golf and Fishing Club,** Mahony's Point, Killarney (00 353 646631034; Fax: 00 353 646633065). *Location:* Killarney town, two miles west on Ring of Kerry road. Undulating parkland courses - lakeside. Mahony's Point: 18 holes, 6152 metres. S.S.S. 72. Killeen: 18 holes, 6474 metres. S.S.S. 73. Lackabane Course, 18 holes, 6410 metres. Practice area. *Green Fees:* information not available. *Eating facilities:* available all day. *Visitors:* welcome at all times, reservations in advance, Handicap Certificate required. *Society Meetings:* welcome. Professional: David Keating. General Manager: Maurice O'Meara.
e-mail: reservations@killarney-golf.com
website: www.killarney-golf.com

KILLARNEY. **Ross Golf Club,** Ross Road, Killarney (064-31125; Fax: 064-31860). *Location*: from town centre follow signs to Muckross House, take first right on Muckross Road to Ross Castle and Ross Golf Club. Parkland, wooded course. 9 holes, 6450 yards, S.S.S. 73. Practice area and putting green. *Green Fees*: information not available. *Eating facilities*: full bar and snack bar serving soup and sandwiches. *Vistors*: welcome. PGA tuition and accommodation can be arranged. *Society Meetings*: welcome, special rates available. Professional & Secretary: Alan O'Meara (064 31125; Fax: 064 31860).*
e-mail: info@rossgolfclub.com
website: www.rossgolfclub.com

18 HOLE PARKLAND CHAMPIONSHIP GOLF COURSE – PAR 71

★ Stone built clubhouse offers a traditional and warm atmosphere
★ Societies, Groups and Visitors welcome 7 days
★ Electric buggies, trolleys, clubs and caddies for hire
★ Golf Professional   ★ Golf shop
★ Bar food and snacks all day

Killarney:10km • Kerry Airport: 20km • Cork Airport: 90km

Tel: 00353 64 44440 • Fax: 00353 64 44752
e-mail: info@beaufortgolfresort.com
www.beaufortgolfclub.com

CHURCHTOWN • BEAUFORT • KILLARNEY • Co KERRY

Kerry / IRELAND

KILLORGLIN. Killorglin Golf Club, Stealroe, Killorglin (066 9761979; Fax: 066 9761437). *Location:* just 20 minutes from Killarney and from Kerry Airport, three kilometres from the bridge at Killorglin on N70 road to the county town of Tralee. Parkland course overlooking Dingle Bay. 18 holes, 6435 yards. S.S.S. 71. *Green Fees:* €35, weekdays and weekends. 9 holes €20. Group rates available. *Eating facilities:* bar and restaurant facilities all day. *Visitors:* always welcome, booking necessary at weekends. Accommodation can be arranged; all major credit cards accepted. *Society Meetings:* all welcome, rates on request. Manager: Billy Dodd.
e-mail: kilgolf@iol.ie
website: www.killorglingolf.ie

SNEEM. Parknasilla Golf Club, Parknasilla, Sneem (064 45195; Fax: 064 45323). *Location:* on the Ring of Kerry route, two miles east of Sneem Village. Hilly seaside course, wooded. 12 holes, 5284 metres. S.S.S. 67. Practice ground. *Green Fees:* information not available. *Eating facilities:* available at Great Southern Hotel, 10 minutes' walk. *Visitors:* welcome, no restrictions. Caddy cars available. *Society Meetings:* contact 064 45195. Secretary/Manager: Maurice Walsh (064 45233).*

TRALEE. The Kerries Golf Club, Kerries East, Tralee (667 122112; Fax: 667 120085). *Location*: one mile from Tralee town. Parkland, overlooking Tralee Bay. 9 holes. S.S.S. 68. *Green Fees:* information not available. *Eating facilities*: snacks and wine bar. *Visitors:* welcome daily except Sundays 8am-12.30 pm. *Society Meetings:* welcome. Secretary: Helen Barrett.*

TRALEE. Tralee Golf Club, West Barrow, Ardfert, Tralee (066 7136379; Fax: 066 7136008). *Location:* Tralee to Barrow via the Spa and Churchill. Seaside links. 18 holes, 6975 yards, S.S.S. 73. *Green Fees:* information not available. 2009 rates (subject to review). *Eating facilities:* bar and restaurant. *Visitors:* welcome except Wednesdays of June, July and August. Other months Wednesdays 7.30-10.30pm, Saturdays 10am-2.30pm, no visitors on Sundays or Bank Holidays. General Manager: Anthony Byrne.*
e-mail: info@traleegolfclub.com
         reservations@traleegolfclub.com
website: www.traleegolfclub.com

WATERVILLE. Waterville House and Golf Links, Waterville (066 947 4102; Fax: 066 947 4482). *Location:* 55 miles from Killarney and Tralee, halfway round the Ring of Kerry. Links course, established in 1889 - Awards: Golf Monthly Top 5 British Isles, Golf Digest Top 100 World, Golf Digest No.1 Ireland, Golf Magazine - Best International Resorts. 7355 yards. S.S.S. 74. *Green Fees:* various rates, contact Waterville Golf Links. *Eating facilities:* bar and restaurant facilities available. *Visitors:* welcome every day. *Society Meetings:* welcome every day. Carts and caddies available on request. Secretary/ Manager: Noel Cronin (066 947 4102; Fax: 066 947 4482).
e-mail: wvgolf@iol.ie
website: www.watervillegolflinks.ie

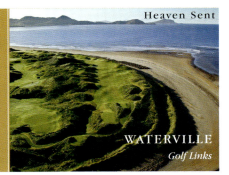

Waterville Golf Links, Waterville, Co Kerry
Tel: 066-9474102
Fax: 066-9474482
wvgolf@iol.ie
www.watervillegolflinks.ie

Location: 55 miles from Killarney and Tralee, half way round the Ring of Kerry. Links Course established in 1889.
Awards: Golf Monthly Top 5 British Isles, Golf Digest Top 100 World, Golf Digest No.1 Ireland, Golf Magazine - Best International Resorts.
7355 yards - SSS 74. Green Fees: contact Waterville Golf Links for various Green Fee rates.).
Visitors welcome every day. Bar and Restaurant facilities available, carts and caddies on request. Secretary/Manager: Noel Cronin.

Heaven Sent

WATERVILLE *Golf Links*

FHG Guides publish a large range of well-known accommodation guides. We will be happy to send you details or you can use the order form at the back of this book.

County Kildare

CARBURY. **Highfield Golf & Country Club** Carbury (046 9731021). *Location*: 10km from N4. One hour Dublin. Nearest town is Edenderry. Family owned. Parkland course in quiet rural location. 18 holes, 6292 yards, 5720 metres, S.S.S. 70. First tee on roof of Canadian Log Clubhouse. Open-air driving range. *Green Fees*: weekday €20; weekend €30. *Eating facilities*: full bar and restaurant. *Visitors*: welcome. Luxury 4* self-catering lodges. *Society Meetings*: welcome.
e-mail: highfieldgolf@eircom.net
website: www.highfield-golf.ie

CLANE. **Millicent Golf & Country Club,** Millicent Road, Clane (045 893279; Fax: 045 868369). *Location*: drive through Clane, take right after Corner House pub. Golf course on left after one mile. Parkland course, playable all year round. 18 holes, 7063 metres, S.S.S. 73. Driving range, chipping and putting greens. *Green Fees*: information not available. *Eating facilities*: bar and restaurant. *Visitors*: welcome every day, except Saturday between 8-9am and Sundays between 8-10am. *Society Meetings*: welcome every day, rates depending on numbers. Secretary: Niamh Killian.*
e-mail: info@millicentgolfclub.com
website: www.millicentgolfclub.com

CURRAGH. **The Curragh Golf Club,** Curragh, Newbridge (045 441238; Fax: 045 442476). Ireland's oldest Golf Club. Revamped over last 3 years. *Location:* three miles south of Newbridge. M7 Exit 12 direction Kilcullen, turn right at first crossroads. Hilly parkland course. 18 holes, 6586 yards. S.S.S. 72. Practice ground. *Green Fees:* €35 per person weekdays. *Eating facilities:* bar and restaurant. *Visitors:* restricted, please check in advance for course availability. *Society Meetings:* by appointment. Society package €60 including meal, minimum 25 players (weekends only). Society weekday green fee only €35. Professional: Gerry Burke (045 441896). Secretary: Ann Culleton (045 441714; Fax: 045 442476).
e-mail: curraghgolf@eircom.net
website: www.curraghgolf.com

DONADEA. **Knockanally Golf and Country Club,** Donadea, North Kildare (Tel & Fax: 045 869322). *Location:* three miles off N4 between Enfield and Kilcock. Parkland, home of the Irish International Professional Championship. 18 holes, 6495 yards. S.S.S. 72. *Green Fees:* information not available. *Eating facilities:* bar and restaurant. *Visitors:* welcome, no restrictions. *Society Meetings:* by arrangement. Professional: Martin Darcy (045 869322). Secretary: Declan M. Monaghan (045 869322).*
e-mail: golf@knockanally.com
website: www.knockanally.com

KILKEA. **Kilkea Castle Golf Resort,** Castledermot (00353 91 45555). *Location:* southbound on N7, onto M9, then N78 to Athy. Before entering Athy look for Ford garage on right. Kilkea is signposted on the left. Championship course. 18 holes. Par 70. *Green Fees:* information not available. *Eating facilities:* restaurant and bar. *Visitors:* welcome. Open all year round. Accommodation available on site.*
e-mail: kilkeagolfclub@eircom.net

KILL. **Killeen Golf Club,** Kill (045 86603; Fax: 045 875881). *Location:* South from Dublin on N7, turn right at Kill village. Parkland course with abundant wildlife. 18 holes, 6732 yards. S.S.S. 72. *Green Fees:* information not available. *Eating facilities:* restaurant and bar. *Visitors:* welcome. *Society Meetings:* welcome. For bookings contact Manager: Maurice Kelly.*
e-mail: admin@killeengc.ie
website: www.killeengolf.com

MAYNOOTH. **Carton House,** Maynooth, Co. Kildare (00353 1 5052000; Fax: 00353 1 6286555). *Location:* from Dublin take the N4. The Lexlip West exit from the N4 and follow signs to Carton House. O'Meara, Parkland course; The Montgomerie, inland links course. The Montgomerie course home to the 2005 & 2006 Nissan Irish Open. O'Meara 18 holes, 6400 metres, S.S.S. 74; Montgomerie 18 holes, 6700 metres, S.S.S. 74. Practice range and putting green. Golfing Union of Ireland Academy. *Green Fees:* information not available. *Eating facilities:* clubhouse restaurant. *Visitors:* always welcome, 165 bedroom hotel with conference and spa facility. *Society Meetings:* always welcome. Professional: Francis Howley. Secretary: John Lawler (00353 1 5052000; Fax: 00353 1 6286555).*
e-mail: golfreservations@cartonhouse.com
website: www.cartonhouse.com

NAAS. **Craddockstown Golf Club,** Blessington Road, Naas (045 897610; Fax: 045 896968). *Location*: off the southbound N7 turn left before Naas and take Blessington road, club one mile on right. Parkland course with meandering fairways, bunkers and many water features. Newly redeveloped golf course opened in May 2004. 18 holes, Par 71. Practice area. *Green Fees:* information not available. *Eating facilities:* Bar/snacks; lunch, dinner. *Visitors:* welcome Mondays, Thursdays and Fridays. Trolley and buggy hire. *Society Meetings*: welcome. Special group rates on request. Trolley and buggy hire. Contact club office (00353 45897610).*
e-mail: enquiries@craddockstown.com

The finest club in Ireland

At the K Club we pride ourselves on the style and comfort we afford our guests. Nestled amid lush green woodlands, just 17 miles from Dublin, The K Club is the most rewarding place to stay. Already acclaimed as one of the finest in the world, this magnificent 5 star Hotel offers you the highest standards of accommodation and service, without losing the elegance and unique charm of an Irish country house.

For incredible relaxation, guests can enjoy our extensive facilities including the K Spa, where with its mix of the very best treatments from around the world you can be lavishly pampered. Or indulge in any of the quality leisure activities available including our two championship golf courses, both designed by Arnold Palmer.

Be it for business or pleasure, at The K Club you can expect the warmest of welcomes in the most luxurious of surroundings.

For further information and reservations:
Hotel Tel: 353 (0)1 601 7200 Fax: 353 (0)1 601 7299
Golf Tel: 353 (0)1 601 7300 Fax: (0)1601 7297
e-mail: resortsales@kclub.ie
The K Club, Straffan, Co. Kildare, Ireland.

Home of the 2006 Ryder Cup Matches in 2006 and Venue for 14 European Opens

NAAS. **Naas Golf Club,** Kerdiffstown, Naas (045 897509; Fax: 045 896109). *Location*: N7 from Dublin, take Sallins exit (No. 8). Approx. one and a half kilometres on right hand side. Parkland. 18 holes, 6232 yards. S.S.S. 71. Practice ground. Public driving range within 200 metres. *Green Fees*: visit website. *Eating facilities:* 10.30am-11.00pm. *Visitors*: welcome. Contact club in advance. Dress code applies. *Society Meetings*: welcome. Manager: Denis Mahon (045 874644).
website: www.naasgolfclub.com

NAAS. **Woodlands Golf Club,** Coill Dubh, Cooleragh (045 860777; Fax: 045 860988). *Location:* From Naas, main Road to Sallins on to Clane village, left onto prosperous village, on to public house (Dagwelds) then turn right one mile ahead. Parkland, wooded with seven lakes. 18 holes. Putting green plus 9 hole pitch & putt course. *Green Fees:* information not available. *Visitors:* welcome except Saturday pm and Sunday am. Always phone in advance. *Society Meetings:* always welcome, rates depend on number playing. Secretary: Pat O'Rourke.*
e-mail: woodlandsgolf@eircom.net

SALLINS. **Bodenstown Golf Club,** Sallins (045 897096). *Location:* take Exit 7 off N7. 36 holes. S.S.S. 72. Practice green. *Green Fees:* from €15. *Eating facilities:* full catering and bar. *Visitors:* welcome, no restrictions. *Society Meetings:* please telephone. Secretary: Bernadette Curtin (045 897096).

STRAFFAN. **Castlewarden Golf and Country Club,** Castlewarden, Straffan (3531 4589254; Fax: 3531 4588972). *Location:* on the N7 Dublin to Naas road, take the second right after Blackchurch Inn. Parkland. 18 holes, 6690 yards. S.S.S. 71. Practice area and putting green. *Green Fees:* information not available. *Eating facilities:* full catering and bar. *Visitors:* welcome, booking advisable. *Society Meetings:* welcome. Professional: Brian O'Brien (3531 4588219). Secretary: Fiona Kane (3531 4589838).*
e-mail: castlewarden@clubi.ie
website: www.castlewardengolfclub.com

STRAFFAN. **The K Club,** Straffan, Co. Kildare (6017300; Fax: 6017399). *Location:* N7 south of Dublin to Kill, turn right, five miles from Junction. Signposted. Parkland course with trees, lakes, River Liffey – absolute Championship course. 18 holes, 7178 yards. S.S.S.76. Driving range. *Green Fees:* on request. Internet tee times available. *Eating facilities:* Legends Restaurant and Bar, The Arnold Palmer Room, Snack Bar and Members' Restaurant. *Visitors:* welcome. Golf shop, trolleys, clubs and shoe hire. The Kildare Hotel (within complex) AA 5 Red Star; 69 bedrooms. Professional: Michael Dixon (6017321; Fax: 6017399). Director of Golf: Bill Donald.
e-mail: bill.donald@kclub.ie
website: www.kclub.ie

Carton House, Maynooth

County Kilkenny

CALLAN. **Callan Golf Club,** Geraldine, Callan (056 772 5136; Fax: 056 7755155). *Location*: One mile from Callan on the Knocktopher Road. Parkland course with many water features. 18 holes, 6400 yards. S.S.S. 70. Practice area. *Green Fees*: weekdays €20, weekends €30 all year round. *Eating facilities*: full bar and catering available, reduced Winter hours. *Visitors*: welcome, advance booking recommended. *Society Meetings*: all welcome. Professional: Michael O'Shea. Secretary /Manager: Deirdre Power.
e-mail: info@callangolfclub.com
website: www.callangolfclub.com

CASTLECOMER. **Castlecomer Golf Club,** Drumgoole, Castlecomer (00 353 564441575; Fax: 00 353 564441139). *Location*: Main Castlecomer to Kilkenny Road. Parkland course beside the River Deen. 18 holes, 6180 metres. S.S.S. 74. Par 72. Practice ground. *Green Fees*: weekdays €20; weekends €25. 2010 rates (subject to review). *Eating facilities*: catering available. *Visitors*: always welcome. *Society Meetings*: welcome, society and group rates available. Secretary: Paul Campion (00 353 567 727480).
e-mail: info@castlecomergolf.com
website: www.castlecomergolf.com

GOWRAN. **Gowran Park,** Gowran (056 7726699). *Location:* on Waterford–Dublin road (N9), half a mile on the Waterford side of Gowran. Parkland, part of old Annally Estate, with woodland and lakes. 18 holes, 6100 metres. S.S.S. 72 (Blue), 70 (White), 68 (Green). Putting green, practice range. *Green Fees:* weekday €30; weekend €40. *Eating facilities:* full catering available daily. *Visitors:* welcome daily (some restrictions at weekends). *Society Meetings:* welcome daily (price on application).
e-mail: golf@gowranpark.ie
website: www.gowranpark.ie

KILKENNY. **Kilkenny Golf Club,** Glendine, Kilkenny (056 7765400; Fax: 056 7723593). *Location:* off Castlecomer Road two kilometres from centre of city. Parkland. 18 holes, 5908 metres. S.S.S. 71. Practice area. *Green Fees:* €30-€45. *Eating facilities*: available. *Visitors*: welcome, weekends by arrangement. *Society Meetings*: welcome, by arrangement. Professional: Jimmy Bolger (056 7761730). Manager: Sean Boland (056 7765400).
e-mail: enquiries@kilkennygolfclub.com

THOMASTOWN. **Mount Juliet Golf & Country Club,** Thomastown (056 7773064; Fax: 056 7773078). *Location:* Thomastown - on main Dublin to Waterford Road. Parkland, designed by Jack Nicklaus, home of the 1993-95 Irish Open. Home of the American Express World Golf Championship 2002 won by Tiger Woods and in 2004 won by Ernie Els. Voted Golf Course of the Year 2003. 18 holes, 7260 yards. S.S.S. 75, 73, 72. Golf academy and driving range, also Europe's first 18 hole putting course with a par of 53. *Green Fees:* information not available. *Eating facilities:* hotel, Spike bar, President's bar, two restaurants. *Visitors:* welcome, no restrictions but please book in advance. Handicap Cards preferred. 59 bedroom de luxe Hotel. *Society Meetings:* please book in advance. Professional: Sean Cotter.*

County Laois

ABBEYLEIX. **Abbeyleix Golf Club,** Rathmoyle, Abbeyleix (057 8731450; Fax: 057 8730108). *Location*: quarter mile outside town of Abbeyleix on Ballyroan Road. Parkland course with many water features. Practice chipping and putting green. 18 holes, 6020 yards. S.S.S. 70. *Green Fees*: Monday-Friday €25, weekends €30. 2010 rates (subject to review). *Eating facilities*: bar/restaurant (by arrangement). *Visitors:* welcome weekdays, weekends after 5pm. Secretary: Gerry O'Hara (057 8730643).
website: www.abbeyleixgolfclub.com

KILLENARD. **The Heritage Golf & Spa Resort,** Killenard (057 864 5500). *Location*: one hour from Dublin. Championship course designed by Seve Ballasteros and Jeff Howes, set amidst beautiful rolling countryside. 18 holes, Par 72. Golf school with driving range, teaching bays, pitching green and practice bunker. 9-hole Par 3 course. *Green Fees:* information not available. *Eating facilities:* Greens Restaurant, clubhouse, Spike Bar. *Visitors:* welcome by arrangement, Handicap Certificate required. *Society Meetings:* welcome by previous arrangement; special rates for groups of 20 or more.*
e-mail: info@theheritage.com
website: www.theheritage.com

MOUNTRATH. **Mountrath Golf Club,** Knockanina, Mountrath (0502 32558 (Public) or 0502 32643 (Office) or Fax: 0502 56735). *Location:* one kilometre off Dublin/Limerick Road, turn left outside Mountrath, signposted. Undulating parkland course with river flowing through it. 18 holes, 5643 metres. S.S.S. 69. Putting green, chipping green and practice area. *Green Fees:* information not available. *Eating facilities:* available everyday and by arrangement. Bar everyday. *Visitors:* welcome weekdays, and weekends after 4pm, phone beforehand. *Society Meetings:* welcome, contact office. Secretary: Lar Scully.*

PORTARLINGTON. **Portarlington Golf Club,** Garry Hinch, Portarlington (057 8623115; Fax: 057 8623044). *Location*: two and a half miles from Portarlington on the Mount Mellick Road. Parkland course with tree lines fairways. Practice ground. 18 holes, 5906 metres. S.S.S. 71. *Green Fees*: information not available. *Eating facilities*: bar and catering facilities available throughout the day. *Visitors:* welcome restricted at weekends. Golf Shop (057 8642916). *Society Meetings:* welcome, rates available.*
e-mail: portarlingtongc@eircom.net
website: www.portarlingtongolf.com

PORTLAOISE. **The Heath Golf Club,** The Heath, Portlaoise (057 86 46533; Fax: 057 86 46735). *Location:* three-and-a-half miles north-east of Portlaoise, off main Dublin road. Relatively flat with furze, gorse and three lakes. 18 holes, 5736 metres. S.S.S. 71. 10 bay all-weather floodlit driving range and practice area. *Green Fees:* information not provided. *Eating facilities:* full bar and catering facilities available. *Visitors:* welcome at all times but advance booking required for weekends and Public Holidays. *Society Meetings:* welcome by prior arrangement. Professional: Mark O'Boyle.

PORTLAOISE. **Rathdowney Golf Club,** Rathdowney, Portlaoise (0505 46170 or Tel & Fax: 0505 46065 office). *Location*: half a mile from Rathdowney, signposted from the square. Parkland course with gentle sloping hills; good test for most golfers (second 9 holes opened June 1997). 18 holes, 5894 metres, S.S.S. 70, Par 71. *Green Fees:* €25. *Eating facilities*: bar open all day, meals available. *Visitors*: welcome any time during the week, Sundays after 4.30pm, Saturday mornings reserved for societies. *Society Meetings:* welcome by appointment through Hon. Secretary. Hon. Secretary: Martin O'Brien.
website: www.rathdowneygolfclub.com

County Leitrim

BALLINAMORE. **Ballinamore Golf Club,** Ballinamore (00353 7 196 44346). *Location:* 1½ miles north-west of town alongside Shannon/Erne waterway. Parkland. 9 holes, 6142 yards, 5514 metres. S.S.S.68. *Green Fees:* information not available. *Eating facilities:* bar with snacks. *Visitors:* welcome with some restrictions on certain weekends. *Society Meetings:* welcome with restrictions on certain weekends. Captain: Martin McCartin (086 6035582). Secretary: Gerry Mahon (071 9644031 or 087 7678392).*

County Limerick

ABBEYFEALE. **Abbeyfeale Golf Club,** Dromtrasna Collins, Abbeyfeale (068 32033). *Location*: two miles from Abbeyfeale. Parkland. 9 holes, 4072 yards. S.S.S. 64. 20 bay indoor driving range, practice putting green. *Green Fees*: information not available. *Eating facilities*: by appointment. *Visitors*: welcome everyday. *Society Meetings*: societies/companies/groups always welcome. Professional: (068 32033). Hon. Secretary: Conleth Dillon (068 31454).*
e-mail: abbeyfealegolf@eircom.net

ADARE. **Adare Golf Club,** Adare Manor Hotel & Golf Resort, Adare (061 605274; Fax: 061 605271). *Location:* from Limerick take the N21. Robert Trent Jones designed Championship parkland course, home to the Irish Open 2007 and 2008 and the J P McManus Invitational Pro-Am 2005 and 2010. 18 holes, 7453 yards. Putting green, short game area and driving range. *Green Fees:* rates on request. *Eating facilities:* clubhouse bar and restaurant. *Visitors:* always welcome. *Society Meetings:* welcome. Professional: Gary Howie.
e-mail: golf@adaremanor.com
website: www.adaregolfclub.com

ADARE. **Adare Manor Golf Club,** Adare (353 61 396204; Fax: 353 61 396800). *Location*: main Limerick to Killarney road, 10 miles from Limerick. Parkland course. 18 holes, 5764 yards. S.S.S. 69. Putting green, chipping area. *Green Fees*: €30 per person. *Eating facilities*: full bar and restaurant. *Visitors*: welcome all year round. Check with club for times at weekends. *Society Meetings:* information not available. Hon. Secretary: Dr. M. Spillane (353 61 396204; Fax: 353 61 396800).
e-mail: info@adaremanorgolfclub.com
website: www.adaremanorgolfclub.com

ARDAGH. **Newcastle West Golf Club,** Ardagh (00-353-6976500; Fax: 00-353-6976511). *Location:* Off N21 roadway linking Shannon, Limerick and Killarney beyond Rathkeale. Parkland course. 18 holes, 6400 yards. S.S.S. 72. Floodlit driving bays, practice green and bunker. *Green Fees:* Monday to Thursday €30, 4 ball €100; Friday to Sunday €35, 4 ball €120. 2010 rates (subject to review). *Eating facilities:* bar and restaurant. *Visitors:* welcome. *Society Meetings:* welcome; green fee reductions. Professional: Conor McCormick (Tel & Fax: 00-353-6976500) Secretary/Manager: John F. Whelan (Tel & Fax: 00-353-6976500).
website: www.newcastlewestgolf.com

For full details of convenient accommodation near clubs and courses
www.holidayguides.com

THE APPEARANCE OF AN ASTERISK (*) AT THE END OF A CLUB OR COURSE ENTRY INDICATES THAT UP-TO-DATE INFORMATION HAS NOT BEEN SUPPLIED

BALLYNEETY. **Limerick County Golf and Country Club,** Ballyneety (061 351881; Fax: 061 351384). *Location:* five miles from Limerick City, R512 direction of Lough Gur/Kilmallock. Championship standard, parkland course with water hazards bordering 8 holes. 18 holes, 5876 metres. S.S.S. 71. Driving range, putting greens, golf school with professional tuition. *Green Fees:* €25. 2010 rates (subject to review). *Eating facilities:* excellent restaurant serving light snacks, lunch and dinner menus, full bar service. *Visitors:* always welcome, online tee times. Professional: Donal McSweeney (061 351881). Manager: Brian McLoghlin (061 351881; Fax: 061 351384).
e-mail: teetimes@limerickcounty.com
website: www.limerickcounty.com

CASTLETROY. **Castletroy Golf Club,** Golf Links Road, Castletroy, Limerick City (061 335753; Fax: 061 335373). *Location:* three miles from Limerick City on N7 (Dublin Road). 18 hole popular parkland course, 6274 metres. Golf Shop. *Green Fees:* €50 Monday to Thursday; €60 Friday to Sunday and Bank Holidays. *Eating facilities:* full catering and bar service. *Visitors:* welcome all week except Tuesday and Thursday - advisable to phone. *Society Meetings:* welcome Monday, Wednesday, Friday and Saturday; group rates available. General Manager: Patrick Keane.
e-mail: golf@castletroygolfclub.ie
website: www.castletroygolfclub.ie

LIMERICK. **Limerick Golf Club,** Ballyclough, Limerick (061 414083; Fax: 061 319219). *Location*: five km from Limerick city on Fedamore Road. Parkland. 18 holes, 5932 metres. S.S.S. 71. *Green Fees:* €50 Monday to Thursday, €70 Friday to Sunday and Bank Holidays. *Eating facilities:* full bar and dining facilities. *Visitors*: welcome Mondays, Wednesdays, Thursdays, Fridays up to 4pm. *Society Meetings*: advance booking required. Professional: Lee Harrington (061 412492). General Manager: Pat Murray (061 415146).
e-mail: information@limerickgolfclub.ie
website: www.limerickgolfclub.ie

County Longford

LONGFORD. **County Longford Golf Club,** Glack, Dublin Road, Longford (043 33 46310; Fax: 043 33 47082). *Location:* one mile from centre of town on Dublin road. 18 holes, 5981 metres. S.S.S. 73. *Green Fees:* information not available. *Eating facilities:* full catering and bar. *Visitors:* welcome at all times subject to availability. Buggies and carts available. *Society Meetings:* all welcome. Secretary: Martina Glennon.*
e-mail: colonggolf@eircom.net

County Louth

ARDEE. **Ardee Golf Club,** Townparks, Ardee (041 6853227; Fax: 041 6856137). Parkland, wooded course with beautiful mature trees and exquisite greens. 18 holes, 6348 yards, S.S.S. 71. Large practice area. *Green Fees:* information not available. *Eating facilities:* restaurant and bar. *Visitors:* welcome. Carts for hire, caddies by arrangement. *Society Meetings:* welcome Mondays to Saturdays. Professional: Scott Kirkpatrick (041 6857472). Hon Secretary: E. Roe. Secretary/Manager: Seamus Rooney (041 6853227; Fax: 041 6856137).*

DROGHEDA. **County Louth Golf Club,** Baltray, Drogheda (041 9881530; Fax: 041 9881531). *Location:* Drogheda, five miles north east. Championship links course. 18 holes, 7035 yards. S.S.S. 74. *Green Fees:* weekdays €100; weekends €135. *Eating facilities:* restaurant, coffee shop and bar. *Visitors:* welcome weekdays except Tuesdays on application, weekends restricted. Residential accommodation available for 20 persons. *Society Meetings:* on application. Professional: Paddy McGuirk (041 9881536). Secretary: Michael Delany (041 9881530; Fax: 041 9881531).

DROGHEDA. **Seapoint Golf Club,** Termonfeckin, Drogheda (041 982333; Fax: 041 982331). *Location:* Dublin–Belfast–Drogheda to Termonfeckin Road. Links course. 18 holes, 6339 metres. S.S.S. 74. Practice range and putting green. *Green Fees:* information not available. *Eating facilities:* restaurant and bar. *Visitors:* welcome at all times; members' tee times 1-2pm daily and up to 10.30am weekends. *Society Meetings:* welcome, discounts available. Trolleys and caddies available. Professional: David Carroll. Secretary: Kevin Carrie.*
e-mail: info@seapointgolfclub.com
website: www.seapointgolfclub.com

DUNDALK. **Dundalk Golf Club,** Blackrock, Dundalk (042 9321731; Fax: 042 9322022). *Location:* Dundalk coast road to Blackrock, two miles. Championship parkland course with tree-lined fairways. Hosted All Ireland Finals in 1997 and 2000. Attracts country's top players to Senior Scratch Cup. Hosts major PGA Pro-Am and Ladies' Home Internationals. Celebrated Centenary in 2005. 18 holes, 6776 yards, 6160 metres. S.S.S. 72 (Par 72). Six-acre field practice ground. *Green Fees:* on request. *Eating facilities:* full restaurant and bar. *Visitors:* welcome Mondays, Wednesdays, Thursdays and Fridays, restrictions weekends and Tuesday Ladies' Day. *Society Meetings:* welcome by appointment. Professional: Leslie Walker (042 9322102).
e-mail: manager@dundalkgolfclub.ie
website: www.dundalkgolfclub.ie

GREENORE. **Greenore Golf Club,** Greenore (042 93 73212/73678; Fax: 042 9383898). *Location:* Dundalk/ Newry, Dundalk 15 miles, Newry 12 miles. Flat semi-links course with heathland features, pine trees, rivers, ponds – very scenic, Carlingford Mountains and Mountains of Mourne. 18 holes, 6647 yards. S.S.S. 73. *Green Fees:* information not provided. *Eating facilities:* full catering and bar facilities (daylight hours). *Visitors:* always welcome, prior booking advisable. Caddies on request, trolley and golf buggy available for hire. *Society Meetings:* very welcome by prior arrangement. Professional: Robert Giles. Secretary: Linda Clarke (042 9373678).
e-mail: greenoregolfclub@eircom.net
website: www.greenoregolfclub.com

KILLIN. **Killin Park Golf & Country Club,** Killin, Dundalk (00353 42 9339303). *Location:* two miles west of Dundalk. Undulating parkland with mature trees. The 4th and 6th holes are surrounded by the Castletown River. 18 holes. Par 69. *Green Fees:* information not available. *Eating facilities:* available from dawn till dusk.*

Co. Mayo

ACHILL. **Achill Golf Club,** Keel, Achill Island (098 43456). *Location:* N59 from Westport and R319 from Mulranny to Achill. Flat seaside links in scenic setting. 9 holes, 2726 metres. S.S.S. 67. *Green Fees:* information not available. *Visitors:* welcome at all times, no restrictions. *Society Meetings:* by prior arrangement. Secretary: Michael McGinty (085 1743571.*

BALLINA. **Ballina Golf Club,** Mossgrove, Shanaghy, Ballina (Tel & Fax: 096 21050). *Location:* on Bonniconlon Road. Parkland course. 18 holes, 6103 yards. S.S.S. 69. *Green Fees:* information not available. *Eating facilities:* bar, snacks. *Visitors:* welcome every day, Sundays 11am to 1.30pm. *Society Meetings:* weekdays to 4pm, Saturdays 10am to 12 noon, Sundays 11am to 1.30pm. Secretary: Padhraig Connolly (096 21050; Fax: 096 2178).*
e-mail: ballinagc@eircom.net
website: www.ballinagolfclub.com

BALLINROBE. **Ballinrobe Golf Club,** Cloonacastle, Ballinrobe (09495 41118; Fax: 09495 41889). *Location:* off N84 at Ballinrobe onto the R331 to Claremorris. Parkland course with trees and man-made lakes. 18 holes, 6354 metres. S.S.S. 73. Practice ground, driving range. *Green Fees:* information not available. *Eating facilities:* catering and bar facilities. *Visitors:* welcome at all times but is advisable to book tee times in advance. Buggies and carts available. Excellent fishing. *Society Meetings:* welcome by arrangement. Secretary: Bernie Murphy.
e-mail: info@ballinrobegolfclub.com
website: www.ballinrobegolfclub.com

BELMULLET. **Carne Golf Links,** Belmullet (097 82292; Fax: 097 81477) *Location:* on N59 three km from centre of Belmullet town. Pure links course - feature holes 9th, 14th and 18th. 18 holes, 6119 metres. Medal S.S.S 72; Championship. S.S.S 72, Par 72. Practice ground and putting green. *Green Fees:* available on request. *Eating facilities:* full restaurant and bar facilities. *Visitors:* very welcome at all times. Buggies and caddies available. *Society Meetings:* by arrangement. Office: (097 82292; Fax: 097 81477).
e-mail: info@carnegolflinks.com
website: www.carnegolflinks.com

CASTLEBAR. **Castlebar Golf Club,** Rocklands, Castlebar (353 94 9021649; Fax: 353 94 9026088). *Location:* situated on the Galway road out of town. Championship, parkland course with abundance of water and trees. 18 holes, 6500 yards, S.S.S. 71. *Green Fees:* Monday to Thursday €25, Friday/ Saturday/Sunday €35. *Eating facilities:* full catering facilities. *Visitors:* welcome every day, except Sunday before 1.30pm. Pro Shop. *Society Meetings:* welcome every day except Sunday. Honorary Secretary: Padraig Corrigan (087 0578584.

CLAREMORRIS. **Claremorris Golf Club,** Castlemacgarrett, Claremorris (094 9371527). *Location:* on N17, Galway 35 miles, Claremorris two miles, Knock airport 20 miles. Parkland/wooded course designed by Tom Craddock; numerous water hazards and excellent sand-based greens. 18 holes, 7000 yards. S.S.S. 72. Practice ground. *Green Fees:* €25. 2010 rates (subject to review). *Visitors:* welcome weekdays, weekends on request. *Society Meetings:* welcome, booking required. Admin Manager: Christina Rush (094 9371527)
e-mail: info@claremorrisgolfclub.com
website: www.claremorrisgolfclub.com

SWINFORD. **Swinford Golf Club,** Brabazon Park, Swinford (094 92 51378). *Location:* on Kiltimagh Road beside Swinford town. Parkland. 9 holes, S.S.S. 68. Practice green and pitching area. *Green Fees:* information not available. *Eating facilities:* bar with catering by arrangement. *Visitors:* welcome with some restrictions. *Society Meetings:* Golf societies welcome, prices on application. Secretary: John Sheahan (087 9100 572).*
e-mail: sheetsjj@eircom.net

WESTPORT. **Westport Golf Club,** Carrowholly, Westport (098 28262/27070; Fax: 098 27217). Parkland championship course. 18 holes. Practice area, 9 bay floodlit driving range. *Green Fees:* information not available. *Eating facilities:* bar and restaurant. *Visitors:* welcome with restrictions. *Society Meetings:* welcome. Professional: Alex Mealia. Club Administrator: Margaret Walsh. Secretary: Karen Walsh. Manager: Paul O'Neil.*
e-mail: info@westportgolfclub.com

Co. Meath

ASHBOURNE. **Ashbourne Golf Club,** Archerstown, Ashbourne (00 353 (0)1835 2005). *Location:* 12 miles from Dublin, on the road to Derry. Parkland course to USGA standards. 18 holes. Par 71. *Green Fee:* information not available. *Eating facilities:* from 11am to 10pm (noon to 4pm during winter). Professional: John Dwyer.*
e-mail: ashgc@iol.ie
website: www.ashbournegolfclub.ie

BETTYSTOWN. **Laytown and Bettystown Golf Club,** Bettystown, Drogheda. *Location:* 25 miles north of Dublin. A traditional links golf course, a good test for any golfer, excellent conditions. 18 holes, 5697 metres. S.S.S. 72. *Green Fees:* Monday to Friday €50; Saturday/Sunday €60. 2010 rates (subject to review). *Eating facilities:* full bar and catering facilities. *Visitors:* welcome but make reservation. *Society Meetings:* welcome; make reservation. Professional: Robert J. Browne (041 9828793). Secretary: Helen Finnegan (041 9827170; Fax: 041 9828506).

DUNSHAUGHLIN. **Black Bush Golf Club,** Thomastown, Dunshaughlin (01-8250021; Fax: 01-8250400). *Location:* situated on the Navan Road, Dunshaughlin. Lush fairways bordered by mature trees with sand based greens. 27 holes, played in a combination. Course A + B 6849 yards, S.S.S. 72; B + C 6434 yards, S.S.S. 70; C + A 6599 yards, S.S.S. 71. *Green Fees:* information not available. *Society Meetings:* welcome. Professional: Shane O'Grady (01-8250793). Secretary: Aiden Burns*.
e-mail: info@blackbushgolfclub.ie

ENFIELD. **Rathcore Golf and Country Club,** Rathcore, Enfield (046 9541855; Fax: 0446 9542916). *Location:* three miles from Enfield, 30 minutes from the M50 and Dublin. Parkland course. 18 holes, 6533 yards, S.S.S. 72. Putting green. *Green Fees:* information not available. *Eating facilities:* restaurant. *Visitors:* welcome at all times, phone to book. Buggy and club hire. *Society Meetings:* all welcome, book in advance. Secretary: Aileen McDonnell.*
e-mail: rathcoregolfandcountryclub.com
website: www.rathcoregolfandcountryclub.com

JULIANSTOWN. **Julianstown Golf Course and Pitch & Putt,** Julianstown, Drogheda (041 9811953). *Location:* located along the R132 immediately south of the River Nanny, overlooking Julianstown Village. Parkland course. Excellently maintained 9 hole course, five par 4s and four par 3s with water, trees and flat terrain. 9 holes - 2107 yards; 18 holes - 4214 yards. S.S.S. 64. Putting green. 18 hole pitch & putt course of equally high standard. *Green Fees:* 9 hole course: 9 holes €12, 18 holes €20. *Eating facilities:* light refreshments available from clubhouse. *Visitors:* welcome everyday. *Society Meetings:* welcome on enquiry. Secretary: D. Berrill (041 9811953 or 087 4178290).

KELLS. **Headfort Golf Club,** Navan Road, Kells (046 9240146; Fax: 046 9249282). *Location:* on N3 from Dublin, bypass Navan and half-a-mile from Kells. Parkland. 18 holes x 2, 6007 metres. S.S.S. 71. Practice area. *Green Fees:* information not provided. *Eating facilities:* bar and full catering. *Visitors:* welcome everyday. *Society Meetings:* welcome by prior arrangement. Professional: Brendan McGovern (Tel. & Fax: 046 9240639). Admin. Secretary: Nora Murphy (046 9282001).

KILCOCK. **Kilcock Golf Club,** Gallow, Kilcock (01 628 7592/628 4074). *Location:* off main Dublin to Galway motorway at Kilcock. Parkland with undulating fairways, light rough, and flat greens. Practice area. 18 holes, 5816 metres. S.S.S.72. *Green Fees:* information not available. *Eating facilities:* catering available. *Visitors:* welcome but some restrictions at weekends. *Society Meetings:* society outings welcome but must book.*
e-mail: kilcockgolfclub@eircom.net
website: www.kilcockgolfclub.com

www.ashbournegolfclub.ie

This beautiful 18-hole parkland course, located on the outskirts of Ashbourne village, welcomes visitors and societies. The three man-made lakes complement the Broadmeadow River in a manner that sees water impact on 9 out of the 18 holes, providing the golfer with quite a challenge. It lies within a 20-minute drive of Dublin Airport, and a full bar and catering service is available in the friendly clubhouse.

Ashbourne Golf Club, Archerstown, Co Meath • Tel: 01835 2005/9261
Pro Shop: 01835 9002 • Fax: 01835 9261 • ashgc@iol.ie

NAVAN. **Royal Tara Golf Club,** Bellinter, Navan (+353 46 9025244/9025508/9026868). *Location*: 25 miles north of Dublin off National Primary Route N3 - close to Hill of Tara. Parkland, private course. 27 holes. 18 hole course, 6457 yards, S.S.S. 71. 9 hole course 3184 yards, S.S.S. 35. Practice ground. *Green Fees*: information not available. *Eating facilities*: full catering facilities all day every day. *Visitors*: welcome, Ladies' Day Tuesdays, please check with club in advance. Carts and caddies on request. *Society Meetings*: welcome except Tuesdays and Sundays. Professional: Mr Adam Whiston (+353 46 902 6009). Hon Secretary: Mr John Byrne. General Manager: Francis Duffy (+353 46 902 5508; Fax: +353 46 902 6684).*
e-mail: info@royaltaragolfclub.com
website: www.royaltaragolfclub.com

TRIM. **Glebe Golf Club,** Dunlever, Trim (Tel: & Fax: 00 353 469431926). *Location:* one mile from Trim on Kildalkey Road. Top quality parkland course in the heart of Meath countryside. Full size practice area. 18 holes, 6466 yards, 5906 metres. S.S.S.71. *Green Fees:* information not available. *Eating facilities:* bar/restaurant. *Visitors:* welcome but some restrictions during society time. Please telephone for availability. *Society Meetings:* welcome, discount for 15 or more persons. Secretary: Patrick Bligh (Tel: & Fax: 00 353 46943 1926).*
e-mail: glebegc@eircom.net
website: www.glebegolfclub.com

TRIM. **Knightsbrook Golf Club,** Dublin Road, Trim (046 9482101). *Location:* from M50 take N3 Navan Road, left at Fairyhouse Cross, left at roundabout at Victorine Abbey . Parkland course. Practice putting and chipping greens. 18 holes, 7270 metres. S.S.S.72. *Green Fees:* information not available. *Eating facilities:* full bar and catering facilities. *Visitors:* welcome everyday, no restrictions. Four-star hotel and self-catering accommodation available on site. *Society Meetings:* welcome everyday, discounts available. Professional: Eugene McEneaney. Director: Gavin Hunt.*
e-mail: golf@knightsbrook.com
website: www.knightsbrook.com

THE APPEARANCE OF AN ASTERISK (*) AT THE END OF A CLUB OR COURSE ENTRY INDICATES THAT UP-TO-DATE INFORMATION HAS NOT BEEN SUPPLIED

Co. Monaghan

CARRICKMACROSS. **Mannan Castle Golf Club,** Donaghmoyne, Carrickmacross ((42) 9663308). *Location:* 3 miles from Carrickmacross on Crossmaglen Road. Wooded parkland course. 18 holes, 6082 yards. S.S.S. 69. *Green Fees:* information not available. *Eating facilities:* full restaurant in operation. *Visitors:* welcome any day except Sunday before 4.00pm. *Society Meetings:* especially welcome, contact Sheila for details.*
e-mail: mannancastlegc@eircom.net

CARRICKMACROSS. **Nuremore Hotel & Country Club,** Carrickmacross (042 9661438). *Location:* 50 miles north of Dublin on N2. *Green Fees:* information not available. *Eating facilities:* bar and catering facilities in hotel and clubhouse. *Visitors:* welcome at all times. Opening hours - daylight hours. All hotel facilities. Professional: Maurice Cassidy (042 9671368; Fax: 042 9661853).*
e-mail: nuremore@eircom.net
website: www.nuremore-hotel.ie

CASTLEBLAYNEY. **Castleblayney Golf Club,** Onomy, Hope Castle Estate, Castleblayney (042 9749485). *Location:* N2 road, Hope Castle Estate, 500 yards from town centre. Scenic parkland course with lakes and forest in centre of Leisure Park. 9 holes, 5345 yards. S.S.S. 66. *Green Fees:* information not available. *Eating facilities:* snacks and bar. *Visitors:* welcome at all times except during major competitions at weekends. Accommodation in Hope Castle Complex. *Society Meetings:* welcome. Secretary: Raymond Kernan (Tel & Fax: 042 9740451).*

CLONES. **Clones Golf Club,** Hilton Demesne, Clones (047 56017). *Location:* three miles from Clones on the Scotshouse Road. Parkland course. 18 holes, 5980 metres. Par 71. S.S.S. - White 70, Yellow 68. Practice area and putting green. *Green Fees:*.information not available. *Eating facilities:* full catering facilities all year round. *Visitors:* welcome at all times, advance booking necessary at weekends. Caddy cars and buggy hire available. *Society Meetings:* welcome. Hon. Secretary: Martin Taylor (049 5552354).*
e-mail: clonesgolfclub@eircom.net
website: www.clonesgolfclub.com

MONAGHAN. **Rossmore Golf Club,** Cootehill Road, Monaghan (047 81613). *Location:* 2 km from Monaghan town. Parkland. 18 holes, 5600 metres. S.S.S. 69. *Green Fees*: information not available. *Eating facilities*: available. *Visitors*: always welcome, golf carts and trolleys available. *Society Meetings*: welcome. Professional: Ciaran Smyth (047 71222). Secretary: Henry Durnin.
e-mail: info@rossmoregc.com

Co. Offaly

BIRR. **Birr Golf Club,** "The Glenns", Birr (0509 20082; Fax: 0509 22155). *Location*: approximately two miles from Birr on the Banagher Road. Parkland/wooded, carved out of natural woodlands, with undulating fairways. The course was originally part of the Estate of the Earl of Rosse, who still lives in Birr Castle. 18 holes, 6317 yards, 5754 metres. S.S.S. 70. Driving range. *Green Fees*: information not available. *Eating facilities*: available; bar. *Visitors*: always welcome; some restrictions on Sundays only. *Society Meetings*: all welcome. Secretary: Mary O'Gorman.*

EDENDERRY. **Edenderry Golf Club,** Kishawanny, Edenderry (0469 731072; Fax: 0469 733911). *Location*: outside Edenderry, quarter of a mile on Dublin Road then turn left after half a mile, on left hand side. Wooded course. 18 holes, S.S.S. 72. *Green Fees*: information not provided. *Eating facilities*: catering available. *Visitors*: welcome Monday, Tuesday, Wednesday and Friday, please telephone for booking. *Society Meetings*: welcome, please book in advance. Hon. Secretary: Noel Usher.*
e-mail: enquiries@edenderrygolfclub.com
website: www.edenderrygolfclub.com

OFFALY. **Castle Barna Golf Club,** Daingean, Tullamore (057 9353384). *Location:* ten miles east of Tullamore and 8 miles south of main N6 Dublin to Galway road. Parkland with mature trees. 18 holes, 6200 yards. S.S.S. 71. *Green Fees*: weekdays €22, weekends €32. *Eating facilities:* meals available. *Visitors*: welcome except Sundays before noon. *Society Meetings:* welcome.
e-mail: info@castlebarna.ie
website: www.castlebarna.ie

TULLAMORE. **Esker Hills Golf Club,** Tullamore (057 93 55999; Fax: 057 93 55021). *Location*: 3 miles from Tullamore, off the Tullamore/Clara Road (N80 Route). A Christy O'ConnorJnr designed parkland course with a distinct links feel. 18 holes, 6618 metres. S.S.S.71. Putting green, practice nets. *Green Fees*: weekdays €35, weekends and Bank Holidays €45. Open Singles every Tuesday from May 2011 to September 2011 €20. *Eating facilities*: available. *Visitors*: welcome. Golf buggies available for hire at €25 per buggy. *Society Meetings*: welcome. Group rates on request. Secretary: Caroline Guinan (057 93 55999; Fax: 057 93 55021).
e-mail: info@eskerhillsgolf.com
website: www.eskerhillsgolf.com

TULLAMORE. **Tullamore Golf Club,** Brookfield, Tullamore (057 9321439; Fax: 057 9341806). *Location:* from Dublin take N4 (signposted Sligo), at Junction 2 continue forward onto the motorway M4 (signposted Sligo) at Toll Plaza, leave the M4 at Junction 11, then at roundabout take 2nd exit N6 (signposted Galway), at roundabout take the 2nd exit onto the N52, (signposted Tullamore, continue on through the next 4 roundabouts (signposted Birr), and at the 5th roundabout, take the first exit for Kinnitty, the R421. Continue on for 1 km, the Golf Club is on your right. Parkland. 18 holes, 6472 yards. S.S.S. 70. Practice area. *Green Fees*: €37 weekdays, €48 weekends. €25 with member. *Eating facilities*: full bar and dining service, order meals before play. *Visitors:* welcome; restrictions Wednesdays; limited availability on Sundays. Local accommodation available. *Society Meetings*: welcome, contact Secretary. Professional: Donagh McArdle (Tel & Fax: 057 9351757). Secretary: Helen Egan (057 9321439) or Ann Marie Cunniffe.
e-mail: tullamoregolfclub@eircom.net
website: www.tullamoregolfclub.ie

Co. Roscommon

ATHLONE. **Athlone Golf Club,** Hodson Bay, Athlone (090 649 2073; Fax: 090 649 4080). *Location*: off the Roscommon road close to the Hodson Bay Hotel. Parkland championship standard course with mature trees and undulating fairways 18 new USGA greens. 18 holes, 5983 metres. S.S.S.71. Practice ground. *Green Fees*: information not provided. Open Day each Wednesday May to October, entry €15. *Eating facilities*: restaurant and bar. *Visitors*: welcome Monday to Saturday, contact club in advance. *Society Meetings*: society outings welcome. Professional: Kevin Grealy. Administrative Secretary: l. Dockery.
e-mail: athlonegolfclub@eircom.net
website: www.athlonegolfclub.ie

CARRICK-ON-SHANNON. **Carrick-on-Shannon Golf Club,** Woodbrook, Carrick-on-Shannon (07196 67015). *Location:* four miles west of Carrick-on-Shannon adjacent to N4. Parkland course overlooking River Shannon, a fine test of golf for low/high handicappers. 18 holes, 5787 metres. S.S.S. 68. *Green Fees:* information not available. *Eating facilities:* full catering facilities available. *Visitors:* welcome midweek and weekends, please phone in advance. Buggy and trolley hire available. *Society Meetings:* welcome by arrangement. Secretary: Liz (07196 67015).*
e-mail: ckgc3@eircom.net
website: www.carrickgolfclub.ie

ROSCOMMON. **Roscommon Golf Club,** Mote Park, Roscommon (090 6626382; Fax: 090 6626043). *Location:* half a mile south of Roscommon town. Rolling parkland, special feature 13th hole over lake Par 3. 18 holes, 6059 metres. S.S.S. 71. Practice ground, putting green. *Green Fees*. information not available. *Eating facilities*: full bar and restaurant. *Visitors*: welcome, restrictions Sundays (competition day). Carts, caddies. *Society Meetings*: welcome. Secretary: Noreen O'Grady (090 6626382).*
e-mail: rosgolfclub@eircom.net

Co. Sligo

BALLYMOTE. **Ballymote Golf Club**, Ballinascarrow, Ballymote (071 9183504/9183089). *Location:* 15 miles south of Sligo town, 12 miles west of Boyle. Undulating parkland with pleasant views. 9 holes, 2651 metres. S.S.S. 67 (for 18 holes). *Green Fees:* information not available. Trolleys available for hire 2 euros, buggies 3 euros. *Society Meetings:* please telephone John O'Connor (087 2187054).*

ENNISCRONE. **Enniscrone Golf Club,** Enniscrone (096 36297 three lines; Fax: 096 36657). *Location:* on coast road from Sligo to Ballina, about 13 km from Ballina. Championship links course - host to the Irish Close Championship 1993 - host to West of Ireland Championship 1997-1999 - host to Senior Inter Provincials 1999. 18 holes, 6857 yards. Par 73. Practice area and putting green. *Green Fees:* information not available. *Eating facilities:* bar and full catering facilities. *Visitors:* welcome, please phone beforehand. Professional: Charlie McGoldrick (096 36666). Hon. Secretary: Brian Casey (096 36414). Administrator: Anne Freeman. Secretary/ Manager: Mick Staunton.*
e-mail: enniscronegolf@eircom.net
website: www.enniscronegolf.com

ROSSES POINT. **County Sligo Golf Club,** Rosses Point (+353 (0)71 9177134; Fax: +353 (0)71 9177460). *Location:* 8km west of Sligo city at Rosses Point village. Championship links course which has hosted all of Ireland's major championships. Rated No 57 in Golf World's 100 Best Courses (2007). 27 holes. Championship course at 6162 metres. S.S.S. 72. Excellent practice facilities. *Green Fees:* information not provided. *Eating facilities:* full 80 seat restaurant and spacious lounge bar overlooking the course. *Visitors:* welcome seven days, Tuesdays Ladies' Day. Bomore 9 hole course Par 35. Electric buggies available for rent at €40 per round. *Society Meetings:* welcome. Professional: Jim Robinson (+353 (0)71 9177171). Reservations: Teresa Banks (+353 (0)71 9177134; Fax: +353 (0)71 9177460).
e-mail: teresa@countysligogolfclub.ie
website: www.countysligogolfclub.ie

SLIGO. **Castle Dargan Estate,** Ballygawley (00353 71 9118080; Fax: 00353 71 9118090). *Location:* ten minutes south of Sligo town. Darren Clarke designed parkland championship course. 18 holes, 7000 metres, S.S.S. 71. Practice academy, driving bays, chipping green and putting green. *Green Fees:* information not available. *Eating facilities:* club bar, restaurant and conference facility. *Visitors:* always welcome. 22-bedroom 4-star hotel and self-catering apartments. *Society Meetings:* welcome all year round. Secretary: David O'Donovan.*
e-mail: golf@castledargan.com
website: www.castledargan.com

Online booking now available at www.enniscronegolf.com

Enniscrone gives the golfer a picture of life as it must have been for a primeval person - rugged dunes, unchanged since time began, a bracing wind, clear sky - the most beautiful beach in Ireland.

Enniscrone Golf Club, Sligo, Ireland
e-mail: enniscronegolf@eircom.net
Tel: 00353 963 6297

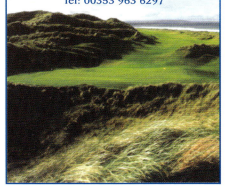

Co. Tipperary

CAHIR. **Cahir Park Golf Club,** Kilcommon, Cahir (052 41474; Fax: 052 42717). *Location:* half-a-mile from Cahir town on Clogheen road. Parkland. 18 holes, 5740 metres. S.S.S. 71. *Green Fees:* information not available. *Eating facilities:* meals available, bar, dining room in new clubhouse. *Visitors:* welcome. Practice area. Locker rooms. Buggy available for hire. *Society Meetings:* welcome. PGA Professional: David Ryan.*

CARRICK-ON-SUIR. **Carrick-on-Suir Golf Club,** Garravoone, Carrick-on-Suir (051 640047; Fax: 051 640558). *Location:* one mile from Carrick-on-Suir on Dungarvan Road. Parkland course set against the backdrop of the Comeragh Mountains on one side and the Suir Valley on the other. 18 holes, 6061 yards. S.S.S. 70, Par 72. *Green Fees:* information not available. *Eating facilities:* full facilities, bar open 9am to 11.30pm. *Visitors:* welcome thoughout the week except during competition times on Wednesday, Tuesday and Sunday. Sean Kelly's (cyclist) home club. One buggy for hire and carts. *Society Meetings:* all welcome by prior arrangement. Secretary/Manager: Aidan Murphy (051 640047).*

Tipperary/Waterford / IRELAND

CLONMEL. **Clonmel Golf Club,** Lyreanearla, Mountain Road, Clonmel (052 6124050; Fax: 052 6183349). *Location:* three miles up the mountain road from Clonmel town. Parkland set on the scenic slopes of the Comeragh Mountains. 18 holes, 6347 (white), 6068 (green) yards. S.S.S. 71 white, 70 green. Practice area. *Green Fees:* information not available. *Eating facilities:* bar food, sit-down meals available on request. *Visitors:* always welcome but contact Secretary/Manager re weekends. Ladies' Day Wednesdays. Golf Buggy available for hire, contact professional. *Society Meetings:* welcome, contact Secretary/Manager for weekends. Course information (052 6183344). Professional: Robert Hayes (052 6124050). Secretary/ Manager: Ms Aine Myles Keating (052 6124050; Fax: 052 6183349).*
e-mail: cgc@indigo.ie
website: www.clonmelgolfclub.com

DUNDRUM. **Co. Tipperary Golf & Country Club,** Dundrum House Hotel, Golf & Leisure Resort, Dundrum (00 353 (0)62 71717; Fax: 00 353 (0)62 71718). *Location:* 7 miles west of Cashel Town. Parkland course. 18 holes, 6800 yards (Championship course). *Green Fees:* information not available. *Eating facilities:* full bar and food facilities available. *Visitors:* welcome anytime. Club house with changing facilities. Putting Green and chipping area. *Society Meetings:* welcome.*

MONARD. **Ballykisteen Hotel and Golf Resort,** Monard, Tipperary (052 33333; Fax: 062 82587). *Location:* on the N24 20 minutes' drive from Limerick City, two miles from Tipperary town and 500 metres from Limerick Junction railway station. 4 Star rated Ballykisteen Hotel and Suites with Leisure Centre and 18 hole Championship golf course. 6765 yards, Par 72. Driving range and practice green. Fully stocked golf shop, PGA coaching. *Green Fees:* information not available. *Eating facilities:* full restaurant and bar facilities. *Visitors:* welcome at all times. *Society Meetings:* all welcome. Bookings to PGA Professional James Harris (062 32117).*
e-mail: info@ballykisteenhotel.com
website: www.ballykisteenhotel.com

TEMPLEMORE. **Templemore Golf Club,** Manna South, Templemore (0504 31400; Fax: 0504 31913). *Location:* beside N62 (South) half-a-mile from town centre. Flat parkland course, short distance between greens and tees, easy to walk. 9 holes, 5443 metres. S.S.S. 68. *Green Fees:* information not available. *Visitors:* welcome at all times, some restrictions Sundays. *Society Meetings:* welcome. Secretary: Jim Tobin (087 6882618).*

THURLES. **Thurles Golf Club,** Turtulla, Thurles (0504 21983; Fax: 0504 24647). *Location:* one mile from town centre on Cork Road. Sloping parkland course. 18 holes, 6465 yards. S.S.S.71. *Green Fees:* information not provided. *Eating facilities:* restaurant and bar. *Visitors:* welcome except Tuesday and Sunday. *Society Meetings:* welcome, special rates available. Professional: Sean Hunt. Hon. Secretary: Michael O'Sullivan (0504 21983; Fax: 0504 90800).

Co. Waterford

DUNGARVAN. **Dungarvan Golf Club,** Knocknagranagh, Dungarvan (00 353 5843310 /5841605; Fax: 00 353 5844113). *Loca*tion: 4km east of Dungarvan on N25 to Waterford. Parkland course adjacent to Dungarvan Bay. 18 holes, 6688 yards, S.S.S. 72. Practice ground. *Green Fees*: weekdays €30, weekends and Bank Holidays €40. *Eating facilities*: full bar and catering services by prior arrangement. *Visitors*: welcome but booking advisable. *Society Meetings*: welcome, special rates. Professional: David Hayes (00 353 5844707). Manager: Irene Howell (00 353 5843310).
e-mail: dungarvangc@eircom.net
website: www.dungarvangolfclub.com

DUNGARVAN. **Gold Coast Golf Club,** Ballinacourty, Dungarvan (Tel & Fax: 00 353 58 44055). *Location*: 45 miles east of Cork city, 30 miles south of Waterford city, on N25, 2 miles from Dungarvan town, on the coast. Scenic and challenging course bordering the Atlantic Ocean with unrivalled panoramic views of Dungarvan Bay and Comeragh Mountains. 18 holes, 6788 yards, 6171 metres. S.S.S. 72. *Green Fees*: weekdays from €20, weekends from €30. *Eating facilities*: full hotel and leisure facilities. *Visitors*: welcome anytime. *Society Meetings*: welcome, special rates available. Secretary: Tom Considine (Tel & Fax: 00 353 58 44055).
e-mail: info@goldcoastgolfclub.com
website: www.goldcoastgolfclub.com

DUNGARVAN. **West Waterford Golf & Country Club,** Dungarvan (058 43216/41475). *Location*: 4km west of Dungarvan, off N25 bypass. Challenging parkland course with natural water hazards, mature trees, abundant wildlife. 18 holes, 6712 yards. S.S.S. 72 blue. Large practice area and putting green. *Green Fees*: weekdays €25; weekends and Bank Holidays €35. Discounts for groups and societies. *Eating facilities*: full restaurant and catering facilities. *Visitors*: always welcome, but reservations are necessary. *Society Meetings*: always welcome, pre-booking essential. Contact (058 43216/41475).
e-mail: info@westwaterfordgolf.com
website: www.westwaterfordgolf.com

DUNMORE EAST. **Dunmore East Golf Club,** Dunmore East (Tel. & Fax: 00 353 51 383151). *Location:* at the entrance to Dunmore village take first left to Strand and follow signpost to Club. Seaside parkland. 18 holes, 6070 metres. S.S.S. 70. *Green Fees:* weekday €30; weekend and Bank Holiday €30. 2010 rates (subject to review). *Eating facilities:* full bar and catering facilities. *Visitors:* always welcome. Self-catering accommodation on-site. *Society Meetings:* welcome, prices on request. Distance membership available. Club Professional: Suzi O'Brien. Secretary: Paul O'Neill (Tel & Fax: 00 353 51 383151).
e-mail: info@dunmoreeastgolfclub.ie
website: www.dunmoreeastgolfclub.ie

THE GOLF GUIDE 2011

IRELAND / Waterford/Westmeath 549

LISMORE. **Lismore Golf Club,** Ballyin, Lismore (058 54026; Fax: 058 53338). *Location:* one kilometre north of Lismore Heritage Town, just off the N72. Undulating parkland with mature trees, course surrounded by woodlands. 9 holes, 5871 metres. S.S.S. 68. *Green Fees:* €20. *Eating facilities:* tea, coffee, snacks. *Visitors:* welcome weekdays, restriction may apply on Wednesday (Ladies' Day) and weekends. *Society Meetings:* welcome. Secretary: Willie F. Henry.

TRAMORE. **Tramore Golf Club,** Newtown, Tramore (051 386170; Fax: 051 390961). *Location:* seven miles from Waterford city. Parkland. 18 holes, 5918 metres. S.S.S. 72. *Green Fees*: information not available. *Eating facilities:* full catering and bar. *Visitors*: welcome Monday to Saturday. No visitors on Sundays. *Society Meetings:* welcome on application. Professional: Deirdre Brennan. Club Manager: Alan Briggs.*
website: www.tramoregolfclub.com

WATERFORD. **Faithlegg Golf Club,** Faithlegg House, Waterford (051 380587; Fax: 051 382010). *Location:* 6 miles from Waterford city centre on Dunmore road; head for Cheek Point. Premier course in the south-east, a challenge to all levels of golfer, with superb views. Ranked in the top ten best new courses in Britain and Ireland by Golf World Magazine in 1993. Hosted Ladies Irish Open in 1999 and 2000, Europro event 2007. 18 holes, 6666 yards. S.S.S. 72. Practice ground and putting green. *Green Fees:* weekday €35; weekend €45. *Eating facilities:* full bar and restaurant facilities available every day. *Visitors:* always welcome. Hotel on site. *Society Meetings:* always welcome, booking advisable. Professional: Derry Kiely (051 380587; Fax: 051 382010). General Manager: Ryan Hunt (051 380588).
e-mail: golf@faithlegg.com
website: www.faithlegg.com

WATERFORD. **Waterford Castle Golf Club,** The Island, Ballinakill, Waterford City (00 353 51 871633; Fax: 00 353 51 871634). *Location*: one mile east of Waterford City on the R683. A unique island course surrounded by River Suir and accessed by private ferry. Parkland course, internal water features, mature woodlands and a Swilken Bridge. 18 holes, 6814 yards, 6231 metres. S.S.S. 73. Driving range, practice ground, chipping area. *Green Fees*: information not available. *Eating facilities*: full bar and bar food. *Visitors*: welcome, no restrictions subject to availability. Accommodation available at five star Waterford Castle Hotel with all its facilities including all-weather tennis courts. Golf buggies, trolleys available. *Society Meetings*: welcome, special rates available. Director of Golf: Michael Garland (051 871633).*
e-mail: directorofgolf@waterfordcastle.com
e-mail: golf@waterfordcastle.com
website: www.waterfordcastle.com

Please mention THE GOLF GUIDE when you enquire about clubs or accommodation

Co. Westmeath

ATHLONE. **Glasson Hotel and Golf Club,** Glasson, Athlone (090 6485120; Fax: 090 6485444). *Location*: take the N55 from Athlone to Glasson village and turn left. Parkland course bordering Lough Ree and the Shannon – spectacular scenery and 555 yard 14th hole. 18 holes, 7215 yards. S.S.S. 74. 3 hole golf academy. *Green Fees*: information not provided. *Eating facilities*: restaurant, spike bar, snack bar and private rooms available. *Visitors*: welcome every day. *Society Meetings*: welcome, no restrictions, all facilities available. Office: Gareth Jones (090 6485120; Fax: 090 6485444).
e-mail: info@glassongolf.ie
website: www.glassongolf.ie

HIGGINSTOWN. **New Forest Golf Club,** Higginstown, Tyrellspass (044 922 1100). *Location:* just off J4 M6, 20 minutes from Mullingar and Tullamore, one hour from Dublin. Mixed parkland designed by Peter McEvoy. 18 holes, 6959 yards, S.S.S. 73. *Visitors*: welcome, Handicap Cerificate required.*

MOATE. **Mount Temple Golf Club,** Mount Temple Village, Moate (09064 81841/81545). *Location:* four miles off N6 Dublin/Galway road signposted to Mount Temple village. Parkland. 18 holes, 5927 metres. S.S.S. 72. Three hole practice area. New Golf Academy/golf range *Green Fees:* information not provided. *Eating facilities:* snacks and farmhouse cuisine, dinner by arrangement, wine licence, pub and restaurant 100 yards. *Visitors:* welcome but possible restrictions at weekends. *Society Meetings:* welcome. Professional: Mel Flanagan (089 4333688). Secretary: Michelle Allen (090 648 1841).
e-mail: mttemple@iol.ie
website: www.mounttemplegolfclub.com

For full details of convenient accommodation near clubs and courses

www.holidayguides.com

Co. Wexford

ENNISCORTHY. **Enniscorthy Golf Club,** Knockmarshall, Enniscorthy (053 92 33191). *Location:* one mile from Enniscorthy town on New Ross Road. Parkland course, renowned for excellent greens. 18 holes, 6115 metres. S.S.S. 72. Practice ground. *Green Fees:* Monday to Thursday €30, Friday to Sunday/Public Holidays €40. *Eating facilities:* bar and restaurant facilities. *Visitors:* welcome. Please telephone for bookings. Golf buggies available, must be pre-booked. Carts available. *Society Meetings:* welcome, must be pre-booked. Professional: (053 92 37600). Hon. Secretary: John Cullen (053 92 33191). e-mail: info@enniscorthygc.ie
website: www.enniscorthygc.ie

GOREY. **Seafield Golf and Country Club,** Ballymoney, Gorey (053 9424777; Fax: 053 9424837). *Location:* in the north Wexford coastal village of Ballymoney. Challenging parkland course with mature woodland and water features and beautiful cliff top holes. 18 holes, 6814 yards, Par 71. *Green Fees:* information not available: *Visitors:* welcome.*
e-mail: info@seafieldgolf.com
website: www.seafieldgolf.com

ROSSLARE. **Rosslare Golf Club,** Rosslare Strand, Wexford (053 91 32203; Fax: 053 91 32363). *Location:* 6 miles from ferry terminal at Rosslare Harbour. 10 miles south of Wexford. Seaside links course, beside Irish Sea. Old Course – 18 holes, 6608 yards. S.S.S. 72. New Course – 12 holes, 3983 yards. S.S.S. 70. Practice ground. *Green Fees:* Old Course: weekday €40, weekend and Bank Holiday €50; New 12 hole course: weekday €20, weekend and Bank Holiday €25. *Eating facilities:* available all day. *Visitors:* welcome, telephone for booking. *Society Meetings:* welcome, telephone for booking. General Manager: J.P. Hanrick (053 91 32203).
e-mail: office@rosslaregolf.com

ROSSLARE HARBOUR. **St Helen's Bay Golf Resort,** St Helens Bay, Kilrane, Rosslare Harbour ((053) 9133234; Fax: (053) 9133803). *Location:* two miles from ferry terminal at Rosslare Harbour, 10 miles south of Wexford. Championship seaside parkland and links course with several water features. Additional 9 hole pay 'n' play course and driving range. 18 holes, 6608 yards, S.S.S. 72. *Green Fees:* information not provided. *Eating facilities:* newly refurbished fully licensed bar and restaurant. *Visitors:* always welcome with no restrictions. Advisable to book in advance, especially in high season. Self-catering cottage and B&B accommodation on site. *Society Meetings:* play and stay specialists. Meetings/conferences welcome. Secretary: Kevin Doherty.
e-mail: info@sthelensbay.com
website: www.sthelensbay.com

Co. Wicklow

ARKLOW. **Coollattin Golf Club,** Shillelagh, Arklow (053 94 29125; Fax: 053 94 29930) *Location*: take N11 from Dublin to Rathnew, then travel to Rathdrum, Aughrim, Tinahely and Coollattin. Parkland with large oak trees being a special feature of the course. 18 holes, 5831 yards, par 70. S.S.S. 68. *Green Fees:* information not available. *Eating facilities*: full bar and catering facilities. *Visitors*: by arrangement with Professional. *Society Meetings*: by arrangement with Dave Masterson. Professional: Peter Jones. Secretary: Billy Stamp (053 94 29938).*
e-mail: coollattingolfclub@eircom.net
website: www.coollattingolfclub.com

BALTINGLASS. **Baltinglass Golf Club,** Stratford Lodge, Baltinglass (059 6481350; Fax: 059 6482842). *Location:* just outside Baltinglass on main Dublin road (N81). Picturesque course with mature trees and breathtaking views. 18 holes, 5912 metres. Par 71. *Green Fees:* information not available. *Eating facilities:* bar and catering facilities available. *Visitors:* welcome. *Society Meetings:* information not available. Contact Hon. Secretary, Genevieve or Patricia at Club Office.*
e-mail: baltinglassgc@eircom.net
website: www.baltinglass.com

BLAINROE. **Blainroe Golf Club,** Blainroe (0404 68168; Fax: 0404 69369). *Location:* three miles south of Wicklow town on coast road. Parkland terrain with extensive views of the sea. 18 holes, 6175 metres, S.S.S. 72. Practice area, putting green. *Green Fees:* summer from €35; winter from €25. *Eating facilities:* full bar and restaurant facilities. *Visitors:* welcome with previous booking. Buggies, carts and caddies available. *Society Meetings:* welcome. Professional: John McDonald (0404 66470). General Manager: Patrick Bradshaw.

BLESSINGTON. **Tulfarris Golf Club,** Blessington Lakes, Blessington (045 867600; Fax: 045 867565). *Location*: through Blessington village take N81, 4 miles outside town, turn left after Poulaphuca House. Parkland course built on 3 peninsulas, surrounded by Poulaphuca Lake. 18 holes, 7116 yards, S.S.S. 72. Practice range, chipping area, putting green. *Green Fees:* information not available. *Society Meetings*: welcome, rates available on request. Director of Golf: David Murray (045 867654).*
e-mail: golf@tulfarris.com
website: www.tulfarris.com

BRAY. **Bray Golf Club**, Greystones Road, Bray (00 353 1 276 3200; Fax: 00 353 1 276 3262). *Location:* from N11 take turnoff for Bray & Greystones. Turn right at roundabout, continue on to Ramada Hotel, turn right at roundabout. Golf club is 700 yards up on the left. Partly wooded, parkland course. 18 holes, 6750 yards, 5645 metres. S.S.S 71. Putting green, chipping green and practice range. *Green Fees:* information not provided. *Eating facilities:* full bar and restaurant. *Visitors:* welcome Mondays, Thursdays and Fridays. No green fees after 4.30pm. Limited on Saturdays.

Lessons available. Meeting rooms for hire. *Society Meetings:* welcome Mondays, Thursdays and Fridays; limited on Saturdays. Rates vary according to numbers - telephone office for details. Professional: Ciaran Carroll (00 353 1 276 3200) Secretary: Alan Threadgold (00 353 1 276 3200; Fax 00 353 1 276 3262).
e-mail: info@braygolfclub.com
alan.threadgold@braygolfclub.com
website: www.braygolfclub.com

BRAY. **Woodbrook Golf Club,** Dublin Road, Bray (003531 2824799; Fax: 003531 2821950). *Location:* Bray, Co Wicklow. Flat parkland course on the cliff above Bray harbour. 18 holes, 6800 yards, S.S.S. 72. *Green Fees:* information not available. *Eating facilities:* bar/restaurant. *Visitors:* welcome Monday, Tuesday and Friday. *Society Meetings:* welcome Monday, Tuesday and Friday. Professional: Billy Kinsella (0035312 820205). Secretary: Jim Melody. *
e-mail: woodbrook@internet-ireland.ie
website: www.woodbrook.ie

BRAY. **Old Conna Golf Club**, Ferndale Road, Bray (01282 6055; Fax: 01282 5611). *Location:* two miles from Bray town, 12 miles south of Dublin route N11. Parkland course set in wooded hillside terrain with panoramic views of Irish Sea and Wicklow. 18 holes, 6650 yards. S.S.S. 72. *Green Fees:* information on application. *Eating facilities:* full catering facilities. *Visitors:* welcome, Tuesdays Ladies' Day, semi open Wednesdays. Hire of clubs/caddy car. *Society Meetings:* society outings welcome Mondays, Thursdays and Fridays. Professional: (Fax: 01282 5611). General Manager: Tom Sheridan.*

BRITTAS BAY. **The European Club,** Brittas Bay, Wicklow (0404 47415). *Location:* one mile south of main Brittas Bay beach on coast road, 40 miles south of Dublin city centre. Rolling linksland overlooking Arklow Bay, designed and owned by Pat Ruddy. Ranked No. 2 among Ireland's 100 greatest golf courses by Golf Digest (2006); 24th Greatest Golf Course of the 20th Century (Golfer's Companion Jan. 2000). 18 holes, 7323 yards. S.S.S. 73. Extensive practice areas. *Green Fees:* information not available. *Eating facilities:* full services. *Visitors:* welcome to all golfers, advisable to book. *Society Meetings:* welcome. Secretary: Sidon Ruddy (0404 47415; Fax: 0404 47449).*
e-mail: info@theeuropeanclub.com

DELGANY. **Delgany Golf Club,** Delgany (01287 4536; Fax: 01287 3977). *Location:* half an hour from Dublin city centre just off the N11 to Wexford in Delgany village. Wooded parkland course with splendid hill and sea views. 18 holes, 5473 metres. S.S.S. 69. *Green Fees:* €45 midweek, €55 weekends. *Eating facilities:* restaurant and bar food. *Visitors:* particularly welcome Mondays, Thursdays and Fridays. Carts for hire, ten motor buggies. Special packages with local hotels, see website. *Society Meetings:* welcome. Professional: Gavin Kavanagh (01287 4697; Fax: 01287 3977). General Manager: Peter Ribeiro.
e-mail: delganygolf@eircom.net
website: www.delganygolfclub.com

Glenview Hotel & Leisure Club
AA/RAC ★★★★
- 70 De luxe en suite bedrooms
- 5 ★ Leisure Centre with indoor pool
- Beauty treatments and therapies
- Award-winning Woodlands Restaurant
- Conservatory Bar
- Snooker room
- Woodland walks and gardens. Golf nearby

e-mail: sales@glenviewhotel.com
www.glenviewhotel.com
GLEN OF THE DOWNS, DELGANY, CO. WICKLOW
TEL: 00353 1287 3399

DELGANY. **Glen of the Downs Golf Club,** Coolnaskeagh, Delgany (01287 6240; Fax: 01287 0063). *Location*: off the N11, 35 minutes from Dublin. Parkland course. 18 holes, 6443 yards. Practice area. *Green Fees:* information not available. *Eating facilities:* Pavilion with restaurant and bar. *Visitors:* welcome. Golf shop, locker rooms; clubs, buggies and caddy cars for hire. *Society Meetings:* welcome.*
e-mail:info@glenofthedowns.com
website: www.glenofthedowns.com

DUNLAVIN. **Rathsallagh Golf Club,** Dunlavin (045 403316; Fax: 045 403295). *Location:* take M7 southbound, turn left 8 miles south of Kilcullen. Set on 270 acres of mature rolling parkland, of which the golf course takes up 252 acres, surrounded by thousands of trees, water on 5 holes. 18 holes, 6920 yards. S.S.S. 72. Practice tees, putting green, driving range. *Green Fees:* midweek: €45, weekends €55. *Eating facilities:* full bar and restaurant. *Visitors:* welcome all week. Reservation essential, no Handicap required. Ireland's Country House of the Year on site - 29 bedrooms, including conference facilities. Best Restaurant in Leinster 2007. Brendan McDaid Golf Academy. *Society Meetings:* welcome all week. Club Professional: Brendan McDaid (045 403316; Fax: 045 403295). Secretary: Joe O'Flynn (045 403316; Fax: 045 403295).
e-mail: info@rathsallagh.com
website: www.rathsallagh.com

ENNISKERRY. Powerscourt Golf Club, Powerscourt Estate, Enniskerry (2046393; Fax: 2761303). *Location:* 12 miles south of Dublin city centre just off N11, south of Bray adjacent to Enniskerry village. Two parkland courses (East designed by Peter McEvoy, West by David McLay Kidd) located in Powerscourt Estate with links characteristics, exceptional tiered greens, selection of 5 tee boxes on each course. Practice range,short game practice area. *Green Fees:* information not available. *Eating facilities:* restaurant and bar food available, full bar facilities. *Visitors:* welcome daily. Buggies, carts and caddies available. Conference facilities available. Professional: Paul Thompson. Manager: Bernard Gibbons.*
website: www.powerscourt.ie

GREYSTONES. Charlesland Golf Club, Greystones. *Location*: 45 minutes south of Dublin just off the M50/N11. Charlesland boasts a magnificent location beside the sea, in the shadow of the Wicklow mountains. 18 hole parkland Championship Course 6169 metres. S.S.S. 72. Large practice area, putting green, public driving range available within 500 metres. *Green Fees*: April to October – weekdays €40, weekends €50; early bird €30. 2010 rates (subject to review). *Eating facilities*: restaurant and bar food available. Full bar facilities. *Visitors*: welcome daily. Please make prior booking. Neat dress essential. Buggies and handcarts for hire from our well-stocked Golf Shop. 12 en suite bedrooms; boardroom and conference facilities. For reservations phone 01-2878200; Fax: 01-2870078. *Society Meetings*: corporate, society and group rates available on request. For golf bookings phone (01-2874350; 01-2874360). Club Administrator: Rosaleen Horan.
e-mail: teetimes@charlesland.com
website: www.charlesland.com

GREYSTONES. Greystones Golf Club, Whitshed Road, Greystones (01-287 4136; Fax: 01-287 3749). Parkland course. 18 holes, 5322 metres, S.S.S. 69. Practice facilities. *Green Fees*: information not available. *Eating facilities*: full catering available. *Visitors*: welcome Monday, Tuesday, Friday and Sunday. *Society Meetings*: especially welcome, please contact the Secretary for details. Professional: Karl Holmes (01-287 5308). Secretary: Angus Murray (01-287 4136).*
e-mail: secretary@greystonesgc.com
website: www.greystonesgc.com

KILCOOLE. Kilcoole Golf Club, Kilcoole (01 2872066; Fax: 01 2010497). *Location:* two miles from Greystones off N11. Flat course one mile from sea. 9 holes, 5506 metres. S.S.S. 69. Practice area. *Green Fees:* information not available. *Eating facilities:* bar with meals available. *Visitors:* welcome, booking advisable. *Society Meetings:* welcome, special rate available. Secretary/Manager: Eddie Lonergan.*

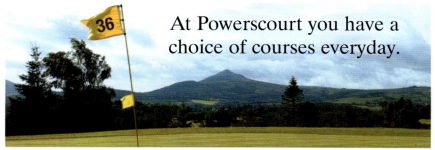

At Powerscourt you have a choice of courses everyday.

Located just 20 minutes from Dublin City Centre and 30 minutes from Dublin Airport in the foothills of the Wicklow Mountains, Powerscourt Golf Club is South Dublin's premier golfing venue. Both our Championship courses are open to visitors daily with a choice of courses everyday. There are a variety of packages available for all your golfing needs.
Isn't it time you paid a visit to Powerscourt?

West Course

POWERSCOURT
GOLF CLUB

East Course

Powerscourt Estate, Enniskerry, Co. Wicklow Tel: +353 1 204 6033 Fax: +353 1 276 1303
www.powerscourt.ie

THE GOLF GUIDE 2011 — IRELAND / Wicklow

NEWTOWNMOUNTKENNEDY. Druids Glen Golf Club, Newtownmountkennedy (00 353 1 287 3600; Fax: 00 353 1 287 3699). *Location*: less than 30 minutes south of Dublin, taking Exit 12 off the N11 southbound. Classical parkland layout known as "The Augusta of the North". 18 holes, 6560 yards, S.S.S. 73, Par 71. Golf academy with practice greens, bunkers and fully enclosed driving range. *Green Fees:* from €90. *Eating facilities:* available. *Visitors:* welcome. Tuition available; also golf and accommodation packages and multi-course passes. Five-star Marriott hotel on site. *Society Meetings:* rates available on request. Professional: George Henry. Resort Manager: Donal Flinn.
e-mail: info@druidsglen.ie
website: www.druidsglen.ie

NEWTOWNMOUNTKENNEDY. Druids Heath Golf Club, Newtownmountkennedy (00 353 1 287 3600; Fax: 00 353 1 287 3699). *Location:* less than 30 minutes south of Dublin, taking Exit 12 of the N11 southbound. Known as "Nature's gift to golf", this heathland course has strong links influences and panoramic views of the Irish Sea and Wicklow Mountains. 18 holes, 6629 yards, S.S.S. 74, Par 71. Golf academy with practice greens, bunkers and fully enclosed driving range. *Green Fees:* from €45. *Eating facilities*: available. *Visitors:* welcome. Golf and accommodation packages and multi-course passes available. Tuition available. Five-star Marriott hotel on site. *Society Meetings:* rates available on request. Professional: George Henry. General Manager: Donal Flinn.
e-mail: info@druidsglen.ie
website: www.druidsglenresort.com

NEWTOWNMOUNTKENNEDY. Roundwood Golf Club, Newtownmountkennedy (01 281 8488; Fax: 01 284 3642). Location: on the Glendalough/Roundwood road, in the heart of County Wicklow, just 35 minutes' drive from the ferry port at Dun Laoghaire. Parkland/heathland course with all-weather greens built to USGA standards. 18 holes, 6685 yards, Par 72. *Green Fees:* information not available. *Eating facilities:* five-star clubhouse catering for all requirements. *Visitors:* welcome. *Society Meetings:* welcome.*
e-mail: rwood@indigo.ie
website: www.roundwoodgolf.com

RATHDRUM. Glenmalure Golf Club, Greenan, Rathdrum (0404 46679). *Location:* two miles west of Rathdrum - signposted. Parkland, hilly course. 18 holes, 5500 yards. S.S.S. 66. *Green Fees:* information not available. *Eating facilities:* full facilities. *Visitors:* welcome, no restrictions. Self catering Scandinavian Lodges available. Buggies, carts available, caddy on notice. *Society Meetings:* welcome weekdays and Saturdays. Secretary: Kathleen Byrne (0404 46679).*

REDCROSS. Millbrook Golf Course, Redcross (0404 41647). *Location:* in Redcross village, two miles off N11, eight miles south of Wicklow town. Parkland, Par 3 course. 18 holes, 2009 yards. S.S.S 55. *Green Fees:* information not available. *Eating facilities:* full bar, restaurant and takeaway. Clubs for hire. River Valley Caravan and Camping Park with mobile homes to let; many other facilities also available.*

Roundwood Golf Club

Situated in the heart of County Wicklow, just 35 minutes' drive from the ferry port at Dun Laoghaire. The spectacular layout maximises the wonderful terrain, with all-weather greens built to USGA standards. With sweeping views of the Irish Sea and Roundwood Lakes, this is a wonderful opportunity to play parkland and heathland in the same round.

NEWTOWNMOUNTKENNEDY, CO WICKLOW
Tel: +353 1 2818488 • Fax: +353 1 2843642
e-mail: rwood@indigo.ie • www.roundwoodgolf.com

PLEASE MENTION THIS GUIDE WHEN YOU ENQUIRE ABOUT CLUBS OR ACCOMMODATION

WICKLOW. Wicklow Golf Club, Dunbur Road, Wicklow. *Location:* Wicklow Town, off N11. Parkland course by the seaside. 18 holes, 5695 metres. S.S.S. 69. *Green Fees:* winter from €20; summer from €30. *Eating facilities:* full facilities available. *Visitors:* welcome; some restrictions Wednesday and Thursday evenings and Sunday. Caddy cars. *Society Meetings:* welcome, prior arrangement with Secretary advisable. Information brochure sent on request. Professional: Enda McLoughlin (00 353 404 66122). Secretary: Joe Kelly (00353 404 67379; Fax: 00353 404 64756).
e-mail: info@wicklowgolfclub.ie
website: www.wicklowgolfclub.ie

For full details of convenient accommodation near clubs and courses
www.holidayguides.com

Wicklow Golf Club

Wicklow Golf Club is a picturesque parkland course which follows the coastline of Wicklow Bay and is situated just outside the historic town of Wicklow. Each of the 18 holes make full use of the contours and natural features of the clifftop terrain, providing a challenging test for even the most ardent golfer. Our new Clubhouse facilities will complete the perfect golfing experience. Panoramic views, excellent golf, bar and dining facilities and a welcome which will make you feel right at home.
But don't take our word for it. So go on...treat yourself, you've no reason not to.
**Dunbur Road, Wicklow Town, Co Wicklow • Tel: 00353 (0) 404 67379
www.wicklowgolfclub.ie • e-mail: info@wicklowgolfclub.ie**

Hunter's Hotel

Hunter's Hotel, the oldest coaching inn in Ireland, is located 45 minutes by car from Dublin City and 30 minutes from the ferry at Dun Laoghaire. It is set in 2 acres of award winning gardens on the banks of the River Vartry. • 16 bedrooms, all with private bathroom, colour TV and telephone.
Local amenities include 15 eighteen hole golf courses within a half hour's drive, notably Druid's Glen and The European.
The Gelletlie Family • Hunter's Hotel
Newrath Bridge, Rathnew, Co. Wicklow, Ireland
Tel: +353 (0)404 40106 • Fax: +353 (0)404 40338
Email: reception@hunters.ie • www.hunters.ie

FHG Guides publish a large range of well-known accommodation guides. We will be happy to send you details or you can use the order form at the back of this book.

Isle of Man

CASTLETOWN. **Castletown Golf Links,** Derbyhaven, Castletown IM9 1UA (01624 822220). *Location:* five minutes from Ronaldsway Airport and 20 minutes from Douglas. Championship links course voted in the Top 100 in the UK by 'Golf World' magazine. Host to the Duke of York Young Champions Trophy in 2003 and 2005. 18 holes, 6734 yards. S.S.S. 72. *Green Fees:* information not provided. *Visitors:* most welcome but must be pre-booked. Contact (01624 822211) to book tee times. *Society Meetings:* welcome, must be pre-booked (01624 822220; Fax: 01624 829661). Professional: Andy Patterson.
website: www.golfiom.com

DOUGLAS. **Douglas Golf Club,** Pulrose Road, Douglas IM2 1AE (01624 675952). *Location*: one mile out of Douglas near Pulrose Power Station. Parkland - 17th hole tee off 200ft above green (214 yards). 18 holes, 5982 yards. S.S.S. 69. *Green Fees:* mid-week £15.00, weekends £19.00 adult, £8.00 junior. *Visitors:* welcome, but not before 10am Sundays. Dress code in bar, no jeans. *Society Meetings:* catered for by arrangement with Pro Shop (01624 661558). Manager/Professional: Mike Vipond. Secretary: Elaine Vincent (Tel & Fax: 01624 616865).

DOUGLAS. **Pulrose Golf Course,** Pulrose Park, Douglas IM2 1AE (01624 675952). *Location:* one mile from town centre. Undulating parkland with memorable 17th hole. 18 holes, 5922 yards. S.S.S. 68. Putting and practice area. *Green Fees:* information not available. *Eating facilities*: bar and restaurant. *Visitors:* welcome, not before 10am on Sundays. Dress code in bar - no jeans. *Society Meetings*: by arrangement with Professional: Mike Vipond (01624 661558).*

ONCHAN. **King Edward Bay Golf Club,** Groudle Road, Howstrake, Onchan (01624 672709). *Location*: north headland of Douglas Bay. Stunning views from Headland links course. Watered greens, excellent fairways. 18 holes, 5450 yards. S.S.S. 67. Practice area. *Green Fees:* information not available. *Eating facilities:* full catering available (except Mondays), three bars. *Visitors:* welcome without reservation but not before 9.30am Sundays. *Society Meetings:* most welcome by arrangement. Special rates. Professional: Donald Jones (01624 672709). Secretary: Cyril Kelly (01624 827726; Fax: 01624 827724).*

PEEL. **Peel Golf Club,** Rheast Lane, Peel IM5 1BG (01624 842227). *Location:* outskirts of Peel on main Douglas Road. Combination of links and heathland. 18 holes, 5850 yards. S.S.S. 69. Practice ground. *Green Fees:* weekdays £22.00, weekends £30.00. *Eating facilities:* full bar service and meals. *Visitors:* welcome, but check in advance for weekend availability. *Society Meetings:* catered for, check in advance. Pro Shop. Professional: Paul O'Reilly (01624 844232). Secretary/Manager: Neil Richmond (01624 843456).
website: www.peelgolfclub.com

PORT ERIN. **Rowany Golf Club,** Rowany Drive, Port Erin IM9 6LN (Tel & Fax: 01624 834072). *Location:* off the Promenade, five minutes from Port Erin. Hilly setting and meadowland. 18 holes, 5774 yards. S.S.S. 69. Practice ground. *Green Fees*: £25.00 per round, 2010 rates (subject to review). *Eating facilities:* restaurant and bar meals. *Visitors:* welcome by arrangement, few restrictions. Accommodation can be arranged. *Society Meetings:* welcome. Secretary: K. O'Loughlin. General Manager: C.A. Corrin (Tel & Fax: 01624 834072).

PORT ST MARY. **Port St Mary Golf Club,** Kallow Point Road, Port St Mary (01624 834932). *Location:* clearly signposted after entering Port St Mary. Seaside links with beautiful panoramic views. 9 holes, 2885 yards. S.S.S. 68. *Green Fees*: information not available. *Eating facilities:* restaurant and bar open all day. *Visitors:* welcome at all times, only restrictions weekends between 8am to 10.30am. Handicap Certificate required. Secretary: N.F. Shimmin (01624 834053; 07624 498848).*

RAMSEY. **Ramsey Golf Club Ltd,** Brookfield Avenue, Ramsey IM8 2AH (01624 812244; Fax: 01624 815833). *Location:* west boundary of Ramsey. Parkland. 18 holes, 5982 yards. S.S.S. 69. Practice area. *Green Fees:* weekdays £22.00, weekends and Bank Holidays £30.00. 2010 rate (subject to review). *Eating facilities:* bar and restaurant. *Visitors:* welcome. *Society Meetings:* welcome weekdays only. Professional: Andrew Dyson (01624 814736).
e-mail: ramseygolfclub@manx.net
website: www.ramseygolfclub.im

**Visit www.holidayguides.com
for convenient accommodation
when playing golf around the regions**

Channel Islands

ALDERNEY. **Alderney Golf Club,** Route des Carrieres, Alderney (01481 822835; Fax: 01481 823609). *Location:* one mile east of St Annes. Seaside links with sea views from every hole. 9 holes, 2528 yards. S.S.S. 65. Putting green and practice range. *Green Fees:* information not available. *Eating facilities:* friendly lounge bar with bar meals all day. *Visitors:* welcome all year, tees reserved for competitions only. *Society Meetings:* welcome by arrangement. Hon. Secretary: Paul Skerritt.*

GUERNSEY. **La Grande Mare Golf Club,** Vazon Bay, Castel, Guernsey GY5 7LL (01481 253544; Fax: 01481 255194). *Location:* on west coast main road. Parkland course. 18 holes, 5112 yards. S.S.S. 67. *Green Fees:* information not available. *Eating facilities:* full hotel facilities, restaurant, bar, leisure club. *Visitors:* welcome at most times by prior booking. La Grande Mare Hotel. Changing facilities and Pro Shop. Trolleys, clubs for hire. *Society Meetings:* welcome. Professional: Matt Groves (01481 253432; Fax: 01481 255194). Secretary: Mr Nick Graham (01481 253544; Fax: 01481 255194).*

GUERNSEY. **Royal Guernsey Golf Club,** L'Ancresse, Vale, Guernsey GY3 5BY (01481 247022). *Location:* three miles north of St Peter Port. Seaside links. 18 holes, 6215 yards. S.S.S. 70. Driving range. *Green Fees:* information not available. *Eating facilities:* restaurant and bar. *Visitors:* welcome except Thursday and Saturday afternoons and Sundays unless playing with a member. Must have Handicap Certificate. Professional: Chris Douglas (01481 245070). Secretary: Roy Bushby (01481 246523; Fax: 01481 243960).*

GUERNSEY. **St Pierre Park Golf Club,** Rohais, St. Peter Port, Guernsey GY1 1FD (01481 727039; Fax: 01481 712041). *Location:* 10 minutes' drive from town centre. Wooded parkland with numerous lakes. 9 holes, 1323 yards, 1210 metres. S.S.S. 50. Driving range, putting green. *Green Fees:* information not available. *Eating facilities:* two restaurants and two bars. *Visitors:* welcome, all times bookable. Subject to rules and regulations on display. Hotel accommodation in 135 luxurious rooms and suites. Tennis. Pro Shop/ Club Manager: G. Roberts.

JERSEY. **St Clements Golf and Sports Centre,** Plat Douet Road, St Clement, Jersey JE2 6PN (01534 721938). *Location:* inner coast road near St Helier. Open all year from sun rise to sun set. Peacefully located in the parish of St Clement, this sports centre boasts the most southerly golf course in the Biritish Isles and is a testing 9 hole parkland golf course, 2585 yards. Par 32. There is also a 3 hole academy course suitable for all ages, a practice putting green. *Green fees:* 9 holes £15.00; 18 holes/All day £24.00. Booking advisable. *Eating facilities:* fully licensed restaurant and bar. *Visitors:* welcome. 12 outdoor tennis courts and 4 squash courts. Golf and tennis equipment is available for hire. Manager: Steven Davison.
website: www.stclementsgolfandsportscentre.co.uk

JERSEY. **La Moye Golf Club,** St Brelade, Jersey JE3 8GQ (01534 743401; Fax: 01534 747289). *Location:* on road to Corbiere Lighthouse at La Moye, St Brelade. Turn right at airport crossroads, right again at crossroads traffic lights. Seaside links championship course. 18 holes, 6664 yards. S.S.S. 72. Practice ground. *Green Fees:* information not available. *Eating facilities:* full restaurant/ snack facilities, three bars. *Visitors:* weekdays 9.30-11am and 2-3.30pm, weekends 2.30pm onwards. Must have Handicap Certificate. *Society Meetings:* by prior appointment only. Professional: Mike Deeley (01534 743130; Fax: 01534 7499565). Secretary/ Manager: Ian Prentice (01534 743401). Course Ranger's Office: (01534 747166).*
e-mail: secretary@lamoyegolfclub.co.uk
website: www.lamoyegolfclub.co.uk

JERSEY. **Les Mielles Golf and Country Club,** St Ouen's Bay, Jersey JE3 7FQ (01534 482787; Fax: 01534 485414). *Location:* centre of St Ouen's Bay. Set in an American styled seaside parkland course with "bent grass" greens and fairways of "dwarf rye". The 18 hole course plays 5758 yards, Par 70 gents, 5253 yards, Par 71 ladies. Other facilities include: 25 bay covered driving range, practice putting green, 75 yard short hole practice hole. *Green Fees:* please telephone for information. *Eating facilities:* Rocco's on site 120- seater restaurant, Rocco's bar, BBQ and seasonal patio area. *Visitors:* always welcome, pre-booking necessary. Smart golfing attire required; no jeans. VAT Free Pro Shop, miniature golf, laser clay pigeon shooting, Segway Rally, hire equipment available - carts, buggies, clubs. *Society Meetings:* welcome, packages available. Professionals: Wayne Osmand and Lynne Cummins (01534 483252). Administration, Enquiries & Corporate Bookings: please call (01534 485984).
e-mail: enquiry@lesmielles.co.je
website & online booking: www.lesmielles.com

JERSEY. **Les Ormes Golf & Leisure Club,** Mont à la Brune, St. Brelade JE3 8FL (01534 497000; Fax: 01534 499122). *Location:* on top of Mont à la Brune, adjacent to the airport. Attractive elevated course with beautiful coastal views. 9 hole course, 2509 yards, S.S.S. 65 white, 63 yellow. 17 bay covered driving range, practice bunkers and putting green. *Green Fees:* information not available. *Eating facilities;* restaurant and bar with terrace. *Visitors:* welcome, pre-booking advisable. Health and fitness complex, eight indoor tennis courts and LTA qualified coaches. Hair and Beauty salon on site. *Society Meetings:* welcome by arrangement. Professional: Andrew Chamberlain (01534 744464). General Manager: Mike Graham (01534 497002). Secretary: Frank Le Quesne (01534 853809).*

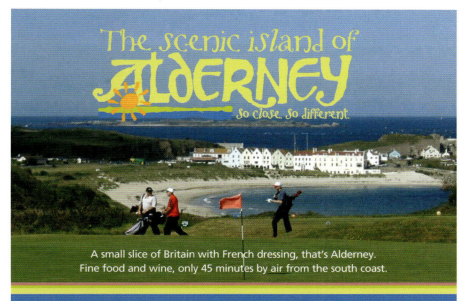

The scenic island of ALDERNEY
so close, so different.

A small slice of Britain with French dressing, that's Alderney. Fine food and wine, only 45 minutes by air from the south coast.

Tel: 01481 822333   Email: brochures@visitalderney.com
www.visitalderney.com/golfguide

ALDERNEY GOLF CLUB

Route des Carrieres, Alderney, Channel Islands
Tel: 01481 822835 • Fax: 01481 823609

- 9 holes, 2528 yards. S.S.S. 65
- Putting green and practice range
- Green Fees: available on request
- Eating facilities: friendly lounge bar with bar meals all day
- Visitors welcome all year, tees reserved for competitions only
- Society Meetings welcome by arrangement
- Secretary: Paul Skerritt

~ Located one mile east of St Annes. ~
Seaside links with sea views from every hole.

Les Mielles Golf & Country Club

Les Mielles is an 18 hole championship golf course, overlooking **St. Ouens Bay, Jersey**. There is also a VAT free Pro Shop, driving range, restaurant and activity centre on site.

www.lesmielles.com
Bookings: 01534 482787, Group Bookings: 01534 485984

Golf in the CHANNEL ISLANDS

JERSEY. **Royal Jersey Golf Club,** Grouville, Jersey JE3 9BD (01534 854416; Fax: 01534 854684). *Location:* take coast road from St Helier, head towards Gorey. Seaside links course. 18 holes, 6120 yards. S.S.S. 70. *Green Fees:* information not provided. *Eating facilities:* restaurant and bar. *Visitors:* welcome weekdays between 10am and 12 noon or 2pm to 4pm; weekends after 2.30pm. Handicap Certificate required. *Society Meetings:* welcome by prior arrangement. Professional: D Morgan (01534 852234; Fax: 01534 854684). Secretary: D.J. Attwood.
e-mail: thesecretary@royaljersey.com
website: www.royaljersey.com

JERSEY. **Wheatlands Golf Course and Country Hotel,** Off Old Beaumont Hill, St Peter, Jersey JE3 7ED (01534 888877; Fax: 01534 69880). *Location:* Le Vieux Beaumont, St Peter. Officially opened by Ryder Cup Captain Ian Woosnam in 1994, Jersey's only inland/parkland course; undulating setting with pond features and extensive countryside views. 9 holes (18 tees), 2767 yards, S.S.S. 54. Practice nets. *Green Fees:* weekdays £13.50 per round, weekends £15.00 per round. *Eating facilities:* "Tenth Hole Bar", "Garden Terrace" - coffee shop/bistro. *Visitors:* always welcome. Accommodation available in 20 en suite rooms. Hire equipment available - clubs, shoes, carts; VAT free shop. Professional tuition. *Society Meetings:* welcome. Professional: Terry Le Brocq.
e-mail: info@wheatlandsjersey.com
website: www.wheatlandsjersey.com

Royal Jersey Golf Club

The Royal Jersey Golf Club is situated on the east coast of Jersey in the Channel Islands.

- Seaside links course – founded in 1876
- 18 holes, 6120 yards, SSS 71.
- Restaurant and bar • Visitors welcome weekdays between 10am and 12 noon or 2pm to 4pm; weekends and Bank Holidays after 2.30pm. Handicap Certificate required.
- Society meetings welcome by prior arrangement.

Grouville, Jersey JE3 9BD • Tel: 01534 854416 • Fax: 01534 854684
e-mail: thesecretary@royaljersey.com • www.royaljersey.com

PLEASE NOTE

All the information regarding Golf Clubs in this guide is given in good faith in the belief that it is correct. However, the publishers cannot guarantee the facts given in these pages, neither are they responsible for changes in ownership or facilities, such as green fees, that may take place after the date of going to press. Readers should always satisfy themselves that the facilities they require are available and that the terms, if quoted, still apply.

DRIVING RANGES

LONDON

CHINGFORD. **Chingford Golf Range,** Waltham Way, Chingford E4 8AQ (020 8529 2409). *Location:* two miles south of Junction 26 M25. 24 bay floodlit, covered two tier driving range. *Prices:* information not available. *Opening hours:* 8am to 10pm. Practice putting green, practice bunker; NI Golf Academy; video, tuition available at all times. Nevada Bob Superstore now open. Professional: Gordon Goldie PGA (020 8529 2409).
e-mail: info@chingfordgolfrange.com
website: www.chingfordgolfrange.com

LONDON. **Dukes Meadows Golf Club and Tennis,** Dukes Meadows, Dan Mason Drive, London W4 2SH (020 8994 3314; Fax: 020 8995 5326). *Location:* Next to Chiswick Bridge on A316, one mile south of the Hogarth Roundabout. Golf Range with 50 covered, floodlit bays. Practice putting green. Indoor digital tuition studio, individual and on-course. Function suite available - catering for up to 300 people. *Prices*: starting from £5.00, no membership required. *Eating facilities:* restaurant area. *Opening hours*: 8am to 10pm.

LONDON. **Ealing Golf Range,** Rowdell Road, Northolt, Middlesex UB5 6AG (Tel & Fax: 020 8845 4967). *Location:* A40 Target roundabout, Northolt. Golf range with 35 floodlit, covered bays. Bunker. Artificial putting green. *Prices:* information not available. *Eating facilities:* bar and snack bar. *Opening hours:* 9.30am to 10pm. Five professionals, video tuition, large golf shop, repair shop. Head Professional: Paul O'Brien (Tel & Fax: 020 8845 4967).*
e-mail: pob.golf@cwco.net

NORTHOLT. **Lime Trees Park Golf Club,** Ruislip Road, Northolt UB5 6QZ (020 8845 3180). *Location:* 500 yards south of Polish War Memorial roundabout off A40, two miles inside M25. 20 bay covered, floodlit, grassed driving range. *Prices*: information not available. *Eating facilities:* two bars and bistro (bar open 11am to 11pm). *Opening Hours*: 10am to 10pm. Two PGA Professionals, 'Geoff Buddis' golf superstore, public golf course. Social club with pool and snooker; functions catered for. Professional: Neil MacDonald. Secretary: Adam Phelps (020 8842 0442; Fax: 020 8842 2097).*

NORTHOLT. **London Golf Centre,** Ruislip Road, Northolt UB5 6QZ (020 8845 3180). *Location:* 500 yards south of Polish War Memorial roundabout off A40, two miles inside M25. 20 bay covered, floodlit, grassed driving range. *Prices:* information not available. *Eating facilities:* full bar and catering facilities (bar open 11am to 11pm). *Opening Hours:* daybreak to sunset. Two PGA Professionals, golf superstore, public golf course. Social club with pool and snooker; functions catered for.*

STANMORE. **Stanmore and Edgware Golf Centre,** Brockley Hill, Stanmore HA7 4LR (020 8420 6222; Fax: 020 8420 6333). *Location:* 200 yards down right hand side from Royal Orthopaedic Hospital, (A5). 38 bay covered floodlit driving range, including automatic "Power Tees". *Prices*: £3.50 range, £6.70 course. *Eating facilities:* drinks and confectionery. *Opening hours:* 8am-10pm daily (open 7 days a week). Direct Golf UK superstore. Group lessons and Academy programmes available. Professionals: Cranfield Golf Academy.

BEDFORDSHIRE

DUNSTABLE. **Tilsworth Golf Centre,** Dunstable Road, Tilsworth, Near Leighton Buzzard LU7 9PU (01525 210721). *Location*: two miles north of Dunstable, off A5 Tilsworth turn. 30 bay covered floodlit range. *Prices*: information not available. *Eating facilities:* restaurant and bar (extensive menu), function suite. *Opening hours:* 10am to 10pm. Large Pro shop, repairs, tuition and group lessons. 18 hole golf course open to public. *Society Meetings*: catered for; prior reservation essential. Professional: Nick Webb (01525 210721; Fax: 01525 210465).*

LEIGHTON BUZZARD. **Aylesbury Vale Golf Club,** Stewkley Road, Wing, Leighton Buzzard LU7 0UJ (01525 240196). *Location:* four miles west of Leighton Buzzard between the villages of Wing and Stewkley. 9 bay covered, floodlit range.18 hole golf course, 6612 yards, Par 72. *Prices:* £2.00 per 35 ball bucket. *Eating facilities:* downstairs bar and restaurant, first floor bar and balcony. *Opening hours*: Daylight hours. Please telephone. Group and individual lessons. Professional: Terry Bunyan (07731 966 749). Secretary/ Manager: Chris Wright (01525 240196).

For full details of convenient accommodation near clubs and courses

www.holidayguides.com

560 DRIVING RANGES — THE GOLF GUIDE 2011

BERKSHIRE

BINFIELD. **Blue Mountain Golf Centre,** Wood Lane, Binfield, Bracknell RG42 4EX (01344 300 200; Fax: 01344 360 960). *Location*: two miles from M4 near Bracknell/Wokingham. 33 bay covered floodlit range. Parkland course with numerous lakes. 18 holes, 6097 yards. S.S.S 70. *Eating facilities:* fully licensed restaurant/bar. New Blues Bar with live jazz and food. *Opening hours*: 7am - 9pm. Manager: Steve Coles (01344 300220).*

MAIDENHEAD. **Bird Hills Golf Centre,** Drift Road, Hawthorn Hill, Near Maidenhead SL6 3ST (01628 771030). *Location*: on A330 Ascot to Maidenhead road. 36 covered, floodlit bays. 18 hole "pay and play" course. Tuition from Professional available. *Prices*: range balls 20 for £1.00. *Opening hours*: 7.30am to 10pm daily. *Eating facilities:* "Elizabethan Restaurant" and Golfers Bar and terrace.

WARGRAVE. **Hennerton Golf Club,** Crazies Hill Road, Wargrave RG10 8LT (01189 401000; Fax: 01189 401042). *Location*: halfway between Maidenhead and Reading off the A321 to Henley. Scenic course overlooking the Thames valley. 18 hole course, Par 65. S.S.S. 62. *Visitors*: welcome. Driving range. *Prices*: information not provided. *Eating facilities:* clubhouse with full facilities. Fully stocked Pro shop. Professional/ Manager: Glenn Johnson (01189 404778).

WOKINGHAM. **Downshire Golf Complex,** Easthampstead Park, Wokingham RG40 3DH (01344 302030; Fax: 01344 301020). *Location*: between Bracknell and Wokingham, off the Nine Mile Ride. 30 bay covered floodlit driving range, with PowerTee® installed in 15 bays. *Prices*: 50 balls for £3.25, 20 balls £1.50. *Eating facilities:* bar and restaurant, bar snacks available. 18 hole course, 9 hole pitch and putt; well stocked golf shop, tuition. Societies welcome. Small meeting room. Events Officer: Emma Evans.
e-mail: downshiregc@bracknell-forest.gov.uk
website: www.bracknell-forest.gov.uk/be

BUCKINGHAMSHIRE

AYLESBURY. **Aylesbury Golf Centre,** Hulcott Lane, Bierton, Aylesbury HP22 5GA (01296 393644). *Location*: north of Aylesbury on the A418 Leighton Buzzard road. 30 bay covered, floodlit driving range. *Prices*: information not available. *Eating facilities*: bar, bar snacks 11am to 11pm. *Opening hours*: weekdays 8am to 10pm; weekends 7am to 10pm. Professional coaching. 18 hole golf course. General Manager: Kevin Partington. Professional: D. MacDonald.

COLNBROOK. **Colnbrook Golf Range,** Galleymead Road, Colnbrook SL3 0EN (01753 682670). *Location*: one mile from Junction 5 M4, one mile Junction 14 M25. 27 bay floodlit, grassed range; 14 covered bays. *Prices*: information not available. *Opening hours*: 9am to 6pm. Professional: Alistair McKay. Full tuition, video assisted lessons given.*

MILTON KEYNES. **Kingfisher Country Club,** Buckingham Road, Deanshanger MK19 6DG (01908 562332; Fax: 01908 260857). *Location*: Between Milton Keynes and Buckingham on A422 opposite Shires Motel. 10 bay covered, grassed driving range. *Prices:* information not available. *Eating facilities:* full clubhouse and lodge facilities. *Opening hours:* 7.30am to 7.30pm Monday to Sunday. Professional tuition by request. Director Golf & Leisure: Major D. M. Barraclough (01908 562332; Fax: 01908 260857).*

MILTON KEYNES. **Windmill Hill Golf Centre,** Tattenhoe Lane, Bletchley, Milton Keynes MK3 7RB (01908 630660; Tee reservations: 01908 631113. 7 days in advance). *Location*: M1 South Junction 14 /M1 North Junction 13, A421 towards Buckingham. 23 bay covered floodlit driving range, 7 grassed bays. Two putting greens; practice area; two pool tables. *Prices*: information not available. *Eating facilities:* carvery restaurant, cafeteria, two bars, function room. *Opening hours*: 7.30am till dusk. *Society Meetings:* welcome (after 11am weekends and Bank Holidays). Three teaching Professionals, tuition, Pro shop. Professional: Colin Clingan (01908 378623). Secretary: Di Allen.*
e-mail: info@golfinmiltonkeynes.co.uk
website: www.golfinmiltonkeynes.com

STOKE POGES. **The Lanes Golf Course & Driving Range,** Stoke Road, Stoke Poges (01753 554840). *Location:* half-a-mile from Slough Railway Station in direction of Stoke Poges. 18 bay covered, floodlit driving range. *Prices:* information not available. *Eating facilities:* small lounge area with snack facilities. *Opening hours*: contact for details. Clubs for hire. Expert tuition available. A Golf Foundation starter centre. Professional: D. Green (01753 554840).*

STOWE. **Silverstone Golf Club,** Silverstone Road, Stowe MK18 5LH (01280 850005; Fax: 01280 850156). *Location*: A43 Oxford-Northampton opposite Grand Prix Circuit. 11 bay covered range. *Prices*: information not provided. *Eating facilities*: Restaurant/bar. *Opening hours*: dawn to dusk. Tuition by teaching Professional is available - group or private. Professional: Rodney Holt.

THE APPEARANCE OF AN ASTERISK (*) AT THE END OF A CLUB OR COURSE ENTRY INDICATES THAT UP-TO-DATE INFORMATION HAS NOT BEEN SUPPLIED

CAMBRIDGESHIRE

CAMBRIDGE. **Cambridge Golf Club,** Station Road, Longstanton, Cambridge CB24 3DS (01954 789388). *Location*: 10 minutes from city, off A14 at Bar Hill, turn right to Longstanton B1050. 12 bay floodlit driving range.. *Prices:* information not available. *Eating facilities:* clubhouse. *Opening hours*: contact for details. Buggies and trolleys for hire. Society meetings catered for. Professional: Geoff Hugget.*

HUNTINGDON. **Edrich Driving Range and Old Nene Golf and Country Club,** Muchwood Lane, Bodsey, Ramsey PE26 2XQ (01487 815622). *Location:* halfway between Ramsey and Ramsey Mereside, three quarters of a mile north of Ramsey, half a mile from Rainbow Supercentre. 24 bay driving range, 12 covered, 24 floodlit. *Prices*: information not available. *Eating facilities*: at adjoining club house, open to all. *Opening hours:* summertime, dawn to 9pm, winter to 7pm weekends. Private and group instruction arranged on 9 hole (18 tee) golf course. Coarse fishing on half acre lake and barbecues for summer months arranged. Secretary/Director: M. & G. Stoneman.*

PETERBOROUGH. **Thorney Golf Centre,** English Drove, Thorney, Peterborough PE6 0TJ (01733 270570). *Location*: Heading from Peterborough to Wisbech, left at the middle roundabout off the Thorney bypass and then 1st right. 13 bay covered, floodlit, grassed range. Two 18 hole courses. *Prices*: £2.00 for 50 balls. *Eating facilities*: full bar and restaurant open to public. *Opening hours*: 8am to 9.30pm seven days.

ST NEOTS. **Abbotsley Golf Hotel & Country Club,** Eynesbury, Hardwicke, St Neots PE19 4XN (01480 474000; Fax: 01480 471018). *Location*: A428 St Neots bypass to Abbotsley, south east of St Neots Junction 13 M11. 21 bay floodlit driving range, 300 yard grass driving range. Two 18 hole courses, 9 hole par 3 course. Abbotsley course is regarded by many as one of the finest golf courses in the county and combines the best of both parkland and woodland features. Excellent drainage makes it an ideal venue for all year round corporate and society days. Home of the Denise Hastings School of Golf. *Prices*: information not available. *Visitors:* welcome. 42 room hotel, gym, squash courts, beauty salon.*

CHESHIRE

ADLINGTON. **Adlington Golf Centre,** Sandy Hey Farm, Adlington, Macclesfield SK10 4NG (01625 850660). *Location*: 2 miles south of Poynton off A523. 24 bay covered, floodlit driving range. *Prices*: information not available. *Eating facilities:* tea and coffee available. *Opening hours*: 9am to 10.00pm Monday to Friday, 8.30am to 9pm weekends. 9 hole Par 3 course plus 9 hole Academy Course. Reductions for Senior Citizens/Juniors. Tuition available all the time. Proprietor: David Moss (01625 850660).*

CHESTER. **Carden Park Hotel, Golf Resort and Spa,** Chester CH3 9DQ (01829 731000; Fax: 01829 731032). *Location*: on A543 east of Wrexham. Golf School. 13 bay covered driving range and short game area. *Prices*: available on request. *Eating facilities*: Full Clubhouse facilites and 196 bedroom four star hotel. Nicklaus Course - 7045 yards. Cheshire Course - 6824 yards.
website: www.cardenpark.co.uk

NORTHWICH. **Hartford Golf Range,** Burrows Hill, Hartford, Northwich CW9 3AP. *Location*: off A556 Northwich, near ICI. 26 bay floodlit driving range, automatic tees. Golf shop. 9 hole pay as you play course now open. *Prices*: information not available. Professional: (01606 871162; Fax: 01606 872182).*

STOCKPORT. **Cranford Golf Centre,** Harwood Road, Heaton Mersey, Stockport SK4 3AW (0161-432 8242; Fax: 01625 827365). *Location*: five minutes from M60 and M56 motorways. 43 all-weather covered tees, fully floodlit. Two indoor bunkers, 9 hole indoor putting course. *Prices*: £4.00 per bucket (50 balls); £6.80 100 balls. No booking or membership required. School, Junior and group concessions. *Eating facilities:* drinks and snacks available. *Opening hours:* Monday to Thursday 10am to 10pm, Friday to Sunday 10am to 9.30pm. Hours may vary during Winter months and Bank Holidays. Changing rooms and golf shop. Group facilities and lessons available. Custom club fitting and repair centre now open. Professionals: Tony Murray, Matt Griffin, Granville Ogden and Rob Eastwood. Director: Jeffrey S. Yates.
e-mail: info@cranfordgolfcentre.co.uk
website: www.cranfordgolfcentre.co.uk

Looking for accommodation near golf clubs?, then visit
www.holidayguides.com
for where to stay when playing golf around the regions

STYAL. **Styal Golf Driving Range and Par 3 Academy Course,** Home of Cheshire Golf Academy, Styal Golf Club, Station Road, Styal SK9 4JN (Office: 01625 530063; Golf Booking Line: 01625 531359; Pro: 01625 530063). *Location*: five minutes from Manchester Airport. Junction 5 M56, near Wilmslow. 24 bay covered floodlit range plus 10 outdoor bays and practice bunker. 20 bays on the existing range have been fitted with power tee self-loading ball dispensers. *Prices*: £4.00 for 50 balls, £7.00 for 100 balls, £18.00 for 300 balls. *Eating facilities*: drinks and snacks available. *Opening hours*: 7.30am to 9.30pm midweek, 7am to 8.30pm weekends. Happy hours are from 10am-12pm and 4pm-6pm Monday to Friday and 5.30pm-7.30pm Saturday and Sunday. Cheshire Golf Academy, tuition available for beginners and established players. Range is fully carpeted with target distances and two-piece premium golf balls. Latest hi-tec teaching and practice facilities. 9 hole deluxe par 3 course, USGA spec greens, 1242 yards, par 27. Professional: Simon Forrest. Secretary: Bill Higham. Golf Director: Glynn Traynor.
e-mail: gtraynor@styalgolf.co.uk
website: www.styalgolf.co.uk

CORNWALL

NEWQUAY. **Merlin Golf Course and Driving Range,** Mawgan Porth, Newquay TR8 4DN (01841 540222). *Location*: on coast road between Newquay and Padstow, after Mawgan Porth take St. Eval Road, golf course and range on right. 6 bay covered, floodlit driving range. *Prices*: £1.50 per token for 25 balls. *Eating facilities*: use of the club facilities. *Opening hours*: 8am till dark. Secretary: Richard Burrough.

REDRUTH. **Radnor Golf and Leisure,** Radnor Road, Treleigh, Redruth TR16 5EL (01209 211059). *Location*: two miles north east of Redruth, signposted from A3047 at Treleigh and North Country crossroads. Purpose-built Par 3 - interesting layout. 9 holes, 18 tees, 1312 yards. S.S.S. 52. Covered driving range. *Prices:* information not available. *Eating facilities:* licensed bar, hot and cold food. *Visitors:* welcome. Indoor ski training machine. Small touring site and static caravans. Professionals: Scott Richards and John Rule.*
website: www.radnorgolfandleisure.co.uk

SALTASH. **China Fleet Country Club,** Saltash PL12 6LJ (01752 848668). *Location*: one mile from Tamar Bridge. Parkland course with beautiful river views. 18 holes, 6551 yards, S.S.S. 72. 28 bay floodlit driving range. *Prices:* information not provided. *Eating facilities:* bars and bar meals, full restaurant facilities, coffee shop. *Visitors:* welcome, Handicap Certificate required. Other facilities include large Pro Shop, full leisure facilities and 40 apartments. *Society Meetings:* welcome, minimum number 12. Professional: Dominic Rehaag (01752 854665; Fax: 01752 848456). Golf Manager: Linda Goddard (01752 848668 extension 657; Fax: 01752 848456).

TRURO. **Killiow Golf Club & Driving Range,** Kea, Truro TR3 6AG (01872 270246; Fax: 01872 240915). *Location*: take A39 Truro to Falmouth Road. Turn right into club at first playing place roundabout (2½ miles). 18 hole golf course (Par 72). All weather floodlit driving range. *Opening hours*: 8am to 9pm weekdays; weekends till 6pm. *Eating facilities*: bar and restaurant. *Visitors*: only restricted by competitions – phone for availability. Secretary: John Crowson (01872 266876).*

CUMBRIA

BRAMPTON. **Brampton Golf Club,** Tarn Road, Brampton CA8 1HN (016977 2000; Fax: 016977 41487). *Location:* situated one and a half miles from Brampton on the B6413 Castle Carrock Road. The town of Brampton is 8 miles to the east of Carlisle on the main A69 to Newcastle. Part of Brampton Golf Club. 6 grassed bays. *Prices:* information not available. *Eating facilities:* use of club's bar and dining facilities. Tuition and practice facilities available. Professional: Stewart Wilkinson (016977 2000; Fax: 016977 41487).*
e-mail: wilkinsonwilf@aol.com
secretary@bramptongolfclub.com
website: www.bramptongolfclub.com

CARLISLE. **The Eden Golf Course,** Crosby-on-Eden, Carlisle CA6 4RA (01228 573003; Fax: 01228 818435). *Location*: M6 Junction 44, A689 to Crosby-on-Eden village. 16 bay floodlit range. *Prices:* Bucket of balls only £1.50. *Eating facilities*: modern clubhouse, Fairway restaurant. *Opening hours:* 10am to 10pm. Professional tuition. Junior school of excellence. 18 hole parkland course, tree lined fairways and numerous water hazards plus 9 hole Hadrian Course, Par 71. *Society Meetings:* welcome. Discounts for societies, company days, etc. Professional/ Manager: Steven Harrison (01228 573003).
website: www.edengolf.co.uk

DERBYSHIRE

BRAILSFORD. **Brailsford Golf Centre,** Pools Head Lane, Brailsford, Near Ashbourne DE6 3BU (01335 360096). *Location*: on the main A52 Derby to Ashbourne road, Derby 6 miles, Ashbourne 5 miles. Parkland course. 12 holes, 5758 yards (18 holes), S.S.S. 70. Practice facilities and 15-bay covered, floodlit driving range. *Prices*: information not available. *Eating facilities*: available. *Visitors*: welcome at any time except Sunday mornings. Tuition available - two teaching Professionals. *Society Meetings*: welcome except Sunday mornings. Special rates available. Professional: David McCarthy (01335 360096). Secretary: K. Wilson (01332 553703).*

BUXTON. **Peak Practice Golf,** Barms Farm, Fairfield, Buxton SK17 7HW (01298 74444; Fax: 01298 78692). *Location:* approximately one mile north of Buxton off A6 on right hand side. Same drive as for Barms Farm Guesthouse. 300 metre floodlit public driving range offering 20 covered bays, 12 outdoor bays, sand bunker and putting green. Top quality two-piece balls and mats used, clubs for hire. *Prices*: £3.50 for 50 balls, £5.50 for 100 balls (Discounted rates for PPG range members). *Eating facilities*: drinks and snacks available. *Opening hours*: Monday to Thursday 10am to 9pm, Friday to Sunday 10am to 6pm. PGA Professionals available for individual and group tuition. Societies very welcome with advance notification.
e-mail: info@peakpracticegolf.co.uk
website: www.peakpracticegolf.co.uk

CHESTERFIELD. **Grassmoor Golf Centre,** North Wingfield Road, Grassmoor, Chesterfield S42 5EA (01246 856044; Fax: 01246 853486). *Location*: 4 miles M1 Junction 29 or A61 near Chesterfield. 26 bay covered, floodlit range, grass landing areas, target greens and electronic tee system. 18 hole pay-as-you-play course. 5723 yards, Par 69. *Prices*: weekdays £12.00, weekends and Bank Holidays £15.00. *Eating facilities:* Bar and Restaurant open daily 8am to 10pm. *Opening hours*: seven days a week 8am to 10pm. Coaching available. Club Membership. Societies welcome, must book in advance. Discount Golf Superstore. Professional: Gary Hagues. Club Manager: Helen Hagues.
website: www.grassmoorgolf.co.uk

DEVON

BARNSTAPLE. **Portmore Golf Range,** Portmore Golf Park, Landkey Road, Barnstaple EX32 9LB (01271 378378). *Location:* one and a half miles east of Barnstaple on A361. 24 floodlit bays with bunkers and putting. 27 holes (9 hole par 3 course, and 18 hole full Barum Course). *Prices:* information not available. *Eating facilities:* full clubhouse open to all. *Opening hours:* 9am to 9pm weekdays, 8am to 9pm weekends. All facilities are pay and play; there is also a membership. PGA Professional: Darren Everett.*

ILFRACOMBE near. **Ilfracombe & Woolacombe Golf Range,** Woolacombe Road, Near Ilfracombe EX34 7HF (01271 866222). *Location*: Woolacombe Road (B3343). 12 covered bays. *Prices*: £2.50 for 50 balls. £4.50 for 18 holes pitch and putt. *Eating facilities*: snacks. *Opening hours:* April to June and September 10am-6pm; July and August 10am-7pm; October 10am-5pm. Facilities include tuition and tennis.
e-mail: DCWRanger@aol.com

DORSET

SHAFTESBURY. **Oak Tree Driving Range,**Twyford, Shaftesbury SP7 0JN (01747 812225; Mobile 07732115581). *Location*: situated 4½ miles south of Shaftesbury between Twyford and Bedchester, 14 bay grassed range, 6 covered. 310 yards long with markers, flags and sand bunker. *Prices*: information not available. *Opening hours:* open 365 days a year, dawn until dusk.*

DURHAM

SEDGEFIELD. **Knotty Hill Golf Centre,** Sedgefield, Stockton-on-Tees TS21 2BB (01740 620320; Fax: 01740 622227). *Location*: A1 (M) Junction 60, one mile north of Sedgefield on A177. Indoor Golf Academy, tuition and video range, 20 bay covered, floodlit range, 14 tees open and grassed, chipping and putting greens, practice bunker, target golf. *Prices*: small baskets £2.00, large basket £3.00 (two-piece balls). *Eating facilities:* restaurant and coffee shop. *Opening hours*: 8am to 9pm. Professional tuition. Secretary: Mrs J. Reynolds (01740 620320).
website: www.knottyhill.com

ESSEX

BRAINTREE. **Towerlands Driving Range,** Panfield Road, Braintree CM7 5BJ (01376 326802; Fax: 01376 552487). *Location*: take A120 into Braintree then B1053. 6 grassed bays. *Prices*: information not available. *Eating facilities:* full bar and restaurant. *Opening hours*: 8.30am till dark. 9 hole course, professional tuition, indoor bowls, squash, full sports hall and equestrian facilities.*

CHADWELL HEATH. **Warren Park Golf Centre,** Whalebone Lane North, Chadwell Heath, Romford RM6 6SB (020 8597 1120; Fax: 020 8590 5457). *Location*: on A12 opposite "Moby Dick" public house. 37 bay covered, floodlit driving range. *Prices*: information not available. *Eating facilities:* bar and snacks; function suite. *Opening hours*: 9am to 9.45pm Monday to Friday, 9am to 8.45pm Saturday and Sunday. Warren Park is a JJB Golf Centre. Seven PGA Professionals. Fully stocked golf shop, golf club repair facilities. Two piece range balls and astroturf mats.*

COLCHESTER. **Colchester Golf Range,** Old Ipswich Road, Ardleigh, Colchester (01206 230974). *Location*: next to the Crown Inn, Old Ipswich Road. Covered, floodlit range, 12 bays. Professional tuition available. Fully stocked Pro shop and repair centre. *Prices*: information not available. *Opening hours*: weekdays 10am to 9pm, weekends 10am to 6pm. *Eating facilities:* The Crown Inn, 50 yards from golf range.*

COLCHESTER. **The Essex Golf and Country Club,** Earls Colne, Colchester CO6 2NS (01787 224466; Fax: 01787 224410). *Location:* A1124 signed from A1124 and B1024. 22 bay covered floodlit driving range. Indoor bunker range. 18 hole and 9 hole courses. *Prices*: information not available. *Eating facilities:* Sports Brasserie and bar facilities. *Opening hours*: weekdays 7am to 11pm, weekends 8am to 9pm. Tuition available from 3 professional teachers. Video studio, Leisure centre - swimming pool, gym, sun beds, aerobics, beauty parlour, spa bath. Six indoor tennis courts and three all-weather outdoor courts. Full day nursery facilities. Sports injury clinic. Hairdresser. Conference and banqueting facilities. 42 bedroom hotel. Professional: Lee Cocker. Golf Secretary: Barry Larcombe.*

COLCHESTER. **Lexden Wood Golf Club,** Bakers Lane, Colchester CO3 4AU (01206 843333; Fax: 01206 854775). *Location*: one mile north west of Colchester off A133. 24 bay driving range (floodlit and covered). *Eating facilities:* home-cooked food and snacks are always available. *Prices*: 50 range balls £3.75, 100 range balls £5.75. *Opening hours*: weekdays 7.30am to 9pm; weekends 7am to 7.30pm. Tuition available. 9 hole Par 3 course and 18 hole main course playing over many water features. Brand new golf superstore now open. *Society Meetings*: welcome by appointment. Professional/Centre Director: Phil Grice.

ILFORD. **Fairlop Waters,** Forest Road, Barkingside, Ilford IG6 3JA (020 8500 9911). *Location*: two miles north of Ilford, half a mile from A12, one and a half miles from southern end of M11. Covered, floodlit range, 36 bays. 18 hole golf course, 9 hole Par 3 course. Individual or group tuition available. *Prices*: information not available. *Opening hours*: 7am to 10pm. *Eating facilities:* bars and diner. Banqueting facilities and conferences. 38 acre sailing lake, 25 acre country park, children's play area. Professional: Paul Davies (020 8501 1881).*

MALDON. **Five Lakes Resort,** Colchester Road, Tolleshunt Knights, Maldon CM9 8HX. *Location*: eight miles from Colchester on the B1026. 10 bay grassed, covered driving range. Mats. *Prices*: information not available. Monthly season ticket available. *Eating facilities*: full catering, bar snacks. *Opening hours*: 7.30am to 10pm weekdays; 7am to 10pm weekends. Lessons given to non-members, group lessons. Professional: Gary Carter.*

GLOUCESTERSHIRE

BRISTOL. **Bristol Golf Centre,** Hambrook Golf Range, Common Mead Lane, Filton Road, Bristol BS16 1QQ (0117-970 1116; Fax: 0117-970 1118). *Location*: by the side of Holiday Inn Hotel on A4174 by Junction 1 of M32. 24 bay covered, floodlit range with power tees. *Prices*: information not available. *Eating facilities:* coffee shop. *Opening hours*: weekdays 9am to 10pm; weekends 9am to 8pm.

Astroturf putting green, bunker and chipping green. 9 PGA Professionals available for group and individual lessons. Award-winning golf shop with club repair facilities. Main Powakaddy repair centre.*
e-mail: nicky@nickylumb.com
website: www.nickylumb.com

CHELTENHAM. **Brickhampton Court Golf Complex,** Cheltenham Road, Churchdown GL2 9QF (01452 859606; Fax: 01452 859333). *Location:* midway between Cheltenham and Gloucester on B4063. 28-bay floodlit and covered Driving Range. Brickhampton Court Golf Complex includes 18 hole Par 71 and 9 hole Par 31 courses. *Prices*: visit website. *Eating facilities*: full catering facilities at Clubhouse. *Opening hours*: weekdays 9am to 9pm; weekends 9am to 5pm. PGA qualified teaching staff available for group and individual lessons. Two fully stocked Pro shops.
e-mail: range@brickhampton.co.uk
website: www.brickhampton.co.uk

GLOUCESTER. **Ramada Hotel & Resort Gloucester,** Robinswood Hill, Matson Lane, Gloucester GL4 6EA (01452 525653). 12 bays covered and floodlit. *Prices*: information not available. *Opening Hours*: 10am to 8.45pm. *Prices*: information not available. *Eating facilities*: available. Professional instructors, private and group tuition available. Sebastian Coe Health Park, dry ski slope, 9 and 18 hole golf course, indoor swimming pool, sauna, solarium, gymnasium, 5 squash courts, two tennis courts, snooker, pool, etc.*

TEWKESBURY. **Sherdons Golf Centre,** Tredington, Tewkesbury GL20 7PB (01684 274782; Fax: 01684 275358). 26 bays; 20 covered, 6 outdoor. Floodlit. Bunker, putting, 9 hole golf course. *Prices*: information not available. Weekday societies special rates. *Opening Hours:* April to October inclusive 8am to 9 pm. October to March weekdays 8am to 9pm; weekends 8am to 6pm. *Eating facilities*: coffee, bar, restaurant. Group and individual tuition, Golf Foundation junior coaching. Meeting room available. Professionals: Philip Clark, John Parker, Chris Gillick and Joanne Lee. Secretary: Richard Chatham.*

HAMPSHIRE

ANDOVER. **The Hampshire Golf Club,** Winchester Road, Goodworth, Clatford, Andover SP11 7TB (01264 357555; Fax: 01264 356606). *Location:* two minutes from the A303 on the A3057 near Andover. Beautiful countryside. Part of the Hampshire Golf Club. 10 covered bays; three practice bunkers. *Prices:* £2.00 for 40 balls. Telephone for special offers. *Opening hours:* 8am to dusk weekdays, 7am to 8pm (or dusk) weekends. *Eating facilities:* restaurant, bar, conference rooms. Tuition available. PGA Professional: (01264 357555; Fax: 01264 356606).
e-mail: enquiry@thehampshiregolfclub.co.uk
website: www.thehampshiregolfclub.co.uk

CRONDALL. **Oak Park Golf Club Driving Range,** Heath Lane, Crondall, Farnham GU10 5PB (01252 850066; Fax: 01252 850851). *Location:* behind the club house at Oak Park Golf Club. 13 covered bays, (five grassed bays for members only); one bunker. *Prices:* information not available. *Opening hours:* open during daylight hours. *Eating facilities:* full clubhouse facilities. Tuition, practice area, pitching etc. Professional: Gavin Grenville-Wood (01252 850850).*
e-mail: oakpark-academy@crown-golf.co.uk
website: www.oakparkgolf.co.uk

ROMSEY. **Paultons Golf Centre,** Old Salisbury Road, Ower, Near Romsey SO51 6AN (023 8081 3992). *Location*: off M27 at Junction 2, A36 towards Salisbury, at first roundabout take first exit then first right at the Vine Public House. 24-bay covered floodlit driving range. *Prices*: information not available. *Eating facilities:* full bar and restaurant. *Opening hours:* 8am until 9pm. Full Professional shop and teaching facilities. 27 holes.*

SOUTHAMPTON. **Chilworth Golf Club,** Main Road, Chilworth, Southampton SO16 7JP (02380 740544). *Location*: on the A27. 22 floodlit bays, 11 grassed, covered driving range. Bunker practice. *Prices*: information not provided. *Eating facilities*: bar. *Opening hours*: Monday to Friday 7.30am till 9.00pm, Saturday and Sunday 7.30am till 6.00pm. Tuition available. Professional: Darren Newing (02380 740544).

HEREFORDSHIRE

LEOMINSTER. **Grove Golf Centre,** Fordbridge, Leominster HR6 0LE (01568 610602). *Location*: adjacent to Leominster Golf Club three miles south of Leominster on A49. 18-bay floodlit driving range, four outdoor bays. 2 x 9-hole loops USGA spec golf course. 9-hole putting green, practice bunker. *Prices*: information not available. *Eating facilities*: full bar and catering facilities every day. *Visitors:* welcome anytime. Hire clubs and shoes available. Also 8-lane ten pin bowling. *Opening hours*: 8am to 9pm. Professional: Peter Lowery (01568 615333).*
e-mail: info@grovegolf.co.uk
website: www.grovegolf.co.uk
            www.peterlowerygolf.co.uk

ROSS-ON-WYE. **South Herefordshire Golf Club,** Twin Lakes, Upton Bishop, Ross-on-Wye HR9 7UA (01989 780535). *Location:* end roundabout of M50. At Ross take B4221 to Upton Bishop. At Upton Bishop turn right half a mile. 12 bay covered, floodlit driving range. Top quality mats and two piece balls. *Prices*: information not available. *Eating facilities:* fully licensed bar serving snacks and full meals. *Opening hours*: 8.30am to last balls 8pm. 9 hole Par 3 £5.00 per round. 18 hole Par 71, S.S.S. 72 Course. £20.00 per round weekdays, £25.00 per round weekends. Fully qualified PGA Professional. Pro shop. Lessons available.
website: www.herefordshiregolf.co.uk

HERTFORDSHIRE

BROXBOURNE. **The Hertfordshire Golf & Country Club,** Broxbournebury Mansion, Broxbourne EN10 7PY (01992 466666; Fax: 01992 470326). *Location*: 10 minutes north on A10 from Junction 25 of M25 take Broxbourne Exit, third left Bell Lane, over A10 right hand side. Driving range with 30 covered floodlit bays and 25 grassed bays. *Prices*: information not available. *Eating facilities:* Spike Bar, Cocktail Bar. Health club, indoor pool, indoor and outdoor tennis courts, golf academy. 18 hole "Nicklaus" design course set around a Grade II Listed country house. 18 holes 6400 yards. Professionals: Adrian Shearn and David Smith.*

ROYSTON. **Whaddon Golf Centre,** Whaddon, Royston SG8 5RX (01223 207325). *Location*: four miles north of Royston off A1198, nine miles south of Cambridge off A603. 14 bays covered, floodlit, and 9 grassed. Putting green and Par 3 9 hole course. *Prices*: £2.00 for 40 balls. £5.00 per round weekday, £6.00 weekends. *Eating facilities:* available. *Opening hours*: 8am to 9pm daily. Video, group and individual tuition available daily. Crazy golf. Professional: Mike Clemmons (01223 207325).

WARE. **Whitehill Golf Centre,** Dane End, Ware SG12 0JS (01920 438495; Fax: 01920 438891). *Location*: turn at 'Raj Villa', High Cross four miles north of Ware. 25 bays covered, floodlit, grassed. *Prices*: information not available. *Eating facilities:* full catering facilities 8am to 6pm. *Opening hours*: Monday to Friday 7am to 10pm, Tuesday 10am to 10pm, weekends 7am to dusk. Professional tuition, 18 hole golf course, practice bunkers, snooker. Professional: Matthew Belsham (01920 438326). Secretary: Andrew Smith.*

WATFORD. **TopGolf Game Centre,** Bushey Mill Lane, Watford WD24 7AB (01923 222045; Fax: 01923 222885). *Location*: off Junction 5 on M1. The latest in golf driving ranges. 44 heated bays with screens giving instant feedback on how far you hit each shot and a points score – thanks to a microchip inside each and every Dunlop LoCo golf ball. *Prices*: information not available. *Eating facilities:* Café/bar. American Golf Discount Centre Adventure Golf Putting Course and TopGolf Academy. As seen on Sky Sports Golf Extra and Tomorrow's World.*
website: www.topgolf.co.uk

WELWYN GARDEN CITY. **Gosling Golf Range,** Gosling Sports Park, Stanborough Road, Welwyn Garden City AL8 6XE (01707 331056). *Location:* A1(M) Junction 4, follow signs for Welwyn Garden City. 22 bays covered floodlit driving range. *Prices:* information not available. *Opening hours*: 10am to 10pm weekdays, weekends 9am to 8pm. *Eating facilities:* extensive bar/catering within Sports Park. Resident Professional, tuition and shop. Extensive facilities with ski-ing, tennis, athletics, bowls, cycling, badminton. Health suite, etc. Brochure available.*

KENT

ASHFORD. **Ashford Great Chart Golf & Leisure Complex,** Great Chart, Ashford TN23 3BZ (01233 645858). *Location*: Junction 9 M20, signposted from Great Chart, Ashford. 26 bay covered floodlit, heated, carpeted driving range, 9 hole full course, 9 hole Par 3 course, practice bunkers. Floodlit beach soccer/volleyball. *Prices*: information not available. *Eating facilities:* bar/café. *Opening hours:* 9am to 10pm 7 days a week. Tuition, video tuition, shop. Juniors and families welcome. Professional: James Sheldrick. Secretaries: Grant Kay/John Kay.*

ASHFORD. **The Homelands Golf Centre,** Ashford Road, Kingsnorth, Ashford TN26 1NJ (01233 661620; Fax: 01233 720934). *Location*: take exit 10 off M20. Signed to international passenger station, at second roundabout turn left, course signposted through Kingsnorth. 14 bay covered floodlit range. 10 grassed bays. 9 hole parkland course, Par 68. Practice ground; bunker, pitching, chipping and putting green. *Prices*: information not provided. *Eating facilities*: licensed bar and hot/cold snacks. *Opening hours*: 7am to 10pm. Head Professional: Howard Bonaccorsi.

CHATHAM. **Chatham Golf Centre,** Street End Road, Chatham ME5 0BG. *Location*: five minutes' drive from Rochester Airport. Covered, floodlit range, 30 bays. Tuition available. *Prices*: information not available. *Opening hours*: weekdays 10am to 9pm, weekends 9am to 7pm. *Eating facilities:* vending area. Fully stocked Pro Shop. Competitive prices. Pro Shop: (01634 848925).*

CHISLEHURST. **World of Golf,** A20 Sidcup Bypass, Chislehurst BR7 6RP (020 8309 0181). *Location:* six miles from Junction 3 on M25 heading towards London on A20. 54 bay floodlit driving range, Golf School and coaching studio. Par 3 9 hole course, floodlit short game practice area, putting green and bunker, golf shop, club repair service. Adventure putting course, tennis courts, cafe/bar. JJB Sports Golf Store. *Prices*: information not available. *Eating facilities:* licensed cafe/bar. *Visitors:* welcome, no restrictions. *Opening hours*: 9am to 10.30pm weekdays; 8am to 10pm weekends. Head Golf Professional: David Young.*
e-mail: sidcup@worldofgolf.biz
website: www.worldofgolf.biz

GRAVESEND **Gravesend Golf Centre,** Thong Lane, Gravesend DA12 4LG (01474 335002; Fax: 01474 335004). *Location*: only one and a half miles from the A2. 30 bay floodlit, covered driving range with power tees. Teaching Academy, 9 hole Par 3 golf course, mini golf, short game area, golf shop, club repair workshop. *Prices*: information not available. *Opening hours:* 9am to 10pm Monday-Friday, 8am-7.30pm Saturday and Sunday. Head Teaching Professional: Stacey Dordoy.*

MAIDSTONE. **Maidstone Golf Centre,** Sutton Road, Langley, Maidstone ME17 3NQ (Tel & Fax: 01622 863163). *Location:* south of Maidstone on A274, first turning after Park Wood Industrial Estate. 26 covered, floodlit bays (two heated). *Prices*: information not available. *Opening hours*: 10am to 10pm weekdays, 9.30 am to 7.30 pm weekends. PGA tuition, video coaching, putting green. Fully stocked golf shop. Caravan Club site for tourists. Professional: Cormac McCarthy.*
e-mail: rashby@lpdr.co.uk
website: lpdr.co.uk

ORPINGTON. **Orpington Golf Centre,** Sandy Lane, St Pauls Cray, Orpington BR5 3HY (01689 871490; Fax: 01689 891428). *Location*: off old A20 at Ruxley Corner. 28 bays, covered, floodlit. *Prices*: information not available. *Opening hours*: 7am to 9pm. *Eating facilities:* breakfast, lunch available, bar open all day. 53 holes, 4 courses.*

RAMSGATE. **Manston Golf Centre,** Manston Road, Manston, Ramsgate CT12 5BE (01843 590005). *Location:* quarter of a mile east of Manston village. 20 covered floodlit bays, plus grassed tees and short game area with real greens and bunkers. 9 hole course open to the public, 4958 yards. Par 66. *Prices:* Midweek 9 holes for £7.50, Weekends 9 holes for £10.00. *Eating facilities:* snacks, coffee, tea, etc. *Opening hours*: 8am till 9.30pm. Specialised teaching unit and short game practice area with real greens and bunkers. Absolute beginners welcome, with four PGA qualified "Positive Impact Coaching" Professionals. Residential coaching courses arranged with local hotels. Professional/Manager: Philip Sparks.
e-mail: info@manstongolf.co.uk
website: www.manstongolf.co.uk

For full details of convenient accommodation near clubs and courses

www.holidayguides.com

THE GOLF GUIDE 2011 — DRIVING RANGES 567

RAMSGATE near. **Stonelees Golf Centre,** Ebbsfleet Lane, Near Ramsgate CT12 5DJ (01843 823133; Fax: 01843 850569). *Location:* near junction of A256 and B2048. 22 bay covered floodlit/carpeted range. Animated and jackpot range targets. 2-piece balls. Practice bunker, putting green and chipping area. *Prices*: information not available. *Eating facilities:* licensed bar/restaurant. *Opening hours:* Centre 8am to 10pm. Range 9am to 10pm. Open every day except Christmas Day. PGA Approved teaching centre, golf simulator, three 9 hole courses. Professional: David Bonthron.*
e-mail: stonelees@stonelees.com
website: www.stonelees.co.uk.

SITTINGBOURNE. **The Oast Golf Centre Ltd,** Church Road, Tonge, Sittingbourne ME9 9AR (01795 473527). *Location*: one mile north A2 between Faversham and Sittingbourne, take the turning to Tonge at Bapchild. 9-hole Par 3 course; 17 bay covered floodlit driving range. *Prices*: information not available. *Eating facilities:* sandwiches, rolls; licensed bar. *Visitors:* Welcome. Tuition available, golf shop. Two short mat bowls facility.*
e-mail: info@oastgolf.co.uk

SWANLEY. **Olympic Golf Range,** Beechenlea Lane, Swanley BR8 8DR (01322 615126). *Location*: Junction 3 M25, take Swanley exit then first on right. 17 covered, 8 open air bays, all floodlit. Putting green and practice bunker. *Prices*: information not available. *Eating facilities:* bar, restaurant and sun terrace, all open to the public. *Opening hours*: 10am to 10pm. Extensive group tuition by PGA qualified staff. Also snooker centre, bowling green and conference rooms.*

SWANLEY. **Pedham Place Golf Centre,** London Road, Swanley BR8 8PP (01322 867000; Fax: 01322 861646). *Location:* off Junction 3 of M25, A20 towards Brands Hatch. 40-bay floodlit driving range, putting green, practice facilities.18-hole and 9-hole golf courses. *Prices:* telephone for offers. *Eating facilities:* bar; food available daily. *Opening hours:* weekdays and weekends 7am to 10pm.
e-mail: carole@ppgc.co.uk
website: www.ppgc.co.uk

TONBRIDGE. **Hilden Golf Centre,** Rings Hill, Hildenborough, Tonbridge TN11 8LX (01732 833607; Fax: 01732 834484). *Location*: take exit off A21 for Tonbridge North/Hildenborough; take second turning right (Watts Cross Road), follow road past station to bottom of the hill, golf centre is on the left. 36 bay covered, floodlit driving range with PowerTee. *Prices:* information not available. *Eating facilities:* fully licensed cafe bar open 8am to 10pm. *Visitors:* open to the public all day every day, memberships available. Health and leisure centre, crèche (9.30am to 11.20am weekdays), French boules (petanque). Teaching academy and large golf discount store stocking all the top brands at discount prices. *Society Meetings:* welcome. Professional: Nicky Way, Nick McNally, Rupert Hunter, Karl Steptoe and Oliver Brown (01732 834404; Fax: 01732 834484). Secretary: Jan Parfett (01732 834404; Fax: 01732 834484).*

LANCASHIRE

BLACKBURN. **Blackburn Golf Centre and Driving Range,** Queens Park Playing Fields, Haslingden Road, Blackburn BB2 3HQ. *Location*: east side of Blackburn, one mile from town centre. 27 bay covered, floodlit range. Two bunkers and two greens for outdoor practice. *Prices*: information not available. *Opening hours*: 9am to 9pm weekdays; 9am to 5pm weekends. PGA Professional/Owner Mark M^{C}Evoy (01254 581996).*

BLACKPOOL. **De Vere Herons' Reach Golf Club,** East Park Drive, Blackpool FY3 8LL (01253 766156; Fax: 01253 798800). Location: leave M55 at Junction 4, follow signs for Stanley Park and Victoria Hospital. Testing championship course with 10 man-made lakes - all year round play course. Herons Reach Course - 18 holes, 6461 yards, S.S.S. 72. 18 bay floodlit driving range, putting and chipping green. *Prices:* information not available. *Eating facilities:* spikes bar serving from 7am to 6pm daily, leisure bar and Cairolis open seven days. *Visitors:* welcome. Handicap Certificate required. 164 bedroomed hotel with extensive conference and banqueting facilities for up to 600 plus leisure complex. *Society Meetings:* welcome. Secretary: Mr P. Heaton.*

LEICESTERSHIRE

BOTCHESTON. **Forest Hill Golf Club,** Markfield Lane, Botcheston LE9 9FH (01455 824800; Fax: 01455 828522). *Location*: M1 Junction 22, take Leicester exit on A50, at first roundabout turn right towards Desford, 3 miles on left. 26-bay floodlit, grassed driving range with Power Tees. 18 hole course, Par 73; 9-hole short game. *Prices*: information not available. *Eating facilities*: food available all day/ evening. *Society Meetings*: welcome; special deals for golf available. PGA Professionals: O. Johnson and R. Hughes.*
website: www.foresthillgolfclub.co.uk

COALVILLE. **Discovery Golf Centre,** Chiswell Drive, Coalville LE67 3SX (01530 812332). *Location:* follow the signs to Snibston Discovery Park at Coalville. 18 covered bays with 10 PowerTees, 6 grassed. *Eating facilities:* licensed bar. *Prices:* information not available. *Opening hours*: Monday to Thursday 10.30am to 9pm, Friday 10.30am to 7pm, Saturday/Sunday and Bank Holidays - 10am to 6pm. Golf shop, tuition, repairs. 9 hole Par 3 golf course. Friendly and pleasant atmosphere.*

Please mention THE GOLF GUIDE when you enquire about clubs or accommodation

LEICESTER. **Humberstone Golf Range,** Gipsy Lane, Leicester LE5 (0116 2740033; Fax: 01509 210185). *Location:* Leicester city location, opposite the Hamilton Retail Site, on ring road 5 minutes from A46, A47 and M1 link road. Part of Humberstone Golf Complex. 30 covered, floodlit and heated bays; two grassed. Automatic Power Tees, video bays, multi-level mats. *Prices:* information not available. *Opening hours:* 7am to 9.30pm. *Eating facilities:* bar and restaurant. Tuition by PGA Professionals available.*

LINCOLNSHIRE

GRIMSBY. **Great Grimsby Golf Centre (incorporating Willow Park Golf Club),** Cromwell Road, Grimsby DN31 2BH (01472 250555; Fax: 01472 267447). *Location:* two miles from A180 and A46. Four-and-a-half miles from A16. Adjacent to Grimsby Leisure Centre/Auditorium. 27 bay covered, floodlit range. *Prices:* information not available. *Opening Hours*: 9am to 9.30 pm. *Society Meetings:* welcome by prior arrangement. 2500 sq ft golf superstore. All club repairs undertaken. Pay and Play and Membership available for Willow Park Golf Club. Reductions for Juniors and Seniors. European Tour Professional: Stephen Bennett. Secretary: B.J. Hoggett. *

LINCOLN. **Welton Manor Golf Centre,** Hackthorn Road, Welton, Lincoln LN2 3PA (01673 862827). *Location:* six miles north of Lincoln. Off A46 to Welton village, through Welton, turn left at mini roundabout signposted Spridlington, entrance half-a-mile on left. 10-bay floodlit driving range. 18 hole course. *Prices:* information not available. *Eating facilities:* licensed bar and restaurant. *Opening hours*: 8am to 9pm. Golf Foundation starter centre. Professional: Gary Leslie.*
e-mail: enquiries@weltonmanorgolfcentre.co.uk
website:www.weltonmanorgolfcentre.co.uk

STAMFORD. **Rutland County Golf Club,** Pickworth, Stamford PE9 4AQ (01780 460330). *Location*: heading north on A1 from Stamford, about one and a quarter miles after Texaco Garage/OK Diner, take Pickworth/Woolfox Depot off-slip, turn right under A1, turn left take second turning on right at mobile telephone masts. Heading south, after Ram Jam Inn, take off-slip marked Pickworth/ Woolfox Depot and turn left at mobile telephone masts. 20-bay floodlit driving range with Power Tees, practice bunker, chipping green, putting green. *Prices:* £2.00 per bucket of 60 balls (subject to review). *Eating facilities:* bar meals, lounge bar, dining room. *Visitors:* very welcome. Academy Professionals: Clive Fromant, Alison Johns and Darren Game (01780 460239). Director: George Lowe.
e-mail: info@rutlandcountygolf.co.uk
website: www.rutlandcountygolf.co.uk

WOODHALL SPA. **National Training Academy,** The Broadway, Woodhall Spa LN10 6PU (01526 351837; Fax: 01526 351817). *Location:* 19 miles south east of Lincoln. Part of Woodhall Spa Golf Club. 18 floodlit bays. *Prices:* £1.00 per basket. *Opening hours:* 7am to 7pm. *Eating facilities:* clubhouse with bar and restaurant. Grass tees and short game academy only available to parties with a PGA Professional, must book in advance on (01526 351809). Professional: please contact (01526 351809) to book lessons.
e-mail: lbrown@englishgolfunion.org
website: www.woodhallspagolf.com

GREATER MANCHESTER

KEARSLEY. **Kearsley Golf Driving Range,** Moss Lane, Kearsley, Bolton BL4 8SF (01204 575726). *Location:* two miles north on A666 from Junction 16 on M60. Driving range, 10 covered, 15 grassed tees. Prices: information not available. *Opening hours:* weekdays 11am to 9pm; weekends 11am to 4pm. *Visitors:* welcome. Bar. Small 3 hole pitch and putt with practice sand bunker. Open to the public. Professional/Owner: E. Raymond Warburton PGA. 18-hole pay-as-you-play course immediately adjacent.*

ROCHDALE. **Castle Hawk Driving Range,** Chadwick Lane, Castleton, Rochdale OL11 3BY (01706 659995). *Location*: five minutes from exit 20 M62. 20 bay covered, floodlit, grassed driving range. 27 hole course. *Prices*: information not available. *Eating facilities:* restaurant available at club. *Opening hours*: 9am to 7.30pm. Professional tuition available. Professionals: Frank Accleton and Craig Bowring.*
e-mail: teeoff@castlehawk.co.uk
website: www.castlehawk.co.uk

MERSEYSIDE

LIVERPOOL. **The Formby Golf Centre**, Moss Side, Formby L37 0AF (01704 875952). *Location:* A565 between Southport and Liverpool. 22-bay floodlit driving range. *Prices:* £2.50 for 50 balls, £4.50 for 100 balls. Digicard £15.00 for 500 balls. *Eating facilities:* cafe. *Opening hours:* weekdays 8.30am to 9.30pm; weekends 8.30am to 7.30pm. 3 golf Professionals, 9-hole pitch and putt course, putting green, bunker. Well stocked Pro Shop specialising in ladies' clothing.

MORETON. **Moreton Hills Golf Centre,** Tarran Way, Moreton, Wirral CH46 4TP (0151-677 6606). *Location:* off Pasture Road, opposite Cadbury's factory. 30 bay covered floodlit driving range. *Prices*: information not available. *Eating facilities:* not available. *Opening hours*: Monday to Thursday 9am to 9pm, Friday to Sunday 9am to 7pm. 6 hole golf course, putting green, practice bunkers, golf shop, PGA Professionals, golf lessons in an undercover academy.*
website: www.moretonhills.co.uk

NORTHAMPTONSHIRE

CHURCH BRAMPTON. **Brampton Heath Golf Centre,** Sandy Lane, Church Brampton, Northampton NN6 8AX (01604 843939; Fax: 01604 843885). *Location:* 2 miles north east of Kingsthorpe off A5009 (Welford Road). 18 bay covered floodlit driving range. *Prices:* information not available. *Eating facilities:* Spike bar/restaurant. *Opening hours:* Summer: weekdays 8am to 10pm. Weekends 7.30am to 9pm. Winter: 8am to 9pm. Weekends 8am to 8.30pm. Group/individual tuition available. 18 hole 6533 yards course and 9 hole Par 3 academy course. Professional: Alan Wright. General Manager: Sally Carter-Jones.*

NORTHAMPTON. **Delapre Golf Centre,** Eagle Drive, Nene Valley Way, Northampton NN4 7DU (01604 764036; Fax: 01604 706378). *Location:* two miles from Junction 15 M1 on A45 towards Wellingborough. 40 bay covered, floodlit range. 18 hole main course Par 70; 9 hole course; two Par 3 courses; pitch and putt course and putting greens. *Prices:* information not provided. *Eating facilities:* licensed bar and restaurant, coffee shop. *Opening hours:* 7am to 10.30pm daily. PGA qualified teaching staff available for private or group tuition; golf schools – video etc. Centre Manager/PGA Professional: Andrew Coleman (01604 764036). website: www.jackbarker.com

NEWARK. **Rufford Park Golf & Country Club,** Rufford Lane, Rufford, Newark NG22 9DG (01623 825253; Fax: 01623 825254). *Location*: situated 400 yards off A614, 2 miles south of Ollerton Roundabout - map available on request. 16-bay floodlit driving range. 18- hole golf course. Practice greens. *Eating facilities*: large function suite and clubhouse available for social functions, restaurant with spectacular views offering a warm and genuine welcome to all who enjoy superb focd. *Opening hours:* 7.30am to 9pm. Tuition available from both professionals. 10 buggies for hire. Corporate hospitality and Society days a speciality. Meeting rooms available. Professionals: James Thompson, John Vaughan. Secretary: Kay Whitehead.
e-mail: enquiries@ruffordpark.co.uk
website: www.ruffordpark.co.uk

NOTTINGHAM. **Cotgrave Place Golf and Country Club,** Cotgrave, Near Stragglethorpe, Radcliffe-on-Trent, Nottingham NG12 3HB (0115 933 3344; Fax: 0115 933 4567). *Location:* two minutes from A52 to Grantham from Nottingham city centre. 10 bay covered, floodlit range. *Prices:* information not available. *Eating facilities:* food available all day in the golf clubhouse. *Opening hours:* 8am to dusk seven days a week. Professional tuition. 36 holes of golf. Ideal for all standards. Buggies available. Golf clinics. Professional: Robert Smith (0115 933 3344; Fax: 0115 933 4567). General Manager: Nick Leuty.*
e-mail: cotgrave@americangolf.com

NOTTINGHAMSHIRE

CALVERTON. **Ramsdale Park Golf Centre,** Oxton Road, Calverton NG14 6NV (01159 655600; Fax: 01159 654105). *Location:* off the A614 from Nottingham to Mansfield. 25 covered, floodlit bays; one bunker. *Prices:* information not provided. *Opening hours:* 8.30am to 10pm. *Eating facilities:* full bar and catering. Tuition available. Professional: Rob Macey (01159 655600; Fax: 01159 654105).
e-mail: info@ramsdaleparkgc.co.uk
website: www.ramsdaleparkgc.co.uk

LONG EATON. **Trent Lock Golf Centre,** Lock Lane, Sawley, Long Eaton, Nottingham NG10 2FY (0115 946 4398; Fax: 0115 946 1183). *Location:* 2 miles from M1 motorway Junction 24 or 25. 22 bay covered, floodlit driving range. 18-hole and 9 hole golf course. *Prices:* information not provided. *Eating facilities:* à la carte restaurant, 200 capacity function suite, bar and bar food area. *Opening hours*: 8am until midnight. Professional tuition available, five PGA staff. River trips and walking available. Online "virtutour". Professional: Mark Taylor (01159 464398; Fax: 01159 461183).
e-mail: trentlockgolf@aol.com
website: www.trentlock.co.uk

OXFORDSHIRE

DRAYTON. **Drayton Park Golf Course**, Steventon Road, Drayton, near Abingdon OX14 4LA (01235 528989). *Location:* A34 Didcot turn off, through Steventon to Drayton. 21 bay covered floodlit driving range. 18 hole Par 70 golf course. 9 hole Par 3 course. *Prices:* information not provided. *Eating facilities:* full facilities available. *Opening hours:* 8am to 9pm. Societies, groups and individual golfers welcome. Professional: Jon Draycott. Secretary: Ian Rhead.

OXFORD. **Oxford Golf Centre,** Binsey Lane, Botley Road, Oxford OX2 0EX (01865 721592). *Location:* just off Botley Road by Halfords. 26 bay covered floodlit driving range. *Prices*: information not available. *Eating facilities:* light refreshments. *Opening Hours:* weekdays 10am to 9pm, weekends 10am-8pm. Lessons available from Professional. Golf superstore, 100s of demonstration clubs, launch monitor, professional club fitting and repairs. Head PGA Professional: Simon Walker.*

570 DRIVING RANGES

OXFORD. **Studley Wood Golf Club,** The Straight Mile, Horton-cum-Studley, Oxford OX33 1BF (01865 351122; Fax: 01865 351166). *Location:* 4 miles east of Oxford. 15 bay covered driving range. *Prices:* information not available. *Eating facilities:* full Clubhouse facilities; bar, restaurant, function room. *Opening hours:* 9am to dusk. Three teaching Professionals, short game academy, putting lab, practice putting green. Eight target greens complete with bunkers, fully irrigated grass practice tee and target greens. Professional: Matt Avann.
e-mail: admin@studleywoodgolfclub.co.uk
website: www.studleywoodgolfclub.co.uk

OXFORD. **Waterstock Golf Club and Driving Range,** Thame Road, Waterstock, Oxford OX33 1HT (01844 338093). *Location:* on Junction 8 M40, one mile from Wheatley, four miles from Oxford, three miles from Thame. 22 bay covered, fully floodlit, open grassed driving range. *Prices:* 50 balls for £3.00, 100 balls for £5.00. *Eating facilities:* full bar and catering facilities. *Opening hours:* weekdays 7.30am to 10pm, Saturdays 7am to 9pm, Sundays 7am to 8pm. Resident Professional offers tuition; large junior and adult golf academy; Pro shop with many demonstration clubs; 18-hole golf course; clubhouse with full facilities (societies and functions catered for).
e-mail: wgc_oxfordgolf@btinternet.com
website: www.waterstockgolf.co.uk

WITNEY. **Witney Lakes Golf Club,** Witney Lakes Resort, Downs Road, Witney OX29 0SY (01993 893011; Fax: 01993 778866). *Location:* two miles west of Witney town centre, turn into Downs Road. from B4095. 22-bay floodlit covered driving range. *Fees:* information not provided. *Opening hours:* 7am to 9pm. *Eating facilities:* Greens Sportsbar and Greens Restaurant, Function/Conference room. Health and fitness club includes swimming pool, gymnasium and sauna. Rawles Hairdresser, Retreat Spa, Beauty Salon, creche facilities. 3 teaching Professionals. Head Professional: John Cook (01993 893011; Fax: 01993 778866). Secretary: (01993 893005; Fax: 01993 778866).
e-mail: golf@witney-lakes.co.uk
website: www.witney-lakes.co.uk

SHROPSHIRE

NEWPORT. **Aqualate Golf Centre,** Stafford Road, Newport TF10 9DB (01952 811699). *Location*: On A518 two miles east of Newport town centre and 400 yards from junction with A41. 20 floodlit bay driving range. *Prices*: information not available. *Opening hours*: weekdays 9.00am to 10.00pm, weekends and Bank Holidays 7.30am to 9.00pm. *Eating facilities*: coffee bar. PGA Professional tuition available by appointment - group and/or personal lessons. Golf Club Memberships available. 9 hole, 18 tee golf course - Pay and Play golf available. Visitors welcome. No handicap restrictions. Professional: Kevin Short. Director: H. Brian Dawes.*

OSWESTRY. **Oswestry Golf Driving Range,** Mile End, Oswestry SY11 4JF (01691 671246; Fax: 01691 670580). *Location:* signposted "Mile End Golf Club" off A5, one mile south-east of Oswestry. New two tier, 16 bay floodlit range. Indoor full custom-fit facilities. *Prices:* from £2.00 for 30 balls. Discount card available. *Eating facilities:* bar/catering available to members and green fee paying visitors who adhere to dress code. *Opening hours*: Summer: 8am until dusk daily; Winter: 8am to 8pm weekdays, 8am to 6pm weekends. Group bookings welcome. Many "Try before you buy" demo days. Professional tuition available, fully stocked Pro shop. Par 71 18 hole golf course. Professional: Scott Carpenter (01691 671246). Proprietor: Richard Thompson.
website: www.mileendgolfclub.co.uk

TELFORD. **The Shropshire,** Granville Park, Muxton, Telford TF2 8PQ (01952 677800; Fax: 01952 677622). *Location:* Take B5060 off M54/A5 heading for Donnington. Take third exit at Granville roundabout. 30 bay covered, floodlit driving range. *Prices*: information not available. *Eating facilities:* Greenkeeper Bar open from 8am serving food. *Opening hours*: 7am to 10pm. 27 hole golf course, 12 hole Par 3 course, 2 putting greens, retail shop. Entertainment nights, four function suites, and conference facilities. *Society Meetings*: welcome. Professional: Mark Sutcliffe (01952 677800).*

SOMERSET

BRISTOL. **Mendip Spring Golf Club,** Honeyhall Lane, Congresbury, Bristol BS49 5JT (01934 852322). *Location:* between A370 and A38. 15 bay covered, floodlit driving range with a grassed area. Practice bunker and putting green. *Prices*: information not provided. *Eating facilities:* none at range but restaurant/bar facilities available at the clubhouse. *Opening hours*: 7.30am to 8pm. Tuition available from our team of Professionals. Buggies for hire April to September. There is also an active members' social club. Societies welcome by arrangement.

LANGPORT. **Long Sutton Golf Club,** Langport TA10 9JU (01458 241017; Fax: 01458 241022). *Location:* three miles north of A303 from Podimore roundabout on A372 to Langport and Taunton. 18 hole golf course and large practice putting green. 12 bay covered, floodlit, grassed range. *Prices:* information not available. *Eating facilities:* snacks in bar, restaurant. *Opening hours:* 8am till dusk. Tuition from Andrew Hayes by appointment. Secretary: T. Tulk.*

TAUNTON. **Oake Manor Driving Range,** Oake Manor Golf Club and Range, Oake, Taunton TA4 1BA (01823 461993). *Location:* Junction 26 M5, take A38 to Taunton, follow signs to Oake, only seven minutes from motorway. 11 bay covered range. *Prices*: information not available. *Eating facilities:* adjacent bar/lounge, food available seven days all day long. *Opening hours:* 8am to dark. *Visitors:* welcome. 18 hole course, tuition by appointment, new golf

academy and 3 practice holes; Pro shop, 4 PGA Professionals; club fitting centre - free equipment advice service and demo clubs.*
e-mail: golf@oakemanor.com
website: www.oakemanor.com

TICKENHAM. **Tickenham Golf Club,** Clevedon Road, Tickenham BS21 6RY (01275 856626). *Location:* M5 Junction 20, follow Nailsea signs, Centre on left after Tickenham village. Golfmark Award. Somerset County Partnership Development Centre. 9 hole course, 24 bay covered, floodlit driving range. Power tees. Practice bunkers. *Prices:* 50 balls for £3.00. *Eating facilities:* 19th hole licensed bar, snacks. *Opening hours*: 8.30am to 8.30pm daily. Professionals available for tuition, group lessons, etc.
website: www.tickenhamgolf.co.uk

STAFFORDSHIRE

BURTON-ON-TRENT. **The Craythorne,** Craythorne Road, Rolleston on Dove, Burton-on-Trent DE13 0AZ (01283 564329). *Location:* Rolleston on Dove, 1½ miles north of Burton – A5121/A38 Junction. 14 bay covered floodlit driving range. *Prices*: £2.00 minimum; Happy Hour 4pm-5pm weekdays. *Eating facilities:* 80-cover restaurant open to public every day, two bars. *Opening Hours*: weekdays 7.30am to 10pm. *Society Meetings:* welcome, rates available. Conference and function facilities available; discounts at local hotels. Professional (PGA): S. Hadfield. Managing Director: A.A. Wright.
website: www.craythorne.co.uk

SUFFOLK

HALESWORTH. **Halesworth Golf Club,** Bramfield Road, Halesworth IP19 9XA (01986 875567; Fax: 01986 874565). *Location:* A12, A144 to and through Bramfield. 13 bays floodlit (10 covered). *Prices*: information not available. *Opening hours:* dawn until dusk (9pm winter months). Professional tuition and fully equipped Pro shop; 27-hole golf course, putting and chipping greens. Professional: Richard Davies. Manager: Chris Aldred.*

IPSWICH. **Fynn Valley Golf Club,** Witnesham, Ipswich IP6 9JA (01473 785267; Fax: 01473 785632). *Location:* two miles due north of Ipswich on B1077. 23 bays floodlit (10 covered). Practice green and bunker. 9 hole par 3 course. 18 hole course. *Prices*: 120 balls £4.80, 90 balls £3.75, 60 balls £2.90, 30 balls £1.80. *Opening hours*: 9am to 9pm Monday to Friday and 8am to 8pm (6pm in winter) Saturday and Sunday. *Eating facilities:* meals available every lunchtime. Evening meals Tuesday to Saturday. *Societies:* welcome. Professional tuition, group lessons, etc. Golf shop. Golf range membership available. Professionals: Alastair Spink, Simon Dainty, Chris Smith. Secretary: A. Tyrrell.
e-mail: enquiries@fynn-valley.co.uk
website: www.fynn-valley.co.uk

WOODBRIDGE. **Seckford Golf Club,** Seckford Hall Road, Great Bealings, Near Woodbridge IP13 6NT (01394 388000; Fax: 01394 382818). *Location:* signposted from A12 near Woodbridge. 12 bay fixed mats driving range. *Prices*: information not available. *Eating facilities:* fully licensed bar and restaurant. Golf lessons available from qualified PGA staff using GASP video analysis system as seen on Sky TV. Hire equipment available. Professional: Simon Jay.*

SURREY,

CARSHALTON. **Oaks Sports Centre,** Woodmansterne Road, Carshalton SM5 4AN (020 8643 8363; Fax: 020 8770 7303). Covered, grassed and floodlit bays with bunkers. 18 hole and 9 hole courses. *Prices*: information not provided. *Opening hours:* 9am to 9.30pm. *Eating facilities:* Cafeteria and bar. Pay and play and membership available. PGA Professional teaching. Professional: Michael Pilkington (020 8643 8363).
e-mail: golf@oaks.sagehost.co.uk
website: www.oaksportscentre.co.uk

CHESSINGTON **Chessington Golf Centre,** Garrison Lane, Chessington KT9 2LW (020 8391 0948). *Location:* off A243, 500 yards from Chessington World of Adventure. Opposite Chessington South Station, Junction 9 M25. Covered, floodlit range, 18 bays. 9 hole course. Private and group tuition available. *Prices:* information not provided. *Opening hours*: 8am to 10pm. *Eating facilities:* bar and catering. Tuition, public course.

COBHAM. **Silvermere Driving Range,** Redhill Road, Cobham KT11 1EF (01932 584300; Fax: 01932 584301). *Location:* half-a-mile from Junction 10 on M25 at A3; 30 minutes from central London. Covered, floodlit range, 34 bays. Public golf course. *Prices:* information not available. *Eating facilities:* full service available. *Opening hours:* 8.30am to 9.30pm. Tuition available. Telephone bookings taken. Administrator: Pauline Devereux (01932 584300; Fax: 01932 584301).*

CROYDON. **World of Golf Croydon,** 175 Long Lane, Addiscombe, Croydon CR0 7TE (020 8656 1690; Fax: 020 8654 7859). *Location:* on A222 about two miles east of Croydon. 22 bay covered, floodlit, driving range. *Prices*: information not provided. *Eating facilities:* snacks/coffee. *Opening hours*: weekdays 9am to 10pm, weekends 9am to 8pm. *Visitors:* very welcome at all times, open to the public. Lessons from 4 PGA qualified instructors, and club repairs available. Head Professional: Paul Smith (020 8656 1690; Fax: 020 8656 3059).

Please mention THE GOLF GUIDE when you enquire about clubs or accommodation

572 DRIVING RANGES

ESHER. **Sandown Golf Centre,** More Lane, Esher KT10 8AN (01372 461234). *Location*: signposted from A3, centre of Sandown Park Racecourse. 33 bay covered floodlit driving range, plus grassed area. Three golf courses. *Prices:* information not available. *Eating facilities:* bar and restaurant. *Opening hours:* 8am to 10pm weekdays; 7am to 8pm weekends. Cranfield Golf Acadamy *Visitors*: visitors and societies welcome. General Manager: David Parr (01372 461234; Fax: 01372 461203).*

GODALMING. **Broadwater Park Golf Club,** Guildford Road, Farncombe, Near Godalming GU7 3BU (01483 429955). 16 bay covered, floodlit driving range. *Prices:* information not available. *Eating facilities:* licensed bar. *Opening hours:* 8am to 10pm. Professional, tuition and 9 hole Par 3 course. Professional: Kevin Milton.*

GUILDFORD. **Roker Park Golf Club,** Fairlands Farm, Aldershot Road, Guildford GU3 3PB (01483 236677; Fax: 01483 232324). *Location*: from A3 Guildford take A323 to Aldershot, course two miles on right. Flat parkland course. 9 holes, 3037 yards. S.S.S. 72. *Prices:* information not available. *Eating facilities*: restaurant and bar. *Visitors*: welcome, pay and play course. *Society Meetings*: welcome weekdays only, reductions for parties over 12. Professional: Adrian Carter. Secretary: G. Barnett (Tel & Fax: 01438 232324).*

LEATHERHEAD. **Pachesham Park Golf Centre,** Oaklawn Road, Leatherhead KT22 0BP (01372 843453). *Location*: half-a-mile outside Leatherhead, just off A244. Junction 9 M25. 33 bay covered floodlit range with Power Tees. 9 hole golf course. New chipping area. *Prices:* 30 balls £3.00, 60 balls £5.00, 90 balls £7.00, 120 balls £8.00. Discount range ball cards available. *Eating facilities:* available. *Opening hours*: April to October, weekdays 9am to 9.30pm, weekends 9am to 9pm; November to March 9am to 8pm. PGA teaching Professionals. Club membership also available. Custom Fit centre.

NEWDIGATE. **Rusper Golf Club and Driving Range,** Rusper Road, Newdigate RH5 5BX (01293 871871). *Location:* Dorking-Horsham A24, Beare Green roundabout, left to Newdigate, in village turn right to Rusper, club approximately one mile on right hand side. 12 bay covered driving range. 18 hole golf course. *Prices*: please contact the club. *Eating facilities:* fresh food and daily specials available every day; bar. *Opening hours*: dawn till dusk. Qualified professional tuition by arrangement; club hire. Membership available. Professional: Janice Arnold. Secretary: Mrs Jill Thornhill.
e-mail: nikki@ruspergolfclub.co.uk
website: www.ruspergolfclub.co.uk

NEW MALDEN. **World of Golf at Beverley Park,** Beverley Way, New Malden KT3 4PH (020 8949 9200; Fax: 020 8336 2856). *Location*: leave the A3 northbound at B282, follow sign to A3 London, entrance on left before rejoining A3. Southbound exit A3 at A298, follow A3 London from roundabout. 60 bay floodlit, covered driving range. Golf School, two coaching studios, floodlit putting green and bunker. *Prices:* information not available. *Eating facilities:* cafe/bar. *Opening hours*: 8am to 11pm daily. JJB Golf Store, club repair service.*
website: www.worldofgolf.biz

OLD WOKING. **Hoebridge Golf Centre,** Old Woking Road, Old Woking GU22 8JH (01483 722611). *Location*: near the A3. 36-bay covered, floodlit range. 75 yard constructed external chipping range. *Prices:* see website for details. *Eating facilities:* full bar and restaurant facilities. *Opening hours:* 7am to 10pm. Golf tuition. Custom fitting and launch monitor testing. Centre Manager: Mike O'Connell.
e-mail: info@hoebridgegc.co.uk
website: www.hoebridgegc.co.uk

REDHILL. **Redhill Golf Centre,** Canada Avenue, Redhill RH1 5BF (01737 770204). *Location*: in the grounds of East Surrey Hospital. 37-bay covered, floodlit driving range. 9-hole golf course. *Prices:* information not provided. *Opening hours*: 8am to 10pm; weekends 9pm. Sponsored by Golf Foundation to give free junior coaching. Professional: Declan Malone. Manager: Steven Furlonger.

EAST SUSSEX

HELLINGLY. **Wellshurst Golf and Country Club,** North Street, Hellingly BN27 4EE (01435 813456). *Location:* two miles from the A22 London to Eastbourne Road on A267. 16 bay covered, floodlit range. 18 hole course, two sand bunker bays. *Prices:* information not available. *Eating facilities:* full bar and catering facilities available at all times. *Opening hours*: 7.30am to 9.30pm. Full leisure and conference facilities. Full professional staff for lessons, well stocked pro shop.*

HORAM. **Horam Park Golf Course and Floodlit Driving Range,** Chiddingly Road, Horam TN21 0JJ (01435 813477, Fax: 01435 813677). *Location:* 13 miles north of Eastbourne, 7 miles east of Uckfield. Covered floodlit driving range, Astroturf range. 15 bays. Pitch and putt course, floodlit putting green, pitch and putt course. 9-hole golf course, 3092 yards, Par 35. *Prices*: information not available. *Eating facilities:* restaurant bar and spike bar, seven days, children welcome. PGA golf Professionals, lessons and tuition available. Golf shop. Professional: Giles Velvick.*

SEDLESCOMBE. **Sedlescombe Golf Club,** Kent Street, Near Battle, TN33 0SD (01424 871700). Home of The James Andrews School of Golf. *Location:* 1066 Country, 5 miles north of Hastings on the A21, 3 miles from Battle. Gently undulating parkland course, 18 holes, 6269 yards. S.S.S. 70. 24 bay floodlit driving range, four practice putting greens, academy hole and bunkers. Residential golf school with 2, 3 and 5 day intensive courses for all ages and abilities. Five PGA Professionals. Facilities include

indoor video and computer analysis centre, on-site hotel, golf shop and tennis courts. *Green Fees:* information not available. *Eating facilities:* bar and restaurant open seven days. *Visitors:* Course open to public. *Society Meetings:* welcome. Head Professional: James Andrews (01424 871700). Club Secretary (01424 871700). Golf School (01424 871717).*
website: www.golfschool.co.uk

WEST SUSSEX

BURGESS HILL. **The Burgess Hill Golf Academy,** Cuckfield Road, Burgess Hill RH15 8RE (01444 258585; Fax: 01444 247318). *Location:* on the B2036 north of Burgess Hill, on the Burgess Hill to Cuckfield road. 28 bay undercover, grassed, floodlit driving range. 9 hole short course. New practice bunker, synthetic grass tees (first in UK), Augusta style putting green. *Prices:* information not available. *Eating facilities:* Bar and restaurant. Tea and coffee. *Opening Hours:* seven days a week 8am to 9pm. Well stocked golf shop. PGA teaching academy including video tuition. Professional: Mark Collins. Secretary: (01444 258585; Fax: 01444 247318).*

CHICHESTER. **Chichester Golf Club,** Hunston Village, Chichester PO20 6AX (01243 528999). *Location:* take B2145 off A27 to Selsey, golf club is on the left after Hunston Village. 27 bay covered, 10 automated Powertee bays, floodlit, grassed driving range. Two 18 hole golf courses, 9 hole Par 3 minigolf. *Prices:* information not available. *Eating facilities:* fully licensed clubhouse. *Opening hours*: 8.30am to 9.30pm, 9.00am to 8.00pm in winter. *Society Meetings:* welcome seven days a week. Video teaching academy. Membership available. Professional: James Willmott.*

CRAWLEY. **Gatwick Manor Golf Club,** Gatwick Manor Hotel, London Road, Lowfield Heath, Crawley RH10 2ST (01293 526301 (Hotel); 01293 538587 (Club)). *Location:* A23 Crawley to Gatwick Airport on London Road on right. 9 grassed tees. *Prices:* information not available. *Eating facilities:* hotel facilities at Gatwick Manor. *Opening hours:* 9am to 8.00pm seven days a week.*

CRAWLEY. **Tilgate Forest Golf Centre,** Titmus Drive, Tilgate, Crawley RH10 5EU (01293 530103; Fax: 01293 523478). 35 floodlit bays. *Prices*: information not provided. *Opening hours:* 7am to 9.15pm. *Eating facilities:* bar and restaurant. Tuition, practice area, putting green etc. Professional: William Easdale (01293 530103).
e-mail: tilgate@glendale-services.co.uk.

RUSTINGTON. **Rustington Golf Centre,** Golfers Lane, Angmering BN16 4NB (01903 850790; Fax: 01903 850982). *Location:* on A259 at Rustington, between Worthing and Littlehampton. 9 holes with 18 tees, 5735 yards. Par 70. 9 hole par 3 course, 3 hole golf academy course, putting green, 30 bay floodlit driving range. *Prices:* information not provided. *Opening hours*: 8am-9pm Monday to Friday, 8am-6pm Saturday and Sunday. *Eating facilities:* coffee shop and licensed bar. *Visitors:* welcome at all times. Cranfield golf academies available for tuition of all standards. *Society Meetings:* societies and corporate days welcome. Centre Manager: Stuart Langmead (01903 850790; Fax: 01903 850982).

TYNE & WEAR

NEWCASTLE UPON TYNE. **Parklands,** High Gosforth Park, Newcastle upon Tyne NE3 5HQ (0191-236 4480). *Location:* off A1 for Gosforth Park. 28 bay covered, floodlit range. *Prices:* infomation not available. *Eating facilities:* bar and restaurant. *Opening hours:* 8am to 10.30pm. Professional tuition, 18-hole golf course, 18-hole American-style putting course. Societies welcome at weekends. Ring for package details.*

WASHINGTON. **George Washington Golf and Country Club,** Stone Cellar Road, High Usworth, District 12, Washington NE37 1PH (0191 4029988; Fax: 0191 4151166). *Location:* just off A1(M), take A194 then exit A195 Washington. 21 bay covered, floodlit, grassed range. 9 hole pitch and putt. *Prices*: information not available. *Eating facilities:* Bunkers Bar – hours vary, serves snacks. Buffets etc by arrangement. Tuition available. Golf buggies. Leisure club with sauna, pool, solarium, multi gym, spa and squash. Professional: Graeme Robinson (0191 417 8346). *

WARWICKSHIRE

COVENTRY. **John Reay Golf Centres,** Sandpits Lane, Keresley, Coventry CV7 8NJ (024 7633 3920). *Location:* three miles from Coventry city centre along A51 Tamworth Road. Covered, floodlit driving range. 60 bays. Golf club repair facility. Teaching professionals using latest video techniques. *Prices*: information not available. *Opening hours:* daily 9am to 10pm. *Eating facilities:* Hogan's Bar & Bistro open every day. *Visitors:* open to the public. Large Golf Shop with all the leading brands of golf equipment. Professional: John Reay (024 7633 3920/3405).*
website: www.johnreaygolf.com

WARWICK. **Warwick Golf Centre,** The Racecourse, Warwick CV34 6HW (01926 494316). *Location:* A46 off the M40 (middle of Warwick). 25 bay covered, floodlit range. 9 hole golf course (Par 34) open to the public. *Prices:* information not provided. *Eating facilities:* bar only. *Opening hours*: driving range 10am to 9pm, 9 hole golf course 8am to 9pm. Professional tuition. Professional: Phil Sharp. Secretary: Roma Dunkley.

WEST MIDLANDS

DUDLEY near. **Swindon Ridge Golf Driving Range, Shop & Golf Club,** Bridgnorth Road, Swindon, Near Dudley DY3 4PU (01902 896191). *Location:* B4176 Bridgnorth/Dudley Road, three miles from Himley A449 Junction. 27 bay floodlit range (22 covered). *Opening hours:* 9.30am to 8.30pm weekdays, 9.30am to 5.30pm weekends and Bank Holidays. *Eating facilities:* licensed bar and restaurant. 18 hole private golf club on site. Snooker table in bar.
website: www.swindongolfclub.co.uk

SUTTON COLDFIELD. **Lea Marston Hotel & Leisure Complex,** Haunch Lane, Lea Marston, Sutton Coldfield B76 0BY (01675 470468; Fax: 01675 470871). *Location:* From Junction 9 of M42, take A4097 towards Kingbury for just over one mile, take second right into Haunch Lane, right after 150 yards approximately. 27 floodlit bays. 9 hole Marston Lakes Par 31 and 9 hole Par 3 pay and play course. *Prices:* information not available. *Eating facilities:* Adderley Restaurant, Sportsmen's Lounge Bar and Conservatories. *Visitors:* welcome. Professional tuition available. Golf simulator with 20 courses including Valderrama and the Belfry's Brabazon. Fully stocked golf shop. 83 bedroom hotel, leisure facilities including indoor swimming pool.*

WOLVERHAMPTON. **3 Hammers Golf Complex,** Old Stafford Road, Coven WV10 7PP (01902 790428). *Location:* Junction 2 M54 north on A449, one mile on right. 23 covered floodlit bays. *Prices:* information not available. *Eating facilities:* bookings taken from 10.30am, details on (01902 791917). *Opening hours:* weekdays 9.30am to 10pm, weekends 9.30am to 9pm. 18 hole Par 3 course, three teaching Professionals.
e-mail: info@3hammers.co.uk
website: 3hammers.co.uk

WILTSHIRE

CALNE. **Bowood Hotel, Spa and Golf Resort,** Derry Hill, Calne SN11 9PQ (01249 822228; Fax: 01249 822218). *Location:* located off A4 between Calne and Chippenham. Signposted from Junction 17. Part of Bowood, a championship course on the beautiful Bowood Estate. 10 covered, floodlit bays. *Prices:* information not provided. *Opening hours:* telephone for details. *Eating facilities:* restaurant and brasserie; bar. Tuition, academy course, putting green. Professional: Paul McLean (01249 822228; Fax: 01249 822218).
e-mail: golfclub@bowood.org
website: www.bowood.org.

SALISBURY. **Hamptworth Academy,** Hamptworth Road, Hamptworth, Near Salisbury SP5 2DU (01794 390155; Fax: 01794 390022). *Location:* halfway between Southampton and Salisbury, one mile off A36. 3 covered bays, 8 grassed bays, bunkers. 18 hole golf course, putting green. *Prices:* information not available. *Opening hours:* 8am till dusk. *Eating facilities:* all-day menu in clubhouse. Tuition, available. Professional: Mark White (01794 390155; Fax: 01794 390022).*
e-mail: info@hamptworthgolf.co.uk
website: www.hamptworthgolf.co.uk

SWINDON. **Broome Manor Golf Complex,** Pipers Way, Swindon SN3 1RG (01793 532403). *Location:* two miles from Junction 15 of M4, follow signs for Golf Complex. 34 bays, 27 covered, seven uncovered, floodlit range (astroturf). *Prices:* information not available. *Eating facilities:* full service available. *Opening hours:* Summer 8am to 10pm, Winter 8am to 9pm. Five PGA professionals - group and individual lessons always available. 18 hole courses, 9 hole course and nearby pitch and putt course. Restaurant available for functions and conferences.*

WORCESTERSHIRE

BROMSGROVE. **Bromsgrove Golf Centre,** Stratford Road, Bromsgrove B60 1LD (01527 575886; Fax: 01527 570964; Course Reception: 01527 570505; Conference & Restaurant 01527 579179). *Location:* easily located at the roundabout junction of the A38 and A448, one mile from Bromsgrove town centre, just five minutes' drive from Junctions 4 and 5 of the M5 and Junction 1 of the M42 (exit west bound only). *Facilities include:* new 29-bay automated driving range, new teaching studio with state-of-the-art computerised video systems. Golf Academy - wide range of tuition available with resident PGA Professionals, including on-course video tuition etc. Tuition price list available on request. 18 hole "Pay and Play" parkland golf course 5969 yards S.S.S. 68. Large multi-level putting green. Conference & function rooms. Large golf shop. *Prices:* available on request. *Eating facilities*: friendly clubhouse with full bar and restaurant facilities. Visitors most welcome. Bar snacks or 'Daily Specials' available in spacious bar/lounge. Sky TV. *Opening hours*: weekdays 8am to 9pm, Saturdays, 7am to 9pm, Sundays 7am to 5pm (Sunday lunch 12 noon to 4pm). Head Professional: Graeme Long. Assistant Professional: Danny Wall. Secretary: John Brothwood.
e-mail: enquiries@bromsgrovegolfcentre.com
website: www.bromsgroveofcentre.com

REDDITCH. **The Abbey Hotel, Golf and Country Club,** Hither Green Lane, Dagnell End Road, Redditch B98 9BE (01527 406500; Fax: 01527 406514). *Location*: leave M42 at Junction 2, take A441 towards Redditch, at end of dual carriageway turn left still keeping on the A441, at petrol station turn left into Dagnell End Road (A4101) - hotel and golf club are approximately 600 yards on right. 12 bay range. *Prices*: information not provided. *Eating facilities*: extended Bramblings Restaurant and

Tawnys Bar. *Opening hours*: 7am until 8.30pm in summer, 7.30am until dusk in winter. Fully stocked golf shop. Golf & Leisure Complex . Professional tuition available. Professional: Rob Davies.

WORCESTER. **Ravenmeadow Golf Club,** Hindlip Lane, Claines, Worcester WR3 8SA (01905 575725; Fax: 01905 458876). *Location:* Junction 6 M5 motorway, take A449 signed Kidderminster, leave at Blackpole exit. At main road turn right, first left into Hindlip Lane, half mile on left. Part of Ravenmeadow Golf Club. Newly refurbished driving range. 6 grass tees, 10 indoor automatic tees. Putting green, chipping green, 9 hole pitch and putt course; finest practice facilities in the country. *Prices*: information not available. *Eating facilities*: bar, snack meals. Professional: Tommy Robinson (01905 575725)*.
e-mail: info@ravenmeadowgolf.co.uk
website: www.ravenmeadowgolf.co.uk

WORCESTER. **Worcester Golf Range,** Weir Lane, Lowerwick WR2 4AY (01905 748788/421213). *Location*: Junction 7 M5 off Malvern Road next to Lowerwick Swimming Pool. 26 bay covered, floodlit, golf range. 9 hole pitch and putt. *Prices*: information not available. *Eating facilities*: cold drinks, free coffee, confectionery and sandwiches. *Opening hours:* 9.30am to 10pm Monday - Friday, 9.30am to 6pm Saturday and Sunday. Three fully qualified PGA professionals always available for teaching. Swimming pool next door. Professional: Mark Dove.*

EAST YORKSHIRE

BEVERLEY. **Cherry Burton Golf Club,** Leconfield Lane, Cherry Burton, Beverley HU17 7LU (Tel & Fax: 01964 550924). *Location*: off the B1248 3 miles north of Beverley. 6 bay covered, grassed, floodlit driving range. One bunker. *Prices*: information not available. *Eating facilities*: licensed bar with snacks and light meals. *Opening hours*: dawn to dusk. Professional: John Gray and John Wells (01964 550924).
website: www.cherryburtongolfclub.co.uk

SCUNTHORPE. **Grange Park Golf Range,** Butterwick Road, Messingham, Scunthorpe DN17 3PP (01724 764478). *Location*: five miles south of Scunthorpe between Messingham and East Butterwick, four miles south of Junction 3 of M180. 20-bay covered floodlit driving range. 9 hole pay and play course on site (£4.70 weekdays, £4.90 weekends). *Prices*: 100 balls £4.80. *Opening hours*: 9am to 9.30pm weekdays, 9am to 8.30pm weekends. Large Pro shop. Professional available.

NORTH YORKSHIRE

HARROGATE. **Rudding Park Golf,** Rudding Park, Harrogate HG3 1JH (01423 872100; Fax: 01423 872286). *Location:* lies just off the A658 linking the A61 from Leeds to the A59 York Road. Parkland course designed to USGA specifications. 18 holes, 6883 yards. Par 72, 6 hole Par 3 short course and Golf Academy incorporating extensive practice facilities. 18 bay floodlit driving range with resident professionals. *Prices*: information not available. *Eating facilities:* Clubhouse open all day everyday, spike bar. *Visitors:* welcome at all times, must have a Handicap Certificate. Shop and buggies available all year round with all year weather buggy tracks, caddies on request. Society and corporate days welcome. Professional: Mark Moore (01423 872100).*
e-mail: golf@ruddingpark.com
website: www.ruddingpark.co.uk

NORTHALLERTON. **Romanby Driving Range,** Romanby Golf Course, Yafforth Road, Northallerton DL7 0PE (01609 778855; Fax: 01609 779084). *Location:* on the North West of Northallerton, easy road access. Part of Romanby Golf Course Ltd. 12 covered, grassed, floodlit bays. Practice bunker. Academy Course. *Prices: Prices*: information not available. *Opening hours:* 8am to 9pm; closes 6pm weekends. *Eating facilities:* Country Club open daily from 8am till 9pm; full bar and restaurant facilities. Lessons available; pro shop. Full disabled facilities. Professional: Richard Wood (01609 760777; Fax: 01609 760660).*
e-mail: richard@romanby.com
marketing: richard.boucher@romanby.com
website: www.romanby.com

SALTBURN. **Hunley Hall Golf Club & Hotel,** Brotton, Saltburn TS12 2QQ (01287 676216; Fax: 01287 678250). *Location:* off A174 at St. Margarets Way in Brotton. Signposted through housing estate, approximately half-a-mile to club. 12 bay floodlit driving range, large practice and chipping area. Picturesque 27 hole coastal courses adjacent to Heritage Coast. *Prices:* information not available. *Eating facilities:* excellent facilities including restaurant, lounge bar, spike bar, golfers' bar; quality food available all day, every day. *Opening hours:* Summer - 8am to 8pm, 6pm weekends and Bank Holidays. Winter - 8am till dusk, floodlit Wednesday, Thursday and Friday to 7.30pm. Three Star Hotel on site. Club hire, buggy hire and tuition available. *Society Meetings:* welcome Monday to Saturday, packages available. Golfing Holidays available. Professional: Andrew Brook (Tel & Fax: 01287 677444). Secretary: Liz Lillie (01287 676216; Fax: 01287 678250).*
e-mail: enquiries@hunleyhall.co.uk
e-mail: andy@asbrook-golf.co.uk
website: www.hunleyhall.co.uk

THE APPEARANCE OF AN ASTERISK (*) AT THE END OF A CLUB OR COURSE ENTRY INDICATES THAT UP-TO-DATE INFORMATION HAS NOT BEEN SUPPLIED

576 DRIVING RANGES

SOUTH YORKSHIRE

DONCASTER. **Bawtry Golf Club Driving Range,** Cross Lane, Austerfield, Bawtry, Doncaster DN10 6RF (01302 710841). *Location:* A614 Doncaster to Blyth Roundabout on the A1. Adjacent to the new Robin Hood Doncaster Airport. 10 covered, grassed, floodlit bays. *Prices:* information not available. *Opening hours:* 8am to 8pm. *Eating facilities:* full clubhouse facilities. Tuition available. Professional: Daniel Gregory (01302 710841).*
e-mail: enquiries@bawtrygolfclub.co.uk
website: www.bawtrygoldclub.co.uk

SHEFFIELD. **Concord Park Driving Range,** Concord Park Golf Club, Shiregreen, Sheffield S5 6AE (Tel & Fax: 0114 257 7378). *Location:* next to Concord Park Golf Club. 30 covered, floodlit bays; 2 bunkers. Putting green. *Prices:* information not available. *Opening hours:* 7am to 9pm. *Eating facilities:* restaurant in the clubhouse, also fully licensed bar. Tuition available. Professional: Warren Allcroft (07968 618766).*

SHEFFIELD. **Rother Valley Golf Centre,** Mansfield Road, Wales Bar, Sheffield S26 5PQ (0114 247 3000; Fax: 0114 247 6000). *Location:* Junction 31 off M1 motorway, follow signs to Rother Valley Country Park. 25 covered, floodlit bays; bunkers. 12 Power Tee mats on range. *Prices*: information not available. *Opening hours:* 9am to 9pm. *Eating facilities:* bar and restaurant. Professional: Jason Ripley.
e-mail: rother@jbgolf.co.uk
website: www.jackbarker.com

WEST YORKSHIRE

BRADFORD. **Shay Grange Golf Centre,** Long Lane, off Bingley Road, Bradford BD9 6RX (01274 491945). *Location:* take the A650 Bradford to Bingley road, turn left at Cottingley lights, the Centre will be found on the left after two miles. 32 bay covered, floodlit, grassed range. *Prices:* information not available. *Eating facilities:* fully licensed bar and catering facilities. *Opening hours:* weekdays 9am to 9pm, weekends and Bank Holidays 7am to 9pm. 9 hole (Par 29) course, Golf Academy, all weather putting green, sand bunker, grass short game area. Tuition. Golf clinics - Juniors, Senior Citizens, Ladies. Golf shop staffed by qualified PGA professionals. Manager: T. Grunwell.*

BRIGHOUSE. **Willow Valley Golf,** Highmoor Lane, off Walton Lane, Clifton, Brighouse HD6 4JB (01274 878624; Fax: 01274 852805). *Location:* Junction 25 off M62 to Brighouse A644, right at roundabout A643, 2 miles on right. Yorkshire's largest golfing venue – 24 bay, covered, floodlit, grassed driving range; two 18-hole and one 9-hole courses. *Prices:* information not available. *Eating facilities:* fully licensed bar and catering. Sunday evening play+stay offer. Junior Golf Foundation courses and 3 hole floodlit golf course. Professional: Julian Haworth.
website: www.wvgc.co.uk

HUDDERSFIELD. **Stadium Golf Driving Range,** The Alfred Macalpine Stadium, Stadium Way, Huddersfield HD1 6PG (01484 452566; Fax: 01484 452540). *Location:* off A62 centre of Huddersfield, signposted the Macalpine Stadium. 30 bay covered, floodlit driving range, range grassed. *Prices:* information not available. *Eating facilities:* snack bar serving sandwiches, etc., licensed bar. *Opening hours:* weekdays 9am to 10pm (last balls 9.30pm). weekends 9am to 7pm (last balls 6.30pm). State of the art Panasonic split screen video lessons with PGA qualified instructors. Corporate and group evenings a speciality. Team and video golf fun for juniors to seniors and all in between. Well stocked shop with all major brands. Professional: Simon Roberts.*

LEEDS. **Cookridge Hall Golf Club,** Cookridge Lane, Leeds LS16 7NL (0113 2300641; Fax: 0113 2030198). *Location*: A6120 ring road, 10 minutes Leeds city centre, Bradford city centre, 20 minutes Harrogate centre. 18 hole Championship course. 22-bay driving range with floodlights. *Prices:* £3.50 for 50 balls, £17.00 for range card and 6 baskets. 2 piece golf balls. *Eating facilities*: sports bar, hot and cold sandwiches and drinks available. *Opening hours*: weekdays 8.30am to 9.30pm, weekends 8.30am to 8pm. PGA tuition 7 days a week. Bunker and chipping area, latest in air-cushioned mats.
e-mail: info@cookridgehall.co.uk
website: www.cookridgehall.co.uk

LEEDS. **Leeds Golf Centre,** Wike Ridge Lane, Shadwell, Leeds LS17 9JW (0113 2886000; Fax: 0113 2886185). *Location:* two miles north of Leeds between A61 and A58 at the village of Wike. 19 bay covered, floodlit range. *Prices:* information not available. *Eating facilities:* bar/brasserie open 8.30am to 10pm. *Opening hours:* 7am to 10pm. Resident teaching professionals, 18 hole championship course, 12 hole Par 3 course. Head Professional: Andrew Herridge. General Manager: Mick Redmond.*
e-mail: info@leedsgolfcentre.com
website: www.leedsgolfcentre.com

THE APPEARANCE OF AN ASTERISK (*) AT THE END OF A CLUB OR COURSE ENTRY INDICATES THAT UP-TO-DATE INFORMATION HAS NOT BEEN SUPPLIED

SCOTLAND

ABERDEEN, BANFF & MORAY

ABERDEEN. **Kings Links Golf Centre,** Golf Road, Aberdeen AB24 1RZ (01224 641577; Fax: 01224 639410). *Location:* in front of Pittodrie football stadium, 56 covered, floodlit bays on two tiers. *Prices:* information not available. *Eating facilities:* vending drinks, vending snacks and sandwiches. *Opening hours*: 9am to 10pm weekdays, 9am to 5.30pm weekends. 5 PGA Professionals available for tuition, club repairs, advise and custom fitting service. Video academy equipped with the latest video analysis equipment. Floodlit outdoor short game area. 3000sq ft golf superstore stocking all the latest golf equipment. Beginners welcome. Director of Golf: Paul Girvan.*
e-mail: info@kings-links.com
website: www.kings-links.com

ANGUS & DUNDEE

DUNDEE. **Ballumbie Castle Golf Club,** 3 Old Quarry Road, Off Ballumbie Road, Dundee DD4 0SY (01382 730026; Fax: 01382 730008). *Location*: one and a half miles north of Claypotts Junction, less than 2 miles from Dundee City Centre. 22 bay floodlit driving range, putting green, chipping green. 18 hole course. *Prices*: information not available. *Eating facilities*: clubhouse facilities with menu and full bar. Public house licence. *Opening hours*: 9am to 9pm weekdays, 9am to 7pm weekends. Tuition available. *Society Meetings*: welcome, please telephone for details. Professional: Lee Sutherland (01382 770028).*
e-mail: ballumbie2000@yahoo.com
website: www.ballumbiecastlegolfclub.com

AYRSHIRE & ARRAN

DAILLY. **Brunston Castle Golf Course,** Dailly, Girvan KA26 9GD (01465 811471). *Location:* five miles north of Girvan on B471, five miles from Turnberry. 10-bay floodlit driving range. *Prices:* information not available. *Eating facilities:* full bar and restaurant facilities. *Opening hours:* 8am to 11pm (Summer). 18 hole championship course in most scenic part of Ayrshire. Full PGA tuition by Professional, full practice facilities. 16-seater minibus and trailer available.*
e-mail: golf@brunstoncastle.co.uk
website: www.brunstoncastle.co.uk

EDINBURGH & LOTHIANS

EDINBURGH. **Braid Hills Shop & Golf Centre,** 91 Liberton Drive, Edinburgh EH16 6NS (0131-658 1111; Fax: 0131-672 1411). *Location:* leave Edinburgh bypass at Straiton Junction, head towards city centre, take left turn at second set of traffic lights, proceed half-a-mile along Liberton Drive. 32 bay covered, floodlit range. Short game area and 3 putting greens. *Prices:* information not available. *Opening Hours:* 10am to 9pm weekdays, 9am to 6pm weekends. Scotland's top Professionals available for group and individual tuition. S.A.S video tuition. Professionals: Ian Young, Colin Brooks, Sandy Stephen, Mark Berrie, Paul Malone, Craig Waddell.*

EDINBURGH. **Port Royal Golf Driving Range,** Eastfield Road, Ingliston, Edinburgh EH28 8TR (0131-333 4377). *Location:* situated next to Edinburgh Airport. Recently refurbished to cater for golfers of every ability. 25 covered, floodlit practice bays, 17 outside bays, double teaching studio with swing analysis software, 100 square yard Himalayan putting green, 9 hole Par 3 golf course. PGA Professionals and tuition. *Prices*: information not available. *Eating facilities:* licensed cafe/bar area, snacks served all day. *Opening hours:* 10am to 10pm summer, 10am to 9pm winter. Open all year. General Manager/Head Professional: Keith Pickard.*

EDINBURGH near. **Melville Golf Centre, Golf Course, Range & Shop,** Lasswade, Near Edinburgh EH18 1AN (0131-663 8038; Fax: 0131-654 0814). *Location:* south of Edinburgh, three minutes from City Bypass on A7 South (signposted). 22 floodlit, covered bays plus 12 bays. 300 yards long. *Prices:* information not available. *Eating facilities:* hot and cold drinks, confectionery. *Opening hours:* weekdays 9am to 10pm, weekends 9am to 8pm. Full equipment and shoe hire. Repairs. Golf shop fully stocked, ladies, gents, and juniors. PGA tuition all levels; practice bunker, putting green, 4 hole practice area, pay & play 9-hole golf course. Children under 14 must be accompanied by an adult. Junior Golf Academy. Owners Mr and Mrs MacFarlane.*
e-mail: golf@melvillegolf.co.uk
website: www.melvillegolf.co.uk

FIFE

CUPAR. **Elmwood,** Stratheden, By Cupar KY15 5RS (01334 658780). *Location:* signposted from A91 and A914 one mile west of Cupar. 9 miles from St Andrews. Grass tees and mats, real green targets, video analysis and club fitting suite. *Prices:* information not available. *Eating facilities:* Fairways Restaurant and Bar. *
e-mail: clubhouse@elmwood.ac.uk
website: www.elmwoodgc.co.uk

578 DRIVING RANGES

ST ANDREWS. **St Andrews Links Golf Practice Centre & Golf Academy,** St Andrews, KY16 9SF (01334 474489; Fax: 01334 479555). *Location:* situated parallel to the Old Course, just ten minutes' walk from the town centre. *Prices:* information not available. *Eating facilities:* light refreshments and seated viewing area. *Opening hours:* 7am to 9pm daily. Floodlit driving range with over 60 bays. Short game area with greens and bunkers. Grass tees. Golf club hire available. Locker rooms: (01334 474489).*

GLASGOW & DISTRICT

GLASGOW. **Mearns Castle Golf Academy,** Waterfoot Road, Newton Mearns, Glasgow G77 5RR (0141 644 8200; Fax: 0141 644 1133). *Location:* near Newton Mearns. 34 covered, floodlit bays; bunkers. *Prices:* information not available. *Eating facilities:* cafe bar. Tuition available; 9 hole pay and play course, short game facility. Memberships available.*
website: www.mcgolfacademy.co.uk

UDDINGSTON. **Clydeway Golf Centre,** Blantyre Farm Road, Uddingston G71 7RR (0141-641 8899). *Location:* near Glasgow Zoo. 25 covered floodlit bays. *Prices:* information not available. Professional tuition. Group rates for parties, schools, colleges, works, offices, etc. Now incorporates Nevada Bob's golf discount superstore, target golf competition. *

HIGHLANDS

INVERNESS. **Fairways Driving Range,** Castle Heather, Inverness IV2 6AA (01463 713335; Fax: 01463 712695). *Location:* on the southern outskirts of Inverness, heading west along the new ring road. 19 bay covered, floodlit driving range. 18 hole golf course and 9-hole course. Practice area. *Prices:* 14 balls £1.00, 50 balls £3.00. *Eating facilities:* restaurant lounge, sports bar. *Opening hours:* Monday to Sunday 8am to 11pm daily. *Visitors:* welcome, buggies, carts available. *Society Meetings:* welcome. Two PGA Professionals, tuition available. Professionals: Martin Piggot, Michael Campbell.
e-mail: info@golflochness.com
website: www.golflochness.com

PERTH & KINROSS

BLAIRGOWRIE. **Strathmore Golf Centre Driving Range.** Leroch, Alyth, Blairgowrie PH11 8NZ (01828 633322; Fax: 01828 633533). *Location:* one mile south of Alyth, (off the A926 Alyth-Kirriemuir Road). 10 bay floodlit driving range. *Prices:* information not provided. *Eating facilities:* restaurant and bar at Clubhouse. *Opening hours:* dawn to 10pm. 18 and 9 hole courses available. Golf Operations Manager: Jane Taylor.
e-mail: enquiries@strathmoregolf.com
website: www.strathmoregolf.com

MIDDLEBANK. **Middlebank Golf Centre,** Middlebank, Errol PH2 7SX (01821 670320). *Location:* midway between Perth and Dundee on the A90. 27 bay floodlit driving range; 7 covered, 20 outdoors. Short game area. *Prices*: £3.50 for 50 balls, £5.00 for 100, 5 credit digicard £12.00. 10-credit digicard £22.00. *Eating facilities:* hot and cold drinks and snacks available. *Opening Hours*: Summer 10am to 8pm Monday-Friday, 10am to 5pm Saturday/Sunday, Winter hours may vary. *Visitors*: open to public. Recently refurbished and under new management. Home of the Andy Lamb Golf Academy. Resident PGA professional Andy Lamb. Extensive golf shop stocks golf equipment including ladies' golf clothing. Titleist Custom Fit Centre.

SCONE. **Murrayshall Golf Range,** Murrayshall Hotel & Golf Courses, Scone PH2 7PH (01738 554804; Fax: 01738 552595). *Location*: 3 miles outside Perth (NE) off A94. 18 bay covered, floodlit driving range, 11 grassed, bunkers. Two 18 hole golf courses. *Prices*: information not provided. *Eating facilities*: 4 Star Hotel and golf clubhouse on site. *Opening hours*: Daylight until 8.30pm. Video analysis tuition. Professional: Alan Reid.
e-mail: golf@murrayshall.co.uk
website: www.murrayshall.co.uk

Other British holiday guides from FHG Guides

**PUBS & INNS · 300 GREAT HOTELS · SHORT BREAK HOLIDAYS
The bestselling and original PETS WELCOME! · 500 GREAT PLACES TO STAY
SELF-CATERING HOLIDAYS · BED & BREAKFAST STOPS
CARAVAN & CAMPING HOLIDAYS · FAMILY BREAKS**

Published annually: available in all good bookshops or direct from the publisher:
**FHG Guides, Abbey Mill Business Centre, Seedhill, Paisley PA1 1TJ
Tel: 0141 887 0428 · Fax: 0141 889 7204
e-mail: admin@fhguides.co.uk · www.holidayguides.com**

WALES

ANGLESEY & GWYNEDD

.ANGLESEY. **Penrhyn Golf Complex,** Llanddaniel - Fâb LL60 6NN (01248 421150). *Location:* A5 turn off at Star Crossroads taking Llanddaniel road. Follow Brown Tourism signs from the village. 14 bay covered and floodlit driving range, 9 hole golf course. *Prices*: information not available. *Visitors*: no restrictions. Professional: Paul Lovell (Visiting). Owner: W.R. Carter.*

PWLLHELI. **Llyn Golf,** Pen-y-Berth, Penrhos, Pwllheli LL53 7HG (01758 701200). *Location:* Situated off the A499 between Pwllheli and Abersoch. 14 covered floodlit bays and bunker practice area. 9-hole pay and play golf course, 1782 yards, Par 3 and 4. Hire clubs available. *Prices:* information not available. *Eating facilities:* refreshments available. *Opening hours:* open daily. *

NORTH WALES

CHESTER near. **Bannel Golf Driving Range,** Mold Road, Penymynydd, Near Chester CH4 0EN (01244 544639). *Location:* A5118 Penymynydd to Mold road, 7 miles from Chester. 10 bay covered floodlit range; three bays open. *Prices:* information not available. *Eating facilities:* light refreshments available. *Opening hours:* 10am-8pm weekdays; 10am-5pm weekends and Bank Holidays. 9 hole putting green, golf shop. Lessons from PGA Professional by appointment. Proprietors: L.J. & J. Povey (01244 544639).*

ST ASAPH. **North Wales Golf Driving Range and 9 hole Course,** Llannerch Park, St Asaph LL17 0BD (01745 730805;). *Location:* on the A525 between St Asaph and Trefnant, one-and-a-quarter miles from St Asaph Cathedral. 14 bay covered, floodlit driving range. New, automatic power-tees. *Prices*: information not available. *Eating facilities:* refreshments, hot and cold drinks, sweets, biscuits, crisps. *Opening hours*: 10am to 9pm seven days a week during Summer, early closing in Winter 5pm Friday to Monday. Lessons with resident Professional by arrangement. 9 hole course also on site - £6.00 pay and play. Non-membership Complex. Secretary: Stephen Mueller (07771 733651 mobile). *

POWYS

CRADOC. **Cradoc Golf Club,** Penoyre Park, Cradoc, Brecon LD3 9LP (01874 623658; Fax: 01874 611711). *Location*: two miles north of the market town of Brecon, off B4520 Upper Chapel Road (signposted) past Brecon Cathedral. 10-bay undercover floodlit driving range. *Prices*: information not provided. *Opening hours*: Monday and Tuesday (1st November to 31st March) 8.30am till 5pm and (1st April to 31st October) 8.30am to 8.45pm. Wednesday to Sunday (inclusive) 8.30am to 8.45pm all year. Professional: R.W. Davies (01874 625524). Club Manager: Robert Southcott (01874 623658).
e-mail: secretary@cradoc.co.uk
website: www.cradoc.co.uk

SOUTH WALES

ABERGAVENNY. **Wernddu Golf Club,** Old Ross Road, Abergavenny NP7 8NG (01873 856223; Fax: 01873 852177). *Location:* one and a half miles east of Abergavenny on B4521 (off A465). 26 bay floodlit driving range. *Prices:* information not provided. *Eating facilities:* lounge bar, bar snacks. *Visitors:* welcome. Professional tuition, 9 hole pitch and putt and 18 hole Par 67 golf course. Contact: Pro Tina Tetley (L.E.T.).
e-mail: info@wernddu-golf-club.co.uk
website: www.wernddu-golf-club.co.uk

BARRY. **South Wales Golf Range and Course,** Port Road East, Barry (Range: 01446 742434; Mobile: 07986 738744). *Location:* A4050 road Cardiff to Barry. 16 covered floodlit bays. *Prices:* information not available. *Opening hours:* weekdays 9am to 8pm; weekends 9am to 6pm. Professional tuition available from Simon Cox (three times Welsh Champion); 9-hole Par 3 course.*

CAERPHILLY. **Virginia Park Golf Club,** Virginia Park, Caerphilly CF8 1LP (029 2086 7891). *Location:* off Pontygwindy Road, next to recreation centre. 20 bay covered, floodlit, grassed driving range. *Prices:* information not available. *Eating facilities:* licensed bar in clubhouse, full catering. Coffee shop in driving range. *Opening hours:* weekdays 10.30am to 10pm; weekends 8am to 7pm seven days a week. Secretary: Graham Taylor.*

FHG Guides publish a large range of well-known accommodation guides. We will be happy to send you details or you can use the order form at the back of this book.

580 DRIVING RANGES

CHEPSTOW. **Dewstow Golf Club,** Caerwent, Chepstow NP26 5AH (01291 430444; Fax: 01291 425816). *Location*: Off A48 at Caerwent, between Chepstow and Newport, four miles from Severn Bridge. 26 bay floodlit, covered golf range. Two 18 hole courses. *Prices*: information not available. *Eating facilities*: restaurant, bars. *Opening hours*: on application. *Society Meetings*: welcome weekdays. Limited weekends. Professional: Jonathan Skuse. Golf Secretary:Dave Bradbury (01291 430444; Fax: 01291 425816). Booking Secretary: Hayley Battle.*

CWMBRAN. **Greenmeadow Golf and Country Club,** Treherbert Road, Croesyceiliog, Cwmbran NP44 2BZ (01633 869321; Fax: 01633 868430). *Location:* M4 Junction 26 five miles north on A4042. Turn right at brown tourist sign. Golf Course & Range next to Gwent Crematorium. 26 bay covered floodlit driving range. *Prices:* information not available. *Eating facilities:* lounge bar, patio coffee lounge and restaurant, private function room. *Opening hours:* 9.30am to 9.00pm all year. *Visitors:* welcome. Professional tuition by appointment. 18 hole parkland golf course, putting green. Range situated with panoramic views, facing easterly. Professional: Dave Woodman (01633 862626. Fax: 01633 868430). Secretary: P. Richardson (01633 869321).*
e-mail: info@greenmeadowgolf.com
website: www.greenmeadowgolf.com

NEWPORT. **Parc Golf Club,** Church Lane, Coedkernew NP10 9TU (01633 680933). *Location:* Junction 28 M4, then A48 towards Cardiff. 38 bay covered, floodlit driving range. Automatic tee system installed. 9 hole Par 3 course. *Prices:* information not available. *Eating facilities:* excellent full facilities. *Opening Hours:* weekdays 7.30am to 10pm, weekends 7.30am to 8.30pm. Three Professionals, individual and group tuition, excellent shop. Function suite, corporate and society days organised. Weddings, seminars, private parties catered for.*

SWANSEA. **Gowerton Golf Range,** Victoria Road, Gowerton, Swansea SA4 3AB (01792 875188). 20 covered bays, all floodlit. *Prices*: information not provided. *Eating facilities*: diner, hot and cold meals available. *Opening hours*: 10am to 9pm, closed at 7pm winter weekends. Tuition available. Putting green, golf course. Professional: Mike Hobbs.
e-mail: waynebattye@yahoo.com
website: www.gowertongolfrange.co.uk

THE GOLF GUIDE 2011

NORTHERN IRELAND

ANTRIM

NEWTOWNABBEY. **Ballyearl Golf and Leisure Centre,** 585 Doagh Road, Newtownabbey BT36 8RZ (028 9084 8287). *Location:* from Belfast take M2 then A8 to Larne, half a mile through second roundabout following exit from motorway turn right to Mossley. Ballyearl one mile on left. 24 bay covered, floodlit range, large grassed area. *Prices:* information not available. *Eating facilities:* squash club with bar facilities. *Opening hours:* 9am to 9.30pm. 9 hole Par 3 course, PGA Golf Professional, tuition, fully stocked golf shop (028 9084 0899), repairs. Squash court, fitness suite, arts theatre.*

ARMAGH

CRAIGAVON. **Craigavon Golf and Ski Club,** Turmoyra Lane, Lurgan, Craigavon (028 3832 6606; Fax: 028 3834 7272). *Location:* half a mile from motorway, one mile from town centre, adjacent to ski slope. Driving range. 18-hole course, 9-hole par 3 course, 12-hole pitch and putt. *Prices:* information not available. *Eating facilities:* full restaurant facilities. *Visitors:* always welcome. Modern clubhouse, showers and lockers. *Society Meetings:* welcome - book beforehand. Professional: D. Paul.*

Co. DOWN

KNOCKBRACKEN. **Mount Ober Golf and Country Club,** 24 Ballymaconaghy Road, Knockbracken, Belfast BT8 6SB (028 9079 5666; Fax: 028 9070 5862). *Location:* outskirts of Belfast, approximately three miles from the centre along Ormeau Road to "Four Winds" public house and restaurant. 36 bays covered, floodlit, and grassed area. *Prices:* £3.50 for 70 balls. *Eating facilities:* bar open seven days a week during normal opening hours, catering available seven days a week 11am to 10pm. *Opening hours*: 10am to 11pm. Tuition available at Knockbracken Golf Academy by PGA professionals. Snooker and pool tables. Professional: (028 9070 1648). Secretary: (028 9079 5666).
e-mail: mt.ober@ukonline.co.uk
website: www.mountober.com

WARRENPOINT. **Pat Trainor's Golf Academy,** Milltown Street, Burren, Warrenpoint BT34 3RJ (028 4177 3247). *Location:* six miles south of Newry, at Warrenpoint roundabout turn left for Burren: approximately one mile. Driving range - 10 covered, 20 grassed bays, all floodlit. 9 hole pitch and putt course. *Prices*: information not available. *Opening hours:* weekdays 10am to 10pm; weekends 10am to 8pm. Tuition available at all times for individuals, groups and schools. Indoor video lessons. Owner/Professional: Pat Trainor. Teacher: Paddy Gribben.*

FERMANAGH

ENNISKILLEN. **Ashwoods Golf Centre,** Sligo Road, Enniskillen (028 6632 5321). *Location:* one and a half miles west of Enniskillen on main Sligo Road. 7 bay covered, floodlit range; 14-hole Par 3 course. *Prices*: information not available. *Eating facilities:* none on site, available 300 yards away. *Opening hours:* 9am to 10pm summer, 9am to 5pm winter. Professional golf shop stocking full range of clubs, clothes and all golf accessories.*

Co. LONDONDERRY

LIMAVADY. **Roe Park Golf Club,** Radisson SAS Roe Park Resort, Roe Park, Limavady BT49 9LB (028 777 60105; Fax: 028 777 22313). *Location:* on main A2 Londonderry-Limavady Road, 16 miles from Londonderry and one mile from Limavady. 10 covered, floodlit, astroturfed and 6 uncovered bays. 18 hole parkland course. *Prices:* information not available. *Eating facilities:* Coach Brasserie. *Opening hours:* 8am until 10pm, golf course open from 8am until 8pm. PGA Tuition available. Professional: Shaun Devenney. Golf Manager: Terry Kelly.*

LONDONDERRY. **Foyle International Golf Centre,** 12 Alder Road, Londonderry BT48 8DB (028 71 352222; Fax: 028 71 353967). *Location*: 1½ miles from Foyle Bridge towards Moville, Co Donegal. 25 bay covered, floodlit driving range with automated tees. 18 hole, par 71 course and 9 hole par 3 course. *Prices*: information not available. *Eating facilities*: Pitchers Wine Bar and Restaurant. *Opening hours*: 8am to 10pm. Tuition available. Professional indoor video analysis. Professionals: Derek Morrison and Sean Young (028 71 352222; Fax: 028 71 353967).*
e-mail: mail@foylegolf.club24.co.uk
website: www.foylegolfcentre.co.uk

REPUBLIC OF IRELAND

Co. CORK

FOTA ISLAND. **Fota Island Resort,** Cork (021 4883700; Fax: 021 4883713). *Location:* take the N25 east from Cork City, turn off Carrigtwohill/Cobh exit. Follow sign for Fota (100m). Venue for the 2001 and 2002 Murphy's Irish Open. 18 hole championship course. Voted golf course of the year in 2002 by the Irish Golf Tour Operators. State of the Art Golf Academy with indoor and outdoor long and short game areas. 5 Star Hotel & Spa plus self-catering lodge all available on the resort. *Prices*: information not available. *Eating facilities:* full bar and restaurant. *Opening hours:* daylight only. PGA professional plus assistants available for tuition. Package deals available. Professional: Kevin Morris.*
e-mail: reservations@fotaisland.ie
website: www.fotaisland.ie

Co. DUBLIN

FOXROCK. **Leopardstown Driving Range,** Foxrock (2895341). *Location:* five miles south of Dublin city centre situated in Leopardstown Race Course. 38 indoor, 38 outdoor floodlit bays. *Opening hours*: 9am to 10pm. *Prices*: information not available. *Eating facilities:* restaurant. Tuition available from three PGA Professionals - practice green. 18 hole golf course. Manager: Michael Hoey.*

ST MARGARET'S. **The Open Golf Centre,** Newtown House, St Margaret's (010 3531 8640324; Fax: 010 3531 8341400). *Location:* 2kms from Dublin Airport, adjacent to N2 (Derry road). 16 bay floodlit, grassed range. *Prices*: information not available. *Eating facilities:* coffee shop. *Opening hours*: 7.30am to dusk. Nine golf professionals on site, groups organised, video, lecture room and club fitting room.*

PLEASE MENTION THIS GUIDE WHEN YOU ENQUIRE ABOUT CLUBS OR ACCOMMODATION

COUNTY KILDARE

NAAS. **Naas Golf Driving Range,** Kerdiffstown, Sallins, Naas (045 897754 or 045 874489; Fax: 045 871321). *Location*: one mile from N7 and Sallins Village, beside Naas Golf Club. Putting green, pitching area, sand bunker. Covered bays and floodlit outdoor bays. Coin operated automatic dispensing machine. *Visitors*: welcome. *Society Meetings*: welcome any time. Professional: Gerry Egan (085 144 8779), Tommy Halpin (087 987 2682), Gavin Lunny (086 832 6676). Secretary: Gus Fitzpatrick (086 255 6105; Fax: 045 871 321).*
e-mail: gusfitzpatrick@eircom.net

COUNTY MONAGHAN

CARRICKMACROSS. **Nuremore Golf Club,** Nuremore Hotel and Country Club, Carrickmacross (042 61438). *Location:* 50 miles from Dublin on N2. *Prices:* information not available. *Eating facilities:* bar and catering facilities in new clubhouse and hotel. *Opening hours:* daylight hours. PGA Professional, all hotel facilities.*

COUNTY WATERFORD

DUNGARVAN. **Gold Coast Golf Club,** Ballinacourty, Dungarvan (058 44055; Fax: 058 43378). *Location:* from Waterford left of N25 two miles before Dungarvan. Parkland bordered by Atlantic. 18 holes, 6788 yards, 6171 metres. S.S.S. 72. *Prices:* information not available. *Eating facilities:* full hotel and leisure facilities. *Visitors:* welcome. *Society Meetings:* welcome, special rates available. Secretary: Tom Considine (Tel & Fax: 058 44055).*
e-mail: info@clonea.com
website: www.clonea.com

CHANNEL ISLANDS

ST OUEN'S. **Les Mielles Golf and Country Club,** St Ouen's Bay, Jersey JE3 7FQ (01534 482787; Fax: 01534 485414). *Location:* centre of St Ouen's Bay. 20 bay covered driving range. *Prices:* information available on line. *Opening hours:* dawn till dusk. *Eating facilities:* restaurant, alfresco eating, kiosk. Public golf facility. Putting green; golf shop. Professional: Wayne Osmand (01534 483699; Fax: 01534 485414). Director of Golf: J.A. Le Brun. website: www.lesmielles.com

---

Other useful guides to holidays in Britain from FHG Guides

PUBS & INNS
300 GREAT HOTELS
SHORT BREAK HOLIDAYS
The original PETS WELCOME!
500 GREAT PLACES TO STAY
SELF-CATERING HOLIDAYS
BED & BREAKFAST STOPS
CARAVAN & CAMPING HOLIDAYS
FAMILY BREAKS

Published annually: available in all good bookshops or direct from the publisher:
FHG Guides, Abbey Mill Business Centre, Seedhill, Paisley PA1 1TJ
Tel: 0141 887 0428 • Fax: 0141 889 7204
e-mail: admin@fhguides.co.uk
www.holidayguides.com

PLEASE NOTE

All the information regarding Golf Clubs in this guide is given in good faith in the belief that it is correct. However, the publishers cannot guarantee the facts given in these pages, neither are they responsible for changes in ownership or facilities, such as green fees, that may take place after the date of going to press. Readers should always satisfy themselves that the facilities they require are available and that the terms, if quoted, still apply.

Index of Clubs & Courses

Abbey Hill Golf Centre MILTON KEYNES 77
Abbey Hotel Golf & Country Club REDDITCH 245, 574
Abbeydale Golf Club SHEFFIELD 323
Abbeyfeale Golf Club ABBEYFEALE 541
Abbeyleix Golf Club ABBEYLEIX 540
Abbotsley Golf Club & Hotel ST NEOTS 155, 561
Aberdare Golf Club ABERDARE 481
Aberdour Golf Club ABERDOUR 404
Aberdovey Golf Club ABERDOVEY 458
Aberfeldy Golf Club ABERFELDY 436
Aberfoyle Golf Club ABERFOYLE 448
Abergele Golf Club ABERGELE 463
Abernethy Golf Club NETHYBRIDGE 430
Aberystwyth Golf Club ABERYSTWYTH 473
Aboyne Golf Club ABOYNE 344
Aboyne Loch Golf Centre ABOYNE 344
Abridge Golf & Country Club STAPLEFORD TAWNEY 162
Accrington and District Golf Club ACCRINGTON 270
Achill Golf Club ACHILL 543
Acre Gate Golf Club FLIXTON 284
Adare Golf Club ADARE 541
Adare Manor Golf Club ADARE 541
Addington Court Golf Ltd CROYDON 117
Addington Golf Club CROYDON 117
Addington Palace Golf Club CROYDON 117
Adlington Golf Centre ADLINGTON 249, 561
Aigas Golf Course BEAULY 428
Airdrie Golf Club AIRDRIE 432
Airlinks Golf Club HOUNSLOW 145
Aldeburgh Golf Club ALDEBURGH 179
Aldenham Golf & Country Club WATFORD 169
Alder Root Golf Club WARRINGTON 255
Alderley Edge Golf Club ALDERLEY EDGE 249
Alderney Golf Club ALDERNEY 556
Aldersey Green Golf Club CHESTER 250

Aldwark Manor Golf Club ALDWARK 311
Aldwickbury Park Golf Club HARPENDEN 165
Alexandra Golf Club GLASGOW 415
Alford Golf Club ALFORD 346
Alfreton Golf Club ALFRETON 185
Alice Springs Golf Club USK 498
Allendale Golf Club ALLENDALE 296
Allerton Park Golf Club LIVERPOOL 292
Allestree Park Golf Club DERBY 187
Alloa Golf Club ALLOA 448
Allt-y-Graban Golf Club SWANSEA 494
Alness Golf Club ALNESS 424
Alnmouth Golf Club Ltd. ALNMOUTH 296
Alnmouth Village Golf Club ALNMOUTH 296
Alnwick Golf Club ALNWICK 296
Alresford Golf Club ALRESFORD 81
Alsager Golf and Country Club ALSAGER 249
Alston Moor Golf Club ALSTON 257
Alton Golf Club ALTON 81
Altrincham Golf Club ALTRINCHAM 281
Alva Golf Club ALVA 448
Alvaston Hall Golf Club NANTWICH 252
Alwoodley Golf Club LEEDS 330
Alyth Golf Club BLAIRGOWRIE 436
Amida Golf Course & Teaching Academy TWICKENHAM 147
Ampfield Golf Club AMPFIELD 81
Andover Golf Club ANDOVER 81
Anglesey Golf Club Ltd RHOSNEIGR 462
Annanhill Golf Club KILMARNOCK 372
Anstruther Golf Club ANSTRUTHER 404
Ansty Golf Centre COVENTRY 235
Antrobus Golf Club NORTHWICH 254
Appleby Golf Club APPLEBY 257
Aqualate Golf Centre NEWPORT 221, 570
Aquarius Golf Club SOUTHWARK 70
Arbroath Golf Course ARBROATH 358

INDEX OF CLUBS & COURSES

Arcot Hall Golf Club Ltd. NEWCASTLE UPON TYNE 300
Ardee Golf Club ARDEE 542
Ardeer Golf Club STEVENSTON 375
Ardglass Golf Club ARDGLASS 512
Arkley Golf Club BARNET 164
Army Golf Club ALDERSHOT 80
Arrowe Park Golf Course BIRKENHEAD 290
Arscott Golf Club SHREWSBURY 222
Ashbourne Golf Club ASHBOURNE 544
Ashbourne Golf Club Ltd ASHBOURNE 185
Ashburnham Golf Club LLANELLI 472
Ashbury Hotel OKEHAMPTON 32
Ashby Decoy Golf Club SCUNTHORPE 204
Ashfield Golf Club CULLYHANNA 511
Ashford (Kent) Golf Club ASHFORD 92
Ashford Great Chart Golf & Leisure Complex ASHFORD 92, 566
Ashford Manor Golf Club ASHFORD 143
Ashley Wood Golf Club BLANDFORD 38
Ashridge Golf Club BERKHAMSTED 164
Ashton & Lea Golf Club Ltd. PRESTON 277
Ashton-in-Makerfield Golf Club Ltd ASHTON-IN-MAKERFIELD 281
Ashton-on-Mersey Golf Club SALE 288
Ashton-Under-Lyne Golf Club ASHTON-UNDER-LYNE 281
Ashwoods Golf Centre ENNISKILLEN 581
Askernish Golf Club LOCHBOISDALE 453
Aspley Guise and Woburn Sands Golf Club ASPLEY GUISE 149
Astbury Golf Club CONGLETON 250
Aston Wood Golf Club SUTTON COLDFIELD 239
Athenry Golf Club ATHENRY 532
Atherstone Golf Club ATHERSTONE 229
Athlone Golf Club ATHLONE 546
Auchenblae Golf Course AUCHENBLAE 346
Auchmill Golf Club ABERDEEN 343
Auchterarder Golf Club AUCHTERARDER 436
Auchterderran Golf Club CARDENDEN 404
Austin Lodge Golf Club EYNSFORD 96
Axe Cliff Golf Club AXMOUTH 26
Aylesbury Park Golf Club AYLESBURY 75, 560
Aylesbury Vale Golf Club LEIGHTON BUZZARD 150, 559

Baberton Golf Club EDINBURGH 394
Backworth Golf Club SHIREMOOR 304
Bacup Golf Club BACUP 270
Badgemore Park Golf Club HENLEY-ON-THAMES 110
Baildon Golf Club BRADFORD 325
Bakewell Golf Club BAKEWELL 185
Bala Golf Club BALA 458
Balbirnie Park Golf Club MARKINCH 410
Balbriggan Golf Club BALBRIGGAN 528
Balcarrick Golf Club DONABATE 528
Balfron Golf Society BALFRON 448
Balgove Course ST ANDREWS 412
Ballachulish House Golf Course BALLACHULISH 365
Ballards Gore Golf and Country Club ROCHFORD 161
Ballater Golf Club BALLATER 348
Ballina Golf Club BALLINA 543
Ballinamore Golf Club BALLINAMORE 541
Ballinasloe Golf Club BALLINASLOE 532
Ballinrobe Golf Club BALLINROBE 543
Ballochmyle Golf Club MAUCHLINE 373
Ballumbie Castle Golf Club DUNDEE 361, 577
Ballybunion Golf Club BALLYBUNION 534
Ballycastle Golf Club BALLYCASTLE 507
Ballyclare Golf Club BALLYCLARE 507
Ballyearl Golf and Leisure Centre NEWTOWNABBEY 509, 580
Ballykisteen Golf and Country Club MONARD 548
Ballyliffin Golf Club BALLYLIFFIN 526
Ballymena Golf Club BALLYMENA 507
Ballymote Golf Club BALLYMOTE 547
Balmoral Golf Club Ltd BELFAST 512
Balmore Golf Club GLASGOW 415
Balnagask Golf Course ABERDEEN 343
Baltinglass Golf Club BALTINGLASS 550
Bamburgh Castle Golf Club BAMBURGH 296
Banbridge Golf Club BANBRIDGE 512
Banbury Golf Club BANBURY 108
Banchory Golf Club BANCHORY 346
Bandon Golf Club BANDON 523
Bangor Golf Club BANGOR 512
Bannel Golf Driving Range CHESTER 579
Banstead Downs Golf Club SUTTON 124

THE GOLF GUIDE 2011 — INDEX OF CLUBS & COURSES 585

Bantry Bay Golf Club BANTRY 523
Bargoed Golf Club BARGOED 481
Barkway Park Golf Club BARKWAY 164
Barlaston Golf Club BARLASTON 224
Barnard Castle Golf Club BARNARD CASTLE 265
Barnehurst Public Pay & Play Golf Course BEXLEYHEATH 69
Barnham Broom Hotel, Golf & Spa NORWICH 175
Barnsley Golf Club BARNSLEY 320
Baron Hill Golf Club Ltd ANGLESEY 458
Barrow Golf Club BARROW-IN-FURNESS 257
Barrow Hills Golf Club CHERTSEY 116
Barshaw Golf Club PAISLEY 447
Barton-on-Sea Golf Club BARTON-ON-SEA 82
Basildon Golf Club BASILDON 156
Basingstoke Golf Club BASINGSTOKE 82
Batchwood Golf and Tennis Centre ST ALBANS 168
Batchworth Park Golf Club RICKMANSWORTH 167
Bath Golf Club BATH 53
Bathgate Golf Club BATHGATE 392
Battle Golf Club BATTLE 126
Bawburgh Golf Club NORWICH 175
Bawtry Golf Club DONCASTER 320, 576
Baxenden & District Golf Club BAXENDEN 270
Beacon Park Golf Club UPHOLLAND 280
Beaconsfield Golf Club BEACONSFIELD 75
Beadlow Manor Hotel, Golf & Country Club BEADLOW 149
Beamish Park Golf Club BEAMISH 265
Bearsden Golf Club GLASGOW 415
Bearsted Golf Club MAIDSTONE 100
Bearwood Golf Club SINDLESHAM 73
Bearwood Lakes Golf Club WOKINGHAM 74
Beau Desert Golf Club CANNOCK 224
Beauchief Golf Club SHEFFIELD 323
Beaufort Golf Club KILLARNEY 535
Beauport Park Golf Course Ltd HASTINGS 131
Beaverstown Golf Club DONABATE 528
Beccles Golf Club BECCLES 179
Beckenham Place Park Golf Club BECKENHAM 92
Bedale Golf Club BEDALE 311
Bedford and County Golf Club BEDFORD 149
Bedford Golf Club BEDFORD 149
Bedfordshire Golf Club BEDFORD 149
Bedlingtonshire Golf Club BEDLINGTON 296
Beech Park Golf Club RATHCOOLE 530
Beedles Lake Golf Centre EAST GOSCOTE 194
Beeston Fields Golf Club NOTTINGHAM 216
Beith Golf Club BEITH 370
Belfairs Golf Club LEIGH-ON-SEA 160
Belford, The BELFORD 296
Belfry, The WISHAW 240
Belhus Park Golf Club OCKENDON 161
Belleisle Golf Course AYR 369
Bellingham Golf Club BELLINGHAM 298
Bellshill Golf Club BELLSHILL 432
Belmont Lodge and Golf BELMONT 190
Belton Park Golf Club GRANTHAM 201
Belturbet Golf Club BELTURBET 521
Belvoir Park Golf Club BELFAST 512
Ben Rhydding Golf Club ILKLEY 329
Benone Golf Course LIMAVADY 515
Bentham Golf Club BENTHAM 311
Bentley Golf Club BRENTWOOD 156
Benton Hall Golf Club WITHAM 163
Berehaven Golf Club and Amenity Park CASTLETOWNBERE 523
Berkhamsted Golf Club BERKHAMSTED 164
Berkshire Golf Club ASCOT 71
Berwick Upon Tweed (Goswick Golf Club) BERWICK-UPON-TWEED 298
Best Western Ufford Park Hotel Golf & Spa WOODBRIDGE 182
Betchworth Park Golf Club DORKING 118
Betws-y-Coed Golf Club BETWS-Y-COED 463
Beverley and East Riding Golf Club BEVERLEY 306
Bexleyheath Golf Club BEXLEYHEATH 94
Bicester Country Club BICESTER 108
Bidford Grange Golf Club BIDFORD 229
Bidston Golf Club Ltd BIDSTON 290
Bigbury Golf Club Ltd. BIGBURY 26
Biggar Golf Club BIGGAR 432
Billingham Golf Club BILLINGHAM 265
Bingley (St. Ives) Golf Club BINGLEY 325
Birch Grove Golf Club COLCHESTER 158
Birch Hall Golf Club CHESTERFIELD 186
Birchwood Golf Club WARRINGTON 256
Bird Hills (UK) Ltd MAIDENHEAD 72, 560

INDEX OF CLUBS & COURSES

Birley Wood Golf Club SHEFFIELD 323
Birr Golf Club BIRR 546
Birstall Golf Club BIRSTALL 193
Birtley Golf Club BIRTLEY 302
Bishop Auckland Golf Club BISHOP AUCKLAND 265
Bishopbriggs Golf Club BISHOPBRIGGS 414
Bishop's Stortford Golf Club BISHOP'S STORTFORD 164
Bishopshire Golf Club KINNESSWOOD 442
Bishopswood Golf Course LLP BASINGSTOKE 82
Blaby Golf Centre BLABY 193
Black Bush Golf Club DUNSHAUGHLIN 544
Blackburn Golf Centre and Driving Range BLACKBURN 567
Blackburn Golf Club BLACKBURN 270
Blackley Golf Club MANCHESTER 284
Blacklion Golf Club BLACKLION 521
Blackmoor Golf Club BORDON 84
Blacknest Golf & Country Club ALTON 81
Blackpool North Shore Golf Club BLACKPOOL 271
Blackpool Park Golf Club BLACKPOOL 271
Blackwater Valley Golf Centre YATELEY 126
Blackwell Golf Club BLACKWELL 243
Blackwell Grange Golf Club DARLINGTON 266
Blackwood Golf Centre BANGOR 512
Blackwood Golf Club BLACKWOOD 482
Blainroe Golf Club BLAINROE 550
Blair Atholl Golf Club BLAIR ATHOLL 436
Blairbeth Golf Club GLASGOW 415
Blairgowrie Golf Club BLAIRGOWRIE 438
Blairmore and Strone Golf Club DUNOON 366
Blankney Golf Club BLANKNEY 199
Blarney Golf Resort BLARNEY 523
Bletchingley Golf Club BLETCHINGLEY 114
Bloxwich Golf Club (1988) Ltd WALSALL 239
Blue Mountain Golf Centre BINFIELD 71, 560
Blundells Hill Golf Club RAINHILL 293
Blyth Golf Club Ltd. BLYTH 298
Boat of Garten Golf and Tennis Club BOAT OF GARTEN 428
Bodenstown Golf Club SALLINS 539
Bognor Regis Golf Club BOGNOR REGIS 133
Boldmere Golf Club SUTTON COLDFIELD 239
Boldon Golf Club Ltd. EAST BOLDON 302
Bolton Golf Club Ltd. BOLTON 281

Bolton Old Links Golf Club Ltd BOLTON 282
Bolton Open Golf Course BOLTON 272
Bon Accord Golf Club ABERDEEN 343
Bonar Bridge-Ardgay Golf Club BONAR BRIDGE 420
Bondhay Golf Club WORKSOP 218
Bonnybridge Golf Club FALKIRK 449
Bonnyton Golf Club GLASGOW 415
Boothferry Golf Club HOWDEN 307
Bootle Golf Club BOOTLE 291
Borris Golf Club BORRIS 519
Borth and Ynyslas Golf Club Ltd BORTH 474
Boston Golf Club. BOSTON 200
Boston West Golf Club BOSTON 200
Bothwell Castle Golf Club GLASGOW 415
Botley Park Golf Club SOUTHAMPTON 89
Boughton Golf Club FAVERSHAM 97
Bovey Castle MORETONHAMPSTEAD 30
Bowenhurst Golf Centre Ltd CRONDALL 117
Bowood Hotel, Spa & Golf Resort CALNE 61, 574
Bowood Park Hotel & Golf Course CAMELFORD 17
Bowring Municipal HUYTON 292
Boxmoor Golf Club HEMEL HEMPSTEAD 166
Boyce Hill Golf Club Ltd BENFLEET 156
Bracken Ghyll Golf Club ILKLEY 329
Brackenwood Golf Club WIRRAL 295
Brackley Golf Club SALFORD 288
Bradford Golf Club, The GUISELEY 328
Bradford Moor Golf Club BRADFORD 326
Bradley Park Municipal Golf Course HUDDERSFIELD 328
Braehead Golf Club ALLOA 448
Braemar Golf Club BRAEMAR 348
Braeside Golf Club BECKENHAM 92
Braid Hills Golf Course EDINBURGH 394, 577
Brailsford Golf Centre BRAILSFORD 185, 562
Braintree Golf Club BRAINTREE 156
Bramall Park Golf Club STOCKPORT 288
Bramcote Waters Golf Course NUNEATON 230
Bramhall Golf Club STOCKPORT 288
Bramley Golf Club GUILDFORD 120
Brampton Golf Club BRAMPTON 258, 562
Brampton Heath Golf Centre NORTHAMPTON 210, 569
Brampton Park Golf Club HUNTINGDON 153

Bramshaw Golf Club LYNDHURST 86
Brancepeth Castle Golf Club BRANCEPETH 266
Brandhall Golf Club BIRMINGHAM 233
Bransford Golf Club BRANSFORD 244
Branshaw Golf Club KEIGHLEY 330
Branston Golf & Country Club BURTON-ON-TRENT 224
Braxted Park Golf Club WITHAM 163
Bray Golf Club BRAY 550
Brayton Park Golf Club ASPATRIA 257
Brean Golf Club at Brean Leisure Park BURNHAM-ON-SEA 55
Brechin Golf and Squash Club BRECHIN 358
Brecon Golf Club BRECON 478
Breightmet Golf Club BOLTON 282
Brent Valley Golf Club HANWELL 145
Brett Vale Golf Club RAYDON 181
Brickendon Grange Golf Club HERTFORD 166
Brickhampton Court Golf Complex CHELTENHAM 47, 564
Bridge of Allan Golf Club STIRLING 450
Bridgend & District Golf Club LINLITHGOW 400
Bridgnorth Golf Club BRIDGNORTH 220
Bridlington Golf Club BRIDLINGTON 306
Bridlington Links, The BRIDLINGTON 306
Bridport & West Dorset Golf Club BRIDPORT 40
Briggens Park Golf Club WARE 169
Brighouse Bay Golf Club & Driving Range KIRKCUDBRIGHT 386
Bright Castle Golf Club DOWNPATRICK 513
Brighton and Hove Golf Club BRIGHTON 127
Bristol and Clifton Golf Club BRISTOL 45
Bristol Golf Centre BRISTOL 564
Broadstone (Dorset) Golf Club BROADSTONE 40
Broadwater Park Golf Club GODALMING 572
Broadway Golf Club BROADWAY 47
Brocket Hall Golf Club WELWYN GARDEN CITY 169
Brocton Hall Golf Club STAFFORD 225
Brodick Golf Club BRODICK 378
Broke Hill Golf Club HALSTEAD 98
Brokenhurst Manor Golf Club BROCKENHURST 84
Bromborough Golf Club BROMBOROUGH 291
Bromley Golf Centre BROMLEY 69
Bromsgrove Golf Centre BROMSGROVE 244, 574
Brookdale Golf Club Ltd. MANCHESTER 284

Brookmans Park Golf Club HATFIELD 166
Broome Manor Golf Complex SWINDON 63, 574
Broome Park Golf club CANTERBURY 94
Broomieknowe Golf Club Ltd BONNYRIGG 392
Brora Golf Club BRORA 419
Brough Golf Club BROUGH 306
Broughty Golf Club MONIFIETH 364
Brown Trout Golf and Country Club COLERAINE 515
Brucefields Family Golf Centre STIRLING 450
Brunston Castle Golf Course DAILLY 370, 577
Bruntsfield Links Golfing Society Ltd EDINBURGH 394
Bryn Meadows Golf Club HENGOED 488
Bryn Morfydd Hotel Golf Club DENBIGH 464
Brynhill (Barry) Golf Club BARRY 482
Buchanan Castle Golf Club GLASGOW 415
Buckingham Golf Club BUCKINGHAM 76
Buckinghamshire Golf Club DENHAM 76
Buckpool Golf Club (Buckie) BUCKIE 350
Bude and North Cornwall Golf Club BUDE 17
Budock Vean Golf and Country House Hotel FALMOUTH 18
Builth Wells Golf Club BUILTH WELLS 478
Bulbury Woods Golf Club POOLE 42
Bull Bay Golf Club Ltd. ANGLESEY 458
Bullpits Golf Course BOURTON 38
Bulwell Forest Golf Club BULWELL 214
Buncrana Golf Club BUNCRANA 526
Bundoran Golf Club BUNDORAN 526
Bungay and Waveney Valley Golf Club BUNGAY 179
Bunsay Downs Golf Club MALDON 160
Burford Golf Club BURFORD 109
Burgess Hill Golf Academy BURGESS HILL 135, 573
Burgham Park Golf & Leisure Club MORPETH 300
Burghill Valley Golf Club HEREFORD 190
Burghley Park Golf Club STAMFORD 206
Burhill Golf Club WALTON-ON-THAMES 124
Burley Golf Club RINGWOOD 88
Burnham and Berrow Golf Club BURNHAM-ON-SEA 56
Burnham Beeches Golf Club BURNHAM 76
Burnham-on-Crouch Golf Club Ltd BURNHAM-ON-CROUCH 157

INDEX OF CLUBS & COURSES

Burnley Golf Club BURNLEY 272
Burntisland Golf House Club BURNTISLAND 404
Burslem Golf Club Ltd. STOKE-ON-TRENT 226
Burstead Golf Club LITTLE BURSTEAD 160
Burstwick Country Golf HULL 308
Burton-on-Trent Golf Club BURTON-ON-TRENT 186
Bury Golf Club BURY 283
Bury St. Edmunds Golf Club BURY ST. EDMUNDS 179
Bush Hill Park Golf Club WINCHMORE HILL 148
Bushey Golf & Country Club BUSHEY 165
Bushey Hall Golf Club BUSHEY 165
Bushfoot Golf Club PORTBALLINTRAE 509
Bute Golf Club ISLE OF BUTE 366
Buxton and High Peak Golf Club BUXTON 186
Caddington Golf Club CADDINGTON 149
Cadmore Lodge Golf & Country Club TENBURY WELLS 246
Caerleon Public Golf Course CAERLEON 484
Caerphilly Golf Club CAERPHILLY 484
Cahir Park Golf Club CAHIR 547
Caird Park Golf Club DUNDEE 361
Cairndhu Golf Club Ltd. LARNE 509
Calcot Park Golf Club READING 73
Caldecott Hall Golf Club & Hotel GREAT YARMOUTH 171
Calderbraes Golf Club UDDINGSTON 435
Calderfields Golf Club WALSALL 240
Caldwell Golf Club UPLAWMOOR 447
Caldy Golf Club Ltd CALDY 291
Caledonian Golf Club ABERDEEN 344
Callan Golf Club CALLAN 540
Callander Golf Club CALLANDER 448
Cally Palace Hotel GATEHOUSE OF FLEET 386
Calverley Golf Club LEEDS 330
Camberley Heath Golf Club CAMBERLEY 114
Cambridge Golf Club CAMBRIDGE 152, 561
Cambridge Medidian Golf Club CAMBRIDGE 152
Cambuslang Golf Club GLASGOW 415
Came Down Golf Club DORCHESTER 40
Camperdown Golf Club DUNDEE 361
Campsie Golf Club LENNOXTOWN 449
Cams Hall Estate Golf Club FAREHAM 85
Canford Magna Golf Club WIMBORNE 44

Canford School Golf Club WIMBORNE 44
Canmore Golf Club DUNFERMLINE 405
Cannington Golf Course BRIDGWATER 54
Cannock Park Golf Club CANNOCK 224
Canons Brook Golf Club HARLOW 159
Canterbury Golf Club CANTERBURY 94
Canwick Park Golf Club LINCOLN 203
Cape Cornwall Golf and Country Club PENZANCE 21
Caprington Golf Club KILMARNOCK 372
Carden Park Hotel, Golf Resort and Spa CHESTER 250, 561
Cardiff Golf Club CARDIFF 484
Cardigan Golf Club CARDIGAN 474
Cardross Golf Club CARDROSS 390
Carholme Golf Club LINCOLN 203
Carlisle Golf Club CARLISLE 258
Carlow Golf Club CARLOW 519
Carluke Golf Club CARLUKE 432
Carlyon Bay Hotel Golf Course CARLYON BAY 17
Carmarthen Golf Club CARMARTHEN 470
Carnalea Golf Club BANGOR 512
Carne Golf Links BELMULLET 543
Carnegie Golf Club at Skibo Castle DORNOCH 420
Carnoustie Golf Links CARNOUSTIE 361
Carnwath Golf Club CARNWATH 432
Carradale Golf Club CARRADALE 366
Carrbridge Golf Club CARRBRIDGE 428
Carrick Knowe Golf Course EDINBURGH 394
Carrickfergus Golf Club CARRICKFERGUS 508
Carrick-on-Shannon Golf Club CARRICK-ON-SHANNON 546
Carrick-on-Suir Golf Club CARRICK-ON-SUIR 547
Carswell Golf and Country Club FARINGDON 109
Carton House MAYNOOTH 537
Carus Green Golf Club KENDAL 259
Carvynick Golf and Country Club NEWQUAY 20
Castell Heights Golf Club CAERPHILLY 484
Casterton Golf Course KIRKBY LONSDALE 260
Castle Barna Golf Club OFFALY 546
Castle Course ST ANDREWS 412
Castle Dargan Estate SLIGO 547
Castle Douglas Golf Club CASTLE DOUGLAS 383
Castle Eden Golf Club HARTLEPOOL 267

Castle Hawk Golf Club ROCHDALE 287, 568
Castle Hume Golf Club ENNISKILLEN 515
Castle Park Golf Club HADDINGTON 398
Castle Point Golf Club CANVEY ISLAND 157
Castle Stuart Golf Links INVERNESS 428
Castlebar Golf Club CASTLEBAR 543
Castleblayney Golf Club CASTLEBLAYNEY 545
Castlecomer Golf Club CASTLECOMER 540
Castlefields Golf Club BRIGHOUSE 327
Castlegregory Golf Club CASTLEGREGORY 534
Castlereagh Hills Golf Club BELFAST 507
Castlerock Golf Club CASTLEROCK 515
Castletown Golf Links CASTLETOWN 555
Castletroy Golf Club CASTLETROY 542
Castlewarden Golf & Country Club STRAFFAN 539
Cathcart Castle Golf Club GLASGOW 415
Cathkin Braes Golf Club GLASGOW 415
Catterick Golf Club CATTERICK 312
Cave Castle Golf Club BROUGH 306
Cavendish Golf Club Ltd BUXTON 186
Cawder Golf Club GLASGOW 415
Cawdor Castle Golf Course CAWDOR CASTLE 428
Celtic Manor Resort NEWPORT 491
Central London Golf Centre WANDSWORTH 148
Chadwell Springs Golf Club WARE 169
Chalgrave Manor Golf Club TODDINGTON 151
Channels Golf Club CHELMSFORD 157
Chapel-en-le-Frith CHAPEL-EN-LE-FRITH 186
Charlesland Golf Club GREYSTONES 552
Charleton Golf Club COLINSBURGH 404
Charleville Golf Club CHARLEVILLE 523
Charminster Golf Club DORCHESTER 40
Charnock Richard Golf & Country Club CHORLEY 272
Charnwood Forest Golf Club LOUGHBOROUGH 196
Chart Hills Golf Club ASHFORD 92
Chartham Park Golf Club EAST GRINSTEAD 136
Chartridge Park Golf Club CHESHAM 76
Chase Golf Club PENKRIDGE 225
Chatham Golf Centre CHATHAM 566
Cheadle Golf Club CHEADLE 249
Chedington Court Golf Club SOUTH PERROTT 42
Chelmsford Golf Club CHELMSFORD 157
Chelsfield Lakes Golf Centre ORPINGTON 100

Cherry Burton Golf Club BEVERLEY 306, 575
Cherry Lodge Golf Club BIGGIN HILL 94
Cherwell Edge Golf Club BANBURY 108
Chesfield Downs Golf Club HITCHIN 167
Chesham and Ley Hill Golf Club CHESHAM 76
Cheshunt Golf Club WALTHAM CROSS 168
Chessington Golf Centre CHESSINGTON 116, 571
Chester Golf Club CHESTER 250
Chesterfield Golf Club Ltd. CHESTERFIELD 186
Chester-Le-Street Golf Club CHESTER-LE-STREET 266
Chesterton Valley Golf Club BRIDGNORTH 220
Chestfield (Whitstable) Golf Club WHITSTABLE 107
Chevin Golf Club DUFFIELD 187
Chichester Golf Club CHICHESTER 135, 573
Chigwell Golf Club CHIGWELL 158
Childwall Golf Club Ltd LIVERPOOL 292
Chiltern Forest Golf Club AYLESBURY 75
Chilwell Manor Golf Club NOTTINGHAM 216
Chilworth Golf Club SOUTHAMPTON 89, 565
China Fleet Country Club SALTASH 22, 562
Chingford Golf Club CHINGFORD 143, 559
Chippenham Golf Club CHIPPENHAM 61
Chipping Norton Golf Club CHIPPING NORTON 109
Chipping Sodbury Golf Club BRISTOL 45
Chipstead Golf Club Ltd CHIPSTEAD 116
Chirk Golf Club CHIRK 463
Chislehurst Golf Club CHISLEHURST 95
Chobham Golf Club WOKING 125
Chorley Golf Club CHORLEY 272
Chorleywood Golf Club Ltd. CHORLEYWOOD 165
Chorlton-cum-Hardy Golf Club MANCHESTER 284
Chulmleigh Golf Course CHULMLEIGH 27
Church Stretton Golf Club CHURCH STRETTON 220
Churchill & Blakedown Golf Club BLAKEDOWN 243
Churston Golf Club Ltd BRIXHAM 26
Cilgwyn Golf Club LAMPETER 474
Cirencester Golf Club CIRENCESTER 48
City of Coventry Brandon Wood Golf Course COVENTRY 229
City of Derry Golf Club PREHEN 516
City of Edinburgh Golf Club EDINBURGH 394
City Of Newcastle Golf Club NEWCASTLE UPON TYNE 33

INDEX OF CLUBS & COURSES

City of Wakefield Golf Club WAKEFIELD 334
Clacton-on-Sea Golf Club CLACTON-ON-SEA 158
Clandeboye Golf Club NEWTOWNARDS 514
Clandon Regis Golf Club Ltd WEST CLANDON 125
Claremorris Golf Club CLAREMORRIS 543
Clayton Golf Club BRADFORD 326
Cleckheaton and District Golf Club Ltd CLECKHEATON 327
Cleethorpes Golf Club (1894) Ltd CLEETHORPES 201
Cleeve Hill Golf Club CHELTENHAM 48
Cleobury Mortimer Golf Club CLEOBURY MORTIMER 220
Clevedon Golf Club CLEVEDON 56
Cleveland Golf Club REDCAR 314
Cliftonville Golf Club BELFAST 507
Clitheroe Golf Club CLITHEROE 273
Clober Golf Club GLASGOW 416
Clones Golf Club CLONES 545
Clonlara Golf & Leisure CLONLARA 522
Clonmel Golf Club CLONMEL 548
Close House Hotel & Golf HEDDON ON THE WALL 302
Club at Mapledurham MAPLEDURHAM 110
Clwb Golff Abersoch ABERSOCH 458
Clwb Golff Ffestiniog FFESTINIOG 460
Clydebank & District Golf Club CLYDEBANK 390
Clydebank Municipal Golf Course CLYDEBANK 390
Clydeway Golf Centre UDDINGSTON 578
Clyne Golf Club SWANSEA 496
Co. Tipperary Golf & Country Club DUNDRUM 548
Cobh Golf Club COBH 524
Cobtree Manor Park Golf Club MAIDSTONE 100
Cochrane Castle Golf Club JOHNSTONE 446
Cockermouth Golf Club EMBLETON 258
Cocks Moors Woods Golf Club BIRMINGHAM 233
Coed-Y-Mwstwr Golf Club BRIDGEND 484
Colchester Golf Club COLCHESTER 158
Colchester Golf Range COLCHESTER 563
Cold Ashby Golf Club NORTHAMPTON 210
College Pines Golf Club WORKSOP 218
Collingtree Park Golf Course Ltd NORTHAMPTON 210
Colmworth and North Bedfordshire Golf Club COLMWORTH 150

Colnbrook Golf Range COLNBROOK 560
Colne Golf Club COLNE 273
Colne Valley Golf Club COLCHESTER 158
Colonsay Golf Club ISLE OF COLONSAY 451
Colvend Golf Club DALBEATTIE 384
Colville Park Golf Club MOTHERWELL 434
Colworth Golf Club SHARNBROOK 151
Comrie Golf Club CRIEFF 440
Concord Park Driving Range SHEFFIELD 576
Concord Park Municipal Golf Course SHEFFIELD 323
Congleton Golf Club CONGLETON 251
Connemara Golf Club CLIFDEN 532
Connemara Isles Golf Club ANNAGHVANE 532
Consett & District Golf Club Ltd CONSETT 266
Conwy (Caernarvonshire) Golf Club CONWY 464
Cooden Beach Golf Club BEXHILL-ON-SEA 127
Cookridge Hall Golf Club LEEDS 330, 576
Coollattin Golf Club ARKLOW 550
Coombe Hill Golf Club KINGSTON-UPON-THAMES 121
Coombe Wood Golf Club KINGSTON-UPON-THAMES 121
Coosheen Golf CLub SCHULL 525
Copsewood Grange Golf Club COVENTRY 236
Copt Heath Golf Club SOLIHULL 238
Copthorne Golf Club CRAWLEY 135
Corballis Golf Links DONABATE 528
Corhampton Golf Club SOUTHAMPTON 89
Cork Golf Club LITTLE ISLAND 524
Corrie Golf Club CORRIE 378
Corrstown Golf Club KILSALLAGHAN 530
Corus (Port Talbot) PORT TALBOT 493
Cosby Golf Club COSBY 194
Costessey Park Golf Course NORWICH 176
Cotgrave Place Golf & Country Club NOTTINGHAM 216, 569
Cotswold Edge Golf Club WOTTON-UNDER-EDGE 51
Cotswold Hills Golf Club CHELTENHAM 48
Cottesmore Golf & Country Club CRAWLEY 136
Cottingham Parks Golf and Country Club HULL 307
Cottrell Park Golf Club CARDIFF 485
Coulsdon Manor Hotel & Golf Centre COULSDON 116

INDEX OF CLUBS & COURSES

County Armagh Golf Club ARMAGH 511
County Cavan Golf Club CAVAN 521
County Longford Golf Club LONGFORD 542
County Louth Golf Club DROGHEDA 542
County Sligo Golf Club ROSSES POINT 547
Coventry Golf Club COVENTRY 236
Coventry Hearsall Golf Club COVENTRY 236
Cowal Golf Club DUNOON 366
Cowdenbeath Golf Club COWDENBEATH 405
Cowdray Park Golf Club COWDRAY PARK 135
Cowes Golf Club COWES 91
Cowglen Golf Club GLASGOW 416
Coxmoor Golf Club MANSFIELD 215
Craddockstown Golf Club NAAS 537
Cradoc Golf Club CRADOC 478, 579
Craggan Golf Club GRANTOWN-ON-SPEY 353
Craibstone Golf Centre BUCKSBURN 350
Craigavon Golf and Ski Club CRAIGAVON 511, 580
Craigentinny Golf Course EDINBURGH 394
Craigie Hill Golf Club (1982) Ltd PERTH 443
Craigieknowes Golf Club KIPPFORD 386
Craigielaw Golf Club ABERLADY 392
Craigmillar Park Golf Club EDINBURGH 394
Craignure Golf Club CRAIGNURE 452
Crail Golfing Society CRAIL 405
Crane Valley Golf Club VERWOOD 42
Cranfield Golf at Sandown ESHER 119
Cranford Golf Centre STOCKPORT 561
Cranleigh Golf & Leisure Club CRANLEIGH 116
Cray Valley Golf Club ORPINGTON 100
Craythorne, The BURTON-ON-TRENT 224, 571
Creigiau Golf Club CARDIFF 485
Cretingham Golf Club FRAMLINGHAM 180
Crewe Golf Club Ltd CREWE 251
Crews Hill Golf Club (1920) Ltd ENFIELD 144
Criccieth Golf Club CRICCIETH 459
Crichton Golf Club DUMFRIES 384
Cricklade Hotel & Country Club CRICKLADE 62
Crieff Golf Club CRIEFF 438
Crimple Valley Golf Club HARROGATE 312
Croham Hurst Golf Club CROYDON 117
Crompton and Royton Golf Club Ltd OLDHAM 287
Crondon Park Golf Club STOCK 162

Crook Golf Club CROOK 266
Crookhill Park (Municipal) Golf Club DONCASTER 320
Crosland Heath Golf Club Ltd HUDDERSFIELD 329
Crow Nest Park Golf Club BRIGHOUSE 327
Crow Wood Golf Club GLASGOW 416
Crowborough Beacon Golf Club CROWBOROUGH 128
Cruden Bay Golf Club CRUDEN BAY 350
Cruit Island Golf Club KINCASSLAGH 526
Cuckfield Golf Centre CUCKFIELD 136
Cuddington (Banstead) Golf Club Ltd BANSTEAD 114
Culcrieff Golf Club CRIEFF 440
Cullen Golf Club CULLEN 350
Cumberwell Park Golf Club BRADFORD-ON-AVON 61
Cupar Golf Club CUPAR 405
Curragh Golf Club CURRAGH 537
Cushendall Golf Club CUSHENDALL 508
Cwmrhydneuadd Golf Club LLANDYSUL 474
Dainton Park Golf Club NEWTON ABOTT 32
Dalbeattie Golf Club DALBEATTIE 384
Dale Hill Golf Club WADHURST 132
Dalmally Golf Club DALMALLY 366
Dalmilling Golf Course AYR 369
Dalmunzie Golf Course BLAIRGOWRIE 438
Dalston Hall Golf Club Holiday Park CARLISLE 258
Dalziel Park Golf & Country Club MOTHERWELL 435
Darenth Valley Golf Course Ltd SEVENOAKS 104
Darlington Golf Club (Members) Ltd DARLINGTON 267
Dartford Golf Club Ltd DARTFORD 95
Dartmouth Golf & Country Club DARTMOUTH 27
Dartmouth Golf Club WEST BROMWICH 240
Darwen Golf Club DARWEN 274
Datchet Golf Club SLOUGH 74
Davenport Golf Club POYNTON 254
Daventry and District Golf Club DAVENTRY 209
Davyhulme Park Golf Club DAVYHULME 283
Dawn Till Dusk Golf Club MILFORD HAVEN 475
De Vere Belton Woods Hotel GRANTHAM 201
De Vere Dunston Hall NORWICH 176
De Vere Heron's Reach Golf Club BLACKPOOL 271, 567

INDEX OF CLUBS & COURSES

De Vere Mottram Hall Golf Course PRESTBURY 254
De Vere Slaley Hall Hotel Golf Resort & Spa NEWCASTLE UPON TYNE 300
Dean Farm Golf Course BORDON 84
Dean Wood Golf Club UPHOLLAND 280
Deane Golf Club BOLTON 282
Deangate Ridge Golf Club DEANGATE 96
Deanwood Park Golf Club NEWBURY 72
Deer Park Golf & Country Club LIVINGSTON 400
Deer Park Golf Hotel & Spa DUBLIN 529
Deeside Golf Club ABERDEEN 344
Delamere Forest Golf Club NORTHWICH 254
Delapre Golf Centre NORTHAMPTON 210, 569
Delgany Golf Club DELGANY 551
Denbigh Golf Club DENBIGH 464
Denham Golf Club DENHAM 77
Denton Golf Club DENTON 283
Derby Golf Club DERBY 187
Dereham Golf Club DEREHAM 171
Derllys Court Golf Club CARMARTHEN 470
Dewlands Manor Golf Course ROTHERFIELD 131
Dewsbury District Golf Club DEWSBURY 327
Dewstow Golf Club CHEPSTOW 486, 580
Dibden Golf Centre DIBDEN 84
Didsbury Golf Club Ltd MANCHESTER 285
Dinas Powis Golf Club DINAS POWIS 488
Dingle Golf Links/Ceann Sibeal BALLYFERRITER 534
Dinsdale Spa Golf Club DARLINGTON 267
Discovery Golf Centre COALVILLE 567
Disley Golf Club Ltd DISLEY 251
Diss Golf Club DISS 171, 179
Dolgellau Golf Club DOLGELLAU 459
Dollar Golf Club DOLLAR 449
Donabate Golf Club BALCARRICK 528
Donaghadee Golf Club DONAGHADEE 513
Doncaster Golf Club DONCASTER 320
Doncaster Town Moor Golf Club DONCASTER 321
Donegal Golf Club DONEGAL 526
Doneraile Golf Club DONERAILE 524
Donnington Grove Country Club NEWBURY 72
Donnington Valley Hotel & Golf Club NEWBURY 72
Dooks Golf Links GLENBEIGH 534
Doon Valley Golf Club PATNA 373

Doonbeg Golf Club DOONBEG 522
Dora Golf Course COWDENBEATH 405
Dore and Totley Golf Club SHEFFIELD 323
Dorking Golf Club DORKING 118
Dorset Golf & Country Club WAREHAM 43
Douglas Golf Club DOUGLAS 524
Douglas Golf Club DOUGLAS (IOM) 555
Douglas Park Golf Club GLASGOW 416
Douglas Valley Golf Club BOLTON 272
Douglas Water Golf Club DOUGLAS WATER 432
Down Royal Park Golf Course MAZE 509
Downes Crediton Golf Club CREDITON 27
Downfield Golf Club DUNDEE 362
Downpatrick Golf Club DOWNPATRICK 513
Downshire Golf Complex WOKINGHAM 560
Drayton Park Golf Club TAMWORTH 227
Drayton Park Golf Course DRAYTON 109, 569
Driffield Golf Club DRIFFIELD 307
Drift Golf Club EAST HORSLEY 118
Droitwich Golf & Country Club Ltd DROITWICH 244
Dromoland Castle Golf & Country Club NEWMARKET-ON-FERGUS 522
Druids Glen Golf Club NEWTOWNMOUNTKENNEDY 553
Druids Heath Golf Club NEWTOWNMOUNTKENNEDY 553
Druids Heath Golf Club WALSALL 240
Drumoig Golf Hotel ST ANDREWS 412
Drumpellier Golf Club COATBRIDGE 432
Dublin City Golf Club DUBLIN 529
Duddingston Golf Club Ltd EDINBURGH 395
Dudley Golf Club LIVERPOOL 292
Dudley Golf Club Ltd DUDLEY 237
Dudmoor Farm Golf Course CHRISTCHURCH 40
Dudsbury Golf Club FERNDOWN 40
Duff House Royal Golf Club BANFF 348
Dufftown Golf Club DUFFTOWN 350
Duke's, The ST ANDREWS 412
Dukes Meadows Golf & Tennis LONDON 146, 559
Dukinfield Golf Club DUKINFIELD 283
Dullatur Golf Club GLASGOW 416
Dulwich & Sydenham Hill Golf Club DULWICH 69
Dumbarton Golf Club DUMBARTON 390
Dumfries & Galloway Golf Club DUMFRIES 384

Dumfries and County Golf Club DUMFRIES 384
Dumfriesshire, The DUMFRIES 384
Dummer Golf Club BASINGSTOKE 84
Dun Laoghaire Golf Club DUN LAOGHAIRE 530
Dunaverty Golf Club SOUTHEND 368
Dunbar Golf Club DUNBAR 392
Dunblane New Golf Club DUNBLANE 440
Dundalk Golf Club DUNDALK 542
Dundas Parks Golf Club SOUTH QUEENSFERRY 402
Dunfanaghy Golf Club DUNFANAGHY 526
Dunfermline Golf Club DUNFERMLINE 406
Dungannon Golf Club DUNGANNON 517
Dungarvan Golf Club DUNGARVAN 548
Dunham Forest Golf & Country Club ALTRINCHAM 281
Dunkeld & Birnam Golf Club DUNKELD 441
Dunloe Golf Club KILLARNEY 535
Dunmore East Golf Club DUNMORE EAST 548
Dunmurry Golf Club BELFAST 508
Dunnerholme Golf Club ASKAM-IN-FURNESS 257
Dunnikier Park Golf Club KIRKCALDY 407
Dunning Golf Club DUNNING 441
Duns Golf Club DUNS 379
Dunscar Golf Club Ltd. BOLTON 282
Dunstable Downs Golf Club DUNSTABLE 150
Dunstanburgh Castle Golf Club EMBLETON 299
Dunwood Manor Golf Club ROMSEY 88
Durham City Golf Club DURHAM 267
Durness Golf Club DURNESS 420
Duxbury Park Golf Club (Municipal)CHORLEY 273
Dyke Golf Club BRIGHTON 127
Eagles Golf Club KING'S LYNN 175
Eaglescliffe Golf Club Ltd EAGLESCLIFFE 267
Ealing Golf Club GREENFORD 144
Ealing Golf Range LONDON 559
Earlsferry Thistle Golf Club ELIE 406
Earlswood Golf Club NEATH 491
Easingwold Golf Club EASINGWOLD 312
East Berkshire Golf Club CROWTHORNE 71
East Bierley Golf Club BRADFORD 326
East Brighton Golf Club BRIGHTON 127
East Cork Golf Club MIDLETON 525
East Devon Golf Club BUDLEIGH SALTERTON 26

East Herts Golf Club Ltd BUNTINGFORD 165
East Kilbride Golf Club GLASGOW 416
East Renfrewshire Golf Club GLASGOW 416
East Sussex National Golf Resort & Spa UCKFIELD 132
Eastbourne Downs Golf Club EASTBOURNE 130
Eastbourne Golfing Park EASTBOURNE 130
Easter Moffat Golf Club AIRDRIE 432
Eastham Lodge Golf Club EASTHAM 291
Eastwood Golf Club GLASGOW 416
Eaton (Norwich) Golf Club NORWICH 176
Eaton Golf Club CHESTER 250
Eccleston Park Golf Club RAINHILL 293
Eden Course ST ANDREWS 412
Eden Golf Course CARLISLE 258, 562
Edenderry Golf Club EDENDERRY 546
Edenmore Golf & Country Club CRAIGAVON 511
Edgbaston Golf Club Ltd BIRMINGHAM 233
Edinburgh Golf Club EDINBURGH 395
Edmondstown Golf Club DUBLIN 529
Edrich Driving Range and Old Nene Golf & Country Club HUNTINGDON 560
Edwalton Golf Courses EDWALTON 214
Edzell Golf Club EDZELL 362
Effingham Golf Club EFFINGHAM 119
Effingham Park Golf Club EFFINGHAM 137
Elderslie Golf Club ELDERSLIE 445
Elemore Golf Course HUTTON-LE-HOLE 302
Elfordleigh Hotel Golf & Leisure Club PLYMOUTH 32
Elgin Golf Club ELGIN 351
Elland Golf Club ELLAND 327
Ellesborough Golf Club AYLESBURY 75
Ellesmere Golf Club MANCHESTER 285
Ellesmere Port Golf Centre SOUTH WIRRAL 255
Elm Lodge Golf Course LUDLOW 220
Elm Park Golf and Sports Club DUBLIN 529
Elmwood CUPAR 405, 577
Elsenham Golf Centre ELSENHAM 159
Elsham Golf Club BRIGG 200
Elstree Golf and Country Club ELSTREE 165
Eltham Warren Golf Club ELTHAM 69
Elton Furze Golf Club PETERBOROUGH 154
Ely City Golf Course Ltd. ELY 153
Enderby Golf Course ENDERBY 195

INDEX OF CLUBS & COURSES

Enfield Golf Club ENFIELD 144
Enmore Park Golf Club BRIDGWATER 54
Ennis Golf Club ENNIS 522
Enniscorthy Golf Club ENNISCORTHY 550
Enniscrone Golf Club ENNISCRONE 547
Enniskillen Golf Club ENNISKILLEN 515
Entry Hill Golf Club BATH 53
Enville Golf Club Ltd STOURBRIDGE 227
Epping Golf Club EPPING 159
Epsom Golf Club EPSOM 119
Erewash Valley Golf Club Ltd ILKESTON 188
Erlestoke Golf Club DEVIZES 62
Erskine Golf Club BISHOPTON 445
Esker Hills Golf Club TULLAMORE 546
Esporta (Dougalston Golf Club) GLASGOW 416
Essex Golf & Country Club COLCHESTER 158, 564
Etchinghill Golf Club ETCHINGHILL 96
European Club BRITTAS BAY 551
Euxton Park Golf Centre CHORLEY 273
Evesham Golf Club EVESHAM 245
Exeter Golf & Country Club EXETER 28
Eyemouth Golf Club EYEMOUTH 379
Fairfield Golf and Sailing Club MANCHESTER 285
Fairhaven Golf Club LYTHAM ST ANNES 275
Fairlop Waters ILFORD 159, 564
Fairways Driving Range INVERNESS 578
Fairwood Park Golf Club Ltd. SWANSEA 496
Faithlegg Golf Club WATERFORD 549
Fakenham Golf Club FAKENHAM 171
Falkirk Golf Club FALKIRK 449
Falkirk Tryst Golf Club LARBERT 449
Falkland Golf Club FALKLAND 406
Falmouth Golf Club FALMOUTH 18
Farleigh Court Golf Club WARLINGHAM 124
Farnham Estate CAVAN 521
Farnham Golf Club Ltd FARNHAM 119
Farnham Park Pay and Play Golf Course SLOUGH 79
Farrington Golf & Country Club BATH/BRISTOL 54
Farthingstone Golf Club and Hotel TOWCESTER 212
Faversham Golf Club Ltd FAVERSHAM 97
Fawkham Valley Golf Club DARTFORD 95
Feldon Valley Golf Course BRAILES 229
Felixstowe Ferry Golf Club FELIXSTOWE 179
Feltwell Golf Club THETFORD 178
Fereneze Golf Club BARRHEAD 445
Fermoy Golf Club FERMOY 524
Ferndown Forest Golf Club FERNDOWN 41
Ferndown Golf Club FERNDOWN 41
Fernhill Golf & Country Club CARRIGALINE 523
Ferrybridge Golf Club KNOTTINGLEY 330
Filey Golf Club FILEY 312
Filton Golf Club BRISTOL 45
Finchley Golf Club FINCHLEY 144
Fingle Glen Hotel, Golf & Country Club EXETER 29
Fintona Golf Club FINTONA 517
Fishwick Hall Golf Club PRESTON 277
Five Lakes Resort MALDON 160, 564
Flackwell Heath Golf Club. HIGH WYCOMBE 77
Flamborough Head Golf Club BRIDLINGTON 307
Fleetlands Golf Club GOSPORT 85
Fleetwood Golf Club Ltd FLEETWOOD 274
Fleming Park Golf Course EASTLEIGH 85
Flempton Golf Club BURY ST EDMUNDS 179
Flint Golf Club FLINT 466
Flixton Golf Club MANCHESTER 285
Forest Hill Golf & Country Club BOTCHESTON 193, 567
Forest Hills Golf Club COLEFORD 48
Forest of Dean Golf Club COLEFORD 49
Forest of Galtres Golf Club YORK 316
Forest Park Golf Club YORK 317
Forest Pines Hotel & Golf Resort BRIGG 200
Forfar Golf Club FORFAR 362
Formby Golf Centre LIVERPOOL 568
Formby Golf Club FORMBY 291
Formby Ladies' Golf Club FORMBY 291
Forres Golf Club FORRES 352
Forrester Park Golf and Tennis Club MALDON 160
Forrester Park Resort DUNFERMLINE 406
Fort Augustus Golf Club FORT AUGUSTUS 428
Fort William Golf Club FORT WILLIAM 428
Fortrose and Rosemarkie Golf Club FORTROSE 424
Fortwilliam Golf Club BELFAST 508
Fosseway Golf Club and Best Western Centurion Hotel BATH 53
Fota Island Resort FOTA ISLAND 524, 581
Foulford Inn Golf Course CRIEFF 440

INDEX OF CLUBS & COURSES

Four Marks Golf Club FOUR MARKS 85
Foxbridge Golf Club BILLINGSHURST 133
Foxhills OTTERSHAW 123
Foyle International Golf Centre LONDONDERRY 516, 581
Fraserburgh Golf Club FRASERBURGH 353
Freshwater Bay Golf Club FRESHWATER 91
Frilford Heath Golf Club ABINGDON 108
Frinton Golf Club FRINTON-ON-SEA 159
Frodsham Golf Club FRODSHAM 251
Fulford (York) Golf Club Ltd. YORK 317
Fulford Heath Golf Club Ltd BIRMINGHAM 233
Fulneck Golf Club Ltd. PUDSEY 334
Fulwell Golf Club HAMPTON HILL 144
Furness Golf Club BARROW-IN-FURNESS 257
Furzeley Golf Club DENMEAD 84
Fynn Valley Golf Club IPSWICH 180, 571
Gainsborough Golf Club GAINSBOROUGH 201
Gairloch Golf Club GAIRLOCH 424
Galashiels Golf Club GALASHIELS 379
Galgorm Castle Golf Club BALLYMENA 507
Galway Bay Golf Resort ORANMORE 532
Galway Golf Club SALTHILL 532
Ganstead Park Golf Club CONISTON 306
Ganton Golf Club Ltd SCARBOROUGH 315
Garesfield Golf Club CHOPWELL 302
Garforth Golf Club Ltd. LEEDS 330
Garmouth & Kingston Golf Club FOCHABERS 352
Gatehouse of Fleet Golf Club GATEHOUSE OF FLEET 386
Gathurst Golf Club WIGAN 289
Gatley Golf Club Ltd. CHEADLE 249
Gatton Manor DORKING 118
Gaudet Luce Golf Club DROITWICH SPA 244
Gay Hill Golf Club BIRMINGHAM 233
Gedney Hill Golf Course SPALDING 206
George Washington Golf & Country Club WASHINGTON 305, 573
Gerrards Cross Golf Club GERRARDS CROSS 77
Ghyll Golf Club BARNOLDSWICK 311
Gifford Golf Club HADDINGTON 399
Gillingham Golf Club Ltd GILLINGHAM 97
Girton Golf Club CAMBRIDGE 152
Girvan Golf Course GIRVAN 371

Glamorganshire Golf Club PENARTH 492
Glasgow Golf Club GLASGOW 417
Glasgow Golf Club IRVINE 371
Glasson Hotel & Golf Club ATHLONE 549
Glebe Golf Club TRIM 545
Gleddoch Golf Club LANGBANK 447
Glen Golf Club NORTH BERWICK 401
Glen Gorse Golf Club OADBY 197
Glen of the Downs Golf Club DELGANY 551
Glenbervie Golf Club Ltd LARBERT 449
Glencorse Golf Club PENICUIK 402
Glencruitten Golf Club OBAN 366
Gleneagles Hotel Golf Courses AUCHTERARDER 436
Glengarriff Golf Club GLENGARRIFF 524
Glenisla Golf Centre ALYTH 436
Glenmalure Golf Club RATHDRUM 553
Glenrothes Golf Club GLENROTHES 406
Glossop and District Golf Club GLOSSOP 187
Glyn Abbey Golf Club KIDWELLY/LLANELLI 471
Glynhir Golf Club AMMANFORD 470
Glynneath Golf Club GLYNNEATH 488
Goal Farm Golf Course PIRBRIGHT 123
Godstone Golf Club GODSTONE 120
Gog Magog Golf Club CAMBRIDGE 152
Gold Coast Golf Club DUNGARVAN 548, 582
Goldenhill Golf Course STOKE-ON-TRENT 226
Golf at Goodwood CHICHESTER 135
Golf House Club ELIE 406
Golspie Golf Club GOLSPIE 422
Goring and Streatley Golf Club STREATLEY ON THAMES 74
Gorleston Golf Club GREAT YARMOUTH 171
Gort Golf Club GORT 532
Gosfield Lake Golf Club HALSTEAD 159
Gosforth Golf Club NEWCASTLE UPON TYNE 33
Gosling Golf Range WELWYN GARDEN CITY 565
Gosport & Stokes Golf Club GOSPORT 85
Gotts Park Municipal Golf Club LEEDS 331
Gourock Golf Club GOUROCK 446
Gower Golf Club SWANSEA 496
Gowerton Golf Range SWANSEA 496, 580
Gowran Park GOWRAN 540
Gracehill Golf Club BALLYMONEY 507
Grange Fell Golf Club GRANGE-OVER-SANDS 259

INDEX OF CLUBS & COURSES

Grange Park Golf Club ROTHERHAM 321
Grange Park Golf Club SCUNTHORPE 204, 575
Grange Park Golf Club ST HELENS 294
Grangemouth Golf Club POLMONT 450
Grange-over-Sands Golf Club GRANGE-OVER-SANDS 259
Grantown-on-Spey Golf Club GRANTOWN-ON-SPEY 422
Grassmoor Golf Centre CHESTERFIELD 186, 563
Gravesend Golf Centre GRAVESEND 566
Great Barr Golf Club BIRMINGHAM 233
Great Grimsby Golf Centre (Willow Park Golf Club) GRIMSBY 568
Great Hadham Golf & Country Club BISHOP'S STORTFORD 164
Great Harwood Golf Club BLACKBURN 271
Great Lever and Farnworth Golf Club Ltd BOLTON 282
Great Salterns Golf Course PORTSMOUTH 88
Great Torrington Golf Club TORRINGTON 35
Great Yarmouth & Caister Golf Club GREAT YARMOUTH 171
Greenacres Golf Club BALLYCLARE 507
Greenburn Golf Club FAULDHOUSE 398
Greenisland Golf Club CARRICKFERGUS 508
Greenmeadow Golf and Country Club CWMBRAN 486, 580
Greenmount Golf Club BURY 283
Greenock Golf Club GREENOCK 446
Greenock Whinhill Golf Club GREENOCK 446
Greenore Golf Club GREENORE 543
Greetham Valley Hotel Golf & Conference Centre RUTLAND 198
Greystones Golf Club GREYSTONES 552
Grim's Dyke Golf Club PINNER 147
Grimsby Golf Club Ltd GRIMSBY 201
Grove Golf & Bowl LEOMINSTER 191, 565
Grove Golf Club Ltd. PORTHCAWL 492
Guildford Golf Club GUILDFORD 120
Gullane Golf Club GULLANE 398
Habberley Golf Club KIDDERMINSTER 245
Hadden Hill Golf Club DIDCOT 109
Haddington Golf Club HADDINGTON 399
Hadley Wood Golf Club BARNET 164
Haggs Castle Golf Club GLASGOW 417
Hagley Golf and Country Club HAGLEY 245

Haigh Hall Golf Club WIGAN 289
Hainault Forest Golf Club CHIGWELL 158
Hainsworth Park Golf Club HORNSEA 307
Hale Golf Club ALTRINCHAM 281
Halesowen Golf Club HALESOWEN 237
Halesworth Golf Club HALESWORTH 180, 571
Halifax Bradley Hall Golf Club HALIFAX 328
Halifax Golf Club Ltd HALIFAX 328
Halifax West End Golf Club Ltd HALIFAX 328
Hall Garth Golf & Country Club Hotel DARLINGTON 267
Hallamshire Golf Club Ltd SHEFFIELD 323
Hallowes Golf Club SHEFFIELD 323
Halstock Golf Club HALSTOCK 41
Haltwhistle Golf Course CARLISLE 299
Ham Manor Golf Club Ltd ANGMERING 133
Hamilton Golf Club HAMILTON 433
Hampshire Golf Club ANDOVER 81, 564
Hampstead Golf Club HAMPSTEAD 145
Hampton Court Palace Golf Club HAMPTON WICK 69
Hamptworth Golf and Country Club SALISBURY 63, 574
Hanbury Manor Golf & Country Club WARE 169
Handsworth Golf Club BIRMINGHAM 233
Hanging Heaton Golf Club DEWSBURY 327
Hankley Common Golf Club FARNHAM 120
Hanover Golf & Country Club RAYLEIGH 161
Harborne (Church Farm) Golf Club BIRMINGHAM 234
Harborne Golf Club BIRMINGHAM 233
Harbour Point Golf Club LITTLE ISLAND 525
Harburn Golf Club WEST CALDER 402
Harewood Downs Golf Club AMERSHAM 75
Harleyford Golf Club MARLOW 77
Harpenden Common Golf Club HARPENDEN 166
Harpenden Golf Club HARPENDEN 165
Harrogate Golf Club Ltd HARROGATE 312
Hartford Golf Club NORTHWICH 254, 561
Hartland Forest Golf Club BIDEFORD 26
Hartlepool Golf Club Ltd HARTLEPOOL 267
Hartley Wintney Golf Club HARTLEY WINTNEY 85
Hartsbourne Golf & Country Club BUSHEY HEATH 165

INDEX OF CLUBS & COURSES

Hartswood Golf Club BRENTWOOD 156
Harwich and Dovercourt Golf Club HARWICH 159
Harwood Golf Club BOLTON 282
Hassocks Golf Club HASSOCKS 137
Hatchford Brook Golf Club BIRMINGHAM 234
Hatfield London Country Club HATFIELD 166
Haverfordwest Golf Club HAVERFORDWEST 475
Haverhill Golf Club Ltd HAVERHILL 180
Hawarden Golf Club HAWARDEN 466
Hawick Golf Club HAWICK 380
Hawkhurst Golf Club HAWKHURST 98
Hawkstone Park SHREWSBURY 222
Haydock Park Golf Club NEWTON-LE-WILLOWS 293
Hayling Golf Club HAYLING ISLAND 86
Hayston Golf Club GLASGOW 417
Haywards Heath Golf Club HAYWARDS HEATH 137
Hazel Grove Golf Club STOCKPORT 288
Hazelwood Golf Club Ltd SUNBURY ON THAMES 70
Hazlehead Golf Course ABERDEEN 343
Hazlemere Golf Club HIGH WYCOMBE 77
Heacham Manor Golf Club HEACHAM 171
Headfort Golf Club KELLS 544
Headingley Golf Club LEEDS 331
Headley Golf Club BRADFORD 326
Heath Golf Club PORTLAOISE 541
Heathpark Golf Club WEST DRAYTON 70
Heaton Moor Golf Club STOCKPORT 288
Heaton Park Golf Centre MANCHESTER 285
Hebden Bridge Golf Club HEBDEN BRIDGE 328
Hedsor Golf Course WOOBURN COMMON 80
Hele Park Golf Club NEWTON ABBOT 32
Helen's Bay Golf Club BANGOR 512
Helensburgh Golf Club HELENSBURGH 391
Hellidon Lakes Golf Club HELLIDON 209
Helmsdale Golf Club HELMSDALE 422
Helsby Golf Club HELSBY 251
Helston Golf HELSTON 18
Hemingford Abbots Golf Club HUNTINGDON 153
Hemsted Forest Golf Club CRANBROOK 95
Henbury Golf Club BRISTOL 45
Hendon Golf Club HENDON 145

Henley Golf & Country Club HENLEY-IN-ARDEN 229
Henley Golf Club HENLEY-ON-THAMES 110
Henlle Park Golf Club OSWESTRY 221
Henllys Golf Course BEAUMARIS 459
Hennerton Golf Club WARGRAVE 74, 560
Herefordshire Golf Club HEREFORD 190
Heritage Golf & Spa Resort KILLENARD 540
Herne Bay Golf Club HERNE BAY 98
Hertfordshire Golf & Country Club BROXBOURNE 165, 565
Hesketh Golf Club SOUTHPORT 294
Hessle Golf Club COTTINGHAM 307
Heswall Golf Club HESWALL 291
Hever Castle Golf Club HEVER 98
Heworth Golf Club GATESHEAD 302
Heworth Golf Club YORK 317
Hexham Golf Club HEXHAM 299
Heydon Grange Golf and Country Club ROYSTON 168
Heyrose Golf Club KNUTSFORD 251
Heysham Golf Club HEYSHAM 274
Hickleton Golf Club DONCASTER 321
High Elms Golf Club FARNBOROUGH 97
High Post Golf Club Ltd SALISBURY 63
High Throston Golf Club HARTLEPOOL 268
Highbullen Hotel Golf & Country Club CHITTLEHAMHOLT 27
Highcliffe Castle Golf Club CHRISTCHURCH 40
Highfield Golf Course CARBURY 537
Highgate Golf Club HIGHGATE 145
Highwoods Golf Club BEXHILL-ON-SEA 127
Highworth Community Golf Centre HIGHWORTH 62
Hilden Golf Centre TONBRIDGE 106, 567
Hill Barn Golf Club WORTHING 138
Hillingdon Golf Club HILLINGDON 145
Hillsborough Golf Club Ltd. SHEFFIELD 323
Hillside Golf Club SOUTHPORT 294
Hilltop Public Golf Course BIRMINGHAM 234
Hilton Park Golf Club GLASGOW 417
Hilton Puckrup Hall TEWKESBURY 51
Hilton Templepatrick Golf Club TEMPLEPATRICK 510
Himley Hall Golf Centre DUDLEY 237
Hinckley Golf Club HINCKLEY 195

INDEX OF CLUBS & COURSES

Hindhead Golf Club HINDHEAD 121
Hindley Hall Golf Club WIGAN 289
Hinksey Heights Golf Club OXFORD 111
Hintlesham Golf Club IPSWICH 180
Hirsel Golf Club COLDSTREAM 379
HMGC Golf Club HEREFORD 191
Hobson Golf Club NEWCASTLE UPON TYNE 303
Hockley Golf Club WINCHESTER 90
Hoddom Castle Golf Course LOCKERBIE 387
Hoebridge Golf Centre WOKING 125, 572
Hollandbush Golf Club LESMAHAGOW 434
Hollingbury Park Golf Club BRIGHTON 128
Hollystown Golf Club HOLLYSTOWN 530
Hollywood Lakes Golf Club BALLYBOUGHAL 528
Holme Hall Golf Club SCUNTHORPE 204
Holsworthy Golf Club HOLSWORTHY 29
Holtye Golf Club EAST GRINSTEAD 136
Holyhead Golf Club TREARDDUR BAY 462
Holywell Bay Golf Club NEWQUAY 20
Holywell Golf Club HOLYWELL 466
Holywood Golf Club HOLYWOOD 513
Homelands Golf Centre ASHFORD 92, 566
Honiton Golf Club HONITON 29
Honourable Company of Edinburgh Golfers GULLANE 398
Hopeman Golf Club ELGIN 351
Horam Park Golf Course HEATHFIELD 131, 572
Horncastle Golf Club HORNCASTLE 202
Hornsea Golf Club HORNSEA 307
Horsenden Hill Golf Club GREENFORD 144
Horsforth Golf Club Ltd. LEEDS 331
Horsham Golf & Fitness HORSHAM 137
Horsley Lodge Golf Club & Hotel HORSLEY 188
Horton Park Golf & Country Club EPSOM 119
Horwich Golf Club HORWICH 284
Houghton-Le-Spring Golf Club HOUGHTON-LE-SPRING 303
Houghwood ST HELENS 278
Houldsworth Golf Club Ltd. MANCHESTER 285
Hounslow Heath Golf Centre HOUNSLOW 145
Howley Hall Golf Club LEEDS 331
Howth Golf Club SUTTON 531
Hoylake Golf Club WIRRAL 295
Hucknall Golf Centre HUCKNALL 214
Huddersfield Golf Club HUDDERSFIELD 329

Hull Golf Club (1921) Ltd HULL 310
Humberstone Golf Range LEICESTER 568
Humberstone Heights Golf Club LEICESTER 195
Hunley Hall Golf Club & Hotel BROTTON 312, 575
Hunstanton Golf Club HUNSTANTON 173
Huntercombe Golf Club HENLEY-ON-THAMES 110
Huntly Golf Club HUNTLY 353
Huntswood Golf Club BURNHAM 71
Hurdwick Golf Club TAVISTOCK 34
Hurlston Hall Golf Club SCARISBRICK 278
Hurst Golf Club READING 73
Hurtmore Golf Club GODALMING 120
Huyton & Prescot Golf Ltd. HUYTON 292
Hylands Golf Complex INGATESTONE 160
Hythe Imperial Hotel, Spa & Golf Club HYTHE 98
Ifield Golf Club CRAWLEY 135
Ilfracombe & Woolacombe Golf Range ILFRACOMBE 30, 563
Ilford Golf Club ILFORD 160
Ilfracombe Golf Club ILFRACOMBE 30
Ilkeston Borough Golf Club ILKESTON 188
Ilkley Golf Club ILKLEY 329
Immingham Golf Club IMMINGHAM 202
Inchmarlo Golf Club BANCHORY 348
Ingestre Park Golf Club STAFFORD 225
Ingol Golf Club PRESTON 277
Ingon Manor Hotel & Golf Club STRATFORD-UPON-AVON 231
Innellan Golf Club DUNOON 366
Innerleithen Golf Club INNERLEITHEN 380
Insch Golf Club INSCH 353
Inverallochy Golf Club INVERALLOCHY 354
Inveraray Golf Club INVERARAY 366
Invergordon Golf Club INVERGORDON 426
Inverness Golf Club INVERNESS 430
Inverurie Golf Club INVERURIE 354
Ipswich Golf Club IPSWICH 180
Irvine Golf Club IRVINE 371
Irvine Ravenspark Golf Club IRVINE 371
Island Golf Club DONABATE 529
Islay Golf Club PORT ELLEN 451
Isle of Gigha Golf Club ISLE OF GIGHA 451
Isle of Harris Golf Club SCARISTA 451

Isle of Purbeck Golf Club STUDLAND 42
Isle Of Seil Golf Club OBAN 366
Isle of Skye Golf Club SCONSER 452
Isle of Wedmore Golf Club WEDMORE 59
Isles of Scilly Golf Club ST MARY'S 25
Iver Golf Club IVER 77
Ivinghoe Golf Club LEIGHTON BUZZARD 150
Izaak Walton Golf Club STONE 227
Jack Barker's Greenway Hall STOKE-ON-TRENT 226
Jack Barker's Keele Golf Centre NEWCASTLE-UNDER-LYME 225
Jedburgh Golf Club JEDBURGH 381
John O'Gaunt Golf Club SANDY 151
John Reay Golf Centres COVENTRY 573
Jubilee Course ST ANDREWS 413
Julianstown Golf Course & Pitch & Putt JULIANSTOWN 544
K Club STRAFFAN 539
Kames Golf Club LANARK 433
Kearsley Golf Driving Range KEARSLEY 568
Kedleston Park Golf Club QUARNDON 189
Keighley Golf Club KEIGHLEY 330
Keith Golf Club KEITH 354
Kelso Golf Club KELSO 381
Kemnay Golf Club KEMNAY 354
Kendal Golf Club KENDAL 259
Kendleshire Golf Club BRISTOL 46
Kenilworth Golf Club Ltd KENILWORTH 229
Kenmare Golf Club KENMARE 534
Kenmore Golf Course KENMORE 442
Kent & Surrey Golf & Country Club EDENBRIDGE 96
Kenwick Park Golf Club LOUTH 203
Kerries Golf Club TRALEE 536
Keswick Golf Club KESWICK 260
Kettering Golf Club KETTERING 209
Kibworth Golf Club LEICESTER 195
Kidderminster Golf Club KIDDERMINSTER 245
Kilbirnie Place Golf Club KILBIRNIE 372
Kilcock Golf Club KILCOCK 544
Kilcoole Golf Club KILCOOLE 552
Kilkea Castle Golf Resort KILKEA 537
Kilkee Golf Club KILKEE 522
Kilkeel Golf Club KILKEEL 514

Kilkenny Golf Club KILKENNY 540
Killarney Golf and Fishing Club KILLARNEY 535
Killeen Golf Club KILL 537
Killerig Golf Club KILLERIG 519
Killin Golf Club KILLIN 442
Killin Park Golf & Country Club KILLIN 543
Killiney Golf Club KILLINEY 530
Killiow Golf Club & Driving Range TRURO 24, 562
Killorglin Golf Club KILLORGLIN 536
Killymoon Golf Club COOKSTOWN 517
Kilmacolm Golf Club KILMACOLM 447
Kilmarnock (Barassie) Golf Club TROON 375
Kilrush Golf Club KILRUSH 522
Kilspindie Golf Club ABERLADY 392
Kilsyth Lennox Golf Club KILSYTH 418
Kilton Forest Golf Club WORKSOP 219
Kilworth Springs Golf club NORTH KILWORTH 197
King Edward Bay Golf Club ONCHAN 555
King James VI Golf Club PERTH 443
Kingfisher Country Club MILTON KEYNES 78, 560
Kinghorn Municipal Golf Club KINGHORN 407
Kings Acre Golf Course & Academy LASSWADE 400
King's Hill Golf Club WEST MALLING 107
King's Links Golf Course ABERDEEN 343, 577
King's Lynn Golf Club KING'S LYNN 174
Kings Norton Golf Club Ltd. BIRMINGHAM 234
Kingsbarns Golf Links KINGSBARNS 407
Kingsdown Golf Club CORSHAM 62
Kingsknowe Golf Club EDINBURGH 395
Kingsthorpe Golf Club NORTHAMPTON 210
Kingswood Golf & Country Club KINGSWOOD 121
Kington Golf Club KINGTON 191
Kingussie Golf Club KINGUSSIE 430
Kingweston Golf Club STREET 58
Kinloss Country Golf Course FORRES 352
Kinmel Park Golf Complex BODELWYDDAN 463
Kinross Golf Courses KINROSS 442
Kinsale Golf Club KINSALE 524
Kinsale Golf Course HOLYWELL 466
Kintore Golf Club KINTORE 355
Kirby Muxloe Golf Club KIRKBY MUXLOE 195

INDEX OF CLUBS & COURSES

Kirkby Lonsdale Golf Club KIRKBY LONSDALE 260
Kirkbymoorside Golf Club KIRKBYMOORSIDE 313
Kirkcaldy Golf Club KIRKCALDY 407
Kirkcudbright Golf Club KIRKCUDBRIGHT 386
Kirkhill Golf Club GLASGOW 417
Kirkintilloch Golf Club KIRKINTILLOCH 391
Kirkistown Castle Golf Club NEWTOWNARDS 514
Kirriemuir Golf Club Ltd. KIRRIEMUIR 362
Kirtlington Golf Club KIRTLINGTON 110
Kirton Holme Golf Club BOSTON 200
Knaresborough Golf Club KNARESBOROUGH 313
Knebworth Golf Club KNEBWORTH 167
Knighton Golf Club KNIGHTON 478
Knighton Heath Golf Club BOURNEMOUTH 38
Knights Grange Sports Complex WINSFORD 256
Knightsbrook Golf Club TRIM 545
Knightswood Golf Club GLASGOW 417
Knock Golf Club BELFAST 512
Knockanally Golf and Country Club DONADEA 537
Knole Park Golf Club SEVENOAKS 103
Knott End Golf Club Ltd BLACKPOOL 272
Knotty Hill Golf Centre STOCKTON-ON-TEES 268, 563
Knowle Bristol Golf Club BRISTOL 46
Knutsford Golf Club KNUTSFORD 251
KP Club KILNWICK PERCY 310
Kyles Of Bute Golf Club TIGHNABRUAICH 368
La Grande Mare Golf Club GUERNSEY 556
La Moye Golf Club JERSEY 556
Ladbrook Park Golf Club Ltd SOLIHULL 238
Ladybank Golf Club LADYBANK 407
Lagganmore Golf Club & Hotel PORTPATRICK 388
Lahinch Golf Club LAHINCH 522
Lakeside Golf Club PORT TALBOT 493
Lakeside Golf Club RUGELEY 225
Lakeside Lodge Golf Centre HUNTINGDON 153
Laleham Golf Club CHERTSEY 116
Lamberhurst Golf Club TUNBRIDGE WELLS 106
Lambourne Golf Club BURNHAM 76
Lamlash Golf Club LAMLASH 378
Lanark Golf Club LANARK 434
Lancaster Golf Club Ltd LANCASTER 274
Lanes Golfing Academy STOKE POGES 79, 560
Langdon Hills Golf & Country Club BULPHAN 157
Langholm Golf Club LANGHOLM 386
Langland Bay Golf Club SWANSEA 496
Langley Park Golf Club BECKENHAM 92
Lanhydrock Hotel & Golf Club BODMIN 17
Lansdown Golf Club BATH 53
Lansil Golf Club LANCASTER 274
Largs Golf Club LARGS 372
Larkhall Golf Club LARKHALL 434
Larne Golf Club LARNE 509
Lauder Golf Club LAUDER 381
Launceston Golf Club LAUNCESTON 19
Lavender Park Golf Centre ASCOT 71
Laytown & Bettystown Golf Club BETTYSTOWN 544
Lea Marston Hotel & Leisure Complex SUTTON COLDFIELD 574
Leadhills Golf Club LEADHILLS 434
Leamington and County Golf Club LEAMINGTON SPA 230
Leaside Golf Club EDMONTON 143
Leasowe Golf Club MORETON 293
Leatherhead Golf Club LEATHERHEAD 122
Lee Park Golf Club LIVERPOOL 292
Lee Valley Golf & Country Club OVENS 525
Lee Valley Leisure Golf Course EDMONTON 143
Leeds Castle Golf Course MAIDSTONE 100
Leeds Golf Centre LEEDS 332, 576
Leeds Golf Club LEEDS 332
Leek Golf Club LEEK 224
Leek Westwood Golf Club LEEK 224
Lee-on-the-Solent Golf Club LEE-ON-THE-SOLENT 86
Lees Hall Golf Club Ltd. SHEFFIELD 324
Leicestershire Golf Club LEICESTER 195
Leigh Golf Club WARRINGTON 256
Leighton Buzzard Golf Club LEIGHTON BUZZARD 150
Lenzie Golf Club LENZIE 391
Leominster Golf Club LEOMINSTER 191
Leopardstown Driving Range FOXROCK 581
Les Mielles Golf and Country Club JERSEY 556, 582
Les Ormes Golf & Leisure Club JERSEY 556
Leslie Golf Club LESLIE 408
Letchworth Golf Club LETCHWORTH 167
Letham Grange Golf Course ARBROATH 358

INDEX OF CLUBS & COURSES

Lethamhill Golf Course GLASGOW 417
Letterkenny Golf Club LETTERKENNY 527
Leven Golfing Society LEVEN 408
Leven Thistle Golf Club LEVEN 408
Lewes Golf Club LEWES 131
Lexden Wood Golf Club COLCHESTER 158, 564
Leyland Golf Club Ltd LEYLAND 275
Libbaton Golf Club Ltd UMBERLEIGH 35
Liberton Golf Club EDINBURGH 395
Lickey Hills Golf Club REDNAL 238
Lightcliffe Golf Club HALIFAX 328
Lilleshall Hall Golf Club NEWPORT 221
Lilley Brook Golf Club CHELTENHAM 48
Lime Trees Park Golf Club NORTHOLT 559
Limerick County Golf & Country Club BALLYNEETY 542
Limerick Golf Club LIMERICK 542
Limpsfield Chart Golf Club OXTED 123
Lincoln Golf Club LINCOLN 203
Lincolnshire Golf Course SCUNTHORPE 205
Lindfield Golf Club LINDFIELD 137
Lindrick Golf Club WORKSOP 219, 324
Lingdale Golf Club WOODHOUSE EAVES 198
Lingfield Park Golf Club LINGFIELD 122
Links Country Park Hotel and Golf Club CROMER 171
Links Golf Club NEWMARKET 181
Linlithgow Golf Club LINLITHGOW 400
Linn Park Golf Club GLASGOW 417
Liphook Golf Club LIPHOOK 86
Lisburn Golf Club LISBURN 509
Lismore Golf Club LISMORE 549
Little Aston Golf Club STREETLY 227
Little Chalfont Golf Club LITTLE CHALFONT 77
Little Hay Golf Complex HEMEL HEMPSTEAD 166
Little Lakes Golf Club BEWDLEY 242
Littlehampton Golf Club LITTLEHAMPTON 138
Littlehill Golf Club GLASGOW 417
Littlestone Golf Club NEW ROMNEY 100
Littlestone Warren NEW ROMNEY 100
Llandrindod Wells Golf Club LLANDRINDOD WELLS 478
Llandudno Golf Club (Maesdu) Ltd LLANDUDNO 466

Llanfairfechan Golf Club LLANFAIRFECHAN 467
Llangefni Public Golf Course LLANGEFNI 460
Llanishen Golf Club CARDIFF 485
Llantrisant and Pontyclun Golf Club TALBOT GREEN 498
Llanwern Golf Club (Est 1929) LLANWERN 488
Llanymynech Golf Club OSWESTRY 220
Llanyrafon Golf Course CWMBRAN 486
Llyn Golf PWLLHELI 461, 579
Lobden Golf Club ROCHDALE 287
Loch Ness Golf Course INVERNESS 430
Lochcarron Golf Club LOCHCARRON 426
Lochgelly Golf Club LOCHGELLY 408
Lochgilphead Golf Club LOCHGILPHEAD 366
Lochmaben Golf Club LOCHMABEN 386
Lochranza Golf LOCHRANZA 378
Lochwinnoch Golf Club LOCHWINNOCH 447
Lockerbie Golf Club LOCKERBIE 387
Lofthouse Hill Golf Club WAKEFIELD 335
London Beach Golf Club TENTERDEN 106
London Golf Centre NORTHOLT 559
London Golf Club ASH 92
London Scottish Golf Club LONDON 69
Long Ashton Golf Club BRISTOL 46
Long Sutton Golf Club LANGPORT 58, 570
Longcliffe Golf Club LOUGHBOROUGH 196
Longhirst Hall Golf Course MORPETH 300
Longley Park Golf Club HUDDERSFIELD 329
Longniddry Golf Club Ltd LONGNIDDRY 401
Longridge Golf Club PRESTON 277
Longside Golf Club PETERHEAD 357
Looe Golf Club LOOE 19
Lostwithiel Hotel Golf & Country Club LOSTWITHIEL 19
Lothianburn Golf Club EDINBURGH 396
Loudoun Gowf Club GALSTON 370
Loughrea Golf Club LOUGHREA 532
Loughton Golf Club LOUGHTON 160
Louth Golf Club LOUTH 204
Low Laithes Golf Club Ltd. WAKEFIELD 335
Lowes Park Golf Club Ltd BURY 283
Lucan Golf Club DUBLIN 529
Ludlow Golf Club LUDLOW 221
Luffenham Heath Golf Club STAMFORD 198

Luffness New Golf Club ABERLADY 392
Lullingstone Park Golf Club ORPINGTON 102
Lumphanan Golf Club BANCHORY 348
Lundin Golf Club LUNDIN LINKS 408
Lundin Ladies Golf Club LUNDIN LINKS 408
Lurgan Golf Club LURGAN 511
Lutterworth Golf Club LUTTERWORTH 196
Luttrellstown Castle Golf and Country Club CASTLEKNOCK 528
Lybster Golf Club LYBSTER 422
Lydd Golf Club & Driving Range LYDD 98
Lydney Golf Club LYDNEY 50
Lyme Regis Golf Club LYME REGIS 41
Lymm Golf Club LYMM 252
Lytham Green Drive Golf Club LYTHAM ST ANNES 275
Macclesfield Golf Club MACCLESFIELD 252
MacDonald Cardrona Hotel, Golf & Country Club PEEBLES 382
MacDonald Hill Valley Hotel, Golf & Country Club WHITCHURCH 223
MacDonald Linden Hall MORPETH 300
Macdonald Portal Golf and Country Club TARPORLEY 255
Machrie Bay Golf Course MACHRIE 378
Machrie Golf Links PORT ELLEN 451
Machrihanish Golf Club CAMPBELTOWN 365
Machynlleth Golf Club MACHYNLLETH 478
Machynys Peninsula Golf & Country Club LLANELLI 472
Macroom Golf Club MACROOM 525
Maesteg Golf Club MAESTEG 488
Magdalene Fields Golf Club BERWICK-UPON-TWEED 298
Magnolia Park Golf & Country Club OXON/BUCKINGHAMSHIRE 112
Magpie Hall Lane Municipal Golf Club BROMLEY 94
Mahee Island Golf Club NEWTOWNARDS 514
Maidenhead Golf Club MAIDENHEAD 72
Maidstone Golf Centre MAIDSTONE 566
Malahide Golf Club MALAHIDE 530
Malden Golf Club NEW MALDEN 123
Maldon Golf Club MALDON 160
Malkins Bank Municipal Golf Course SANDBACH 255

Mallow Golf Club MALLOW 525
Malone Golf Club BELFAST 508
Malton and Norton Golf Club MALTON 313
Manchester Golf Club Ltd MANCHESTER 286
Mannan Castle Golf Club CARRICKMACROSS 545
Mannings Heath Golf Club HORSHAM 137
Manor Golf Club BRADFORD 326
Manor Golf Club GRIMSBY 202
Manor Golf Club UTTOXETER 228
Manor House Golf Club at Castle Combe CASTLE COMBE 61
Manor of Groves SAWBRIDGEWORTH 168
Mansfield Woodhouse Golf Club MANSFIELD 215
Manston Golf Centre RAMSGATE 102, 566
Mapperley Golf Club MAPPERLEY 216
March Golf Club Ltd MARCH 153
Market Drayton Golf Club MARKET DRAYTON 221
Market Harborough Golf Club MARKET HARBOROUGH 196
Market Rasen and District Golf Club MARKET RASEN 204
Market Rasen Racecourse 9 hole Pay & Play Course MARKET RASEN 204
Marlborough Golf Club MARLBOROUGH 62
Marple Golf Club MARPLE 287
Marriott Breadsall Priory Hotel & Country Club DERBY 187
Marriott Dalmahoy Hotel and Country Club KIRKNEWTON 400
Marriott Forest of Arden Hotel & Country Club COVENTRY 229, 236
Marriott Hollins Hall Hotel & Country Club SHIPLEY 334
Marriott Meon Valley Hotel and Country Club SHEDFIELD 89
Marriott Sprowston Manor Hotel & Country Club NORWICH 176
Marriott St Pierre Hotel & Country Club CHEPSTOW 486
Marriott Tudor Park Hotel and Country Club MAIDSTONE 100
Marriott Worsley Park Hotel & Country Club WORSLEY 289
Marsden Golf Club HUDDERSFIELD 329
Marston Lakes Golf Club SUTTON COLDFIELD 232
Martin Moor Golf Club BLANKNEY 199

INDEX OF CLUBS & COURSES

Maryport Golf Club Ltd MARYPORT 260
Masham Golf Club RIPON 314
Massereene Golf Club ANTRIM 507
Matfen Hall Golf Club MATFEN 300
Matlock Golf Club MATLOCK 188
Mattishall Golf Club MATTISHALL 175
Maxstoke Park Golf Club BIRMINGHAM 234
Maybole Golf Course MAYBOLE 373
Maylands Golf and Country Club ROMFORD 161
Maywood Golf Club RISLEY 189
McCaulays Fitness & Golf IVYBRIDGE 30
McDonald-Ellon Golf Club ELLON 351
Mearns Castle Golf Academy GLASGOW 578
Mellor and Townscliffe Golf Club STOCKPORT 288
Melrose Golf Club MELROSE 381
Meltham Golf Club HUDDERSFIELD 329
Melton Mowbray Golf Club MELTON MOWBRAY 197
Melville Golf Centre Golf Course Range & Shop EDINBURGH 396, 577
Mendip Golf Club Ltd. SHEPTON MALLET 58
Mendip Spring Golf Club BRISTOL 54, 570
Mentmore Golf and Country Club LEIGHTON BUZZARD 150
Menzies Cambridgeshire Hotel & Golf Club CAMBRIDGE 152
Menzies Thistle Roseholm Golf Course IRVINE 371
Menzies Welcombe Hotel & Golf Course STRATFORD-UPON-AVON 231
Merchants of Edinburgh Golf Club EDINBURGH 396
Mere Golf and Country Club KNUTSFORD 252
Merlin Golf Course and Driving Range NEWQUAY 20, 562
Merrist Wood Golf Club GUILDFORD 120
Mersey Valley Golf & Country Club WIDNES 256
Merthyr Tydfil Golf Club MERTHYR TYDFIL 488
Meyrick Park Golf Club BOURNEMOUTH 38
Mickleover Golf Club MICKLEOVER 188
Mid Yorkshire Golf Club PONTEFRACT 334
Middlebank Golf Centre MIDDLEBANK 578
Middlesbrough Golf Club MIDDLESBROUGH 314
Middlesbrough Municipal Golf Centre MIDDLESBROUGH 314
Middleton Hall Golf Club KING'S LYNN 175
Middleton Park (Municipal) Golf Club LEEDS 332
Mid-Herts Golf Club ST ALBANS 168
Mid-Kent Golf Club GRAVESEND 98
Mid-Sussex Golf Club DITCHLING 128
Mile End Golf Club OSWESTRY 222
Milford Golf Club MILFORD 122
Milford Haven Golf Club Ltd MILFORD HAVEN 475
Mill Green Golf Club WELWYN GARDEN CITY 170
Mill Hill Golf Club LONDON 146
Mill Ride Golf & Country Club ASCOT 71
Millbrook Golf Club AMPTHILL 149
Millbrook Golf Course REDCROSS 553
Millicent Golf & Country Club CLANE 537
Millport Golf Club MILLPORT 451
Milnathort Golf Club Ltd MILNATHORT 442
Milngavie Golf Club GLASGOW 417
Minchinhampton Golf Club (New Course) MINCHINHAMPTON 50
Minchinhampton Golf Club (Old Course) MINCHINHAMPTON 50
Minto Golf Club HAWICK 380
Mitcham Golf Club MITCHAM 122
Mitchelstown Golf Club MITCHELSTOWN 525
Mobberley Golf Club KNUTSFORD 252
Moffat Golf Club MOFFAT 387
Mold Golf Club MOLD 467
Mollington Grange Golf Club CHESTER 250
Monifieth Golf Links MONIFIETH 364
Monkstown Golf Club MONKSTOWN 525
Monkton Park Golf Course CHIPPENHAM 61
Monmouth Golf Club MONMOUTH 490
Monmouthshire Golf Club ABERGAVENNY 481
Montrose Golf Links Ltd MONTROSE 364
Moor Allerton Golf Club LEEDS 332
Moor Hall Golf Club Ltd SUTTON COLDFIELD 239
Moor Park Golf Club RICKMANSWORTH 167
Moore Place Golf Club ESHER 119
Moorpark Golf Club STEVENSTON 375
Moors Valley Golf Course RINGWOOD 88
Moortown Golf Club LEEDS 332
Moray Golf Club LOSSIEMOUTH 355
Morecambe Golf Club Ltd. MORECAMBE 275
Moreton Hills Golf Centre MORETON 568

Morlais Castle Golf Club MERTHYR TYDFIL 488
Morley Hayes Golf Club MORLEY 189
Morpeth Golf Club Ltd MORPETH 300
Morriston Golf Club SWANSEA 497
Mortehoe & Woolacombe Golf Club WOOLACOMBE 36
Mortonhall Golf Club EDINBURGH 396
Moseley Golf Club BIRMINGHAM 235
Moss Valley Golf Club WREXHAM 469
Mossock Hall Golf Club ORMSKIRK 275
Mount Ellen Golf Club GARTCOSH 433
Mount Juliet Golf & Country Club THOMASTOWN 540
Mount Ober Golf & Country Club KNOCKBRACKEN 514, 580
Mount Oswald Manor and Golf Course DURHAM 267
Mount Pleasant Golf Course HENLOW 150
Mount Temple Golf Club MOATE 549
Mount Wolsey Golf Club TULLOW 520
Mountain Ash Golf Club MOUNTAIN ASH 490
Mountain Lakes Golf Club CAERPHILLY 484
Mountrath Golf Club MOUNTRATH 540
Mouse Valley Golf Course LANARK 434
Mowsbury Golf Club BEDFORD 149
Moyola Park Golf Club MAGHERAFELT 516
Muckhart Golf Club MUCKHART 450
Muir of Ord Golf Club MUIR OF ORD 426
Muirkirk Golf Club MUIRKIRK 373
Mullion Golf Club HELSTON 18
Mundesley Golf Club NORWICH 176
Murcar Links Golf Club ABERDEEN 344
Murrayfield Golf Club Ltd EDINBURGH 397
Murrayshall Golf Course SCONE 444, 578
Muskerry Golf Club MUSKERRY 525
Musselburgh Golf Club MUSSELBURGH 401
Musselburgh Old Course Golf Club MUSSELBURGH 401
Muswell Hill Golf Club MUSWELL HILL 146
Muthill Golf Club CRIEFF 440
Mytton Fold Hotel & Golf Complex BLACKBURN 271
Naas Golf Club NAAS 539, 582
Nailcote Hall Golf Club BERKSWELL 229
Nairn Dunbar Golf Club NAIRN 430

Nairn Golf Club NAIRN 355
Narin and Portnoo Golf Club NAIRN/PORTNOO 527
National Golf Centre WOODHALL SPA 208, 568
Naunton Downs Golf Club Ltd CHELTENHAM 48
Nazeing Golf Club NAZEING 160
Neath Golf Club NEATH 491
Nefyn and District Golf Club NEFYN 460
Nelson Golf Club NELSON 275
Nevill Golf Club TUNBRIDGE WELLS 106
New Course ST ANDREWS 413
New Cumnock Golf Club NEW CUMNOCK 373
New Forest Golf Club HIGGINSTOWN 549
New Forest Golf Club Ltd LYNDHURST 86
New Galloway Golf Club NEW GALLOWAY 388
New Malton Golf ROYSTON 168
New Mills Golf Club STOCKPORT 189
New North Manchester Golf Club Ltd MANCHESTER 286
New Zealand Golf Club WEYBRIDGE 125
Newark Golf Club NEWARK 216
Newbattle Golf Club Ltd DALKEITH 392
Newbiggin-by-the-Sea Golf Club NEWBIGGIN-BY-THE-SEA 300
Newbold Comyn Golf Club LEAMINGTON SPA 230
Newburgh-on-Ythan Golf Club NEWBURGH 355
Newbury & Crookham Golf Club NEWBURY 73
Newbury Racecourse Golf Centre NEWBURY 73
Newcastle United Golf Club NEWCASTLE UPON TYNE 33
Newcastle West Golf Club ARDAGH 541
Newcastleton Golf Club NEWCASTLETON 381
Newcastle-under-Lyme Golf Club NEWCASTLE-UNDER-LYME 225
Newmachar Golf Club NEWMACHAR 356
Newport (I.O.W.) Golf Club NEWPORT 91
Newport Golf Club NEWPORT 491
Newport Links Golf Club Ltd NEWPORT 476
Newquay Golf Club NEWQUAY 19
Newton Abbot (Stover) Golf Club NEWTON ABBOT 30
Newton Green Golf Club SUDBURY 181
Newton Stewart Golf Club NEWTON STEWART 388
Newtonmore Golf Club NEWTONMORE 430

INDEX OF CLUBS & COURSES

Newtownstewart Golf Club NEWTOWNSTEWART 517
Niddry Castle Golf Club WINCHBURGH 402
Nigg Bay Golf Club ABERDEEN 344
Nizels Golf Club TONBRIDGE 106
Norfolk Golf & Country Club REYMERSTON 177
Normanby Hall Golf Club SCUNTHORPE 205
Normanton Golf Club WAKEFIELD 335
North Berwick Golf Club NORTH BERWICK 402
North Downs Golf Club WOLDINGHAM 126
North Foreland Golf Club BROADSTAIRS 94
North Hants Golf Club FLEET 85
North Inch Golf Course PERTH 443
North Middlesex Golf Club BARNET 143
North Oxford Golf Club OXFORD 112
North Shore Hotel and Golf Club SKEGNESS 205
North Wales Golf Club Ltd LLANDUDNO 466
North Wales Golf Driving Range & 9 Hole Course ST ASAPH 579
North Warwickshire Golf Club Ltd COVENTRY 236
North Weald Golf Club EPPING 159
North West Golf Club BUNCRANA 526
North Wilts Golf Club DEVIZES 62
North Worcestershire Golf Club BIRMINGHAM 235
Northampton Golf Club NORTHAMPTON 211
Northamptonshire County Golf Club NORTHAMPTON 211
Northcliffe Golf Club BRADFORD 326
Northenden Golf Club MANCHESTER 286
Northern Golf Club ABERDEEN 344
Northop Country Park Golf Club CHESTER 463
Northumberland Golf Club Ltd NEWCASTLE UPON TYNE 33
Northwood Golf Club Ltd NORTHWOOD 146
Norton Golf Course STOCKTON-ON-TEES 269
Norwood Park Golf Course Ltd SOUTHWELL 218
Nottingham City Golf Club NOTTINGHAM 217
Notts. Golf Club Ltd. KIRKBY-IN-ASHFIELD 215
Nuneaton Golf Club NUNEATON 230
Nuremore Hotel & Country Club CARRICKMACROSS 545, 582
Oadby Golf Course OADBY 197
Oak Leaf Golf Complex NEWTON AYCLIFFE 268
Oak Park Golfing Complex CRONDALL 84, 565
Oak Tree Driving Range SHAFTESBURY 563

Oakdale Golf Club HARROGATE 312
Oakdale Golf Course OAKDALE 492
Oake Manor Golf Club TAUNTON 58, 570
Oakland Park Golf Club CHALFONT ST GILES 76
Oakmere Park Golf Club NOTTINGHAM 217
Oakridge Golf Club NUNEATON 230
Oaks Golf Club and Spa YORK 318
Oaks Sport Centre Ltd CARSHALTON 114, 571
Oast Golf Centre Ltd SITTINGBOURNE 104, 567
Oastpark Golf Course SNODLAND 105
Ogbourne Downs Golf Club SWINDON 64
Okehampton Golf Club OKEHAMPTON 32
Old Colwyn Golf Club COLWYN 464
Old Conna Golf Club BRAY 551
Old Course ST ANDREWS 411
Old Course Ranfurly Golf Club Ltd BRIDGE OF WEIR 445
Old Fold Manor Golf Club BARNET 143
Old Head Golf Links KINSALE 524
Old Nene Golf Club RAMSEY 155
Old Padeswood Golf Club Ltd PADESWOOD 467
Old Rectory Hotel & Golf Club CRICKHOWELL 478
Old Thorns Golf & Country Estate LIPHOOK 86
Oldham Golf Club OLDHAM 287
Oldmeldrum Golf Club OLDMELDRUM 356
Olton Golf Club Ltd. SOLIHULL 238
Olympic Golf Range SWANLEY 567
Omagh Golf Club OMAGH 517
Ombersley Golf Club DROITWICH 244
Onneley Golf Club CREWE 251
Open Golf Centre ST MARGARET'S 531, 582
Orchardleigh Golf Club FROME 56
Orkney Golf Club KIRKWALL 452
Ormeau Golf Club BELFAST 513
Ormonde Fields Golf Club CODNOR 187
Ormskirk Golf Club ORMSKIRK 277
Orpington Golf Centre ORPINGTON 102, 566
Orsett Golf Club ORSETT 161
Orton Meadows Golf Course PETERBOROUGH 154
Osborne Golf Club EAST COWES 91
Oswestry Golf Club OSWESTRY 222
Oswestry Golf Driving Range OSWESTRY 570
Otley Golf Club OTLEY 333
Otter Valley Golf Centre HONITON 29

606 INDEX OF CLUBS & COURSES — THE GOLF GUIDE 2011

Otterbourne Golf Centre WINCHESTER 90
Otway Golf Club RATHMULLAN 527
Oughterard Golf Club OUGHTERARD 532
Oulton Park LEEDS 332
Oundle Golf Club OUNDLE 211
Outlane Golf Club OUTLANE 333
Overstone Park Golf and Country Club NORTHAMPTON 211
Owston Hall DONCASTER 321
Oxford Golf Centre OXFORD 569
Oxfordshire Golf Club THAME 112
Oxley Park Golf Club Ltd WOLVERHAMPTON 240
Pachesham Park Golf Centre LEATHERHEAD 122, 572
Padbrook Park Golf Club CULLOMPTON 27
Padeswood & Buckley Golf Club MOLD 467
Painswick Golf Club PAINSWICK 50
Paisley Golf Club PAISLEY 447
Palacerigg Golf Club CUMBERNAULD 414
Palleg and Swansea Valley Golf Course SWANSEA 497
Panmure Golf Club BARRY 358
Pannal Golf Club HARROGATE 312
Panshanger Golf Complex WELWYN GARDEN CITY 170
Parc Golf Club NEWPORT 491, 580
Park Golf Course WINCHESTER 90
Park Hill Golf Club LOUGHBOROUGH 196
Park Resort BRISTOL/BATH 47, 54
Park Wood Golf Club TATSFIELD 105
Parkhall Golf Course STOKE ON TRENT 226
Parklands Golf Club NEWCASTLE UPON TYNE 304, 573
Parknasilla Golf Club SNEEM 536
Parkstone Golf Club POOLE 41
Parley Court Golf Club CHRISTCHURCH 40
Pastures Golf Club MICKLEOVER 188
Pat Trainor's Golf Academy WARRENPOINT 581
Patshull Park Hotel, Golf and Country Club WOLVERHAMPTON 223
Paultons Golf Centre ROMSEY 88, 565
Pavenham Park Golf Club BEDFORD 149
Peacehaven Golf Club NEWHAVEN 131
Peak Practice Golf BUXTON 563
Pease Pottage Golf Centre CRAWLEY 135

Pedham Place Golf Centre SWANLEY 105, 567
Peebles Golf Club PEEBLES 382
Peel Golf Club PEEL 555
Penmaenmawr Golf Club PENMAENMAWR 460
Penn Golf Club Ltd WOLVERHAMPTON 241
Pennard Golf Club SWANSEA 498
Pennington Golf Club (Municipal) LEIGH 284
Pennyhill Park Country Club BAGSHOT 114
Penrhos Golf and Country Club LLANRHYSTYD 474
Penrhyn Golf Complex ANGLESEY 458, 579
Penrith Golf Club PENRITH 260
Penwortham Golf Club Ltd PRESTON 277
Peover Golf Club KNUTSFORD 252
Percy Wood Golf & Country Retreat SWARLAND 301
Perdiswell Park Golf Club WORCESTER 246
Perivale Park Golf Club GREENFORD 144
Perranporth Golf Club PERRANPORTH 21
Perton Golf Club WOLVERHAMPTON 241
Peterborough Milton Golf Club PETERBOROUGH 154
Peterculter Golf Club PETERCULTER 356
Peterhead Golf Club PETERHEAD 356
Petersfield Golf Club PETERSFIELD 88
Peterstone Lakes Golf Club CARDIFF 486
Petworth Golf Course PETWORTH 138
Phoenix Golf Club ROTHERHAM 322
Pike Fold Golf Club BURY 283
Pike Hills Golf Club YORK 318
Piltdown Golf Club UCKFIELD 132
Pincents Manor Golf READING 73
Pinner Hill Golf Club PINNER 147
Piperdam Golf and Leisure Resort, Osprey Club DUNDEE 362
Pitcheroak Golf Course REDDITCH 246
Pitlochry Golf Ltd PITLOCHRY 443
Pitreavie (Dunfermline) Golf Club DUNFERMLINE 406
Plassey Oaks Golf Complex WREXHAM 469
Pleasington Golf Club BLACKBURN 271
Polkemmet Golf Course WHITBURN 402
Pollok Golf Club GLASGOW 418
Polmont Golf Club FALKIRK 449
Pontardawe Golf Club SWANSEA 498
Pontefract & District Golf Club PONTEFRACT 334

Ponteland Golf Club NEWCASTLE UPON TYNE 301
Pontypool Golf Club PONTYPOOL 492
Pontypridd Golf Club PONTYPRIDD 492
Port Bannatyne Golf Club ROTHESAY 368
Port Glasgow Golf Club PORT GLASGOW 447
Port Royal Golf Driving Range EDINBURGH 577
Port St Mary Golf Club PORT ST MARY 555
Portadown Golf Club PORTADOWN 511
Portal, The Premier Course TARPORLEY 255
Portarlington Golf Club PORTARRLINGTON 540
Porters Park Golf Club RADLETT 167
Porthmadog Golf Club MORFA BYCHAN 460
Portlethen Golf Club PORTLETHEN 357
Portmarnock Hotel & Golf Links PORTMARNOCK 530
Portmore Golf Park BARNSTAPLE 26, 563
Portobello Golf Course EDINBURGH 397
Portpatrick Golf Club PORTPATRICK 388
Portsalon Golf Club PORTSALON 527
Portsmouth Golf Club (1926) PORTSMOUTH 88
Portstewart Golf Club PORTSTEWART 516
Pottergate Golf Club LINCOLN 203
Potters Bar Golf Club POTTERS BAR 167
Poult Wood Public Golf Centre TONBRIDGE 106
Poulton Park Golf Club Ltd. WARRINGTON 256
Poulton-le-Fylde Golf Club BLACKPOOL 271
Powerscourt Golf Club ENNISKERRY 552
Powfoot Golf Club ANNAN 383
Praa Sands Golf Club PENZANCE 21
Prenton Golf Club BIRKENHEAD 290
Prestatyn Golf Club PRESTATYN 468
Prestbury Golf Club PRESTBURY 254
Preston Golf Club PRESTON 278
Prestonfield Golf Club EDINBURGH 397
Prestwich Golf Club MANCHESTER 286
Prestwick Golf Club PRESTWICK 373
Prestwick St Cuthbert Golf Club PRESTWICK 375
Prestwick St Nicholas Golf Club PRESTWICK 375
Prince's Golf Club SANDWICH BAY 103
Princes Golf Course EDINBURGH 397
Princes Risborough Golf Club PRINCES RISBOROUGH 78
Priors Hall Golf Club CORBY 209
Priskilly Forest Golf Club DINAS POWIS 475

Prudhoe Golf Club PRUDHOE 301
Pryors Hayes Golf Club CHESTER 250
Pulrose Golf Course DOUGLAS 555
Pumpherston Golf Club LIVINGSTON 400
Purley Chase Golf Club NORTH WARWICKSHIRE 230
Purley Downs Golf Club PURLEY 123
Puttenham Golf Club GUILDFORD 120
Pwllheli Golf Club PWLLHELI 468
Pyecombe Golf Club BRIGHTON 133
Pyle & Kenfig Golf Club PORTHCAWL 492
Pype Hayes Golf Club SUTTON COLDFIELD 239
Pyrford Golf Club 1993 WOKING 125
Queens Park (Bournemouth) Golf Club BOURNEMOUTH 38
Queens Park Golf Course CREWE 251
Queensbury Golf Club BRADFORD 326
RAF Coningsby Golf Club LINCOLN 203
RAF St Athan Golf Club BARRY 482
Radcliffe-on-Trent Golf Club RADCLIFFE-ON-TRENT 218
Radnor Golf and Leisure REDRUTH 21, 562
Radyr Golf Club CARDIFF 486
Raglan Parc Golf Club RAGLAN 494
Ralston Golf Club PAISLEY 447
Ramada Hotel & Golf Resort GLOUCESTER 49, 564
Ramsdale Park Golf Centre CALVERTON 214, 569
Ramsey Golf and Bowls Club HUNTINGDON 153
Ramsey Golf Club RAMSEY 555
Ramside Hall Hotel & Golf Club DURHAM 267
Ramsnest Golf Club CHIDDINGFOLD 116
Ranfurly Castle Golf Club Ltd BRIDGE OF WEIR 445
Rathcore Golf and Country Club ENFIELD 544
Rathdowney Golf Club PORTLAOISE 541
Rathmore Golf Club PORTRUSH 509
Ratho Park Golf Club Ltd EDINBURGH 397
Rathsallagh Golf Club DUNLAVIN 551
Ravelston Golf Club Ltd EDINBURGH 397
Raven Meadow Golf Club WORCESTER 246, 575
Ravensworth Golf Club Ltd. GATESHEAD 302
Rawdon Golf & Lawn Tennis Club LEEDS 333
Reading Golf Club READING 73

INDEX OF CLUBS & COURSES

Reaseheath Golf Club NANTWICH 254
Reay Golf Club REAY 422
Redbourn Golf Club REDBOURN 167
Redcastle Golf Club REDCASTLE 527
Reddish Vale Golf Club STOCKPORT 288
Redditch Golf Club REDDITCH 246
Redditch Kingfisher Golf Club REDDITCH 246
Redhill and Reigate Golf Club REDHILL 123
Redhill Golf Centre REDHILL 123, 572
Redlibbets Golf Club ASH 92
Regent Park Golf Club Ltd BOLTON 282
Regiment Way Golf Centre CHELMSFORD 157
Reigate Heath Golf Club REIGATE 123
Reigate Hill Golf Club REIGATE 124
Renfrew Golf Club RENFREW 447
Renishaw Park Golf Club SHEFFIELD 189
Retford Golf Club Ltd. RETFORD 218
Rhondda Golf Club RHONDDA 494
Rhosgoch Golf Club RHOSGOCH 480
Rhos-on-Sea Residential Golf Club LLANDUDNO 466
Rhuddlan Golf Club RHUDDLAN 468
Rhyl Golf Club RHYL 468
Richings Park Golf Club IVER 77
Richmond (Yorkshire) Golf Club RICHMOND 314
Richmond Golf Club RICHMOND 124
Richmond Park Golf Club LONDON 69
Richmond Park Golf Club WATTON 178
Rickmansworth Public Golf Course RICKMANSWORTH 167
Riddlesden Golf Club KEIGHLEY 330
Ridge Golf Club MAIDSTONE 100
Ridgeway Golf Club CAERPHILLY 484
Ring Of Kerry Golf & Country Club KENMARE 534
Ringway Golf Club Ltd ALTRINCHAM 281
Ripon City Golf Club RIPON 314
Risebridge Golf Centre ROMFORD 161
Rishton Golf Club BLACKBURN 271
Riverside Golf Centre LENTON LANE 215
RNAS Culdrose Golf Club HELSTON 18
Robin Hood Golf Club SOLIHULL 238
Rochdale Golf Club ROCHDALE 288
Rochester and Cobham Park Golf Club ROCHESTER 103

Rochford Hundred Golf Club ROCHFORD 161
Rodway Hill Golf Course GLOUCESTER 50
Roe Park Golf Club LIMAVADY 515, 581
Roehampton Club ROEHAMPTON 70
Roker Park Golf Club GUILDFORD 120, 572
Rolls of Monmouth Golf Club MONMOUTH 490
Romanby Golf Course NORTHALLERTON 304, 575
Romiley Golf Club Ltd STOCKPORT 289
Romsey Golf Club Ltd SOUTHAMPTON 89
Rookery Park Golf Club LOWESTOFT 180
Rosapenna Hotel & Golf Links DOWNINGS 526
Roscommon Golf Club ROSCOMMON 546
Rose Hill Golf Club BIRMINGHAM 235
Roseberry Grange Golf Club CHESTER-LE-STREET 266
Rosehearty Golf Club ROSEHEARTY 357
Roserrow Golf & Country Club WADEBRIDGE 24
Ross Golf Club KILLARNEY 535
Rossendale Golf Club Ltd. ROSSENDALE 278
Rosslare Golf Club ROSSLARE 550
Rossmore Golf Club MONAGHAN 545
Ross-on-Wye Golf Club ROSS-ON-WYE 192
Rothbury Golf Club ROTHBURY 301
Rother Valley Golf Centre SHEFFIELD 324, 576
Rotherham Golf Club Ltd ROTHERHAM 322
Rothes Golf Club ROTHES 357
Rothesay Golf Club ROTHESAY 368
Rothley Park Golf Club ROTHLEY 197
Rouken Glen Golf Centre GLASGOW 418
Roundhay Golf Club LEEDS 333
Roundwood Golf Club NEWTOWNMOUNTKENNEDY 553
Roundwood Golf Club ROTHERHAM 322
Routenburn Golf Club LARGS 372
Rowany Golf Club PORT ERIN 555
Rowlands Castle Golf Club HAVANT 86
Roxburghe Golf Club KELSO 381
Royal Aberdeen Golf Club ABERDEEN 344
Royal Ascot Golf Club ASCOT 71
Royal Ashdown Forest Golf Club (Old Course) FOREST ROW 130
Royal Ashdown Forest Golf Club (West Course) FOREST ROW 130
Royal Belfast Golf Club HOLYWOOD 513

Royal Birkdale Golf Club SOUTHPORT 294
Royal Blackheath Golf Club ELTHAM 69
Royal Burgess Golfing Society of Edinburgh EDINBURGH 397
Royal Cinque Ports Golf Club DEAL 95
Royal County Down Golf Club NEWCASTLE 514
Royal Cromer Golf Club CROMER 171
Royal Dornoch Golf Club DORNOCH 420
Royal Dublin Golf Club DUBLIN 529
Royal Eastbourne Golf Club EASTBOURNE 130
Royal Epping Forest Golf Club CHINGFORD 143
Royal Guernsey Golf Club GUERNSEY 556
Royal Jersey Golf Club JERSEY 558
Royal Liverpool Gol Club HOYLAKE 292
Royal Lytham & St Annes Golf Club LYTHAM ST ANNES 275
Royal Mid-Surrey Golf Club RICHMOND 124
Royal Montrose Golf Club MONTROSE 364
Royal Musselburgh Golf Club PRESTONPANS 402
Royal North Devon Golf Club WESTWARD HO! 36
Royal Norwich Golf Club NORWICH 176
Royal Porthcawl Golf Club PORTHCAWL 492
Royal Portrush Golf Club PORTRUSH 510
Royal St David's Golf Club HARLECH 460
Royal St George's Golf Club SANDWICH 103
Royal Tara Golf club NAVAN 545
Royal Tarlair Golf Club MACDUFF 355
Royal Town of Caernarfon Golf Club CAERNARFON 459
Royal Troon Golf Club TROON 376
Royal West Norfolk Golf Club KING'S LYNN 175
Royal Wimbledon Golf Club WIMBLEDON 70
Royal Winchester Golf Club WINCHESTER 90
Royal Worlington and Newmarket Golf Club MILDENHALL 181
Royston Golf Club (Founded 1892) ROYSTON 168
Rudding Park Golf HARROGATE 313, 575
Ruddington Grange Golf Club NOTTINGHAM 217
Rufford Park Golf & Country Club RUFFORD 218, 569
Rugby Golf Club RUGBY 230
Ruislip Golf Club RUISLIP 147
Runcorn Golf Club RUNCORN 255
Rushcliffe Golf Club EAST LEAKE 214
Rushden Golf Club RUSHDEN 212
Rushmere Golf Club IPSWICH 180
Rushmore Golf Club SALISBURY 63
Rusper Golf Club & Driving Range NEWDIGATE 122, 572
Rustington Golf Centre RUSTINGTON 138, 573
Rutherford Castle Golf Club WEST LINTON 382
Ruthin-Pwllglas Golf Club RUTHIN 469
Rutland County Golf Club STAMFORD 206, 568
Ryburn Golf Club HALIFAX 328
Ryde Golf Club RYDE 91
Rye Golf Club RYE 131
Rye Hill Golf Club BANBURY 108
Ryston Park Golf Club DOWNHAM MARKET 171
Ryton Golf Club RYTON 304
St Andrews Links Golf Practice Centre & Golf Academy ST ANDREWS 578
St Andrews Major Golf Club BARRY 482
St Annes Old Links Golf Club LYTHAM ST ANNES 275
St Augustine's Golf Club RAMSGATE 102
St Austell Golf Club ST. AUSTELL 22
St Bees Golf Club ST BEES 260
St Boswells Golf Club ST BOSWELLS 382
St Clements Golf & Sports Centre JERSEY 556
St Cleres Hall Golf Club STANFORD LE HOPE 162
St Davids City Golf Club ST DAVIDS 476
St Deiniol Golf Club BANGOR 459
St Enodoc Golf Club WADEBRIDGE 25
St Fillans Golf Club ST FILLANS 444
St George's Hill Golf Club WEYBRIDGE 125
St Giles Golf Club NEWTOWN 480
St Helen's Bay Golf Resort ROSSLARE HARBOUR 550
St Idloes Golf Club LLANIDLOES 478
St Ives (Hunts) Golf Club ST. IVES 155
St Kew Golf Club WADEBRIDGE 25
St Margaret's Golf & Country Club ST MARGARET'S 531
St Mary's Golf Club PENCOED 492
St Medan Golf Club PORT WILLIAM 388
St Mellion Hotel International Resort SALTASH 22
St Mellons Golf Club CARDIFF 485
St Melyd Golf Club PRESTATYN 468

INDEX OF CLUBS & COURSES

St Michaels Golf Club LEUCHARS 408
St Neots Golf Club ST. NEOTS 155
St Pierre Park Golf Club GUERNSEY 556
St Thomas Priory RUGELEY 225
Saddleworth Golf Club OLDHAM 287
Saffron Walden Golf Club SAFFRON WALDEN 161
Sale Golf Club SALE 288
Saline Golf Club DUNFERMLINE 406
Salisbury & South Wilts Golf Club SALISBURY 63
Saltburn by the Sea Golf Club Ltd SALTBURN BY THE SEA 315
Saltford Golf Club SALTFORD 58
Sand Martins Golf Club WOKINGHAM 74
Sand Moor Golf Club LEEDS 333
Sandbach Golf Club SANDBACH 255
Sandford Springs Golf Club BASINGSTOKE 82
Sandhill Golf Club BARNSLEY 320
Sandilands Golf Club MABLETHORPE 204
Sandiway Golf Club NORTHWICH 254
Sandown Golf Centre ESHER 572
Sandwell Park Golf Club WEST BROMWICH 240
Sandy Lodge Golf Club NORTHWOOD 146
Sandyhills Golf Club GLASGOW 418
Sanquhar Golf Club SANQUHAR 388
Sapey Golf Club BROMYARD 244
Saron Golf Course LLANDYSUL 471
Saunton Golf Club SAUNTON 34
Scarborough North Cliff Golf Club SCARBOROUGH 315
Scarborough South Cliff Golf Club Ltd SCARBOROUGH 315
Scarcroft Golf Club LEEDS 333
Scarthingwell Golf Course TADCASTER 316
Scoonie Golf Club LEVEN 408
Scotscraig Golf Club TAYPORT 413
Scrabo Golf Club NEWTOWNARDS 514
Scraptoft Golf Club LEICESTER 195
Seacroft Golf Club SKEGNESS 205
Seafield Golf & Country Club GOREY 550
Seafield Golf Course AYR 370
Seaford Golf Club SEAFORD 132
Seaford Head Golf Club SEAFORD 132
Seaham Golf Club SEAHAM 268
Seahouses Golf Club SEAHOUSES 301

Seapoint Golf Club DROGHEDA 542
Searles Resort Golf Course HUNSTANTON 174
Seascale Golf Club SEASCALE 260
Seaton Carew Golf Club HARTLEPOOL 268
Seckford Golf Club WOODBRIDGE 182, 571
Sedbergh Golf Club SEDBERGH 262
Sedgley Golf Centre DUDLEY 237
Sedlescombe Golf Club SEDLESCOMBE 132, 572
Seedy Mill Golf Club LICHFIELD 224
Selby Golf Club SELBY 315
Selkirk Golf Club SELKIRK 382
Selsdon Park Hotel & Golf Club CROYDON 118
Selsey Golf Club CHICHESTER 135
Sene Valley Golf Club FOLKESTONE 97
Serlby Park Golf Club DONCASTER 321
Settle Golf Club SETTLE 315
Severn Meadows Golf Club BRIDGNORTH 220
Shandon Park Golf Club BELFAST 513
Shanklin & Sandown Golf Club SANDOWN 91
Shannon Golf Club SHANNON 522
Shaw Hill Hotel Golf & Country Club CHORLEY 273
Shay Grange Golf Centre BRADFORD 576
Sheerness Golf Club SHEERNESS 104
Shendish Manor Hotel & Golf Course HEMEL HEMPSTEAD 166
Sherborne Golf Club SHERBORNE 42
Sherdley Park Municipal Golf Course & Driving Range ST HELENS 294
Sherdons Golf Centre TEWKESBURY 51, 564
Sheringham Golf Club SHERINGHAM 177
Sherwood Forest Golf Club MANSFIELD 216
Shetland Golf Club SHETLAND 452
Shifnal Golf Club SHIFNAL 222
Shipley Golf Club BINGLEY 325
Shipley Golf Club BRADFORD 325
Shirehampton Park Golf Club BRISTOL 47
Shirland Golf Club SHIRLAND 189
Shirley Golf Club SOLIHULL 238
Shirley Park Golf Club Ltd. CROYDON 117
Shiskine Golf & Tennis Club BLACKWATERFOOT 377
Shooters Hill Golf Club Ltd SHOOTERS HILL 70
Shortlands Golf Club BROMLEY 94

Shortwood Lodge Golf Club BRISTOL 47
Shotts Golf Club SHOTTS 435
Shrewsbury Golf Club SHREWSBURY 222
Shrigley Hall Hotel Golf & Country Club POYNTON 254
Shriveham Park Golf Club SHRIVENHAM 63
Shropshire (The) TELFORD 570
Shropshire Golf Centre TELFORD 223
Sickleholme Golf Club SHEFFIELD 189
Sidcup Golf Club SIDCUP 104
Sidmouth Golf Club SIDMOUTH 34
Silecroft Golf Club SILECROFT 262
Silkstone Golf Club BARNSLEY 320
Silloth On Solway Golf Club SILLOTH 262
Silsden Golf Club KEIGHLEY 330
Silverdale Golf Club SILVERDALE 262, 278
Silverknowes Golf Course EDINBURGH 398
Silvermere Golf & Leisure Complex COBHAM 116, 571
Silverstone Golf Club STOWE 80, 560
Singing Hills Golf Course Ltd ALBOURNE 133
Sittingbourne and Milton Regis SITTINGBOURNE 104
Sitwell Park Golf Club ROTHERHAM 322
Six Hills Golf Club MELTON MOWBRAY 197
Skeabost Golf Club SKEABOST BRIDGE 452
Skelmorlie Golf Club SKELMORLIE 375
Skerries Golf Club SKERRIES 531
Skipton Golf Club Ltd SKIPTON 315
Slade Valley Golf Club BRITTAS 528
Sleaford Golf Club SLEAFORD 206
Slieve Russell Hotel, Golf & Country Club BALLYCONNELL 521
Slinfold Golf and Country Club HORSHAM 137
Solent Meads Golf Centre BOURNEMOUTH 38
Solway Links Golf Club SOUTHERNESS 389
Sonning Golf Club READING 73
South Beds. Golf Club LUTON 151
South Bradford Golf Club BRADFORD 326
South County Golf Club BRITTAS 528
South Essex Golf & Country Club BRENTWOOD 156
South Herefordshire Golf Club ROSS-ON-WYE 192, 565
South Herts Golf Club TOTTERIDGE 147

South Kyme Golf Club SOUTH KYME 206
South Leeds Golf Club LEEDS 333
South Moor Golf Club STANLEY 269
South Pembrokeshire Golf Club PEMBROKE DOCK 475
South Shields Golf Club Ltd. SOUTH SHIELDS 304
South Staffordshire Golf Club WOLVERHAMPTON 242
South Wales Golf Range and Course BARRY 579
South Winchester Golf Club WINCHESTER 90
Southampton Golf Club SOUTHAMPTON 90
Southend-on-Sea Golf Club SOUTHEND-ON-SEA 162
Southern Valley Golf Course GRAVESEND 98
Southerndown Golf Club SOUTHERNDOWN 494
Southerness Golf Club DUMFRIES 386
Southfield Golf Club OXFORD 111
Southport & Ainsdale Golf Club SOUTHPORT 294
Southport Municipal Golf Club SOUTHPORT 295
Southport Old Links Golf Club SOUTHPORT 295
Southview Golf Club SKEGNESS 205
Southwell Golf Club SOUTHWELL 218
Southwick Park Golf Club FAREHAM 85
Southwold Golf Club SOUTHWOLD 181
Southwood Golf Course FARNBOROUGH 85
Spa Golf Club BALLYNAHINCH 512
Spalding Golf Club SPALDING 206
Spanish Point Golf Club MILTON MALBAY 522
Sparkwell Golf Club PLYMOUTH 32
Spean Bridge Golf Club SPEAN BRIDGE 430
Spey Bay Golf Club SPEY BAY 357
Sportscotland National Centre LARGS 372
Springfield Park Golf Club ROCHDALE 288
Springhead Park Golf Club HULL 310
Springs Hotel & Golf Club WALLINGFORD 113
Springwater Golf Club CALVERTON 214
Stackstown Golf Club RATHFARNHAM 530
Staddon Heights Golf Club PLYMOUTH 32
Stadium Golf Driving Range HUDDERSFIELD 576
Stafford Castle Golf Club STAFFORD 225
Stamford Golf Club STALYBRIDGE 255
Stand Golf Club MANCHESTER 286
Stanedge Golf Club CHESTERFIELD 186
Stanmore & Edgware Golf Centre STANMORE 147, 559

Stanmore Golf Club STANMORE 147

Stanton-on-the-Wolds Golf Club STANTON-ON-THE-WOLDS 218

Stapleford Abbotts Golf Club STAPLEFORD ABBOTTS 162

Staverton Park Golf Club DAVENTRY 209

Stevenage Golf Centre STEVENAGE 168

Stinchcombe Hill Golf Club DURSLEY 49

Stirling Golf Club STIRLING 450

Stock Brook Golf & Country Club BILLERICAY 156

Stockley Park Golf Club UXBRIDGE 148

Stockport Golf Club Ltd STOCKPORT 289

Stocksbridge and District Golf Club Ltd SHEFFIELD 324

Stocksfield Golf Club STOCKSFIELD 301

Stockwood Park Golf Club LUTON 151

Stockwood Vale Golf Club BRISTOL 55

Stoke Albany Golf Club MARKET HARBOROUGH 210

Stoke by Nayland Golf & Spa STOKE BY NAYLAND 163, 181

Stoke Park Club STOKE POGES 79

Stoke Rochford Golf Club GRANTHAM 201

Stone Golf Club STONE 227

Stonebridge MERIDEN 230

Stoneham Golf Club SOUTHAMPTON 89

Stonehaven Golf Club STONEHAVEN 357

Stonelees Golf Centre RAMSGATE 103, 567

Stoneleigh Deer Park Golf Club STONELEIGH 231

Stoney Holme Municipal Golf Course CARLISLE 258

Stornoway Golf Club STORNOWAY 451

Storws Wen Golf Club BRYNTEG 459

Stourbridge Golf Club STOURBRIDGE 239

Stowe Golf Club STOWE 79

Stowmarket Golf Club Ltd STOWMARKET 181

Strabane Golf Club STRABANE 517

Stranraer Golf Club STRANRAER 389

Stratford-on-Avon Golf Club STRATFORD-UPON-AVON 231

Strathaven Golf Club STRATHAVEN 435

Strathclyde Park Golf Club HAMILTON 433

Strathendrick Golf Club DRYMEN 449

Strathlene Golf Club BUCKIE 350

Strathmore Golf Centre BLAIRGOWRIE 438, 578

Strathpeffer Spa Golf Club STRATHPEFFER 427

Strathtay Golf Club STRATHTAY 444

Strathtyrum Course ST ANDREWS 413

Strawberry Hill Golf Club TWICKENHAM 148

Stressholme Golf Club DARLINGTON 267

Stromness Golf Club Ltd STROMNESS 452

Studley Wood Golf Club OXFORD 111, 570

Sturminster Marshall Golf Club WIMBORNE 44

Styal Golf Club STYAL 255, 562

Sudbrook Moor Golf Club GRANTHAM 201

Sudbury Golf Club Ltd. WEMBLEY 148

Suffolk Hotel Golf & Country Club BURY ST. EDMUNDS 179

Summerhill Golf Course HAY-ON-WYE 190

Sunbury Golf Centre SHEPPERTON 147

Sundridge Park Golf Club BROMLEY 94

Sunningdale Golf Club SUNNINGDALE 124

Sunningdale Ladies' Golf Club SUNNINGDALE 74

Surbiton Golf Club CHESSINGTON 116

Surrey National Golf Club CATERHAM 114

Sutton Bridge Golf Club SPALDING 206

Sutton Coldfield Golf Club SUTTON COLDFIELD 239

Sutton Green Golf Club GUILDFORD 120

Sutton Hall Golf Club SUTTON WEAVER 255

Sutton Park Golf Club HULL 310

Swaffham Golf Club SWAFFHAM 177

Swansea Bay Golf Club NEATH 491

Swanston Golf Course EDINBURGH 398

Sweetwoods Park Golf Club EAST GRINSTEAD 130

Swindon Golf Club DUDLEY 237

Swindon Ridge Golf Driving Range, Shop and Golf Club DUDLEY 574

Swinford Golf Club SWINFORD 543

Swinley Forest Golf Club ASCOT 71

Swinton Park Golf Club MANCHESTER 286

Swords Open Golf Course SWORDS 531

Tadmarton Heath Golf Club BANBURY 108

Tain Golf Club TAIN 427

Tall Pines Golf Club BRISTOL 55

Tamworth Golf Centre Ltd TAMWORTH 227

Tandragee Golf Club TANDRAGEE 511

Tandridge Golf Club OXTED 123
Tankersley Park Golf Club Ltd SHEFFIELD 324
Tapton Park Golf & Leisure Centre CHESTERFIELD 186
Tarbat Golf Club PORTMAHOMACK 426
Tarbert Golf Club TARBERT 368
Tarland Golf Club ABERDEEN 344
Taunton & Pickeridge Golf Club TAUNTON 58
Taunton Vale Golf Club TAUNTON 59
Tavistock Golf Club TAVISTOCK 35
Tawe Vale Golf Club SWANSEA 498
Taymouth Castle Golf Course KENMORE 442
Taynuilt Golf Club TAYNUILT 368
Teesside Golf Club STOCKTON-ON-TEES 269, 316
Tehidy Park Golf Club CAMBORNE 17
Teign Valley Golf Club EXETER 29
Teignmouth Golf Club TEIGNMOUTH 35
Telford Golf & Spa Hotel TELFORD 223
Temple Golf Club HURLEY 72
Temple Newsam Golf Club LEEDS 333
Templemore Golf Club TEMPLEMORE 548
Tenby Golf Club TENBY 476
Tenterden Golf Club TENTERDEN 106
Test Valley Golf Club BASINGSTOKE 82
Tewkesbury Park Hotel Golf & Country Club TEWKESBURY 51
Thames Ditton & Esher Golf Club ESHER 119
Thamesview Golf Centre LONDON 69
Thetford Golf Club THETFORD 178
Theydon Bois Golf Club EPPING 159
Thirsk and Northallerton Golf Club THIRSK 316
Thornbury Golf Centre BRISTOL 46
Thorndon Park Golf Club Ltd. BRENTWOOD 156
Thorne Golf Club DONCASTER 321
Thorney Golf Centre PETERBOROUGH 154, 561
Thornhill Golf Club THORNHILL 389
Thornhurst Park Golf Course DONCASTER 321
Thornton Golf Club THORNTON 413
Thorpe Hall Golf Club SOUTHEND-ON-SEA 162
Thorpe Wood Golf Course PETERBOROUGH 154

Thorpeness Golf Club & Hotel THORPENESS 182
Three Hammers Golf Complex WOLVERHAMPTON 574
Three Locks Golf Club MILTON KEYNES 78
Three Rivers Golf & Country Club CHELMSFORD 157
Thurles Golf Club THURLES 548
Thurlestone Golf Club THURLESTONE 35
Thurso Golf Club THURSO 422
Tickenham Golf Club TICKENHAM 59, 571
Tidbury Green Golf Club SOLIHULL 238
Tidworth Garrison Golf Club TIDWORTH 64
Tilgate Forest Golf Centre CRAWLEY 135, 573
Tillicoultry Golf Club STIRLING 450
Tilsworth Golf Centre DUNSTABLE 150, 559
Tinsley Park Golf Club (Municipal) SHEFFIELD 324
Tiverton Golf Club TIVERTON 35
Tobermory Golf Club TOBERMORY 452
Todmorden Golf Club TODMORDEN 334
Toft Hotel Golf Club BOURNE 200
Toot Hill Golf Club ONGAR 161
Top Meadow Golf Club & Hotel UPMINSTER 163
Topgolf Game Centre WATFORD 565
Torphin Hill Golf Club EDINBURGH 398
Torphins Golf Club TORPHINS 357
Torquay Golf Club TORQUAY 35
Torrance House Golf Club EAST KILBRIDE 433
Torvean Golf Club INVERNESS 428
Torwoodlee Golf Club GALASHIELS 380
Towerlands Driving Range BRAINTREE 563
Towerlands Golf Club BRAINTREE 156
Towneley Golf Club BURNLEY 272
Traditions Golf Course 1999 WOKING 125
Traigh Golf Course ARISAIG 428
Tralee Golf Club TRALEE 536
Tramore Golf Club TRAMORE 549
Tredegar & Rhymney Golf Club RHYMNEY 494
Tredegar Park Golf Club Ltd NEWPORT 492
Trefloyne Golf Club TENBY 476
Tregenna Castle Hotel Golf & Country Club ST IVES 22
Treloy Golf Club NEWQUAY 19
Trent Lock Golf Centre LONG EATON 215, 569
Trent Park Public Golf Course LONDON 146

Trentham Golf Club STOKE-ON-TRENT 226
Trentham Park Golf Club STOKE-ON-TRENT 227
Trethorne Golf Club LAUNCESTON 19
Trevose Golf and Country Club PADSTOW 20
Troon Municipal Golf Courses TROON 376
Truro Golf Club TRURO 24
Tulfarris Golf Club BLESSINGTON 550
Tullamore Golf Club TULLAMORE 546
Tulliallan Golf Club KINCARDINE 406
Tunbridge Wells Golf Club TUNBRIDGE WELLS 106
Tunshill Golf Club Ltd ROCHDALE 278
Turnberry, A Luxury Collection Resort, Scotland TURNBERRY 376
Turnhouse Golf Club EDINBURGH 398
Turriff Golf Club TURRIFF 357
Turton Golf Club BOLTON 283
Tydd St Giles Golf & Leisure Estate WISBECH 155
Tylney Park HOOK 86
Tynedale Golf Club HEXHAM 300
Tynemouth Golf Club Ltd. TYNEMOUTH 305
Tyneside Golf Club Ltd NEWCASTLE UPON TYNE 304
Tyrrells Wood Golf Club Ltd LEATHERHEAD 122
Tytherington Club MACCLESFIELD 252
Ullapool Golf Club ULLAPOOL 427
Ullenwood Manor Golf Course CHELTENHAM 48
Ullesthorpe Court Golf Club LUTTERWORTH 196
Ulverston Golf Club Ltd ULVERSTON 262
Upavon Golf Club UPAVON 64
Upchurch River Valley Golf Courses SITTINGBOURNE 104
Uphall Golf Club UPHALL 402
Upminster Golf Club UPMINSTER 163
Upton-By-Chester Golf Club CHESTER 250
Uttoxeter Golf Club UTTOXETER 228
Uxbridge Golf Course UXBRIDGE 148
Vale Golf Club PERSHORE 245
Vale Hotel Golf & Spa Resort HENSOL 488
Vale of Leven Golf Club ALEXANDRIA 390
Vale of Llangollen Golf Club Ltd LLANGOLLEN 467
Vale Royal Abbey Golf Club NORTHWICH 254
Vaul Golf Club SCARINISH 453
Ventnor Golf Club UPPER VENTNOR 91
Verulam Golf Club ST ALBANS 168

Vicars Cross Golf Club CHESTER 250
Virginia Park Golf Club CAERPHILLY 484, 579
Vivary Golf Course TAUNTON 59
Wakefield Golf Club WAKEFIELD 335
Waldringfield Golf Club WOODBRIDGE 182
Wallasey Golf Club WALLASEY 295
Wallsend Golf Club WALLSEND 305
Walmer and Kingsdown Golf Club DEAL 96
Walmersley Golf Club BURY 283
Walmley Golf Club SUTTON COLDFIELD 239
Walsall Golf Club WALSALL 240
Waltham Windmill Golf Club GRIMSBY 202
Walton Hall Golf Club WARRINGTON 256
Walton Heath Golf Club TADWORTH 124
Wanstead Golf Club WANSTEAD 148
Wareham Golf Club WAREHAM 43
Warkworth Golf Club WARKWORTH 301
Warley Park Golf Club BRENTWOOD 157
Warley Woods Golf Club WARLEY 240
Warren Golf Club DAWLISH 28
Warren Golf Club MALDON 160
Warren Golf Club WALLASEY 295
Warren Park Golf Centre CHADWELL HEATH 563
Warrenpoint Golf Club WARRENPOINT 514
Warrington Golf Club APPLETON 249
Warwick Golf Club WARWICK 232, 573
Warwickshire, The WARWICK 232
Waterbridge Golf Course CREDITON 27
Waterford Castle Golf Club WATERFORD 549
Waterhall Golf Club BRIGHTON 128
Waterlooville Golf Club PORTSMOUTH 88
Waterstock Golf Club & Driving Range OXFORD 112, 570
Waterville House & Golf Links WATERVILLE 536
Wath Golf Club ROTHERHAM 323
Wavendon Golf Centre MILTON KEYNES 78
Weald of Kent Golf Course HEADCORN 98
Weald Park Golf Club BRENTWOOD 157
Wearside Golf Club SUNDERLAND 304
Wellingborough Golf Club WELLINGBOROUGH 212
Wellow Golf Club ROMSEY 88
Wells (Somerset) Golf Club Ltd WELLS 59
Wellshurst Golf and Country Club HAILSHAM 131, 572

Welsh Border Golf CLub WELSHPOOL 480
Welshpool Golf Club WELSHPOOL 480
Welton Manor Golf Centre LINCOLN 203, 568
Welwyn Garden City Golf Club Ltd WELWYN GARDEN CITY 170
Wensum Valley Hotel Golf & Country Club NORWICH 176
Wentworth Club Ltd VIRGINIA WATER 124
Wenvoe Castle Golf Club CARDIFF 486
Wergs Golf Club WOLVERHAMPTON 242
Wernddu Golf Club ABERGAVENNY 481, 579
Werneth Golf Club OLDHAM 287
Werneth Low Golf Club HYDE 284
Wessex Golf Centre WEYMOUTH 44
West Berkshire Golf Course NEWBURY 73
West Bradford Golf Club Ltd BRADFORD 326
West Byfleet Golf Club WEST BYFLEET 125
West Chiltington Golf Club WEST CHILTINGTON 138
West Cornwall Golf Club ST IVES 22
West Derby Golf Club LIVERPOOL 293
West Essex Golf Club CHINGFORD 143
West Herts Golf Club WATFORD 169
West Hill Golf Club WOKING 126
West Hove Golf Club Ltd HOVE 131
West Kent Golf Club ORPINGTON 102
West Kilbridge Golf Club WEST KILBRIDE 376
West Lancashire Golf Club BLUNDELLSANDS 291
West Linton Golf Club WEST LINTON 382
West Lothian Golf Club BO'NESS 392
West Malling Golf Club MAIDSTONE 100
West Middlesex Golf Club SOUTHALL 147
West Midlands Golf Club SOLIHULL 238
West Monmouthshire Golf Club NANTYGLO 490
West Surrey Golf Club GODALMING 120
West Sussex Golf Club PULBOROUGH 138
West Waterford Golf & Country Club DUNGARVAN 548
West Wilts Golf Club WARMINSTER 64
Westerham Golf Club WESTERHAM 106
Westerhope Golf Club NEWCASTLE UPON TYNE 304
Western Gailes Golf Club IRVINE 371
Western Park Golf Club LEICESTER 196
Westerwood Hotel Golf & Country Club CUMBERNAULD 414
Westgate and Birchington Golf Club WESTGATE ON SEA 107
Westhill Golf Club WESTHILL 357
Westhoughton Golf Club WESTHOUGHTON 289
Weston Park Golf Club NORWICH 177
Weston Turville Golf AYLESBURY 75
Westonbirt Golf Course TETBURY 50
Weston-Super-Mare Golf Club WESTON-SUPER-MARE 59
Westport Golf Club WESTPORT 543
Westray Golf Club WESTRAY 452
Wetherby Golf Club WETHERBY 335
Wexham Park Golf Course WEXHAM 79
Weybrook Park Golf Club BASINGSTOKE 82
Weymouth Golf Club Ltd WEYMOUTH 44
Whaddon Golf Centre ROYSTON 565
Whalley Golf Club CLITHEROE 273
Whalsay Golf Club WHALSAY 452
Wharton Park Golf Club BEWDLEY 243
Wheathill Golf Club SOMERTON 58
Wheatlands Golf Course & Country Hotel JERSEY 558
Wheatley Golf Club DONCASTER 321
Whetstone Golf Club and Driving Range LEICESTER 196
Whickham Golf Club Ltd.NEWCASTLE UPON TYNE 304
Whipsnade Park Golf Club WHIPSNADE 170
Whiston Hall Golf Club & Mansion Court Hotel CHEADLE 224
Whitburn Golf Club Ltd SOUTH SHIELDS 304
Whitby Golf Club WHITBY 316
Whitchurch (Cardiff) Golf Club CARDIFF 486
Whitecraigs Golf Club GLASGOW 418
Whitefield Golf Club WHITEFIELD 289
Whitefields Golf Club & Draycote Hotel RUGBY 230
Whitehall Golf Club NELSON 491
Whitehaven Golf Club WHITEHAVEN 262
Whitehead Golf Club CARRICKFERGUS 508
Whitehill Golf Club WARE 169, 565
Whitehill House Golf Club EDINBURGH (SOUTH) 398
Whitekirk Golf & Country Club WHITEKIRK 402

INDEX OF CLUBS & COURSES

Whiteleaf Golf Club Ltd PRINCES RISBOROUGH 79
Whitemoss Golf Club DUNNING 442
Whitewebbs Golf Club ENFIELD 144
Whiting Bay Golf Club WHITING BAY 378
Whitley Bay Golf Club WHITLEY BAY 305
Whitsand Bay Hotel Golf Club TORPOINT 22
Whitstable and Seasalter Golf Club WHITSTABLE 107
Whittaker Golf Club LITTLEBOROUGH 284
Whittington Heath Golf Club LICHFIELD 225
Whittlebury Park Golf & Country Club TOWCESTER 212
Wick Golf Club WICK 422
Wickham Park Golf Club FAREHAM 85
Wicklow Golf Club WICKLOW 554
Widnes Golf Club WIDNES 256
Widney Manor Golf Club SOLIHULL 239
Wigan Golf Club WIGAN 280
Wigtown and Bladnoch Golf Club WIGTOWN 389
Wigtownshire County Golf Club NEWTON STEWART 388
Wildernesse Club SEVENOAKS 103
Wildwood Country Club CRANLEIGH 117
Willesley Park Golf Club ASHBY DE LA ZOUCH 193
William Wroe Municipal Golf Club TRAFFORD 289
Williamwood Golf Club GLASGOW 418
Willingcott Valley Golf Club WOOLACOMBE 36
Willingdon Golf Club EASTBOURNE 130
Willow Valley Golf BRIGHOUSE 327, 576
Wilmslow Golf Club KNUTSFORD 252
Wilpshire Golf Club Ltd BLACKBURN 271
Wilton Golf Club REDCAR 314
Wiltshire, The SWINDON 64
Wimbledon Common Golf Club WIMBLEDON 70
Wimbledon Park Golf Club WIMBLEDON 70
Wincanton Golf Club WINCANTON 60
Windermere Golf Club WINDERMERE 263
Windlemere Golf Club WOKING 125
Windlesham Golf Club BAGSHOT 114
Windmill Hill Golf Centre MILTON KEYNES 78, 560
Windmill Village Hotel, Golf & Leisure COVENTRY 236
Windwhistle Golf Club Ltd CHARD 56
Windyhill Golf Club GLASGOW 418
Winter Hill Golf Club MAIDENHEAD 72
Winterfield Golf Club DUNBAR 394
Wirral Ladies' Golf Club Ltd BIRKENHEAD 290
Wishaw Golf Club WISHAW 435
Withernsea Golf Club WITHERNSEA 310
Withington Golf Club MANCHESTER 287
Witney Lakes Golf Club WITNEY 113, 570
Woburn Golf Club MILTON KEYNES 78
Wokefield Park Golf Club READING 73
Woking Golf Club WOKING 126
Woldingham Golf Club CATERHAM 114
Woll Golf Course ASHKIRK 379
Wollaton Park Golf Club NOTTINGHAM 217
Wolstanton Golf Club WOLSTANTON 228
Woodbridge Golf Club WOODBRIDGE 182
Woodbrook Golf Club BRAY 551
Woodbury Park Hotel & Golf Club EXETER 29
Woodcote Park Golf Club COULSDON 116
Woodford Golf Club WOODFORD GREEN 163
Woodhall Hills Golf Club Ltd. PUDSEY 334
Woodham Golf & Country Club NEWTON AYCLIFFE 268
Woodlake Park Golf and Country Club PONTYPOOL 492
Woodlands Golf and Country Club BRISTOL 47
Woodlands Golf Club NAAS 539
Woodlands Manor Golf Club SEVENOAKS 104
Woodsome Hall Golf Club HUDDERSFIELD 329
Woodspring Golf & Country Club BRISTOL 55
Woodstock Golf and Country Club ENNIS 522
Woodthorpe Hall Golf Club ALFORD 199
Wooler Golf Club WOOLER 301
Woolley Park Golf Club WAKEFIELD 335
Woolston Manor Golf Club CHIGWELL 158
Woolton Golf Club LIVERPOOL 293
Worcester Golf and Country Club WORCESTER 246
Worcester Golf Range WORCESTER 575
Worcestershire Golf Club MALVERN WELLS 245
Worfield Golf Club WORFIELD 223
Workington Golf Club Ltd WORKINGTON 263
Worksop Golf Club WORKSOP 219

World of Golf CHISLEHURST 95, 566
World of Golf at Beverley Park NEW MALDEN 572
World of Golf Croydon CROYDON 571
Worldham Golf Club ALTON 81
Worlebury Golf Club WESTON-SUPER-MARE 60
Worplesdon Golf Club WOKING 126
Worsley Golf Club ECCLES 284
Worthing Golf Club WORTHING 138
Wortley Golf Club SHEFFIELD 324
Wrag Barn Golf and Country Club HIGHWORTH 62
Wrangaton Golf Club SOUTH BRENT 34
Wrekin Golf Club TELFORD 223
Wrexham Golf Club WREXHAM 469

Wrotham Heath Golf Club SEVENOAKS 104
Wyboston Lakes Golf Course WYBOSTON 151
Wychwood Golf Club CHIPPING NORTON 109
Wychwood Park Golf Club WESTON 256
Wycombe Heights Golf Centre HIGH WYCOMBE 77
Wyke Green Golf Club ISLEWORTH 146
Wyre Forest Golf Club KIDDERMINSTER 245
Yelverton Golf Club YELVERTON 36
Yeovil Golf Club YEOVIL 60
York Golf Club YORK 318
Youghal Golf Club YOUGHAL 525

Index of Advertisers

Aaran Luxury Apartments	399
Abbotsford Hotel	370
Aberdeen City Golf	343
Aberdour Hotel	385
Abernethy Golf Club	430
Aberystwyth Golf Club	473
Aldenham Golf & Country Club	169
Alderney Golf Club	557
Alderney Tourism	557
Alford Golf Club	346
Alice Springs Golf Club	498
Allandale House	378
Allestree Park Golf Course	187
Alnmouth Golf Club	297
Alnwick Golf Club	297
Alresford Golf Club	81
Alsager Golf & Country Club	249
Altonwood Golf Group	115
Alyth Hotel	437
Anglesey Golf Club	462
Ansty Golf Centre	235
Aquaterra Leisure	53
Ardeer Golf Club	375
Arran Golf	377
Ashbourne Golf Club (Derbyshire)	185
Ashbourne Golf Club (Co. Meath)	544
Ashburnham Hotel	472
Ashley Wood Golf Club	39
Ashton Under Lyne Golf Club	281
Aston Hotel	385
Auchterarder Golf Club	437
Baginton Oak	236
Balbirnie Park Golf Club	410
Ballochmyle Golf Club	373
Ballyearl Arts & Leisure Centre	509
Banchory Lodge Hotel	347
Barnham Broom Hotel, Golf & Spa	175
Beacon Park Golf Club	280
Beaufort Golf Club	535
Bedale Golf Club	311
Beedles Lake Golf Centre	194
Beeston Fields Golf Club	216
Bell Hotel	103
Belmont Lodge & Golf	190
Berrow Links House	56
Berwick Upon Tweed Goswick Golf Club	299
Best Western Diplomat Hotel	472
Best Western Keavil House Hotel	407
Best Western Scores Hotel	411
Betws-y-Coed Golf Club	463
Bingley St Ives Golf Club	325
Bishop Auckland Golf Club	265
Bishopbriggs Golf Club	414
Blackwell Golf Club	243
Blairgowrie Golf Club	439
Blankney Golf Club	199
Blyth Golf Club	299
Boat of Garten Golf Club	429
Borth & Ynyslas Golf Club	474
Bourne Hall Hotel	38
Bovey Castle	30
Bradford (Hawksworth) Golf Club	328
Brampton Golf Club	259
Brampton Park Golf Club	153
Brancepeth Castle Golf Club	266
Brean Golf Club	55
Brecon Castle Hotel	479
Brighouse Bay Golf & Leisure Complex	387
Bristol & Clifton Golf Club	45
Broadway Golf Club	47
Broome Park Golf Club	94
Brora Golf Club	419
Brynhill Golf Club	482
Buck Inn	311
Builth Wells Golf Club	479
Bulwell Forest Gollf Club	214
Bunchrew House Hotel	431
Burford Golf Club	109
Burghill Valley Golf Club	190
Burnham & Berrow Golf Club	57
Burnham Beeches Golf Club	76
Burnside Guest House	373
Caerwylan Hotel	459
Cairndale Hotel	386
Cairndhu Golf Club	508
Cairndow Stagecoach Inn	367
Caledonian Hotel & Bar	409
Callander Golf Club	448
Cambridge Meridian Golf Club	152
Cambus O'May Hotel	348
Came Down Golf Club	40
Canwick Park Golf Club	202
Cardigan Golf Club	474
Carlton George Hotel	414
Carlton Hotel	374
Carlyon Bay Hotel	17
Carmarthen Golf Club	470
Carnoustie Country	341, 360
Charleville Golf Club	523
Chart Hills Golf Club	93

Cleobury Mortimer Golf Club	220	East Fife Letting Company	411
Clyne Golf Club	496	East Neuk Cottage	404
Coach House Bed & Breakfast	361	Eaton Golf Club	250
Comrie Golf Club	440	Eden Golf Club & Driving Range	258
Connemara Golf Club	533	Edzell Golf Club	363
Conwy (Caernarfonshire) Golf Club	465	Eglinton Guest House	369
Cookridge Hall Golf Club	331	Elfordleigh Hotel, Golf & Country Club	33
Cosby Golf Club	194	Elmwood Golf Course	6, 405
Cotswold Hills Golf Club	48	Enmore Park Golf Club	55
Cottesmore Golf & Country Club	136	Enniscrone Golf Club	547
Cottingham Parks Golf & Leisure Club	309	Erskine Golf Club	445
Cottrell Park Golf Resort	483	Falmouth Golf Club	18
Cowal Golf Club	367	Farm & Cottage Holidays	16
Cradoc Golf Club	479	Farnham Golf Club	119
Craigmillar Park Golf Club	394	Farnham Park Golf Course	79
Crews Hill Golf Club	144	Farthingstone Hotel & Golf Course	212
Crowborough Beacon Golf Club	128	Filey Golf Club	312
Crusoe Hotel	410	Five Roads Caravan Park	437
Cullen Golf Club	350	Fleetwood Golf Course	274
Culloden House Hotel	431	Forest Hills Golf Club	49
Cutkive Wood Holiday Lodges	23	Forest of Galtres Golf Club	316
Dale Head Hall Lakeside Hotel	261	Forfar Golf Club	363
Dalmunzie Golf Course	438	Fort Augustus Golf Club	429
Darenth Valley Golf Course	104	Fort William Golf Club	429
Dart Valley Cottages	27	Fortrose & Rosemarkie Golf Club	425
Darwen Golf Club	274	Foxhunters Inn	34
Dawlish Warren Golf Club	28	Fraserburgh Golf Club	353
Deer Park Golf & Country Club	400	Frilford Heath Golf Club	108
Deer Park Spa Hotel & Golf	529	Fulford Golf Club	317
Denbigh Golf Club	464	Gairloch Golf Club	425
Dewstow Golf Club	487	Galloway Arms Hotel	385
Didsbury Golf Club	285	Garesfield Golf Club	302
Dingle Golf Links	534	George Hotel	261
Dochlaggie	429	Gifford Golf Club	399
Donaghadee Golf Club	513	Gillingham Golf Club	97
Dornoch Castle Hotel	420	Glen Golf Club	401
Dorset Golf & Country Club	43	Glenbrae Knitwear	8
Downfield Golf Club	362	Glenview Hotel	551
Drumoig Golf Hotel	412	Glyn Abbey Golf Club	Inside Front Cover, 457, 472
Duff House Royal Golf Club	349	Golf Hotel	262
Dumfries & County Golf Club	384	Golfers (Scotland) Ltd	339
Dumfries & Galloway Golf Club	385	Golspie Golf Club	423
Dunbar Golf Club	393	Goodwood Golf	134
Dunblane New Golf Club	441	Gordon Arms Hotel	353
Dyke Golf Club	127		

Looking for accommodation near golf clubs?, then visit
www.holidayguides.com
for where to stay when playing golf around the regions

INDEX OF ADVERTISERS

Gort Golf Club	533
Gourock Golf Club	446
Gowerton Golf Range	497
Grange & Links Hotel	204
Grange Park Golf Club	205
Grantown-on-Spey Golf Club	423
Great Bodieve Farm Barns	25
Great Yarmouth & Caister Golf Club	172
Green Acre Public House & Motel	484
Green Hotel	442
Greenbank Hotel	18
Greenock Golf Club	446
Grove Golf Club	493
Haddington Golf Club	399
Hainsworth Park Golf Club	309
Halesowen Golf Club	237
Haverfordwest Golf Club	475
Heacham Manor	173
Heatherdale Bed & Breakfast	425
Henbury Golf Club	45
Henllys Hall Apartments	458
Herefordshire Golf Club	191
Hesketh Golf Club	294
Hessle Golf Club	309
Hever Castle Golf Club	99
High Post Golf Club	63
Highgate Golf Club	145
Hilton Puckrup Hall	52
Hinckley Golf Club	195
Hinksey Heights Golf Course	110
Hirsel Golf Club	379
Holly-Wood Guest House	263
Holywell Bay Golf Club	20
Hopeman Golf Club	351
Hornsea Golf Club	309
Horsforth Golf Club	331
Horsley Lodge	188
Hull Golf Club	310
Hunter's Hotel	554
Hurlston Hall Golf & Country Club	279
Immingham Golf Club	202
Imperial Hotel	383
Inchmurrin Island Self Catering Holidays	367
Ingon Manor Hotel & Golf Club	231
Inverurie Golf Club	354
Jedburgh Golf Club	380
K Club	538
Kames Country Club	433
Kent & Surrey Golf & Country Club	97
Kettering Golf Club	209
Kildrummy Castle Hotel	346
Killerig Golf Resort	519
Killiow Golf	24
Kilmorie Smallholding	50
Kincraig Castle Hotel	426
Kings Hill Golf Club	107
King's Lynn Golf Club	174
Kings Norton Golf Club	234
Kingsknowe Golf Club	395
Kington Golf Club	191
Kinloch Hotel	377
Kirkby Lonsdale Golf Club	260
Knott End Golf Club	272
Langland Bay Golf Club	497
Largs Golf Club	372
Le Strange Arms Hotel	173
Lea Gate Inn	199
Learney Arms Hotel	349
Leatherhead Golf Club	122
Lenzie Golf Club	391
Les Mielles Golf & Country Club	557
Letham Grange	359
Leven Links	409
Lilleshall Hall Golf Club	221
Lincoln Golf Club	203
Links Country Park Hotel & Golf Club	171
Littlestone Golf Club	101
Llandrindod Wells Golf Club	479
Loch Ness Golf Course	431
Loch Tay Lodges	436
Lodge on the Loch of Aboyne	345
Longridge Golf Club	278
Loudoun Gowf Club	371
Lundin Golf Club	409
Lyme Regis Golf Club	41
Lyn Leven Guest House	365
Lytham Green Drive Golf Club	276
Lythe Hill Hotel & Spa	121
Machrihanish Golf Club	365
Machynlleth Golf Club	479
Magdalene Fields Golf Club	299
Malahide Golf Club	530
Malton & Norton Golf Club	313
Manor Golf Club	228
Manor House & Ashbury Hotels	31
Manor House Hotel	42
Manston Golf Centre	102
Market Drayton Golf Club	221
Marriott St Pierre Hotel & Country Club	487
McDonald Golf Club	352
Meldrum House Country Hotel & Golf Course	356
Melton Mowbray Golf Club	197
Menzies Welcombe Hotel Spa & Golf Club	231
Mercure Newcastle George Washington Hotel, Golf & Spa	305
Mere Golf & Country Club Inside Back Cover,	253
Mid Yorkshire Golf Club	334
Minehead & West Somerset Golf Club	58
Monifieth Golf Links	364
Monmouth Golf Club	490

THE GOLF GUIDE 2011 — INDEX OF ADVERTISERS 621

Monmouthshire Golf Club	481	Pumpherston Golf Club	401
Moortown Golf Club	332	Purbeck House Hotel & Louisa Lodge	43
Moray Golf Club	355	Pwllheli Golf Club	461
Morley Hayes Golf Club	189	Queenwood Lodge	61
Morton Golf Holidays	7	Raglan Parc Golf Club	495
Mortonhall Golf Club	396	Ravenswood Residential Club	349
Moseley Golf Club	235	Red House Hotel	437
Mount Wolseley Hotel Spa & Country Club	520	Redcoats Farmhouse Hotel & Restaurant	166
Muir of Ord Golf Club	427	Revelstoke Hotel	307
Muirhouses Farm	363	Rhuddlan Golf Club	469
Munro Inn	441	Riverdale Hall Hotel	298
Murcar Links Golf Club	345	Rolls of Monmouth Golf Club	490
Mycoal Warm Packs	7	Rossborough Hotel	393
Mytton Fold Hotel & Golf Complex	270	Rother Valley Golf Centre	324
Nairn Dunbar Golf Club	431	Roundwood Golf Club	553
New Close Farm	315	Roxburghe Hotel & Golf Course	381
New North Manchester Golf Club	286	Royal Ashdown Forest Golf Club	66, 130
Newbattle Golf Club	393	Royal Cinque Ports Golf Club	95
Newport Links Golf Club	476	Royal Dornoch Golf Club	421
North Berwick Golf Club	403	Royal Dunkeld Hotel	441
North Shore Hotel & Golf Club	205	Royal Jersey Golf Club	558
Northumberland Golf Tours	7	Royal Liverpool Golf Club	292
Oakmere Park Golf Club	217	Royal Marine Hotel	419
Oaks Golf Club & Spa	319	Royal North Devon Golf Club	36
Ogbourne Downs Golf Club	64	Royal St David's Golf Club	460
Old Colwyn Golf Club	464	Rudding Park	313
Old Thorns Manor Hotel	Front Cover, 83	Ruddington Grange Golf Club	217
Orton Meadows Golf Course	154	SAC Auchincruive	370
Overstone Park Hotel, Golf & Leisure Resort	211	St Augustines Golf Club	102
Painswick Golf Club	51	St Margaret's Golf & Country Club	531
Palace Hotel	356	St Mellion Golf Breaks	23
Panmure Golf Club	358	St Mellion International Resort	22
Park Resort, The	54	St Mellons Golf Club	485
Park Wood Golf Club	105	Saltburn-by-the-Sea Golf Club	314
Patshull Park Hotel, Golf & Country Club	223	Sandhill Golf Club	320
Penmaenmawr Golf Club	468	Sandilands Golf Club	204
Penny Farthing Inn	208	Saron Golf Course	471
Peover Golf Club	252	Saunton Golf Club	34
Penwortham Golf Club	277	Scarthingwell Golf Course	316
Perranporth Golf Club	21	Scotscraig Golf Club	413
Petwood Hotel	208	Seabraes Self Catering Flats	361
Pine Lodge Hotel	215	Seaford Golf Club	132
Pitcairlie House	411	Seahouses Golf Club	301
Pitlochry Golf Course	443	Searles Leisure Resort	174
Plough (Rhosmaen)	470	Seascale Golf Club	261
Point Cottages	297	Selsdon Park Hotel & Golf Club	118
Pollaughan Cottages	24	Shannon Region Golf	518
Pontypool Golf Club	493	Shaw Hill Hotel, Golf & Country Club	273
Port Gaverne Hotel	24	Sherdons Driving Range & Golf Centre	51
Porthmadog Golf Club	460	Sheringham Golf Club	177
Powerscourt Golf Club	552	Shipley Golf Club	325
Prestatyn Golf Club	468	Shotts Golf Club	434
Prestonfield Golf Club	397	Sinfin Golf Course	187
Prestwick St Cuthbert Golf Club	374	Sittingbourne & Milton Regis Golf Club	105
Prestwick St Nicholas Golf Club	374	Sitwell Park Golf Club	322

INDEX OF ADVERTISERS

Skidby Lakes Golf Club	309
Solway Links Golf Club	389
South Beach Hotel	376
South Staffordshire Golf Club	241
Southfield Golf Club	110
Springs Hotel & Golf Club	113
Stafford Castle Golf Club	226
Stapleford Abbotts Golf Club	162
Stinchcombe Hill Golf Club	49
Stoke Albany Golf Club	210
Stoneham Golf Club	89
Stover Golf Club	30
Strathmore Golf Centre	438
Studley Wood Golf Club	111
Sunninghill Hotel	351
Swaffham Golf Club	177
Sweetswoods Park Golf Club	129
Tarbat Golf Club	427
Taunton Vale Golf Club	59
Taynuilt Golf Club	368
Tayside Hotel	444
Teign Valley Golf and Hotel	29
Teignmouth Golf Club	35
Tenby Golf Club	476
Thornbury Golf Centre	46
Thornhill Golf Club	389
Thornton Golf Club	413
Thorpe Wood Golf Course	154
Thorpeness Hotel & Golf Club	182
Toft Country House Hotel & Golf Club	200
Torwodlee Golf Club	380
Trefloyne Golf, Bar & Restaurant	477
Treglos Hotel	20
Trent Lock Golf Centre	215
Trentham Golf Club	227
Trethorne Golf Club	19
Trevose Golf and Country Club	21
Tulliallan Golf Club	407
Turton Golf Club	282
Tylney Park	87
Upavon Golf Club	64
Uttoxeter Golf Club	228
Vale of Leven Golf Club	390
Valleys Golf Breaks	489
Vine House Bed & Breakfast	466
Walmer & Kingsdown Golf Club	96
Walsall Golf Club	240
Wareham Golf Club	43
Waren Lea Hall	297
Watersplash Hotel	84
Waterville Golf Links	536
Wavendon Golf Centre	78
Wellingborough Golf Club	213
Welshpool Golf Club	480
Wenvoe Castle Golf Club	487
Wernddu Golf Club	481
West Derby Golf Club	293
West Fenton Court Cottages	403
West Kilbride Golf Club	376
West Lancashire Golf Club	290
West Midlands Golf Club	238
West Wilts Golf Club	65
Weston Turville Golf Club	75
Wetherby Golf Club	335
Weybrook Park Golf Club	82
Whitchurch (Cardiff) Golf Club	487
Whittlebury Park Golf & Country Club	213
Wicklow Golf Club	500, 554
Widnes Golf Club	256
Wigtownshire County Golf Club	388
Wild Boar	264
Willingcott Valley	37
Willowbank Hotel	372
Windermere Golf Club	263
Windmill Village Hotel, Golf & Leisure Club	237
Winston Hotel	497
Wishaw Golf Club	435
Withington Golf Club	287
Wolfedale Golf Course	41
Woodbury Park Hotel and Golf Club	28
Woodford Golf Club	163
Woodhall Spa (National Golf Centre)	207
Woodham Golf & Country Club	268
Woodland Holiday Lodges	412
Wrag Barn Golf & Country Club	62
Wrangaton Golf Club	34
Wyke Green Golf Club	146
York Golf Club	318

For full details of convenient accommodation near clubs and courses

www.holidayguides.com

Other FHG titles for 2011

FHG Guides Ltd have been publishing an attractive range of holiday accommodation guides for over 50 years. For all kinds of holiday opportunities, they make useful gifts at any time of year. Our guides are available in most bookshops and larger newsagents but we will be happy to post you a copy direct if you have any difficulty. POST FREE for addresses in the UK.
We will also post abroad but have to charge separately for post or freight.

 £7.99

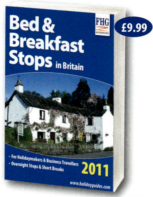 £9.99

 £9.99

500 Great Places to Stay in Britain
- Coast & Country Holidays
- Full range of family accommodation

Bed & Breakfast Stops in Britain
- For holidaymakers and business travellers
- Overnight stops and Short Breaks

The Original Pets Welcome!
- The bestselling guide to holidays for pets and their owners
- Including Holidays in France

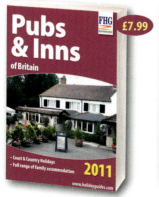 £7.99

 £7.99

 £7.99

Pubs & Inns of Britain
- Including Dog-friendly Pubs
- Accommodation, food and traditional good cheer

300 Great Hotels of Britain
- Hotels with Conference, Leisure and Wedding Facilities

Caravan & Camping Holidays in Britain
- Campsites and Caravan parks
- Facilities fully listed

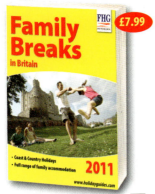

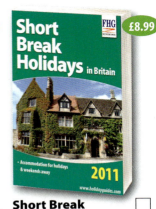

Family Breaks
in Britain
- Accommodation, attractions and resorts
- Suitable for those with children and babies

Self-Catering Holidays
in Britain
- Cottages, farms, apartments and chalets
- Over 400 places to stay
- Pet-Friendly accommodation

Short Break Holidays
in Britain
- Accommodation for holidays and weekends away

Tick your choice above and send your order and payment to

**FHG Guides Ltd. Abbey Mill Business Centre
Seedhill, Paisley, Scotland PA1 1TJ
TEL: 0141- 887 0428 • FAX: 0141- 889 7204
e-mail: admin@fhguides.co.uk**

Deduct 10% for 2/3 titles or copies; 20% for 4 or more.

Send to: NAME..

ADDRESS ....

....

....

POST CODE ....

I enclose Cheque/Postal Order for £ ....

SIGNATURE ....DATE ....

Please complete the following to help us improve the service we provide.
How did you find out about our guides?:

☐ Press   ☐ Magazines   ☐ TV/Radio   ☐ Family/Friend   ☐ Other